MCGRAW-HILL
ONLINE RESOURCES

IMPORTANT:

HERE IS YOUR REGISTRATION CODE TO ACCESS
YOUR PREMIUM McGRAW-HILL ONLINE RESOURCES.

For key premium online resources you need THIS CODE to gain access. Once the code is entered, you will be able to use the Web resources for the length of your course.

If your course is using **WebCT** or **Blackboard**, you'll be able to use this code to access the McGraw-Hill content within your instructor's online course.

Access is provided if you have purchased a new book. If the registration code is missing from this book, the registration screen on our Website, and within your WebCT or Blackboard course, will tell you how to obtain your new code.

Registering for McGraw-Hill Online Resources

TO gain access to your McGraw-Hill web resources simply follow the steps below:

1. USE YOUR WEB BROWSER TO GO TO: **www.mhhe.com/santrockcd10**

2. CLICK ON **FIRST TIME USER**.

3. ENTER THE REGISTRATION CODE* PRINTED ON THE TEAR-OFF BOOKMARK ON THE RIGHT.

4. AFTER YOU HAVE ENTERED YOUR REGISTRATION CODE, CLICK **REGISTER**.

5. FOLLOW THE INSTRUCTIONS TO SET-UP YOUR PERSONAL UserID AND PASSWORD.

6. WRITE YOUR UserID AND PASSWORD DOWN FOR FUTURE REFERENCE.
   KEEP IT IN A SAFE PLACE.

TO GAIN ACCESS to the McGraw-Hill content in your instructor's **WebCT** or **Blackboard** course simply log in to the course with the UserID and Password provided by your instructor. Enter the registration code exactly as it appears in the box to the right when prompted by the system. You will only need to use the code the first time you click on McGraw-Hill content.

Thank you, and welcome to your McGraw-Hill online Resources!

* YOUR REGISTRATION CODE CAN BE USED ONLY ONCE TO ESTABLISH ACCESS. IT IS NOT TRANSFERABLE.

0-07-292373-3 T/A SANTROCK: CHILD DEVELOPMENT, 10/E

HMIG-1KLU-B0QT-OJA7-UL3U

REGISTRATION CODE

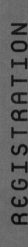

Higher Education

Child Development

TENTH EDITION

John W. Santrock
University of Texas at Dallas

Boston   Burr Ridge, IL   Dubuque, IA   Madison, WI   New York   San Francisco   St. Louis
Bangkok   Bogotá   Caracas   Kuala Lumpur   Lisbon   London   Madrid   Mexico City
Milan   Montreal   New Delhi   Santiago   Seoul   Singapore   Sydney   Taipei   Toronto

Higher Education

Published by McGraw-Hill, a business unit of The McGraw-Hill Companies, Inc., 1221 Avenue of the Americas, New York, NY 10020. Copyright © 2004, 2001, 1998, 1996, 1994, 1992, 1989, 1987, 1982 by The McGraw-Hill Companies, Inc. All rights reserved. No part of this publication may be reproduced or distributed in any form or by any means, or stored in a database or retrieval system, without the prior written consent of The McGraw-Hill Companies, Inc., including, but not limited to, in any network or other electronic storage or transmission, or broadcast for distance learning.

Some ancillaries, including electronic and print components, may not be available to customers outside the United States.

 This book is printed on recycled, acid-free paper containing 10% postconsumer waste.

International   1 2 3 4 5 6 7 8 9 0 QPD/QPD 0 9 8 7 6 5 4 3
Domestic   1 2 3 4 5 6 7 8 9 0 QPD/QPD 0 9 8 7 6 5 4 3

ISBN 0-07-282038-1
ISBN 0-07-121508-5 (ISE)

Vice president and editor-in-chief: *Thalia Dorwick*
Publisher: *Stephen D. Rutter*
Senior sponsoring editor: *Rebecca H. Hope*
Developmental editor: *Mary Kate Hanley*
Marketing manager: *Melissa Caughlin*
Senior project manager: *Marilyn Rothenberger*
Manager, New book production: *Sandra Hahn*
Media technology producer: *Ginger Bunn*
Design coordinator: *Gino Cieslik*
Cover/interior designer: *Ellen Pettengell*
Cover image: *© Getty Images*
Art editor: *Robin Mouat*
Photo research coordinator: *Alexandra Ambrose*
Photo research: *LouAnn Wilson*
Senior supplement producer: *David A. Welsh*
Compositor: *The GTS Companies*
Typeface: *9.5/12 Meridien*
Printer: *Quebecor World, Dubuque, IA*

The credits section for this book begins on page C-1 and is considered an extension of the copyright page.

Library of Congress Cataloging-in-Publication Data

Santrock, John W.
  Child development/ John w. Santrock.—10th ed.
  p. cm.
  Includes bibliographical references and index.
  ISBN 0-07-282038-1 (alk. paper) – ISBN 0-07-121508-5 (alk paper)
 1. child development. 2. Child psychology. I. Title

RJ131.S264 2004
305.231—dc21
                                        2003046356

INTERNATIONAL EDITION ISBN 0-07-121508-5
Copyright © 2004. Exclusive rights by The McGraw-Hill Companies, Inc., for manufacture and export. This book cannot be re-exported from the country to which it is sold by McGraw-Hill. The International Edition is not available in North America.

www.mhhe.com

*With special appreciation to my wife
Mary Jo, my children Tracy and Jennifer,
and my granddaughter Jordan.*

About the Author

John W. Santrock

John Santrock received his PH.D. from the University of Minnesota in 1973. He taught at the University of Charleston and the University of Georgia before joining the Program on Psychology and Human Development at the University of Texas at Dallas, where he currently teaches a number of undergraduate courses in developmental psychology.

John has been a member of the editorial boards of Child Development and Developmental Psychology. His research on father custody is widely cited and used in expert witness testimony to promote flexibility and alternative considerations in custody disputes. John has also authored these exceptional McGraw-Hill texts: Psychology (7th edition), Children (7th edition), Adolescence (9th edition), Life-Span Development (9th edition), and Educational Psychology (2nd edition).

For many years, John was involved in tennis as a player, teaching professional, and coach of professional tennis players. He has been married for more than 35 years to his wife, Mary Jo, who is a realtor. He has two daughters—Tracy, who is a medical sales specialist at Nortel in Raleigh, North Carolina, and Jennifer, who is a medical sales specialist at Medtronic in San Antonio, Texas. He has one granddaughter, Jordan, age 11. Tracy recently competed in the New york Marathon, and Jennifer was in the top 100 ranked players on the Women's Professional Tennis Tour. In the last decade, John has also spent time painting expressionist art.

John Santrock, teaching in his undergraduate course.

Brief Contents

SECTION 1

The Nature of Child Development 3

1 Introduction 5
2 The Science of Child Development 27

SECTION 2

Biological Processes, Physical Development, and Perceptual Development 63

3 Biological Beginnings 65
4 Prenatal Development and Birth 93
5 Physical Development in Infancy 129
6 Physical Development in Childhood and Adolescence 167

SECTION 3

Cognition and Language 203

7 Cognitive Developmental Approaches 205
8 Information Processing 241
9 Intelligence 279
10 Language Development 313

SECTION 4

Socioemotional Development 343

11 Emotional Development 345
12 The Self and Identity 383
13 Gender 409
14 Moral Development 435

SECTION 5

Social Contexts of Development 469

15 Families 471
16 Peers 509
17 Schools 539
18 Culture 577

Contents

Preface xvii

Expert Consultants xxix

Student-Driven Pedagogy xxxii

Prologue 1

SECTION 1

The Nature of Child Development 3

CHAPTER 1

Introduction 5

The Stories of Jeffrey Dahmer and Alice Walker 6

Child Development—Yesterday and Today 7

Historical Views of Childhood 7

The Modern Study of Child Development 8

Today's Children: Some Contemporary Concerns 10

Careers in Child Development *Luis Vargas, Clinical Child Psychologist 11*

Social Policy and Children's Development 14

Explorations in Child Development *Resilience, Prevention, and Competence 16*

Developmental Processes and Periods 17

Biological, Cognitive, and Socioemotional Processes 17

Periods of Development 18

Developmental Issues 19

Nature and Nurture 19

Continuity and Discontinuity 20

Early and Later Experience 20

Evaluating the Developmental Issues 21

Reach Your Learning Goals 22

Summary 23

Key Terms 24

Key People 24

Taking It to the Net 25

E-Learning Tools 25

CHAPTER 2

The Science of Child Development 27

The Stories of Erik Erikson and Jean Piaget 28

Theories of Development 29

Psychoanalytic Theories 30

Cognitive Theories 33

Behavioral and Social Cognitive Theories 36

Ethological Theory 38

Ecological Theory 40

An Eclectic Theoretical Orientation 41

Research in Child Development 43

Types of Research 43

Time Span of Research 48

Research Journals 49

Explorations in Child Development *Being a Wise Consumer of Information About Children's Development 52*

Facing Up to Research Challenges 53

Conducting Ethical Research 53

Minimizing Bias 54

Careers in Child Development *Pam Reid, Educational and Developmental Psychologist 55*

Reach Your Learning Goals 58

Summary 59

Key Terms 60

Key People 60

Taking It to the Net 61

E-Learning Tools 61

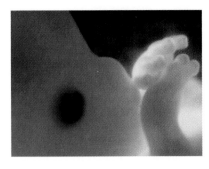

S E C T I O N   2

Biological Processes, Physical Development, and Perceptual Development 63

C H A P T E R   3

Biological Beginnings 65

The Stories of the Jim and Jim Twins 66

The Evolutionary Perspective 67
  Natural Selection and Adaptive Behavior 67
  Evolutionary Psychology 67

Genetic Foundations 69
  What Are Genes? 70
  Mitosis and Meiosis 70
  Genetic Principles 71
  Behavior Genetics 74
  Molecular Genetics 74
  The Collaborative Gene 75

  Explorations in Child Development *Genetic Counseling 76*
  Chromosome- and Gene-Linked Abnormalities 77

  Careers in Child Development *Holly Ishmael, Genetic Counselor 80*

Reproductive Challenges and Choices 81
  Prenatal Diagnostic Tests 81
  Infertility 81
  Adoption 83

Heredity-Environment Interaction 84
  Heredity-Environment Correlations 84
  Shared and Nonshared Environmental Experiences 85
  The Epigenetic View 86
  Conclusions About Heredity-Environment Interaction 86

Reach Your Learning Goals 88

Summary 89

Key Terms 90

Key People 90

Taking It to the Net 91

E-Learning Tools 91

C H A P T E R   4

Prenatal Development and Birth 93

The Story of Tanner Roberts' Birth: A Fantastic Voyage 94

Prenatal Development 95
  The Course of Prenatal Development 95
  Teratology and Hazards to Prenatal Development 99
  Prenatal Care 107

  Careers in Child Development *Rachel Thompson, Obstetrician/Gynecologist 107*
  Cultural Beliefs About Pregnancy 108
  Positive Prenatal Development 109

Birth 109
  The Birth Process 109

  Careers in Child Development *Linda Pugh, Perinatal Nurse 113*
  Low Birth Weight Infants 114

  Explorations in Child Development *The Power of Touch and Massage in Development 117*
  Measures of Neonatal Health and Responsiveness 118

The Postpartum Period 119
  What Is the Postpartum Period? 119
  Physical Adjustments 120
  Emotional and Psychological Adjustments 120

  Careers in Child Development *Diane Sanford, Clinical Psychologist and Postpartum Expert 122*
  Bonding 122

Reach Your Learning Goals 124

Summary 125

Key Terms 126

Key People 126

Taking It to the Net 127

E-Learning Tools 127

C H A P T E R   5

Physical Development in Infancy 129

The Stories of Latonya and Ramona: Bottlefeeding and Breastfeeding in Africa 130

Physical Growth and Development in Infancy 131
  Cephalocaudal and Proximodistal Patterns 131
  Height and Weight 132
  The Brain 132
  Sleep 137
  Nutrition 139

  Careers in Child Development *Barbara Deloin, Pediatric Nurse 141*

  Explorations in Child Development *A Healthy Start 142*
  Toilet Training 143

  Careers in Child Development *T. Berry Brazelton, Pediatrician 143*

Motor Development 144
Reflexes 144
Gross and Fine Motor Skills 146
Dynamic Systems Theory 151

Sensory and Perceptual Development 152
What Are Sensation and Perception? 152
The Ecological View 152
Visual Perception 153
Other Senses 157
Intermodal Perception 159
Perceptual-Motor Coupling 159

Reach Your Learning Goals 162

Summary 163

Key Terms 164

Key People 164

Taking It to the Net 165

E-Learning Tools 165

Handedness 172
The Brain 172

Health and Illness 174
A Developmental Perspective 175
Explorations in Child Development *Life Science and Life Skills Education 176*
Nutrition and Obesity 176
Exercise and Sports 179
Children's Health and Illness in the United States and Around the World 180
Careers in Child Development *Sharon McLeod, Child Life Specialist 182*

Puberty and Adolescence 183
Puberty and Sexuality 183
Careers in Child Development *Lynn Blankinship, Family and Consumer Science Educator 191*
Substance Use and Abuse 192
The Interrelation of Problems and Successful Programs 195
Today's Youth 196

Reach Your Learning Goals 198

Summary 199

Key Terms 200

Key People 200

Taking It to the Net 201

E-Learning Tools 201

CHAPTER 6

Physical Development in Childhood and Adolescence 167

The Story of Zhang Liyin 168

Physical Growth in Childhood 169
Child Growth Patterns 169
Motor Development 170

SECTION 3

Cognition and Language 203

CHAPTER 7

Cognitive Developmental Approaches 205

The Stories of Laurent, Lucienne, and Jacqueline 206

Piaget's Cognitive Developmental Theory 207
Jean Piaget and His Place in Developmental Psychology 207
Cognitive Developmental Theory and Processes 207

Piaget's Stages 209
Sensorimotor Thought 209
Preoperational Thought 214
Concrete Operational Thought 220
Formal Operational Thought 221

Applying and Evaluating Piaget's Theory 226
Piaget and Education 226

Evaluating Piaget's Theory 227

Vygotsky's Theory of Cognitive Development 229
The Zone of Proximal Development 230
Scaffolding 230
Explorations in Child Development *Apprenticeship Training 231*
Language and Thought 232
Vygotsky and Education 232
Careers in Child Development *Donene Polson, Elementary School Teacher 233*
Evaluating and Comparing Vygotsky's Theory and Piaget's Theory 234

Reach Your Learning Goals 236

Summary 237

Key Terms 238

Key People 238

Taking It to the Net 239

E-Learning Tools 239

CHAPTER 8

Information Processing 241

The Story of Laura Bickford 242

The Information-Processing Approach 242

Processes 242

Comparison with the Cognitive Developmental Approach 243

Memory 244

What Is Memory? 244

Encoding 244

Storage 250

Retrieval and Forgetting 256

Personal Trauma and Memory 257

Explorations in Child Development *Repressed Memories, Child Abuse, and Reality* 259

Thinking 260

What Is Thinking? 260

Forming Concepts 260

Solving Problems 261

Careers in Child Development *Helen Schwe, Developmental Psychologist and Toy Designer* 262

Thinking Critically 267

Careers in Child Development *Laura Martin, Science Museum Educator and Research Specialist* 269

Thinking Scientifically 270

Metacognition 270

Developmental Changes 271

Strategies 271

Self-Regulatory Learning 272

Reach Your Learning Goals 274

Summary 275

Key Terms 276

Key People 276

Taking It to the Net 277

E-Learning Tools 277

CHAPTER 9

Intelligence 279

The Story of Project Spectrum 280

The Nature of Intelligence 281

Intelligence Testing 281

Approaches to Testing 282

Criteria of a Good Intelligence Test 285

Cultural Bias in Testing 287

The Use and Misuse of Intelligence Tests 288

Theories of Multiple Intelligence 289

Factor Analysis, Two-Factor Theory, and Multiple-Factor Theory 289

Gardner's Theory of Eight Intelligences 290

Sternberg's Triarchic Theory 291

Emotional Intelligence 293

Evaluating the Multiple-Intelligences Approach 293

Do Children Have a General Intelligence? 294

Intelligence in Infancy and Developmental Transformations 294

Infant Intelligence Tests 295

Careers in Child Development *Toosje Thyssen Van Beveren, Infant Assessment Specialist* 296

Stability and Change in Intelligence 296

Information-Processing Tasks as Predictors of Intelligence 297

The Extremes of Intelligence and Creativity 298

Mental Retardation 298

Giftedness 299

Creativity 300

Careers in Child Development *Sterling Jones, Supervisor of Gifted and Talented Education* 301

The Influence of Heredity and Environment 303

Hereditary Influences 303

Explorations in Child Development *The Abecedarian Intervention Program* 304

Environmental Influences 304

Group Comparisons 305

Reach Your Learning Goals 308

Summary 309

Key Terms 310

Key People 310

Taking It to the Net 311

E-Learning Tools 311

CHAPTER 10

Language Development 313

The Story of Helen Keller 314

What Is Language? 314

Defining Language 314

Language's Rule Systems 315

Biological and Environmental Influences 318

Biological Influences 318

Behavioral and Environmental Influences 320

An Interactionist View of Language 322

Explorations in Child Development *How Parents Can Facilitate Children's Language Development* 323

Language and Cognition 324

How Language Develops 326

Infancy 326

Early Childhood 329

Middle and Late Childhood 332

Bilingualism 336

　Careers in Child Development *Salvador Tamayo, Bilingual
　　Education Teacher 337*

Reach Your Learning Goals 338

Summary 339

Key Terms 340

Key People 340

Taking It to the Net 341

E-Learning Tools 341

SECTION 4

Socioemotional Development 343

C H A P T E R　11

Emotional Development 345

The Story of Tom's Fathering 346

Exploring Emotion 346
　Defining Emotion 346
　Functionalism in Emotion 347
　Relational Emotion 347
　Regulation of Emotion 348
　Emotional Competence 349

Development of Emotion 350
　Infancy 350
　Early Childhood 353
　Middle and Late Childhood 354
　Adolescence 355

Emotional Problems, Stress, and Coping 356
　Depression 356
　Suicide 357
　Stress and Coping 358

Temperament 363
　Defining and Classifying Temperament 363
　Goodness of Fit 365
　Developmental Connections and Contexts 365
　Gender, Culture, and Temperament 366
　Parenting and the Child's Temperament 367

Attachment 368
　What Is Attachment? 368
　Individual Differences 370
　Caregiving Styles and Attachment Classification 371
　Attachment, Temperament, and the Wider Social World 372
　Fathers as Caregivers of Infants 373
　Child Care 374

　Explorations in Child Development *Child-Care Policy Around the
　　World 374*

　Careers in Child Development *Rashmi Nakhre, Child-Care
　　Director 376*

Reach Your Learning Goals 378

Summary 379

Key Terms 380

Key People 380

Taking It to the Net 381

E-Learning Tools 381

C H A P T E R　12

The Self and Identity 383

The Story of a Fifteen-Year-Old Girl's Self-Description 384

Self-Understanding 384
　What Is Self-Understanding? 385
　Developmental Changes 385

　Explorations in Child Development *Multiple Selves and
　　Sociocultural Contexts 389*

Self-Esteem and Self-Concept 391
　What Are Self-Esteem and Self-Concept? 391
　Assessment 392
　Parent-Child Relationships 393
　Developmental Changes 393
　Consequences of Low Self-Esteem 393
　Increasing Children's Self-Esteem 393

Identity 395
　Erikson's View 395
　Some Contemporary Thoughts 397
　Identity Statuses 398
　Developmental Changes 400
　Social Contexts 400

　Careers in Child Development *Armando Ronquillo, High School
　　Counselor 402*

Reach Your Learning Goals 404

Summary 405

Key Terms 406

Key People 406

Taking It to the Net 407

E-Learning Tools 407

C H A P T E R   1 3

Gender 409

The Story of Jerry Maguire: Gender, Emotion, and Caring 410

Influences on Gender Development 411

Biological Influences 411

Social Influences 414

Careers in Child Development *Eleanor Maccoby, Professor 417*

Cognitive Influences 418

Gender Stereotypes, Similarities, and Differences 420

Gender Stereotyping 420

Gender Similarities and Differences 421

Gender-Role Classification 424

What Is Gender-Role Classification? 425

Androgyny and Education 425

Masculinity in Childhood and Adolescence 426

Gender-Role Transcendence 426

Gender in Context 426

Explorations in Child Development *Gender Roles in Iran and China 427*

Developmental Windows of Gender Opportunity and Asymmetric Gender Socialization 428

Developmental Windows 428

Asymmetric Gender Socialization 429

Reach Your Learning Goals 430

Summary 431

Key Terms 432

Key People 432

Taking It to the Net 433

E-Learning Tools 433

C H A P T E R   1 4

Moral Development 435

The Story of Pax, the Make-Believe Planet 436

Domains of Moral Development 437

Moral Thought 437

Moral Behavior 445

Moral Feeling 448

Contexts of Moral Development 452

Parenting 452

Schools 453

Prosocial and Antisocial Behavior 456

Altruism 456

Juvenile Delinquency 457

Careers in Child Development *Rodney Hammond, Health Psychologist 461*

Explorations in Child Development *Why Youth Kill 462*

Reach Your Learning Goals 464

Summary 465

Key Terms 466

Key People 466

Taking It to the Net 467

E-Learning Tools 467

S E C T I O N   5

Social Contexts of Development 469

C H A P T E R   1 5

Families 471

The Story of a Mother with Multiple Sclerosis 472

Family Processes 473

Reciprocal Socialization and the Family as a System 473

The Developmental Construction of Relationships 474

Adapting Parenting to Developmental Changes in the Child 476

Sociocultural and Historical Changes 477

The Roles of Cognition and Emotion in Family Relationships 478

Parenting 479

The Parental Role 479

Parents as Managers 480

Careers in Child Development *Janis Keyser, Parent Educator 481*

Parenting Styles 481

Punishment 482

Child Maltreatment 484

Careers in Child Development *Darla Botkin, Marriage and Family Therapist 485*

Parenting Takes Time and Effort 486

Siblings 487

Sibling Relationships 487

Birth Order 487

Families and Adolescents 489

Autonomy and Attachment 489

Parent-Adolescent Conflict 490

The Changing Family in a Changing Social World 493
Working Mothers 493
Effects of Divorce on Children 495
Stepfamilies 496
Gay and Lesbian Parents 497
Cultural, Ethnic, and Socioeconomic Variations in Families 498
Gender and Parenting 499
Explorations in Child Development *Acculturation and Ethnic Minority Parenting 500*

Reach Your Learning Goals 504

Summary 505

Key Terms 506

Key People 506

Taking It to the Net 507

E-Learning Tools 507

C H A P T E R   1 6
Peers 509

The Stories of Young Adolescent Girls' Friends and Relational Worlds 510

Peer Relations 511
Peer Group Functions 511
The Distinct but Coordinated Worlds of Parent-Child and Peer Relations 512
The Developmental Course of Peer Relations in Childhood 513
Social Cognition 514
Peer Statuses 515
Bullying 516
Gender and Peer Relations 517

Play 518
Play's Functions 518
Parten's Classic Study of Play 519
Types of Play 520
The Sociocultural Contexts of Play 521

Friendship 522
Friendship's Functions 522
Sullivan's Ideas 523
Intimacy and Similarity 524
Mixed-Age Friendships 525

Adolescence, Peers, and Romantic Relationships 526
Peer Pressure and Conformity 526
Cliques and Crowds 527
Adolescent Groups Versus Child Groups 527
Dating and Romantic Relationships 528
Explorations in Child Development *Ethnic Minority Adolescents' Peer Relations 530*

Reach Your Learning Goals 534

Summary 535

Key Terms 536

Key People 536

Taking It to the Net 537

E-Learning Tools 537

C H A P T E R   1 7
Schools 539

The Story of Reggio Emilia's Children 540

Exploring Children's Schooling 541
Contemporary Approaches to Children's Schooling 541
Schools' Changing Social Developmental Contexts 541

Schools and Developmental Status 543
Early Childhood Education 543
Careers in Child Development *Yolanda Garcia, Director of Children's Services/Head Start 548*
The Transition to Elementary School 549
Careers in Child Development *Susan Bradburn, Elementary School Teacher 550*
Schools for Adolescents 550
Careers in Child Development *Mark Fodness, Middle School Teacher 553*

Socioeconomic Status and Ethnicity in Schools 555
Socioeconomic Status 555
Ethnicity 556
Careers in Child Development *James Comer, Child Psychiatrist 558*

Children with Disabilities 559
Who Are Children with Disabilities? 559
Learning Disabilities 560
Attention Deficit Hyperactivity Disorder (ADHD) 562
Educational Issues 563

Achievement 564
Need for Achievement 564
Extrinsic and Intrinsic Motivation 565
Mastery Motivation 567
Explorations in Child Development *Teachers Who Care 568*
Self-Efficacy 568
Goal Setting, Planning, and Self-Monitoring 569
Ethnicity and Culture 570

Reach Your Learning Goals 572

Summary 573

Key Terms 574

Key People 574

Taking It to the Net 575

E-Learning Tools 575

C H A P T E R   1 8
Culture 577

The Stories of Sonya's and Michael's Cultural Conflicts 578

Culture and Children's Development 578
What Is Culture? 579

The Relevance of Culture to the Study of Children 579
Cross-Cultural Comparisons 580

Socioeconomic Status and Poverty 583
What Is Socioeconomic Status? 583
Socioeconomic Variations in Families, Neighborhoods, and Schools 584
Poverty 585

Ethnicity 588
Immigration 588
Ethnicity and Socioeconomic Status 588
Careers in Child Development *Carola Suarez-Orozco, Lecturer, Researcher, and Codirector of Immigration Projects 589*
Differences and Diversity 590
Prejudice, Discrimination, and Bias 591
Assimilation and Pluralism 592
America: A Nation of Blended Cultures 592
Explorations in Child Development *Canada 593*

Technology 594
Television 594
Computers and the Internet 597

Reach Your Learning Goals 600

Summary 601

Key Terms 602

Key People 602

Taking It to the Net 603

E-Learning Tools 603

Appendix A-1

Glossary G-1

References R-1

Credits C-1

Name Index NI-1

Subject Index SI-1

Preface

Preparing a new edition of *Child Development* is both a joy and a challenge. I enjoy revising this text because the feedback from instructors and students on each edition has been consistently enthusiastic. The challenge of revising a successful text is always to continue meeting readers' needs and expectations, while keeping the material fresh and up to date. For the tenth edition of *Child Development*, the revision focuses on three areas to meet this challenge:

- Research and content
- Applications
- Accessibility and interest

Here I describe the thrust of these changes in general terms. A list of chapter-by-chapter changes subsequently provides more detail.

> John Santrock's book offers professors and students the most comprehensive coverage of child development. The new edition balances cultural/diversity issues, current research, and the latest information on behavior genetics in an easy-to-understand format. The engaging writing style and illustrations capture and maintain student interest. The addition of chapter goals and section reviews facilitates the retention of information for students with various learning styles.
> —MEGAN E. BRADLEY *Frostburg State University*

> There is a wonderful flow to this book and the organization is great.
> —SUSAN N. SIAW *California State Polytechnic Institute–Pomona*

RESEARCH AND CONTENT

Above all, a text on child development must include a solid research foundation. This edition of *Child Development* presents the latest, most contemporary research. *Child Development*, tenth edition, has more than 800 citations from the past three years, making it truly a twenty-first century rendition of the field of child development.

More Depth in Research Descriptions and More Supporting Data

In response to instructors' requests for greater depth of research coverage, I have expanded discussions of research, but with a careful eye toward explaining theory and research in a very understandable way. For example, in chapter 8, there is a new description of a research study on habituation and dishabituation, along with a figure (figure 8.2) illustrating the findings.

Reviewers recommended that I include more graphs and tables to show how researchers visually present their data. I took this recommendation to heart. There are more than 60 new figures and tables of data in *Child Development*, tenth edition. Special care was taken to make sure that these illustrations are designed clearly so that students can interpret and understand them.

New and Expanded Content

Many new content areas have been added to the tenth edition of *Child Development* and many others updated and expanded. The details of these content changes will be described shortly on a chapter-by-chapter basis. Two content areas, though, deserve to be singled out: the brain and diversity.

Considerable progress is being made in charting developmental changes in the brain. These changes are highlighted in chapters 5 and 6.

> I was excited to see the addition of material on the development of the brain.
> —KRISTA SCHOENFELD *Colby Community College*

Also it is very important to examine the many aspects of diversity in the study of children's development. This text has always taken the discussion of diversity seriously and in the tenth edition this coverage has been significantly updated.

> This text includes great coverage of ethnicity.
> —KEVIN MACDONALD *California State University*

> Overall, I think John Santrock has done an excellent job with diversity issues.
> —K. LAURIE DICKSON *Northern Arizona University*

Expert Research Consultants

Child development has become an enormous, complex field, and no single author can possibly be an expert in all areas of the field. To solve this problem, I have sought the input of the world's leading experts in many different areas of child development. They provided me with detailed recommendations on new research to include in every chapter. The experts for this book literally are a who's who in the field of child development, and their photographs and biographies appear on pages xxix-xxxi of the Preface.

> *The coverage is wonderfully broad, the topics appropriate, the selection of resources exceptional, and the links to practical issues thoughtful and interesting. The level and fluency of the writing are impressive as well, as are the boxed features and other pedagogical features. I especially like the framing of the chapter summary as points that meet the learning goals set out at the beginning of the chapter.*
>
> —W. ANDREW COLLINS *University of Minnesota*

> *John Santrock has done a very admirable job in distilling the often confusing and contradictory field of developmental psychology into a textbook for undergraduate courses in child development.*
>
> —CAROLYN SAARNI *Sonoma State University*

> *I am impressed by the effort to bring students up-to-date know-how (such as Gilbert Gottlieb's probabilistic epigenesis, developments in modern genetics). It is also very refreshing to see a repeated focus on issues usually not emphasized in such textbooks (role of massage, tactile contact, and so on).*
>
> —JEAN VALISNER *University of North Carolina–Chapel Hill*

APPLICATIONS

It is important not only to present the scientific foundations of child development to students, but also to demonstrate that research has real-world applications, to include many applied examples of concepts, and to give students a sense that the field of child development has personal meaning for them. For example, a new addition to chapter 11, "Emotional Development," focuses on recommendations for helping children cope effectively with terrorist attacks.

> *John Santrock provides thorough coverage of how the topics presented relate to everyday life. The examples that he uses emphasize application. I think students learn more when they see connections to the 'real world.'*
>
> —K. LAURIE DICKSON *Northern Arizona University*

In addition to giving special attention throughout the text to health, parenting, and educational applications, the tenth edition emphasizes careers. Every chapter has one or more Careers in Child Development inserts that profile an individual whose career relates to the chapter's content. Most of these inserts include a photograph of the person at work. In addition, a new Careers Appendix describes a number of careers in the education/research, clinical/counseling, medical/nursing/physical development, and families/relationships categories. Numerous Web links provide students with opportunities to read about these careers in greater depth.

> *I think the Careers in Child Development feature is an EXCELLENT addition. This helps to show students possibilities related to an in-depth study of an area.*
>
> —SHIRLEY-ANNE HENSCH *University of Wisconsin*

> *The Careers in Child Development inserts are GREAT! They really help to keep the book current, accessible, and unique.*
>
> —KATHY E. JOHNSON *Indiana University–Purdue University–Indianapolis*

Improved Accessibility and Interest

I strongly believe that students not only should be challenged to study hard and think more deeply and productively about child development, but also should be provided with an effective learning system. Instructors and students alike have commented on many occasions about how student-friendly this text is. However, I strive to keep making the learning system better, and I am truly excited about the improvements for this edition.

Now more than ever, students struggle to find the main ideas in their courses, especially in courses like child development, which includes so much material. The new learning headings and learning system centers on learning goals that, together with the main text headings, keep the key ideas in front of the reader from the beginning to the end of a chapter. Each chapter has no more than six main headings and corresponding learning goals, which are presented side-by-side on the chapter-opening spread. At the end of each main section of a chapter, the learning goal is repeated in a new feature called Review and Reflect, which prompts students to review the key topics in the section and poses a question to encourage them to think critically about what they have read. At the end of the chapter, under the heading Reach Your Learning Goals, the learning goals guide students through the bulleted chapter review.

> *I especially appreciated the learning goals/cognitive maps.*
>
> —RICHARD A. SPROTT *California State University*

> *I found the learning goals to be very useful and I prefer to have visuals like cognitive maps whenever possible. I particularly like the Reflect questions. I think the Reach Your Learning Goals section is a good way to visually review what was covered in the chapter. I also like having learning goals with the answers. This is a great review for readers.*
>
> —KRISTA SCHOENFELD *Colby Community College*

In addition to the verbal tools just described, maps that link up with the learning goals are presented at the beginning of each major section in the chapter. At the end of each chapter, the section maps are assembled into a complete map of the chapter that provides a visual review guide. The complete learning system, including many additional features not mentioned here, is presented later in the Preface in a section titled To the Student.

As important as it is to provide students with an effective learning system, it is imperative to present theories and research at a level that students can understand them and are motivated to learn about them. In each edition of the book, I have carefully rewritten much of the material to make sure it is at a level that challenges students but is also clearly written so they can understand it. I also continually seek better examples of concepts and material that will interest students.

> *It is hard to beat John Santrock's writing style and the text is written at just the right level for average college students.*
>
> —ROBERT PASHAK *George Mason University*

CHAPTER-BY-CHAPTER CHANGES

A number of changes were made in each of the 18 chapters of *Child Development*, tenth edition. The highlights of these changes include:

CHAPTER 1
Introduction

Addition of research descriptions to each section of contemporary concerns: health and well-being, families and parenting, education, and sociocultural contexts. Each of the research studies described is from the twenty-first century.

New figure 1.3 illustrating that the main differences in the home environments of children from different ethnic groups are due to poverty rather than ethnicity (Bradley & others, 2001)

New Careers in Child Development insert on Luis Vargas, child clinical psychologist

> *I like the addition of specific research projects in different areas (such as poverty).*
>
> —MEGAN E. BRADLEY *Frostburg State University*

CHAPTER 2
The Science of Child Development

Extensive reworking of section on research methods

Reorganization of types of research; new headings are Descriptive Research, Correlational Research, and Experimental Research

New discussion of naturalistic observation research (Crowley & others, 2001) and new figure 2.8 which illustrates the results of this research

Expanded presentation of surveys and interviews with new research example

Expanded material on standardized tests

New discussion of correlation coefficient

Expanded and updated coverage of ethics

Extensively revised discussion of Vygotsky's theory for better student understanding

Two new photographs to illustrate how research might produce different results depending on how homogeneous or diverse the sample is

> *This chapter does an excellent job of simplifying some pretty complicated constructs and making them more accessible.*
>
> —KATHY E. JOHNSON *Indiana University–Purdue University–Indianapolis*

> *The sections that talk about research journals and being a wise consumer are WONDERFUL!*
>
> —KRISTA SCHOENFELD *Colby Community College*

CHAPTER 3
Biological Beginnings

Reorganization of heredity section with the discussion of abnormalities now following genetic principles

New section on Reproduction Choices and Challenges

Important new section, The Collaborative Gene, that discusses why DNA does not determine heredity in a completely independent manner (Gottlieb, 2001)

Clear, improved discussion of mitosis and meiosis

New section on genetic imprinting

Expanded, updated coverage of sex-linked genes

New discussion of phenylketonuria in terms of the nature-nurture issue (Luciana, Sullivan, & Nelson, 2001)

Updated description of test-tube babies with new recent research studies (Golombok, MaCallum, & Goodman, 2001; Hahn & Dipietro, 2001) and new figure 3.10 on research data

New Careers in Child Development insert on Holly Ishmael, a genetic counselor

Expanded, contemporary discussion of the Human Genome Project, including the finding that humans only have about 30,000 to 35,000 genes

New high-interest figure 3.5, Exploring Your Genetic Future

New figure 3.10 to illustrate the three types of genotype-environment correlations with new examples

Deleted section on intelligence so that heredity-environment issues in intelligence can be more fully explored in chapter 9, "Intelligence"

... I found much to like with the chapter in terms of coverage, scope, and applications... John Santrock has expanded and updated previous versions of the chapter, including discussions of several recent advances from genetics (genetic imprinting), developmental biology (the dependent gene), and psychobiology (canalization).

—ROBERT LICKLITER *Florida International University*

A strength is the discussion of current findings, such as dependent genes and environmental influences on cellular processes. I'm glad the intelligence discussion was moved to the intelligence chapter.

—K. LAURIE DICKSON *Northern Arizona University*

I love Dr. Santrock's writing style, which was especially effective for the biological material that is typically not the interest/strength area of my students.

—SUSAN N. Siaw *California State Polytechnic Institute–Pomona*

CHAPTER 4
Prenatal Development and Birth

Expanded coverage of teratogens in terms of dose, time of exposure, and genetic susceptibility

Updated research on cocaine babies

New teratology section on incompatibility of blood types

New discussion of cultural variations in childbirth

New coverage of small for date infants and their comparison to preterm infants

New discussion of low birth weight infant rates around the world and up-to-date information about this topic, including new figure 4.7 (UNICEF, 2001)

New figure 4.8 to illustrate research on the positive effects of massage therapy on low birth weight infants conducted by Tiffany Field

New Careers in Child Development inserts on Linda Pugh, a perinatal nurse, and Diane Sanford, clinical psychologist and postpartum expert

New material on reduced risk of neonatal death and delivery of low birth weight baby when baby is delivered by certified nurse midwives compared to physicians

Good, up to date discussion of the effects of prematurity. I liked the chapter a lot.

—KEVIN MACDONALD *California State University*

CHAPTER 5
Physical Development in Infancy

Considerable expansion of material on the development of the brain, including new figure 5.4 on synaptic pruning

New discussion of Charles Nelson's infant brain research and intriguing photo of his brain research with infants

Extensive research updating of breastfeeding

New figure 5.9 on plasticity in the human brain; also new, the fascinating story of Michael Rehbein's loss of his left hemisphere and how his right hemisphere started taking over the functions of speech

New research on the stressful aspects of co-sleeping (Hunsley & Thoman, 2002)

Expanded discussion of cultural variations in infants' motor skills

Research updating of toilet training

Updated, expanded discussion of dynamic systems theory

Expanded coverage of motor skills, including links between perception and the development of motor skills

New Careers in Child Development insert on T. Berry Brazelton, pediatrician

The chapter is comprehensive. Nice improvement on the brain development section, dynamic systems theory, and Gipsonian theory. Good examples throughout the chapter.

—K. LAURIE DICKSON *Northern Arizona University*

CHAPTER 6
Physical Development in Childhood and Adolescence

Extensive reorganization of chapter to reflect a stronger topical approach (e.g., all of the nutrition and eating problems material discussed together)

Much expanded coverage of developmental changes in the brain

Revised and updated coverage of handedness, including new material on handedness, language, and the brain's hemispheres

Gross motor skills through childhood now discussed together rather than separate sections; same for fine motor skills

New longitudinal studies on the increase in obesity in children and adolescents in the United States, including new figure 6.4

Considerably updated and revised discussion of eating problems and disorders in adolescence, including new research (Dowda & others, 2001; Field & others, 2001; Stice, 2002)

Updated and revised coverage of exercise including new figure 6.5 on the decrease in P.E. programs since the 1960s (Health Management Resources, 2001)

New Careers in Child Development insert on Sharon McLeod, child life specialist

Substantially revised section on illness and health in the world's children, including very recent data and a discussion of the increased problem of AIDS (UNICEF, 2002)

New sections on developing a sexual identity in adolescence and the progression of adolescent sexual behaviors

Recent data on adolescent pregnancy around the world (Centers for Disease Control and Prevention, 2001)

New Careers in Child Development insert on Lynn Blankinship, a family and consumer science educator

Very recent data on trends in adolescent drug use (Johnston, O'Malley, & Bachman, 2001)

New coverage of the increasing problem of Ecstasy use by adolescents and new figure 6.14 showing Ecstasy's effect on the brain

New research on the role of parents in adolescent drug use (National Center for Addiction and Substance Abuse, 2001)

New cross-cultural research showing the poor health habits of U.S. adolescents compared to adolescents in many other countries (World Health Organization, 2000)

> *Big improvements. Last edition, I recommended that chapters 5 and 6 be combined; however, after reading this edition, I'm impressed and think they should remain as separate, distinct chapters. Great emphasis on the long-term effects of health behaviors (continuity of behavior).*
>
> —K. LAURIE DICKSON *Northern Arizona University*

> *Overall, this is a strong chapter. The depth of coverage is very good. The illustrations are GREAT.*
>
> —RICHARD A. SPROTT *California State University*

CHAPTER 7
Cognitive Developmental Approaches

New section on infants' understanding of physical reality, including discussion of object permanence and causality

Description of research and new figure 7.3 on infants' understanding of physical reality

Updated coverage of Barbara Rogoff's ideas on cognitive apprenticeship and research conclusions about this topic

New Careers in *Child Development* insert on elementary school teacher, Donene Polson, who teaches in a Vygostky-based school

New entry in figure 7.15 comparing Piaget and Vygotsky, focusing on sociocultural context

Added criticisms of Vygotsky's approach

> *My rating of this chapter: Excellent.*
>
> —KATHY E. JOHNSON *Indiana University–Purdue University–Indianapolis*

CHAPTER 8
Information Processing

New description of research study on habituation and dishabituation and new figure 8.2 to illustrate the findings

New figure 8.3 on planning and attention

New discussion of verbal elaboration and new figure 8.4 to illustrate the results of a study on this topic

New coverage of developmental changes in imagery and new figure 8.5 to illustrate the results of a study on children's use of imagery

New figure 8.6 on developmental changes in memory span

New discussion of research on working memory and reading comprehension and new figure 8.8 to illustrate research on this topic

Coverage of recent study linking speed of information processing, working memory, and problem solving (Demetriou & others, 2002)

New coverage of recent research by Loftus and Pickrell (2001) on false memories

New figure 8.11 showing developmental changes in false-belief performance in theory of mind (Wellman & Cross, 2001)

New Careers in Child Development insert on Helen Schwe, developmental psychologist and toy designer

Extensively revised, updated, and expanded coverage of expertise

New Careers in Child Development insert on Laura Martin, science museum educator and research specialist

Updated, revised coverage of math education controversy

New figure 8.17 on the link between calculator use at different grade levels and math achievement

Updated coverage of research on children's scientific thinking

> *This is a very strong chapter on information processing. Although some students get confused by various research projects and findings, Santrock does an excellent job of clarifying this information.*
>
> —MEGAN E. BRADLEY *Frostburg State University*

> *The new section on expertise is great; very useful.*
>
> —RICHARD A. SPROTT *California State University*

CHAPTER 9
Intelligence

Extensive reorganization of chapter with topics now in this sequence: The Nature of Intelligence, Intelligence Testing, Theories of Multiple Intelligence, Intelligence in Infancy and Developmental Transformations, The Extremes of Intelligence and Creativity, and The Influence of Heredity and Environment

New section on emotional intelligence and new figure 9.5 that compares Gardner's, Sternberg's, and Salovy/Mayer/Goleman's views

New coverage of the Fagan Test of Infant Intelligence

New Careers in Child Development insert on Toosje Thyssen Van Beveren, infant assessment specialist

New Careers in Child Development insert on Sterling Jones, supervisor of gifted and talented education

New figure 9.8 on the correlation between intelligence test scores and twin status

Much expanded coverage of heredity and environment on intelligence—some of this material was in chapter 3 in the last edition and now it is located in one place—chapter 9

Updated coverage of the Abcedarian Intervention program (Ramey, Ramey, & Lanzi, 2001) and new figure 9.9 on early intervention and retention in school

New discussion of heritability

New section on group comparisons, including new material on gender and intelligence

New coverage of changes in the SAT that will take place in 2005

New section: Do Children Have a General Intelligence?

I like the reorganization of this chapter.

—**K. Laurie Dickson** *Northern Arizona University*

An excellent chapter. The reorganization of the chapter is a great improvement.

—**Richard A. Sprott** *California State University*

New figure 10.7, which summarizes language milestones in infancy

Considerably updated coverage of the best way to teach children to read, including recommendations of the National Reading Panel (2000)

New figure 10.10 showing the results of a national assessment of reading achievement and its relation to how much children read daily

Updated coverage of bilingualism and bilingual education, including recent research by Kenji Hakuta and his colleagues (2000) on how long it takes children to develop reading proficiency in a second language

New Careers in Child Development insert on Salvador Tamayo, bilingual education teacher

New figure 10.11 on grammar proficiency and age at arrival in the United States

Updated, expanded discussion of language development in early and middle/late childhood

The chapter's coverage of language theories was well done . . . the chapter does a good job of integrating issues related to culture and diversity, and the discussion of bilingual education is well presented.

—**Shirley-Anne Hensch** *University of Wisconsin*

This chapter provides a comprehensive overview of the research and theories that comprise the foundation for the study of language development. It also offers the student plenty of opportunities to place language and communication into an overall picture of the whole child.

—**Virginia Marchman** *University of Texas at Dallas*

CHAPTER 10
Language Development

Expanded discussion of poverty effects on language development, including new figure 10.3 on language input from professional and welfare families and young children's vocabulary development

Expanded coverage of language and cognitive development with an in-depth discussion of Williams syndrome and Wendy Verougstraete, an individual with Williams syndrome; new figure 10.4 on the disparity in the verbal and motor skills of an individual with Williams syndrome

Considerable expansion of the material on the development of language in infancy with new subsections on babbling and other vocalizations, recognizing language sounds, first words, two-word utterances, and language production/comprehension

Dramatic figure 10.5 showing an infant's brain waves being monitored as the infant listens to different sounds in Patricia Kuhl's research

New figure 10.6 showing variation in language milestones

CHAPTER 11
Emotional Development

New section on social referencing

New discussion of Kagan's research on inhibition to the unfamiliar and recent research on continuity and change in inhibition and lack of inhibition (Pfeifer & others, 2002)

New section on self-regulation of emotion and coping in infancy

Expanded coverage of temperament classification in terms of positive affect and approach, negative affectivity, and effortful control (self-regulation)

New discussion of separation protest, including new figure 11.2 on cross-cultural aspects of separation protest

New graph showing dramatic results of Harlow cloth and wire monkey study (figure 11.6)

Expanded coverage of attachment and culture, including new figure 11.8 on attachment in the United States, Germany, and Japan

New Careers in Child Development insert, on Rashmi Nakhre, child-care director

New discussion of the importance of context and developmental change in temperament, including new figure 11.5

New section on what constitutes emotional competence based on Carolyn Saarni's (1999, 2000) views

New examples of attachment categories tied to the Ainsworth Strange Situation

New research on children of depressed parents (Beardslee, 2002)

New section on gender, culture, and temperament (Putnam, Sanson, & Rothbart, 2002)

Expanded coverage of concept of goodness of fit, including Grazyna Kochanska's research

Added recent cross-cultural study on sensitivity in parenting and secure attachment in infancy (Carbonell & others, 2002)

> *The depth of coverage was excellent. Everything I thought should be covered was presented and the level of detail was good without being too detailed.*
>
> —RICHARD A. SPROTT *California State University*

> *This chapter's coverage of theories of attachment and also the coverage of emotional development were extremely well done.*
>
> —SHIRLEY-ANNE HENSCH *University of Wisconsin*

CHAPTER 12
The Self and Identity

New figure 12.4, Evaluating Self-Esteem, that lets students assess their self-esteem

New section on developmental changes in self-esteem including new figure 12.5 showing the decline of self-esteem in adolescence (Robins & others, 2002)

New figure 12.8, Exploring Your Identity, that lets students assess their identity status in a number of areas

Expanded coverage of identity statuses, including new examples of each status

Updated and expanded discussion of culture, ethnicity, and identity

New Careers in Child Development insert on Armando Ronquillo, high school counselor, who guides Latino students in exploring their identity

> *I thought this chapter was especially good. The information was presented in an interesting manner that was easy to understand.*
>
> —K. LAURIE DICKSON *Northern Arizona University*

> *I rate this chapter an 'A.' It flowed and was easy to read. The balance was great!*
>
> —SUSAN N. SIAW *California State Polytechnic Institute–Pomona*

CHAPTER 13
Gender

New figure 13.2 on expectations for boys and girls

New figure 13.3 on developmental changes in time spent in same-sex and mixed-sex groups

New Careers in Child Development insert on Eleanor Maccoby, professor

Extensively revised and updated coverage of genetic and hormonal influences on gender development, including some fascinating sex reassignment cases (Lippa, 2002)

Extensive revision and updating of material on gender and the brain (Goldstein & others, 2001; Swaab & others, 2001)

New research on gender, reading, and writing (Coley, 2001)

New discussion of relational aggression (Crick & others, 2001; Underwood, 2002)

Research updating of gender and achievement (DeZolt & Hull, 2001)

New discussion of William Pollack's concerns about the "boy code," based on his book *Real Boys*

Extensively revised and updated coverage of gender in school and interactions with teachers (DeZolt & Hull, 2001)

New section on stereotyping of occupations (Liben, Bigler, & Krogh, 2001)

> *This chapter is well done—concrete, clearly written, interesting research studies.*
>
> —JULIA GUTTMAN *Iowa Wesleyan College*

CHAPTER 14
Moral Development

Substantial revision of chapter organization to focus on three main areas: domains of moral development; contexts of moral development; and prosocial and antisocial behavior

Expanded discussion of how moral thoughts can be used to justify immoral behavior with examples from 9/11/01 and the war on terrorism (Bandura, 2002)

Added figure 14.2 showing typical responses of individuals at each of Kohlberg's stages to the Heinz and the druggist story

New research figure on developmental changes in responses to the Kohlberg dilemmas

Substantial updating of the social cognitive theory of moral development based on Bandura's (2002) recent theorizing

New discussion of research on guilt (Koshanska & others, 2002)

New research on the link between maternal warmth and children's empathy (Zhou & others, 2002)

Added coverage of study of caring and prosocial behavior in a highly impoverished group of adolescents

New Careers in Child Development insert on Rodney Hammond, health psychologist, who works with delinquents and alienated youth

New discussion of the Pittsburgh Youth Study

New research on the role of siblings in delinquency

Expansion of material on the antecedents of delinquency to include cognitive distortions, authority conflict, and other factors

Updates on youth and violence, including school violence

New discussion of Fast Track, an extensive delinquency prevention study (The Conduct Problems Prevention Research Group, 2002)

Research update on the values of college students

> *This chapter continues John Santrock's tradition of providing an excellent introduction to the topic of moral development and its relevance to child development and adolescence. The style is engaging; the pedagogical aids pique interest; the balance among theory, research, and application is exemplary; there is a good mix of classic studies and new research; and the material provides a a good basis for more advanced material in graduate courses or professional training.*
>
> —Lawrence Walker *University of British Columbia*

> *The criticism of Kohlberg's theory was impressive. The moral education and service learning discussions are great. I have not seen this type of discussion in other books.*
>
> —K. Laurie Dickson *Northern Arizona University*

CHAPTER 15
Families

New chapter opening story of a mother with multiple sclerosis

New section on marital relationships and parenting (Grych, 2002)

New section on punishment, including new figure 15.3 on attitudes toward corporal punishment in different countries, as well as recent theory and research on punishment (Greven, 2002)

Recent research on child maltreatment on children's emotional regulation and adjustment (Maughan & Cicchetti, 2002)

New section: Parenting Takes Time and Effort

New material from the National Longitudinal Study on Adolescent Health (2000) that focuses on parental involvement and adolescent problems

Two new Careers in Child Development inserts, one on Janis Keyser, a parent educator, the other on Darla Batkin, a marriage and family therapist

Extensively revised and updated section on working mothers, including recent research (Brooks-Gunn, Han, & Waldfogel, 2002)

Updated research on the effects of divorce on children (Hetherington & Kelly, 2002; Hetherington & Stanley-Hagan, 2002),

including new research figure 15.6 on children's emotional problems in divorced and nondivorced families

Updated research on stepfamilies (Hetherington & Stanley-Hagan, 2002)

New section on gay and lesbian families (Patterson, 2002)

Expanded and updated coverage of socioeconomic status and parenting (Hoff, Laursen, & Tardif, 2002)

New Explorations in Child Development box on acculturation and ethnic minority parenting (Coll & Pachter, 2002)

Updated and expanded coverage of fathers and children's development, including new figure 15.7 on fathers' involvement in children's lives (Yeung & others, 2001)

New section on coparenting, including recent research (McHale & others, 2002)

> *Chapter rating: A. The depth of coverage is excellent.*
>
> —Richard A. Sprott *California State University*

CHAPTER 16
Peers

Important new section on gender and peer relations (Maccoby, 1998, 2002)

Revised organization of peer relations with social cognition discussed earlier in the section, followed by peer statuses, bullying, and gender and peer relations

New research on bullying, including new figure 16.3 on bullying behaviors among U.S. youth (Nansel & others, 2001)

New figure 16.4 on developmental changes in self-disclosing conversations with friends and parents

Extensively revised and updated discussion of cliques and crowds with new definitions and more accurate distinction between these social groups

Expanded and updated discussion of adolescent dating and romantic relationships

New figure 16.7 on the age of onset of different types of romantic activity (Buhrmester, 2001)

> *This chapter is successful in providing a clear, compelling account of peer relations in childhood. This chapter reflects John Santrock's careful scholarship; descriptions of topics are precise, accurate, and presented at a good level of detail for a text covering child development. Another important strength is the attention to culture throughout. . . . The prose in this chapter is clear, direct, compelling, and authoritative.*
>
> —Marian Underwood *University of Texas at Dallas*

> *A strong chapter—consistent in its focus on development, easily understandable, relevant research. . . . The chapter is well written and smooth.*
>
> —Julia Guttman *Iowa Wesleyan College*

CHAPTER 17
Schools

Three new Careers in Child Development inserts: Yolanda Garcia, Director of Children's Services/Head Start; Susan Bradburn, elementary school teacher; and Mark Fodness, middle school teacher, including a description of how he helped students cope with the terrorist attack of 9/11/01

Updated coverage of school dropouts, including new figure 17.3 on ethnic variations in school dropout rates

Updated, expanded coverage of the education of students from low-income backgrounds (Bradley & Corwyn, 2002)

Expanded information about strategies for improving relationships among ethnically diverse students, including the role of the teacher as a cultural mediator

Extensively updated, revised coverage of intrinsic and extrinsic motivation (Cameron, 2001), including new section on developmental shifts (Eccles & Wigfield, 2002)

New Explorations in Child Development box on teachers who care, including new figure 17.5 on students' perceptions of caring teachers

New figure 17.6 on behaviors that suggest learned helplessness

New figure 17.7 on mothers' beliefs about the factors responsible for children's math achievement in three countries

Updated coverage of children with disabilities

> *Great chapter. Great discussion about the influence of socioeconomic status relative to culture. Nice coverage of motivation and education.*
> —**K. LAURIE DICKSON** *Northern Arizona University*

> *This chapter does a great job of focusing on the changing demands and roles in schools as children developmentally grow.*
> —**KRISTA SCHOENFELD** *Colby Community College*

CHAPTER 18
Culture

New material on individualistic and collectivist cultures, including new figure 18.1, research on self-conceptions in Chinese and U.S. students

Recent research on the importance of family processes in the social adjustment of children from low-income families (Mistry & others, 2001) and research on providing benefits to low-income families and how this links up with children's development (Gennetian & Miller, 2002; Houston & others, 2001)

Important new section on immigration, including recent theory and research (Fulgini & Yoshikawa, 2003; Roosa & others, 2002; Suarez-Orozco, 2002)

New Careers in Child Development insert on Carola Suarez-Orozco, lecturer, researcher, and codirector of immigration projects

New discussion of recent research on ethnic variations in home environments of European, American, African American, Latino, and Asian American children (Bradley & others, 2001)

Description of recent longitudinal study linking early childhood TV watching with adolescent grades, achievement, and aggression (Anderson & others, 2001), including new figure 18.6 which presents data from the study

Updating of statistics on the amount of TV children watch (National Center for Children Exposed to TV Violence, 2001)

New figure 18.3 on the reading and TV habits of students from low- and middle-SES families

> *Overall, this chapter is well done. It touches on several controversies in child development and discusses them in a thorough, evaluative manner.*
> —**SHIRLEY-ANNE HENSCH** *University of Wisconsin*

ACKNOWLEDGMENTS

I very much appreciate the support and guidance provided to me by many people at McGraw-Hill. Steve Debow, President, and Thalia Dorwick, Editor-in-Chief, have been truly outstanding in their administration of the social sciences area of McGraw-Hill Higher Education. Steve Rutter, Publisher, has brought a wealth of publishing knowledge and vision to bear on improving this book. Rebecca Hope is a wonderful editor who has made very competent decisions and provided valuable advice about many aspects of the tenth edition. This new edition has considerably benefited from developmental editor Mary Kate Hanley's efforts. Melissa Caughlin, Marketing Manager, has contributed in numerous creative ways to this book. Marilyn Rothenberger was a superb project manager and Beatrice Sussman did a stellar job in copyediting the book.

EXPERT RESEARCH CONSULTANTS

I gratefully acknowledge the invaluable feedback and recommendations of the expert research consultants for the tenth edition of this book:

Carolyn Saarni, *Sonoma State University*
W. Andrew Collins, *University of Minnesota*
Susan Harter, *University of Denver*
Craig Hart, *Brigham Young University*
Marian Underwood, *University of Texas at Dallas*
Jaan Valsiner, *University of North Carolina/Clarke University*
Virginia Marchman, *University of Texas at Dallas*
Robert Lickliter, *Florida International University*

Deanna Kuhn, *Columbia University*
Lawrence Walker, *University of British Columbia*

The biographies and photos of the expert research consultants appear on pages xxix-xxxi.

GENERAL TEXT REVIEWERS

I also owe a special gratitude to the instructors teaching the Child Development course who have provided detailed feedback about the book. Many of the changes in *Child Development*, tenth edition, are based on their feedback. In this regard, I thank these individuals.

User-Nonuser Pre-Revision Reviewers

Dara Musher-Eizenman, *Bowling Green State University*
Claire Etaugh, *Bradley University*
Janet A. Fuller, *Mansfield University*
John P. Murray, *Kansas State University*
Randall E. Osborne, *Southwest Texas State University*
Robert Pasnak, *George Mason University*
Alan Russell, *Flinders University*
Frederic Wynn, *County College of Morris*

Tenth Edition Reviewers

Megan E. Bradley, *Frostburg State University*
K. Laurie Dickson, *Northern Arizona University*
Julia Guttman, *Iowa Wesleyan College*
Joyce Hemphill, *University of Wisconsin*
Shirley-Anne Hensch, *University of Wisconsin*
Kathy E. Johnson, *Indiana University–Purdue University Indianapolis*
Krista Schoenfeld, *Colby Community College*
Susan Siaw, *California Polytechnic Institute–Pomona*
Mildred D. Similton, *Pfeiffer University*
Richard Sprott, *California State University*

General Text Reviewers of Previous Editions

I also remain indebted to these individuals who reviewed previous editions and whose recommendations have been carried forward into the present edition:

Ruth L. Ault, *Davidson College*
Mary Ballard, *Appalachian State University*
William H. Barber, *Midwestern State University*
Wayne Benenson, *Illinois State University*
Michael Bergmire, *Jefferson College*
David Bernhardt, *Carleton University*
Kathryn Norcross Black, *Purdue University*
Elaine Blakemore, *Indiana University*
Susan Bland, *Niagara County Community College*
Amy Booth, *Northwestern University*

Marc Bornstein, *National Institute of Child Health and Human Development*
Maureen Callahan, *Webster University*
D. Bruce Carter, *Syracuse University*
Elaine Cassel, *Marymount University, Lord Fairfax Community College*
Steven Ceci, *Cornell University*
Theodore Chandler, *Kent State University*
Dante Cicchetti, *University of Rochester*
Audrey E. Clark, *California State University, Northridge*
Debra E. Clark, *SUNY–Cortland*
Robert Cohen, *The University of Memphis*
John D. Coie, *Duke University*
Cynthia Garcia Coll, *Wellesley College*
Robert C. Coon, *Louisiana State University*
Roger W. Coulson, *Iowa State University*
Fred Danner, *University of Kentucky*
Denise M. DeZolt, *Kent State University*
Daniel R. DiSalvi, *Kean College*
Diane C. Draper, *Iowa State University*
Beverly Brown Dupré, *Southern University at New Orleans*
Glen Elder, Jr., *University of North Carolina*
Dennis T. Farrell, *Luzerne County Community College*
Saul Feinman, *University of Wyoming*
Tiffany Field, *University of Miami (Florida)*
Jane Goins Flanagan, *Lamar University*
L. Sidney Fox, *California State University–Long Beach*
Irma Galejs, *Iowa State University*
Mary Gauvain, *University of California, Riverside*
Colleen Gift, *Highland Community College*
Margaret S. Gill, *Kutztown State College*
Hill Goldsmith, *University of Wisconsin*
Cynthia Graber, *Columbia University*
Nira Grannott, *University of Texas at Dallas*
Donald E. Guenther, *Kent State University*
Robert A. Haaf, *University of Toledo*
Daniel Hart, *Rutgers University*
Elizabeth Hasson, *Westchester University*
Rebecca Heikkinen, *Kent State University*
Stanley Henson, *Arkansas Technical University*
Alice Honig, *Syracuse University*
Helen L. Johnson, *Queens College*
Seth Kalichman, *Loyola University*
Kenneth Kallio, *SUNY–Geneseo*
Maria Kalpidou, *Assumption College*
Daniel W. Kee, *California State University, Fullerton*
Melvyn B. King, *SUNY–Cortland*
Claire Kopp, *UCLA*
Deanna Kuhn, *Columbia University*
John W. Kulig, *Northern Illinois University*
Janice Kupersmidt, *University of North Carolina*
Michael Lamb, *National Institute of Child Health and Human Development*
Daniel K. Lapsley, *University of Notre Dame*
David B. Liberman, *University of Houston*
Marianna Footo Linz, *Marshall University*

Kevin MacDonald, *California State University, Long Beach*
Dottie McCrossen, *University of Ottawa*
Sheryll Mennicke, *Concordia College, St. Paul*
Carolyn Meyer, *Lake Sumter Community College*
Dalton Miller-Jones, *NE Foundation for Children*
Marilyn Moore, *Illinois State University*
Jose E. Nanes, *University of Minnesota*
Sherry J. Neal, *Oklahoma City Community College*
Larry Nucci, *University of Illinois at Chicago*
Daniel J. O'Neill, *Bristol Community College*
Margaret Owen, *Timberlawn Research Foundation*
Elizabeth Pemberton, *University of Delaware*
Herb Pick, *University of Minnesota*
Kathy Lee Pillow, *Arkansas State University, Beebe*
Nan Ratner, *University of Maryland*
Brenda Reimer, *Southern Missouri State*
Cosby Steel Rogers, *Virginia Polytechnic Institute and State University*
Kimberly A. Gordon Rouse, *Ohio State University*
Douglas B. Sawin, *University of Texas, Austin*
Ed Scholwinski, *Southwest Texas State University*
Dale Schunk, *Purdue University*
Bill M. Seay, *Louisiana State University*
Matthew J. Sharps, *University of Colorado*
Marilyn Shea, *University of Maine, Farmington*
Robert Siegler, *Carnegie Mellon University*
Evelyn D. Silva, *Cosumnes River College*
Dorothy Justus Sluss, *Virginia Polytechnic Institute and State University*
Janet Spence, *University of Texas, Austin*
Melanie Spence, *University of Texas at Dallas*
Mark S. Strauss, *University of Pittsburgh*
Donna J. Tyler Thompson, *Midland College*
Cherie Valeithian, *Kent State University*
Lawrence Walker, *University of British Columbia*
Kimberlee L. Whaley, *Ohio State University*
Belinda M. Wholeben, *Northern Illinois University*

SUPPLEMENTS

The tenth edition of *Child Development* is accompanied by a comprehensive and fully integrated array of supplemental materials, both print and electronic, written specifically for instructors and students of child development. In addition, a variety of generic supplements are available to further aid in the teaching and learning of child development.

For the Instructor

Based on comprehensive and extensive feedback from instructors, we spent considerable time and effort in expanding and improving the supplementary materials.

Instructor's Manual By Cosby Steele Rogers and Bonnie Graham, Virginia Polytechnic Institute and State University

This extensively revised and expanded manual provides a variety of useful tools for both the seasoned instructors and those new to the child development course. New features include: the integration of in-class activities for the Lifespan Development course by Dr. Patricia A. Jarvis and Dr. Gary Creasy at Illinois State University, activities and suggestions for encouraging student's critical thinking, and references to additional assets on the Online Learning Center. Instructors will find that all of the course resources have been correlated to the new learning goals system as appropriate. Useful tools from the previous edition have been updated and expanded and include suggested lecture material and research topics, key terms, and essay questions. The Instructor's Manual is available only in electronic format on the Online Learning Center (www.mhhe. com/santrockcd10) and on the Instructor's Resource CD-ROM.

Printed Test Bank By Marilyn Moore, Illinois State University

This comprehensive Test Bank has been extensively revised to include over 2,200 multiple-choice and short-answer/brief essay questions for the text's 18 chapters. Each multiple-choice item is classified as factual, conceptual, or applied, as defined by Benjamin Bloom's taxonomy of educational objectives. New to this edition, each test question is now keyed to a chapter learning goal, and the test bank notes which learning goal each item addresses. In response to customer feedback, this Test Bank also provides page references that indicate where in the text the answer to each item can be found.

Instructor's Resource CD-ROM This CD-ROM offers instructors the opportunity to customize McGraw-Hill materials to prepare for and create their lecture presentations. Among the resources included on the CD-ROM are the Instructor's Manual, Test Bank (In Word, Rich Text, and computerized formats), PowerPoint Presentation, and the *Child Development* Image Gallery.

PowerPoint Presentations The chapter-by-chapter PowerPoint lectures for this edition integrate the text's learning goals, and provide key text material and illustrations, as well as additional illustrations and images not found in the textbook. These presentations are designed to be useful in both small and large lecture settings, and are easily tailored to suit an individual instructor's lectures. This PowerPoint presentation can be found on the Instructor's Resource CD-ROM and on the Instructor's side of the Online Learning Center.

Computerized Test Bank on CD-ROM The computerized Test Bank contains all of the questions in the printed Test Bank and can be used in both Windows and Macintosh platforms. This CD-ROM provides a fully functioning editing feature that enables instructors to integrate their own questions, scramble items, and modify questions.

The McGraw-Hill Developmental Psychology Image Bank This set of 200 full-color images was developed using the best selection of our human development art and tables and is available online for both instructors and students on the text's Online Learning Center.

Online Learning Center This extensive website is designed specifically to accompany the tenth edition of Santrock's *Child Development*, and offers an array of resources for both instructor and student. For instructors, this password-protected website includes a full set of PowerPoint Presentations, hotlinks for the text's topical web links that appear in margins, and for the Taking It to the Net exercises that appear at the end of each chapter. These resources and more can be found by logging on to the website at www.mhhe.com/santrockcd10.

McGraw-Hill's Visual Assets Database (VAD) for Lifespan Development By Jasna Jovanovic, University of Illinois–Urbana-Champaign

McGraw-Hill's Visual Assets Database is a password-protected online database of hundreds of multimedia resources for use in classroom presentations, including original video clips, audio clips, photographs, and illustrations—all designed to bring to life concepts in developmental psychology. In addition to offering ready-made multimedia presentations for every stage of the life span, the VAD's search engine and unique "My Modules" program allows instructors to select from the database's resources to create their own customized presentations, or "modules." These customized presentations are saved in an instructor's folder on the McGraw-Hill site, and the presentation is then run directly from the VAD to the internet-equipped classroom. For information about this unique resource, contact your McGraw-Hill representative.

Multimedia Courseware for Child Development This state-of-the-art interactive CD-ROM set, created by Charlotte Patterson of the University of Virginia, covers central phenomena and classic experiments in child development. It includes hours of video footage of classic and contemporary experiments, detailed viewing guides, related websites, graduated developmental charts, and much more. The content focuses on integrating digital media to better explain physical, cognitive, social, and emotional development throughout childhood and adolescence. This CD-ROM is compatible with both Macs and PCs.

Annual Editions There are two Annual Editions that work nicely with the tenth edition of Santrock's *Child Development*. Published by Dushkin/McGraw-Hill, *Child Growth and Development* and *Early Childhood Education* each contain collections of articles related to the latest research and thinking in the field of child development. These editions are updated annually and contain helpful features including a topic guide, an annotated table of contents, unit overviews, and a topical index. For more

information on these annual editions and many more, please visit the Dushkin/McGraw-Hill website: www.dushkin.com or ask your McGraw-Hill representative.

Taking Sides *Clashing Views on Controversial Issues in Childhood and Society*. This debate-style reader is designed to introduce students to controversial viewpoints on the field's most crucial issues. Each issue is carefully framed for the student, and the pro and con essays represent the arguments of leading scholars and commentators in their fields. An Instructor's Guide containing testing material is available. For more information on this *Taking Sides* and many more, please visit the Dushkin/McGraw-Hill website: www.dushkin.com or ask your McGraw-Hill representative.

For the Student

Student Study Guide By Megan E. Bradley, Frostburg State University

The Study Guide provides a complete introduction for students studying child development, beginning with How to Use This Study Guide and Time Management features. This fully revised study guide includes key terms with definitions, a guided review, self tests, and section tests that provide a variety of study and quizzing opportunities for the student. The Study Guide also now thoroughly integrates the learning goals provided in each text chapter. The self-test sections contain multiple-choice questions and comprehensive essays with suggested answers, all of which are keyed to the learning goals.

Interactive CD-ROM for Students This user-friendly CD-ROM gives students an opportunity to test their comprehension of the course material. Prepared specifically to accompany Santrock's *Child Development*, tenth edition, this CD-ROM provides 25 multiple-choice questions for each chapter to help students further test their understanding of key concepts. Feedback is provided for each question's answer. In addition, the CD-ROM provides a Learner Assessment questionnaire to help students discover which type of learner they are, of the three types covered in the program.

Online Learning Center This extensive website, designed specifically to accompany Santrock's *Child Development*, tenth edition, offers an array of resources for instructors and students. For students, the website includes interactive quizzes and exercises, key terms, chapter outlines and summaries, as well as hotlinks for the text's topical web links that appear in the margins and for the *Taking It to the Net* exercises that appear at the end of the chapter. These resources and more can be found by logging on to the website at www.mhhe.com/santrockcd10.

Expert Consultants

Carolyn Saarni
Sonoma State University

Carolyn Saarni is one of the world's leading experts on children's emotional development. She received her Ph.D. from the University of California at Berkeley and her first academic appointment was at New York University. Since 1980 Saarni has been a Professor and subsequently Chair of the Graduate Department of Counseling at Sonoma State University in California where she trains prospective marriage, family, child, and school counselors. Her research has focused on how children learn that they can adopt an emotional front—that is, what they express emotionally does not need to match what they really feel. She has also investigated how children use this knowledge strategically in their interpersonal relations with others as well as when coping with aversive feelings. Her research has been funded by the National Science Foundation and the Spencer Foundation, among others. Saarni has co-edited several books on children's emotional development and most recently published *The Development of Emotional Competence*. The thesis of this book is that the skills of emotional competence are contextualized by culture, including moral values and beliefs about "how emotion works." She has also authored numerous chapters and articles on children's emotional development and is regularly consulted by the popular media on topics concerning emotional development in children and youth.

W. Andrew Collins
University of Minnesota

Andrew Collins is one of the leading experts on developmental pathways, parenting, and adolescent development.

Trajectories and processes of change in close relationships are the focus of Dr. Collins' current research. This work is part of the Minnesota Longitudinal Study of Parents and Children. His research team is currently examining two aspects of development and close relationships. In one line of work, they are conducting intensive interviews and observation with the participants in the project, who are now in their mid-twenties, and with their romantic partners. The goal is to examine functioning in these intimate relationships as a manifestation of competence appropriate to young adulthood. They have documented links between the characteristics of these relationships and earlier history of relationships with parents and with peers from infancy through adolescence. Recently, this team has discovered that these earlier histories also predict patterns of consistency, change, and qualities of romantic experiences between the ages of 16 and 23. Work is continuing to examine trajectories of romantic experience in connection with the transition to parenthood and with competence in work and other adult roles.

In addition, this research team is studying developmental pathways leading to competencies traditionally associated with adolescent development. For example, they have documented links between competence in early and middle childhood and patterns of both behavioral and emotional autonomy in late adolescence. They also have shown that a history of positive social relationships with parents and with friends is associated with constructive patterns of identity exploration in middle adolescence. Ongoing studies focus on links between these aspects of adolescent competence and subsequent participation and competence in romantic relationships and young adult work roles.

Susan Harter
University of Denver

Susan Harter is recognized as one of the world's foremost experts on the self. Dr. Harter is a Professor of Psychology and Head of the Developmental Psychology Program (both graduate and postdoctoral components) at the University of Denver. She received her Ph.D. from Yale University in 1966. She remained at Yale, as the first faculty woman in the Psychology Department. Her research, focusing on self-esteem, the construction of multiple-selves, false-self behavior, classroom motivation, and emotional development, has been funded by NICHD for the past 25 years. Most recently, she has turned her attention to school violence and the role of the self-system in provoking both depressive and violent ideation.

Her research has resulted in the development of a battery of assessment instruments that are in widespread use in this country and abroad. She has published numerous scholarly articles and chapters, and recently completed a book entitled *The Construction of the Self: Developmental Perspectives* (Guilford, 1999). Dr. Harter has served on NIMH study sections, including chairing the committee on Cognition, Emotion, and Personality. She is also a member of several editorial boards (*Developmental Psychology, Child Development, Psychological Review, Psychological Bulletin, Development and Psychopathology,* and the *American Education Research Journal*).

Craig H. Hart
Brigham Young University

Craig Hart is a leading expert on family processes and developmentally appropriate education. He received his Ph.D. from Purdue University in 1987, and is Professor and Chair of Marriage, Family, and Human Development in the School of Family Life at Brigham Young University. He was formerly an Associate Professor in the School of Human Ecology at Louisiana State University. Dr. Hart has authored and coauthored fifty scientific articles/book chapters and has presented numerous papers at national and international conferences on parenting/familial linkages with children's social development and on developmentally appropriate practices in early childhood education. His work has appeared in leading human development scientific journals such as *Child Development* and *Developmental Psychology,* and in early childhood education research journals including *Early Childhood Research Quarterly* and *Journal of Research in Childhood Education.* He has also published two edited books entitled *Children on Playgrounds: Research Perspectives and Applications* and *Integrated Curriculum and Developmentally Appropriate Practice: Birth to Age Eight.* He currently serves as associate editor for *Early Childhood Research Quarterly* and is co-editor of *Blackwell's Handbook of Childhood Social Development* (2002).

Marion K. Underwood
University of Texas at Dallas

Marion K. Underwood is a leading researcher in children's socioemotional development. She obtained her undergraduate degree from Wellesley College and her doctoral degree in clinical psychology from Duke University. Underwood began her faculty career at Reed College in Portland, Oregon, and is currently a Professor at the University of Texas at Dallas. Her research examines anger, aggression, and gender, with special attention to the development of social aggression among girls. Underwood's research has been published in numerous scientific journals and her research program has been supported by the National Institutes of Mental Heath. She authored the forthcoming book, *Ice and Fire: Social Aggression in Girls.* Underwood also received the 2001 University of Texas Chancellor's Council Outstanding Teacher of the Year Award.

Jaan Valsiner
University of North Carolina/Clarke University

Jaan Valsiner is a leading expert on the role of culture in children's development. Dr. Valsiner received his higher education in Estonia and taught at the University of Tartu until 1980. He left Estonia (which was then part of the USSR) and established himself at the University of North Carolina at Chapel Hill. He has been at Clark since 1997 and is currently the Chair of the Psychology Department. He won the Alexander-von-Humboldt Research Prize in Germany in 1995, and is affiliated with research groups in Brazil, The Netherlands, Australia, and Estonia.

Dr. Valsiner's general interests are in the cultural organization of mental and affective processes in human development across the whole life span. He is also interested in psychology's history as a resource of ideas for contemporary advancement of the discipline, and in theoretical models of human development. He is the editor of *Culture & Psychology* and *From Past to Future,* as well as of the *Handbook of Developmental Psychology* (London: Sage, 2003).

Virginia A. Marchman
University of Texas at Dallas

Virginia Marchman is a leading researcher in children's language development. Dr. Marchman is an Associate Professor in the School of Behavioral and Brain Sciences at the University of Texas at Dallas. Dr. Marchman holds M.A. and Ph.D. degrees from the University of California, Berkeley, in developmental psychology. She has conducted research in several areas of language and cognitive development, language disorders, and early childhood development. Her most recent work focuses on the identification of precursors of language delay and individual differences in lexical and morphological development in monolingual English and bilingual (Spanish and English) speakers. She is on the editorial board of the *Journal of Speech, Language, and Hearing Research* and was named a Distinguished Scholar at the Callier Center for Communication Disorders. Dr. Marchman is also a member of the Advisory Board for the MacArthur Communicative Development Inventories, a set of parent report instruments used to assess the development of language and communication in infants and toddlers.

Robert Lickliter
Florida International University

Robert Lickliter is a leading expert on biological foundations of early development. Dr. Lickliter conducts research on the development of intersensory perception in animal and human infants. In particular his work focuses on prenatal sensory experience and its role in early perception, learning, and memory. Dr. Lickliter currently serves on the editorial boards of *Infancy* and *Developmental Psychobiology* and is the President-Elect of the International Society for Developmental Psychobiology. He teaches courses on biopsychology, developmental psychology, and animal behavior.

Deanna Kuhn
Columbia University

Deanna Kuhn is a leading expert on children's cognition. Professor Kuhn (Ph. D. University of California, Berkeley, 1969) teaches courses in cognitive development, critical thinking, research methods in developmental psychology, and the application of developmental psychology to education.

She is involved in the study of critical thinking and reasoning from a developmental perspective and its implications for education. Her research has involved a wide range of age groups from middle childhood through old age.

Lawerence Walker
University of British Columbia

Lawrence Walker is one of the world's leading experts on moral development. Dr. Walker's primary research interests and activities concern the development of moral functioning: reasoning, personality, character, and moral action. Earlier research focused on an examination of the validity of the central assumptions of a stage theory of moral development, and the processes in developmental progression. Other research has examined the issue of gender and cultural differences in moral reasoning and the role of family and peer interactions in the development of moral reasoning. Current research focuses on four issues: (1) individuals' conceptions of morality and the moral domain, (2) the psychological functioning of moral exemplars, (3) models of developmental stage transition, and (4) the development of the moral personality.

Student-Driven Pedagogy

This book provides you with important study tools to help you more effectively learn about child development. Especially important is the learning goals system that is integrated throughout each chapter. In the visual walk-through of features, pay special attention to how the learning goals system works.

THE LEARNING GOALS SYSTEM

Using the learning goals system will help you to learn more material more easily. Key aspects of the learning goals system are the learning goals, chapter maps, review and reflect, and Reach Your Learning Goals sections, which are all linked together.

At the beginning of each chapter, you will see a page that includes both a chapter outline and three to six learning goals that preview the chapter's main themes and underscore the most important ideas in the chapter. Then, at the beginning of each major section of a chapter, you will see a mini–chapter map that provides you with a visual organization of the key topics you are about to read in the section. At the end of each section is Review and Reflect, in which the learning goal for the section is restated, a series of review questions related to the mini–chapter map are asked, and a question that encourages you to think critically about a topic related to the section appears. At the end of the chapter, you will come to a section titled Reach Your Learning Goals. This includes an overall chapter map that visually organizes all of the main headings, a restatement of the chapter's learning goals, and a summary of the chapter's content that is directly linked to the chapter outline at the beginning of the chapter and the questions asked in the Review part of Review and Reflect within the chapter. The summary essentially answers the questions asked in the within-chapter Review sections.

Chapter Opening Outline and Learning Goals

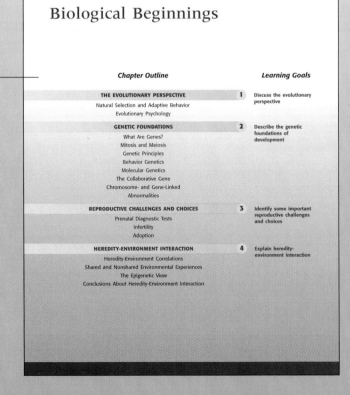

Biological Beginnings

Chapter Outline		Learning Goals
THE EVOLUTIONARY PERSPECTIVE	**1**	Discuss the evolutionary perspective
Natural Selection and Adaptive Behavior		
Evolutionary Psychology		
GENETIC FOUNDATIONS	**2**	Describe the genetic foundations of development
What Are Genes?		
Mitosis and Meiosis		
Genetic Principles		
Behavior Genetics		
Molecular Genetics		
The Collaborative Gene		
Chromosome- and Gene-Linked Abnormalities		
REPRODUCTIVE CHALLENGES AND CHOICES	**3**	Identify some important reproductive challenges and choices
Prenatal Diagnostic Tests		
Infertility		
Adoption		
HEREDITY-ENVIRONMENT INTERACTION	**4**	Explain heredity-environment interaction
Heredity-Environment Correlations		
Shared and Nonshared Environmental Experiences		
The Epigenetic View		
Conclusions About Heredity-Environment Interaction		

Mini–Chapter Map

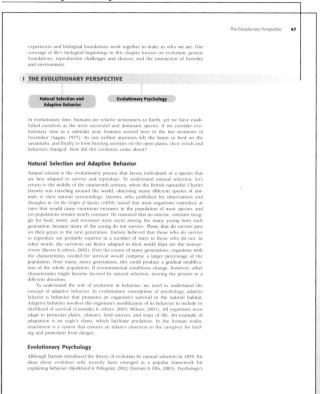

Review and Reflect

Reach Your Learning Goals

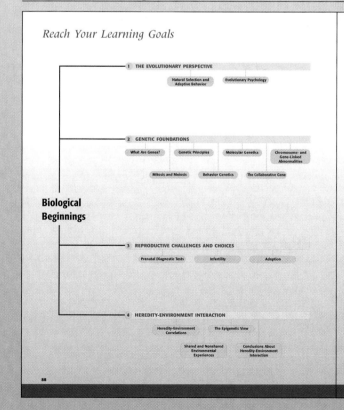

OTHER LEARNING SYSTEM FEATURES

Explorations in Child Development

These boxes provide more in-depth discussion of child development with ethnicity, and many of them focus on high-interest applications and the sociocultural worlds of children.

Images of Child Development

Each chapter opens with a high-interest story that is linked to the chapter's content.

Careers in Child Development

Every chapter has one or more Careers in Child Development inserts, which feature a person working in a life-span field related to the chapter's content.

A Careers in Child Development Appendix that describes a number of careers appears after chapter 18.

Key Terms and Glossary

Key terms appear in boldface. Their definitions appear in the margin near where they are introduced.

70 Chapter 3 Biological Beginnings

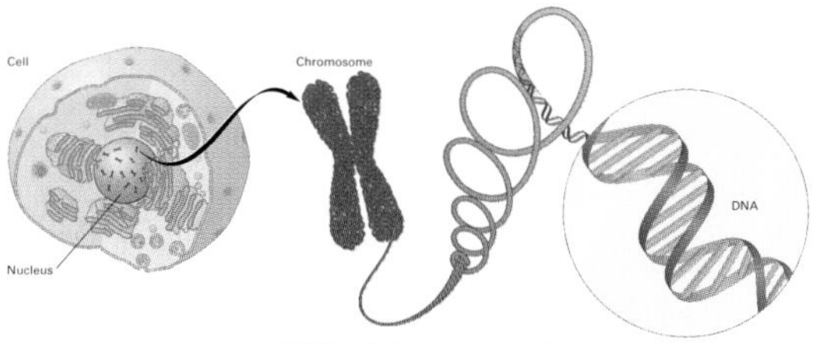

FIGURE 3.1 Cells, Chromosomes, Genes, and DNA

(*Left*) The body contains trillions of cells, which are the basic structural units of life. Each cell contains a central structure, the nucleus. (*Middle*) Chromosomes and genes are located in the nucleus of the cell. Chromosomes are made up of threadlike structures composed of DNA molecules. (*Right*) A gene is a segment of DNA that contains the hereditary code. The structure of DNA is a spiraled double chain of molecules.

What Are Genes?

Each of us began life as a single cell weighing about one twenty-millionth of an ounce! This tiny piece of matter housed our entire genetic code—information about who we would become. These instructions orchestrated growth from that single cell to a person made of trillions of cells, each containing a perfect replica of the original genetic code (Wilson, 2003).

The nucleus of each human cell contains 46 **chromosomes,** which are threadlike structures that come in 23 pairs, one member of each pair coming from each parent. Chromosomes are made up of deoxyribonucleic acid, or **DNA,** a complex molecule that contains genetic information. DNA's "double helix" shape looks like a spiral staircase. **Genes,** the units of hereditary information, are short segments of DNA. Genes carry information that enables cells to reproduce and manufacture the proteins needed to sustain life. Chromosomes, DNA, and genes can be mysterious. To gain a better understanding of this mystery, see figure 3.1.

chromosomes Threadlike structures that come in 23 pairs, one member of each pair coming from each parent. Chromosomes contain the genetic substance DNA.

DNA A complex molecule that contains genetic information.

genes Units of hereditary information composed of DNA. Genes carry information that enables cells to reproduce themselves and manufacture the proteins that maintain life.

mitosis The process by which each chromosome in a cell's nucleus duplicates itself.

meiosis The process by which cells in the reproductive organs divide into gametes (sperm in males, eggs in females), which have half of the genetic material of the parent cell.

Mitosis and Meiosis

Mitosis and meiosis are processes of cellular reproduction by which DNA is distributed to new cells. **Mitosis** is the process of cell division by which each chromosome in the cell's nucleus duplicates itself. The resulting 46 chromosomes move to the opposite sides of the cell, then the cell separates, and two new daughter cells are formed with each now containing 46 identical chromosomes. Thus the process of mitosis allows DNA to duplicate itself.

A specialized division of chromosomes occurs during the formation of reproductive cells. **Meiosis** is the process by which cells in the reproductive organs divide into gametes (sperm in males, eggs in females), which have half the genetic material of the parent cell. Here are differences between mitosis and meiosis:

- In mitosis, the focus is on cell growth and repair, whereas meiosis involves sexual reproduction.

Key terms also are listed and page-referenced at the end of each chapter.

Key Terms

evolutionary psychology 68
chromosomes 70
DNA 70
genes 70
mitosis 70
meiosis 70
reproduction 71
zygote 71
genotype 73
phenotype 73
reaction range 73
canalization 73
behavior genetics 74
twin study 74
adoption study 74
Down syndrome 78
Klinefelter syndrome 78
fragile X syndrome 78
Turner syndrome 78
XYY syndrome 78
phenylketonuria (PKU) 78
sickle-cell anemia 79
passive genotype-environment correlations 85
evocative genotype-environment correlations 85
active (niche-picking) genotype-environment correlations 85
shared environmental experiences 85
nonshared environmental experiences 86
epigenetic view 86

Key terms are alphabetically listed, defined, and page-referenced in a Glossary at the end of the book.

G-2 Glossary

basic-skills-and-phonetics approach An approach that emphasizes that reading instruction should teach phonetics and its basic rules for translating written symbols into sounds. 334

Bayley Scales of Infant Development Widely used scales in assessing infant development with three main components: a Mental Scale, a Motor Scale, and a Behavior Rating Scale. 295

behavior genetics The study of the degree and nature of behavior's basis in heredity. 74

biological processes Changes in an individual's body. 17

blastocyst The inner layer of cells that develops during the germinal period. These cells later develop into the embryo. 95

bonding The formation of a close connection, especially a physical bond between parents and their newborn in the period shortly after birth. 122

brainstorming A technique in which children are encouraged to come up with creative ideas in a group, play off each other's ideas, and say practically whatever comes to mind. 301

Brazelton Neonatal Behavioral Assessment Scale A test given several days after birth to assess newborns' neurological development, reflexes, and reactions to people. 118

breech position The baby's position in the uterus that causes the buttocks to be the first part to emerge from the vagina. 113

Broca's area An area of the brain's left frontal lobe that directs the muscle movements involved in speech production. 318

bulimia nervosa An eating disorder that involves a binge-and-purge sequence on a regular basis. 179

C

canalization The process by which certain characteristics take a narrow path or developmental course. Apparently, preservative forces help to protect a person from environmental extremes. 73

care perspective The moral perspective, emphasized by Carol Gilligan, that views people in terms of their connectedness with others and emphasizes interpersonal communication, relationships with others, and concern for others. 444

case study An in-depth look at a single individual. 46

centration The focusing of attention on one characteristic to the exclusion of all others. 217

cephalocaudal pattern The sequence in which the greatest growth occurs at the top—the head—with physical growth in size, weight, and feature differentiation gradually working from top to bottom. 131

character education A direct approach that involves teaching students a basic moral literacy to prevent them from engaging in immoral behavior and doing harm to themselves or others. 453

child-centered kindergarten Education that involves the whole child by considering both the child's physical, cognitive, and social development and the child's needs, interests, and learning styles. 544

child-directed speech The kind of speech often used by adults to talk to babies and young children—in a higher pitch than normal and with simple words and sentences. 321

chromosomes Threadlike structures that come in 23 pairs, one member of each pair coming from each parent. Chromosomes contain the genetic substance DNA. 70

cliques Small groups that range from 2 to about 12 individuals and average about 5 to 6 individuals. Cliques can form because of friendship or because individuals engage in similar activities, and members usually are of the same sex and about the same age. 527

cognitive appraisal Lazarus' term for children's interpretations of events in their lives as harmful, threatening, or challenging, and their determination of whether they have the resources to effectively cope with the event. 359

cognitive constructivist approaches Approaches that emphasize the child's active, cognitive construction of knowledge and understanding; Piaget's theory is an example of this approach. 541

cognitive developmental theory of gender In this view, children's gender-typing occurs after they have developed a concept of gender. Once they begin to consistently conceive of themselves as male or female, children often organize their world on the basis of gender. 419

cognitive moral education A concept based on the belief that students should learn to value things like democracy and justice as their moral reasoning develops. 454

cognitive processes Changes in an individual's thought, intelligence, and language. 17

collectivism Emphasizing values that serve the group by subordinating personal goals to preserve group integrity, interdependence of members, and harmonious relationships. 581

commitment The part of identity development in which adolescents show a personal investment in what they are going to do. 398

concepts Categories used to group objects, events, and characteristics on the basis of common properties. 260

conduct disorder The psychiatric diagnosis category used when multiple behaviors occur over a six-month period. These behaviors include truancy, running away, fire setting, cruelty to animals, breaking and entering, excessive fighting, and others. When three or more of these behaviors co-occur before the age of 15, and the child or adolescent is considered unmanageable or out of control, the clinical diagnosis is conduct disorder. 458

connectedness An important element in adolescent identity development. It consists of two dimensions: mutuality, sensitivity to and respect for others' views; and permeability, openness to others' views. 400

conservation The idea that an amount stays the same regardless of how its container changes. 217

constructive play Play that combines sensorimotor/practice repetitive activity with symbolic representation of ideas. Constructive play occurs when children engage in self-regulated creation or construction of a product or a problem solution. 521

context The settings, influenced by historical, economic, social, and cultural factors, in which development occurs. 12

continuity view A developmental view that emphasizes the role of early parent-child relationships in constructing a basic way of relating to people throughout the life span. 474

continuity-discontinuity issue The issue regarding whether development involves gradual, cumulative change (continuity) or distinct stages (discontinuity). 20

controversial children Children who are frequently nominated both as someone's best friend and as being disliked. 516

conventional reasoning The second, or intermediate, level in Kohlberg's theory of moral development. Internalization is intermediate. Individuals abide by certain standards (internal), but they are the standards of

genes, there is no person; without environment, there is no person (Scarr & Weinberg, 1980). Heredity and environment operate together—or cooperate—to produce a person's intelligence, temperament, height, weight, ability to pitch a baseball, ability to read, and so on (Gottlieb, 2001, 2002; Gottlieb, Wahlsten, & Lickliter, 1998; Maccoby, 2002). page 21 If an attractive, popular, intelligent girl is elected president of her senior class in high school, is her success due to heredity or to environment? Of course, the answer is both. Because the environment's influence depends on genetically endowed characteristics, we say the two factors *interact* (Mader, 2002).

The relative contributions of heredity and environment are not additive. That is, we can't say that such-and-such a percentage of nature and such-and-such a percentage of experience make us who we are. That's the old view. Nor is it accurate to say that full genetic expression happens once, around conception or birth, after which we carry our genetic legacy into the world to see how far it takes us. Genes produce proteins throughout the life span, in many different environments. Or they don't produce these proteins, depending on how harsh or nourishing those environments are.

nonshared environmental experiences The child's own unique experiences, both within the family and outside the family, that are not shared by another sibling. Thus, experiences occurring within the family can be part of the "nonshared environment."

epigenetic view Emphasizes that development is the result of an ongoing bidirectional interchange between heredity and environment.

Cross-Linkage

This refers you to the primary discussion of key concepts. A specific page reference appears in the text with a backward-pointing arrow each time a key concept occurs in a chapter subsequent to its initial coverage. When you see the cross-linkage, go back to the page listed to obtain a foundation for the concept.

Quotations

These appear at the beginning of the chapter and occasionally in the margins to stimulate further thought about a topic.

Critical Thinking and Content Questions in Photograph Captions

Most photographs have a caption that ends with a critical thinking or knowledge question in italics to stimulate further thought about a topic.

The Internet

Web icons appear a number of times in each chapter. They signal you to go to the book's website where you will find connecting links that provide additional information on the topic discussed in the text. The labels under the Web icon appear as web links at the Santrock *Child Development*, tenth edition website, under that chapter for easy access.

Taking It to the Net, which appears at the end of each chapter, asks questions that you can answer by exploring the Internet. By going to the Santrock website under *Taking It to the Net*, you will be able to connect to other websites, where you can find information that will help you to think more deeply about the question posed.

Key Terms

evolutionary psychology 68	phenotype 73	Turner syndrome 78	active (niche-picking)
chromosomes 70	reaction range 73	XYY syndrome 78	genotype-environment
DNA 70	canalization 73	phenylketonuria (PKU) 78	correlations 85
genes 70	behavior genetics 74	sickle-cell anemia 79	shared environmental
mitosis 70	twin study 74	passive genotype-environment	experiences 85
meiosis 70	adoption study 74	correlations 85	nonshared environmental
reproduction 71	Down syndrome 78	evocative genotype-	experiences 86
zygote 71	Klinefelter syndrome 78	environment correlations	epigenetic view 86
genotype 73	fragile X syndrome 78	85	

Key People

Thomas Bouchard 66	Albert Bandura 69	David Moore 76	Robert Plomin 86
Charles Darwin 67	Steven Jay Gould 69	Barry Commoner 77	Judith Harris 87
David Buss 68	Gilbert Gottlieb 74	Sandra Scarr 84	

Key People

The most important theorists and researchers in the chapter are listed and page-referenced at the end of each chapter.

Online Learning Center

This directs you to the Online Learning Center for this book, where you will find many learning activities to improve your knowledge and understanding of the chapter.

Taking It to the Net

1. Ahmahl, a biochemistry major, is writing a psychology paper on the potential dilemmas that society and scientists may face as a result of the decoding of the human genome. What are some of the main issues or concerns that Ahmahl should address in his class paper?

2. Brandon and Katie are thrilled to learn that they are expecting their first child. They are curious about the genetic makeup of their unborn child and want to know (a) what disorders might be identified through prenatal genetic testing, and (b) which

tests, if any, Katie should undergo to help determine this information.

3. Greg and Courtenay have three boys. They would love to have a girl. Courtenay read that there is a clinic in Virginia where you can pick the sex of your child. How successful are such efforts? Would you want to have this choice available to you?

Connect to **www.mhhe.com/santrockcd10** to research the answers and complete these exercises.

E-Learning Tools

To help you master the material in this chapter, you'll find a number of valuable study tools on the Student CD-ROM that accompanies this book. Also visit the Online Learning Center for *Child Development*, tenth edition (**www.mhhe.com/santrockcd10**) where you'll find these additional resources:

• Build your decision-making skills by trying your hand at the parenting, nursing, and education "Scenarios" on the Online Learning Center.

91

If I Had My Child to Raise Over Again

If I had my child to raise all over again,

I'd finger paint more, and point the finger less.

I'd do less correcting, and more connecting.

I'd take my eyes off my watch, and watch with my eyes.

I would care to know less, and know to care more.

I'd take more hikes and fly more kites.

I'd stop playing serious, and seriously play.

I would run through more fields, and gaze at more stars.

I'd do more hugging, and less tugging.

I would be firm less often, and affirm much more.

I'd build self-esteem first, and the house later.

I'd teach less about the love of power,

And more about the power of love.

DIANE LOOMANS

The Nature of Child Development

In every child who is born, under no matter what circumstances, and of no matter what parents, the potentiality of the human race is born again.

—JAMES AGEE
American Writer, 20th Century

Examining the shape of childhood allows us to understand it better. Every childhood is distinct, the first chapter of a new biography in the world. This book is about children's development, its universal features, its individual variations, its nature at the beginning of the twenty-first century. *Child Development* is about the rhythm and meaning of children's lives, about turning mystery into understanding, and about weaving together a portrait of who each of us was, is, and will be. In Section 1, you will read two chapters: "Introduction" (chapter 1) and "The Science of Child Development" (chapter 2).

CHAPTER

1

*We reach backward to
our parents and forward
to our children and
through their children to
a future we will never
see, but about which we
need to care.*

—CARL JUNG
Swiss Psychoanalyst, 20th Century

Introduction

Chapter Outline

CHILD DEVELOPMENT—YESTERDAY AND TODAY

Historical Views of Childhood

The Modern Study of Child Development

Today's Children: Some Contemporary Concerns

Social Policy and Children's Development

DEVELOPMENTAL PROCESSES AND PERIODS

Biological, Cognitive, and Socioemotional Processess

Periods of Development

DEVELOPMENTAL ISSUES

Nature and Nurture

Continuity and Discontinuity

Early and Later Experience

Evaluating the Developmental Issues

Learning Goals

1 Describe the past and the present in the field of child development

2 Identify the most important developmental processes and periods

3 Describe three key developmental issues

Alice Walker

Jeffrey Dahmer's senior portrait in high school.

The Stories of Jeffrey Dahmer and Alice Walker

Jeffrey Dahmer had a troubled childhood. His parents constantly bickered before they divorced, his mother had emotional problems and doted on his younger brother, and he felt that his father neglected him. When he was 8 years old, Jeffrey was sexually abused by an older boy. But most individuals who suffer through such childhood pains never go on to commit Dahmer's grisly crimes.

In 1991, a man in handcuffs dashed out of Dahmer's bizarrely cluttered apartment in a tough Milwaukee neighborhood, called the police, and stammered that Dahmer had tried to kill him. At least 17 other victims did not get away.

Alice Walker was born in 1944. She was the eighth child of Georgia sharecroppers who earned $300 a year. When Walker was 8, her brother accidentally shot her in the left eye with a BB gun. By the time her parents got her to the hospital a week later (they had no car), she was blind in that eye and it had developed a disfiguring layer of scar tissue.

Despite the counts against her, Alice Walker went on to become an essayist, a poet, and an award-winning novelist. She won the Pulitzer Prize for her book *The Color Purple*. Like her characters, especially the women, Alice Walker overcame pain and anger to celebrate the human spirit. Walker writes about people who "make it, who come out of nothing. People who triumph."

What leads one child to grow up and commit brutal acts of violence and another to turn poverty and trauma into a rich literary harvest? How can we explain how one child picks up the pieces of a life shattered by tragedy, while another becomes unhinged by life's stress? Why is it that some children are whirlwinds—full of energy, successful in school, and able to get along well with their peers—while others stay on the sidelines, mere spectators of life? If you ever have wondered about why children turn out the way they do, you have asked yourself the central questions we will explore in this book.

Why study children? Perhaps you are or will be a parent or teacher, and responsibility for children is or will be a part of your everyday life. The more you learn about children, the better you can guide them. Perhaps you hope to gain an understanding of your own history—as an infant, as a child, and as an adolescent. Perhaps you accidentally came across the course description and found it intriguing. Whatever your reasons, you will discover that the study of child development *is* provocative, intriguing, and informative.

This chapter previews the themes and issues that we will explore throughout our study of children's development. First, we will familiarize ourselves with how children were thought of and studied in the past and how they are perceived and studied today. Then we will examine the processes and periods that characterize children's development. Finally, we will examine the primary issues that developmentalists debate, issues that will come up repeatedly in the text.

As you might imagine, understanding children's development, and our own personal journey through childhood, is a rich and complicated undertaking. You will discover that various experts approach the study of children in many different ways and ask many different questions. Amid this richness and complexity we seek to understand how children change as they grow up and the forces that contribute to this change.

1 CHILD DEVELOPMENT—YESTERDAY AND TODAY

- **Historical Views of Childhood**
- **Today's Children: Some Contemporary Concerns**
- **The Modern Study of Child Development**
- **Social Policy and Children's Development**

Everywhere an individual turns in contemporary society, the development and well-being of children capture public attention, the interest of scientists, and the concern of policymakers. Historically, though, interest in the development of children has been uneven.

Historical Views of Childhood

Childhood has become such a distinct period that it is hard to imagine that it was not always thought of in that way. However, in medieval times, laws generally did not distinguish between child and adult offenses. After analyzing samples of art along with available publications, historian Philippe Ariès (1962) concluded that European societies did not accord any special status to children prior to 1600. In paintings, children were often dressed in adultlike clothing (see figure 1.1).

Were children actually treated as miniature adults with no special status in medieval Europe? Ariès' interpretation has been criticized. He primarily sampled aristocratic, idealized subjects, which might have been misleading. In medieval times, children often worked and their emotional bond with parents might not have been as strong as it is for many children today. However, childhood probably was recognized as a distinct phase of life more than Ariès believed. Also, we know that the ancient Egyptians, Greeks, and Romans held rich conceptions of children's development.

Throughout history, philosophers have speculated at length about the nature of children and how they should be reared. Three influential philosophical views portray children in terms of original sin, tabula rasa, and innate goodness:

- In the **original sin view,** especially advocated during the Middle Ages, children were perceived as being basically bad, born into the world as evil beings. The goal of child rearing was to provide salvation, to remove sin from the child's life.
- Toward the end of the seventeenth century, the **tabula rasa view** was proposed by English philosopher John Locke. He argued that children are not innately bad but, instead, are like a "blank tablet." Locke believed that childhood experiences are important in determining adult characteristics. He advised parents to spend time with their children and to help them become contributing members of society.
- In the eighteenth century, the **innate goodness view** was presented by Swiss-born French philosopher Jean-Jacques Rousseau. He stressed that children are inherently good. Because children are basically good, said Rousseau, they should be permitted to grow naturally, with little parental monitoring or constraint.

In the past century and a half, our view of children has changed dramatically. We now conceive of childhood as a highly eventful and unique period of life that lays an important foundation for the adult years and is highly differentiated from them. In most approaches to childhood, distinct periods are identified, in which children master special skills and confront new life tasks. Childhood is no longer

FIGURE 1.1 Historical Perception of Children

This artistic impression shows how children were viewed as miniature adults earlier in history. Artists' renditions of children as miniature adults may have been too stereotypical.

original sin view Advocated during the Middle Ages, the belief that children were born into the world as evil beings and were basically bad.

tabula rasa view The idea, proposed by John Locke, that children are like a "blank tablet."

innate goodness view The idea, presented by Swiss-born philosopher Jean-Jacques Rousseau, that children are inherently good.

*A*h! What would the world
be to us
If the children were no more?
We should dread the desert
behind us
Worse than the dark before.

—HENRY WADSWORTH
LONGFELLOW
American Poet, 19th Century

History of Childhood

seen as an inconvenient "waiting" period during which adults must suffer the incompetencies of the young. We now value childhood as a special time of growth and change, and we invest great resources in caring for and educating our children. We protect them from the stresses and responsibilities of adult work through strict child labor laws. We treat their crimes against society under a special system of juvenile justice. We also have governmental provisions for helping children when ordinary family support systems fail or when families seriously interfere with children's well-being.

The Modern Study of Child Development

The modern era of studying children has a history that spans only a little more than a century (Cairns, 1983, 1998). This era began with some important developments in the late 1800s. Why is this past century so special? During the past century, the study of child development has evolved into a sophisticated science. A number of major theories, along with elegant techniques and methods of study, help organize our thinking about children's development (Lerner, 2002). New knowledge about children—based on direct observation and testing—is accumulating at a breathtaking pace.

During the last quarter of the nineteenth century, a major shift took place—from a strictly philosophical perspective on human psychology to a perspective that includes direct observation and experimentation. Most of the influential early psychologists were trained either in the natural sciences (such as biology or medicine) or in philosophy. In the field of child development, this was true of such influential thinkers as Charles Darwin, G. Stanley Hall, James Mark Baldwin, and Sigmund Freud. The natural scientists, even then, underscored the importance of conducting experiments and collecting reliable observations of what they studied. This approach had advanced the state of knowledge in physics, chemistry, and biology; however, these scientists were not at all sure that people, much less children or infants, could be profitably studied in this way. Their hesitation was due, in part, to a lack of examples to follow in studying children. In addition, philosophers of the time debated, on both intellectual and ethical grounds, whether the methods of science were appropriate for studying people.

The deadlock was broken when some daring thinkers began to study infants, children, and adolescents, trying new methods of study. For example, near the turn of the century, French psychologist Alfred Binet invented many tasks to study attention and memory. He used them to study his own daughters, other normal children, children with mental retardation, extremely gifted children, and adults. Eventually, he collaborated in the development of the first modern test of intelligence, which is named after him (the Binet test). At about the same time, G. Stanley Hall pioneered the use of questionnaires with large groups of children and popularized psychology's findings. In one investigation, Hall tested 400 children in the Boston schools to find out how much they "knew" about themselves and the world, asking them such questions as "Where are your ribs?"

Later, during the 1920s, a large number of child development research centers were created (White, 1995), and their professional staffs began to observe and chart a myriad of behaviors in infants and children. The centers at the Universities of Minnesota, Iowa, California at Berkeley, Columbia, and Toronto became famous for their investigations of children's play, friendship patterns, fears, aggression and conflict, and sociability. This work became closely associated with the so-called child study movement, and a new organization, the Society for Research in Child Development, was formed at about the same time.

Another ardent observer of children was Arnold Gesell. With his photographic dome, Gesell (1928) could systematically observe children's behavior without interrupting them (see figure 1.2). The direct study of children, in which investigators directly observe children's behavior, conduct experiments, and obtain information

FIGURE 1.2 Gesell's Photographic Dome
Cameras rode on metal tracks at the top of the dome and were moved as needed to record the child's activities. Others could observe from outside the dome without being seen by the child.

about children by questioning their parents and teachers, had an auspicious start in the work of these child study experts. The flow of information about children, based on direct study, has not slowed since that time.

Gesell not only developed sophisticated observational strategies for studying children, but he also had some provocative views on the nature of children's development. He theorized that certain characteristics of children simply "bloom" with age because of a biological, maturational blueprint. Gesell strove for precision in charting what a child is like at a specific age. Gesell's views, as well as G. Stanley Hall's, were strongly influenced by Charles Darwin's evolutionary theory (Darwin had made the scientific study of children respectable when he developed a baby journal for recording systematic observations of children). Hall (1904) believed that child development follows a natural evolutionary course that can be revealed by child study. He also theorized that child development unfolds in stages, with distinct motives and capabilities at each stage. Hall had much to say about adolescence, arguing that it is full of "storm and stress."

Sigmund Freud's psychoanalytic theory was prominent in the early part of the twentieth century. Freud believed that children are rarely aware of the motives and reasons for their behavior and that the bulk of their mental life is unconscious. His ideas were compatible with Hall's, emphasizing conflict and biological influences on development, although Freud did stress that a child's experiences with parents in the first five years of life are important determinants of later personality development. Freud envisioned the child moving through a series of psychosexual stages, filled with conflict between biological urges and societal demands. Freud's theory has had a profound influence on the study of children's personality development and socialization, especially in the areas of gender, morality, family processes, and problems and disturbances.

During the 1920s and 1930s, John Watson's (1928) theory of behaviorism influenced thinking about children. Watson proposed a view of children very different from Freud's, arguing that children can be shaped into whatever society wishes by examining and changing the environment. One element of Watson's view, and of behaviorism in general, was a strong belief in the systematic observation of children's behavior under controlled conditions. Watson had some provocative views about child rearing as well. He claimed that parents are too soft on children; quit cuddling and smiling at babies so much, he told parents.

Whereas John Watson was observing the environment's influence on children's behavior and Sigmund Freud was probing the depths of the unconscious mind to discover clues about our early experiences with our parents, others were more concerned about the development of children's conscious thoughts—that is, the thoughts of which they are aware. James Mark Baldwin was a pioneer in the study of children's thought (Cairns, 1998). **Genetic epistemology** was the term that Baldwin gave to the study of how children's knowledge changes over the course of their development. (The term *genetic* at that time was a synonym for "developmental," and the term *epistemology* means "the nature or study of knowledge.") Baldwin's ideas initially were proposed in the 1880s. Later, in the twentieth century, Swiss psychologist Jean Piaget adopted and elaborated on many of Baldwin's themes, keenly observing the development of thoughts in his own children and devising clever experiments to investigate how children think. Piaget became a giant in developmental psychology. Some of you, perhaps, are already familiar with his view that children pass through a series of cognitive, or thought, stages from infancy through adolescence. According to Piaget, children think in a qualitatively different manner than adults do.

Our introduction to several influential and diverse theories of children's development has been brief, designed to give you a glimpse of some of the different ways children have been viewed as the study of child development unfolded. You will read more about theoretical perspectives later in the text. For example, much of chapter 7, "Cognitive Developmental Approaches," is devoted to Piaget's theory.

genetic epistemology The study of how children's knowledge changes over the course of their development.

Today's Children: Some Contemporary Concerns

Consider some of the topics you read about every day in newspapers, magazines, and on the Internet: health and well-being, families and parenting, education, culture and ethnicity, and gender. What child development researchers are discovering in each of these areas has direct and significant consequences for understanding children and for improving their lives (Zigler & Hall, 2000). An important theme of this book is to provide up-to-date coverage of the roles that health and well-being, families and parenting, education, and culture, ethnicity, and gender play in improving children's lives.

*C*hildren are the legacy we leave for the time we will not live to see.

—ARISTOTLE
Greek Philosopher, 4th Century B.C.

Children's Issues
Prevention Programs

Health and Well-Being   Although we have become a nation obsessed with health and well-being, the health and well-being of our nation's children and children in many countries around the world are jeopardized by many factors, including

- poverty
- the AIDS epidemic
- starvation
- poor-quality health care
- inadequate nutrition and exercise
- alcohol and drug abuse in adolescence
- sexual abuse of children

Asian physicians around 2600 B.C. and Greek physicians around 500 B.C. recognized that good habits are essential for good health. They did not blame the gods for illness and think that magic would cure it. They realized that people have some control over their health and well-being. A physician's role was as guide, assisting patients in restoring a natural and emotional balance.

At the beginning of the twenty-first century, once again we recognize the power of lifestyles and psychological states in promoting health and well-being (Hahn & Payne, 2003; Melamed, Roth, & Fogel, 2001; Weiss, 2000). We are returning to the ancient view that the ultimate responsibility for our health and well-being, both ours and our children's, rests in our hands. Parents, teachers, nurses, physicians, and other adults serve as important models of health and well-being for children. They also can communicate effective strategies for health and well-being to children and monitor how effectively children are following these strategies (Weissberg & Greenberg, 1998).

Luis Vargas is a child clinical psychologist who has a deep concern about helping children who have become juvenile delinquents and/or substance abusers get their lives back on track. You can read further about Luis Vargas and his work in the Careers in Child Development insert.

Research on Premature Infants   Tiffany Field's (2001) research focuses on how massage therapy can facilitate weight gain in premature infants. In their original research, Field and her colleagues (1986) found that massage therapy conducted three times per day for 15 minutes with preterm infants led to 47 percent greater weight gain than standard medical treatment. The massaged infants also showed improved social and motor skills. The same positive results for massage therapy has been found in the Phillipines and Israel (Goldstein-Ferber, 1997; Jinon, 1996). We will further discuss Field's massage therapy in chapter 4, "Prenatal Development and Birth."

Families and Parenting   Experts increasingly describe the pressures on contemporary families (Bornstein & Bradley, 2003; Hetherington & Kelly, 2002). The number of families in which both parents work is increasing; at the same time, the number of one-parent families has risen over the past two decades as a result of a climbing divorce rate. With more children being raised by single parents or by two working parents, the time parents have to spend with their children is being squeezed and the quality of child care is of concern to many (Scarr, 2000). Are working parents more effectively using the decreased time with their children? Do day-care arrangements provide high-quality alternatives for parents? How concerned should we be about the increasing number of latchkey children—those at home alone after school, waiting for their parents to return from work? Answering these questions requires several different kinds of information obtained by experts in child development. For example, information comes from studies of the way working parents use time with their children, studies of the ways various day-care arrangements influence children's social and intellectual growth in relation to home-care arrangements, and examination of the consequences of a child being without adult supervision for hours every day after school (Gottfried, Gottfried, & Bathurst, 2002; Honig, 2002).

Twentieth-century Irish playwright George Bernard Shaw once commented that, although parenting is a very important profession, no test of fitness for it is ever imposed. If a test were imposed, some parents would turn out to be more fit than others. Parents want their children to grow into socially mature individuals, but they often are not sure about what to do to help their children reach this goal. One reason for parents' frustration is that they often get conflicting messages about how to deal with their children. One "expert" might urge them to be more permissive with their children. Another might tell them to place stricter controls on them or they will grow up to be spoiled brats.

You might be a parent someday or might already be one. You should take seriously the importance of rearing your children, because they are the future of our society. Good parenting takes considerable time. If you plan to become a parent, commit yourself day after day, week after week, month after month, and year after year to providing your children with a warm, supportive, safe, and stimulating environment that will make them feel secure and allow them to reach their full potential as human beings.

Understanding the nature of children's development can help you become a better parent (Borkowski, Ramey, & Bristol-Power, 2002; Maccoby, 2001). Many parents learn parenting practices and how to care for their children from their parents—some practices they accept but some they discard. Unfortunately, when parenting practices and child-care strategies are passed from one generation to the next, both desirable and undesirable ones are usually perpetuated. This book and your instructor's lectures in this course can help you become much more knowledgeable about children's development and sort through which practices in your own upbringing you should continue with your own children and which you should abandon.

Careers in Child Development

Luis Vargas, *Clinical Child Psychologist*

Luis Vargas is Director of the Clinical Child Psychology Internship Program and a professor in child and adolescent psychiatry at the University of New Mexico School of Medicine. Luis obtained an undergraduate degree in psychology from Trinity University in Texas and a Ph.D. in clinical psychology at the University of Nebraska–Lincoln.

Luis' work includes assessing and treating children, adolescents, and their families, especially when a child or adolescent has a serious mental disorder. Luis also trains mental health professionals to provide culturally responsive and developmentally appropriate mental health services. In addition, he is interested in cultural and assessment issues with children, adolescents, and their families. He recently co-authored (with Joan Koss-Chiono, a medical anthropologist) (1999) *Working with Latino Youth: Culture, Context, and Development.*

Luis' clinical work is heavily influenced by contextual and ecological theories of development (which we will discuss in chapter 2, "The Science of Child Development"). His first undergraduate course in human development, and subsequent courses in development, contributed to his decision to pursue a career in clinical child psychology.

In the Appendix at the end of this chapter you can read about many careers in child development, including more about the field of child clinical psychology. Also, to provide you with a better sense of the breadth of careers in child development, throughout the book at appropriate places in various chapters we will provide profiles of individuals in various child development careers.

Luis Vargas (*left*) conducting a child therapy session.

Children learn to love when they are loved

Research on Family and Peer Relations One issue that interests researchers who study families focuses on links between family and peer functioning (Ladd & Pettit, 2002). In one recent study of maltreated chidren (children who have been abused) and nonmaltreated children, the maltreated children were more likely to be repeatedly rejected by peers across the childhood and adolescent years (Bolger & Patterson, 2001). The main reason for the rejection was the high rate of aggressive behavior shown by the children who had been abused by their parents. Why do you think the abuse by parents resulted in more aggression toward their peers by the children? We will have more to say about maltreated children in chapter 15, "Families."

Education Like parenting, education is an extremely important dimension of children's lives (Sadker & Sadker, 2003). Education takes place not only in schools. Children learn from their parents, from their siblings, from their peers, from books, from watching television, and from computers.

You might look back on your own education and think of ways it could have been a lot better. Some, or even most, of your school years might have been spent in classrooms in which learning was not enjoyable but boring, stressful, and rigid. Some of your teachers might have not adequately considered your unique needs and skills. On the other hand, you might remember some classrooms and teachers that made learning exciting, something you looked forward to each morning you got up. You liked the teacher and the subject, and you learned.

There is widespread agreement that something needs to be done to improve the education of our nation's children (Oates & Lipton, 2003). What can we do to make the education of children more effective? What can we do to make schools more productive and enjoyable contexts for children's development? Should we make the school days longer or shorter? the school year longer or shorter? or keep it the same and focus more on changing the curriculum itself? Should we emphasize less memorization and give more attention to the development of children's ability to process information more efficiently? Have schools become too soft and watered down? Should they make more demands on, and have higher expectations of, children? Should schools focus only on developing the child's knowledge and cognitive skills, or should they pay more attention to the whole child and consider the child's socioemotional and physical development as well? Should more tax dollars be spent on schools, and should teachers be paid more to educate our nation's children? Should schools be dramatically changed so that they serve as a locus for a wide range of services, such as primary health care, child care, preschool education, parent education, recreation, and family counseling, as well as the traditional educational activities, such as learning in the classroom?

Research on Mentoring Mentoring programs are increasingly being advocated as a strategy for improving the achievement of children and adolescents who are at risk for failure. One study focused on 959 adolescents who had a applied to the Big Brothers/Big Sisters program (Rhodes, Grossman, & Resch, 2000). Half of the adolescents were mentored through extensive discussions about school, careers, and life, as well as participation in leisure activities with other adolescents. The other half were not mentored. Mentoring led to reduced unexcused absences from school, improvements in classroom performance, and better relationships with parents.

Sociocultural Contexts: Culture, Ethnicity, and Gender Sociocultural contexts of development involve four important concepts: contexts, culture, ethnicity, and gender. These concepts are central to our discussion of children's development in this book, so we need to define them clearly. **Context** refers to the setting in which development occurs, a setting that is influenced by historical, economic, social, and cultural factors. To sense how important context is in understanding children's development, consider a researcher who wants to discover whether children today are more racially tolerant than children were a decade ago. Without

context The settings, influenced by historical, economic, social, and cultural factors, in which development occurs.

reference to the historical, economic, social, and cultural aspects of race relations, students' racial tolerance cannot be fully understood. Every child's development occurs in numerous contexts (Eccles, 2002; Valsiner, 2000). Contexts include homes, schools, peer groups, churches, cities, neighborhoods, communities, and countries—each with meaningful historical, economic, social, and cultural legacies (Matsumoto, 2001).

Culture encompasses the behavior patterns, beliefs, and all other products of a particular group of people that are passed on from generation to generation. The products result from the interaction between groups of people and their environment over many years. A cultural group can be as large as the United States or as small as an African hunter-gatherer group. Whatever its size, the group's culture influences the identity, learning, and social behavior of its members.

Cross-cultural studies—comparisons of one culture with one or more other cultures—provide information about the degree to which children's development is similar, or universal, across cultures and to what degree it is culture-specific. A special concern in comparing the United States with other cultures is our nation's unsatisfactory record in caring for its children, especially in terms of poverty. For example, the United States is an achievement-oriented culture with a strong work ethic. However, recent cross-cultural studies of American and Japanese children revealed that the Japanese are better at math, spend more time working on math in school, and spend more time doing homework than do Americans (Stevenson, 1995, 2000).

Race and ethnicity are sometimes misrepresented. *Race* is a controversial classification of people according to real or imagined biological characteristics such as skin color and blood group membership (Corsini, 1999). An individual's ethnicity can include his or her race but also many other characteristics (Chun, Organista, & Marín, 2003). Thus, an individual might be White (a racial category) and a fifth-generation Texan who is Catholic and speaks English and Spanish fluently.

Ethnicity (the word *ethnic* comes from the Greek word for "nation") is rooted in cultural heritage, nationality characteristics, race, religion, and language. Ethnicity is central to the development of an **ethnic identity,** which is a sense of membership in an ethnic group, based on shared language, religion, customs, values, history, and race. You are a member of one or more ethnic groups. Your ethnic identity reflects your deliberate decision to identify with an ancestor or ancestral group (Phinney, 2000, 2003). If you are of Native American and African slave ancestry, you might choose to align yourself with the traditions and history of Native Americans, although an outsider might believe that your identity is African American.

The tapestry of American culture has changed dramatically in recent years. Nowhere is the change more noticeable than in the increasing ethnic diversity of America's citizens. Non-White ethnic minority groups—African American, Latino, Native American (American Indian), and Asian American, for example—made up 20 percent of all children and adolescents under the age of 17 in 1989. As we begin the twenty-first century, one-third of all school-age children fall into this category. This changing demography promises not only the richness that diversity produces but also difficult challenges in extending the American dream to individuals of all ethnic groups (Cushner, 2003; McLoyd, 2000). Historically, immigrant and non-White ethnic minorities have found themselves at the bottom of the economic and social order. They have been disproportionately represented among the poor and the inadequately educated (Fuligni & Yoshikawa, 2003; Suárez-Orozco, 2002). Half of all African American children and one-third of all Latino children live in poverty. School dropout rates for minority youth reach the alarming rate of 60 percent in some urban areas. These population trends and our nation's inability to prepare minority individuals for full participation in American life have produced an imperative for the social institutions that serve minorities (Diaz, 2003). Schools, social services, health and mental health agencies, juvenile probation services, and other programs need to become more sensitive to ethnic issues and to provide improved services to ethnic minority and low-income individuals (Banks, 2002, 2003).

Shown here are two Korean-born children on the day they became U.S. citizens. Asian American children are the fastest-growing group of ethnic minority children.

culture The behavior patterns, beliefs, and all other products of a group that are passed on from generation to generation.

cross-cultural studies Comparisons of one culture with one or more other cultures. These provide information about the degree to which children's development is similar, or universal, across cultures, and to the degree to which it is culture-specific.

ethnicity A characteristic based on cultural heritage, nationality characteristics, race, religion, and language.

ethnic identity A sense of membership in an ethnic group, based upon shared language, religion, customs, values, history, and race.

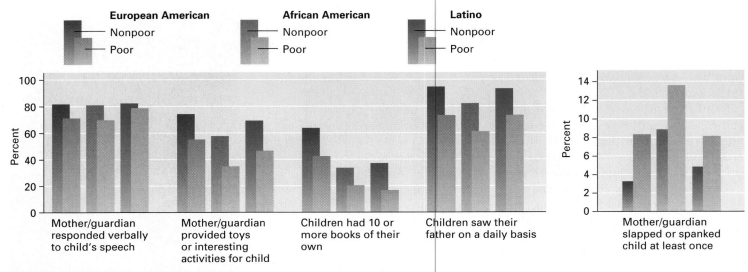

FIGURE 1.3 Home Environments of Infants by Ethnicity and Poverty Status

The above data are based on home observations and maternal interviews obtained in the first three years of children's lives. Although there were some differences across ethnic groups, the most consistent differences were found between families classified as poor and nonpoor. For example, regardless of their ethnic group, children growing up in nonpoor home environments were more likely to have their speech responded to, be provided with toys or interesting activities, have 10 or more books of their own, see their father on a daily basis, and be less likely to be slapped or spanked. Similar findings occurred when children were older.

AskERIC

Education Resources

Diversity

Trends in the Well-Being of Children and Youth

Children Now

Children and Advocacy

An especially important idea in considering minority groups is that, not only is there ethnic diversity within a culture such as the United States, but there is also considerable diversity within each ethnic group (Pang, 2001). Not all African American children come from low-income families. Not all Latino children are members of the Catholic Church. Not all Asian American children are academically gifted. Not all Native American children drop out of school. It is easy to make the mistake of stereotyping the members of an ethnic minority group as all being the same. Keep in mind, as we describe children from ethnic groups, that each group is heterogeneous.

Gender involves the psychological and sociocultural dimensions of being female or male. *Sex* refers to the biological dimension of being female or male. Few aspects of our development are more central to our identity and social relationships than gender (Eagly, 2001). Our society's attitudes about gender are changing, but how much? We will explore many aspects of gender throughout the text.

Research on Children's Ethnicity, Poverty, and Type of Home Environment One study recently examined the home environments of three ethnic groups: European American, African American, and Latino (Bradley & others, 2001). The home environments were assessed by a combination of observations and maternal interviews at five points in children's lives from infancy through early adolescence. There were some ethnic differences but the most consistent results involved poverty, which was a more powerful indicator of the type of home environment children experienced than ethnicity was (See figure 1.3).

Social Policy and Children's Development

Social policy is a national government's course of action designed to promote the welfare of its citizens. The shape and scope of social policy related to children are tied to the political system. The values held by individual lawmakers, the nation's economic strengths and weaknesses, and partisan politics all influence the policy

gender The psychological and sociocultural dimension of being female or male.

social policy A national government's approach to promoting the welfare of its citizens.

agenda. Periods of comprehensive social policy are often the outgrowth of concern over broad social issues. Child labor laws were established in the early twentieth century to protect children and jobs for adults as well; federal day-care funding during World War II was justified by the need for women laborers in factories; and Head Start and other War on Poverty programs in the 1960s were implemented to decrease intergenerational poverty (Zigler & Styfco, 1994).

Out of concern that policymakers are doing too little to protect the well-being of children, researchers increasingly are undertaking studies that they hope will lead to wise and effective decision making in the area of social policy (Maccoby, 2001). When more than 15 percent of all children and almost half of all ethnic minority children are being raised in poverty, when between 40 and 50 percent of all children born today can expect to spend at least five years in a single-parent home, when children and young adolescents are giving birth, when the use and abuse of drugs are widespread, and when the specter of AIDS is present, our nation needs revised social policy (Pittman & others, 2003; Zigler & Hall, 2000).

Among the groups that have worked to improve the lives of children are UNICEF in New York and the Children's Defense Fund in Washington, D.C. At a United Nations convention, a number of children's rights were declared (Limber & Wilcox, 1996). Marian Wright Edelman, president of the Children's Defense Fund, has been a leading advocate of children's rights. Especially troubling to Edelman (1997) are the indicators that rank the United States as one of the worst industrialized nations in terms of social neglect of its children. Edelman says that we need a better health-care system for families, safer schools and neighborhoods, better parent education, and improved family support systems.

At the beginning of the twenty-first century, the well-being of children is one of America's foremost concerns. We all cherish the future of our children, because they are the future of any society. Children who do not reach their potential, who are unable to contribute effectively to society, and who do not take their place as productive adults diminish the power of society's future (Horowitz & O'Brien, 1989). To read about the characteristics that help children be resilient in the face of adversity, and about strategies for preventing problems and enhancing competency, see the Explorations in Child Development box.

If our American way of life fails the child, it fails us all.

—**PEARL BUCK**
American Author, 20th Century

Marian Wright Edelman, president of the Children's Defense Fund (shown here interacting with some young children), has been a tireless advocate of children's rights and has been instrumental in calling attention to the needs of children. *What are some of these needs?*

Explorations in Child Development

Resilience, Prevention, and Competence

Even when children are faced with adverse conditions, such as poverty, there are buffers that help make them resilient and improve their chances of successful development. Some children do triumph over life's adversities (Germezy, 1993). Ann Masten and her colleagues (2001; Masten & Coatsworth, 1998; Masten & Reed, 2002) analyzed the research literature on resilience and concluded that a number of individual factors (such as good intellectual functioning), family factors (close relationship to a caring parent), and extrafamilial factors (bonds to prosocial adults outside the family) characterize resilient children (see figure 1.4).

Norman Garmezy (1993) described a setting in a Harlem neighborhood of New York City to illustrate resilience. In the foyer of the walkup apartment building is a large frame that displays photographs of children who live in the building and a written request that if anyone sees any of the children endangered on the street to bring them back to the apartment house. Garmezy commented that this is an excellent example of adult competence and concern for the safety and well-being of children.

Among the prevention programs aimed at promoting children's competence are those that attempt to build a specific skill in children. These have included programs to teach children interpersonal problem-solving skills, assertiveness training, and other life skills. Recently, prevention programs aimed at improving children's competence have increasingly placed more emphasis on developmental issues, social contexts, and multiple causes (Masten, 2001). A competence en-

hancement program might be two-generational (for example, working to help a child's parents find good jobs and health care, in addition to focusing on the child), include health education for the child, and seek to improve the child's socioemotional skills. For example, broadly applicable social skills such as self-control, stress management, problem solving, decision making, communication, peer resistance, and assertiveness have been found to reduce children's aggressive behavior and improve their adjustment and competence (Weisberg & Greenberg, 1998). Such prevention programs support the concept that effective programs focus not just on a reduction of problems alone but also on competence enhancement.

Children who have a close relationship to a caring parent often show resiliency.

Source	Characteristic
Individual	Good intellectual functioning
	Appealing, sociable, easygoing disposition
	Self-confidence, high self-esteem
	Talents
	Faith
Family	Close relationship to caring parent figure
	Authoritative parenting: warmth, structure, high expectations
	Socioeconomic advantages
	Connections to extended supportive family networks
Extrafamilial Context	Bonds to caring adults outside the family
	Connections to positive organizations
	Attending effective schools

FIGURE 1.4 Characteristics of Resilient Children and Their Contexts

Review and Reflect: Learning Goal 1

1 Describe the past and the present in the field of child development

REVIEW

- How has childhood been discussed through history?
- What is the modern study of child development like?
- What are some contemporary concerns about today's children?
- What is social policy, and what is its status in regard to America's children?

REFLECT

- Imagine what your development as a child would have been like in a culture that offered fewer or distinctly different choices than your own. How might your development have been different if your family has been significantly richer or poorer than it was?

2 DEVELOPMENTAL PROCESSES AND PERIODS

Biological, Cognitive, and Socioemotional Processes

Periods of Development

Each of us develops in certain ways like all other individuals, like some other individuals, and like no other individuals. Most of the time, our attention is directed to a person's uniqueness, but psychologists who study development are drawn to our shared characteristics as well as what makes us unique. As humans, we all have traveled some common paths. Each of us—Leonardo da Vinci, Joan of Arc, George Washington, Martin Luther King, Jr., and you—walked at about the age of 1, engaged in fantasy play as a young child, and became more independent as a youth.

What do psychologists mean when they speak of an individual's development? **Development** is the pattern of change that begins at conception and continues through the life span. Most development involves growth, although it also includes decay (as in death and dying). The pattern of movement is complex because it is the product of several processes—biological, cognitive, and socioemotional.

Biological, Cognitive, and Socioemotional Processes

Biological processes produce changes in an individual's body. Genes inherited from parents, the development of the brain, height and weight gains, motor skills, and the hormonal changes of puberty all reflect the role of biological processes in development.

Cognitive processes refer to changes in an individual's thought, intelligence, and language. The tasks of watching a colorful mobile swinging above a crib, putting together a two-word sentence, memorizing a poem, solving a math problem, and imagining what it would be like to be a movie star all involve cognitive processes.

Socioemotional processes involve changes in an individual's relationships with other people, changes in emotions, and changes in personality. An infant's smile in response to her mother's touch, a young boy's aggressive attack on a playmate, a girl's development of assertiveness, and an adolescent's joy at the senior prom all reflect socioemotional development.

Biological, cognitive, and socioemotional processes are intricately intertwined. For example, consider a baby smiling in response to its mother's touch. This response depends on biological processes (the physical nature of the touch and responsiveness to it), cognitive processes (the ability to understand intentional acts), and socioemotional processes (the act of smiling often reflects a positive emotional feeling and smiling helps to connect infants in positive ways with other human beings).

We typically will study the various processes involved in children's development in separate sections of the book. However, keep in mind that you are studying the development of an integrated human child who has only one interdependent mind and body (see figure 1.5 on page 18).

development The pattern of change that begins at conception and continues through the life cycle.

biological processes Changes in an individual's body.

cognitive processes Changes in an individual's thought, intelligence, and language.

socioemotional processes Changes in an individual's relationships with other people, emotions, and personality.

PEANUTS reprinted by permission of United Features Syndicate, Inc.

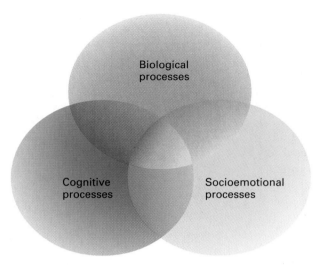

FIGURE 1.5 Changes in Development Are the Result of Biological, Cognitive, and Socioemotional Processes.
The processes interact as individuals develop.

Periods of Development

For the purposes of organization and understanding, development is commonly described in terms of periods. The most widely used classification of developmental periods involves the following sequence: the prenatal period, infancy, early childhood, middle and late childhood, and adolescence. Approximate age ranges are placed on the periods to provide a general idea of when a period first appears and when it ends.

The **prenatal period** is the time from conception to birth, roughly a nine-month period. It is a time of tremendous growth—from a single cell to an organism, complete with a brain and behavioral capabilities.

Infancy is the developmental period that extends from birth to about 18 to 24 months of age. Infancy is a time of extreme dependence on adults. Many psychological activities are just beginning—language, symbolic thought, sensorimotor coordination, and social learning, for example.

Early childhood is the developmental period that extends from the end of infancy to about 5 to 6 years of age; sometimes this period is called the preschool years. During this time, young children learn to become more self-sufficient and to care for themselves, they develop school readiness skills (following instructions, identifying letters), and they spend many hours in play and with peers. First grade typically marks the end of this period.

Middle and late childhood is the developmental period that extends from about 6 to 11 years of age; sometimes this period is referred to as the elementary school years. Children master the fundamental skills of reading, writing, and arithmetic, and they are formally exposed to the larger world and its culture. Achievement becomes a more central theme of the child's world, and self-control increases.

Adolescence is the developmental period of transition from childhood to early adulthood, entered at approximately 10 to 12 years of age and ending at 18 to 22 years of age. Adolescence begins with rapid physical changes—dramatic gains in height and weight; changes in body contour; and the development of sexual characteristics such as enlargement of the breasts, development of pubic and facial hair, and deepening of the voice. At this point in development, the pursuit of independence and an identity are prominent. Thought is more logical, abstract, and idealistic. More and more time is spent outside of the family during this period.

Today, developmentalists do not believe that change ends with adolescence (Baltes, 2000; Santrock, 2002). They describe development as a lifelong process. However, the purpose of this text is to describe the changes in development that take place from conception through adolescence.

The periods of development from conception through adolescence are shown in figure 1.6, along with the processes of development—biological, cognitive, and socioemotional. The interplay of biological, cognitive, and socioemotional processes produces the periods of development.

prenatal period The time from conception to birth.

infancy The developmental period that extends from birth to about 18 to 24 months.

early childhood The developmental period that extends from the end of infancy to about 5 to 6 years of age, sometimes called the preschool years.

middle and late childhood The developmental period that extends from about 6 to 11 years of age, sometimes called the elementary school years.

adolescence The developmental period of transition from childhood to early adulthood, entered at approximately 10 to 12 years of age and ending at 18 to 22 years of age.

Review and Reflect: Learning Goal 2

2 Identify the most important developmental processes and periods

REVIEW

- What are three key developmental processes?
- What are five main developmental periods?

REFLECT

- At what age did you become an adolescent? Were you physically, cognitively, and socioemotionally different when you became an adolescent? If so, how?

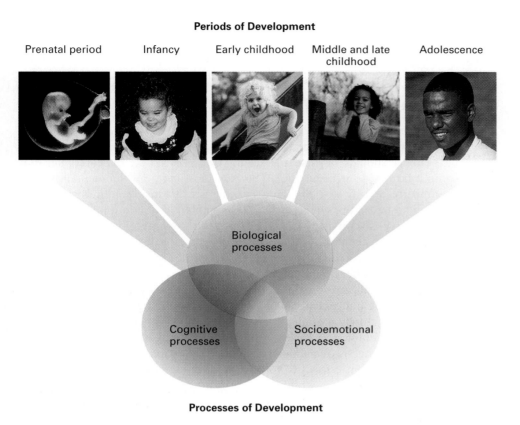

Periods of Development

| Prenatal period | Infancy | Early childhood | Middle and late childhood | Adolescence |

Biological processes

Cognitive processes

Socioemotional processes

Processes of Development

FIGURE 1.6 Processes and Periods of Development

Development moves through the prenatal, infancy, early childhood, middle and late childhood, and adolescence periods. These periods of development are the result of biological, cognitive, and socioemotional processes. Development is the creation of increasingly complex forms.

3 DEVELOPMENTAL ISSUES

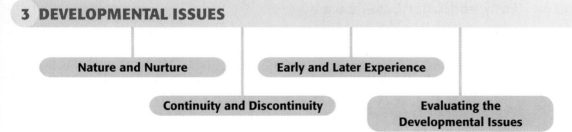

Nature and Nurture

Early and Later Experience

Continuity and Discontinuity

Evaluating the Developmental Issues

The most important issues in the study of children's development include nature and nurture, continuity and discontinuity, and early and later experience.

Nature and Nurture

The **nature-nurture issue** involves the debate about whether development is primarily influenced by nature or by nurture (Rutter, 2002). Nature refers to an organism's biological inheritance, nurture to its environmental experiences. "Nature" proponents claim that the most important influence on development is biological inheritance. "Nurture" proponents claim that environmental experiences are the most important influence.

According to the nature advocates, just as a sunflower grows in an orderly way—unless defeated by an unfriendly environment—so does the human grow in an orderly way. The range of environments can be vast, but the nature approach argues that a genetic blueprint produces commonalities in growth and development. We walk before we talk, speak one word before two words, grow rapidly in infancy and less so in early childhood, and experience a rush of sexual hormones in puberty. The nature proponents acknowledge that extreme environments—those that are psychologically barren or hostile—can depress development. However, they believe that basic growth tendencies are genetically wired into humans.

nature-nurture issue *Nature* refers to an organism's biological inheritance, *nurture* to environmental influences. The "nature" proponents claim biological inheritance is the most important influence on development; the "nurture" proponents claim that environmental experiences are the most important.

Continuity

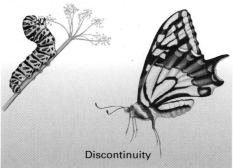

Discontinuity

FIGURE 1.7 Continuity and Discontinuity in Development

Is human development more like that of a seedling gradually growing into a giant oak or more like that of a caterpillar suddenly becoming a butterfly?

continuity-discontinuity issue The issue regarding whether development involves gradual, cumulative change (continuity) or distinct stages (discontinuity).

early-later experience issue The issue of the degree to which early experiences (especially infancy) or later experiences are the key determinants of the child's development.

By contrast, other psychologists emphasize the importance of nurture, or environmental experiences, in development. Experiences run the gamut from the individual's biological environment (nutrition, medical care, drugs, and physical accidents) to the social environment (family, peers, schools, community, media, and culture).

Continuity and Discontinuity

Think about your own development for a moment. Did you become the person you are gradually, like the seedling that slowly, cumulatively grows into a giant oak? Or did you experience sudden, distinct changes in your growth, like the caterpillar that changes into a butterfly (see figure 1.7)? For the most part, developmentalists who emphasize nurture usually describe development as a gradual, continuous process. Those who emphasize nature often describe development as a series of distinct stages.

The **continuity-discontinuity issue** focuses on the extent to which development involves gradual, cumulative change (continuity) or distinct stages (discontinuity). In terms of continuity, as the oak grows from seedling to giant oak, it becomes *more* oak—its development is continuous. Similarly, a child's first word, though seemingly an abrupt, discontinuous event, is actually the result of weeks and months of growth and practice. Puberty, another seemingly abrupt, discontinuous occurrence, is actually a gradual process occurring over several years.

In terms of discontinuity, each person is described as passing through a sequence of stages in which change is qualitatively rather than quantitatively different. As the caterpillar changes to a butterfly, it is not just more caterpillar, it is a *different kind* of organism—its development is discontinuous. Similarly, at some point a child moves from not being able to think abstractly about the world to being able to. This is a qualitative, discontinuous change in development, not a quantitative, continuous change.

Early and Later Experience

Another important developmental topic is the **early-later experience issue,** which focuses on the degree to which early experiences (especially in infancy) or later experiences are the key determinants of the child's development. That is, if infants experience negative, stressful circumstances in their lives, can those experiences be overcome by later, more-positive experiences? Or are the early experiences so critical—possibly because they are the infant's first, prototypical experiences—that they cannot be overridden by a later, better environment?

The early-later experience issue has a long history and continues to be hotly debated among developmentalists (Gottlieb, 2002). Some believe that, unless infants experience warm, nurturant caregiving in the first year or so of life, their development will never be optimal (Bowlby, 1989; Sroufe, Egeland, & Carlson, 1999). Plato was sure that infants who were rocked frequently become better athletes. Nineteenth-century New England ministers told parents in Sunday sermons that the way they handled their infants would determine their children's future character. The emphasis on the importance of early experience rests on the belief that each life is an unbroken trail on which a psychological quality can be traced back to its origin (Kagan, 1992, 2000).

The early-experience doctrine contrasts with the later-experience view that development, like a river, ebbs and flows continuously. The later-experience advocates argue that children are malleable throughout development and that later sensitive caregiving is just as important as earlier sensitive caregiving. A number of life-span developmentalists, who focus on the entire life span rather than only on child development, stress that too little attention has been given to later experiences in development (Baltes, 2000). They accept that early experiences are important contributors to development, but no more important than later experiences. Jerome Kagan (2000) points out that even children who show the qualities of an inhibited temperament, which is linked to heredity, have the capacity to change their behavior. In his research, almost one-third of a group of children who had an inhibited temperament at 2 years of age were not unusually shy or fearful when they were 4 years of age (Kagan & Snidman, 1991).

People in Western cultures, especially those steeped in the Freudian belief that the key experiences in development are children's relationships with their parents in the first five years of life, have tended to support the idea that early experiences are more important than later experiences (Chan, 1963; Lamb & Sternberg, 1992). By contrast, the majority of people in the world do not share this belief. For example, people in many Asian countries believe that experiences occurring after about 6 to 7 years of age are more important to development than are earlier experiences. This stance stems from the long-standing belief in Eastern cultures that children's reasoning skills begin to develop in important ways in the middle childhood years.

One recent book—*The Myth of the First Three Years* (Bruer, 1999)—supports the later-experience argument. The argument is made, based on the available research evidence, that learning and cognitive development do not occur only in the first three years of life but rather are lifelong. The author concludes that too many parents act as though their a switch goes off when a child turns 3, after which further learning either does not take place or is greatly diminished. That is not to say that experiences in the first three years are unimportant, but rather that later experiences are too. This book has been controversial with early experience advocates being especially critical of it (Bornstein, 2000).

What is the nature of the early and later experience issue?

Evaluating the Developmental Issues

Most developmentalists recognize that it is unwise to take an extreme position on the issues of nature and nurture, continuity and discontinuity, and early and later experiences. Development is not all nature or all nurture, not all continuity or all discontinuity, and not all early or later experiences (Rutter, 2002). Nature and nurture, continuity and discontinuity, and early and later experiences all characterize development through the human life span. With respect to the nature-nurture issue, then, the key to development is the *interaction* of nature and nurture rather than either factor alone. Thus, an individual's cognitive development is the result of heredity-environment interaction, not heredity or environment alone. Much more about heredity-environment interaction appears in chapter 3.

Although most developmentalists do not take extreme positions on these three important issues, this consensus has not meant the absence of spirited debate about how strongly development is influenced by each of these factors (Waters, 2001). Are girls less likely to do well in math because of their "feminine" nature or because of society's masculine bias? Can enriched experiences in adolescence remove the "deficits" resulting from childhood experiences of poverty, neglect by parents, and poor schooling? The answers given by developmentalists to such questions depend on their stances on the issues of nature and nurture, continuity and discontinuity, and early and later experience. The answers to these questions also have a bearing on social policy decisions about children and adolescents, and consequently on each of our lives.

Review and Reflect: Learning Goal 3

3 Describe three key developmental issues

REVIEW

- What is the nature and nurture issue?
- What is the continuity and discontinuity issue?
- What is the early and later experience issue?
- What is a good strategy for evaluating the developmental issues?

REFLECT

- Can you identify an early experience that you believe contributed in important ways to your development? Can you identify a recent or current (later) experience that you think had (is having) a strong influence on your development?

Reach Your Learning Goals

Introduction

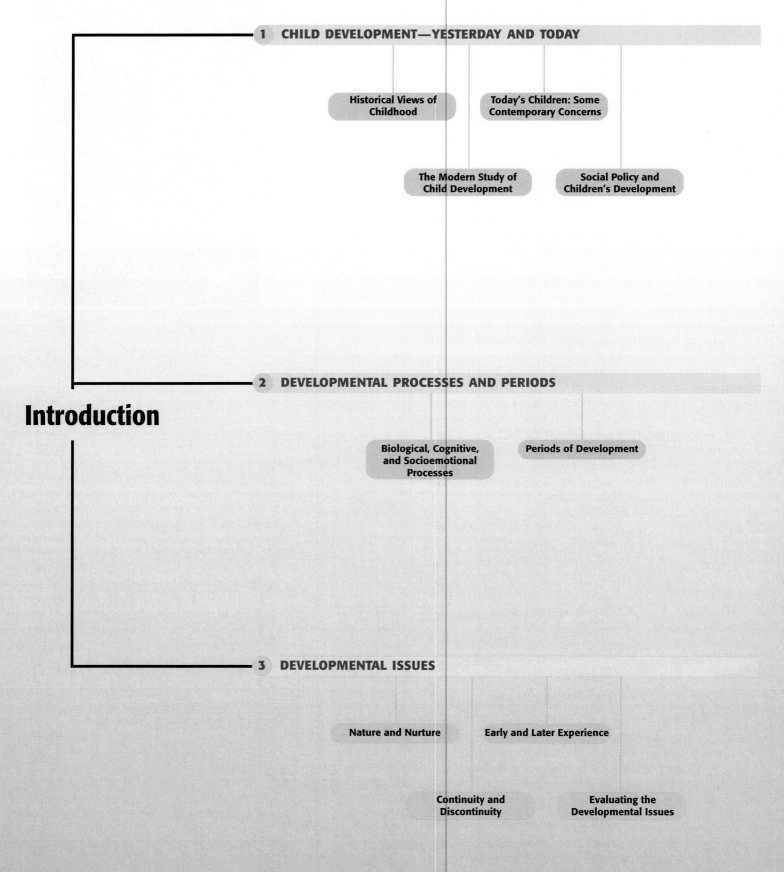

1 CHILD DEVELOPMENT—YESTERDAY AND TODAY

- Historical Views of Childhood
- Today's Children: Some Contemporary Concerns
- The Modern Study of Child Development
- Social Policy and Children's Development

2 DEVELOPMENTAL PROCESSES AND PERIODS

- Biological, Cognitive, and Socioemotional Processes
- Periods of Development

3 DEVELOPMENTAL ISSUES

- Nature and Nurture
- Early and Later Experience
- Continuity and Discontinuity
- Evaluating the Developmental Issues

Summary

1 Discuss the past and the present in the field of child development

- The history of interest in children is long and rich. Prior to the nineteenth century, philosophical views of childhood were prominent, including the notions of original sin, *tabula rasa*, and innate goodness.
- Today, we conceive of childhood as an important time of development. The modern era of studying children spans a little more than a century, an era in which the study of child development has become a sophisticated science. Methodological advances in observation and theoretical views— among them psychoanalytic, behavioral, and cognitive developmental—characterize this scientific theme.
- Four important contemporary concerns in children's development are health and well-being, families and parenting, education, and the sociocultural contexts of the culture, ethnicity, and gender.
- Social policy is a national government's course of action designed to promote the welfare of its citizens. The shape and scope of social policy are influenced by the political system.

2 Identify the most important developmental processes and periods

- Development is the pattern of movement or change that occurs throughout the life span. Development is influenced by an interplay of biological, cognitive, and socioemotional processes.
- Development is commonly divided into the following periods from conception through adolescence: prenatal, infancy, early childhood, middle and late childhood, and adolescence.

3 Describe three key developmental issues

- The nature-nurture issue focuses on the extent to which development is mainly influenced by nature (biological inheritance) or nurture (experience).
- Some developmentalists describe development as continuous (gradual, cumulative change), others describe it as discontinuous (a sequence of abrupt stages).
- The early-later experience issue focuses on whether early experiences (especially in infancy) are more important in development than later experiences.
- Most developmentalists recognize that extreme positions on the nature-nurture, continuity-discontinuity, and early-later experience issues are unwise. Despite this consensus, these issues continue to be spiritedly debated.

Key Terms

original sin view 7
tabula rasa view 7
innate goodness view 7
genetic epistemology 9
context 12
culture 13

cross-cultural studies 13
ethnicity 13
ethnic identity 13
gender 14
social policy 14
development 17

biological processes 17
cognitive processes 17
socioemotional processes 17
prenatal period 18
infancy 18
early childhood 18

middle and late childhood 18
adolescence 18
nature-nurture issue 19
continuity-discontinuity
   issue 20
early-later experience issue 20

Key People

Philippe Ariès 7
John Locke 7
Jean-Jacques Rousseau 7

G. Stanley Hall 8
Charles Darwin 8
Arnold Gesell 8

Sigmund Freud 8
John Watson 9
James Mark Baldwin 9

Jean Piaget 9
Marian Wright Edelman 15
Jerome Kagan 20

Taking It to the Net

1. George is teaching fourth grade. He wants his students to learn about the difficulties and challenges of being a child in colonial America. What was life like for children in the early history of our country?
2. Janice thinks that better and stricter gun control laws will help decrease violent crime among children. Her husband, Elliott, disagrees. Janice found a March 2000 Department of Justice study that provides support for her argument. What facts in the report can she point to in order to convince Elliott?

3. For his political science class, Darren has to track federal funding appropriations in the most recent Congress for any issue of his choice. He has chosen children's issues. How did children and families fare in terms of congressional appropriations in the first half of the 106th Congress?

Connect to **www.mhhe.com/santrockcd10** to research the answers and complete these exercises.

E-Learning Tools

To help you master the material in this chapter, you'll find a number of valuable study tools on the Student CD-ROM that accompanies this book. Also visit the Online Learning Center for *Child Development,* tenth edition (**www.mhhe.com/santrockcd10**) where you'll find these additional resources:

- Build your decision-making skills by trying your hand at the parenting, nursing, and education "Scenarios" on the Online Learning Center.

CHAPTER 2

There is nothing quite so practical as a good theory.

—KURT LEWIN
*American Social Psychologist,
20th Century*

The Science of Child Development

Chapter Outline	***Learning Goals***

THEORIES OF DEVELOPMENT

Psychoanalytic Theories

Cognitive Theories

Behavioral and Social Cognitive Theories

Ethological Theory

Ecological Theory

An Eclectic Theoretical Orientation

1 Describe theories of child development

RESEARCH IN CHILD DEVELOPMENT

Types of Research

Time Span of Research

Research Journals

2 Explain how research on child development is conducted

FACING UP TO RESEARCH CHALLENGES

Conducting Ethical Research

Minimizing Bias

3 Discuss research challenges in child development

The Stories of Erik Erikson and Jean Piaget

Imagine that you have developed a major theory of development. What would influence you to construct this theory? A person interested in developing such a theory usually goes through a long university training program that culminates in a doctoral degree. As part of the training, the future theorist is exposed to many ideas about a particular area of development, such as biological, cognitive, or socioemotional development. Another factor that could explain why someone develops a particular theory is that person's life experiences. Two important developmental theorists, whose views will be described later in the chapter, are Erik Erikson and Jean Piaget. Let's examine a portion of their lives as they were growing up to discover how their experiences might have contributed to the theories they developed.

Erik Homberger Erikson (1902–1994) was born near Frankfurt, Germany, to Danish parents. Before Erik was born, his parents separated, and his mother left Denmark to live in Germany. At age 3, Erik became ill, and his mother took him to see a pediatrician named Homberger. Young Erik's mother fell in love with the pediatrician, married him, and named Erik after his new stepfather.

Erik attended primary school from the ages of 6 to 10 and then the gymnasium (high school) from 11 to 18. He studied art and a number of languages. Erik did not like the atmosphere of formal schooling, and this attitude was reflected in his grades. Rather than going to college at age 18, the adolescent Erikson wandered around Europe, keeping a diary about his experiences. After a year of travel through Europe, he returned to Germany and enrolled in art school, became dissatisfied, and enrolled in another. Later he traveled to Florence, Italy. Psychiatrist Robert Coles described Erikson at this time:

> To the Italians he was the young, tall, thin Nordic expatriate with long, blond hair. He wore a corduroy suit and was seen by his family and friends as not odd or "sick" but as a wandering artist who was trying to come to grips with himself, a not unnatural or unusual struggle. (Coles, 1970, p. 15)

Contrast Erikson's experiences with those of Jean Piaget. Piaget (1896–1980) was born in Neuchâtel, Switzerland. Jean's father was an intellectual who taught young Jean to think systematically. Jean's mother was also very bright. His father had an air of detachment from his mother, whom Piaget described as prone to frequent outbursts of neurotic behavior.

In his autobiography, Piaget detailed why he chose to study cognitive development rather than social or abnormal development:

> I started to forego playing for serious work very early. Indeed, I have always detested any departure from reality, an attitude which I relate to . . . my mother's poor health. It was this disturbing factor which at the beginning of my studies in psychology made me keenly interested in psychoanalytic and pathological psychology. Though this interest helped me to achieve independence and widen my cultural background, I have never since felt any desire to involve myself deeper in that particular direction, always much preferring the study of normalcy and of the workings of the intellect to that of the tricks of the unconscious. (Piaget, 1952a, p. 238)

These snapshots of Erikson and Piaget illustrate how personal experiences might influence the direction in which a particular theorist goes. Erikson's wanderings and search for self contributed to his theory of identity development, and Piaget's intellectual experiences with his parents and schooling contributed to his emphasis on cognitive development.

Theories are part of the science of child development. Some individuals have difficulty thinking of child development as a science like physics, chemistry, and biology. Can a discipline that studies how parents nurture children, how peers interact, the developmental changes in children's thinking, and whether watching TV long hours is linked with being overweight be equated with disciplines that study the molecular structure of a compound and how gravity works? The answer is yes. Science is defined not by *what* it investigates, but by *how* it investigates. Whether you're studying photosynthesis, butterflies, Saturn's moons, or children's development, it is the way you study that makes the approach scientific or not.

This chapter introduces the theories and methods that are the foundation of the science of child development. At the end of the chapter we will explore some of the ethical challenges and biases that researchers must guard against to protect the integrity of their results and repect the rights of the participants in their studies.

1 THEORIES OF DEVELOPMENT

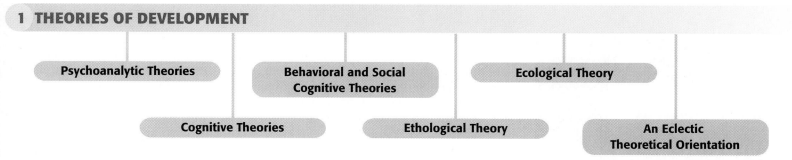

All scientific knowledge stems from a rigorous, systematic method of investigation (Salkind, 2003). The *scientific method* is essentially a four-step process:

1. Conceptualize a process or problem to be studied.
2. Collect research information (data).
3. Analyze data.
4. Draw conclusions.

In step 1, when researchers are formulating a problem to study, they often draw on *theories* and develop *hypotheses* (Miller, 2001). A **theory** is an interrelated, coherent set of ideas that helps to explain and make predictions. **Hypotheses** are specific assumptions and predictions that can be tested to determine their accuracy. For example, a theory on mentoring might attempt to explain and predict why sustained support, guidance, and concrete experience make a difference in the lives of children from impoverished backgrounds. The theory might focus on children's opportunities to model the behavior and strategies of mentors, or it might focus on the effects of individual attention, which might be missing in the children's lives.

The diversity of theories makes understanding children's development a challenging undertaking. Just when you think one theory has the correct explanation of children's development, another theory crops up and makes you rethink your earlier conclusion. To keep from getting frustrated, remember that child development is a complex, multifaceted topic. No single theory has been able to account for all aspects of it. Each theory contributes an important piece to the child development puzzle. Although the theories sometimes disagree about certain aspects of child development, much of their information is complementary rather than contradictory. Together they let us see the total landscape of child development in all its richness.

We will briefly explore five major theoretical perspectives on development: psychoanalytic, cognitive, behavioral and social cognitive, ethological, and ecological. In chapter 1, we described the three major processes involved in children's development: biological, cognitive, and socioemotional. The theoretical approaches that we will describe reflect these processes. Biological processes are very important in Freud's psychoanalytic and ethological theory, cognitive processes in Piaget's,

theory An interrelated, coherent set of ideas that helps to explain and to make predictions.

hypotheses Specific assumptions and predictions that can be tested to determine their accuracy.

Vygotsky's, information-processing, and social cognitive theories. Socioemotional processes are important in Freud's and Erikson's psychoanalytic theories, Vygotsky's sociocultural cognitive theory, behavioral and social cognitive theories, and ecological theory. You will read more about these theories and processes at different points in later chapters in the book.

Psychoanalytic Theories

Psychoanalytic theory describes development as primarily unconscious (beyond awareness) and colored by emotion. Psychoanalytic theorists believe that behavior is merely a surface characteristic and that a true understanding of development requires analyzing the symbolic meanings of behavior and the deep inner workings of the mind. Psychoanalytic theorists also stress that early experiences with parents extensively shape development. These characteristics are highlighted in the main psychoanalytic theory, that of Sigmund Freud.

Freud's Psychosexual Theory Freud (1856–1939) developed his ideas about psychoanalytic theory while working with mental patients. He was a medical doctor who specialized in neurology. He spent most of his years in Vienna, though he moved to London near the end of his career because of Nazi anti-Semitism.

Freud (1917) believed that personality has three structures: the id, the ego, and the superego. The *id*, he said, consists of instincts, which are an individual's reservoir of psychic energy. In Freud's view, the id is totally unconscious; it has no contact with reality. As children experience the demands and constraints of reality, a new part of personality emerges—the *ego*, the Freudian personality structure that deals with the demands of reality. The ego is called the executive branch of personality because it uses reasoning to make decisions. The id and the ego have no morality. They do not take into account whether something is right or wrong. The *superego* is the Freudian structure of personality that is the moral branch of personality. The superego decides whether something is right or wrong. Think of the superego as what we often refer to as our "conscience." You probably are beginning to sense that both the id and the superego make life rough for the ego. Your ego might say, "I will have sex only occasionally and be sure to take the proper precautions because I don't want the intrusion of a child in the development of my career." However, your id is saying, "I want to be satisfied; sex is pleasurable." Your superego is at work, too: "I feel guilty about having sex."

As Freud listened to, probed, and analyzed his patients, he became convinced that their problems were the result of experiences early in life. Freud believed that we go through five stages of psychosexual development, and that at each stage of development we experience pleasure in one part of the body more than in others.

Freud thought that our adult personality is determined by the way we resolve conflicts between these early sources of pleasure—the mouth, the anus, and then the genitals—and the demands of reality. When these conflicts are not resolved, the individual may become fixated at a particular stage of development. Fixation occurs when the individual remains locked in an earlier developmental stage because needs are under- or overgratified. For example, a parent might wean a child too early, be too strict in toilet training the child, punish the child for masturbation, or "smother" the child with too much attention. Figure 2.1 illustrates the five Freudian stages.

The *oral stage* is the first Freudian stage of development, occurring during the first 18 months of life, in which the infant's pleasure centers around the mouth. Chewing, sucking, and biting are the chief sources of pleasure. These actions reduce tension in the infant.

The *anal stage* is the second Freudian stage of development, occurring between $1\frac{1}{2}$ and 3 years of age, in which the child's greatest pleasure involves the anus or the eliminative functions associated with it. In Freud's view, the exercise of anal muscles reduces tension.

Sigmund Freud, the pioneering architect of psychoanalytic theory. *What are some characteristics of Freud's theory?*

www.mhhe.com/santrockcd10

Freud's Theory

psychoanalytic theory Describes development as primarily unconscious and heavily colored by emotion. Behavior is merely a surface characteristic, and the symbolic workings of the mind have to be analyzed to understand behavior. Early experiences with parents are emphasized.

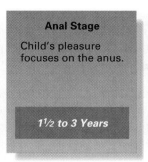

Oral Stage

Infant's pleasure centers on the mouth.

Birth to 1½ Years

Anal Stage

Child's pleasure focuses on the anus.

1½ to 3 Years

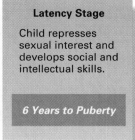

Phallic Stage

Child's pleasure focuses on the genitals.

3 to 6 Years

Latency Stage

Child represses sexual interest and develops social and intellectual skills.

6 Years to Puberty

Genital Stage

A time of sexual reawakening; source of sexual pleasure becomes someone outside the family.

Puberty Onward

FIGURE 2.1 Freudian Stages

The *phallic stage* is the third Freudian stage of development. The phallic stage occurs between the ages of 3 and 6; its name comes from the Latin word *phallus,* which means "penis." During the phallic stage, pleasure focuses on the genitals as both boys and girls discover that self-manipulation is enjoyable.

In Freud's view, the phallic stage has a special importance in personality development because it is during this period that the Oedipus complex appears. This name comes from Greek mythology, in which Oedipus, the son of the King of Thebes, unwittingly kills his father and marries his mother. The *Oedipus complex,* according to Freudian theory, is the young child's development of an intense desire to replace the same-sex parent and enjoy the affections of the opposite-sex parent.

How is the Oedipus complex resolved? At about 5 to 6 years of age, children recognize that their same-sex parent might punish them for their incestuous wishes. To reduce this conflict, the child identifies with the same-sex parent, striving to be like him or her. If the conflict is not resolved, though, the individual may become fixated at the phallic stage.

The *latency stage* is the fourth Freudian stage of development, which occurs between approximately 6 years of age and puberty. During this period, the child represses all interest in sexuality and develops social and intellectual skills. This activity channels much of the child's energy into emotionally safe areas and helps the child forget the highly stressful conflicts of the phallic stage.

The *genital stage* is the fifth and final Freudian stage of development, occurring from puberty onward. The genital stage is a time of sexual reawakening; the source of sexual pleasure now becomes someone outside of the family. Freud believed that unresolved conflicts with parents reemerge during adolescence. When these conflicts have been resolved, the individual is capable of developing a mature love relationship and functioning independently as an adult.

Freud's theory has undergone significant revisions by a number of psychoanalytic theorists (Eagle, 2000). Many contemporary psychoanalytic theorists place less emphasis on sexual instincts and more emphasis on cultural experiences as determinants of an individual's development. Unconscious thought remains a central theme, but most contemporary psychoanalysts believe that conscious thought makes up more of the mind than Freud envisioned. Next, we will explore the ideas of an important revisionist of Freud's ideas—Erik Erikson.

Erikson's Psychosocial Theory

Erik Erikson recognized Freud's contributions but believed that Freud misjudged some important dimensions of human development. For one thing, Erikson (1950, 1968) said we develop in *psychosocial* stages, rather than in *psychosexual* stages, as Freud maintained. For Freud, the primary motivation for human behavior was sexual in nature; for Erikson it was social and reflected a desire to affiliate with other people. Erikson emphasized developmental change throughout the human life span, whereas Freud argued that our basic personality is shaped in the first five years of life. In **Erikson's theory,** eight stages of development unfold as we go through the life span (see figure 2.2). Each stage

Erik Erikson with his wife, Joan, an artist. Erikson generated one of the most important developmental theories of the twentieth century. *Which stage of Erikson's theory are you in? Does Erikson's description of this stage characterize you?*

Erikson's theory Includes eight stages of human development. Each stage consists of a unique developmental task that confronts individuals with a crisis that must be faced.

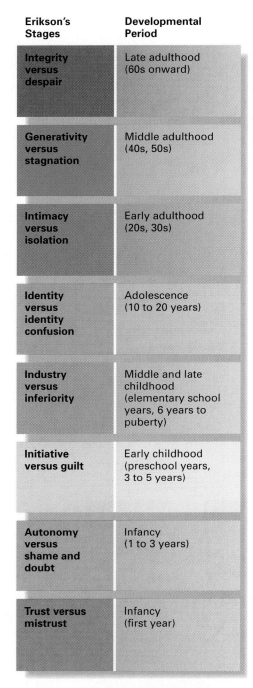

Erikson's Stages	Developmental Period
Integrity versus despair	Late adulthood (60s onward)
Generativity versus stagnation	Middle adulthood (40s, 50s)
Intimacy versus isolation	Early adulthood (20s, 30s)
Identity versus identity confusion	Adolescence (10 to 20 years)
Industry versus inferiority	Middle and late childhood (elementary school years, 6 years to puberty)
Initiative versus guilt	Early childhood (preschool years, 3 to 5 years)
Autonomy versus shame and doubt	Infancy (1 to 3 years)
Trust versus mistrust	Infancy (first year)

FIGURE 2.2 Erikson's Eight Life-Span Stages

www.mhhe.com/santrockcd10

Erikson's Theory

consists of a unique developmental task that confronts individuals with a crisis that must be resolved. According to Erikson, this crisis is not a catastrophe but a turning point of increased vulnerability and enhanced potential. The more successfully an individual resolves the crisis, the healthier development will be (Hopkins, 2000).

Trust versus mistrust is Erikson's first psychosocial stage, which is experienced in the first year of life. A sense of trust requires a feeling of physical comfort and a minimal amount of fear and apprehension about the future. Trust in infancy sets the stage for a lifelong expectation that the world will be a good and pleasant place to live.

Autonomy versus shame and doubt is Erikson's second stage of development. This stage occurs in late infancy and toddlerhood (1 to 3 years). After gaining trust in their caregivers, infants begin to discover that their behavior is their own. They start to assert their sense of independence, or autonomy. They realize their *will*. If infants are restrained too much or punished too harshly, they are likely to develop a sense of shame and doubt.

Initiative versus guilt, Erikson's third stage of development, occurs during the preschool years. As preschool children encounter a widening social world, they are challenged more than when they were infants. Active, purposeful behavior is needed to cope with these challenges. Children are asked to assume responsibility for their bodies, their behavior, their toys, and their pets. Developing a sense of responsibility increases initiative. Uncomfortable guilt feelings may arise, though, if the child is irresponsible and is made to feel too anxious. Erikson has a positive outlook on this stage. He believes that most guilt is quickly compensated for by a sense of accomplishment.

Industry versus inferiority is Erikson's fourth developmental stage, occurring approximately in the elementary school years. Children's initiative brings them in contact with a wealth of new experiences. As they move into middle and late childhood, they direct their energy toward mastering knowledge and intellectual skills. At no other time is the child more enthusiastic about learning than at the end of early childhood's period of expansive imagination. The danger in the elementary school years is that the child can develop a sense of inferiority—feeling incompetent and unproductive. Erikson believed that teachers have a special responsibility for children's development of industry. Teachers should "mildly but firmly coerce children into the adventure of finding out that one can learn to accomplish things which one would never have thought of by oneself" (Erikson, 1968, p. 127).

Identity versus identity confusion is Erikson's fifth developmental stage, which individuals experience during the adolescent years. At this time, individuals are faced with finding out who they are, what they are all about, and where they are going in life. Adolescents are confronted with many new roles and adult statuses—vocational and romantic, for example. Parents need to allow adolescents to explore many different roles and different paths within a particular role. If the adolescent explores such roles in a healthy manner and arrives at a positive path to follow in life, then a positive identity will be achieved. If an identity is pushed on the adolescent by parents, if the adolescent does not adequately explore many roles, and if a positive future path is not defined, then identity confusion reigns.

Intimacy versus isolation is Erikson's sixth developmental stage, which individuals experience during the early adulthood years. At this time, individuals face the developmental task of forming intimate relationships with others. Erikson describes intimacy as finding oneself yet losing oneself in another. If the young adult forms healthy friendships and an intimate relationship with another individual, intimacy will be achieved; if not, isolation will result.

Generativity versus stagnation is Erikson's seventh developmental stage, which individuals experience during middle adulthood. A chief concern is to assist the younger generation in developing and leading useful lives—this is what Erikson means by generativity. The feeling of having done nothing to help the next generation is stagnation.

Integrity versus despair is Erikson's eighth and final stage of development, which individuals experience in late adulthood. During this stage, a person reflects on the past and either pieces together a positive review or concludes that life has not been spent well. Through many different routes, the older person may have developed a positive outlook in most or all of the previous stages of development. If so, the retrospective glances will reveal a picture of a life well spent, and the person will feel a sense of satisfaction—integrity will be achieved. If the older adult resolved many of the earlier stages negatively, the retrospective glances likely will yield doubt or gloom—the despair Erikson talks about.

Erikson did not believe that the proper solution to a stage crisis is always completely positive. Some exposure or commitment to the negative side of the person's conflict is sometimes inevitable—you cannot trust all people under all circumstances and survive, for example. Nonetheless, in the healthy solution to a stage crisis, the positive resolution dominates (Hopkins, 2000). We will discuss Erikson's theory again on a number of occasions in the chapters on socioemotional development in this book.

Evaluating the Psychoanalytic Theories   Here are some contributions of psychoanalytic theories:

- Early experiences play an important part in development.
- Family relationships are a central aspect of development.
- Personality can be better understood if it is examined developmentally.
- The mind is not all conscious; unconscious aspects of the mind need to be considered.
- Changes take place in adulthood as well as the childhood (Erikson).

Here are some criticisms of psychoanalytic theories:

- The main concepts of psychoanalytic theories have been difficult to test scientifically.
- Much of the data used to support psychoanalytic theories come from individuals' reconstruction of the past, often the distant past, and are of unknown accuracy.
- The sexual underpinnings of development are given too much importance (especially in Freud's theory).
- The unconscious mind is given too much credit for influencing development.
- Psychoanalytic theories present an image of humans that is too negative (especially in Freud's theory).
- Psychoanalytic theories are culture- and gender-biased.

Cognitive Theories

Whereas psychoanalytic theories stress the importance of children's unconscious thoughts, cognitive theories emphasize their conscious thoughts. Three important cognitive theories are Piaget's cognitive developmental theory, Vygotsky's sociocultural cognitive theory, and the information-processing theory.

Piaget's theory will be covered in detail later in this book, when we discuss cognitive development in infancy, early childhood, middle and late childhood, and adolescence. Here we briefly present the main ideas of his theory.

Piaget's Cognitive Developmental Theory   **Piaget's theory** states that children actively construct their understanding of the world and go through four stages of cognitive development. Two processes underlie this cognitive construction of the world: organization and adaptation. To make sense of our world, we organize our

Horney's Theory

Piaget's theory States that children actively construct their understanding of the world and go through four stages of cognitive development.

Sensorimotor Stage	Preoperational Stage	Concrete Operational Stage	Formal Operational Stage
The infant constructs an understanding of the world by coordinating sensory experiences with physical actions. An infant progresses from reflexive, instinctual action at birth to the beginning of symbolic thought toward the end of the stage.	The child begins to represent the world with words and images. These words and images reflect increased symbolic thinking and go beyond the connection of sensory information and physical action.	The child can now reason logically about concrete events and classify objects into different sets.	The adolescent reasons in more abstract, idealistic, and logical ways.
Birth to 2 Years of Age	*2 to 7 Years of Age*	*7 to 11 Years of Age*	*11 Years of Age through Adulthood*

FIGURE 2.3 Piaget's Four Stages of Cognitive Development

Jean Piaget, the famous Swiss developmental psychologist, changed the way we think about the development of children's minds. *What are some key ideas in Piaget's theory?*

assimilation Occurs when children incorporate new information into their existing knowledge.

accommodation Occurs when children adjust to new information.

experiences. For example, we separate important ideas from less important ideas. We connect one idea to another. In addition to organizing our observations and experiences, we *adapt* our thinking to include new ideas because additional information furthers understanding.

Piaget (1954) believed that we adapt in two ways: assimilation and accommodation. **Assimilation** occurs when children incorporate new information into their existing knowledge. **Accommodation** occurs when children adjust to new information. Consider a circumstance in which a 9-year-old girl is given a hammer and nails to hang a picture on the wall. She has never used a hammer, but from observation and vicarious experience she realizes that a hammer is an object to be held, that it is swung by the handle to hit the nail, and that it is usually swung a number of times. Recognizing each of these things, she fits her behavior into the information she already has (assimilation). However, the hammer is heavy, so she holds it near the top. She swings too hard and the nail bends, so she adjusts the pressure of her strikes. These adjustments reveal her ability to alter slightly her conception of the world (accommodation).

Piaget thought that assimilation and accommodation operate even in the very young infant's life. Newborns reflexively suck everything that touches their lips (assimilation), but, after several months of experience, they construct their understanding of the world differently. Some objects, such as fingers and the mother's breast, can be sucked, but others, such as fuzzy blankets, should not be sucked (accommodation).

Piaget also believed that we go through four stages in understanding the world (see figure 2.3). Each of the stages is age-related and consists of distinct ways of thinking. Remember, it is the *different* way of understanding the world that makes one stage more advanced than another; knowing *more* information does not make the child's thinking more advanced, in the Piagetian view. This is what Piaget meant when he said the child's cognition is *qualitatively* different in one stage compared to another (Vidal, 2000). What are Piaget's four stages of cognitive development like?

The *sensorimotor stage,* which lasts from birth to about 2 years of age, is the first Piagetian stage. In this stage, infants construct an understanding of the world by coordinating sensory experiences (such as seeing and hearing) with physical, motoric actions—hence the term *sensorimotor.* At the beginning of this stage, newborns have little more than reflexive patterns with which to work. At the end of the stage, 2-year-olds have complex sensorimotor patterns and are beginning to operate with primitive symbols.

The *preoperational stage,* which lasts from approximately 2 to 7 years of age, is the second Piagetian stage. In this stage, children begin to represent the world with words, images, and drawings. Symbolic thought goes beyond simple connections of sensory information and physical action. However, although preschool children can symbolically represent the world, according to Piaget, they still lack the ability to perform *operations,* the Piagetian term for internalized mental actions that allow children to do mentally what they previously did physically.

The *concrete operational stage,* which lasts from approximately 7 to 11 years of age, is the third Piagetian stage. In this stage, children can perform operations, and logical reasoning replaces intuitive thought as long as reasoning can be applied to specific or concrete examples. For instance, concrete operational thinkers cannot imagine the steps necessary to complete an algebraic equation, which is too abstract for thinking at this stage of development.

The *formal operational stage,* which appears between the ages of 11 and 15, is the fourth and final Piagetian stage. In this stage, individuals move beyond concrete experiences and think in abstract and more logical terms. As part of thinking more abstractly, adolescents develop images of ideal circumstances. They might think about what an ideal parent is like and compare their parents to this ideal standard. They begin to entertain possibilities for the future and are fascinated with what they can be. In solving problems, formal operational thinkers are more systematic, developing hypotheses about why something is happening the way it is, then testing these hypotheses in a deductive manner. We will examine Piaget's cognitive developmental theory further in chapter 7.

Piaget's Theory
Vygotsky's Theory

Vygotsky's Sociocultural Cognitive Theory

Like Piaget, the Russian developmentalist Lev Vygotsky (1896–1934) also believed that children actively construct their knowledge. However, Vygotsky gave social interaction and culture far more important roles in cognitive development than Piaget did. **Vygotsky's theory** is a sociocultural cognitive theory that emphasizes how culture and social interaction guide cognitive development. Vygotsky was born the same year as Piaget, but he died much earlier, at the age of 37. Both Piaget's and Vygotsky's ideas remained virtually unknown to American scholars until the 1960s. In the past several decades, American psychologists and educators have shown increased interest in Vygotsky's (1962) views.

Vygotsky portrayed the child's development as inseparable from social and cultural activities. He believed that the development of memory, attention, and reasoning involves learning to use the inventions of society, such as language, mathematical systems, and memory strategies. In one culture, this might consist of learning to count with the help of a computer. In another, it might consist of counting on one's fingers or using beads.

Vygotsky's theory has stimulated considerable interest in the view that knowledge is *collaborative* (Greeno, Collins, & Resnick, 1996; Kozulin, 2000; Rogoff, 2001). In this view, knowledge is not generated from within the individual but rather is constructed through interaction with other people and objects in the culture, such as books. This suggests that knowing can best be advanced through interaction with others in cooperative activities.

Vygotsky believed that children's social interaction with more-skilled adults and peers is indispensable in advancing cognitive development. It is through this interaction that less-skilled members of the culture learn to use the tools that will help them adapt and be successful in the culture. For example, when a skilled reader regularly helps a child learn how to read, this not only advances a child's reading skills but also communicates to the child that reading is an important activity in the culture.

Vygotsky articulated unique and influential ideas about cognitive development. In chapter 7, "Cognitive Developmental Approaches," we will further explore Vygotsky's contributions to our understanding of children's development.

There is considerable interest today in Lev Vygotsky's sociocultural cognitive theory of child development. *What were Vygotsky's basic ideas about children's development?*

Vygotsky's theory A sociocultural cognitive theory that emphasizes how culture and social interaction guide cognitive development.

Information-Processing Theory **Information-processing theory** emphasizes that children manipulate information, monitor it, and strategize about it. Central to this approach are the processes of memory and thinking. According to information-processing theory, children develop a gradually increasing capacity for processing information, which allows them to acquire increasingly complex knowledge and skills (Bjorklund & Rosenbaum, 2000; Chen & Siegler, 2000; Siegler, 2001). Unlike Piaget's cognitive developmental theory, information-processing theory does not describe development as stagelike.

Although a number of factors stimulated the growth of information-processing theory, none was more important than the computer, which demonstrated that a machine could perform logical operations. Psychologists began to wonder if the logical operations carried out by computers might tell us something about how the human mind works. They drew analogies to computers to explain the relation between cognition or thinking and the brain. The physical brain is said to be analogous to the computer's hardware, cognition is said to be analogous to its software. Although computers and software are not perfect analogies for brains and cognitive activities, the comparison contributed to our thinking about the mind as an active information-processing system.

Robert Siegler (1998), a leading expert on children's information processing, believes that thinking is information processing. He says that when individuals perceive, encode, represent, store, and retrieve information, they are thinking. Siegler especially thinks that an important aspect of development is to learn good strategies for processing information. For example, becoming a better reader might involve learning to monitor the key themes of the material being read.

Evaluating the Cognitive Theories Here are some contributions of cognitive theories:

- The cognitive theories present a positive view of development, emphasizing conscious thinking.
- The cognitive theories (especially Piaget's and Vygotsky's) emphasize the individual's active construction of understanding.
- Piaget's and Vygotsky's theories underscore the importance of examining developmental changes in children's thinking.
- Information-processing theory offers detailed descriptions of cognitive processes.

Here are some criticisms of cognitive theories:

- There is skepticism about the pureness of Piaget's stages.
- The cognitive theories do not give adequate attention to individual variations in cognitive development.
- Information-processing theory does not provide an adequate description of developmental changes in cognition.
- Psychoanalytic theorists argue that the cognitive theories do not give enough credit to unconscious thought.

Behavioral and Social Cognitive Theories

Behaviorists essentially believe that scientifically we can study only what can be directly observed and measured. At about the same time as Freud was interpreting patients' unconscious minds through their early childhood experiences, Ivan Pavlov and John B. Watson were conducting detailed observations of behavior in controlled laboratory settings. Out of the behavioral tradition grew the belief that development is observable behavior that can be learned through experience with the environment. The three versions of the behavioral approach that we will explore are Pavlov's classical conditioning, Skinner's operant conditioning, and social cognitive theory.

information-processing theory Emphasizes that children manipulate information, monitor it, and strategize about it. Central to this approach are the processes of memory and thinking.

Pavlov's Classical Conditioning In the early 1900s, the Russian physiologist Ivan Pavlov (1927) knew that dogs innately salivate when they taste food. He became curious when he observed that dogs salivate to various sights and sounds before eating their food. For example, when an individual paired the ringing of a bell with the food, the bell ringing subsequently elicited the salivation response from the dogs when it was presented by itself. With this experiment, Pavlov discovered the principle of *classical conditioning*, in which a neutral stimulus (in our example, ringing a bell) acquires the ability to produce a response originally produced by another stimulus (in our example, food).

In the 1920s, John Watson wanted to show that Pavlov's concept of classical conditioning could be applied to human beings. He showed an infant named Albert a white rat to see if he was afraid of it. He was not. As Albert played with the rat, a loud noise was sounded behind his head. As you might imagine, the noise caused little Albert to cry. After several pairings of the loud noise and the white rat, Albert begin to fear the rat even when the noise was not sounded (Watson & Rayner, 1920). Today, we could not ethically conduct such an experiment, for reasons that we will discuss later in the chapter.

Many of our fears—fear of the dentist from a painful experience, fear of driving from being in an automobile accident, fear of heights from falling off a high chair when we were infants, and fear of dogs from being bitten—can be learned through classical conditioning.

B. F. Skinner was a tinkerer who liked to make new gadgets. The younger of his two daughters, Deborah, was raised in Skinner's enclosed Air-Crib, which he invented because he wanted to control her environment completely. The Air-Crib was soundproofed and temperature-controlled. Debbie, shown here as a child with her parents, is currently a successful artist, is married, and lives in London. *What do you think about Skinner's Air-Crib?*

Skinner's Operant Conditioning In B. F. Skinner's (1938) *operant conditioning,* the consequences of a behavior produce changes in the probability of the behavior's occurrence. If a behavior is followed by a rewarding stimulus it is more likely to recur, but if a behavior is followed by a punishing stimulus it is less likely to recur. For example, when a person smiles at a child after the child has done something, the child is more likely to engage in the activity than if the person gives the child a nasty look.

For Skinner, such rewards and punishments shape individuals' development. For example, Skinner's approach argues that shy people learned to be shy as a result of experiences they had while growing up. It follows that modifications in an environment can help a shy person become more socially oriented.

Behavioral and Social Cognitive Theories

Social Cognitive Theory Some psychologists believe that the behaviorists basically are right when they say development is learned and is influenced strongly by environmental interactions. However, they believe that Skinner went too far in declaring that cognition is unimportant in understanding development. **Social cognitive theory** is the view of psychologists who emphasize behavior, environment, and cognition as the key factors in development.

American psychologists Albert Bandura (1986, 2000, 2001, 2002) and Walter Mischel (1973, 1995) are the main architects of social cognitive theory's contemporary version, which Mischel (1973) initially labeled *cognitive* social learning theory. Both Bandura and Mischel believe that cognitive processes are important mediators of environment-behavior connections. Bandura's early research program focused heavily on observational learning, learning that occurs through observing what others do. Observational learning is also referred to as imitation or modeling. What is *cognitive* about observational learning in Bandura's view? Bandura (1925–) believes that people cognitively represent the behavior of others and then sometimes

social cognitive theory The view of psychologists who emphasize behavior, environment, and cognition as the key factors in development.

Albert Bandura has been one of the leading architects of social cognitive theory. *What is the nature of his theory?*

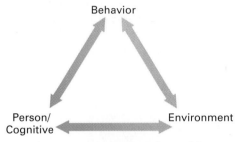

FIGURE 2.4 Bandura's Social Cognitive Model

The arrows illustrate how relations between behavior, person/cognitive, and environment are reciprocal rather than unidirectional.

Albert Bandura

ethology Stresses that behavior is strongly influenced by biology, is tied to evolution, and is characterized by critical or sensitive periods.

adopt this behavior themselves. For example, a young boy might observe his father's aggressive outbursts and hostile interchanges with people; when observed with his peers, the young boy's style of interaction is highly aggressive, showing the same characteristics as his father's behavior. A girl might adopt the dominant and sarcastic style of her teacher. When observed interacting with her younger brother, she says, "You are so slow. How can you do this work so slowly?" Social cognitive theorists believe that children acquire a wide range of such behaviors, thoughts, and feelings through observing others' behavior and that these observations form an important part of their development.

Bandura's (1986, 2001, 2002) most recent model of learning and development involves behavior, the person/cognition, and the environment. A child's confidence that she can control her success is an example of a person factor and thinking is an example of a cognitive factor. As shown in figure 2.4, behavior, person/cognitive, and environmental factors operate interactively. Behavior can influence person factors and vice versa. The person's cognitive activities can influence the environment, the environment can change the person's cognition, and so on.

Evaluating the Behavioral and Social Cognitive Theories Contributions of the behavioral and social cognitive theories include:

- The importance of scientific research
- The environmental determinants of behavior
- The importance of observational learning (Bandura)
- Person and cognitive factors (social cognitive theory)

Criticisms of the behavioral and social cognitive theories include:

- Too little emphasis on cognition (Pavlov, Skinner)
- Too much emphasis on environmental determinants
- Inadequate attention to developmental changes
- Too mechanical and inadequate consideration of the spontaneity and creativity of humans

Behavioral and social cognitive theories emphasize the importance of environmental experiences in human development. Next we turn our attention to a theory that underscores the importance of biological foundations of development—ethological theory.

Ethological Theory

Ethology stresses that behavior is strongly influenced by biology, is tied to evolution, and is characterized by critical or sensitive periods. Ethologists believe that the presence or absence of certain experiences at particular times in the life span influences individuals well beyond the time they first occur, and that most psychologists underestimate the importance of these special time frames in early development. Ethologists also stress the powerful roles that evolution and biological foundations play in development (Rosenzweig, 2000).

Ethology emerged as an important view because of the work of European zoologists, especially Konrad Lorenz (1903–1989). Working mostly with greylag geese, Lorenz (1965) studied a behavior pattern that was considered to be programmed within the birds' genes. A newly hatched gosling seemed to be born with the instinct to follow its mother. Observations showed that the gosling was capable of such behavior as soon as it hatched. Lorenz proved that it was incorrect to assume that such behavior was programmed in the animal. In a remarkable set of experiments, Lorenz separated the eggs laid by one goose into two groups. One group he returned to the goose to be hatched by her. The other group was hatched in an incubator. The goslings in the first group performed as predicted. They followed their mother

Konrad Lorenz, a pioneering student of animal behavior, is followed through the water by three imprinted greylag geese. Describe Lorenz's experiment with the geese. *Do you think his experiment would have the same results with human babies? Explain.*

as soon as they hatched. However, those in the second group, which saw Lorenz when they first hatched, followed him everywhere, as though he were their mother. Lorenz marked the goslings and then placed both groups under a box. Mother goose and "mother" Lorenz stood aside as the box lifted. Each group of goslings went directly to its "mother." Lorenz called this process *imprinting,* the rapid, innate learning within a limited critical period of time that involves attachment to the first moving object seen.

The ethological view of Lorenz and the European zoologists forced American developmental psychologists to recognize the importance of the biological basis of behavior. However, the ethological research and theory lacked some ingredients that would elevate it to the ranks of the other theories discussed so far in this chapter. In particular, there was little or nothing in the classical ethological view about the nature of social relationships across the human life span, something that any major theory of development must explain. Also, its concept of *critical period,* a fixed time period very early in development during which certain behaviors optimally emerge, seemed to be overdrawn. Classical ethological theory was weak in stimulating studies with humans. Recent expansion of the ethological view has improved its status as a viable developmental perspective.

One of the most important applications of ethological theory to human development involves John Bowlby's (1969, 1989) theory of attachment. Bowlby argued that attachment to a caregiver over the first year of life has important consequences throughout the life span. In his view, if this attachment is positive and secure, the individual will likely develop more positively in childhood and adulthood. If this attachment is negative and insecure, life-span development will likely not be optimal. In chapter 11, "Emotional Development," we will explore the concept of infant attachment in much greater detail.

Contributions of ethological theory include:

- Increased focus on the biological and evolutionary basis of development
- Use of careful observations in naturalistic settings
- Emphasis on sensitive periods of development

Here are some criticisms of ethological theory:

- The concepts of critical and sensitive periods might be too rigid.
- It places too strong an emphasis on biological foundations.
- It gives inadequate attention to cognition.
- The theory has been better at generating research with animals than with humans.

Exploring Ethology

Bronfenbrenner's Theory

Bronfenbrenner and a Multicultural Framework

Another theory that emphasizes the biological aspects of human development—evolutionary psychology—will be presented in chapter 3, "Biological Beginnings," along with views on the role of heredity in development.

Ecological Theory

While ethological theory stresses biological factors, ecological theory emphasizes environmental factors. One ecological theory that has important implications for understanding child development was created by Urie Bronfenbrenner (1917–).

Ecological theory is Bronfenbrenner's (1986, 2000; Bronfenbrenner & Morris, 1998) environmental system of development. It consists of five environmental systems ranging from the fine-grained inputs of direct interactions with people to the broad-based inputs of culture (see figure 2.5):

- *Microsystem*: the setting in which the individual lives. These contexts include the person's family, peers, school, and neighborhood. It is in the microsystem that the most direct interactions with social agents take place—with parents, peers, and teachers, for example. The individual is viewed not as a passive recipient of experiences in these settings, but as someone who helps to construct the settings.
- *Mesosystem:* involves relations between microsystems or connections between contexts. Examples are the relation of family experiences to school experiences, school experiences to church experiences, and family experiences to peer experiences. For example, children whose parents have rejected them may have difficulty developing positive relations with teachers.

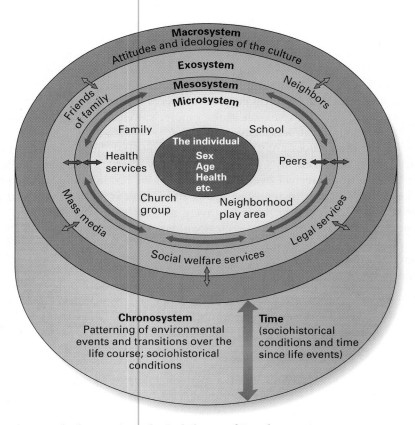

FIGURE 2.5 Bronfenbrenner's Ecological Theory of Development

Bronfenbrenner's ecological theory consists of five environmental systems: microsystem, mesosystem, exosystem, macrosystem, and chronosystem.

ecological theory Bronfenbrenner's environmental systems theory that focuses on five environmental systems: microsystem, mesosystem, exosystem, macrosystem, and chronosystem.

- *Exosystem:* when experiences in another social setting—in which the individual does not have an active role—influence what the individual experiences in an immediate context. For example, work experiences can affect a woman's relationship with her husband and their child. The mother might receive a promotion that requires more travel, which might increase marital conflict and change patterns of parent-child interaction. Another example is the federal government through its role in the quality of medical care and support systems for older adults.
- *Macrosystem:* the culture in which individuals live. Remember from chapter 1 that culture refers to the behavior patterns, beliefs, and all other products of a group of people that are passed on from generation to generation.  **page 13** Remember also that cross-cultural studies—the comparison of one culture with one or more other cultures—provide information about the generality of development. **page 13**
- *Chronosystem:* the patterning of environmental events and transitions over the life course, as well as sociohistorical circumstances. For example, in studying the effects of divorce on children, researchers have found that the negative effects often peak in the first year after the divorce. The effects also are more negative for sons than for daughters (Hetherington, 1993). By two years after the divorce, family interaction is less chaotic and more stable. With regard to sociocultural circumstances, women today are much more likely to be encouraged to pursue a career than they were 20 or 30 years ago.

Urie Bronfenbrenner developed ecological theory, a perspective that is receiving increased attention. *What is the nature of ecological theory?*

Bronfenbrenner (2000; Bronfenbrenner & Morris, 1998) has added biological influences to his theory and now describes it as a bioecological theory. Nonetheless, ecological, environmental contexts still predominate in Bronfenbrenner's theory (Ceci, 2000).

The contributions of ecological theory include:

- A systematic examination of macro and micro dimensions of environmental systems
- Attention to connections between environmental settings (mesosystem)
- Consideration of sociohistorical influences on development (chronosystem)

Here are some criticisms of ecological theory:

- Even with the added discussion of biological influences in recent years, there is still too little attention to biological foundations of development.
- It may give inadequate attention to cognitive processes.

An Eclectic Theoretical Orientation

An **eclectic theoretical orientation** does not follow any one theoretical approach, but rather selects from each theory whatever is considered its best features. No single theory described in this chapter can explain entirely the rich complexity of children's development. Each of the theories has made important contributions to our understanding of development, but none provides a complete description and explanation. Psychoanalytic theory best explains the unconscious mind. Erikson's theory best describes the changes that occur in adult development and the life tasks that children's parents face. Piaget's, Vygotsky's, and the information-processing views provide the most complete description of cognitive development. The behavioral and social cognitive and ecological theories have been the most adept at examining the environmental determinants of development. The ethological theories have made us aware of biology's role and the importance of sensitive periods in development. It is important to recognize that, although theories are helpful guides, relying on a single theory to explain development is probably a mistake.

An attempt was made in this chapter to present five theoretical perspectives objectively. The same eclectic orientation will be maintained throughout the book.

eclectic theoretical orientation An orientation that does not follow any one theoretical approach, but rather selects from each theory whatever is considered the best in it.

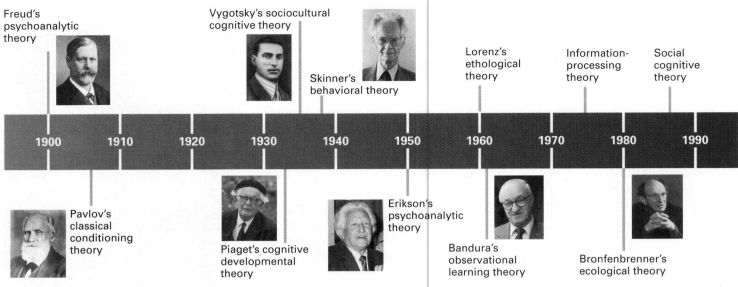

FIGURE 2.6 Time Line for Major Developmental Theories

In this way, you can view the study of development as it actually exists—with different theorists making different assumptions, stressing different empirical problems, and using different strategies to discover information.

The theories that we have discussed were conceived at different points in the twentieth century. For a chronology of their development, see figure 2.6. Figure 2.7 compares the main theoretical perspectives in terms of how they view important developmental issues and the methods used to study child development. ◀ page 19

Theory	Issues		
	Continuity/discontinuity, early versus later experiences	Biological and environmental factors	Importance of cognition
Psychoanalytic	Discontinuity between stages—continuity between early experiences and later development; early experiences very important; later changes in development emphasized in Erikson's theory	Freud's biological determination interacting with early family experiences; Erikson's more balanced biological-cultural interaction perspective	Emphasized, but in the form of unconscious thought
Cognitive	Discontinuity between stages in Piaget's theory; continuity between early experiences and later development in Piaget's and Vygotsky's theory; no stages in Vygotsky's theory or information-processing theory	Piaget's emphasis on interaction and adaptation; environment provides the setting for cognitive structures to develop; information-processing view has not addressed this issue extensively but mainly emphasizes biological-environmental interaction	The primary determinant of behavior
Behavioral and social cognitive	Continuity (no stages); experience at all points of development important	Environment viewed as the cause of behavior in both views	Strongly deemphasized in the behavioral approach but an important mediator in social cognitive theory
Ethological	Discontinuity but no stages; critical or sensitive periods emphasized; early experiences very important	Strong biological view	Not emphasized
Ecological	Little attention to continuity/discontinuity; change emphasized more than stability	Strong environmental view	Not emphasized

FIGURE 2.7 A Comparison of Theories and Issues in Child Development

Review and Reflect: Learning Goal 1

1 Describe theories of child development

REVIEW

- What are the four steps in the scientific method? What is the relationship between a theory and hypotheses?
- What are two main psychoanalytic theories? What are some of the terms, contributions, and criticisms of the psychoanalytic theories?
- What are three main cognitive theories? What are some of the terms, contributions, and criticisms of the cognitive theories?
- What are three main behavioral and social cognitive theories? What are some of the terms, contributions, and criticisms of the behavioral and social cognitive theories?
- What is the nature of ethological theory? What are some of its terms, contributions, and criticisms?
- What is the nature of ecological theory? What are some of its terms, contributions, and criticisms?
- What is an eclectic theoretical orientation?

REFLECT

- Which of the theories do you think best explains your own development? Why?

2 RESEARCH IN CHILD DEVELOPMENT

| Types of Research | Time Span of Research | Research Journals |

Generally, research in child development is designed to test hypotheses, which in some cases, are derived from the theories just described. Through research, theories are modified to reflect new data and occasionally new theories arise. What types of research are conducted in child development? If researchers want to study people of different ages, what research designs can they use? These are the questions that we will examine next.

Types of Research

This section describes the major methods used to gather data about child development. For this purpose, there are three basic types of research: descriptive, correlational, and experimental. Each has strengths and weaknesses.

Descriptive Research   Some important theories have grown out of **descriptive research,** which has the purpose of observing and recording behavior. For example, a psychologist might observe the extent to which children are altruistic or aggressive toward each other. By itself, descriptive research cannot prove what causes some phenomenon, but it can reveal important information about children's behavior. Descriptive research methods include observation, surveys and interviews, standardized tests, and case studies.

Observation   Scientific observation requires an important set of skills (McMillan & Wergin, 2002). Unless we are trained observers and practice our skills regularly, we might not know what to look for, we might not remember what we saw, we might not realize that what we are looking for is changing from one moment to the next, and we might not communicate our observations effectively.

*S*cience refines everyday thinking.

—**Albert Einstein**
German-born American Physicist, 20th Century

descriptive research A type of research whose purpose is to observe and record behavior.

In this research study, mother-child interaction is being videotaped. Later, researchers will code the interaction using precise categories.

For observations to be effective, they have to be systematic (Elmes, Kantowitz, & Roedinger, 2003). We have to have some idea of what we are looking for. We have to know whom we are observing, when and where we will observe, and how the observations will be made. In what form will they be recorded: In writing? Tape recording? Video?

Where should we make our observations? We have two choices: the laboratory and the everyday world.

When we observe scientifically, we often need to control certain factors that determine behavior but are not the focus of our inquiry (Hoyle & Judd, 2002; Pittenger, 2003). For this reason, some research in child development is conducted in a **laboratory,** a controlled setting with many of the complex factors of the "real world" removed.

An experiment conducted by Albert Bandura (1965) found that children behaved more aggressively after observing a model being rewarded for aggression. Bandura conducted this study in a laboratory with adults the child did not know. Thus, he controlled when the child witnessed aggression, how much aggression the child saw, and what form the aggression took. Bandura would not have had as much control over the experiment, or as much confidence in the results, if the study had been conducted in the children's homes and if familiar people had been present, such as the child's parents, siblings, or friends.

Laboratory research does have some drawbacks. First, it is almost impossible to conduct research without the participants' knowing they are being studied. Second, the laboratory setting is unnatural and therefore can cause the participants to behave unnaturally.

Another drawback of laboratory research is that people who are willing to come to a university laboratory may not fairly represent groups from diverse cultural backgrounds. Those who are unfamiliar with university settings, and with the idea of "helping science," may be intimidated by the setting.

Still another problem is that some aspects of child development are difficult if not impossible to examine in the laboratory. Laboratory studies of certain types of stress may even be unethical.

Naturalistic observation provides insights that we sometimes cannot achieve in the laboratory (Billman, 2003; Langston, 2002). **Naturalistic observation** means

laboratory A controlled setting in which many of the complex factors of the "real world" are removed.

naturalistic observation Observing behavior in real-world settings.

observing behavior in real-world settings, making no effort to manipulate or control the situation. Researchers conduct naturalistic observations in homes, at schools, at sporting events, at day-care centers, in malls, and in other settings where people live and frequent.

Naturalistic observation was used in one study that focused on conversations in a children's science museum (Crowley & others, 2001). Parents were three times as likely to engage boys than girls in explanatory talk while visiting different exhibits at the science museum, suggesting a gender bias that encourages boys more than girls in science (see figure 2.8). In another study, Mexican American parents who had completed high school used more explanations with their children when visiting a science museum than Mexican American parents who had not completed high school (Tenenbaum & others, 2002).

Survey and Interview   Sometimes the best and quickest way to get information about people is to ask them for it. One technique is to *interview* them directly. A related method that is especially useful when information from many people is needed is the *survey*, sometimes referred to as a questionnaire. A standard set of questions is used to obtain people's self-reported attitudes or beliefs about a particular topic. In a good survey, the questions are clear and unbiased, allowing respondents to answer unambiguously.

Some survey and interview questions are unstructured and open-ended, such as "What do you think could be done to improve America's schools?" They allow for unique responses from each person surveyed. Other survey and interview questions are more structured and ask about more specific things. For example, one national poll on beliefs about what needs to be done to improve U.S. schools asked: "Of the following four possibilities, which one do you think offers the most promise for improving public schools in the community: a qualified, competent teacher in every classroom; free choice for parents among a number of private, church-related, and public schools; rigorous academic standards; the elimination of social promotion; or don't know?" (Rose & Gallup, 2000). More than half of the respondents said that the most important way to improve schools is to have a qualified, competent teacher in every classroom.

One problem with surveys and interviews is the tendency of participants to answer questions in a way that they think is socially acceptable or desirable rather than telling what they truly think or feel (Best & Kahn, 2003). For example, on a survey or in an interview some individuals might say that they do not take drugs even though they do.

Standardized Test   A **standardized test** has uniform procedures for administration and scoring. Many standardized tests allow a person's performance to be compared with the performance of other individuals (Aiken, 2003). One widely used standardized test in psychology is the Stanford-Binet intelligence test, which is described in chapter 9, "Intelligence."

Scores on standardized tests are often stated in percentiles. Suppose that you scored in the 92nd percentile on the SAT when you were in high school. This score would mean that 92 percent of a large group of individuals who previously took the test received scores lower than yours.

The main advantage of standardized tests is that they provide information about individual differences among people. One problem with standardized tests is that they do not always predict behavior in nontest situations. Another problem is that standardized tests are based on the belief that a person's behavior is consistent and stable, yet personality and intelligence—two primary targets of standardized

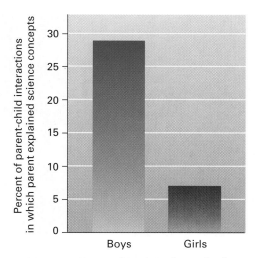

FIGURE 2.8 Parents' Explanations of Science to Sons and Daughters at a Science Museum

In a naturalistic observation study at a children's science museum, parents were three times more likely to explain science to boys than to girls (Crowley & others, 2001). The gender difference occurred regardless of whether the father, the mother, or both parents were with the child, although the gender difference was greatest for fathers' science explanations to sons and daughters.

"Would you say Attila is doing an excellent job, a good job, a fair job, or a poor job?"

standardized test A test with uniform procedures for administration and scoring. Many standardized tests allow a person's performance to be compared with the performance of other individuals.

Mahatma Gandhi was the spiritual leader of India in the middle of the twentieth century. Erik Erikson conducted an extensive case study of his life to determine what contributed to his identity development. *What are some limitations of the case study approach?*

testing—can vary with the situation. For example, children may perform poorly on a standardized intelligence test in the office of a school psychologist but score much higher at home, where they are less anxious.

This criticism is especially relevant for members of minority groups, some of whom have been inaccurately classified as mentally retarded on the basis of their scores on intelligence tests (Valencia & Suzuki, 2001). In addition, cross-cultural psychologists caution that many psychological tests developed in Western cultures might might not be appropriate in other cultures (Cushner, 1999). People in other cultures may have had experiences that cause them to interpret and respond to questions much differently from the people on whom the test was standardized.

Case Study   A **case study** is an in-depth look at a single individual. Case studies are performed mainly by mental health professionals when, for either practical or ethical reasons, the unique aspects of an individual's life cannot be duplicated and tested in other individuals (Dattilio, 2001). A case study provides information about one person's fears, hopes, fantasies, traumatic experiences, upbringing, family relationships, health, or anything that helps the psychologist understand the person's mind and behavior.

An example of a case study is Erik Erikson's (1969) analysis of India's spiritual leader Mahatma Gandhi. Erikson studied Gandhi's life in great depth to discover insights about how his positive spiritual identity developed, especially during his adolescence. In putting the pieces of Gandhi's identity development together, Erikson described the contributions of culture, history, family, and various other factors that might affect the way other people develop an identity.

Other vivid case studies appear in chapters 5 and 10. One involves Michael Rehbein, who had much of the entire left side of his brain removed at 7 years of age to end severe epileptic seizures. Another concerns a modern-day wild child named Genie, who lived in near isolation during her childhood.

Case histories provide dramatic, in-depth portrayals of people's lives, but remember that we must be cautious when generalizing from this information. The subject of a case study is unique, with a genetic makeup and personal history that no one else shares. In addition, case studies involve judgments of unknown reliability. Psychologists who conduct case studies rarely check to see if other psychologists agree with their observations.

Correlational Research   In **correlational research,** the goal is to describe the strength of the relationship between two or more events or characteristics. The more strongly the two events are correlated (or related or associated), the more effectively we can predict one event from the other (Whitley, 2002). For example, if researchers find that low-involved, permissive parenting is correlated with a child's lack of self-control, it suggests that low-involved, permissive parenting might be one source of the lack of self-control. This form of research is a key method of data analysis, which you may recall, is the third step in the scientific method.

A caution is in order, however. Correlation does not equal causation. The correlational finding just mentioned does not mean that permissive parenting necessarily causes low self-control in children. It could mean that, but it also could mean that a child's lack of self-control caused the parents to simply throw up their hands in despair and give up trying to control the child. It also could mean that other factors, such as heredity or poverty, caused the correlation between permissive parenting and low self-control in children. Figure 2.9 illustrates these possible interpretations of correlational data.

case study An in-depth look at a single individual.

correlational research A type of research whose goal is to describe the strength of the relationship between two or more events or characteristics.

Observed correlation   Possible explanations for this correlation

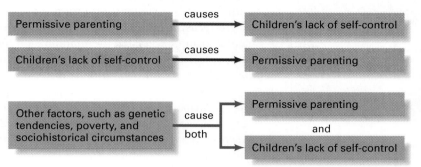

FIGURE 2.9 Possible Explanations for Correlational Data

An observed correlation between two events cannot be used to conclude that one event caused the other. Some possibilities are that the second event caused the first event or that a third, unknown event caused the correlation between the first two events.

Throughout this book you will read about numerous correlational research studies. Keep in mind how easy it is to assume causality when two events or characteristics merely are correlated.

The **correlation coefficient** is a number based on a statistical analysis that is used to describe the degree of association between two variables. The correlation coefficient ranges from +1.00 to −1.00. A negative number means an inverse relation. For example, researchers often find a *negative* correlation between permissive parenting and children's self-control. By contrast, they often find a *positive* correlation between parental monitoring of children and children's self-control. The higher the correlation coefficient (whether positive or negative), the stronger the association between the two variables. A correlation of 0 means that there is no association between the variables. A correlation of −.40 is stronger than a correlation of +.20 because we disregard whether the correlation is positive or negative in determining the strength of the correlation.

Experimental Research   An **experiment** is a carefully regulated procedure in which one or more factors believed to influence the behavior being studied are manipulated while all other factors are held constant. If the behavior under study changes when a factor is manipulated, we say that the manipulated factor has caused the behavior to change. In other words, the experiment has demonstrated cause and effect. The cause is the factor that was manipulated. The effect is the behavior that changed because of the manipulation. Nonexperimental research methods (descriptive and correlational research) cannot establish cause and effect because they do not involve manipulating factors in a controlled way.

Independent and Dependent Variables   Experiments include two types of changeable factors, or variables: independent and dependent. An *independent variable* is a manipulated, influential, experimental factor. It is a potential cause. The label *independent* is used because this variable can be manipulated independently of other factors to determine its effect. Researchers have a vast array of options open to them in selecting independent variables, and one experiment may include several independent variables.

A *dependent variable* is a factor that can change in an experiment, in response to changes in the independent variable. As researchers manipulate the independent variable, they measure the dependent variable for any resulting effect.

Experimental and Control Groups   Experiments can involve one or more experimental groups and one or more control groups.

Correlational Research

Experimental Research

correlation coefficient A number based on statistical analysis used to describe the degree of association between two variables.

experiment A carefully regulated procedure in which one or more of the factors believed to influence the behavior being studied are manipulated while all other factors are held constant.

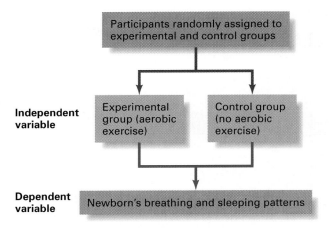

FIGURE 2.10 Principles of Experimental Research
Imagine that you decide to conduct an experimental study of the effects of aerobic exercise by pregnant women on their newborns' breathing and sleeping patterns. You would randomly assign pregnant women to experimental and control groups. The experimental group women would engage in aerobic exercise over a specified number of sessions and weeks. The control group would not. Then, when the infants are born, you would assess their breathing and sleeping patterns. If the breathing and sleeping patterns of newborns whose mothers were in the experimental group are more positive than those of the control group, you would conclude that aerobic exercise caused the positive effects.

cross-sectional approach A research strategy in which individuals of different ages are compared at one time.

longitudinal approach A research strategy in which the same individuals are studied over a period of time, usually several years or more.

An *experimental group* is a group whose experience is manipulated. A *control group* is a comparison group that is as much like the experimental group as possible and that is treated in every way like the experimental group except for the manipulated factor (independent variable). The control group serves as a baseline against which the effects of the manipulated condition can be compared.

Random assignment is an important principle for deciding whether each participant will be placed in the experimental group or in the control group (Shaughnessy, Zechmeister, & Zechmeister, 2003). *Random assignment* means that researchers assign participants to experimental and control groups by chance. It reduces the likelihood that the experiment's results will be due to any preexisting differences between groups. Figure 2.10 illustrates the nature of experimental research.

Time Span of Research

A special concern of developmentalists is the time span of a research investigation (Miller, 2001). Studies that focus on the relation of age to some other variable are common in child development. We have several options: Researchers can study different individuals of different ages and compare them; they can study the same individuals as they age over time; or they can use some combination of these two approaches.

Cross-Sectional Approach The **cross-sectional approach** is a research strategy in which individuals of different ages are compared at one time. A typical cross-sectional study might include a group of 5-year-olds, 10-year-olds, and 15-year-olds. The different groups can be compared with respect to a variety of dependent variables: IQ, memory, peer relations, attachment to parents, hormonal changes, and so on. All of this can be accomplished in a short time. In some studies data are collected in a single day. Even in large-scale cross-sectional studies with hundreds of participants, data collection does not usually take longer than several months to complete.

The main advantage of the cross-sectional study is that the researcher does not have to wait for the individuals to grow up or become older. Despite its time efficiency, the cross-sectional approach has its drawbacks. It gives no information about how individuals change or about the stability of their characteristics. The increases and decreases of development—the hills and valleys of growth and development—can become obscured in the cross-sectional approach. For example, in a cross-sectional study of self-esteem, average increases and decreases might be revealed. But the study would not show how the life satisfaction of individual children waxed and waned over the years. It also would not tell us whether younger children who had high or low self-esteem as young adults continued to have high or low self-esteem, respectively, when they became older.

Longitudinal Approach The **longitudinal approach** is a research strategy in which the same individuals are studied over a period of time, usually several years or more. For example, if a study of self-esteem were conducted longitudinally, the same children might be assessed at the ages of 5, 10, and 15. Figure 2.11 compares the cross-sectional and longitudinal approaches.

Although longitudinal studies provide a wealth of information about such important issues as stability and change in development and the importance of early experience for later development, they are not without their problems (Raudenbush, 2001). They are expensive and time-consuming. The longer the study lasts, the more participants drop out—they move, get sick, lose interest, and so forth. Participants can bias the outcome of a study, because those who remain may be dissimilar to those who drop out. Those individuals who remain in a longitudinal study

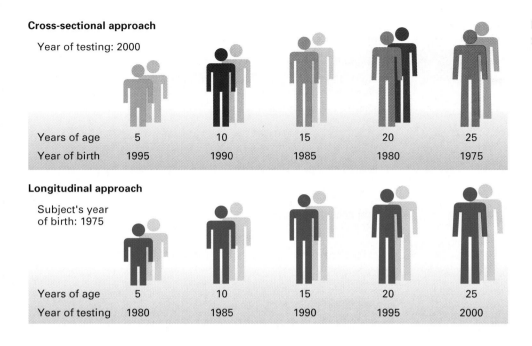

Cross-sectional approach

Year of testing: 2000

| Years of age | 5 | 10 | 15 | 20 | 25 |
| Year of birth | 1995 | 1990 | 1985 | 1980 | 1975 |

Longitudinal approach

Subject's year of birth: 1975

| Years of age | 5 | 10 | 15 | 20 | 25 |
| Year of testing | 1980 | 1985 | 1990 | 1995 | 2000 |

FIGURE 2.11 A Comparison of Cross-Sectional and Longitudinal Approaches

over a number of years may be more compulsive and conformity-oriented, for example, or they might have more stable lives.

A point that is important to make is that theories often are linked with a particular research method or methods. Thus, method(s) researchers use are associated with their particular theoretical approach. Figure 2.12 illustrates the connections between research methods and theories.

Research Journals

Regardless of whether you pursue a career in child development, education, psychology, nursing, or a related field, you can benefit by learning about research journals. Possibly as a student you will be required to look up original research in journals as part of writing a term paper. As a parent, teacher, or nurse you might want to consult journals to obtain information that will help you understand and work more effectively with children. And, as an inquiring person, you might want to look up information in journals after you have heard or read something that piqued your curiosity.

A *journal* publishes scholarly and academic information, usually in a specific domain, such as physics, math, sociology, or, in the case of our interest, child development. Scholars in these fields publish most of their research in journals, which are the core information source in virtually every academic discipline.

Journal articles are usually written for other professionals in the same field as the journal's focus—such as geology, anthropology, or child development. Because the articles are written for other professionals, they often contain technical language and specialized terms related to a specific discipline that are difficult for nonprofessionals to understand. You have probably already had one or more courses in psychology, and you will be learning a great deal more about the specialized field of child development in this course, which should improve your ability to understand journal articles in this field.

An increasing number of journals publish information about children's development. Among the leading journals of child development are *Child Development, Developmental Psychology, Infant Behavior and Development, Pediatric Nursing, Pediatrics, Early Childhood Research Quarterly,* and *Journal of Research on Adolescence.* Also, a number of journals that do not focus solely on development include articles on children's

FIGURE 2.12 Connections of Research Methods to Theories

Research Method	Theory
Observation	• All theories emphasize some form of observation. • Behavioral and social cognitive theories place the strongest emphasis on laboratory observation. • Ethological theory places the strongest emphasis on naturalistic observation.
Interview/survey	• Psychoanalytic and cognitive studies (Piaget, Vygotsky) often use interviews. • Behavioral, social cognitive, and ethological theories are the least likely to use surveys or interviews.
Case study	• Psychoanalytic theories (Freud, Erikson) are the most likely to use this method.
Standardized test	• None of the theories discussed emphasize the use of this method.
Physiological research and research with animals	• Non of the theories discussed address physiological research to any significant degree. • Behavioral and ethological theories are the most likely to conduct animal research.
Correlational research	• All of the theories use this research method, although psychoanalytic theories are the least likely to use it.
Experimental research	• The behavioral and social cognitive theories and the information-processing theories are the most likely to use the experimental method. • Psychoanalytic theories are the least likely to use it.
Cross-sectional/ longitudinal/ sequential methods	• No theory described uses these methods more than any other. • The sequential method is the least likely to be used by any theory.

development, such as *Journal of Educational Psychology, Sex Roles, Journal of Cross-Cultural Psychology, Journal of Marriage and the Family,* and *Journal of Consulting and Clinical Psychology.*

In psychology and the field of child development, most journal articles are reports of original research. Many journals also include review articles that present an overview of different studies on a particular topic, such as a review of day care, a review of the transition to elementary school, or a review of adolescent depression.

Many journals are highly selective about what they publish. Every journal has a board of experts that evaluates articles submitted for publication. One or more of the experts carefully examine the submitted paper and accept or reject it on such factors as its contribution to the field, its theoretical relevance, its methodological excellence, and its clarity of writing. Some of the most prestigious journals reject as many as 80 to 90 percent of the articles that are submitted because they fail to meet the journal's standards.

Where can you find research journals? Your college or university library likely has one or more of the journals listed. Some public libraries also carry journals. An increasing number of research journals can be accessed on the Internet.

An *abstract* is a brief summary that appears at the beginning of a journal article. The abstract lets readers quickly determine whether the article is relevant to their interests and if they want to read the entire article. The *introduction,* as its title suggests, introduces the problem or issue that is being studied. It includes a concise

Research journals are the core of information in virtually every academic discipline. Those shown here are among the increasing number of research journals that publish information about child development. *What are the main parts of a research article that presents findings from original research?*

review of research relevant to the topic, theoretical ties, and one or more hypotheses to be tested. The *method* section consists of a clear description of the subjects evaluated in the study, the measures used, and the procedures followed. The method section should be sufficiently clear and detailed so that, by reading it, another researcher could repeat, or replicate, the study. The *results* section reports the analysis of the data collected. In most cases, the results section includes statistical analyses that are difficult for nonprofessionals to understand. The *discussion* section describes the author's conclusions, inferences, and interpretation of the findings. Statements are usually made about whether the hypotheses presented in the introduction were supported, the limitations of the study, and suggestions for future research. The last part of a journal article is called *references*, which lists bibliographic information for every source cited in the article. The references section is often a good source for finding other articles relevant to the topic you are interested in.

We live in a society that generates a vast amount of information about children in various media ranging from the research journals we just described to newspaper and television accounts. The information varies greatly in quality. To read about some strategies for evaluating media reports of research, see the Explorations in Child Development box.

www.mhhe.com/santrockcd10

Child Development
Developmental Psychology
Ethics

Explorations in Child Development

Being a Wise Consumer of Information About Children's Development

Be Cautious About What Is Reported in the Popular Media
Television, radio, newspapers, and magazines frequently report research on child development. Many researchers regularly supply the media with information about children. In some cases, this research has been published in professional journals or presented at national meetings and then is picked up by the popular media. And most colleges have a media relations department, which contacts the press about current faculty research.

However, not all research on children that appears in the media comes from professionals with excellent credentials and reputations. Journalists, television reporters, and other media personnel generally are not scientifically trained. It is not an easy task for them to sort through the avalanche of material they receive and to make sound decisions about which information to report.

Unfortunately, the media often tend to focus on sensational, dramatic findings. They want you to stay tuned or buy their publication. When the information they gather from research journals is not sensational, they may embellish it and sensationalize it, going beyond what the researcher intended.

Another problem with research reported in the media is a lack of time or space to go into important details about a study. They often have only a few lines or a few minutes to summarize as best they can what may be complex findings. Too often this means that what is reported is overgeneralized and stereotyped.

Don't Assume Group Research Applies to an Individual
Most research on children focuses on children as a group. Individual variations in how children behave is usually not a main focus. However, in many instances, parents, teachers, and others want to know about how to help one particular child cope and learn more effectively.

Don't Overgeneralize About a Small or Clinical Sample
There often isn't space or time in media presentations to go into detail about the nature of the sample of the children on which a study was based. In many cases, samples are too small to let us generalize to a larger population.

Don't Generally Take a Single Study as the Defining Word
The media might identify an interesting research study and claim that it is something phenomenal with far-reaching implications. As a competent consumer of information, be aware that it is extremely rare for a single study to have earth-shattering, conclusive answers that apply to all children. In fact, where there are large numbers of studies that focus on a particular issue, it is not unusual to find conflicting results from one study to the next. Reliable answers about children's development usually emerge only after many researchers have conducted similar studies and have drawn similar conclusions.

Don't Accept Causal Conclusions from Correlational Studies   Drawing causal conclusions from correlational studies is one of the most common mistakes made by the media. In nonexperimental studies (remember that, in an experiment, participants are randomly assigned to treatments or experiences), two variables or factors might be related to each other. However, causal conclusions cannot be drawn when two or more factors simply are correlated; we cannot say that one causes the other.

An insightful exercise is to select a topic from this book and course—such as day care, adolescent problems, or parenting. Find an article in a research journal (for example, *Child Development* or *Developmental Psychology*) and an article in a newspaper or magazine on the same topic. How are the journal article and the newspaper/magazine article different?

Review and Reflect: Learning Goal 2

2 Explain how research on child development is conducted

REVIEW

- What are three main types of research? What are four types of descriptive research? What is correlational research like? How can experimental research be characterized?
- What are some ways that researchers study the time span of people's lives?
- What are research journals like? What are the main sections of a research journal article?

REFLECT

- You have learned that correlation does not equal causation. Develop an example of two variables (two sets of observations) that are correlated but that you believe almost certainly have no causal relationship.

3 FACING UP TO RESEARCH CHALLENGES

| Conducting Ethical Research | | Minimizing Bias |

The scientific foundation of research in child development helps to minimize the effect of individual researchers' biases and to maximize the objectivity of the results. Still, some subtle challenges remain to be fully resolved. One is to ensure that research is conducted in an ethical way; another is to recognize, and try to overcome, researchers' deeply buried personal biases.

Conducting Ethical Research

Ethics is an important part of your understanding of the science of child development. Even if you have no formal exposure to child development beyond this course, you will find that scientific research in this field and related disciplines affects our everyday life. For one thing, decision makers in government, schools, and many other institutions use the results of research in child development to help children and the adults who care for them lead happier, healthier, more productive lives.

The explosion in technology has forced society to grapple with looming ethics questions that were unimaginable only a few decades ago. The same line of research that enables previously sterile couples to have children might also let prospective parents "call up and order" the characteristics they prefer in their children and someday tip the balance of males and females in the world. Should embryos left over from procedures for increasing fertility be saved or discarded? The line of research that enables previously sterile couples to have children has also led to the spectacle of frozen embryos being passed about in the courts as a part of divorce settlements.

Ethics in research may affect you more personally if you serve at some point, as is quite likely, as a participant in a study. In that event, you need to know about your rights as a participant and about the responsibilities researchers have in assuring that these rights are safeguarded. The failure to consider participants' well-being can have life-altering consequences for them. For example, one investigation of young dating couples asked them to complete a questionnaire that coincidentally stimulated some of the participants to think about potentially troublesome issues (Rubin & Mitchell, 1976). One year later, when the researchers followed up with the original sample, 9 of 10 participants said they had discussed their answers with their dating partner. In most instances, the discussions helped to strengthen the relationships. In some cases, though, the participants used the questionnaire as a springboard to discuss previously hidden problems or concerns. One participant said, "The study definitely played a role in ending my relationship with Larry." In this case, the couple had different views about how long they expected to be together. She was thinking of a short-term dating relationship only, while he was thinking in terms of a lifetime. Their answers to the questions brought the disparity in their views to the surface and led to the end of their relationship. Researchers have a responsibility to anticipate the personal problems their study might cause and to at least inform the participants of the possible fallout.

If you ever become a researcher in child development yourself, you will need an even deeper understanding of ethics. You may never become a researcher in the field of child development, but you may conduct one or more studies in this or other courses. Even smart, conscientious students frequently do not consider the rights of the participants who serve in their experiments. A student might think, "I volunteer in a home for the mentally retarded several hours per week. I can use the residents of the home in my study to see if a particular treatment helps improve their memory for everyday tasks." But without proper permissions the most well-meaning, kind, and considerate studies still violate the rights of the participants.

Ethics Guidelines Safeguarding the rights of research participants is a challenge because the potential harm is not always obvious (Gall, Borg, & Gall, 2003). At first glance, you might not imagine that a questionnaire on dating relationships would have any substantial impact. However, researchers increasingly recognize that lasting harm might come to the participants in a study of children's development.

Today colleges and universities have review boards that evaluate the ethical nature of research conducted at their institutions. Proposed research plans must pass the scrutiny of a research ethics committee before the research can be initiated.

In addition, the American Psychological Association (APA) has developed ethics guidelines for its members. The code of ethic instructs psychologists to protect their participants from mental and physical harm. The participants' best interests need to be kept foremost in the researcher's mind (Rosnow, 1995). APA's guidelines address four important issues:

- **Informed Consent** All participants, if they are old enough (typically 7 years or older), must give their consent to participate. If they are not old enough, their parents' or guardians' consent must be attained. Informed consent means that the participants (and/or their parents or legal guardians) have been told what their participation will entail and any risks that might be involved. For example, if researchers want to study the effects of conflict in divorced families on children's self-esteem, the participants should be informed that in some instances discussion of a family's experiences might improve family relationships, but in other cases might raise unwanted stress. After informed consent is given, participants have the right to withdraw at any time.
- **Confidentiality** Researchers are responsible for keeping all of the data they gather on individuals completely confidential and when possible, completely anonymous.
- **Debriefing** After the study has been completed, participants should be informed of its purpose and the methods that were used. In most cases, the experimenter also can inform participants in a general manner beforehand about the purpose of the research without leading participants to behave in a way they think that the experimenter is expecting. When preliminary information about the study is likely to affect the results, participants can at least be debriefed after the study has been completed.
- **Deception** This is an ethical issue that psychologists debate extensively (Hoyle & Judd, 2002; Whitley, 2002). In some circumstances, telling the participant beforehand what the research study is about substantially alters the participant's behavior and invalidates the researcher's data. In all cases of deception, however, the researcher must ensure that the deception will not harm the participant and that the participant will be told the complete nature of the study (debriefed) as soon as possible after the study is completed.

Psychologists' Ethical Principles

Minimizing Bias

Studies of children's development are most useful when they are conducted without bias or prejudice toward any particular group of people. Of special concern is bias based on gender and bias based on culture or ethnicity.

Gender Bias For decades, society has had a strong gender bias, a preconceived notion about the abilities of females and males that prevented individuals from pursuing their own interests and achieving their potential. But gender bias also has had a less obvious effect within the field of child development (Etaugh & Bridges, 2001; Paludi, 2002; Shields & Eyssell, 2001). For example, it is not unusual for conclusions to be drawn about females' attitudes and behaviors from research conducted with males as the only participants.

Florence Denmark and her colleagues (1988) argue as well that when gender differences are found, they sometimes are unduly magnified. For example, a researcher might report in a study that 74 percent of the boys had high achievement expectations versus only 67 percent of the girls and go on to talk about the differences in some detail. In reality, this might be a rather small difference. It also might disappear if the study were repeated, or the study might have methodological problems that don't allow such strong interpretations.

Researchers giving females equal rights in research have raised some new questions (Tetreault, 1997):

- How might gender bias influence the choice of hypotheses, participants, and research design? For example, the most widely known theory of moral development was proposed by a male (Lawrence Kohlberg) in a male-dominant society (the United States), and males were the main participants in research used to support the theory for many years.
- How might research on topics of primary interest to females, such as relationships, feelings, and empathy, challenge existing theory? For example, in the study of moral development, the highest level has often been portrayed as based on a principle of "justice for the individual" (Kohlberg, 1976). However, more recent theorizing notes individuality and autonomy tend to be male concerns and suggests that a principle based on relationships and connections with others be added to our thinking about high-level moral development (Brabeck, 2000; Gilligan, 1982, 1996).
- How has research that has exaggerated gender differences between females and males influenced the way the people think about females? For example, some researchers believe that gender differences in mathematics have often been exaggerated and have been fueled by societal bias (Hyde & Mezulis, 2001; Hyde & Plant, 1995). Such exaggeration of differences can lead to negative expectations for females' math performance.

Cultural and Ethnic Bias The realization that research on child development needs to include more people from diverse ethnic groups has also been building (Graham, 1992). Historically, people from ethnic minority groups (African American, Latino, Asian American, and Native American) have been discounted from most research in the United States and simply thought of as variations from the norm or average. Because their scores don't always fit neatly into measures of central tendency (such as a mean score to reflect the average performance of a group of participants),

Careers in Child Development

Pam Reid, *Educational and Developmental Psychologist*

As a child, Pam Reid played with chemistry sets, and at the university she was majoring in chemistry, planning on becoming a medical doctor. Because some of her friends signed up for a psychology course as an elective, she decided to join them. She was so intrigued by learning more about how people think, behave, and develop that she changed her major to psychology. She says, "I fell in love with psychology." Pam went on to obtain her Ph.D. in educational psychology.

Today, Pamela Trotman Reid is a professor of education and psychology at the University of Michigan. She is also a research scientist for the UM Institute for Research on Women and Gender. Her main interest is how children and adolescents develop social skills, and especially how gender, socioeconomic status, and ethnicity are involved in development (Reid & Zalk, 2001). Because many psychological findings have been based on research with middle-socioeconomic-status non-Latino White populations, Pam believes it is important to study people from different ethnic groups. She stresses that by understanding the expectations, attitudes, and behavior of diverse groups, we enrich the theory and practice of psychology. Currently Pam is working with her graduate students on a project involving middle school girls. She is interested in why girls, more often than boys, stop taking classes in mathematics.

Pam Reid *(center, back row)* with some of the graduate students she mentors at the University of Michigan.

Look at these two photographs, one of all White male children, the other of a diverse group of girls and boys from different ethnic groups, including some White children. Consider a topic in child development, such as parenting, cultural values, or independence seeking. *If you were conducting research on this topic, might the results of the study be different depending on whether the participants in your study were the children in the bottom or top photograph?*

minority individuals have been viewed as confounds or "noise" in data. Consequently, researchers have deliberately excluded them from the samples they have selected (Ryan-Finn, Cauce, & Grove, 1995). Given the fact that individuals from diverse ethnic groups were excluded from research on child development for so long, we might reasonably conclude that children's real lives are perhaps more varied than research data have indicated in the past (Ponterotto & others, 2001; Stevenson, 1995).

Researchers also have tended to overgeneralize about ethnic groups (Trimble, 1989). **Ethnic gloss** is using an ethnic label such as African American or Latino in a superficial way that portrays an ethnic group as being more homogeneous than it really is. For example, a researcher might describe a research sample like this: "The participants were 20 Latinos and 20 Anglo-Americans." A more complete description of the Latino group might be something like this: "The 20 Latino participants were Mexican Americans from low-income neighborhoods in the southwestern area of Los Angeles. Twelve were from homes in which Spanish is the dominant language spoken, 8 from homes in which English is the main language spoken. Ten were born in the United States, 10 in Mexico. Ten described themselves as Mexican American, 5 as Mexican, 3 as American, 2 as Chicano, and 1 as Latino." Ethnic gloss can cause researchers to obtain samples of ethnic groups that are not representative of the group's diversity, which can lead to overgeneralization and stereotyping.

Pam Reid is a leading researcher who studies gender and ethnic bias in development. To read about Pam's interests, see the Careers in Child Development insert on page 55.

Review and Reflect: Learning Goal 3

3 Discuss research challenges in child development

REVIEW

- What are researchers' ethical responsibilities to the people they study?
- How can gender, cultural, and ethnic bias affect the outcome of a research study?

REFLECT

- Imagine that you are conducting a research study on the sexual attitudes and behaviors of adolescents. What ethical safeguards should you use in conducting the study?

ethnic gloss Using an ethnic label such as African American or Latino in a superficial way that portrays an ethnic group as being more homogeneous than it really is.

Reach Your Learning Goals

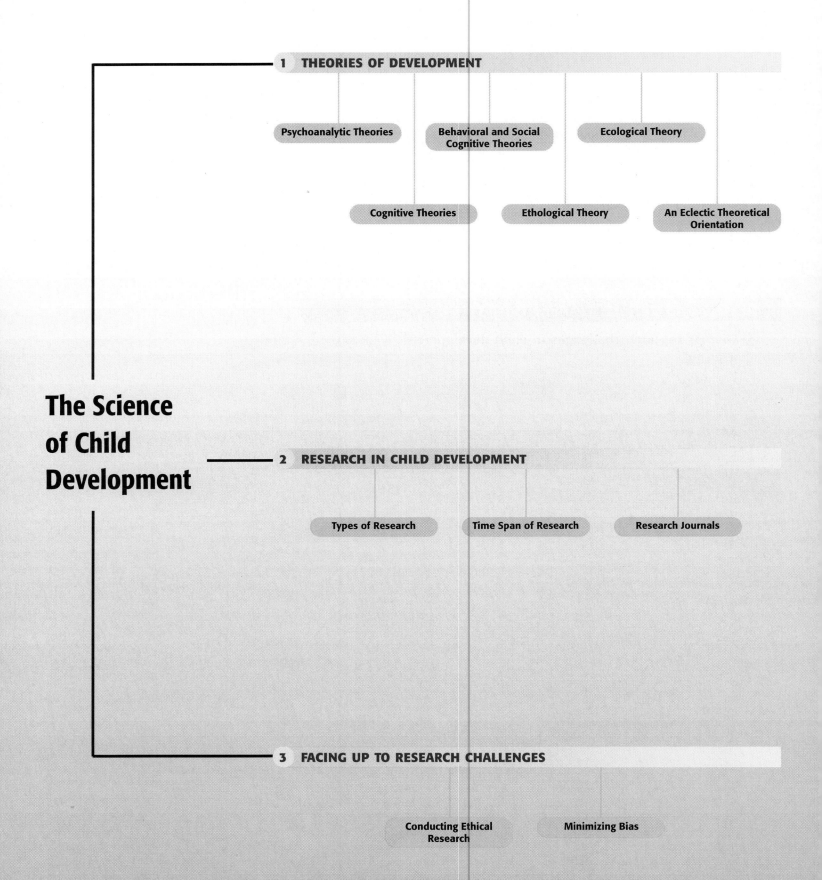

The Science of Child Development

1 THEORIES OF DEVELOPMENT

- Psychoanalytic Theories
- Behavioral and Social Cognitive Theories
- Ecological Theory
- Cognitive Theories
- Ethological Theory
- An Eclectic Theoretical Orientation

2 RESEARCH IN CHILD DEVELOPMENT

- Types of Research
- Time Span of Research
- Research Journals

3 FACING UP TO RESEARCH CHALLENGES

- Conducting Ethical Research
- Minimizing Bias

Summary

1 Describe theories of child development

- The scientific method involves four main steps: (1) conceptualize a problem, (2) collect data, (3) analyze data, and (4) draw conclusions. Theory is often involved in conceptualizing a problem. A theory is an interrelated, coherent set of ideas that helps to explain and to make predictions. Hypotheses are specific assumptions and predictions, often derived from theory, that can be tested to determine their accuracy.

- Psychoanalytic theory describes development as primarily unconscious and as heavily colored by emotion. Psychoanalytic theorists believe that behavior is merely a surface characteristic and that early experiences with parents shape development. Freud said that personality is made up of three structures—id, ego, and superego. The conflicting demands of these structures produce anxiety. Freud also believed that individuals go through five psychosexual stages—oral, anal, phallic, latency, and genital. Erikson's theory emphasizes these eight psychosocial stages of development: trust versus mistrust, autonomy versus shame and doubt, initiative versus guilt, industry versus inferiority, identity versus identity confusion, intimacy versus isolation, generativity versus stagnation, and integrity versus despair. Contributions of psychoanalytic theories include an emphasis on a developmental framework. One criticism is that they often lack scientific support.

- Cognitive theories emphasize conscious thoughts. Piaget proposed a cognitive developmental theory in which children use the processes of organization and adaptation (assimilation and accommodation) to understand their world. In Piaget's theory, children go through four cognitive stages: sensorimotor, preoperational, concrete operational, and formal operational. Vygotsky's sociocultural cognitive theory emphasizes how culture and social interaction guide cognitive development. The information-processing theory emphasizes that children manipulate information, monitor it, and strategize about it. Contributions of cognitive theories include an emphasis on the active construction of understanding. One criticism is that they give too little attention to individual variations in cognitive development.

- Three versions of the behavioral approach are Pavlov's classical conditioning, Skinner's operant conditioning, and Bandura's social cognitive theory. In Pavlov's classical conditioning, a neutral stimulus acquires the ability to produce a response originally produced by another stimulus. In Skinner's operant conditioning, the consequences of a behavior produce changes in the probability of the behavior's occurrence. In Bandura's social cognitive theory, observational learning is a key aspect of development. Bandura emphasizes reciprocal interactions among the person/cognition, behavior, and environment. Contributions of the behavioral and social cognitive theories include an emphasis on scientific research. One criticism is that they give inadequate attention to developmental changes.

- Ethology stresses that behavior is strongly influenced by biology, is tied to evolution, and is characterized by critical or sensitive periods. Contributions of ethological theory include a focus on the biological and evolutionary basis of development. Criticisms include a belief that the critical and sensitive period concepts are too rigid.

- Ecological theory is Bronfenbrenner's environmental systems view of development. It consists of five environmental systems: microsystem, mesosystem, exosystem, macrosystem, and chronosystem. Contributions of the theory include a systematic examination of macro and micro dimensions of environmental systems. One criticism is that it gives inadequate attention to biological and cognitive factors.

- An eclectic theoretical orientation does not follow any one theoretical approach, but rather selects from each theory whatever is considered the best in it.

2 Explain how research on child development is conducted

- Three main types of research are (1) descriptive, (2) correlational, and (3) experimental. Four types of descriptive research are observation (in a laboratory or a naturalistic setting), survey (questionnaire) or interview, standardized test, and case study. In correlational research, the goal is to describe the strength of the relationship between two or more events or characteristics. Experimental research involves conducting an experiment, which can determine cause and effect. An independent variable is the manipulated, influential, experimental factor. A dependent variable is a factor that can change in an experiment, in response to changes in the independent variable. Experiments can involve one or more experimental groups and control groups. In random assignment, researchers assign participants to experimental and control groups by chance.

- When researchers decide about the time span of their research, they can conduct cross-sectional or longitudinal studies.

- A journal publishes scholarly and academic information, and an increasing number of journals publish information about child development. Most journal articles are reports of original research. Most research journal articles follow this format: abstract, introduction, methods, results, discussion, and references.

3 Discuss research challenges in child development

- Researchers' ethical responsibilities include seeking participants' informed consent, ensuring their confidentiality, debriefing them about the purpose and potential personal consequences of participating, and avoiding unnecessary deception of participants.

- Researchers need to guard against gender, cultural, and ethnic bias in research. Every effort should be made to make research equitable for both females and males. More children from ethnic minority backgrounds need to be included in child development research.

Key Terms

theory 29
hypotheses 29
psychoanalytic theory 30
Erikson's theory 31
Piaget's theory 33
assimilation 34
accommodation 34
Vygotsky's theory 35

information-processing theory 36
social cognitive theory 37
ethology 38
ecological theory 40
eclectic theoretical orientation 41
descriptive research 43

laboratory 44
naturalistic observation 44
standarized test 45
case study 46
correlational research 46
correlation coefficient 47
experiment 47
cross-sectional approach 48

longitudinal approach 48
ethnic gloss 56

Key People

Sigmund Freud 30
Erik Erikson 31
Jean Piaget 34

Lev Vygotsky 35
Robert Siegler 36
Ivan Pavlov 37

B. F. Skinner 37
Albert Bandura 37
Walter Mischel 37

Konrad Lorenz 38
Urie Bronfenbrenner 40

Taking It to the Net

1. Erika has never put much faith in Freud's theories, especially the one about the Oedipus complex and how it accounts for differences in male and female moral development. Her child development teacher challenged her to find out if there is any empirical evidence to back up Freud's claims.

2. Sean has to do a presentation in his psychology class on how ethological theories can be utilized to understand some aspects of child development. Sean found a report that compares and contrasts how and why nonhuman primates and human beings imitate others of their species.

3. For her senior psychology project, Doris wants to study the effect on self-esteem of mandatory school uniforms. She wants to limit her study to fourth-graders. She has located a school with a mandatory uniform policy and one without such a policy. What type of research design should she use?

Connect to **www.mhhe.com/santrockcd10** to research the answers and complete these exercises.

E-Learning Tools

To help you master the material in this chapter, you'll find a number of valuable study tools on the Student CD-ROM that accompanies this book. Also visit the Online Learning Center for *Child Development,* tenth edition (**www.mhhe.com/santrockcd10**) where you'll find these additional resources:

- View video clips by key developmental psychology experts, including Judy Dunn discussing how to design a study on children.

- Use the interactive Prism exercises to learn more about independent and dependent variables.
- Build your decision-making skills by trying your hand at the parenting, nursing, and education "Scenarios" on the Online Learning Center.

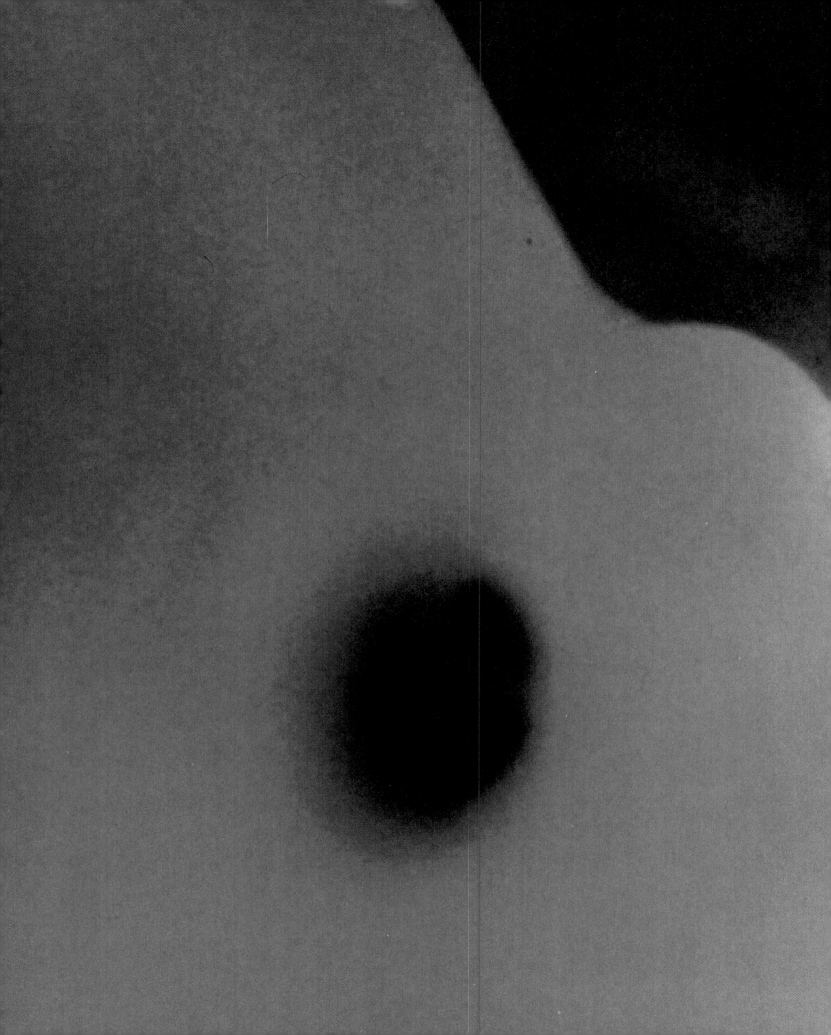

Biological Processes, Physical Development, and Perceptual Development

What endless questions vex the thought, of whence and whither, when and how.

—SIR RICHARD BURTON
British Explorer, 19th Century

The rhythm and meaning of life involve beginnings. Questions are raised about how, from so simple a beginning, endless forms develop, grow, and mature. What was this organism, what is this organism, and what will this organism be? In Section 2, you will read four chapters: "Biological Beginnings" (chapter 3), "Prenatal Development and Birth" (chapter 4), "Physical Development in Infancy" (chapter 5), and "Physical Development in Childhood and Adolescence" (chapter 6).

There are one hundred and ninety-three living species of monkeys and apes. One hundred and ninety-two of them are covered with hair. The exception is the naked ape, self-named Homo sapiens.

—DESMOND MORRIS
British Zoologist, 20th Century

Biological Beginnings

Chapter Outline

THE EVOLUTIONARY PERSPECTIVE

Natural Selection and Adaptive Behavior

Evolutionary Psychology

GENETIC FOUNDATIONS

What Are Genes?

Mitosis and Meiosis

Genetic Principles

Behavior Genetics

Molecular Genetics

The Collaborative Gene

Chromosome- and Gene-Linked Abnormalities

REPRODUCTIVE CHALLENGES AND CHOICES

Prenatal Diagnostic Tests

Infertility

Adoption

HEREDITY-ENVIRONMENT INTERACTION

Heredity-Environment Correlations

Shared and Nonshared Environmental Experiences

The Epigenetic View

Conclusions About Heredity-Environment Interaction

Learning Goals

1 Discuss the evolutionary perspective

2 Describe the genetic foundations of development

3 Identify some important reproductive challenges and choices

4 Explain heredity-environment interaction

The Stories of the Jim and Jim Twins

Jim Lewis (*left*) and Jim Springer (*right*).

Jim Springer and Jim Lewis are identical twins. They were separated at 4 weeks of age and did not see each other again until they were 39 years old. Both worked as part-time deputy sheriffs, vacationed in Florida, drove Chevrolets, had dogs named Toy, and married and divorced women named Betty. One twin named his son James Allan, and the other named his son James Alan. Both liked math but not spelling, enjoyed carpentry and mechanical drawing, chewed their fingernails down to the nubs, had almost identical drinking and smoking habits, had hemorrhoids, put on 10 pounds at about the same point in development, first suffered headaches at the age of 18, and had similar sleep patterns.

But Jim and Jim have some differences. One wears his hair over his forehead, the other slicks it back and has sideburns. One expresses himself best orally; the other is more proficient in writing. But, for the most part, their profiles are remarkably similar.

Another pair, Daphne and Barbara, are called the "giggle sisters" because, after being reunited, they were always making each other laugh. A thorough search of their adoptive families' histories revealed no gigglers. And the identical sisters handled stress by ignoring it, avoided conflict and controversy whenever possible, and showed no interest in politics.

Two other identical twin sisters were separated at 6 weeks and reunited in their fifties. Both had nightmares, which they describe in hauntingly similar ways: both dreamed of doorknobs and fishhooks in their mouths as they smothered to death! The nightmares began during early adolescence and stopped within the past 10 to 12 years. Both women were bed wetters until about 12 or 13 years of age, and their educational and marital histories are remarkably similar.

These sets of twins are part of the Minnesota Study of Twins Reared Apart, directed by Thomas Bouchard and his colleagues. The study brings identical twins (identical genetically because they come from the same fertilized egg) and fraternal twins (dissimilar genetically because they come from different fertilized eggs) from all over the world to Minneapolis to investigate their lives. There the twins complete a number of personality tests and provide detailed medical histories, including information about diet and smoking, exercise habits, chest X rays, heart stress tests, and EEGs (brain-wave tests). The twins are interviewed and asked more than 15,000 questions about their family and childhood environment, personal interests, vocational orientation, values, and aesthetic judgments. They also are given ability and intelligence tests (Bouchard & others, 1990).

Critics of the Minnesota identical twins study point out that some of the separated twins were together for several months prior to their adoption, that some of the twins had been reunited prior to their testing (in some cases, a number of years earlier), that adoption agencies often place twins in similar homes, and that even strangers who spend several hours together and start comparing their lives are likely to come up with some coincidental similarities (Adler, 1991). Still, the Minnesota study of identical twins indicates the increased interest scientists have recently shown in the genetic basis of human development and points to the need for further research on genetic and environmental factors (Bouchard, 1995).

The examples of Jim and Jim, the giggle sisters, and the identical twins who had the same nightmares stimulate us to think about our genetic heritage and the biological foundations of our existence. Organisms are not like billiard balls, moved by simple, external forces to predictable positions on life's pool table. Environmental experiences and biological foundations work together to make us who we are. Our coverage of life's biological beginnings in this chapter focuses on evolution, genetic foundations, reproduction challenges and choices, and the interaction of heredity and environment.

1 THE EVOLUTIONARY PERSPECTIVE

| Natural Selection and Adaptive Behavior | Evolutionary Psychology |

In evolutionary time, humans are relative newcomers to Earth, yet we have established ourselves as the most successful and dominant species. If we consider evolutionary time as a calendar year, humans arrived here in the last moments of December (Sagan, 1977). As our earliest ancestors left the forest to feed on the savannahs, and finally to form hunting societies on the open plains, their minds and behaviors changed. How did this evolution come about?

Natural Selection and Adaptive Behavior

Natural selection is the evolutionary process that favors individuals of a species that are best adapted to survive and reproduce. To understand natural selection, let's return to the middle of the nineteenth century, when the British naturalist Charles Darwin was traveling around the world, observing many different species of animals in their natural surroundings. Darwin, who published his observations and thoughts in *On the Origin of Species* (1859), noted that most organisms reproduce at rates that would cause enormous increases in the population of most species, and yet populations remain nearly constant. He reasoned that an intense, constant struggle for food, water, and resources must occur among the many young born each generation, because many of the young do not survive. Those that do survive pass on their genes to the next generation. Darwin believed that those who do survive to reproduce are probably superior in a number of ways to those who do not. In other words, the survivors are better adapted to their world than are the nonsurvivors (Raven & others, 2002). Over the course of many generations, organisms with the characteristics needed for survival would comprise a larger percentage of the population. Over many, many generations, this could produce a gradual modification of the whole population. If environmental conditions change, however, other characteristics might become favored by natural selection, moving the process in a different direction.

To understand the role of evolution in behavior, we need to understand the concept of adaptive behavior. In evolutionary conceptions of psychology, *adaptive behavior* is behavior that promotes an organism's survival in the natural habitat. Adaptive behavior involves the organism's modification of its behavior to include its likelihood of survival (Cosmides & others, 2003; Wilson, 2003). All organisms must adapt to particular places, climates, food sources, and ways of life. An example of adaptation is an eagle's claws, which facilitate predation. In the human realm, attachment is a system that ensures an infant's closeness to the caregiver for feeding and protection from danger.

Evolutionary Psychology

Although Darwin introduced the theory of evolution by natural selection in 1859, his ideas about evolution only recently have emerged as a popular framework for explaining behavior (Bjorklund & Pellegrini, 2002; Durrant & Ellis, 2003). Psychology's newest approach, **evolutionary psychology,** emphasizes the importance of adaptation, reproduction, and "survival of the fittest" in explaining behavior. Evolution favors organisms that are best adapted to survive and reproduce in a particular environment. The evolutionary psychology approach focuses on conditions that allow individuals to survive or to fail. In this view, the evolutionary process of natural selection favors behaviors that increase organisms' reproductive success and their ability to pass their genes to the next generation (Bjorklund & Bering, 2001; Caporael, 2001; Cosmides & others, 2003; Kenrick & Butner, 2003).

David Buss' (1995, 1999, 2000; Larsen & Buss, 2002) ideas on evolutionary psychology have ushered in a whole new wave of interest in how evolution can explain human behavior. He believes that just as evolution shapes our physical features, such as body shape and height, it also pervasively influences how we make decisions, how aggressive we are, our fears, and our mating patterns.

Evolutionary Developmental Psychology   Much of the thinking about evolutionary psychology has not had a developmental focus. Recently, however, considerable interest has been generated in discovering how evolutionary psychology can improve our understanding of the changes that take place as people develop. Among the views proposed by evolutionary developmental psychologists are (Bjorklund & Pellegrini, 2002):

- *An extended "juvenile" period is needed to develop a large brain and learn the complexity of human social communities.* Humans spend more time prior to when they are reproductively mature than any other mammal. The benefits of this extended "juvenile" period can be seen in the development of a large brain and the experiences required for mastering the complexities of human society.
- *Many aspects of childhood function as preparations for adulthood and were selected over the course of evolution.* For example, children learn much about their physical and social worlds through childhood play that can help them adapt as adults. Sex differences in childhood play have especially been highlighted in this regard. Beginning in the preschool years, boys in all cultures engage in more rough-and-tumble play as preparation for adult fighting and hunting, based on the similarity between child play and adult behavior. Girls engage in more play parenting (such as doll play) and less physical dominance than boys do, a difference that evolutionary psychologists believe is an evolved tendency related to females being the primary caregivers for offspring.
- *Some child characteristics were selected to be adaptive at specific points in development and not as preparation for adulthood.* We just described how play can serve as a preparation for adulthood. However, some aspects of play may function to help children adapt in their immediate circumstances. For example, play provides a context for children to engage in physical exercise and to learn about their current environment.
- *Many evolved psychological mechanisms are domain-specific.* A basic theme of evolutionary psychology is that domain-specific information processing has evolved to help people deal with recurring problems faced by their ancestors. In this view, the mind is not a general-purpose device that can be applied equally well to a vast array of problems. Rather, it consists of a set of specialized modules (Geary & Huffman, 2002). Also in this view, infants enter the world prepared to learn some information more readily than other information, and these preparations serve as a foundation for social and cognitive development across the childhood and adolescent years. Modules have been proposed for physical knowledge (such as the concept that objects are permanent), mathematics, and language. In chapter 9, "Intelligence," we will examine the issue of whether intelligence is a general ability or consists of a number of specific intelligences.
- *Evolved mechanisms are not always adaptive in contemporary society.* Just because some behaviors were adaptive for our prehistoric ancestors does not mean they will

Evolutionary Psychology
Handbook of Evolutionary Psychology
Evolutionary Psychology Resources

evolutionary psychology A contemporary approach that emphasizes the importance of adaptation, reproduction, and "survival of the fittest" in explaining behavior.

serve us well today. For example, being physically dominant and aggressive was adaptive and necessary for survival for prehistoric males. However, just because some tendencies (such as violence among adolescent males) might be "natural" based on evolution does not mean they are morally "good" or inevitable today.

Evaluating Evolutionary Psychology   Albert Bandura (1998), whose social cognitive theory was described in chapter 2, addressed the "biologizing" of psychology and evolution's role in social cognitive theory.   ◀ page 37 Bandura acknowledges the important influence of evolution on human adaptation and change. However, he rejects what he calls "one-sided evolutionism," which sees social behavior as the product of evolved biology, in favor of a bidirectional view. According to this view, evolutionary pressures created changes in biological structures for the use of tools, which enabled organisms to manipulate, alter, and construct new environmental conditions. Environmental innovations of increasing complexity produced, in turn, new selection pressures for the evolution of specialized biological systems for consciousness, thought, and language.

Human evolution gave us body structures and biological potentialities, in other words, not behavioral dictates. Having evolved, advanced biological capacities can be used to produce diverse cultures—aggressive, pacific, egalitarian, or autocratic. As American scientist Stephen Jay Gould (1981) concluded, in most domains of human functioning, biology allows a broad range of cultural possibilities. Bandura (1998) points out that the pace of social change shows that biology does permit a range of possibilities.

Review and Reflect: Learning Goal 1

1 Discuss the evolutionary perspective

REVIEW

- How can natural selection and the concept of adaptive behavior be defined?
- What is evolutionary psychology? What are some key ideas in evolutionary developmental psychology? How can evolutionary psychology be evaluated?

REFLECT

- Are you more inclined to support the views of evolutionary psychologists or their critics? Why?

---

2 GENETIC FOUNDATIONS

| What Are Genes? | Genetic Principles | Molecular Genetics | Chromosome- and Gene-Linked Abnormalities |

| Mitosis and Meiosis | Behavior Genetics | The Collaborative Gene |

Every species must have mechanisms for transmitting characteristics from one generation to the next. These mechanisms often involve the principles of genetics (Cummings, 2003). Each of us carries a genetic code that we inherited from our parents. This code is located within every cell in our bodies. Our genetic codes are alike in one important way—they all contain the human genetic code. Because of the human genetic code, a fertilized human egg cannot grow into an egret, eagle, or elephant.

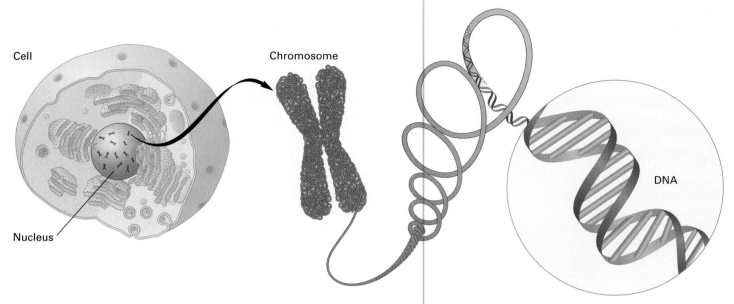

Cell

Nucleus

Chromosome

DNA

FIGURE 3.1 Cells, Chromosomes, Genes, and DNA

(*Left*) The body contains trillions of cells, which are the basic structural units of life. Each cell contains a central structure, the nucleus. (*Middle*) Chromosomes and genes are located in the nucleus of the cell. Chromosomes are made up of threadlike structures composed of DNA molecules. (*Right*) A gene is a segment of DNA that contains the hereditary code. The structure of DNA is a spiraled double chain of molecules.

What Are Genes?

Each of us began life as a single cell weighing about one twenty-millionth of an ounce! This tiny piece of matter housed our entire genetic code—information about who we would become. These instructions orchestrated growth from that single cell to a person made of trillions of cells, each containing a perfect replica of the original genetic code (Wilson, 2003).

The nucleus of each human cell contains 46 **chromosomes,** which are thread-like structures that come in 23 pairs, one member of each pair coming from each parent. Chromosomes are made up of deoxyribonucleic acid, or **DNA,** a complex molecule that contains genetic information. DNA's "double helix" shape looks like a spiral staircase. **Genes,** the units of hereditary information, are short segments of DNA. Genes carry information that enables cells to reproduce and manufacture the proteins needed to sustain life. Chromosomes, DNA, and genes can be mysterious. To gain a better understanding of this mystery, see figure 3.1.

Mitosis and Meiosis

Mitosis and meiosis are processes of cellular reproduction by which DNA is distributed to new cells. **Mitosis** is the process of cell division by which each chromosome in the cell's nucleus duplicates itself. The resulting 46 chromosomes move to the opposite sides of the cell, then the cell separates, and two new daughter cells are formed with each now containing 46 identical chromosomes. Thus the process of mitosis allows DNA to duplicate itself.

A specialized division of chromosomes occurs during the formation of reproductive cells. **Meiosis** is the process by which cells in the reproductive organs divide into gametes (sperm in males, eggs in females), which have half the genetic material of the parent cell. Here are differences between mitosis and meiosis:

- In mitosis, the focus is on cell growth and repair, whereas meiosis involves sexual reproduction.

chromosomes Threadlike structures that come in 23 pairs, one member of each pair coming from each parent. Chromosomes contain the genetic substance DNA.

DNA A complex molecule that contains genetic information.

genes Units of hereditary information composed of DNA. Genes carry information that enables cells to reproduce themselves and manufacture the proteins that maintain life.

mitosis The process by which each chromosome in a cell's nucleus duplicates itself.

meiosis The process by which cells in the reproductive organs divide into gametes (sperm in males, eggs in females), which have half of the genetic material of the parent cell.

- In mitosis, the number of chromosomes present in the new cells remains the same as in the original cell (the chromosomes copy themselves), whereas in meiosis, the number of chromosomes is cut in half.
- In mitosis, two daughter cells are formed from the dividing cell; in meiosis, four daughter cells are produced as a result of two meiotic divisions.

Each human gamete has 23 unpaired chromosomes. The process of human **reproduction** begins when a female gamete, or ovum (egg), is fertilized by a male gamete, or sperm (see figure 3.2). A **zygote** is the single cell formed through fertilization. In the zygote, two sets of unpaired chromosomes combine to form one set of paired chromosomes—one member of each pair from the mother and the other member from the father. In this manner, each parent contributes 50 percent of the offspring's genes.

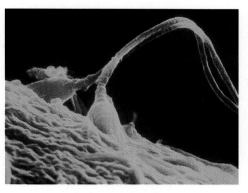

FIGURE 3.2 Union of Sperm and Egg

Genetic Principles

Genetic determination is a complex affair, and much is still unknown about the way genes work (Lewis, 2003). The known genetic principles include dominant-recessive genes, sex-linked genes, genetic imprinting, polygenic inheritance reaction range, and canalization.

Dominant-Recessive Genes Principle   According to the *dominant-recessive genes principle,* some genes are dominant and will always override so-called recessive genes. In other words, if one gene of a pair is dominant and one is recessive, the dominant gene will be expressed in the characteristic it governs. A recessive gene exerts its influence only if the two genes of a pair are both recessive. If you inherit a recessive gene for a trait from each of your parents, you will show the trait. If you inherit a recessive gene from only one parent, you may never know you carry the gene.

Brown hair and dimples rule over blond hair and freckles in the world of dominant-recessive genes. Can two brown-haired parents have a blond-haired child? Yes, they can. Suppose that in each parent the gene pair that governs hair color includes a dominant gene for brown hair and a recessive gene for blond hair. Since dominant genes override recessive genes, the parents have brown hair, but both are carriers of blondness and can pass on their recessive genes for blond hair. With no dominant gene to override them, if a child receives a gene for blond hair from each parent, the pair of recessive genes will make the child's hair blond. Figure 3.3 illustrates the dominant-recessive genes principle.

reproduction The process that, in humans, begins when a female gamete (ovum) is fertilized by a male gamete (sperm).

zygote The single cell formed through fertilization.

FIGURE 3.3 How Brown-Haired Parents Can Have a Blond-Haired Child

Although both parents have brown hair, each parent can have a recessive gene for blond hair. In this example, both parents have brown hair, but each parent carries the recessive gene for blond hair. Therefore, the odds of their child having blond hair are one in four—the probability the child will receive a recessive gene (*b*) from each parent.

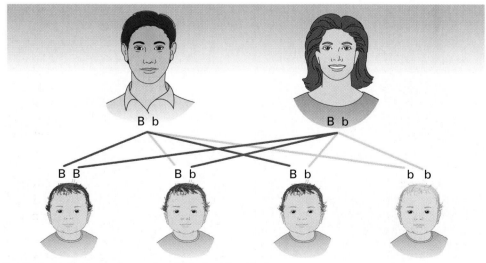

B b   B b

B B   B b   B b   b b

B = Gene for brown hair   b = Gene for blond hair

Sex-Linked Genes For thousands of years, people wondered what determined whether we become male or female. Aristotle believed that the father's arousal during intercourse determines the offspring's sex. The more excited the father was, the more likely it would be a son, he reasoned. Of course, he was wrong, but it was not until the 1920s that researchers confirmed the existence of human sex chromosomes, 2 of the 46 chromosomes human beings normally carry. Ordinarily females have two X chromosomes, so-named for their shape, and males have one X and a smaller Y chromosome. Figure 3.4 shows the chromosome makeup of a male and a female.

A number of disorders have been traced to the sex chromosomes. *X-linked inheritance* is the term used to describe the inheritance of a defective or mutated gene that is carried on the X chromosome (Trappe & others, 2001). Because males have only one X chromosome, when there is a mutant gene on the X chromosome, males have no "backup" copy and therefore may carry an X-linked disease. Females will be less likely to have an X-linked problem because their second X chromosome is not likely to carry the altered gene. Thus, most individuals who have X-linked diseases are males. Females who have one changed copy of the X gene are known as "carriers," and they usually do not show any signs of the X-linked disease. Hemophilia and fragile X syndrome, which we will discuss later in the chapter, are examples of X-linked inheritance (Gonzalez-del Angel & others, 2000; O'Donnell & Warren, 2002).

Genetic Imprinting *Genetic imprinting* is a mechanism in which genes have been modified in one of the parents and have differing effects depending on whether they are transmitted to the offspring through the egg or sperm (Haig, 2003; Jirtle, Sander, & Barrett, 2000). An imprinted gene dominates one that has not been imprinted. Genetic imprinting may explain why individuals who inherit Huntington disease from their fathers show symptoms of the disease at an earlier age than when they inherit from their mother (Navarette, Martinez, & Salamanca, 1994). Also, when individuals inherit Turner syndrome (which is characterized by underdeveloped sex organs) from their fathers they tend to show better cognitive and social skills than when they inherit the disorder from their mothers (Martinez-Pasarell & others, 1999). We will further discuss Huntington disease and Turner syndrome later in chapter.

Polygenic Inheritance Genetic transmission is usually more complex than the simple examples we have examined thus far (Lewis, 2003). *Polygenic inheritance* is the genetic principle by which many genes can interact to produce a particular characteristic. Few psychological characteristics are associated with single pairs of genes. Most are related to the interaction of many different genes. There are about 30,000 to 35,000 human genes in the human genome, so you can imagine that possible combinations of these are staggering in number. Traits affected by this mixing of genes are said to be polygenically determined.

Landmarks in the History of Genetics

Heredity Resources

Genetic Journals and News

FIGURE 3.4 The Genetic Difference Between Males and Females

Set (*a*) shows the chromosome structure of a male, and set (*b*) shows the chromosome structure of a female. The last pair of 23 pairs of chromosomes is in the bottom right box of each set. Notice that the Y chromosome of the male is smaller than the X chromosome of the female. To obtain this kind of chromosomal picture, a cell is removed from a person's body, usually from the inside of the mouth. The chromosomes are stained by chemical treatment, magnified extensively, and then photographed.

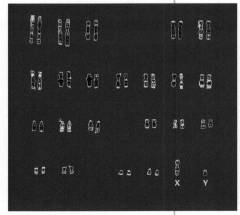

(a)

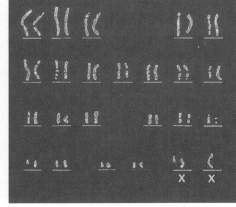

(b)

Calvin and Hobbes   by Bill Watterson

No one possesses all the characteristics that our genetic structure makes possible. A **genotype** is the person's genetic heritage, the actual genetic material. However, not all of this genetic material is apparent in our observed and measurable characteristics. A **phenotype** is the way an individual's genotype is expressed in observable and measurable characteristics. Phenotypes include physical traits (such as height, weight, eye color, and skin pigmentation) and psychological characteristics (such as intelligence, creativity, personality, and social tendencies).

For each genotype, a range of phenotypes can be expressed. Imagine that we could identify all of the genes that would make a person introverted or extraverted. Would measured introversion-extraversion be predictable from knowledge of the specific genes? The answer is no, because even if our genetic model were adequate, introversion-extraversion is a characteristic shaped by experience throughout life. For example, parents may push an introverted child into social situations and encourage the child to become more gregarious.

To understand how introverted a child is, think about a series of genes that predispose the child to develop in a particular way, and imagine environments that are responsive or unresponsive to this development. For instance, the genotype of some persons may predispose them to be introverted in an environment that promotes a turning inward of personality, yet in an environment that encourages social interaction and outgoingness, these individuals may become more extraverted. However, it would be unlikely for the individual with this introverted genotype to become a strong extravert.

Reaction Range   **Reaction range** is the range of possible phenotypes for each genotype. The actual phenotype depends on an environment's restrictiveness or richness. Sandra Scarr (1984) explains reaction range this way: Each of us has a range of potential. For example, an individual with "medium-tall" genes for height who grows up in a poor environment may be shorter than average; however, in an excellent nutritional environment, the individual may grow up to be taller than average. No matter how well fed a person is, though, someone with "short" genes will never be taller than average. Scarr believes that characteristics such as intelligence and introversion work the same way. That is, there is a range within which the environment can modify intelligence, but intelligence is not completely malleable. Reaction range gives us an estimate of how modifiable intelligence is.

Canalization   Although some traits have a wide reaction range, others are somewhat immune to extensive changes in the environment. These characteristics seem to stay on a particular developmental course, regardless of the environmental assaults on them (Waddington, 1957). **Canalization** is the term used to describe the narrow path, or developmental course, that certain characteristics take. Apparently, preservative forces help to protect, or buffer, a person from environmental extremes (Stearns, 2002). For example Jerome Kagan (1984) points to his research on Guatemalan infants who had experienced extreme malnutrition as infants yet showed normal social and cognitive development later in childhood.

genotype A person's genetic heritage; the actual genetic material.

phenotype The way an individual's genotype is expressed in observable and measurable characteristics.

reaction range The range of possible phenotypes for each genotype, suggesting the importance of an environment's restrictiveness or richness.

canalization The process by which certain characteristics take a narrow path, or developmental course. Apparently, preservative forces help to protect a person from environmental extremes.

Although the genetic influence of canalization keeps organisms on a particular developmental path, genes alone do not directly determine human behavior. Developmentalist Gilbert Gottlieb (2000, 2001) points out that genes are an integral part of the organism but that their activity (genetic expression) can be affected by the organism's environment. For example, hormones that circulate in the blood make their way into the cell, where they influence the cell's activity by turning genes "on" and "off." The flow of hormones themselves can be affected by environmental events, such as light, day length, nutrition, and behavior.

Behavior Genetics

At the beginning of the chapter, we described the Minnesota Study of Twins Reared Apart. Comparing twins reared apart is one of a number of methods used to examine heredity's influence on behavior. **Behavior genetics** is the study of the degree and nature of behavior's hereditary basis. Behavior geneticists assume that behaviors are jointly determined by the interaction of heredity and environment (Durrant & Ellis, 2003; Eaves & Silberg, 2003; Rowe, 2001; Wahlsten, 2000). It is important to note that studies involving behavior genetics refer to groups of people (populations) and not to individuals.

In conducting research on the link between heredity and behavior, behavior geneticists often use either twin studies or adoption studies (Maxon, 2003). In the most common type of **twin study,** the behavioral similarity of identical twins is compared with the behavioral similarity of fraternal twins. *Identical twins* (called monozygotic twins) develop from a single fertilized egg that splits into two genetically identical replicas, each of which becomes a person. *Fraternal twins* (called dizygotic twins) develop from separate eggs and separate sperm, making them genetically no more similar than ordinary siblings. Although fraternal twins share the same womb, they are no more alike genetically than are nontwin brothers and sisters, and they may be of different sexes. By comparing groups of identical and fraternal twins, behavior geneticists capitalize on the basic knowledge that identical twins are more similar genetically than are fraternal twins (Jacob & others, 2001). In one twin study, 7,000 pairs of Finnish identical and fraternal twins were compared on the personality traits of extraversion and neuroticism (psychological instability) (Rose & others, 1998). On both of these personality traits, the identical twins were much more similar than the fraternal twins were, suggesting the role of heredity in both traits. However, several issues crop up as a result of twin studies. Adults might stress the similarities of identical twins more than those of fraternal twins, and identical twins might perceive themselves as a "set" and play together more than fraternal twins do. If so, observed similarities in identical twins could be environmentally influenced.

In an **adoption study,** investigators seek to discover whether, in behavior and psychological characteristics, adopted children are more like their adoptive parents, who have provided a home environment, or more like their biological parents, who contributed their heredity. Another form of the adoption study involves comparing adoptive and biological siblings. In one investigation, the educational levels attained by the biological parents were better predictors of the adopted children's IQ scores than were the IQs of the children's adoptive parents (Scarr & Weinberg, 1983). Because of the genetic relation between the adopted children and their biological parents, the implication is that heredity influences children's IQ scores. However, keep in mind that adoption studies are correlational, so we cannot conclude that heredity alone causes variations in the behavior or psychological characteristics of adopted and biological children.

Molecular Genetics

Studies of behavior genetics do not focus on the molecular makeup of genes. Rather, behavior geneticists study heredity at a more global level by such methods as

behavior genetics The study of the degree and nature of behavior's basis in heredity.

twin study A study in which the behavioral similarity of identical twins is compared with the behavioral similarity of fraternal twins.

adoption study A study in which investigators seek to discover whether, in behavior and psychological characteristics, adopted children are more like their adoptive parents, who provided a home environment, or more like their biological parents, who contributed their heredity. Another form of the adoption study is to compare adoptive and biological siblings.

comparing the behavior of identical and fraternal twins. Today, there is a great deal of enthusiasm about the use of molecular genetics to discover the specific locations on genes that are linked to an individual's susceptibility to many diseases and other aspects of health and well-being (Klug & Cummings, 2003; Venter, 2003). The human genome consists of tightly coiled threads of DNA. The Human Genome Project, begun in the 1970s, has made stunning progress in mapping the human genome (Polychronakos, 2003; U.S. Department of Energy, 2001). The Human Genome Project has already linked specific DNA mutations with the increased risk of a number of diseases and conditions, including Huntington disease (in which the central nervous system deteriorates), some forms of cancer, asthma, diabetes, hypertension, and Alzheimer's disease (Davies, 2001; Goodstadt & Pointing, 2001; Zvara & others, 2003).

Every individual carries a number of DNA mutations that might lead to serious physical disease or mental disorder. Identifying the flaws could enable doctors to predict an individual's disease risks, recommend healthy lifestyle regimens, and prescribe the safest and most effective drugs. A decade or two from now, parents of a newborn baby may be able to leave the hospital with a full genome analysis of their offspring that reveals disease risks.

However, mining DNA mutations to discover health risks might increasingly threaten an individual's ability to land and hold jobs, obtain insurance, and keep his genetic profile private. For example, should an airline pilot or neurosurgeon who one day will develop a hereditary disorder that makes her hands shake be required to leave that job early? To think further about such issues, see figure 3.5.

Behavior Genetics
Twin Research
Human Genome Project

The Collaborative Gene

The hope of many biologists was that the Human Genome Project would yield such precise information about the configuration of DNA that virtually a one-to-one connection between genes and behavior could be documented. I remember a conversation I had in the late 1990s with a biologist who had discovered the identity of several genes as part of the Human Genome Project. He strongly believed that the behavior of his two adolescents was solely due to the genes they inherited and had nothing to do with the myriad of experiences they had while they were growing up.

	Yes	No	Undecided
1. Would you want you or your loved one to be tested for a gene that increases your risk for a disease, but does not determine whether you will actually develop the disease?	☐	☐	☐
2. Would you want you and your mate to be tested before having offspring to determine your risk for having a child who is likely to contract various diseases?	☐	☐	☐
3. Should testing of unborn children be restricted to traits that are commonly considered to have negative outcomes, such as disease?	☐	☐	☐
4. Should altering a newly conceived person's genes to improve qualities such as intelligence, appearance, and strength be allowed?	☐	☐	☐
5. Should employers be permitted access to your genetic information?	☐	☐	☐
6. Should life insurance companies have access to your genetic information?	☐	☐	☐

FIGURE 3.5 Exploring Your Genetic Future

Genetic Counseling

In 1978, Richard Davidson was an athletic 37-year-old. A slip on an icy driveway landed him in the hospital for minor surgery for a broken foot. The day after the operation, he died. The cause was malignant hyperthermia (MH), a fatal allergy-like reaction to certain anesthetics. The condition is hereditary and preventable—if the anesthesiologist is aware of the patient's susceptibility, alternative drugs can be used. Richard's death inspired his parents, Owen and Jean Davidson, to search their family tree for others with the MH trait. They mailed 300 letters to relatives, telling them of their son's death and warning about the hereditary risk. The gene, it turned out, came from Jean's side of the family. When her niece, Suellen Gallamore, informed the hospital where she was going to have infertility surgery about the MH in her bloodline, the doctors refused to treat her. In 1981, she cofounded the Malignant Hyperthermia Association to educate medical providers about MH, so that people at risk, like her sons, would not suffer as she had—or lose their lives, as her cousin had (Adato, 1995).

Consider also Bob and Mary Sims, who have been married for several years. They would like to start a family, but they are frightened. The newspapers and popular magazines are full of stories about infants who are born prematurely and don't survive, infants with debilitating physical defects, and babies found to have congenital mental retardation. The Simses feel that to have such a child would create a social, economic, and psychological strain on them and on society.

Accordingly, the Simses turn to a genetic counselor for help. Genetic counselors are usually physicians or biologists who are well versed in the field of medical genetics. The Simses tell their counselor that there has been a history of mental retardation in Bob's family. Bob's younger sister was born with Down syndrome, a form of mental retardation. Mary's older brother has hemophilia, a condition in which bleeding is difficult to stop. They wonder what the chances are that a child of theirs might also be retarded or have hemophilia and what measures they can take to reduce their chances of having a mentally or physically defective child.

The counselor probes more deeply, because she understands that these facts in isolation do not give her a complete picture of the possibilities. She learns that no other relatives in Bob's family are retarded and that Bob's mother was in her late forties when his younger sister was born. She concludes that the retardation was probably due to the age of Bob's mother and not to some general tendency for members of his family to inherit retardation. It is well known that women over 40 have a much higher probability of giving birth to retarded children than are younger women. Apparently, in women over 40 the ova (egg cells) are not as healthy as in women under 40.

In Mary's case the counselor determines that there is a small but clear possibility that Mary might be a carrier of hemophilia and might transmit that condition to a son. Otherwise the counselor can find no evidence from the family history to indicate genetic problems.

The decision is then up to the Simses. In this case, the genetic problem will probably not occur, so the choice is fairly easy. But what should parents do if they face the strong probability of having a child with a major birth defect? Ultimately, the decision depends on the couple's ethical and religious beliefs (Wilfond, 1999).

Suellen Gallamore with her sons, Scott and Greg Vincent. Among her immediate family, only Suellen has had the painful muscle biopsy for the MH gene. Scott, 24, and Greg, 26, assume that they carry the gene and protect against MH by alerting doctors about their family's medical history.

One of the big surprises in the Human Genome Project was the recent finding that humans have only about 30,000 to 35,000 genes (U.S. Department of Energy, 2001). Previously, biologists were sure that humans had 50,000 to 100,000 or more genes. They also believed that there was a one-to-one correspondence between the number of genes and the number of proteins. However, with the recent finding that humans have only 30,000 to 35,000 genes, it is now accepted that humans have far more proteins (300,000 to 500,000) than they have genes, and thus there cannot be a one-to-one correspondence between them (Commoner, 2002; Moore, 2001).

Developmental psychologist David Moore (2001) titled his recent book *The Dependent Gene* to underscore the concept that DNA does not determine traits in an independent manner. Rather, genes and the environment together influence our characteristics. DNA contains the genetic instructions needed for growth and development. However, DNA information can be modified within the cell as small pieces of DNA are mixed, matched, and linked with RNA (ribonucleic acid) in a process called *RNA editing*. RNA transmits the information for further processing in protein synthesis.

DNA clearly exerts an important influence on inheritance, but it acts only in collaboration with many protein-based processes that prevent and repair incorrect sequences, transform proteins into an active form, and provide genetic information beyond that originating in the gene itself (Commoner, 2002; Gottlieb, 1998). Numerous studies have shown that external sensory and internal neural events can excite or inhibit gene expression (Gottlieb, Wahlsten, & Lickliter, 1998; Mauro & others, 1994; Rusak & others, 1990). In sum, according to an increasing number of developmental psychologists who study molecular genetics, no single gene is solely responsible for a given protein and therefore for the inherited trait (Gottlieb, 2001; Moore, 2001). Rather than being an independent gene, DNA is a collaborative gene.

Most molecular biologists operate under the assumption that DNA is the secret of life. However, environmental scientist Barry Commoner (2002) argues that DNA likely did not create life but instead life created DNA. He concluded that when life was first formed on the Earth, proteins must have appeared before DNA because, unlike DNA, proteins have the ability to generate the chemical energy necessary to assemble small molecules into larger ones like DNA. According to Commoner, DNA is a mechanism created by the cell to store information produced in the cell. Once produced by the primitive cell, DNA could become a stable place to store information about the cell's chemistry, not unlike the minutes a secretary takes at a busy meeting. Thus, in Commoner's view, the fundamental unit of life is not DNA but rather the cell of which DNA is a component.

Chromosome- and Gene-Linked Abnormalities

Earlier in this chapter, we saw that abnormal genes are linked with a number of disorders. Here we will examine some of the abnormalities that can occur in chromosomes and genes.

Chromosome Abnormalities   When gametes are formed, the 46 chromosomes do not always divide evenly. In this case, the resulting sperm or ovum does not have the normal 23 chromosomes. The most notable outcomes of this error are Down syndrome and abnormalities of the sex chromosomes (see figure 3.6).

Name	Description	Treatment	Incidence
Down syndrome	An extra chromosome causes mild to severe retardation and physical abnormalities.	Surgery, early intervention, infant stimulation, and special learning programs	1 in 1,900 births at age 20 1 in 300 births at age 35 1 in 30 births at age 45
Klinefelter syndrome	An extra X chromosome causes physical abnormalities.	Hormone therapy can be effective	1 in 800 males
Fragile X syndrome	An abnormality in the X chromosome can cause mental retardation, learning disabilities, or short attention span.	Special education, speech and language therapy	More common in males than in females
Turner syndrome	A missing X chromosome in females can cause mental retardation and sexual underdevelopment.	Hormone therapy in childhood and puberty	1 in 2,500 female births
XYY syndrome	An extra Y chromosome can cause above-average height.	No special treatment required	1 in 1,000 male births

FIGURE 3.6 Some Chromosome Abnormalities

Note: Treatment does not necessarily erase the problem but may improve the individual's adaptive behavior and quality of life.

These athletes, many of whom have Down syndrome, are participating in a Special Olympics competition. Notice the distinctive facial features of the individuals with Down syndrome, such as a round face and a flattened skull. *What causes Down syndrome?*

Genetic Disorders

Prenatal Testing and Down Syndrome

Down syndrome A form of mental retardation, caused by the presence of an extra or altered 21st chromosome.

Klinefelter syndrome A disorder in which males have an extra X chromosome, making them XXY instead of XY.

fragile X syndrome A disorder involving an abnormality in the X chromosome, which becomes constricted and often breaks.

Turner syndrome A disorder in females in which either an X chromosome is missing, making the person XO instead of XX, or the second X chromosome is partially deleted.

XYY syndrome A disorder in which males have an extra Y chromosome.

phenylketonuria (PKU) A genetic disorder in which an individual cannot properly metabolize a substance needed for production of proteins in the body. PKU is now easily detected but, if left untreated, results in mental retardation and hyperactivity.

Down Syndrome **Down syndrome** is a chromosomally transmitted form of mental retardation that is caused by the presence of an extra or altered 21st chromosome. An individual with Down syndrome has a round face, a flattened skull, an extra fold of skin over the eyelids, a protruding tongue, short limbs, and retardation of motor and mental abilities. It is not known why the extra chromosome is present, but the health of the male sperm or female ovum may be involved (Davisson, Gardiner, & Costa, 2001; MacLean, 2000). Women between the ages of 18 and 38 are less likely to give birth to a child with Down syndrome than are younger or older women (Morris & others, 2003). Down syndrome appears approximately once in every 700 live births. African American children are rarely born with Down syndrome.

A large number of special programs exist to help children with Down syndrome (Uyanik, Bumin, & Kayihan, 2003). One such program was developed by Janet Marchese, an adoptive mother of a baby with Down syndrome. She began putting the parents of children with Down syndrome together with couples who wanted to adopt the children. Her adoption network has placed more than 1,500 children with Down syndrome and has a waiting list of couples who want to adopt.

Abnormalities of the Sex Chromosomes Each newborn has at least one X chromosome. However, approximately 1 in every 500 infants either is missing a second X chromosome, or has an X chromosome that is combined with two more sex chromosomes. Four such sex-linked chromosomal disorders are Klinefelter syndrome, fragile X syndrome, Turner syndrome, and XYY syndrome (Baum, 2000).

Klinefelter syndrome is a disorder in which males have an extra X chromosome, making them XXY instead of XY (Bojesen, Juul, & Gravholt, 2003; Lowe & others, 2001). Males with this disorder have undeveloped testes, and they usually have enlarged breasts and become tall. Klinefelter syndrome occurs approximately once in every 800 live male births.

Fragile X syndrome is a disorder that results from an abnormality in the X chromosome, which becomes constricted and often breaks. Mental deficiency often is an outcome, but its form may vary considerably (mental retardation, learning disability, short attention span) (Lewis, 2003). This disorder occurs more frequently in males than in females, possibly because the second X chromosome in females negates the disorder's negative effects.

Turner syndrome is a disorder in females in which either an X chromosome is missing, making the person XO instead of XX, or the second chromosome is partially deleted (Bramswig, 2001; Frias & Davenport, 2003). These females are short in stature and have a webbed neck. They might be infertile and have difficulty in mathematics, but their verbal ability is often facilitated. Turner syndrome occurs in approximately 1 of every 2,500 live female births.

The **XYY syndrome** is a disorder in which a male has an extra Y chromosome (Parmar, Muranjan, & Swami, 2003). Early interest in this syndrome focused on the belief that the extra Y chromosome found in some males contributed to their aggression and violence. It was then reasoned that if a male had an extra Y chromosome, he would likely be extremely aggressive and possibly develop a violent personality. However, researchers subsequently found that XYY males are no more likely to commit crimes than are XY males (Witkin & others, 1976).

Gene-Linked Abnormalities Not only can abnormalities be produced by an uneven number of chromosomes, but they also can result from harmful genes (Croyle, 2000). More than 7,000 such genetic disorders have been identified, although most of them are rare.

Phenylketonuria (PKU) is a genetic disorder in which the individual cannot properly metabolize a substance needed for production of proteins in the body.

Phenylketonuria is now easily detected, but if it is left untreated, mental retardation and hyperactivity result. The disorder is treated by diet to prevent an excess accumulation of the substance, phenylalanine (Schulpis & others, 2003). Phenylketonuria involves a recessive gene and occurs about once in every 10,000 to 20,000 live births. Phenylketonuria accounts for about 1 percent of institutionalized mentally retarded individuals, and it occurs primarily in Whites.

The story of phenylketonuria has important implications for the nature-nurture issue. Although phenylketonuria is a genetic disorder (nature), how or whether a gene's influence in phenylketonuria is played out can depend on environmental influences since the disorder can be treated (nurture). That is, when the usual diet (environment) is altered and replaced with a different diet, mental retardation is avoided (Bendelius, 2003). Thus, phenylketonuria is an excellent example of the interaction of heredity and environment (Merrick, Aspler, & Schwartz, 2001).

Sickle-cell anemia, which occurs most often in African Americans, is a genetic disorder that deforms the body's red blood cells. A red blood cell is usually shaped like a disk, but in sickle-cell anemia, a change in a recessive gene modifies its shape to a hook-shaped "sickle." These cells die quickly, causing anemia, crippling pain in bones and joints, and early death of the individual because they cannot carry oxygen to other cells in the body (Fixler & Styles, 2002). About 1 in 400 African American babies is born with sickle-cell anemia. One in 10 African Americans is a carrier, as is 1 in 20 Latin Americans. Treatment of individuals with sickle-cell anemia starts with early diagnosis, preferably in the newborn period and includes penicillin (Luffy & Grove, 2003). Treatment of complications often includes antibiotics, pain management, and blood transfusions.

Other disorders that can result from harmful genes include cystic fibrosis, diabetes, hemophilia, spina bifida, and Tay-Sachs disease. Figure 3.7 provides information about these conditions.

During a physical examination for a college football tryout, Jerry Hubbard, 32, learned that he carried the gene for sickle-cell anemia. Daughter Sara is healthy but daughter Avery (in the print dress) has sickle-cell anemia. *If you were a genetic counselor, would you recommend that this family have more children? Explain.*

sickle-cell anemia A genetic disorder that affects the red blood cells and occurs most often in people of African descent.

Name	Description	Treatment	Incidence
Cystic fibrosis	Glandular dysfunction that interferes with mucus production; breathing and digestion are hampered, resulting in a shortened life span.	Physical and oxygen therapy, synthetic enzymes, and antibiotics; most individuals live to middle age.	1 in 2,000 births
Diabetes	Body does not produce enough insulin, which causes abnormal metabolism of sugar.	Early onset can be fatal unless treated with insulin.	1 in 2,500 births
Hemophilia	Delayed blood clotting causes internal and external bleeding.	Blood transfusions/injections can reduce or prevent damage due to internal bleeding.	1 in 10,000 males
Phenylketonuria (PKU)	Metabolic disorder that, left untreated, causes mental retardation.	Special diet can result in average intelligence and normal life span.	1 in 14,000 births
Sickle-cell anemia	Blood disorder that limits the body's oxygen supply; it can cause joint swelling, as well as heart and kidney failure.	Penicillin, medication for pain, antibiotics, and blood transfusions.	1 in 400 African American children (lower among other groups)
Spina bifida	Neural tube disorder that causes brain and spine abnormalities.	Corrective surgery at birth, orthopedic devices, and physical/medical therapy.	2 in 1,000 births
Tay-Sachs disease	Deceleration of mental and physical development caused by an accumulation of lipids in the nervous system.	Medication and special diet are used, but death is likely by 5 years of age.	One in 30 American Jews is a carrier.

FIGURE 3.7 Some Gene-Linked Abnormalities

Careers in Child Development

Holly Ishmael, *Genetic Counselor*

Holly Ishmael is a genetic counselor at Children's Mercy Hospital in Kansas City. She obtained an undergraduate degree in psychology from Sarah Lawrence College and then a master's degree in genetic counseling from the same college. Holly uses many of the principles discussed in this chapter in her genetic counseling work.

Genetic counselors have specialized graduate degrees in the areas of medical genetics and counseling. They enter graduate school in these areas with undergraduate backgrounds from a variety of disciplines, including biology, genetics, psychology, public health, and social work. Genetic counselors, like Holly, work as members of a health-care team, providing information and support to families with birth defects or genetic disorders. They identify families at risk by analyzing inheritance patterns and explore options with the family. Genetic counselors may serve as educators and resource people for other health-care professionals and the public. Some genetic counselors also work in administrative positions or conduct research. Some genetic counselors, like Holly, became specialists in prenatal and pediatric genetics; others might specialize in cancer genetics or psychiatric genetic disorders.

Holly says, "Genetic counseling is a perfect combination for people who want to do something science-oriented, but need human contact and don't want to spend all of their time in a lab or have their nose in a book."

There are approximately 30 graduate genetic counseling programs in the United States. If you are interested in this profession, you can obtain further information from the National Society of Genetic Counselors at this website: **www.nsgc.org.**

Holly Ishmael (*left*) in a genetic counseling session.

Some genetic disorders, such as spina bifida, can be diagnosed before birth. Genetic counselors, usually physicians or biologists who are well versed in the field of medical genetics, are familiar with the kinds of problems just described, the odds of encountering them, and helpful strategies for offseting some of their effects (Frezzo & others, 2003). To read about the career and work of a genetic counselor, see the Careers in Child Development insert. Further information about genetic counseling is presented in the Explorations in Child Development box on page 76.

Review and Reflect: Learning Goal 2

2 Describe the genetic foundations of development

REVIEW

- What are genes?
- What are mitosis and meiosis?
- What are some important genetic principles?
- What is behavior genetics?
- What is molecular genetics?
- What is the nature of the collaborative gene?
- What are some key chromosome- and gene-linked abnormalities?

REFLECT

- What are some possible ethical issues regarding genetics and development that might arise in the future?

3 REPRODUCTIVE CHALLENGES AND CHOICES

| Prenatal Diagnostic Tests | Infertility | Adoption |

Earlier in this chapter we discussed several principles of genetics, including the role of meiosis in reproduction. Having also examined a number of genetic abnormalities that can occur, we now have some background to consider some of the challenges and choices facing prospective parents.

Prenatal Diagnostic Tests

Scientists have developed a number of tests to determine whether a fetus is developing normally, among them amniocentesis, ultrasound sonography, chorionic villus sampling, and the maternal blood test.

Amniocentesis is a prenatal medical procedure in which a sample of amniotic fluid is withdrawn by syringe and tested for any chromosome or metabolic disorders (Tercyak & others, 2001; Welch, Blessed, & Lacoste, 2003). The amnionic fluid is in the amnion, a thin, membranous sac in which the embryo is suspended. Amniocentesis is performed between the 12th and 16th weeks of pregnancy. The later amniocentesis is performed, the better its diagnostic potential. The earlier it is performed, the more useful it is in deciding whether to terminate a pregnancy. There is a small risk of miscarriage when amniocentesis is performed; about 1 woman in every 200 to 300 miscarries after amniocentesis.

Ultrasound sonography is a prenatal medical procedure in which high-frequency sound waves are directed into the pregnant woman's abdomen. The echo from the sounds is transformed into a visual representation of the fetus' physical structures. This technique can detect such disorders as microencephaly, a form of mental retardation involving an abnormally small brain (Bahado-Singh & others, 2003). Ultrasound sonography is often used in conjunction with amniocentesis to determine the precise location of the fetus in the mother's abdomen. When ultrasound sonography is used five or more times, the risk of low birth weight may be increased.

As scientists have searched for more accurate, safer assessments of high-risk prenatal conditions, they have developed a new test. *Chorionic villi sampling* is a prenatal medical procedure in which a small sample of the placenta (the vascular organ that links the fetus to the mother's uterus) is removed at some point between the 8th and 11th weeks of pregnancy (Zoppi & others, 2001). Diagnosis takes approximately 10 days. Chorionic villi sampling allows a decision about abortion to be made near the end of the first 12 weeks of pregnancy, a point when abortion is safer and less traumatic than after amniocentesis. Chorionic villi sampling has a slightly higher risk of miscarriage than amniocentesis and is linked with a slight risk of limb deformities. Both techniques provide valuable information about the presence of birth defects, but they also raise issues pertaining to whether an abortion should be obtained if birth defects are present (Papp & Papp, 2003).

The *maternal blood test (alpha-fetoprotein—AFP)* is a prenatal diagnostic test that is used to assess blood alpha-fetoprotein level, which is associated with neural-tube defects (Erdem & others, 2002). This test is administered to women 14 to 20 weeks into pregnancy only when they are at risk for bearing a child with defects in the formation of the brain and spinal cord.

Infertility

Approximately 10 to 15 percent of couples in the United States experience *infertility,* which is defined as the inability to conceive a child after 12 months

www.mhhe.com/santrockcd10

Amniocentesis
Obstetric Ultrasound
Chorionic Villus Sampling
Genetic Counseling

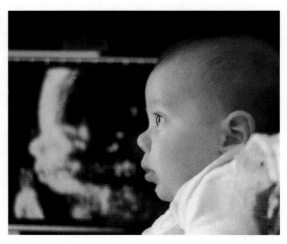

A 6-month-old infant poses with the ultrasound sonography record taken 4 months into the baby's prenatal development. *What is ultrasound sonography?*

of regular intercourse without contraception. The cause of infertility can rest with the woman or the man (Pasch, 2001). The woman may not be ovulating (releasing eggs to be fertilized), she may be producing abnormal ova, her fallopian tubes by which ova normally reach the womb may be blocked, or she may have a disease that prevents implantation of the ova. The man may produce too few sperm, the sperm may lack mobility (the ability to move adequately), or he may have a blocked passageway (El-Ghobashy & West, 2003; Feng, 2003; Oehningner, 2001). In one study, long-term use of cocaine by men was related to low sperm count, low motility, and a higher number of abnormally formed sperm (Bracken & others, 1990). Cocaine-related infertility appears to be reversible if users stop taking the drug for at least one year.

In some cases, surgery may correct the cause of infertility. In others, hormone-based drugs may improve the probability of having a child. However, in some instances, fertility drugs have caused superovulation, producing three or more babies at a time. A summary of some of infertility's causes and solutions is presented in figure 3.8.

In the United States, more than 2 million couples seek help for infertility every year. Of those, about 40,000 try high-tech assisted reproduction. The five most common techniques are these:

- *In vitro fertilization (IVF).* An egg and a sperm are combined in a laboratory dish. If the egg is fertilized, the resulting embryo is transferred into the woman's uterus, or womb (Spandorfer & others, 2003). The success rate is just under 20 percent.
- *Gamete intrafallopian transfer (GIFT).* A doctor inserts eggs and sperm directly into a woman's fallopian tube (Fountain & Krulewitch, 2002). The success rate is almost 30 percent.
- *Intrauterine insemination (IUI).* Frozen sperm—that of the husband or an unknown donor—is placed directly into the uterus (Isaza & others, 2003). The success rate is 10 percent.
- *Zygote intrafallopian transfer (ZIFT).* This is a two-step procedure. First, eggs are fertilized in the laboratory. Then, any resulting zygotes are transferred to a fallopian tube (Levran & others, 2002). The success rate is approximately 25 percent.

Infertility Resources

FIGURE 3.8 Fertility Problems, Possible Causes, and Treatments

Men

Problem	Possible causes	Treatment
Low sperm count	Hormone imbalance, varicose vein in scrotum, possibly environmental pollutants Drugs (cocaine, marijuana, lead, arsenic, some steroids and antibiotics) Y chromosome gene deletions	Hormone therapy, surgery, avoiding excessive heat
Immobile sperm	Abnormal sperm shape Infection Malfunctioning prostate	None Antibiotics Hormones
Antibodies against sperm	Problem in immune system	Drugs

Women

Problem	Possible causes	Treatment
Ovulation problems	Pituitary or ovarian tumor Underactive thyroid	Surgery Drugs
Antisperm secretions	Unknown	Acid or alkaline douche, estrogen therapy
Blocked fallopian tubes	Infection caused by IUD or abortion or by sexually transmitted disease	Eggs surgically removed from ovary and placed in uterus
Endometriosis (tissue buildup in uterus)	Delayed parenthood until the thirties	Hormones, surgical removal of uterine tissue buildup

• *Intracytoplasmic sperm injection (ICSI).* A doctor uses a microscopic pipette to inject a single sperm from a man's ejaculate into an egg in a laboratory dish. The zygote is returned to the uterus (Li & others, 2003). The success rate is approximately 25 percent.

The creation of families by means of the new reproductive technologies raises important questions about the psychological consequences for children. Studies support the idea that "test-tube" babies function well and typically do not differ from naturally conceived children in various behaviors and psychological characteristics (Golombok, MacCallum, & Goodman, 2001; Hahn & DiPietro, 2001) (see figure 3.9).

One consequence of fertility treatments is an increase in multiple births. Twenty-five to 30 percent of pregnancies achieved by fertility treatments—including in vitro fertilization—now result in multiple births. Though parents may be thrilled at the prospect of having children, they also face serious risks. Any multiple birth increases the likelihood that the babies will have life-threatening and costly problems, such as extremely low birth weight.

The McCaughey septuplets, born in 1998. *Why has there been such a dramatic increase in multiple births?*

Adoption

Although surgery and fertility drugs can sometimes solve an infertility problem, another choice is to adopt a child (Moody, 2001; Smit, 2002). Adoption is the social and legal process by which a parent-child relationship is established between persons unrelated at birth. Researchers have found that adopted children and adolescents often show more psychological and school-related problems than nonadopted children (Brodzinsky & others, 1984; Brodzinsky, Lang, & Smith, 1995). Adopted adolescents are referred to psychological treatment two to five times as often as their nonadopted peers (Grotevant & McRoy, 1990).

In one study of 4,682 adopted adolescents and the same number of nonadopted adolescents, adoptees showed lower levels of adjustment (Sharma, McGue, & Benson, 1996). In another study, adopted adolescents had more school adjustment problems, were more likely to use illicit drugs, and were more likely to engage in delinquent behavior (Sharma, McGue, & Benson, 1998). However, adopted siblings were less withdrawn and engaged in more prosocial behavior (such as being altruistic, caring, and supportive of others) than nonadopted siblings. In one study of 1,587 adopted and 87,165 nonadopted adolescents, the adopted adolescents were at higher risk for all of the domains sampled, including school achievement and problems, substance abuse, psychological well-being, and physical health (Miller & others, 2000). In this study, the effects of adoption were more negative when the adopted parents had low levels of education. Also, in this study, when a subsample consisting of the most negative problem profiles was examined, the differences between adopted and nonadopted adolescents widened with the adopted adolescents far more likely to have the most problems.

In one of these studies, the later adoption occurred, the more problems the adoptees had. Infant adoptees had the fewest adjustment difficulties; those adopted after they were 10 years of age had the most problems (Sharma, McGue, & Benson, 1996). Other research has documented that early adoption often has better outcomes for the child than later adoption. At age 6, children adopted from an orphanage in the first 6 months of their lives showed no lasting negative effects of their early experience. However, children from the orphanage who were adopted

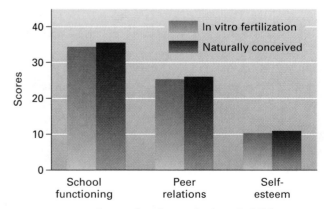

FIGURE 3.9 Socioemotional Functioning of Children Conceived Through In Vitro Fertilization or Naturally Conceived

In one study, comparisons of the socioemotional functioning of young adolescents who had either been conceived through in vitro fertilization (IVF) or naturally conceived revealed no differences between the two groups (Golombok, MacCallum, & Goodman, 2001). Although the means for the naturally conceived group were slightly higher, this is likely due to chance. The mean scores shown for the different measures are in the normal range of functioning.

after they were 6 months of age had abnormally high levels of cortisol, a stress-regulating hormone, indicating that their stress regulation had not developed adequately (Chisholm, 1998).

These results have policy implications, especially for the thousands of children who are relegated to the foster-care system after infancy. Most often, older children are put up for adoption due to parental abuse or neglect. The process of terminating the birth parents' parental rights can be lengthy. In the absence of other relatives, children are turned over to the foster-care system, where they must wait for months or even years to be adopted.

A question that virtually every adoptive parent wants answered is, "Should I tell my adopted child that he or she is adopted? If so, when?" Most psychologists believe that adopted children should be told that they are adopted, because they will eventually find out anyway. Many children begin to ask where they came from when they are approximately 4 to 6 years of age. This is a natural time to begin to respond in simple ways to children about their adopted status. Clinical psychologists report that one problem that sometimes surfaces is the desire of adoptive parents to make life too perfect for the adoptive child and to present a perfect image of themselves to the child. The result too often is that adopted children feel that they cannot release any angry feelings and openly discuss problems (Warshak, 2001).

Review and Reflect: Learning Goal 3

3 Identify some important reproductive challenges and choices

REVIEW

*   What are some common prenatal diagnostic tests?
*   What are some causes of infertility?
*   How does adoption affect children's development?

REFLECT

*   We discussed a number of studies indicating that adoption is linked with negative outcomes for children. Does that mean that all adopted children have more negative outcomes than all nonadopted children? Explain.

---

4 HEREDITY-ENVIRONMENT INTERACTION

Heredity-Environment Correlations		The Epigenetic View
	Shared and Nonshared Environmental Experiences	Conclusions About Heredity-Environment Interaction

In our discussion of adoption, we indicated that children who are adopted later in their development often have more problems than those who are adopted very early in their lives. This finding suggests that the environment plays an important role in children's development. Indeed, heredity and environment interact to produce development (McGuire, 2001). First, we will explore an approach that gives heredity a very strong role in this interaction, then turn to approaches that give heredity a less dominant role.

Heredity-Environment Correlations

The notion of heredity-environment correlations involves the concept that individuals' genes influence the types of environments to which they are exposed. That is,

Heredity-Environment Correlation	Description	Examples
Passive	Children inherit genetic tendencies from their parents and parents also provide an environment that matches their own genetic tendencies.	Musically inclined parents usually have musically inclined children and they are likely to provide an environment rich in music for their children.
Evocative	The child's genetic tendencies elicit stimulation from the environment that supports a particular trait. Thus genes evoke environmental support.	A happy, outgoing child elicits smiles and friendly responses from others.
Active (niche-picking)	Children actively seek out "niches" in their environment that reflect their own interests and talents and are thus in accord with their genotype.	Libraries, sports fields, and a store with musical instruments are examples of environmental niches children might seek out if they have intellectual interests in books, talent in sports, or musical talents, respectively.

FIGURE 3.10 **Exploring Heredity-Environment Correlations**

individuals inherit environments that are related or linked to their genetic propensities (Plomin & DeFries, 1998). Behavior geneticist Sandra Scarr (1993) described three ways that heredity and environment are correlated: passively, evocatively, and actively (see figure 3.10).

- **Passive genotype-environment correlations** occur because biological parents provide an environment that matches their own genetic tendencies, and their children inherit genetic tendencies from their parents. For example, the parents might have a genetic predisposition to be intelligent and read skillfully. Because they read well and enjoy reading, they provide their children with books to read. The likely outcome is that their children, given their own inherited predispositions from their parents, will become skilled readers.
- **Evocative genotype-environment correlations** occur because a child's genotype elicits certain types of physical and social environments. For example, active, smiling children receive more social stimulation than passive, quiet children do. Cooperative, attentive adolescents evoke more pleasant and instructional responses from the adults around them than uncooperative, distractible adolescents do. Athletically inclined youth tend to elicit encouragement to engage in school sports. As a consequence, these adolescents tend to be the ones who try out for sport teams and go on to participate in athletically oriented activities.
- **Active (niche-picking) genotype-environment correlations** occur when children seek out environments that they find compatible and stimulating. Niche-picking refers to finding a niche or setting that is suited to one's abilities. Adolescents select from their surrounding environment some aspect that they respond to, learn about, or ignore. Their active selections of environments are related to their particular genotype. For example, attractive adolescents tend to seek out attractive peers. Adolescents who are musically inclined are likely to select musical environments in which they can successfully perform their skills.

Scarr believes that the relative importance of the three genotype-environment correlations changes as children develop from infancy through adolescence. In infancy, much of the environment that children experience is provided by adults. Thus, passive genotype-environment correlations are more common in the lives of infants and young children than they are for older children and adolescents who can extend their experiences beyond the family's influence and create their environments to a greater degree.

Shared and Nonshared Environmental Experiences

Behavior geneticists also believe that another way to study the environment's role in heredity-environment interaction is to consider the experiences that children have in common with other children living in the same home, as well as experiences that are not shared (Rowe, 2002). **Shared environmental experiences** are

passive genotype-environment correlations Correlations that occur because biological parents provide an environment that matches their own genetic tendencies, and their children inherit genetic tendencies from their parents.

evocative genotype-environment correlations Correlations that exist when the child's genotype elicits certain types of physical and social environments.

active (niche-picking) genotype-environment correlations Correlations that exist when children seek out environments they find compatible and stimulating.

shared environmental experiences Children's common environmental experiences that are shared with their siblings, such as their parents' personalities and intellectual orientation, the family's social class, and the neighborhood in which they live.

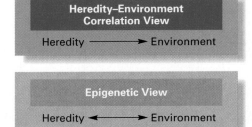

FIGURE 3.11 Comparison of the Heredity-Environment Correlation and Epigenetic Views

*T*he interaction of heredity and environment is so extensive that to ask which is more important, nature or nurture, is like asking which is more important to a rectangle, height or width.

—WILLIAM GREENOUGH
Contemporary Developmental Psychologist, University of Illinois at Urbana

nonshared environmental experiences The child's own unique experiences, both within the family and outside the family, that are not shared by another sibling. Thus, experiences occurring within the family can be part of the "nonshared environment."

epigenetic view Emphasizes that development is the result of an ongoing bidirectional interchange between heredity and environment.

children's common experiences, such as their parents' personalities or intellectual orientation, the family's socioeconomic status, and the neighborhood in which they live. Behavior geneticist Robert Plomin (1993) has found that common rearing, or shared environment, accounts for little of the variation in children's personality or interests. In other words, even though two children live under the same roof with the same parents, their personalities are often very different.

Nonshared environmental experiences are a child's unique experiences, both within the family and outside the family, that are not shared with another sibling. Thus, experiences occurring within the family can be part of the "nonshared environment." Parents often interact differently with each sibling, and siblings interact differently with parents (Hetherington, Reiss, & Plomin, 1994; Rowe, 2002). Siblings often have different peer groups, different friends, and different teachers at school.

Further, some behavior geneticists argue that heredity influences the nonshared environments of siblings in the manner we described earlier in the concept of heredity-environment correlations (Plomin & DeFries, 1998). For example, a child who has inherited a genetic tendency to be athletic is likely to spend more time in environments related to sports, while a child who has inherited a tendency to be musically inclined is more likely to spend time in environments related to music.

The Epigenetic View

Earlier in the chapter we discussed the collaborative gene. Recall that DNA does not determine an individual's traits in an independent matter. DNA is influenced by activity in the cell and by external sensory and neural events, which can excite or inhibit gene expression. Indeed, DNA is an inert molecule that requires a signal to be activated (Gottlieb, 2003).

The **epigenetic view** emphasizes that development is the result of an ongoing, bidirectional interchange between heredity and the environment (Gottlieb, 1998, 2002, 2003). Figure 3.11 compares the heredity-environment correlation and epigenetic views of development.

Let's look at an example that reflects the epigenetic view. A baby inherits genes from both parents at conception (called the *genotype*). During prenatal development, toxins, nutrition, and stress can influence some genes to stop functioning while others become stronger or weaker. During infancy, environmental experiences such as toxins, nutrition, stress, learning, and encouragement continue to modify genetic activity.

Conclusions About Heredity-Environment Interaction

Both genes and environment are necessary for a person to even exist. Without genes, there is no person; without environment, there is no person (Scarr & Weinberg, 1980). Heredity and environment operate together—or cooperate—to produce a person's intelligence, temperament, height, weight, ability to pitch a baseball, ability to read, and so on (Gottlieb, 2001, 2002; Gottlieb, Wahlsten, & Lickliter, 1998; Maccoby, 2002). ◀ page 21 If an attractive, popular, intelligent girl is elected president of her senior class in high school, is her success due to heredity or to environment? Of course, the answer is both. Because the environment's influence depends on genetically endowed characteristics, we say the two factors *interact* (Mader, 2002).

The relative contributions of heredity and environment are not additive. That is, we can't say that such-and-such a percentage of nature and such-and-such a percentage of experience make us who we are. That's the old view. Nor is it accurate to say that full genetic expression happens once, around conception or birth, after which we carry our genetic legacy into the world to see how far it takes us. Genes produce proteins throughout the life span, in many different environments. Or they don't produce these proteins, depending on how harsh or nourishing those environments are.

The emerging view is that many complex behaviors likely have some genetic loading that gives people a propensity for a particular developmental trajectory (Plomin & DeFries, 1998). However, the actual development requires more: an environment (Maccoby, 2002). And that environment is complex, just like the mixture of genes we inherit (Sternberg & Grigorenko, 2001). Environmental influences range from the things we lump together under "nurture" (such as parenting, family dynamics, schooling, and neighborhood quality) to biological encounters (such as viruses, birth complications, and even biological events in cells) (Greenough, 1997, 1999; Greenough & others, 2001).

Imagine for a moment that there is a cluster of genes somehow associated with youth violence (this example is hypothetical because we don't know of any such combination). The adolescent who carries this genetic mixture might experience a world of loving parents, regular nutritious meals, lots of books, and a series of masterful teachers. Or the adolescent's world might include parental neglect, a neighborhood where gunshots and crime are everyday occurrences, and inadequate schooling. In which of these environments are the adolescent's genes likely to manufacture the biological underpinnings of criminality?

The most recent nature-nurture controversy erupted when Judith Harris (1998) published *The Nurture Assumption*. In this provocative book, she argued that what parents do does not make a difference in their children's and adolescents' behavior. Yell at them. Hug them. Read to them. Ignore them. Harris says it won't influence how they turn out. She argues that genes and peers are far more important than parents in children's and adolescents' development.

Harris is right that genes matter and she is right that peers matter, although her descriptions of peer influences do not take into account the complexity of peer contexts and developmental trajectories (Hartup, 1999). In addition to not adequately considering peer complexities, Harris is wrong that parents don't matter. For example, in the early child years, parents play an important role in selecting children's peers and indirectly influencing children's development (Baumrind, 1999).

Child development expert T. Berry Brazelton (1998) commented, "*The Nurture Assumption* is so disturbing it devalues what parents are trying to do. . . . Parents might say, 'If I don't matter, why should I bother?' That's terrifying and it's coming when children and youth need a stronger home base." Even Jerome Kagan (1998), a champion of the view that biology strongly influences development, when commenting about Harris' book, concluded that whether children are cooperative or competitive, achievement-oriented or not, they are strongly influenced by their parents for better or for worse.

There is a huge parenting literature with many research studies documenting the importance of parents in children's development (Collins & others, 2000, 2001; Maccoby, 2002). We will discuss parents' important roles throughout this book.

What is the theme of Judith Harris' controversial book, The Nurture Assumption? *What is the nature of the controversy?*

Genes and Parenting

Review and Reflect: Learning Goal 4

4 Explain heredity-environment interaction

REVIEW

- What are three types of heredity-environment correlations?
- What are shared and nonshared experiences?
- What conclusions can be reached about heredity-environment interaction?
- What is the epigenetic view?

REFLECT

- Someone tells you that he has analyzed his genetic background and environmental experiences and reached the conclusion that environment definitely has had little influence on his intelligence. What would you say to this person about his ability to make this self-diagnosis?

Reach Your Learning Goals

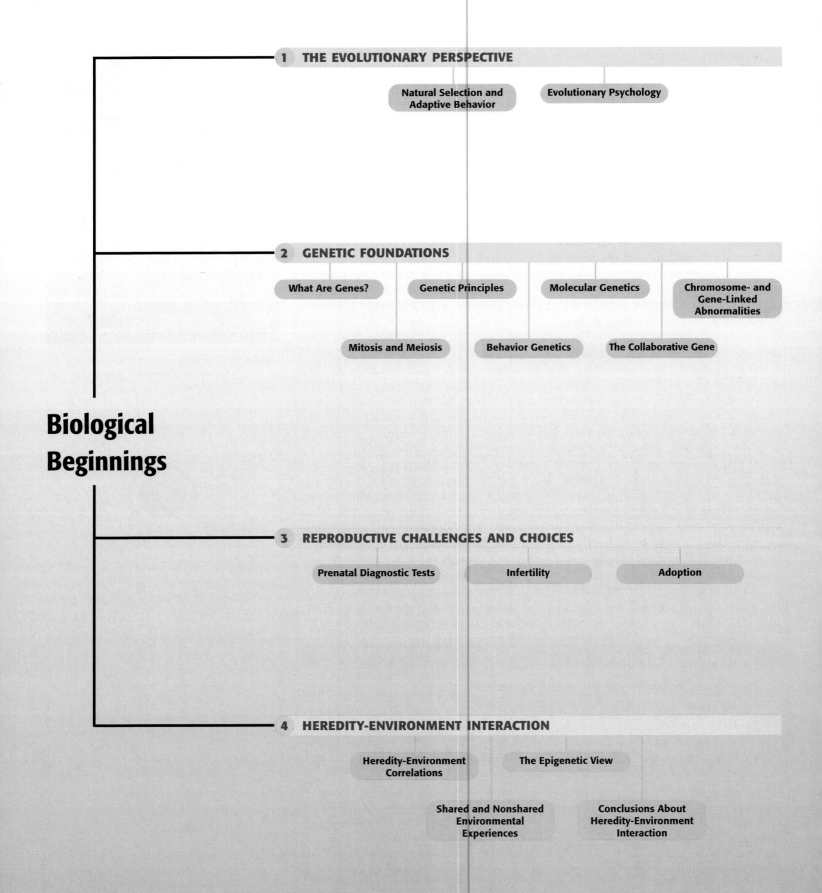

Biological Beginnings

1 THE EVOLUTIONARY PERSPECTIVE

Natural Selection and Adaptive Behavior

Evolutionary Psychology

2 GENETIC FOUNDATIONS

What Are Genes?

Genetic Principles

Molecular Genetics

Chromosome- and Gene-Linked Abnormalities

Mitosis and Meiosis

Behavior Genetics

The Collaborative Gene

3 REPRODUCTIVE CHALLENGES AND CHOICES

Prenatal Diagnostic Tests

Infertility

Adoption

4 HEREDITY-ENVIRONMENT INTERACTION

Heredity-Environment Correlations

The Epigenetic View

Shared and Nonshared Environmental Experiences

Conclusions About Heredity-Environment Interaction

Summary

1 Discuss the evolutionary perspective

- Natural selection is the process that favors the individuals of a species that are best adapted to survive and reproduce. The process of natural selection was originally described by Charles Darwin. In evolutionary theory, adaptive behavior is behavior that promotes the organism's survival in a natural habitat. Biological evolution shaped human beings into a culture-making species.
- Evolutionary psychology is the view that adaptation, reproduction, and "survival of the fittest" are important in explaining behavior. Evolutionary developmental psychology has proposed a number of ideas, including the view that an extended "juvenile" period is needed to develop a large brain and learn the complexity of human social communities. Social cognitive theorist Albert Bandura acknowledges evolution's important role in human adaptation and change but argues for a bidirectional view that enables organisms to manipulate, alter, and construct new environmental conditions. Biology allows for a broad range of cultural possibilities.

2 Describe the genetic foundations of development

- The nucleus of each human cell contains 46 chromosomes, which are composed of DNA. Genes are short segments of DNA that provide information to help cells to reproduce and manufacture proteins that sustain life.
- Mitosis is the process of cell division in which each chromosome duplicates itself so that the two daughter cells each have 46 identical chromosomes. Meiosis is the process of gamete formation in the reproductive organs by which one parent cell splits into four daughter cells. Genes are transmitted from parents to offspring by gametes, or sex cells, which contain only half the full complement of chromosomes (23). Reproduction takes place when a female gamete (ovum) is fertilized by a male gamete (sperm) to create a single-celled zygote.
- Genetic principles include those involving dominant-recessive genes, sex-linked genes, genetic imprinting, polygenic inheritance, reaction range, and canalization.
- Behavior genetics is the field concerned with the degree and nature of behavior's hereditary basis. Methods used by behavior geneticists include twin studies and adoption studies.
- The field of molecular genetics seeks to discover the precise locations of genes that determine an individual's susceptibility to various diseases and other aspects of health and well-being. The Human Genome Project has made stunning progress in mapping the human genome.
- It is important to recognize that there is not a one-to-one correspondence between DNA, a protein, and a human trait or behavior. Thus, DNA does not act independently to produce a trait or behavior. Rather, it acts collaboratively.

- Chromosome abnormalities occur when chromosomes do not divide evenly. Down syndrome is the result of a chromosome abnormality caused by the presence of an extra or altered 21st chromosome. Gene-linked disorders caused by harmful genes include phenylketonuria (PKU) and sickle-cell anemia. Abnormalities of the sex chromosomes include Klinefelter syndrome, fragile X syndrome, Turner syndrome, and XYY syndrome.

3 Identify some important reproductive challenges and choices

- Amniocentesis, ultrasound sonography, chorionic villi sampling, and the maternal blood test are used to determine the presence of defects once pregnancy has begun. Genetic counseling has increased in popularity as more couples desire information about their risk of having a child with defective characteristics.
- Approximately 15 percent of U.S. couples have infertility problems, some of which can be corrected through surgery or fertility drugs. Additional options include in vitro fertilization and other more recently developed techniques.
- Adopted children and adolescents have more problems than their nonadopted counterparts. When adoption occurs very early in development, the outcomes for the child are improved.

4 Explain heredity-environment interaction

- Passive genotype-environment, evocative genotype-environment, and active (niche-picking) genotype-environment are three correlations. Scarr believes the relative importance of these three genotype-environment correlations changes as children develop. She argues that the environments parents select for their children depend on the parents' genotypes.
- Shared environmental experiences refer to siblings' common experiences, such as their parents' personalities and intellectual orientation, the family's socioeconomic status, and the neighborhood in which they live. Nonshared environmental experiences involve the child's unique experiences, both within a family and outside a family, that are not shared with a sibling. Many behavior geneticists argue that differences in the development of siblings are due to nonshared environmental experiences (and heredity) rather than shared environmental experiences.
- The epigenetic view emphasizes that development is the result of an ongoing, bidirectional interchange between heredity and environment.
- Many complex behaviors have some genetic loading that gives people a propensity for a particular developmental trajectory. Actual development also requires an environment and that environment is complex. The interaction of heredity and environment is extensive.

Key Terms

evolutionary psychology 68
chromosomes 70
DNA 70
genes 70
mitosis 70
meiosis 70
reproduction 71
zygote 71
genotype 73

phenotype 73
reaction range 73
canalization 73
behavior genetics 74
twin study 74
adoption study 74
Down syndrome 78
Klinefelter syndrome 78
fragile X syndrome 78

Turner syndrome 78
XYY syndrome 78
phenylketonuria (PKU) 78
sickle-cell anemia 79
passive genotype-environment
    correlations 85
evocative genotype-
    environment correlations
    85

active (niche-picking)
    genotype-environment
    correlations 85
shared environmental
    experiences 85
nonshared environmental
    experiences 86
epigenetic view 86

Key People

Thomas Bouchard 66
Charles Darwin 67
David Buss 68

Albert Bandura 69
Steven Jay Gould 69
Gilbert Gottlieb 74

David Moore 76
Barry Commoner 77
Sandra Scarr 84

Robert Plomin 86
Judith Harris 87

Taking It to the Net

1. Ahmahl, a biochemistry major, is writing a psychology paper on the potential dilemmas that society and scientists may face as a result of the decoding of the human genome. What are some of the main issues or concerns that Ahmahl should address in his class paper?

2. Brandon and Katie are thrilled to learn that they are expecting their first child. They are curious about the genetic makeup of their unborn child and want to know (a) what disorders might be identified through prenatal genetic testing, and (b) which tests, if any, Katie should undergo to help determine this information.

3. Greg and Courtenay have three boys. They would love to have a girl. Courtenay read that there is a clinic in Virginia where you can pick the sex of your child. How successful are such efforts? Would you want to have this choice available to you?

Connect to **www.mhhe.com/santrockcd10** to research the answers and complete these exercises.

E-Learning Tools

To help you master the material in this chapter, you'll find a number of valuable study tools on the Student CD-ROM that accompanies this book. Also visit the Online Learning Center for *Child Development*, tenth edition (**www.mhhe.com/santrockcd10**) where you'll find these additional resources:

- Build your decision-making skills by trying your hand at the parenting, nursing, and education "Scenarios" on the Online Learning Center.

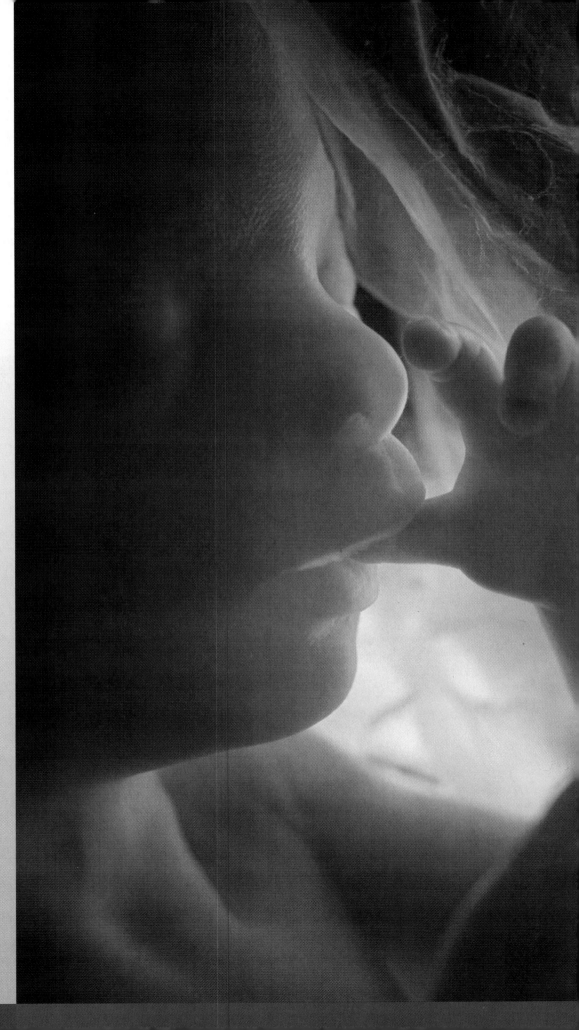

*There was a star danced,
and under that I was
born.*

—WILLIAM SHAKESPEARE
English Playwright, 17th Century

Prenatal Development and Birth

Chapter Outline

Learning Goals

PRENATAL DEVELOPMENT

The Course of Prenatal Development
Teratology and Hazards to Prenatal Development
Prenatal Care
Cultural Beliefs About Pregnancy
Positive Prenatal Development

1 Describe prenatal development

BIRTH

The Birth Process
Low Birth Weight Infants
Measures of Neonatal Health and Responsiveness

2 Discuss the birth process

THE POSTPARTUM PERIOD

What Is the Postpartum Period?
Physical Adjustments
Emotional and Psychological Adjustments
Bonding

3 Explain the changes that take place in the postpartum period

The Story of Tanner Roberts' Birth: A Fantastic Voyage

Tanner Roberts was born in a suite at St. Joseph's Medical Center in Burbank, California (Warrick, 1992). Let's examine what took place in the hours leading up to his birth. It is day 266 of his mother Cindy's pregnancy. She is in the frozen-food aisle of a convenience store and feels a sharp pain, starting in the small of her back and reaching around her middle, which causes her to gasp. For weeks, painless Braxton Hicks spasms (named for the gynecologist who discovered them) have been flexing her uterine muscles. But these practice contractions were not nearly as intense and painful as the one she just experienced. After six hours of irregular spasms, her uterus settles into a more predictable rhythm.

At 3 A.M., Cindy and her husband, Tom, are wide awake. They time Cindy's contractions with a stopwatch. The contractions are now only six minutes apart. It's time to call the hospital. At the hospital, Cindy goes to a labor-delivery suite. The nurse puts a webbed belt and fetal monitor around Cindy's middle to measure the labor. The monitor picks up the fetal heart rate. With each contraction of the uterine wall, Tanner's heartbeat jumps from its resting state of about 140 beats to 160 to 170 beats per minute. When the cervix is dilated to more than 4 centimeters, or almost half open, Cindy is given her first medication. As Demerol begins to drip in her veins, she becomes more relaxed. Tanner's heart rate dips to 130 and then 120.

Contractions are now coming every three to four minutes, each one lasting about 25 seconds. The Demerol does not completely obliterate Cindy's pain. She hugs her husband as the nurse urges her to "relax those muscles. Breathe deep. Relax. You are almost done."

Each contraction briefly cuts off Tanner's source of oxygen. However, the minutes of rest between each contraction resupply the oxygen, and Cindy's deep breathing helps rush fresh blood to the fetal heart and brain.

At 8 A.M., Cindy's obstetrician arrives and determines that her cervix is almost completely dilated. Using a tool made for the purpose, he reaches into the birth canal and tears the membranes of the amnio sac, and about half a liter of clear fluid flows out. Contractions are now coming every two minutes, and each one is lasting a full minute.

By 9 A.M., the labor suite has been transformed into a delivery room. Tanner's body is compressed by his mother's contractions and pushes. As he nears his entrance into the world, the compressions help press the fluid from his lungs in preparation for his first breath.

Squeezed tightly in the birth canal, the top of Tanner's head emerges. His face is puffy and scrunched. Although fiercely squinting because of the sudden light, Tanner's eyes are open. Tiny bubbles of clear mucus are on his lips. Before any more of his body emerges, the obstetrician cradles Tanner's head and suctions his nose and mouth. Tanner takes his first breath, a large gasp followed by whimpering, and then a loud cry. Tanner's body is wet but only slightly bloody as the doctor lifts him onto his mother's abdomen. The umbilical cord, still connecting Tanner with his mother, slows and stops pulsating. The obstetrician cuts it, severing Tanner's connection to his mother's womb. Now Tanner's blood flows not to his mother's blood for nourishment, but to his own lungs, intestines, and other organs. This chapter chronicles the truly remarkable developments from conception through birth. Imagine . . . at one time you were an organism floating in a sea of fluid in your mother's womb. Let's now explore what your development was like from the time you were conceived through the time you were born.

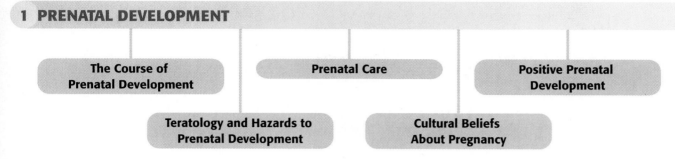

1 PRENATAL DEVELOPMENT

- The Course of Prenatal Development
- Prenatal Care
- Positive Prenatal Development
- Teratology and Hazards to Prenatal Development
- Cultural Beliefs About Pregnancy

Imagine how Tanner Roberts came to be. Out of thousands of eggs and millions of sperm, one egg and one sperm united to produce him. Had the union of sperm and egg come a day or even an hour earlier or later, he might have been very different— maybe even of the opposite sex. Conception occurs when a single sperm cell from the male unites with an ovum (egg) in the female's fallopian tube in a process called fertilization. Remember from chapter 3 that the fertilized egg is called a zygote.

The Course of Prenatal Development

The course of prenatal development lasts approximately 266 days, beginning with fertilization and ending with birth. Prenatal development is divided into three periods: germinal, embryonic, and fetal.

The Germinal Period   The **germinal period** is the period of prenatal development that takes place in the first two weeks after conception. It includes the creation of the zygote, continued cell division, and the attachment of the zygote to the uterine wall. By approximately one week after conception, the differentiation of cells has already commenced, as inner and outer layers of the organism are formed. The **blastocyst** is the inner layer of cells that develops during the germinal period. These cells later develop into the embryo. The **trophoblast** is the outer layer of cells that develops during the germinal period. It later provides nutrition and support for the embryo. *Implantation*, the attachment of the zygote to the uterine wall, takes place about 10 to 14 days after conception. Figure 4.1 illustrates some of the most significant developments during the germinal period.

The Embryonic Period   The **embryonic period** is the period of prenatal development that occurs from two to eight weeks after conception. During the embryonic period, the rate of cell differentiation intensifies, support systems for cells form, and organs appear. As the zygote attaches to the uterine wall, its cells form two layers. At this time, the name of the mass of cells changes from *zygote* to *embryo*. The embryo's *endoderm* is the inner layer of cells, which will develop into the digestive and respiratory systems. The outer layer of cells is divided into two parts. The *ectoderm* is the outermost layer, which will become the nervous system, sensory receptors (ears, nose, and eyes, for example), and skin parts (hair and nails, for example). The *mesoderm* is the middle layer, which will become the circulatory system, bones, muscles, excretory system, and reproductive system. Every body part eventually develops from these three layers. The endoderm primarily produces internal body parts, the mesoderm primarily produces parts that surround the internal areas, and the ectoderm primarily produces surface parts.

As the embryo's three layers form, life-support systems for the embryo mature and develop rapidly. These life-support systems include the placenta, the umbilical cord, and the amnion. The **placenta** is a life-support system that consists of a disk-shaped group of tissues in which small blood vessels from the mother and the offspring intertwine but do not join. The **umbilical cord** is a life-support system, containing two arteries and one vein, that connects the baby to the placenta. Very small

germinal period The period of prenatal development that takes place in the first two weeks after conception. It includes the creation of the zygote, continued cell division, and the attachment of the zygote to the uterine wall.

blastocyst The inner layer of cells that develops during the germinal period. These cells later develop into the embryo.

trophoblast The outer layer of cells that develops in the germinal period. These cells provide nutrition and support for the embryo.

embryonic period The period of prenatal development that occurs two to eight weeks after conception. During the embryonic period, the rate of cell differentiation intensifies, support systems for the cells form, and organs appear.

placenta A life-support system that consists of a disk-shaped group of tissues in which small blood vessels from the mother and offspring intertwine.

umbilical cord A life-support system, containing two arteries and one vein, that connects the baby to the placenta.

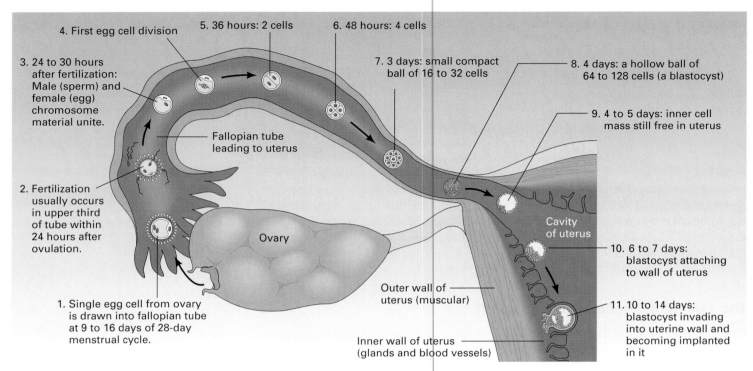

FIGURE 4.1 Significant Developments in the Germinal Period

The numbered steps shown in the figure are:

1. Single egg cell from ovary is drawn into fallopian tube at 9 to 16 days of 28-day menstrual cycle.

2. Fertilization usually occurs in upper third of tube within 24 hours after ovulation.

3. 24 to 30 hours after fertilization: Male (sperm) and female (egg) chromosome material unite.

4. First egg cell division

5. 36 hours: 2 cells

6. 48 hours: 4 cells

7. 3 days: small compact ball of 16 to 32 cells

8. 4 days: a hollow ball of 64 to 128 cells (a blastocyst)

9. 4 to 5 days: inner cell mass still free in uterus

10. 6 to 7 days: blastocyst attaching to wall of uterus

11. 10 to 14 days: blastocyst invading into uterine wall and becoming implanted in it

Fallopian tube leading to uterus

Ovary

Cavity of uterus

Outer wall of uterus (muscular)

Inner wall of uterus (glands and blood vessels)

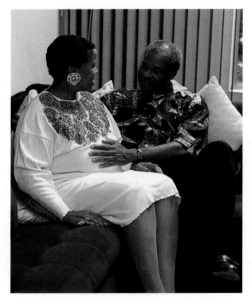

Lines of communication should be open between the expectant mother and her partner during pregnancy. *What are some examples of good partner communication during pregnancy?*

amnion The life-support system that is a bag or envelope that contains a clear fluid in which the developing embryo floats.

organogenesis Organ formation that takes place during the first two months of prenatal development.

molecules—oxygen, water, salt, food from the mother's blood, as well as carbon dioxide and digestive wastes from the embryo's blood—pass back and forth between the mother and infant. Large molecules cannot pass through the placental wall; these include red blood cells and harmful substances, such as most bacteria, maternal wastes, and hormones. The mechanisms that govern the transfer of substances across the placental barrier are complex and are still not entirely understood (Garcia-Bournissen, Feig, & Koren, 2003; Gielchinsky & others, 2002; Weeks & Mirembe, 2002). Figure 4.2 provides an illustration of the placenta, the umbilical cord, and the nature of blood flow in the expectant mother and developing child in the uterus. The **amnion,** a bag or an envelope that contains a clear fluid in which the developing embryo floats, is another important life-support system. Like the placenta and umbilical cord, the amnion develops from the fertilized egg, not from the mother's own body. At approximately 16 weeks, the kidneys of the fetus begin to produce urine. This fetal urine remains the main source of the amniotic fluid until the third trimester, when some of the fluid is excreted from the lungs of the growing fetus. Although the amniotic fluid increases in volume tenfold from the 12th to the 40th week of pregnancy, it is also removed in various ways. Some is swallowed by the fetus, and some is absorbed through the umbilical cord and the membranes covering the placenta. The amniotic fluid provides an environment that is temperature and humidity controlled, as well as shockproof.

Before most women even know they are pregnant, some important embryonic developments take place. In the third week, the neural tube that eventually becomes the spinal cord forms. At about 21 days, eyes begin to appear, and at 24 days the cells for the heart begin to differentiate. During the fourth week, the urogenital system becomes apparent, and arm and leg buds emerge. Four chambers of the heart take shape, and blood vessels appear. From the fifth to the eighth week, arms and legs differentiate further; at this time, the face starts to form but still is not very recognizable. The intestinal tract develops and the facial structures fuse. At eight weeks, the developing organism weighs about 1/30 ounce and is just over 1 inch long. **Organogenesis** is the process of organ formation that takes place during the first two months of prenatal development. When organs are being formed,

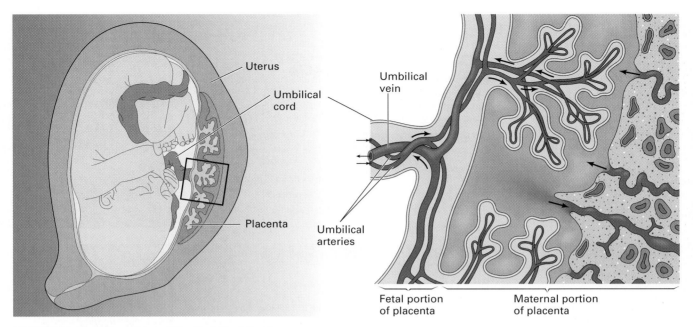

FIGURE 4.2 The Placenta and the Umbilical Cord

Maternal blood flows through the uterine arteries to the spaces housing the placenta, and it returns through the uterine veins to maternal circulation. Fetal blood flows through the umbilical arteries into the capillaries of the placenta and returns through the umbilical veins to the fetal circulation. The exchange of materials takes place across the layer separating the maternal and fetal blood supplies, so the bloods never come into contact. *Note:* The area bound by the square is enlarged in the right half of the illustration. Arrows indicate the direction of blood flow.

they are especially vulnerable to environmental changes. Later in the chapter, we will describe the environmental hazards that can adversely affect organogenesis.

The Fetal Period The **fetal period** is the prenatal period of development that begins two months after conception and lasts for seven months, on the average. Growth and development continue their dramatic course during this time. Three months after conception, the fetus is about 3 inches long and weighs about 1 ounce. It has become active, moving its arms and legs, opening and closing its mouth, and moving its head. The face, forehead, eyelids, nose, and chin are distinguishable, as are the upper arms, lower arms, hands, and lower limbs. The genitals can be identified as male or female. By the end of the fourth month, the fetus has grown to 6 inches in length and weighs 4 to 7 ounces. At this time, a growth spurt occurs in the body's lower parts. Prenatal reflexes are stronger; arm and leg movements can be felt for the first time by the mother.

By the end of the fifth month, the fetus is about 12 inches long and weighs close to a pound. Structures of the skin have formed—toenails and fingernails, for example. The fetus is more active and shows a preference for a particular position in the womb. By the end of the sixth month, the fetus is about 14 inches long and has gained another half pound to a pound. The eyes and eyelids are completely formed, and a fine layer of hair covers the head. A grasping reflex is present and irregular breathing movements occur. By the end of the seventh month, the fetus is about 16 inches long, and having gained another pound, now weighs about 3 pounds. During the eighth and ninth months, the fetus grows longer and gains substantial weight— about another 4 pounds. At birth, the average American baby weighs $7\frac{1}{2}$ pounds and is about 20 inches long. In these last two months, fatty tissues develop, and the functioning of various organ systems—heart and kidneys, for example—steps up.

We have described a number of changes in prenatal development in terms of germinal, embryonic, and fetal periods. Another way to divide prenatal development is in terms of equal periods of three months, called trimesters. An overview of some

www.mhhe.com/santrockcd10

The Visible Embryo

The Trimesters

fetal period The prenatal period of development that begins two months after conception and lasts for seven months, on the average.

First trimester (first 3 months)			
Prenatal growth	**Conception to 4 weeks** • Is less than $\frac{1}{10}$ inch long • Beginning development of spinal cord, nervous system, gastro-intestinal system, heart, and lungs • Amniotic sac envelopes the preliminary tissues of entire body • Is called a "zygote"	**8 weeks** • Is less than 1 inch long • Face is forming with rudimentary eyes, ears, mouth, and tooth buds • Arms and legs are moving • Brain is forming • Fetal heartbeat is detectable with ultrasound • Is called an "embryo"	**12 weeks** • Is about 3 inches long and weighs about 1 ounce • Can move arms, legs, fingers, and toes • Fingerprints are present • Can smile, frown, suck, and swallow • Sex is distinguishable • Can urinate • Is called a "fetus"	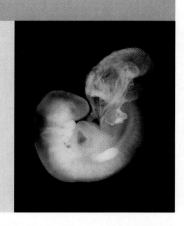

Second trimester (middle 3 months)			
Prenatal growth	**16 weeks** • Is about $5\frac{1}{2}$ inches long and weighs about 4 ounces • Heartbeat is strong • Skin is thin, transparent • Downy hair (lanugo) covers body • Fingernails and toenails are forming • Has coordinated movements; is able to roll over in amniotic fluid	**20 weeks** • Is 10 to 12 inches long and weighs $\frac{1}{2}$ to 1 pound • Heartbeat is audible with ordinary stethoscope • Sucks thumb • Hiccups • Hair, eyelashes, eyebrows are present	**24 weeks** • Is 11 to 14 inches long and weighs 1 to $1\frac{1}{2}$ pounds • Skin is wrinkled and covered with protective coating (vernix caseosa) • Eyes are open • Waste matter is collected in bowel • Has strong grip	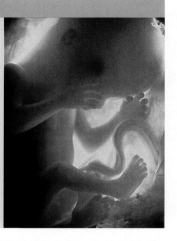

Third trimester (last 3 months)			
Prenatal growth	**28 weeks** • Is 14 to 17 inches long and weighs $2\frac{1}{2}$ to 3 pounds • Is adding body fat • Is very active • Rudimentary breathing movements are present	**32 weeks** • Is $16\frac{1}{2}$ to 18 inches long and weighs 4 to 5 pounds • Has periods of sleep and wakefulness • Responds to sounds • May assume the birth position • Bones of head are soft and flexible • Iron is being stored in liver	**36 to 38 weeks** • Is 19 inches long and weighs 6 pounds • Skin is less wrinkled • Vernix caseosa is thick • Lanugo is mostly gone • Is less active • Is gaining immunities from mother	

FIGURE 4.3 The Three Trimesters of Prenatal Development

of the main changes in prenatal development in the three trimesters is presented in figure 4.3. Remember that the three trimesters are not the same as the three prenatal periods we have discussed—germinal, embryonic, and fetal. The germinal and embryonic periods occur in the first trimester. The fetal period begins two months into the first trimester and continues through the second and third trimesters. An important point that needs to be made is that the first time a fetus has a chance of surviving outside of the womb is the beginning of the third trimester (at about seven months). Even when infants are born in the seventh month, they usually need assistance in breathing.

Teratology and Hazards to Prenatal Development

Some expectant mothers carefully tiptoe about in the belief that everything they do and feel has a direct effect on their unborn child. Others behave casually, assuming that their experiences will have little effect. The truth lies somewhere between these two extremes. Although living in a protected, comfortable environment, the fetus is not totally immune to the larger world surrounding the mother. The environment can affect the child in many well-documented ways. Thousands of babies born deformed or mentally retarded every year are the result of events that occurred in the mother's life, as early as one or two months before conception (Bailey, Forget, & Koren, 2002).

A **teratogen** (the word comes from the Greek word *tera* meaning "monster") is any agent that causes a birth defect. The field of study that investigates the causes of birth defects is called *teratology*. Teratogens include drugs, incompatible blood types, environmental pollutants, infectious diseases, nutritional deficiencies, maternal stress, and advanced maternal and paternal age. So many teratogens exist that practically every fetus is exposed to at least some teratogens. For this reason, it is difficult to determine which teratogen causes which birth defect. In addition, it may take a long time for the effects of a teratogen to show up. Only about half of all potential effects appear at birth.

The dose, the time of exposure to a particular agent, and genetic susceptibility influence the severity of the damage to an unborn child and the type of defect that occurs:

- *Dose* The dose effect is rather obvious—the greater the dose of an agent, such as a drug, the greater the effect.
- *Time of Exposure* Teratogens do more damage when they occur at some points in development than at others (Brent & Fawcett, 2000). In general, the embryonic period is a more vulnerable time than the fetal period. As figure 4.4 shows, sensitivity to teratogens begins about three weeks after conception. The probability of a structural defect is greatest early in the embryonic period, when organs are being formed. After organogenesis is complete, teratogens are less likely to cause anatomical defects. Exposure later, during the fetal period, is more likely to stunt growth or to create problems in the way organs function. The precision of organogenesis is evident; teratologists point out that the vulnerability of the eyes is greatest at 24 to 40 days, the heart at 20 to 40 days, and the legs at 24 to 36 days.

In chapter 2, we introduced the concept of *critical period* in our discussion of Lorenz' ethological theory. Recall that a critical period is a fixed time period very early in development during which certain experiences or events can have a long-lasting effect on development. As shown in figure 4.4, each body structure has its own critical period of formation. Thus, the critical period for the central nervous system (week 3) is earlier than for arms and legs (weeks 4 and 5).

- *Genetic Susceptibility* The type or severity of abnormalities caused by a teratogen is linked to the genotype of the pregnant woman and the genotype of the fetus (Frayling & Hattersley, 2002). For example, variation in maternal metabolism of a particular drug can influence the degree to which the drug effects are transmitted to the fetus. Differences in placental membranes and placental transport also affect fetal exposure. The genetic susceptibility of the fetus to a particular teratogen can also affect the extent to which the fetus is vulnerable.

Prescription and Nonprescription Drugs
Some pregnant women take prescription and nonprescription drugs without thinking about the possible effects on the fetus (Addis, Magrini, & Mastroiacovo, 2001). Occasionally, a rash of deformed babies is born, bringing to light the damage drugs can have on a developing baby. This happened in 1961, when many pregnant women took a popular tranquilizer,

> *T*he history of man for nine months preceding his birth would, probably, be far more interesting, and contain events of greater moment than all three score and ten years that follow it.
>
> —SAMUEL TAYLOR COLERIDGE
> *English Poet, Essayist, 19th Century*

www.mhhe.com/santrockcd10

Health and Prenatal Development

Exploring Teratology

High-Risk Situations

teratogen From the Greek word TERA, meaning "monster." Any agent that causes a birth defect. The field of study that investigates the causes of birth defects is called teratology.

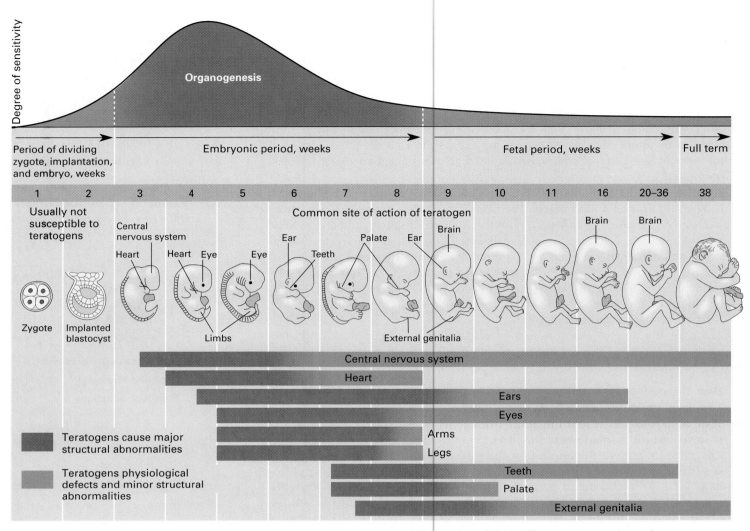

FIGURE 4.4 Teratogens and the Timing of Their Effects on Prenatal Development
The danger of structural defects caused by teratogens is greatest in embryonic development. The period of organogenesis (red color) lasts for about six weeks. Later assaults by teratogens (blue color) mainly occur in the fetal period and instead of causing structural damage are more likely to stunt growth or cause problems of organ function.

thalidomide, to alleviate their morning sickness. In adults, the effects of thalidomide are mild; in babies, however, they are devastating. Not all infants were affected in the same way. If the mother took thalidomide on day 26 (probably before she knew she was pregnant), an arm might not grow. If she took the drug two days later, the arm might not grow past the elbow. The thalidomide tragedy shocked the medical community and parents into the stark realization that the mother does not have to be a chronic drug user for the fetus to be harmed. Taking the wrong drug at the wrong time is enough to physically handicap the offspring for life (Sorokin, 2002).

Because of the devastating effects of thalidomide on embryos, its use in the United States and some other countries was banned. However, thalidomide is once again being used to treat a number of diseases, including cancer and leprosy (Chaudhry & others, 2002; Jin & others, 2002; Thompson & Hansen, 2003). The renewed availability of thalidomide is controversial because of the fear that it may be misused and once again harm embryos.

Prescription drugs that can function as teratogens include antibiotics, such as streptomycin and tetracycline; some antidepressants; certain hormones, such as progestin and synthetic estrogen; and Accutane (which often is prescribed for acne) (Committee on Drugs, 2000).

Nonprescription drugs that can be harmful include diet pills, aspirin, and caffeine (Christian & Brent, 2002; Cnattingius & others, 2000). Let's explore the research on caffeine. A review of studies on caffeine consumption during pregnancy concluded that a small increase in the risks for spontaneous abortion and low birth weight occurs for pregnant women consuming more than 150 milligrams of caffeine (approximately two cups of brewed coffee or two to three 12-ounce cans of cola) per day (Fernandes & others, 1998). In one study, pregnant women who drank caffeinated coffee were more likely to have preterm deliveries and newborns with a lower birth weight than their counterparts who did not drink caffeinated coffee (Eskenazi & others, 1999). In this study, no effects were found for pregnant women who drank decaffeinated coffee. However, in another study, there were no associations between caffeine consumption during pregnancy and birth weight (Clausson & others, 2002). Overall, despite such inconsistencies in research results, the Food and Drug Administration recommends that pregnant women either not consume caffeine or consume it sparingly.

Psychoactive Drugs   *Psychoactive drugs* are drugs that act on the nervous system to alter states of consciousness, modify perceptions, and change moods. A number of psychoactive drugs, including alcohol and nicotine, as well as illegal drugs such as cocaine, marijuana, and heroin have been studied to determine their links to prenatal and child development (Caulfield, 2001; Fogel, 2001; Obel & others, 2002).

Alcohol   Heavy drinking by pregnant women can be devastating to offspring (Barr & Streissguth, 2001; Enoch & Goldman, 2002; Committee on Substance Abuse, 2000). **Fetal alcohol syndrome (FAS)** is a cluster of abnormalities that appears in the offspring of mothers who drink alcohol heavily during pregnancy (Archibald & others, 2001). The abnormalities include facial deformities and defective limbs, face, and heart. Most of these children are below average in intelligence, and some are mentally retarded (Bookstein & others, 2002; Olson, 2000; Riley & others, 2003). Although many mothers of FAS infants are heavy drinkers, many mothers who are heavy drinkers do not have children with FAS or have one child with FAS and other children who do not have it. Figure 4.5 shows a child with fetal alcohol syndrome. Although no serious malformations such as those produced by FAS are found in infants born to mothers who are moderate drinkers, in one study, children whose mothers drank moderately (one to two drinks a day) during pregnancy were less attentive and alert, even at four years of age (Streissguth & others, 1984). In one study, prenatal alcohol exposure was a better predictor of adolescent alcohol use and its negative consequences than was a family history of alcohol problems (Baer & others, 1998). And in another study, adults with fetal alcohol syndrome had a high incidence of mental disorders, such as depression or anxiety (Famy, Streissguth, & Unis, 1998).

What are some guidelines for alcohol use during pregnancy? The U.S. Surgeon General recommends that *no* alcohol be consumed during pregnancy.

Nicotine   Cigarette smoking by pregnant women can also adversely influence prenatal development, birth, and postnatal development. Fetal and neonatal deaths are higher among smoking mothers. There also are higher incidences of preterm births and lower birth weights (Bush & others, 2001; Wang & others, 2000).

In one study, urine samples from 22 of 31 newborns of smoking mothers contained substantial amounts of one of the strongest carcinogens (NNK) in tobacco smoke; the urine samples of the newborns whose mothers did not smoke were free of the carcinogen (Lackmann & others, 1999). In another study, prenatal exposure to cigarette smoking was related to poorer language and cognitive skills at 4 years of age (Fried & Watkinson, 1990). Respiratory problems and sudden infant death syndrome (also known as crib death) are more common among the offspring of mothers who smoked during pregnancy (Schoendorf & Kiely, 1992). Intervention

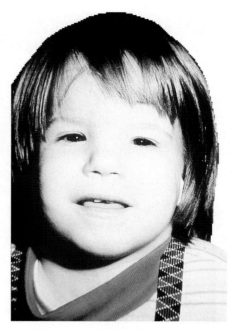

FIGURE 4.5 Fetal Alcohol Syndrome
Notice the wide-set eyes, flat bones, and thin upper lip.

www.mhhe.com/santrockcd10

Fetal Alcohol Syndrome
Smoking and Pregnancy

fetal alcohol syndrome (FAS) A cluster of abnormalities that appears in the offspring of mothers who drink alcohol heavily during pregnancy.

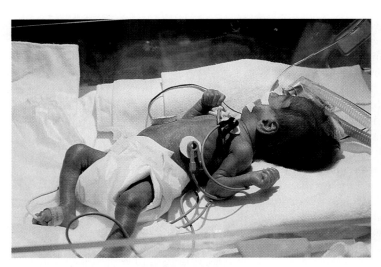

This baby was born addicted to cocaine because its mother was a cocaine addict. *What do we know about the effects of cocaine on children's development?*

programs designed to help pregnant women stop smoking can reduce some of smoking's negative effects, especially by raising birth weights (Klesges & others, 2001; Lightwood, Phibbs, & Glantz, 1999).

Illegal Drugs   Among the illegal drugs that have been studied to determine their effects on prenatal and child development are cocaine, marijuana, and heroin (Fifer & Grose-Fifer, 2001).

Cocaine   With the increased use of cocaine in the United States, there is concern about its effects on the embryos, fetuses, and infants of pregnant cocaine users (Hand & others, 2001). Cocaine use during pregnancy has recently attracted considerable attention because of possible harm to the developing embryo and fetus (Butz & others, 2001; Smith & others, 2001; Zeskind & others, 1999). The most consistent finding is that cocaine exposure during prenatal development is associated with reduced birth weight, length, and head circumference. Also, in one study, prenatal cocaine exposure was associated with impaired motor development at 2 years of age (Arendt & others, 1999). In another recent study that controlled for the use of other drugs, at 1 month of age cocaine exposure during pregnancy was related to lower arousal, less effective self-regulation, higher excitability, and lower quality of reflexes (Lester & others, 2002).

Researchers increasingly are finding that fetal cocaine exposure is linked with impaired information processing (Singer & others, 1999). In one study, prenatal cocaine exposure was moderately related to poor attentional skills through 5 years of age (Bandstra & others, 2000). In another study, prenatal cocaine exposure was related to impaired processing of auditory information after birth (Potter & others, 2000).

Although researchers are finding such deficits in children who are prenatally exposed to cocaine, a cautious interpretation of these findings is in order (Chavkin, 2001; Frank & others, 2001; Potter & others, 2000). Why? Because other factors (such as poverty, malnutrition, and other substance abuse) in the lives of pregnant women who use cocaine often cannot be ruled out as possible contributors to the negative effects on children (Kaugers, Russ, & Singer, 2000). For example, cocaine users are more likely than nonusers to smoke cigarettes, use marijuana, drink alcohol, and take amphetamines. Teasing apart these potential influences from the effects of cocaine itself has not yet been adequately accomplished. Obtaining valid information about the frequency and type of drug use by mothers is complicated because many mothers fear prosecution and loss of child custody because of their drug use.

Indeed, there is still controversy about the effects on the offspring of cocaine use by women during pregnancy (Frank & others, 2002). One recent review concluded that prenatal exposure to cocaine by itself has not been demonstrated to have negative effects on the offspring (Frank & others, 2001).

Marijuana   In spite of marijuana being used by a number of women of reproductive age, there has not been extensive research investigation of its effects on the offspring. In a recent review of the research that has been done, it was concluded that marijuana use during pregnancy is not linked to the offspring's general intelligence but that the child's attention may be impaired (Fried & Smith, 2001). Also, the National Institute of Drug Abuse's (2001) review of marijuana effects concludes that babies born to mothers who used marijuana during pregnancy are smaller than babies born to mothers who did not use the drug. Further, in a longitudinal study, prenatal marijuana exposure was related to learning and memory difficulties at age 11 (Richardson & others, 2002). Nonetheless, because of the small numbers of studies, it is difficult to reach conclusions about the effects of marijuana use by mothers during pregnancy on the child's development.

Heroin It is well documented that infants whose mothers are addicted to heroin show several behavioral difficulties (Hulse & others, 2001). The young infants of these mothers are addicted and show withdrawal symptoms characteristic of opiate abstinence, such as tremors, irritability, abnormal crying, disturbed sleep, and impaired motor control. Behavioral problems are still often present at the first birthday, and attention deficits may appear later in the child's development. The most common treatment for heroin addiction, methadone, is associated with very severe withdrawal symptoms in newborns (Dashe & others, 2002).

Incompatible Blood Types The incompatibility of the mother's and the father's blood types is another risk to prenatal development. Variations in the surface structure of red blood cells distinguish different blood types. One type of surface marker borne by red blood cells identifies a person's blood group as A, B, O, or AB. The second type, called the *Rh factor,* is said to be positive if the Rh marker is present or negative if the individual's red blood cells do not carry this marker. If a pregnant woman is Rh negative and her partner is Rh positive, the fetus may be Rh positive (Weiss, 2001). When the fetus' blood is Rh positive and the mother's is Rh negative, the mother's immune system may produce antibodies that will attack the fetus. This can result in any number of problems, including miscarriage or stillbirth, anemia, jaundice, heart defects, brain damage, or death soon after birth (Narang & Jain, 2001).

Generally, the first Rh-positive baby of an Rh-negative mother is not at risk, but with each subsequent pregnancy the risk becomes greater. A vaccine (RhoGAM) may be given to the mother within three days of the child's birth to prevent her body from making antibodies that will attack future Rh-positive fetuses. Also, babies affected by Rh incompatibility can be given blood transfusions before or right after birth (Mannessier & others, 2000).

Environmental Hazards Radiation, chemicals, and other hazards in our modern industrial world can endanger the fetus (Grigorenko, 2001; Ostrea, Whitehall, & Laken, 2000; Timins, 2001). For instance, radiation can cause a gene mutation (an abrupt, permanent change in genetic material). Chromosomal abnormalities are higher among the offspring of fathers exposed to high levels of radiation in their occupations (Schrag & Dixon, 1985). Radiation from X rays also can affect the developing embryo and fetus, especially in the first several weeks after conception, when women do not yet know they are pregnant (Barnett & Maulik, 2001). It is important for women and their physicians to weigh the risk of an X ray when an actual or potential pregnancy is involved (Shaw, 2001).

Environmental pollutants and toxic wastes are also sources of danger to unborn children. Researchers have found that various hazardous wastes and pesticides cause defects in animals exposed to high doses. Among the dangerous pollutants and wastes are carbon monoxide, mercury, and lead. Some children are exposed to lead because they live in houses in which lead-based paint flakes off the walls or near busy highways, where there are heavy automobile emissions from leaded gasoline. Researchers believe that early exposure to lead affects children's mental development (Markowitz, 2000). For example, in one study, 2-year-olds who prenatally had high levels of lead in their umbilical-cord blood performed poorly on a test of mental development (Bellinger & others, 1987).

Researchers also have found that manufacturing chemicals known as PCBs are harmful to prenatal development (Vreugdenhil & others, 2002). Although banned in the 1970s in the United States, PCBs continue to be present in landfills, sediments, and wildlife. In one study, the extent to which pregnant women ate PCB-polluted fish from Lake Michigan was examined, and subsequently their children

An explosion at the Chernobyl nuclear power plant in the Ukraine produced radioactive contamination that spread to surrounding areas. Thousands of infants were born with health problems and deformities as a result of the nuclear contamination, including this boy whose arm did not form. *Other than radioactive contamination, what are some other types of environmental hazards to prenatal development?*

were observed as newborns, young children, and at 11 years of age (Jacobson & others, 1984; Jacobson & Jacobson, 2002). The women who had eaten more PCB-polluted fish were more likely to have smaller, preterm infants who were more likely to react slowly to stimuli. As preschool children, their exposure to PCBs was linked with less effective short-term memory, and at age 11 with lower verbal intelligence and reading comprehension.

A current environmental concern is the low-level electromagnetic radiation emitted by computer monitors. The fear is that women who spend long hours in front of the monitors might risk adverse effects to their offspring, should they become pregnant. Researchers have not found exposure to computer monitors to be related to miscarriage (Schnorr & others, 1991).

Yet another recent environmental concern for expectant mothers is prolonged exposure to heat produced by saunas or hot tubs. By raising the mother's body temperature, a sauna or a hot tub can cause a fever that endangers the fetus. The high temperature of a fever may interfere with cell division and may cause birth defects or even fetal death if the fever occurs repeatedly for prolonged periods of time. If the expectant mother wants to take a sauna or bathe in a hot tub, prenatal experts recommend that she take her oral temperature while she is exposed to the heat. When the expectant mother's body temperature rises a degree or more, she should get out and cool down. Ten minutes is a reasonable length of time for expectant mothers to spend in a sauna or hot tub, since the body temperature does not usually rise in this length of time. If the expectant mother feels uncomfortably hot in a sauna or hot tub, she should get out, even if she has been there only for a short time.

Other Maternal Factors So far we have discussed a number of drugs and environmental hazards that have harmful effects on prenatal and child development. Here we will explore these other potentially harmful maternal factors: infectious diseases, nutrition, emotional states and stress, and age.

Infectious Diseases Maternal diseases and infections can produce defects in offspring by crossing the placental barrier, or they can cause damage during the birth process itself. Rubella (German measles) is one disease that can cause prenatal defects. The greatest damage occurs if a mother contracts rubella in the third or fourth week of pregnancy, although infection during the second month is also damaging. A rubella outbreak in 1964–1965 resulted in 30,000 prenatal and neonatal (newborn) deaths, and more than 20,000 affected infants were born with malformations, including mental retardation, blindness, deafness, and heart problems. Elaborate preventive efforts ensure that rubella will never again have such disastrous effects. A vaccine that prevents German measles is now routinely administered to children, and women who plan to have children should have a blood test before they become pregnant to determine whether they are immune to the disease (Signore, 2001; Ward, Lambert, & Lester, 2001).

Syphilis (a sexually transmitted infection) is more damaging later in prenatal development—four months or more after conception. Rather than affecting organogenesis, as rubella does, syphilis damages organs after they have formed. Damage includes eye lesions, which can cause blindness, and skin lesions. When syphilis is present at birth, problems can develop in the central nervous system and gastrointestinal tract (Hollier & others, 2001). Most states require that pregnant women be given a blood test to detect the presence of syphilis.

Another infection that has received widespread attention recently is genital herpes. Newborns contract this virus when they are delivered through the birth canal of a mother with genital herpes (Tyring, Baker, & Snowden, 2002; Qutub & others, 2001; Watts & others, 2003). About one-third of babies delivered through an infected birth canal die; another one-fourth become brain damaged. If an active case of genital herpes is detected in a pregnant woman close to her delivery date, a cesarean section can be performed (in which the infant is delivered through an incision in the mother's abdomen) to keep the virus from infecting the newborn.

AIDS is a sexually transmitted infection that is caused by the human immunodeficiency virus (HIV), which destroys the body's immune system. In the early 1990s, before preventive treatments were available, 1,000 to 2,000 infants were born with HIV infection each year in the United States. Since then, dramatic reductions in the transmission of AIDS from mothers to the fetus/newborn have occurred. Only about one-third as many cases of newborns with AIDS appear today as in the early 1990s. This decline is due to the increase in counseling and voluntary testing of pregnant women for HIV and to the use of zidovudine (AZT) by infected women during pregnancy, and for the infant after birth (Capparelli & others, 2003; Centers for Disease Control and Prevention, 2000; Committee on Pediatric AIDS, 2000; Rovira & others, 2001).

A mother can infect her offspring with AIDS in three ways: (1) during gestation across the placenta, (2) during delivery through contact with maternal blood or fluids, and (3) postpartum (after birth) through breastfeeding. The transmission of AIDS through breastfeeding is especially a problem in many developing countries (Semba & Neville, 1999).

Babies born to HIV-infected mothers can be (1) infected and symptomatic (show AIDS symptoms), (2) infected but asymptomatic (not show AIDS symptoms), or (3) not infected at all. An infant who is infected and asymptomatic may still develop HIV symptoms until 15 months of age.

Nutrition   A developing fetus depends completely on its mother for nutrition, which comes from the mother's blood. The nutritional status of the fetus is determined by the mother's total calorie intake, and also by appropriate levels of proteins, vitamins, and minerals (Udipi, Ghugre, & Antony, 2000). The mother's nutrition even influences her ability to reproduce. In extreme instances of malnutrition, women stop menstruating, thus precluding conception. Children born to malnourished mothers are more likely to be malformed.

Researchers have also found that being overweight before and during pregnancy can be risk factors for the fetus. In two recent studies, obese women had a significant risk of late fetal death, although the risk of preterm delivery was reduced in these women (Cnattingius & others, 1998; Kumari, 2001).

One aspect of maternal nutrition that is important for normal prenatal development is folic acid, a B-complex vitamin (Callender, Rickard, & Rinsky-Eng, 2001; Langley-Evans & Langley-Evans, 2002). A lack of folic acid is linked with neural-tube defects in offspring, such as spina bifida (Honein & others, 2001). The U.S. Public Health Service now recommends that pregnant women consume a minimum of 400 micrograms of folic acid per day (that is about twice the amount the average woman gets in one day). It also is a good idea for women planning to become pregnant to begin taking a a multivitamin with folic acid several months in advance of trying to conceive. Orange juice and spinach are examples of foods rich in folic acid.

Emotional States and Stress   Tales abound about how a pregnant woman's emotional state affects the fetus. For centuries it was thought that frightening experiences—such as a severe thunderstorm or a family member's death—leave birthmarks on the child or affect the child in more serious ways. Today, we believe that the mother's stress can be transmitted to the fetus, but we have a better grasp of how this takes place (Monk

Because the fetus depends entirely on its mother for nutrition, it is important for the pregnant woman to have good nutritional habits. In Kenya, this government clinic provides pregnant women with information about how their diet can influence the health of their fetus and offspring. *What might the information about diet be like?*

& others, 2000; Relier, 2001). We now know that, when a pregnant woman experiences intense fears, anxieties, and other emotions, physiological changes occur—among them, changes in respiration and glandular secretions. For example, producing adrenaline in response to fear restricts blood flow to the uterine area and can deprive the fetus of adequate oxygen.

The mother's emotional state during pregnancy can influence the birth process too. An emotionally distraught mother might have irregular contractions and a more difficult labor, which can cause irregularities in the baby's oxygen supply or can produce irregularities after birth. Babies born after extended labor also may adjust more slowly to their world and be more irritable.

Maternal anxiety during pregnancy is related to less than optimal outcomes (Brouwers, van Baar, & Pop, 2001). Circumstances that are linked with maternal anxiety during pregnancy include marital discord, death of a husband, and unwanted pregnancy (Field, 1990).

In studies on stress, prenatal development, and birth, Christine Dunkel-Schetter (1998) and her colleagues (Dunkel-Schetter & others, 2001) have found that women under stress are about four times as likely to deliver their babies prematurely as are their low-stress counterparts. In another study, maternal stress increased the level of corticotrophin-releasing hormone (CRH) early in pregnancy (Hobel & others, 1999). CRH has been linked with premature delivery. There also is a connection between stress and unhealthy behaviors, such as smoking, drug use, and poor prenatal care (Dunkel-Schetter, 1999). Also, in one recent study, maternal depression was linked with increased fetal activity, possibly as a result of elevated stress hormones in the mother (Dieter & others, 2001). Further, researchers have found that pregnant women who are optimistic thinkers have less-adverse birth outcomes than pregnant women who are pessimistic thinkers (Loebel & Yali, 1999). Optimists believe that they have more control over the outcome of their pregnancy.

Maternal Age Consideration of possible harmful effects of the mother's age on the fetus and infant focuses on adolescence and the thirties and beyond (Abel, Kruger, & Burd, 2002; Blickstein, 2003). Approximately one of every five births is to an adolescent; in some urban areas, the figure reaches as high as one in every two births. Infants born to adolescents are often premature (Ekwo & Moawad, 2001). In one recent study, low birth weight delivery increased 11 percent and preterm delivery increased 14 percent for women 35 years and older (Tough & others, 2002). The mortality rate of infants born to adolescent mothers is double that of infants born to mothers in their twenties. Although such figures probably reflect the mothers' immature reproductive system, they also may involve poor nutrition, lack of prenatal care, and low socioeconomic status (Lenders, McElrath, & Scholl, 2000). Prenatal care decreases the probability that a child born to an adolescent girl will have physical problems. However, adolescents are the least likely of women in all age groups to obtain prenatal assistance from clinics, pediatricians, and health services.

Increasingly, women seek to establish their careers before beginning a family, delaying childbearing until their thirties. Down syndrome, a form of mental retardation, is related to the mother's age (Holding, 2002). A baby with Down syndrome rarely is born to a mother under the age of 30, but the risk increases after the mother reaches 30. By age 40, the probability is slightly over 1 in 100, and by age 50 it is almost 1 in 10. The risk also is higher before age 18.

Women also have more difficulty becoming pregnant after the age of 30. One study in a French fertility clinic focused on women whose husbands were sterile (Schwartz & Mayaux, 1982). To make it possible for the women to have a child, women were artificially inseminated once a month for one year. Each woman had 12 chances to become pregnant. Seventy-five percent of the women in their twenties became pregnant, 62 percent of the women 31 to 35 years old became pregnant, and only 54 percent of the women over 35 years old became pregnant.

What are some of the risks for infants born to adolescent mothers?

We still have much to learn about the role of the mother's age in pregnancy and childbirth. As women remain active, exercise regularly, and are careful about their nutrition, their reproductive systems may remain healthier longer than was thought possible in the past.

Paternal Factors So far, we have been considering maternal factors during pregnancy that can influence prenatal development and the development of the child. Might there also be some paternal risk factors? Indeed, there are several. Men's exposure to lead, radiation, certain pesticides, and petrochemicals may cause abnormalities in sperm that lead to miscarriage or diseases, such as childhood cancer (Lindbohm, 1991; Trasler, 2000; Trasler & Doerksen, 2000). When fathers have a diet low in vitamin C, their offspring have a higher risk of birth defects and cancer (Fraga & others, 1991). Also, it has been speculated that, when fathers take cocaine, it may attach itself to sperm and cause birth defects, but the evidence for this is not yet strongly established. In some studies, chronic marijuana use has been shown to reduce testosterone levels and sperm counts, although the results have been inconsistent (Fields, 1998; Nahas, 1984).

The father's smoking during the mother's pregnancy also can cause problems for the offspring. In one investigation, the newborns of fathers who smoked during their wives' pregnancy were 4 ounces lighter at birth for each pack of cigarettes smoked per day than were the newborns whose fathers did not smoke during their wives' pregnancy (Rubin & others, 1986). In another study, in China, the longer the fathers smoked, the stronger the risk was for their children to develop cancer (Ji & others, 1997). In such studies, it is very difficult to tease apart prenatal and postnatal effects.

As is the case with older mothers, older fathers also may place their offspring at risk for certain birth defects. These include Down syndrome (about 5 percent of these children have older fathers), dwarfism, and Marfan's syndrome, which involves head and limb deformities. In one recent study, the risk of an adverse pregnancy outcome, such as miscarriage, was much greater when the woman was 35 years or older and the man was 40 years of age or older (de la Rochebrochard & Thonneau, 2002).

Careers in Child Development

Rachel Thompson, *Obstetrician/Gynecologist*

Rachel Thompson is the senior member of Houston Women's Care Associates, which specializes in health care for women. She has one of Houston's most popular obstetrics/gynecology (OB/GYN) practices. Rachel's medical degree is from Baylor College of Medicine, where she also completed her internship and residency. Rachel's work focuses on many of the topics we discuss in this chapter on prenatal development, birth, and the postpartum period.

In addition to her clinical practice, Rachel also is a clinical instructor in the Department of Obstetrics and Gynecology at Baylor College of Medicine. Rachel says that one of the unique features of their health-care group is that the staff is comprised only of women who are full-time practitioners.

Rachel Thompson (*right*), talking with one of her patients at Houston Women's Care Associates.

Prenatal Care

Prenatal care varies enormously, but usually involves a package of medical care services in a defined schedule of visits (McCormick, 2001). In addition to medical care, prenatal care programs often include comprehensive educational, social, and nutritional services (Nichols & Humenick, 2000; Shiono & Behrman, 1995). Women who are pregnant can benefit from the information and advice they receive from health-care personnel, such as Rachel Thompson, an obstetrician/gynecologist whose work is described in the Careers in Child Development insert.

Prenatal care usually includes screening for manageable conditions and/or treatable diseases that can affect the baby or the mother. The education an expectant woman receives about pregnancy, labor and delivery, and caring for the newborn

Early prenatal education classes focus on such topics as changes in the development of the fetus. Later classes focus on preparation for the birth and care of the newborn. *To what extent should fathers, as well as mothers, participate in these classes?*

Reproductive Health Links

Exploring Pregnancy

Childbirth Classes

Prenatal Care

Health-Care Providers

can be extremely valuable, especially for first-time mothers (Cosey & Bechtel, 2001). Prenatal care is also very important for women in poverty because it links them with other social services. The legacy of prenatal care continues after birth, because women who receive this type of care are more likely to seek preventive care for their infants (Bates & others, 1994).

Inadequate prenatal care can occur for a variety of reasons, including the health-care system, provider practices, and individual and social characteristics (Howell, 2001). In one national study, 71 percent of low-income women experienced problems obtaining prenatal care (U.S. General Accounting Office, 1987). Lack of transportation and child care, as well as financial difficulties, were commonly cited as barriers to getting prenatal care. Motivating positive attitudes toward pregnancy is also important. Women who have unplanned or unwanted pregnancies, or who have negative attitudes about being pregnant, are more likely to delay prenatal care or to miss appointments (Joseph, 1989).

Despite the advances made in prenatal care and technology in the United States, the availability of high-quality medical and educational services still needs much improvement. Some countries, especially in Scandinavia and Western Europe, provide more consistent, higher-quality prenatal care than the United States does.

Cultural Beliefs About Pregnancy

A woman's behavior during pregnancy is often determined by cultural beliefs. Certain behaviors are expected if a culture views pregnancy as a medical condition, whereas other behaviors are expected if pregnancy is viewed as a natural occurrence. For example, prenatal care may not be a priority for expectant mothers who view pregnancy as a natural occurrence. Thus, health-care providers need to become aware of the health practices of various cultural groups, including health beliefs about pregnancy and prenatal development. Cultural assessment is an important dimension of providing adequate health care for expectant mothers from various cultural groups. Cultural assessment includes identifying the main beliefs, values, and behaviors related to pregnancy and childbearing. In particular, ethnic background, degree of affiliation with the ethnic group, patterns of decision making, religious preference, language, communication style, and common etiquette practices can significantly affect women's attitudes about the type of medical care needed during pregnancy.

Health-care practices during pregnancy are influenced by numerous factors. Some cultures emphasize traditional home care remedies and folk beliefs and the impor-

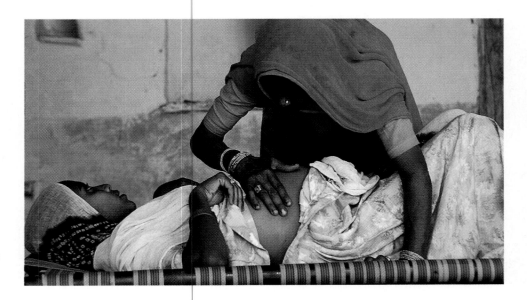

In India, a midwife checks on the size, position, and heartbeat of a fetus. Midwives deliver babies in many cultures around the world. *What are some cultural variations in prenatal care?*

tance of indigenous healers. Others stress the use of professional health-care workers. Many Mexican American mothers are strongly influenced by their mothers and older women in their culture, often seeking and following their advice during pregnancy. In Mexican American culture, the indigenous healer is called a *curandero*. In some Native American tribes, the medicine woman or man fulfills the healing role. Herbalists are often found in Asian cultures, and faith healers, root doctors, and spiritualists are sometimes found in African American culture. When health-care providers come into contact with expectant mothers, they need to assess whether such cultural practices pose a threat to the expectant mother and the fetus. If they pose no threat, there is no reason to try to change them. On the other hand, if certain cultural practices do pose a threat to the health of the expectant mother or the fetus, the health-care provider should consider a culturally sensitive way to handle the problem. For example, some Filipinos will not take any medication during pregnancy.

Positive Prenatal Development

Much of our discussion so far in this chapter has focused on what can go wrong with prenatal development. It is important to keep in mind that most of the time, prenatal development does not go awry and development occurs along the positive path that we described at the beginning of the chapter (Lester, 2000). That said, it is still important for prospective mothers and those who are pregnant to avoid the vulnerabilities to fetal development that we have described.

Review and Reflect: Learning Goal 1

1 Describe prenatal development

REVIEW

- What is the course of prenatal development?
- What is teratology? What are some of the main hazards to prenatal development?
- What are some good prenatal care strategies?
- What are some cultural beliefs about pregnancy?
- Why is it important to take a positive approach to prenatal development?

REFLECT

- What can be done to convince women who are pregnant not to smoke or drink? Consider the role of health-care providers, the role of insurance companies, and specific programs targeted at women who are pregnant.

2 BIRTH

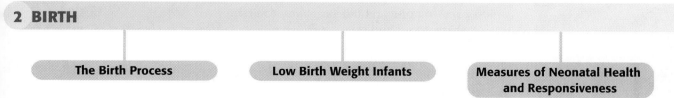

The Birth Process | Low Birth Weight Infants | Measures of Neonatal Health and Responsiveness

As we saw in the opening story about Tanner Roberts, many changes take place during the birth of a baby (Verklan, 2002). Let's further explore the birth process.

The Birth Process

Here we will examine the stages of birth, the transition from fetus to newborn, childbirth strategies, low birth weight infants, and measures of neonatal (newborn) health and responsiveness.

FIGURE 4.6 The Stages of Birth

(*a*) First stage: cervix is dilating; (*b*) late first stage (transition stage): cervix is fully dilated, and the amniotic sac has ruptured, releasing amniotic fluid; (*c*) second stage: birth of the infant; (*d*) third stage: delivery of the placenta (afterbirth).

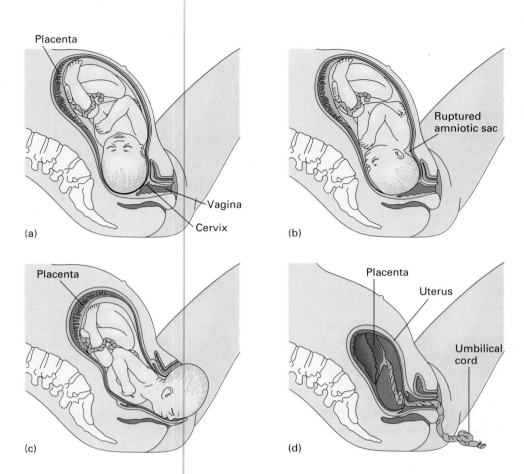

(a)   (b)

(c)   (d)

Preparing for Birth

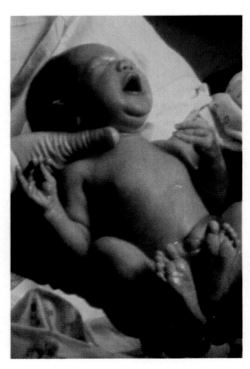

After the long journey of prenatal development, birth takes place. During birth the baby is on a threshold between two worlds. *What is the fetus/newborn transition like?*

Stages of Birth   Childbirth—or labor—occurs in three stages (see figure 4.6). For a woman having her first child, the first stage lasts an average of 12 to 24 hours; it is the longest of the three stages. In the first stage, uterine contractions are 15 to 20 minutes apart at the beginning and last up to a minute. These contractions cause the woman's cervix, the opening into the birth canal, to stretch and open. As the first stage progresses, the contractions come closer together, appearing every 2 to 5 minutes. Their intensity increases too. By the end of the first birth stage, contractions dilate the cervix to an opening of about 4 inches, so that the baby can move from the uterus to the birth canal.

The second birth stage begins when the baby's head starts to move through the cervix and the birth canal. It terminates when the baby completely emerges from the mother's body. For a first birth, this stage lasts approximately 1½ hours. With each contraction, the mother bears down hard to push the baby out of her body. By the time the baby's head is out of the mother's body, the contractions come almost every minute and last for about a minute.

Afterbirth is the third stage, at which time the placenta, umbilical cord, and other membranes are detached and expelled. This final stage is the shortest of the three birth stages, lasting only minutes.

The Transition from Fetus to Newborn   Being born involves considerable stress for the baby. During each contraction, when the placenta and umbilical cord are compressed as the uterine muscles draw together, the supply of oxygen to the fetus is decreased. If the delivery takes too long, anoxia can develop (Mohan, Golding, & Paterson, 2001). *Anoxia* is the condition in which the fetus/newborn has an insufficient supply of oxygen. Anoxia can cause brain damage (Cowan & others, 2003).

The baby has considerable capacity to withstand the stress of birth. Large quantities of adrenaline and noradrenaline, hormones that protect the fetus in the event of oxygen deficiency, are secreted in stressful circumstances. These hormones increase the heart's pumping activity, speed up the heart rate, channel blood flow to the brain, and raise the blood-sugar level. Never again in life will such large amounts of these hormones be secreted. This circumstance underscores how stressful it is to be born and also how well prepared and adapted the fetus is for birth (Committee on Fetus and Newborn, 2000; Mishell, 2000; Van Beveren, 2003).

As we saw in the case of Tanner Roberts at the beginning of the chapter, the umbilical cord is cut immediately after birth, and the baby is on its own. Now 25 million little air sacs in the lungs must be filled with air. Until now, these air sacs have held fluid, but this fluid is rapidly expelled or enters the bloodstream. The first breaths may be the hardest ones an individual takes. Before birth, oxygen came from the mother via the umbilical cord, but now the baby has to be self-sufficient and breathe on its own.

At the time of birth, the baby is covered with what is called *vernix caseosa,* a protective skin grease. This vernix consists of fatty secretions and dead cells, thought to function in protecting the baby's skin against heat loss before and during birth. After the baby and mother have met and become acquainted with each other, the baby is taken to be cleaned, examined, weighed, and evaluated. Later in the chapter, we will discuss several measures that are used to examine the newborn's health and responsiveness.

Childbirth Strategies   Among the childbirth decisions that need to be made are what the setting will be, who the attendants will be, and which childbirth technique will be used. Here we will discuss the options available to expectant parents.

Childbirth Setting and Attendants   In the United States, 99 percent of births take place in hospitals, and more than 90 percent are attended by physicians (Ventura & others, 1997). Many hospitals now have birthing centers, where fathers or birth coaches may be with the mother during labor and delivery. Some people believe this so-called alternative birthing center offers a good compromise between a technological, depersonalized hospital birth (which cannot offer the emotional experience of a home birth) and a birth at home (which cannot offer the medical backup of a hospital). A birthing room approximates a home setting as much as possible and allows for a full range of birth experiences, from a totally unmedicated, natural birth to the most complex, intensive medical care. Some women with good medical histories and low risk for problem delivery choose a home delivery or a delivery in a freestanding birthing center, which is usually staffed by nurse-midwives (Wong, Perry, & Hockenberry, 2001). Regardless of the childbirth setting, there is increasing research evidence that supportive care improves the outcomes for both the mother and the baby (Sauls, 2002).

Approximately 6 percent of women who deliver a baby in the United States are attended by a midwife (Ventura & others, 1997). Most midwives are nurses who have been specially trained in delivering babies (Oshio, Johnson, & Fullerton, 2002; Moyo, 2003). One study found that the risk of neonatal mortality (an infant death occurring in the first 28 days of life) was 33 percent lower and the risk of a low birth weight baby was 31 percent lower for births attended by a certified nurse-midwife than for births attended by physicians (MacDorman & Singh, 1998). Compared to physicians, certified nurse-midwives generally spend more time with patients during prenatal visits, place more emphasis on patient counseling and education, provide more emotional support, and are more likely to be with the patient one-on-one during the entire labor and delivery process, which may explain the more positive outcomes for babies delivered by certified nurse-midwives.

In many countries around the world, babies are more likely to be delivered at home than they are in the United States. For example, in Holland, 35 percent of the babies are born at home, and more than 40 percent are delivered by midwives rather than doctors (Treffers & others, 1990).

> *W*e must respect this instant of birth, this fragile moment. The baby is between two worlds, on a threshold, hesitating . . .
> —FREDERICK LEBOYER
> *French Obstetrician, 20th Century*

A woman in the African !Kung culture giving birth in a sitting position. Notice the help and support being given by another woman. *What are some cultural variations in childbirth?*

Childbirth Strategies

Childbirth Setting and Attendants

Midwifery

Doula

Fathers and Childbirth

Siblings and Childbirth

doula A caregiver who provides continuous physical, emotional, and educational support to the mother before, during, and just after childbirth.

In many countries, a doula attends a childbearing woman. *Doula* is a Greek word that means "a woman who helps." A **doula** is a caregiver who provides continuous physical, emotional, and educational support for the mother before, during, and after childbirth. Doulas remain with the mother throughout labor, assessing and responding to her needs (Gilliland, 2002). In one study, the mothers who received doula support reported less labor pain than the mothers who did not receive doula support (Klaus, Kennell, & Klaus, 1993). Doulas typically function as part of a "birthing team," serving as an adjunct to the midwife or the hospital obstetric staff (McGrath & others, 1999; Pascali-Bonaro, 2002).

In the United States, most doulas work as independent providers hired by the expectant woman. Managed-care organizations are increasingly offering doula support as a part of regular obstetric care. In many cultures, the practice of a knowledgeable woman helping a mother in labor is not officially labeled "doula" support but is simply an ingrained, centuries-old custom.

In many cultures, several people attend the mother during labor and delivery. Which persons attend the mother may vary across cultures. In the East African Nigoni culture, men are completely excluded from the childbirth process. In this culture, women even conceal their pregnancy from their husband as long as possible. In the Nigoni culture, when a woman is ready to give birth, female relatives move into the woman's hut and the husband leaves, taking his belongings (clothes, tools, weapons, and so on) with him. He is not permitted to return until after the baby is born.

In some cultures, childbirth is a more open, community affair than in the United States. For example, in the Pukapukan culture in the Pacific Islands, women give birth in a shelter that is open for villagers to observe.

Methods of Delivery Among the methods of delivery are medicated, natural and prepared, and cesarean. The American Academy of Pediatrics recommends the least possible medication during delivery, although it is up to the mother or attending medical personnel to decide whether drugs are needed (Hotchner, 1997).

There are three basic kinds of drugs that are used for labor: analgesia, anesthesia, and oxytocics. *Analgesia* is used to relieve pain. Analgesics include tranquilizers, barbiturates, and narcotics (such as Demerol). *Anesthesia* is used in late first-stage labor and during expulsion of the baby to block sensation in an area of the body or to block consciousness. There is a trend toward not using general anesthesia, which blocks consciousness, in normal births because it can be transmitted through the placenta to the fetus (Ransjo-Arvidson & others, 2002). However, epidural anesthesia does not cross the placenta (Howell & others, 2002). An *epidural block* is regional anesthesia that numbs the woman's body from the waist down. Even this drug, thought to be relatively safe, has come under recent criticism because it is associated with fever, extended labor, and increased risk for cesarean delivery (Ransjo-Arvidson & others, 2001). *Oxytocics* are synthetic hormones that are used to stimulate contractions. Pitocin is the most commonly used oxytocic (Carbonne, Tsatsarius, & Goffinet, 2001; Gard & others, 2002; Oboro & Tabowei, 2003).

Predicting how a particular drug will affect an individual pregnant woman and the fetus is difficult. Though we have many commonalities as human beings, we also vary a great deal. Thus, a particular drug might have only a minimal effect on one fetus yet have a much stronger effect on another fetus. The drug's dosage also is a factor. Stronger doses of tranquilizers and narcotics given to decrease the mother's pain have a potentially more negative effect on the fetus than mild doses. It is important for the mother to assess her level of pain and have a voice in the decision of whether she should receive medication or not (Young, 2001).

Though the trend at one time was toward a natural childbirth without any medication, today the emphasis is on using some medication but keeping it to a minimum when possible. The emphasis today also is on broadly educating the pregnant woman so that she can be reassured and confident. This emphasis on education is reflected in the techniques of natural childbirth and prepared childbirth.

Natural childbirth was developed in 1914 by an English Obstetrician, Grantley Dick-Read. Its purpose is to reduce the mother's pain by decreasing her fear through education about childbirth and by teaching her to use breathing methods and relaxation techniques during delivery. Dick-Read believed that the doctor's relationship with the mother is an important dimension of reducing her perception of pain. He said the doctor should be present during her active labor prior to delivery and should provide reassurance.

Prepared childbirth was developed by French obstetrician Ferdinand Lamaze. This childbirth strategy is similar to natural childbirth but includes a special breathing technique to control pushing in the final stages of labor, as well as a more detailed anatomy and physiology course. The Lamaze method has become very popular in the United States. The pregnant woman's husband or a friend usually serves as a coach, who attends childbirth classes with her and helps her with her breathing and relaxation during delivery.

Many other prepared childbirth techniques also have been developed (Samuels & Samuels, 1996). They usually include elements of Dick-Read's natural childbirth or Lamaze's method, plus one or more other components. For instance, the Bradley method places special emphasis on the father's role as a labor coach. Virtually all of the prepared childbirth methods emphasize some degree of education, relaxation and breathing exercises, and support. In recent years, new ways of teaching relaxation have been offered, including guided mental imagery, massage, and meditation. In sum, the current belief in prepared childbirth is that, when information and support are provided, women *know* how to give birth. To read about one nurse whose research focuses on discovering ways to prevent and reduce fatigue during childbearing and the use of breathing exercises during labor, see the Careers in Child Development insert.

Careers in Child Development

Linda Pugh, *Perinatal Nurse*

Perinatal nurses work with childbearing women to support health and growth during the childbearing experience. Linda Pugh (Ph.D., R.N.C.) is a perinatal nurse on the faculty at the Johns Hopkins University School of Nursing. She is certified as an inpatient obstetric nurse and specializes in the care of women during labor and delivery. Linda teaches nursing to both undergraduate and graduate students. In addition to educating professional nurses and conducting research, Linda consults with hospitals and organizations about women's health issues.

Linda's research interests include nursing interventions with low-income breastfeeding women, discovering ways to prevent and ameliorate fatigue during childbearing, and using effective breathing exercises during labor.

Linda Pugh (*right*) with a mother and her newborn.

In a *cesarean delivery,* the baby is removed from the mother's uterus through an incision made in her abdomen. This method also is sometimes known as a cesarean section. A cesarean section is usually performed if the baby is in a **breech position,** which causes the baby's buttocks to be the first part to emerge from the vagina (Hauth & Cunningham, 2002). Normally, the crown of the baby's head comes through the vagina first, but in 1 of every 25 deliveries, the baby's head is still in the uterus when the rest of the body is out. Breech births can cause respiratory problems (Vidaeff & Yeomans, 2002).

Cesarean deliveries also are performed if the baby is lying crosswise in the uterus, if the baby's head is too large to pass through the mother's pelvis, if the baby develops complications, or if the mother is bleeding vaginally.

The benefits and risks of cesarean sections continue to be debated (Green & others, 2001; Morrison & MacKenzie, 2003; Peskin & Reine, 2002). Cesarean deliveries are safer than breech deliveries, but they involve a higher infection rate, longer hospital stay, and greater expense and stress that accompany any surgery.

Some critics believe that in the United States too many babies are delivered by cesarean section. The cesarean delivery rate jumped 7 percent from 2000 to 2001

natural childbirth Developed in 1914 by Dick-Read, this method attempts to reduce the mother's pain by decreasing her fear through education about childbirth and relaxation techniques during delivery.

prepared childbirth Developed by French obstetrician Ferdinand Lamaze, this childbirth strategy is similar to natural childbirth but includes a special breathing technique to control pushing in the final stages of labor and a more detailed anatomy and physiology course.

breech position The baby's position in the uterus that causes the buttocks to be the first part to emerge from the vagina.

A "kilogram kid," weighing less than 2.3 pounds at birth. *What are some long-term outcomes for weighing so little at birth?*

in the United States to 24.4 percent of all births, the highest level reported since these data began being reported on birth certificates in 1989 (MacDorman & others, 2002). Indeed, more cesarean sections are performed in the United States than in any other country in the world (National Center for Health Statistics, 2002).

Low Birth Weight Infants

A **low birth weight infant** weighs less than $5\frac{1}{2}$ pounds at birth. Two subgroups are those that are very low birth weight (under 3 pounds) and extremely low birth weight (under 2 pounds).

Another way of classifying low birth weight babies involves whether they are preterm or small for date. **Preterm infants** are those born three weeks or more before the pregnancy has reached its full term. This means that the term *preterm* is given to an infant who is born at 35 or less weeks after conception. Most preterm babies are also low birth weight babies. For the first time in almost a decade the preterm birth rate declined (to 11.6 percent) in 2001 (MacDorman & others, 2002).

A short gestation period does not necessarily harm an infant. It is distinguished from retarded prenatal growth, in which the fetus has been damaged (Kopp, 1992). The neurological development of the preterm baby continues after birth on approximately the same timetable as if the infant were still in the womb. For example, consider a preterm baby born 30 weeks after conception. At 38 weeks, approximately two months after birth, this infant shows the same level of brain development as a 38-week fetus who is yet to be born.

Small for date infants (also called *small for gestational age infants*) are those whose birth weight is below normal when the length of the pregnancy is considered. Small for date infants may be preterm or full-term. They weigh less than 90 percent of all babies of the same gestational age. Inadequate nutrition and smoking by pregnant women are among the main factors in producing small for date infants (Chan, Keane, & Robinson, 2001; England & others, 2001).

There has been an increase in low birth weight infants in the United States in the last two decades (Hall, 2000). The increase is thought to be due to the increasing number of adolescents having babies, drug abuse, and poor nutrition. The incidence of low birth weight varies considerably from country to country (see figure 4.7). As shown in figure 4.7, the United States low birth weight rate of 7.6 percent is considerably higher than for many other developed countries (UNICEF, 2001). In 2000, 66 percent of all infant deaths in the United States occurred among the 7.6 percent of infants born with low birth weight (MacDorman & others, 2002).

In the developing world, low birth weight stems mainly from the mother's poor health and nutrition. Diseases such as diarrhea and malaria, which are common in developing countries, can impair fetal growth if the mother becomes infected while she is pregnant. In developed countries, cigarette smoking during pregnancy is the leading cause of low birth weight (UNICEF, 2001). In both developed and developing countries, adolescents who give birth when their bodies have yet to fully mature are at risk for having low birth weight babies.

Although most low birth weight infants are normal and healthy, as a group they have more health and developmental problems than normal birth weight infants (Hack & others, 2002; Rickards & others, 2001; Sweet & others, 2003). The number and severity of these problems increase as birth weight decreases (Kilbride, Thorstad, & Daily, 2000). With the improved survival rates for infants who are born very early and very small have come increases in severe brain damage (Yu, 2000). Cerebral palsy and other forms of brain injury are highly correlated with brain weight—the lower the brain weight, the greater the likelihood of brain injury (Watemberg & others, 2002). Approximately 7 percent of moderately low birth weight infants (3 pounds 5 ounces to 5 pounds 8 ounces) have brain injuries. This figure increases to 20 percent for the smallest newborns (1 pound 2 ounces to 3 pounds 5 ounces).

low birth weight infant An infant who weighs less than $5\frac{1}{2}$ pounds at birth.

preterm infant An infant born three weeks or more before the pregnancy has reached its full term.

small for date infant Also called a small for gestational age infant, this infant's birth weight is below normal when the length of pregnancy is considered. A small for date infant may be preterm or full-term.

Low birth weight infants are also more likely than normal birth weight infants to have lung or liver diseases.

At school age, children who were born low birth weight infants are more likely than their normal birth weight counterparts to have a learning disability, attention deficit hyperactivity disorder, or breathing problems such as asthma (Taylor, Klein, & Hack, 1994). Very low birth weight children have more learning problems and lower levels of achievement in reading and math than moderately low birth weight children. These problems are reflected in much higher percentages of low birth weight children being enrolled in special education programs. Approximately 50 percent of all low birth weight children are enrolled in special education programs.

Do these negative outcomes of low birth weight continue into adolescence? In one recent study, the outcomes in middle school students of being low birth weight were examined (Taylor & others, 2000). When compared with a control group that was born at full-term, the low birth weight adolescents had lower cognitive skills, weaker academic records, and showed more behavioral problems (see figure 4.8).

Not all of these adverse consequences can be attributed solely to low birth weight. Some of the less severe but more common developmental and physical delays occur because many low birth weight children come from disadvantaged environments (Fang, Madhaven, & Alderman, 1999).

Intervention   A number of efforts to improve the outcomes of low birth weight infants have been developed. These include enrichment programs, the best level of stimulation, massage, and kangaroo care.

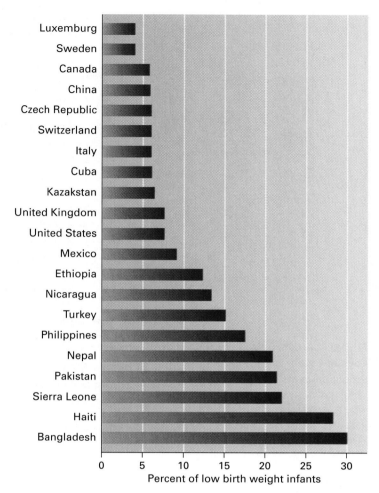

FIGURE 4.7 Low Birth Weight Rates by Country

The graph shows the percentage of children born with low birth weight in a wide range for countries around the world (UNICEF, 2001).

Enrichment   Some of the devastating effects of low birth weight can be reversed (Blair & Ramey, 1996; Shino & Behrman, 1995). Intensive enrichment programs that provide medical and educational services for both the parents and the child have been shown to improve short-term developmental outcomes for low birth weight children. Federal laws mandate that services for school-age children with a disability (which include medical, educational, psychological, occupational, and physical care) be expanded to include family-based care for infants. At present, these services are aimed at children born with severe congenital disabilities. The availability of services for moderately low birth weight children who do not have severe physical problems varies from state to state, but generally these services are not available.

Level of Stimulation   Just three decades ago, preterm infants were perceived to be too fragile to cope well with environmental stimulation, and the recommendation was to handle such infants as little as possible. The climate of opinion changed when the adverse effects of maternal deprivation (mothers' neglect of their infants) became known and was interpreted to include a lack of stimulation. A number of research studies followed that indicated a "more is better" approach in the stimulation of preterm infants. Today, however, experts on infant development argue that preterm infant care is far too complex to be described only in terms of amount of stimulation (Liaw, 2000).

Here are some conclusions about the stimulation of preterm infants (Lester & Tronick, 1990):

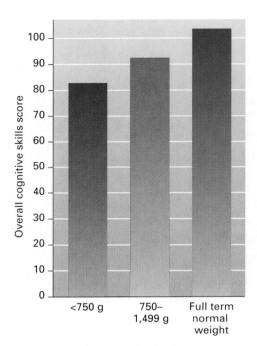

FIGURE 4.8 Comparison of the Overall Cognitive Processing Skills of Middle School Students Who Were Born Low Birth Weight or Normal Birth Weight

The overall cognitive skills score was a composite score arrived at by combining students' scores on several cognitive measures such as the Kaufman Assessment Battery for Children (an intelligence test), analogies (a task that requires individuals to understand how concepts are similar), and other tests.

1. Preterm infants' responses to stimulation vary with their conceptual age, illness, and individual makeup. The immature brain of the preterm infant may be more vulnerable to excessive, inappropriate, or mistimed stimulation. The very immature infant should probably be protected from stimulation that could destabilize its condition.
2. As the healthy preterm infant becomes less fragile and approaches term, the issue of what is appropriate stimulation should be considered. Infants' behavioral cues can be used to determine appropriate interventions. An infant's signs of stress or avoidance behaviors indicate that stimulation should be terminated. Positive behaviors indicate that stimulation is appropriate.
3. Intervention with the preterm infant should be organized in the form of an individualized developmental plan. This plan should be constructed as a psychosocial intervention to include the parents and other immediate family members and to acknowledge the socioeconomic, cultural, and home environmental factors that will determine the social context in which the infant will be reared. The developmental plan should also include assessing the infant's behavior, working with the parents to help them understand the infant's medical and behavioral status, and helping the parents deal with their own feelings.

Massage Throughout history and in many cultures, infant massage has been used by caregivers. In India, Africa, and Asia, infants are routinely massaged by parents or other family members for several months after birth.

Many preterm infants experience less touch than full-term infants because they are isolated in temperature-controlled incubators. However, the research of Tiffany Field (1998, 2001, 2002) has led to a surge of interest in the role that massage might play in improving the developmental outcomes of preterm infants. To read about her research, see the Explorations in Child Development box.

Why might massage improve the developmental outcomes of preterm infants? The precise mechanism behind the positive effects of massaging preterm infants is not completely known. However, massage directly stimulates the musculoskeletal, nervous, and circulatory systems. Further, massage promotes weight gain, moderates infants' stress hormones (such as cortisol), and improves immune system functioning.

Kangaroo Care Kangaroo care is a way of holding a preterm infant so that there is skin-to-skin contact (Ludington-Hoe & Golant, 1993). The baby, wearing only a diaper, is held upright against the parent's bare chest. Kangaroo care is typically practiced for two to three hours per day, skin-to-skin, over an extended time period in early infancy.

The label *kangaroo care* was chosen to describe this strategy because the method is similar to how a kangaroo is carried by its mother. It is estimated that more than 200 neonatal intensive care units practice kangaroo care today compared to less than 70 in the early 1990s. One recent survey found that 82 percent of neonatal intensive care units use kangaroo care in the United States today (Engler & others, 2002).

Why use kangaroo care with preterm infants? Researchers have found that the close physical contact with the parent can help to stabilize the preterm infant's heartbeat, temperature, and breathing (Bohnhorst & others, 2002; Feldman & Eidelman, 2003). Preterm infants often have difficulty coordinating their breathing and heart rate. Researchers also have found that mothers who use kangaroo care often have more success with breastfeeding and improve their milk supply (Charpak & others, 1997). Further, researchers have found that preterm infants who experience kangaroo care have longer periods of sleep, gain more weight, decrease their crying, have longer periods of alertness, and earlier hospital discharge (Charpak & others, 2001; Chwo &

New mothers learning how to practice kangaroo care. *What is kangaroo care?*

kangaroo care A way of holding a preterm infant so that there is skin-to-skin contact.

The Power of Touch and Massage in Development

In an early study by Field and her colleagues (1986), massage therapy conducted three times per day for 15-minute periods led to 47 percent greater weight gain than standard medical treatment (Field & others, 1986) (see figure 4.9). The massaged infants also were more active and alert, and they performed better on developmental tests.

In another study, Field (1992) gave the same kind of massage (firm stroking with the palms of the hands) to preterm infants who were exposed to cocaine in utero. The infants also showed significant weight gain and improved scores on developmental tests. In another study, 28 newborns born to HIV-positive mothers were randomly assigned to massage therapy or to a control group (Scafidi & Field, 1996). The treatment-group infants were given three 15-minute massages daily for 10 days. The massaged group showed superior performance on a wide range of infant assessments, including daily weight gain.

Field also has conducted a number of studies of infants born to depressed mothers. In one study, Field and her colleagues (Field, Grizzle, & others, 1996) investigated 1- to 3-month-old infants born to depressed adolescent mothers. The infants were given 15 minutes of either massage or rocking for two days per week for a six-week period. The infants who received massage therapy had lower stress, as well as improved emotionality, sociability, and soothability, when compared with the rocked infants.

Field and her colleagues also have demonstrated the benefits of massage therapy with women in reducing their labor pain (Field, Hernandez-Reif, Taylor, & others, 1997), with children who have arthritis (Field, Hernandez-Reif, Seligman, & others, 1997), with children who have asthma (Field & others, 1998a), with autistic children's attentiveness (Field, Lasko, & others, 1997), with alleviating stress in children following a hurricane (Field, Seligman, & others, 1996), and with adolescents who have attention deficit hyperactivity disorder (Field & others, 1998b).

FIGURE 4.9 Weight Gain Comparison of Premature Infants Who Were Massaged or Not Massaged

The graph shows that the mean daily weight gain of premature infants who were massaged was greater than for premature infants who were not massaged.

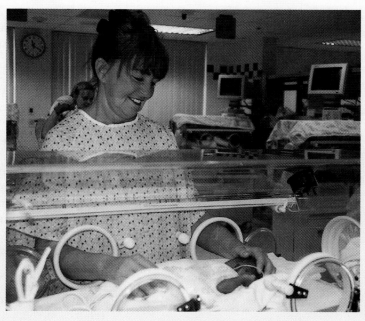

Shown here is Dr. Tiffany Field massaging a newborn infant. *What types of infants has massage therapy been shown to help?*

others, 2002; Ludington-Hoe, Cong, & Hashemi, 2002). One recent study compared 26 low birth weight infants who received kangaroo care with 27 low birth weight infants who received standard medical/nursing care (Ohgi & others, 2002). At both 6 and 12 months of age, the kangaroo care infants were able to better regulate their body states, showed better orientation, and had more positive mood. Another recent study found that kangaroo care preterm infants had better control of their arousal, more effectively attended to stimuli, and showed sustained exploration in a toy

Score	0	1	2	
Heart rate	Absent	Slow—less than 100 beats per minute	Fast—100 to 140 beats per minute	
Respiratory effort	No breathing for more than one minute	Irregular and slow	Good breathing with normal crying	
Muscle tone	Limp and flaccid	Weak, inactive, but some flexion of extremities	Strong, active motion	
Body color	Blue and pale	Body pink, but extremities blue	Entire body pink	
Reflex irritability	No response	Grimace	Coughing, sneezing, and crying	

FIGURE 4.10 The Apgar Scale

session than a control group of preterm infants who did not receive kangaroo care (Feldman & others, 2002). Increasingly kangaroo care is being recommended for full-term infants as well.

Measures of Neonatal Health and Responsiveness

Almost immediately after birth, a newborn is weighed, cleaned up, and tested for signs of developmental problems that might require urgent attention. The **Apgar Scale** is widely used to assess the health of newborns at one and five minutes after birth. The Apgar Scale evaluates infants' heart rate, respiratory effort, muscle tone, body color, and reflex irritability. An obstetrician or a nurse does the evaluation and gives the newborn a score, or reading, of 0, 1, or 2 on each of these five health signs (see figure 4.10). A total score of 7 to 10 indicates that the newborn's condition is good. A score of 5 indicates there may be developmental difficulties. A score of 3 or below signals an emergency and indicates that the baby might not survive. The Apgar Scale is especially good at assessing the newborn's ability to respond to the stress of delivery, labor, and the new environment (Casey, McIntire, & Leveno, 2001). The Apgar Scale also identifies high-risk infants who need resuscitation.

To evaluate the newborn more thoroughly, the **Brazelton Neonatal Behavioral Assessment Scale** is performed within 24 to 36 hours after birth. This scale measures the newborn's neurological development, reflexes, and reactions to people. When the Brazelton is given, the newborn is treated as an active participant, and the score attained is based on the newborn's best performance. Sixteen reflexes, such as sneezing, blinking, and rooting, are assessed, along with reactions to circumstances, such as the infant's reaction to a rattle. (We will have more to say about reflexes in chapter 5, when we discuss physical development in infancy.) The examiner rates the newborn on each of 27 categories. As an indication of how detailed the ratings are, consider item 15: "cuddliness." Nine categories are involved in assessing this item, and scoring is done on a continuum that ranges from the infant's being very resistant to being held to the infant's being extremely cuddly and clinging. The Brazelton scale is used not only as a sensitive index of neurological competence in the week after birth, but also as a measure in many research studies on infant development. In scoring the Brazelton scale, T. Berry Brazelton and his colleagues (Brazelton, Nugent, & Lester, 1987) categorize the 27 items into four categories—physiological, motoric, state, and interaction. They also classify the baby in global terms, such as "worrisome," "normal," or "superior," based on these categories (Nugent & Brazelton, 2000).

Apgar Scale A widely used method to assess the health of newborns at one and five minutes after birth. The Apgar Scale evaluates infants' heart rate, respiratory effort, muscle tone, body color, and reflex irritability.

Brazelton Neonatal Behavioral Assessment Scale A test given several days after birth to assess newborns' neurological development, reflexes, and reactions to people.

A very low Brazelton score can indicate brain damage, or it can reflect stress to the brain that may heal in time. However, if an infant merely seems sluggish in responding to social circumstances, parents are encouraged to give the infant attention and become more sensitive to the infant's needs. Parents are shown how the newborn can respond to people and how to stimulate such responses. Researchers have found that the social interaction skills of both high-risk infants and healthy, responsive infants can be improved through such communication with parents (Worobey & Belsky, 1982).

Review and Reflect: Learning Goal 2

2 Discuss the birth process

REVIEW

- What are the three stages of birth? What is the transition from fetus to newborn like for the infant? What are some different childbirth strategies?
- What are the outcomes for children who are born with a low birth weight?
- What are two measures of neonatal health and responsiveness?

REFLECT

- If you are a female, which birth strategy do you prefer? Why? If you are a male, how involved would you want to be in helping your partner through pregnancy and the birth of your baby?

---

3 THE POSTPARTUM PERIOD

What Is the Postpartum Period?	Emotional and Psychological Adjustments
Physical Adjustments	Bonding

The weeks immediately following childbirth present a number of challenges for new parents and their offspring. Many health professionals believe that the best way to meet these challenges is with a family-centered approach that uses the family's resources to support an early and smooth adjustment to the newborn by all family members.

What Is the Postpartum Period?

The **postpartum period** is the period after childbirth or delivery. It is a time when the woman adjusts, both physically and psychologically, to the process of child-bearing. It lasts for about six weeks or until the body has completed its adjustment and has returned to a nearly prepregnant state. Some health professionals refer to the postpartum period as the "fourth trimester." Though the time span of the postpartum period does not necessarily cover three months, the term of "fourth trimester" suggests continuity and the importance of the first several months after birth for the mother.

The postpartum period is influenced by what preceded it. During pregnancy, the woman's body gradually adjusted to physical changes, but now it is forced to respond quickly. The method of delivery and circumstances surrounding the

postpartum period The period after childbirth when the mother adjusts, both physically and psychologically, to the process of childbirth. This period lasts for about six weeks or until her body has completed its adjustment and returned to a near prepregnant state.

The postpartum period is a time of considerable adjustment and adaptation for both the mother and the father. Fathers can provide an important support system for mothers, especially in helping mothers care for young infants. *As part of supporting the mother, what kinds of tasks might the father of a newborn do?*

Postpartum Adjustment

Postpartum Resources

delivery affect the speed with which the woman's body readjusts during the postpartum period.

The postpartum period involves a great deal of adjustment and adaptation (Plackslin, 2000). The baby has to be cared for; the mother has to recover from childbirth; the mother has to learn how to take care of the baby; the mother needs to learn to feel good about herself as a mother; the father needs to learn how to take care of his recovering wife; the father needs to learn how to take care of the baby; and the father needs to learn how to feel good about himself as a father.

Physical Adjustments

A woman's body makes numerous physical adjustments in the first days and weeks after childbirth. She may have a great deal of energy or feel exhausted and let down. Most new mothers feel tired and need rest. Though these changes are normal, the fatigue can undermine the new mother's sense of well-being and confidence in her ability to cope with a new baby and a new family life.

Involution is the process by which the uterus returns to its prepregnant size five or six weeks after birth. Immediately following birth, the uterus weighs 2 to 3 pounds. By the end of five or six weeks, the uterus weighs 2 to $3\frac{1}{2}$ ounces. Nursing the baby helps contract the uterus at a rapid rate.

After delivery, a woman's body undergoes sudden and dramatic changes in hormone production. When the placenta is delivered, estrogen and progesterone levels drop steeply and remain low until the ovaries start producing hormones again. The woman will probably begin menstruating again in four to eight weeks if she is not breastfeeding. If she is breastfeeding, she might not menstruate for several months to a year or more, though ovulation can occur during this time. The first several menstrual periods following delivery might be heavier than usual, but periods soon return to normal.

Some women and men want to resume sexual intercourse as soon as possible after the birth. Others feel constrained or afraid. A sore perineum (the area between the anus and vagina in the female), a demanding baby, lack of help, and extreme fatigue affect a woman's ability to relax and to enjoy making love. Physicians often recommend that women refrain from having sexual intercourse for approximately six weeks following the birth of the baby.

If the woman regularly engaged in conditioning exercises during pregnancy, exercise will help her recover her former body contour and strength during the postpartum period. With a caregiver's approval, the new mother can begin some exercises as soon as one hour after delivery. In addition to recommending exercise in the postpartum period for women, health professionals also increasingly recommend that women practice the relaxation techniques they used during pregnancy and childbirth. Five minutes of slow breathing on a stressful day in the postpartum period can relax and refresh the new mother, as well as the new baby.

Emotional and Psychological Adjustments

Emotional fluctuations are common for mothers in the postpartum period. These emotional fluctuations may be due to any of a number of factors: hormonal changes, fatigue, inexperience or lack of confidence with newborn babies, or the extensive time and demands involved in caring for a newborn. For some women, the emotional fluctuations decrease within several weeks after the delivery and are a minor aspect of their motherhood. For others, they are more long-lasting and can produce feelings of anxiety, depression, and difficulty in coping with stress (Barnes, 2002; Troisi & others, 2002). Mothers who have such feelings, even when they are getting adequate rest, may benefit from professional help in dealing with their problems (Olson & others, 2002; Strass, 2002).

As shown in figure 4.11, about 70 percent of new mothers have what are called "baby blues." About two to three days after birth, they begin to feel depressed, anxious, and upset. These feelings may come and go for several days after the birth, often peaking about three to five days after the birth. However, they usually go away after one or two weeks without treatment. However, women with **postpartum depression** have such strong feelings of sadness, anxiety, or despair that they have trouble coping with their daily tasks. Postpartum depression involves a major depressive episode that typically occurs about four weeks after delivery. Without treatment, postpartum depression may become worse and last for many months. As shown in figure 4.11, postpartum depression occurs in approximately 10 percent of new mothers. Between 25 to 50 percent of these depressed new mothers have episodes that last six months or longer (Beck, 2002). If untreated, approximately 25 percent of these women are still depressed a year later.

Here are some of the signs that may indicate a need for professional help in treating postpartum depression:

- Excessive worrying
- Depression
- Extreme changes in appetite
- Crying spells
- Inability to sleep

The father also undergoes considerable adjustment in the postpartum period, although in many cases he will be away at work all day, whereas the mother will be at home, at least in the first few weeks. One of the most common reactions of the husband is the feeling that the baby comes first and gets all of the attention. In some marriages, the man may have had that relationship with his wife and now feels that he has been replaced by the baby.

Though the hormonal changes occurring after childbirth are believed to play a role in postpartum depression, the precise nature of this hormonal role has not been identified (Flores & Hendrick, 2002). Estrogen has been shown to have positive effects in treating postpartum depression for some women, but some possible negative side effects of estrogen are problematic (Grigoriadis & Kennedy, 2002; Tsigos & Chrousos, 2002). Several antidepressant drugs have been shown to be effective in treating postpartum depression and appear to be safe for breastfeeding women (Sharma, 2002). Psychotherapy, especially cognitive therapy, has also been found to be an effective treatment of postpartum depression (Beck, 2002; Kennedy, Beck, & Driscoll, 2002).

One recent study found that postpartum depression not only affects the new mother but also her child (Righetti-Veltema & others, 2002). A sample of 570 women and their infants was assessed three months after delivery. Ten percent of the mothers were classified as experiencing postpartum depression on the basis of their responses to the Edinburgh Postnatal Depression Scale (Cox & others, 1987). The negative effects on the infant involved eating or sleeping problems. The depressed mothers had less vocal and visual communication with their infant, touched the infant less, and smiled less at the infant than nondepressed mothers.

One strategy to help the man's postpartum reaction is for the parents to set aside some special time to be together with each other. The father's postpartum reaction also likely will be improved if he has taken childbirth classes with his wife and is an active participant in caring for the baby.

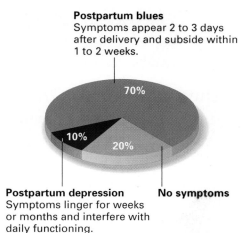

Postpartum blues
Symptoms appear 2 to 3 days after delivery and subside within 1 to 2 weeks.

70%

10%   20%

Postpartum depression   **No symptoms**
Symptoms linger for weeks or months and interfere with daily functioning.

FIGURE 4.11 Percentage of U.S. Women Who Experience Postpartum Blues and Postpartum Depression

postpartum depression Strong feelings of sadness, anxiety, or despair in new mothers that make it difficult for them to carry out daily tasks.

Careers in Child Development

Diane Sanford, *Clinical Psychologist and Postpartum Expert*

Diane Sanford has a doctorate in clinical psychology and never set out to become a specialist in women's health. For many years she had a private practice in clinical psychology with a focus on marital and family issues. Then she began collaborating with a psychiatrist whose clients included women with postpartum depression.

For the last 16 years, Diane has specialized in postpartum problems and other related aspects of female development, including infertility, pregnancy loss, and menopause.

Diane provides clients with practical advice that she believes helps women effectively cope with their problems. She begins by guiding them to think about concrete steps they can take to ease their emotional turmoil during this important postpartum transition. For example, new mothers may need help in figuring out ways to get partners and others to help with their infants. Or they may just need to be reassured that they can handle the responsibilities they face as parents.

After years of practicing on her own, Diane and a women's health nurse formed Women's Healthcare Partnership. In addition to the two partners, the staff now includes a full-time

counselor in marriage and family relationships, and a social worker. Nurse educators, a dietician, and a fitness expert work on a consulting basis. Diane also has co-authored *Postpartum Survival Guide* (Dunnewold & Sanford, 1994), which reflects her strategies for helping women cope with postpartum issues.

Diane Sanford holding an infant of one of the mothers who comes to her for help in coping with postpartum issues.

Important factors for both the mother and the father are the time and thought that go into being a competent parent of a young infant (Cowan & Cowan, 2000; McVeigh, Baafi, & Williamson, 2002). It is important for both the mother and the father to become aware of the young infant's developmental needs—physical, psychological, and emotional. Both the mother and the father need to develop a sensitive, comfortable relationship with the baby.

Some health-care professionals specialize in the postpartum period. To read about the work and career of postpartum specialist Diane Sanford, see the Careers in Child Development insert.

Bonding

A special component of the parent-infant relationship is **bonding,** the formation of a connection, especially a physical bond between parents and the newborn in the period shortly after birth. Some physicians believe that the period shortly after birth is critical in development. During this time, the parents and child need to form an important emotional attachment that provides a foundation for optimal development in years to come (Kennell & McGrath, 1999). Special interest in bonding stems from concern by pediatricians that the circumstances surrounding delivery often separate mothers and their infants, preventing or making difficult the development of a bond. The pediatricians argued that giving the mother drugs to make her delivery less painful can contribute to the lack of bonding. The drugs can make the mother drowsy, thus interfering with her ability to respond to and stimulate the newborn. Advocates of bonding also assert that preterm infants are isolated from

bonding The formation of a close connection, especially a physical bond between parents and their newborn in the period shortly after birth.

their mothers to an even greater degree than are full-term infants, thereby increasing their difficulty in bonding.

Is there evidence that such close contact between mothers and newborns is critical for optimal development later in life? Although some research supports the bonding hypothesis (Klaus & Kennell, 1976), a body of research challenges the significance of the first few days of life as a critical period (Bakeman & Brown, 1980; Rode & others, 1981). Indeed, the extreme form of the bonding hypothesis—that the newborn must have close contact with the mother in the first few days of life to develop optimally—simply is not true.

Nonetheless, the weakness of the maternal-infant bonding research should not be used as an excuse to keep motivated mothers from interacting with their infants in the postpartum period. Such contact brings pleasure to many mothers. In some mother-infant pairs—including preterm infants, adolescent mothers, or mothers from disadvantaged circumstances—the practice of bonding may set in motion a climate for improved interaction after the mother and infant leave the hospital.

In recognition of the belief that bonding may have a positive effect on getting the parental-infant relationship off to a good start, many hospitals now offer a *rooming-in* arrangement, in which the baby remains in the mother's room most of the time during its hospital stay. However, if parents choose not to use this rooming-in arrangement, the weight of the research evidence suggests that it will not harm the infant emotionally (Lamb, 1994).

Review and Reflect: Learning Goal 3

3 Explain the changes that take place in the postpartum period

REVIEW

- What does the postpartum period involve?
- What physical adjustments does the woman's body make in this period?
- What emotional and psychological adjustments characterize the postpartum period?
- How critical is bonding in development?

REFLECT

- If you are a female, what can you do to adjust effectively in the postpartum period? If you are a male, what can you do to help in the postpartum period?

Reach Your Learning Goals

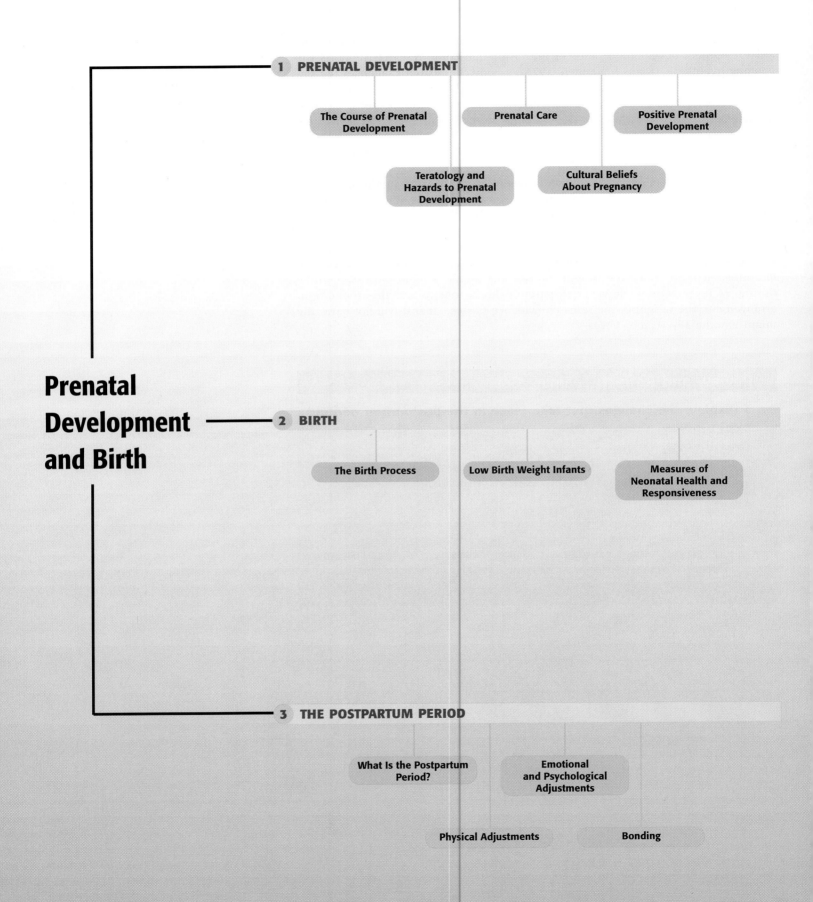

Prenatal Development and Birth

1 PRENATAL DEVELOPMENT

The Course of Prenatal Development

Prenatal Care

Positive Prenatal Development

Teratology and Hazards to Prenatal Development

Cultural Beliefs About Pregnancy

2 BIRTH

The Birth Process

Low Birth Weight Infants

Measures of Neonatal Health and Responsiveness

3 THE POSTPARTUM PERIOD

What Is the Postpartum Period?

Emotional and Psychological Adjustments

Physical Adjustments

Bonding

Summary

1 Describe prenatal development

- Prenatal development is divided into three periods: germinal (conception until 10 to 14 days later), which ends when the zygote (a fertilized egg) attaches to the uterine wall; embryonic (two to eight weeks after conception), during which the embryo differentiates into three layers, life-support systems develop, and organ systems form (organogenesis); and fetal (two months after conception until about nine months, or when the infant is born), a time when organ systems have matured to the point at which life can be sustained outside of the womb.

- Teratology is the field that investigates the causes of congenital (birth) defects. Any agent that causes birth defects is called a teratogen. The dose, time of exposure, and genetic susceptibility influence the severity of the damage to an unborn child and the type of defect that occurs. Prescription drugs that can be harmful include antibiotics. Nonprescription drugs that can be harmful include diet pills, aspirin, and coffee. Fetal alcohol syndrome is a cluster of abnormalities that appear in offspring of mothers who drink heavily during pregnancy. Even when pregnant women drink moderately (one to two drinks a day), negative effects on their offspring have been found. Cigarette smoking by pregnant women has serious adverse effects on prenatal and child development (such as low birth weight). Illegal drugs that are potentially harmful to offspring include marijuana, cocaine, and heroin. Incompatibility of the mother's and the father's blood types can also be harmful to the fetus. Potential environmental hazards include radiation, environmental pollutants, toxic wastes, and prolonged exposure to heat in saunas and hot tubs. Rubella (German measles) can be harmful. Syphilis, genital herpes, and AIDS are other teratogens. A developing fetus depends entirely on its mother for nutrition. One nutrient that is especially important very early in development is folic acid. High anxiety and stress in the mother are linked with less than optimal prenatal and birth outcomes. Maternal age can negatively affect the offspring's development if the mother is an adolescent or over 30. Paternal factors that can adversely affect prenatal development include exposure to lead, radiation, certain pesticides, and petrochemicals.

- Prenatal care varies extensively but usually involves medical care services with a defined schedule of visits.

- Specific actions in pregnancy are often determined by cultural beliefs. Certain behaviors are expected if a culture views pregnancy as a medical condition or a natural occurrence. Some cultures emphasize traditional home care remedies and folk beliefs and the importance of indigenous healers. Others emphasize the use of professional health-care workers.

- It is important to remember that, although things can and do go wrong during pregnancy, most of the time pregnancy and prenatal development go well. Avoiding teratogens helps ensure a positive outcome.

2 Discuss the birth process

- Childbirth occurs in three stages. In the first stage, which lasts about 12 to 24 hours for a woman having her first child, the cervix dilates to about 4 inches. The second stage begins when the baby's head moves through the cervix and ends with the baby's complete emergence. The third stage is afterbirth. Being born involves considerable stress for the baby, but the baby is well prepared and adapted to handle the stress. Anoxia—insufficient oxygen supply to the fetus/newborn—is a potential hazard. Childbirth strategies involve the childbirth setting (for example, home birth or hospital birth) and attendants (for example, nurse-midwife or physician). In many countries, a doula attends a childbearing woman. Methods of delivery include medicated, natural and prepared, and cesarean.

- Low birth weight infants weigh less than $5\frac{1}{2}$ pounds at birth and they may be preterm (born 3 weeks or more before the pregnancy has reached full-term) or small for date (also called small for gestational age, which refers to infants whose birth weight is below normal when the length of pregnancy is considered). Small for date infants may be preterm or full-term. Although most low birth weight infants are normal and healthy, as a group they have more health and developmental problems than normal birth weight infants. Enrichment programs can benefit low birth weight infants. Preterm infant care is much too complex to only be described in terms of amount of stimulation. Preterm infants' responses vary according to their conceptual age, illness, and individual makeup. Intervention should be organized in the form of an individualized developmental plan. Massage therapy is increasingly being used with preterm infants and has positive outcomes. Kangaroo care, a way of holding a preterm infant so that there is skin-to-skin contact, has positive effects on preterm infants.

- For many years, the Apgar Scale has been used to assess the newborn's health. The Brazelton Neonatal Behavioral Assessment Scale examines the newborn's neurological development, reflexes, and reactions to people.

3 Explain the changes that take place in the postpartum period

- The postpartum period is the name given to the period after childbirth or delivery. In this period, the woman adjusts physically and psychologically to the process of childbearing. The period lasts for about six weeks or until the body has completed its adjustment.

- Physical adjustments in the postpartum period include involution (the process by which the uterus returns to its prepregnant size five or six weeks after birth), hormonal changes, dealing with fatigue, and deciding when to resume sexual intercourse and when to begin exercises to recover body contour and strength.

- The mother's emotional fluctuation is common in the postpartum period. These fluctuations may be due to hormonal changes, fatigue, inexperience or lack of confidence in caring for a newborn, or the extensive demands involved in caring for a newborn. For some, these fluctuations are minimal and disappear in several weeks, but for others they can be more long-lasting. Postpartum depression, which involves such strong feelings of sadness, anxiety, or despair that new mothers have difficulty carrying out daily tasks, characterizes approximately 10 percent of U.S. women. The father also goes through a postpartum adjustment. Another adjustment for both the mother and the father is the time and thought that go into being a competent parent of a young infant.

• Bonding is the formation of a close connection, especially a physical bond between parents and the newborn shortly after birth. Early bonding has not been found to be critical in the development of a competent infant, but it may benefit some mothers, such as those living in poverty and adolescent mothers.

Key Terms

germinal period 95
blastocyst 95
trophoblast 95
embryonic period 95
placenta 95
umbilical cord 95
amnion 96

organogenesis 96
fetal period 97
teratogen 99
fetal alcohol syndrome (FAS) 101
doula 112
natural childbirth 113

prepared childbirth 113
breech position 113
low birth weight infant 114
preterm infant 114
small for date infant 114
kangaroo care 116
Apgar Scale 118

Brazelton Neonatal Behavioral Assessment Scale 118
postpartum period 119
postpartum depression 121
bonding 122

Key People

Christine Dunkel-Schetter 106

Grantley Dick-Read 113

Ferdinand Lamaze 113

T. Berry Brazelton 118

Taking It to the Net

1. Denise's sister, Doreen, is pregnant for the first time. Doreen is not particularly known for her healthy lifestyle. What particular things can Denise encourage Doreen to do in order to give birth to a healthy baby?

2. Sienne told her fiancé, Jackson, that he had better stop smoking before they begin trying to conceive a child. Why is Sienne concerned about Jackson's smoking and its effect on their children before they have even started planning their family?

3. Hannah, who gave birth to a healthy baby boy—her first child—two weeks ago, appears to her husband Sean to be sad, lethargic, and is having trouble sleeping. How can Sean determine if Hannah is just going through a natural period of post-baby "blues" or if she might be suffering from postpartum depression?

Connect to **www.mhhe.com/santrockcd10** to research the answers and complete these exercises.

E-Learning Tools

To help you master the material in this chapter, you'll find a number of valuable study tools on the Student CD-ROM that accompanies this book. Also visit the Online Learning Center for *Child Development*, tenth edition (**www.mhhe.com/santrockcd10**) where you'll find these additional resources:

- Build your decision-making skills by trying your hand at the parenting, nursing, and education "Scenarios" on the Online Learning Center.

A baby is the most complicated object made by unskilled labor.

—Anonymous

Physical Development in Infancy

Chapter Outline

PHYSICAL GROWTH AND DEVELOPMENT IN INFANCY

Cephalocaudal and Proximodistal Patterns

Height and Weight

The Brain

Sleep

Nutrition

Toilet Training

MOTOR DEVELOPMENT

Reflexes

Gross and Fine Motor Skills

Dynamic Systems Theory

SENSORY AND PERCEPTUAL DEVELOPMENT

What Are Sensation and Perception?

The Ecological View

Visual Perception

Other Senses

Intermodal Perception

Perceptual-Motor Coupling

Learning Goals

1 Discuss physical growth and development in infancy

2 Describe infants' motor development

3 Explain sensory and perceptual development in infancy

The Stories of Latonya and Ramona:
Bottle- and Breastfeeding in Africa

Latonya is a newborn baby in the African country of Ghana. The culture of the area in which she was born discourages breastfeeding. She has been kept apart from her mother and bottlefed in her first days of infancy. Manufacturers of infant formula provide the hospital where she was born with free or subsidized milk powder. Her mother has been persuaded to bottlefeed rather than breastfeed her.

When her mother bottlefeeds Latonya, she overdilutes the milk formula with unclean water. Latonya's feeding bottles also have not been sterilized. Latonya starts getting sick, very sick. She dies before her first birthday.

By contrast, Ramona lives in the African country of Nigeria. Her mother is breastfeeding her. Ramona was born at a Nigerian hospital where a "baby-friendly" program had been initiated. In this program, babies are not separated from their mothers when they are born, and the mothers are encouraged to breastfeed them. The mothers are told of the perils that bottlefeeding can bring because of unsafe water and unsterilized bottles. They also are informed about the advantages of breast milk, which include its nutritious and hygienic qualities, its ability to immunize babies against common illnesses, and its role in reducing the mother's risk of breast and ovarian cancer. At 1 year of age, Ramona is very healthy.

For the past 10 to 15 years, the World Health Organization and UNICEF have been trying to reverse the trend toward bottlefeeding of infants, which emerged in many impoverished countries. They have instituted the "baby-friendly" program in many countries. They also have persuaded the International Association of Infant Formula Manufacturers to stop marketing their baby formulas to hospitals in countries where the governments support the baby-friendly initiatives. For the hospitals themselves, costs actually will be reduced as infant formula, feeding bottles, and separate nurseries become unnecessary.

For example, baby-friendly Jose Fabella Memorial Hospital in the Philippines already has reported saving 8 percent of its annual budget.

Hospitals play a vital role in getting mothers to breastfeed their babies. For many years, maternity units were on the side of bottlefeeding babies and failed to give mothers adequate information about the benefits of breastfeeding. Fortunately, with the initiatives of the World Health Organization and UNICEF, that is beginning to change, but there still are many impoverished places in the world where the baby-friendly initiatives have not been implemented (Grant, 1993).

It is very important for infants to get a healthy start. In this chapter we will explore these aspects of the infant's development: physical growth, motor development, and sensory and perceptual development.

1 PHYSICAL GROWTH AND DEVELOPMENT IN INFANCY

Cephalocaudal and Proximodistal Patterns

The Brain

Nutrition

Height and Weight

Sleep

Toilet Training

Infants' physical development in the first two years of life is extensive. At birth, neonates have a gigantic head (relative to the rest of the body), which flops around uncontrollably. They also possess reflexes that are dominated by evolutionary movements. In the span of 12 months, infants become capable of sitting anywhere, standing, stooping, climbing, and usually walking. During the second year, growth decelerates, but rapid increases in such activities as running and climbing take place. Let's now examine in greater detail the sequence of physical development in infancy.

Cephalocaudal and Proximodistal Patterns

The **cephalocaudal pattern** is the sequence in which the greatest growth always occurs at the top—the head—with physical growth in size, weight, and feature differentiation gradually working its way down from top to bottom (for example, shoulders, middle trunk, and so on). This same pattern occurs in the head area, because the top parts of the head—the eyes and brain—grow faster than the lower parts, such as the jaw. An extraordinary proportion of the total body is occupied by the head during prenatal development and early infancy (see figure 5.1). Later in the chapter you will see that sensory and motor development proceed according to the cephalocaudal principle. For example, infants see objects before they can control their trunk, and they can use their hands long before they can crawl or walk.

The **proximodistal pattern** is the sequence in which growth starts at the center of the body and moves toward the extremities. An example of this is the early

> **cephalocaudal pattern** The sequence in which the greatest growth occurs at the top—the head—with physical growth in size, weight, and feature differentiation gradually working from top to bottom.
>
> **proximodistal pattern** The sequence in which growth starts at the center of the body and moves toward the extremities.

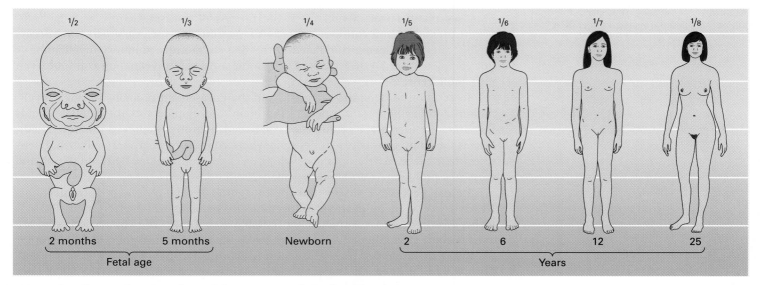

| 1/2 | 1/3 | 1/4 | 1/5 | 1/6 | 1/7 | 1/8 |

| 2 months | 5 months | Newborn | 2 | 6 | 12 | 25 |

Fetal age

Years

FIGURE 5.1 Changes in Proportions of the Human Body During Growth
As individuals develop from infancy through adulthood, one of the most noticeable physical changes in that the head becomes smaller in relation to the rest of the body. The fractions listed refer to head size as a proportion of total body length at different ages.

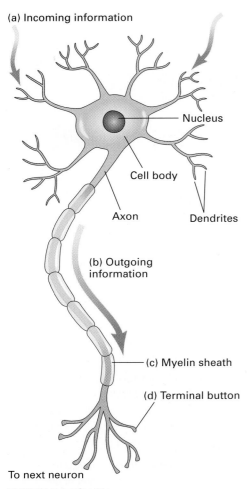

(a) Incoming information

Nucleus

Cell body

Axon

Dendrites

(b) Outgoing information

(c) Myelin sheath

(d) Terminal button

To next neuron

FIGURE 5.2 The Neuron

(*a*) The dendrites of the cell body receive information from other neurons, muscles, or glands through the axon. (*b*) Axons transmit information away from the cell body. (*c*) A myelin sheath covers most axons and speeds information transmission. (*d*) As the axon ends, it branches out into terminal buttons.

neuron Nerve cell that handles information processing at the cellular level.

maturation of muscular control of the trunk and arms, as compared with that of the hands and fingers. Further, infants use their whole hand as a unit before they can control several fingers.

Height and Weight

The average North American newborn is 20 inches long and weighs $7\frac{1}{2}$ pounds. Ninety-five percent of full-term newborns are 18 to 22 inches long and weigh between $5\frac{1}{2}$ and 10 pounds.

In the first several days of life, most newborns lose 5 to 7 percent of their body weight before they learn to adjust to neonatal feeding. Once infants adjust to sucking, swallowing, and digesting, they grow rapidly, gaining an average of 5 to 6 ounces per week during the first month. They have doubled their birth weight by the age of 4 months and have nearly tripled it by their first birthday. Infants grow about 1 inch per month during the first year, reaching approximately $1\frac{1}{2}$ times their birth length by their first birthday.

Infants' rate of growth is considerably slower in the second year of life. By 2 years of age, infants weigh approximately 26 to 32 pounds, having gained about a quarter to half a pound per month during the second year; now they have reached about one-fifth of their adult weight. At 2 years of age, the average infant is 32 to 35 inches in height, which is nearly one-half of their adult height.

The Brain

As an infant walks, talks, runs, shakes a rattle, smiles, and frowns, changes are occurring in its brain. Consider that the infant began life as a single cell and nine months later was born with a brain and nervous system that contained approximately 100 billion nerve cells, or neurons. A **neuron** is a nerve cell that handles information processing at the cellular level (see figure 5.2).

The Brain's Development Among the most dramatic changes in the brain in the first 2 years of life are the spreading connections of dendrites to each other. Figure 5.3 illustrates these changes.

A myelin sheath, which is a layer of fat cells, encases most axons (review figure 5.2). Not only does the myelin sheath insulate nerve cells, but it also helps nerve impulses travel faster. Myelination, the process of encasing axons with fat cells, begins prenatally and continues after birth. Myelination for visual pathways occurs rapidly after birth, being completed in the first six months. Auditory myelination is not completed until 4 or 5 years of age. Some aspects of myelination continue even into adolescence.

In addition to dendritic spreading and the encasement of axons through myelination, another important aspect of the brain's development at the cellular level is the dramatic increase in connections between neurons (Ramey & Ramey, 2000). *Synapses* are tiny gaps between neurons where connections between axons and dendrites take place. As the infant develops, synaptic connections between axons and dendrites proliferate (Neville & Bavelier, 2002).

Researchers have discovered an intriguing aspect of synaptic connections. Nearly twice as many of these connections are made as will ever be used (Huttenlocher & others, 1991; Huttenlocher & Dabholkar, 1997). The connections that are used become strengthened and survive while the unused ones are replaced by other pathways or disappear (Casey, Durston, & Fossella, 2001). That is, these connections will be "pruned," in the language of neuroscience. Figure 5.4 vividly illustrates the dramatic growth and later pruning of synapses in the visual, auditory, and prefrontal cortex areas of the brain (Huttenlocher & Dabholkar, 1997). These areas are critical for higher-level cognitive functioning in areas like learning, memory, and reasoning.

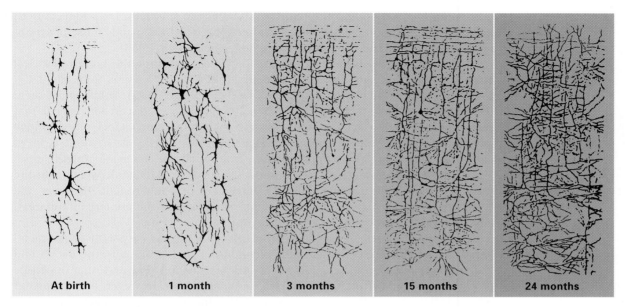

FIGURE 5.3 The Development of Dendritic Spreading

Note the increase in connectedness between neurons over the course of the first two years of life.

As shown in Figure 5.4, "blooming and pruning" vary considerably by brain region in humans (Thompson & Nelson, 2001). For example, the peak of synaptic overproduction in the visual cortex occurs at about the fourth postnatal month, followed by a gradual retraction until the middle to end of the preschool years (Huttenlocher & Dabholkar, 1997). In areas of the brain involved in hearing and language, a similar, though somewhat later, course is detected. However, in the prefrontal cortex (the area of the brain where higher-level thinking and self-regulation occur), the peak of overproduction takes place at about 1 year of age and it is not

Neural Processes

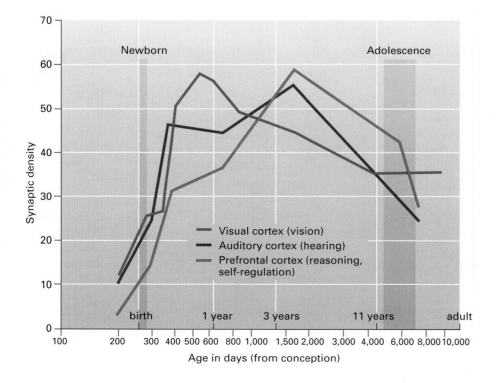

FIGURE 5.4 Synaptic Density in the Human Brain from Infancy to Adulthood

The graph shows the dramatic increase and then pruning in synaptic density for three regions of the brain: visual cortex, auditory cortex, and prefrontal cortex. Synaptic density is believed to be an important indication of the extent of connectivity between neurons.

until middle to late adolescence that the adult density of synapses is achieved. Both heredity and environment are thought to influence the timing and course of synaptic overproduction and subsequent retraction (Greenough, 2000).

Using the electroencephalogram (EEG), which measures the brain's electrical activity, researchers have found that a spurt in EEG activity occurs from about $1\frac{1}{2}$ to 2 years of age (Fischer & Bidell, 1998; Fischer & Rose, 1995). Other spurts seem to take place at about 9, 12, 15, and 18 to 20 years of age. Researchers believe that these spurts of brain activity may coincide with important changes in cognitive development. For example, the increase in EEG brain activity at $1\frac{1}{2}$ to 2 years of age is likely associated with an increase in conceptual and language growth.

At birth, the newborn's brain is about 25 percent of its adult weight. By the second birthday, the brain is about 75 percent of its adult weight. However, the brain's areas do not mature uniformly. Some areas, such as the primary motor areas, develop earlier than others, such as the primary sensory areas.

Studying the brain's development in infancy is not as easy as it might seem, because even the latest brain-imaging technologies can't make out fine details and they can't be used on babies. PET scans pose a radiation risk, and infants wriggle too much for an MRI (Marcus, Mulrine, & Wong, 1999). However, one researcher who is making strides in finding out more about the brain's development in infancy is Charles Nelson (1999; deHaan & Nelson, 1999). His research involves attaching 16 to 128 electrodes to a baby's scalp (see figure 5.5). He has found that even newborns produce distinctive brain waves that reveal they can distinguish their mother's voice from another woman's, even while they are asleep. In other research, Nelson has found that by 8 months of age babies can distinguish the picture of a wooden toy they were allowed to feel, but not see, from pictures of other toys. This achievement coincides with the development of neurons in the brain's hippocampus (an important structure in memory), allowing the infant to remember specific items and events.

The Brain's Lobes and Hemispheres   The forebrain is the highest level of the brain. It consists of a number of structures, including the *cerebral cortex*, which makes up about 80 percent of the brain's volume and covers the lower portions of the brain like a cap. The cerebral cortex plays a critical role in many important human functions, such as perception, language, and thinking.

FIGURE 5.5 Measuring the Brain's Activity in Research on Infant Memory

In Charles Nelson's research, electrodes are attached to a baby's scalp to measure the brain's activity to determine its role in the development of an infant's memory. *Why is it so difficult to measure infants' brain activity?*

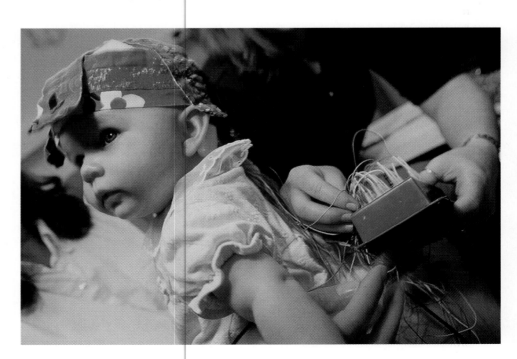

The cerebral cortex is divided into four main areas called lobes (see figure 5.6):

- The *frontal lobe* is involved in voluntary movement and thinking.
- The *occipital lobe* is involved in vision.
- The *temporal lobe* is involved in hearing.
- The *parietal lobe* is involved in processing information about body sensations.

The frontal lobe is immature in the newborn. However, as neurons in the frontal lobes become myelinated and interconnected during the first year of life, infants develop an ability to regulate their physiological states (such as sleep) and gain more control over their reflexes. Cognitive skills that require deliberate thinking don't emerge until later (Bell & Fox, 1992). Indeed, as we saw earlier, the prefrontal region of the frontal lobe has the most prolonged development of any brain region with changes detectable at least into the adolescent years (Johnson, 2001).

The cerebral cortex is divided into two halves, or hemispheres (see figure 5.7). **Lateralization** is the specialization of function in one hemisphere of the cerebral cortex or the other. There continues to be considerable interest in the degree to which each is involved in various aspects of thinking, feeling, and behavior.

The most extensive research on the brain's hemispheres has focused on language. At birth, the hemispheres already have started to specialize: Newborns show greater electrical brain activity in the left hemisphere than the right hemisphere when they are listening to speech sounds (Hahn, 1987). A common misconception is that virtually all language processing is carried out in the left hemisphere. Speech and grammar are localized to the left hemisphere in most people; however, some aspects of language, such as appropriate language use in different contexts and the use of metaphor and humor, involve the right hemisphere. Thus, language does not occur exclusively in the brain's left hemisphere (Johnson, 2000, 2001).

It is a popular myth that the left hemisphere is the exclusive location of logical thinking and the right hemisphere the exclusive location of creative thinking. However, most neuroscientists agree that complex functions, such as reading, performing music, and creating art, involve both hemispheres. They believe that labeling people as "left-brained" because they are logical thinkers and "right-brained" because they are creative thinkers does not correspond to the way the brain's hemispheres actually work. Such complex thinking in normal people is the outcome of communication between both sides of the brain.

Early Experience and the Brain   Until the middle of the twentieth century, scientists believed that the brain's development was determined almost exclusively by genetic factors. ◄ **page 69** Researcher Mark Rosenzweig (1969) was curious about whether early experiences change the brain's development. He conducted a number of experiments with rats and other animals to investigate this possibility. Animals were randomly assigned to grow up in different environments. Animals in an enriched early environment lived in cages with stimulating features, such as wheels to rotate, steps to climb, levers to press, and toys to manipulate. In contrast, other animals had the early experience of growing up in standard cages or in barren, isolated conditions.

The results were stunning. The brains of the animals growing up in the enriched environment developed better than the brains of the animals reared in standard or isolated conditions. The brains of the "enriched" animals weighed more, had thicker layers, had more neuronal connections, and had higher levels of neurochemical activity.

Similar findings occurred when older animals were reared in vastly different environments, although the results were not as strong as for the younger animals.

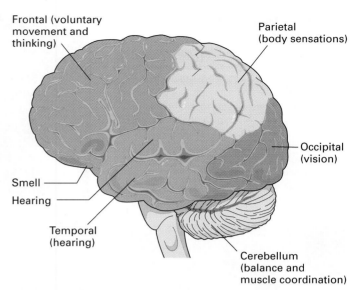

FIGURE 5.6 The Brain's Four Lobes

Shown here are the locations of the brain's four lobes: frontal, occipital, temporal, and parietal.

Development of the Brain

Early Development of the Brain

Early Experience and the Brain

FIGURE 5.7 The Human Brain's Hemispheres

The two halves (hemispheres) of the human brain are clearly seen in this photograph.

lateralization Specialization of function in one hemisphere of the cerebral cortex or the other.

FIGURE 5.8 Early Deprivation and Brain Activity

These two photographs are PET (positron emission tomography) scans—which use radioactive tracers to image and analyze blood flow and metabolic activity in the body's organs—of the brains of (a) a normal child and (b) an institutionalized Romanian orphan who experienced substantial deprivation since birth. In PET scans, the highest to lowest brain activity is reflected in the colors of red, yellow, green, blue, and black, respectively. As can be seen, red and yellow show up to a much greater degree in the PET scan of the normal child than the deprived Romanian orphan.

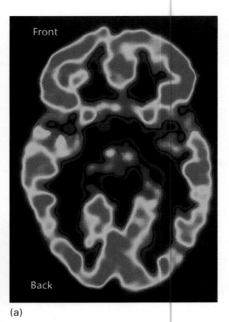

(a)

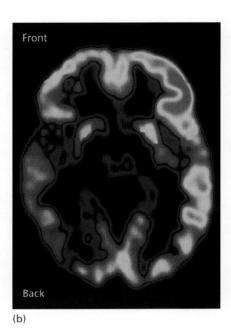

(b)

(a)

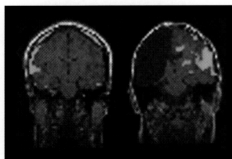

(b)

FIGURE 5.9 Plasticity in the Brain's Hemispheres

(a) Michael Rehbein at 14 years of age.
(b) Michael's right hemisphere (*near left*) has reorganized to take over the language functions normally carried out by corresponding areas in the left hemisphere of an intact brain (*far left*). However, the right hemisphere is not as efficient as the left, and more areas of the brain are recruited to process speech.

Such results give hope that enriching the lives of infants and young children who live in impoverished environments can produce positive changes in their development. ◀ **page 20**

Depressed brain activity has recently been found in children who grow up in a deprived environment (Cicchetti, 2001). As shown in figure 5.8, a child who grew up in the unresponsive and unstimulating environment of a Romanian orphanage showed considerably depressed brain activity compared with a normal child (Begley, 1997).

Scientists also now know that, starting shortly after birth, a baby's brain produces trillions more connections between neurons than it can possibly use. The brain eliminates connections that are seldom or never used. This pruning of brain connections continues at least until about 10 years of age.

The profusion of connections provides the growing brain with flexibility and resilience. Consider 14-year-old Michael Rehbein. At age 7, he began to experience uncontrollable seizures—as many as 400 a day. Doctors said the only solution was to remove the left hemisphere of his brain where the seizures were occurring. Recovery was slow but his right hemisphere began to reorganize and take over functions that normally occur in the brain's left hemisphere. One of these functions was speech (see figure 5.9).

Neuroscientists believe that what wires the brain—or rewires it, in the case of Michael Rehbein—is repeated experience (Nash, 1997). Each time a baby tries to touch an attractive object or gazes intently at a face, tiny bursts of electricity shoot through the brain, knitting together neurons into circuits. The results are some of the behavioral milestones we discuss in this and other chapters. For example, at about 2 months of age, the motor-control centers of the brain develop to the point at which infants can suddenly reach out and grab a nearby object. At about 4 months, the neural connections necessary for depth perception begin to form. And at about 12 months, the brain's speech centers are poised to produce one of infancy's magical moments: when the infant utters its first word.

In sum, neural connections are formed early in life. The infant's brain literally is waiting for experiences to determine how connections are made (Greenough, 2000, 2001; Johnson, 2000, 2001). Before birth, it appears that genes mainly direct how the brain establishes basic wiring patterns. Neurons grow and travel to distant places awaiting further instructions. After birth, environmental experiences are important in the brain's development. The inflowing stream of sights, sounds, smells, touches, language, and eye contact help shape the brain's neural connections (Black, 2001).

Sleep

When we were infants, sleep consumed more of our time than it does now. Newborns sleep 16 to 17 hours a day, although some sleep more and others less. The range is from a low of about 10 hours to a high of about 21 hours, although the longest period of sleep is not always between 11 P.M. and 7 A.M. Although total sleep remains somewhat consistent for young infants, their sleep during the day does not always follow a rhythmic pattern. An infant might change from sleeping several long bouts of 7 or 8 hours to three or four shorter sessions only a few hours in duration. By about 1 month of age, most infants have begun to sleep longer at night, and, by about 4 months of age, they usually have moved closer to adultlike sleep patterns, spending the most time sleeping at night and the most time awake during the day (Daws, 2000).

There are cultural variations in infant sleeping patterns. For example, in the Kipsigis culture in the African country of Kenya, infants sleep with their mothers at night and are permitted to nurse on demand (Super & Harkness, 1997). During the day they are strapped to their mother's back, accompanying them on their daily rounds of chores and social activities. As a result, the Kipsigis infants do not sleep through the night until much later than American infants. During the first eight months of postnatal life, Kipsigis infants rarely sleep longer than three hours at a stretch, even at night. This contrasts with American infants, many of whom begin to sleep up to eight hours a night by eight months of age.

REM Sleep   Researchers are intrigued by the various forms of infant sleep. They are especially interested in *REM (rapid eye movement) sleep*. Most adults spend about one-fifth of their night in REM sleep, and REM sleep usually appears about one hour after non-REM sleep. However, about one-half of an infant's sleep is REM sleep, and infants often begin their sleep cycle with REM sleep rather than non-REM sleep. By the time infants reach 3 months of age, the percentage of time they spend in REM sleep falls to about 40 percent, and REM sleep no longer begins their sleep cycle. The large amount of REM sleep may provide infants with added self-stimulation, since they spend less time awake than do older children. REM sleep also might promote the brain's development in infancy. Figure 5.10 illustrates the average number of total hours spent in sleep, and the amount of time spent in REM sleep, across the human life span. As can be seen, infants sleep far more than children and adults do, and a much greater amount of time is taken up by REM sleep in infancy than at any other point in the life span.

Shared Sleeping   There is considerable variation across cultures in newborns' sleeping arrangements. Sharing a bed with a mother is a common practice in many cultures, whereas in others newborns sleep in a crib, either in the same room as the parents or in a separate room. In the United States, sleeping in a crib in a separate room is the most frequent sleeping arrangement for an infant. In one cross-cultural study, American mothers said they have their infants sleep in a separate room to promote the infant's self-reliance and independence (Morelli & others, 1992). By contrast, Mayan mothers in rural Guatemala had infants sleep in their bed until the birth of a new sibling, at which time the infant would sleep with another family member or in a separate bed in the mother's room. The Mayan mothers believed that the co-sleeping arrangement with their infants enhances the closeness of their relationship with the infants and were shocked when told that American mothers have their baby sleep alone.

Some child experts believe there are benefits to shared sleeping, such as promoting breastfeeding, responding more quickly to the baby's cries, and detecting potentially dangerous breathing pauses in the baby (McKenna, Mosko, & Richard, 1997). However, the American Academy of Pediatrics (AAP) Task Force on Infant Positioning and SIDS (2000; Cohen, 2000) discourages shared sleeping. The Task

*S*leep that knits up the ravelled sleave of care . . . Balm of hurt minds, nature's second course. Chief nourisher in life's feast.

—WILLIAM SHAKESPEARE
English Playwright, 17th Century

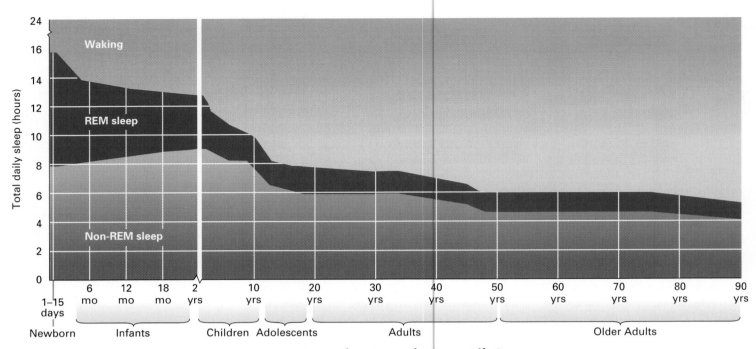

FIGURE 5.10 Sleep Across the Human Life Span

Force concluded that in some instances bed sharing might lead to sudden infant death syndrome (SIDS), as could be the case if a sleeping mother rolls over on her baby. One recent study found physiological responses indicative of greater stress in co-sleeping infants than non-co-sleeping infants (Hunsley & Thoman, 2002). Thus, shared sleeping remains a controversial issue, with some experts recommending it, others arguing against it.

SIDS **Sudden infant death syndrome (SIDS)** is a condition that occurs when infants stop breathing, usually during the night, and suddenly die without an apparent cause. Since 1992, the American Academy of Pediatrics has recommended that infants be placed to sleep on their backs to reduce the risk of SIDS. Since that time, the frequency of prone sleeping has decreased from 70 percent to 20 percent of U.S. infants (American Academy of Pediatrics Task Force on Infant Sleep Positioning and SIDS, 2000). Some researchers now believe that an inability to swallow effectively in the prone (face down) sleeping position is an important reason SIDS occurs (Jeffery & others, 2000; Moon & others, 2000). Researchers have found that SIDS decreases when infants sleep on their backs rather than on their stomachs or sides (Smith & Hattersley, 2000). However, SIDS still remains the highest cause of infant death in the United States with nearly 3,000 infant deaths due to SIDS. Risk of SIDS is highest at 4 to 6 weeks of age. Among the reasons given for prone sleeping being a high risk factor for SIDS are that it impairs arousal from sleep and restricts the ability to swallow effectively (Horne & others, 2002; Kahn & others, 2002).

In addition to sleeping in a prone position, researchers have also found these risk factors for SIDS (AAP Task Force on Infant Sleep Positioning and SIDS, 2000; Goldwater, 2001; Maas, 1998):

- Low birth weight infants are 5 to 10 times more likely to die of SIDS than are their normal weight counterparts (Horne & others, 2002; Sowter & others, 1999).
- Infants whose siblings have died of SIDS are two to four times as likely to die of it (Lenoir, Mallet, & Calenda, 2000).
- Six percent of infants with sleep apnea, a temporary cessation of breathing in which the airway is completely blocked, usually 10 seconds or longer, die of SIDS (McNamara & Sullivan, 2000).

SIDS

sudden infant death syndrome (SIDS) A condition that occurs when an infant stops breathing, usually during the night, and suddenly dies without an apparent cause.

- African American and Eskimo infants are two to six times as likely as all others to die of SIDS (Pollack & Frohna, 2001). One recent study found that prone sleeping was linked to SIDS in African American infants, suggesting the importance of educational outreach to African American families regarding the importance of placing infants on their back while sleeping (Hauck & others, 2002).
- SIDS is more common in lower socioeconomic groups (Mitchell & others, 2000).
- SIDS is more common in infants who are passively exposed to cigarette smoke (Pollack, 2001).
- Soft bedding is not recommended (Flick & others, 2001).

Nutrition

Our coverage of infant nutrition begins with information about nutritional needs and eating behavior, then turns to the issue of breast- versus bottlefeeding, and concludes with an overview of malnutrition.

Nutritional Needs and Eating Behavior   The importance of adequate energy and nutrient intake consumed in a loving and supportive environment during the infant years cannot be overstated (Samour, Helm, & Lang, 2000). From birth to 1 year of age, human infants have nearly tripled their weight and increased their length by approximately 50 percent. Individual differences among infants in terms of their nutrient reserves, body composition, growth rates, and activity patterns make defining actual nutrient needs difficult. However, because parents need guidelines, nutritionists recommend that infants consume approximately 50 calories per day for each pound they weigh—more than twice an adult's requirement per pound.

Some years ago, controversy surrounded the issue of whether a baby should be fed on demand or on a regular schedule. Behaviorist John Watson (1928) argued that scheduled feeding is superior because it increases the child's orderliness. An example of a recommended schedule for newborns was 4 ounces of formula every six hours. In recent years, demand feeding—in which the timing and amount of feeding are determined by the infant—has become more popular.

Today, Americans are extremely nutrition-conscious. Does the same type of nutrition that makes us healthy adults also make young infants healthy? Some affluent, well-educated parents almost starve their babies by feeding them the low-fat, low-calorie diet they eat themselves. Diets designed for adult weight loss and prevention of heart disease may actually retard growth and development in babies. Fat is very important for babies. Nature's food—breast milk—is not low in fat or calories. No child under the age of 2 should be consuming skim milk.

In one investigation, seven babies 7 to 22 months of age were found to be undernourished by their unwitting health-conscious parents (Lifshitz & others, 1987). In some instances, the parents had been fat themselves and were determined that their child was not going to be. The well-meaning parents substituted vegetables, skim milk, and other low-fat foods for what they called junk food. However, for growing infants, high-calorie, high-energy foods are part of a balanced diet.

Breastfeeding Versus Bottlefeeding   Human milk or an alternative formula is the baby's source of nutrients and energy for the first four to six months of life. For years, debate has focused on whether breastfeeding is better for the infant than bottlefeeding. The growing consensus is that breastfeeding is better for the baby's health (Blum, 2000; Cronin, 2003; Hanson & others, 2002).

Information on breastfeeding in the United States has been collected for a number of decades by Abbott Laboratories. As shown in figure 5.11, in 2001, the prevalence of initiating breastfeeding in the

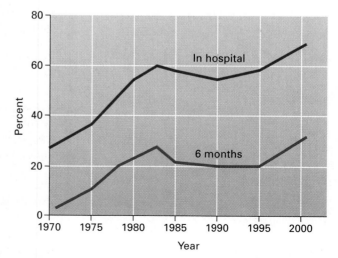

FIGURE 5.11 Trends in Breastfeeding in the United States: 1970–2001

Human milk or an alternative formula is a baby's source of nutrients for the first 4 to 6 months. The growing consensus is that breastfeeding is better for the baby's health, although controversy still swirls about the issue of breastfeeding versus bottlefeeding. *Why is breastfeeding strongly recommended by pediatricians?*

hospital and breastfeeding at six months after birth reached an all-time high of 69.5 percent and 32.5 percent, respectively (Ryan, Wenjun, & Acosta, 2002).

What are some of the benefits of breastfeeding? They include these benefits during the first two years of life and later (AAP Work Group on Breastfeeding, 1997; Eiger & Olds, 1999; London & others, 2000):

- Appropriate weight gain
- Fewer allergies (Arshad, 2001; Hoppu & others, 2001; Miyake, Yura, & Iki, 2003)
- Prevention or reduction of diarrhea, respiratory infections (such as pneumonia and bronchitis), bacterial and urinary tract infections, and otitis media (a middle ear infection) (AAP Work Group on Breastfeeding, 1997; Hanson & Korotkova, 2002; Kramer & others, 2001)
- Denser bones in childhood and adulthood (Gibson & others, 2000; Jones, Riley, & Dwyer, 2000)
- Reduced childhood cancer and reduced incidence of breast cancer in mothers and their female offspring (Bernier & others, 2000)
- Lower incidence of SIDS—in one study, for every month of exclusive breastfeeding, the rate of SIDS was cut in half (Fredrickson, 1993)
- Higher levels of neurological and cognitive development (Brody, 1994)
- Better visual acuity (Makrides & others, 1995)

Which women are least likely to breastfeed? They include mothers who work full-time outside of the home, mothers under age 25, mothers without a high school education, African American mothers, and mothers in low-income circumstances (Ryan, 1997). In one study of low-income mothers in Georgia, interventions (such as counseling focused on the benefits of breastfeeding and the free loan of a breast pump) increased the incidence of breastfeeding (Ahluwalia & others, 2000). Increasingly, mothers who return to work in the infant's first year of life use a breast pump to extract breast milk that can be stored for later feeding of the infant when the mother is not present.

The American Pediatric Association strongly endorses breastfeeding throughout the first year of life (AAP Work Group on Breastfeeding, 1997). Are there circumstances when mothers should not breastfeed? Yes, they are (1) if the mother is infected with AIDS, which can be transmitted through her milk, or has another infectious disease; (2) if she has active tuberculosis; or (3) if she is taking any drug that might not be safe for the infant (AAP Committee on Drugs, 1994; AAP Work Group on Breastfeeding, 1997). To read about the work of a pediatric nurse who works in a pediatric oral feeding clinic, see the Careers in Child Development insert.

Some women cannot breastfeed their infants because of physical difficulties; others feel guilty if they terminate breastfeeding early (Mozingo & others, 2000). They might worry that they are depriving their infants of important emotional and psychological benefits. Some researchers have found that there are no psychological differences between breastfed and bottlefed infants (Ferguson, Harwood, & Shannon, 1987; Young, 1990).

Malnutrition in Infancy   Early weaning from breast milk to inadequate nutrients, such as unsuitable and unsanitary cow's milk formula, can cause protein deficiency and malnutrition. Something that looks like milk but is not, usually a form of tapioca or rice, also might be used. In many of the world's developing countries, mothers used to breastfeed their infants for at least two years. To become more modern, they stopped breastfeeding much earlier and replaced it with bottlefeeding.

Careers in Child Development

Barbara Deloin, *Pediatric Nurse*

Barbara Deloin is a pediatric nurse in Denver, Colorado. She practices nursing in the Pediatric Oral Feeding Clinic and is involved in research as part of an irritable infant study for the Children's Hospital in Denver. She also is on the faculty of nursing at the Colorado Health Sciences Center. Barbara previously worked in San Diego where she was coordinator of the Child Health Program for the County of San Diego.

Her research interests focus on children with special health-care needs, especially high-risk infants and children and promoting positive parent-child experiences. She was elected president of the National Association of Pediatric Nurse Associates and Practitioners for the 2000–2001 term.

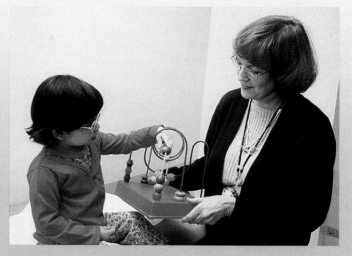

Barbara Deloin, working with a child with special health-care needs.

Comparisons of breastfed and bottlefed infants in such countries as Afghanistan, Haiti, Ghana, and Chile document that the death rate of bottlefed infants is as much as five times that of breastfed infants (Grant, 1997).

Two diseases that can result from infant malnutrition are marasmus and kwashiorkor. **Marasmus** is a wasting away of body tissues in the infant's first year, caused by severe protein-calorie deficiency. The infant becomes grossly underweight, and its muscles atrophy. **Kwashiorkor** is a condition caused by a deficiency in protein in which the child's abdomen and feet swell with water. This disease usually appears between 1 to 3 years of age. Kwashiorkor makes children sometimes appear to be well-fed even though they are not. Kwashiorkor causes a child's vital organs to collect the nutrients that are present and deprive other parts of the body of them. The child's hair also becomes thin, brittle, and colorless. And the child's behavior often becomes listless.

In the United States, there is concern about the energy and nutrient intakes of infants from low-income families. One recent study found low intakes of vitamin D, zinc, and iron, especially at 12 and 18 months (Nolan & others, 2002). In this study, high protein intake was noted at all of the ages the infants were assessed: 3, 6, 9, 12, 18, and 24 months.

Even if not fatal, severe and lengthy malnutrition is detrimental to physical, cognitive, and social development (Grantham-McGregor, Ani, & Fernald, 2001). In some cases, even moderate malnutrition can produce subtle difficulties in development. In one investigation, two groups of extremely malnourished 1-year-old South African infants were studied (Bayley, 1970). The children in one group were given adequate nourishment during the next six years; no intervention took place in the lives of the other group. After the seventh year, the poorly nourished group of children performed much worse on tests of intelligence than did the adequately nourished group. Another study linked the diets of rural Guatemalan infants with their social development at the time they entered elementary school (Barrett, Radke-Yarrow, & Klein, 1982). Children whose mothers had been given nutritious supplements during pregnancy and who themselves had been given more nutritious,

This Honduran child has kwashiorkor. Notice the tell-tale sign of kwashiorkor—a greatly expanded abdomen. *What are some other characteristics of kwashiorkor?*

marasmus A wasting away of body tissues in the infant's first year, caused by severe protein-calorie deficiency.

kwashiorkor A condition caused by a deficiency in protein in which the child's abdomen and feet become swollen with water.

A Healthy Start

The Hawaii Family Support/Healthy Start Program began in 1985 (Allen, Brown, & Finlay, 1992). It was designed by the Hawaii Family Stress Center in Honolulu, which had been making home visits to improve family functioning and reduce child abuse for more than a decade. Participation is voluntary. Families of newborns are screened for family risk factors, including unstable housing, histories of substance abuse, depression, parents' abuse as children, late or no prenatal care, fewer than 12 years of schooling, poverty, and unemployment. Early identification workers screen and interview new mothers in the hospital. They also screen families referred by physicians, nurses, and others. Because the demand for services outstrips available resources, only families with a substantial number of risk factors can participate.

Each new participating family receives a weekly visit from a family support worker. Each of the program's eight home visitors works with approximately 25 families at a time. The worker helps the family cope with any immediate crisis, such as unemployment or substance abuse. The family also is linked directly with a pediatrician to ensure that the children receive regular health care. Infants are screened for developmental delays and are immunized on schedule. Pediatricians have been educated about the program. They are notified when a child is enrolled in Healthy Start and when a family at risk stops participating.

The Family Support/Healthy Start Program recently hired a child development specialist to work with families of children with special needs. And in some instances, the program's male family support worker visits a father to talk specifically about his role in the family. The support workers encourage parents to participate in group activities held each week at the program center located in a neighborhood shopping center.

Over time, parents are encouraged to assume more responsibility for their family's health and well-being. Families can participate in Healthy Start until the child is 5 and enters public school.

The Hawaii Family Support/Health Start Program provides many home-visitor services for overburdened families of newborns and young children. This program has been very successful in reducing abuse and neglect in families. *What are some examples of the home-visitor services in this program?*

high-calorie foods in their first two years of life were more active, more involved, more helpful with their peers, less anxious, and happier than their counterparts who had not been given nutritional supplements. The results suggest how important it is for parents to be attentive to the nutritional needs of their infants.

In further research on early supplementary feeding and children's cognitive development, Ernesto Pollitt and his colleagues (1993) conducted a longitudinal investigation over two decades in rural Guatemala. They found that early nutritional supplements in the form of protein and increased calories can have positive long-term effects on cognitive development. The researchers also found that the relation of nutrition to cognitive performance is moderated both by the time period during which the supplement is given and by the sociodemographic context. For example, the children in the lowest socioeconomic groups benefited more than did the children in higher socioeconomic groups. Although there still was a positive nutritional influence when supplementation began after 2 years of age, the effect on cognitive development was less powerful. To read about a program that gives infants a healthy start in life, see the Explorations in Child Development box.

To adequately develop physically, as well as cognitively and socioemotionally, caregivers need to provide a nurturant, supportive environment. One individual who has stood out as an advocate of caring for children is T. Berry Brazelton, who is featured in the Careers in Child Development insert.

www.mhhe.com/santrockcd10

Malnutrition in Infancy

Toilet Training

Toilet Training

The ability to control elimination depends on both muscular maturation and motivation. Children must be able to control their muscles to eliminate at the appropriate time, and they must want to eliminate in the toilet or potty, rather than in their pants. Many toddlers are physically able to do this by the time they are about 2 years of age (Maizels, Rosenbaum, & Keating, 1999). When toilet training is initiated, it should be accomplished in a warm, relaxed, supportive manner (Michel, 2000).

Many parents today are being encouraged to use a "readiness" approach to toilet training—that is, wait until children show signs that they are ready for toilet training. One recent survey of 103 U.S. pediatricians found that a majority endorsed a gradual, passive rather than intensive, active approach to toilet training (Polaha, Warzak, & Dittmer-Memahon, 2002). However, almost 30 percent advocated the more intense approach.

Pediatricians note that toilet training is being delayed until an older age today more than in earlier generations (American Academy of Pediatrics, 2001). One recent study of almost 500 U.S. children found that 50 percent of the girls were toilet trained by 35 months and 50 percent of the boys by 39 months (Schum & others, 2001). Some developmentalists argue that delaying toilet training until the twos and threes can make it a battleground because many children at these ages are pushing so strongly for autonomy. Another argument is that late toilet training can be difficult for children who go to day care, because older children in diapers or training pants can be stigmatized by peers. Also, one study found that the later toilet training began the more it was associated with daytime and nighttime wetting in the elementary school years (Bakker & others, 2002). In sum, there still is controversy about when to initiate toilet training, and more research is needed in this area.

Careers in Child Development

T. Berry Brazelton, *Pediatrician*

T. Berry Brazelton is America's best-known pediatrician as a result of his numerous books, television appearances, and newspaper and magazine articles about parenting and children's health. He takes a family-centered approach to child development issues and communicates with parents in easy-to-understand ways.

Brazelton founded the Child Development Unit at Boston Children's Hospital and created the Brazelton Neonatal Behavioral Assessment Scale, a widely used measure of the newborn's health and well-being (which you read about in chapter 4). He also has conducted a number of research studies on infants and children and has been President of the Society for Research in Child Development, a leading research organization.

T. Berry Brazelton, pediatrician, with a young child.

Review and Reflect: Learning Goal 1

1 Discuss physical growth and development in infancy

REVIEW

- What are cephalocaudal and proximodistal patterns?
- What changes in height and weight take place in infancy?
- What are some key features of the brain and its development in infancy?
- What characterizes sleep during infancy?
- What are infants' nutritional needs?
- When should toilet training be attained?

REFLECT

- What three pieces of advice about the infant's physical development would you want to give a friend who has just had a baby? Why those three?

2 MOTOR DEVELOPMENT

| Reflexes | Gross and Fine Motor Skills | Dynamic Systems Theory |

The study of motor development has seen a renaissance in the past decade. New insights are being made into the ways in which infants acquire motor skills. We will begin our exploration of motor development by examining reflexes, then turn our attention to gross and fine motor skills. To conclude, we will cover dynamic systems theory, which is responsible for the awakened interest in the ways in which infants acquire motor skills.

Reflexes

The newborn is not a passive, unresponsive organism. Among other things, it has some basic reflexes, which are genetically endowed survival mechanisms. For example, the newborn has no fear of water, naturally holding its breath and contracting its throat to keep water out if it is submerged in water. Reflexes can serve as important building blocks for subsequent purposeful motor activity.

Reflexes govern the newborn's movements, which are automatic and beyond the newborn's control. They are built-in reactions to stimuli. Reflexes provide infants adaptive responses to the environment before infants have had the opportunity to learn. Let's look at several of these reflexes:

- The **sucking reflex** occurs when newborns automatically suck an object placed in their mouth. The sucking reflex enables newborns to get nourishment before they have associated a nipple with food. The sucking reflex is an example of a reflex that is present at birth but later disappears.
- The **rooting reflex** occurs when the infant's cheek is stroked or the side of the mouth is touched. In response, the infant turns its head toward the side that was touched in an apparent effort to find something to suck. The sucking and rooting reflexes disappear when the infant is 3 to 4 months old. They are replaced by the infant's voluntary eating. The sucking and rooting reflexes have survival value for newborn mammals, who must find the mother's breast to obtain nourishment.
- The **Moro reflex** is a neonatal startle response that occurs in response to a sudden, intense noise or movement. When startled, the newborn arches its back, throws back its head, and flings out its arms and legs. Then the newborn rapidly closes its arms and legs to the center of its body. The Moro reflex is a vestige from our primate ancestry, and it also has survival value—it leads the newborn to grab for support while falling. This reflex, which is normal in all newborns, also tends to disappear at 3 to 4 months of age. Steady pressure on any part of the infant's body calms the infant after it has been startled. Holding the infant's arm flexed at the shoulder will quiet the infant.
- The **grasping reflex** occurs in the first three months of life when something touches the infant's palms. The infant responds by grasping tightly.

Some reflexes present in the newborn—coughing, blinking, and yawning, for example—persist throughout life. They are as important for the adult as they are for the infant. Other reflexes, though, disappear several months following birth, as the infant's brain functions mature, and voluntary control over many behaviors develops. The movements of some reflexes eventually become incorporated into more complex, voluntary actions. One example is the grasping reflex. By the end of the third month, the grasping reflex diminishes, and the infant displays a more voluntary grasp, which is often produced by visual stimuli. For example, when an

sucking reflex A newborn's built-in reaction of automatically sucking an object placed in its mouth. The sucking reflex enables the infant to get nourishment before it has associated a nipple with food.

rooting reflex A newborn's built-in reaction that occurs when the infant's cheek is stroked or the side of the mouth is touched. In response, the infant turns its head toward the side that was touched, in an apparent effort to find something to suck.

Moro reflex A neonatal startle response that occurs in reaction to a sudden, intense noise or movement. When startled, the newborn arches its back, throws its head back, and flings out its arms and legs. Then the newborn rapidly closes its arms and legs to the center of the body.

grasping reflex A neonatal reflex that occurs when something touches the infant's palms. The infant responds by grasping tightly.

Reflex	Stimulation	Infant's Response	Developmental Pattern
Blinking	Flash of light, puff of air	Closes both eyes	Permanent
Babinski	Sole of foot stroked	Fans out toes, twists foot in	Disappears after 9 months to 1 year
Grasping	Palms touched	Grasps tightly	Weakens after 3 months, disappears after 1 year
Moro (startle)	Sudden stimulation, such as hearing loud noise or being dropped	Startles, arches back, throws head back, flings out arms and legs and then rapidly closes them to center of body	Disappears after 3 to 4 months
Rooting	Cheek stroked or side of mouth touched	Turns head, opens mouth, begins sucking	Disappears after 3 to 4 months
Stepping	Infant held above surface and feet lowered to touch surface	Moves feet as if to walk	Disappears after 3 to 4 months
Sucking	Object touching mouth	Sucks automatically	Disappears after 3 to 4 months
Swimming	Infant put face down in water	Makes coordinated swimming movements	Disappears after 6 to 7 months
Tonic neck	Infant placed on back	Forms fists with both hands and usually turns head to the right (sometimes called the "fencer's pose" because the infant looks like it is assuming a fencer's position)	Disappears after 2 months

FIGURE 5.12 Infant Reflexes

infant sees a mobile whirling above its crib, it may reach out and try to grasp it. As its motor development becomes smoother, the infant will grasp objects, carefully manipulate them, and explore their qualities.

An overview of the main reflexes we have discussed, along with others, is given in figure 5.12.

Sucking is an especially important reflex: It is the infant's route to nourishment. The sucking capabilities of newborns vary considerably. Some newborns are efficient at forceful sucking and obtaining milk; others are not as adept and get tired before they are full. Most newborns take several weeks to establish a sucking style that is coordinated with the way the mother is holding the infant, the way milk is coming out of the bottle or breast, and the infant's sucking speed and temperament.

A study by pediatrician T. Berry Brazelton (1956) involved observations of infants for more than a year to determine the incidence of their sucking when they were nursing and how their sucking changed as they grew older. Over 85 percent of the infants engaged in considerable sucking behavior unrelated to feeding. They sucked their fingers, their fists, and pacifiers. By the age of 1 year, most had stopped the sucking behavior.

Parents should not worry when infants suck their thumb, their fist, or even a pacifier. Many parents, though, do begin to worry when thumb sucking persists into the preschool and elementary school years. As much as 40 percent of children continue to suck their thumbs after they have started school (Kessen, Haith, & Salapatek, 1970). Most developmentalists do not attach a great deal of significance to this behavior and are not aware of parenting strategies that might contribute to it. Individual differences in children's biological makeup may be involved to some degree in the continuation of sucking behavior.

The experiences of the first three years of life are almost entirely lost to us, and when we attempt to enter into a small child's world, we come as foreigners who have forgotten the landscape and no longer speak the native tongue.

—SELMA FRAIBERG
Developmentalist and Child Advocate, 20th Century

Gross and Fine Motor Skills

Gross motor skills involve large muscle activities, such as moving one's arms and walking. **Fine motor skills** involve more finely tuned movements, such as finger dexterity. Let's examine the changes in gross and fine motor skills in the first two years of life.

Gross Motor Skills   Ask any parents about their baby, and sooner or later you are likely to hear about one or more motor milestones, such as "Cassandra just learned to crawl," "Jesse is finally sitting alone," or "Shauna took her first step last week." It is no wonder that parents proudly announce such milestones. New motor skills are the most dramatic and observable changes in the infant's first year of life. These motor progressions transform babies from being unable to even lift their head to being able to grab things off the grocery store shelf, to chase the cat, and to participate actively in the family's social life (Thelen, 1995, 2000).

The Development of Posture   In Thelen's (1995, 2000) view, postural control is critical for engaging in adaptive activities. Infants need to control their heads to stabilize their gaze and to track moving objects. They also must have strength and balance in their legs to walk. Posture is more than just holding still and straight though. Posture, like other movements, is a dynamic process that is linked with a number of converging sensory modalities: proprioception from the skin, joints, and muscles; vestibular organs in the inner ear that regulate balance and equilibrium; and cues from vision and hearing.

Newborn infants cannot voluntarily control their posture. Within a few weeks, though, they can hold their head erect, and then lifting their head while prone soon follows. By 2 months of age, babies can sit while supported on a lap or an infant seat, but sitting independently is not accomplished until 6 or 7 months of age. Standing also develops gradually across the first year of life. By about 8 months of age, infants can usually learn to pull themselves up and hold on to a chair, and they often can stand alone by about 10 to 12 months of age.

Keeping with our theme of linking perception with action, one question that can be asked is this: Do infants use visual information to control posture? Researchers have constructed a "moving room" to investigate this question (Bertenthal, Rose, & Bai, 1997; Rose & Bertenthal, 1995). An infant stands on a stationary floor surrounded by walls that can move back and forth. The visual perception created by the moving walls produces the illusion that it is the infants who are moving, not the walls. The same type of illusion occurs when a moving train passes a stationary train you are sitting in. Infants who have just learned to walk are highly susceptible to the illusion. They sway and sometimes fall, suggesting that they recognize the link between visual perception and self-movement. Even infants as young as 7 months of age experience the illusion, but 5-month-olds don't. It may be that the younger infants detect the visual illusion but do not yet have the motor skills to control their posture and respond to the visual information.

Learning to Walk   Locomotion and postural control are closely linked, especially in walking upright (Adolph & Eppler, 2002). Walking upright requires being able both to balance on one leg as the other is swung forward and to shift the weight from one leg to the other (Thelen, 2000).

Although infants usually learn to walk about their first birthday, the neural pathways that control the leg alternation component of walking are in place from a very early age, possibly even at birth or before. Infants engage in frequent alternating kicking movements throughout the first 6 months of life when they are lying on their backs. Also when 1- to 2-month-olds are given support with their feet in contact with a motorized treadmill, they show well-coordinated, alternating steps.

gross motor skills Motor skills that involve large muscle activities, such as walking.

fine motor skills Motor skills that involve more finely tuned movements, such as finger dexterity.

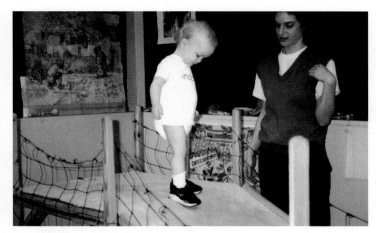

FIGURE 5.13 The Role of Experience in Crawling and Walking Infants' Judgments of Whether to Go Down A Slope

Karen Adolph (1997) found that locomotor experience rather than age was the primary predictor of adaptive responding on slopes of varying steepness. Newly crawling and walking infants could not judge the safety of the various slopes. With experience, they learned to avoid slopes where they would fall. When expert crawlers began to walk, they again made mistakes and fell, even though they had judged the same slope accurately when crawling. Adolph referred to this as the *specificity of learning* because it does not transfer across crawling and walking.

If infants can produce forward stepping movements so early, why does it take them so long to learn to walk? The key skills in learning to walk appear to be stabilizing balance on one leg long enough to swing the other forward and shifting the weight without falling. This is a difficult biomechanical problem to solve, and it takes infants about a year to do it.

In learning to locomote, infants learn what kinds of places and surfaces afford safe locomotion. Karen Adolph's research (1997) investigated how experienced and inexperienced crawling infants and walking infants go down steep slopes (see figure 5.13). Newly crawling infants, who averaged about $8\frac{1}{2}$ months in age, rather indiscriminately went down the steep slopes, often falling in the process (with their mothers next to the slope to catch them). However, with further weeks of practice, the crawling babies became more adept at judging which slopes were too steep to crawl down and which ones they could navigate safely. Newly walking infants also could not judge the safety of the various slopes but infants who were experienced walkers accurately matched locomotor skills with the steepness of the slopes. They rarely fell downhill, either refusing to go down the steep slopes or going down backward in a cautious manner. Experienced walkers perceptually assessed the situation—looking, swaying, touching, and thinking before they moved down the slope. With experience both the crawlers and the walkers learned to avoid the risky slopes where they would fall, integrating perceptual information with the development of a new motor behavior.

Summary and Further Development A summary of some important developmental accomplishments in gross motor skills during the first year is shown in figure 5.14. The timing of milestones varies by as much as two to four months, especially among older infants. What remains fairly uniform, however, is the sequence of accomplishments. An important implication of these infant motor accomplishments is the increasing degree of independence they bring. Older infants can explore their environment more extensively and initiate social interaction with caregivers and peers more readily than when they were younger.

In the second year of life, toddlers become more motorically skilled and mobile. They are no longer content with being in a playpen and want to move all over the place. Child development experts believe that motor activity during the second year

A baby is an angel whose wings decrease as his legs increase.
—FRENCH PROVERB

Developmental Milestones
Physical Development in Infancy

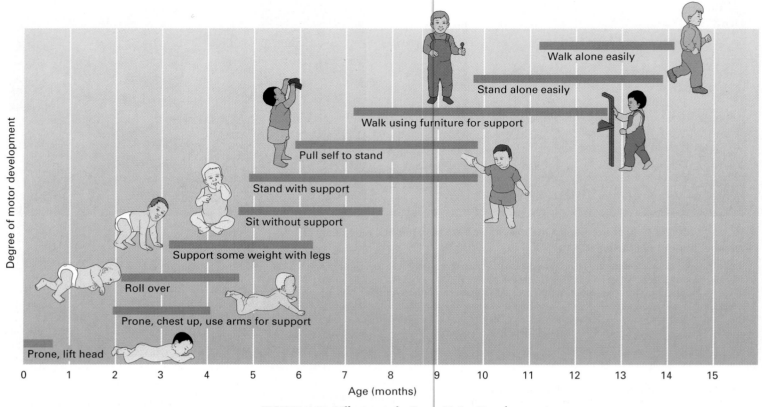

FIGURE 5.14 Milestones in Gross Motor Development

is vital to the child's competent development and that few restrictions, except for safety purposes, should be placed on their motoric adventures (Fraiberg, 1959).

By 13 to 18 months, toddlers can pull a toy attached to a string, use their hands and legs to climb up a number of steps, and ride four-wheel wagons. By 18 to 24 months, toddlers can walk quickly or run stiffly for a short distance, balance on their feet in a squat position while playing with objects on the floor, walk backward without losing their balance, stand and kick a ball without falling, stand and throw a ball, and jump in place.

Should Babies Be Placed in Fitness Classes? With the increased interest of today's adults in aerobic exercise and fitness, some parents have tried to give their infants a head start on becoming physically fit and physically talented. However, most infancy experts recommend against structured exercise classes for babies. Pediatricians are seeing more bone fractures and dislocations and more muscle strains in babies now than in the past. They point out that when an adult is stretching and moving an infant's limbs, it is easy for them to go beyond the infant's physical limits without knowing it.

Physical fitness classes for infants range from passive fare—with adults putting infants through the paces—to programs called "aerobic" because they demand crawling, tumbling, and ball skills. However, pediatricians recommend that exercise for infants should not be of the intense, aerobic variety. They argue that babies cannot adequately stretch their bodies to achieve aerobic benefits.

Culture and Gross Motor Skills In most cultures, infants are not exposed to structured physical fitness classes like the ones that are showing up in the United States. However, when parents or other caregivers provide babies with physical guidance by physically handling them in special ways (such as stroking, massaging, or stretching) or providing them with opportunities for exercise, the infants often attain motor milestones earlier than infants whose caregivers have not provided these physical activities. For example, Jamaican mothers expect their infants to sit and walk alone two to three months earlier than English mothers do (Hopkins & Westra, 1990). Also, Jamaican mothers regularly massage their infants and stretch their arms and legs, and this is linked with advanced motor development (Hopkins, 1991). In the Gusii culture of Kenya, mothers encourage vigorous movement in their babies (Hopkins & Westra, 1998).

In developing countries, mothers often attempt to stimulate their infants' motor skills more than mothers in more advanced cultures (Hopkins, 1991). This stimulation of infants' motor skills in developing countries may be necessary to improve the infants' chances of survival. In some cases, the emphasis on early stimulation may occur because the caregivers recognize that motor skills are required for important jobs in the culture. Other factors such as climate and spiritual beliefs also may influence the way that caregivers guide their infants' motor development.

Although infants in some cultures, such as Jamaica, reach motor milestones earlier than infants in many cultures, nonetheless, regardless of how much practice takes place, infants around the world reach these motor milestones within the same age range. For example, Algonquin infants in Quebec, Canada, spend much of their first year strapped to a cradle board. Despite such inactivity, these infants still sit up, crawl, and walk within an age range similar to infants in other cultures who have much greater opportunity for activity. In sum, there are slight variations in the age at which infants reach motor milestones depending on their activity opportunities in different cultures, but the variations are not substantial and they are within normal ranges.

Fine Motor Skills   Infants have hardly any control over fine motor skills at birth, although they have many components of what later become finely coordinated arm, hand, and finger movements (Rosenblith, 1992). The onset of reaching and grasping marks a significant achievement in infants' functional interactions with their surroundings (McCarty & Ashmead, 1999).

For many years it was believed that reaching for an object is visually guided—that is, the infant must continuously have sight of the hand and the target (White, Castle, & Held, 1964). However, in one study, Rachel Clifton and her colleagues (1993) demonstrated that infants do not have to see their own hands when reaching for an object. They concluded that, because the infants could not see their hand or arm in the dark in the experiment, proprioceptive (muscle, tendon, joint sense) cues, not sight of limb, guided the early reaching of the 4-month-old infants.

The development of reaching and grasping becomes more refined during the first two years of life. Initially, infants show only crude shoulder and elbow movements, but later they show wrist movements, hand rotation, and coordination of the thumb and forefinger. The maturation of hand-eye coordination over the first two years of life is reflected in the improvement of fine motor skills. Figure 5.15 provides an overview of the development of fine motor skills in the first two years of life.

The infant's grasping system is very flexible, and the environment plays a stronger role in grasping than previously thought. One way to show that the environment influences grasping is to vary the motor task and examine if this influences

(*Top*) In the Algonquin culture in Quebec, Canada, babies are strapped to a cradle board for much of their infancy. (*Bottom*) In Jamaica, mothers massage and stretch their infants' arms and legs. *To what extent do cultural variations in the activity infants engage in influence the time at which they reach motor milestones?*

Birth to 6 months	
2 months	Holds rattle briefly
2½ months	Glances from one object to another
3 to 4 months	Plays in simple way with rattle; inspects fingers; reaches for dangling ring; visually follows ball across table
4 months	Carries object to mouth
4 to 5 months	Recovers rattle from chest; holds two objects
5 months	Transfers object from hand to hand
5 to 6 months	Bangs in play; looks for object while sitting

6 to 12 months	
6 months	Secures cube on sight; follows adult's movements across room; immediately fixates on small objects and stretches out to grasp them; retains rattle
6½ months	Manipulates and examines an object; reaches for, grabs, and retains rattle
7 months	Pulls string to obtain an object
7½ to 8½ months	Grasps with thumb and finger
8 to 9 months	Persists in reaching for toy out of reach on table; shows hand preference, bangs spoon; searches in correct place for toys dropped within reach of hands; may find toy hidden under cup
10 months	Hits cup with spoon; crude release of object
10½ to 11 months	Picks up raisin with thumb and forefinger; pincer grasp; pushes car along
11 to 12 months	Puts three or more objects in a container

12 to 18 months	
	Places one 2-inch block on top of another 2-inch block (in imitation)
	Scribbles with a large crayon on large piece of paper
	Turns two to three pages in a large book with cardboard pages while sitting in an adult's lap
	Places three 1-inch cube blocks in a 6-inch diameter cup (in imitation)
	Holds a pencil and makes a mark on a sheet of paper
	Builds a four-block tower with 2-inch cube blocks (in imitation)

18 to 24 months	
	Draws an arc on a piece of unlined paper with a pencil after being shown how
	Turns a doorknob that is within reach, using both hands
	Unscrews a lid put loosely on a small jar after being shown how
	Places large pegs in a pegboard
	Connects and takes apart a pop bead string of five beads
	Zips and unzips a large zipper after being shown how

FIGURE 5.15 The Development of Fine Motor Skills in Infancy

the infant's responses. This can be done by changing the size and shape of the objects for the infant to grasp. Indeed, infants vary their grip on an object depending on its size and shape, as well as the size of their own hands relative to the object's size. Infants grip small objects with their thumb and forefinger (and sometimes their middle finger too), while they grip large objects with all of the fingers of one hand or both hands.

In studies of grasping, age differences occur in regard to which perceptual system is most likely to be used in coordinating grasping. Four-month-olds rely more on touch to determine how they will grip an object; eight-month-olds are more likely to use vision as a guide (Newell & others, 1989). This developmental change is efficient because vision lets infants preshape their hands as they reach for an object. As we see next, such perceptual-motor coupling is an important aspect of dynamic systems theory.

Dynamic Systems Theory

The study of motor development has seen a renaissance in the last decade. Historically, researcher Arnold Gesell (1934), as well as others, gave rich descriptions of motor milestones, but they assumed that they were unfolding as a consequence of a genetic plan. In recent years, it has become recognized that motor development is not the result of nature alone or nurture alone. And there has been a shift to focus on *how* motor skills develop.

Esther Thelen (1995, 2000, 2001) has presented a new theory that reflects the new perspective in motor development. **Dynamic systems theory** seeks to explain how motor behaviors are assembled for perceiving and acting. In this theory, "assembly" means the coordination or convergence of a number of factors, such as the development of the nervous system, the body's physical properties and movement possibilities, the goal the infant is motivated to reach, and the environmental support for the skill. This theory also emphasizes that perception and action work together in the infant's mastery of a skill.

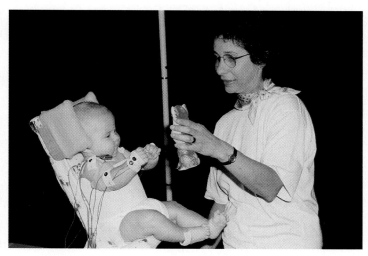

Esther Thelen is shown conducting an experiment to discover how infants learn to control their arms to reach and grasp for objects. A computer device is used to monitor the infant's arm movements and to track muscle patterns. Thelen's research is conducted from a dynamic systems perspective. *What is the nature of this perspective?*

The dynamic systems view contrasts with the traditional maturational view by proposing that even the universal milestones, such as crawling, reaching, and walking, are learned through a process of adaptation. It emphasizes exploration and selection in finding solutions to new task demands. In other words, infants modify their movement patterns to fit a new task by exploring and selecting various configurations. The assumption is that the infant is motivated by the new challenge—a desire to get a new toy in one's mouth or to cross the room to join other family members. It is the new task, the challenge of the context, not a genetic program that represents the driving force for change.

Let's look at two babies—Gabriel and Hannah—to see how dynamic systems theory describes and explains their behavior and development (Bower, 1999). Each child improvises ways to reach out with one of their arms from a sitting position and wrap their fingers around a new toy. Gabriel and Hannah make all sorts of split-second adjustments to keep each reaching motion on course. Their rapid arm extension requires holding their body steady so that their arm and upper torso don't plow into the toy. Muscles in their arm and shoulder contract and stretch in a host of combinations and exert a variety of forces. Their arm movements are not exact, machinelike motions that can be precisely planned out in advance but rather adapt to the goal and context at hand—how to pick up the new toy.

Review and Reflect: Learning Goal 2

2 Describe infants' motor development

REVIEW

- What are some reflexes that infants have?
- What characterizes gross and fine motor skills in infancy?
- What is dynamic systems theory?

REFLECT

- Which view of infant motor development do you prefer—the traditional maturational view or or the dynamic systems view? Why?

dynamic systems theory The new perspective on motor development in infancy that seeks to explain how motor behaviors are assembled for perceiving and acting.

3 SENSORY AND PERCEPTUAL DEVELOPMENT

What Are Sensation and Perception?	Visual Perception	Intermodal Perception

The Ecological View	Other Senses	Perceptual-Motor Coupling

A key theme in the dynamic systems view that we just discussed is that perception and action are coupled when new skills are learned. Keep this idea in mind as you read about sensory and perceptual development (Slater, 2001).

What Are Sensation and Perception?

How does a newborn know that her mother's skin is soft rather than rough? How does a 5-year-old know what color his hair is? How does an 8-year-old know that summer is warmer than winter? How does a 10-year-old know that a firecracker is louder than a cat's meow? Infants and children "know" these things because of their senses. All information comes to the infant through the senses. Without vision, hearing, touch, taste, smell, and other senses, the infant's brain would be isolated from the world; the infant would live in dark silence, a tasteless, colorless, feelingless void.

Sensation occurs when information interacts with sensory receptors—the eyes, ears, tongue, nose, and skin. The sensation of hearing occurs when waves of pulsating air are collected by the outer ear and transmitted through the bones of the inner ear to the auditory nerve. The sensation of vision occurs as rays of light contact the eyes and become focused on the retina.

Perception is the interpretation of what is sensed. The information about physical events that contacts the ears may be interpreted as musical sounds, for example. The physical energy transmitted to the retinas may be interpreted as a particular color, pattern, or shape.

The Ecological View

For the past several decades, much of the research on perceptual development in infancy has been guided by the ecological view of Eleanor and James J. Gibson (E. Gibson, 1969, 1989, 2001; J.P. Gibson, 1966, 1979). They argue that we do not have to take bits and pieces of data from sensations and build up representations of the world in our minds. The environment itself is rich with information; our perceptual system selects from that rich output (Cohen & Sashon, 2003).

According to the Gibsons' **ecological view,** we directly perceive information that exists in the world around us. Perception brings us into contact with the environment in order to interact with and adapt to it. Perception is designed for action. Perception gives people such information as when to duck, when to turn their bodies through a narrow passageway, and when to put their hands up to catch something.

In the Gibsons' view, all objects have **affordances,** which are opportunities for interaction offered by objects that are necessary to perform activities. A pot may afford you something to cook with, and may afford a toddler something to bang. Adults immediately know when a chair is appropriate for sitting, when a surface is safe for walking, or when an object is within reach. We directly and accurately perceive these affordances by sensing information from the environment—the light or sound reflecting from the surfaces of the world—and from our own bodies through muscle receptors, joint receptors, and skin receptors, for example.

The infant is by no means as helpless as it looks and is quite capable of some very complex and important actions.

—HERB PICK
Contemporary Developmental Psychologist, University of Minnesota

www.mhhe.com/santrockcd10

Perceptual Development

Newborns' Senses

Richard Aslin's Research

International Society on Infant Studies

---

sensation The product of the interaction between information and the sensory receptors—the eyes, ears, tongue, nose, and skin.

perception The interpretation of what is sensed.

ecological view The view that perception functions to bring organisms in contact with the environment and to increase adaptation.

affordances Opportunities for interaction offered by objects that are necessary to perform functional activities.

Through perceptual development, children become more efficient at discovering and using affordances. An important developmental question is, What affordances can infants or children detect and use? In one study, for example, when babies who could walk were faced with a squishy waterbed, they stopped and explored it, then chose to crawl rather than walk across it (Gibson & others, 1987). They combined perception and action to adapt to the demands of the task.

Similarly, as we described earlier in the section on motor development, infants who were just learning to crawl or just learning to walk were less cautious when confronted with a steep slope than experienced crawlers or walkers were (Adolph, 1997). The more experienced crawlers and walkers perceived that a slope *affords* the possibility for not only faster locomotion but also for falling. Again, infants coupled perception and action to make a decision about what do in their environment.

Visual Perception

Can newborns see? How does visual perception develop in infancy?

Visual Acuity and Color   Psychologist William James (1890/1950) called the newborn's perceptual world a "blooming, buzzing confusion." Was James right? A century later, we can safely say that he was wrong. The infant's perception of visual information is far more advanced than was once thought (Slater, 2001).

Just how well can infants see? The newborn's vision is estimated to be 20/400 to 20/800 on the well-known Snellen chart, with which you are tested when you have your eyes examined (Haith, 1991). This is about 10 to 30 times lower than normal adult vision (20/20). By 6 months of age, though, vision is 20/100 or better, and, by about the first birthday, the infant's vision approximates that of an adult (Banks & Salapatek, 1983). Figure 5.16 shows a computer estimation of what a picture of a face looks like to an infant at different points in development from a distance of about 6 inches.

Can newborns see color? At birth, babies can distinguish between green and red (Adams, 1989). Adultlike functioning in all three types (red, blue, green) of color-sensitive receptors is present by 2 months of age.

Visual Preferences   Robert Fantz (1963) is a pioneer in the study of visual perception in infants. Fantz made an important discovery that advanced the ability of researchers to investigate infants' visual perception: Infants look at different things

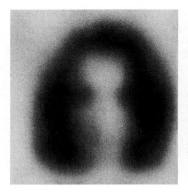 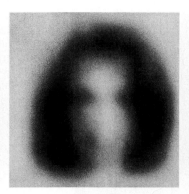  

FIGURE 5.16 Visual Acuity During the First Months of Life

The four photographs represent a computer estimation of what a picture of a face looks like to a 1-month-old, 2-month-old, 3-month-old, and 1-year-old (which approximates the visual acuity of an adult).

for different lengths of time. Fantz placed infants in a "looking chamber," which had two visual displays on the ceiling above the infant's head. An experimenter viewed the infant's eyes by looking through a peephole. If the infant was fixating on one of the displays, the experimenter could see the display's reflection in the infant's eyes. This allowed the experimenter to determine how long the infant looked at each display. In figure 5.17, you can see Fantz's looking chamber and the results of his experiment. The infants preferred to look at patterns rather than at color or brightness. For example, they preferred to look at a face, a piece of printed matter, or a bull's-eye longer than at red, yellow, or white discs. In another experiment, Fantz found that younger infants—only 2 days old—look longer at patterned stimuli, such as faces and concentric circles, than at red, white, or yellow discs. Based on these results, it is likely that pattern perception has an innate basis, or at least is acquired after only minimal environmental experience. The newborn's visual world is not the blooming, buzzing confusion William James imagined.

Perceiving a World of Objects   Some perceptual accomplishments are especially intriguing because they indicate that the infant's perception is better than it should be based on sensory information (Bower, 2002; Cohen & Sashon, 2003; Slater, Field, & Hernandez, 2002). This is the case in *perceptual constancy*, in which sensory stim-

FIGURE 5.17 Fantz's Experiment on Infants' Visual Perception

(*a*) Infants 2 to 3 months old preferred to look at some stimuli more than others. In Fantz's experiment, infants preferred to look at patterns rather than at color or brightness. For example, they looked longer at a face, a piece of printed matter, or a bull's-eye than at red, yellow, or white discs. (*b*) Fantz used a "looking chamber" to study infants' perception of stimuli.

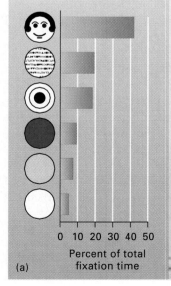 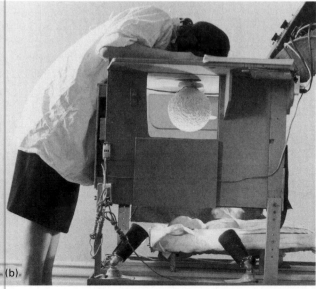

Percent of total fixation time

(a)   (b)

ulation is changing but perception of the physical world remains constant. Two types of perceptual constancy are size constancy and shape constancy.

Size constancy is the recognition that an object remains the same even though the retinal image of the object changes. The size of an object on the retina is not sufficient to determine its actual size. The farther away from us an object is, the smaller its image is on our eyes. For example, a bicycle standing right in front of a child appears smaller than the car parked across the street, even though the bicycle casts a larger image on the child's eyes than the car does.

But what about babies? Do they have size constancy? Researchers have found that babies as young as 3 months of age show size constancy (Bower, 1966; Day & McKenzie, 1973). However, at 3 months of age, this ability is not full-blown and continues to develop. As infants' binocular vision develops between 4 and 5 months of age, their ability to perceive size constancy improves (Aslin, 1987). Further progress in perceiving size constancy continues until 10 or 11 years of age (Kellman & Banks, 1998).

Shape constancy is the recognition that an object remains the same shape even though its orientation to us changes. Look around the room you are in right now. You likely see objects of varying shapes, such as tables and chairs. If you get up and walk around the room, you will see these objects from different sides and angles. Even though your retinal image of the objects changes as you walk and look, you will still perceive the objects as the same shape.

Do babies have shape constancy? As with size constancy, researchers have found that babies as young as 3 months of age have shape constancy (Bower, 1966; Day & McKenzie, 1973). Three-month-old infants, however, do not have shape constancy for irregularly shaped objects, such as tilted planes (Cook & Birch, 1984).

Why is it important for infants to develop perceptual constancy early in their lives? If infants did not develop perceptual constancy, each time they saw an object at a different distance or in a different orientation, they would perceive it as a different object. Thus, the development of perceptual constancy allows the infant to perceive its world as stable.

The human face is the object that has been studied the most in infant perception research. Researchers have found that as soon as 12 hours after birth, infants spend more time looking at their mother's face than at a stranger's face (Bushnell, 2001).

How do young infants scan the human face? In one study, researchers showed human faces to 1- and 2-month-old infants (Maurer & Salapatek, 1976). By use of a special mirror arrangement, the faces were projected as images in front of the infant's eyes so that the infant's eye movements could be photographed. Figure 5.18 shows the plotting of eye fixations of a 1-month-old and a 2-month-old infant. Notice that the 1-month-old scanned only a few portions of the entire face—a narrow segment of the chin and two spots on the head. The 2-month-old scanned a much wider area of the face—the mouth, the eyes, and a large portion of the head. The older infant also spent more time examining the internal details of the face, while the younger infant concentrated more on the outer contour of the face.

Infants' perception of objects continues to develop as they get older. For example, by 6 to 8 months, they have learned to perceive gravity and support—that an object hanging on the end of a table should fall, that ball-bearings will travel farther when rolled down a longer rather than a shorter ramp, and that cup handles will not fall when attached to a cup (Slater, Field, & Hernandez-Reif, 2002). As infants develop, their experiences of and actions on the world help them to understand physical laws.

Even following infancy, children's perception of the physical world continues to develop. In one study, 2- to 4½-year-old children were given a task in which the goal was to find a toy ball that had been dropped through an opaque tube (Hood,

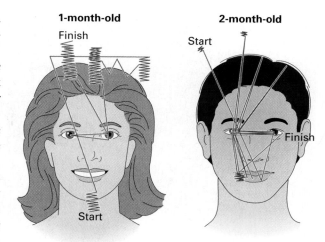

FIGURE 5.18 How 1- and 2-Month-Old Infants Scan the Human Face

size constancy Recognition that an object remains the same even though the retinal image of the object changes.

shape constancy Recognition that an object remains the same even though its orientation to us changes.

FIGURE 5.19 Gravity Rules

Even when toddlers see a ball dropped into the tube they will search for it immediately below the dropping point.

1995) (see figure 5.19). As shown in the figure, if the ball is dropped into the tube at the top left it will land in the container at the bottom right. However, in this task, most of the 2-year-olds, and even some of the 4-year-olds, persisted in searching in the box immediately beneath the dropping point. For them, gravity ruled and they had failed to perceive the end location of the curved tube.

Depth Perception How early can infants perceive depth? To investigate this question, infant perception researchers Eleanor Gibson and Richard Walk (1960) conducted a classic experiment. They constructed a miniature cliff with a drop-off covered by glass. The motivation for this experiment arose when Gibson was eating a picnic lunch on the edge of the Grand Canyon. She wondered whether an infant looking over the canyon's rim would perceive the dangerous drop-off and back up. In their laboratory, Gibson and Walk placed infants on the edge of a visual cliff and had their mothers coax them to crawl onto the glass (see figure 5.20). Most infants would not crawl out on the glass, choosing instead to remain on the shallow side, indicating that they could perceive depth. However, because the 6- to 14-month-old infants had extensive visual experience, this research did not answer the question of whether depth perception is innate.

Exactly how early in life does depth perception develop? Since younger infants do not crawl, this question is difficult to answer. Research with 2- to 4-month-old infants shows differences in heart rate when they are placed directly on the deep side of the visual cliff instead of on the shallow side (Campos, Langer, & Krowitz, 1970). However, an alternative interpretation is that young infants respond to differences in some visual characteristics of the deep and shallow cliffs, with no actual knowledge of depth.

Visual Expectations Infants not only see forms and figures at an early age but also develop expectations about future events in their world by the time they are 3 months of age. Marshall Haith and his colleagues (Canfield & Haith, 1991; Haith, Hazen, & Goodman, 1988) studied whether babies would form expectations about where an interesting picture would appear. The pictures were presented to the infants in either a regular alternating (such as left, right, left, right) or an unpredictable sequence (such as right, right, left, right). When the sequence was predictable, the 3-month-old infants began to anticipate the location of the picture, looking at the side on which it was expected to appear. The young infants formed this visual expectation in less than 1 minute. However, younger infants did not develop expectations about where a picture would be presented.

Elizabeth Spelke (1991, 2000; Spelke & Hespos, 2001) also has demonstrated that young infants form visual expectations. She placed babies before a puppet stage and showed them a series of unexpected actions—for example, one ball seemed to roll through a solid barrier, another seemed to leap between two platforms, and a third appeared to hang in midair (Spelke, 1979). Spelke measured the babies' looking times and recorded longer intervals for unexpected than expected actions. She concluded that, by 4 months of age, even though infants do not yet have the ability to talk about objects, move around objects, manipulate objects, or even see objects with high resolution, they can recognize the solidity of objects and the continuity of objects. However, she has found that at 4 months of age,

FIGURE 5.20 Examining Infants' Depth Perception on the Visual Cliff

Eleanor Gibson and Richard Walk (1960) found that most infants would not walk out on the glass, which indicated that they had depth perception.

(a)

(b)

FIGURE 5.21 Hearing in the Womb

(*a*) Pregnant mothers read *The Cat in the Hat* to their fetuses during the last few months of pregnancy. (*b*) When they were born, the babies preferred listening to a recording of their mothers reading *The Cat in the Hat,* as evidenced by their sucking on a nipple that produced this recording, rather than another story, *The King, The Mice and the Cheese.*

infants do not expect an object to obey gravitational constraints (Spelke & others, 1992).

Other Senses

Considerable development also takes place in other sensory systems during infancy. We will explore development in hearing, touch and pain, smell, and taste.

Hearing   During the last two months of pregnancy, the fetus can hear sounds as it nestles in its mother's womb: It hears the mother's voice, music, and so on (Kisilevsky, 1995; Smith, Muir, & Kisilevsky, 2001). Two psychologists wanted to find out if a fetus that heard Dr. Seuss' classic story *The Cat in the Hat* while still in the mother's womb would prefer hearing the story after birth (DeCasper & Spence, 1986). During the last months of pregnancy, sixteen women read *The Cat in the Hat* to their fetuses. Then shortly after they were born, the mothers read to them either *The Cat in the Hat* or a story with a different rhyme and pace, *The King, the Mice, and the Cheese* (which was not read to them during prenatal development). The infants sucked on a nipple in a different way when the mothers read the two stories, suggesting that the infants recognized the pattern and tone of *The Cat in the Hat* (see figure 5.21). This study illustrates that an infant's brain has a remarkable ability to learn even before birth and reflects the ingenuity of researchers in assessing development.

Hearing changes in infancy involve a sound's loudness, pitch, and localization. Immediately after birth, infants cannot hear soft sounds quite as well as adults can; a stimulus must be louder to be heard by a newborn than by an adult (Trehub & others, 1991). For example, an adult can hear a whisper from about 4 to 5 feet away but a newborn requires that sounds be closer to a normal conversational level to be heard at that distance. Infants are also less sensitive to the pitch of a sound than adults are. *Pitch* is the perception of the frequency of a sound. A soprano voice sounds high pitched, a bass voice low pitched. Infants are less sensitive to low-pitched sounds and are more likely to hear high-pitched sounds (Aslin & others, 1998). By two years of age, infants have considerably improved their ability to distinguish sounds with different pitches. It is important to be able to *localize* sounds,

Elizabeth Spelke's Research

detecting their origins. Even newborns can determine the general location from where a sound is coming but by 6 months of age, they are more proficient at localizing sounds and this ability continues to improve in the second year (Litovsky & Ashmead, 1997; Morrongiello, Fenwick, & Chance, 1990).

Newborns are especially sensitive to the sounds of human speech. They will suck more rapidly on a nipple in order to listen to some sounds rather than others. Their sucking behavior indicates that they prefer a recording of their mother's voice to the voice of an unfamiliar woman, their mother's native language to a foreign language, and the classical music of Beethoven to the rock music of Aerosmith (Flohr & others, 2001; Mehler & others, 1988; Spence & DeCasper, 1987).

Our sensory-perceptual system seems built to give a special place to the sounds of language. Babies are born into the world prepared to respond to the sounds of any human language. Even young infants can discriminate subtle phonetic differences, such as those between the speech sounds of *ba* and *ga*. Experience with the native language, however, has an effect on speech perception. In the second half of the first year of life, infants become "native listeners," especially attuned to the sounds of their native language (Jusczyk, 2002). In chapter 10, Language Development, we will further discuss infants' development of infants' ability to distinguish the sounds they need for speech.

Touch and Pain   Do newborns respond to touch? Can newborns feel pain?

Touch   Newborns respond to touch. A touch to the cheek produces a turning of the head, whereas a touch to the lips produces sucking movements. An important ability that develops in infancy is to connect information about vision with information about touch. One-year-olds clearly can do this, and it appears that 6-month-olds can, too (Acredolo & Hake, 1982). Whether still younger infants can coordinate vision and touch is yet to be determined.

Pain   It once was thought that newborns are indifferent to pain, but we now know that is not true. The main research that has documented newborns' sensitivity to pain involves male infants' stressful reactions to being circumcised (Gunnar, Malone, & Fisch, 1987). For example, newborn males show a higher level of cortisol (a hormonal response to stress) after circumcision than prior to the surgery. As a consequence, anesthesia now is used in some cases of circumcision (Taddio & others, 1997).

For many years, doctors have performed operations on newborns without anesthesia. This medical practice was accepted because of the dangers of anesthesia and the supposition that newborns do not feel pain. Recently, as researchers have convincingly demonstrated that newborns can feel pain, the long-standing practice of operating on newborns without anesthesia is being challenged.

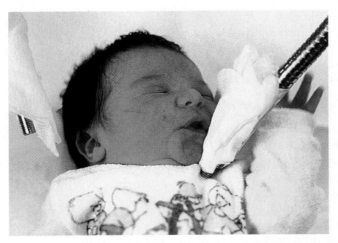

FIGURE 5.22 Newborns' Preference for the Smell of Their Mother's Breast Pad

In the experiment by MacFarlane (1975), 6-day-old infants preferred to smell their mother's breast pad rather than a clean one that had never been used, but 2-day-old infants did not show this preference, indicating that this odor preference requires several days of experience to develop.

Smell   Newborns can differentiate odors. For example, by the expressions on their faces, they seem to indicate that they like the smell of vanilla and strawberry but do not like the smell of rotten eggs and fish (Steiner, 1979). In one investigation, young infants who were breastfed showed a clear preference for smelling their mother's breast pad when they were 6 days old (MacFarlane, 1975) (see figure 5.22). However, when they were 2 days old, they did not show this preference (compared to a clean breast pad), indicating that they require several days of experience to recognize this odor.

Taste   Sensitivity to taste might be present before birth. When saccharin was added to the amniotic fluid of a near-term fetus, increased swallowing was observed (Windle, 1940). In one study, even at only

2 hours of age, babies made different facial expressions when they tasted sweet, sour, and bitter solutions (Rosenstein & Oster, 1988) (see figure 5.23). At about 4 months of age, infants begin to prefer salty tastes, which as newborns they were averse to (Harris, Thomas, & Booth, 1990).

Intermodal Perception

Imagine yourself playing basketball or tennis. You are experiencing many visual inputs: the ball coming and going, other players moving around, and so on. You are also experiencing many auditory inputs: the sound of the ball bouncing or being hit, the grunts and groans, and so on. There is good correspondence between much of the visual and auditory information: When you see the ball bounce, you hear a bouncing sound; when a player stretches to hit a ball, you hear a groan.

We live in a world of objects and events that can be seen, heard, and felt. When mature observers simultaneously look and listen to an event, they experience a unitary episode. All of this is so commonplace that it scarcely seems worth mentioning, but consider the task of very young infants with little practice at perceiving. Can they put vision and sound together as precisely as adults do?

Intermodal perception is the ability to relate and integrate information about two or more sensory modalities, such as vision and hearing. To test intermodal perception, Elizabeth Spelke (1979) showed 4-month-old infants two films simultaneously. In each film, a puppet jumped up and down, but in one of the films the sound track matched the puppet's dancing movements; in the other film, it did not. By measuring the infants' gaze, Spelke found that the infants looked more at the puppet whose actions were synchronized with the sound track, suggesting that they recognized the visual-sound correspondence. Young infants can also coordinate visual-auditory information involving people (Condry, Smith, & Spelke, 2001). In one study, infants as young as $3\frac{1}{2}$ months old looked more at their mother when they also heard her voice and longer at their father when they also heard his voice (Spelke & Owsley, 1979).

Might auditory-visual relations be coordinated even in newborns? Newborns do turn their eyes and their head toward the sound of a voice or rattle when the sound is maintained for several seconds (Clifton & others, 1981), but the newborn can localize a sound and look at an object only in a crude way (Bechtold, Bushnell, & Salapatek, 1979). Improved accuracy at auditory-visual coordination likely requires a sharpening through experience with visual and auditory stimuli. Nonetheless, although at a crude level, auditory-visual intermodal perception appears to be present at birth, likely having evolutionary value.

In sum, crude exploratory forms of intermodal perception exist in newborns. These exploratory forms of intermodal perception become sharpened with experience in the first year of life. In the first six months, infants have difficulty forming mental representations that connect sensory input from different modes, but in the second half of the first year they show an increased ability to make this connection mentally. Thus, babies come into the world with some innate abilities to perceive relations among sensory modalities, but their intermodal abilities improve considerably through experience. As with all aspects of development, in perceptual development, nature and nurture interact and cooperate.

Perceptual-Motor Coupling

For the most part, our discussion of motor development and sensory/perceptual development have been separated in this chapter. Indeed, the main thrust of research in many studies has been to discover how perception guides action. A less well studied but important issue is how action shapes perception. Motor activities might be crucial because they provide the means for exploring the world and learning about its properties. Only by moving one's eyes, head, hands, and arms and by

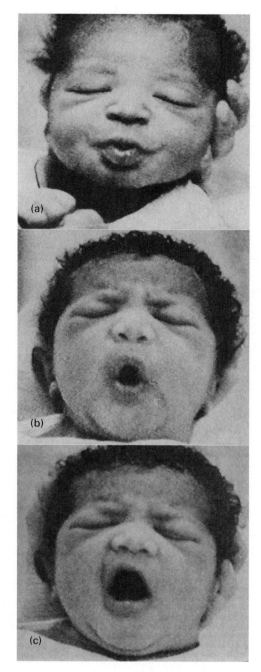

FIGURE 5.23 Newborns' Facial Responses to Basic Tastes

Facial expression elicited by (*a*) a sweet solution, (*b*) a sour solution, and (*c*) a bitter solution.

intermodal perception The ability to relate and integrate information about two or more sensory modalities, such as vision and hearing.

traversing from one location to another can individuals fully experience their environment and learn to effectively adapt to it.

The distinction between perceiving and doing has been a time-honored tradition in psychology. However, a number of contemporary experts on perceptual and motor development question this distinction (Bornstein & Arterberry, 1999; Pick, 1997; Thelen, 2000, 2001). For example, Esther Thelen (1995) argues that individuals perceive in order to move and move in order to perceive. Thus, there is an increasing belief that perceptual and motor development do not occur in isolation from one another but, rather, are coupled.

Babies are continually coordinating their movements with concurrent perceptual information to learn how to maintain balance, reach for objects in space, and locomote across various surfaces and terrains (Thelen, 2001). To illustrate how infants are motivated to move by what they perceive, consider the sight of an attractive object across the room. In this situation, infants must perceive the current state of their bodies and learn how to use their limbs to get to the goal object. Although their movements at first are awkward and uncoordinated, babies soon learn to select patterns that are appropriate for reaching their goals. Equally important is the other part of the perception-action coupling: action educates perception. For example, watching an object while exploring it manually helps infants to visually discriminate its properties of texture, size, and hardness. Locomoting in the environment teaches babies how objects and people look from different perspectives or whether surfaces will support their weight.

Also think about how often during each day you need to coordinate perceptual input with motor actions to accomplish what you want to do. For example, right now I am looking at my computer screen (perceiving) to make sure the words are appearing accurately as I am typing them (motorically). We develop this ability by physically exploring the world revealed to us by sensation and perception, thus experiencing new sensations and perceptions to be explored.

Review and Reflect: Learning Goal 3

3 Explain sensory and perceptual development in infancy

REVIEW

- What are sensation and perception?
- How can the ecological view of perception be described?
- How does visual perception develop in infancy?
- How do hearing, touch and pain, smell, and taste develop in infancy?
- What is intermodal perception?
- How is perceptual-motor development coupled?

REFLECT

- How much sensory stimulation should caregivers provide for infants? A little? A lot? Could an infant be given too much sensory stimulation? Explain.

Reach Your Learning Goals

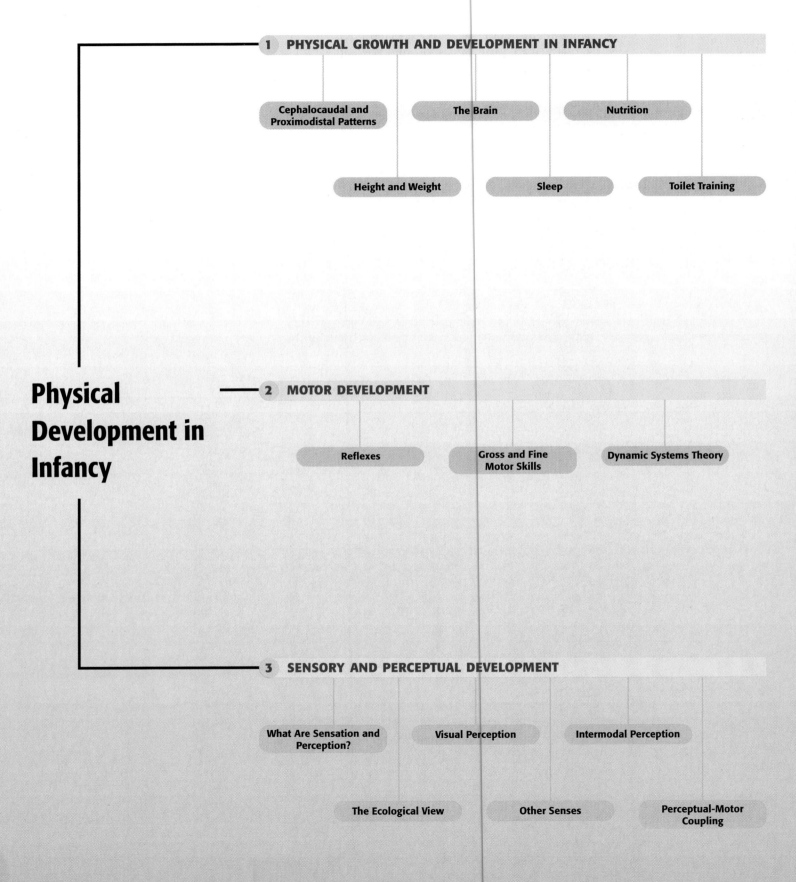

Physical Development in Infancy

1 PHYSICAL GROWTH AND DEVELOPMENT IN INFANCY

- Cephalocaudal and Proximodistal Patterns
- The Brain
- Nutrition
- Height and Weight
- Sleep
- Toilet Training

2 MOTOR DEVELOPMENT

- Reflexes
- Gross and Fine Motor Skills
- Dynamic Systems Theory

3 SENSORY AND PERCEPTUAL DEVELOPMENT

- What Are Sensation and Perception?
- Visual Perception
- Intermodal Perception
- The Ecological View
- Other Senses
- Perceptual-Motor Coupling

Summary

1 Discuss physical growth and development in infancy

- The cephalocaudal pattern is the sequence in which the greatest growth occurs at the top—the head—and gradually proceeds from top to bottom. The proximodistal pattern is the sequence in which growth starts at the center of the body and moves toward the extremities.
- The average North American newborn is 20 inches long and weights $7\frac{1}{2}$ pounds. Infants grow about 1 inch per month in the first year and nearly triple their weight by their first birthday. The rate of growth slows in the second year.
- One of the most dramatic changes in the brain in the first two years of life is dendritic spreading. Myelination continues through infancy and into childhood. The cerebral cortex has two hemispheres (left and right). Lateralization refers to the specialization of function in one hemisphere or the other. Research with animals suggests that the environment plays a key role in early brain development. Neural connections are formed early in an infant's life. Before birth, genes mainly direct neurons to different locations. After birth, the inflowing stream of sights, sounds, smells, touches, language, and eye contact help shape the brain's neural connections.
- Newborns usually sleep 16 to 17 hours a day. By 4 months of age, many American infants approach adultlike sleeping patterns. REM sleep—during which dreaming occurs—is present more in early infancy than in childhood and adulthood. Sleeping arrangements for infants vary across cultures. In America, infants are more likely to sleep alone than in many other cultures. Some experts believe shared sleeping can lead to sudden infant death syndrome (SIDS), a condition that occurs when a sleeping infant suddenly stops breathing and dies without an apparent cause.
- Infants need to consume about 50 calories per day for each pound they weigh. The growing consensus is that breastfeeding is superior to bottlefeeding. Severe infant malnutrition is still prevalent in many parts of the world. Two diseases that can result from infant malnutrition are marasmus or kwashiorkor.
- Toilet training is expected to be attained by about 3 years of age in North America. Toilet training should be carried out in a relaxed, supportive manner.

2 Describe infants' motor development

- The newborn is not a passive organism. Reflexes (automatic movements) govern the newborn's behavior. For infants, sucking is an especially important reflex because it provides a means of obtaining nutrition. Other reflexes include the rooting reflex, Moro reflex, and grasping reflex.
- Gross motor skills involve large muscle activities (such as moving one's arms and walking). The development of posture and learning to walk illustrate the complexity of motor development and the importance of perceptual-motor coupling. A number of gross motor milestones are reached in infancy. Although there are cultural variations in the type and amount of activity infants experience, infants in these cultures typically reach motor milestones within the same range.
- Fine motor skills involve finely tuned movements, such as finger dexterity. Infants reach a number of fine motor milestones. The onset of reaching and grasping represents a significant accomplishment.
- Dynamic systems theory seeks to explain how motor behaviors are assembled for perceiving and acting. This approach emphasizes the importance of exploration and selection in finding solutions to new task demands. A key theme is that perception and action are coupled when new skills are learned.

3 Explain sensory and perceptual development in infancy

- Sensation occurs when information interacts with the sensory receptors—the eyes, ears, tongue, nose, and skin. Perception is the interpretation of what is sensed.
- In the ecological view, perception functions to bring organisms in contact with the environment and increase adaptation.
- William James was wrong in his belief that the newborn's visual world is a "blooming, buzzing confusion." Newborns can see and can distinguish colors, and they prefer to look at patterns rather than at color or brightness. In Fantz's pioneering research, infants only 2 days old looked longer at patterned stimuli, such as faces, than at single-colored discs. Although young infants' vision is much poorer than adults', their visual world is organized. Size constancy and shape constancy develop early, and young infants systematically scan human faces. Visual perception continues to develop as their experiences and actions in a world of objects help them to understand physical laws. A classic study by Gibson and Walk demonstrated through the use of the visual cliff that infants as young as 6 months of age have depth perception. As visual perception develops, infants develop visual expectations.
- The fetus can hear several weeks before birth. Immediately after birth, the newborn can hear, although its sensory threshold is higher than that of adults. Developmental changes in the perception of loudness, pitch, and localization of sound occur in infancy. Newborns respond to touch and can feel pain. They can also distinguish between different tastes.
- Intermodal perception is the ability to relate and integrate information about two or more sensory modalities, such as vision and hearing. Spelke's research demonstrated that infants as young as $3\frac{1}{2}$ months of age can link visual and auditory stimuli.
- A time-honored belief in psychology has been that perceptual and motor development are distinct. Increasingly, it is believed that perceptual-motor development is coupled. Perception can guide action and action can shape perception. Babies are continually coordinating their movements with concurrent perceptual information to learn how to maintain balance, reach for objects in space, and locomote across various surfaces and terrains.

Key Terms

cephalocaudal pattern 131
proximodistal pattern 131
neuron 132
lateralization 135
sudden infant death syndrome
    (SIDS) 138

marasmus 141
kwashiorkor 141
sucking reflex 144
rooting reflex 144
Moro reflex 144
grasping reflex 144

gross motor skills 146
fine motor skills 146
dynamic systems theory 151
sensation 152
perception 152
ecological view 152

affordances 152
size constancy 155
shape constancy 155
intermodal perception 159

Key People

Charles Nelson 134
Mark Rosenzweig 135
Ernesto Pollitt 142
T. Berry Brazelton 144

Rachel Clifton 149
Esther Thelen 151
Eleanor and James J. Gibson
    152

William James 153
Robert Fantz 153
Richard Walk 156

Marshall Haith 156
Elizabeth Spelke 156

Taking It to the Net

1. Professor Samuels asked his child development students to write a one-page report explaining how a child's brain develops during infancy and what role parents play in fostering maximal brain development. What should this report contain to provide a concise but comprehensive summary of the research found to date?

2. One of the families in a community day-care center lost a 4-month-old child to SIDS. Laura, the center's director, is planning to conduct an in-service training for her employees about the effect of a SIDS-related death on the deceased child's par-

ents and siblings. What information should they have in order to help them deal with this family?

3. Marianne has landed a part-time job as a nanny for Jack, a 2-month-old boy. What can Marianne expect to see in terms of the child's sensory and motor development as she interacts with and observes Jack over the next six months?

Connect to **www.mhhe.com/santrockcd10** to research the answers and complete these exercises.

E-Learning Tools

To help you master the material in this chapter, you'll find a number of valuable study tools on the Student CD-ROM that accompanies this book. Also visit the Online Learning Center for *Child Development*, tenth edition (**www.mhhe.com/santrockcd10**) where you'll find these additional resources:

- Build your decision-making skills by trying your hand at the parenting, nursing, and education "Scenarios" on the Online Learning Center.

That energy which makes a child hard to manage is the energy which afterward makes him a manager of life.

—HENRY WARD BEECHER
American Author, 19th Century

Physical Development in Childhood and Adolescence

Chapter Outline

PHYSICAL GROWTH IN CHILDHOOD

Child Growth Patterns

Motor Development

Handedness

The Brain

HEALTH AND ILLNESS

A Developmental Perspective

Nutrition and Obesity

Exercise and Sports

Children's Health and Illness in the United
States and Around the World

PUBERTY AND ADOLESCENCE

Puberty and Sexuality

Substance Use and Abuse

The Interrelation of Problems
and Successful Programs

Today's Youth

Learning Goals

1 Discuss physical growth
in childhood

2 Describe children's and
adolescents' health and
illness

3 Explain the changes of
puberty and adolescence

The Story of Zhang Liyin

Zhang Liyin was playing in a kindergarten class in Beijing, China, when a coach from a sports school spotted her and invited her to attend the school. Zhang was selected because of her broad shoulders, narrow hips, straight legs, symmetrical limbs, open-minded attitude, vivaciousness, and outgoing personality. Zhang's parents accepted the invitation, and now she attends the sports school in the afternoon.

Attending the sports school is a privilege given to only 260,000 of China's 200 million students from elementary school to college age. China spends lavishly on its sports schools, which are the only road to Olympic stardom in China.

Today, at age 6, Zhang is standing on the balance beam, stretching her arms outward as she gets ready to perform a back flip. She wears the bright red gymnastic suit of the elite—a suit given to only the 10 best girls in her class of 6- to 8-year-olds. However, her face wears a fearful expression. She can't drum up enough confidence to do the flip. Maybe it is because she has had a rough week. A purple bruise decorates her one leg, a nasty gash disfigures the other.

Because of her young age, Zhang stays at home during the mornings and goes to the sports school from noon until 6 P.M. If she continues to perform well, next year, at age 7, she will live and study at the sports school like many of the other students. The development of these children is closely monitored. If at any point, a child shows a decline in potential, the child is asked to leave the sports school.

As children develop, they go through many physical changes. In chapter 5, we saw that some dramatic changes characterize the physical growth of infants. In this chapter, we will explore the physical changes that occur in childhood and adolescence.

Six-year-old Zhang Liyin (*third from left*) hopes to someday become an Olympic gymnastics champion. Attending the sports school is considered an outstanding privilege; only 260,000 of China's 200 million children are given this opportunity. *What positive and negative outcomes might children experience from playing sports? Are some sports programs, such as China's sports schools, too intense for children? Should children experience a more balanced life? Is there too much emphasis on sports in the United States?*

1 PHYSICAL GROWTH IN CHILDHOOD

- Child Growth Patterns
- Motor Development
- Handedness
- The Brain

Remember from chapter 5 that the infant's growth in the first year is rapid and follows cephalocaudal and proximodistal patterns. ◀ page 131 At some point around the first birthday, most infants begin to walk. During the infant's second year, the growth rate begins to slow down, but both gross and fine motor skills progress rapidly. ◀ page 148 The infant develops a sense of mastery through increased proficiency in gross motor skills—such as walking and running—and in fine motor skills—such as being able to turn the pages of a book one at a time in the second year of life. The growth rate continues to slow down in early childhood. Otherwise, we would be a species of giants.

Child Growth Patterns

What are some changes in physical growth in early childhood? Middle and late childhood?

Early Childhood The average child grows $2^1/_2$ inches in height and gains between 5 and 7 pounds a year during early childhood. As the preschool child grows older, the percentage of increase in height and weight decreases with each additional year. Girls are only slightly smaller and lighter than boys during these years, a difference that continues until puberty. During the preschool years, both boys and girls slim down as the trunks of their bodies lengthen. Although their heads are still somewhat large for their bodies, by the end of the preschool years most children have lost their top-heavy look. Body fat also shows a slow, steady decline during the preschool years. The chubby baby often looks much leaner by the end of early childhood. Girls have more fatty tissue than boys; boys have more muscle tissue.

Growth patterns vary individually. Think back to your preschool years. This was probably the first time you noticed that some children were taller than you, some shorter; some were fatter, some thinner; some were stronger, some weaker. Much of the variation is due to heredity, but environmental experiences are involved to some extent. A review of the height and weight of children around the world concluded that the two most important contributors to height differences are ethnic origin and nutrition (Meredith, 1978). The urban, middle-socioeconomic-status (middle-SES), and firstborn children were taller than rural, lower-SES, and later-born children. The children whose mothers smoked during pregnancy were half an inch shorter than the children whose mothers did not smoke during pregnancy. In the United States, African American children are taller than White children.

Why are some children unusually short? The culprits are congenital factors (genetic or prenatal problems), a physical problem that develops in childhood, or an emotional difficulty. In many cases, children with congenital growth problems can be treated with hormones. Usually this treatment is directed at the pituitary, the body's master gland, located at the base of the brain. This gland secretes growth-related hormones. With regard

The bodies of 5-year-olds and 2-year-olds are different. Notice how the 5-year-old not only is taller and weighs more, but also has a longer trunk and legs than the 2-year-old. *What might be some other physical differences in 2- and 5-year-olds?*

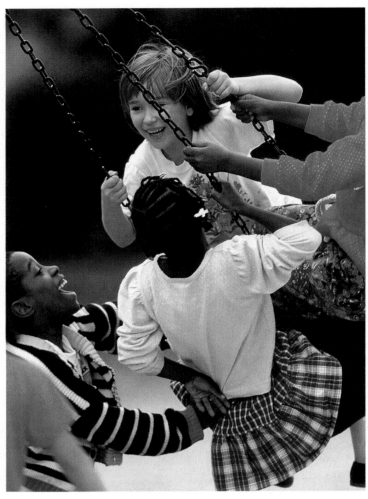

As children move through the elementary school years, they gain greater control over their bodies. Physical action is essential for them to refine their developing skills.

All the sun long I was running . . .

—DYLAN THOMAS
Welsh Poet and Writer, 20th Century

deprivation dwarfism A type of growth retardation caused by emotional deprivation; when children are deprived of affection, they experience stress, which alters the release of hormones by the pituitary gland.

to physical problems that develop during childhood, malnutrition and chronic infections can stunt growth. However, if the problems are properly treated, normal growth usually is attained. **Deprivation dwarfism** is a type of growth retardation caused by emotional deprivation; children are deprived of affection, which causes stress and alters the release of hormones by the pituitary gland. Some children who are not dwarfs may also show the effects of an impoverished emotional environment, although most parents of these children say they are small and weak because they have a poor body structure or constitution (Gardner, 1972).

Middle and Late Childhood   The period of middle and late childhood involves slow, consistent growth. This is a period of calm before the rapid growth spurt of adolescence. In middle and late childhood, important developmental changes occur in the skeletal and muscular systems.

During the elementary school years, children grow an average of 2 to 3 inches a year until, at the age of 11, the average girl is 4 feet $10\frac{3}{4}$ inches tall and the average boy is 4 feet 9 inches tall. Children's legs become longer and their trunks slimmer. During the middle and late childhood years, children gain about 5 to 7 pounds a year. The weight increase is due mainly to increases in the size of the skeleton and muscular systems, as well as the size of some body organs. Muscle mass and strength gradually increase as "baby fat" decreases. The loose movements and knock-knees of early childhood give way to improved muscle tone. The increase in muscular strength is due to heredity and to exercise. Children double their strength capabilities during these years. Because of their greater number of muscle cells, boys are usually stronger than girls.

Proportional changes are among the most pronounced physical changes in middle and late childhood. Head circumference, waist circumference, and leg length decrease in relation to body height (Hockenberry, 2003; Wong, 2002).

Motor Development

Running as fast as you can, falling down, getting right back up and running just as fast as you can . . . building towers with blocks . . . scribbling . . . cutting paper with scissors . . . During your preschool years, you probably developed the ability to perform all of these activities. First, we will explore gross motor skills in the childhood years, then fine motor skills.

Gross Motor Skills   The preschool child no longer has to make an effort simply to stay upright and to move around. As children move their legs with more confidence and carry themselves more purposefully, moving around in the environment becomes more automatic.

At 3 years of age, children enjoy simple movements, such as hopping, jumping, and running back and forth, just for the sheer delight of performing these activities. They delight in showing how they can run across a room and jump all of 6 inches. The run-and-jump will win no Olympic gold medals, but for the 3-year-old the activity is a source of considerable pride and accomplishment.

By 4 years of age, children are still enjoying the same kinds of activities, but they have become more adventurous. They scramble over low jungle gyms as they display their athletic prowess. Although they have been able to climb stairs with one foot on each step for some time now, they are just beginning to be able to come down the same way. They still often revert to marking time on each step. By 5 years of age, children are even more adventuresome than when they were 4. Five-year-olds run hard and enjoy races with each other and their parents.

You probably have arrived at one important conclusion about preschool children: They are very, very active. Indeed, 3-year-old children have the highest activity level of any age in the entire human life span. They fidget when they watch television. They fidget when they sit at the dinner table. Even when they sleep, they move around quite a bit. Because of their activity level and the development of large muscles, especially in the arms and legs, preschool children need daily exercise.

During middle and late childhood, children's motor development becomes much smoother and more coordinated than it was in early childhood. For example, only one child in a thousand can hit a tennis ball over the net at the age of 3, yet by the age of 10 or 11 most children can learn to play the sport. Running, climbing, skipping rope, swimming, bicycle riding, and skating are just a few of the many physical skills elementary school children can master. And, when mastered, these physical skills are a source of great pleasure and accomplishment for children. In gross motor skills involving large muscle activity, boys usually outperform girls.

As children move through the elementary school years, they gain greater control over their bodies and can sit and attend for longer periods of time. However, elementary school children are far from having physical maturity, and they need to be active. Elementary school children become more fatigued by long periods of sitting than by running, jumping, or bicycling. Physical action is essential for these children to refine their developing skills, such as batting a ball, skipping rope, or balancing on a beam. An important principle of practice for elementary school children, therefore, is that they should be engaged in *active*, rather than passive, activities.

Fine Motor Skills Children make considerable progress in fine motor skills in early childhood. Then, further advancements are made in middle and late childhood.

At 3 years of age, children are still emerging from the infant ability to place and handle things. Although they have had the ability to pick up the tiniest objects between their thumb and forefinger for some time, they are still somewhat clumsy at it. Three-year-olds can build surprisingly high block towers, each block placed with intense concentration but often not in a completely straight line. When 3-year-olds play with a form board or a simple jigsaw puzzle, they are rather rough in placing the pieces. Even when they recognize the hole a piece fits into, they are not very precise in positioning the piece. They often try to force the piece in the hole or pat it vigorously.

By 4 years of age, children's fine motor coordination has improved substantially and becomes much more precise. Sometimes 4-year-old children have trouble building high towers with blocks because, in their desire to place each of the blocks perfectly, they may upset those already stacked. By age 5, children's fine motor coordination has improved further. Hand, arm, and body all move together under better command of the eye. Mere towers no longer interest the 5-year-old, who now wants to build a house or a church, complete with steeple, though adults may still need to be told what each finished project is meant to be.

In middle and late childhood, children use their hands more adroitly as tools. Six-year-olds can hammer, paste, tie shoes, and fasten clothes. By 7 years of age, children's hands become steadier. At this age, children prefer a pencil to a crayon for printing, and reversal of letters is less common. Printing becomes smaller. Between 8 and 10 years of age, the hands can be used independently with more ease and precision. Fine motor coordination develops to the point where children can write rather than print words. Letter size continues to decrease and becomes more even. By 10 to 12 years of age, children's manipulative skills begin to approximate those of adults'. Children begin to master complex, intricate, and rapid

Preschool Growth and Development
Developmental Milestones

Today, most teachers let children write with the hand they favor. *What are the main reasons children became left- or right-handed?*

Handedness

movements needed to produce fine-quality crafts, or a difficult piece on a musical instrument can be mastered. One final point: Girls usually outperform boys in fine motor skills.

Handedness

For centuries, left-handers have suffered unfair discrimination in a world designed for right-handers. For many years, teachers forced all children to write with their right hand, even if they had a left-hand tendency. Fortunately, today most teachers let children write with the hand they favor.

Origin and Development of Handedness What is the origin of hand preference? Genetic inheritance is likely strong. In one study, the handedness of adopted children was not related to the handedness of their adoptive parents but was related to the handedness of their biological parents (Carter-Saltzman, 1980).

Right-handedness is dominant in all cultures (it appears in a ratio of about 90 percent right-handers and 10 percent left-handers), and it appears before the impact of culture. For example, in one study, ultrasound observations of fetal thumb sucking showed that 9 of 10 fetuses were more likely to be sucking their right hand's thumb (Hepper, Shahidullah, & White, 1990). Newborns also show a preference for one side of their body over the other. In one study, 65 percent of the infants turned their head to the right when they were lying on their back in a crib (Michel, 1981). Fifteen percent preferred to face toward the left. These preferences for the right or the left were linked with handedness later in development.

Handedness, the Brain, and Language Approximately 95 percent of right-handed individuals primarily process speech in the brain's left hemisphere (Springer & Deutsch, 1985). However, left-handed individuals show more variation. More than one-half of left-handers process speech in their left hemisphere, just like right-handers. However, about one-fourth of left-handers process speech equally in both hemispheres (Knecht & others, 2000).

Are there differences in the language development of left- and right-handers? The most consistent finding is that left-handers are more likely to have reading problems (Geschwind & Behan, 1984; Natsopoulos & others, 1998).

Handedness and Other Abilities Although there is a tendency for left-handers to have more reading problems than right-handers, left-handers are more common among mathematicians, musicians, architects, and artists (Michelangelo, Leonardo da Vinci, and Picasso were all left-handed) (Schacter & Ransil, 1996). Architects and artists who are left-handed benefit from the tendency of left-handers to have unusually good visual spatial skills and be able to imagine spatial layouts (Holtzen, 2000). Also, in one study of more than 100,000 students taking the Scholastic Aptitude Test (SAT), 20 percent of the top-scoring group was left-handed, twice the rate of left-handedness found in the general population (10 percent) (Bower, 1985).

The Brain

One of the most important physical developments during childhood is the continuing development of the brain and nervous system (Byrnes, 2001). Does a child's brain just get bigger than an infant's brain or are there other changes in the brain that take place?

Brain Size and Growth While the brain continues to grow in early childhood, it does not grow as rapidly as in infancy. ◀ **page 132** By the time children have reached 3 years of age, the brain is three-quarters of its adult size. By age 5, the brain has reached about nine-tenths of its adult size.

The brain and the head grow more rapidly than any other part of the body. The top parts of the head, the eyes, and the brain grow faster than the lower portions, such as the jaw. Figure 6.1 reveals how the growth curve for the head and brain advances more rapidly than the growth curve for height and weight. At 5 years of age, when the brain has attained approximately 90 percent of its adult weight, the 5-year-old's total body weight is only about one-third of what it will be when the child reaches adulthood.

Changes in Neurons Communication in the brain is characterized by the transmission of information between neurons, or nerve cells. Some of the brain's increase in size is due to the increase in the number and size of nerve endings within and between areas of the brain. These nerve endings continue to grow at least until adolescence.

Neurons communicate with each other through *neurotransmitters* (chemical substances) that carry information across *synapses* (gaps) between the neurons. The concentration of the neurotransmitter dopamine increases considerably from 3 to 6 years of age (Diamond, 2001). We will return to a discussion of dopamine shortly.

Some of the brain's increase in size also is due to the increase in **myelination,** in which nerve cells are covered and insulated with a layer of fat cells. This has the effect of increasing the speed of information traveling through the nervous system. Some developmentalists believe myelination is important in the maturation of a number of children's abilities. For example, myelination in the areas of the brain related to hand-eye coordination is not complete until about 4 years of age. Myelination in the areas of the brain related to focusing attention is not complete until the end of middle or late childhood.

Changes in Brain Structures Until recently, scientists have not had adequate technology to detect and map sensitive changes in the human brain as it develops. However, the creation of sophisticated brain-scanning techniques is allowing better detection of these changes (Blumenthal & others, 1999). Using these techniques, scientists recently have discovered that children's brains undergo dramatic anatomical changes between the ages of 3 and 15 (Thompson & others, 2000). By repeatedly obtaining brain scans of the same children for up to four years, they have found that children's brains experience rapid, distinct spurts of growth. The amount of brain material in some areas can nearly double in as little as a year, followed by a drastic loss of tissue as unneeded cells are purged and the brain continues to reorganize itself. The scientists found that the overall size of the brain did not increase dramatically from age 3 to 15. However, what did dramatically change were local patterns within the brain.

Researchers have found that from 3 to 6 years of age the most rapid growth takes place in the frontal lobe areas involved in planning and organizing new actions, and in maintaining attention to tasks. From age 6 through puberty, the most growth takes place in the temporal and parietal lobes, especially areas that play major roles in language and spatial relations.

Development of the brain in adolescence also may be linked to changes in emotional development. In one study, researchers used magnetic resonance imaging (MRI) to discover if the brain activity of adolescents (10 to 18 years of age) differed from that of adults (20 to 40 years of age) (Baird & others, 1999). Participants were asked to view pictures of faces displaying fearful expressions while undergoing an MRI. When adolescents (especially the younger ones) processed emotional information, brain activity in the amygdala was more pronounced than in the frontal lobe, but the reverse occurred in adults. The amygdala is highly involved in emotion, while the frontal lobe is more involved in reasoning and thinking. The researchers concluded that adolescents might respond with "gut" reactions to emotional stimuli, whereas adults are more

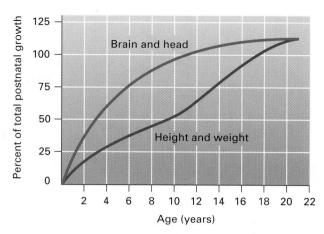

FIGURE 6.1 Growth Curves for the Head and Brain and for Height and Weight

The more rapid growth of the brain and head can easily be seen. Height and weight advance more gradually over the first two decades of life.

myelination A process in which nerve cells are insulated with a layer of fat cells, which increases the speed at which information travels through the nervous system.

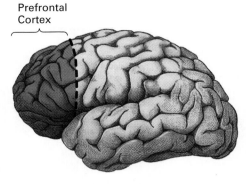

Prefrontal
Cortex

FIGURE 6.2 The Prefrontal Cortex

This evolutionarily advanced portion (shaded in purple) of the brain shows extensive development from 3 to 6 years of age and is believed to play important roles in attention and working memory.

likely to respond with rational, reasoned responses. They also concluded that these changes are linked with growth in the frontal lobe of the brain from adolescence to adulthood. However, more research is needed to clarify the developmental changes in the brain during adolescence and their link to behavior (Dahl, 2001).

The Brain and Cognitive Development The increasing maturation of the brain, combined with opportunities to experience a widening world, contribute to children's emerging cognitive abilities. Consider a child who is learning to read aloud. Input from the child's eyes is transmitted to the child's brain, then passed through many brain systems, which translate (process) the patterns of black and white into codes for letters, words, and associations. The output occurs in the form of messages to the child's lips and tongue. The child's own gift of speech is possible because brain systems are organized in ways that permit language processing.

The brain is organized in many neural circuits, which consist of neurons with certain functions. One neural circuit has an important function in attention and working memory (a type of memory similar to short-term memory that is like a mental workbench in performing many cognitive tasks) (Krimer & Goldman-Rakic, 2001). This neural circuit involves the *prefrontal cortex* and the neurotransmitter dopamine (Casey, Durston, & Fossella, 2001; Diamond, 2001) (see figure 6.2).

In sum, scientists are beginning to chart connections between children's cognitive development (attention and memory, for example), brain structures (prefrontal cortex, for example), and the transmission of information at the level of the neuron (the neurotransmitter dopamine, for example). As advances in technology allow scientists to "look inside" the brain to observe its activity, we will likely see increased precision in understanding the brain's functioning in cognitive development.

Review and Reflect: Learning Goal 1

1 Discuss physical growth in childhood

REVIEW

- What is the nature of children's physical growth?
- How do children's gross and fine motor skills develop?
- Why are some children right-handed and others left-handed? How is handedness linked with the brain, language, and other abilities?
- How does the brain change in childhood and adolescence?

REFLECT

- Since left-handed individuals perform better on the SAT than right-handers, should parents train their children to be left-handed? Explain.

2 HEALTH AND ILLNESS

A Developmental Perspective

Nutrition and Obesity

Exercise and Sports

Children's Health and Illness in the United States and Around the World

Although we have become a health-conscious nation, aware of the importance of nutrition and exercise in our lives, many of us still eat junk food, have extra flab hanging around our middles, and spend too much time as couch potatoes. All too often, this description fits children as well as adults.

A Developmental Perspective

Although there has been great national interest in the psychological aspects of adult health, only recently has a developmental perspective on the psychological aspects of children's health been proposed. Adolescence also is increasingly recognized as a critical juncture in the development of health behaviors.

Children's Health-Care Needs The uniqueness of young children's health-care needs is evident when we consider their motor, cognitive, and social development (Maddux & others, 1986). For example, think about the infant's and preschool child's motor development—it is inadequate to ensure personal safety while riding in an automobile. Adults must take preventive measures to restrain infants and young children in car seats. Young children might lack the intellectual skills—including reading ability—to discriminate between safe and unsafe household substances, and they might lack the impulse control to keep them from running out into a busy street while chasing after a ball or toy.

Playgrounds for young children need to be designed with their safety in mind. The initial step in ensuring children's safety is to walk with children through the existing playground or the site where the playground is to be developed, talking with them about possible safety hazards, letting them assist in identifying hazards, and indicating how they can use the playground safely. The outdoor play environment should enhance children's motor, cognitive, and social development.

Health education programs for preschool children need to be cognitively simple. There are three simple but important goals for health education programs for preschool children (Parcel & others, 1987): (1) to help children identify feelings of wellness and illness and be able to express them to adults, (2) to help children identify appropriate sources of assistance for health-related problems, and (3) to help children independently initiate the use of sources of assistance for health problems.

Caregivers have an important health role for young children (Tinsley, Finley, & Ortiz, 1999). For example, by controlling the speed of the vehicles they drive, by decreasing their drinking, and by not smoking around children, caregivers enhance children's health (Gergen & others, 1998). In one investigation, it was found that if a mother smokes, her children are twice as likely to have respiratory ailments (Etzel, 1988). The young children of single, unemployed, smoking mothers are also three times more likely to be injured. Smoking may serve as a marker to identify mothers less able to supervise young children. In sum, caregivers can actively affect young children's health and safety by training them and monitoring their recreational safety, self-protection skills, proper nutrition, and dental hygiene.

Illnesses, especially those that are not life threatening, provide an excellent opportunity for young children to expand their development (Deluca, 1999). The preschool period is a peak time for such illnesses as respiratory infections (colds, flu) and gastrointestinal upsets (nausea, diarrhea). These illnesses usually are of short duration and are often handled outside the medical community through the family, day care, or school. Such minor illnesses can increase the young child's knowledge of health and illness and sense of empathy.

Adolescence: A Critical Juncture in Health Adolescence is a critical juncture in the adoption of behaviors relevant to health (Maggs, Schulenberg, & Hurrelmann, 1997; Roth & Brooks-Gunn, 2000; Spear & Kulbok, 2001). Many of the factors linked to poor health habits and early death in the adult years begin during adolescence.

The early formation of healthy behavioral patterns, such as eating foods low in fat and cholesterol and engaging in regular exercise in childhood and adolescence, not only has immediate health benefits but contributes to the delay or prevention of major causes of premature disability and mortality in adulthood—heart disease, stroke, diabetes, and cancer (Jessor, 1998).

Many adolescents reach a level of strength and energy that they will never match in the remainder of their lives. They also have a sense of uniqueness and

Pediatrics

Health Links

MEDLINE Plus

Harvard Center for Children's Health

Maternal and Child Health Resources

Life Science and Life Skills Education

Early adolescence is a time when many health-compromising behaviors—drug abuse, unprotected sex, poor dietary habits, and lack of exercise, for example—either occur for the first time or intensify. As children move through puberty and often develop a feeling that they should be able to engage in adultlike behaviors, they essentially ask, "How should I use my body?" According to David Hamburg and his colleagues (1993), any responsible education must answer that basic question with a substantial life science curriculum that provides adolescents with accurate information about their own bodies, including what the consequences are for engaging in health-compromising behaviors.

Most adolescent health experts believe that a life science education program should be an important part of the curriculum in all middle schools (Hamburg, 1990, 1997; Kolbe, Collins, & Cortese, 1997). This education involves providing adolescents with a better understanding of adolescent development, including puberty (its biological and social ramifications), the reproductive system, sexual behavior, sexually transmitted infections, nutrition, diet, and exercise. In addition, young adolescents should have readily accessible health services, nutritious food in the cafeteria, a smoke-free and physically safe environment, and appropriate physical fitness activities.

Many adolescent health experts also believe that life skills training should be part of the life science curriculum (Hamburg & others, 1993). Life skills training programs teach young adolescents

how to make informed, deliberate, and constructive decisions that will reduce their health-compromising behaviors. Life skills training programs also can improve the interpersonal skills of young adolescents, helping them relate better with others and solve interpersonal problems more effectively.

One new school-based model for enhancing the life opportunities of adolescents is the full-service school, which encompasses school-based primary health clinics, youth service programs, and other innovative services to improve access to health and social services. These programs have in common the use of school facilities for delivering services through partnerships with community agencies, a shared vision of youth development, and financial support from sources outside of school systems, especially states and foundations. Organizing a full-service school requires careful planning to involve school personnel, community agencies, parents, and students. Evaluation of the full-service school's effectiveness is still scattered, although some recent results are encouraging with regard to adolescents' health and mental health care, dropout rates, substance abuse, pregnancy prevention, and improved attendance (Dryfoos, 1995).

It is also important to remember that health promotion in adolescence should not be solely the responsibility of schools. Adolescent health can benefit from the cooperation and integration of a number of societal institutions: the family, schools, the health-care system, the media, and community organizations.

Adolescent Health

National Longitudinal Study of Adolescent Health

invulnerability which can lead them to think that poor health will never enter their lives, or that if it does, they will quickly recoup it. Given this combination of physical and cognitive factors, it is not surprising that many adolescents have poor health habits. To read about one strategy for improving adolescent health, see the Explorations in Child Development box.

In a recent comparison of adolescent health behavior in 28 countries, U.S. adolescents exercised less and ate more junk food than adolescents in most other countries (World Health Organization, 2000). Just two-thirds of U.S. adolescents exercised at least twice a week, compared to 80 percent or more of adolescents in Ireland, Austria, Germany, and the Slovak Republic. U.S. adolescents were more likely to eat fried food and less likely to eat fruits and vegetables than adolescents in most other countries studied. U.S. adolescents' eating choices were similar to those of adolescents in England. Eleven-year-olds in the United States were as likely as European 11-year-olds to smoke, but by age 15 U.S. adolescents were less likely to smoke.

Many health experts believe that improving adolescent health involves far more than trips to a doctor's office when sick. The health experts increasingly recognize that whether adolescents will develop a health problem or be healthy is primarily based on their behavior. The goals are to (1) reduce adolescents' health-compromising behaviors, such as drug abuse, violence, unprotected sexual intercourse, and dangerous driving; and (2) increase health-enhancing behaviors, such as eating nutritiously, exercising, and wearing seat belts.

Nutrition and Obesity

What are children's energy needs? What are some eating problems that can arise during childhood and adolescence?

Age	Weight (kg)	Height (cm)	Energy needs (calories)	Calorie ranges
1 to 3	13	90	1,300	900 to 1,800
4 to 6	20	112	1,700	1,300 to 2,300
7 to 10	28	132	2,400	1,650 to 3,300

FIGURE 6.3 Recommended Energy Intakes for Children Ages 1 Through 10

Energy Needs Feeding and eating habits are important aspects of development during early childhood. What children eat affects their skeletal growth, body shape, and susceptibility to disease. Recognizing that nutrition is important for the child's growth and development, the federal government provides money for school lunch programs. An average preschool child requires 1,700 calories per day. In the middle and late childhood years, children's average body weight doubles, and they expend considerable energy in motor activities. Because of their increased size, weight, and motor activity, children need to consume more calories in middle and late childhood than in early childhood. Figure 6.3 shows the increasing energy needs of children as they grow through the childhood years.

Energy requirements for individual children are determined by the **basal metabolism rate (BMR),** which is the minimum amount of energy a person uses in a resting state. Energy needs of individual children of the same age, sex, and size vary. Reasons for these differences remain unexplained. Differences in physical activity, basal metabolism, and the efficiency with which children use energy are among the candidates for explanation.

Eating Behavior and Obesity Within a recommended calorie range, it is important to impress on children the importance of a balanced diet. A special concern is the appropriate amount of fat in young children's diets (Troiano & Flegal, 1998). While some health-conscious parents may be providing too little fat in their infants' and children's diets, many parents are raising their children on diets in which the percentage of fat is far too high. Our changing lifestyles, in which we often eat on the run and pick up fast-food meals, contribute to the increased fat levels in children's diets. The American Heart Association recommends that the daily limit for calories from fat should be approximately 35 percent, and many fast-food meals have fat content that is too high for good health.

In one recent analysis, the prevalence of being overweight from 6 to 11 years of age in the United States increased from approximately 5 percent in 1970 to almost 15 percent in 1999 (NHANES, 2001). Girls are more likely than boys to be obese. Obesity at 6 years of age results in approximately a 25 percent probability that the child will be obese as an adult; obesity at age 12 results in approximately a 75 percent chance that the adolescent will be obese as an adult.

Obesity is a risk factor for many medical and psychological problems (Kiess & others, 2001; Kimm & Obarzanek, 2002; Polivy & Herman, 2002). Obese children can develop pulmonary problems involving upper airway obstruction, and hip problems also are common in obese children (Li & others, 2003). Obese children also are prone to have high blood pressure and elevated blood cholesterol levels. Low self-esteem and depression also are common outgrowths of obesity. In one recent study, the relation of weight status and self-esteem in 5-year-old girls was examined (Davison & Birth, 2001). The girls who were overweight had lower body self-esteem than those who were not overweight.

The context in which children eat can influence their eating habits and weight. In one recent study, children who ate with their families were more likely to eat low-fat foods (such as low-fat milk and salad dressing and lean meats), more vegetables, and to drink fewer sodas than children who ate alone (Cullen, 2001). In this study, overweight children ate 50 percent of their meals in front of a TV, compared to only 35 percent of normal-weight children.

*S*pinach: Divide into little piles. Rearrange again into new piles. After five or six maneuvers, sit back and say you are full.

—DELIA EPHRON
*American Writer and Humorist,
20th Century*

www.mhhe.com/santrockcd10

Exploring Childhood Obesity

Helping an Overweight Child

Preschoolers' Health

Harvard Center for Children's Health

Child Health Guide

basal metabolism rate (BMR) The minimum amount of energy an individual uses in a resting state.

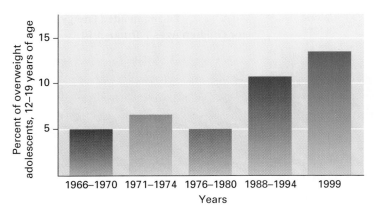

FIGURE 6.4 The Increase in Adolescent Obesity from 1968 to 1999 in the United States

In this study, being overweight was determined by body mass index (BMI), which is computed by a formula that takes into account height and weight (National Center for Health Statistics, 2000). Only adolescents above the 95th percentile in the overweight category were included in the study. There was a substantial increase in the percentage of adolescents who were overweight from 1968 to 1999.

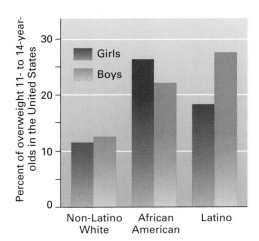

FIGURE 6.5 Percentage of Overweight U.S. Adolescent Boys and Girls in Different Ethnic Groups

anorexia nervosa An eating disorder that involves the relentless pursuit of thinness through starvation.

Inadequate levels of exercise are linked with being overweight (Ribeiro & others, 2003). A child's activity level is influenced by heredity but also by a child's motivation to engage in energetic activities and by caregivers who model an active lifestyle and provide children with opportunities to be active (French, Story, & Jeffery, 2001).

Prevention of obesity in children includes helping children and parents see food as a way to satisfy hunger and nutritional needs, not as proof of love or as a reward for good behavior (Hill & Trowbridge, 1998; Hodges, 2003). Routine physical activity should be a daily occurrence. The child's life should be centered around activities, not meals (Rotenstein, 2001; Schwartz & Puhl, 2003).

Eating Problems and Disorders in Adolescence Eating disorders have become increasing problems in adolescence (Garner & Desai, 2001). Here are some research findings involving adolescent eating disorders:

- Girls who felt negatively about their bodies in early adolescence were more likely to develop eating disorders two years earlier than their counterparts who felt more positively about their bodies (Attie & Brooks-Gunn, 1989).
- Negative parent-adolescent relationships were linked with increased dieting by girls over a one-year period (Archibald, Graber, & Brooks-Gunn, 1999).
- Girls who were both sexually active with their boyfriends and in pubertal transition were the most likely to be dieting or engaging in disordered eating patterns (Cauffman, 1994).
- Girls who were making a lot of effort to look like same-sex figures in the media were more likely than their peers to become very concerned about their weight (Field & others, 2001).
- Adolescent girls who watched four hours of television or more per day were more likely to be overweight than those who watched less than four hours a day (Dowda & others, 2001).
- A number of studies have revealed that adolescent girls have a strong desire to weigh less (Graber & Brooks-Gunn, 2001). One recent review found that social pressure to be thin fosters body dissatisfaction, which places individuals at risk for dieting and eating problems (Stice, 2002).
- In the last 40 years, an increasing percentage of adolescents have become overweight (see figure 6.4). A recent survey by the National Center for Health Statistics (2002) found that African American girls and Latino boys have especially high risks of being overweight during adolescence (see figure 6.5). Another recent study of 2,379 girls from 9 to 19 years of age found that the prevalence of being overweight was considerably higher for African American girls than non-Latino White girls (Kimm & others, 2002).

Let's now examine two eating disorders that may appear in adolescence: anorexia nervosa and bulimia nervosa.

Anorexia Nervosa Anorexia nervosa is an eating disorder that involves the relentless pursuit of thinness through starvation. Anorexia nervosa eventually can lead to death. Three main characteristics of persons with anorexia nervosa are these (Davison & Neale, 2001):

- Weighing less than 85 percent of what is considered normal for their age and height.
- Having an intense fear of gaining weight. The fear does not decrease with weight loss.
- Having a distorted image of their body shape (Smolak & Striegel-Moore, 2001). Even when they are extremely thin, they see themselves as too fat. They never

think they are thin enough, especially in the abdomen, buttocks, and thighs. They usually weigh themselves frequently, often take their body measurements, and gaze critically at themselves in mirrors.

Anorexia nervosa typically begins in the early to middle teenage years, often following an episode of dieting and the occurrence of some type of life stress. It is about ten times more likely in females than in males. When anorexia nervosa does occur in males, the symptoms and other characteristics (such as family conflict) are usually similar to those reported by females who have the disorder.

Most anorexics are White adolescent or young adult females from well-educated, middle- and upper-income families that are competitive and high-achieving (Fairburn & Harrison, 2003). They set high standards, become stressed about not being able to reach the standards, and are intensely concerned about how others perceive them (Striegel-Moore, Silberstein, & Rodin, 1993). Unable to meet these high expectations, they turn to something they can control: their weight.

The fashion image in the American culture that emphasizes "thin is beautiful" contributes to the incidence of anorexia nervosa. This image is reflected in the saying "You never can be too rich or too thin." The media portrays thin as beautiful in their choice of fashion models, which many adolescent girls want to emulate (Andrist, 2003).

Bulimia Nervosa   Anorexics control their eating by restricting it. Most bulimics cannot. **Bulimia nervosa** is an eating disorder in which the individual consistently follows a binge-and-purge eating pattern. The bulimic goes on an eating binge and then purges by self-inducing vomiting or using a laxative. Most binge-purge eaters are female in their late teens or early twenties. As with anorexics, most bulimics are preoccupied with food, have a strong fear of becoming overweight, and are depressed or anxious (Davison & Neale, 2001; May & Bacaltchuk, 2002). Unlike anorexia nervosa, the binge-and-purging of bulimia nervosa occurs within a normal weight range, which means that it often is difficult to detect (Orbanic, 2001).

Although many people binge and purge occasionally and some experiment with it, for a person to be considered to have a serious bulimic disorder, the episodes must occur at least twice a week for three months. Many bulimics once were somewhat overweight and began binging and purging during an episode of dieting (Schwitzer & others, 2001).

Exercise and Sports

How much exercise do children get? What are children's sports like?

Exercise   Are children getting enough exercise? In a 1997 national poll, only 22 percent of children in grades 4 through 12 were physically active for 30 minutes every day of the week (Harris, 1997). Their parents said their children were too busy watching TV, spending time on the computer, or playing video games to exercise much. Boys were more physically active at all ages than girls. In one historical comparison, the percentage of children involved in daily P.E. programs in schools decreased from 80 percent in 1969 to 20 percent in 1999 (Health Management Resources, 2001) (see figure 6.6).

In one recent study, activity habits of more than 1,000 African American and more than 1,000 non-Latino White girls were examined annually from 9 to 10 years of age to 18 to 19 years of age (Kimm & others, 2002). The study did not examine boys because it was designed to determine why more African American women than non-Latino White women become obese. At 9 to 10 years of age, most girls reported that they were engaging in some physical activity outside of school. However, by 16 to 17 years of age, 56 percent of African American girls and 31 percent of non-Latino White girls were not engaging in any regular physical activity in their spare time. By 18 to 19 years of age, the figures were 70 percent and 29 percent, respectively. In sum, substantial declines in physical activity occur during adolescence in

Anorexia nervosa has become an increasing problem for adolescent girls and young adult women. *What are some possible causes of anorexia nervosa?*

Eating Disorders

Anorexia Nervosa and Other Eating Disorders

bulimia nervosa An eating disorder that involves a binge-and-purge sequence on a regular basis.

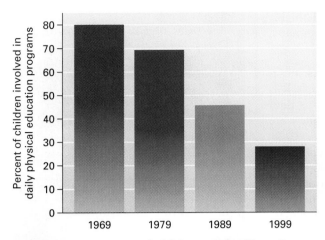

FIGURE 6.6 Percentage of Children Involved in Daily Physical Education Programs in the United States from 1969 to 1999

There has been a dramatic drop in the percentage of children participating in daily physical education programs in the United States from 80 percent in 1969 to only 20 percent in 1999.

girls and are greater in African American than non-Latino White girls (Kimm & Obarzanek, 2002).

Here are some ways to get children and adolescents to exercise more:

- Offer more physical activity programs run by volunteers at school facilities.
- Improve physical fitness activities in schools.
- Have children plan community and school activities that really interest them.
- Encourage families to focus more on physical activity and parents to exercise more (in the national poll more than 50 percent of the parents engaged in no vigorous physical activities on a regular basis).

Sports Sports have become an integral part of American culture. Thus, it is not surprising that more and more children become involved in sports every year. Both in public schools and in community agencies, children's sports programs that involve baseball, soccer, football, basketball, swimming, gymnastics, and other activities have grown to the extent that they have changed the shape of many children's lives.

Participation in sports can have both positive and negative consequences for children. Children's participation in sports can provide exercise, opportunities to learn how to compete, self-esteem, and a setting for developing peer relations and friendships. However, sports also can have negative outcomes for children: the pressure to achieve and win, physical injuries, a distraction from academic work, and unrealistic expectations for success as an athlete (Cheng & others, 2000; Committee on Sports Medicine and Fitness, 2000). Few people challenge the value of sports for children when conducted as part of a school physical education or intramural program. However, some critics question the appropriateness of highly competitive, win-oriented sports teams in schools and communities (Kelm & others, 2001; Washington & others, 2001).

The negative consequences of children's sports was tragically played out when Thomas Junta beat to death another father after their sons' ice hockey game in July 2001. He was sentenced to 6 to 10 years in prison in January 2002.

Children's Health and Illness in the United States and Around the World

In the United States, if a pediatrician stopped practicing 50 years ago and observed the illness and health of young children today, the sight might seem to be more science fiction than medical fact. The story of children's health in the past 50 years is a shift toward prevention and outpatient care. However, in many impoverished countries today, children's illnesses have not been reduced that much.

The United States How has children's illness changed in early childhood? What is the main cause of death in middle and late childhood? In adolescence?

Early Childhood In recent decades, vaccines have nearly eradicated disabling bacterial meningitis and have become available to prevent measles, rubella, mumps, and chicken pox. From 1950 to the present, there has been a dramatic decline in deaths of children under the age of 5 from birth immaturity, birth defects, accidents, cancer, homicide, and heart disease. The disorders still most likely to be fatal during early childhood today are birth defects, cancer, and heart disease. Although the dangers of many diseases for children have been greatly diminished, it still is important for parents to keep young children on an immunization schedule.

Accidents are the leading cause of death in young children (National Vital Statistics Reports, 2001) (see figure 6.7). Motor vehicle accidents, drowning, falls, and poisoning are high on the list of causes of death in young children (Brenner & others, 2001).

A special concern about children's illness and health is exposure to parental smoking. Estimates indicate that approximately 22 percent of children and adolescents in the United States are exposed to tobacco smoke in the home. An increasing number of studies reach the conclusion that children are at risk for health problems if they live in homes in which a parent smokes (Ehrlich & others, 2001):

- *Respiratory problems.* In one study, if the mother smoked, her children were twice as likely to have respiratory problems (Etzel, 1988). Research studies have found that children exposed to tobacco smoke in the home are more likely to experience wheezing symptoms and asthma than children in nonsmoking homes (Jaakkola, Nafstad, & Magnus, 2001; Mannino & others, 2001).
- *Vitamin C.* Environmental tobacco smoke also affects the amount of vitamin C in children and adolescents. In a recent study, when parents smoked at home their 4- to 18-year-old children and adolescents had significantly lower levels of vitamin C in their blood than their counterparts in nonsmoking homes (Strauss, 2001). And the more parents smoked, the less vitamin C the children and adolescents had.

Of special concern in the United States is the poor health status of many young children from low-income families. Approximately 11 million preschool children in the United States are malnourished, which places their health at risk. Many have less resistance to diseases, including minor ones, such as colds, and major ones, such as influenza.

There also is concern about lead poisoning in young children with an estimated 3 million children under 6 years of age estimated to be at risk for lead poisoning that might harm their development (Geltman, Brown, & Cochran, 2001). Children in poverty are at higher risk for lead poisoning than children living in higher socioeconomic conditions. Lead can get into children's bloodstreams through food or water that is contaminated by lead, from putting lead-contaminated fingers in their mouths, or from inhaling dust from lead-based paint. The negative effects of high lead levels in children's blood are found in lower intelligence and achievement, and children with attention deficit hyperactivity disorder (Soong & others, 1999).

Middle and Late Childhood

For the most part, middle and late childhood is a time of excellent health. Disease and death are less prevalent in this period than in others in childhood and adolescence.

The most common cause of severe injury and death in middle and late childhood is motor vehicle accidents, either as a pedestrian or as a passenger (Wong & others, 2001). The use of safety-belt restraints is important in reducing the severity of motor vehicle injuries. The school-age child's motivation to ride a bicycle increases the risk of accidents. Other serious injuries involve skateboards, roller skates, and other sports equipment.

Most accidents occur in or near the child's home or school. The most effective prevention strategy is to educate the child about the hazards of risk taking and improper use of equipment. Appropriate safety helmets, protective eye and mouth shields, and protective padding are recommended for children who engage in active sports.

Cancer is the second leading cause of death (with motor vehicle accidents the leading cause) in children 5 to 14 years of age. Three percent of all children's deaths in this age period are due to cancer. In the 15- to 24-year-old age group, cancer accounts for 13 percent of all deaths. Currently, 1 in every 330 children in the United States develops cancer before the age of 19. Morover, the incidence of cancer in children is increasing (Neglia & others, 2001).

Child cancers have a different profile from adult cancers. Adult cancers attack mainly the lungs, colon, breast, prostate, and pancreas. Child cancers mainly attack the white blood cells (leukemia), brain, bone, lymph system, muscles, kidneys, and nervous system. All are characterized by an uncontrolled proliferation of abnormal cells.

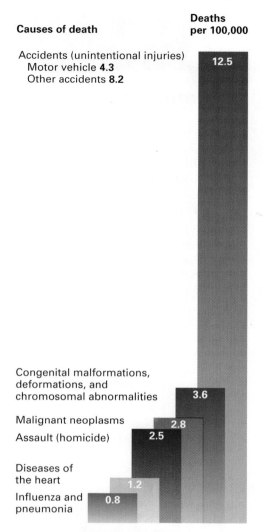

FIGURE 6.7 **Main Causes of Death in U.S. Children 1 Through 4 Years of Age**

These figures are based on the number of deaths per 100,000 children 1 through 4 years of age in the United States in 1999 (National Vital Statistics Reports, 2001).

Diseases and Illnesses

Medical Links

Cancer in Children

Careers in Child Development

Sharon McLeod, *Child Life Specialist*

Sharon McLeod is a child life specialist who is clinical director of the Child Life and Recreational Therapy Department at the Children's Hospital Medical Center in Cincinnati.

Under Sharon's direction, the goals of the Child Life Department are to promote children's optimal growth and development, reduce the stress of health-care experiences, and provide support to child patients and their families. These goals are accomplished through therapeutic play and developmentally appropriate activities, educating and psychologically preparing children for medical procedures, and serving as a resource for parents and other professionals regarding child development and health-care issues.

In Sharon's view, "Human growth and development coping theory, and play provide the foundation for the profession of child life. My most beneficial moments as a student were during my fieldwork and internship when I experienced hands-on theories and concepts learned in courses."

Sharon McLeod, child life specialist, working with a child at Children's Hospital Medical Center in Cincinnati.

As indicated in figure 6.8, the most common cancer in children is leukemia, a cancer of the tissues that make blood cells. In leukemia, the bone marrow makes an abundance of white blood cells that don't function properly. They invade the marrow and crowd out normal cells, making the child susceptible to bruising and infection. Lymphomas arise in the lymph system. Childhood lymphomas spread to the central nervous system and bone marrow.

Child life specialists are among the health professionals who try to make the lives of children with diseases such as cancer less stressful. To read about the work of child life specialist Sharon Mcleod, see the Careers in Child Development insert.

Adolescence Medical improvements have increased the life expectancy of today's adolescents compared to their counterparts who lived earlier, in the twentieth century. Still, life-threatening factors continue to exist in adolescents' lives.

The three leading causes of death in adolescence are accidents, homicide, and suicide. More than half of all deaths in adolescents ages 10 to 19 are due to accidents, and most of those involve motor vehicles, especially for older adolescents. Risky driving habits, such as speeding, tailgating, and driving under the influence of alcohol or other drugs, may be more important causes of these accidents than is lack of driving experience. In about 50 percent of the motor vehicle fatalities involving an adolescent, the driver has a blood alcohol level of 0.10 percent, twice the level needed to be "under the influence" in some states. A high rate of intoxication is also often present in adolescents who die as pedestrians or while using recreational vehicles.

Homicide is the second leading cause of death in adolescence (National Center for Health Statistics, 2001). Homicide is especially high among African American male adolescents, who are three times more likely to be killed by guns than by natural causes (Simons, Finlay, & Yang, 1991).

Suicide accounts for 6 percent of the deaths in the 10- to 14-year-old age group, a rate of 1.3 per 100,000 population. In the 15- to 19-year-old age group, suicide accounts for 12 percent of deaths or 9 per 100,000 population. Since the 1950s, the adolescent suicide rate has tripled.

Health and Illness in the World's Children A special concern is the state of children's illness and health in developing countries around the world. The most devastating effects occur in countries where poverty rates are high. The poor are the majority in nearly one of every five nations in the world (UNICEF, 2002). They often experience lives of hunger, malnutrition, illness, inadequate access to health care, unsafe water, and inadequate protection from harm.

A leading cause of child death in impoverished countries is diarrhea produced by dehydration. Giving the child a large volume of water and liquids usually prevents dehydration. Measles, tetanus, and whooping cough also still lead to the deaths of many children around the world, although increased immunization programs in the last several decades have led to a decrease in deaths due to these diseases (Foege, 2000).

In the last decade, there has been a dramatic increase in the number of children who have died because of HIV/AIDS transmitted to them by their parents (UNICEF, 2002). The uneducated are four times more likely to believe there is no way to avoid AIDS and three times more likely to be unaware that the virus can be transmitted from mother to child (UNICEF, 2002).

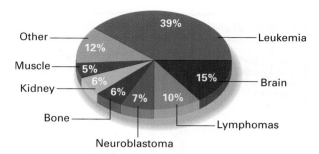

FIGURE 6.8 Types of Cancer in Children

Review and Reflect: Learning Goal 2

2 Describe children's and adolescents' health and illness

REVIEW

- What are children's health-care needs? Why is adolescence a critical juncture in health?
- What are children's energy needs? What types of eating problems can develop in childhood and adolescence?
- How much exercise do children get? What role does sports play in children's lives?
- What are children's health and illness like in the United States and around the world?

REFLECT

- What were your eating habits like as a young child? In what ways are they similar or different to your current eating habits? Were your early eating habits a forerunner of whether or not you have weight problems today?

---

3 PUBERTY AND ADOLESCENCE

- **Puberty and Sexuality**
- **Substance Use and Abuse**
- **The Interrelation of Problems and Successful Programs**
- **Today's Youth**

We already have discussed several aspects of physical development in adolescence, such as eating problems and adolescence as a critical juncture in health. Let's now explore the changes of puberty and further dimensions of adolescence. After the slow, methodical growth of middle and late childhood, children grow more rapidly during pubertal change. In this section we explore the nature of pubertal change as well as some important dimensions of adolescent development.

Puberty and Sexuality

One father remarked that the problem with his teenage son was not that he grew, but that he did not know when to stop growing. As we will see, there is considerable variation in the timing of the adolescent growth spurt.

Puberty　Puberty can be distinguished from adolescence. For most of us, puberty has ended long before adolescence is exited, although puberty is the most important

From *Penguin Dreams and Stranger Things,* by Berke Breathed. Copyright © 1985 by The Washington Post Company. By permission of Little, Brown & Company, Inc. Reprinted by permission of International Creative Management, Inc. Copyright © 1985 by Berkeley Breathed.

marker of the beginning of adolescence. What is puberty? **Puberty** is a period of rapid physical maturation involving hormonal and bodily changes that occur primarily during early adolescence.

Imagine a toddler displaying all the features of puberty—a 3-year-old girl with fully developed breasts or a boy just slightly older with a deep voice. That is what we would see by the year 2250 if the age at which puberty arrives kept getting younger at its present pace. In Norway, **menarche**—a girl's first menstruation—occurs at just over 13 years of age, compared to 17 years of age in the 1840s. In the United States—where children mature up to a year earlier than children in European countries—the average age of menarche has declined significantly since the mid nineteenth century (see figure 6.9). Fortunately, however, we are unlikely to see pubescent toddlers, since what has happened in the past century is likely the result of a higher level of nutrition and health. The available information suggests that menarche began to occur earlier at about the time of the Industrial Revolution, a period associated with increased standards of living and advances in medical science (Petersen, 1979).

Genetic factors also are involved in puberty. Puberty is not simply an environmental accident. As indicated earlier, while nutrition, health, and other factors affect puberty's timing and variations in its makeup, the basic genetic program is wired into the nature of the species (Plomin, 1993).

Another key factor in puberty's occurrence is body mass. Menarche occurs at a relatively consistent weight in girls. A body weight approximating 106 +/− 3 pounds can trigger menarche and the end of the pubertal growth spurt. For menarche to begin and continue, fat must make up 17 percent of the girl's body weight. Both teenage anorexics whose weight drops dramatically and female athletes in certain sports (such as gymnastics) may become amenorrheic (having an absence or suppression of menstrual discharge).

In summary, puberty's determinants include nutrition, health, heredity, and body mass. So far, our discussion of puberty has emphasized its dramatic changes. Keep in mind, though, that puberty is not a single, sudden event. We know when a young boy or girl is going through puberty, but pinpointing its beginning and its end is difficult. Except for menarche, which occurs rather late in puberty, no single marker heralds puberty. For boys, the first whisker or first wet dream is an event that could mark its appearance, but both may go unnoticed.

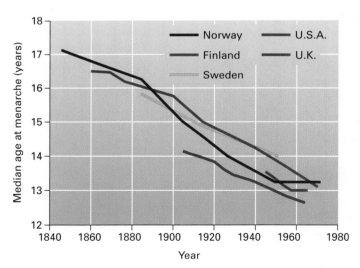

FIGURE 6.9 Median Ages at Menarche in Selected Northern European Countries and the United States from 1845 to 1969
Notice the steep decline in the age at which girls experienced menarche in five different countries. Recently the age at which girls experience menarche has been leveling off.

puberty A period of rapid physical maturation involving hormonal and bodily changes that occur mainly in early adolescence.

menarche A girl's first menstruation.

Hormonal Changes Behind the first whisker in boys and the widening of hips in girls is a flood of **hormones,** powerful chemical substances secreted by the endocrine glands and carried through the body by the bloodstream. The endocrine system's role in puberty involves the interaction of the hypothalamus, the pituitary gland, and the gonads (sex glands). The **hypothalamus** is a structure in the higher portion of the brain that monitors eating, drinking, and sex. The **pituitary gland** is an important endocrine gland that controls growth and regulates other glands. The **gonads** are the sex glands—the testes in males, the ovaries in females. How does this hormonal system work? The pituitary sends a signal via gonadotropins (hormones that stimulate the testes or ovaries) to the appropriate gland to manufacture the hormone. Then the pituitary gland, through interaction with the hypothalamus, detects when the optimal level of hormones is reached and responds by maintaining gonadotropin secretion.

The concentrations of certain hormones increase dramatically during adolescence (Dorn & Lucas, 1995; Steiner, Dunn, & Born, 2003; Susman & others, 1995). Testosterone is a hormone associated in boys with the development of genitals, an increase in height, and a change in voice. Estradiol is a hormone associated in girls with breast, uterine, and skeletal development. In one study, testosterone levels increased eighteenfold in boys but only twofold in girls during puberty; estradiol increased eightfold in girls but only twofold in boys (Nottelmann & others, 1987) (see figure 6.10). Note that both testosterone and estradiol are present in the hormonal makeup of both boys and girls but that testosterone dominates in male pubertal development, estradiol in female pubertal development.

The same influx of hormones that puts hair on a male's chest and imparts curvature to a female's breast may contribute to psychological development in adolescence (Dorn & Lucas, 1995). In one study of 108 normal boys and girls ranging in age from 9 to 14, a higher concentration of testosterone was present in boys who rated themselves more socially competent (Nottelmann & others, 1987). In another study of 60 normal boys and girls in the same age range, girls with higher estradiol levels expressed more anger and aggression (Inoff-Germain & others, 1988). However, hormonal effects by themselves do not account for adolescent development. For example, in one study, social factors accounted for two to four times as much variance as did hormonal factors in young adolescent girls' depression and anger (Brooks-Gunn & Warren, 1989). Also, behavior and moods can affect hormones (Paikoff, Buchanan, & Brooks-Gunn, 1991). Stress, eating patterns, exercise, sexual activity, tension, and depression can activate or suppress various aspects of the hormonal system. In sum, the hormone-behavior link is complex.

One additional aspect of the pituitary gland's role in development still needs to be described. Not only does the pituitary gland release gonadotropins that stimulate the testes and ovaries, but through interaction with the hypothalamus the pituitary gland also secretes hormones that either directly lead to growth and skeletal maturation or produce such growth effects through interaction with the thyroid gland, located in the neck region.

Height, Weight, and Sexual Maturation Among the most noticeable physical changes in adolescence are those that involve height and weight, as well as sexual maturation.

Height and Weight As indicated in figure 6.11, the growth spurt occurs approximately two years earlier for girls than for boys (Abbassi, 1998). The mean beginning of the growth spurt in girls is 9 years of age; for boys, it is 11 years of age.

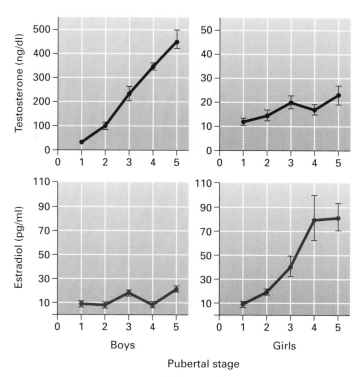

FIGURE 6.10 Hormone Levels by Sex and Pubertal Stage for Testosterone and Estradiol

The five stages range from the early beginning of puberty (stage 1) to the most advanced stage of puberty (stage 5). Notice the significant increase in testosterone in boys and the significant increase in estradiol in girls.

Pubertal Changes

hormones Powerful chemical substances secreted by the endocrine glands and carried through the body by the bloodstream.

hypothalamus A structure in the higher portion of the brain that monitors eating, drinking, and sex.

pituitary gland An important endocrine gland that controls growth and regulates other glands.

gonads The sex glands—the testes in males and the ovaries in females.

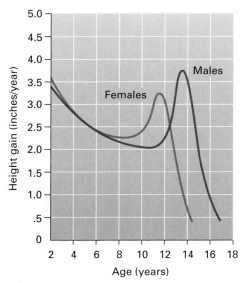

FIGURE 6.11 Pubertal Growth Spurt

On the average, the peak of the growth spurt that characterizes pubertal change occurs 2 years earlier for girls (11$\frac{1}{2}$) than for boys (13$\frac{1}{2}$).

Biological Changes

The peak rate of pubertal change occurs at 11$\frac{1}{2}$ years for girls and 13$\frac{1}{2}$ years for boys. During their growth spurt, girls increase in height about 3$\frac{1}{2}$ inches per year, boys about 4 inches.

Boys and girls who are shorter or taller than their peers before adolescence are likely to remain so during adolescence. In our society, there is a stigma attached to short boys. At the beginning of the adolescent period, girls tend to be as tall as or taller than boys of their age, but by the end of the middle school years most boys have caught up or, in many cases, have even surpassed girls in height. And, even though height in the elementary school years is a good predictor of height later in adolescence, there is still room for the individual's height to change in relation to the height of his or her peers. As much as 30 percent of the height of late adolescence is unexplained by height in the elementary school years.

The rate at which adolescents gain weight follows approximately the same developmental timetable as the rate at which they gain height. Marked weight gains coincide with the onset of puberty. During early adolescence, girls tend to outweigh boys, but, just as with height, by about age 14 boys begin to surpass girls.

Sexual Maturation   Think back to the onset of your puberty. Of the striking changes that were taking place in your body, what was the first change that occurred? Researchers have found that male pubertal characteristics develop in this order: increase in penis and testicle size, appearance of straight pubic hair, minor voice change, first ejaculation (which usually occurs through masturbation or a wet dream), appearance of kinky pubic hair, onset of maximum growth, growth of hair in armpits, more detectable voice changes, and growth of facial hair. Three of the most noticeable areas of sexual maturation in boys are penis elongation, testes development, and growth of facial hair. The normal range and average age of development for these sexual characteristics, along with height spurt, are shown in figure 6.12.

What is the order of appearance of physical changes in females? First, either the breasts enlarge or pubic hair appears. Later, hair appears in the armpits. As these changes occur, the female grows in height, and her hips become wider than her shoulders. Her first menstruation comes rather late in the pubertal cycle. Initially, her menstrual cycles may be highly irregular. For the first several years, she might not ovulate every menstrual cycle. Some girls do not become fertile until two years after the period begins. No voice changes comparable to those in pubertal males occur in pubertal females. By the end of puberty, the female's breasts have become more fully rounded. Two of the most noticeable aspects of female pubertal change are pubic hair and breast development. Figure 6.12 shows the normal range and average development of these sexual characteristics and also provides information about menarche and height gain.

Individual Variations in Puberty   The pubertal sequence may begin as early as 10 years of age or as late as 13$\frac{1}{2}$ for most boys. It may end as early as 13 years or as late as 17 years for most boys. The normal range is wide enough that, given two boys of the same chronological age, one might complete the pubertal sequence before the other one has begun it. For girls, the age range of the first menstrual period is even wider. Menarche is considered within a normal range if it appears between the ages of 9 and 15.

Body Image   One psychological aspect of physical change in puberty is certain: Adolescents are preoccupied with their bodies and develop individual images of what their bodies are like (McCabe & Ricciardelli, 2003). Perhaps you looked in the mirror on a daily and sometimes even hourly basis to see if you could detect anything different about your changing body. Preoccupation with one's body image is strong throughout adolescence, but it is especially acute during puberty, a time when adolescents are more dissatisfied with their bodies than in late adolescence (Wright, 1989).

There are gender differences in adolescents' perceptions of their bodies. In general, girls are less happy with their bodies and have more negative body images, compared with boys, throughout puberty (Brooks-Gunn & Paikoff, 1993). Also, as pubertal change proceeds, girls often become more dissatisfied with their bodies, probably because their body fat increases, while boys become more satisfied as they move through puberty, probably because their muscle mass increases.

Early and Late Maturation   Some of you entered puberty early, others late, and yet others on time. When adolescents mature earlier or later than their peers, might they perceive themselves differently? In the Berkeley Longitudinal Study some years ago, early-maturing boys perceived themselves more positively and had more successful peer relations than did their late-maturing counterparts (Jones, 1965). The findings for early-maturing girls were similar but not as strong as for boys. When the late-maturing boys were in their thirties, however, they had developed a stronger sense of identity than the early-maturing boys had (Peskin, 1967). Possibly this occurred because the late-maturing boys had more time to explore life's options or because the early-maturing boys continued to focus on their advantageous physical status instead of on career development and achievement.

More recent research confirms, though, that at least during adolescence it is advantageous to be an early-maturing rather than a late-maturing boy (Simmons & Blyth, 1987). The more recent findings for girls suggest that early-maturing girls experience more problems in school but also more independence and popularity with boys. The time that maturation is assessed also is a factor. In the sixth grade, early-maturing girls show greater satisfaction with their figures than do late-maturing girls, but by the tenth grade late-maturing girls are more satisfied (Simmons & Blyth, 1987) (see figure 6.13). The reason for this is that, in late adolescence, early-maturing girls are shorter and stockier, whereas late-maturing girls are taller and thinner. Late-maturing girls in late adolescence have bodies that more closely approximate the current American ideal of feminine beauty—tall and thin.

In the past decade, an increasing number of researchers have found that early maturation increases girls' vulnerability to a number of problems (Brooks-Gunn & Paikoff, 1993). Early-maturing girls are more likely to smoke, drink, be depressed, have an eating disorder, request earlier independence from their parents, and have older friends; and their bodies are likely to elicit responses from males that lead to earlier dating and earlier sexual experiences. In one study, the early-maturing girls had lower educational and occupational attainment in adulthood (Stattin & Magnusson, 1990). Apparently as a result of their social and cognitive immaturity, combined with early physical development, early-maturing girls are easily lured into problem behaviors, not recognizing the possible long-term effects of these on their development (Petersen, 1993; Sarigiani & Petersen, 2000).

Some researchers now question whether the effects of puberty are as strong as once believed (Petersen, 1993). Puberty affects some adolescents more strongly than others and some behaviors more strongly than others. Body image, dating interest, and sexual behavior are affected by pubertal change. The recent questioning of puberty's effects suggests that, in terms of overall development and adjustment in the human life span, pubertal variations (such as early and late maturation) are less dramatic than is commonly thought. In thinking about puberty's effects, keep in mind that an adolescent's world involves cognitive and socioemotional changes, as well as physical changes. As with all periods of development, these processes work in concert to produce who we are in adolescence.

Adolescent Sexuality   Adolescence is a time of sexual exploration and experimentation, of sexual fantasies and realities, of incorporating sexuality into one's identity. Adolescents have an almost insatiable curiosity about sexuality's mysteries. They think about whether they are sexually attractive, how to do sex, and what the future holds for their sexual lives. The majority of adolescents eventually manage to

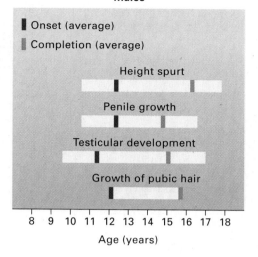

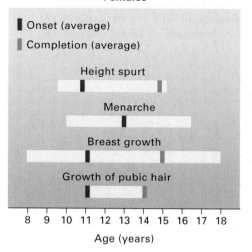

FIGURE 6.12 Normal Range and Average Development of Sexual Characteristics in Males and Females

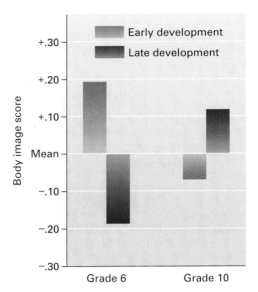

FIGURE 6.13 Early- and Late-Maturing Adolescent Girls' Perceptions of Body Image in Early and Late Adolescence

develop a mature sexual identity, but for most there are times of vulnerability and confusion along life's sexual journey.

Adolescence is a bridge between the asexual child and the sexual adult (Feldman, 1999). Every society gives some attention to adolescent sexuality. In some societies, adults clamp down and protect adolescent females from males by chaperoning them. Other societies promote very early marriage. Yet other societies, such as found in the United States, allow some sexual experimentation, although there is controversy about just how far sexual experimentation should be allowed to go.

An important point to keep in mind as you read about adolescent sexuality is that sexual development and interest are normal aspects of adolescent development and that the majority of adolescents have healthy sexual attitudes and engage in sexual practices that will not compromise their development (Feldman, 1999). In our discussion of adolescent sexuality, we will focus on developing a sexual identity, the progression of adolescent sexual behaviors, risk factors for sexual problems, contraceptive use, sexually transmitted infections, and adolescent pregnancy.

Developing a Sexual Identity Mastering emerging sexual feelings and forming a sense of sexual identity is multifaceted (Brooks-Gunn & Graber, 1999). This lengthy process involves learning to manage sexual feelings (such as sexual arousal and attraction), developing new forms of intimacy, and learning the skills to regulate sexual behavior to avoid undesirable consequences. Developing a sexual identity also involves more than just sexual behavior. It includes interfaces with other developing identities. Sexual identities emerge in the context of physical factors, social factors, and cultural factors, with most societies placing constraints on the sexual behavior of adolescents.

An adolescent's sexual identity involves an indication of sexual orientation (homosexual, heterosexual, bisexual), and it also involves activities, interests, and styles of behavior (Buzwell & Rosenthal, 1996). For example, some adolescents have a high anxiety level about sex, others a low level. Some adolescents are strongly aroused sexually, others less so. Some adolescents are very active sexually, others are virgins. Some adolescents are sexually inactive because of a strong religious upbringing, others go to church regularly and it does not inhibit their sexual activity (Thorton & Camburn, 1989).

Although the development of gay or lesbian identity has been widely studied in adults, few researchers have investigated the gay or lesbian identity (often referred to as the coming-out process) in adolescents. In one comprehensive survey of adolescent sexual orientation in almost 35,000 junior and senior high school students in Minnesota, 4.5 percent reported predominantly homosexual attractions (Remafedi & others, 1992). Homosexual identities, attractions, and behaviors increased with age. More than 6 percent of the 18-year-olds said they had predominantly homosexual attractions. How many of these youths later become gay is not known, although it is widely accepted that many adolescents who engage in homosexual behavior in adolescence do not continue the practice into adulthood.

One of the harmful aspects of the stigmatization of homosexuality is the self-devaluation engaged in by gay individuals (Savin-Williams, 2001). The common form of self-devaluation is called *passing*, the process of hiding one's real social identity. Passing strategies include giving out information that hides one's homosexual identity or avoiding one's true sexual identity. Passing behaviors include lying to others and saying, "I'm straight and attracted to opposite-sex individuals." Such defenses against self-recognition are heavily entrenched in our society. Without adequate support, and with fear of stigmatization, many gay and lesbian youth return to the closet and then reemerge at a safer time later, often in college. A special concern is the lack of support gay adolescents receive from parents, teachers, and counselors.

The Progression of Adolescent Sexual Behaviors Adolescents engage in a rather consistent progression of sexual behaviors (DeLamater & MacCorquodale, 1979). Necking usually comes first, followed by petting. Next comes intercourse, or, in some cases, oral sex, which has increased substantially in adolescence in recent years. In one recent study, 452 individuals 18 to 25 years of age were asked about their own past sexual experiences (Feldman, Turner, & Araujo, 1999). The following progression of sexual behaviors occurred: kissing preceded petting which preceded sexual intercourse and oral sex. Male adolescents reported engaging in these sexual behaviors approximately one year earlier than female adolescents.

Here is information from a national survey of adolescents that further reveals the timing of their sexual activities (Alan Guttmacher Institute, 1998):

What is the progression of sexual behaviors in adolescence?

- Most young adolescents have not had sexual intercourse: 8 in 10 girls and 7 in 10 boys are virgins at age 15.
- The probability that adolescents will have sexual intercourse increases steadily with age, but 1 in 5 individuals have not yet had sexual intercourse by age 19.
- Initial sexual intercourse occurs in the mid- to late-adolescent years for a majority of teenagers, about 8 years before they marry.
- The majority of adolescent females' first voluntary sexual partner are younger, the same age, or no more than 2 years older; 27 percent are 3 to 4 years older; and 12 percent are 5 or more years older.

In some areas of the United States, the percentages of sexually active young adolescents may be even greater. In an inner-city area of Baltimore, 81 percent of the males at age 14 said that they already had engaged in sexual intercourse. Other surveys in inner-city, low-income areas also reveal a high incidence of early sexual intercourse (Clark, Zabin, & Hardy, 1984).

In sum, by the end of adolescence the majority of U.S. adolescents have had sexual intercourse. Male, African American, and inner-city adolescents report being the most sexually active (Feldman, Turner, & Araujo, 1999). Although sexual intercourse can be a meaningful experience for older, mature adolescents, many adolescents are not emotionally prepared to handle sexual experiences, especially in early adolescence.

The timing of teenage sexual initiation varies by country and gender. In one study, among females, the proportion having first intercourse by age 17 ranged from 72 percent in Mali to 47 percent in the United States and 45 percent in Tanzania (Singh & others, 2000). The percentage of males who had their first intercourse by age 17 ranged from 76 percent in Jamaica to 64 percent in the United States and 63 percent in Brazil.

Risk Factors for Sexual Problems Although most adolescents become sexually active at some point during adolescence, some adolescents engage in sex at early ages (before age 16) and experience a number of partners over time. These adolescents are the least effective users of contraception and are at risk for early, unintended pregnancy and for sexually transmitted infections. Early sexual activity is also linked with other risky behaviors such as excessive drinking, drug use, delinquency, and school-related problems (Dryfoos, 1990). In one recent longitudinal study, sexual involvement by girls at an early age was linked with lower self-esteem, greater depression, greater sexual activity, and lower grades in high school (Buhrmester, 2001). Early sexual involvement by boys was related to greater substance abuse and sexual activity in the high school years in this study.

Risk factors for sexual problems in adolescence include contextual factors such as socioeconomic status (SES) and family/parenting circumstances. One recent research review found that living in a dangerous and/or low-income neighborhood were risk factors for adolescent pregnancy (Miller, Benson, & Galbraith, 2001). Also in this review, these aspects of parenting were linked with reduced risk of adolescent pregnancy: parent-adolescent closeness or connectedness, parental supervision or regulation of the adolescent's activities, and parental values against intercourse or unprotected intercourse in adolescence.

Contraceptive Use Sexual activity is a normal activity necessary for procreation, but it involves considerable risks if appropriate safeguards are not taken. There are two kinds of risks that youth encounter: unintended/unwanted pregnancy and sexually transmitted infections. Both of these risks can be reduced significantly by using contraception and barriers (such as condoms) (Moos, Bartholomew, & Lohr, 2003). Gay and lesbian youth who do not experiment with heterosexual intercourse are spared the risk of pregnancy, but, like their heterosexual peers, they still face the risk of sexually transmitted infections.

The good news is that adolescents are increasing their use of contraceptives (Child Trends, 2000). Adolescent girls' contraceptive use at first intercourse rose from 48 percent to 65 percent during the 1980s (Forrest & Singh, 1990). By 1995, use at first intercourse reached 78 percent, with two-thirds of that figure involving condom use. A sexually active adolescent who does not use contraception has a 90 percent chance of pregnancy within one year (Alan Guttmacher Institute, 1998). The method adolescent girls use most frequently is the pill (44 percent), followed by the condom (38 percent). About 10 percent use an injectable form of contraception, 4 percent use withdrawal, and 3 percent use an implant (Alan Guttmacher Institute, 1998). Approximately one-third of adolescent girls who rely on condoms also take the pill or practice withdrawal.

Although adolescent contraceptive use is increasing, many sexually active adolescents still do not use contraceptives, or they use them inconsistently (Ford, Sohn, & Lepkowski, 2001; Paukku & others, 2003). Sexually active younger adolescents are less likely than older adolescents to take contraceptive precautions. Younger adolescents are more likely to use a condom or withdrawal, whereas older adolescents are more likely to use the pill or a diaphragm. In one study, adolescent females reported changing their behavior in the direction of safer sex practices more than did adolescent males (Rimberg & Lewis, 1994).

The Alan Guttmacher Institute
CDC National Prevention Network
American Social Health Association
HIV/AIDS and Adolescents
Adolescent Pregnancy

Sexually Transmitted Infections   Sexually transmitted infections (STIs) are contracted primarily through sexual contact, which is not limited to sexual intercourse. Oral-genital and anal-genital contact also can transmit STIs.

Every year more than 3 million American adolescents (about one-fourth of those who are sexually experienced) acquire an STI (Centers for Disease Control and Prevention, 2002). In a single act of unprotected sex with an infected partner, a teenage girl has a 1 percent risk of getting HIV, a 30 percent risk of acquiring genital herpes, and a 50 percent chance of contracting gonorrhea (Glei, 1999). Chlamydia (which can spread by sexual contact and infects the genitals of both sexes) is more common among adolescents than among young adults. In some areas, as many as 25 percent of sexually active adolescents have contracted chlamydia (Donovan, 1993). In one recent cross-cultural study of sixteen developed countries, the incidence of chlamydia was high among adolescents in all of the countries (Panchaud & others, 2000). Adolescents also have a higher incidence of gonorrhea than young adults.

A special concern is the high incidence of AIDS in sub-Saharan Africa (World Health Organization, 2000). Adolescent girls in many African countries are vulnerable to infection with the HIV virus by adult men. Approximately six times as many adolescent girls as boys have AIDS in these countries, while in the United States adolescent males are more likely to have AIDS than their female counterparts (Centers for Disease Control and Prevention, 2002). In Kenya, 25 percent of the 15- to 19-year-old girls are HIV positive compared with 4 percent of the boys.

There continues to be great concern about AIDS in many parts of the world, not just sub-Saharan Africa. In the United States, prevention targets high-risk groups, such as individuals with other sexually transmitted infections, intravenous drug users, homosexual males, those living in poverty, and Latinos and African Americans (Centers for Disease Control and Prevention, 2002).

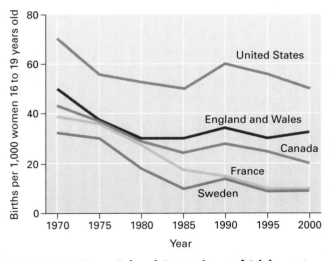

FIGURE 6.14 Cross-Cultural Comparisons of Adolescent Pregnancy Rates

sexually transmitted infections (STIs) Infections that are contracted primarily through sexual contact, which is not limited to sexual intercourse. Oral-genital and anal-genital contact also can transmit STIs.

Adolescent Pregnancy   In a recent cross-cultural comparison, the United States continued to have one of the highest adolescent pregnancy and childbearing rates in the industrialized world, despite a considerable decline in the 1990s (Alan Guttmacher Institute, 2002; Centers for Disease Control and Prevention, 2002). In 2000, U.S. adolescent birth rates for women ages 15 to 19 were higher than those in England and Wales and nearly five times the rates in Sweden and France (see figure 6.14 on page 190). The U.S. adolescent pregnancy rate is eight times as high as in the Netherlands. While U.S. adolescents are no more sexually active than their counterparts in the Netherlands, their adolescent pregnancy rate is dramatically higher.

There are encouraging trends, though, in U.S. adolescent pregnancy rates (Ventura & others, 2001). In 2000, births to adolescent girls fell to a record low (Centers for Disease Control and Prevention, 2002). For every 1,000 girls 15 to 19 years of age, there were 49 births—the lowest rate in six decades that the statistic has been kept. The rate of births to adolescent girls has dropped 22 percent since 1991. Reasons for the decline include increased contraceptive use, fear of sexually transmitted infections such as AIDS, and the economic prosperity of the 1990s, which may have motivated adolescents to delay starting a family so that they could take jobs. The greatest drop in U.S. adolescent pregnancy rates in the 1990s was for 15- to 17-year-old girls. There is a special concern about the continued high rate of adolescent pregnancy in Latinas (Child Trends, 2001).

The consequences of adolescent pregnancy are cause for concern (Koniak-Griffin & others, 2003). Adolescent pregnancy creates health risks for both the offspring and the mother. Infants born to adolescent mothers are more likely to have low birth weights—a prominent factor in infant mortality—as well as neurological problems and childhood illness (Dryfoos, 1990). Adolescent mothers often drop out of school. However, often it is not pregnancy alone that leads to negative consequences for an adolescent mother and her offspring (Brooks-Gunn & Paikoff, 1997; Feldman, 1999; Leadbeater & Way, 2001). Adolescent mothers are more likely to come from low-income backgrounds (Hoffman, Foster, & Furstenberg, 1993). Many adolescent mothers also were not good students before they became pregnant. One recent study found that adolescent childbearers were more likely to have a history of conduct problems, less educational attainment, and lower childhood socioeconomic status than later childbearers (Jaffee, 2002). However, early childbearing increased the difficulties associated with these risks.

Keep in mind that not every adolescent female who bears a child lives a life of poverty and low achievement. Thus, while adolescent pregnancy is a high-risk circumstance and in general adolescents who do not become pregnant fare better than those who do, some adolescent mothers do well in school and have positive outcomes (Ahn, 1994; Whitman & others, 2001). Serious, extensive efforts are needed to help pregnant adolescents and young mothers enhance their educational and occupational opportunities. Adolescent mothers also need extensive help in obtaining competent day care and in planning for the future.

Family and consumer science educators teach life skills to adolescents. Among the life skills they teach adolescents involves working with them to increase their responsibility for making effective decisions about sexuality. To read about the work of one family and consumer science educator, see the Careers in Child Development insert.

Careers in Child Development

Lynn Blankinship, *Family and Consumer Science Educator*

Lynn Blankinship is a family and consumer science educator. She has an undergraduate degree in this area from the University of Arizona. She has taught for more than 20 years, the last 14 at Tucson High Magnet School.

Lynn was awarded the Tucson Federation of Teachers Educator of the Year Award for 1999–2000 and the Arizona Teacher of the Year Award in 1999.

Lynn especially enjoys teaching life skills to adolescents. One of her favorite activities is having students care for an automated baby that imitates the needs of real babies. Lynn says that this program has a profound impact on students because the baby must be cared for around the clock for the duration of the assignment. Lynn also coordinates real-world work experiences and training for students in several child-care facilities in the Tucson area.

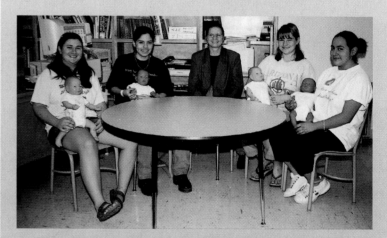

Lynn Blankinship (*center*), family and consumer science educator, with students caring for automated babies.

FIGURE 6.15 Trends in Drug Use by U.S. Eighth-, Tenth-, and Twelfth-Grade Students

This graph shows the percentage of U.S. eighth-, tenth-, and twelfth-grade students who reported having taken an illicit drug in the last 12 months from 1991 to 2002 for eighth- and tenth-graders, and from 1975 to 2002 for twelfth-graders (Johnston, O'Malley, & Bachman, 2003).

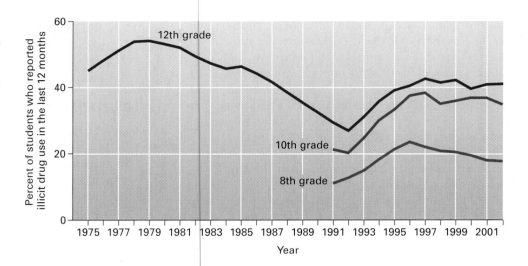

Substance Use and Abuse

The 1960s and 1970s were a time of marked increases in the use of illicit drugs. During the social and political unrest of those years, many youth turned to marijuana, stimulants, and hallucinogens. Increases in adolescent alcohol consumption during this period also were noted (Robinson & Greene, 1988). More precise data about drug use by adolescents have been collected in recent years.

Each year since 1975, Lloyd Johnston, Patrick O'Malley, and Gerald Bachman, working at the Institute of Social Research at the University of Michigan, have carefully monitored the drug use of America's high school seniors in a wide range of public and private high schools. Since 1991, they also have surveyed drug use by eighth- and tenth-graders. The University of Michigan study is called the Monitoring the Future Study. In 2002, the study surveyed approximately 44,000 students in nearly 400 secondary schools.

The use of drugs among U.S. secondary school students declined in the 1980s but began to increase in the early 1990s (Johnston, O'Malley, & Bachman, 2001). In the late 1990s and the first two years of the twenty-first century, the proportions of tenth- and twelfth-grade students' use of any illicit drug had been holding fairly steady, while eighth-graders were showing a slight decline in use (Johnston, O'Malley, & Bachman, 2003). In 2002, the proportion of students reporting the use of any illicit drug in the past 30 days declined at all three grade levels, significantly so in grades 8 and 10. Figure 6.15 shows the overall trends in drug use by U.S. high school seniors since 1975 and for tenth- and eighth-graders since 1991.

A special concern in recent years is the increase in the use of "club drugs," so labeled because they are popular at nightclubs and all-night dance parties called "raves." The main club drug is Ecstasy, a methamphetamine that also has hallucinogenic properties (see figure 6.16). Ecstasy use by U.S. adolescents peaked in the first two years of the twenty-first century but declined in 2002 (Johnston, O'Malley, & Bachman, 2003). Thirty-day prevalence of use in 2002, by eighth-, tenth-, and twelfth-graders was 1.4, 1.8, and 2.4 percent (down from 1.8, 2.6, and 2.8 percent in 2001). The downturn in reported use of Ecstasy in 2002 coincides with adolescents' increasing belief that Ecstasy can be dangerous (Johnston, O'Malley, & Bachman, 2003).

Nonetheless, even with the recent leveling off in use, the United States still has the highest rate of adolescent drug use of any industrialized nation. Also, the University of Michigan survey likely underestimates the percentage of adolescents who take drugs because it does not include high school dropouts, who have a higher rate of drug use than do students who are still in school. Johnston, O'Malley, and Bachman (1999) believe that "generational forgetting" contributed to the rise of adolescent drug use in the 1990s, with adolescents' beliefs about the dangers of drugs eroding considerably. The recent downturn in drug use by U.S. adolescents has been

 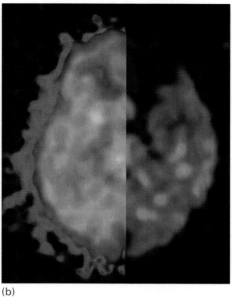

(a)   (b)

FIGURE 6.16 Ecstasy and the Adolescent's Brain

(*a*) In recent years, the use of Ecstasy by adolescents has become increasingly popular at nightclubs and all-night dance parties called "raves." (*b*) Ecstasy stimulates the release of the neurotransmitter serotonin in the brain, producing a euphoric high that lasts for several hours. However, Ecstasy also destroys nerve cells and affects areas of the brain responsible for learning and memory. The images show a brain scan of a normal brain (*left*) and a brain under the influence of Ecstasy (*right*). Notice the dramatic differences in cerebral activity in the two brains as reflected in their different coloring in the brain scans.

attributed to such factors as an increase in perceived dangers of drug use and the tragedy of the terrorist attacks of 9/11/01 having a sobering effect on youth (Johnston, O'Malley, & Bachman, 2003). Let's now consider separately a number of drugs that are used by adolescents.

Alcohol is the drug most widely used by U.S. adolescents. It has produced many enjoyable moments and many sad ones as well. Alcoholism is the third leading killer in the United States. Each year, approximately 25,000 individuals are killed and 1.5 million injured, by drunk drivers. In 65 percent of the aggressive male acts against females, the offender has been under the influence of alcohol (Goodman & others, 1986). In numerous instances of drunk driving and assaults on females, the offenders have been adolescents. More than 13 million individuals are classified as alcoholics, many of whom established their drinking habits during adolescence.

Alcohol use by eighth-, tenth-, and twelfth-graders dropped significantly at all three grade levels in the percentage of U.S. students saying that they had any alcohol to drink in the past 30 days (Johnston, O'Malley, & Bachman, 2003). The 30-day prevalence of alcohol use by eighth-graders has fallen from a 1996 high of 26 percent to 20 percent in 2002. From 2001 to 2002, 30-day prevalence among tenth-graders fell from 39 to 35 percent. Monthly prevalence among high school seniors was 72 percent in 1980 but had declined to 49 percent in 2002. Binge drinking (defined in the University of Michigan surveys as having five or more drinks in a row in the last two weeks) fell from 41 percent to 30 percent in 2002. Binge drinking by eighth- and tenth-graders also dropped in 2002 (7 percent of eighth-graders, 18 percent of tenth-graders). While still high, these rates are down from 1 to 4 percent from 2001. A consistent sex difference occurs in binge drinking, with males engaging in this more than females. In 1997, 39 percent of male high school seniors said they had been drunk in the last two weeks, compared to 29 percent of their female counterparts.

Cigarette Smoking Cigarette smoking (in which the active drug is nicotine) is one of the most serious yet preventable health problems. Smoking is likely to begin in grades 7 through 9, although sizable portions of youth are still establishing regular smoking habits during high school and college. Since the national surveys by Johnston, O'Malley, and Bachman began in 1975, cigarettes have been the substance most frequently used on a daily basis by high school seniors.

Smoking often begins in early adolescence. The peer group especially plays an important role in smoking (McRee & Gebelt, 2001). In one recent study, the risk of current smoking was linked with peer networks in which at least half of the

National Clearinghouse for Alcohol and Drug Information

Monitoring the Future

National Institute of Drug Abuse

FIGURE 6.17 Trends in Cigarette Smoking by U.S. Secondary School Students

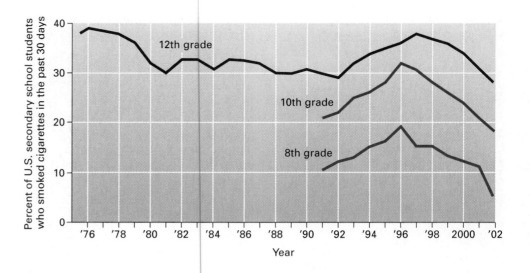

members smoked, one or two best friends smoked, and smoking was common in the school (Alexander & others, 2001).

The good news is that cigarette smoking is decreasing among adolescents. In the national survey by the Institute of Social Research, the percentage of U.S. adolescents who are current cigarette smokers continued to decline in 2002 (Johnston, O'Malley, & Bachman, 2003). Cigarette smoking peaked in 1996 and 1997 and since then had been gradually declining through 2001. In 2002, the decline in cigarette smoking by adolescents was substantial. For example, the percentage of eighth-, tenth-, and twelfth-graders who said they had ever smoked cigarettes dropped by 4 to 5 percentage points—more than any recent year. Following peak use in 1996, smoking rates for U.S. eighth-graders have fallen by 50 percent. Smoking in the past 30 years fell from 10.4 percent to 5.1 percent. As shown in figure 6.17, percentage declines in upper grades have been smaller, although the picture for older adolescents should improve in the next few years as a result of the current eighth-graders becoming older.

There are a number of explanations for the decline in cigarette use by U.S. youth. These include increasing prices, less tobacco advertising reaching adolescents, more antismoking advertisements, and an increase in negative publicity about the tobacco industry. Since the mid-1990s, an increasing percentage of adolescents have reported that they perceive cigarette smoking as dangerous, that they disapprove of it, that they are less accepting of being around smokers, and that they prefer to date nonsmokers (Johnston, O'Malley, & Bachman, 2003).

The devastating effects of early smoking were brought home in a research study that found that smoking in the adolescent years causes permanent genetic changes in the lungs and forever increases the risk of lung cancer, even if the smoker quits (Weincke & others, 1999). The damage was much less likely among smokers in the study who started in their twenties. One of the remarkable findings in the study was that the early age of onset of smoking was more important in predicting genetic damage than how much the individuals smoked.

The Roles of Development, Parents, and Peers Most adolescents become drug users at some point in their development, whether limited to alcohol, caffeine, and cigarettes or extended to marijuana, cocaine, and hard drugs. A special concern involves adolescents using drugs as a way of coping with stress, which can interfere with the development of competent coping skills and responsible decision making. Researchers have found that drug use in childhood or early adolescence has more detrimental long-term effects on the development of responsible, competent behavior than when drug use occurs in late adolescence (Newcomb & Bentler, 1988). When they use drugs to cope with stress, many young adolescents enter adult roles of marriage and work prematurely, without adequate socioemotional growth, and experience greater failure in adult roles.

How early are adolescents beginning drug use? National samples of eighth- and ninth-grade students were included for the first time in 1991 in the Institute for Social Research survey of drug use (Johnston, O'Malley, & Bachman, 1992). Early in the drug use increase in the United States (late 1960s, early 1970s), drug use was much higher among college students than among high school students, who in turn had much higher rates of drug use than middle or junior high school students. However, today the rates for college and high school students are similar, and the rates for young adolescents are not as different from those for older adolescents as might be anticipated.

Parents, peers, and social support play important roles in preventing adolescent drug abuse (Dishion, 2001; Reifman, 2001; Simons-Morton & others, 2001; Windle & Windle, 2003). Positive relationships with parents and others are important in reducing adolescents' drug use (Brody & Ge, 2001). In one recent study, low parental involvement, peer pressure, and associating with problem-behaving friends were linked with higher use of drugs by adolescents (Simons-Morton & others, 2001). Also, in a recent national survey, parents who were more involved in setting limits (such as where adolescents went after school and what they were exposed to on TV and the Internet) were more likely to have adolescents who did not use drugs (National Center for Addiction and Substance Abuse, 2000).

The Interrelation of Problems and Successful Programs

We have described some of the major adolescent problems in this chapter: substance abuse, adolescent pregnancy and sexually transmitted infections, and suicide. We also will discuss depression in chapter 11, "Emotional Development," examine juvenile delinquency in chapter 14, "Moral Development," and explore school-related problems in chapter 17, "Schools."

The most at-risk adolescents have more than one problem. Researchers are increasingly finding that problem behaviors in adolescence are interrelated (Tubman & Windle, 1995). For example, heavy substance abuse is related to early sexual activity, lower grades, dropping out of school, and delinquency. Early initiation of sexual activity is associated with the use of cigarettes and alcohol, the use of marijuana and other illicit drugs, lower grades, dropping out of school, and delinquency. Delinquency is related to early sexual activity, early pregnancy, substance abuse, and dropping out of school. As many as 10 percent of all adolescents in the United States have serious multiple-problem behaviors (for example, adolescents who have dropped out of school, are behind in their grade level, are users of heavy drugs, regularly use cigarettes and marijuana, and are sexually active but do not use contraception). Many, but not all, of these very high-risk youth "do it all." Another 15 percent of adolescents participate in many of these behaviors but with slightly lower frequency and less deleterious consequences. These high-risk youth often engage in two- or three-problem behaviors (Dryfoos, 1990).

In addition to understanding that many adolescents engage in multiple-problem behaviors, it also is important to develop programs that reduce adolescent problems. In a review of the programs that have been successful in preventing or reducing adolescent problems, adolescent researcher Joy Dryfoos (1990) described the common components of these successful programs:

1. *Intensive individualized attention.* In successful programs, high-risk children are attached to a responsible adult, who gives the child attention and deals with the child's specific needs. This theme occurs in a number of programs. In a successful substance-abuse program, a student assistance counselor is available full-time for individual counseling and referral for treatment.
2. *Community-wide multiagency collaborative approaches.* The basic philosophy of community-wide programs is that a number of different programs and services have to be in place. In one successful substance-abuse program, a community-wide health promotion campaign has been implemented that uses local media and community education, in concert with a substance-abuse curriculum in the schools.

3. *Early identification and intervention.* Reaching children and their families before children develop problems, or at the beginning of their problems, is a successful strategy (Botvin, 1999). One preschool program serves as an excellent model for the prevention of delinquency, pregnancy, substance abuse, and dropping out of school. Operated by the High Scope Foundation in Ypsilanti, Michigan, the Perry Preschool has had a long-term positive impact on its students. This enrichment program, directed by David Weikart, serves disadvantaged African American children. They attend a high-quality two-year preschool program and receive weekly home visits from program personnel. Based on official police records, by age 19, individuals who had attended the Perry Preschool program were less likely to have been arrested and reported fewer adult offenses than a control group. The Perry Preschool students also were less likely to drop out of school, and teachers rated their social behavior as more competent than that of a control group who had not received the enriched preschool experience.

Today's Youth

Today's adolescents face demands and expectations, as well as risks and temptations, that appear to be more numerous and complex than those faced by adolescents only a generation ago. Nonetheless, contrary to the popular stereotype of adolescents as highly stressed and incompetent, the vast majority of adolescents successfully negotiate the path from childhood to adulthood. By some criteria, today's adolescents are doing better than their counterparts from a decade or two earlier. Today, more adolescents complete high school, especially African American adolescents. The majority of adolescents today have a positive self-concept and positive relationships with others.

A cross-cultural study by Daniel Offer and his colleagues (1988) supported the contention that most adolescents have positive images of themselves and contradicted the stereotype that most adolescents have problems or are disturbed in some way. The self-images of adolescents around the world were sampled—in the United States, Australia, Bangladesh, Hungary, Israel, Italy, Japan, Taiwan, Turkey, and West Germany. A healthy self-image characterized at least 73 percent of the adolescents studied. They appeared to be moving toward adulthood with a healthy integration of previous experiences, self-confidence, and optimism about the future. Although there were some differences among the adolescents, they were happy most of the time, they enjoyed life, they perceived themselves as able to exercise self-control, they valued work and school, they expressed confidence about their sexual selves, they expressed positive feelings toward their families, and they felt they had the capability to cope with life's stresses.

According to adolescent researchers Shirley Feldman and Glen Elliott (1990), public attitudes about adolescence emerge from a combination of personal experience and media portrayals, neither of which produce an objective picture of how normal adolescents develop. Some of the readiness to assume the worst about adolescents likely involves the short memories of adults. Many adults measure their current perceptions of adolescents by their memories of their own adolescence. Adults may portray today's adolescents as more troubled, less respectful, more self-centered, more assertive, and more adventurous than they were.

However, in matters of taste and manners, the young people of every generation have seemed radical, unnerving, and different from adults—different in how they look, in how they behave, in the music they enjoy, in their hairstyles, and in the clothing they choose. It is an enormous error, though, to confuse adolescents' enthusiasm for trying on new identities and enjoying moderate amounts of outrageous behavior with hostility toward parental and societal standards. Acting out and boundary testing are time-honored ways in which adolescents move toward accepting, rather than rejecting, parental values.

Although the majority of adolescents experience the transition from childhood to adulthood more positively than is portrayed by many adults and the media, too

Growing up has never been easy. However, adolescence is not best viewed as a time of rebellion, crisis, pathology, and deviance. A far more accurate vision of adolescence describes it as a time of evaluation, of decision making, of commitment, and of carving out a place in the world. Most of the problems of today's youth are not with the youth themselves. What adolescents need is access to a range of legitimate opportunities and to long-term support from adults who deeply care about them. *What might be some examples of such support and caring?*

many adolescents today are not provided with adequate opportunities and support to become competent adults. In many ways, today's adolescents are presented with a less stable environment than adolescents of a decade or two ago. High divorce rates, high adolescent pregnancy rates, and increased geographic mobility of families contribute to this lack of stability in adolescents' lives. Today's adolescents are exposed to a complex menu of lifestyle options through the media, and, although the rate of adolescent drug use is beginning to show signs of decline, the rate of adolescent drug use in the United States is higher than that of any other country in the industrialized Western world. Many of today's adolescents face these temptations, as well as sexual activity, at increasingly younger ages.

Our discussion underscores an important point about adolescents: They do not make up a homogeneous group (Damon, 2003; Perkins & Borden, 2003). Most adolescents negotiate the lengthy path to adult maturity successfully, but too large a group does not. Ethnic, cultural, gender, socioeconomic, age, and lifestyle differences influence the actual life trajectory of every adolescent. Different portrayals of adolescence emerge, depending on the particular group of adolescents being described.

www.mhhe.com/santrockcd10

Practical Resources and Research

Adolescent Issues

Profile of America's Youth

Trends in the Well-Being of America's Youth

Review and Reflect: Learning Goal 3

3 Explain the changes of puberty and adolescence

REVIEW

- What changes take place in puberty? What characterizes adolescent sexuality?
- What is the extent of substance use and abuse in adolescence?
- How are adolescent problems interrelated, and what are the key components of successful programs for preventing or intervening in adolescent problems?
- How can today's youth be characterized?

REFLECT

- Did you experience puberty on time or off time (early or late)? How did this affect your development?

Reach Your Learning Goals

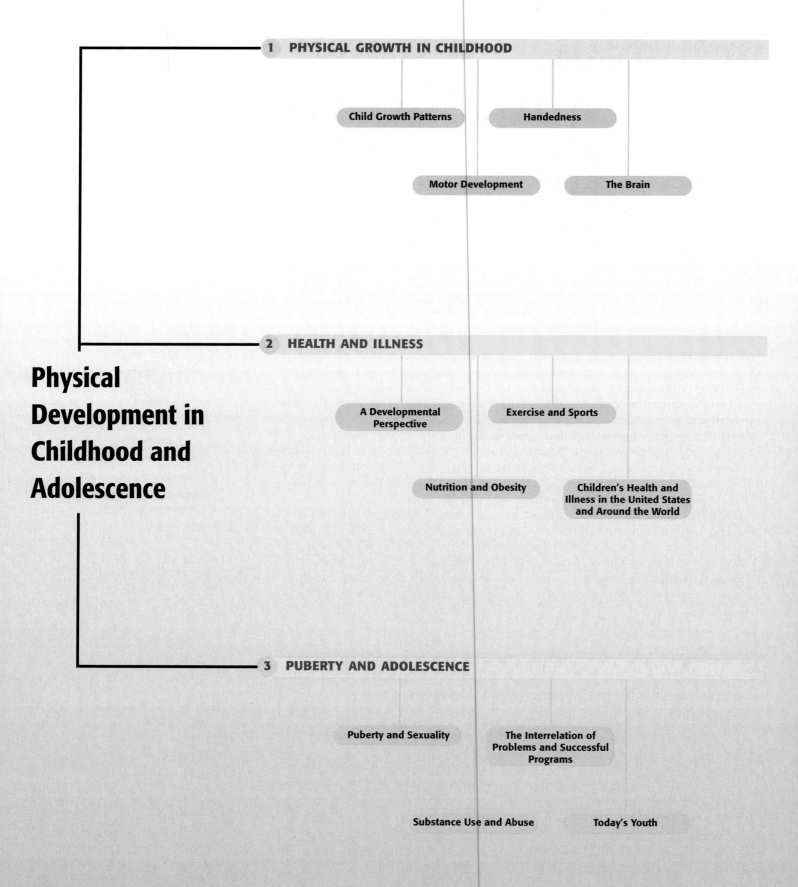

Physical Development in Childhood and Adolescence

1 PHYSICAL GROWTH IN CHILDHOOD

- Child Growth Patterns
- Handedness
- Motor Development
- The Brain

2 HEALTH AND ILLNESS

- A Developmental Perspective
- Exercise and Sports
- Nutrition and Obesity
- Children's Health and Illness in the United States and Around the World

3 PUBERTY AND ADOLESCENCE

- Puberty and Sexuality
- The Interrelation of Problems and Successful Programs
- Substance Use and Abuse
- Today's Youth

Summary

1 Discuss physical growth in childhood

- The average child grows $2^{1}/_{2}$ inches in height and gains 5 to 7 pounds a year during early childhood. Growth patterns, though, vary individually. Some children are unusually short because of congenital (physical) problems, others possibly because of emotional problems.
- Children's motor development becomes much smoother and more coordinated. Gross and fine motor skills improve considerably in early childhood. Boys are usually better at gross motor skills, girls are often better at fine motor skills.
- In today's world, the strategy is to let children use the hand they prefer. Handedness likely has a genetic link. About 90 percent of children are right-handed, 10 percent left-handed. Left-handers are more likely to process speech in the right hemisphere of the brain than right-handers, and left-handers have more reading problems. Left-handers often show up in higher than expected numbers as mathematicians, musicians, architects, and artists. Left-handers tend to have unusually good visuospatial skills.
- By age 5, the brain has reached nine-tenths of its adult size. The neurotransmitter dopamine increases considerably from 3 to 6 years of age. Some of the increase in the brain's size is due to increases in the size and number of nerve endings, some to myelination. Development of the brain in adolescence may be linked to changes in emotional development. Increasing brain maturation contributes to improved cognitive abilities.

2 Describe children's and adolescents' health and illness

- Only recently have researchers applied a developmental perspective to children's health. Children's health-care needs involve their motor, cognitive, and social development. Adolescence is a critical juncture in health because many of the factors linked to poor health habits and early death in the adult years begin in adolescence.
- In the middle and late childhood years, children's average body weight doubles and children expend considerable energy in various motor activities. Because of their increased size, weight, and motor activity, children need to consume more calories than when they were younger. Energy requirements for individual children are influenced by basal metabolism rate. Within a recommended calorie range, it is important to impress on children the value of a balanced diet. However, obesity is an increasing problem in childhood and it is related to a number of physical problems, as well as lower self-esteem and increased depression. Eating disorders have become increasing problems in adolescence, especially anorexia nervosa and bulimia nervosa.
- Every indication is that North America's children are not getting enough exercise. Television viewing, parents being poor role models for exercise, and the lack of adequate physical education classes might be the culprits. Children's participation in sports can have positive and negative consequences.
- In recent decades, vaccines have eradicated many diseases that once were responsible for many child deaths. The disorders most likely to be fatal for children today are birth defects, cancer, and heart disease. Accidents are the number one cause of death in young children followed by cancer. Children are at risk for health problems if they live in a home in which a parent smokes. A special concern is the poor health status of many children from low-income families. For the most part, middle and late childhood is a time of excellent health. The three leading causes of death in adolescence are accidents, homicide, and suicide. A special concern are children's illness and health in impoverished countries. A leading cause of child death in these countries is diarrhea produced by dehydration. There also has been a dramatic increase in the number of children who have died because of HIV/AIDS transmitted to them by their parents in low-income countries.

3 Explain the changes of puberty and adolescence

- Puberty is a period of rapid skeletal and sexual maturation that involves hormonal and bodily changes that occur mainly in early adolescence. Puberty's determinants include nutrition, health, heredity, and body mass. The endocrine system's influence on puberty involves an interaction with the hypothalamus, the pituitary gland, and the gonads (sex glands). Testosterone plays an important role in male pubertal development; estradiol plays an important role in female pubertal development. The initial onset of pubertal growth occurs, on the average, at 9 years for girls, 11 years for boys, reaching a peak change at $11^{1}/_{2}$ for girls and $13^{1}/_{2}$ for boys. Sexual maturation is a predominant feature of pubertal change. Adolescents show a heightened interest in body image. Girls have more negative body images in adolescence than boys do. Early maturation favors boys over girls, at least during adolescence. As adults, though, men who were late-maturing achieve more competent identities than men who were early-maturing. Researchers are increasingly finding that early-maturing girls are vulnerable to a number of problems. Mastering emerging sexual feelings and forming a sense of sexual identity involve multiple factors. National U.S. data indicate that by age 19, four of five individuals have had sexual intercourse. Risk factors for sexual problems include poverty and early sexual activity. Contraceptive use by U.S. adolescents is increasing. About one in four U.S. adolescents has a sexually transmitted infection (STI). America's adolescent pregnancy rate is one of the world's highest but it has been decreasing in recent years.
- The 1960s and 1970s were a time of marked increase in the use of illicit drugs. Drug use began to decline in the 1980s

but increased again in the 1990s. Since the mid-1990s, there has been a decline in the overall use of illicit drugs by U.S. adolescents. The United States has one of the highest rates of adolescent drug use of any industrialized nation. A special recent concern is the increased use of Ecstasy by youth. Alcohol abuse is a major adolescent problem, although its rate, as well as the rate of cigarette smoking, has been dropping in recent years. Drug use in childhood or early adolescence is linked with more negative outcomes than drug use that begins in late adolescence. Parents and peers are important influences on drug use by adolescents.

- At-risk adolescents often have more than one major problem. Common components of successful programs include individualized attention, community-wide intervention, and early identification and intervention.
- Many stereotypes of adolescents are too negative. The majority of adolescents successfully negotiate the path from childhood to adulthood. Too many of today's youth, though, are not provided with adequate opportunities and support. Different portraits of adolescents emerge depending on the particular set of adolescents being described.

Key Terms

deprivation dwarfism 170
myelination 173
basal metabolism rate
   (BMR) 177

anorexia nervosa 178
bulimia nervosa 179
puberty 184
menarche 184

hormones 185
hypothalamus 185
pituitary gland 185
gonads 185

sexually transmitted infections
   (STIs) 190

Key People

David Hamburg 176
Lloyd Johnston, Patrick O'Malley, and Gerald Bachman 192

Joy Dryfoos 195
Daniel Offer 196

Shirley Feldman and Glenn
   Elliott 196

Taking It to the Net

1. Janice and Derek are both left-handed. What are the chances that their son, Kyle, will be left-handed?
2. Rashad and Gloria are overcome with guilt over the news that their 5-year-old daughter, Briana, has leukemia. They can't stop thinking that they had it in their genes and passed it on to her. Their friends, Tom and Nancy, want to find some facts to reassure Rashad and Gloria that they aren't responsible for Briana's cancer.
3. Dana's part-time job involves helping in a community center's after-school program for inner-city elementary school chil-

dren. Many of the children eat too much junk food, have low energy levels, and are overweight. She wants to institute an exercise program as part of each day's activities. What are some things that Dana should keep in mind?

Connect to **www.mhhe.com/santrockcd10** to research the answers and complete these exercises.

E-Learning Tools

To help you master the material in this chapter, you'll find a number of valuable study tools on the Student CD-ROM that accompanies this book. Also visit the Online Learning Center for *Child Development*, tenth edition (**www.mhhe.com/santrockcd10**) where you'll find these additional resources:

- Build your decision-making skills by trying your hand at the parenting, nursing, and education "Scenarios" on the Online Learning Center.

Cognition and Language

Learning is an ornament in prosperity, a refuge in adversity.

—ARISTOTLE
Greek Philosopher, 4th Century B.C.

Children thirst to know and understand. In their effort to know and understand, they construct their own ideas about the world around them. They are remarkable for their curiosity and their intelligence. In Section 3, you will read four chapters: "Cognitive Developmental Approaches" (chapter 7), "Information Processing" (chapter 8), "Intelligence" (chapter 9), and "Language Development" (chapter 10).

We are born capable of learning.

—JEAN-JACQUES ROUSSEAU
*Swiss-Born French Philosopher,
18th Century*

Cognitive Developmental Approaches

Chapter Outline

Learning Goals

PIAGET'S COGNITIVE DEVELOPMENTAL THEORY

Jean Piaget and His Place in Developmental Psychology

Cognitive Developmental Theory and Processes

1 Discuss Piaget's place in developmental psychology and the key dimensions of his theory

PIAGET'S STAGES

Sensorimotor Thought

Preoperational Thought

Concrete Operational Thought

Formal Operational Thought

2 Describe Piaget's four stages of cognitive development

APPLYING AND EVALUATING PIAGET'S THEORY

Piaget and Education

Evaluating Piaget's Theory

3 Apply Piaget's theory to education and evaluate his theory

VYGOTSKY'S THEORY OF COGNITIVE DEVELOPMENT

The Zone of Proximal Development

Scaffolding

Language and Thought

Vygotsky and Education

Evaluating and Comparing Vygotsky's Theory and Piaget's Theory

4 Summarize Vygotsky's theory and compare it with Piaget's theory

The Stories of Laurent, Lucienne, and Jacqueline

Jean Piaget, the famous Swiss psychologist, was a meticulous observer of his three children—Laurent, Lucienne, and Jacqueline. His books on cognitive development are filled with these observations. Here are a few of Piaget's observations of his children's cognitive development in infancy (Piaget, 1952).

- At 21 days of age, Laurent finds his thumb after three attempts; once he finds his thumb, prolonged sucking begins. But, when he is placed on his back, he doesn't know how to coordinate the movement of his arms with that of his mouth; his hands draw back, even when his lips seek them.
- During the third month, thumb sucking becomes less important to Laurent because of new visual and auditory interests. But, when he cries, his thumb goes to the rescue.
- Toward the end of Lucienne's fourth month, while she is lying in her crib, Piaget hangs a doll above her feet. Lucienne thrusts her feet at the doll and makes it move. Afterward, she looks at her motionless foot for a second, then kicks at the doll again. She has no visual control of her foot because her movements are the same whether she only looks at the doll or it is placed over her head. By contrast, she does have tactile control of her foot; when she tries to kick the doll and misses, she slows her foot movements to improve her aim.
- At 11 months, while seated, Jacqueline shakes a little bell. She then pauses abruptly so she can delicately place the bell in front of her right foot; then she kicks the bell hard. Unable to recapture the bell, she grasps a ball and places it in the same location where the bell was. She gives the ball a firm kick.
- At 1 year, 2 months, Jacqueline holds in her hands an object that is new to her: a round, flat box that she turns over and shakes; then she rubs it against her crib. She lets it go and tries to pick it up again. She succeeds only in touching it with her index finger, being unable to fully reach and grasp it. She keeps trying to grasp it and presses to the edge of her crib. She makes the box tilt up, but it nonetheless falls again. Jacqueline shows an interest in this result and studies the fallen box.
- At 1 year, 8 months, Jacqueline arrives at a closed door with a blade of grass in each hand. She stretches her right hand toward the doorknob but detects that she cannot turn it without letting go of the grass, so she puts the grass on the floor, opens the door, picks up the grass again, and then enters. But, when she wants to leave the room, things get complicated. She puts the grass on the floor and grasps the doorknob. Then she perceives that, by pulling the door toward her, she simultaneously chases away the grass that she had placed between the door and the threshold. She then picks up the grass and places it out of the door's range of movement.

For Piaget, these observations reflect important changes in the infant's cognitive development. Later in the chapter, you will learn that Piaget believed that infants go through six substages of development and that the behaviors you have just read about characterize those substages.

This chapter focuses on two main cognitive developmental approaches—Piaget's theory and Vygotsky's theory. These two major approaches share some basic ideas about how children's development proceeds but also differ in their views on some key aspects of development.

1 PIAGET'S COGNITIVE DEVELOPMENTAL THEORY

| Jean Piaget and His Place in Developmental Psychology | Cognitive Developmental Theory and Processes |

What is Piaget's place in developmental psychology? What are the key dimensions of his theory?

Jean Piaget and His Place in Developmental Psychology

In discussing Sigmund Freud's contribution to psychology, Edwin Boring (1950) remarked that it is not likely that a history of general psychology could be written in the next three centuries without mention of Freud's name and still claim to be a general history of psychology. Indeed, the best criterion of greatness might be posthumous fame. Four decades after Boring published his book, it seems likely that his judgment was accurate—Freud is still a dominating presence in psychology. However, Jean Piaget's contribution to developmental psychology may be as important as Freud's contribution to personality and abnormal behavior. Piaget's death was rather recent (he died in 1980), so it may be too early to judge, but Piaget's contributions will be strongly felt for the foreseeable future. He truly is a giant in the field of developmental psychology.

Shortly after Piaget's death, John Flavell (1980, p. 1), a leading Piagetian scholar, described what we owe Piaget:

> First, we owe him a host of insightful concepts of enduring power and fascination . . . concepts of object permanence, conservation, assimilation, accommodation, and decentration, for example. Second, we owe him a vast conceptual framework that has highlighted key issues and problems in human cognitive development. This framework is the now-familiar vision of the developing child, who, through its own active and creative commerce with its environment, builds an orderly succession of cognitive structures en route to intellectual maturity. These two debts add up to a third, more general one: We owe him the present field of cognitive development. . . . Our task is now to extend and go beyond what he began so well.

Cognitive Developmental Theory and Processes

What characterizes cognitive developmental theory? What cognitive processes are responsible for changes in a child's development in this theory?

Piaget stressed that children construct their own cognitive worlds. Information is not just poured into their minds from the environment. Children use schemas to make sense of what they experience. A **schema** is a concept or framework that already exists at a given moment in a child's mind and that organizes information and provides a structure for interpreting it. Schemas are expressed as various behaviors and skills that the child can exercise in relation to objects or situations. For example, sucking is an early, simple schema. Later, more complex schemas might include licking, blowing, crawling, hiding, and so on. Piaget's interest in schemas had to do with how they help in organizing and making sense out of current experience.

Piaget (1954) said that two processes, which we first described in chapter 2, "The Science of Child Development," are responsible for how children use and adapt their schemas: assimilation and accommodation. page 34 Recall that *assimilation* occurs when children incorporate new information. That is, children *assimilate* the environment into a schema. For example, a schema in a child's mind might provide the information that some objects can be picked up. The first time a child realizes

www.mhhe.com/santrockcd10

The Jean Piaget Society

Jean Piaget, the famous Swiss developmental psychologist, dramatically changed the way we think about children's cognitive development.

schema A concept or framework that already exists at a given moment in a child's mind and that organizes information and provides a structure for organizing it.

that she might pick up a set of keys, she is assimilating the category "keys" into the schema of "picking up."

Accommodation occurs when children adjust their schemas to new information. That is, children *accommodate* their schemas to the environment. For example, a child might possess the schema of "picking up." With experience, the child might learn that some things can be picked up easily between two fingers, that other things might require both hands and strong use of the arms, and that still other things cannot be picked up at all because they are too hot, for example, or too heavy. Thus, the schema "picking up" becomes modified into different schemas that *accommodate* the realities of different types of objects.

Piaget also emphasized that, to make sense out of their world, children cognitively organize their experiences. **Organization** is Piaget's concept of grouping isolated behaviors into a higher-order, more smoothly functioning cognitive system. Every level of thought is organized. Continual refinement of this organization is an inherent part of development. A boy who has only a vague idea about how to use a hammer might also have a vague idea about how to use other tools. After learning how to use each one, he must interrelate these uses, or organize his knowledge, if he is to become skilled in using tools. In the same way, children continually integrate and coordinate the many other branches of knowledge that often develop independently. Organization occurs within stages of development as well as across them.

Equilibration is a mechanism that Piaget proposed to explain how children shift from one stage of thought to the next. The shift occurs as children experience cognitive conflict or disequilibrium in trying to understand the world. Eventually, the child resolves the conflict and reaches a balance, or equilibrium, of thought. Piaget believed there is considerable movement between states of cognitive equilibrium and disequilibrium as assimilation and accommodation work in concert to produce cognitive change. For example, if a child believes that an amount of liquid changes simply because it is poured into a container with a different shape (from a container that is short and wide into a container that is tall and narrow), she might be puzzled by such issues as where the "extra" liquid came from and whether there is actually more liquid to drink. The child will eventually resolve these puzzles as her thought becomes more advanced. In the everyday world, the child is constantly faced with such counterexamples and inconsistencies.

Piaget also believed that we go through four stages in understanding the world. ◀ **page 34** Each of the stages is age related and consists of distinct ways of thinking. Remember, it is the *different* way of understanding the world that makes one stage more advanced than another; knowing *more* information does not make a child's thinking more advanced, in the Piagetian view. This is what Piaget meant when he said a child's cognition is *qualitatively* different in one stage compared with another.

organization Piaget's concept of grouping isolated behaviors into a higher-order, more smoothly functioning cognitive system; the grouping or arranging of items into categories.

equilibration A mechanism that Piaget proposed to explain how children shift from one stage of thought to the next. The shift occurs as children experience cognitive conflict or disequilibrium in trying to understand the world. Eventually, they resolve the conflict and reach equilibrium of thought.

Review and Reflect: Learning Goal 1

1 Discuss Piaget's place in developmental psychology and the key dimensions of his theory

REVIEW

- What is Piaget's place in developmental psychology?
- What are the key dimensions and processes in Piaget's theory?

REFLECT

- Try to come up with two examples of assimilation and two examples of accommodation beyond those described in the text.

2 PIAGET'S STAGES

> **Sensorimotor Thought**

> **Concrete Operational Thought**

> **Preoperational Thought**

> **Formal Operational Thought**

Piaget proposed that cognitive development consists of four main stages: sensorimotor, preoperational, concrete operational, and formal operational. We briefly discussed these four stages in chapter 2, "The Science of Child Development." Here we will cover the stages in greater depth.

Sensorimotor Thought

Poet Nora Perry asked, "Who knows the thoughts of the child?" As much as anyone, Piaget knew. Through careful, inquisitive interviews and observations of his own three children—Laurent, Lucienne, and Jacqueline—Piaget changed our perceptions of the way infants think about their world. Two of the most important features of sensorimotor thought involve the child's coordination of sensation and action and the nonsymbolic aspects of the period.

According to Piaget, the sensorimotor stage lasts from birth to about 2 years of age, corresponding to the period of infancy. During this time, mental development is characterized by considerable progression in the infant's ability to organize and coordinate sensations with physical movements and actions—hence the name *sensorimotor* (Piaget, 1952).

At the beginning of the sensorimotor stage, the infant has little more than reflexive patterns with which to work. By the end of the stage, the 2-year-old has complex sensorimotor patterns and is beginning to operate with a primitive system of symbols. Unlike other stages, the sensorimotor stage is subdivided into six substages, each of which involves qualitative changes in sensorimotor organization.

As we saw earlier, the concept of *schema* is an important one in Piaget's theory. Within a substage, there can be different schemas. For example, substage 1 includes sucking, rooting, and blinking. In substage 1, the schemas are basically reflexive. From substage to substage, the schemas change in organization. This change is at the heart of Piaget's description of the stages. The six substages of sensorimotor development are (1) simple reflexes; (2) first habits and primary circular reactions; (3) secondary circular reactions; (4) coordination of secondary circular reactions; (5) tertiary circular reactions, novelty, and curiosity; and (6) internalization of schemes.

Simple reflexes is Piaget's first sensorimotor stage, which corresponds to the first month after birth. In this substage, the basic means of coordinating sensation and action is through reflexive behaviors. These include rooting and sucking, which the infant has at birth. In substage 1, the infant exercises these reflexes. More important, the infant develops an ability to produce behaviors that resemble reflexes in the absence of obvious reflexive stimuli. The newborn may suck when a bottle or nipple is only nearby, for example. When the baby was just born, the bottle or nipple would have produced the sucking pattern only when placed directly in its mouth or touched to the lips. Reflexlike actions in the absence of a triggering stimulus are evidence that the infant is initiating action and is actively structuring experiences in the first month of life.

First habits and primary circular reactions is Piaget's second sensorimotor substage, which develops between 1 and 4 months of age. In this substage, the infant learns to coordinate sensation and types of schemes or structures—that is, habits and primary circular reactions. A *habit* is a scheme based on a simple reflex, such as sucking, that has become completely separated from its eliciting stimulus. For

Piaget's Stages
Sensorimotor Development
Cognitive Milestones

simple reflexes Piaget's first sensorimotor substage, which corresponds to the first month after birth. The basic means of coordinating sensation and action is through reflexive behaviors, such as rooting and sucking, which infants have at birth.

first habits and primary circular reactions Piaget's second sensorimotor substage, which develops between 1 and 4 months of age. Infants learn to coordinate sensation and types of schemes or structures—that is, habits and primary circular reactions.

example, an infant in substage 1 might suck when orally stimulated by a bottle or when visually shown the bottle. However, an infant in substage 2 might exercise the sucking scheme even when no bottle is present. A **primary circular reaction** is a scheme based on the infant's attempt to reproduce an interesting or pleasurable event that initially occurred by chance. In a popular Piagetian example, a child accidentally sucks his fingers when they are placed near his mouth. Later, he searches for his fingers to suck them again, but the fingers do not cooperate in the search because the infant cannot coordinate visual and manual actions. Habits and circular reactions are stereotyped, in that the infant repeats them the same way each time. The infant's own body remains the center of attention. There is no outward pull by environmental events. Next, you will see that Piaget's second substage of infant development also involves the concept of "circular reaction," which Piaget used to describe repetitive actions that take different forms.

Secondary circular reactions is Piaget's third sensorimotor substage, which develops between 4 and 8 months of age. In this substage, the infant becomes more object-oriented or focused on the world, moving beyond preoccupation with the self in sensorimotor interactions. The chance shaking of a rattle, for example, may fascinate the infant. The infant will repeat this action for the sake of experiencing fascination. The infant imitates some simple actions of others, such as the baby talk or burbling of adults, and some physical gestures. However, these imitations are limited to actions the infant is already able to produce. Although directed toward objects in the world, the infant's schemes lack an intentional, goal-directed quality.

Coordination of secondary circular reactions is Piaget's fourth sensorimotor substage, which develops between 8 and 12 months of age. In this substage, several significant changes take place that involve the coordination of schemes and intentionality. Infants readily combine and recombine previously learned schemes in a *coordinated way.* They might look at an object and grasp it simultaneously, or they might visually inspect a toy, such as a rattle, and finger it simultaneously in obvious tactile exploration. Actions are even more outwardly directed than before. Related to this coordination is the second achievement—the presence of *intentionality,* the separation of means and goals in accomplishing simple feats. For example, infants might manipulate a stick (the means) to bring a desired toy within reach (the goal). They might knock over one block to reach and play with another one.

Tertiary circular reactions, novelty, and curiosity is Piaget's fifth sensorimotor substage, which develops between 12 and 18 months of age. In this substage, infants become intrigued by the variety of properties that objects possess and by the many things they can make happen to objects. A block can be made to fall, spin, hit another object, and slide across the ground. **Tertiary circular reactions** are schemes in which the infant purposely explores new possibilities with objects, continually changing what is done to them and exploring the results. Piaget says that this stage marks the developmental starting point for human curiosity and interest in novelty. Previous circular reactions have been devoted exclusively to reproducing former events, with the exception of imitation of novel acts, which occurs as early as substage 4. The tertiary circular act is the first to be concerned with novelty.

Internalization of schemes is Piaget's sixth and final sensorimotor substage, which develops between 18 and 24 months of age. In this substage, the infant's mental functioning shifts from a purely sensorimotor plane to a symbolic plane, and the infant develops the ability to use primitive symbols. For Piaget, a *symbol* is an internalized sensory image or word that represents an event. Primitive symbols permit the infant to think about concrete events without directly acting them out or perceiving them. Moreover, symbols allow the infant to manipulate and transform the represented events in simple ways. In a favorite Piagetian example, Piaget's young daughter saw a matchbox being opened and closed. Sometime later, she mimicked the event by opening and closing her mouth. This was an obvious expression of her image of the event. In another example, a child opened a door slowly to avoid dis-

primary circular reactions Schemes based on the infant's attempt to reproduce an interesting or pleasurable event that initially occurred by chance.

secondary circular reactions Piaget's third sensorimotor substage, which develops between 4 and 8 months of age. Infants become object-oriented or focused on the world, moving beyond preoccupation with the self in sensorimotor interactions.

coordination of secondary circular reactions Piaget's fourth sensorimotor substage, which develops between 8 and 12 months of age. In this substage, several significant changes take place involving the coordination of schemes and intentionality.

tertiary circular reactions, novelty, and curiosity Piaget's fifth sensorimotor substage, which develops between 12 and 18 months of age. Infants become intrigued by the variety of properties that objects possess and by the multiplicity of things they can make happen to objects.

tertiary circular reactions Schemes in which the infant purposely explores new possibilities with objects, continually changing what is done to them and exploring the results.

internalization of schemes Piaget's sixth sensorimotor substage, which develops between 18 and 24 months of age. In this substage, infants' mental functioning shifts from a purely sensorimotor plane to a symbolic plane, and they develop the ability to use primitive symbols.

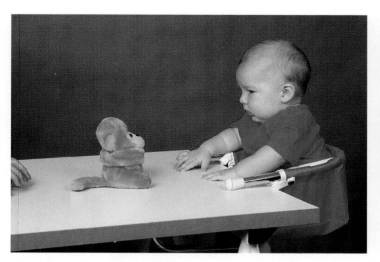 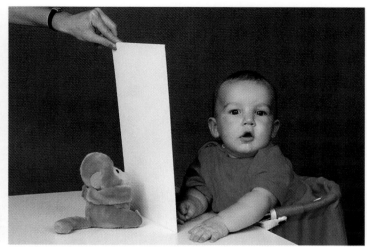

FIGURE 7.1 Object Permanence

Piaget thought that object permanence is one of infancy's landmark cognitive accomplishments. For this 5-month-old boy, "out-of-sight" is literally out of mind. The infant looks at the toy monkey (*left*), but, when his view of the toy is blocked (*right*), he does not search for it. Several months later, he will search for the hidden toy monkey, reflecting the presence of object permanence.

turbing a piece of paper lying on the floor on the other side. Clearly, the child had an image of the unseen paper and what would happen to it if the door opened quickly. However, developmentalists have debated whether 2-year-olds really have such representations of action sequences at their command (Corrigan, 1981).

Understanding Physical Reality   Piaget thought that children, even infants, are much like little scientists, examining the world to see how it works. Developmentalists are interested in how infants' knowledge of the physical world develops (Bremner, 2002). Two aspects of infants' understanding of physical reality involve the permanence of objects and cause and effect.

Object Permanence   **Object permanence** is the Piagetian term for one of an infant's most important accomplishments: understanding that objects and events continue to exist even when they cannot directly be seen, heard, or touched. Imagine what thought would be like if you could not distinguish between yourself and your world. Your thought would be chaotic, disorganized, and unpredictable. This is what the mental life of a newborn is like, according to Piaget. There is no self-world differentiation and no sense of object permanence. By the end of the sensorimotor period, however, both are present.

The principal way that object permanence is studied is by watching an infant's reaction when an interesting object or event disappears (see figure 7.1). If infants show no reaction, it is assumed they believe the object no longer exists. By contrast, if infants are surprised at the disappearance and search for the object, it is assumed they believe it continues to exist.

In one research study focused on object permanence, Renée Baillargeon (1986) showed 6- and 8-month-old infants a toy car that moved down an inclined track, disappeared behind a screen, and then reemerged at the other end, still on the track. After this same sequence was repeated several times, the infants then saw something different take place. A box was placed behind the screen, in one instance next to the track (a possible event), in another instance directly on the track (an impossible event). Then the infants watched the toy car go from one side of the screen to the other. Infants looked longer at the impossible event than at the possible event. This indicated they remembered not only that the box still existed (object permanence) but its location.

> *I* wish I could travel by the road that crosses the baby's mind, and out beyond all bounds; where messengers run errands for no cause between the kingdoms of kings of no history; where reason makes kites of her laws and flies them, and truth sets facts free from its fetters.
>
> —RABINDRANATH TAGORE
> *Bengali Poet, Essayist, 20th Century*

object permanence The Piagetian term for one of an infant's most important accomplishments: understanding that objects and events continue to exist even when they cannot directly be seen, heard, or touched.

FIGURE 7.2 The Six Substages of Object Permanence

Sensorimotor Stage	Behavior
Substage 1	There is no apparent object permanence. When a spot of light moves across the visual field, an infant follows it but quickly ignores its disappearance.
Substage 2	A primitive form of object permanence develops. Given the same experience, the infant looks briefly at the spot where the light disappeared, with an expression of passive expectancy.
Substage 3	The infant's sense of object permanence undergoes further development. With the newfound ability to coordinate simple schemes, the infant shows clear patterns of searching for a missing object, with sustained visual and manual examination of the spot where the object apparently disappeared.
Substage 4	The infant actively searches for a missing object in the spot where it disappeared, with new actions to achieve the goal of searching effectively. For example, if an attractive toy has been hidden behind a screen, the infant may look at the screen and try to push it away with a hand. If the screen is too heavy to move or is permanently fixed, the infant readily substitutes a secondary scheme—for example, crawling around it or kicking it. These new actions signal that the infant's belief in the continued existence of the missing object is strengthening.
Substage 5	The infant now is able to track an object that disappears and reappears in several locations in rapid succession. For example, a toy may be hidden under different boxes in succession in front of the infant, who succeeds in finding it. The infant is apparently able to hold an image of the missing object in mind longer than before.
Substage 6	The infant can search for a missing object that disappeared and reappeared in several locations in succession, as before. In addition, the infant searches in the appropriate place even when the object has been hidden from view as it is being moved. This activity indicates that the infant is able to "imagine" the missing object and to follow the image from one location to the next.

According to Piaget, object permanence develops in a series of substages that correspond to the six substages of sensorimotor development. Figure 7.2 shows how the six substages of object permanence reflect Piaget's substages of sensorimotor development.

Although Piaget's stage sequence is the best summary of what might happen as an infant fathoms the permanence of things in the world, some contradictory findings have emerged (Baillargeon, 1995; Xu & Carey, 1995). Piaget's stages broadly describe the interesting changes reasonably well, but an infant's life is not neatly packaged into distinct areas of organization as Piaget believed. Some of Piaget's explanations for the causes of change are debated.

Piaget claimed that certain processes are crucial in stage transitions, but the data do not always support his explanations. For example, according to Piaget the critical requirement for an infant to progress into sensorimotor substage 4 is the coordination of vision and the sense of touch, or hand-eye coordination. Another important feature in the progression into substage 4 is an infant's inclination to search for an object hidden in a familiar location rather than to look for the object in a new location. The **AB̄ error** is the Piagetian object-permanence concept in which an infant progressing into substage 4 makes frequent mistakes, selecting the familiar hiding place (A) rather than new hiding places (B̄). Researchers have found, however, that the AB̄ error does not show up consistently (Corrigan, 1981; Sophian, 1985). There is also accumulating evidence that AB̄ errors are sensitive to the delay between hiding an object at B̄ and the infant's attempt to find it (Diamond, 1985). Thus, the

AB̄ error The Piagetian object-permanence concept in which an infant progressing into substage 4 makes frequent mistakes, selecting the familiar hiding place (A) rather than the new hiding place (B̄).

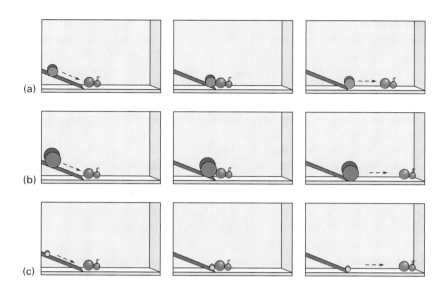

FIGURE 7.3 The Infants' Understanding of Causality

After young infants saw how far the medium-sized cylinder (*a*) pushed a toy bug, they showed more surprise at the event in (*c*) that showed a very small cylinder pushing the toy bug as far as the large cylinder (*b*). Their surprise, indicated by looking at (*c*) longer than (*b*), indicated that they understood the size of a cylinder was a causal factor in determining how far the toy bug would be pushed when it was hit by the cylinder.

A$\overline{\text{B}}$ error might be partly due to the failure of memory. And the A$\overline{\text{B}}$ error might be due to a lack of maturation of the frontal cortex of the brain (Diamond, 1995).

Causality   Piaget was very interested in infants' knowledge of cause and effect. His conclusions about infants' understanding of cause and effect were based mainly on his observations of the extent to which infants acted to produce a desired outcome, such as pushing aside an obstacle to reach a goal.

One study focused on understanding of causality found that even young infants comprehend that the size of a moving object determines how far it will move a stationary object if it collides with it (Kotovsky & Baillargeon, 1994) (see figure 7.3). In this research, a cylinder rolls down a ramp and hits a toy bug that is located at the bottom of the ramp. By 5½ to 6½ months of age, infants understand that the bug will roll farther if it is hit by a large cylinder than if it is hit by a small cylinder after they have observed how far it will be pushed by a medium-sized cylinder. Thus, by the middle of the first year of life, these infants understood that the size of the cylinder was a causal factor in determining how far the bug would move if it was hit by the cylinder.

At this point we have discussed a number of characteristics of Piaget's stage of sensorimotor development. To help you remember the main characteristics of sensorimotor thought, see figure 7.4.

Evaluating Piaget's Sensorimotor Stage   Piaget opened up a whole new way of looking at infants by describing how their main task is to coordinate their sensory impressions with their motor activity. However, some cognitive changes occur earlier than Piaget thought, and some of Piaget's explanations for the cause of change are debated.

Piaget constructed his view of infancy mainly by observing the development of his own three children. Few laboratory techniques were available at the time. In the past several decades, sophisticated experimental techniques have been devised to study infants, and there have been a large number of research studies on infant development. Much of the new research suggests that Piaget's view of sensorimotor development needs to be modified (Meltzoff, 2000). The two research areas that have led researchers to a somewhat different understanding of infant development are (1) perceptual development and (2) conceptual development.

Ability to organize and coordinate sensations with physical movements

Is nonsymbolic through most of its duration

Consists of six sub-stages of cognitive development

Object permanence develops

FIGURE 7.4 The Main Characteristics of Sensorimotor Thought, According to Piaget

Perceptual Development   A number of theorists, such as Eleanor Gibson (2001) and Elizabeth Spelke (1991; Spelke & Newport, 1998), believe that infants' perceptual abilities are highly developed very early in development.   ◀ **page 152** For example, Spelke has demonstrated that infants as young as 4 months of age have intermodal perception—the ability to coordinate information from two or more sensory modalities, such as vision and hearing. Other research, by Renée Baillargeon (1995), documents that infants as young as 4 months expect objects to be substantial (in the sense that other objects cannot move through them) and permanent (in the sense that objects continue to exist when they are hidden). In sum, researchers believe that infants see objects as bounded, unitary, solid, and separate from their background, possibly at birth or shortly thereafter, but definitely by 3 to 4 months of age. Young infants still have much to learn about objects, but the world appears both stable and orderly to them and, thus, capable of being conceptualized. Infants are continually trying to structure and make sense of their world (Meltzoff & Gopnik, 1997).

Conceptual Development   It is more difficult to study what infants are thinking about than to study what they see. Still, researchers have devised ways to assess whether or not infants are thinking. One strategy is to look for symbolic activity, such as using a gesture to refer to something. Piaget (1952) used this strategy to document infants' motor recognition. For example, he observed his 6-month-old daughter make a gesture when she saw a familiar toy in a new location. She was used to kicking at the toy in her crib. When she saw it across the room, she made a brief kicking motion. However, Piaget did not consider this to be true symbolic activity because it was a motor movement, not a purely mental act. Nonetheless, Piaget suggested that his daughter was referring to, or classifying, the toy through her actions (Mandler, 1998). In a similar way, infants whose parents use sign language have been observed to start using conventional signs at about 6 to 7 months of age (Bonvillian, Orlansky, & Novack, 1983).

In summary, many of today's researchers believe that Piaget wasn't specific enough about how infants learn about their world and that infants are far more competent than Piaget envisioned (Meltzoff, 2000). Recent research on infants' perceptual and conceptual development suggests that infants have more sophisticated perceptual abilities and can begin to think earlier than Piaget envisioned. These researchers believe that infants either are born with or acquire these abilities early in their development (Mandler, 1998).

Piaget's view is a general, unifying story of how biology and experience sculpt the infant's cognitive development: Assimilation and accommodation always take the infant to higher ground through a series of substages. And for Piaget, the motivation for change is general, an internal search for equilibrium. However, like much of the modern world, today the field of infant cognition is very specialized. There are many researchers working on different questions, with no general theory emerging that can connect all of the different findings (Nelson, 1999). Their theories are local theories, focused on specific research questions, rather than grand theories like Piaget's (Kuhn, 1998). If there is a unifying theme, it is that investigators in infant development struggle with the big issue of nature and nurture.

Preoperational Thought

The cognitive world of the preschool child is creative, free, and fanciful. The imagination of preschool children works overtime and their mental grasp of the world improves. When Piaget described the preschool child's cognition as *preoperational,* what did he mean?

Because this stage of thought is called preoperational, it might seem that not much of importance occurs until full-fledged operational thought appears. Not so. The preoperational stage stretches from approximately 2 to 7 years of age. It is a time when stable concepts are formed, mental reasoning emerges, egocentrism begins strongly and then weakens, and magical beliefs are constructed. Preopera-

www.mhhe.com/santrockcd10

Cognitive Milestones

Challenges to Piaget

Infant Cognition

*I*nfants are creating concepts and organizing their world into conceptual domains that will form the backbone of their thought throughout life.

—JEAN MANDLER
Contemporary Psychologist,
University of California–San Diego

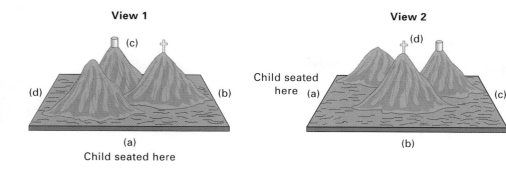

View 1

View 2

Child seated here (a)

Child seated here

FIGURE 7.5 The Three Mountains Task

View 1 shows the child's perspective from where he or she is sitting. View 2 is an example of the photograph the child would be shown, mixed in with others from different perspectives. To correctly identify this view, the child has to take the perspective of a person sitting at spot (b). Invariably, a preschool child who thinks in a preoperational way cannot perform this task. When asked what a view of the mountains looks like from position (b), the child selects a photograph taken from location (a), the child's view at the time.

tional thought is anything but a convenient waiting period for concrete operational thought. However, the label *preoperational* emphasizes that the child at this stage does not yet think in an operational way. What are operations? **Operations** are internalized sets of actions that allow children to do mentally what before they did physically. Operations are highly organized and conform to certain rules and principles of logic. The operations appear in one form in concrete operational thought and in another form in formal operational thought. Thought in the preoperational stage is flawed and not well organized. Preoperational thought is the beginning of the ability to reconstruct at the level of thought what has been established in behavior. Preoperational thought also involves a transition from primitive to more sophisticated use of symbols. Preoperational thought can be divided into two substages: the symbolic function substage and the intuitive thought substage.

Symbolic Function Substage

The **symbolic function substage** is the first substage of preoperational thought, occurring roughly between the ages of 2 and 4. In this substage, the young child gains the ability to mentally represent an object that is not present. The ability to engage in such symbolic thought is called *symbolic function,* and it vastly expands the child's mental world. Young children use scribbled designs to represent people, houses, cars, clouds, and so on. Other examples of symbolism in early childhood are language and the prevalence of pretend play. In sum, the ability to think symbolically and to represent the world mentally predominates in this early substage of preoperational thought. However, although young children make distinct progress during this substage, their thought still has several important limitations, two of which are egocentrism and animism.

Egocentrism is an important characteristic of preoperational thought. It is the inability to distinguish between one's own perspective and someone else's perspective. This telephone conversation between 4-year-old Mary, who is at home, and her father, who is at work, typifies Mary's egocentric thought:

Father: Mary, is Mommy there?
Mary: (Silently nods)
Father: Mary, may I speak to Mommy?
Mary: (Nods again silently)

Mary's response is egocentric in that she fails to consider her father's perspective before replying. A nonegocentric thinker would have responded verbally.

Piaget and Barbel Inhelder (1969) initially studied young children's egocentrism by devising the three mountains task (see figure 7.5). The child walks around the model of the mountains and becomes familiar with what the mountains look like from different perspectives, and they can see that there are different objects on the mountains. The child is then seated on one side of the table on which the mountains are placed. The experimenter moves a doll to different locations around the table, at each location asking the child to select, from a series of photos, the one photo that most accurately reflects the view the doll is seeing. Children in the preoperational stage often pick their view from where they are sitting, rather than the doll's view. Perspective taking does not develop uniformly in preschool children, who frequently show perspective skills on some tasks but not others.

Symbolic Thinking

www.mhhe.com/santrockcd10

operations Internalized sets of actions that allow children to do mentally what before they had done physically.

symbolic function substage The first substage of preoperational thought, occurring roughly between the ages of 2 and 4. In this substage, the young child gains the ability to represent mentally an object that is not present.

egocentrism A salient feature of preoperational thought, the inability to distinguish between one's own and someone else's perspective.

FIGURE 7.6 The Symbolic Drawings of Young Children

(*a*) A 3½-year-old's symbolic drawing. Halfway into this drawing, the 3½-year-old artist said it was "a pelican kissing a seal." (*b*) This 11-year-old's drawing is neater and more realistic but also less inventive.

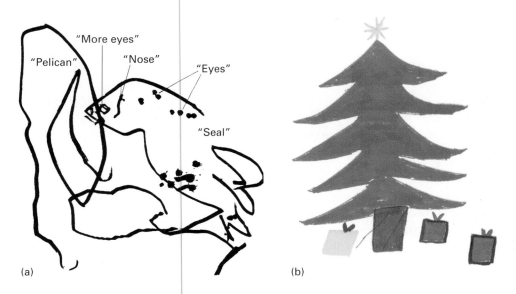

(a)
(b)

Animism, another limitation within preoperational thought, is the belief that inanimate objects have "lifelike" qualities and are capable of action (Gelman & Opfer, 2002). A young child might show animism by saying, "That tree pushed the leaf off, and it fell down," or "The sidewalk made me mad; it made me fall down." A young child who uses animism fails to distinguish the appropriate occasions for using human and nonhuman perspectives.

Possibly because young children are not very concerned about reality, their drawings are fanciful and inventive. Suns are blue, skies are yellow, and cars float on clouds in their symbolic, imaginative world. One 3½-year-old looked at a scribble he had just drawn and described it as a pelican kissing a seal (see figure 7.6a). The symbolism is simple but strong, like abstractions found in some modern art. As Picasso commented, "I used to draw like Raphael but it has taken me a lifetime to draw like young children." In the elementary school years, a child's drawings become more realistic, neat, and precise (see figure 7.6b). Suns are yellow, skies are blue, and cars travel on roads (Winner, 1986).

Intuitive Thought Substage Tommy is 4 years old. Although he is starting to develop his own ideas about the world he lives in, his ideas are still simple, and he is not very good at thinking things out. He has difficulty understanding events he

animism A facet of preoperational thought, the belief that inanimate objects have "lifelike" qualities and are capable of action.

FIGURE 7.7 Arrays

(*a*) A random array of objects. (*b*) An ordered array of objects.

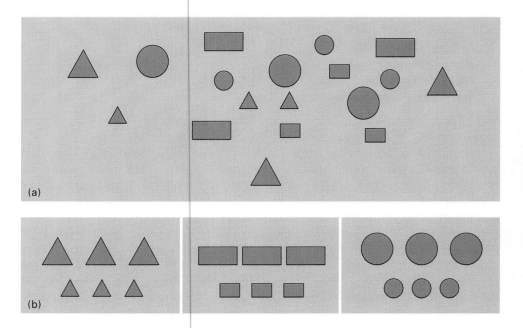

(a)

(b)

knows are taking place but which he cannot see. His fantasized thoughts bear little resemblance to reality. He cannot yet answer the question "What if . . . ?" in any reliable way. For example, he has only a vague idea of what would happen if a car were to hit him. He also has difficulty negotiating traffic because he cannot do the mental calculations necessary to estimate whether an approaching car will hit him when he crosses the road.

The **intuitive thought substage** is the second substage of preoperational thought, occurring approximately between 4 and 7 years of age. In this substage, children begin to use primitive reasoning and want to know the answers to all sorts of questions. Piaget called this time period *intuitive* because, on the one hand, young children seem so sure about their knowledge and understanding, yet they are so unaware of how they know what they know. That is, they say they know something but know it without the use of rational thinking.

An example of young children's reasoning ability is the difficulty they have putting things into correct categories. Faced with a random collection of objects that can be grouped together on the basis of two or more properties, preoperational children are seldom capable of using these properties consistently to sort the objects into appropriate groupings. Look at the collection of objects in figure 7.7a. You would respond to the direction "Put the things together that you believe belong together" by sorting according to the characteristics of size and array. Your sorting might look something like that shown in figure 7.7b. In the social realm, a 4-year-old girl might be given the task of dividing her peers into groups according to whether they are friends and whether they are boys or girls. She would be unlikely to arrive at the following classification: friendly boys, friendly girls, unfriendly boys, unfriendly girls. Another example of classification shortcomings involves the preoperational child's understanding of religious concepts (Elkind, 1976). When asked "Can you be a Protestant and an American at the same time?" 6- and 7-year-olds usually say no. Nine-year-olds often say yes, understanding that objects can be cross-classified simultaneously.

Many of these examples show a characteristic of preoperational thought called **centration**—the focusing or centering of attention on one characteristic to the exclusion of all others. Centration is most clearly evidenced in young children's lack of **conservation**—the idea that an amount stays the same regardless of how its container changes. To adults, it is obvious that a certain amount of liquid stays the same, regardless of a container's shape. But this is not at all obvious to young children. Instead, they are struck by the height of the liquid in the container. In the conservation task—Piaget's most famous test—a child is presented with two identical beakers, each filled to the same level with liquid (see figure 7.8). The child is asked if these

intuitive thought substage The second substage of preoperational thought, occurring approximately between 4 and 7 years of age. Children begin to use primitive reasoning and want to know the answers to all sorts of questions.

centration The focusing of attention on one characteristic to the exclusion of all others.

conservation The idea that an amount stays the same regardless of how its container changes.

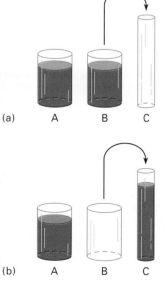

FIGURE 7.8 Piaget's Conservation Task

The beaker test is a well-known Piagetian test to determine whether a child can think operationally—that is, can mentally reverse actions and show conservation of the substance. (*a*) Two identical beakers are presented to the child. Then, the experimenter pours the liquid from B into C, which is taller and thinner than A or B. (*b*) The child is asked if these beakers (A and C) have the same amount of liquid. The preoperational child says no. When asked to point to the beaker that has more liquid, the preoperational child points to the tall, thin beaker.

beakers have the same amount of liquid, and she usually says yes. Then the liquid from one beaker is poured into a third beaker, which is taller and thinner than the first two. The child is then asked if the amount of liquid in the tall, thin beaker is equal to that which remains in one of the original beakers. Children who are less than 7 or 8 years old usually say no and justify their answers in terms of the differing height or width of the beakers. Older children usually answer yes and justify their answers appropriately ("If you poured the milk back, the amount would still be the same").

In Piaget's theory, failing the conservation of liquid task is a sign that children are at the preoperational stage of cognitive development. Passing this test is a sign that they are at the concrete operational stage. In Piaget's view, the preoperational child fails to show conservation not only of liquid but also of number, matter, length, volume, and area (see figure 7.9).

The child's inability to mentally reverse actions is an important characteristic of preoperational thought. For example, in the conservation of matter task shown in figure 7.9, preoperational children say that the longer shape has more clay because they assume that "longer is more." Preoperational children cannot mentally reverse the clay-rolling process to see that the amount of clay is the same in both the shorter ball shape and the longer stick shape.

Some developmentalists do not believe Piaget was entirely correct in his estimate of when children's conservation skills emerge. For example, Rochel Gelman (1969) showed that, when the child's attention to relevant aspects of the conservation task

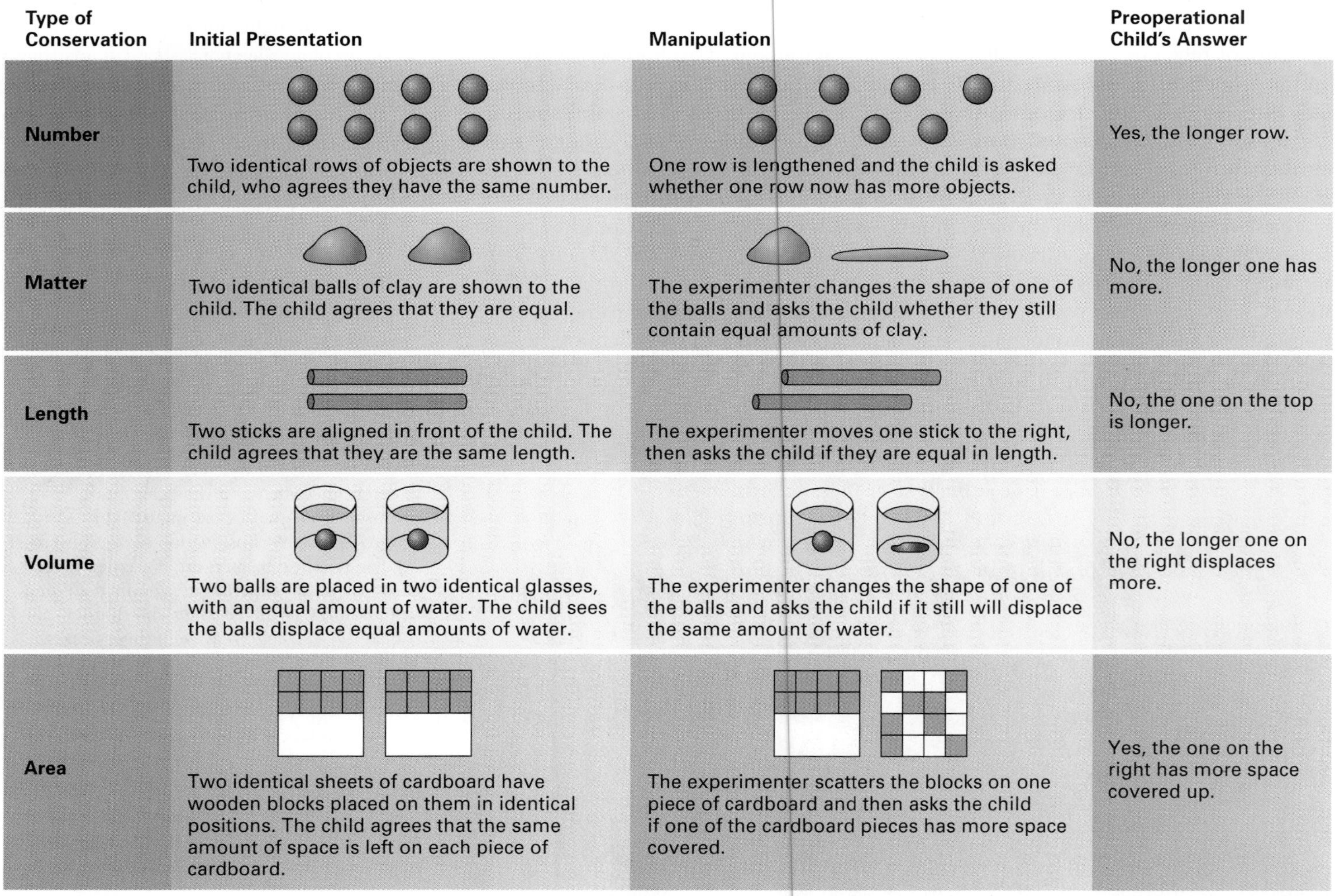

Type of Conservation	Initial Presentation	Manipulation	Preoperational Child's Answer
Number	Two identical rows of objects are shown to the child, who agrees they have the same number.	One row is lengthened and the child is asked whether one row now has more objects.	Yes, the longer row.
Matter	Two identical balls of clay are shown to the child. The child agrees that they are equal.	The experimenter changes the shape of one of the balls and asks the child whether they still contain equal amounts of clay.	No, the longer one has more.
Length	Two sticks are aligned in front of the child. The child agrees that they are the same length.	The experimenter moves one stick to the right, then asks the child if they are equal in length.	No, the one on the top is longer.
Volume	Two balls are placed in two identical glasses, with an equal amount of water. The child sees the balls displace equal amounts of water.	The experimenter changes the shape of one of the balls and asks the child if it still will displace the same amount of water.	No, the longer one on the right displaces more.
Area	Two identical sheets of cardboard have wooden blocks placed on them in identical positions. The child agrees that the same amount of space is left on each piece of cardboard.	The experimenter scatters the blocks on one piece of cardboard and then asks the child if one of the cardboard pieces has more space covered.	Yes, the one on the right has more space covered up.

FIGURE 7.9 Some Dimensions of Conservation: Number, Matter, Length, Volume, and Area

is improved, the child is more likely to conserve. Gelman has also demonstrated that attentional training on one dimension, such as number, improves the preschool child's performance on another dimension, such as mass. Thus, Gelman believes that conservation appears earlier than Piaget thought and that attention is especially important in explaining conservation.

Yet another characteristic of preoperational children is that they ask a barrage of questions. Children's earliest questions appear around the age of 3, and by the age of 5 they have just about exhausted the adults around them with "why" questions. The child's questions yield clues about mental development and reflect intellectual curiosity. These questions signal the emergence of the child's interest in reasoning and figuring out why things are the way they are. Here are some samples of the questions children ask during the questioning period of 4 to 6 years of age (Elkind, 1976):

- "What makes you grow up?"
- "What makes you stop growing?"
- "Why does a lady have to be married to have a baby?"
- "Who was the mother when everybody was a baby?"
- "Why do leaves fall?"
- "Why does the sun shine?"

At this point we have discussed a number of characteristics of preoperational thought. To help you remember these characteristics, see figure 7.10.

Earlier, we mentioned that Gelman's research demonstrated that children may fail a Piagetian task because they do not attend to relevant dimensions of the task—length, shape, density, and so on. Gelman and other developmentalists also believe that many of the tasks used to assess cognitive development may not be sensitive to the child's cognitive abilities. Thus, any apparent limitations on cognitive development may be due to the tasks used to assess that development. Gelman's research reflects the thinking of information-processing psychologists who place considerable importance on the tasks and procedures involved in assessing children's cognition.

"I still don't have all the answers, but I'm beginning to ask the right questions."

More symbolic than sensorimotor thought

Inability to engage in operations; can't mentally reverse actions; lacks conservation skills

Egocentric (inability to distinguish between own perspective and someone else's)

Intuitive rather than logical

FIGURE 7.10 Preoperational Thought's Characteristics

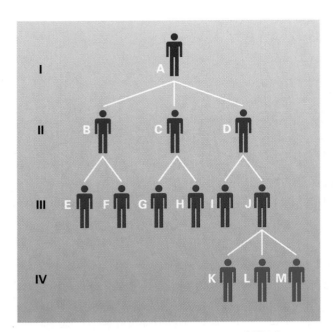

FIGURE 7.11 Classification: An Important Ability in Concrete Operational Thought

A family tree of four generations (*I to IV*): The preoperational child has trouble classifying the members of the four generations; the concrete operational child can classify the members vertically, horizontally, and obliquely (up and down and across). For example, the concrete operational child understands that a family member can be a son, a brother, and a father, all at the same time.

horizontal décalage Piaget's concept that similar abilities do not appear at the same time within a stage of development.

seriation The concrete operation that involves ordering stimuli along a quantitative dimension (such as length).

Concrete Operational Thought

In the well-known test of reversibility of thought involving conservation of matter, a child is presented with two identical balls of clay. An experimenter rolls one ball into a long, thin stick; the other remains in its original ball shape. The child is then asked if there is more clay in the ball or in the long, thin stick of clay. By the time children reach the age of 7 or 8, most answer that the amount of clay is the same. To answer this problem correctly, children have to imagine the clay stick rolling back into a ball. This type of imagination involves a reversible mental action. Thus, a concrete operation is a reversible mental action on real, concrete objects. Concrete operations allow children to coordinate several characteristics rather than focus on a single property of an object. In the clay example, a preoperational child is likely to focus on height or width; a concrete operational child coordinates information about both dimensions. We can get a better understanding of concrete operational thought by considering further ideas about conservation and the nature of classification.

We already have highlighted some of Piaget's basic ideas on conservation in our discussion of preoperational children's failure to answer questions correctly about such circumstances as the beaker task. Remember that conservation involves the recognition that the length, number, mass, quantity, area, weight, and volume of objects and substances do not change by transformations that alter their appearance. An important point that needs to be made about conservation is that children do not conserve all quantities or on all tasks simultaneously. The order of their mastery is number, length, liquid quantity, mass, weight, and volume. **Horizontal décalage** is Piaget's concept that similar abilities do not appear at the same time within a stage of development. As we have just seen, during the concrete operational stage, conservation of number usually appears first and conservation of volume last. Also, an 8-year-old child might know that a long stick of clay can be rolled back into a ball but not understand that the ball and the stick weigh the same. At about 9 years of age, the child recognizes that they weigh the same, and eventually, at about 11 to 12 years of age, the child understands that the clay's volume is unchanged by rearranging it. Children initially master tasks in which the dimensions are more salient and visible, only later mastering those not as visually apparent, such as volume.

Many of the concrete operations identified by Piaget involve the ways children reason about the properties of objects. One important skill that characterizes concrete operational children is the ability to classify or divide things into sets or subsets and to consider their interrelationships. An example of concrete operational classification skills involves a family tree of four generations (Furth & Wachs, 1975) (see figure 7.11). This family tree suggests that the grandfather (A) has three children (B, C, and D), each of whom has two children (E through J), and that one of these children (J) has three children (K, L, and M). The concrete operational child understands that person J can, at the same time, be father, brother, and grandson. A child who comprehends this classification system can move up and down a level (vertically), across a level (horizontally), and up and down and across (obliquely) within the system.

Some Piagetian tasks require children to reason about relations between classes. One such task is **seriation,** the concrete operation that involves ordering stimuli along a quantitative dimension (such as length). To see if students can serialize, a teacher might haphazardly place eight sticks of different lengths on a table. The teacher then asks the students to order the sticks by length. Many young children end up with two or three small groups of "big" sticks or "little" sticks, rather than a correct ordering of all eight sticks. Another mistaken strategy they use is to evenly

| Can use operations, mentally reversing action; shows conser-vation skills | Logical reasoning replaces intuitive reasoning, but only in concrete circumstances | Not abstract (can't imagine steps in algebraic equation, for example) | Classification skills—can divide things into sets and subsets and reason about their interrelations |

FIGURE 7.12 Characteristics of Concrete Operational Thought

line up the tops of the sticks but ignore the bottoms. The concrete operational thinker simultaneously understands that each stick must be longer than the one that precedes it and shorter than the one that follows it.

Another aspect of reasoning about the relations between classes is **transitivity.** This involves the ability to logically combine relations to understand certain conclusions. In this case, consider three sticks (A, B, and C) of differing lengths. A is the longest, B is intermediate in length, and C is the shortest. Does the child understand that, if A > B and B > C, then A > C? In Piaget's theory, concrete operational thinkers do; preoperational thinkers do not.

Although concrete operational thought is more advanced than preoperational thought, it has its limitations. Logical reasoning replaces intuitive thought as long as the principles can be applied to specific or *concrete* examples. For example, a concrete operational child cannot imagine the steps necessary to complete an algebraic equation, which is too abstract for thinking at this stage of cognitive development. A summary of the characteristics of concrete operational thought is shown in figure 7.12.

Formal Operational Thought

Adolescents' developing power of thought opens up new cognitive and social horizons. Their thought becomes more abstract, logical, and idealistic. Adolescents are more capable of examining their own thoughts, others' thoughts, and what others are thinking about them, and more likely to interpret and monitor the social world.

Characteristics of Formal Operational Thought Piaget believed that formal operational thought comes into play between the ages of 11 and 15. Formal operational thought is more *abstract* than a child's thinking. Adolescents are no longer limited to actual, concrete experiences as anchors for thought. They can conjure up make-believe situations, events that are purely hypothetical possibilities or strictly abstract propositions, and can try to reason logically about them.

The abstract quality of the adolescent's thought at the formal operational level is evident in the adolescent's verbal problem-solving ability. Whereas the concrete operational thinker needs to see the concrete elements A, B, and C to be able to

transitivity In concrete operational thought, a mental concept that underlies the ability to logically combine relations to understand certain conclusions. It focuses on reasoning about the relations between classes.

Might adolescents' ability to reason hypothetically and to evaluate what is ideal versus what is real lead them to engage in demonstrations, such as this protest related to better ethnic relations? What other causes might be attractive to adolescents' newfound cognitive abilities of hypothetical-deductive reasoning and idealistic thinking?

The thoughts of youth are long, long thoughts.

—HENRY WADSWORTH
LONGFELLOW
American Poet, 19th Century

hypothetical-deductive reasoning Piaget's formal operational concept that adolescents have the cognitive ability to develop hypotheses about ways to solve problems and can systematically deduce which is the best path to follow in solving the problem.

make the logical inference that, if A = B and B = C, then A = C, the formal operational thinker can solve this problem when it is merely presented verbally.

Another indication of the abstract quality of adolescents' thought is their increased tendency to think about thought itself. One adolescent commented, "I began thinking about why I was thinking what I was. Then I began thinking about why I was thinking about what I was thinking about what I was." If this sounds abstract, it is, and it characterizes the adolescent's enhanced focus on thought and its abstract qualities.

Accompanying the abstract nature of formal operational thought in adolescence is thought full of idealism and possibilities. Whereas children frequently think in concrete ways, or in terms of what is real and limited, adolescents begin to engage in extended speculation about ideal characteristics—qualities they desire in themselves and in others. Such thoughts often lead adolescents to compare themselves with others in regard to such ideal standards. And adolescents' thoughts are often fantasy flights into future possibilities. It is not unusual for the adolescent to become impatient with these newfound ideal standards and to become perplexed over which of many ideal standards to adopt.

At the same time that adolescents think more abstractly and idealistically, they also think more logically. Adolescents begin to think more as a scientist thinks, devising plans to solve problems and systematically testing solutions. This type of problem solving has an imposing name. **Hypothetical-deductive reasoning** is Piaget's formal operational concept that adolescents have the cognitive ability to develop hypotheses, or best guesses, about ways to solve problems, such as algebraic equations. Then, they systematically deduce, or conclude, which is the best path to follow in solving the problem. By contrast, children are more likely to solve problems in a trial-and-error fashion.

One example of hypothetical-deductive reasoning involves a modification of the familiar game Twenty Questions. Individuals are shown a set of 42 color pictures, displayed in a rectangular array (six rows of seven pictures each) and are asked to determine which picture the experimenter has in mind (that is, which is "correct"). The subjects are allowed to ask only questions to which the experimenter can answer yes or no. The object of the game is to select the correct picture by asking as few questions as possible. Adolescents who are deductive hypothesis testers formulate a plan and test a series of hypotheses, which considerably narrows the field

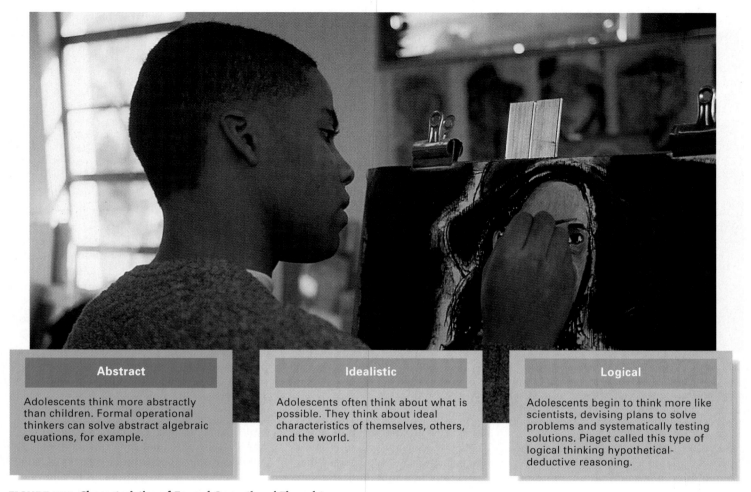

Abstract	Idealistic	Logical
Adolescents think more abstractly than children. Formal operational thinkers can solve abstract algebraic equations, for example.	Adolescents often think about what is possible. They think about ideal characteristics of themselves, others, and the world.	Adolescents begin to think more like scientists, devising plans to solve problems and systematically testing solutions. Piaget called this type of logical thinking hypothetical-deductive reasoning.

FIGURE 7.13 Characteristics of Formal Operational Thought

Adolescents begin to think more as scientists think, devising plans to solve problems and systematically testing solutions. Piaget gave this type of thinking the imposing name of hypothetical-deductive reasoning.

of choices. The most effective plan is a "halving" strategy (*Q:* Is the picture in the right half of the array? *A:* No. *Q:* OK. Is it in the top half? And so on.). A correct halving strategy guarantees the answer in seven questions or less. By contrast, concrete operational thinkers may persist with questions that continue to test some of the same possibilities that previous questions could have eliminated. For example, they may ask whether the correct picture is in row 1 and are told that it is not. Later, they ask whether the picture is *x*, which is in row 1.

Thus, formal operational thinkers test their hypotheses with judiciously chosen questions and tests. By contrast, concrete operational thinkers often fail to understand the relation between a hypothesis and a well-chosen test of it, stubbornly clinging to ideas that already have been discounted.

Piaget believed that formal operational thought is the best description of how adolescents think. A summary of formal operational thought's characteristics is shown in figure 7.13. As we will see next, though, formal operational thought is not a homogeneous stage of development.

Some of Piaget's ideas on formal operational thought are being challenged (Byrnes, 2001; Overton & Byrnes, 1991). There is much more individual variation in formal operational thought than Piaget envisioned. Only about one in three young adolescents is a formal operational thinker. Many American adults never become formal operational thinkers, and neither do many adults in other cultures.

Many adolescent girls spend long hours in front of the mirror, depleting cans of hairspray, tubes of lipstick, and jars of cosmetics. *How might this behavior be related to changes in adolescent cognitive and physical development?*

Consider this conversation between a researcher and an illiterate Kpelle farmer in the West African country of Liberia (Scribner, 1977):

> **Researcher:** All Kpelle men are rice farmers. Mr. Smith is not a rice farmer. Is he a Kpelle man?
> **Kpelle farmer:** I don't know the man. I have not laid eyes on the man myself.

Members of the Kpelle culture who had gone through formal schooling answered the researcher in a logical way. Thus, cultural experiences influence whether individuals reach a Piagetian stage of thought. Education in the logic of science and mathematics is an important cultural experience that promotes the development of formal operational thinking.

Also, for adolescents who become formal operational thinkers, assimilation (incorporating new information into existing knowledge) dominates the initial development of formal operational thought, and the world is perceived subjectively and idealistically. Later in adolescence, as intellectual balance is restored, these individuals accommodate (adjust to new information) to the cognitive upheaval that has occurred.

In addition to thinking more logically, abstractly, and idealistically, which characterize Piaget's formal operational thought stage, what other ways does adolescent cognition change? One important way involves adolescent egocentrism.

Adolescent Egocentrism   "Oh, my gosh! I can't believe it. Help! I can't stand it!" Tracy desperately yells. "What is wrong? What is the matter?" her mother asks. Tracy responds, "Everyone in here is looking at me." The mother queries, "Why?" Tracy says, "Look, this hair just won't stay in place," as she rushes to the rest room of the restaurant. Five minutes later, she returns to the table in the restaurant after she has depleted an entire can of hairspray.

During a conversation between two 14-year-old girls, the one named Margaret says, "Are you kidding, I won't get pregnant." And 13-year-old Adam describes himself, "No one understands me, particularly my parents. They have no idea of what I am feeling."

Adolescent egocentrism is the heightened self-consciousness of adolescents, which is reflected in adolescents' belief that others are as interested in them as the adolescents are in themselves, and in adolescents' sense of personal uniqueness and invulnerability.

David Elkind (1978) believes that adolescent egocentrism can be dissected into two types of social thinking—imaginary audience and personal fable. The term **imaginary audience** refers to the heightened self-consciousness of adolescents that is reflected in their belief that others are as interested in them as they are themselves. The imaginary audience involves attention-getting behavior—the attempt to be noticed, visible, and "on stage." Tracy's comments and behavior above reflect the imaginary audience. Another adolescent might think that others are as aware of a small spot on his trousers as he is, possibly knowing that he has masturbated. Another adolescent, an eighth-grade girl, walks into her classroom and thinks that all eyes are riveted on her complexion. Adolescents especially sense that they are "on stage" in early adolescence, believing they are the main actors and all others are the audience.

According to Elkind, the **personal fable** is the part of adolescent egocentrism that involves an adolescent's sense of personal uniqueness and invincibility. Adolescents' sense of personal uniqueness makes them feel that no one can understand how they really feel. For example, an adolescent girl thinks that her mother cannot possibly sense the hurt she feels because her boyfriend has broken up with her.

adolescent egocentrism The heightened self-consciousness of adolescents, which is reflected in their belief that others are as interested in them as the adolescents are in themselves, and in adolescents' sense of personal uniqueness and vulnerability.

imaginary audience An adolescent's belief that others are as preoccupied with her as she is.

personal fable An adolescent's sense of personal uniqueness and indestructibility.

As part of their effort to retain a sense of personal uniqueness, adolescents might craft stories about themselves that are filled with fantasy, immersing themselves in a world that is far removed from reality. Personal fables frequently show up in adolescent diaries.

Adolescents also often show a sense of invincibility—feeling that although others might be vulnerable to tragedies, such as a terrible car wreck, these things won't happen to them. Some developmentalists believe that the sense of uniqueness and invincibility that egocentrism generates is responsible for some of the seemingly wreckless behavior of adolescents, including drag racing, drug use, suicide, and failure to use contraceptives during intercourse (Dolcini & others, 1989). For example, one study found that eleventh- and twelfth-grade females who were high in adolescent egocentrism were more likely to say they would not get pregnant from engaging in sex without contraception than were their counterparts who were low in adolescent egocentrism (Arnett, 1990).

Early and Late Formal Operational Thought   Formal operational thought has been conceptualized as occurring in two phases. In the first phase, the increased ability to think hypothetically produces unconstrained thoughts with unlimited possibilities. This early formal operational thought submerges reality (Broughton, 1978). Reality is overwhelmed. Idealism and possibility dominate. During the middle years of adolescence, an intellectual balance is restored; adolescents test the products of their reasoning against experience and develop a consolidation of formal operational thought.

Piaget's (1952) early writings seemed to indicate that the onset and consolidation of formal operational thought is completed during early adolescence, from about 12 to 15 years of age. Later, Piaget (1972) concluded that formal operational thought is not achieved until later in adolescence, between approximately 15 and 20 years of age.

Piaget's concepts of assimilation and accommodation help us understand the two phases of formal operational thought. Remember that *assimilation* occurs when adolescents incorporate new information into their existing knowledge; *accommodation* occurs when adolescents adjust to new information. During early adolescence, there is an excess of assimilation as the world is perceived too subjectively and idealistically. In the middle years of adolescence, an intellectual balance is restored, as the individual accommodates to the cognitive change that has taken place. In this view, the assimilation of formal operational thought marks the transition to adolescence; accommodation marks a later consolidation of thought (Lapsley, 1989).

Variations in Adolescent Cognition   Piaget's theory emphasizes universal and consistent patterns of formal operational thought; his theory does not adequately account for the unique differences that characterize the cognitive development of adolescents. These individual variations in adolescents' cognitive development have been documented in a number of investigations (Neimark, 1982).

Some individuals in early adolescence are formal operational thinkers; others are not. A review of formal operational thought investigations revealed that only about one of every three eighth-grade students is a formal operational thinker (Strahan, 1983). Some investigators have found that formal operational thought increases with age in adolescence (Martorano, 1977); others have not (Strahan, 1987). Many college students and adults do not think in formal operational ways, either. For example, investigators have found that from 17 percent to 67 percent of all college students think in formal operational ways (Elkind, 1961; Tomlinson-Keasey, 1972).

Many young adolescents are at the point of consolidating their concrete operational thought, using it more consistently than in childhood. At the same time, many young adolescents are just beginning to think in a formal operational manner. By

In any consideration of adolescent cognition it is important to recognize the wide variation in performance among them.
—DANIEL KEATING
Contemporary Psychologist, University of Toronto

late adolescence, many adolescents have begun to consolidate their formal operational thought, using it more consistently, and there often is variation across the content areas of formal operational thought, just as there is in concrete operational thought in childhood. A 14-year-old might reason at the formal operational level when it comes to analyzing algebraic equations but not do so with verbal problem solving or when reasoning about interpersonal relations.

Formal operational thought is more likely to be used in areas in which adolescents have the most experience and knowledge (Carey, 1988). Children and adolescents gradually build up elaborate knowledge through extensive experience and practice in various sports, games, hobbies, and school subjects such as math, English, and science. The development of expertise in different domains of life may make possible high-level, developmentally mature-looking thought. In some instances, the sophisticated reasoning of formal operational thought might be responsible. In other instances, however, the thought might be largely due to the accumulation of knowledge that allows more automatic, memory-based processes to function. Some developmentalists wonder if the acquisition of knowledge accounts for all cognitive growth. Most, however, argue that *both* cognitive changes in such areas as concrete and formal operational thought *and* the development of expertise through experience are at work in understanding the adolescent's cognitive world.

Review and Reflect: Learning Goal 2

2 Describe Piaget's four stages of cognitive development

REVIEW

- What are the main characteristics of sensorimotor thought? How can the sensorimotor stage be evaluated?
- What are the main characteristics of preoperational thought?
- What are the main characteristics of concrete operational thought?
- What are the main characteristics of formal operational thought?

REFLECT

- Do you consider yourself to be a formal operational thinker? Do you still sometimes feel like a concrete operational thinker? Give examples.

3 APPLYING AND EVALUATING PIAGET'S THEORY

Piaget and Education   Evaluating Piaget's Theory

What are some applications of Piaget's theory to education? What are the main contributions and criticisms of Piaget's theory?

Piaget and Education

Piaget was not an educator and never pretended to be. However, he provided a sound conceptual framework from which to view learning and education. Here are some ideas in Piaget's theory that can be applied to teaching (Elkind, 1976; Heuwinkel, 1996):

1. *Take a constructivist approach.* In a constructivist vein, Piaget emphasized that children learn best when they are active and seek solutions for themselves. Piaget opposed teaching methods that imply that children are passive receptacles. The

www.mhhe.com/santrockcd10

Piaget and Education

educational implication of Piaget's view is that, in all subjects, students learn best by making discoveries, reflecting on them, and discussing them, rather than blindly imitating the teacher or doing things by rote.

2. *Facilitate rather than direct learning.* Effective teachers design situations that allow students to learn by doing. These situations promote students' thinking and discovery. Teachers listen, watch, and question students to help them gain better understanding. Don't just examine *what* students think and the product of their learning. Rather, carefully observe them as they find out *how* they think. Ask relevant questions to stimulate their thinking and ask them to explain their answers.

3. *Consider the child's knowledge and level of thinking.* Students do not come to class with empty heads. They have many ideas about the physical and natural world. They have concepts of space, time, quantity, and causality. These ideas differ from the ideas of adults. Teachers need to interpret what a student is saying and respond in a mode of discourse that is not too far from the student's level.

4. *Use ongoing assessment.* Individually constructed meanings cannot be measured by standardized tests. Evaluate students' progress with such tools as math and language portfolios (which contain work in progress as well as finished products) and individual conferences in which students discuss their thinking strategies. Students' written and verbal explanations of their reasoning also can be used to evaluate progress.

5. *Promote the student's intellectual health.* When Piaget came to lecture in the United States, he was asked, "What can I do to get my child to a higher cognitive stage sooner?" He was asked this question so often here compared with other countries that he called it the American question. For Piaget, children's learning should occur naturally. Children should not be pushed and pressured into achieving too much too early in their development, before they are maturationally ready. Some parents spend long hours every day holding up large flash cards with words on them to improve their baby's vocabulary. In the Piagetian view, this is not the best way for infants to learn. It places too much emphasis on speeding up intellectual development, involves passive learning, and will not work.

6. *Turn the classroom into a setting of exploration and discovery.* What do actual classrooms look like when the teachers adopt Piaget's views? Several first- and second-grade math classrooms provide some good examples (Kamii, 1985, 1989). The teachers emphasize students' own exploration and discovery. The classrooms are less structured than what we think of as a typical classroom. Workbooks and predetermined assignments are not used. Rather, the teachers observe the students' interests and natural participation in activities to determine what the course of learning will be. For example, a math lesson might be constructed around counting the day's lunch money or dividing supplies among students. Often, games are prominently used in the classroom to stimulate mathematical thinking. For example, a version of dominoes teaches children about even-numbered combinations. A variation on tic-tac-toe involves replacing Xs and Os with numbers. Teachers encourage peer interaction during the lessons and games because students' different viewpoints can contribute to advances in thinking.

Evaluating Piaget's Theory

What were Piaget's main contributions? Has his theory withstood the test of time?

Contributions   Piaget was a giant in the field of developmental psychology, the founder of the present field of children's cognitive development. Psychologists owe him a long list of masterful concepts of enduring power and fascination: assimilation, accommodation, object permanence, egocentrism, conservation, and others. Psychologists also owe him the current vision of children as active, constructive thinkers.

Jean Piaget, the main architect of the field of cognitive development, at age 27.

Piaget with his wife and three children; he often used his observations of his children to provide examples of his theory.

Infants know that objects are substantial and permanent at an earlier age than Piaget envisioned.

—RENÉE BAILLARGEON
*Contemporary Psychologist,
University of Illinois*

An outstanding teacher and education in the logic of science and mathematics are important cultural experiences that promote the development of operational thought. Schooling and education likely play more important roles in the development of operational thought than Piaget envisioned. *What are some other criticisms of Piaget's theory?*

Piaget also was a genius when it came to observing children. His careful observations showed us inventive ways to discover how children act on and adapt to their world. Piaget showed us some important things to look for in cognitive development, such as the shift from preoperational to concrete operational thinking. He also showed us how children need to make their experiences fit their schemas (cognitive frameworks) yet simultaneously adapt their schemas to experience. Piaget also revealed how cognitive change is likely to occur if the context is structured to allow gradual movement to the next higher level and that a concept does not emerge suddenly, full-blown but, rather, through a series of partial accomplishments that lead to increasingly comprehensive understanding (Haith & Benson, 1998).

Criticisms Piaget's theory has not gone unchallenged. Questions are raised about his estimates of children's competence at different developmental levels; his view of stages; his ideas about the training of children to reason at higher levels; and his downplayed views of culture and education.

- *Estimates of children's competence.* Some cognitive abilities emerge earlier than Piaget thought (Meltzoff, 2000). For example, as previously noted, some aspects of object permanence emerge earlier than he believed. Even 2-year-olds are nonegocentric in some contexts. When they realize that another person will not see an object, they investigate whether the person is blindfolded or looking in a different direction. Some understanding of the conservation of number has been demonstrated as early as age 3, although Piaget did not think it emerged until 7. Young children are not as uniformly "pre-" this and "pre-" that (precausal, preoperational) as Piaget thought. Other cognitive abilities also can emerge later than Piaget thought. Many adolescents still think in concrete operational ways or are just beginning to master formal operations. Even many adults are not formal operational thinkers. In sum, recent theoretical revisions highlight more cognitive competencies of infants and young children and more cognitive shortcomings of adolescents and adults (Flavell, Miller, & Miller, 2002).
- *Stages.* Piaget conceived of stages as unitary structures of thought. Thus, his theory assumes developmental synchrony; that is, various aspects of a stage should

emerge at the same time. However, some concrete operational concepts do not appear in synchrony. For example, children do not learn to conserve at the same time as they learn to cross-classify. Thus, most contemporary developmentalists agree that children's cognitive development is not as stagelike as Piaget thought.

- *The training of children to reason at higher levels.* Some children who are at one cognitive stage (such as preoperational) can be trained to reason at a higher cognitive stage (such as concrete operational). This poses a problem for Piaget's theory. He argued that such training is only superficial and ineffective, unless the child is at a maturational transition point between the stages (Gelman & Williams, 1998).
- *Culture and education.* Culture and education exert stronger influences on children's development than Piaget believed (Gelman & Brenneman, 1994). The age at which children acquire conservation skills is related to the extent to which their culture provides relevant practice. An outstanding teacher and education in the logic of math and science can promote concrete and formal operational thought.

Still, some developmental psychologists believe we should not throw out Piaget altogether. These **neo-Piagetians** argue that Piaget got some things right but that his theory needs considerable revision. In their revisions of Piaget, more emphasis is given to how children process information through attention, memory, and strategy use (Case, 1987, 1999). They especially believe that a more accurate vision of children's thinking requires more emphasis on strategies, the speed at which children process information, the particular cognitive task involved, and the division of cognitive problems into smaller, more precise steps.

neo-Piagetians Developmentalists who have elaborated on Piaget's theory, believing that children's cognitive development is more specific in many respects than he thought.

Review and Reflect: Learning Goal 3

3 Apply Piaget's theory to education and evaluate his theory

REVIEW

- How can Piaget's theory be applied to children's education?
- What are some key contributions and criticisms of Piaget's theory?

REFLECT

- How might thinking in formal operational ways rather than concrete operational ways help students to develop better study skills?

4 VYGOTSKY'S THEORY OF COGNITIVE DEVELOPMENT

The Zone of Proximal Development	Language and Thought	Evaluating and Comparing Vygotsky's Theory and Piaget's Theory
Scaffolding	Vygotsky and Education	

In chapter 2, we described the basic ideas in Vygotsky's theory. ◀ page 35 Here we expand on Vygotsky's theory of development, beginning with his unique ideas about the zone of proximal development.

Upper limit

Level of additional responsibility child can accept with assistance of an able instructor

Zone of proximal development (ZPD)

Lower limit

Level of problem solving reached on these tasks by child working alone

FIGURE 7.14 Vygotsky's Zone of Proximal Development

Lev Vygotsky (1896–1934), shown here with his daughter, believed that children's cognitive development is advanced through social interaction with skilled individuals embedded in a sociocultural backdrop. *How is Vygotsky's theory different from Piaget's theory?*

zone of proximal development (ZPD) Vygotsky's term for the range of tasks that are too difficult for children to master alone but that can be mastered with the guidance and assistance of adults or more-skilled children.

scaffolding Changing the level of support over the course of a teaching session in which a more-skilled individual (teacher or more-advanced peer of the child) adjusts the amount of guidance to fit the child's current performance level.

The Zone of Proximal Development

Zone of proximal development (ZPD) is Vygotsky's term for the range of tasks too difficult for children to master alone but which can be learned with the guidance and assistance of adults or more-skilled children. Thus, the lower limit of the ZPD is the level of problem solving reached by the child working independently. The upper limit is the level of additional responsibility the child can accept with the assistance of an able instructor (see figure 7.14). Vygotsky's emphasis on the ZPD underscores his belief in the importance of social influences, especially instruction, on children's cognitive development.

The ZPD captures the child's cognitive skills that are in the process of maturing and can be accomplished only with the assistance of a more-skilled person (Kozulin, 2000). Vygotsky (1962) called these the "buds" or "flowers" of development, to distinguish them from the "fruits" of development, which the child already can accomplish independently.

Scaffolding

Closely linked to the idea of zone of proximal development is the concept of **scaffolding.** Scaffolding means changing the level of support. Over the course of a teaching session, a more-skilled person (teacher or more-advanced peer of the child) adjusts the amount of guidance to fit the student's current performance level. When the task the student is learning is new, the more-skilled person may use direct instruction. As the student's competence increases, less guidance is given.

Dialogue is an important tool of scaffolding in the zone of proximal development (Tappan, 1998). Vygotsky viewed children as having rich but unsystematic, disorganized, and spontaneous concepts. These meet with the skilled helper's more systematic, logical, and rational concepts. As a result of the meeting and dialogue between the child and the skilled helper, the child's concepts become more systematic, logical, and rational.

Closely related to the concept of scaffolding is *cognitive apprenticeship,* which involves an expert stretching and supporting a novice's understanding and use of a culture's skills. To read further about the role of cognitive apprenticeship in children's development, see the Explorations in Child Development box.

Apprenticeship Training

Barbara Rogoff (1990, 1998; Rogoff, Turkanis, & Bartlett, 2001) believes that children's cognitive development is an apprenticeship that occurs through participation in social activity, guided by companions who stretch and support children's understanding of and skill in using the "tools" of the culture. Some of the technologies that are important tools for handling information in a culture are (1) language systems that organize categories of reality and structure ways of approaching situations, (2) literate practices to record information and transform it through written exercises, (3) mathematical systems that handle numerical and spatial problems, and (4) memory strategies to preserve information in memory over time. Some of these technologies have material supports, such as pencil and paper, word-processing programs, alphabets, calculators, abacus and slide rule, notches on sticks, and knots on ropes. These tools provide a mechanism for transmitting information from one generation to the next.

Cognitive apprenticeships are important in the classroom. Researchers have found that students' learning benefits when teachers think of their relationship with the student as a cognitive apprenticeship, using scaffolding and guided participation to help the student learn (Englert, Berry, & Dunsmore, 2001).

The general processes of guided participation appear around the world. Caregivers and children arrange children's activities and revise children's responsibilities as they gain skill and knowledge. With guidance, children participate in cultural activities that socialize them into skilled activities. For example, Mayan mothers in Guatemala help their daughters learn to weave in a process of guided participation. In the United States and in many other nations, the development of prominent and creative thinkers is promoted through interaction with a knowledgeable person as well as by studying books and attending classes and exhibits.

Children begin to practice the skills for using cultural tools, such as literacy, even before the children have contact with the technology. For example, most middle-socioeconomic-status American parents involve their children in extensive conversation long before they go to kindergarten or elementary school, and they provide their young children with picture books and read stories to them at bedtime as part of their daily routine. Most middle-socioeconomic-status American parents embed their children in a way of life in which reading and writing are integral parts of communication, recreation, and livelihood (Rogoff, 1990).

By contrast, consider the practices of two communities whose children have trouble reading (Heath, 1989). Parents in an Appalachian mill town taught their children respect for the written word but did not involve book characters or information in the children's everyday lives. Their children did well in the first several years of learning to read but had difficulty when required to *use* these literate skills to express themselves or interpret text. Children of rural origin in another mill town learned the skillful and creative use of language but were not taught about books or the style of communication and language used in school. These children had difficulty learning to read, which kept them from using their creative skills with language in the school setting. Early childhood in both of these communities did not include school-style reading and writing in the context of daily life and, not surprisingly, the children experienced difficulties with literacy in school.

In sum, Rogoff argues that guided participation—the participation of children in skilled cultural activities with other people of varying levels of skill and status—is an important aspect of children's development.

What is the nature of a cognitive apprenticeship? When teachers think of their relationship with students as a cognitive apprenticeship, how is teaching likely to proceed?

Language and Thought

Vygotsky (1962) believed that young children use language not only for social communication but also to plan, guide, and monitor their behavior in a self-regulatory fashion. The use of language for self-regulation is called *inner speech* or *private speech*. For Piaget, private speech is egocentric and immature, but for Vygotsky it is an important tool of thought during the early childhood years.

Vygotsky believed that language and thought initially develop independently of each other and then merge. He said that all mental functions have external, or social, origins. Children must use language to communicate with others before they can focus inward on their own thoughts. Children also must communicate externally and use language for a long period of time before the transition from external to internal speech takes place. This transition period occurs between 3 and 7 years of age and involves talking to oneself. After a while, the self-talk becomes second nature to children, and they can act without verbalizing. When this occurs, children have internalized their egocentric speech in the form of inner speech, which becomes their thoughts. Vygotsky believed that children who use a lot of private speech are more socially competent than those who don't. He argued that private speech represents an early transition in becoming more socially communicative.

Vygotsky's view challenged Piaget's ideas on language and thought. Vygotsky said that language, even in its earliest forms, is socially based (Kozulin, 2000; Santiago-Delefosse, Delefosse, & Oderic, 2002). By contrast, Piaget emphasized young children's egocentric and nonsocial speech. For Vygotsky, when young children talk to themselves, they are using language to govern their behavior and guide themselves. Piaget believed that such self-talk reflects immaturity. However, researchers have found support for Vygotsky's view of the positive role of private speech in children's development (Winsler, Diaz, & Montero, 1997).

Vygotsky and Education

Here are some ways that Vygotsky's theory can be incorporated in the classroom:

1. *Use the child's zone of proximal development in teaching.* Teaching should begin toward the zone's upper limit, where the child is able to reach the goal only through close collaboration with the instructor. With adequate continuing instruction and practice, the child organizes and masters the behavioral sequences required to perform the target skill. As the instruction continues, the performance transfers from the teacher to the child. The teacher gradually reduces the explanations, hints, and demonstrations until the student is able to perform the skill alone. Once the goal is achieved, it may become the foundation for the development of a new ZPD.

2. *Use scaffolding.* Look for opportunities to use scaffolding when children need help with self-initiated learning activities (Elicker, 1996). Also use scaffolding to help children move to a higher level of skill and knowledge. Offer just enough assistance. You might ask, "What can I do to help you?" Or simply observe the child's intentions and attempts, smoothly providing support when needed. When the child hesitates, offer encouragement. And encourage the child to practice the skill. You may watch and appreciate the child's practice or offer support when the child forgets what to do.

3. *Use more-skilled peers as teachers.* It is not just adults that Vygotsky believed are important in helping children learn important skills. Children also benefit from the support and guidance of more-skilled children.

4. *Monitor and encourage children's use of private speech.* Be aware of the developmental change from externally talking to oneself when solving a problem during the preschool years to privately talking to oneself in the early elementary school years. In the elementary school years, encourage children to internalize and self-regulate their talk to themselves.

www.mhhe.com/santrockcd10

Lev Vygotsky:
Revolutionary Scientist
Vygotsky Links
Scaffolding
Cognitive Apprenticeship

5. *Assess the child's ZPD, not IQ.* Like Piaget, Vygotsky did not believe that formal, standardized tests are the best way to assess children's learning. Rather, Vygotsky argued that assessment should focus on determining the child's zone of proximal development. The skilled helper presents the child with tasks of varying difficulty to determine the best level at which to begin instruction. The ZPD is a measure of learning potential. IQ, also a measure of learning potential, emphasizes that intelligence is a property of the child. By contrast, ZPD emphasizes that learning is interpersonal. It is inappropriate to say that the child *has* a ZPD. Rather, a child *shares* a ZPD with a more-skilled individual.

6. *Transform the classroom with Vygotskian ideas.* What does a Vygotskian classroom look like? The Kamehameha Elementary Education Program (KEEP) is based on Vygotsky's theory (Tharp, 1994). The zone of proximal development is the key element of instruction in this program. Children might read a story and then interpret its meaning. Many of the learning activities take place in small groups. All children spend at least 20 minutes each morning in an activity setting called "Center One." In this context, scaffolding is used to improve children's literary skills. The instructor asks

Careers in Child Development

Donene Polson, *Elementary School Teacher*

Donene Polson teaches at Washington Elementary School in Salt Lake City, Utah. Washington is an innovative school that emphasizes the importance of people learning together as a community of learners. Children as well as adults plan learning activities. Throughout the school day, children work in small groups.

Donene says that she loves working in a school in which students, teachers, and parents work together as a community to help children learn. Before the school year begins, Donene meets with parents at the family's home to prepare for the upcoming year, getting acquainted, and establishing schedules to determine when parents can contribute to classroom instruction. At monthly parent-teacher meetings, Donene and the parents plan the curriculum and discuss how children's learning is progressing. They brainstorm about resources in the community that can be used effectively to promote children's learning.

In Vygotsky's theory, an important point is that children need to learn the skills that help them do well in their culture. Vygotsky believed that this should be accomplished through interaction with more-skilled members of the culture, such as this Mexican American girl learning to read with the guidance of her mother.

questions, responds to students' queries, and builds on the ideas that students generate. Thousands of low-income children have attended KEEP public schools in Hawaii, on an Arizona Navajo Indian reservation, and in Los Angeles. Compared with a control group of non-KEEP children, the KEEP children participate more actively in classroom discussion, are more attentive in class, and have higher reading achievement (Tharp & Gallimore, 1988). To read further about a Vygotsky-based classroom and its teacher, see the Careers in Child Development insert.

In one recent study with a foundation in Vygotsky's theory, pairs of children from two U.S. public schools worked together (Matusov, Bell, & Rogoff, 2001). One member of the pair was always from a school with a traditional format involving only occasional opportunities for children to cooperate in their schoolwork. The other member of the pair was always from a school that emphasizes collaboration throughout the school day. The children with the collaborative school background more often built on each other's ideas in a collaborative way than did the children with the traditional school background. The traditional school children primarily used a "quizzing" form of guidance based on asking known-answer questions and withholding information to test the learner's understanding.

Evaluating and Comparing Vygotsky's Theory and Piaget's Theory

Vygotsky's theory became known later than Piaget's theory, so it has not yet been evaluated as thoroughly. However, Vygotsky's theory already has been embraced by many teachers and has been successfully applied to education. His view of the importance of sociocultural influences on children's development fits with the cur-

	Vygotsky	**Piaget**
Sociocultural Context	Strong Emphasis	Little Emphasis
Constructivism	Social constructivist	Cognitive constructivist
Stages	No general stages of development proposed	Strong emphasis on stages (sensorimotor, preoperational, concrete operational, and formal operational)
Key Processes	Zone of proximal development, language, dialogue, tools of the culture	Schema, assimilation, accommodation, operations, conservation, classification, hypothetical-deductive reasoning
Role of Language	A major role; language plays a powerful role in shaping thought	Language has a minimal role; cognition primarily directs language
View on Education	Education plays a central role, helping children learn the tools of the culture.	Education merely refines the child's cognitive skills that have already emerged.
Teaching Implications	Teacher is a facilitator and guide, not a director; establish many opportunities for children to learn with the teacher and more-skilled peers	Also views teacher as a facilitator and guide, not a director; provide support for children to explore their world and discover knowledge

FIGURE 7.15 Comparison of Vygotsky's and Piaget's Theories

rent belief that it is important to evaluate contextual factors in learning (Bearison & Dorval, 2002; Gojdamaschko, 1999; Rowe & Wertsch, 2002).

Criticisms of Vygotsky's approach have surfaced. For example, some critics say that he overemphasizes the role of language in thinking. Also, might facilitators ever be too helpful (as when an a parent becomes too overbearing and controlling)? Further, some children might become lazy and expect help when they actually can do something on their own.

We already have mentioned several comparisons of Vygotsky's and Piaget's theories, such as Vygotsky's emphasis on the importance of inner speech in development and Piaget's view that such speech is immature. We also said earlier that both Vygotsky's and Piaget's theories are constructivist, emphasizing that children actively construct knowledge and understanding, rather than being passive receptacles.

Although both theories are constructivist, Vygotsky's is a **social constructivist approach,** which emphasizes the social contexts of learning and the idea that knowledge is mutually built and constructed. Moving from Piaget to Vygotsky, the conceptual shift is from the individual to collaboration, social interaction, and sociocultural activity (Rogoff, 1998). For Piaget, children construct knowledge by transforming, organizing, and reorganizing previous knowledge. For Vygotsky, children construct knowledge through social interaction with others. The implication of Piaget's theory for teaching is that children need support to explore their world and discover knowledge. The main implication of Vygotsky's theory for teaching is that students need many opportunities to learn with the teacher and more-skilled peers. In both Piaget's and Vygotsky's theories, teachers serve as facilitators and guides, rather than as directors and molders of learning. Figure 7.15 compares Vygotsky's and Piaget's theories.

social constructivist approach Emphasizes the social contexts of learning and that knowledge is mutually built and constructed.

Review and Reflect: Learning Goal 4

4 Summarize Vygotsky's theory and compare it with Piaget's theory

REVIEW

- What is the zone of proximal development?
- What is scaffolding?
- What is Vygotsky's view of language and thought?
- How can Vygotsky's view be applied to educating children?
- What are some contributions and criticisms of Vygotsky's theory? How can Vygotsky's theory and Piaget's theory be compared?

REFLECT

- Which theory do you like best—Piaget's or Vygotsky's? Why?

Reach Your Learning Goals

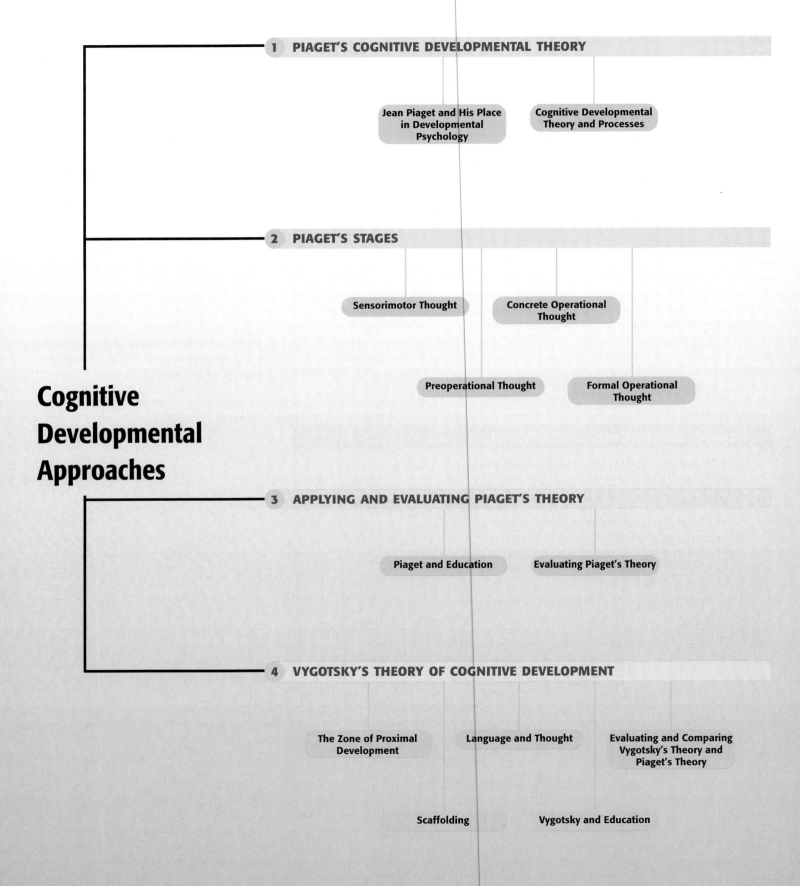

Cognitive Developmental Approaches

1 PIAGET'S COGNITIVE DEVELOPMENTAL THEORY

Jean Piaget and His Place in Developmental Psychology

Cognitive Developmental Theory and Processes

2 PIAGET'S STAGES

Sensorimotor Thought

Concrete Operational Thought

Preoperational Thought

Formal Operational Thought

3 APPLYING AND EVALUATING PIAGET'S THEORY

Piaget and Education

Evaluating Piaget's Theory

4 VYGOTSKY'S THEORY OF COGNITIVE DEVELOPMENT

The Zone of Proximal Development

Language and Thought

Evaluating and Comparing Vygotsky's Theory and Piaget's Theory

Scaffolding

Vygotsky and Education

Summary

1 Discuss Piaget's place in developmental psychology and the key dimensions of his theory

- Piaget's contribution to developmental psychology might be as important as Freud's to personality and abnormal psychology. We owe to Piaget the present field of cognitive development.
- In Piaget's theory, the development of the child's rational thinking and stages of thought are emphasized. Thoughts are the primary determinant of the child's actions. Children use schemas to make sense of what they experience. A schema is a concept or framework that exists at a given moment in a child's mind and that organizes information and provides a structure for interpreting it. Two processes are responsible for how children use and adapt their schemas: assimilation and accommodation. Assimilation occurs when children incorporate new information into their existing knowledge. Accommodation refers to children's adjustment to new information. Through the process of organization, Piaget believed that children group isolated behaviors into a higher-order, more smoothly functioning cognitive system. Every level of thought is organized. Equilibration is a mechanism Piaget proposed to explain how children shift from one cognitive stage to the next. The shift occurs as the child experiences cognitive conflict or disequilibrium in trying to understand the world. Eventually the child resolves the conflict and reaches a new balance of thought.

2 Describe Piaget's four stages of cognitive development

- In sensorimotor thought, the first of Piaget's four stages, the infant organizes and coordinates sensations with physical movements. The stage lasts from birth to about 2 years of age and is nonsymbolic throughout, according to Piaget. Sensorimotor thought has six substages: simple reflexes; first habits and primary circular reactions; secondary circular reactions; coordination of secondary circular reactions; tertiary circular reactions, novelty, and curiosity; and internalization of schemes. Piaget and other developmentalists have been interested in the infant's understanding of physical reality. One aspect of this reality is object permanence, the ability to understand that objects continue to exist even though the infant is no longer observing them. Another aspect involves the infant's understanding of cause and effect. Piaget opened up a whole new way of looking at infant development in terms of coordinating sensory input with motoric actions. However, in the past two decades, many research studies have suggested that revision of Piaget's view is needed. In perceptual development, researchers have found that a stable and differentiated perceptual world is established earlier than Piaget envisioned. In conceptual development, researchers have found that memory and other forms of symbolic activity occur at least by the second half of the first year of life, also much earlier than Piaget believed. Some developmentalists argue that it is hard to tell a unifying story about infant cognitive development today the way Piaget did many years ago. Debate flourishes about many issues, such as whether a concept is innate and whether a concept emerges full-blown or gradually.
- Preoperational thought is the beginning of the ability to reconstruct at the level of thought what has been established in behavior. It involves a transition from a primitive to a more sophisticated use of symbols. In preoperational thought, the child does not yet think in an operational way. The symbolic function substage occurs roughly from 2 to 4 years of age and is characterized by symbolic thought, egocentrism, and animism. The intuitive thought substage stretches roughly from 4 to 7 years of age. It is called intuitive because, on the one hand, children seem so sure about their knowledge, yet, on the other hand, they are unaware of how they know what they know. The child lacks conservation and asks a barrage of questions.
- Concrete operational thought occurs roughly from 7 to 11 years of age. It involves operations, conservation, classification, seriation, and transitivity. Thought is not as abstract as later in development.
- Piaget believed that formal operational thought appears between 11 and 15 years of age. Formal operational thought is more abstract, idealistic, and logical than concrete operational thought. Piaget believed that adolescents become capable of engaging in hypothetical-deductive reasoning. Adolescents develop a special kind of egocentrism that involves an imaginary audience and a personal fable about being unique and invulnerable. Formal operational thought has two phases—an assimilation phase in which reality is overwhelmed (early adolescence) and an accommodation phase in which intellectual balance is restored (late adolescence). Piaget did not give adequate attention to individual variation in adolescent thinking. Many young adolescents do not think in hypothetical-deductive ways but rather are consolidating their concrete operational thinking.

3 Apply Piaget's theory to education and evaluate his theory

- Piaget was not an educator, but his constructivist views have been applied to teaching.
- We owe to Piaget the field of cognitive development. He was a genius at observing children, and he gave us a number of masterful concepts. Critics question his estimates of competence at different developmental levels, his stage concept, and other ideas. Neo-Piagetians believe that children's cognition is more specific than Piaget thought.

4 Summarize Vygotsky's theory and compare it with Piaget's theory

- Zone of proximal development (ZPD) is Vygotsky's term for the range of tasks that are too difficult for children to master alone but that can be learned with the guidance and assistance of more-skilled adults and peers.

- Scaffolding involves changing the level of support over the course of a teaching session, with the more-skilled person adjusting guidance to fit the child's current performance level. Dialogue is an important aspect of scaffolding.
- Vygotsky believed that language plays a key role in cognition. Language and thought initially develop independently, but then children internalize their egocentric speech in the form of inner speech, which becomes their thoughts. This transition to inner speech occurs from 3 to 7 years of age. Vygotsky's view contrasts with Piaget's view that young children's speech is immature and egocentric.
- Applications to education include using the child's zone of proximal development, using scaffolding, monitoring and encouraging children's use of private speech, assessing the ZPD instead of IQ, and transforming the classroom with Vygotskian ideas. Vygotsky's view increasingly has been applied to education.
- Especially important are Vygotsky's ideas related to sociocultural influences on children's development. Some critics say Vygotsky overestimated the role of the language. Comparison of Vygotsky's and Piaget's theories involves culture, constructivism, stages, key processes, role of language, views on education, and teaching implications.

Key Terms

schema 207
organization 208
equilibration 208
simple reflexes 209
first habits and primary
    circular reactions 209
primary circular reactions 210
secondary circular reactions
    210
coordination of secondary
    circular reactions 210

tertiary circular reactions,
    novelty, and curiosity 210
tertiary circular reactions 210
internalization of schemes 210
object permanence 211
A$\overline{\text{B}}$ error 212
operations 215
symbolic function substage
    215
egocentrism 215

animism 216
intuitive thought substage 217
centration 217
conservation 217
horizontal décalage 220
seriation 220
transitivity 221
hypothetical-deductive
    reasoning 222
adolescent egocentrism 224

imaginary audience 224
personal fable 224
neo-Piagetians 229
zone of proximal development
    (ZPD) 230
scaffolding 230
social constructivist approach
    235

Key People

Jean Piaget 207
Renée Baillargeon 211

Barbel Inhelder 215
Rochel Gelman 218

David Elkind 224
Lev Vygotsky 229

Barbara Rogoff 231

Taking It to the Net

1. Francesca is surveying *Time* magazine's list of the top 100 people of the twentieth century. She notices that Piaget made the list. Why would Piaget be on the list?
2. Ellen is majoring in interdisciplinary studies. She is preparing a report on famous thinkers who engaged in cross-disciplinary study and teaching and how this influenced their theories. She has heard that Piaget was adept at several disciplines. She wants to know what they were and how they might have influenced his theory of cognitive development.

E-Learning Tools

To help you master the material in this chapter, you'll find a number of valuable study tools on the Student CD-ROM that accompanies this book. Also visit the Online Learning Center for *Child Development*, tenth edition (**www.mhhe.com/santrockcd10**) where you'll find these additional resources:

3. Theo has to write a compare-and-contrast paper for his English class. His teacher has encouraged the class to write about something they are studying in another class. Theo thinks it would be interesting to compare and contrast Vygotsky's and Piaget's theories of cognitive development. Would a paper on their beliefs about how culture influences cognitive development be a good choice?

Connect to **www.mhhe.com/santrockcd10** to research the answers and complete these exercises.

- View video clips by key developmental psychology experts including Charles Nelson on the benefits of studying brain development.
- Build your decision-making skills by trying your hand at the parenting, nursing, and education "Scenarios" on the Online Learning Center.

*The mind is an enchant-
ing thing.*

—MARIANNE MOORE
American Poet, 20th Century

Information Processing

Chapter Outline	*Learning Goals*

THE INFORMATION-PROCESSING APPROACH   **1**

Processes

Comparison with the Cognitive
Developmental Approach

1 Discuss the basic ideas in the information-processing approach and compare it with the cognitive developmental approach

MEMORY   **2**

What Is Memory?

Encoding

Storage

Retrieval and Forgetting

Personal Trauma and Memory

2 Describe the way that memory works in children

THINKING   **3**

What Is Thinking?

Forming Concepts

Solving Problems

Thinking Critically

Thinking Scientifically

3 Explain how children think

METACOGNITION   **4**

Developmental Changes

Strategies

Self-Regulatory Learning

4 Summarize developmental changes and processes involved in children's metacognition

The Story of Laura Bickford

Laura Bickford is a master teacher and chairs the English Department at Nordoff High School in Ojai, California. She recently spoke about how she encourages her students to think:

> I believe the call to teach is a call to teach students how to think. In encouraging critical thinking, literature itself does a good bit of work for us but we still have to be guides. We have to ask good questions. We have to show students the value in asking their own questions, in having discussions and conversations. In addition to reading and discussing literature, the best way to move students to think critically is to have them write. We write all the time in a variety of modes: journals, formal essays, letters, factual reports, news articles, speeches, or other formal oral presentations. We have to show students where they merely scratch the surface in their thinking and writing. I call these moments "hits and runs." When I see this "hit and run" effort, I draw a window on the paper. I tell them it is a "window of opportunity" to go deeper, elaborate, and clarify. Many students don't do this kind of thinking until they are prodded to do so.
>
> I also use metacognitive strategies all the time—that is, helping students know about knowing. These include asking students to comment on their learning after we have finished particular pieces of projects and asking them to discuss in advance what we might be seeking to learn as we *begin* a new project or activity. I also ask them to keep reading logs so they can observe their own thinking as it happens. For example, they might copy a passage from a reading selection and comment on it. Studying a passage from J. D. Salinger's *The Catcher in the Rye,* a student might write: "I've never thought about life the way that Holden Caulfield does. Maybe I see the world differently than he does. He always is so depressed. I'm not depressed. Salinger is good at showing us someone who is usually depressed. How does he manage to do that?" In addition, I ask students to comment on their own learning by way of grading themselves. This year a student gave me one of the most insightful lines about her growth as a reader I have ever seen from a student. She wrote, "I no longer think in a monotone when I'm reading." I don't know if she grasps the magnitude of that thought or how it came to be that she made that change. It is magic when students see themselves growing like this.

1 THE INFORMATION-PROCESSING APPROACH

Processes

Comparison with the Cognitive Developmental Approach

What are some of the basic ideas in the information-processing approach? How is it similar to and different from the cognitive developmental approaches we described in chapter 7?

Processes

information-processing approach The approach that focuses on the ways children process information about their world—how they manipulate information, monitor it, and strategize about it.

The **information-processing approach** focuses on the ways that children process information about their world—how they manipulate the information, monitor it, and strategize about it. ◀ **page 36** Central to this approach are the processes of memory and thinking. According to the information-processing approach, children develop a gradually increasing capacity for processing information, which allows them to acquire increasingly complex knowledge and skills. Robert Siegler (1998) described three main characteristics of the information-processing approach: thinking, change mechanisms, and self-modification.

Thinking In Siegler's view, thinking is information processing. In this regard, Siegler provides a broad perspective on thinking. He says that when children perceive, encode, represent, and store information from the world, they are engaging in thinking. Siegler believes that thinking is highly flexible, which allows individuals to adapt and adjust to many changes in circumstances, task requirements, and goals. However, there are some limits on the human's remarkable thinking abilities. Individuals can pay attention to only a limited amount of information at any one moment, and there are limits on how fast we can process information. Later in the chapter we will explore children's powers of attention.

Change Mechanisms Siegler argues that in information processing the main focus should be on the role of mechanisms of change in development. He believes that the following mechanisms work together to create changes in children's cognitive skills: encoding, automaticity, and strategy construction.

- **Encoding** is the process by which information gets into memory. Siegler states that a key aspect of solving problems is to encode the relevant information and ignore the irrelevant parts. Because it often takes time and effort to construct new strategies, children must practice them in order to eventually execute them automatically and maximize their effectiveness.
- **Automaticity** refers to the ability to process information with little or no effort. With age and experience, information processing becomes increasingly automatic on many tasks, allowing children to detect new connections among ideas and events that they otherwise would miss.
- **Strategy construction** involves the discovery of new procedures for processing information. Siegler (2001) says that children need to encode key information about a problem and coordinate the information with relevant prior knowledge to solve the problem.

Self-Modification The contemporary information-processing approach argues that children play an active role in their development. They use knowledge and strategies that they have learned in previous circumstances to adapt their responses to a new learning situation. In this manner, children build newer and more sophisticated responses from prior knowledge and strategies. The importance of self-modification in processing information is exemplified in **metacognition,** which means cognition about cognition, or "knowing about knowing" (Flavell, 1999; Flavell, Miller, & Miller, 2002). We will study metacognition in the final section of this chapter and especially will emphasize how self-awareness can enable children to adapt and manage their strategies during problem solving and thinking.

Comparison with the Cognitive Developmental Approach

The information-processing and cognitive developmental approaches have quite a bit in common. Both try to identify children's cognitive capabilities and limits at various points in development. Both seek to describe ways in which children do and do not understand important concepts at different points in life and try to explain how later, more advanced understandings grow out of earlier, more primitive ones. Both also emphasize the impact that existing understandings can have on children's ability to acquire new understandings.

However, the two approaches differ in some important ways. The information-processing approach places greater emphasis on the role of processing limitations, strategies for overcoming the limitations, and knowledge about specific content. It also focuses on more precise analysis of change and on the contribution of ongoing

Strategies

encoding The process by which information gets into memory.

automaticity The ability to process information with little or no effort.

strategy construction The process of discovering a new procedure for processing information.

metacognition Cognition about cognition, or "knowing about knowing."

cognitive activity to that change. These differences have led to a greater use of formal descriptions, such as computer simulations and flow diagrams, that allow information-processing theorists to determine in detail how thinking proceeds.

The information-processing approach does not describe cognition as unfolding in stages like Piaget did. ◀ **page 36** Rather, for information-processing psychologists, development is more continuous. Also, for information-processing psychologists, children socially construct knowledge to a lesser degree than Vygotsky suggests.

Review and Reflect: Learning Goal 1

1 Discuss the basic ideas in the information-processing approach and compare it with the cognitive developmental approach

REVIEW

• What are the key cognitive processes in the information-processing approach?
• How is the information-processing approach similar to and different from the cognitive developmental approach?

REFLECT

• In terms of ability to learn, are there ways that a child processes information similar to the way that a computer does? What might be some differences in the way that children and computers process information?

---

2 MEMORY

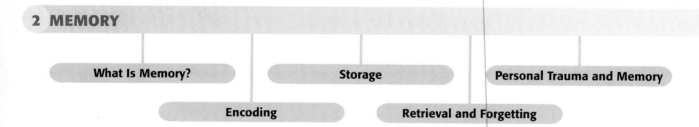

What Is Memory?   Storage   Personal Trauma and Memory

Encoding   Retrieval and Forgetting

Twentieth-century playwright Tennessee Williams once commented that life is all memory except for that one present moment that goes by so quickly that you can hardly catch it going. Just what is memory?

What Is Memory?

Memory is the retention of information over time and involves encoding, storage, and retrieval. As we indicated earlier, *encoding* is the mechanism by which information gets into memory. **Storage** consists of the retention of information over time. **Retrieval** takes place when information is taken out of storage.

Memory anchors the self in continuity. Without memory children would not be able to connect what happened to them yesterday with what is going on in their lives today. Contemporary developmentalists and educators emphasize that it is important not to view memory in terms of how children add something to it but rather underscore how children actively construct their memory (Schacter, 2001; Schneider & Bjorklund, 1998). Thinking about memory in terms of encoding, storage, and retrieval should help you to understand it better (see figure 8.1).

Encoding

Encoding clearly is a critical process for memory. We will explore a number of aspects of encoding, beginning with attention.

www.mhhe.com/santrockcd10

Memory Links

memory The retention of information over time, involving encoding, storage, and retrieval.

storage The retention of information over time.

retrieval Taking information out of storage.

Attention In everyday language, encoding has much in common with attention and learning. When children are listening to a teacher, watching a movie, listening to music, or talking with a friend, they are encoding information into memory. Although children can perform some activities automatically, many others require them to pay **attention,** which refers to concentrating and focusing mental resources.

Habituation and Dishabituation Closely linked with attention are the processes of habituation and dishabituation. If a stimulus—a sight or sound—is presented to infants several times in a row, they usually pay less attention to it each time. This suggests they are bored with it. This is the process of **habituation**—repeated presentation of the same stimulus, which causes reduced attention to the stimulus. **Dishabituation** is an increase in responsiveness after a change in stimulation. Among the measures researchers use to study whether habituation is occurring are sucking behavior (sucking behavior stops when the young infant attends to a novel object), heart and respiration rates, and the length of time the infant looks at an object. Newborn infants can habituate to repetitive stimulation in virtually every stimulus modality—vision, hearing, touch, and so on (Rovee-Collier, 1987). However, habituation becomes more acute over the first three months of life. Figure 8.2 shows the results of one study of habituation and dishabituation with newborns (Slater, Morison, & Somers, 1988).

Habituation can be used to tell us much about infants' perception, such as the extent to which they can see, hear, smell, taste, and experience touch (Slater, Field, & Hernandez-Reif, 2002). Habituation also can be used to tell whether infants recognize something they have previously experienced.

The extensive assessment of habituation in recent years has resulted in its use as a measure of an infant's maturity and well-being. Infants who have brain damage or have suffered birth traumas, such as lack of oxygen, do not habituate well and might later have developmental and learning problems.

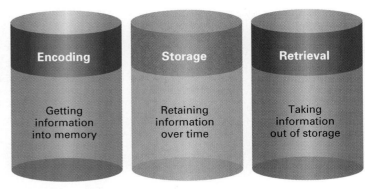

FIGURE 8.1 Processing Information in Memory

As you read about the many aspects of memory in this chapter, think about the organization of memory in terms of these three main activities.

attention Concentrating and focusing mental resources.

habituation Repeated presentation of the same stimulus, which causes reduced attention to the stimulus.

dishabituation Increase in responsiveness after a change in stimulation.

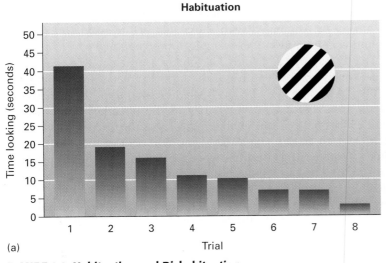

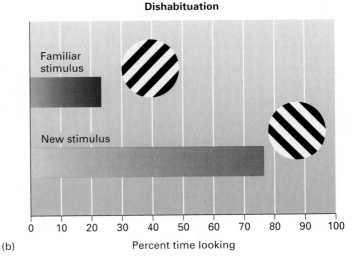

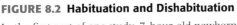

FIGURE 8.2 Habituation and Dishabituation

In the first part of one study, 7-hour-old newborns were shown the stimulus in (*a*). As indicated, the newborns looked at it an average of 41 seconds when it was first presented to them (Slater, Morison, & Somers, 1988). Over seven more presentations of the stimulus, they looked as it less and less. In the second part of study, infants were presented with both the familiar stimulus to which they had just become habituated to (*a*) and a new stimulus (shown in *b*, which was rotated 90 degrees). The newborns looked at the new stimulus three times as much as the familiar stimulus.

What are some good strategies teachers might use to get students' attention?

A knowledge of habituation and dishabituation can benefit parent-infant interaction. Infants respond to changes in stimulation. If stimulation is repeated often, the infant's response will decrease to the point that the infant no longer responds to the parent. In parent-infant interaction, it is important for parents to do novel things and to repeat them often until the infant stops responding. The wise parent senses when the infant shows an interest and that many repetitions of the stimulus may be necessary for the infant to process the information. The parent stops or changes behaviors when the infant redirects her attention (Rosenblith, 1992).

Developmental Changes in Childhood   Toddlers wander around, shift attention from one activity to another, and seem to spend little time focused on any one object or event. By comparison, the preschool child might be observed watching television for a half hour. In one study, young children's attention to television in the natural setting of the home was videotaped (Anderson & others, 1985). Ninety-nine families comprising 460 individuals were observed for 4,672 hours. Visual attention to television dramatically increased during the preschool years.

One deficit in attention during the preschool years concerns those dimensions that stand out, or are *salient*, compared with those that are relevant to solving a problem or performing well on a task. For example, a problem might have a flashy, attractive clown that presents the directions for solving a problem. Preschool children are influenced strongly by the features of the task that stand out, such as the flashy, attractive clown. After the age of 6 or 7, children attend more efficiently to the dimensions of the task that are relevant, such as the directions for solving a problem. Developmentalists believe this change reflects a shift to cognitive control of attention, so that children act less impulsively and reflect more.

One reason older children are better than younger children at deploying attention is that they are more likely to construct a plan of action to guide their attentional efforts when they are trying to solve a problem. However, younger children often can use attention-focusing strategies when such strategies are provided to them. Possibly school experiences help children become more aware of their own attentional capabilities; or as children develop, perhaps they come to understand that their mind works best when it is active and constructive. Thus, attending to something relevant is an active, effortful process that draws on mental resources rather than a passive process of receiving the available information.

When experimenters ask children to judge whether two complex pictures are the same, preschool children tend to use a haphazard comparison strategy, not examining all of the details before making a judgment. By comparison, elementary

(a)   (b)

FIGURE 8.3 The Planfulness of Attention

In one study, children were given pairs of houses to examine, like the ones shown here (Vurpillot, 1968). For three pairs of houses, what was in the windows was identical (*a*). For the other three pairs, the windows had different items in them (*b*). By filming the reflection in the children's eyes, it could be determined what they were looking at, how long they looked, and the sequence of their eye movements. Children under 6 examined only a fragmentary portion of each display and made their judgments on the basis of insufficient information. By contrast, older children scanned the windows in more detailed ways and were more accurate in their judgments of which windows were identical.

school age children are more likely to systematically compare the details across the pictures, one detail at a time (Vurpillot, 1968) (see figure 8.3).

A critical skill in paying attention is doing it *selectively*. For example, as a teacher gives instructions for completing a task, students need to pay attention to what she is saying and not be distracted by other students who are talking. As students study for a test, they need to focus selectively on the book they are reading and tune out or eliminate other stimuli, such as the sound of a television. In one research study, 8-year-old children tended to use exhaustive attentional searches to find information, whereas 11-year-olds used more selective attentional strategies in searching for information (Davidson, 1996).

Being able to *shift* from one activity to another when called for is another challenge related to attention. For example, learning to write good stories requires shifting among the competing tasks of forming letters, composing grammar, structuring paragraphs, and conveying the story as a whole. Older children and adolescents are better than younger children at shifting attention when it is required.

Rehearsal   In addition to attention, rehearsal is another process involved in encoding. *Rehearsal* is the conscious repetition of information over time that increases the length of time that information stays in memory. Rehearsal does not hold more information in memory, it just keeps the same information in memory longer. Rehearsal works best when individuals need to remember a list of items over a brief period of time. When they must retain information over long periods of time, as when studying for a test the next week, other strategies usually work better than rehearsal. A main reason rehearsal does not work well for retaining information over the long term is that rehearsal often involves just rotely repeating information without imparting any meaning to it. When children construct their memory in meaningful ways, they remember better.

A classic study by John Flavell and his colleagues (Flavell, Beach, & Chinsky, 1966) illustrates the importance of rehearsal and developmental changes in its use. Children from 5 to 10 years old were given the task of remembering the names of a set of two to five pictures for 15 seconds. The novel feature of the experiment was that the experimenter was a trained lip-reader. Although not many children said anything aloud, a number of children made lip movements that indicated rehearsal of names and pictures. The percentage of children making lip movements increased with age: 10 percent of the 5-year-olds, 60 percent of the 7-year-olds, and 85 percent of the 10-year-olds made lip movements. In a later study of 6-year-olds, the research team found that children who rehearsed showed better recall than those who did not. When nonrehearsers were taught to rehearse, their performance rivaled that of the spontaneous rehearsers (Keeney, Cannizzo, & Flavell, 1967).

Subsequent investigations made the interesting point that rudimentary, rehearsal-like processes begin to appear at very young ages (DeLoache, Cassidy, & Brown, 1985). In one study, 3- and 4-year-old children watched a toy dog being hidden under one of three cups. Instructed to remember where the dog was hidden, the children looked at, pointed to, and touched the appropriate cup (Wellman, Ritter, & Flavell, 1975). Even 1½-year-olds, under certain circumstances, use rehearsal—when they see an object hidden in a room, they will point to it, touch it, and repeat its name while they wait to be able to retrieve it (DeLoache, 1984).

If using rehearsal is so helpful in short-term remembering, why do young children so often not rehearse? One simple reason is that young children both benefit less and incur greater costs by using the strategy than do older children. When children begin to use rehearsal (and other new strategies), executing the new strategy requires greater mental resources than it will later (Kee & Howell, 1988). Similarly, when the experimental procedure makes it easier to execute the strategy, the difference between the performances produced by older and younger children's use of the strategy decreases (DeMarie-Dreblow & Miller, 1988). The point is that children need a reasonable amount of experience with a strategy before they can gain the full potential benefit from using it.

A second reason why young children tend not to rehearse, even when they have been taught to do so and have benefited from doing so, is that they often attribute their success to other factors—luck, greater effort, or being smart. Those children who attribute their success to the new strategy they used tend to use it again in the future, but those who think other factors were responsible tend not to use the new approach again (Fabricius & Hagen, 1984).

Deep Processing Following the discovery that rehearsal is not an efficient way to remember information over the long term, Fergus Craik and Robert Lockhart (1972) proposed that individuals process information at different levels. Their theory, *levels of processing theory,* states that memory is on a continuum from shallow to deep, with deeper processing producing better memory. The sensory or physical features of stimuli are analyzed first at a *shallow* level. This might involve detecting the lines, angles, and contours of a printed word's letters, or a spoken word's frequency, duration, and loudness. At an *intermediate* level of processing, the stimulus is recognized and given a label. For example, a four-legged, barking object is identified as a dog. Then, at the *deepest* level, information is processed semantically, in terms of its meaning. For example, if a child sees the word *boat,* at the shallow level she might notice the shapes of the letters, at the intermediate level she might think of the characteristics of the word (such as it rhymes with *coat*), and at the deepest level she might think about the last time she went fishing with her dad on a boat and the kind of boat it was. Researchers have found that individuals remember information better when they process it at a deeper level (Hunt & Ellis, 1999).

Elaboration Cognitive psychologists soon recognized, however, that there is more to good memory than just depth of processing. They discovered that individuals have better memory if they use elaboration in their encoding of information. *Elaboration* involves more extensive information processing. Thus, when a teacher presents the concept of democracy to students, they likely will remember it better if they come up with good examples of it. Thinking of examples is a good way to elaborate information. Self-reference is also an effective way to elaborate information. A person will be more likely to remember the concept of fairness if he can generate personal examples of inequities and equities he has personally experienced; a person will be more likely to remember the concept of a symphony if she associates it with the last time she attended a symphony concert rather than merely rehearses the words that define what a symphony is. Thinking about personal associations with information makes the information more meaningful and helps students remember it.

One reason elaboration works so well in producing good memory is that it adds to the *distinctiveness* of memory code (Ellis, 1987). To remember a piece of information such as a name, an experience, or a fact about geography, children need to search for the code that contains this information among the mass of codes in long-term memory. The search process is easier if the memory code is unique (Hunt & Kelly, 1996). The situation is not unlike searching for a friend at a crowded airport. A friend who is 6 feet 3 inches tall and has flaming red hair will be easier to find in the crowd than someone who has more common features. Also, as a person elaborates information, more information is stored, making it easier to differentiate the memory from others. For example, if a child witnesses another child being hit by a car that speeds away, the child's memory of the car will be far better if she deliberately encodes that the car is a red 1995 Pontiac with tinted windows and spinners on the wheels than if she encodes only that it is a red car.

The use of elaboration changes developmentally (Schneider & Pressley, 1997). Adolescents are more likely to use elaboration spontaneously than children. Elementary school children can be taught to use elaboration strategies on learning tasks, but they are less likely than adolescents to use the strategies on other learning tasks in the future. In one study, elaboration involved the experimenter telling second-and fifth-grade children to construct a meaningful sentence for a key word (such as "The postman carried a letter in his cart" for the key word *cart*). As shown in figure 8.4, both second- and fifth-grade children remembered the key words better when they constructed a meaningful sentence containing the word than when the key word and its definition were told to the children (Pressley, Levin, & McCormick, 1980).

Constructing Images When we construct an image of something, we are elaborating the information. For example, think of a house or apartment where you have spent a lot of time—do you know how many windows are in it? Few of us ever memorize this information, but you probably can come up with a good answer, especially if you reconstruct a mental image of each room. Take a "mental walk" through the house or apartment, counting the windows as you go.

Allan Paivio (1971, 1986) believes that memories are stored in two ways: as a verbal code or as an image code. For example, you can remember a picture by a label (*The Last Supper*, a verbal code) or by a mental image. Paivio says that the more detailed and distinctive the image code, the better your memory of the information will be.

Researchers have found that encouraging children to use imagery to remember verbal information works better for older children than younger children (Schneider & Pressley, 1997). In one study, 20 sentences were presented to first- through sixth-grade children to remember (such as "The angry bird shouted at the white dog" and "The policeman painted the circus tent on a windy day") (Pressley & others, 1987). Children were randomly assigned to an imagery condition (make a picture in your head for each sentence) and a control condition (children were just told to try hard). Figure 8.5 shows that the imagery instructions improved memory for the sentences in the older elementary school children (grades 4 through 6) but not for the younger elementary school children (grades 1 through 3). Researchers have found that young elementary school children can use imagery to remember pictures better than they can verbal materials, such as sentences (Schneider & Pressley, 1997).

Organization If children organize information when they are encoding it, their memory benefits. To understand the importance of organization in encoding, complete the following exercise. Recall the 12 months of the year as quickly as you can.

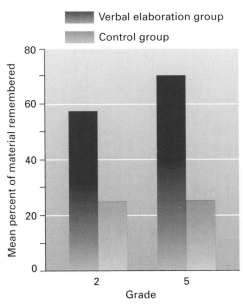

FIGURE 8.4 Verbal Elaboration and Memory

Both second- and fifth-grade children remembered words better when they constructed a meaningful sentence for the word (verbal elaboration group) than when they merely heard the word and its definition (control group). The verbal elaboration worked better for the fifth-graders than the second-graders.

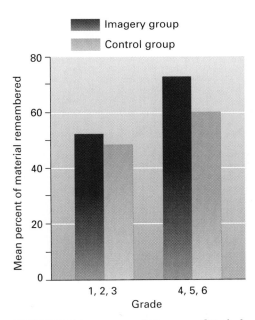

FIGURE 8.5 Imagery and Memory of Verbal Information

Imagery improved older elementary school children's memory for sentences more than younger elementary school children's memory for sentences.

FRANK AND ERNEST by Bob Thaves

FRANK & ERNEST reprinted by permission of Newspaper Enterprise Association, Inc.

How long did it take you? What was the order of your recall? Your probable answer: a few seconds and in natural order (January, February, March, and so on). Now try to remember the months in alphabetical order. Did you make any errors? How long did it take you? There is a clear distinction between recalling the months in natural order and alphabetically. This exercise is a good one to use with children to help them understand the importance of organizing their memories in *meaningful* ways.

The more adults present information in an organized way, the easier it will be for children to remember it. This is especially true if adults organize information hierarchically or outline it. Also, simply encouraging children to organize information helps them to remember it better than if they are given no instructions about organizing (Mandler, 1980).

Children show increased organization in middle and late childhood. In one investigation, children were presented with a circular array of pictures from four categories: clothing, furniture, animals, and vehicles (Moely & others, 1969). The children were told to study the pictures so that later they could say their names back to the experimenter. They also were told they could move the pictures around to remember them better. The 10- and 11-year-olds performed such groupings; the younger children did not. When younger children were put through a brief training procedure that encouraged grouping, they were able to follow this strategy, and their memory for the pictures improved.

The development of organizational strategies in many ways parallels that of rehearsal. Organization is used far less often by 5- and 6-year-olds than by 9- and 10-year-olds and older children. The quality of the younger children's execution of the strategy is also lower than that of older ones. Executing the strategy also requires more of the younger children's cognitive resources, so it often yields poorer recall among younger than among older children (Bjorklund & Harnishfeger, 1987). Thus, it is not altogether surprising that young children use these strategies less often than older children do—they have more difficulty executing the strategies, and realize smaller benefits from using them.

Chunking is an organizational strategy that benefits memory. Chunking involves grouping or "packing" information into "higher-order units" that can be remembered as single units. Chunking works by making large amounts of information more manageable and more meaningful. For example, consider this simple list of words: *hot, city, book, forget, tomorrow,* and *smile.* Try to hold these in memory for a moment, then write them down. If you recalled all six words, you succeeded in holding 30 letters in your memory.

Storage

After children encode information, they need to retain or store the information. The most prominent aspects of memory storage include the three main stores that vary according to time: sensory memory, short-term memory, and long-term memory.

Memory Time Frames Children remember some information for less than a second, some for about half a minute, and other information for minutes, hours, years, even a lifetime. The three types of memory that vary according to their time frames are *sensory memory* (which lasts a fraction of a second to several seconds); *working memory, or short-term memory* (which lasts about 30 seconds); and *long-term memory* (which lasts up to a lifetime).

Sensory Memory   **Sensory memory** holds information from the world in its original sensory form for only an instant, not much longer than the brief time a child is exposed to visual, auditory, and other sensations. Its information is quickly lost unless the child engages in mental processes like rehearsal to transfer it into short-term or long-term memory.

Children have a sensory memory for sounds up to several seconds, sort of like a brief echo. However, their sensory memory for visual images lasts only for about one-fourth of a second. Because sensory information lasts for only a fleeting moment or two, an important task for the child is to attend to the sensory information that is important for learning.

The sensory memories of children as young as 5 years old have the same capacity as those of adults (Morrison, Holmes, & Haith, 1974). However, young children form sensory-level representations at a slower speed than adults do. Under ideal viewing conditions, adults can represent objects at a sensory level for a tenth of a second, while 7-year-olds take about one-seventh of a second to form similar representations (Hoving & others, 1978). Although this difference is small, when multiplied by the huge amount of sensory-level processing that people do every day, the differences likely have large cumulative effects.

Short-Term Memory   Much information goes no further than the sensory memories of sounds and sights. This information is retained only for a brief instant. However, some of the information, especially that to which we pay attention, is transferred to short-term memory. **Short-term memory** is a limited-capacity memory system in which information is usually retained for only as long as 30 seconds unless strategies are used to retain it longer. Compared with sensory memory, short-term memory is limited in capacity, but it can store information for a relatively longer time.

One way to illustrate the growth of working, or short-term, memory is to present children of different ages with memory tasks. If you have taken an intelligence test, you probably were exposed to one of these tasks. A short list of stimuli, usually digits, is presented at a rapid pace (for example, one item per second). Using this type of memory-span task, researchers have found that short-term memory increases over time in childhood (Case, 1985; Dempster, 1981) (see figure 8.6). The increase is from about two digits in 2- to 3-year-old children, to about five digits in 7-year-old children, to about seven digits in 12- to 13-year-old children. Not every child of a given age has the same short-term memory capacity, however, which is why these items are often used on intelligence tests. In general, children who have larger short-term memory spans do better in school than do their counterparts of the same age who have smaller spans (Siegler, 1998).

Just as the capacity of short-term memory increases with age, so does the speed of processing (Schneider, 2002). This has been the finding with virtually every task that has been used to study memory. For example, children are sometimes shown two shapes, such as those in figure 8.7, and asked whether the shape on the left is just a rotated form of the shape on the right or whether they are different shapes. For children and adults of all ages, the greater the amount of rotation, the longer it takes to tell that the shapes are the same (on trials in which they are the same). However, the rate of rotation is slower for younger children and gradually increases with age, reaching adultlike levels only at about 15 years of age.

Because the growth of processing speed is similar on many different tasks, some investigators have concluded that the speedup reflects a

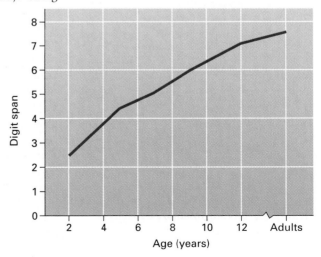

"Can we hurry up and get to the test? My short-term memory is better than my long-term memory."

Copyright © 1999. Reprinted courtesy of Bunny Hoest and *Parade Magazine*.

Short-Term Memory

sensory memory The memory system that holds information from the world in its original sensory form for only an instant.

short-term memory The limited-capacity memory system in which information is retained for as long as 30 seconds, unless the information is rehearsed, in which case it can be retained longer.

FIGURE 8.6 Developmental Changes in Memory Span

In one study, memory span increased about three digits from 2 years of age to five digits in 7 years of age (Dempster, 1981). By 12 years of age, memory span had increased on average another 1½ digits.

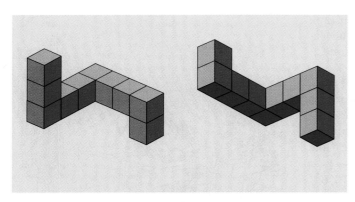

FIGURE 8.7 Cubes Used to Study Mental Rotation Abilities

Both children and adults attempt to determine whether the Lego-like figures are identical by rotating one of them into the same orientation as the other. For all age groups, the more discrepant the initial position of the two figures, the longer this rotation process takes. However, from age 5 to adulthood, the older the individual, the faster their rate of mental rotation.

working memory A kind of mental "work-bench" where information is manipulated and assembled when making decisions, solving problems, and comprehending language.

long-term memory A type of memory that holds enormous amounts of information for a long period of time in a relatively permanent fashion.

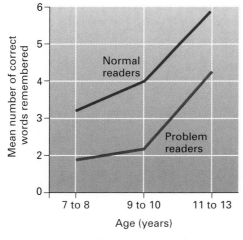

FIGURE 8.8 Working Memory Capacity in Normal and Problem Readers

As they increased in age, the working memory capacity of both normal readers and problem readers improved (Siegel & Ryan, 1989). However, problem readers had a lower working memory capacity than normal readers at each age level.

basic maturation of the central nervous system (Hale, 1990; Kail, 1993). Other researchers have reviewed the same data and concluded that they reflect the greater amount of practice that older children engage in, rather than changes in physiological maturation (Stigler, Nusbaum, & Chalip, 1988).

Developmental changes in processing speed are intertwined with changes in processing capacity. For example, in one study, the faster that 6-year-olds repeated auditorially presented words, the longer their memory spans for those words were (Case, Kurland, & Goldberg, 1982). When speed of word presentation was controlled, though, the memory spans of the 6-year-olds were equal to those of young adults. Thus, the greater memory spans usually observed in older children might be due in large part to the fact that older children can process the material more quickly.

Many cognitive psychologists today prefer the term *working memory* over short-term memory. **Working memory** is a kind of mental "workbench" where individuals manipulate and assemble information when they make decisions, solve problems, and comprehend written and spoken language (Baddeley, 1990, 1998, 2001). While short-term memory is more like a passive storehouse with shelves to store information until it moves to long-term memory, working memory is thought of as far more active and powerful in modifying information. One recent study found that speed of processing information was linked to working memory, which in turn was related to problem-solving effectiveness (Demetriou & others, 2002).

Working memory is linked with children's reading comprehension (Bjorklund, 2000). It is important to retain information in working memory as long as possible so that each newly read word in a passage can be interpreted with the words and concepts that just preceded it. Children who are competent at reading have a greater working memory capacity than children who have problems in reading. In one study, 7- to 13-year-old children who either were normal readers or had reading problems were given a series of incomplete sentences that required them to supply the final word of each sentence (Siegel & Ryan, 1989). For example, one sentence was: "In the summer it is very _____." Another sentence was: "With dinner, we sometimes eat bread and _____." After being presented with a series of such sentences, children were asked to repeat the final word that they had generated for each sentence earlier. As shown in figure 8.8, as children got older, working memory capacity improved for both the normal and the problem readers, but the problem readers had lower working memory capacity (shorter memory spans) than the normal readers at each age level.

Long-Term Memory **Long-term memory** is a type of memory that holds enormous amounts of information for a long period of time in a relatively permanent fashion. A typical human's long-term-memory capacity is staggering. Consider how efficiently individuals can retrieve information. It often takes only a moment to search through this vast storehouse to find the information we want. Think about your own long-term memory. Who wrote the Gettysburg Address? Who was your first-grade teacher? When were you born? Where do you live? You can answer thousands of such questions instantly. Of course, not all information is retrieved so easily from long-term memory.

Memory's Contents Just as memory can be distinguished by how long it lasts, it can also be differentiated on the basis of its *content*. For long-term memory, many contemporary psychologists accept the hierarchy of contents described in figure 8.9. In this hierarchy, long-term memory is divided into the subtypes of declarative memory and procedural memory. Declarative memory is subdivided into episodic memory and semantic memory.

Declarative and Procedural Memory *Declarative memory* is the conscious recollection of information, such as specific facts or events that can be verbally communicated. Declarative memory has been called "knowing that," and more recently has been labeled "explicit memory." Demonstrations of children's declarative memory could include recounting an event they have witnessed or describing a basic principle of math. However, children do not need to be talking to be using declarative memory. If children simply sit and reflect on an experience, their declarative memory is involved.

Procedural memory refers to knowledge in the form of skills and cognitive operations (Schacter, 2001). Procedural memory cannot be consciously recollected, at least not in the form of specific events or facts. This makes procedural memory difficult, if not impossible, to communicate verbally. Procedural memory is sometimes called "knowing how," and recently it also has been described as "implicit memory." When children apply their abilities to perform a dance, ride a bicycle, or type on a computer keyboard, their procedural memory is at work. It also is at work when they speak grammatically correct sentences without having to think about how to do it.

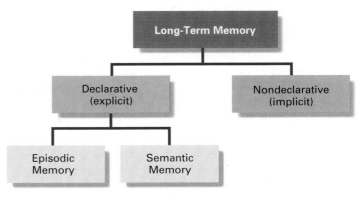

FIGURE 8.9 Classification of Long-Term Memory's Contents

Explicit and implicit memory are involved in a controversy about what infants can remember. Some infant researchers, such as Carolyn Rovee-Collier, argue that infants as young as 2 to 6 months of age can remember some experiences through 1½ to 2 years of age (Rovee-Collier, 2002).

However, Jean Mandler (2000) criticizes Rovee-Collier for failing to distinguish implicit memory (remembering a perceptual-motor skill involved in a conditioning task, such as kicking a mobile) and explicit memory (consciously recalling the past). According to Mandler, when people think about what memory is, they are referring to explicit memory, which most researchers have found does not occur until the second half of the first year (Mandler & McDonough, 1995).

By 9 months of age, infants' explicit memory is readily apparent. For example, in one study, 9-month-old infants' long-term recall of a two-step sequence (such as "Make Big Bird turn on the light") occurred (Carver & Bauer, 1999). Five weeks after experiencing such two-step sequences, 45 percent of the infants demonstrated their long-term memory by producing the two actions in the sequence. The other 55 percent did not show evidence of remembering the sequence of actions, reflecting individual differences in infant memory. Also, in a related assessment of these infants, researchers demonstrated changes in the brain activity of the infants as they engaged in recall of the sequences they had experienced five weeks earlier (Carver, Bauer, & Nelson, 2000).

While explicit memory emerges in the second half of the first year of life, the results of other research reveal that it undergoes substantial development and consolidation over the course of the second year of life (Carver & Bauer, 2001). In one longitudinal study, infants were assessed several times during the second year of life (Bauer & others, 2000). These older infants showed more accurate memory and required fewer prompts to demonstrate their memory than infants under the age of 1.

Most adults cannot remember anything from the first three years of their life; this is referred to as *infantile amnesia*. When adults seem to be able to recall something from their infancy, it likely is something they have been told about by relatives or something they saw in a photograph or home movie. One explanation of infantile amnesia focuses on the maturation of the brain, especially in the frontal lobes, which occurs after infancy (Boyer & Diamond, 1992).

Episodic and Semantic Memory Cognitive psychologist Endel Tulving (2000) distinguishes between two subtypes of declarative memory: episodic and semantic. *Episodic memory* is the retention of information about the where and when of life's happenings. Children's memories of the first day of school, who they had lunch with, or the guest who came to talk with their class last week are all episodic.

Semantic memory is a child's general knowledge about the world. It includes:

- Knowledge of the sort learned in school (such as knowledge of geometry)
- Knowledge in different fields of expertise (such as knowledge of chess, for a skilled chess player)
- "Everyday" knowledge about meanings of words, famous people, important places, and common things (such as what being "street smart" means or who Nelson Mandela or Mahatma Gandhi is)

Semantic memory knowledge is independent of the person's identity with the past. For example, children might access a fact—such as "Lima is the capital of the country of Peru"—and not have the foggiest idea of when and where they learned it.

Content Knowledge and How It Is Represented in Long-Term Memory

Does what children already know about a subject affect their ability to remember new information about it? How do children represent information in their memory?

Content Knowledge Our ability to remember new information about a subject does depend considerably on what we already know about it. For example, a child's ability to recount what she has seen on a trip to the library is largely governed by what she already knows about libraries, such as where books on certain topics are located, how to check books out, and so on. With little knowledge of libraries, the child would have a much harder time recounting what she saw there.

The contribution of content knowledge to memory is especially evident in the memory of individuals who are experts or novices in a particular knowledge domain. An expert is the opposite of a novice (someone who is just beginning to learn a content area). Experts demonstrate especially impressive memory in their areas of expertise. One reason children remember less than adults is that they are far less expert in most areas.

What is it, exactly, that experts do? They (National Research Council, 1999):

1. Notice features and meaningful patterns of information that novices don't.
2. Have acquired a great deal of content knowledge that is organized in a manner that reflects a deep understanding of the subject.
3. Can retrieve important aspects of their knowledge with little effort.

Experts have superior recall of information in their area of expertise. The process of chunking that we discussed earlier is one way they accomplish this superior recall. For example, chess masters perceive chunks of meaningful information, which affects their memory of what they see on a chess board. Lacking a hierarchical, highly organized structure for the domain, novices can't use this chunking strategy.

In areas where children are experts, their memory is often extremely good. In fact, it often exceeds that of adults who are novices in that content area. This was documented in a study of 10-year-old chess experts (Chi, 1978). These children were excellent chess players, but not especially brilliant in other ways. As with most 10-year-olds, their memory spans for digits were shorter than an adult's. However, when they were presented chess boards, they remembered the configurations far better than did the adults who were novices at chess (see figure 8.10).

Experts' knowledge is organized around important ideas or concepts more than novices' knowledge is (National Research Council, 1999). This provides experts with a much deeper understanding of knowledge than novices.

Experts in a particular area usually have far more elaborate networks of information about that area than novices do. The information they represent in memory has more nodes, more interconnections, and better hierarchical organization.

Retrieval of relevant information can range from taking a lot of effort to being fluent and almost effortless (National Research Council, 1999). Experts retrieve information in an almost effortless, automatic manner while novices expend a great deal of effort in retrieving information. Consider expert and novice readers. Expert

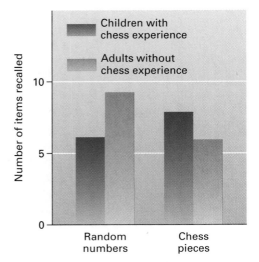

FIGURE 8.10 Memory for Numbers and Chess Pieces

readers can quickly scan the words of a sentence and paragraph, which allows them to devote attention to understanding what they are reading. However, novice readers' ability to decode words is not yet fluent, so they have to allocate considerable attention and time to this task, which restricts the time they can give to understanding a passage.

What determines whether someone becomes an expert or not? Can motivation and practice get someone to expert status? Or does expertise also require a great deal of talent? (Sternberg & Ben-Zeev, 2001).

One view of expertise is that *deliberate practice* is required to become an expert. This is not just any kind of practice. Rather, it involves practice in which the task is at an appropriate level of difficulty for the individual; provides informative feedback; allows opportunities for repetition; and permits correction of mistakes (Ericsson, 1996).

In one study of violinists at a music academy, the main difference between students at different levels of expertise was the amount of their deliberate practice (Ericsson, Krampe, & Tesch-Römer, 1993). The top violinists averaged 7,500 hours of deliberate practice by age 18, the good violinists only 5,300 hours. Many individuals give up on becoming an expert because they are unwilling to commit to extensive levels of deliberate practice over a number of years.

Such extensive practice requires considerable motivation. Students who are not motivated to practice long hours are unlikely to become experts in a particular area. Thus, a student who complains about all of the work, doesn't persevere, and doesn't extensively practice solving math problems over a number years is not going to become an expert in math.

A number of psychologists who study expertise believe it not only requires deliberate practice and motivation, but also talent (Bloom, 1985; Shiffrin, 1996; Sternberg & Ben-Zeev, 2001). Many types of abilities—music and athletic, for example—seem to have some heritable component (Plomin, 1997). For example, is it likely that Mozart could have become such an outstanding musical composer just because he practiced long hours? Is it likely that Michael Jordan became such a fantastic basketball player just because he was motivated to do so? Many individuals have attempted to become as great as Mozart or Jordan but have given up trying after only mediocre performances. Nonetheless, Mozart and Jordan would not have developed expertise in their fields without being highly motivated and engaging in extensive deliberate practice. Talent alone does not make an expert.

Network Theories   *Network theories* describe how information in memory is organized and connected. They emphasize nodes in the memory network. The nodes stand for labels or concepts. Consider the concept "bird." One of the earliest network theories described memory representation as being hierarchically arranged, with more concrete concepts ("canary," for example) nestled under more abstract concepts (like "bird"). However, it soon was realized that such hierarchical networks are too neat to fit the way memory representation really works. For example, students take longer to answer the question "Is an ostrich a bird?" than to answer the question "Is a canary a bird?" Thus, today memory researchers envision the memory network as more irregular and distorted. A *typical bird,* such as a canary, is closer to the node or center of the category *bird* than is the atypical *ostrich.*

Schema Theories   Long-term memory has been compared to a library of books. The idea is that our memory stores information just as a library stores books. In this analogy, the way children retrieve information is said to be similar to the process they use to locate and check out a book. However, the process of retrieving information from long-term memory is not as precise as the library analogy suggests. When children search through their long-term memory storehouse, they don't always find the *exact* "book" they want, or they might find the "book" they want but discover that only "several pages" are intact. They have to *reconstruct* the rest.

Schema theories state that when individuals reconstruct information, they fit it into information that already exists in their minds (Terry, 2003). A *schema* is information—

concepts, events, knowledge—that already exists in a person's mind. You might recall our description of schemas in Piaget's theory (chapter 7, "Cognitive Developmental Approaches"). Schemas from prior experiences influence the way children encode, make inferences about, and retrieve information. Unlike network theories, which assume that retrieval involves specific facts, schema theory claims that long-term memory searches are not very exact. Children often don't find precisely what they want. Hence, as we just indicated, children have to reconstruct the rest. Often when asked to retrieve information, they fill in the gaps between their fragmented memories with varying accuracies and inaccuracies (Mayer, 2003).

Children have schemas for all sorts of information. If a teacher tells a story to a class and then asks the students to write down what the story was about, she likely will get many different versions. That is, the students won't remember every detail of the story the teacher told and will reconstruct stories with their own particular stamps on them. For example, imagine that a teacher tells a class a story about two men and two women who were involved in a train crash in France. One student might reconstruct the story as being about a plane crash, another might say it involved three men and three women, another might say it took place in Germany, and so on. The reconstruction and distortion of memory is nowhere more apparent than in the memories given by people involved in a trial. In criminal court trials like that of O. J. Simpson, the variations in people's memories of what happened underscores the fact that we reconstruct the past rather than take an exact photograph of it.

A *script* is a schema for an event. Scripts often have information about physical features, people, and typical occurrences. This kind of information is helpful when children need to figure out what is happening around them. In a script for an art activity, children likely will remember that the teacher has told them what to draw, that they are supposed to put on smocks over their clothes, that they must get the art paper and paints from the cupboard, that they are to clean the brushes when they are finished, and so on. For example, a child who comes in late to the art activity likely knows much of what to do because of his art activity script.

As children develop, their scripts become more sophisticated. For example, a 4-year-old's script for a restaurant might include only information about sitting down and eating food. In middle and late childhood, the child adds information to the restaurant script about the types of people who serve food, about paying the cashier, and so on. The process of elaborating this type of information in long-term memory continues throughout life.

Retrieval and Forgetting

After children have encoded information and then represented it in memory, they might be able to retrieve some of it but might also forget some of it.

Retrieval   When children retrieve something from their mental "data bank," they search their store of memory to find the relevant information. Just as with encoding, this search can be automatic or it can require effort. For example, if children are asked what month it is, the answer might immediately spring to their lips. That is, the retrieval might be automatic. But if children are asked to name the guest speaker who came to the class two months earlier, the retrieval process likely will require more effort.

An item's position on a list also affects how easy or difficult the item will be to remember. The *serial position effect* is that recall is better for items at the beginning and end of a list than for items in the middle (see figure 8.11). Suppose a child is given these directions about where to go to get tutoring help:

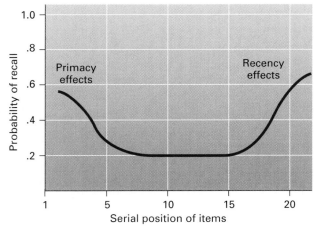

FIGURE 8.11 The Serial Position Effect

When a person is asked to memorize a list of words, the words memorized last usually are recalled best, those at the beginning next best, and those in the middle least efficiently.

"Left on Mockingbird, right on Central, left on Balboa, left on Sandstone, and right on Parkside." The child likely will remember "Left on Mockingbird" and "Right on Parkside" better than "Left on Balboa." The *primacy effect* is that items at the beginning of a list tend to be the easiest to remember. The *recency effect* is that items at the end of the list tend to be remembered the easiest.

Yet another aspect of retrieval is the nature of the retrieval task itself. *Recall* is a memory task in which individuals must retrieve previously learned information, as when students are given fill-in-the-blank or essay questions. *Recognition* is a memory task in which individuals only have to identify ("recognize") learned information, as is often the case on multiple-choice tests. Many students prefer multiple-choice items because they have good retrieval cues, whereas fill-in-the-blank and essay items don't.

Forgetting   One form of forgetting involves the cues we just discussed. *Cue-dependent forgetting* is retrieval failure caused by a lack of effective retrieval cues. Cue-dependent forgetting explains why students might fail to retrieve a needed fact for an exam even when the student is sure she "knows" the information. For example, if you are studying for a test in this course and are asked a question about a distinction between recall and recognition in retrieval, you likely will remember the distinction better if you possess the cues of fill-in-the-blank and multiple-choice, respectively.

The principle of cue-dependent forgetting is consistent with *interference theory,* which states that we forget not because we actually lose memories from storage, but rather because other information gets in the way of what we are trying to remember. Thus, if a student studies for a biology test, then studies for a history test, and then takes the biology test, the information about history will interfere with remembering the information about biology. Thus, interference theory implies that a good study strategy is to study last what you are going to be tested on next if you have multiple courses to study for. That is, the student taking the biology test would have benefited from studying history first, then biology just before taking the biology test. This strategy also fits with the recency effect we described earlier. Take a moment and think about how you might use your knowledge of interference theory in terms of reviewing for students what you plan to test them on next.

Another source of forgetting is memory decay. *Decay theory* states that when something new is learned, a neurochemical "memory trace" is formed that will disintegrate. Thus, decay theory suggests that the passage of time is responsible for forgetting. Memories decay at different speeds. Some memories are vivid and last for long periods of time, especially when they have emotional ties. These "flashbulb" memories—such as memory of a car accident you were in or witnessed, the night of your high school graduation, an early romantic experience, where you were when you heard about Princess Diana's death—can have considerable accuracy and vivid imagery, and chances are you can retrieve such information even when the events happened a long time ago.

Personal Trauma and Memory

In 1890, American psychologist William James said that an experience can be so arousing emotionally as to almost leave a scar on the brain's tissue. Personal traumas can have such an effect. Some psychologists argue that memory for emotionally traumatic events is accurately retained, possibly forever, in considerable detail (Langer, 1991). There is good evidence that memory for traumatic events is usually more accurate than memory for ordinary events (Schacter, 2001). But consider the traumatic experience of children who were kidnapped at gunpoint on a school bus in Chowchilla, California, then buried underground for 16 hours before escaping. On the one hand, the children had the classic signs of traumatic memory—detailed and vivid recollections. On the other hand, when a child psychiatrist interviewed them four or five years after the chilling episode, she noted some striking errors and distortions in half of the children's memories of it (Terr, 1988).

Four-year-old Jennifer Royal was the only eyewitness to one of her play-mates being shot to death. She was allowed to testify in open court, and the clarity of her statements helped to convict the gunman. *What are some issues involved in whether young children should be allowed to testify in court?*

Children's Eyewitness Testimony

How can a traumatic memory be so vivid and detailed, yet at the same time have inaccuracies? A number of factors can be involved. Some children might have made perceptual errors at the time of encoding information because the episode was so shocking. Others might have distorted the information and recalled the episode as being less traumatic than it actually was, in order to reduce their anxiety about what happened. Others, in discussing the traumatic event with various people, might have incorporated bits and pieces of these persons' recollections of what happened into their own version of the event.

In sum, memories of real-life traumas are usually more accurate and long-lasting than everyday events. However, memories of traumas are subject to some deterioration and distortion. In traumatic memories, the central part of the memory is almost always effectively remembered. Where distortion often arises is in the details of the traumatic episode.

Some cases of memory for personal trauma involve a mental disorder called *post-traumatic stress disorder*, which includes severe anxiety symptoms that can immediately follow the trauma or be delayed by months or even years until onset. This mental disorder can emerge as a consequence of exposure to any of several traumatic events, such as war, severe abuse (as in rape), and accidental disasters (such as a plane crash). The symptoms of this disorder can include "flashbacks" in which the individual relives the traumatic event in nightmares, or in an awake but dissociative-like state. They also can include difficulties with memory and concentration.

The emotional blows of personal trauma can produce distortions of memory or vivid reenactments of the event in memory (Kassin & others, 2001). In the case of post-traumatic stress disorder, the event might be pushed beneath awareness only to reappear in vivid flashbacks months or even years later. Repression takes place when something shocking happens and the mind pushes all memory of the occurrence into some inaccessible part of the unconscious mind. At some later point, the memory might emerge in consciousness, as in the case of post-traumatic stress disorder.

In psychoanalytic theory, which we initially discussed in chapter 2, repression's main function is to protect the individual from threatening information. Repression doesn't erase a memory, it just makes it extremely difficult to remember consciously. To read further about repressed memories, see the Explorations in Child Development box.

Review and Reflect: Learning Goal 2

2 Describe the way that memory works in children

REVIEW

- What is memory?
- How do children encode information?
- How do children store information?
- How do children retrieve information, and why do they forget?
- How does personal trauma influence memory?

REFLECT

- What is your earliest memory? Why do you think you remember this particular situation?

Repressed Memories, Child Abuse, and Reality

There has been a dramatic increase in reported memories of childhood sexual abuse that were allegedly repressed for many years. With recent changes in legislation, people with recently discovered memories are suing alleged perpetrators for events that occurred 20, 30, even 40 or more years earlier.

In 1991, popular actress Roseanne was on the cover of *People* magazine. She reported that her mother had abused her from the time Roseanne was an infant until she was 6 or 7 years of age, but that she had become aware of the abuse only recently during therapy. Other highly publicized cases of repressed memories of child abuse coming into awareness during therapy dot the pages of popular magazines and self-help books.

There is little doubt that actual childhood abuse is tragically common. Memory experts such as Elizabeth Loftus (1993, 2002) and others (Kutchinsky, 1992) don't dispute that child abuse is a serious problem. What they take issue with is the way therapists get their clients to recall abuse. Therapists might help their clients to reconstruct a memory that is not real. Some clients who originally claimed they were abused later have recanted their accusations, blaming their abuse report on the therapist's leading inquiries.

In recent years, there has been an increasing number of court cases entailing allegations of sexual improprieties involving children. Many cases that end up in the legal system likely involve true claims of sexual abuse but questions are raised about whether children's reports are reliable.

Is there a time in childhood when children are especially susceptible to misleading suggestions? Recent studies have confirmed that preschool children are disproportionately vulnerable to suggestive influences about such things as bodily touching, emotional events, and participatory events (Bruck & Ceci, 1999). Nonetheless, concerns remain about the reliability of older children's, adolescents', and even adults' testimony when they are subjected to suggestive interviews (Poole & Lindsey, 1996). Also, individual variations in preschool children suggest that some preschool children are resistant to interviewers' suggestions.

One study focused on 329 students in the third/fourth, seventh/eighth, and eleventh/twelfth grades (Lindberg, Keiffer, & Thomas, 2000). Participants saw a 3.5-minute videotape about two boys aged 5 and 11 coming home from school and playing video games. The older boy exited to call a friend, at which time the mother came home and spilled a bag of groceries. She asked the younger boy to help her pick them up, and he repeatedly ignored her and continued to play the video game. She then apparently hit him with a blow to head that knocked him to the floor crying. She picked him up in a rough fashion, took him to the kitchen, and apparently hit him again. The experimenters manipulated a number of factors to determine their effects on the way the children interpreted the video. For example, one question that was posed to the children was: "How many drops of blood fell from Mark's (the younger boy's) nose? Actually no drops of blood fell. The results indicated that the children in the third and fourth grades (combined as grade 3.5) reported more drops of blood than older children (see figure 8.12), indicating

greater suggestibility in the elementary school children. Notice also in figure 8.12 that when the question about drops of blood was used (labeled as "Led"), individuals at all grade levels were more likely to report seeing blood falling from the boy's nose than when the question was not included (labeled "Not Led").

Few research studies offer convincing evidence about the extent to which repression of abuse actually occurs. At present, there are no satisfactory methods that can help us discover the answer. Although Loftus has demonstrated the ease with which memories can be implanted in unsuspecting individuals, her critics say that her research might not accurately capture the actual trauma that occurs in abuse episodes.

Therapists and their clients are left with the chilling possibility that not all abuse memories recovered in therapy are real. In the absence of corroboration, some recollections might be authentic and others might not be.

According to Loftus (1993, 2002), psychotherapists, counselors, social service agencies, and law enforcement personnel need to be careful about probing for horrors on the other side of some amnesiac barrier. They should be cautious in their interpretation of uncorroborated repressed memories that return. Clarification, compassion, and gentle confrontation along with a demonstration of empathy are techniques that can be used to help individuals in their painful struggle to come to grips with their personal truths.

There is a final tragic risk involved in suggestive probing and uncritical acceptance of all allegations made by clients. These activities increase the probability that society in general will disbelieve the actual cases of child abuse that deserve extensive attention and evaluation. In general, any careless or uncritical acceptance of unreplicated findings in psychology, especially when they have a colorful element that attracts media attention, harms public attitudes toward the contributions of psychological research.

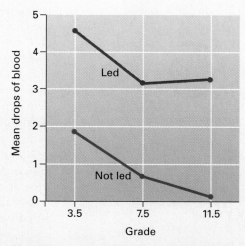

FIGURE 8.12 Suggestibility of Children at Different Grade Levels

3 THINKING

What Is Thinking?	Solving Problems	Thinking Scientifically

Forming Concepts	Thinking Critically

What does it mean to "think"? What are some good strategies for helping children become better thinkers?

What Is Thinking?

Thinking involves manipulating and transforming information in memory. This often is done to form concepts, reason, think critically, and solve problems—topics that we will explore shortly. Children can think about the concrete, such as a vacation at the beach or how to win at a video game; as adolescents, they can think in more abstract ways, such as pondering the meaning of freedom or identity. They can think about the past (what happened to them last month) and the future (what their life will be like next year). They can think about reality (such as how to do better on the next test in a subject area) and fantasy (what it might be like to meet Elvis Presley or land a spacecraft on Mars).

Forming Concepts

Forming concepts is an important aspect of constructing information.

What Are Concepts? **Concepts** are categories that are used to group objects, events, and characteristics on the basis of common properties. Concepts are elements of cognition that help to simplify and summarize information (Medin, 2000). In a world without concepts, each object would be unique, no generalization would be possible. Without concepts, the most trivial problem would be time-consuming and even impossible. Consider the concept of a book. If a child were not aware that a book is sheets of paper of uniform size, all bound together along one edge, and full of printed words and pictures in some meaningful order, each time the child encountered a new book she would have to figure out what it was. In a way, then, concepts keep us from "reinventing the wheel" each time we come across a new piece of information.

Concepts also aid the process of remembering, making it more efficient. When children group objects to form a concept, they can remember the concept, then retrieve the concept's characteristics. Thus, when a teacher assigns math homework, she probably doesn't need to go through the details of what math is or what homework is. Children will have embedded in their memory a number of associations with concepts of math and homework. In ways such as this, concepts not only help to jog memory, they also make communication more efficient. If a teacher says, "It's time for art," students know what this concept means. One doesn't have to go into a lengthy explanation of what art is. Thus, concepts help children to simplify and summarize information, as well as improve the efficiency of memory, communication, and time use.

Many of children's concepts embody implicit theories about the world (Carey & Gelman, 1991). Children often are not able to state these theories explicitly, but their use of the concepts shows many of the features characteristic of concepts within the theories of adult scientists. One aspect of children's theories that has been extensively studied involves their theory of mind.

The Young Child's Theory of Mind **Theory of mind** refers to awareness of one's own mental processes and the mental processes of others. Even young children are curious about the nature of the human mind, and developmentalists have

Forming Concepts

thinking Manipulating and transforming information in memory.

concepts Categories used to group objects, events, and characteristics on the basis of common properties.

theory of mind Awareness of one's own mental processes and the mental processes of others.

shown a flurry of interest in children's thoughts about what the human mind is like (Flavell, 1999; Wellman, 2000, 2002).

Children's theory of mind changes as they go through the childhood years (Flavell, Miller, & Miller, 2002):

1. *Two to three years of age.* Children begin to understand three mental states:
   - *Perceptions.* Children realize that another person sees what is in front of their eyes and not necessarily in front of the children's eyes.
   - *Desires.* Children understand that if someone wants something, he or she will try to get it. A child might say, "I want my mommy."
   - *Emotions.* Children can distinguish between positive (for example, "happy") and negative (for example, "sad") emotions. A child might say, "Tommy feels bad." Despite these advances, at 2 to 3 years of age, children have only a minimal understanding of how mental life can be linked to behavior. They think that people are at the mercy of their desires and don't understand how beliefs influence behavior.

2. *Four to five years of age.* Children begin to understand that the mind can represent objects and events accurately or inaccurately. The realization that people have *false beliefs*—beliefs that are not true—develops in a majority of children by the time they are 5 years old (Wellman, Cross, & Watson, 2001) (see figure 8.13). One study of false beliefs involved showing young children a Band-Aid box and asking them what was inside (Jenkins & Astington, 1996). To the children's surprise, the box actually contained pencils. When asked what a child who had never seen the box would think was inside, 3-year-olds typically responded "pencils." However, the 4- and 5-year-olds, grinning at the anticipation of other children's false-belief beliefs who had not seen what was inside the box were more likely to say "Band-Aids."

Some developmental psychologists use their training in areas such as cognitive development to pursue careers in applied areas. To read about the work of one individual who followed this path, see the Careers in Child Development insert.

Forming concepts is an important aspect of thinking. As we see next, so is solving problems.

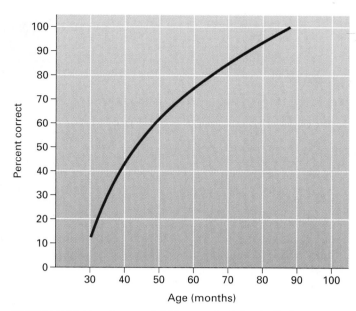

FIGURE 8.13 Developmental Changes in False-Belief Performance

False-belief performance dramatically increases from 2½ years of age through the middle of the elementary school years. In a summary of the results of many studies, 2½-year-olds gave incorrect responses about 80 percent of the time (Wellman, Cross, & Watson, 2001). At 3 years, 8 months, they were correct about 50 percent of the time, and after that, gave increasingly correct responses.

Solving Problems

Problem solving involves finding an appropriate way to attain a goal. Consider these problems that require students to engage in problem solving: getting to a club meeting at a new location or creating a project for a science fair.

Efforts have been made to specify the steps that individuals go through in effectively solving problems. Here are four such steps.

(1) Find and Frame Problems   Before a problem can be solved, it has to be recognized. In the past, most problem-solving exercises given to students have involved well-defined problems with well-defined solutions and operations for attaining the solutions. Schools need to place more emphasis on encouraging students to identify problems instead of just trying to solve well-defined textbook problems. Many real-life problems are ill-defined: They are vague and don't have clearly defined ways of being solved. Consider a child's problem of having to get to a club meeting that is being held at a new location an hour after the last class at school. First, the child needs to identify the existence of a problem to be solved, such as what time to leave to make the club meeting on time. To solve this general problem the child has to solve several subproblems, such as these: Where is the new location? How far away is it? Can I get there in time by riding my bike? Will I have to take a bus? And so on.

problem solving Finding an appropriate way to attain a goal.

Careers in Child Development

Helen Schwe, *Developmental Psychologist and Toy Designer*

Helen Schwe obtained a Ph.D. from Stanford University in developmental psychology. She now spends her days talking with computer engineers and designing "smart" toys for children. Smart toys are designed to improve children's problem-solving and symbolic thinking skills.

During graduate school Helen worked part-time for Hasbro Toys, testing its children's software on preschoolers. Her first job after graduate school was with Zowie Intertainment, which recently was purchased by LEGO.

While with Zowie and now LEGO, Helen helped to design the pirate game called "Redbeard's Pirate Quest" and many other toys for children. Helen says that even in a toy's most primitive stage of development, you see children's creativity in responding to challenges and their joy when they solve a problem. Along with conducting experiments and focus groups at different stages of a toy's development, Helen also helps assess the age-appropriateness of a toy. Most of her current work focuses on 3- to 5-year-old children (Schlegel, 2000).

Helen Schwe, a developmental psychologist, with some of the "smart" toys she designed.

subgoaling Setting intermediate goals that put one in a better position to reach the final goal or solution.

algorithms Strategies that guarantee a solution to a problem.

heuristics Strategies that can suggest a solution to a problem but don't guarantee a solution.

(2) Develop Good Problem-Solving Strategies Once children find a problem and clearly define it, they need to develop strategies for solving it. Effective strategies include setting subgoals, using algorithms, and calling on heuristics.

Subgoaling involves setting intermediate goals that put students in a better position of reaching the final goal or solution. Children might do poorly at solving problems because they don't generate subproblems or subgoals. Let's consider a 14-year-old girl who is doing a science fair project that focuses on the reliability of people's memory for traumatic events they have experienced. What might be some subgoaling strategies? One might be locating the right books and research journals on thinking, another might be interviewing teachers about the strategies they use to encourage deep thinking. At the same time as this subgoaling strategy is taking place, the girl likely will benefit from establishing further subgoals in terms of what she needs to accomplish along the way to her final goal of a finished science project. If the science project is due in three months, she might set a subgoal of finishing the first draft of the project two weeks before it is due, another subgoal of completing the research a month before the project is due, being halfway through the research two months before the project is due, having three teacher interviews done two weeks from today, and starting library research tomorrow.

Notice that in establishing the subgoals, we worked backward in time. Working backward in establishing subgoals is often a good strategy. Children first create a subgoal that is closest to the final goal and then work backward to the subgoal that is closest to the beginning of the problem-solving effort.

Algorithms are strategies that guarantee an answer to a problem. When children solve a multiplication problem by a set procedure, they are using an algorithm. When they follow the directions for diagramming a sentence, they are using an algorithm. Life would be easy if all its problems could be solved by algorithms. But many real-world problems are not so straightforward. They require the use of heuristics.

Heuristics are strategies that can suggest a solution to a problem but do not guarantee a solution. Consider an adolescent who has just gotten his driver's license. He is going to drive over to a friend's house he has never been to before. He drives through an unfamiliar part of town and soon realizes that he is lost. If he knows that the correct direction to turn is north, he might use the heuristic of turning onto the road that goes in that direction. This strategy might work, but it also might fail. The road might end or it might veer east.

Means-end analysis is the heuristic in which the goal (end) of a problem is identified, the current situation is assessed, and what needs to be done (means) to decrease the difference between the two conditions is evaluated. Another name for the means-end analysis is "difference reduction." Means-end analysis also can involve the use of subgoaling, which we described earlier. Means-end analysis is commonly used in solving problems. Consider the girl who is working on the science project (the end). She initially assessed her current state, when she was just starting to think about the project. Then she mapped out a plan to reduce the difference between her current state and the goal (end). Her "means" included talking to several scientists in the community about potential projects, going to the library to study about the topics, and exploring the Internet for potential projects and ways to carry them out.

Infants less than 1 year of age exhibit such means-end analysis in some situations. For example, in one study, 9-month-olds were presented with a foam-rubber barrier, behind which was hidden a cloth (Willatts, 1990). Some of the babies saw a small toy on the far end of the cloth, others saw the toy beside, rather than on top of, the cloth. When the toy was on the cloth rather than beside it, the 9-month-olds were much more likely to knock down the barrier and pull the cloth to them. Means-end analysis later is extended to much more complex situations, involving more numerous and complex subgoals and requiring the discipline to resist the lure of short-term goals to pursue longer-term ones.

means-end analysis A heuristic in which one identifies the goal (end) of a problem, assesses the current situation, and determines what needs to be done (means) in order to attain the goal.

(3) Evaluate Solutions   Once we think we have solved a problem, we won't really know how effective our solution is until we find out if it actually works. It helps to have in mind a clear criterion for effectiveness. For example, what will be the girl's criterion for the science fair project? Will it be simply getting it completed? Receiving positive feedback about the project? Winning an award? Winning first place? The self-satisfaction of having set a goal, planned for it, and reached it?

(4) Rethink and Redefine Problems and Solutions over Time   An important final step in problem solving is to continually rethink and redefine problems and solutions over time (Bereiter & Scardamalia, 1993). People who are good at problem solving are motivated to improve on their past performances and to make original contributions. Thus, the girl who completed the science fair project can look back at the project and think about ways that the project can be improved. She might use feedback from judges or information from others who talked with her about the project to tinker with and fine-tune it.

Using Rules to Solve Problems   Much of information-processing research on problem solving has been aimed at identifying the rules children use to solve problems. The balance scale problem is useful for illustrating this research. The type of balance scale that has been used to examine children's understanding is shown in figure 8.14. The scale includes a fulcrum and an arm that can rotate around it. The arm can tip left or right or remain level, depending on how weights (metal disks with holes in the center) are arranged on the pegs on each side of the fulcrum. The child's task is to look at the configuration of weights on the pegs on each problem and then predict whether the left side will go down, the right side will go down, or the arm will balance.

Robert Siegler (1976) hypothesized that children would use one of the four rules depicted in figure 8.15:

Rule I. If the weight is the same on both sides, predict that the scale will balance. If the weight differs, predict that the side with more weight will go down.

Rule II. If the weight is greater on one side, say that that side will go down. If the weights on the two sides are equal, choose the side on which the weight is farther from the fulcrum.

Rule III. Act as in Rule II, except that if one side has more weight and the weight on the other side is farther from the fulcrum, then guess.

Rule IV. Proceed as in Rule III, unless one side has more weight and the other more distance. In that case, calculate torques by multiplying weight times distance on each side. Then predict that the side with the greater torque will go down.

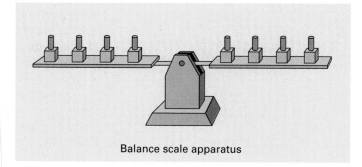

Balance scale apparatus

FIGURE 8.14 The Type of Balance Scale Used by Siegler (1976)
Weights could be placed on pegs on each side of the fulcrum; the torque (the weight on each side times the distance of that weight from the fulcrum) determined which side would go down.

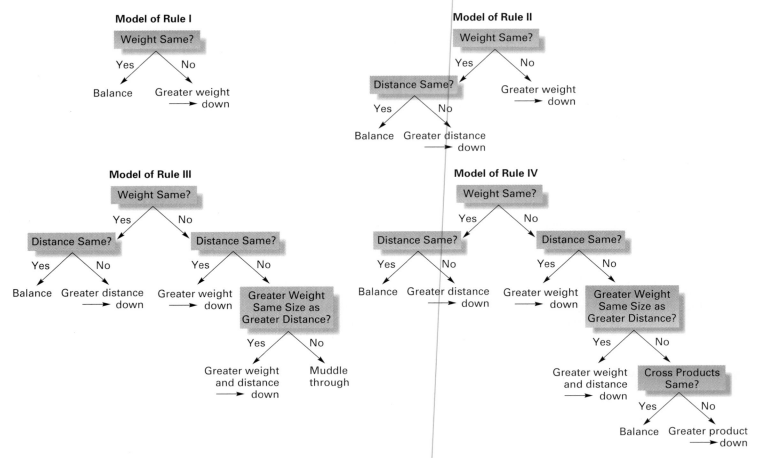

FIGURE 8.15 Four Rules for Solving the Balance Scale Task

Children following Rule I would always pick the side with more weight as the one that would go down, and would say that the scale would balance whenever the two sides had the same amount of weight. Children using Rule II would do the same, except that if the two sides had the same amount of weight, they would base their judgments on the distance of the weights from the fulcrum. Children using Rule III would always consider both weight and distance, and would respond correctly if one or both were equal. However, they would muddle through or guess if one side had more weight and the other had its weight farther from the fulcrum. Finally, children using Rule IV would act the same as those using Rule III, except that they would compute torques when one side had more weight and the other had its weight farther from the fulcrum.

But how could it be determined which rule, if any, a given child was using? Siegler reasoned that presenting problems on which different rules would generate different outcomes would allow assessment of each child's rules. For example, suppose there were four weights on the third peg to the left of the fulcrum and three weights on the fourth peg to the right of the fulcrum. A child using Rule I or Rule II would say that the left side will go down, because it has more weight; a child using Rule III would guess and therefore sometimes say one answer and sometimes another; and a child using Rule IV would compute torques and realize that the two sides would balance. Through a child's pattern of correct answers and errors on a set of such problems, that child's underlying rule could be inferred.

This *rule assessment approach* demonstrated that almost 90 percent of children aged 5 to 17 years used one of the four rules. Almost all 5-year-olds used Rule I, almost all 9-year-olds used either Rule II or Rule III, and both 13-year-olds and 17-year-olds generally used Rule III. Interestingly, despite the 17-year-olds' having studied balance scales in their physics course, almost none of them used the only rule that generated consistently correct answers, Rule IV. Discussions with their teachers revealed why; the balance scale the students had studied was a pan balance, on which small pans could be hung from various locations along the arm, rather than an arm balance, with pegs extending upward. Retesting the children showed that most could consistently solve the problems when the familiar pan balance was used. The example illustrates a set of lessons that frequently has emerged from studies of problem solving—learning is often quite narrow, generalization beyond one's existing knowledge is difficult, and even analogies that seem straightforward are often missed.

The development of problem solving does not start at age 5. Certain basic problem-solving abilities are already present in infancy. Next we consider some of these, as well as the subsequent development of a number of other key problem-solving capabilities.

Using Analogies to Solve Problems   When people encounter new problems, often they interpret them with reference to better-understood, previously encountered ones. For example, in one study college students were presented with a problem in which a physician needed to destroy a patient's tumor, and the only way to do so was with massive amounts of radiation (Duncker, 1945). However, the amount of radiation was sufficiently large that it would also destroy healthy tissue on the way to the tumor. Half the dosage of radiation would not kill the healthy tissue, though it also would not destroy the tumor. What should the physician do?

Most people find this problem difficult. They are more likely to solve it, however, if they first learn the solution to another problem in which an attacking army cannot travel in one large group, because the attack route is too narrow, but instead must divide into separate units, come from different directions, and converge at a central location. This suggests to many the idea of sending half the desired amount of radiation from each of two directions, with the two converging at the site of the tumor. Such extrapolation from better-understood to less-understood problems is the key to analogical problem solving.

The development of analogical problem solving resembles that of scientific reasoning. Even very young children can draw reasonable analogies under some circumstances and use them to solve problems (Freeman & Gehl, 1995). Under other circumstances, even college students fail to draw seemingly obvious analogies (as in the example of the high school students' difficulty in extrapolating from the familiar pan balance to the unfamiliar arm balance, described earlier). This resemblance is not coincidental, since scientific reasoning often depends on drawing useful analogies.

Ann Brown and her collaborators (Brown, 1990; Brown, Kane, & Echols, 1986) have demonstrated some of the types of analogical reasoning that occur at ages 1 through 5 years. When 1- and 2-year-olds are shown that a curved stick can be used as a tool to pull in a toy that is too far away to be reached unaided, they draw the correct analogy in choosing which stick to use the next time. They do not choose sticks on the basis of their being of the same color as the stick they used before. They also do not just choose objects that look exactly like the tool they saw demonstrated to be effective (such as a curved cane); instead they identify the essential property and will choose whichever objects have it (they will choose a straight rake as well as the curved cane). The 2-year-olds were more likely than the 1-year-olds to learn the initial task without any help, but once they learned the task, both 1- and 2-year-olds drew the right analogy to new problems.

Successful analogical problem solving often involves tools more abstract than curved sticks for hauling in objects that are beyond one's reach (DeLoache, 2002). Maps and verbal descriptions of routes, for example, often help us to figure out how to get where we want to go (DeLoache, Miller, & Pierroutsakos, 1997). Recent studies of toddlers' abilities to use scale models to guide their problem-solving activities show that dramatic developments occur in such tool use quite early in development.

Judy DeLoache (1989) created a situation in which 2½- and 3-year-olds were shown a small toy hidden within a scale model of a room. The child was then asked to find the toy in a real room that was a bigger version of the scale model. If the toy was hidden under the armchair in the scale model, it was also hidden under

Judy DeLoache *(left)* has conducted research that focuses on young children's developing cognitive abilities. She has demonstrated that children's symbolic representation between 2½ and 3 years of age enables them to find a toy in a real room that is a much bigger version of the scale model.

the armchair in the real room. Considerable development occurred between 2½ and 3 years of age on this task. Thirty-month-old children rarely could solve the problem; by 36 months they generally could.

What was the source of the 2½-year-olds' difficulty on the task? It was not inability to understand how any type of symbol could represent another situation. Shown line drawings or photographs of the larger room, 2½-year-olds had no difficulty finding the object. Instead, the difficulty seemed to come from the toddlers' simultaneously viewing the scale model as a symbol of the larger room and as an object in itself. Surprising consequences followed from this insight. Allowing children to play with the scale model before using it as a symbol worsened their performance, presumably because playing with it made them think of it more as an object in itself. Conversely, putting the scale model in a glass case, where the children could not handle it at all, resulted in the children's more often being able to use it successfully to find the object hidden in the larger room. The general lesson is that young children can use a variety of tools to draw analogies, but they easily can forget that an object is being used as a symbol of something else and instead take it as being of interest as an object in its own right.

We have studied a number of ways infants and young children learn and solve problems. Next we explore another very important way infants, as well as children and adults, solve problems—by imitation.

Infant Imitation   One of the most important ways to solve problems is to imitate the actions of more-knowledgeable others who are confronted with similar problems (Call, 1995). This is especially true for young children, who have less experience solving problems and fewer general problem-solving strategies than older individuals have. Copying its mother's problem-solving strategies has, clearly, survival value for an infant. Thus, it is not surprising that basic imitative abilities are present from early in life.

Just how early certain imitative capacities are present became apparent in an intriguing experiment conducted by Tiffany Field and her colleagues (1982). They examined the capabilities of newborns within 36 hours of their birth. An adult held each newborn in front of her, with its head upright, 10 inches from herself. With her face she expressed one of the three emotions: happiness, sadness, or surprise. Infants were most likely to imitate the model's display of surprise by widely opening their mouths. When the infants observed a happy expression, they frequently widened their lips. When the adult's face looked sad, the infant's lips moved into a pouting expression.

Infant development researcher Andrew Meltzoff (1995) has conducted numerous studies of infants' imitative abilities. He believes that these abilities are biologically based, because infants can imitate a facial expression within the first few days after birth, before they have had the opportunity to observe social agents in their environment engage in tongue protrusion and other behaviors. He also believes that infants' imitative abilities do not fit the ethologists' concept of a hardwired, reflexive, innate releasing mechanism, but rather that these abilities are flexible and adaptable to the demands of particular situations (Meltzoff, 2000). In Meltzoff's observations of infants in the first 72 hours of life, the infants gradually displayed a full imitative response to an adult's facial expressions, such as tongue protrusion or a wide opening of the mouth (see figure 8.16). Initially, a young infant might only get its tongue to the edge of its lips, but after a number of attempts and observations of adult behavior, the infant displays a more full-blown imitation.

FIGURE 8.16 Infant Imitation

Infant development researcher Andrew Meltzoff protrudes his tongue in an attempt to get the infant to imitate his behavior.

Meltzoff also has studied deferred imitation, imitation that occurs hours or days after the original event. In one investigation, Meltzoff (1988) demonstrated that 9-month-old infants can imitate actions they saw performed 24 hours earlier. Each action consisted of an unusual gesture, such as pushing a recessed button in a box (which produced a beeping sound). Piaget had concluded that deferred imitation was impossible until about 18 months of age, because he believed that until then infants lacked basic representational abilities needed to maintain the memory of the earlier event. Meltzoff's research suggests that infants can form such representations much earlier in development.

Current debate focuses on what is implied by the rich initial state of early imitation. One view is that the innate psychological structures involved in early imitation are adultlike. This approach argues that newborns remain virtually unchanged during the course of development. However, Meltzoff and his colleague M. Keith Moore (1999) argue that evolution equipped infants not with adult concepts but with early mental structures that allow imitation to be deployed as a discovery mechanism for understanding persons.

So far in our focus on children's thinking we have explored what thinking is, how children form concepts, and how they solve problems. Next, we will examine the importance of guiding children to become better critical thinkers.

Thinking Critically

Currently, there is considerable interest in critical thinking among psychologists and educators, although it is not an entirely new idea. The famous educator John Dewey (1933) proposed a similar idea when he talked about the importance of getting students to think reflectively. The well-known psychologist Max Wertheimer (1945) talked about the importance of thinking productively rather than just guessing at a correct answer. **Critical thinking** involves thinking reflectively and productively, and evaluating the evidence. In this book, the Review and Reflect section that appears a number of times in each chapter includes an item that encourages you to think critically about a topic or issue related to the section.

We can consciously build critical thinking in children by modeling or encouraging these behaviors:

- Asking not only *what* happened but *how* and *why* it happened
- Examining supposed "facts" to determine if there is evidence to support them
- Arguing in a reasoned way rather than through emotions
- Recognizing that there is sometimes more than one good answer or explanation
- Comparing various answers to a question and judging which is really the best answer
- Evaluating and possibly questioning what other people say rather than immediately accepting it as the truth
- Asking questions and speculating beyond what we already know to create new ideas and new information

Jacqueline and Martin Brooks (1993, 2001) lament that so few schools really teach students to think critically. In their view, schools spend too much time getting students to give a single correct answer in an imitative way rather than encouraging students to expand their thinking by coming up with new ideas and rethinking earlier conclusions. They believe that too often teachers ask students to recite, define, describe, state, and list—rather than to analyze, infer, connect, synthesize, criticize, create, evaluate, think, and rethink.

Brooks and Brooks point out that many successful students complete their assignments, do well on tests, and get good grades, yet don't ever learn to think critically and deeply. They believe our schools turn out students who think too superficially, staying on the surface of problems rather than stretching their minds and becoming deeply engaged in meaningful thinking.

critical thinking Thinking reflectively and productively, and evaluating the evidence.

"We did that last year—how come we have to do it again this year?

Used by permission of the Estate of W. A. Vanselow

David Perkins and Sarah Tishman (1997) work with teachers to incorporate critical thinking into classrooms. Here are some of the critical-thinking skills they encourage teachers to help their students develop:

- *Open-mindedness.* This involves getting students to avoid narrow thinking and to explore options. For example, when teaching American literature, teachers might ask students to generate multiple critiques of Aldous Huxley's *Brave New World*.
- *Intellectual curiosity.* This involves encouraging students to wonder, probe, question, and inquire. Getting students to recognize problems and inconsistencies also is an aspect of intellectual curiosity. In history class, this might mean looking beyond culturally biased views of American history by reading British or Native American views on the American Revolution.
- *Planning and strategy.* Teachers can work with students to help them develop plans, set goals, find direction, and seek outcomes. In physical education, this might involve determining the best strategy for winning a basketball or softball game.
- *Intellectual carefulness.* Teachers can encourage students to check for inaccuracies and errors, to be precise, and to be organized. For example, when students write a paper, they can learn to structure the content and check the facts that they include.

For many years, a major debate in teaching critical thinking has been whether it should involve teaching critical-thinking skills as general entities or in the context of specific subject matter instruction (math, English, or science, for example). Experts on children's thinking continue to debate whether instruction in critical thinking should be embedded in a rich subject matter or should be taught in a more general manner (Kuhn, 1999; Mayer, 2003).

Today, another debate regarding critical thinking has emerged. On the one side are traditionalists who see critical thinking as a set of mental competencies that reside in children's heads. On the other side are advocates of a collaborative approach to critical thinking, who regard intellectual skills as social entities that are exercised and shared within a community (Rogoff, 1998). This ongoing debate has not yet been resolved.

An innovative program that encourages critical thinking, Fostering a Community of Learners (FCL), was created by Ann Brown and Joe Campione (1996; Brown, 1997, 1998). The program focuses on literacy development and biology. As currently established, it is set in inner-city elementary schools and is appropriate for 6- to 12-year-old children. Reflection and discussion are key dimensions of the program. Constructive commentary, questioning, querying, and criticism are the mode rather than the exception. Three strategies that encourage reflection and discussion are (1) having children teach children, (2) implementing online computer consultation, and (3) using adults as role models.

reciprocal teaching A teaching method in which students take turns leading small-group discussions.

A Fostering a Community of Learners classroom. *What is the nature of this approach to education?*

- *Children Teaching Children*

    Brown says that children as well as adults enrich the classroom learning experience by contributing their particular expertise. Cross-age teaching, in which older students teach younger students, is used in FCL. This occurs both face-to-face and via electronic mail (e-mail). Older students often serve as discussion leaders. Cross-age teaching provides students with invaluable opportunities to talk about learning, gives students responsibility and purpose, and fosters collaboration among peers.

    Reciprocal teaching, in which students take turns leading a small-group discussion, is used in FCL. Reciprocal teaching requires students to discuss complex passages, collaborate, and share their individual expertise and perspectives on a particular topic. Reciprocal teaching can involve a teacher and a student as well as student-student interaction.

FCL also uses a modified version of the jigsaw classroom (students cooperate by doing different parts of a project to reach a common goal). As students create preliminary drafts of reports, they participate in "cross-talk" sessions. These are whole-class activities in which groups periodically summarize where they are in their learning activity and get input from the other groups. "Mini-jigsaws" (small groups) also are used. At both the whole-class level and mini-jigsaw level, if group members can't understand what someone is saying or writing about, the students have to revise their product and present it again later. Students are then grouped into reciprocal teaching seminars in which each student is an expert on one subtopic, teaches the part to the others, and also participates in constructing test questions based on the subunit.

- *Online Computer Consultation*

  Face-to-face communication is not the only way to build community and expertise. FCL classrooms also use electronic mail. Through e-mail, experts provide coaching and advice, as well as commentary about what it means to learn and understand. Online experts function as role models of thinking. They wonder, query, and make inferences based on incomplete knowledge.

- *Adults as Role Models*

  Visiting experts and classroom teachers introduce the big ideas and difficult principles at the beginning of a unit. The adult models how to think and reflect in the process of finding a topic or reasoning with given information. The adults continually ask students to justify their opinions and then support them with evidence, to think of counterexamples to rules, and so on.

One example of a teaching theme used in the FCL program is "changing populations." Outside experts and/or teachers introduce this lesson and ask students to generate as many questions about it as possible—it is not unusual for students to come up with more than a hundred questions. The teacher and the students categorize the questions into subtopics according to the type of population they refer to (usually about five categories), such as extinct, endangered, artificial, assisted, and urbanized populations. About six students make up a learning group, and each group takes responsibility for one of the subtopics.

A culture of learning, negotiating, sharing, and producing work that is displayed to others is at the heart of FCL. The educational experience involves an interpretive community that encourages active exchange and reciprocity. This approach has much in common with what Jerome Bruner (1996) recommended for improving the culture of education. Research evaluation of the Fostering a Community of Learners approach suggests that it benefits students' understanding and flexible use of content knowledge, resulting in improved achievement in reading, writing, and problem solving.

Careers in Child Development

Laura Martin, *Science Museum Educator and Research Specialist*

After taking a psychology course as an undergraduate, Laura Martin obtained a master's degree from Bank Street College of Education in New York. Laura then worked as a teacher of young children for several years. That experience challenged her to learn more about how children think, so she applied to graduate school in child development and eventually obtained her Ph.D. from the University of California–San Diego. She later returned to Bank Street College and orchestrated projects on technology and learning. Then Laura joined Children's Television Workshop, which produces *Sesame Street,* as research director. Later, she became Vice President for Productions Research at Children's Television Workshop.

Interesting opportunities continued to be presented to her, including offers from a software developer, the government, and colleges. She took a job as a science museum education and research specialist at the Arizona Science Center. At the center, she conceptualizes exhibits and researches whether the layout designs are communicating effectively. She organizes programs, classes, and resources. She says that as she does these things, her education and training in child development are extremely helpful.

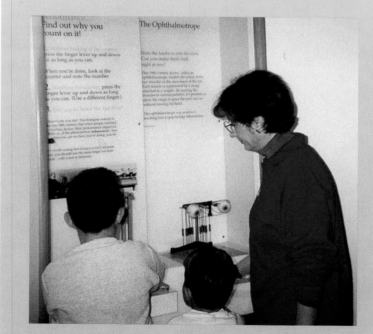

Laura Martin with children visiting the Arizona Science Center.

Thinking Scientifically

Children's problem solving is often compared to that of scientists. Both children and scientists ask fundamental questions about the nature of reality. Both also seek answers to problems that often seem utterly trivial or unanswerable to other people (such as, Why is the sky blue?). Both also are granted by society the time and freedom to pursue answers to the problems they find interesting. This "child as scientist" metaphor has led researchers to ask whether children generate hypotheses, perform experiments, and reach conclusions concerning the meaning of their data in ways resembling those of scientists (Clinchy, Mansfield, & Schott, 1995).

Scientific reasoning often is aimed at identifying causal relations. Like scientists, children often emphasize causal mechanisms (Frye & others, 1996). However, preadolescents have much greater difficulty in separating their prior theories from the evidence that they have obtained. Often, when they try to learn about new phenomena, they maintain their old theories regardless of the evidence (Kuhn, Schauble, & Garcia-Mila, 1992).

Another difference between scientists and children is that children are influenced more by happenstance events than by the overall pattern of occurrences (Kuhn, Amsel, & O'Laughlin, 1988). Children also have difficulty designing new experiments that can distinguish conclusively among alternative causes. Instead, they tend to bias the experiments in favor of whichever hypothesis they began with, and sometimes they will see the results as supporting their original hypothesis even when the results directly contradict it (Schauble, 1996). Thus, although there are important similarities between children and scientists, in their basic curiosity and in the kinds of questions they ask, there are also important differences in the degree to which they can separate theory and evidence and in their ability to design conclusive experiments (Lehrer, Schauble, & Petrosino, 2001; Schauble, 1996).

One setting in which thinking is often stimulated is a children's museum. To read about the work of one individual who works in a children's science museum, see the Careers in Child Development insert on page 269.

Review and Reflect: Learning Goal 3

3 Explain how children think

REVIEW

- What is thinking?
- What are concepts? What is theory of mind?
- How do children solve problems?
- What are some key aspects of children's ability to think critically?
- How do children's and scientists' thinking differ?

REFLECT

- Choose an area in which you feel at least somewhat of an expert. Compare your ability to learn in that field with the ability of a novice.

4 METACOGNITION

| Developmental Changes | Strategies | Self-Regulatory Learning |

At the beginning of the chapter we defined *metacognition* as cognition about cognition, or "knowing about knowing" (Flavell, 1999; Flavell & Miller, 2002). One expert on children's thinking, Deanna Kuhn (1999), believes that metacognition should be a stronger focus of efforts to help children become better critical thinkers, especially at the middle school and high school levels. She distinguishes between first-order cognitive skills that enable children to know about the world (which have been the main focus of critical-thinking programs) and second-order cognitive skills—*meta-knowing skills*—that entail knowing about one's own (and others') knowing.

A distinction can be made between metacognitive knowledge and metacognitive activity. **Metacognitive knowledge** involves monitoring and reflecting on one's current or recent thoughts. This includes both *factual knowledge,* such as knowledge about the task, one's goals, or oneself, and *strategic knowledge,* such as how and when to use specific procedures to solve problems. **Metacognitive activity** occurs when individuals use self-awareness to adapt to and manage strategies during actual problem solving and thinking. Thus, a child's awareness and use of self-regulatory learning strategies involve metacognition.

Developmental Changes

The majority of developmental studies classified as "metacognitive" have focused on metamemory, or knowledge about memory. This includes general knowledge about memory, such as knowing that recognition tests are easier than recall tests. It also encompasses knowledge about one's own memory, such as a student's ability to monitor whether she has studied enough for a test that is coming up next week.

By 5 or 6 years of age, children usually know that familiar items are easier to learn than unfamiliar ones, that short lists are easier than long ones, that recognition is easier than recall, and that forgetting is more likely to occur over time (Lyon & Flavell, 1993). However, in other ways young children's metamemory is limited. They don't understand that related items are easier to remember than unrelated ones or that remembering the gist of a story is easier than remembering information verbatim (Kreutzer, Leonard, & Flavell, 1975). By fifth grade, students understand that gist recall is easier than verbatim recall. Young children also have an inflated opinion of their memory abilities. For example, in one study a majority of young children predicted that they would be able to recall all 10 items of a list of 10 items. When tested for this, none of the young children managed this feat (Flavell, Friedrichs, & Hoyt, 1970). As they move through the elementary school years, children give more realistic evaluations of their memory skills (Schneider & Pressley, 1997).

Young children also have little appreciation for the importance of "cognitive cueing," for memory. Cognitive cueing involves being reminded of something by an external cue or phrase, such as "Don't you remember, it helps you to learn a concept when you can think of an example of it." By 7 or 8 years of age, children better appreciate the importance of such cognitive cueing in memory.

Strategies

In Michael Pressley's view (Pressley, 1983, 2003; McCormick & Pressley, 1997; Pressley & others, 2003), the key to education is helping students learn a rich repertoire of strategies that result in solutions of problems (Kuhn, 2000). Good thinkers routinely use strategies and effective planning to solve problems. Good thinkers also know when and where to use strategies (they have metacognitive knowledge about strategies). Understanding when and where to use strategies often results from the learner's monitoring of the learning situation.

Pressley argues that when students are given instruction about effective strategies, they often can apply these strategies that they previously have not used on their own. However, some strategies are not effective for young children. For example, young children cannot competently use mental imagery. Pressley emphasizes that students benefit when the teacher models the appropriate strategy and overtly verbalizes the steps in the strategy. Then, students subsequently practice the strategy. Their practice of the strategy is guided and supported by the teacher's feedback until the students can effectively execute the strategy autonomously. When instructing students about employing the strategy, it also is a good idea to tell them how using the strategy will benefit them.

*T*he developing cognitive competencies that are the most relevant to critical thinking are metacognitive competencies.
—DEANNA KUHN
Contemporary Psychologist,
Columbia University

www.mhhe.com/santrockcd10

Metacognition
Metacognition and Reading

metacognitive knowledge Monitoring and reflecting on one's current or recent thoughts.

metacognitive activity Using self-awareness to adapt to and manage strategies during problem solving and thinking.

Practice alone will not guarantee that students will continue to use the new strategy and transfer it to new situations. For effective maintenance and transfer, encourage students to monitor the effectiveness of the new strategy relative to their use of old strategies by comparing their performance on tests and other assessments. Pressley says that it is not enough to say "Try it, you will like it"; you need to say "Try it and compare."

Learning how to effectively use strategies often takes time. Initially, executing the strategies is usually slow and requires guidance and support from the teacher. With practice, strategies are executed faster and more competently. This means using the effective strategy over and over again until it is automatically performed. For learners to execute the strategies effectively, they need to have the strategies in long-term memory, and extensive practice makes this possible. Learners also need to be motivated to use the strategies.

Let's examine an example of how strategy instruction can be effective. Good readers extract the main ideas from text and summarize them. In contrast, novice readers (for example, most children) usually don't store the main ideas of what they read. One intervention based on what is known about the summarization strategies of good readers consisted of instructing children to (1) ignore trivial information, (2) ignore redundant information, (3) replace less-inclusive terms with more-inclusive ones, (4) combine a series of events with a more-inclusive action term, and (5) choose a topic sentence (Brown & Day, 1983). Researchers have found that instructing elementary school students to use these summarization strategies benefits their reading performance (Rinehart, Stahl, & Erickson, 1986).

Do children use one strategy or multiple strategies in memory and problem solving? They often use more than one strategy (Schneider & Bjorklund, 1998; Siegler, 1998). Most children benefit from generating a variety of alternative strategies and experimenting with different approaches to a problem, discovering what works well, when, and where (Schneider & Bjorklund, 1998). This is especially true for children from the middle elementary school grades on, although some cognitive psychologists believe that even young children should be encouraged to practice varying strategies (Siegler, 1998).

In this discussion, we have indicated that self-monitoring and self-regulatory skills are important aspects of metacognition. Next, we will explore self-regulatory skills in greater detail.

Self-Regulatory Learning

Self-Regulatory Learning

Self-regulatory learning consists of the self-generation and self-monitoring of thoughts, feelings, and behaviors to reach a goal. These goals might be academic (improving comprehension while reading, becoming a more organized writer, learning how to do multiplication, asking relevant questions) or they might be socioemotional (controlling one's anger, getting along better with peers). What are some of the characteristics of self-regulated learners? Self-regulatory learners (Winne, 1997, 2001):

- Set goals for extending their knowledge and sustaining their motivation
- Are aware of their emotional makeup and have strategies for managing their emotions
- Periodically monitor their progress toward a goal
- Fine-tune or revise their strategies based on the progress they are making
- Evaluate obstacles that arise and make the necessary adaptations

Researchers have found that high-achieving students are often self-regulatory learners (Pintrich, 2003; Pressley, 1995; Schunk & Zimmerman, 2003; Zimmerman & Schunk, 2001). For example, compared with low-achieving students, high-achieving students set more-specific learning goals, use more strategies to learn, self-monitor their learning more, and more systematically evaluate their progress toward a goal.

self-regulatory learning Generating and monitoring thoughts, feelings, and behaviors to reach a goal.

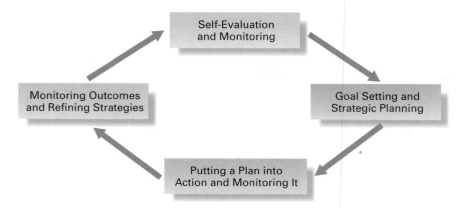

FIGURE 8.17 A Model of Self-Regulatory Learning

A Model of Self-Regulatory Learning   Teachers, tutors, mentors, counselors, and parents can help children become self-regulatory learners. Barry Zimmerman, Sebastian Bonner, and Robert Kovach (1996) developed a model for turning low-self-regulatory students into students who engage in these multistep strategies: (1) self-evaluation and self-monitoring, (2) goal setting and strategic planning, (3) putting a plan into action and monitoring it, and (4) monitoring outcomes and refining strategies (see figure 8.17).

They describe a seventh-grade student who is doing poorly in history and apply their self-regulatory model to her situation. In step 1, she self-evaluates her studying and test preparation by keeping a detailed record of them. The teacher gives her some guidelines for keeping these records. After several weeks, the student turns the records in and traces her poor test performance to low comprehension of difficult reading material.

In step 2, the student sets a goal, in this case of improving her reading comprehension, and plans how to achieve the goal. The teacher helps her break down the goal into components such as locating main ideas and setting specific goals for understanding a series of paragraphs in her textbook. The teacher also provides the student with strategies, such as focusing initially on the first sentence of each paragraph and then scanning the others as a means of identifying main ideas. Another support the teacher might offer the student is adult or peer tutoring in reading comprehension if it is available.

In step 3, the student puts the plan into action and begins to monitor her progress. Initially, she might need help from the teacher or tutor in identifying main ideas in the reading. This feedback can help her monitor her reading comprehension more effectively on her own.

In step 4, the student monitors her improvement in reading comprehension by evaluating whether it has had any impact on her learning outcomes. Most importantly: Has her improvement in reading comprehension led to better performance on history tests?

Review and Reflect: Learning Goal 4

4 Summarize developmental changes and processes involved in children's metacognition

REVIEW

- What are some developmental changes that take place in metacognition?
- How do children use strategies as part of their metacognition?
- What is self-regulatory learning?

REFLECT

- How might changes in metacognition be involved in the ability of college students to have better study skills than children?

Reach Your Learning Goals

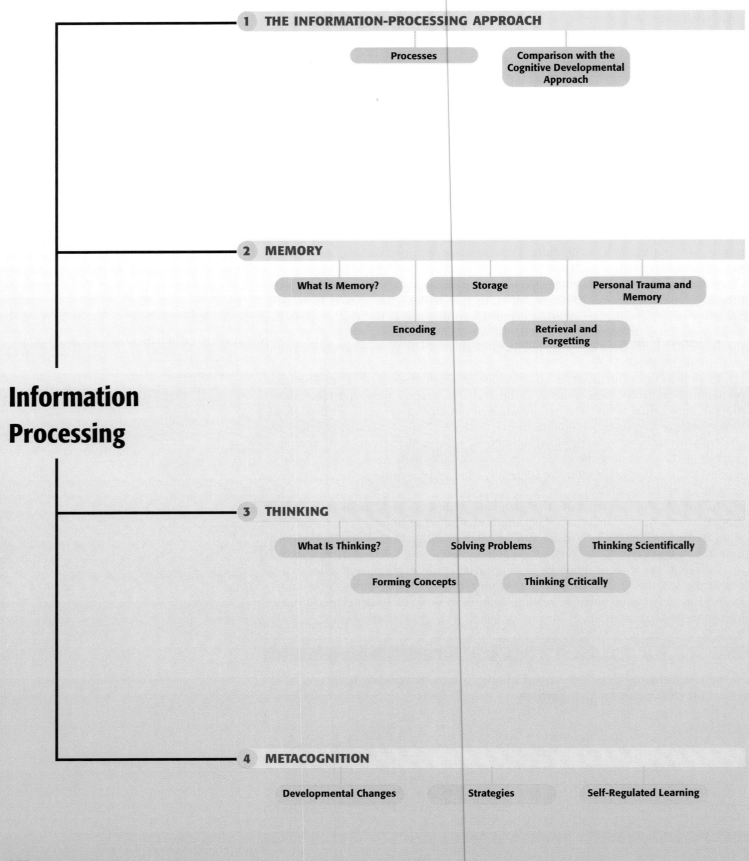

Information Processing

1 THE INFORMATION-PROCESSING APPROACH

Processes

Comparison with the Cognitive Developmental Approach

2 MEMORY

What Is Memory?

Storage

Personal Trauma and Memory

Encoding

Retrieval and Forgetting

3 THINKING

What Is Thinking?

Solving Problems

Thinking Scientifically

Forming Concepts

Thinking Critically

4 METACOGNITION

Developmental Changes

Strategies

Self-Regulated Learning

Summary

1   Discuss the basic ideas in the information-processing approach and compare it with the cognitive developmental approach

- The information-processing approach emphasizes that children manipulate information, monitor it, and strategize about it. Siegler described three main characteristics of the information-processing approach: (1) thinking, (2) change mechanisms (include encoding, automaticity, and strategy construction), and (3) self-modification.

- Both the information-processing and cognitive developmental approaches try to identify children's cognitive capacities and limits at various points in development. The information-processing approach places more emphasis on processing limitations, strategies for overcoming limitations, knowledge about specific content, and precise analysis of change. Piaget's theory underscores the importance of cognitive stages and Vygotsky's theory the social construction of knowledge, while the information-processing approach does not.

2   Describe the way that memory works in children

- Memory is the retention of information over time. Memory involves encoding (how information gets into memory), storage (how the information is stored over time), and retrieval (taking information out of memory).

- In everyday language, encoding has much in common with attention and learning. Habituation and dishabituation are closely linked with attention and widely studied in infants. As children become older, they are better at attending to the relevant rather than the salient dimensions of a task, are more likely to construct a plan for attending, attend selectively, and shift attention from one activity to another when it is called for. Rehearsal, deep processing, elaboration, constructing images, and organization are other processes that are involved in encoding.

- One way that memory varies involves the time frames of sensory memory, short-term memory, and long-term memory. However, many contemporary psychologists prefer the term *working memory* to *short-term memory* because of its active, constructivist nature and because it fits the research results better.

  Many cognitive psychologists accept this hierarchy of long-term memory's contents: division into declarative (explicit) and procedural (implicit) subtypes, with declarative memory further subdivided into episodic and semantic memory. One controversy about infant memory involves explicit and implicit memory. Children's ability to remember new information about a subject depends extensively on what they already know about it. The contribution of content knowledge is especially relevant in the memory of experts. Experts have a number of characteristics that can explain why they solve problems better than novices do. Becoming an expert requires deliberate practice, motivation,

and talent. Two major approaches to how memory is represented are in terms of networks and schemas. A script is a schema for an event.

- Retrieval is influenced by the serial position effect, how effective retrieval cues are, and the memory task. Forgetting can be explained in terms of cue-dependent forgetting, interference theory, and decay theory.

- Some cases of personal trauma involve post-traumatic stress disorder. Personal trauma can cause children to repress emotionally laden information. Repression doesn't erase memory, it just makes it extremely hard to remember consciously. Controversy surrounds the accuracy of recovered memories in such situations as when child abuse has allegedly occurred.

3   Explain how children think

- Thinking involves manipulating and transforming information in memory. Thinking is often carried out to form concepts, reason, think critically, and solve problems.

- Concepts are categories used to group objects, events, and characteristics on the basis of common properties. Concepts are elements of cognition that help to simplify and summarize information. They also improve memory, communication, and time use. One aspect of concept formation in children involves their theory of mind, which refers to awareness of one's own mental processes and the mental processes of others.

- Problem solving involves finding an appropriate way to attain a goal. Four steps in problem solving are (1) finding and framing problems, (2) developing good problem-solving strategies, (3) evaluating solutions, and (4) rethinking and redefining problems over time. Much of the information-processing research on problem solving has focused on identifying the rules that children use in solving problems. Even very young children can draw reasonable analogies in some circumstances.

- Critical thinking involves thinking reflectively and productively, and evaluating the evidence. Fostering a Community of Learners is an example of a program that seeks to improve children's critical-thinking skills.

- Children's thinking shares certain characteristics with scientists but also differs in certain ways. Both scientists and children ask fundamental questions about the nature of reality. Children are influenced more by happenstance events than by the overall pattern of occurrences than scientists are.

4   Identify developmental changes and processes involved in children's metacognition

- Metacognition is cognition about cognition, or knowing about knowing. Metacognition involves both metacognitive knowledge and metacognitive activity. Most studies focus on metamemory, or what children know about how memory works. Children's metamemory improves considerably during the elementary school years.

- In Pressley's view, the key to education is helping children learn a rich repertoire of strategies that result in solutions to problems. Students benefit when teachers model effective strategies and give students opportunities to practice strategies, when students are encouraged to monitor the effectiveness of their new strategy, and when students are motivated to use the strategy. It takes considerable time to learn a new strategy and use it independently. Most children benefit from using multiple strategies, exploring when and where they work well.

- Self-regulatory learning consists of the self-generation and self-monitoring of thoughts, feelings, and behaviors to reach a goal. High-achieving students are often self-regulatory learners. One model of self-regulatory learning involves these components: self-evaluation and self-monitoring; goal setting and strategic planning; putting a plan into action; and monitoring outcomes and refining strategies. Self-regulatory learning gives children responsibility for their learning.

Key Terms

information-processing approach 242
encoding 243
automaticity 243
strategy construction 243
metacognition 243
memory 244
storage 244

retrieval 244
attention 245
habituation 245
dishabituation 245
sensory memory 251
short-term memory 251
working memory 252
long-term memory 252

thinking 260
concepts 260
theory of mind 260
problem solving 261
subgoaling 262
algorithms 262
heuristics 262
means-end analysis 263

critical thinking 267
reciprocal teaching 268
metacognitive knowledge 271
metacognitive activity 271
self-regulatory learning 272

Key People

Robert Siegler 242
John Flavell 247
Fergus Craik and Robert Lockhart 248
Allan Paivio 249
Carolyn Rovee-Collier 253
Endel Tulving 253

Elizabeth Loftus 259
Judy DeLoache 265
Andrew Meltzoff and Keith Moore 267
John Dewey 267
Max Wertheimer 267

Jacqueline and Martin Brooks 267
David Perkins and Sarah Tishman 268
Ann Brown and Joe Campione 268

Deanna Kuhn 270
Michael Pressley 271
Barry Zimmerman, Sebastian Bonner, and Robert Kovach 273

Taking It to the Net

1. Nancy, who is 14, is talking to her older sister, Joanne, age 20. Joanne insists that when Nancy was 6, she got lost at the circus and Joanne and their parents searched frantically for her for two hours. Joanne says that they finally found her hanging out by the concession stand, just watching the people. At first, Nancy had no recollection of this, but the more Joanne talked about it, the more Nancy started to recall some of the details. Is it possible that Nancy is imaging a false "memory"?

2. A group of parents have called a special PTA meeting to discuss the math curriculum at their children's elementary school. Apparently students are using computers and calculators, and working in groups on math "projects." The parents are alarmed that their children don't seem to be learning old-fashioned arithmetic. What happened to multiplication tables and long division?

3. Bill Harris, grandfather to fourth-grader Kevin and sixth-grader Jocelyn, is looking for a volunteer opportunity at Kevin and Jocelyn's school. A retired chemical engineer, he would like to help the school beef up its science education program. How could he help?

Connect to **www.mhhe.com/santrockcd10** to research the answers and complete these exercises.

E-Learning Tools

To help you master the material in this chapter, you'll find a number of valuable study tools on the Student CD-ROM that accompanies this book. Also visit the Online Learning Center for *Child Development*, tenth edition (**www.mhhe.com/santrockcd10**) where you'll find these additional resources:

- Build your decision-making skills by trying your hand at the parenting, nursing, and education "Scenarios" on the Online Learning Center.

CHAPTER 9

As many people, as many minds, each in his own way.

—TERENCE
Roman Playwright, 2nd Century B.C.

Intelligence

Chapter Outline

Learning Goals

THE NATURE OF INTELLIGENCE **1**

1. Describe what intelligence is

INTELLIGENCE TESTING **2**

Approaches to Testing
Criteria of a Good Intelligence Test
Cultural Bias in Testing
The Use and Misuse of Intelligence Tests

2. Explain how intelligence is measured and the limitations of intelligence tests

THEORIES OF MULTIPLE INTELLIGENCE **3**

Factor Analysis, Two-Factor Theory, and Multiple-Factor Theory
Gardner's Theory of Eight Intelligences
Sternberg's Triarchic Theory
Emotional Intelligence
Evaluating the Multiple-Intelligences Approach
Do Children Have a General Intelligence?

3. Evaluate theories of multiple intelligence

INTELLIGENCE IN INFANCY AND DEVELOPMENTAL TRANSFORMATIONS **4**

Infant Intelligence Tests
Stability and Change in Intelligence
Information-Processing Tasks as Predictors of Intelligence

4. Summarize the testing of intelligence in infancy and developmental transformations

THE EXTREMES OF INTELLIGENCE AND CREATIVITY **5**

Mental Retardation
Giftedness
Creativity

5. Discuss characteristics of mental retardation, giftedness, and creativity

THE INFLUENCE OF HEREDITY AND ENVIRONMENT **6**

Hereditary Influences
Environmental Influences
Group Comparisons

6. Analyze the contributions of heredity and environment to intelligence

The Story of Project Spectrum

Project Spectrum is an innovative educational attempt by Howard Gardner (1993) to encourage the development of a range of intelligences in young children. Spectrum begins with the basic idea that every child has the potential to develop strengths in one or more areas. It provides a context in which to see the strengths and weaknesses of individual children more clearly.

What is a Spectrum classroom like? The classroom has rich and engaging materials that can stimulate a range of intelligences. Teachers do not try to evoke an intelligence directly by using materials that are separated under labels like *sensory* or *verbal*. Rather, materials that relate to a combination of intelligence domains are used. For example, a naturalist corner houses biological specimens that children can explore and compare. This area elicits children's sensory capacities, logical analytic skills, and naturalist skills. In a storytelling area, children create imaginative tales with stimulating props and design their own storyboards. This area encourages children to use their skills in language, drama, and imagery. In a building corner, children can construct a model of their classroom and arrange small-scale photographs of the children and teachers in their class. This area encourages the use of spatial and personal skills. In all, the Spectrum classroom has twelve such areas designed to improve children's multiple intelligences.

The Spectrum classroom can identify skills that are typically missed in a regular classroom. In one first-grade Spectrum classroom, a boy who was the product of a highly conflicted home was at risk for school failure. However, when Project Spectrum was introduced, the boy was identified as the best student in the class at taking apart and putting together common objects, like a food grinder or a doorknob. His teacher became encouraged when she found that he possessed this skill, and his overall school performance began to improve.

In addition to identifying unexpected strengths in children, Project Spectrum also can identify weaknesses. Gregory was doing very well in first grade, being especially skilled in math computation and conceptual knowledge. However, he performed poorly in a number of Spectrum areas. He did well only in the areas in which he needed to give the correct answer and a person in authority gave it to him. As a result of the Spectrum program, Gregory's teacher began to search for ways to encourage him to take risks on more open-ended tasks, to try things out in innovative ways, and to realize that it is okay to make mistakes.

Project Spectrum has evolved to include the development of theme-related kits that tap a range of intelligences. Two such themes are "Night and Day" and "About Me." Children experience the basics of reading, writing, and calculating in the context of the themes and materials with which they are motivated to work.

In this chapter, we will continue our discussion of children's cognition by examining the nature of intelligence. We will see that the concept of intelligence is broad, and that there is controversy over how intelligence should be conceptualized and measured. Gardner's theory of multiple intelligences is part of the controversy. We will explore infant intelligence and developmental transformations in intelligence. We will also discuss creativity, both as a component of intelligence and as a separate process. Other topics we will explore are the extremes of intelligence—mental retardation and giftedness—as well as the contributions of heredity and environment to intelligence.

1 THE NATURE OF INTELLIGENCE

What does the term *intelligence* mean? Some experts describe intelligence as the ability to solve problems. Others describe it as the capacity to adapt and learn from experience. Still others argue that defining intelligence in these cognitive terms ignores other dimensions of intelligence, such as creativity, and practical and interpersonal intelligence (Gardner, 2003; Sternberg, 2003a).

The problem with intelligence is that, unlike height, weight, and age, intelligence cannot be directly measured. We can't peel back a person's scalp and see how much intelligence he or she has. We can evaluate intelligence only *indirectly* by studying and comparing the intelligent acts that people perform.

The primary components of intelligence are similar to the cognitive processes of problem solving, thinking, and memory that we discussed in chapter 8. ◄ **page 236** The differences in how we described these cognitive processes in chapter 8 and how we will discuss intelligence lie in the concepts of individual differences and assessment. *Individual differences* are the stable, consistent ways in which people are different from one another. Individual differences in intelligence generally have been measured by intelligence tests designed to tell us whether a person can reason better than others who have taken the test. Intelligence is one of the areas of psychology in which individual differences have been extensively examined (Sternberg, Lautrey, & Lubart, 2003). As you will see later in the chapter, though, the use of intelligence tests to assess intelligence is controversial. However, we'll temporarily set aside the contentions of psychologists who believe that the conventional intelligence tests are inadequate measures of intelligence and use as our definition of **intelligence** the ability to solve problems and to adapt and learn from experience.

Review and Reflect: Learning Goal 1

1 **Describe what intelligence is**

REVIEW

- What is intelligence? How is intelligence linked to the concepts of individual differences and assessment?

REFLECT

- What do you think makes a child intelligent?

---

2 INTELLIGENCE TESTING

Approaches to Testing

Cultural Bias in Testing

Criteria of a Good Intelligence Test

The Use and Misuse of Intelligence Tests

If you took the SAT exam before entering college, you might understand psychologist Robert Sternberg's (1997) childhood anxieties about intelligence tests. Because he got so stressed out about taking the tests, he did very poorly on them. Fortunately, a fourth-grade teacher worked with Robert and helped instill the confidence in him to overcome his anxieties. He not only began performing better on them, but when he was 13, he devised his own intelligence test and began using it to

intelligence The ability to solve problems and to adapt to and learn from life's everyday experiences.

Alfred Binet constructed the first intelligence test after being asked to create a measure to determine which children could benefit from instruction in France's schools and which could not.

Alfred Binet
Mental Measurements Yearbook

assess classmates—until the school principal found out and scolded him. Sternberg became so fascinated by intelligence that he made its study a lifelong pursuit. Later in the chapter, we will discuss his approach to intelligence.

Approaches to Testing

Early psychologists completely ignored the "higher mental processes," such as thinking and problem solving, that we equate with intelligence today. They believed that simple sensory, perceptual, and motor processes were the key dimensions of intelligence. Sir Frances Galton, an English psychologist who is considered the father of mental tests, shared this point of view. However, in the late nineteenth century, he set out to demonstrate that there are systematic individual differences in these processes. Although his research provided few conclusive results, Galton raised many important questions about intelligence—how it should be measured, what its components are, and the degree to which it is inherited—that we continue to study today.

The Binet Tests In 1904 the French Ministry of Education asked psychologist Alfred Binet to devise a method that would determine which students did not profit from typical school instruction. School officials wanted to reduce overcrowding by placing those who did not benefit from regular classroom teaching in special schools. Binet and his student Theophile Simon developed an intelligence test to meet this request. The test consisted of 30 items ranging from the ability to touch one's nose or ear when asked to the ability to draw designs from memory and to define abstract concepts.

Binet developed the concept of **mental age (MA),** which is an individual's level of mental development relative to others. Binet reasoned that a mentally retarded child would perform like a normal child of a younger age. He developed norms for intelligence by testing 50 nonretarded children from the ages of 3 to 11. Children suspected of mental retardation were given the test, and their performance was compared with children of the same chronological age in the normal sample. Average mental age (MA) scores correspond to chronological age (CA), which is age from birth. A bright child has an MA considerably above CA; a dull child has an MA considerably below CA.

The term **intelligence quotient (IQ)** was devised in 1912 by William Stern. IQ consists of an individual's mental age divided by chronological age multiplied by 100:

$$IQ = \frac{MA}{CA} \times 100$$

If mental age is the same as chronological age, then the individual's IQ is 100; if mental age is above chronological age, the IQ is more than 100; if mental age is below chronological age, the IQ is less than 100. Scores noticeably above 100 are considered above average; those considerably below are considered below average. For example, a 6-year-old child with a mental age of 8 would have an IQ of 133, whereas a 6-year-old child with a mental age of 5 would have an IQ of 83.

The Binet scales represented a major advance over earlier efforts to measure intelligence. Binet stressed that the core of intelligence consists of complex cognitive processes, such as memory, imagery, comprehension, and judgment. In addition, he believed that a developmental approach was crucial for understanding the concept of intelligence. His developmental interest was underscored by the emphasis on the child's mental age compared to chronological age.

The Binet test has been revised many times to incorporate advances in the understanding of intelligence and intelligence testing. Many of the revisions were carried out by Lewis Terman, who applied Stern's IQ concept to the test, developed extensive norms, and provided detailed, clear instructions for each problem on the

mental age (MA) An individual's level of mental development relative to others.

intelligent quotient (IQ) Devised by William Stern in 1912, consists of an individual's mental age divided by chronological age multiplied by 100.

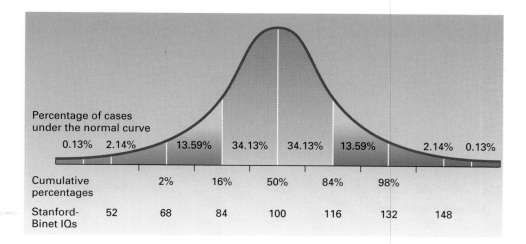

FIGURE 9.1 The Normal Curve and Stanford-Binet IQ Scores

The distribution of IQ scores approximates a normal curve. Most of the population falls in the middle range of scores. Notice that extremely high and extremely low scores are very rare. Slightly more than two-thirds of the scores fall between 84 & 116. Only about 1 in 50 individuals has an IQ of more than 132 and only about 1 in 50 individuals has an IQ of less than 68.

test. In 1985, the test, now called the Stanford-Binet (Stanford University is where the revisions were done), was revised to analyze an individual's responses in four content areas: verbal reasoning, quantitative reasoning, abstract/visual reasoning, and short-term memory. A general composite score also is obtained to reflect overall intelligence.

The current Stanford-Binet is given to individuals from the age of 2 through adulthood. It includes a wide variety of items, some requiring verbal responses, others nonverbal responses. For example, items that characterize a 6-year-old's performance on the test include the verbal ability to define at least six words, such as *orange* and *envelope,* and the nonverbal ability to trace a path through a maze. Items that reflect the average adult's intelligence include defining such words as *disproportionate* and *regard,* explaining a proverb, and comparing idleness and laziness.

Over the years, the Stanford-Binet test has been given to thousands of children and adults of different ages selected at random from different parts of the United States. By administering the test to large numbers of individuals and recording the results, it has been found that intelligence measured by the Stanford-Binet approximates a normal distribution (see figure 9.1). A **normal distribution** is a symmetrical, bell-shaped curve with a majority of the cases falling in the middle of the range of possible scores and few scores appearing toward the extremes of the range. The Stanford-Binet continues to be one of the most widely used individual tests of intelligence.

The Wechsler Scales   Besides the Stanford-Binet, the most widely used intelligence tests are the Wechsler scales, developed by David Wechsler. In 1939, Wechsler introduced the first of his scales, designed for use with adults. Now in its third edition, the Wechsler Adult Intelligence Scale–III (WAIS-III) was followed by the Wechsler Intelligence Scale for Children–III (WISC-III) for children between the ages of 6 and 16, and the Wechsler Preschool and Primary Scale of Intelligence (WPPSI) for children from the ages of 4 to $6^{1}/_{2}$.

The Wechsler scales not only provide an overall IQ score, but also yields scores on six verbal and five nonverbal measures. This allows the examiner to separate verbal and nonverbal IQ scores and to see quickly the areas of mental performance in which the individual is below average, average, or above average. The inclusion of a number of nonverbal subscales makes the Wechsler test more representative of verbal and nonverbal intelligence; the Stanford-Binet test includes some nonverbal items, but not as many as the Wechsler scales. Several of the Wechsler subscales are shown in figure 9.2.

Group Tests of Intelligence   The Stanford-Binet and Wechsler tests are individually administered intelligence tests. A psychologist approaches the testing situation

normal distribution A symmetrical, bell-shaped curve with a majority of the cases falling in the middle of the possible range of scores and few scores appearing toward the extremes of the range.

FIGURE 9.2 Sample Subscales of the Wechsler Intelligence Scale for Children–Revised

Verbal Subscales

Similarities

A child must think logically and abstractly to answer a number of questions about how things might be similar.

Examples: "In what way are a saw and a hammer alike?"
"In what way are a circle and a triangle alike?"

Comprehension

This subscale is designed to measure an individual's judgment and common sense.

Examples: "What should you do if you see someone forget his book when he leaves a restaurant?"
"What is the advantage of keeping money in a bank?"

Nonverbal Subscales

Block Design

An child must assemble a set of multicolored blocks to match designs that the examiner shows. Visual-motor coordination, perceptual organization, and the ability to visualize spatially are assessed.

Example: "Use the four blocks on the left to make the pattern on the right."

The Wechsler includes 11 subscales, 6 verbal and 5 nonverbal. Three of the subscales are shown here.

as a structured interaction between the psychologist and the individual being tested. This provides an opportunity to sample the individual's behavior. During testing the psychologist observes the ease with which rapport is established, the level of energy and enthusiasm the individual expresses, and the degree of frustration tolerance and persistence the individual shows in performing difficult tasks. Each of these observations helps the psychologist understand the individual.

Though economical and convenient, group tests have some significant disadvantages. When a test is given to a large group, the examiner cannot establish rapport, determine the level of anxiety, and so on. Most testing experts recommend that, when important decisions are to be made about an individual, a group intelligence test should be supplemented by other information about the individual's abilities. For example, many children take ability tests at school in a large group. If a decision is to be made about placing a child in a special education class, it is a legal requirement that the decision not be based on a group intelligence test. The psychologist must administer an individual intelligence test, such as the Stanford-Binet or Wechsler, and obtain extensive additional information about the child's abilities outside the testing situation.

The Scholastic Aptitude Test (SAT), a group test taken each year by more than 1 million high school seniors, measures some of the same abilities as intelligence tests. However, it does not yield an overall IQ score; rather, the SAT provides separate scores for verbal and mathematical ability. The SAT is similar to the original Binet test in that it was developed to predict success in school. Beginning in 2005, the SAT will be changed to include an essay, higher-level math problems, new reading comprehension passages, and the elimination of analogy items. These changes were made in the face of criticism that the SAT does not adequately measure what students actually learn.

The SAT is used widely as a predictor of success in college, but it is only one of many pieces of information that determine whether a college admits a student. High school grades, the quality of the student's high school, letters of recommendation, individual interviews with the student, and special circumstances in the student's life that might have impeded academic ability are taken into account along with the SAT scores.

In recent years, a controversy has developed over whether private coaching can raise a student's SAT scores. The student's verbal and mathematical abilities, which the SAT assesses, have been built over years of experience and instruction. Research shows that private coaching on a short-term basis does not raise SAT scores substantially. Researchers have found that, on the average, SAT preparation courses raise a student's scores only 15 points on the SAT's 200 to 800 scale (Kulik, Bangert-Drowns, & Kulik, 1984).

Another controversy focuses on possible gender bias in the SAT. In 2000, males outscored females by 42 points on the average—35 points higher in the math section and 8 points in the verbal section (College Board, 2001). This represents a 4 point increase in the SAT gender gap from 1999, and only a slight narrowing of the gap since the early 1990s. Educational Testing Service claims that the SAT is supposed to predict college success, especially in terms of first-year grades. However, females make better grades than males in their first year of college, so it would appear that the SAT underpredicts the first-year success of females and overpredicts the first-year success of males.

Aptitude and Achievement Tests Psychologists distinguish between aptitude tests and achievement tests. **Aptitude tests** predict an individual's ability to learn a skill or what the individual can accomplish with training. **Achievement tests** measure what a person has learned or the skills the person has mastered. Because the SAT is used to predict college success, it usually is referred to as an aptitude test. The tests you take in this and other college courses that assess what you have learned are achievement tests. Aptitude tests typically measure future performance; achievement tests assess current performance.

In many cases, the distinction between aptitude and achievement tests becomes blurred. Although the SAT is used along with other information to predict college success (which makes it an aptitude test), it also examines what you have learned and the skills that you have mastered, such as math and vocabulary skills (characteristics of an achievement test). Indeed, the name of the SAT recently was changed from Scholastic Aptitude Test to Scholastic Assessment Test to acknowledge that the test measures both aptitude and achievement.

Criteria of a Good Intelligence Test

Measurement and testing have been components of human decision making for centuries. The Chinese first developed formal oral tests of knowledge as early as 2200 B.C., when the Chinese emperor Ta Yü conducted a three-year cycle of "competency testing" of government officials. After three examinations, the officials were either promoted or fired (Sax, 1997). In today's world, tests have become commonplace as psychologists have sought more precise measurement of psychology's concepts (Aiken, 2003).

Psychometrists specialize in the psychological testing, possibly creating tests, administering them, or interpreting them. Most psychometrists have at least a minimum of a master's degree in psychology and have completed extensive coursework in psychological testing. Psychometrists work in education, business, and clinical fields. For example, a school psychometrist might test children who are having difficulties in school to determine their weaknesses, as well as their strengths. Psychometrists are generally quite knowledgeable about the tests they administer. They know that a good test must meet these three criteria—validity, reliability, and standardization. Let's explore each of these criteria.

aptitude tests Tests that predict an individual's ability to learn a skill or what the individual can accomplish with training.

achievement tests Tests that measure what a person has learned or the skills that a person has mastered.

Validity   **Validity** is the extent to which a test measures what it is intended to measure. If a test is supposed to measure intelligence, then it should measure intelligence, not some other characteristic of the person, such as anxiety.

There are a number of ways to establish a test's validity. One is making sure that the test samples a broad range of the content that is to be measured. For example, a final exam in this class, if it is to cover the entire book, should sample items from each of the chapters rather than just two or three chapters. If an intelligence test purports to measure both verbal ability and problem-solving ability, the items should include a liberal sampling of items that reflects both of these domains, rather than, say, mostly vocabulary items, but did not require you to reason logically in solving a number of problems.

One of the most important measures of validity is the degree to which it predicts an individual's performance when assessed by other measures, or criteria, of the attribute (Haladyna, 2002). For example, a psychologist might validate an intelligence test by asking the employers of the individuals who took the intelligence test how intelligent they are at work. The employers' perceptions would be another criterion for measuring intelligence. It is not unusual for the validation of an intelligence test to be another intelligence test. When the scores on the two measures overlap substantially, we say the test has high *criterion validity*. Of course, we may use more than one other measure to establish criterion validity. We might give the individuals a second intelligence test, get their employer's perceptions of their intelligence, and observe their behavior in real-life problem-solving situations ourselves.

Reliability and Validity

Reliability   A test that is stable and consistent should not fluctuate significantly because of chance factors, such as how much sleep you get the night before the test, who the examiner is, the temperature in the room where you take the test, and so on. **Reliability** is the extent to which a test yields a consistent, reproducible measure of performance. Ideally, a test should yield the same measure of performance when an individual is given the test on two different occasions. Thus, if we gave an intelligence test to a group of children today and then gave them the same test in six months, the test would be considered reliable if those who scored high on the test today generally score high on the test in six months. However, individuals sometimes do better the second time they take the test because they are familiar with it (McMillan, 2001).

Alternate forms reliability involves giving alternate forms of the same test on two different occasions. The test items on the two forms of the test are similar but not identical. This strategy eliminates the chance of individuals performing better due to familiarity with the items, but it does not eliminate an individual's familiarity with the procedures and strategies involved in the testing. It is also difficult to create two truly parallel alternate forms of the test in which the items are similar but not identical.

In considering reliability and validity, a test that is <u>valid</u> <u>is</u> <u>reliable,</u> but a test that is <u>reliable</u> <u>is</u> <u>not</u> necessarily <u>valid</u>. People can respond consistently on a test but the test might not be measuring what it purports to measure (Carey, 2001).

Standardization   Good tests are not only reliable and valid, but they are standardized as well. **Standardization** involves developing uniform procedures for administering and scoring a test, as well as creating *norms* or performance standards for the test. Uniform testing procedures require that the testing environment be as similar as possible for all individuals. Without standardization, it is difficult to compare scores across individuals. If individuals take the SAT in a room where loud music is playing, they are at a disadvantage compared to others who take the test in a quiet room. The test directions and the amount of time allowed to complete the test should be the same, for example.

Norms are created by giving the test to a large group of individuals representative of the population for whom the test is intended. This allows the test constructor

validity The extent to which a test measures what it is intended to measure.

reliability The extent to which a test yields a consistent, reproducible measure of performance.

standardization Involves developing uniform procedures for administering and scoring a test, as well as creating norms for the test.

to determine the distribution of test scores. Norms inform us which scores are considered high, low, or average. For example, suppose you receive a score of 120 on an intelligence test; that number alone has little meaning. The score takes on meaning when we compare it with the other scores. If only 20 percent of the standardized group scored above 120, then we can interpret your score as high rather than low or average. Many tests of intelligence are designed for individuals from diverse groups. So that the tests are applicable to such different groups, many of them have norms for individuals of different ages, socioeconomic statuses, and ethnic groups (Popham, 2002). Figure 9.3 summarizes the three criteria for test construction and evaluation.

Cultural Bias in Testing

Many of the early intelligence tests were culturally biased, favoring people who were from urban rather than rural environments, middle-socioeconomic status rather than low-socioeconomic status, and White rather than African American (Miller-Jones, 1989; Provenzo, 2002; Watras, 2002). For example, one question on an early test asked what you should do if you find a 3-year-old child in the street. The correct answer was "call the police." But children from inner-city families who perceive the police as adversaries are unlikely to choose this answer. Similarly, children from rural areas might not choose this answer if there is no police force nearby. Such questions clearly do not measure the knowledge necessary to adapt to one's environment or to be "intelligent" in an inner-city neighborhood or in rural America (Scarr, 1984). Also, members of minority groups often do not speak English or may speak nonstandard English. Consequently, they may be at a disadvantage in trying to understand verbal questions that are framed in standard English, even if the content of the test is appropriate (Gibbs & Huang, 1989).

A specific case illustrating how cultural bias in intelligence tests can affect people is that of Gregory Ochoa. When Gregory was a high school student, he and his classmates took an IQ test. When Gregory looked at the test questions, he understood only a few words because he did not speak English very well and spoke Spanish at home. Several weeks later, Gregory was placed in a special class for mentally retarded students. Many of the students in the class, it turns out, had last names such as Ramirez and Gonzales. Gregory lost interest in school, dropped out, and eventually joined the Navy. In the Navy, Gregory took high school courses and earned enough credits to attend college later. He later graduated from San Jose City College as an honor student, continued his education, and became a professor of social work at the University of Washington in Seattle.

As a result of such cases as Gregory Ochoa's, researchers have tried to develop tests that accurately reflect a person's intelligence. **Culture-fair tests** are intelligence tests that are intended not to be culturally biased. Two types of culture-fair tests have been developed. The first includes questions that are familiar to people from all socioeconomic and ethnic backgrounds. For example, a child might be asked how a bird and a dog are different, on the assumption that virtually all children are familiar with birds and dogs. The second type of culture-fair test contains no verbal questions. Figure 9.4 shows a sample question from the Raven Progressive Matrices Test. Even though tests such as the Raven Progressive Matrices are designed to be culture-fair, people with more education still score higher than those with less education do.

One test that takes into account the socioeconomic background of children is the SOMPA, which stands for System of Multicultural Pluralistic Assessment (Mercer & Lewis, 1978). This test can be given to children from 5 to 11 years of age, and was especially designed for children from low-income families. Instead of relying on a single test, SOMPA is based on information from four different areas of a child's life: (1) verbal and nonverbal intelligence, assessed by the

Validity

Does the test measure what it purports to measure?

Reliability

Is test performance consistent?

Standardization

Are uniform procedures for administering and scoring the test used?

FIGURE 9.3 Test Construction and Evaluation

Cultural Bias and Testing

culture-fair tests Intelligence tests that are intended not to be culturally biased.

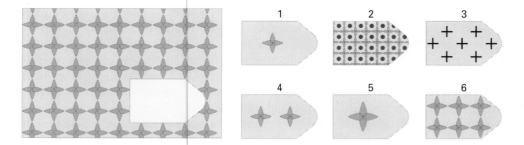

WISC-III; (2) social and economic background, obtained through a one-hour parent interview; (3) social adjustment to school, determined through a questionnaire that parents complete; and (4) physical health, assessed by a medical examination.

Why is it so hard to create culture-fair tests? Most tests tend to reflect what the dominant culture thinks is important (Sax, 1997). If tests have time limits, that will bias the test against groups not concerned with time. If languages differ, the same words might have different meanings for different language groups. Even pictures can produce bias because some cultures have less experience with drawings and photographs (Anastasi & Urbina, 1996). Within the same culture, different groups could have different attitudes, values, and motivation, and this could affect their performance on intelligence tests. Items that ask why buildings should be made of brick are biased against children who have little or no experience with brick houses. Questions about railroads, furnaces, seasons of the year, distances between cities, and so on can be biased against groups who have less experience than others with these contexts.

The Use and Misuse of Intelligence Tests

Psychological tests are tools. Like all tools, their effectiveness depends on the knowledge, skill, and integrity of the user. A hammer can be used to build a beautiful kitchen cabinet or it can be used as a weapon of assault. Like a hammer, psychological tests can be used for positive purposes or they can be abused. It is important for both the test constructor and the test examiner to be familiar with the current state of scientific knowledge about intelligence and intelligence tests. Even though they have limitations, tests of intelligence are among psychology's most widely used tools. To be effective, they should be used in conjunction with other information about an individual, not relied on as the sole indicator of intelligence. For example, an intelligence test alone should not determine whether a child is placed in a special education or gifted class. The child's developmental history, medical background, performance in school, social competencies, and family experiences should be taken into account too.

The single number provided by many IQ tests can easily lead to stereotypes and expectations about an individual (Rosnow & Rosenthal, 1996). Many people do not know how to interpret the results of intelligence tests, and sweeping generalizations are too often made on the basis of an IQ score. For example, imagine that you are a teacher in the teacher's lounge the day after school has started in the fall. You mention a student—Johnny Jones—and a fellow teacher remarks that she had Johnny in class last year; she comments that he was a real dunce and points out that his IQ is 78. You cannot help but remember this information, and it might lead to thoughts that Johnny Jones is not very bright so it is useless to spend much time teaching him. In this way, IQ scores are misused and stereotypes are formed (Rosenthal & Jacobsen, 1968).

Ability tests can help a teacher group together children who function at roughly the same level in math or reading so they can be taught the same concepts together. However, extreme caution is necessary when test scores are used to place children in tracks, such as "advanced," "intermediate," and "low." Periodic assessment of the groups, especially the "low" group, is required. Ability tests measure *current* perfor-

"How are her scores?"

mance, and maturational changes or enriched environmental experiences may advance a child's intelligence, indicating that she should be moved to a higher-level group.

Despite their limitations, when used judiciously by a competent examiner, intelligence tests provide valuable information about individuals. There are not many alternatives to these tests. Subjective judgments about individuals simply reintroduce the bias the tests were designed to eliminate.

Review and Reflect: Learning Goal 2

2 Explain how intelligence is measured and the limitations of intelligence tests

REVIEW

- How can these aspects of intelligence testing be distinguished: early approaches, the Stanford-Binet tests, the Wechsler scales, and group tests?
- What are the criteria for a good test of intelligence?
- How can intelligence testing be culturally biased?
- What are some uses and misuses of intelligence tests?

REFLECT

- A CD-ROM is being sold to parents for testing their child's IQ and how the child is performing in relation to his or her grade in school. The company that makes the CD-ROM says that it helps to get parents involved in their child's education. What might be some problems with parents giving their children an IQ test and interpreting the results?

3 THEORIES OF MULTIPLE INTELLIGENCE

Factor Analysis, Two-Factor Theory, and Multiple-Factor Theory

Sternberg's Triarchic Theory

Evaluating the Multiple-Intelligences Approach

Gardner's Theory of Eight Intelligences

Emotional Intelligence

Do Children Have a General Intelligence?

The concept of mental age and IQ is based on the idea that intelligence is a general ability. So although the early Binet tests assessed some different cognitive skills (such as memory and comprehension), performance measures of these skills were combined to describe an individual's general intellectual ability. The Wechsler scales provide scores on a number of different intellectual skills, as well as an indication of a person's general intelligence.

Wechsler was not the first psychologist to break down intelligence into a number of abilities. Nor was he the last. A number of contemporary psychologists continue to search for specific components that make up intelligence. Unlike Wechsler and other intelligence theorists, however, they do not rely on traditional intelligence tests in their conceptualization of intelligence. Let's explore several key alternative conceptions of intelligence, beginning with Wechsler's predecessor, Charles Spearman.

Factor Analysis, Two-Factor Theory, and Multiple-Factor Theory

Some time before Wechsler analyzed intelligence in terms of general and specific abilities, Charles Spearman (1927) proposed that intelligence has two factors. **Two-factor theory** is Spearman's theory that individuals have both general intelligence,

two-factor theory Spearman's theory that individuals have both general intelligence (g) and a number of specific abilities (s).

which he called *g*, and a number of specific abilities, or *s*. Spearman believed that these two factors accounted for a person's performance on an intelligence test.

Spearman developed his theory by applying a technique called **factor analysis** to a number of intelligence tests. Factor analysis is a statistical procedure that correlates test scores to identify clusters, or factors, that measure a specific ability, such as verbal or mathematical reasoning.

L. L. Thurstone (1938) also used factor analysis in analyzing a number of intelligence tests, but he concluded that the tests measure only a number of specific factors, and not general intelligence. **Multiple-factor theory** is Thurstone's theory that intelligence consists of seven primary mental abilities: verbal comprehension, number ability, word fluency, spatial visualization, associative memory, reasoning, and perceptual speed.

Gardner's Theory of Eight Intelligences

Imagine someone who has great musical skills but does not do well in math or English. Just such a person was the famous musical composer, Ludwig van Beethoven. Would you call Beethoven "unintelligent"? Unlikely! Recently, Howard Gardner has considerably expanded the components of intelligence to include even musical skills.

From Verbal Intelligence to Naturalist Intelligence Gardner (1983, 1993, 2001, 2002) believes there are eight types of intelligence. They are described here along with examples of the occupations in which they are reflected as strengths (Campbell, Campbell, & Dickinson, 1999):

- *Verbal Skills* The ability to think in words and use language to express meaning. Occupations: authors, journalists, speakers.
- *Mathematical Skills* The ability to carry out mathematical operations. Occupations: scientists, engineers, accountants.
- *Spatial Skills* The ability to think three-dimensionally. Occupations: architects, artists, sailors.
- *Bodily-Kinesthetic Skills* The ability to manipulate objects and be physically adept. Occupations: surgeons, craftspeople, dancers, athletes.
- *Musical Skills* A sensitivity to pitch, melody, rhythm, and tone. Occupations: composers, musicians, and sensitive listeners.
- *Interpersonal Skills* The ability to understand and effectively interact with others. Occupations: successful teachers, mental health professionals.
- *Intrapersonal Skills* The ability to understand oneself. Occupations: theologians, psychologists.
- *Naturalist Skills* The ability to observe patterns in nature and understand natural and human-made systems. Occupations: farmers, botanists, ecologists, landscapers.

Gardner believes that each of the eight intelligences can be destroyed by brain damage, that each involves unique cognitive skills, and that each shows up in exaggerated fashion in both the gifted and individuals who have mental retardation or autism (a psychological disorder marked by deficits in social interaction and interests). Dustin Hoffman portrayed an individual with autism who had a remarkable computing ability in the movie *Rain Man*. In one scene, Hoffman's character helped his brother successfully gamble in Las Vegas by keeping track of all the cards that had been played.

Multiple Intelligences in the Classroom Currently there is considerable interest in applying Gardner's theory of multiple intelligences to children's education. We described one educational application of Gardner's theory at the beginning of the

factor analysis A statistical procedure that examines various items or measures and identifies factors that are correlated with each other.

multiple-factor theory Thurstone's theory that intelligence consists of seven primary mental abilities: verbal comprehension, number ability, word fluency, spatial visualization, associative memory, reasoning, and perceptual speed.

Children in the Key School form "pods," in which they pursue activities of special interest to them. Every day, each child can choose from activities that draw on Gardner's eight frames of mind. The school has pods that range from gardening to architecture to gliding to dancing.

chapter—Project Spectrum. Another application is the Key School, a K–6 elementary school in Indianapolis (Goleman, Kaufman, & Ray, 1993). Each day every student is exposed to materials that are designed to stimulate a whole range of human abilities. These include art, music, language skills, math skills, and physical games. In addition, attention is given to understanding oneself and others.

Like other public schools, the Key School is open to any child in Indianapolis, but it is so popular that its students have to be chosen by lottery. The teachers are selected with an eye toward special abilities in certain domains. For example, one teacher is competent at signing for the deaf, a skill in both linguistic and kinesthetic domains.

The Key School's goal is to allow students to discover where they have natural curiosity and talent, then let them explore these domains. Gardner says that if teachers give students the opportunities to use their bodies, imaginations, and different senses, almost every student finds that she or he is good at something. Even students who are not outstanding in a any single area will still find that they have relative strengths.

Every nine weeks, the school emphasizes different themes, such as the Renaissance in sixteenth-century Italy and "Renaissance Now" in Indianapolis. Students develop projects related to the theme. The projects are not graded. Instead, students present them to their classmates, explain them, and answer questions. Collaboration and teamwork are emphasized in the theme projects and in all areas of learning.

Multiple Intelligences
Multiple Intelligence Links
Sternberg's Theory

Sternberg's Triarchic Theory

In his **triarchic theory,** Robert J. Sternberg (1986, 1999, 2003a, 2003b) proposes that there are three main types of intelligence: analytical, creative, and practical. Recall from earlier in the chapter that Sternberg had some very stressful experiences when he had to take traditional intelligence tests as a child. As an adult, he concluded that those intelligence tests did not adequately assess several important dimensions of intelligence.

Analytical, Creative, and Practical Intelligence   Let's explore further what analytical, creative, and practical intelligence mean and look at examples of people who reflect these three types of intelligence.

triarchic theory Sternberg's theory that there are three main types of intelligence: analytical, creative, and practical.

"You're wise, but you lack tree smarts."

Analytical Intelligence   Consider Latisha, who scores high on traditional intelligence tests such as the Stanford-Binet and is a star analytical thinker. Sternberg calls Latisha's analytical thinking and abstract reasoning *analytical intelligence*. It is the closest to what has traditionally been called intelligence and what is commonly assessed by intelligence tests.

In Sternberg's view of analytical intelligence, the basic unit in intelligence is a component, simply defined as a basic unit of information processing. Sternberg believes such components include the ability to acquire or store information; to retain or retrieve information; to transfer information; to plan, make decisions, and solve problems; and to translate our thoughts into performance.

Creative Intelligence   Todd does not have the best test scores but has an insightful and creative mind. The type of thinking at which Todd excels is called *creative intelligence* by Sternberg. According to Sternberg, creative people like Todd have the ability to solve new problems quickly, but they also learn how to solve familiar problems in an automatic, rote way so their minds are free to handle other problems that require insight and creativity.

Practical Intelligence   Consider Emanuel, a street-smart person who learned to deal in practical ways with his world, although his scores on traditional IQ tests are low. Emanuel's street smarts and practical know-how indicate that he has what Sternberg calls *practical intelligence*. Practical intelligence includes the ability to get out of trouble, an aptitude for replacing a fuse, and a knack for getting along with people. Sternberg describes practical intelligence as all of the important information about getting along in the world that you are not taught in school. He believes practical intelligence is sometimes more important than analytical intelligence, the book knowledge that is taught in school.

Triarchic Intelligence in the Classroom   Sternberg (1997) says that students with different triarchic patterns look different in school. Students with high analytic ability tend to be favored in conventional schools. They often do well in direct instruction classes in which the teacher lectures and gives objective tests. They often are considered smart students, typically get good grades, do well on traditional IQ tests and the SAT, and later gain admission to competitive colleges. Students who are high in creative intelligence often are not in the top rung of their class. Sternberg says that many teachers have expectations about how assignments should be done and creatively intelligent students might not conform to those expectations. Instead of giving conformist answers, they give unique answers, for which they might get reprimanded or marked down. Like students high in creative intelligence, students who are practically intelligent often do not relate well to the demands of school. However, these students frequently do well outside of the classroom's walls. They may have excellent social skills and good common sense. As adults, they sometimes become successful managers, entrepreneurs, or politicians, despite undistinguished school records.

Sternberg (1999) believes that few tasks are purely analytic, creative, or practical. Most tasks require some combination of these skills. For example, when students write a book report, they might (1) analyze the book's main themes, (2) generate new ideas about how the book could have been written better, and (3) think about how the book's themes can be applied to people's lives. Sternberg argues that it is important to balance classroom instruction with respect to all three types of intelligence. That is, students should be given opportunities to learn through analytical, creative, and practical thinking, in addition to the conventional strategy of memorization.

Emotional Intelligence

Both Gardner's and Sternberg's theories include one or more categories of social intelligence. In Gardner's theory, the categories are interpersonal intelligence and intrapersonal intelligence. In Sternberg's theory, the category is practical intelligence. Another theory that captures the importance of the interpersonal, intrapersonal, and practical aspects of intelligence has generated a great deal of interest recently. It is called **emotional intelligence,** defined by Peter Salovey and John Mayer (1990) as the ability to monitor one's own and others' feelings and emotions, to discriminate among them, and to use this information to guide one's thinking and action.

The concept of emotional intelligence has been popularized by Daniel Goleman (1995). Goleman believes that when it comes to predicting a person's competence, IQ as measured by traditional intelligence tests matters less than emotional intelligence. In Goleman's view, emotional intelligence involves these four areas:

- *Developing emotional awareness* (such as the ability to separate feelings from actions)
- *Managing emotions* (such as being able to control anger)
- *Reading emotions* (such as taking the perspective of others)
- *Handling relationships* (such as the ability to solve relationship problems)

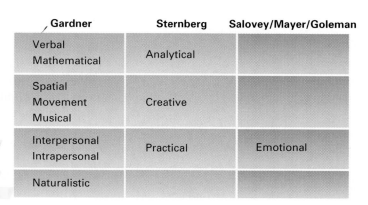

Gardner	Sternberg	Salovey/Mayer/Goleman
Verbal Mathematical	Analytical	
Spatial Movement Musical	Creative	
Interpersonal Intrapersonal	Practical	Emotional
Naturalistic		

FIGURE 9.5 Comparison of Gardner's, Sternberg's, and Salovey/Mayer/Goleman's Views of Intelligence

Evaluating the Multiple-Intelligences Approach

The multiple-intelligence theories have much to offer. They have stimulated us to think more broadly about what makes up people's intelligence and competence. And they have motivated educators to develop programs that instruct students in different domains.

Figure 9.5 provides a comparison of Gardner's, Sternberg's, and Salovey/Mayer/Goleman's views. Notice that Gardner includes a number of types of intelligence that are not addressed by the other views, and that Sternberg is unique in emphasizing creative intelligence.

Some critics say that Gardner's classification of such domains as musical skills as a type of intelligence is off-base. They ask whether there might not be other skill domains that Gardner has left out. For example, there are outstanding chess players, prizefighters, writers, politicians, lawyers, ministers, and poets. Yet we don't refer to chess intelligence, prizefighter intelligence, and so on. Other critics say that the research base to support the eight intelligences of Gardner, the three intelligences of Sternberg, and the emotional intelligence of Salovey/Mayer/Goleman as the best way to characterize intelligence has not yet been developed.

Gardner (1998)—the ultimate multiple-intelligences advocate—has himself even criticized the emotional intelligence advocates as going too far in including emotions in the concept of intelligence. He also believes that creativity should not be included in the concept of intelligence. Although he believes that understanding emotions and being creative are important aspects of human competence and functioning, Gardner says he just thinks that emotional understanding and creativity are different from intelligence.

There also are a number of psychologists who still support Spearman's concept of g (general intelligence), and many of them believe that the multiple-intelligences views have taken the concept of s (specific intelligences) too far. For example, one expert on intelligence, Nathan Brody (2000), argues that people who excel at one type of intellectual task are likely to excel in other intellectual tasks. Thus, individuals who do well at memorizing lists of digits are also likely to be good at solving verbal problems and spatial layout problems.

emotional intelligence The ability to monitor one's own and others' emotions and feelings, to discriminate among them, and to use this information to guide one's thinking and action.

Do Children Have a General Intelligence?

Recall the mention of a general intelligence factor called *g* from the start of our discussion of general intelligences. With all of the interest in multiple intelligences, it might seem that it is unwise to think about children having a general intelligence. However, a number of experts argue that not only do individuals have a general intelligence but that it has real-world applications as a predictor of school and job success (Brody, 2000). For example, scores on what are claimed to be tests of general intelligence are substantially correlated with academic achievement and moderately correlated with work performance (Lubinski, 2000). Individuals with higher scores on tests designed to measure general intelligence tend to get higher-paying, more prestigious jobs (Wagner, 1997).

However, general IQ tests predict only about one-fourth of the variation in job success with the majority of job success due to other factors such as motivation, education, and other factors (Wagner & Sternberg, 1986). Further, the correlations between IQ and achievement decrease the longer people work at a job, presumably because as they gain more job experience they perform better (Hunt, 1995).

Experts on general intelligence agree that it includes abstract reasoning or thinking, the capacity to acquire knowledge, and problem-solving ability (Brody, 2000; Carroll, 1993). And, as we noted earlier, some experts who argue for the importance of general intelligence believe that individuals also have specific intellectual abilities (Brody, 2000). In one study, John Carroll (1993) conducted an extensive examination of intellectual abilities and concluded that while all intellectual abilities are related to each other, which supports the concept of general intelligence, there are many specialized abilities as well. Some of these specialized abilities, such as spatial abilities and mechanical abilities, are not adequately reflected in the curriculum of most schools.

Review and Reflect: Learning Goal 3

3 Evaluate theories of multiple intelligence

REVIEW

- What role did factor analysis play in the development of two-factor theory and multiple-factor theory?
- What is Gardner's theory of eight intelligences?
- How would you describe Sternberg's triarchic theory?
- What is emotional intelligence?
- Evaluate the multiple-intelligences approach.
- Discuss whether children have a general intelligence.

REFLECT

- Apply Gardner's and Sternberg's multiple intelligences to yourself (or someone else you know well). Write a narrative description of yourself based on each of these theorists' views.

---

4 INTELLIGENCE IN INFANCY AND DEVELOPMENTAL TRANSFORMATIONS

| Infant Intelligence Tests | Stability and Change in Intelligence | Information-Processing Tasks as Predictors of Intelligence |

In chapter 7, "Cognitive Developmental Approaches," we saw that Piaget characterized infants as being at the sensorimotor stage of development. Let's now explore the kinds of questions that have been posed on tests of infant intelligence and the extent to which intelligence changes or remains stable throughout the childhood years.

Infant Intelligence Tests

In chapter 4, we discussed the Brazelton Neonatal Behavioral Assessment Scale, which is widely used to evaluate newborns. ◀ **page 118** Developmentalists want to know how development proceeds during the course of infancy as well. If an infant advances at an especially slow rate, then enrichment may be necessary. If an infant develops at an advanced pace, parents may be advised to provide toys that on average would stimulate cognitive growth in slightly older infants.

The infant-testing movement grew out of the tradition of IQ testing with older children. However, the measures that assess infants are necessarily less verbal than IQ tests that assess the intelligence of older children. The infant developmental scales contain far more items related to perceptual motor development. They also include measures of social interaction.

The most important early contributor to the developmental testing of infants was Arnold Gesell (1934). He developed a measure that served as a clinical tool to help sort out potentially normal babies from abnormal ones. This was especially useful to adoption agencies, which had large numbers of babies awaiting placement. Gesell's examination was used widely for many years and still is frequently employed by pediatricians in their assessment of normal and abnormal infants. The current version of the Gesell test has four categories of behavior: motor, language, adaptive, and personal-social. The **developmental quotient (DQ)** is an overall developmental score that combines subscores in the motor, language, adaptive, and personal-social domains in the Gesell assessment of infants. Overall scores on such tests as the Gesell do not correlate highly with IQ scores obtained later in childhood. This is not surprising, since the nature of the items on the developmental scales is considerably less verbal than the items on intelligence tests given to older children.

The **Bayley Scales of Infant Development** are widely used in assessing infant development. They have three components: a Mental Scale, a Motor Scale, and a Behavior Rating Scale. Initially created by Nancy Bayley (1969), the second edition of the Bayley scales was recently developed.

The Behavior Rating Scale, which assesses the infant's behavior during testing, was formerly called the Infant Behavior Record. Among the uses of the scales are the diagnosis of developmental delays and the planning of intervention strategies. The Bayley scales can be used to assess infants from 1 to 42 months of age.

According to the Bayley scales, at approximately 6 months of age an average baby should be able to do these:

- Accept a second cube—the baby holds one cube, while the examiner places a second cube within easy reach of the infant
- Grasp the edge of a piece of paper when it is presented
- Vocalize pleasure and displeasure
- Persistently reach for objects placed just out of immediate reach
- Turn her or his head toward a spoon the experimenter suddenly drops on the floor
- Approach a mirror when the examiner places it in front of the infant

At approximately 12 months of age, an average baby should be able to do these:

- Inhibit behavior when commanded to do so—for example, when the infant puts a block in his or her mouth and the examiner says, "No, no," the infant should cease the activity
- Repeat an action if she or he is laughed at
- Imitate words the experimenter says, such as *mama* and *dada*
- Imitate the experimenter's actions—for example, if the experimenter rattles a spoon in a cup, the infant should imitate this action
- Respond to simple requests, such as "Take a drink"

The Fagan Test of Infant Intelligence is increasingly being used (Fagan, 1992). This test focuses on the infant's ability to process information, including encoding the attributes of objects, detecting similarities and differences between objects,

**Bayley Scales of
Infant Development (2nd ed.)**

developmental quotient (DQ) An overall developmental score that combines subscores in the motor, language, adaptive, and personal-social domains in the Gesell assessment of infants.

Bayley Scales of Infant Development
Widely used scales in assessing infant development with three main components: a Mental Scale, a Motor Scale, and a Behavior Rating Scale.

Careers in Child Development

Toosje Thyssen Van Beveren, *Infant Assessment Specialist*

Toosje Thyssen Van Beveren is a developmental psychologist at the University of Texas Medical Center in Dallas. She has a master's degree in child clinical psychology and a Ph.D. in human development.

Her main current work is in a program called New Connections. This 12-week program is a comprehensive intervention for young children (0 to 6 years of age) who were affected by substance abuse prenatally and for their caregivers.

In the New Connections program, Toosje conducts assessments of infants' developmental status and progress, identifying delays and deficits. She might refer the infants to a speech, physical, or occupational therapist and monitor the infants' therapeutic services and developmental progress. Toosje trains the program staff and encourages them to use the exercises she recommends. She also discusses the child's problems with the primary caregivers, suggests activities they can carry out with their children, and assists them in enrolling their infants in appropriate programs.

During her graduate work at the University of Texas at Dallas, Toosje was author John Santrock's teaching assistant for four years in his undergraduate course on development. As a teaching assistant, she attended classes, graded exams, counseled students, and occasionally gave lectures. Each semester, Toosje returns to give a lecture on prenatal development and infancy. Toosje also teaches part-time in the psychology department at UT-Dallas. She teaches an undergraduate course, "The Child in Society," and a graduate course, "Infant Development."

In Toosje's words, "My days are busy and full. The work is often challenging. There are some disappointments but mostly the work is enormously gratifying."

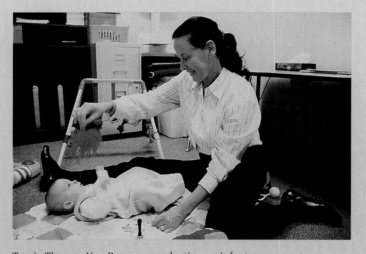

Toosje Thyssen Van Beveren conducting an infant assessment.

forming mental representations, and retrieving these representations.

The Fagan Test of Infant Intelligence estimates babies' intelligence by comparing the amount of time they look at a new object with the amount of time they spend looking at a familiar object. This test elicits similar performances from infants in different cultures and is correlated with measures of intelligence in older children.

Some developmental psychologists specialize in infant assessment. To read about the work of infant assessment specialist Toosje Thyssen Van Beveren, see the Careers in Child Development insert.

Stability and Change in Intelligence

In one study conducted by Nancy Bayley, no relation was found between the Bayley scales and intelligence as measured by the Stanford-Binet at the ages of 6 and 7 (Bayley, 1943). Another investigation found correlations of only .01 between intelligence measured at 3 months and at 5 years of age and .05 between measurements at 1 year and at 5 years (Anderson, 1939). These findings indicate virtually no relation between infant development scales and intelligence at 5 years of age. Again, it should be remembered that one of the reasons for this finding is that the components of intelligence tested in infancy are not the same as the components of intelligence tested at the age of 5.

There is a strong relation between IQ scores obtained at the ages of 6, 8, and 9 and IQ scores obtained at the age of 10. For example, in one study, the correlation between IQ at the age of 8 and IQ at the age of 10 was .88. The correlation between IQ at the age of 9 and IQ at the age of 10 was .90. These figures show a very high relation between IQ scores obtained in these years. The correlation of IQ in the preadolescent years and IQ at the age of 18 is slightly less but still statistically significant. For example, the correlation between IQ at the age of 10 and IQ at the age of 18 was .70 in one study (Honzik, MacFarlane, & Allen, 1948).

What has been said so far about the stability of intelligence has been based on measures of groups of individuals. The stability of intelligence also can be evaluated through studies of individuals. As we will see next, there can be considerable variability in an individual's scores on IQ tests.

Let's look at an example of the absence of a relation between intelligence in infancy and intelligence in later years for two children in the same family. The first child learned to speak at a very early age. She displayed the characteristics of an extravert, and her advanced motor coordination was indicated by her ability to walk at a very early age. The second child learned speech very late, saying very few words until she was $2^{1}/_{2}$ years old. Both children were given standardized tests of intelligence during infancy and then later, during the elementary school years. In the earlier test, the first child's scores were higher than her sister's. In the later test, their scores were reversed. What are some of the possible reasons for the reversal in the IQ scores of the two girls? When the second child did begin to speak, she did so prolifically, and the complexity of her language increased rapidly, undoubtedly as a result of her biological readiness to talk. Her sensorimotor coordination had never been as competent as the first child's, perhaps also accounting in part for her lower scores on the infant intelligence tests. The parents recognized that they had initially given the first child extensive amounts of their time. They were not able to give the second child as much of their time, but when the second child was about 3 years old, they made every opportunity to involve her in physical and academic activities. They put her in a Montessori preschool program, gave her dancing and swimming lessons, and frequently invited other children of her age in to play with her. There may have been other reasons as well for the changes in scores, but these demonstrate that infant intelligence tests may not be good predictors of intelligence in later years.

Robert McCall and his associates (McCall, Applebaum, & Hogarty, 1973) studied 140 children between the ages of $2\frac{1}{2}$ and 17. They found that the average range of IQ scores was more than 28 points. The scores of one out of three children changed by as much as 30 points and one out of seven by as much as 40 points. These data suggest that intelligence test scores can fluctuate dramatically across the childhood years and that intelligence is not as stable as the original intelligence theorists envisioned.

Information-Processing Tasks as Predictors of Intelligence

The explosion of interest in infant development has produced many new measures, especially tasks that evaluate the ways infants process information. Evidence is accumulating that measures of habituation and dishabituation predict intelligence in childhood and adolescence (Bornstein & Sigman, 1986; Sigman, Cohen, & Beckwith, 2000). ⬅ **page 245** Quicker decays or less cumulative looking in the habituation situation and greater amounts of looking in the dishabituation situation reflect more-efficient information processing. Both types of attention—decrement and recovery—when measured in the first six months of infancy, are related to higher IQ scores on standardized intelligence tests given at various times between infancy and adolescence. In sum, more-precise assessment of infant cognition with information-processing tasks involving attention has led to the conclusion that continuity between infant and childhood intelligence is greater than was previously believed (Bornstein & Krasnegor, 1989).

What can we conclude about the nature of stability and change in childhood intelligence? Children are adaptive beings. They have the capacity for intellectual changes but they do not become entirely new intelligent beings. In a sense, children's intelligence changes but has connections to earlier points in development—amid intellectual changes is some underlying coherence and continuity.

Review and Reflect: Learning Goal 4

4 **Summarize the testing of intelligence in infancy and developmental transformations**

REVIEW

- What are infant intelligent tests like?
- To what extent does intelligence stay the same or change as children develop?
- Can information-processing tasks in infancy predict intelligence? Explain.

REFLECT

- As a parent, would you want your infant's intelligence tested? Why or why not?

5 THE EXTREMES OF INTELLIGENCE AND CREATIVITY

| Mental Retardation | Giftedness | Creativity |

Mental retardation and intellectual giftedness are the extremes of intelligence. Often intelligence tests are used to identify exceptional individuals. Keeping in mind that an intelligence test should not be used as the sole basis for decisions about intelligence, let's explore the nature of mental retardation and giftedness. Then, we'll explore how creativity differs from intelligence.

Mental Retardation

Mental Retardation

The most distinctive feature of mental retardation is inadequate intellectual functioning. Long before formal tests were developed to assess intelligence, individuals with mental retardation were identified by a lack of age-appropriate skills in learning and caring for themselves. Once intelligence tests were developed, numbers were assigned to indicate degrees of mental retardation. It is not unusual to find that, of two individuals with mental retardation with the same low IQ, one is married, employed, and involved in the community and the other requires constant supervision in an institution. Such differences in social competence led psychologists to include deficits in adaptive behavior in their definition of mental retardation.

Mental retardation is a condition of limited mental ability in which the individual has a low IQ, usually below 70 on a traditional intelligence test, has difficulty adapting to everyday life, and first exhibits these characteristics during the so-called developmental period—by age 18. The reason for including developmental period in the definition of mental retardation is that we don't usually think of a college student who suffers massive brain damage in a car accident, resulting in an IQ of 60 as "mentally retarded." The low IQ and low adaptiveness should be evident in childhood, not following a long period of normal functioning that is interrupted by an insult of some form. About 5 million Americans fit this definition of mental retardation.

There are several classifications of mental retardation (Hallahan & Kaufmann, 2003). As indicated in figure 9.6, mental retardation may be mild, moderate, severe, or profound. Note that a large majority of individuals diagnosed with mental retardation fits into the mild category. Most school systems still use the classifications shown in figure 9.6. However, because these categories are based on IQ ranges, they are not perfect predictors of functioning. The American Association of Mental Retardation (1992) developed a different classification based on the degree of support required for a person with mental retardation to function at the highest level. As shown in figure 9.7, these categories of support are: intermittent, limited, extensive, and pervasive.

mental retardation A condition of limited mental ability in which the individual has a low IQ, usually below 70, has difficulty adapting to everyday life, and has an onset of these characteristics in the so-called developmental period.

Mental retardation may have an organic cause, or it may be social and cultural in origin (Das, 2000). *Organic retardation* is mental retardation caused by a genetic disorder or by brain damage; "organic" refers to the tissues or organs of the body, so there is some physical damage in organic retardation. Down syndrome, one form of organic mental retardation, occurs when an extra chromosome is present in the individual's genetic makeup. ◀ **page 78** It is not known why the extra chromosome is present, but it may involve the health or age of the female ovum or male sperm. Most people who suffer from organic retardation have IQs between 0 and 50.

Cultural-familial retardation is a mental deficit in which no evidence of organic brain damage can be found. Individuals with this type of retardation have IQs between 55 and 70. Psychologists suspect that such mental deficits result from the distribution of people along the range

Type of Mental Retardation	IQ Range	Percentage
Mild	55–70	89
Moderate	40–54	6
Severe	25–39	4
Profound	Below 25	1

FIGURE 9.6 Classification of Mental Retardation Based on IQ

Intermittent	Supports are provided "as needed." The individual may need episodic or short-term support during life-span transitions (such as job loss or acute medical crisis). Intermittent supports may be low or high intensity when provided.
Limited	Supports are intense and relatively consistent over time. They are time-limited but not intermittent. Require fewer staff members and cost less than more intense supports. These supports likely will be needed for adaptation to the changes involved in the school-to-adult period.
Extensive	Supports are characterized by regular involvement (e.g., daily) in at least some setting (such as home or work) and are not time-limited (for example, extended home-living support).
Pervasive	Supports are constant, very intense, and are provided across settings. They may be of a life-sustaining nature. These supports typically involve more staff members and intrusiveness than the other support categories.

FIGURE 9.7 Classification of Mental Retardation Based on Levels of Support Needed

of intelligence scores above 55, combined with growing up in a below-average intellectual environment. As children, those who are familially retarded can be identified in schools, where they often fail, need tangible rewards (candy rather than praise), and are highly sensitive to what others—both peers and adults—expect of them. However, as adults, the familially retarded are usually invisible, perhaps because adult settings don't tax their cognitive skills as sorely. It may also be that the familially retarded increase their intelligence as they move toward adulthood.

Giftedness

There have always been children whose abilities and accomplishments outshine others'—the whiz kid in class, the star athlete, the natural musician. Children who are **gifted** have high intelligence (an IQ of 130 or higher) and/or superior talent for something. When it comes to programs for the gifted, most school systems select children who have intellectual superiority and academic aptitude. Children who are talented in the visual and performing arts (arts, drama, dance) or in athletics, or who have other special aptitudes tend to be overlooked.

Until recently, giftedness and emotional distress were thought to go hand in hand. English novelist Virginia Woolf suffered from severe depression, for example, and eventually committed suicide. And Sir Isaac Newton, Vincent van Gogh, Ann Sexton, Socrates, and Sylvia Plath all had emotional problems. However, these individuals are the exception rather than the rule; in general, no relation between giftedness and mental disorder has been found. Recent studies support the conclusion that gifted children tend to be more mature and have fewer emotional problems than others, and to grow up in a positive family climate (Feldhusen, 1999; Feldman, 1997).

Lewis Terman (1925) conducted an extensive study of 1,500 children whose Stanford-Binet IQs averaged 150. A popular myth is that gifted children are maladjusted, but Terman found in his study that they were not only academically gifted but also socially well adjusted. Many of these gifted children went on to become successful doctors, lawyers, professors, and scientists.

Ellen Winner (1996) described three criteria that characterize gifted children, whether in art, music, or academic domains:

1. *Precocity.* Gifted children are precocious. They begin to master an area earlier than their peers. Learning in their domain is more effortless for them than for

This young boy has Down syndrome. *What causes a child to develop Down syndrome? In what major classification of mental retardation does the condition fall?*

gifted Describes individuals who have a high IQ (130 or higher) and/or superior talent for something.

ordinary children. In most instances, these gifted children are precocious because they have an inborn high ability in a particular domain or domains.

2. *Marching to their own drummer.* Gifted children learn in a qualitatively different way than ordinary children. For one thing, they need minimal help, or scaffolding, from adults to learn. In many cases, they resist any kind of explicit instruction. They also often make discoveries on their own and solve problems in unique ways.

3. *A passion to master.* Gifted children are driven to understand the domain in which they have high ability. They display an intense, obsessive interest and an ability to focus. They are not children who need to be pushed by their parents. They motivate themselves, says Winner.

As a 10-year-old, Alexandra Nechita was described as a child prodigy. She paints quickly and impulsively on large canvases, some as large as 5 feet by 9 feet. It is not unusual for her to complete several of these large paintings in a week's time. Her paintings—in the modernist tradition—sell for up to $80,000 apiece. When she was only 2 years of age, Alexandra colored in coloring books for hours. She had no interest in dolls or friends. Once she started school, she would start painting as soon as she got home. And she continues to paint—relentlessly and passionately. It is, she says, what she loves to do.

Is giftedness, like Alexandria Nechita's artistic talent, a product of heredity or environment? Likely both (Winner, 2000). Experts who study giftedness point out that gifted individuals recall that they had signs of high ability in a particular area at a very young age, prior to or at the beginning of formal training (Howe & others, 1995). This suggests the importance of innate ability in giftedness. However, researchers also have found that the individuals who enjoy world-class status in the arts, mathematics, science, and sports all report strong family support and years of training and practice (Bloom, 1985). Recall our distinction between experts and novices in chapter 8, where we saw that deliberate practice is an important characteristic of individuals who become experts in a particular domain. For example, in one study, the best musicians engaged in twice as much deliberate practice over their lives as the least successful ones did (Ericsson, Krampe, & Tesch-Romer, 1993).

Do gifted children become gifted and highly creative adults? In Terman's research, children typically became experts in a well-established domain, such as medicine, law, or business. However, although they may have been creative in coming up with innovative ideas in these well-established domains, Ellen Winner (2000) points out that they did not become major creators. That is, they did not create a new domain or revolutionize an old domain.

Thus, while being gifted as a child is linked with also being this way as an adult, only a fraction of gifted children eventually become revolutionary adult creators. Those who do must make a difficult transition from a child prodigy (who learns rapidly and effortlessly in an established domain) to an adult creator (who disrupts and ultimately remakes a domain or creates a new one).

One reason that some gifted children do not become gifted adults or even adult creators is that they have been pushed too hard by overzealous parents and teachers and they lose their intrinsic (internal) motivation (Winner, 1996). As adolescents, they may ask themselves, "Who am I doing this for?" If the answer is not for one's self, they may not want to do it anymore.

A number of individuals work with children who are gifted in various capacities in school systems. To read about the work of gifted children specialist Sterling Jones, see the Careers in Child Development insert.

Creativity

We've used the term *creativity* a number of times in this chapter. What does it mean to be creative? **Creativity** is the ability to think about something in novel and

Children Who Are Gifted
National Association of Gifted Children
Exploring Gifted Education
Miseducation of Children Who Are Gifted

creativity The ability to think about something in novel and unusual ways and come up with unique solutions to problems.

unusual ways and come up with unique solutions to problems.

Creativity and Intelligence   Creativity and intelligence are not the same thing. Sternberg (1999), who included creativity in his triarchic theory of intelligence, says that many highly intelligent people produce large numbers of products but they are not necessarily novel. He also believes that highly creative people defy the crowd, whereas people who are highly intelligent but not creative often try to simply please the crowd.

Creative people tend to be divergent thinkers (Guilford, 1967). **Divergent thinking** produces many answers to the same question. In contrast, the kind of thinking required on conventional intelligence tests is **convergent thinking.** For example, a typical item on a conventional intelligence test is, "How many quarters will you get in return for 60 dimes?" There is only one correct answer to this question. However, the following question has many possible answers: What image comes to mind when you hear the phrase "sitting alone in a dark room"?

Thinking further about intelligence and creativity, most creative people are quite intelligent, but the reverse is not necessarily true. Many highly intelligent people (as measured by high scores on conventional tests of intelligence) are not very creative.

Guiding Children's Creativity   An important goal is to help children become more creative. What are the best strategies for accomplishing this goal? They include:

- *Have children engage in brainstorming and come up with as many ideas as possible.* **Brainstorming** is a technique in which children are encouraged to come up with creative ideas in a group, play off each other's ideas, and say practically whatever comes to mind.

  Children are usually told to hold off from criticizing others' ideas at least until the end of the brainstorming session. Whether in a group or individually, a good creativity strategy is to come up with as many new ideas as possible. Famous twentieth-century Spanish artist Pablo Picasso produced more than 20,000 works of art. Not all of them were masterpieces. The more ideas children produce, the better their chance of creating something unique. Creative children are not afraid of failing or getting something wrong. They may go down twenty dead-end streets before they come up with an innovative idea. They recognize that it's okay to win some and lose some. They are willing to take risks, just as Picasso was.

- *Provide children with environments that stimulate creativity.* Some settings nourish creativity; others depress it (Nakamura & Csikszentmihalyi, 2003). People who encourage children's creativity often rely on their natural curiosity. They provide exercises and activities that stimulate children to find insightful solutions to problems, rather than asking a lot of questions that require rote answers. Adults also encourage creativity by taking children to locations where creativity is valued. Howard Gardner (1993) believes that science,

Careers in Child Development

Sterling Jones, *Supervisor of Gifted and Talented Education*

Sterling Jones is program supervisor for gifted and talented children in the Detroit Public School System. Sterling has been working for more than three decades with children who are gifted. He believes that students' mastery of skills mainly depends on the amount of time devoted to instruction and the length of time allowed for learning. Thus, he believes that many basic strategies for challenging children who are gifted to develop their skills can be applied to a wider range of students than once believed. He has rewritten several pamphlets for use by teachers and parents, including *How to Help Your Child Succeed* and *Gifted and Talented Education for Everyone*.

Sterling has undergraduate and graduate degrees from Wayne State University and taught English for a number of years before becoming involved in the program for gifted children. He also has written materials on African Americans, such as *Voices from the Black Experience*, that are used in the Detroit schools.

Sterling Jones with some of the children in the gifted program in the Detroit Public School System.

divergent thinking Thinking that produces many answers to the same question; characteristic of creativity.

convergent thinking Thinking that produces one correct answer; characteristic of the type of thinking required on traditional intelligence tests.

brainstorming A technique in which children are encouraged to come up with creative ideas in a group, play off each other's ideas, and say practically whatever comes to mind.

"What do you mean 'What is it?' It's the spontaneous, unfettered expression of a young mind not yet bound by the restraints of narrative or pictorial representation."

© Sidney Harris

Teresa Amabile's Research

Harvard Project Zero

Kids' Space

discovery, and children's museums offer rich opportunities to stimulate children's creativity.

- *Don't overcontrol.* Teresa Amabile (1993) says that telling children exactly how to do things leaves them feeling that any originality is a mistake and any exploration is a waste of time. Letting children select their interests and supporting their inclinations are less likely to destroy their natural curiosity than dictating which activities they should engage in. Amabile also believes that, when adults constantly hover over children, the children feel they are being watched while they are working. When children are under constant surveillance, their creative risk taking and adventurous spirit wane. Another strategy that can harm creativity is to have grandiose expectations for a child's performance and expect the child to do something perfectly, according to Amabile.
- *Encourage internal motivation.* The excessive use of prizes, such as gold stars, money, or toys, can stifle creativity by undermining the intrinsic pleasure children derive from creative activities. Creative children's motivation is the satisfaction generated by the work itself. Competition for prizes and formal evaluations often undermine intrinsic motivation and creativity (Amabile & Hennesey, 1992).
- *Foster flexible and playful thinking.* Creative thinkers are flexible and play with problems, which gives rise to a paradox. Although creativity takes effort, the effort goes more smoothly if students take it lightly. In a way, humor can grease the wheels of creativity (Goleman, Kaufman, & Ray, 1993). When children are joking around, they are more likely to consider unusual solutions to problems. Having fun helps disarm the inner censor that can condemn a child's ideas as off-base. As one clown named Wavy Gravy put it, "If you can't laugh about it, it just isn't funny anymore."
- *Introduce children to creative people.* You may not know a clown named Wavy Gravy whom you can ask to stimulate a child's creativity, but it is a good strategy to think about the identity of the most creative people in your community. Teachers can invite these people to their classrooms and ask them to describe what helps them become creative or to demonstrate their creative skills. A writer, poet, musician, scientist, and many others can bring their props and productions to the class, turning it into a theater for stimulating students' creativity. Poet Richard Lewis (1997) visits classrooms in New York City. He brings with him only a large clear glass marble. He lifts it above his head, so that every student can see the spectrum of colors the marble produces. He asks, "Who can see something playing inside?" Then he asks students to write about what they see. One student named Snigdha wrote that she sees the rainbow rising, the sun moving a lot, and the sun sleeping with the stars. She also wrote that she saw the rain dropping on the ground, stems breaking, apples falling from trees, and wind blowing the leaves.

Review and Reflect: Learning Goal 5

5 **Discuss characteristics of mental retardation, giftedness, and creativity**

REVIEW

- What is mental retardation? What causes mental retardation?
- What makes children gifted?
- What characteristics are associated with creativity?

REFLECT

- If you were an elementary school teacher, what would you do to encourage students' creativity?

6 THE INFLUENCE OF HEREDITY AND ENVIRONMENT

Hereditary Influences   **Environmental Influences**   **Group Comparisons**

One of the hottest areas in the study of intelligence centers on the extent to which intelligence is influenced by genetics and the extent to which it is influenced by environment. In chapter 3, we indicated how difficult it is to tease apart these influences, but that has not kept psychologists from trying to unravel them. ◀ **page 86**

Hereditary Influences

Arthur Jensen (1969) sparked a lively and at times hostile debate when he presented his thesis that intelligence is primarily inherited. Jensen believes that environment and culture play only a minimal role in intelligence. Jensen reviewed the research on intelligence, much of which involved comparisons of identical and fraternal twins. Identical twins have exactly the same genetic makeup. If intelligence is genetically determined, Jensen reasoned, identical twins' IQs should be similar. Fraternal twins and ordinary siblings are less similar genetically, so their IQs should be less similar.

The studies on intelligence in identical twins that Jensen reviewed had an average correlation of .82, a very high positive association. Investigations of fraternal twins, however, produced an average correlation of .50, a moderately high positive correlation. The difference of .32 is substantial.

Many scholars have criticized Jensen's work. One criticism concerns his definition of intelligence itself. Jensen believes that IQ as measured by standardized intelligence tests is a good indicator of intelligence. Critics argue that IQ tests tap only a narrow range of intelligence. Everyday problem solving, work, and social adaptability, say the critics, are important aspects of intelligence not measured in the traditional IQ tests used in Jensen's review of studies. A second criticism is that most investigations of heredity and environment do not include environments that differ radically. Thus, it is not surprising that many heredity studies show environment to be a fairly weak influence on intelligence. Further, in a much more recent review than Jensen's, the difference in intelligence between identical and fraternal twins was only .15, substantially less than what Jensen found (Grigorenko, 2000) (see figure 9.8).

How strong is the correlation between parental IQ and children's IQ? The concept of heritability seeks to separate the effects of heredity and environment in a population. **Heritability** refers to the fraction of the variance in IQ in a population that is attributed to genetics. The heritability index is computed using correlational statistical techniques. Thus, the highest degree of heritability is 1.00 and correlations of .70 and above suggest a strong genetic influence. A committee of respected researchers convened by the American Psychological Association concluded that by late adolescence, the heritability of intelligence is about .75, which reflects a strong genetic influence (Neisser & others, 1996).

Interestingly, researchers have found that the heritability of intelligence increases from childhood to adulthood (from as low as 35 percent in childhood to as high as 75 percent in adulthood) (McGue & others, 1993). Why might hereditary influences on intelligence increase with age? Possibly as we grow older, our interactions with the environment are shaped less by the influence of others and the environment on us and more by our ability to choose our environments to allow the expression of genetic tendencies we have inherited (Neisser & others, 1996). For example, sometimes parents push children into environments that are not compatible with their genetic inheritance (wanting to be a doctor or an engineer, for

heritability The fraction of the variance in IQ in a population that is attributed to genetics.

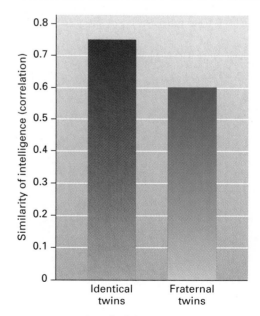

FIGURE 9.8 Correlation Between Intelligence Test Scores and Twin Status

The graph represents a summary of research findings that have compared the intelligence test scores of identical and fraternal twins. An approximate .15 difference has been found, with a higher correlation (.75) for identical twins and a lower correlation (.60) for fraternal twins.

Explorations in Child Development

The Abecedarian Intervention Program

Each morning a young mother waited with her child for the bus that would take the child to school. The unusual part of this is that the child was only 2 months old and "school" was an experimental program at the University of North Carolina at Chapel Hill. There the child experienced a number of interventions designed to improve her intellectual development—everything from bright objects dangled in front of her eyes while she was a baby to language instruction and counting activities when she was a toddler (Wickelgren, 1999).

This child was part of the Abecedarian Intervention Program conducted by Craig Ramey and his associates (Ramey & Campbell, 1984; Ramey & Ramey, 1998; Ramey, Ramey, & Lanzi, 2001). They randomly assigned 111 young children from low-income, poorly educated families either to an intervention group, which experienced full-time, year-round day care along with medical and social work services, or to a control group, which got medical and social benefits but no day care. The day-care program included gamelike learning activities aimed at improving language, motor, social, and cognitive skills. The success of the program in improving IQ was evident by the time the children were 3 years old, at which time the children in the experimental group showed normal IQs averaging 101, a 17-point advantage over the control group. Recent follow-up results suggest that the effects are long-lasting. More than a decade later, at age 15, children from the intervention group still maintained an IQ advantage of 5 points over the control-group children (97.7 to 92.6) (Ramey, Campbell, & Blair, 2001). They also did better on standardized tests of reading and math, and they were less likely to be held back a year in school (see figure 9.9). The greatest IQ gains were in the children whose mothers had especially low IQs—below 70. At age 15, these children showed a 10-point IQ advantage over a group of children whose mothers had IQs below 70 but did not experience the day-care intervention.

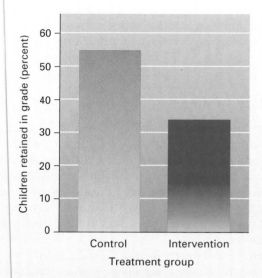

FIGURE 9.9 Early Intervention and Retention in School

When the children in the Abecedarian Intervention Program were 15 years of age, those who experienced the preschool intervention were less likely to have been retained in a grade (30 percent) than the children in the control group (55 percent).

example), but as adults these individuals may make their own choices about career and intellectual interests.

An important point to keep in mind about heritability is that it refers to groups (populations), not to individuals (Okagaki, 2000). Researchers rely on the concept of heritability to describe why people differ, not to explain the effects of heredity on a single individual's intelligence.

Environmental Influences

Today, most researchers agree that heredity does not determine intelligence to the extent Jensen claimed (Sternberg & Grigorenko, 2001). For most people, this means modifications in environment can change their IQ scores considerably. It also means that programs designed to enrich a person's environment can have a considerable impact, improving school achievement and fostering the acquisition of skills needed for employment. While genetic endowment may always influence a person's intellectual ability, the environmental influences and opportunities we provide children and adults do make a difference.

Researchers increasingly are interested in manipulating the early environment of children who are at risk for impoverished intelligence (Ramey, Ramey, & Lanzi, 2001). Their emphasis is on prevention rather than remediation. Many low-income parents have difficulty providing an intellectually stimulating environment for their children. Programs that educate parents to be more sensitive caregivers and train them to be better teachers, as well as support services, such as high-quality child-

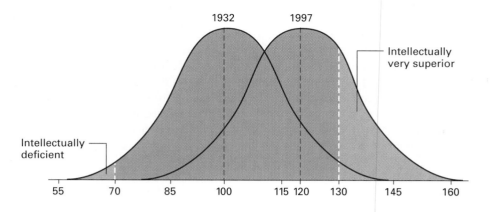

FIGURE 9.10 The Increase in IQ Scores from 1932 to 1997

As measured by the Stanford-Binet intelligence test, American children seem to be getting smarter. Scores of a group tested in 1932 fell along a bell-shaped curve with half below 100 and half above. Studies show that if children took that same test today, using the 1932 scale, half would score above 120. Few of them would score in the "intellectually deficient" range and about one-fourth would rank in the "very superior" range.

care programs, can make a difference in a child's intellectual development. To read about one such early intervention program, see the Explorations in Child Development box.

Studies of schooling also reveal effects on intelligence (Ceci & Gilstrap, 2000; Christian, Bachnan, & Morrison, 2001). The biggest effects have been found when large groups of children have been deprived of formal education for an extended period of time, resulting in lower intelligence. In one study, the intellectual functioning of Indian children in South Africa whose schooling was delayed for four years because of the unavailability of teachers was investigated (Ramphal, 1962). Compared with children in nearby villages who had teachers, the Indian children whose entry into school was delayed by four years experienced a decrement of five IQ points for every year of delay.

Another possible effect of education on intelligence can be seen in rapidly rising IQ test scores around the world (Flynn, 1999). Scores on these tests have been rising so fast that a high percentage of people regarded as having average intelligence at the turn of century would be considered below average in intelligence today (Howard, 2001) (see figure 9.10). If a representative sample of people today took an intelligence test in 1932, about one-fourth would be defined as having very superior intelligence, a label usually accorded to fewer than 3 percent of the population. Because the change has taken place in a relatively short period of time, it can't be due to heredity, but rather may be due to increasing levels of education attained by a much greater percentage of the world's population or to other environmental factors, such as the explosion of information to which people are exposed. The worldwide increase in intelligence test scores that has occurred over a short time frame has been called the *Flynn effect*, after the researcher who discovered it—James Flynn.

Keep in mind that environmental influences are complex. Growing up with all the "advantages," for example, does not necessarily guarantee success. Children from wealthy families may have easy access to excellent schools, books, travel, and tutoring, but they may take such opportunities for granted and fail to develop the motivation to learn and to achieve. By the same token, "poor" or "disadvantaged" does not automatically equal "doomed." Many impoverished children and youth make the best of the opportunities available to them and learn to seek out advantages that can help them improve their lives.

Group Comparisons

Among the ways that groups can be linked to intelligence include comparisons of cultures, ethnic groups, and males and females.

Cross-Cultural Comparisons Cultures vary in the way they define intelligence (Rogoff, 1990; Serpell, 2000). Most European Americans, for example, think of intelligence in terms of reasoning and thinking skills, but people in Kenya consider

"You can't build a hut, you don't know how to find edible roots and you know nothing about predicting the weather. In other words, you do terribly on our I.Q. test."

© by Sidney Harris.

www.mhhe.com/santrocked7o

The Bell Curve

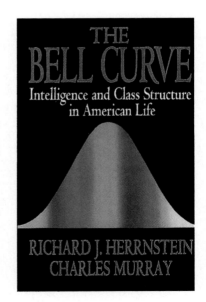

Herrnstein and Murray's book, *The Bell Curve*, advocates a strong role for heredity in intelligence and claims that a large portion of under-class individuals, especially African Americans, are doomed because of their heredity. *What are some of the criticisms that have been leveled at Herrnstein and Murray?*

responsible participation in family and social life an integral part of intelligence. Similarly, an intelligent person in Uganda is someone who knows what to do and then follows through with appropriate action. Intelligence to the Iatmul people of Papua, New Guinea, involves the ability to remember the names of 10,000 to 20,000 clans, and the residents of the widely dispersed Caroline Islands incorporate the talent of navigating by the stars in their definition of intelligence. In a cross-cultural context, then, intelligence depends a great deal on environment.

Ethnic Comparisons   In the United States, children from African American and Latino families score below children from White families on standardized intelligence tests. On the average, African American schoolchildren score 10 to 15 points lower on standardized intelligence tests than White American schoolchildren do (Brody, 2000; Lynn, 1996). We are talking about average scores, though. Estimates also indicate that 15 to 25 percent of all African American schoolchildren score higher than half of all White schoolchildren do, and many Whites score lower than most African Americans. The reason is that the distribution of scores for African Americans and Whites overlap.

How extensively are ethnic differences in intelligence influenced by heredity and environment? In one of his most provocative statements, Arthur Jensen (1969) claimed that genetics account for clear-cut differences in the average intelligence between races, nationalities, and socioeconomic groups. When Jensen published an article in the *Harvard Educational Review* stating that lower intelligence probably was the reason that African Americans do not perform as well in school as Whites, he was called naive and racist. He received hate mail by the bushel, and police had to escort him to his classes at the University of California at Berkeley.

A more recent controversy about heredity and intelligence focuses on the book *The Bell Curve: Intelligence and Class Structure in American Life* (1994) by Richard Herrnstein and Charles Murray. The authors argued that America is rapidly evolving a huge underclass that consists of intellectually deprived individuals whose cognitive abilities will never match the future needs of most employers. They believe that this underclass, a large proportion of which is African American, may be doomed by their shortcomings to welfare dependency, poverty, crime, and lives devoid of any hope of ever reaching the American dream.

Why do Herrnstein and Murray call their book *The Bell Curve?* A bell curve is the shape of a normal distribution graph (see figure 9.1). The normal distribution graph is used to represent large numbers of people who are sorted according to some shared characteristic, such as weight, exposure to asbestos, taste in clothes, or IQ.

Herrnstein and Murray often refer to bell curves to make a point: that predictions about any individual based exclusively on the person's IQ are virtually useless. Weak correlations between intelligence and job success have predictive value only when they are applied to large groups of people. Within such large groups, say Herrnstein and Murray, the pervasive influence of IQ on human society becomes apparent. Significant criticisms have been leveled at *The Bell Curve* as well as at Jensen's work. Experts on intelligence generally agree that African Americans score lower than Whites on IQ tests. However, many of these experts raise serious questions about the ability of IQ tests to accurately measure a person's intelligence. For instance, we saw earlier in this chapter that the tests are culturally biased toward European Americans. In 1971, the Supreme Court endorsed such criticism and ruled that tests of general intelligence, in contrast to tests that solely measure fitness for a particular job, are discriminatory and cannot be administered as a condition of employment. Cognitive psychologist Robert J. Sternberg (1994) said that using one index—IQ—as a basis for policy judgment is not only irresponsible, but also dangerous. Another criticism is that most research on heredity and environment does not include environments that differ radically. Thus, it is not surprising that many genetic studies show environment to be a fairly weak influence on intelligence (Fraser, 1995).

As African Americans have gained social, economic, and educational opportunities, the gap between African Americans and Whites on standardized intelligence tests has begun to narrow (Ogbu & Stern, 2001). This gap especially narrows in college, where African American and White students often experience more similar educational environments than in the elementary and high school years (Myerson & others, 1998). Also, when children from disadvantaged African American families are adopted into more-advantaged middle-socioeconomic status families, their scores on intelligence tests more closely resemble national averages for middle-socioeconomic-status children than for lower-socioeconomic-status children (Scarr & Weinberg, 1983).

Gender Comparisons   The average scores of males and females do not differ on intelligence tests, but variability in their scores does differ (Brody, 2000). For example, males are more likely than females to have extremely high or extremely low scores.

There also are gender differences in specific intellectual abilities (Brody, 2000). Males score better than females in some nonverbal areas, such as spatial reasoning, and females score better than males in some verbal areas, such as the ability to find synonyms for words. However, there often is extensive overlap in the scores of females and males in these areas, and there is debate about how strong the differences are (Eagly, 2001; Hyde & Mezulis, 2001).

Review and Reflect: Learning Goal 6

6 Analyze the contributions of heredity and environment to intelligence

REVIEW

- How does heredity influence intelligence?
- How can the environment influence intelligence?
- How are cultural, ethnic, and gender differences linked with intelligence?

REFLECT

- Someone tells you that he or she has analyzed his or her genetic background and environmental experiences and reached the conclusion that environment definitely has had little influence on his or her intelligence. What would you say to this person about his or her ability to make this self-diagnosed conclusion?

Reach Your Learning Goals

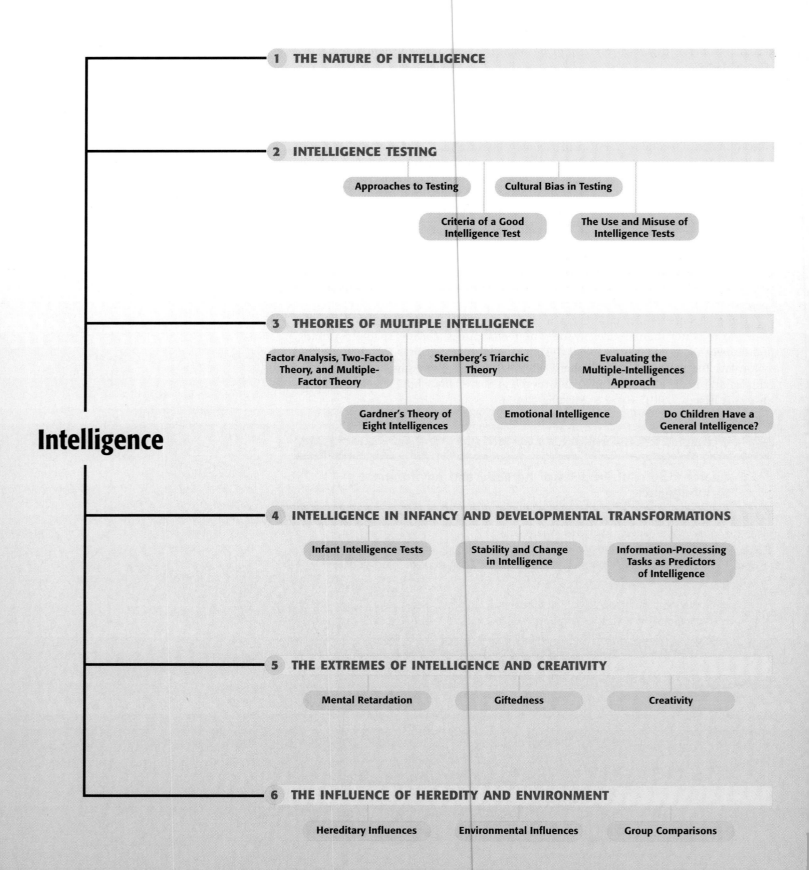

Intelligence

1 THE NATURE OF INTELLIGENCE

2 INTELLIGENCE TESTING

Approaches to Testing

Cultural Bias in Testing

Criteria of a Good Intelligence Test

The Use and Misuse of Intelligence Tests

3 THEORIES OF MULTIPLE INTELLIGENCE

Factor Analysis, Two-Factor Theory, and Multiple-Factor Theory

Sternberg's Triarchic Theory

Evaluating the Multiple-Intelligences Approach

Gardner's Theory of Eight Intelligences

Emotional Intelligence

Do Children Have a General Intelligence?

4 INTELLIGENCE IN INFANCY AND DEVELOPMENTAL TRANSFORMATIONS

Infant Intelligence Tests

Stability and Change in Intelligence

Information-Processing Tasks as Predictors of Intelligence

5 THE EXTREMES OF INTELLIGENCE AND CREATIVITY

Mental Retardation

Giftedness

Creativity

6 THE INFLUENCE OF HEREDITY AND ENVIRONMENT

Hereditary Influences

Environmental Influences

Group Comparisons

Summary

1 Describe what intelligence is

- Intelligence consists of the ability to solve problems and to adapt and learn from everyday experiences. A key aspect of intelligence focuses on its individual variations. Traditionally, intelligence has been measured by tests designed to compare people's performance on cognitive tasks.

2 Explain how intelligence is measured and the limitations of intelligence tests

- Sir Frances Galton is the father of mental tests. Alfred Binet developed the first intelligence test and created the concept of mental age. William Stern developed the concept of IQ for use with the Binet test. Revisions of the Binet test are called the Stanford-Binet. The test scores on the Stanford-Binet approximate a normal distribution. The Wechsler scales, created by David Wechsler, are the other main intelligence assessment tool. These tests provide an overall IQ, verbal and performance IQs, and information about 11 subtests. Group intelligence tests are convenient and economical, but they do not allow an examiner to monitor the testing closely. The SAT is a group test used in conjunction with information about a high school student's performance to predict academic success in college.
- A good test of intelligence meets three criteria: validity, reliability, and standardization. Validity is the extent to which a test measures what it is intended to measure. Reliability is the extent to which a test yields a consistent, reproducible measure of performance. Standardization focuses on uniform procedures for administering and scoring a test; it also involves norms.
- Early intelligence tests favored White, middle-socioeconomic-status urban individuals. Culture-fair tests are intelligence tests that are intended to be culturally unbiased. Many psychologists believe that such culture-fair tests cannot replace traditional intelligence tests.
- When used by a judicious examiner, tests can be valuable tools for determining individual differences in intelligence. Test scores should be only one type of information used to evaluate an individual. IQ scores can produce unfortunate stereotypes and expectations. Ability tests can help divide children into homogeneous groups, but periodic testing should be done to ensure that the groupings are appropriate.

3 Evaluate theories of multiple intelligence

- Factor analysis is a statistical procedure that compares various items or measures and identifies factors that are correlated with each other. Spearman (two-factor theory of g and s) and Thurstone (multiple-factor theory) used factor analysis in developing their views of intelligence.
- Gardner believes there are eight types of intelligence: verbal skills, mathematical skills, spatial skills, bodily-kinesthetic skills, musical skills, interpersonal skills, intrapersonal skills, and naturalist skills. Project Spectrum applies Gardner's view to educating children.
- Sternberg's triarchic theory states that there are three main types of intelligence: analytical, creative, and practical.
- Emotional intelligence is the ability to monitor one's own and others' feelings and emotions, to discriminate among them, and to use this information to guide one's thinking and action. Goleman popularized emotional intelligence.
- The multiple-intelligences approaches have broadened the definition of intelligence and motivated educators to develop programs that instruct students in different domains. Critics maintain that the multiple-intelligence theories include factors that really aren't part of intelligence, such as musical skills and creativity. Critics also say that there isn't enough research to support the concept of multiple intelligences.
- A number of experts on intelligence believe that children have a general intelligence as well as specific intellectual abilities. Among the characteristics of general intelligence are abstract reasoning or thinking, the capacity to acquire knowledge, and problem-solving ability.

4 Summarize the testing of intelligence in infancy and developmental transformations

- Many standardized intelligence tests do not assess infant intelligence. Intelligence tests designed to assess infant intelligence are often called developmental scales, the most widely used being the Bayley scales. Gesell was an important early contributor to the developmental testing of infants. The developmental quotient (DQ) is an overall score in the Gesell assessment of infants. The Fagan Test of Infant Intelligence, which assesses the infant's information-processing skills, is increasingly being used.
- Although intelligence is more stable across the childhood years than many other attributes are, many children's scores on intelligence tests fluctuate considerably.
- Developmentalists have found that infant information-processing tasks that involve attention—especially habituation and dishabituation—are related to standardized intelligence test scores in childhood.

5 Discuss characteristics of mental retardation, giftedness, and creativity

- Mental retardation is a condition of limited mental ability in which the individual has a low IQ, usually below 70, has difficulty adapting to everyday life, and has an onset of these characteristics during the so-called developmental period. Most affected individuals have an IQ in the 55 to 70 range (mild retardation). Mental retardation can have an organic cause (called organic retardation) or be social and cultural in origin if there is no evidence of organic brain damage (called cultural-familial retardation).
- Children who are gifted have high intelligence (an IQ of 130 or higher) and/or superior talent for something. Three characteristics of gifted children are precocity, marching to one's

own drummer, and a passion to master. Giftedness is likely a consequence of both heredity and environment.

- Creativity is the ability to think about something in novel and unusual ways and come up with unique solutions to problems. The difference between intelligence and creativity is the ability to produce something original or unique. Creative people tend to be divergent thinkers who can see more than one possible answer to a question. Traditional intelligence test questions have only one correct answer and thus measure convergent thinking. Some good strategies for encouraging children's creativity are brainstorming, providing environments that stimulate creativity, not overcontrolling and criticizing too much, encouraging internal motivation, fostering flexible and playful thinking, and introducing children to creative people.

6 Analyze the contributions of heredity and environment to intelligence

- Genetic similarity might explain why identical twins show stronger correlations on intelligence tests than fraternal twins do. Many studies show that intelligence has a reasonably strong heritability component. Criticisms of the heritability concept have been made.

- Environmental influences on intelligence have been demonstrated in studies of the effects of parenting, intervention programs for children at risk for having low IQs and dropping out of school, and sociohistorical changes. Ramey's research revealed the positive effects of educational child care on intelligence. Intelligence test scores have risen considerably around the world in recent decades—called the Flynn effect—and this supports the role of environment in intelligence.

- Among the ways that group influences can be linked with intelligence include comparisons of cultures, ethnic groups, and males and females. Cultures vary in the way they define intelligence. In the United States, children from African American and Latino families score below children from White families on standardized intelligence tests and the extent to which such differences are caused by heredity or environment is wrapped in controversy. The average scores of males and females do not differ on intelligence tests, but variability in their scores does differ. For example, males are more likely than females to have extremely high or extremely low scores. There also are gender differences in specific intellectual abilities.

Key Terms

intelligence 281
mental age (MA) 282
intelligence quotient (IQ) 282
normal distribution 283
aptitude tests 285
achievement tests 285
validity 286

reliability 286
standardization 286
culture-fair tests 287
two-factor theory 289
factor analysis 290
multiple-factor theory 290
triarchic theory 291

emotional intelligence 293
developmental quotient (DQ) 295
Bayley Scales of Infant Development 295
mental retardation 298

gifted 299
creativity 300
divergent thinking 301
convergent thinking 301
brainstorming 301
heritability 303

Key People

Sir Frances Galton 282
Alfred Binet 282
William Stern 282
David Wechsler 283
Charles Spearman 289
L. L. Thurstone 290

Howard Gardner 290
Robert J. Sternberg 291
Peter Salovey and John Mayer 293
Daniel Goleman 293
Nathan Brody 293

John Carroll 294
Arnold Gesell 295
Nancy Bayley 295
Robert McCall 297
Lewis Terman 299
Ellen Winner 299

Teresa Amabile 302
Arthur Jensen 303
Craig Ramey 304
Richard Herrnstein and Charles Murray 306

Taking It to the Net

1. Terry and Lauren are on a debating team. They have to argue for the proposition "Intelligence is hereditary." Another pair of members will argue for the opposite proposition, "Intelligence is not related to heredity." What facts do Terry and Lauren need to know as they prepare for the debate?

2. Motabi is from the Congo. He is arguing with his developmental psychology classmates about the meaning of intelligence. Motabi insists that different cultures construct their own paradigms of intelligence and that intelligence in the Congo is a very different concept from intelligence in Illinois. Is there any evidence to support Motabi's argument?

3. Maureen and Harry received a letter from the elementary school principal suggesting that they enroll their daughter, Jasmine, in the gifted program. They know that Jasmine's IQ score is 125—certainly not in the genius category. Is there more to giftedness than IQ score? What talents might Jasmine's teachers have noticed in her that might qualify her as being gifted?

Connect to **www.mhhe.com/santrockcd10** to research the answers and complete these exercises.

E-Learning Tools

To help you master the material in this chapter, you'll find a number of valuable study tools on the Student CD-ROM that accompanies this book. Also visit the Online Learning Center for *Child Development,* tenth edition (**www.mhhe.com/santrockcd10**) where you'll find these additional resources:

- View video clips by key developmental psychology experts including Steve Ceci on the relationship between context and intelligence and on intelligence testing.

- Build your decision-making skills by trying your hand at the parenting, nursing, and education "Scenarios" on the Online Learning Center.

- Use the interactive Prism exercises to learn more about formal operational thought.

*Words not only affect us
temporarily; they change
us, they socialize us, and
they unsocialize us.*

—DAVID REISMAN
American Social Scientist, 20th Century

Language Development

Chapter Outline

Learning Goals

WHAT IS LANGUAGE?

Defining Language

Language's Rule Systems

1 Define language and describe its rule systems

BIOLOGICAL AND ENVIRONMENTAL INFLUENCES

Biological Influences

Behavioral and Environmental Influences

An Interactionist View of Language

2 Discuss the biological and environmental aspects of language

LANGUAGE AND COGNITION

3 Evaluate how language and cognition are linked

HOW LANGUAGE DEVELOPS

Infancy

Early Childhood

Middle and Late Childhood

4 Describe how language develops in children

BILINGUALISM

5 Summarize what is known about bilingualism and bilingual education

The Story of Helen Keller

One of the most stunning portrayals of children isolated from the mainstream of language is the case of Helen Keller (1880–1968). At 18 months of age, Helen was an intelligent toddler in the process of learning her first words. Then she developed an illness that left her both deaf and blind, suffering the double affliction of sudden darkness and silence. For the next five years she lived in a world she learned to fear because she could not see or hear.

Even with her fears, Helen spontaneously invented a number of gestures to reflect her wants and needs. For example, when she wanted ice cream, she turned toward the freezer and shivered. When she wanted bread and butter, she imitated the motions of cutting and spreading. But this homemade language system severely limited her ability to communicate with the surrounding community, which did not understand her idiosyncratic gestures.

Alexander Graham Bell, the famous inventor of the telephone, suggested to her parents that they hire a tutor named Anne Sullivan to help Helen overcome her fears. By using sign language, Anne was able to teach Helen to communicate. Anne realized that language learning needs to occur naturally, so she did not force Helen to memorize words out of context as in the drill methods that were in vogue at the time. Sullivan's success depended not only on the child's natural ability to organize language according to form and meaning but also on introducing language in the context of communicating about objects, events, and feelings about others.

Helen Keller eventually graduated from Radcliffe with honors, became a very successful educator, and crafted books about her life and experiences. She had this to say about language: "Whatever the process, the result is wonderful. Gradually from naming an object we advance step by step until we have traversed the vast distance between our first stammered syllable and the sweep of thought in a line of Shakespeare."

1 WHAT IS LANGUAGE?

Defining Language   **Language's Rule Systems**

In 1799, a nude boy was observed running through the woods in France. The boy was captured when he was 11 years old. He was called the Wild Boy of Aveyron and was believed to have lived in the woods alone for six years. When found, he made no effort to communicate. Even after a number of years, he never learned to communicate effectively. Sadly, a modern-day wild child named Genie was discovered in Los Angeles in 1970. Despite intensive intervention, Genie has never acquired more than a primitive form of language. We will discuss Genie's development in greater detail later in the chapter. Both cases—the Wild Boy of Aveyron and Genie—raise questions about the biological and environmental determinants of language, topics that we also will examine in greater detail later in the chapter. First, though, we need to define language.

Defining Language

language A form of communication, whether spoken, written, or signed, that is based on a system of symbols.

Language is a form of communication, whether spoken, written, or signed, that is based on a system of symbols. Language consists of the words used by a community and the rules for varying and combining them. Think how important language is in

314

our everyday lives. We need language to speak with others, listen to others, read, and write. Our language enables us to describe past events in detail and to plan for the future. Language lets us pass down information from one generation to the next and create a rich cultural heritage.

All human languages have some common characteristics. These include infinite generativity and organizational rules. **Infinite generativity** is the ability to produce an endless number of meaningful sentences using a finite set of words and rules. This quality makes language a highly creative enterprise. Language is characterized by a number of organizational rules that include phonology, morphology, syntax, semantics, and pragmatics which we will discuss next.

Language's Rule Systems

When nineteenth-century American writer Ralph Waldo Emerson said, "The world was built in order and the atoms march in tune," he must have had language in mind. The truly elegant system of language is highly ordered and organized (Berko Gleason, 2000). What are this order and organization like? The order and organization of language involve five rule systems: phonology, morphology, syntax, semantics, and pragmatics.

Phonology   Language is made up of basic sounds, or phonemes. Thus, phonemes are based on how a sound is pronounced rather than how it is spelled. **Phonology** refers to a language's sound system. Phonological rules ensure that certain sound sequences occur (for example, *sp, ba,* or *ar*) and others do not (for example, *zx* or *qp*). A good example of a phoneme in the English language is /k/, the sound represented by the letter *k* in the word *ski* and the letter *c* in the word *cat*. Although the /k/ sound is slightly different in these two words, the variation is not distinguished, and the /k/ sound is described as a single phoneme. In some languages, such as Arabic, this kind of variation represents separate phonemes.

Imagine what language would be like if there were no phonology. Each word in the language would have to be represented by a signal—a sound, for example—that differed from the signals of all other words. The obvious consequence is that the number of words could be no larger than the number of different signals that an individual could efficiently produce and perceive. We do not know precisely what that number is, but we do know that it is very small, especially in the case of speech, in contrast to the hundreds of thousands of words that commonly constitute a language.

Phonology provides a basis for constructing a large and expandable set of words—all that are or ever will be in that language—out of two or three dozen phonemes. We do not need 500,000 phonemes, we need only a few dozen.

Morphology   **Morphology** refers to the units of meaning involved in word formation. A *morpheme* is a unit of sound that conveys a specific meaning. Every word in the English language is made up of one or more morphemes. Some words consist of a single morpheme (for example, *help*), whereas others are made up of more than one morpheme (for example, *helper,* which has two morphemes, *help + er,* with the morpheme *-er* meaning "one who," in this case "one who helps"). Thus, not all morphemes are words by themselves (for example, *pre-, -tion,* and *-ing*). Just as the rules that govern phonemes ensure that certain sound sequences occur, the rules that govern morphemes ensure that certain strings of sounds occur in meaningful sequences.

Morphemes have many different jobs in grammar, such as marking tense (for example, she walks versus he walked) and number (she walks versus they walk). In certain instances, it is straightforward to see the different morphemes that comprise a word—such as, she *walked = walk + ed*. However, sometimes the resulting word does not follow the regular rule; there are irregular forms, such as *fall + ed = fell*. Sometimes children make errors with morphemes, such as overgeneralizing *ed* to

infinite generativity The ability to produce an endless number of meaningful sentences using a finite set of words and rules.

phonology A language's sound system.

morphology Units of meaning involved in word formation.

FRANK & ERNEST reprinted by permission of Newspaper Enterprise Association, Inc.

produce words like *falled*. These errors tell us that children are being creative and producing a word that they do not hear adults use.

Syntax   **Syntax** involves the ways words are combined to form acceptable phrases and sentences. If someone says to you, "Bob slugged Tom" or "Bob was slugged by Tom," you know who did the slugging and who was slugged in each case because you have a syntactic understanding of these sentence structures. You also understand that the sentence "You didn't stay, did you?" is a grammatical sentence but that "You didn't stay, didn't you?" is unacceptable and ambiguous.

If you learn another language, it will soon be clear to you that your English syntax will not get you very far. For example, in English an adjective usually precedes a noun (as in *blue sky*), whereas in Spanish the adjective usually follows the noun *(cielo azul)*. In fact, the difficulty of learning new syntactic patterns is one of the main complaints of a second-language learner. Despite the differences in their syntactic structures, however, the world's languages have much in common. For example, consider these short sentences:

The cat killed the mouse.
The mouse ate the cheese.
The farmer chased the cat.

In many languages it is possible to combine these sentences into more-complex sentences. For example:

The farmer chased the cat that killed the mouse.
The mouse the cat killed ate the cheese.

However, no language in the world permits sentences like this one:

The mouse the cat the farmer chased killed ate the cheese.

Can you make sense of this sentence? If you can, you probably can do it only after wrestling with it for several minutes. You likely could not understand it at all if someone uttered it during a real conversation. It appears that language users cannot process subjects and objects arranged in too complex a fashion in a sentence. That is good news for language learners, because it means there is some common ground that all syntactic systems adhere to. Such findings are also considered important by researchers who are interested in the universal properties of syntax (Maratsos, 1998).

Semantics   **Semantics** refers to the meaning of words and sentences. Every word has a set of semantic features. *Girl* and *woman,* for example, share many of the semantic features as the word *female,* but differ semantically in regard to age. Words have semantic restrictions on how they can be used in sentences. The sentence *The bicycle talked the boy into buying a candy bar* is syntactically correct but semantically incorrect. The sentence violates our semantic knowledge that bicycles do not talk.

Pragmatics   A final set of language rules involves **pragmatics,** the use of appropriate conversation and knowledge of how to effectively use language in context.

syntax The ways words are combined to form acceptable phrases and sentences.

semantics The meanings of words and sentences.

pragmatics The use of appropriate conversation and knowledge of how to effectively use language in context.

Rule System	Description	Examples
Phonology	The sound system of a language. A phoneme is the smallest sound unit in a language.	The word *chat* has three phonemes or sounds: /ch/ /a/ /t/. An example of phonological rule in the English language is while the phoneme /r/ can follow the phonemes /t/ or /d/ in an English consonant cluster (such as *track* or *drab*), the phoneme /l/ cannot follow these letters.
Morphology	The system of meaningful units involved in word formation.	The smallest sound units that have a meaning are called morphemes, or meaning units. The word *girl* is one morpheme, or meaning unit; it cannot be broken down any further and still have meaning. When the suffix *s* is added, the word becomes *girls* and has two morphemes because the *s* changed the meaning of the word, indicating that there is more than one girl.
Syntax	The system that involves the way words are combined to form acceptable phrases and sentences.	Word order is very important in determining meaning in the English language. For example, the sentence, "Sebastian pushed the bike" has a different meaning than "The bike pushed Sebastian."
Semantics	The system that involves the meaning of words and sentences.	Knowing the meaning of individual words—that is, vocabulary. For example, semantics includes knowing the meaning of such words as *orange*, *transportation*, and *intelligent*.
Pragmatics	The system of using appropriate conversation and knowledge of how to effectively use language in context.	An example is using polite language in appropriate situations, such as being mannerly when talking with one's teacher. Taking turns in a conversation involves pragmatics.

FIGURE 10.1 The Rule Systems of Language

The domain of pragmatics is broad, covering such circumstances as (a) taking turns in discussions instead of everyone talking at once; (b) using questions to convey commands ("Why is it so noisy in here?" "What is this, Grand Central Station?"); (c) using words like *the* and *a* in a way that enhances understanding ("I read *a* book last night. *The* plot was boring"); (d) using polite language in appropriate situations (for example, when talking to one's teacher); and (e) telling stories that are interesting, jokes that are funny, and lies that convince.

Pragmatic rules can be complex and differ from one culture to another. If you were to study the Japanese language, you would come face-to-face with countless pragmatic rules about conversing with individuals of various social levels and with various relationships to you. Some of these pragmatic rules concern the ways of saying thank you. Indeed, the pragmatics of saying thank you are complex even in our own culture. Preschoolers' use of the phrase *thank you* varies with sex, socioeconomic status, and the age of the individual they are addressing. Through pragmatics, children learn to convey meaning with words, phrases, and sentences. Pragmatics helps children communicate more smoothly with others.

At this point, we have discussed five important rule systems involved in language. An overview of these rule systems is presented in figure 10.1.

Pragmatics

Review and Reflect: Learning Goal 1

1 Define language and describe its rule systems

REVIEW

- What is language?
- What are language's five main rule systems?

REFLECT

- How good are the people you regularly interact with, such as your family members and friends, at the pragmatics of language? Describe an example in which one of the individuals showed pragmatic skills and another in which he or she did not.

2 BIOLOGICAL AND ENVIRONMENTAL INFLUENCES

Biological Influences

Behavioral and Environmental Influences

An Interactionist View of Language

Is the ability to generate rules for language and then use them to create an infinite number of words the product of biological factors and evolution? Or is language learned and influenced by the environment?

In the wild, chimps communicate through calls, gestures, and expressions, which evolutionary psychologists believe might be the roots of true language.

www.mhhe.com/santrockcd10

Brain and Language Development

aphasia A language disorder, resulting from brain damage, that involves a loss of the ability to use words.

Broca's area An area of the brain's left frontal lobe that directs the muscle movements involved in speech production.

Wernicke's area An area of the temporal lobe in brain's left hemisphere that is involved in language comprehension.

Biological Influences

All people who communicate must in some way "know" the rules for language and have the ability to create an infinite number of words and sentences. Where do these rules come from? Are they the product of biological factors and evolution? Or, are those rules learned in the context of interacting with others, and thus, influenced by the environment?

Some language scholars view the remarkable similarities that exist in children's language acquisition all over the world, despite the vast variation in the language input they receive, as strong evidence for the biological basis of language. However, on closer examination, it is clear that the individual preferences of the child, the particular language to be learned, and the context in which learning takes place can strongly influence language acquisition.

Biological Evolution Estimates vary as to how long ago humans acquired language—but many experts pick a period of about 100,000 years ago. In evolutionary time, then, language is a very recent acquisition. A number of experts believe that biological evolution undeniably shaped humans into linguistic creatures (Chomsky, 1957). The brain, nervous system, and vocal apparatus of our predecessors changed over hundreds of thousands of years. Physically equipped to do so, *Homo sapiens* went beyond grunting and shrieking to develop abstract speech. Language clearly gave humans an enormous edge over other animals and increased the chances of human survival (Pinker, 1994).

The Brain's Role in Language There is evidence that the brain contains particular regions that are predisposed to be used for language (Wartenburger & others, 2003). ← page 135 For example, accumulating evidence suggests that language processing occurs primarily in the brain's left hemisphere (Gazzaniga, 1986; Gazzaniga, Ivry, & Magnum, 2002). Studies of language in brain-damaged individuals have pinpointed two areas of the left hemisphere that are especially critical. In 1861, a patient of Paul Broca, a French surgeon and anthropologist, received an injury to the left side of his brain. The patient became known as Tan, because that was the only word he could speak after his brain injury. Tan suffered from **aphasia,** a language disorder resulting from brain damage that involves a loss of the ability to use words (Leger & others, 2002). Tan died several days after Broca evaluated him, and an autopsy revealed the location of the injury. Today, we refer to the part of the brain in which Broca's patient was injured as **Broca's area,** an area of the left frontal lobe of the brain that directs the muscle movements involved in speech production. Another place in the brain where an injury can seriously impair language is **Wernicke's area,** an area of the temporal lobe in the brain's left hemisphere involved in language comprehension. Individuals with damage to Wernicke's area often babble words in a meaningless way. The locations of Broca's area and Wernicke's area are shown in figure 10.2.

Although the brain's left hemisphere is especially important in language, keep in mind that in most activities there is an interplay between the brain's two hemispheres (Grodzinsky, 2001; Hellige, 1990; Nocentini & others, 2001). For example, in reading, the left hemisphere comprehends syntax and grammar, which the right hemisphere does not. However, the right hemisphere is better at understanding a story's intonation and emotion.

Biological Prewiring   Linguist Noam Chomsky (1957) believes humans are biologically prewired to learn language at a certain time and in a certain way. He said that children are born into the world with a **language acquisition device (LAD),** a biological endowment that enables the child to detect certain language categories, such as phonology, syntax, and semantics. The LAD is a theoretical construct that flows from evidence about the biological basis of language.

Is there evidence for the existence of a LAD? Supporters of the LAD concept cite the uniformity of language milestones across languages and cultures, biological substrates for language, and evidence that children create language even in the absence of well-formed input.

Is There a Critical Period for Learning Language?   Have you ever encountered young children serving as unofficial "translators" for their non-English-speaking parents? Doctors and nurses sometimes encounter this when treating patients. Does this indicate that young children are able to easily learn language, while their parents have lost this ability? Such an explanation fits the view that there is a **critical period,** a period in which there is learning readiness. Beyond this period, learning is difficult or impossible. The concept of a critical period applies nicely to certain varieties of songbirds. For example, baby white-crowned sparrows learn the song of their species quite well if they are exposed to it during a specific time as a chick. After this time, they can never develop a fully formed song pattern. But whether this notion can be extended to humans learning language is much less certain.

Almost all children learn one or more languages during their early years of development, so it is difficult to determine whether there is a critical period for language development (Obler, 1993). In the 1960s, Eric Lenneberg (1967) proposed a biological theory of language acquisition. He said that language is a maturational process and that there is a critical period between about 18 months of age and puberty, during which a first language must be acquired. Central to Lenneberg's thesis is the idea that language develops rapidly and with ease during the preschool years as a result of maturation. Lenneberg provided support for the critical-period concept from studies of several atypical populations. These included children with left-hemisphere brain damage, deaf children, and children with mental retardation (Tager-Flusberg, 1994). With regard to brain damage, Lenneberg believed that adults had already passed the critical period during which plasticity of brain function allows language skills to be relearned.

Remember from chapter 2, "The Science of Child Development," that a case study involves an in-depth study of a single individual. ◀ **page 46** The case study of Genie, a modern-day "wild child" with stunted language development, supports the concept of a critical period in language. In 1970, a California social worker made a routine visit to the home of a partially blind woman who had applied for public assistance. The social worker discovered that the woman and her husband had kept their 13-year-old daughter, Genie, locked away in almost total isolation during her childhood. Genie could not speak or stand erect. She had spent every day bound naked to a child's potty seat. She could move only her hands and feet. At night she was placed in a kind of straightjacket and caged in a crib with wire mesh sides and a cover. Whenever Genie made a noise, her father beat her. He never communicated with her in words but growled and barked at her instead (Rymer, 1992).

After she was rescued from her parents, Genie spent a number of years in extensive rehabilitation programs, such as speech and physical therapy (Curtiss, 1977). She eventually learned to walk, although with a jerky motion, and to use the toilet.

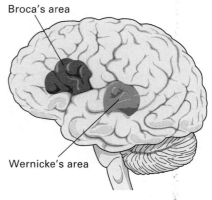

FIGURE 10.2 Broca's Area and Wernicke's Area

Broca's area is located in the frontal lobe of the brain's left hemisphere, and it is involved in the control of speech. Individuals with damage to Broca's area have problems saying words correctly. Also shown is Wernicke's area, a portion of the left hemisphere's temporal lobe that is involved in understanding language. Individuals with damage to this area cannot comprehend words; that is, they hear the words but don't know what they mean.

MIT linguist Noam Chomsky. *What is Chomsky's view of language?*

language acquisition device (LAD) Chomsky's theoretical concept of a biological endowment that enables the child to detect certain language categories, such as phonology, syntax, and semantics.

critical period A period in which there is learning readiness. Beyond this period, learning is difficult or impossible.

What were Genie's (shown above) *experiences like? What implications do they have for language acquisition?*

Critical Period Hypothesis in Language

Genie

Genie also learned to recognize many words and to speak in rudimentary sentences. At first, she spoke in one-word utterances. Later she was able to string together two-word combinations, such as "Big teeth," "Little marble," and "Two hand." Consistent with the language development of most children, three-word combinations (such as "Small two cup") followed. As far as we know, unlike normal children, Genie did not learn to ask questions and did not develop a language system that allowed her to understand English grammar. Four years after she began stringing words together, Genie's speech still sounded like a garbled telegram. As an adult, she speaks in short, mangled sentences, such as "Father hit leg," "Big wood," and "Genie hurt."

Children like Genie, who are abandoned, abused, and not exposed to language for many years, rarely speak normally. Such tragic evidence supports the critical-period hypothesis in language development. However, because these children also suffer severe emotional trauma and possible neurological deficits, the issue is still far from clear.

Let's go back to our "child translator" example. Why is it that children seem to do better than older people in learning language? Many researchers have proposed that the preschool years (until age 5) may be a critical period for language acquisition. Evidence for this notion comes from studies of brain development in young children, and from the amount of language learned by preschool children. However, other evidence suggests that we do not have a critical period for language learning. First of all, although much language learning takes place during the preschool years, learning continues well into the later school years and adulthood (Hakuta, Bialystok, & Wiley, 2003). In other words, young children's proficiency in language, while impressive, does not seem to involve a biologically salient critical period that older children and adults have passed.

Behavioral and Environmental Influences

Behaviorists view language as a complex learned skill, much like learning to play the piano or learning to dance. They argue that language represents chains of responses (Skinner, 1957) or imitation (Bandura, 1977). The difficulty with this argument is that many of the sentences we produce are novel; we have not heard them or spoken them before. For example, a child hears the sentence "The plate fell on the floor" and then says, "My mirror fell on the blanket," after dropping the mirror on the blanket. The behavioral mechanisms of reinforcement and imitation cannot completely explain this.

While spending long hours observing parents and their young children, child language researcher Roger Brown (1973) found that parents did not pay attention to the grammatical form of their children's utterances. Brown concluded that no evidence exists that reinforcement is responsible for language's rule systems.

Another criticism of the behavioral view is that it fails to explain the extensive orderliness of language. The behavioral view predicts that vast individual differences should appear in children's speech development because of each child's unique learning history. But, as we have seen, a compelling fact about language is its orderly development. All infants coo before they babble. All toddlers produce one-word utterances before two-word utterances. All children state sentences in the active form before they state them in a passive form.

Today most language acquisition researchers believe that children from a wide variety of cultural contexts acquire their native language without explicit teaching. In some cases, they do so without apparent encouragement. Thus, there appear to be very few aids that are necessary for learning a language. However, the support and involvement of caregivers and teachers greatly facilitate a child's language learning (MacWhinney, 1999; Snow, 1999). Of special concern are

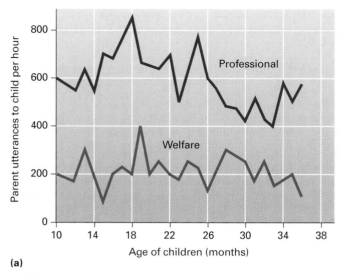

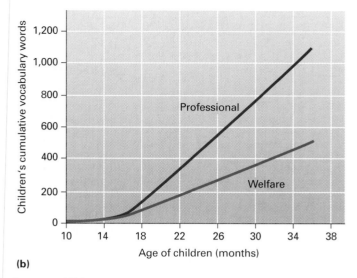

(a)   **(b)**

FIGURE 10.3 Language Input in Professional and Welfare Families and Young Children's Vocabulary Development

(*a*) Parents from professional families talked with their young children more than parents from welfare families. (*b*) Children from professional families developed vocabularies that were twice as large as those from welfare families. Thus, by the time children go to preschool, they already have experienced considerable differences in language input in their families and developed different levels of vocabulary that are linked to the socioeconomic context in which they have lived.

children who grow up in poverty areas and are not exposed to guided participation in language.

One study compared the home language environments of 3-year-old children from professional and welfare families (Hart & Risley, 1995). All of the children developed normally in terms of learning to talk and acquiring all of the forms of English and basic vocabulary. However, there were enormous differences in the sheer amount of language to which the children were exposed and the level of language development the children eventually attained. As can be seen in figure 10.3, professional parents talked much more to their young children than welfare parents talked with their young children, and this difference was linked with the vocabulary development of the children. Further, the style of talk varied across these parents. The parents of the children from welfare families heard fewer descriptions, less talk about past events, and less elaboration. Not only were the early variations in language input (10 to 36 months) related to outcomes at 36 months but also outcomes in IQ and standardized language assessments at 6 to 9 years of age. Thus, the impact of the early language experiences had long-term consequences.

One intriguing component of the young child's linguistic environment is **child-directed speech,** the kind of speech often used by adults to talk to babies and young children—in a higher pitch than normal and with simple words and sentences. Child-directed speech captures the baby's attention. It is hard to use child-directed speech when not in the presence of a baby. As soon as you start talking to a baby, though, you immediately shift into child-directed speech. Much of this is automatic and something most parents are not aware they are doing. Child-directed speech has the important functions of capturing the infant's attention and maintaining communication. When parents are asked why they use baby talk, they point out that it is designed to teach their baby to talk. Older children also modify their speech when talking to babies and younger children who are learning language in much the same way as adults. Even 4-year-olds speak in simpler ways to 2-year-olds than they do to their 4-year-old friends.

Communicating with Babies

child-directed speech The kind of speech often used by adults to talk to babies and young children—in a higher pitch than normal and with simple words and sentences.

Are there strategies other than infant-directed speech that adults use to enhance the child's acquisition of language? Three candidates are recasting, expanding, and labeling:

- **Recasting** is rephrasing something the child has said in a different way, perhaps turning it into a question. For example, if the child says, "The dog was barking," the adult can respond by asking, "When was the dog barking?" The effects of recasting fit with suggestions that "following in order to lead" helps a child learn language. That is, letting a child initially indicate an interest and then proceeding to elaborate that interest—commenting, demonstrating, and explaining—improve communication and help language acquisition. In contrast, an overly active, directive approach to communicating with the child may be harmful.
- **Expanding** is restating, in a linguistically sophisticated form, what a child has said.
- **Labeling** is identifying the names of objects. Young children are forever being asked to identify the names of objects. Roger Brown (1986) identified this as "the great word game" and claimed that much of the early vocabulary acquired by children is motivated by this adult pressure to identify the words associated with objects.

The strategies just described—recasting, expanding, and labeling—are used naturally and in meaningful conversations. Parents do not (and should not) use any deliberate method to teach their children to talk. Even for children who are slow in learning language, the experts agree that intervention should occur in natural ways, with the goal of being able to convey meaning.

Children usually benefit when parents guide their children's discovery of language rather than overloading them with language in an authoritarian manner. If children are not ready to take in some information, they are likely to tell you (as by turning away). Thus, giving the child more information is not always better.

It is important to recognize that children vary in their ability to acquire language and that this variation cannot be readily explained by differences in environmental input alone (Rice, 1996). For children who are slow in developing language skills, opportunities to talk and be talked with are important. Children whose parents provide them with a rich verbal environment show many positive language benefits. Parents who pay attention to what their children are trying to say and expand their children's utterances, who read to them, who label things in the environment, are all providing valuable, if unintentional, language benefits (Berko Gleason, 2002).

Remember, though, that the encouragement of language development, not drill and practice, is the key. Language development is not a simple matter of imitation and reinforcement, a fact acknowledged even by most behaviorists today. To read further about ways that parents can facilitate children's language development, see the Explorations in Child Development box.

An Interactionist View of Language

We have seen that language has very strong biological foundations. The view that language has a biological base was especially promoted by Chomsky (1957), who, as we have noted, proposed the existence of a language acquisition device (LAD) to account for the complexity and speed of young children's understanding of grammar. We have also seen that children all over the world acquire language milestones at about the same time developmentally and in about the same order, despite the vast variation in language input they receive, which is also evidence for a strong biological influence in language development.

However, children do not learn language in a social vacuum. American psychologist Jerome Bruner (1983, 1996) recognized this important point when he proposed that the sociocultural context is extremely important in understanding

recasting Rephrasing a statement that a child has said, perhaps turning it into a question.

expanding Restating, in a linguistically sophisticated form, what a child has said.

labeling Identifying the names of objects.

How Parents Can Facilitate Children's Language Development

In *Growing Up with Language,* linguist Naomi Baron (1992) provides a number of ideas to help parents facilitate their child's language development. Here is a summary of her ideas:

Infants

- *Be an active conversational partner.* Initiate conversation with the infant. If the infant is in a daylong child-care program, ensure that the baby gets adequate language stimulation from adults.
- *Talk as if the infant understands what you are saying.* Parents can generate self-fulfilling prophecies by addressing their young children as if they understand what is being said. The process may take four to five years, but children gradually rise to match the language model presented to them.
- *Use a language style with which you feel comfortable.* Don't worry about how you sound to other adults when you talk with your child. Your affect, not your content, is more important when talking with an infant. Use whatever type of baby talk with which you feel comfortable.

Toddlers

- *Continue to be an active conversational partner.* Engaging toddlers in conversation, even one-sided conversation, is the most important thing a parent can do to nourish a child linguistically.
- *Remember to listen.* Since toddlers' speech is often slow and laborious, parents are often tempted to supply words and thoughts for them. Be patient and let toddlers express themselves, no matter how painstaking the process is or how great a hurry you are in.
- *Use a language style with which you are comfortable, but consider ways of expanding your child's language abilities and horizons.* For example, using long sentences need not be problematic. Don't be afraid to use ungrammatical language to imitate the toddler's novel forms (such as "No eat"). Use rhymes. Ask questions that encourage answers other than "Yes" and "No." Actively repeat, expand, and recast the child's utterances. Introduce new topics. And use humor in your conversation.
- *Adjust to your child's idiosyncrasies instead of working against them.* Many toddlers have difficulty pronouncing words and making

themselves understood. Whenever possible, make toddlers feel that they are being understood.

- *Avoid sexual stereotypes.* Don't let the toddler's sex unwittingly determine your amount or style of conversation. Many American mothers are more linguistically supportive of girls than of boys, and many fathers talk less with their children than mothers do. Active and cognitively enriching initiatives from both mothers and fathers benefit both boys and girls.
- *Resist making normative comparisons.* Be aware of the ages at which your child reaches specific milestones (first word, first 50 words, first grammatical combination). However, be careful not to measure this development rigidly against children of neighbors or friends. Such social comparisons can bring about unnecessary anxiety.

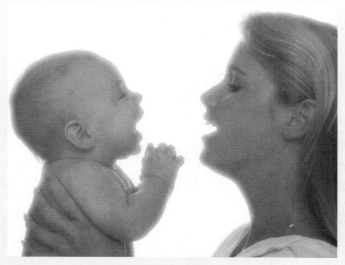

It is a good idea for parents to begin talking to their babies at the start. The best language teaching occurs when the talking is begun before the infant becomes capable of its first intelligible speech.

children's language development. Like Vygotsky, Bruner stresses the role of parents and teachers in constructing a child's communication environment. Bruner developed the concept of a language acquisition support system (LASS) to describe the behaviors of a language-skilled individual, especially a parent, in structuring and supporting the child's language development. Bruner's concept has much in common with Vygotsky's concept of a zone of proximal development, which was discussed in chapter 7. ◀ **page 230**

In sum, children are neither exclusively biological linguists nor exclusively social architects of language (Gleason & Ratner, 1998). No matter how long you converse with a dog, it won't learn to talk, and unfortunately some children fail to develop good language skills even in the presence of very good role models and social stimulation. An interactionist view emphasizes the contributions of both biology and experience in language: It sees children as biologically prepared to learn language as they and their caregivers communicate.

Think for a moment about the longitudinal study described earlier that was conducted by Betty Hart and Todd Risley (1995). They observed the language environments of children from professional and welfare backgrounds. All of the children heard the basic forms and functions of English. Furthermore, all of the children acquired the basic forms and functions of the English language and the universals of language. However, there was extensive variation in the sheer amount of language they were exposed to and the level of language development they attained.

Review and Reflect: Learning Goal 2

2 Discuss the biological and environmental aspects of language

REVIEW

- What are the biological foundations of language?
- What are the behavioral and environmental aspects of language?
- How does an interactionist view describe language?

REFLECT

- How should parents respond to children's grammatical mistakes in conversation? Should parents allow the mistakes to continue and assume their young children will grow out of them, or should they closely monitor their children's grammar and correct mistakes whenever they hear them?

---

3 LANGUAGE AND COGNITION

As a teenager, Wendy Verougstraete felt that she was on the road to becoming a professional author. "You are looking at a professional author," she said. "My books will be filled with drama, action, and excitement. And everyone will want to read them. I am going to write books, page after page, stack after stack."

Overhearing her remarks, you might have been impressed not only by Wendy's optimism and determination, but also by her expressive verbal skills. In fact, at a young age Wendy showed a flair for writing and telling stories. Wendy has a rich vocabulary, creates lyrics for love songs, and enjoys telling stories. You probably would not be able to immediately guess that she has an IQ of only 49, and cannot tie her shoes, cross the street by herself, read or print words beyond the first-grade level, and cannot do even simple arithmetic.

Wendy Verougstraete has *Williams syndrome*, a genetic birth disorder that was first described in 1961 and affects about 1 in 20,000 births. The most noticeable features of the syndrome include a unique combination of expressive verbal skills with an extremely low IQ and limited spatial and motor control (Osborne & Pober, 2001; Vicari, Bellucci, & Carlesimo, 2001). Figure 10.4 shows the great disparity in the verbal and motor skills of one person with Williams syndrome. Individuals with Williams syndrome often have good musical skills and interpersonal skills. The syndrome also includes a number of physical characteristics as well, such as heart defects and a pixielike facial appearance. Despite having excellent verbal skills and competent interpersonal skills, most individuals with Williams syndrome cannot live independent lives (American Academy of Pediatrics, 2001a). For example, Wendy Verougstraete lives in a group home for adults who are mentally retarded.

The verbal abilities of individuals with Williams syndrome are very distinct from those shown by individuals with Down syndrome, a type of mental retardation that we discussed in chapters 3 and 9 (Bellugi & Wang, 1996). On vocabulary tests, children with Williams syndrome show a liking for unusual words. When asked to name as many animals as they can think of in one minute, Williams children come up with creatures like ibex, chihuahua, saber-toothed tiger, weasel, crane, and newt.

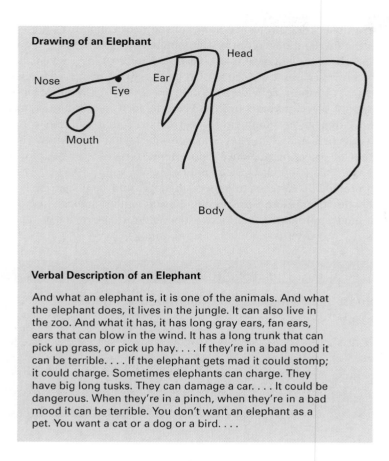

Drawing of an Elephant

Nose

Eye

Ear

Head

Mouth

Body

Verbal Description of an Elephant

And what an elephant is, it is one of the animals. And what the elephant does, it lives in the jungle. It can also live in the zoo. And what it has, it has long gray ears, fan ears, ears that can blow in the wind. It has a long trunk that can pick up grass, or pick up hay. . . . If they're in a bad mood it can be terrible. . . . If the elephant gets mad it could stomp; it could charge. Sometimes elephants can charge. They have big long tusks. They can damage a car. . . . It could be dangerous. When they're in a pinch, when they're in a bad mood it can be terrible. You don't want an elephant as a pet. You want a cat or a dog or a bird. . . .

FIGURE 10.4 Disparity in the Verbal and Motor Skills of an Individual with Williams Syndrome

Children with Down syndrome give simple examples like dog, cat, and mouse. When children with Williams syndrome tell stories, their voices come alive with drama and emotion, punctuating the dialogue with audience-attention grabbers like "Gadzooks" or "lo and behold!" By contrast, children with Down syndrome tell very simple stories with little emotion.

Aside from being an interesting genetic disorder, Williams syndrome offers insights into the normal development of thinking and language. In our society, verbal ability is generally associated with high intelligence. But Williams syndrome raises the possibility that thinking and language might not be so closely related. Williams disorder is due to a defective gene that seems to protect expressive verbal ability but not reading and many other cognitive skills (Schultz, Grelotti, & Pober, 2001). Thus, cases like Wendy Verougstraete's cast some doubt on the general categorization of intelligence as verbal ability and prompts the question, "What is the relation between thinking and language?"

There are essentially two basic and separate issues involved in exploring connections between language and cognition. The first is this: Is cognition necessary for language? Although some researchers have noted that certain aspects of language development typically follow mastery of selected cognitive skills in both normally developing children and children with mental retardation, it is not clear that language development depends upon any specific aspect of cognitive abilities (Lenneberg, 1967). Some experts believe that it is more likely that language and cognitive development occur in parallel but dissociated fashions (Cromer, 1987). Thus, according to research and experts' judgments, cognition is not necessary for language development.

The second issue is this: Is language necessary for (or important to) cognition? This issue is addressed by studies of deaf children. On a variety of thinking and problem-solving skills, deaf children perform at the same level as children of the same age who have no hearing problems. Some of the deaf children in these studies do not even have command of written or sign language (Furth, 1973). Thus, based on studies of deaf children, language is not necessary for cognitive development.

There is, however, some evidence of related activity in the cognitive and language worlds of children (de Villiers & de Villiers, 1999; Goldin-Meadow, 2000). Piaget's concept of object permanence has been the focus of some research that links cognitive and language development. Piaget believed that children come to learn about the world first and then they learn to label what they know. Infants may need a concept of object permanence before they start to use words for disappearance, such as *all gone* (Gopnik & Meltzoff, 1997).

In sum, thought likely can influence language, and language likely can influence thought. However, there is increasing evidence that language and thought are not part of a single, automated cognitive system, but rather evolved as separate modular, biologically prepared components of the mind.

Review and Reflect: Learning Goal 3

3 Evaluate how language and cognition are linked

REVIEW

- To what extent are language and cognition linked? Are they part of a single, automated cognitive system?

REFLECT

- Do children always think in words? Explain.

4 HOW LANGUAGE DEVELOPS

Infancy	Early Childhood	Middle and Late Childhood

In the thirteenth century, the Holy Roman Emperor Frederick II had a cruel idea. He wanted to know what language children would speak if no one talked to them. He selected several newborns and threatened their caregivers with death if they ever talked to the infants. Frederick never found out what language the children spoke because they all died. As we move forward in the twenty-first century, we are still curious about infants' development of language, although our experiments and observations are, to say the least, far more humane than the evil Frederick's.

Infancy

As infants develop, they reach a number of language milestones. What are some of these milestones?

Babbling and Other Vocalizations Babies actively produce sounds from birth onward. The purpose of these early communications is to attract attention from caregivers and others in the environment. In the first year, the production of sound and gesture goes through this sequence:

- *Crying.* This is present even at birth and can signal distress. However, as you will discover in chapter 11, there are different types of cries that can signal different things.
- *Cooing.* This first occurs at about 1 to 2 months. These are *oo* sounds such as *coo* or *goo* that usually occur during interaction with the caregiver.

- *Babbling.* This first occurs in the middle of the first year and includes strings of consonant-vowel combinations.
- *Gestures.* Infants start using gestures, such as showing and pointing, at about 8 to 12 months of age. Some examples of gestures are waving bye-bye, nodding one's head to mean "yes," showing an empty cup to want more milk, and pointing to a dog to draw attention to it.

Deaf infants, born to deaf parents who use sign language, babble with their hands and fingers at about the same age as hearing children babble vocally (Bloom, 1998). Such similarities in timing and structure between manual and vocal babbling indicate the presence of a unified language capacity that underlies signed and spoken language.

Recognizing Language Sounds   As we saw earlier, language is made up of basic sounds or phonemes. Patricia Kuhl's (1993, 2000) research reveals that, long before they actually begin to learn words, infants can sort through a number of spoken sounds in search of the ones that have meaning. Kuhl argues that from birth to about 4 months of age, infants are "universal linguists" who are capable of distinguishing each of the 150 sounds that make up human speech. But by about 6 months of age, they have started to specialize in the speech sounds of their native language (see figure 10.5).

By 8 to 9 months of age, comprehension is more noticeable. For example, babies look at a ball when their mothers say "ball." Language experts say that it is impossible to determine how many words babies understand at this point, but research with only slightly older children suggests that comprehension might outpace expression by a factor of as much as one hundred to one. Researchers have found that although some babies are slow in beginning to talk, comprehension is often about equal between the early and late talkers (Bates & Thal, 1991).

An important language task for infants is to fish out individual words from the nonstop stream of sound that comprises ordinary speech (Brownlee, 1998; Jusczyk, 2000). To do so, they have to find the boundaries between words, which is very difficult for infants because adults don't pause between words when they speak. Still, researchers have found that infants begin to detect word boundaries by 8 months of age. For example, in one study, 8-month-old infants listened at home to recorded stories that contained unusual words, such as *hornbill* and *python* (Jusczyk

> *I*nfants have learned the sounds of their native language by the age of six months.
> —PATRICIA KUHL,
> *Contemporary Psychologist,*
> *University of Washington*

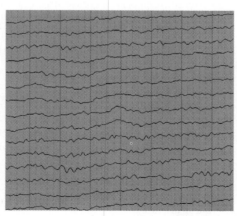

FIGURE 10.5 From Universal to Specialized Linguist

The people of the world speak thousands of languages and babies are born with the ability to learn any of them. In her research, Patricia Kuhl monitors infants' brain waves as they listen to different sounds. She has discovered that up to about the age of 7 months, infants can distinguish between two sounds in a language such as Mandarin Chinese—a subtle difference that English-speaking parents cannot detect. However, by 11 months of age, unused neuronal connections have begun to be pruned away. As infants' brains process a single language over time, they cease to be "universal linguists."

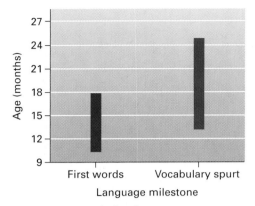

FIGURE 10.6 Variation in Language Milestones

Language Milestones
The Naming Explosion

& Hohne, 1997). Two weeks later, the researchers tested the infants with two lists of words, one made up of words they had already heard in the stories, the other of new, unusual words that did not appear in the stories. The infants listened to the familiar words for a second longer, on average, than to new words.

First Words Spoken vocabulary begins when the infant utters its first word, a milestone eagerly anticipated by every parent. This event usually occurs at about 10 to 15 months of age. However, as we saw earlier, long before babies say their first words, they have been communicating with their parents and making their intentions known, often by pointing, gesturing, and using their own special sounds. The appearance of first words is a continuation of this communication process, rather than a totally new event (Berko Gleason, 2002).

The infant's spoken vocabulary rapidly increases once the first word is spoken (Camaioni, 2002). The *vocabulary spurt* is a label that has been given to the rapid increase in an infant's vocabulary that begins to occur at approximately 18 months of age (Bloom, Lifter, & Broughton, 1985). The average 18-month-old can speak about 50 words, but by the age of 2 years can speak about 200 words.

A child's first words include those that name important people *(dada)*, familiar animals *(kitty)*, vehicles *(car)*, toys *(ball)*, food *(milk)*, body parts *(eye)*, clothes *(hat)*, household items *(clock)*, and greeting terms *(bye)*. These were the first words of babies 50 years ago. They are the first words of babies today. Children often express various intentions with their single words, so that "cookie" might mean "That's a cookie" or "I want a cookie."

There is variation in the timing at which children say their first word and in their vocabulary spurt (Bloom, 1998). Figure 10.6 shows the range for these two language milestones in 14 children. The average ages of these children at the time they reached these milestones were: first word (13 months) and vocabulary spurt (19 months). However, the individual children ranged from 10 to 17 months for their first word and from 13 to 25 months for their vocabulary spurt.

Children sometimes overextend or underextend the meanings of the words they use (Woodward & Markman, 1998). *Overextension* is the tendency of children to misuse words by extending one word's meaning to include objects that are not related to, or are inappropriate for, the word's meaning. For example, when children learn to say the word *dada* for "father," they often apply the word beyond the individual it was intended to represent, using it for other men, strangers, or boys. With time, such overextensions decrease and eventually disappear. *Underextension* occurs when children fail to use a word to name a relevant event or object. For example, a child might learn to use the word *boy* to describe a 5-year-old neighbor but not apply the word to a male infant or a 9-year-old male.

Two-Word Utterances By the time children are 18 to 24 months of age, they usually utter two-word statements. To convey meaning with two-word utterances, the child relies heavily on gesture, tone, and context. The wealth of meaning children can communicate with a two-word utterance includes these (Slobin, 1972):

Around the world, young children learn to speak in two-word utterances, in most cases at about 18 to 24 months of age. *What implications does this have for the biological basis of language?*

- Identification: "See doggie."
- Location: "Book there."
- Repetition: "More milk."
- Nonexistence: "Allgone thing."
- Negation: "Not wolf."
- Possession: "My candy."
- Attribution: "Big car."
- Agent-action: "Mama walk."

- Action-direct object: "Hit you."
- Action-indirect object: "Give Papa."
- Action-instrument: "Cut knife."
- Question: "Where ball?"

These examples are from children whose first language is English, German, Russian, Finnish, Turkish, or Samoan. Although these two-word sentences omit many parts of speech, they are remarkably succinct in conveying many messages. In fact, in every language, a child's first combinations of words have this economical quality. **Telegraphic speech** is the use of short and precise words without grammatical markers to communicate. Young children's two- and three-word utterances are characteristically telegraphic. As a result, articles, auxiliary verbs, and other connectives usually are omitted. Of course, telegraphic speech is not limited to two-word phrases. "Mommy give ice cream" and "Mommy give Tommy ice cream" also are examples of telegraphic speech. As children leave the two-word stage, they move rather quickly into three-, four-, and five-word combinations.

Age	Language Milestones
Birth	Crying
1 to 2 months	Cooing begins
6 months	Babbling begins
8 to 12 months	Use gestures, such as showing and pointing Comprehension of words appears
13 months	First word spoken
18 months	Vocabulary spurt starts
18 to 24 months	Uses two-word utterances Rapid expansion of understanding of words

FIGURE 10.7 Some Language Milestones in Infancy

Language Production and Language Comprehension A distinction is made between language production and language comprehension. *Language production* refers to the words and sentences that children use. *Language comprehension* refers to the language children understand. At about 8 to 12 months, infants often indicate their first word comprehension (Bloom, 1993). However, recall that they don't say their first word (language production) until an average of about 13 months. On the average, infants understand about 50 words at about 13 months but can't say this many words until about 18 months (Menyuk, Liebergott, & Schultz, 1995). Thus, in infancy, receptive vocabulary (words the child understands) considerably exceeds spoken vocabulary (words the child uses).

We have discussed a number of language milestones in infancy. Figure 10.7 summarizes the time at which infants typically reach these milestones.

Early Childhood

Young children's understanding sometimes gets way ahead of their speech. One 3-year-old, laughing with delight as an abrupt summer breeze stirred his hair and tickled his skin, commented, "I got breezed!" Many of the oddities of young children's language sound like mistakes to adult listeners. However, from the children's point of view, they are not mistakes. They represent the way young children perceive and understand their world at that point in their development. As children go through their early childhood years, their grasp of the rule systems that govern language increases.

During the preschool years, most children gradually become sensitive to the sounds of spoken words (National Research Council, 1999). They show this phonological awareness in such ways as noticing rhymes, enjoying poems, making up silly names for things by substituting one sound for another (such as *bubblegum, bubblebum, bubbleyum*), breaking long words into syllables or clapping along with each syllable in a phrase, and noticing that the pronunciations of several words (such as *dog, dark,* and *dusty*) all begin the same way.

Regarding morphology, there is clear evidence that, as they move beyond two-word utterances, children know morphological rules. Children begin using the plural and possessive forms of nouns (*dogs* and *dog's*); putting appropriate endings on verbs (*-s* when the subject is third-person singular, *-ed* for the past tense, and *-ing* for the present progressive tense); and using prepositions (*in* and *on*), articles (*a* and *the*), and various forms of the verb *to be* ("I *was going* to the store"). Some of the best evidence for morphological rules appears in the form of *overgeneralizations* of

telegraphic speech The use of short and precise words without grammatical markers to communicate; it characterizes young children's two- or three-word combinations.

This is a wug.

Now there is another one.
There are two of them.
There are two _____.

FIGURE 10.8 Stimuli in Berko's Study of Young Children's Understanding of Morphological Rules

In Jean Berko's (1958) study, young children were presented cards, such as this one with a "wug" on it. Then the children were asked to supply the missing word; in supplying the missing word, they had to say it correctly too. "Wugs" is the correct response here.

these rules. Have you ever heard a preschool child say "foots" instead of "feet" or "goed" instead of "went"? If you do not remember having heard such things, talk to some parents who have young children or to the young children themselves. You will hear some interesting errors in the use of morphological rule endings.

In a classic experiment, children's language researcher Jean Berko (1958) presented preschool and first-grade children with cards such as the one shown in figure 10.8. Children were asked to look at the card while the experimenter read the words on it aloud. Then the children were asked to supply the missing word. This might sound easy, but Berko was interested not just in the children's ability to recall the right word but also in their ability to say it "correctly" (with the ending that was dictated by morphological rules). *Wugs* would be the correct response for the card in figure 10.8. Although the children were not perfectly accurate, they were much better than chance would dictate. Moreover, they demonstrated their knowledge of morphological rules not only with the plural forms of nouns ("There are two wugs") but also with possessive forms of nouns and with the third-person singular and past-tense forms of verbs. And Berko's study demonstrated not only that the children relied on rules, but also that they had *abstracted* the rules from what they had heard and could apply them to novel situations. What makes Berko's study impressive is that all of the words were fictional; they were created especially for the experiment. Thus, the children could not base their responses on remembering past instances of hearing the words. It seems, instead, that they were forced to rely on *rules*. Their performance suggested that they did so successfully.

Similar evidence that children learn and actively apply rules can be found at the level of syntax (Budwig, 1993). After advancing beyond two-word utterances, the child speaks word sequences that show a growing mastery of complex rules for how words should be ordered. Consider the case of *wh-* questions: "Where is Daddy going?" and "What is that boy doing?" for example. To ask these questions properly, the child has to know two important differences between *wh-* questions and simple affirmative statements (for instance, "Daddy is going to work" and "That boy is waiting for the school bus"). First, a *wh-* word must be added at the beginning of the sentence. Second, the auxiliary verb must be "inverted"—that is, exchanged with the subject of the sentence. Young children learn quite early where to put the *wh-* word, but they take much longer to learn the auxiliary-inversion rule. Thus, it is common to hear preschool children asking such questions as "Where Daddy is going?" and "What that boy is doing?"

As children move into the elementary school years, they become skilled at using syntactical rules to construct lengthy and complex sentences. Utterances such as "The man who fixed the house went home" and "I don't want you to use my bike" are impressive demonstrations of how the child can use syntax to combine ideas into a single sentence. Just how a young child achieves the mastery of such complex rules, while at the same time may be struggling with relatively simple arithmetic rules, is a mystery we have yet to solve.

Regarding semantics, as children move beyond the two-word stage, their knowledge of meanings also rapidly advances (Bloom, 2002). The speaking vocabulary of a 6-year-old child ranges from 8,000 to 14,000 words (Carey, 1977; Clark, 2000). Assuming that word learning began when the child was 12 months old, this translates into a rate for new word meanings of 5 to 8 words a day between the ages of 1 and 6. After 5 years of word learning, the 6-year-old child does not slow down. According to some estimates, the average child of this age is moving along at the awe-inspiring rate of 22 words a day (Miller, 1981). How would you fare if you were given the task of learning 22 new words every day? It is truly miraculous how quickly children learn language (Fenson & others, 1994).

How do children's language abilities develop during early childhood?

Until recently, the wide variation in children's vocabulary was attributed to their inborn, hereditary abilities to learn language. However, in research conducted by Janellen Huttenlocher and her colleagues (Huttenlocher, Levine, & Vevea, 1998), the importance of environmental input in children's vocabulary development was revealed. They taped extensive conversations between 22 toddlers and their mothers during the children's typical daily activities. Tapings were carried out every two to four months, when the children were 16 to 26 months of age. They found a remarkable link between the size of a child's vocabulary and the talkativeness of her or his mother. The mothers varied as much as tenfold in how much they talked. The toddlers of the most talkative mother had a vocabulary more than four times the size of the vocabulary of the child with the quietest mother. Possibly this link might be due at least partly to genes for verbal ability shared by the mother and the child. However, Huttenlocher believes that is not the case, because the mothers in the study did not vary much in terms of their verbal IQs. Also, the children clearly were picking up what their mothers were saying, because the words each child used the most often mirrored those favored by the mother. In another recent study, 18- to 30-month-old African American children from more stimulating and responsive homes were reported to have larger vocabularies and longer utterances than those from less responsive homes (Roberts, Burchinal, & Durham, 1999).

In other research, socioeconomic differences in vocabulary have been documented. In one study, high-socioeconomic-status 2-year-old children used more different words in their spontaneous speech than middle-socioeconomic-status children, even when the size of the speech sample was held constant (Hoff-Ginsberg & Lerner, 1999). Researchers have found that this type of difference is due to differences in the quantity and nature of language input that children experience (Hoff-Ginsberg, 1999). This research provides similar conclusions to the research of Betty Hart and Todd Risley (1995) with welfare and professional families—that the socioeconomic status and the language environment experienced by the children strongly influence their language development.

In yet another study, the importance of the language environment in the home was documented for speech syntax, or grammar, an aspect thought to develop similarly in all children due to the shared mental machinery of language (Huttenlocher & Cymerman, 1999). The speech of 34 parents and their 4-year-old children was taped to determine the proportion of complex, multiclause sentences, such as "I am going to go to the store because we need to get some food," versus simple, single-clause ones, such as "Go to your room." A significant relation was found between the proportion of complex sentences spoken by the parents and the proportion of such sentences spoken by the children (both at home and at school). Although, as in the previous study, parents and children shared some language genes, the researchers concluded that a syntax gene alone is unlikely to account for the close similarity in the language use of the child and his or her parents. Such research demonstrates the important effect that early speech input can have on the development of a child's language skills.

Changes in pragmatics also characterize young children's language development. A 6-year-old is simply a much better conversationalist than a 2-year-old is. What are some of the improvements in pragmatics that are made in the preschool years? At about 3 years of age, children improve in their ability to talk about things that are not physically present—that is, they improve their command of an aspect of language known as *displacement*. Displacement is revealed in games of pretend. Although a 2-year-old might know the word *table*, he is unlikely to use this word to refer to an imaginary table that he pretends is standing in front of him. A child over 3 years of age is more likely to do so. There are large individual differences in preschoolers' talk about imaginary people and things.

At about 4 years of age, children develop a remarkable sensitivity to the needs of others in conversation. One way in which they show such sensitivity is their use of the articles *the* and *an* (or *a*). When adults tell a story or describe an event, they

> *C*hildren pick up words as pigeons peas.
>
> —JOHN RAY
> *English Naturalist,*
> *17th Century*

generally use *an* (or *a*) when they first refer to an animal or an object, and then use *the* when referring to it later (for example, "Two boys were walking through the jungle when *a* fierce lion appeared. *The* lion lunged at one boy while the other ran for cover."). Even 3-year-olds follow part of this rule (they consistently use the word *the* when referring to previously mentioned things). However, the use of the word *a* when something is initially mentioned develops more slowly. Although 5-year-old children follow this rule on some occasions, they fail to follow it on others.

Another pragmatic ability that appears around 4 to 5 years of age involves speech style. As adults, we have the ability to change our speech style in accordance with social situations and persons with whom we are speaking. An obvious example is that adults speak in a simpler way to a 2-year-old child than to an older child or to an adult. Interestingly, even 4-year-old children speak differently to a 2-year-old than to a same-aged peer (they "talk down" to the 2-year-old, using shorter utterance lengths). They also speak differently to an adult than to a same-aged peer, using more polite and formal language with the adult (Shatz & Gelman, 1973).

As we have just seen, language unfolds sequentially. Language expert Lois Bloom (1998) concluded that three sequential frameworks help us better understand early language development:

- The emergence of words and a basic vocabulary, which begins toward the end of the first year and continues through the second year
- The transition from saying one word at a time to combining words and phrases into simple sentences, which begins to take place toward the end of the second year
- The transition from simple sentences expressing a single proposition to complex sentences, which begins between 2 and 3 years of age and continues into the elementary school years

Middle and Late Childhood

Children gain new skills as they enter elementary school that make it possible for them to read and write. These skills include increasingly using language in a displaced manner, learning what a word is, and how to recognize and talk about sounds (Berko Gleason, 2002). They have to learn the alphabetic principle—that the alphabet letters represent sounds of the language. As children develop during middle and late childhood, changes take place in their vocabulary and grammar. Reading assumes a prominent role in their language world, as do writing and the importance of literacy. An increasingly important consideration is bilingualism.

Vocabulary and Grammar During middle and late childhood, a change occurs in the way children think about words. They become less tied to the actions and perceptual dimensions associated with words, and they become more analytical in their approach to words.

When asked to say the first thing that comes to mind when they hear a word, young children typically provide a word that often follows the word in a sentence. For example, when asked to respond to "dog," the young child may say "barks," or to the word "eat" say "lunch." At about 7 years of age, children begin to respond to a word that is the same part of speech as the stimulus word. For example, a child may now respond to the word "dog" with the word "cat" or "horse." To "eat," they might now say "drink." This is evidence that children now have begun to categorize their vocabulary by parts of speech (Berko Gleason, 2002).

An important point needs to be made about vocabulary development. Children who begin elementary school with a small vocabulary are at risk when it comes to learning to read (Berko Gleason, 2002).

Children make similar advances in grammar. The elementary school child's improvement in logical reasoning and analytical skills helps in the understanding of such constructions as the appropriate use of comparatives *(shorter, deeper)* and sub-junctives ("*If* I *were* president . . .").

Reading, Writing, and Literacy   In the twenty-first century, literacy (the ability to read and write) will become even more critical than it was in the previous century. The biggest increase in jobs and the best jobs will be in the professional and technical sectors. These jobs require good reading, writing, and communication skills.

A Developmental Model of Reading   One view of reading skills describes their development in five stages (Chall, 1979). The age boundaries are approximate and do not apply to every child. For example, some children learn to read before they enter first grade. Nonetheless, the stages convey a general sense of the developmental changes involved in learning to read.

- *Stage 0.* From birth to first grade, children master several prerequisites for reading. Many learn the left-to-right progression and order of reading, how to identify the letters of the alphabet, and how to write their names. Some learn to read words that appear on signs. As a result of TV shows like *Sesame Street* and attending preschool and kindergarten programs, many young children today develop greater knowledge about reading earlier than in the past.
- *Stage 1.* In first and second grades, many children learn to read. In doing so, they acquire the ability to sound out words (that is, translate letters into sounds and blend sounds into words). They also complete their learning of letter names and sounds during this stage.
- *Stage 2.* In second and third grades, children become more fluent at retrieving individual words and other reading skills. However, at this stage reading is still not used much for learning. The mechanical demands of learning to read are so taxing at this point that children have few resources left over to process the content.
- *Stage 3.* In fourth through eighth grade, children become increasingly able to obtain new information from print. In other words, they read to learn. They still have difficulty understanding information presented from multiple perspectives within the same story. When children don't learn to read, a downward spiral unfolds that leads to serious difficulties in many academic subjects.
- *Stage 4.* In the high school years, many students become fully competent readers. They develop the ability to understand material told from many different perspectives. This allows them to engage in sometimes more sophisticated discussions of literature, history, economics, and politics. It is no accident that great novels are not presented to students until high school, because understanding the novels requires advanced reading comprehension.

Approaches to Reading   What are some approaches to teaching children how to read? Education and language experts continue to debate how children should be taught to read. The debate focuses on the whole-language approach versus the basic-skills-and-phonetics approach:

- The **whole-language approach** stresses that reading instruction should parallel children's natural language learning. Reading materials should be whole and meaningful. That is, in early reading instruction, children should be presented with materials in their complete form, such as stories and poems. In this way, say the whole-language advocates, children learn to understand language's communicative function. In the whole-language approach, reading is integrated with other skills and subjects. Reading should be connected with listening and writing skills. Although there are variations in whole-language programs, most share the premise that reading should be integrated with other skills and subjects, such as science and social studies, and that it should focus on real-world,

whole-language approach An approach that stresses that reading instruction should parallel children's natural language learning. Reading materials should be whole and meaningful.

*C*hildren most at risk for reading difficulties in the first grade are those who began school with less verbal skill, less phonological awareness, less letter knowledge, and less familiarity with the basic purposes and mechanisms of reading.

—CATHERINE SNOW
Contemporary Psychologist,
Harvard University

basic-skills-and-phonetics approach An approach that emphasizes that reading instruction should teach phonetics and its basic rules for translating written symbols into sounds.

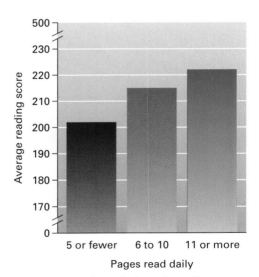

FIGURE 10.9 The Relation of Reading Achievement to Number of Pages Read Daily

In the recent analysis of reading in the fourth grade in the National Assessment of Educational Progress (2000), reading more pages daily in school and as part of homework assignments was related to higher scores on a reading test in which scores ranged from 0 to 500.

relevant material. Thus, a class might read newspapers, magazines, or books, then write about them and discuss them.

- The **basic-skills-and-phonetics approach** emphasizes that reading instruction should teach phonetics and its basic rules for translating written symbols into sounds. Early reading instruction should involve simplified materials. Only after they have learned phonological rules should children be given complex reading materials, such as books and poems. Advocates of the basic-skills-and-phonetics approach often point to low reading achievement scores occurring as an outgrowth of the recent emphasis on holistic, literature-based instruction and the consequent lack of attention to basic skills and phonetics.

Which approach is best? Researchers have found that children can benefit from both approaches. They have found strong evidence that the basic-skills-and-phonetics approach should be used in teaching children to read but that students also benefit from the whole-language approach of being immersed in a natural world of print (Fox & Hull, 2002; Heilman, Blair, & Rupley, 2002; Wilson & others, 2001).

These were the conclusions of the National Reading Panel (2000), which conducted a very comprehensive review of research on reading. The panel, which included a number of leading experts on reading, found that phonological awareness is especially effective when combined with letter training and is part of a total literacy program. The most effective phonological awareness training involves two main skills:

- *Blending,* which involves listening to a series of separate spoken sounds and blending them (such as /g/ /o/ = go).
- *Segmentation,* which consists of tapping out/counting out the sounds in a word, such as /g/ /o/ = go, which is two sounds.

Researchers also have found that phonological awareness improves when it is integrated with reading and writing, is simple, and is conducted in small groups rather than a whole class (Stahl, 2002). Other conclusions reached by the National Reading Panel (2000) suggest that children's reading benefits from guided oral reading (having children practice what they have learned by reading aloud with guidance and feedback) and applying reading comprehension strategies to guide and improve reading instruction.

Reading is like other important skills that children need to develop. It takes time and effort to become a proficient reader. In a national assessment, children in the fourth grade had higher scores on a national reading test when they read 11 or more pages daily for school and homework (National Assessment of Educational Progress, 2000) (see figure 10.9). Teachers who required students to read a great deal on a daily basis had students who were more proficient at reading than teachers who required little reading by their students.

In the cognitive approach, researchers have focused not so much on whether one teaching approach, such as whole language, is better than another, such as phonics. Rather, they have searched for the underlying cognitive processes that explain reading. The search has led to an interest in strategies, especially the strategies of expert readers compared with those of novice readers. Researchers have found that monitoring one's reading progress is an important strategy. Summarizing also is thought to be an important reading strategy.

Writing Children's writing emerges out of their early scribbles, which appear at around 2 to 3 years of age. In early childhood, children's motor skills usually develop to the point at which they can begin printing letters. Most 4-year-olds can print their first name. Five-year-olds can reproduce letters and copy several short words. As they develop their printing skills, they gradually learn to distinguish between the distinctive characteristics of letters, such as whether the lines are curved or straight, open or closed, and so on. Through the early elementary grades, many children continue to reverse letters such as *b* and *d* and *p* and *q*. At this point in development, if other aspects of the child's development are normal, these letter reversals are not a predictor of literacy problems.

As they begin to write, children often invent spellings of words. They usually do this by relying on the sounds of words they hear and using those as the basis of forming the words they write (Hughey & Slack, 2001).

Parents and teachers should encourage children's early writing but not be overly concerned about the proper formation of letters or correct conventional spelling. I (your author) once had a conference with my youngest daughter's first-grade teacher when she brought home a series of papers with her printing of words all marked up and sad faces drawn on the paper. Fortunately, the teacher agreed to reduce her criticism of Jennifer's print skills. Such printing errors should be viewed as a natural part of the child's growth. Spelling and printing corrections can be made selectively in positive ways and in the context of maintaining early writing and spontaneity.

Like becoming a good reader, becoming a good writer takes many years and lots of practice. Children should be given many writing opportunities in the elementary and secondary school years. As their language and cognitive skills improve with good instruction, so will their writing skills. For example, developing a more sophisticated understanding of syntax and grammar serves as an underpinning for better writing.

Cognitive skills such as organization and logical reasoning also provide an improved foundation for writing. Through the course of elementary, middle, and high school, students develop increasingly sophisticated methods of organizing their ideas. In early elementary school, they narrate and describe or write short poems. In late elementary and middle school, they move to projects such as book reports that combine narration with more reflection and analysis. In high school, they become more skilled at forms of exposition that do not depend on narrative structure.

Literacy Learning to both read and write should occur in a supportive environment in which children can generate a positive perception of themselves and develop a positive attitude toward both skills (Pressley, 2003; Schmidt & Mosenthal, 2001). The National Association for the Education of Young Children (NAEYC) (the leading organization of early childhood educators) believes that, unfortunately, in the push to develop a nation of literate people, too many preschool children are being subjected to rigid, formal prereading programs with expectations and experiences that are too advanced (Bredekamp & Rosegrant, 1996). Learning to read and continuing to read should be an enjoyable experience for children, not a stressful one. So should writing.

Teachers and parents should take time to read to children from a wide variety of poetry, fiction, and nonfiction (Pianta, Mambre, & Stuhlman, 2003). They should present models for children to emulate by using language appropriately, listening and responding to children's talk, and engaging in their own reading and writing (Mathes & Torgesen, 1999).

There is concern about the literacy of children who watch TV heavily. Recently the American Academy of Pediatrics (2001b) recommended that the number of hours that children under 2 years of age should be watching TV is zero. Why zero? Because children under 2 years of age who watch TV are not likely spending time in other preliteracy activities with the caregiver, such as book reading.

For children who have participated extensively in print-related interactions in their homes and communities, literacy often comes quickly in school. However, many children who have not participated extensively in lap reading and similar literacy events in the preschool years will take longer to develop literacy skills (Hiebert & Raphael, 1996). A positive school-home partnership provides teachers with opportunities to involve parents in helping children improve their literacy skills.

Review and Reflect: Learning Goal 4

4 **Describe how language develops in children**

REVIEW

- How does language develop in infancy?
- How does language develop in early childhood?
- How does language develop in middle and late childhood?

REFLECT

- How did you learn to read? Was it an effective approach? Explain.

5 BILINGUALISM

As many as 10 million children in the United States come from homes in which English is not the primary language. One major concern regarding such children is to find the best way to help them to succeed in a culture where English is dominant, in school and beyond (Garcia & Willis, 2001; Nieto, 2002).

Bilingual education, which has been the preferred strategy of schools for the last two decades, aims to teach academic subjects to immigrant children in their native languages (most often Spanish), and slowly and simultaneously teach them English (Garcia & others, 2002; Peregoy & Boyle, 2001). Bilingual education continues to be controversial.

Some states have passed laws declaring English to be their official language, eliminating the obligation for schools to teach minority children in the languages other than English. In California, voters repealed bilingual education altogether.

How long does it take language-minority students to learn English? Kenji Hakuta and his colleagues (2000) collected data on children in four different school districts to determine how long it takes language-minority students to speak and read English effectively. Speaking proficiency took three to five years, while reading proficiency took four to seven years.

A common fear is that early exposure to English will lead to children's loss of their native language. However, researchers have found that bilingualism (the ability to speak two languages) is not detrimental to the child's performance in either language (Hakuta, 2000; Hakuta & Garcia, 1989). In studies of Latino American children, there was no evidence of a loss in Spanish proficiency (productive language, receptive language, and language complexity) for children attending a bilingual preschool (Rodriguez & others, 1995; Winsler & others, 1999). Children who attended bilingual preschool, compared to those who remained at home, showed significant and parallel gains in both English and Spanish.

Researchers have also found that bilingualism has a positive effect on children's cognitive development. Children who are fluent in two languages perform better than their single language counterparts on tests of attentional control, concept formation, analytical reasoning, cognitive flexibility, and cognitive complexity (Bialystok, 1999, 2001). They also are more conscious of spoken and written language structure and better at noticing errors of grammar and meaning, skills that benefit their reading ability (Bialystok, 1997). To read about the work of a bilingual education teacher, see the Careers in Child Development insert.

Is it better to learn a second language as a child or as an adult? Adults make faster initial progress but their eventual success in the second language is not as great as children's. For example, in one study Chinese and Korean adults who immigrated to the United States at different ages were given a test of grammatical knowledge (Johnson & Newport, 1991). Those who began learning English from 3 to 7 years of age scored as well as native speakers on the test, but those whose arrived in the

Careers in Child Development

Salvador Tamayo, *Bilingual Education Teacher*

Salvador Tamayo teaches bilingual education in the fifth grade at Turner Elementary School in West Chicago. He recently was given a National Educator Award by the Milken Family Foundation for his work in bilingual education. Salvador especially is adept at integrating technology into his bilingual education classes. He and his students have created several award-winning websites about the West Chicago City Museum, the local Latino community, and the history of West Chicago. His students also developed an "I Want to Be an American Citizen" website to assist family and community members in preparing for the U.S. Citizenship Test. Salvador also teaches a bilingual education class at Wheaton College.

United States (and started learning English) in later childhood or adolescence had lower test scores (see figure 10.10). Children's ability to pronounce a second language with the correct accent also decreases with age, with an especially sharp decline occurring after the age of about 10 to 12 (Asher & Garcia, 1969). Adolescents and adults can become competent at a second language but this is a more difficult task than learning it as a child. However, these findings do not mean that there is a critical period for learning a second language. Indeed, in a recent study, no evidence was found of a critical period in which, beyond a certain age, learning a second language was severely hampered (Hakuta, Bialystok, & Wiley, in press). In this study, the more education individuals had experienced, the more readily they learned a second language.

The United States is one of the few countries in the world in which most students graduate from high school knowing only their own language. For example, in Russia schools have 10 grades, called forms, which roughly correspond to the 12 grades in American schools. Children begin school at age 7 in Russia and begin learning English in the third form. Because of the emphasis on teaching English in Russian schools, most Russian citizens under the age of 40 today are bilingual, able to speak at least some English in addition to their native language.

Bilingual Education

Bilingualism and Bilingual Education

Multilingual Multicultural Research

Improving Schooling for Language-Minority Children: A Research Agenda

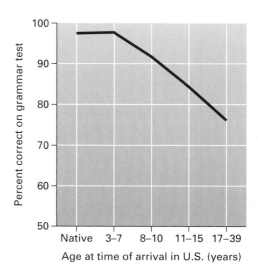

FIGURE 10.10 Grammar Proficiency and Age at Arrival in the United States

In one study, ten years after arriving in the United States, individuals from China and Korea took a grammar test (Johnson & Newport, 1991). People who arrived before the age of 8 had a better grasp of grammar than those who arrived later.

Review and Reflect: Learning Goal 5

5 Summarize what is known about bilingualism and bilingual education

REVIEW

- What is bilingualism, and how does it affect language development? Is it easier to learn a second language as a child or an adolescent?

REFLECT

- Should children in the United States be required to learn more than one language? Explain.

Reach Your Learning Goals

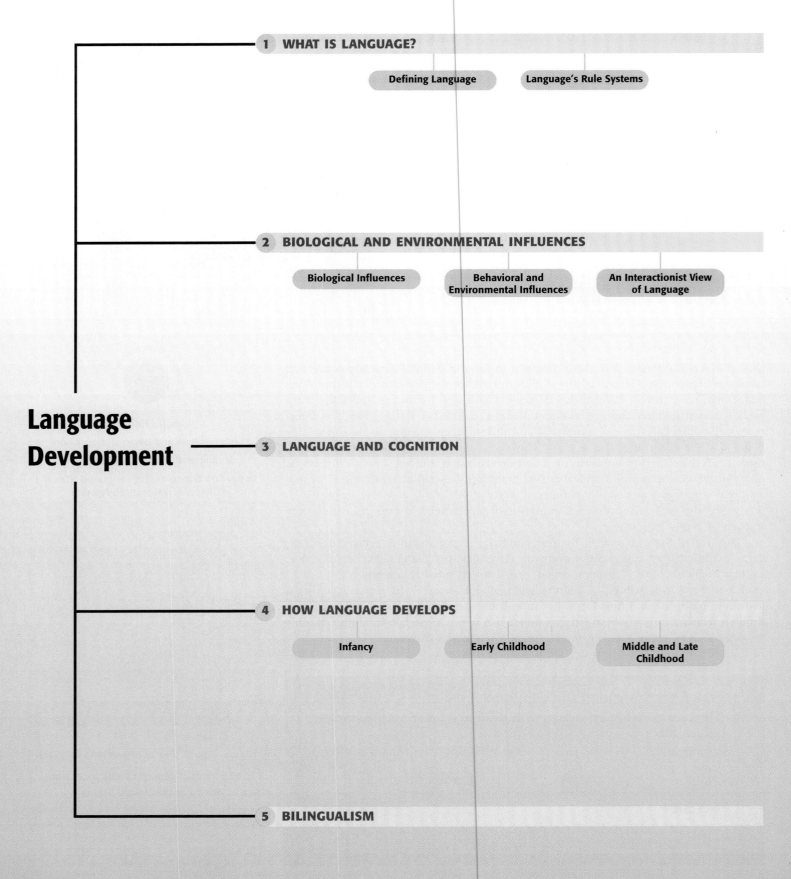

Language Development

1 WHAT IS LANGUAGE?

- Defining Language
- Language's Rule Systems

2 BIOLOGICAL AND ENVIRONMENTAL INFLUENCES

- Biological Influences
- Behavioral and Environmental Influences
- An Interactionist View of Language

3 LANGUAGE AND COGNITION

4 HOW LANGUAGE DEVELOPS

- Infancy
- Early Childhood
- Middle and Late Childhood

5 BILINGUALISM

Summary

1 Define language and describe its rule systems

- Language is a form of communication, whether spontaneous, written, or signed, that is based on a system of symbols. Language consists of all the words used by a community and the rules for varying and combining them. Infinite generativity is the ability to produce an endless number of meaningful sentences using a finite set of words and rules.
- Phonology is a language's sound system. Morphology refers to the meaningful units involved in word formation. Syntax is the way words are combined to form acceptable phrases and sentences. Semantics involves the meaning of words and sentences. Pragmatics is the use of appropriate conversation and knowledge underlying the use of language in context.

2 Discuss the biological and environmental aspects of language

- In evolution, language clearly gave humans an enormous edge over other animals and increased their chance of survival. A substantial portion of language processing occurs in the brain's left hemisphere, with Broca's area and Wernicke's area being important left-hemisphere locations. Chomsky's concept of a language acquisition device (LAD) flows from the evidence about the biological foundations of language. The stunted growth of "wild children" such as Genie support the concept of a critical period in language acquisition. However, the idea that there is a critical period in language development is still controversial.
- The behavioral view—that language reinforcement and imitation are the factors in language acquisition—has not been supported. In the environmental view, among the ways that adults teach language to children are child-directed speech, recasting, expanding, and labeling. Parents should talk extensively with an infant, especially about what the baby is attending to. Talk primarily should be live talk, not mechanical talk.
- One interactionist view is that both Chomsky's LAD and Bruner's LASS are involved in language acquisition. An interactionist view emphasizes the contributions of both biology and experience in language.

3 Evaluate how language and cognition are linked

- Two basic and separate issues are these: (1) Is cognition necessary for language? (2) Is language necessary for cognition? At an extreme, the answer likely is no to these questions, but there is evidence of linkages between language and cogni-

tion. There is increasing evidence that language and thought are not part of a single, automated cognitive system, but rather evolved as separate, modular, biological prepared components of the mind. The disorder of Williams syndrome supports this modular view.

4 Describe how language develops in children

- Among the milestones in infant language development are crying (birth), cooing (1 to 2 months), specializing in the speech sounds of one's native language (6 months), using gestures (8 to 12 months), comprehension of words (8 to 12 months), first word spoken (10 to 15 months), vocabulary spurt (18 months), rapid expansion of understanding words (18 to 24 months), and two-word utterances (18 to 24 months).
- Advances in phonology, morphology, syntax, semantics, and pragmatics continue in early childhood. Three important sequential frameworks of infancy and early childhood are: (1) the emergence of words and basic vocabulary (toward end of first year and through second year); (2) the transition to combining words and phrases into simple sentences (end of second year); and (3) the transition to complex sentences (begins at 2 or 3 years and continues through the elementary school years).
- In middle and late childhood, children become more analytical and logical in their approach to words and grammar. Chall's model proposes five stages in reading, ranging from birth/first grade to high school. Current debate involving how to teach children to read focuses on the whole-language approach versus the basic-skills-and-phonics approach. Many experts today recommend a balance of these two approaches in teaching children to read. Children's writing follows a developmental timetable, emerging out of scribbling. Advances in children's language and cognitive development provide the underpinnings for improved writing. Literacy involves learning to read and write; this should occur in a supportive atmosphere.

5 Summarize what is known about bilingualism and bilingual education

- Bilingual education aims to teach academic subjects to immigrant children in their native languages (most often in Spanish) while gradually adding English instruction. Researchers have found that bilingualism does not interfere with performance in either language. Success in learning a second language is greater in childhood than in adolescence.

Key Terms

language 314
infinite generativity 315
phonology 315
morphology 315
syntax 316
semantics 316

pragmatics 316
aphasia 318
Broca's area 318
Wernicke's area 318
language acquisition device
    (LAD) 319

critical period 319
child-directed speech 321
recasting 322
expanding 322
labeling 322

telegraphic speech 329
whole-language approach 333
basic-skills-and-phonetics
    approach 334

Key People

Helen Keller 314
Paul Broca 318
Noam Chomsky 319

Eric Lenneberg 319
Roger Brown 320
Jerome Bruner 322

Naomi Baron 323
Patricia Kuhl 327
Jean Berko 330

Janellen Huttenlocher 331
Lois Bloom 332
Catherine Snow 334

Taking It to the Net

1. Clarissa wants to be a speech therapist. In her child development class, she learned that Vygotsky believed that linguistic and cognitive development go hand in hand after a certain age. She wants to know more about his theory, because it might give her insight into children's language problems.

2. Todd is working in a day-care center after school. He notices that there is a wide range in the children's use of language, even within age groups. He wonders if there are guidelines that can indicate whether a child is delayed in language development.

3. Jared is concerned because his 7-year-old son, Damion, does not like to read. Damion's second-grade teacher says he is about average for his age, but she has to prod him to do his reading assignments at school. What can Jared do to help Damion become a better reader?

Connect to **www.mhhe.com/santrockcd10** to research the answers and complete these exercises.

E-Learning Tools

To help you master the material in this chapter, you'll find a number of valuable study tools on the Student CD-ROM that accompanies this book. Also visit the Online Learning Center for *Child Development*, tenth edition (**www.mhhe.com/santrockcd10**) where you'll find these additional resources:

- Build your decision-making skills by trying your hand at the parenting, nursing, and education "Scenarios" on the Online Learning Center.

Socioemotional Development

I am what I hope and give.

—ERIK ERIKSON
European-Born American Psychotherapist, 20th Century

As children develop, they need the meeting eyes of love. They split the universe into two halves: "me" and "not me." They juggle the need to curb their own will with becoming what they can will freely. They also want to fly but discover that first they have to learn to stand and walk and climb and dance. As they become adolescents, they try on one face after another, looking for a face of their own. In Section 4 you will read four chapters: "Emotional Development" (chapter 11), "The Self and Identity" (chapter 12), "Gender" (chapter 13), and "Moral Development" (chapter 14).

Blossoms are scattered by the wind
And the wind cares noth-ing, but
The Blossoms of the heart,
No wind can touch.

—YOUSHIDA KENKO
Buddhist Monk, 14th Century

Emotional Development

Chapter Outline		Learning Goals
EXPLORING EMOTION	**1**	**Discuss basic aspects of emotion**
Defining Emotion		
Functionalism in Emotion		
Relational Emotion		
Regulation of Emotion		
Emotional Competence		
DEVELOPMENT OF EMOTION	**2**	**Describe the development of emotion**
Infancy		
Early Childhood		
Middle and Late Childhood		
Adolescence		
EMOTIONAL PROBLEMS, STRESS, AND COPING	**3**	**Summarize the nature of depression, suicide, stress, and coping**
Depression		
Suicide		
Stress and Coping		
TEMPERAMENT	**4**	**Characterize temperament**
Defining and Classifying Temperament		
Goodness of Fit		
Developmental Connections and Contexts		
Gender, Culture, and Temperament		
Parenting and the Child's Temperament		
ATTACHMENT	**5**	**Explain attachment and its development**
What Is Attachment?		
Individual Differences		
Caregiving Styles and Attachment Classification		
Attachment, Temperament, and the Wider Social World		
Fathers as Caregivers of Infants		
Child Care		

The Story of Tom's Fathering

Many fathers are spending more time with their infants today than in the past.

Tom is a 1-year-old infant who is being reared by his father during the day. His mother works full-time at her job away from home, and his father is a writer who works at home; they prefer this arrangement over putting Tom in day care. Tom's father is doing a great job of caring for him. Tom's father keeps Tom nearby while he is writing and spends lots of time talking to him and playing with him. From their interactions, it is clear that they genuinely enjoy each other.

Tom's father is a far cry from the emotionally distant, conformist, traditional-gender-role fathers of the 1950s. He looks to the future and imagines the Little League games Tom will play in and the many other activities he can enjoy with Tom. Remembering how little time his own father spent with him, he is dedicated to making sure that Tom has an involved, nurturing experience with his father.

When Tom's mother comes home in the evening, she spends considerable time with him. Tom shows a positive attachment to both his mother and his father. His parents have cooperated and have successfully juggled their careers and work schedules to provide 1-year-old Tom with excellent child care. Later in this chapter we will explore many aspects of fathering and child care. To begin, though, we will examine the nature of children's emotions.

1 EXPLORING EMOTION

- **Defining Emotion**
- **Relational Emotion**
- **Emotional Competence**
- **Functionalism in Emotion**
- **Regulation of Emotion**

Emotion plays a powerful role in children's development (Bruce, Olen, & Jensen, 1999). But just what is emotion?

Defining Emotion

Defining *emotion* is difficult because it is not easy to tell when a child or an adult is in an emotional state. Is a child in an emotional state when her heart beats fast, her palms sweat, and her stomach churns? Or is she in an emotional state when she smiles or grimaces? The body and face play important roles in understanding children's emotion. However, psychologists debate how important each is in determining whether a child is in an emotional state. For our purposes, we will define **emotion** as feeling, or affect, that can involve physiological arousal (a fast heartbeat, for example), conscious experience (thinking about being in love with someone, for example), and behavioral expression (a smile or grimace, for example). Psychologists debate which of these components is the most important aspect of emotion and how they mix to produce emotional experiences (Izard, 2000).

emotion Feeling, or affect, that can involve physiological arousal, conscious experience, and behavioral expression.

When we think about children's emotions, a few dramatic feelings, such as rage, fear, and glorious joy, usually spring to mind. But emotions can be subtle as well—the feeling a mother has when she holds her baby, the mild irritation of boredom, or the uneasiness of being in a new situation.

Psychologists classify emotions in many different ways, but one characteristic of almost all classifications is the designation of an emotion as positive or negative:

- **Positive affectivity (PA)** refers to the range of positive emotions, from high energy, enthusiasm, and excitement to being calm, quiet, and withdrawn.
- **Negative affectivity (NA)** refers to the range emotions that are negatively toned, such as anxiety, anger, guilt, and sadness.

Functionalism in Emotion

A number of developmentalists view the nature of emotion differently today than their predecessors did (Campos, 1994, 2001). The new view proposes that emotions arise from individuals' attempts to adapt to specific contextual demands with the result that a person's emotional responses cannot be separated from the situations in which they are evoked (Halle, 2003). In this sense, emotions are viewed as relational rather than as strictly intrapsychic phenenomena. In many instances, emotions are elicited in interpersonal contexts. Thus, emotional expressions serve the important functions of signaling to others how one feels, regulating one's own behavior, and playing pivotal roles in social exchange.

In the functionalist view, emotions derive their meaning from the individual's goals. Goals are related to emotion in a variety of ways. Regardless of what the goal is, an individual who overcomes an obstacle to attain a goal experiences happiness. By contrast, a person who must relinquish a goal as unattainable experiences sadness. And a person who faces difficult obstacles in pursuing a goal often experiences anger. The specific nature of the goal can affect the experience of a given emotion. For example, the avoidance of threat is linked with fear, the desire to atone is related to guilt, and the wish to avoid the scrutiny of others is associated with shame. Many of the functionalists focus their work on goal-related emotions.

Relational Emotion

In our description of the functionalist view of emotion, we underscored the links between emotion, relationships, and development. Let's explore the role of emotion in parent-child and peer relationships.

Parent-Child Relationships
Expressions of emotion are the first language with which parents and infants communicate before the infant acquires speech (Maccoby, 1992). Infants react to their parents' facial expressions and tone of voice. In return, parents "read" what the infant is trying to communicate, responding appropriately when their infants are either distressed or happy.

The initial aspects of infant attachment to parents are based on affectively toned interchanges, as when an infant cries and the caregiver sensitively responds. By the end of the first year, a mother's facial expression—either smiling or fearful—influences whether an infant will explore an unfamiliar environment. And, when children hear their parents quarreling, they often react with distressed facial expressions and inhibited play (Cummings, 1987). Exceptionally well-functioning families often include humor in their interactions, sometimes making each other laugh and developing light, pleasant mood states to defuse conflicts. When a positive mood has been induced in the child, the child is more likely to comply with a parent's directions.

Infant and adult affective communicative capacities make possible coordinated infant-adult interactions. The face-to-face interactions of even 3-month-old infants

Exploring Emotion
**International Society
for Research on Emotions**

positive affectivity (PA) The range of positive emotions, from high energy, enthusiasm, and excitement to being calm, quiet, and withdrawn.

negative affectivity (NA) The range of negatively toned emotions, such as anxiety, anger, guilt, and sadness.

and their adults are bidirectional (mutually regulated). That is, infants modify their affective displays and behaviors on the basis of their appreciation of their parents' affective displays and behaviors. This coordination has led to characterizations of the mother-infant interaction as "reciprocal" or "synchronous." These terms are attempts to capture the quality of interaction when all is going well.

Parents differ in how they talk with their children about emotion (Halle, 2003). In this regard, parents can be described as having an *emotion-coaching* or an *emotion-dismissing* philosophy. Emotion-coaching parents monitor their children's emotions, view their children's negative emotions as opportunities for teaching, assist them in verbally labeling emotions, and coach them in how to effectively deal with emotions. In contrast, emotion-dismissing parents view their role as needing to deny, ignore, or change negative emotions. Researchers have found that emotion-coaching parents showed less hostility in their marital relationship, and their marriage was less likely to end in a divorce (Gottman, Katz, & Hooven, 1997). When interacting with their children, they were less rejecting, used more scaffolding and praise, and were more nurturant than were emotion-dismissing parents. The children of emotion-coaching parents were better at physiologically soothing themselves when they got upset, were better at regulating their negative affect, could focus their attention better, and had fewer behavior problems than the children of emotion-dismissing parents.

Peer Relationships Emotions play a strong role in whether a child's peer relationships are successful or not. Emotional regulation is an important aspect of getting along with peers. Moody and emotionally negative children experience greater rejection by their peers, whereas emotionally positive children are more popular (Stocker & Dunn, 1990).

In one study conducted in the natural context of young children's everyday peer interactions, self-regulation of emotion enhanced children's social competence (Fabes & others, 1999). Children who made an effort to control their emotional responses were more likely to respond in socially competent ways in an emotionally provocative peer situation (as when a peer made a hostile comment or took something away from the child). In sum, the ability to modulate and control one's emotions is an important self-regulatory skill that benefits children in their relationships with peers.

Regulation of Emotion

As we just saw, self-regulation of emotion plays an important role in peer relationships. Indeed, the ability to control one's emotions is increasingly recognized as a key dimension of development (Graziano & Tobin, 2003; Mischel & Mendoza-Denton, 2003). Nancy Eisenberg (1998) described these developmental trends in regulating emotion:

- With increasing age in infancy and early childhood, regulation of emotion shifts gradually from external sources in the world (for example, parents) to self-initiated, internal resources. Caregivers soothe young children, manage young children's emotion by choosing the contexts in which they behave, and provide children with information (facial cues, narratives, and so on) to help them interpret events. With age and advances in cognitive development, children are better equipped to manage emotion themselves. For example, older children might minimize the escalation of negative emotion in an interpersonal conflict by monitoring their facial expressions (for example, avoiding sneering or looks of contempt).
- Cognitive strategies for regulating emotions, such as thinking about situations in a positive light, cognitive avoidance, and the ability to shift the focus of one's attention, increase with age.
- With greater maturity, children develop greater capacity to modulate their emotional arousal (such as controlling angry outbursts).

- With age, individuals become more adept at selecting and managing situations and relationships in ways that minimize negative emotion.
- With age, children become more capable of selecting effective ways to cope with stress.

In thinking about these developmental trends in emotional regulation, keep in mind that there are wide individual variations in children's ability to modulate their emotions and, indeed, a prominent feature of adolescents with problems is that they often have difficulty managing their emotions.

Emotional Competence

In chapter 9, we briefly described the concept of emotional intelligence. Here we will examine a closely related concept, emotional competence, that focuses on the adaptive nature of emotional experience. ◀ **page 293** Carolyn Saarni (1999, 2000) believes that becoming emotionally competent involves developing a number of skills in social contexts:

SKILL	EXAMPLE
• *Awareness of one's emotional states*	Being able to differentiate whether one feels sad or anxious
• *Discerning others' emotions*	Understanding when another person is sad rather than afraid
• *Using the vocabulary of emotion terms in socially and culturally appropriate ways*	Appropriately describing a social situation in one's culture when a person is feeling distress
• *Empathic and sympathetic sensitivity to others' emotional experiences*	Being sensitive to others when they are feeling distressed
• *Understanding that inner emotional states do not have to correspond to outer expressions; with maturity, understanding how one's emotionally expressive behavior may impact others and taking this into account in the way one presents oneself*	Recognizing that one can feel very angry yet manage one's emotional expression so that it appears more neutral
• *Adaptively coping with negative emotions by using self-regulatory strategies that reduce the intensity or duration of such emotional states*	Reducing anger by walking away from an aversive situation and engaging in an activity that takes one's mind off of the aversive situation
• *Awareness that the expression of emotions plays a major role in the nature of relationships*	Knowing that expressing anger toward a friend on a regular basis is likely to harm the friendship
• *Viewing oneself overall as feeling the way one wants to feel*	Wanting to feel that one can cope effectively with the stress in one's life and feeling that one is successfully doing this

As children acquire these emotional competence skills in a variety of contexts, they are more likely to effectively manage their emotions (which is crucial for navigating through interpersonal interchanges), develop a sense of well-being, and become resilient in the face of stressful circumstances (Denham & others, 2003; Saarni, 1999). The skills of emotional competence are learned in contexts that are characterized by mutual responsivity and respect. The skills also change developmentally. In young children, they are more concrete and situationally bound, and less likely to be articulated by the child. By adolescence, they are more integrated with social competencies and issues of identity, moral character, and aspirations (Saarni, 2000). As we discuss various aspects of emotion in the remainder of the chapter, we will revisit many of these emotional competence skills.

2 DEVELOPMENT OF EMOTION

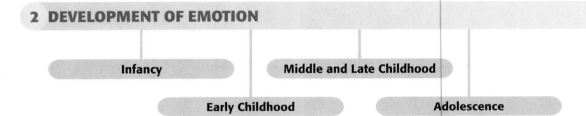

- Infancy
- Early Childhood
- Middle and Late Childhood
- Adolescence

In our discussion of the self-regulation of emotion, we described some important developmental trends. Let's further explore some of the key developmental changes in emotion in infancy, early childhood, middle/late childhood, and adolescence.

Infancy

What functions do an infant's cries serve? When do infants begin to smile? What is the developmental timetable for the appearance of emotions?

Early Developmental Changes in Emotion   In research on emotional development, two broad types of emotions are studied (Lewis, 2002):

- **Primary emotions,** those that are present in humans and other animals. The primary emotions include surprise, interest, joy, anger, sadness, fear, and disgust. They appear in the first six to eight months of life.
- **Self-conscious emotions,** those that require cognition, especially consciousness. The self-conscious emotions include empathy, jealousy, and embarrassment, which first appear at about 1 1/2 years (in the middle of the second year of life following the emergence of consciousness) and pride, shame, and guilt, which first appear at about 2 1/2 years of age (in the middle of the third year of life). In developing this second set of self-conscious emotions (referred to as *self-conscious evaluative emotions*), children acquire and are able to use societal standards and rules to evaluate their behavior.

Figure 11.1 shows the age at which various emotions first appear (Lewis, 2002).

primary emotions Emotions that are present in humans and other animals, including surprise, interest, joy, anger, sadness, fear, and disgust; appear in first six to eight months of life.

self-conscious emotions Emotions that require cognition, especially consciousness, including empathy, jealousy, embarrassment, pride, shame, and guilt; appear for the first time from the middle of the second year through the middle of the third year of life.

Crying Crying is the most important mechanism newborns have for communicating with their world. This is true for the first cry, which tells the mother and doctor the baby's lungs have filled with air. Cries also may tell physicians and researchers something about the central nervous system. Babies don't have just one type of cry. They have at least three:

- The **basic cry** is a rhythmic pattern that usually consists of a cry, followed by a briefer silence, then a shorter inspiratory whistle that is somewhat higher in pitch than the main cry, then another brief rest before the next cry. Some infancy experts believe that hunger is one of the conditions that incites the basic cry.
- The **anger cry** is a variation of the basic cry. However, in the anger cry, which is associated with exasperation or rage, more excess air is forced through the vocal cords.
- The **pain cry,** which is stimulated by high-intensity stimuli, differs from other types of cries. It is characterized by the sudden appearance of loud crying without preliminary moaning and a long initial cry followed by an extended holding of breath.

Most parents, and adults in general, can determine whether an infant's cries signify anger or pain (Zeskind, Klein, & Marshall, 1992). Parents also can distinguish the cries of their own baby better than those of a strange baby.

To soothe or not to soothe—should a crying baby be given attention and soothed, or does this spoil the infant? Many years ago, famous behaviorist John Watson (1928) argued that parents spend too much time responding to infant crying. As a consequence, he said, parents are actually rewarding infant crying and increasing its incidence. By contrast, more recently, infancy experts Mary Ainsworth (1979) and John Bowlby (1989) stressed that you can't respond too much to infant crying in the first year of life. They believe that the caregiver's quick, comforting response to the infant's cries is an important ingredient in the development of secure attachment. In one of Ainsworth's studies, the mothers who responded quickly to their infants when they cried at 3 months of age had infants who cried less later in the first year of life (Bell & Ainsworth, 1972). On the other hand, behaviorist Jacob Gerwirtz (1977) found that a caregiver's quick, soothing response to crying increased subsequent crying.

First appearance	Emotion
Primary Emotions	
3 months	Joy Sadness Disgust
2 to 6 months	Anger
First 6 months	Surprise
6 to 8 months	Fear (peaks at 18 months)
Self-Conscious Emotions	
1½ to 2 years	Empathy Jealousy Embarrassment
2½ years	Pride Shame Guilt

FIGURE 11.1 The First Appearance of Different Emotions

Infant Crying
Learning from Infants' Cries
Exploring Infant Crying

What are some developmental changes in emotion during infancy? What are some different types of crying that infants display?

basic cry A rhythmic pattern usually consisting of a cry, a briefer silence, a shorter inspiratory whistle that is higher pitched than the main cry, and then a brief rest before the next cry.

anger cry A cry similar to the basic cry, with more excess air forced through the vocal chords (associated with exasperation or rage).

pain cry A sudden appearance of loud crying without preliminary moaning and a long initial cry followed by an extended period of breath holding.

*H*e who binds himself to joy
Does the winged life destroy;
But he who kisses the joy as it
Flies lives in eternity's sun rise.
—WILLIAM BLAKE
English Poet, 19th Century

reflexive smile A smile that does not occur in response to external stimuli. It appears during the month after birth, usually during irregular patterns of sleep, not when the infant is in an alert state.

social smile A smile in response to an external stimulus, which, early in development, typically is in response to a face.

stranger anxiety An infant's fear and wariness of strangers; it tends to appear in the second half of the first year of life.

separation protest An infant's distress at being separated from his or her caregiver.

Controversy, then, still swirls about the issue of whether parents should respond to an infant's cries (Lewis & Ramsay, 1999). However, developmentalists increasingly argue that an infant cannot be spoiled in the first year of life, which suggests that parents should soothe a crying infant rather than be unresponsive; in this manner, infants will likely develop a sense of trust and secure attachment to the caregiver in the first year of life.

Smiling Smiling is another important communicative affective behavior of the infant. Two types of smiling can be distinguished in infants—reflexive and social:

- A **reflexive smile** does not occur in response to external stimuli. It appears during the first month after birth, usually during irregular patterns of sleep, not when the infant is in an alert state.
- A **social smile** occurs in response to an external stimulus, which, early in development, is typically a face. Social smiling does not occur until 6 to 10 weeks of age (Emde, Gaensbauer, & Harmon, 1976), although some researchers believe that infants grin in response to voices as early as 3 weeks of age (Sroufe & Waters, 1976). The power of the infant's smiles was appropriately captured by British attachment theorist John Bowlby (1969): "Can we doubt that the more and better an infant smiles the better he is loved and cared for? It is fortunate for their survival that babies are so designed by nature that they beguile and enslave mothers."

Fear The most frequent expression of an infant's fear involves **stranger anxiety,** in which an infant shows a fear and wariness of strangers. This tends to appear in the second half of the first year of life. There are individual variations in stranger anxiety, with not all infants showing distress when they encounter a stranger. Stranger anxiety usually emerges gradually, first appearing at about 6 months of age in the form of wary reactions. By age 9 months, the fear of strangers is often more intense and continues to escalate through the infant's first birthday (Emde, Gaensbauer, & Harmon, 1976).

A number of factors can influence whether an infant shows stranger anxiety, including the social context and the characteristics of the stranger. In terms of the social context, infants show less stranger anxiety when they are in familiar settings. For example, in one study, 10-month-olds showed little stranger anxiety when they met a stranger in their own home but much greater fear when they encountered a stranger in a research laboratory (Sroufe, Waters, & Matas, 1974). Also, infants show less stranger anxiety when they are sitting on their mother's lap than when placed in an infant seat several feet away from their mother (Bohlin & Hagekull, 1993). Thus, it appears that, when infants have a sense of security, they are less likely to show stranger anxiety.

Who the stranger is and how the stranger behaves also influence stranger anxiety in infants. Infants are less fearful of child strangers than adult strangers. They also are less fearful of friendly, outgoing, smiling strangers than of passive, unsmiling strangers (Bretherton, Stolberg, & Kreye, 1981).

Separation protest is a reflection of the infant's fear of being separated from his or her caregiver. Separation protest tends to peak at about 15 months in U.S. infants. Notice in figure 11.2 that in one study, separation protest peaked at about 13 to 15 months in four different cultures (Kagan, Kearsley, & Zelazo, 1978). Although the percentage of infants who engaged in separation protest varied across cultures, the infants reached a peak of protest at about the same age—just before the middle of the second year of life.

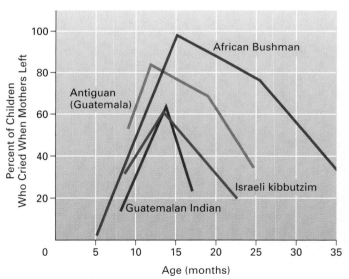

FIGURE 11.2 Separation Protest in Four Cultures

Note that separation protest peaked at about the same time in all four cultures in this study (13 to 15 months of age). However, a higher percentage (100 percent) of infants in an African Bushman culture engaged in separation protest compared to only about 60 percent of infants in Guatemalan Indian and Israeli kibbutzim cultures.

Social Referencing **Social referencing** involves "reading" emotional cues in others to help determine how to act in a particular situation. The development of social referencing helps infants to interpret ambiguous situations more accurately, as when they encounter a stranger and need to know whether to fear the person (Mumme, Fernald, & Herrera, 1996). Infants especially become better at social referencing in the second year of life. In their second year, they have a tendency to "check" with their mother before they act. That is, they look at her to see if she is happy, angry, or fearful. For example, in one study, 14- to 22-month-old infants were more likely to look at their mother's face as a source of information for how to act in a situation than were 6- to 9-month-old infants (Walden, 1991).

Emotional Regulation and Coping Earlier in the chapter, we discussed the importance of emotional regulation in peer relationships and developmental trends in emotional regulation across the childhood years. Here we focus more in depth on the nature of emotional regulation in infancy.

Emotional regulation consists of effectively managing arousal to adapt and reach a goal. Arousal involves a state of alertness or activation, which can reach levels that are too high for effective functioning. Crying and anger are two emotions that often require regulation.

During the first year of life, the infant gradually develops an ability to inhibit, or minimize, the intensity and duration of emotional reactions (Eisenberg, 2001). At the same time, infants acquire a greater diversity of emotional responses. Examples of early emotional regulation are infants' soothing themselves by sucking or by their withdrawing from excessive stimulation. Equally important is caregivers' assisting infants in learning how to regulate their emotions by attending to their distress and providing them with comfort.

From early in infancy, babies put their thumbs in their mouth as a self-soothing strategy. In the early part of infancy, infants mainly depend on caregivers to help them soothe their emotions, as when a caregiver rocks an infant to sleep, sings lullabies to the infant, gently strokes the infant, and so on. Many developmentalists believe it is a good strategy for a caregiver to soothe an infant before the infant gets into an intense, agitated, uncontrolled state (Thompson, 1994). Later in infancy, when they become aroused, infants sometimes redirect their attention to something else or distract themselves in order to reduce their arousal (Grolnick, Bridges, & Connell, 1996). By 2 years of age, toddlers can use language to define their feeling states and the context that is upsetting them (Kopp & Neufeld, 2002). A toddler might say, "Feel bad. Dog scare." The communication of this type of information about feeling states and context may help caregivers to more effectively assist the child in regulating emotion.

Contexts can influence emotional regulation (Gunnar & Davis, 2003; Kopp & Neufeld, 2002; Saarni, 2000). Infants are often affected by such factors as fatigue, hunger, time of day, which people are around them, and where they are. Infants must learn to increasingly adapt to different contexts that require emotional regulation. Further, new context demands appear as the infant becomes older and parents modify their expectations. For example, a parent may not expect a 1½-year-old to scream loudly in a restaurant but may not have been as bothered by this when the infant was 6 months old.

Early Childhood

Young children, like adults, experience many emotions during the course of a day. At times, young children also try to make sense of other people's emotional reactions and feelings. The most important changes in emotional development in early childhood include an increased ability to talk about emotion and an increased understanding of emotion (Kuebli, 1994). Preschoolers become more adept at talking about their own and others' emotions. Between 2 and 4 years of age, children

social referencing "Reading" emotional cues in others to help determine how to act in a particular situation.

considerably increase the number of terms they use to describe emotion (Ridgeway, Waters, & Kuczaj, 1985; Saarni, 2002). However, in the preschool years, children are learning more than just the "vocabulary" of emotion terms; they also are learning about the causes and consequences of feelings.

From 5 to 10 years, children show an increased ability to reflect on emotions. At this age, they also begin to understand that the same event can elicit different feelings in different people. Moreover, they show a growing awareness about controlling and managing emotions to meet social standards. Figure 11.3 summarizes the characteristics of young children's talk about emotion and their understanding of it.

Parents, teachers, and other adults can help children understand emotions (Cummings, Braungart-Rieker, & DuRocher-Schudlich, 2003; Saarni, 2000). They can talk with children to help them cope with their feelings of distress, sadness, anger, or guilt. By being sensitive to children's emotional feelings and needs, adults can help children control their emotions and understand them. Learning to express some feelings and mask others are common, everyday lessons in children's lives. This has been called learning how to do "emotion work" (Hochschild, 1983).

Getting along with others often means handling emotions in a socially acceptable way. Children who get angry because they have to wait their turn or who laugh at a crying child who has fallen and skinned his knee can be encouraged to consider other children's feelings. Children who boast about winning something can be reminded how sad it feels to lose.

Middle and Late Childhood

Here are some important developmental changes in emotions during the middle and late childhood years (Kuebli, 1994; Wintre & Vallance, 1994):

- An increased ability to understand such complex emotions as pride and shame (Kuebli, 1994). These emotions become more internalized and integrated with a sense of personal responsibility
- Increased understanding that more than one emotion can be experienced in a particular situation
- An increased tendency to take into fuller account the events leading to emotional reactions
- Marked improvements in the ability to suppress or conceal negative emotional reactions
- The use of self-initiated strategies for redirecting feelings

Approximate Age of Child	Description
2 to 4 years	Increase emotion vocabulary most rapidly
	Correctly label simple emotions in self and others and talk about past, present, and future emotions
	Talk about the causes and consequences of some emotions and identify emotions associated with certain situations
	Use emotion language in pretend play
5 to 10 years	Show increased capacity to reflect verbally on emotions and to consider more complex relations between emotions and situations
	Understand that the same event may call forth different feelings in different people and that feelings sometimes persist long after the events that caused them
	Demonstrate growing awareness about controlling and managing emotions in accord with social standards

FIGURE 11.3 Some Characteristics of Young Children's Language for Talking About Emotion and Their Understanding of It

Adolescence

Adolescence has long been described as a time of emotional turmoil (Hall, 1904). In its extreme form, this view is too stereotypical because adolescents are not constantly in a state of "storm and stress." Nonetheless, early adolescence is a time when emotional highs and lows increase (Galambos & Costigan, 2003; Rosenblum & Lewis, 2003). Young adolescents can be on top of the world one moment and down in the dumps the next. In many instances, the intensity of their emotions seems out of proportion to the events that elicit them (Steinberg & Levine, 1997). Young adolescents might sulk a lot, not knowing how to adequately express their feelings. With little or no provocation, they might blow up at their parents or siblings, which could involve using the defense mechanism of displacing their feelings onto another person.

In one study, Reed Larson and Maryse Richards (1994) used the *experience sampling method* (in which participants are given electronic pagers, then beeped at random times during their waking hours, and asked to report various aspects of their current situation) to discover the emotions that adolescents and their parents were experiencing. Across the thousands of times they reported their emotions, adolescents experienced emotions that were more extreme but more fleeting than their parents did. For example, adolescents were five times more likely to report being "very happy" than their parents when they were beeped, but also three times more likely to report being "very unhappy" (see figure 11.4). These findings lend support to the perception of adolescents as moody and changeable (Rosenblum & Lewis, 2003).

Researchers have also found that from the fifth through the ninth grades, both boys and girls experience a 50 percent decrease in being "very happy" (Larson & Lampman-Petraitis, 1989). In this same study, adolescents were more likely than preadolescents to report mildly negative mood states.

It is important for adults to recognize that moodiness is a *normal* aspect of early adolescence, and most adolescents make it through these moody times to become competent adults. Nonetheless, for some adolescents, such emotions can reflect serious problems. For example, rates of depressed moods become more elevated for girls during adolescence (Nolen-Hoeksema, 2004).

In adolescence, individuals are more likely to become aware of their emotional cycles, such as feeling guilty about being angry, which may improve their ability to cope with a situation. Adolescents also become more skillful at self-presentation of their emotions to impress others. For example, they become more aware of how important it is for them to cover up their anger in their social relationships. And they are more likely to understand the importance of being able to communicate their emotions to improve the quality of a relationship (Saarni, 1999).

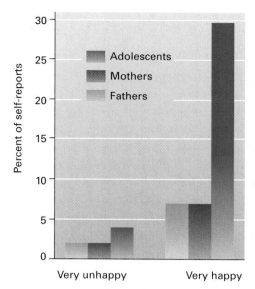

FIGURE 11.4 Self-Reported Extremes of Emotion by Adolescents, Mothers, and Fathers Using the Experience Sampling Method

In the study by Reed Larson and Maryse Richards (1994), adolescents and their mothers and fathers were beeped at random times by researchers using the experience sampling method. The researchers found that adolescents were more likely to report more emotional extremes than their parents.

Review and Reflect: Learning Goal 2

2 Describe the development of emotion

REVIEW

- How does emotion develop in infancy?
- What characterizes emotional development in early childhood?
- What changes take place in emotion during middle and late childhood?
- How does emotion change in adolescence?

REFLECT

- The mother and father of an 8-month-old baby are having difficulty getting sleep at night because the baby wakes up in the middle of night crying. What would you recommend to them regarding how they should deal with this situation?

3 EMOTIONAL PROBLEMS, STRESS, AND COPING

| Depression | Suicide | Stress and Coping |

In chapter 6, "Physical Development in Childhood and Adolescence," we described some problems in adolescence and some programs that have been used to effectively prevent or intervene in these problems. ◀ **page 189** Here we will focus on two other problems—depression and suicide. We also will explore stress in children's lives and ways they can effectively cope with it.

Depression

Depression is a mood disorder in which the individual is unhappy, demoralized, self-derogatory, and bored. The individual does not feel well, loses stamina easily, often has a poor appetite, and is listless and unmotivated.

Depression in Childhood In childhood, the features of depression are often mixed with a broader array of behaviors than in adulthood. During childhood, depression is often associated with aggression, school failure, anxiety, antisocial behavior, and poor peer relations, which makes its diagnosis more difficult (Weiner, 1980). Depression is more likely to occur during adolescence than during childhood and is more pervasive among females than among males (Nolen-Hoeksema, 2001).

Why does depression occur in childhood? Biogenetic, cognitive, and environmental causes have been proposed. Among the views currently being given special attention are Bowlby's developmental theory, Beck's cognitive theory, and Seligman's learned helplessness theory.

John Bowlby (1969, 1989) believes that insecure attachment, a lack of love and affection in child rearing, or the actual loss of a parent in childhood leads to a negative cognitive schema. The schema that is built up during early experiences causes children to interpret later losses as yet other failures in producing enduring and close positive relationships. In Bowlby's view, early experiences, especially those involving loss, create cognitive schemas that are carried forward to influence the way later experiences are interpreted. When the later experiences involve further loss, the loss precipitates depression.

In Aaron Beck's (1973) cognitive view, individuals become depressed because early in their development they acquire cognitive schemas that are characterized by self-devaluation and lack of confidence about the future. These habitual negative thoughts magnify and expand a depressed person's negative experiences. Depressed children blame themselves far more than is warranted, in Beck's view. In one expansion of Beck's view, depression in children is viewed as an outgrowth of attending to negative cues in the environment and identifying the source of negative outcomes as being within one's self (Quiggle & others, 1992).

Martin Seligman's theory is that depression is **learned helplessness**—when individuals are exposed to negative experiences, such as prolonged stress or pain, over which they have no control, they are likely to become depressed (Seligman, 1975). In a reformulation of this view, depression follows the experience of a negative event when the individual explains the event with self-blaming attributions (Abramson, Metalsky, & Alloy, 1989). This explanatory style results in the expectation that no action will control the outcome of similar events in the future, resulting in helplessness, hopelessness, passivity, and depression.

Depression in Parents Depression has traditionally been perceived as a problem of the individual, but today we believe that this view is limited. Researchers have

learned helplessness Seligman's theory of depression—that it occurs when individuals are exposed to negative experiences, especially prolonged stress or pain, over which they have no control.

found an interdependence between depressed persons and their social contexts—this is especially true in the case of parents' depression and children's adjustment (Downey & Coyne, 1990). Depression is a highly prevalent disorder—so prevalent it has been called the "common cold of mental disorders." It occurs often in the lives of women of childbearing age—at a rate of about 8 percent; the rate is 12 percent for women who have recently given birth. As a result, large numbers of children are exposed to depressed parents.

Research on the children of depressed parents clearly documents that depression in parents is associated with problems of adjustment and disorders, especially depression, in their children (Radke-Yarrow & others, 1992). Depressed mothers show lower rates of behavior and show constricted affect, adopt less-effortful control strategies with their children, and sometimes act hostile and negative toward them as well. In considering the effects of parental depression on children, it is important to evaluate the social context of the family. For example, marital discord and stress may precede, precipitate, or co-occur with maternal depression. In such instances, it may be marital turmoil that is the key factor that contributes to children's adjustment problems, not parental depression per se (Gelfand, Teti, & Fox, 1992).

Researchers have found that when a parent is depressed, it is important for children to develop strong friendships outside the home and find success in school and the community (Beardslee, 2002). Children also benefit from understanding events in the family and developing a capacity for self-reflection and self-understanding.

Depression in Adolescence   In adolescence, pervasive symptoms of depression may lead adolescents to wear black clothes, write poetry with morbid themes, or be preoccupied with music that has depressive themes. Sleep problems may be linked with difficulty in getting up for school or sleeping during the day. Lack of motivation and energy may show up in missed classes. Boredom may be a result of feeling depressed. Adolescent depression also may occur in conjunction with conduct disorder, substance abuse, or an eating disorder.   pages 178, 192

How serious a problem is depression in adolescence? Surveys have found that approximately one-third of adolescents who go to a mental health clinic suffer from depression (Fleming, Boyle, & Offord, 1993). Estimates indicate that depression is twice as common in adolescence as in childhood (Compas & Grant, 1993). And adolescent girls have a much higher rate of depression than their male counterparts. Reasons proposed for this sex difference include these:

- Females tend to ruminate in their depressed mood and amplify it.
- Females' self-images, especially their body images, are more negative than males'.
- Females face more discrimination than males.

Treatment of adolescent depression has been carried out through drug therapy and psychotherapy. Antidepressant drugs, such as Elavil, reduce the symptoms of depression in some adolescents. However, some critics argue that such drugs are given to adolescents too indiscriminately. They recommend these guidelines for the use of medication with adolescents who are depressed: absence of environmental determinants for being depressed (family conflict, for example), the depressive symptoms are severe and have pronounced physiological features (body complaints, sleep disturbance), poor response to psychotherapy after a dozen sessions, and if the youth expresses a clear desire for medication rather than psychotherapy (Schroeder & Gordon, 2002). Cognitive therapy has been effective in treating adolescent depression (Beck, 1993).

Suicide

Suicide behavior is rare in childhood but escalates in early adolescence. Suicide is the third leading cause of death today among adolescents 13 through 19 years of age in the United States (National Center for Health Statistics, 2000). Although the

Depression Research

Depression Treatments

Exploring Adolescent Depression

Pathways to Depression in Adolescent Girls

incidence of suicide in adolescence has increased in recent decades, it still is a relatively rare event. In 2000, 1,921 individuals from 10 to 19 years of age committed suicide in the United States (National Center for Health Statistics, 2002).

Far more adolescents contemplate suicide or attempt suicide unsuccessfully (Borowsky, Ireland, & Resnick, 2001). In a national study, one-fifth of U.S. high school students said that they had seriously considered or attempted suicide in the last 12 months (National Center for Health Statistics, 2000). Less than 3 percent reported a suicide attempt that resulted in an injury, poisoning, or drug overdose that had been treated by a doctor. Females were more likely to attempt suicide than males, but males were more likely to commit suicide. Males use more lethal means, such as a gun, in their suicide attempts, while adolescent females are more likely to cut their wrists or take an overdose of sleeping pills, which is less likely to result in death.

There is controversy about whether homosexual adolescents are more vulnerable to suicide than heterosexual adolescents. Early reports suggested that homosexual youth were three to seven times more likely to attempt suicide than heterosexual youth (Fergusson, Horwood, & Beautrais, 1999; Herrill & others, 1999). In one recent study of 12,000 adolescents, approximately 15 percent of gay and lesbian youth said that they had attempted suicide compared to 7 percent of heterosexual youth (Russell & Joyner, 2001). However, in another recent study, gay and lesbian adolescents were only slightly more likely than heterosexual adolescents to attempt suicide (Savin-Williams, in press). According to a leading researcher on gay youth, Richard Savin-Williams (2001), the earlier studies likely exaggerated the suicide rates for gay adolescents because they only surveyed the most disturbed youth who were attending support groups or hanging out at shelters for gay youth.

Distal, or earlier, experiences often are involved in suicide attempts as well. The adolescent might have a long-standing history of family instability and unhappiness. Just as a lack of affection and emotional support, high control, and pressure for achievement by parents during childhood are related to adolescent depression, such combinations of family experiences are also likely to show up as distal factors in suicide attempts. The adolescent might also lack supportive friendships.

Just as genetic factors are associated with depression, they are also associated with suicide. The closer a person's genetic relationship to someone who has committed suicide, the more likely that person is to also commit suicide.

What is the psychological profile of the suicidal adolescent? Suicidal adolescents often have depressive symptoms (American Academy of Pediatrics, 2001). Although not all depressed adolescents are suicidal, depression is the most frequently cited factor associated with adolescent suicide. A sense of hopelessness, low self-esteem, and high self-blame are also associated with adolescent suicide (Harter & Whitesell, 2001).

Stress and Coping

Stress is the response of individuals to the circumstances and events (called stressors) that threaten and tax their coping abilities. Let's explore the roles of cognitive factors, life events and daily hassles, and sociocultural factors in children's stress, as well as how children can effectively cope with stress or the death of someone close to them.

Cognitive Factors Most of us think of stress as environmental events that place demands on an individual's life, events such as an approaching test, being in a car wreck, or losing a friend. While these are some common sources of stress, not everyone perceives the same events as equally stressful or experiences stress in the same way. For example, one child might perceive an approaching test as threatening, another child might perceive it as challenging. To some degree, then, what is stressful for children depends on how they cognitively appraise and interpret events. This

stress The response of individuals to the circumstances and events (called stressors) that threaten them and tax their coping abilities.

view has been presented most clearly by stress researcher Richard Lazarus (1996). **Cognitive appraisal** is Lazarus' term for children's interpretations of events in their lives that are harmful, threatening, or challenging, and their determination of whether they have the resources to effectively cope with the event. In Lazarus' view, events are appraised in two steps:

- In **primary appraisal,** individuals interpret whether an event involves harm or loss that has already occurred, a threat that involves some future danger, or a challenge to be overcome. *Harm* is the child's appraisal of the damage the event has already inflicted. For example, if a child failed a test in school yesterday, the harm has already been done. *Threat* is the child's appraisal of potential future damage an event may bring. For example, failing the test may lower the teacher's opinion of the child and increase the probability the child will get a low grade at the end of the year. *Challenge* is the child's appraisal of the potential to overcome the adverse circumstances of an event and ultimately profit from the event. After failing a test in school, the child may develop a commitment to never get into that situation again and become a better student.
- After children cognitively appraise an event for its harm, threat, or challenge, Lazarus says, they engage in secondary appraisal. In **secondary appraisal,** individuals evaluate their resources and determine how effectively they can cope with the event. This appraisal is called *secondary* because it comes after primary appraisal and depends on the degree to which the event has been appraised as harmful, threatening, or challenging. Coping involves a wide range of potential strategies, skills, and abilities for effectively managing stressful events. In the example of failing the exam, children who learn that their parents will get a tutor to help them likely will be more confident in coping with the stress than if their parents provide no support.

Lazarus believes a child's experience of stress is a balance of primary and secondary appraisal. When harm and threat are high, and challenge and resources are low, stress is likely to be high; when harm and threat are low, and challenge and resources are high, stress is more likely to be moderate or low.

Martin Seligman (1995) also believes that cognitive factors play an important role in coping with stress. He distinguishes between optimistic and pessimistic children. Compared to optimistic children, pessimistic children are more likely to become depressed, feel hopeless, underachieve at school, and have poor health. Young pessimists believe there are permanent reasons why bad things happen to them. Young optimists perceive bad experiences as temporary. If self-blame is appropriate, the optimists blame their behavior, which is changeable; pessimists are more likely to say that their negative experiences are due to innate qualities in themselves. Figure 11.5 shows how some experiences are interpreted differently by pessimistic and optimistic children.

Seligman believes that pessimistic children can be turned into optimistic ones by adults who model optimistic ways of handling themselves. Also, when pessimistic children falter, adults should provide explanations that encourage further effort. Seligman has developed a program to correct distorted explanations of problems and teach realistic ways of interpreting setbacks. The program includes role playing and discussion. In Seligman's research, this program has been very effective in turning pessimistic thinkers into optimistic ones.

Life Events and Daily Hassles   Children can experience a spectrum of stresses, ranging from ordinary to severe. At the ordinary end are experiences that occur in most children's lives and for which there are reasonably well-defined coping patterns. For example, most parents are aware that siblings are jealous of each other and that when one sibling does well at something the other sibling(s) will be jealous. They know how jealousy works and know ways to help children cope with it. More severe stress occurs when children become separated from their parents.

cognitive appraisal Lazarus' term for children's interpretations of events in their lives as harmful, threatening, or challenging, and their determination of whether they have the resources to effectively cope with the event.

primary appraisal Lazarus' concept that individuals interpret whether an event involves harm or loss that already has occurred, a threat that involves some future danger, or a challenge to be overcome.

secondary appraisal Lazarus' concept that individuals evaluate their resources and determine how effectively they can cope with an event.

Bad Events

Pessimistic	Optimistic
• Teachers are unfair.	• Mrs. Carmine is unfair.
• I'm a total clod at sports.	• I stink at kickball.
• Tony hates me and will never hang out with me again.	• Tony is mad at me today.
• Nobody will ever want to be friends with me here at a new school.	• It takes time to make a new best friend when you're at a new school.
• I got grounded because I'm a bad kid.	• I got grounded because I hit Michelle.
• I got a C because I'm stupid.	• I got a C because I didn't study enough.

Good Events

Pessimistic	Optimistic
• I'm smart at math.	• I'm smart.
• I was voted safety patrol captain because the other kids wanted to do a nice thing for me.	• I was voted safety patrol captain because the other kids like me.
• Dad is spending time with me because he's in a good mood.	• Dad loves to spend time with me.
• The only reason I won the spelling bee is because I practiced hard this time.	• I won because I'm a hard worker and I study my lessons.

FIGURE 11.5 Optimistic and Pessimistic Children's Interpretations of Bad and Good Events

Healthy coping patterns for this stressful experience are not as well spelled out. Some children are well cared for; others are ignored when there is a separation caused by divorce, death, illness, or foster placement. Even more severe are the experiences of children who have lived for years in situations of neglect or abuse (Pfeffer, 1996). Victims of incest also experience severe stress, with few coping guidelines.

Recently, psychologists have emphasized that life's daily experiences as well as life's major events may be the culprits in stress (Crnic, 1996). Enduring a tense family life and living in poverty do not show up on scales of major life events in children's development, yet the everyday pounding children take from these living conditions can add up to a highly stressful life and, eventually, psychological disorders or physical illnesses (Pillow, Zautra, & Sandler, 1996).

Sociocultural Factors Sociocultural factors involved in stress include acculturative stress and poverty. **Acculturation** is cultural change that results from continuous, firsthand contact between two distinctive cultural groups. Acculturative stress is the negative consequence of acculturation. Members of ethnic minority groups have historically encountered hostility, prejudice, and lack of effective support during crises, which contributes to alienation, social isolation, and heightened stress. As upwardly mobile ethnic minority families have attempted to penetrate all-White neighborhoods, interethnic tensions often mount. Similarly, racial tensions and hostility often emerge among the various ethnic minorities as they each struggle for limited housing and employment opportunities, seeking a fair share of a limited market. Clashes become inevitable as Latino family markets spring up in African American urban neighborhoods; as Vietnamese extended families displace Puerto Rican apartment dwellers; as the increasing enrollment of Asian students on college campuses is perceived as a threat to affirmative action policies by other non-White ethnic minority students. While race relations in the United States have historically been conceptualized as Black/White, this is no longer the only combination producing ethnic animosity.

As the number of Latinos and Asians has increased dramatically, and as Native Americans have crossed the boundaries of their reservations, the visibility of these groups has brought them in contact not only with mainstream White society, but with one another as well. Depending on the circumstances, this contact has been sometimes harmonious, sometimes antagonistic.

acculturation Cultural change that results from continuous, firsthand contact between two distinctive cultural groups. Acculturative stress is the negative consequence of acculturation.

Poverty imposes considerable stress on children and their families (McLoyd, 2000). Chronic life conditions such as inadequate housing, dangerous neighborhoods, burdensome responsibilities, and economic uncertainties are potent stressors in the lives of the poor (Brooks-Gunn, Leventhal, & Duncan, 2000). The incidence of poverty is especially pronounced among ethnic minority children and their families. For example, African American women heading families face a risk of poverty that is more than 10 times that of White men heading families. Puerto Rican female family heads face a poverty rate that is almost 15 times that found among White male family heads (National Advisory Council on Economic Opportunity, 1980). Many individuals who become poor during their lives remain poor for one or two years. However, African Americans and female family heads are at risk for experiencing persistent poverty. The average poor African American child experiences poverty that will last almost 20 years (Wilson & Neckerman, 1986).

Poverty is related to threatening and uncontrollable events in children's lives (Russo, 1990). For example, poor females are more likely to experience crime and violence than middle-class females are. Poverty also undermines sources of social support that can help buffer the effects of stress.

Coping with Stress   An important aspect of children's emotional lives is learning how to cope effectively with stress (Bridges, 2003). In our discussion of stress, we described some strategies that will help children cope with stress. Among these are Lazarus' ideas about cognitive appraisal and challenge and Seligman's view that children who are optimistic are likely to cope more effectively than those who are pessimistic.

Most researchers also believe that children benefit when they make an effort to approach stress with a problem-solving strategy rather than avoiding the stress (Bridges, 2003; Lazarus & Folkman, 1984). For example, children who respond to low test scores by increasing their study time or developing improved study techniques are likely to cope more effectively and improve their test performance.

It is important for caregivers to help children cope more effectively. They can encourage children to use active, problem-solving strategies in coping with stress. Two other effective strategies are to (1) remove at least one stressor from the child's life and (2) teach children multiple coping strategies.

Based on Michael Rutter's (1979) research on the multiple effects of stress, it makes sense that removing one stressor or hassle can help children feel stronger and more competent. For example, consider Lisa, who had been coming to school hungry each morning. Her teacher arranged for Lisa to have hot breakfasts at school, which improved her concentration in school. This in turn helped Lisa suppress for a time her anxieties about her parents' impending divorce.

Children who have a number of coping techniques have the best chance of adapting and functioning competently in the face of stress. By learning new coping techniques, children might no longer feel as incompetent, and their self-confidence may improve. For example, Kim was relieved when a clinical psychologist helped her anticipate what it would be like to visit her seriously ill sister. She was frightened by the hospital and used withdrawal to cope. She said she did not want to see her sister, even though she missed her a great deal. Children tend to apply their coping strategies only in the situations in which stress develops. Adults can show children how to use these coping skills to their best advantage in many other situations as well. For example, Jennifer used altruism to cope when her mother was hospitalized for cancer. She coped with the separation by mothering her father, her little brother, and her classmates. Her classmates quickly became annoyed with her and began to tease her. Jennifer's teacher at school recognized the problem and helped Jennifer express her altruism by taking care of the pet animals in the class and by being responsible for some daily cleanup chores. Her mothering of the children stopped, and so did the teasing.

As children get older, they are able to more accurately appraise a stressful situation and determine how much control they have over it. Older children generate more coping alternatives to stressful conditions and use more cognitive coping strategies (Compas & others, 2001; Saarni, 1999). For example, older children are better at intentionally shifting their thoughts to something that is less stressful than younger children are. Older children are better at reframing (changing one's perception of a stressful situation). For example, younger children may be very disappointed that their teacher did not say hello to them when they arrived at school. Older children may reframe this type of situation and think, "She might have been busy with other things and just forgot to say hello."

By 10 years of age, most children are able to use these cognitive strategies to cope with stress (Saarni, 1999). However, in families that have not been supportive and are characterized by turmoil or trauma, children may be so overwhelmed by stress that they do not use such strategies.

The terrorist attacks on the World Trade Center in New York City and the Pentagon in Washington, D.C., on September 11, 2001, raised special concerns about how to help children cope with such stressful events (La Greca & others, 2002). Children who have a number of coping techniques have the best chance of adapting and functioning competently in the face of such traumatic events. Here are some recommendations for helping children cope with the stress of these types of events (Gurwitch & others, 2001):

- *Reinforce ideas of safety and security.* This may need to be done a number of times.
- *Listen to and tolerate children retelling events.*
- *Encourage children to talk about confusing feelings, worries, daydreams, and disruptions of concentration.* Listen carefully and remind them that these are normal reactions following a scary event.
- *Help children make sense of what happened.* Children may misunderstand what took place. For example, young children may blame themselves. Children may believe things happened that did not happen, believe that terrorists are coming to their home or school, and so on. Gently help children to develop a realistic understanding of the stressful event.
- *Provide reassurance to children so that they will be able to handle stressful feelings over time.*
- *Protect children from reexposure to frightening situations and reminders of the trauma.* This includes limiting conversations about the event in front of children.

Coping with Death Children who have healthy and positive relationships with their parents before a parent dies cope with the death more effectively than children with unhappy prior relationships with the parent. The years of warmth and caring have probably taught the child effective ways of coping with such a traumatic event. Also, children who are given high-quality care by surviving family members during the mourning period, or who are effectively helped by caregivers in other contexts, experience less separation distress.

Sometimes the death of a sibling is even more difficult for children to understand and accept than the loss of a parent. Many children believe that only old people die, so the death of a child can stimulate children to think about their own immortality. The majority of children, though, seem to be able to cope with a sibling's death effectively if they are helped through a mourning period.

Knowing what children think about death can help adults understand their behavior in the period following the loss of a parent or sibling. When a 3-year-old boy creeps from his bed every night and runs down the street, searching for his mother who has just died, is he mourning for her? When a 6-year-old girl spends an entire afternoon drawing pictures of graveyards and coffins, is she grieving? When a 9-year-old boy can't wait to go back to school after the funeral so he can tell his classmates about how his sister died, is he denying grief? All of these are ways in which children cope with death. And all follow children's logic.

Children 3 to 5 years old think that dead people continue to live, but under changed circumstances. The missing person is simply missing, and young children expect the person to return at some point. When the person does not come back,

How can adults help children cope with terrorist attacks, such as 9/11/01?

they might feel hurt or angry at being abandoned. They might declare that they want to go to heaven to bring the dead person home. They might ask their caregivers where the dead person's house is, where the dead person eats, and why the dead person won't be cold if the person is buried without a coat and hat in winter.

Though children vary somewhat in the age at which they begin to understand death, the limitations of preoperational thought make it difficult for a child to comprehend death before the age of 7 or 8. Young children blame themselves for the death of someone they knew well, believing that the event may have happened because they disobeyed the person who died. Children under 6 rarely understand that death is universal, inevitable, and final. Instead, young children usually think that only people who want to die, or who are bad or careless, actually do die. At some point around the middle of the elementary school years, children begin to grasp the concept that death is the end of life and is not reversible. They come to realize that they, too, will die someday.

Review and Reflect: Learning Goal 3

3 **Summarize the nature of depression, suicide, stress, and coping**

REVIEW

- What causes depression in childhood and adolescence?
- Why do adolescents attempt and commit suicide?
- What is the nature of stress and coping in children?

REFLECT

- What advice would you give to a parent whose child is experiencing a great deal of stress and having difficulty coping?

---

4 TEMPERAMENT

Defining and Classifying Temperament	Developmental Connections and Contexts	Parenting and the Child's Temperament

Goodness of Fit	Gender, Culture, and Temperament

Infants show different emotional responses. One infant may be cheerful and happy much of the time; another baby may cry a lot and more often display a negative mood. These behaviors reflect differences in their temperament. Let's explore a definition of *temperament,* the ways in which it can be classified, goodness of fit, developmental connections and contexts, and the implications of temperamental variations for parenting.

Defining and Classifying Temperament

Temperament is an individual's behavioral style and characteristic way of emotionally responding. Developmentalists are especially interested in the temperament of infants.

A widely debated issue is just what the key dimensions of temperament are. Psychiatrists Alexander Chess and Stella Thomas (Chess & Thomas, 1977; Thomas & Chess, 1991) believe there are three basic types, or clusters, of temperament:

temperament An individual's behavioral style and characteristic way of emotional response.

"Oh, he's cute, all right, but he's got the temperament of a car alarm."

- **Easy child.** This child is generally in a positive mood, quickly establishes regular routines in infancy, and adapts easily to new experiences.
- **Difficult child.** This child reacts negatively and cries frequently, engages in irregular daily routines, and is slow to accept change.
- **Slow-to-warm-up child.** This child has a low activity level, is somewhat negative, and displays a low intensity of mood.

Various dimensions make up these three basic clusters of temperament. In their longitudinal investigation, Chess and Thomas found that 40 percent of the children they studied could be classified as easy, 10 percent as difficult, and 15 percent as slow to warm up (35 percent did not fit any of the three patterns). Researchers have found that these three basic clusters of temperament are moderately stable across the childhood years.

Some critics argue that 35 percent of children not fitting into any temperament category is important (Saarni, 2002). They believe that too often we are prone to pigeon-holing children into categories and traits without examining the context in which temperament occurs (Rothbart & Bates, 1998; Wachs, 2000). We will discuss contextual influences on temperament later.

One way of classifying temperament involves comparing a shy, subdued, timid child with a sociable, extraverted, bold child. Jerome Kagan (1997, 2000, 2002, 2003; Kagan & Snidman, 1991) regards shyness with strangers, whether peers or adults, as one feature of a broader temperament category called *inhibition to the unfamiliar.* Inhibited children react to many aspects of unfamiliarity with initial avoidance, distress, or subdued affect, especially beginning about 7 to 9 months of age. Kagan has found that inhibition shows considerable stability across the infant and early childhood years. One recent study classified toddlers into extremely inhibited, extremely uninhibited, and intermediate groups (Pfeifer & others, 2002). Follow-up assessments occurred at 4 and 7 years of age. Continuity was demonstrated for both inhibition and lack of inhibition, although a substantial number of the inhibited children moved into the intermediate groups at 7 years of age.

New classifications of temperament continue to be forged (Bornstein, 2000; Rothbart, 1999; Wachs & Kohnstamm, 2001). In a review of temperament research, Mary Rothbart and John Bates (1998) concluded that the best framework for classifying temperament involves a revision of Chess and Thomas' categories of easy, difficult, and slow to warm up. The general classification of temperament now focuses more on:

- *Positive affect and approach.* This category is much like the personality trait of extraversion/introversion. This category is closely related to Kagan's concept of inhibition to the unfamiliar.
- *Negative affectivity.* This involves being easily distressed. Children with a temperament that involves negative affectivity may fret and cry often. Negative affectivity is closely related to the personality trait of introversion, which involves the extent to which a child is shy and inhibited. This category also fits Kagan's concept of inhibition.
- *Effortful control (self-regulation).* This involves the child's ability to control his or her emotions and reflects the concept of emotional regulation that we discussed earlier in the chapter. Thus, infants who are high on effortful control show an ability to keep their arousal from getting too high and have strategies for soothing themselves. By contrast, children low on effortful control often show an inability to control their arousal, and they become easily agitated and intensely emotional (Eisenberg & others, 2002).

A number of scholars conceive of temperament as a stable characteristic of newborns, which comes to be shaped and modified by the child's later experiences. This

easy child A child who is generally in a positive mood, who quickly establishes regular routines in infancy, and who adapts easily to new experiences.

difficult child A child who tends to react negatively and cry frequently, who engages in irregular daily routines, and who is slow to accept change.

slow-to-warm-up child A child who has a low activity level, is somewhat negative, and displays a low intensity of mood.

raises the question of heredity's role in temperament (Goldsmith, 1988). Twin and adoption studies have been conducted to answer this question (Plomin & others, 1994). The researchers have found a heritability index in the range of .50 to .60, suggesting a moderate influence of heredity on temperament. However, the strength of the association usually declines as infants become older (Goldsmith & Gottesman, 1981). This finding supports the belief that temperament becomes more malleable with experience. Alternatively, it may be that, as a child becomes older, behavior indicators of temperament are more difficult to spot.

Goodness of Fit

Goodness of fit refers to the match between a child's temperament and the environmental demands the child must cope with (Bates, 2001; Matheny & Phillips, 2001). Goodness of fit can be important to the child's adjustment. For example, consider an active child who is made to sit still for long periods of time or lives in a small apartment. Consider also a slow-to-warm-up child who is abruptly pushed into new situations on a regular basis. Such lacks of fit between the child's temperament and these environmental demands can produce adjustment problems for the child. In our discussion of parenting and the child's temperament, many of the recommendations involve consideration of goodness of fit.

What are some ways that developmentalists have classified infants' temperaments? Which classification makes the most sense to you, based on your observations of infants?

In a longitudinal study, Grazyna Kochanska (1997) found that when children were fearful as 2- and 3-year-olds, gentle discipline by mothers was linked with a stronger conscience at age 4. By contrast, when children were fearless (bold) at ages 2 and 3, secure attachment to mothers was linked with a stronger conscience at age 4. These results support the belief that there are multiple pathways to conscience for children, which depend on how parents respond to children with different temperaments. This notion reflects the goodness-of-fit concept.

Developmental Connections and Contexts

How stable is temperament from childhood to adulthood? Do young adults show the same behavioral style and characteristic emotional responses as when they were infants or young children?

Activity level is an important dimension of temperament. Are children's activity levels linked to their personality in early adulthood? In one longitudinal study, children who were highly active at age 4 were likely to be very outgoing at age 23, which reflects continuity (Franz, 1996). From adolescence into early adulthood, most individuals show fewer emotional mood swings, become more responsible, and engage in less risk-taking behavior, which reflects discontinuity (Caspi, 1998).

Is temperament in childhood linked with adjustment in adulthood? Here is what we know based on the few longitudinal studies that have been conducted on this topic (Caspi, 1998). In one longitudinal study, children who had an easy temperament at 3 to 5 years of age were likely to be well adjusted as young adults (Chess & Thomas, 1977). In contrast, many children who had a difficult temperament at 3 to 5 years of age were not well adjusted as young adults. Also, other researchers have found that boys with a difficult temperament in childhood are less likely as adults to continue their formal education; girls with a difficult temperament in childhood are more likely to experience marital conflict as adults (Wachs, 2000).

Infant Temperament

goodness of fit Refers to the match between a child's temperament and the environmental demands the child must cope with.

Inhibition is another temperament characteristic that has been studied extensively (Kagan, 2000). Researchers have found that individuals with an inhibited temperament in childhood are less likely as adults to be assertive or experience social support, and more likely to delay entering a stable job track (Wachs, 2000).

Yet another aspect of temperament involves emotionality and the ability to control one's emotions. In one longitudinal study, when 3-year-old children showed good control of their emotions and were resilient in the face of stress, they were likely to continue to handle emotions effectively as adults (Block, 1993). By contrast, when 3-year-olds had low emotional control and were not very resilient, they were likely to show problems in these areas as young adults.

In sum, these studies reveal some continuity between certain aspects of temperament in childhood and adjustment in early adulthood. However, keep in mind that these connections between childhood temperament and adult adjustment are based on only a small number of studies, and more research is needed to verify these linkages. Indeed, Theodore Wachs (1994, 2000) proposed ways that linkages between temperament in childhood and personality in adulthood might vary depending on the intervening contexts in individuals' experience (see figure 11.6).

Gender, Culture, and Temperament

Parents might react differently to a child's temperament depending on whether the child is a boy or a girl and on the culture in which they live. For example, in one study, mothers were more responsive to the crying of irritable girls than to the crying of irritable boys (Crockenberg, 1986).

Children's temperament can also vary across cultures (Putnam, Sanson, & Rothbart, 2002). For example, an active temperament might be valued in some cultures (such as in the United States) but not in other cultures (such as in China). Indeed, behavioral inhibition is more highly valued in China than in North America, and researchers have found that Chinese children are more inhibited than Canadian children (Chen & others, 1998). The cultural differences in temperament were linked

Initial Temperament Trait: Inhibition

	Child A	Child B
Intervening Context		
Caregivers	Caregivers (parents) who are sensitive and accepting, and let child set his or her own pace	Caregivers who use inappropriate "low level control" and attempt to force the child into new situations
Physical Environment	Presence of "stimulus shelters" or "defensible spaces" that the children can retreat to when there is too much stimulation	Child continually encounters noisy, chaotic environments that allow no escape from stimulation.
Peers	Peer groups with other inhibited children with common interests, so the child feels accepted	Peer groups consist of athletic extroverts, so the child feels rejected.
Schools	School is "undermanned" so inhibited children are more likely to be tolerated and feel they can make a contribution.	School is "overmanned" so inhibited children are less likely to be tolerated and more likely to feel undervalued.
Personality Outcomes		
	As an adult, individual is closer to extroversion (outgoing, sociable) and is emotionally stable.	As an adult, individual is closer to introversion and has more emotional problems.

FIGURE 11.6 Temperament in Childhood, Personality in Adulthood, and Intervening Contexts

Varying experiences with caregivers, the physical environment, peers, and schools may modify links between temperament in childhood and personality in adulthood. The example given here is for inhibition.

to parent attitude and behaviors. Canadian mothers of inhibited 2-year-olds were less accepting of their infants' inhibited temperament while Chinese mothers were more accepting.

Parenting and the Child's Temperament

Many parents don't become believers in temperament's importance until the birth of their second child. Many parents view the first child's behavior as being solely a result of how they socialized the child. However, management strategies that worked with the first child might not be as effective with the second child. Problems experienced with the first child (such as those involved in feeding, sleeping, and coping with strangers) might not exist with the second child, but new problems might arise. Such experiences strongly suggest that nature as well as nurture influence the child's development, that children differ from each other from very early in life, and that these differences have important implications for parent-child interaction (Kwak & others, 1999; Rothbart & Putnam, 2002).

What are some good strategies for parents to adopt when responding to their infant's temperament?

What are the implications of temperamental variations for parenting? Although answers to this question necessarily are speculative because of the incompleteness of the research literature, these conclusions were reached by temperament experts Ann Sanson and Mary Rothbart (1995):

- *Attention to and respect for individuality.* An important implication of taking children's individuality seriously is that it becomes difficult to generate prescriptions for "good parenting," other than possibly specifying that parents need to be sensitive and flexible. Parents need to be sensitive to the infant's signals and needs. A goal of parenting might be accomplished in one way with one child and in another way with another child, depending on the child's temperament.

     Some temperament characteristics pose more parenting challenges than others, at least in modern Western societies. Children's proneness to distress, as exhibited by frequent crying and irritability, can contribute to the emergence of avoidant or coercive parental responses. In one research study, though, extra support and training for mothers of distress-prone infants improved the quality of mother-infant interaction (van den Boom, 1989).

- *Structuring the child's environment.* Crowded, noisy environments can pose greater problems for some children (such as a "difficult" child) than others (such as an "easygoing" child). We might also expect that a fearful, withdrawing child would benefit from slower entry into new contexts.

- *The "difficult" child and packaged parenting programs.* Some books and programs for parents focus specifically on temperament (Cameron, Hansen, & Rosen, 1989; Turecki & Tonner, 1989). These programs usually focus on children with "difficult" temperaments. Acknowledgment that some children are harder to parent is often helpful, and advice on how to handle particular difficult temperament characteristics can also be useful.

     However, weighted against these programs' potential advantages are several disadvantages. Whether a particular characteristic is difficult depends on its fit with the environment, whereas the notion of difficult temperament suggests that the problem rests solely with the child. To label a child "difficult" also has the danger of becoming a self-fulfilling prophecy. If a child is identified as "difficult," the labeling may maintain that categorization.

Children's temperament needs to be taken into account when considering caregiving behavior. Research does not yet allow for many highly specific recommendations, but, in general, caregivers should (1) be sensitive to the individual characteristics of the child, (2) be flexible in responding to these characteristics, and (3) avoid negative labeling of the child.

Review and Reflect: Learning Goal 4

4 Characterize temperament

REVIEW

- How can temperament be defined and classified?
- What does "goodness of fit" mean?
- What are some developmental connections and contextual influences on temperament?
- How might gender and culture be linked to temperament?
- What are parenting strategies for dealing with a child's temperament?

REFLECT

- Consider your own temperament. We described a number of different temperament categories. Which one best describes your temperament? Has your temperament changed as you have gotten older, or is it about the same as when you were a child or an adolescent? If your temperament has changed, what factors contributed to the changes?

5 ATTACHMENT

| What Is Attachment? | Caregiving Styles and Attachment Classification | Fathers as Caregivers of Infants |
| Individual Differences | Attachment, Temperament, and the Wider Social World | Child Care |

A small curly-haired girl named Danielle, age 11 months, begins to whimper. After a few seconds, she begins to wail. The psychologist observing Danielle is conducting a research study on the nature of attachment between infants and their mothers. Subsequently, the mother reenters the room, and Danielle's crying ceases. Quickly, Danielle crawls over to where her mother is seated and reaches out to be held. The situation is one of the main ways that psychologists study the nature of attachment during infancy.

What Is Attachment?

In everyday language, attachment is a relationship between two individuals who feel strongly about each other and do a number of things to continue the relationship. Many pairs of people are attached: relatives, lovers, a teacher and student. In the language of developmental psychology, though, attachment is often restricted to a relationship between particular social figures and a particular phenomenon that is thought to reflect unique characteristics of the relationship. In this case, the developmental period is infancy, the social figures are the infant and one or more adult caregivers, and the phenomenon is a bond (Bowlby, 1969, 1989). To summarize, **attachment** is a close emotional bond between an infant and a caregiver.

There is no shortage of theories about infant attachment. Freud believed that infants become attached to the person or object that provides oral satisfaction. For most infants, this is the mother, since she is most likely to feed the infant.

Is feeding as important as Freud thought? A classic study by Harry Harlow (1958) reveals that the answer is no (see figure 11.7). These researchers evaluated whether feeding or contact comfort was more important to infant attachment. Infant

attachment A close emotional bond between an infant and a caregiver.

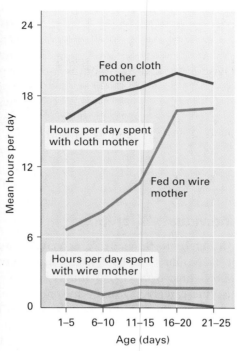

FIGURE 11.7 Contact Time with Wire and Cloth Surrogate Mothers

Regardless of whether the infant monkeys were fed by a wire or a cloth mother, they overwhelmingly preferred to spend contact time with the cloth mother.

monkeys were removed from their mothers at birth and reared for six months by surrogate (substitute) "mothers." One of the mothers was made of wire, the other of cloth. Half of the infant monkeys were fed by the wire mother, half by the cloth mother. Periodically, the amount of time the infant monkeys spent with either the wire or the cloth monkey was computed. Regardless of whether they were fed by the wire or the cloth mother, the infant monkeys spent far more time with the cloth mother. This study clearly demonstrated that feeding is not the crucial element in the attachment process and that contact comfort is important.

Erik Erikson (1968) believed that the first year of life is the key time frame for the development of attachment. Recall his proposal—also discussed in chapter 2— that the first year of life represents the stage of trust versus mistrust. ◀ page 32 A sense of trust requires a feeling of physical comfort and a minimal amount of fear and apprehension about the future. Trust in infancy sets the stage for a lifelong expectation that the world will be a good and pleasant place to be. Erikson also believed that responsive, sensitive parenting contributes to an infant's sense of trust.

The ethological perspective of British psychiatrist John Bowlby (1969, 1989) also stresses the importance of attachment in the first year of life and the responsiveness of the caregiver. Bowlby believes that an infant and its primary caregiver form an attachment. He argues that the newborn is biologically equipped to elicit attachment behavior (Weizmann, 2000). The baby cries, clings, coos, and smiles. Later, the infant crawls, walks, and follows the mother. The infant's goal is to keep the primary caregiver nearby.

Attachment does not emerge suddenly but rather develops in a series of phases, moving from a baby's general preference for human beings to a partnership with primary caregivers. Here are four such phases based on Bowlby's conceptualization of attachment (Schaffer, 1996):

Phase 1:   Birth to 2 months   Infants instinctively direct their attachment to human figures. Strangers, siblings, and parents are equally likely to elicit smiling or crying from the infant.

Phase 2:	2 to 7 months	Attachment becomes focused on one figure, usually the primary caregiver, as the baby gradually learns to distinguish familiar from unfamiliar people.
Phase 3:	7 to 24 months	Specific attachments develop. With increased locomotor skills, babies actively seek contact with regular caregivers, such as the mother or father.
Phase 4:	24 months onward	A goal-corrected partnership is formed in which children become aware of others' feelings, goals, and plans and begin to take these into account in forming their own actions.

Individual Differences

Although attachment to a caregiver intensifies midway through the first year, isn't it likely that some babies have a more positive attachment experience than others? Mary Ainsworth (1979) thinks so. She says that, in **secure attachment,** infants use the caregiver, usually the mother, as a secure base of attachment from which to explore the environment. Ainsworth believes that secure attachment in the first year of life provides an important foundation for psychological development later in life. The caregiver's sensitivity to the infant's signals increases secure attachment (de Wolff & van IJzendoorn, 1997). The securely attached infant moves freely away from the mother but processes her location through periodic glances. The securely attached infant responds positively to being picked up by others and, when put back down, freely moves away to play. An insecurely attached infant, by contrast, avoids the mother or is ambivalent toward her, fears strangers, and is upset by minor, everyday separations.

secure attachment The infant uses a caregiver as a secure base from which to explore the environment. Ainsworth believes that secure attachment in the first year of life provides an important foundation for psychological development later in life.

FIGURE 11.8 The Ainsworth Strange Situation

Mary Ainsworth developed the Strange Situation to assess whether infants are securely or insecurely attached to their caregiver.

Episode	Persons present	Duration of episode	Description of setting
1	Caregiver, baby, and observer	30 seconds	Observer introduces caregiver and baby to experimental room, then leaves. (Room contains many appealing toys scattered about.)
2	Caregiver and baby	3 minutes	Caregiver is nonparticipant while baby explores; if necessary, play is stimulated after 2 minutes.
3	Stranger, caregiver, and baby	3 minutes	Stranger enters. First minute: Stranger is silent. Second minute: Stranger converses with caregiver. Third minute: Stranger approaches baby. After 3 minutes caregiver leaves unobtrusively.
4	Stranger and baby	3 minutes or less	First separation episode. Stranger's behavior is geared to that of baby.
5	Caregiver and baby	3 minutes or more	First reunion episode. Caregiver greets and/or comforts baby, then tries to settle baby again in play. Caregiver then leaves, saying "bye-bye."
6	Baby alone	3 minutes or less	Second separation episode.
7	Stranger and baby	3 minutes or less	Continuation of second separation. Stranger enters and gears behavior to that of baby.
8	Caregiver and baby	3 minutes	Second reunion episode. Caregiver enters, greets baby, then picks baby up. Meanwhile stranger leaves unobtrusively.

Ainsworth created the **Strange Situation,** an observational measure of infant attachment that requires the infant to move through a series of introductions, separations, and reunions with the caregiver and an adult stranger in a prescribed order (see figure 11.8). In using the Strange Situation, researchers hope that their observations will provide them with information about the infant's motivation to be near the caregiver and the degree to which the caregiver's presence provides the infant with security and confidence. For example, when in the presence of their caregiver, securely attached infants explore the room and examine toys that have been placed in it. When the caregiver departs, securely attached infants might mildly protest, and when the caregiver returns these infants reestablish positive interaction with her, perhaps by smiling or climbing on her lap. Subsequently, the securely attached infant often resumes playing with the toys in the room.

Three types of insecurely attached infants have been described:

- **Insecure avoidant babies** show insecurity by avoiding the caregiver. In the Strange Situation, these babies engage in little interaction with the caregiver, often display distress by crying when she leaves the room, usually do not reestablish contact with her on her return, and may even turn their back on her at this point. If contact is established, the infant usually leans away or looks away.
- **Insecure resistant babies** often cling to the caregiver and then resist her by fighting against the closeness, perhaps by kicking or pushing away. In the Strange Situation, these babies often cling anxiously to the caregiver and don't explore the playroom. When the caregiver leaves, they often cry loudly and push away if she tries to comfort them on her return.
- **Insecure disorganized babies** show insecurity in being disorganized and disoriented. In the Strange Situation, these babies might appear dazed, confused, and fearful. To be classified as disorganized, strong patterns of avoidance and resistance must be shown or certain select behaviors, such as extreme fearfulness around the caregiver, must be present.

Although the Strange Situation has been used in a large number of studies of infant attachment, some critics believe that the isolated, controlled events of the setting might not necessarily reflect what would happen if infants were observed with their caregiver in a natural environment. The issue of using controlled, laboratory assessments versus naturalistic observations is widely debated in child development circles.

If early attachment to a caregiver is important, it should relate to a child's social behavior later in development. Researchers have found that for some children, early attachments seem to foreshadow later functioning (Schneider, Atkinson, & Tardif, 2001; Sroufe, 2002; Sroufe, Egeland, & Carlson, 1999). For other children, there is little continuity (Thompson, 2000). Consistency in caregiving over a number of years is likely an important factor in connecting early attachment and the child's functioning later in development (Thompson, Easterbrooks, & Walker, 2003).

Caregiving Styles and Attachment Classification

Attachment is defined as a close emotional bond between the infant and caregiver. Is the parent's caregiving style linked with this close emotional bond called attachment? Securely attached babies have caregivers who are sensitive to their signals and are consistently available to respond to their infants' needs (Gao, Elliott, & Waters, 1999; Main, 2000). These caregivers often let their babies have an active part in determining the onset and pacing of interaction in the first year of life. One recent study found that maternal sensitivity in parenting was linked with secure attachment in infants in two different cultures: the United States and Columbia (Carbonell & others, 2002).

How do the caregivers of insecurely attached babies interact with them? Caregivers of insecure avoidant babies tend to be unavailable or rejecting (Berlin &

What is the nature of secure and insecure attachment?

www.mhhe.com/santrockcd10

Forming a Secure Attachment

Attachment Research

*E*arly attachment experiences do not directly or solely cause later problems but yet have special roles in framing subsequent experiences.

—L. ALAN SROUFE
*Contemporary Psychologist,
University of Minnesota*

Strange Situation An observational measure of infant attachment that requires the infant to move through a series of introductions, separations, and reunions with the caregiver and an adult stranger in a prescribed order.

insecure avoidant babies Babies that show insecurity by avoiding the caregiver.

insecure resistant babies Babies that might cling to the caregiver, then resist her by fighting against the closeness, perhaps by kicking or pushing away.

insecure disorganized babies Babies that show insecurity by being disorganized and disoriented.

Attachment Theory and Research

Mary Ainsworth

Recent Attachment Research

Responsive Care and Attachment

Cassidy, 2000). They often don't respond to their babies' signals and have little physical contact with them. When they do interact with their babies, they may behave in an angry and irritable way toward them. Caregivers of insecure resistant babies tend to be inconsistently available to their babies. That is, sometimes they respond to their babies' needs, and sometimes they don't. In general, they tend not to be very affectionate with their babies and show little synchrony when interacting with them. Caregivers of insecure disorganized babies often neglect or physically abuse their babies (Barnett, Ganiban, & Cicchetti, 1999). In some cases, these caregivers also have depression (Levy, 1999).

Attachment, Temperament, and the Wider Social World

Not all research reveals the power of infant attachment to predict subsequent development. In one longitudinal study, attachment classification in infancy did not predict attachment classification at 18 years of age (Lewis, 1997). In this study, the best predictor of an insecure attachment classification at 18 was the occurrence of parent divorce in intervening years.

Thus, not all developmentalists believe that attachment in infancy is the only path to competence in life. Indeed, some developmentalists believe that too much emphasis is placed on the importance of the attachment bond in infancy. Jerome Kagan (1987, 2000), for example, believes that infants are highly resilient and adaptive; he argues that they are evolutionarily equipped to stay on a positive developmental course, even in the face of wide variations in parenting. Kagan and others stress that genetic and temperament characteristics play more important roles in a child's social competence than the attachment theorists, such as Bowlby, Ainsworth, and Sroufe, are willing to acknowledge (Chauhuri & Williams, 1999; Young & Shahinfar, 1995). For example, infants may have inherited a low tolerance for stress. This, rather than an insecure attachment bond, may be responsible for their inability to get along with peers.

Also, researchers have found cultural variations in attachment. German and Japanese babies often show different patterns of attachment than American infants. As shown in figure 11.9, German infants are more likely to show an avoidant attachment pattern and Japanese infants are less likely to show this pattern than U.S. infants (van IJzendoorn & Kroonenberg, 1988). The avoidant pattern in German babies likely occurs because their caregivers encourage them to be more independent (Grossmann & others, 1985). Also as shown in figure 11.9, Japanese babies are more likely than American babies to be categorized as resistant. This may have more to do with the Ainsworth Strange Situation as a measure of attachment than with attachment insecurity itself. Japanese mothers rarely let anyone unfamiliar with their babies care for them. Thus, the Ainsworth Strange Situation might create considerably more stress for Japanese infants than for American infants, who are more accustomed to separation from their mothers (Takahashi, 1990). Even though there are cultural variations in attachment classification, the most frequent classification in every culture studied so far is secure attachment (van IJzendoorn & Kroonenberg, 1988).

Another criticism of attachment theory is that it ignores the diversity of socializing agents and contexts that exists in an infant's world. In some cultures, infants show attachments to many people. Among the Hausa (who live in Nigeria), both grandmothers and siblings provide a significant amount of care for infants (Harkness & Super, 1995). Infants in agricultural societies tend to form attachments to older siblings, who are assigned

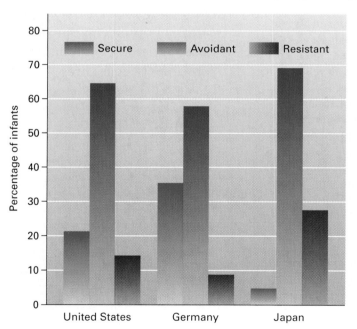

FIGURE 11.9 Cross-Cultural Comparison of Attachment

In one study, infant attachment in three countries—the United States, Germany, and Japan—was measured in the Ainsworth Strange Situation (van IJzendoorn & Kroonenberg, 1988). The dominant attachment pattern in all three countries was secure attachment. However, German infants were more avoidant and Japanese infants were less avoidant and more resistant than U.S. infants.

a major responsibility for younger siblings' care. The attachments formed by infants in group care in Israeli kibbutzim provide another challenge to the singular attachment thesis.

Researchers recognize the importance of competent, nurturant caregivers in an infant's development (Maccoby, 1999; McHale & others, 2001; Parke, 2001). At issue, though, is whether or not secure attachment, especially to a single caregiver, is critical (Thompson, 2000; Thompson, Easterbrooks, & Walker, 2003).

Fathers as Caregivers of Infants

Can fathers take care of infants as competently as mothers can? Observations of fathers and their infants suggest that fathers have the ability to act sensitively and responsively with their infants (Parke, 1995, 2000, 2001). The strongest evidence of the plasticity of male caregiving abilities is based on male primates, which are notoriously low in their interest in offspring. When forced to live with infants whose female caregivers are absent, the adult male competently rears the infants. Remember, however, that, although fathers can be active, nurturant, involved caregivers with their infants, many do not choose to follow this pattern (Eggebeen & Knoester, 2001; Silverstein, 2001).

Do fathers behave differently toward infants than mothers do? Maternal interactions usually center around child-care activities—feeding, changing diapers, bathing. Paternal interactions are more likely to include play. Fathers engage in more rough-and-tumble play. They bounce infants, throw them up in the air, tickle them, and so on (Lamb, 1986, 2000; Lamb & others, 1982). Mothers do play with infants, but their play is less physical and arousing than that of fathers.

In stressful circumstances, do infants prefer their mother or father? In one study, 20 12-month-olds were observed interacting with their parents (Lamb, 1977). With both parents present, the infants preferred neither their mother nor their father. The same was true when the infants were alone with the mother or the father. However, the entrance of a stranger, combined with boredom and fatigue, produced a shift in the infants' social behavior toward the mother. In stressful circumstances, then, infants show a stronger attachment to the mother.

In one study, fathers were interviewed about their caregiving responsibilities when their children were 6, 15, 24, and 36 months of age (NICHD Early Child Care Research Network, 2000). A subset was videotaped during father-child play at 6 and 36 months. Caregiving activities (such as bathing, feeding, and dressing the child, and taking the child to day care) and sensitivity during play interactions (such as being responsive to the child's signals and needs, and expressing positive feelings) with their children were predicted by several factors. Fathers were more involved in caregiving when they worked fewer hours and mothers worked more hours, when fathers and mothers were younger, when mothers reported greater marital intimacy, and when the children were boys. Fathers who had less-traditional child-rearing beliefs and reported more marital intimacy were more sensitive during play.

Might the nature of parent-infant interaction be different in families that adopt nontraditional gender roles? This question was investigated by Michael Lamb and his colleagues (1982). They studied Swedish families in which the fathers were the primary caregivers of their firstborn, 8-month-old infants. The mothers were working full-time. In all observations, the mothers were more likely to discipline, hold, soothe, kiss, and talk to the infants than were the fathers. These mothers and fathers dealt with their infants differently, along the lines of American fathers and mothers following traditional gender roles. Having fathers assume the primary caregiving role did not substantially alter the way they

In the Hausa culture, siblings and grandmothers provide a significant amount of care for infants. *How might these variations in care affect attachment?*

Child-Care Policy Around the World

Sheila Kammerman (1989, 2000a, b) has conducted extensive examinations of parental leave policies around the world. Parental leaves were first enacted as maternity policies more than a century ago to protect the physical health of working women at the time of childbirth. More recently, child-rearing, parental, and paternity leaves were created in response not only to the needs of working women (and parents), but also because of concern for the child's well-being. The European Union (EU) mandated a paid 14-week maternity leave in 1992 and a 3-month parental leave in 1998.

Across cultures, policies vary in eligibility criteria, leave duration, benefit level, and the extent to which parents take advantage of these policies. The European policies just mentioned lead the way in creating new standards of parental leave. The United States is alone among advanced industrialized countries in the briefness of parental leave granted and among the few countries with unpaid leave (Australia and New Zealand are the others).

There are five different types of parental leave from employment:

- *Maternity leave.* In some countries the prebirth leave is compulsory as is a 6- to 10-week leave following birth.
- *Paternity leave.* This is usually much briefer than maternity leave. It especially may be important when a second child is born and the first child requires care.
- *Parental leave.* This is a gender-neutral leave that usually follows a maternity leave and allows either women or men to take advantage of the leave policy and share it or choose which of them will use it.
- *Child-rearing leave.* In some countries, this is a supplement to a maternity leave or a variation on a parental leave. A child-rearing leave is usually longer than a maternity leave and is typically paid at a much lower level.
- *Family leave.* This covers reasons other than the birth of a new baby and can allow time off from employment to care for an ill child or other family members, time to accompany a child to school for the first time, or time to visit a child's school.

Sweden has one of the most extensive leave policies. Paid for by the government at 80 percent of wages, one year of parental leave is allowed (including maternity leave). Maternity leave may begin 60 days prior to expected birth of the baby and ends six weeks after birth. Another six months of parental leave can be used until the child's eighth birthday (Kammerman, 2000a). Virtually all eligible mothers take advantage of the leave policy and approximately 75 percent of eligible fathers take at least some part of the leave they are allowed. In addition, employed grandparents now also have the right to take time off to care for an ill grandchild.

Spain is an example of a relatively poor country that still provides substantial parental leave. Spain allows a 16-week paid maternity leave (paid at 100 percent of wages) at childbirth with up to 6 weeks prior to childbirth allowed. Fathers are permitted two days of leave.

interacted with their infants. This may be for biological reasons or because of deeply ingrained socialization patterns in cultures.

Child Care

Many parents worry whether care of their child by other people will adversely affect their children. They fear that child care by others will reduce their infants' emotional attachment to them, retard the infants' cognitive development, fail to teach them how to control anger, and allow them to be unduly influenced by their peers. How extensive is child care by people other than parents? Are the worries of these parents justified?

Today far more young children are in child care than at any other time in history; about 2 million children currently receive formal, licensed child care, and more than 5 million children attend kindergarten. Also, uncounted millions of children are cared for by unlicensed baby-sitters.

In Sweden, mothers or fathers are given paid maternity or paternity leave for up to one year. Sweden and many other European countries have well-developed child-care policies. To learn about these policies, see the Explorations in Child Development box. In Sweden, day care for infants under 1 year of age is usually not a major concern because one parent is on paid leave for child care.

Because the United States does not have a policy of paid leave for child care, child care in the United States has become a major national concern. The type of child care that young children receive varies extensively (Burchinal & others, 1996; Scarr, 2000). Many child-care centers house large groups of children and have elaborate facilities. Some are commercial operations; others are nonprofit centers run

What constitutes quality child care? These recommendations were made by the National Association for the Education of Young Children (1986). They are based on a consensus arrived at by experts in early childhood education and child development. It is especially important for parents to meet the adults who will care for their child. Caregivers are responsible for every aspect of the program's operation.

1. The adult caregivers

   - The adults should enjoy and understand how infants and young children grow.

   - There should be enough adults to work with a group and to care for the individual needs of children. The recommended ratios of adult caregivers to children of different ages are:

Age of children	Adult to children ratio
0 to 1 Year	1:3
1 to 2 Years	1:5
2 to 3 Years	1:6
3 to 4 Years	1:8
4 to 5 Years	1:10

   - Caregivers should observe and record each child's progress and development.

2. The program activities and equipment

   - The environment should foster the growth and development of young children working and playing together.

   - A good center should provide appropriate and sufficient equipment and play materials and make them readily available.

   - Infants and children should be helped to increase their language skills and to expand their understanding of the world.

3. The relation of staff to families and the community

   - A good program should consider and support the needs of the entire family. Parents should be welcome to observe, discuss policies, make suggestions, and work in the activities of the center.

   - The staff in a good center should be aware of and contribute to community resources. The staff should share information about community recreational and learning opportunities with families.

4. The design of the facility and the program to meet the varied demands of infants and young children, their families, and the staff

   - The health of children, staff, and parents should be protected and promoted. The staff should be alert to the health of each child.

   - The facility should be safe for children and adults.

   - The environment should be spacious enough to accommodate a variety of activities and equipment. More specifically, there should be a minimum of 35 square feet of usable playroom floor space indoors per child and 75 square feet of play space outdoors per child.

FIGURE 11.10 What Is High-Quality Child Care?

by churches, civic groups, and employers. Child care is frequently provided in private homes, at times by child-care professionals, at other times by mothers who want to earn extra money.

A special contemporary interest of researchers who study child care is the role of poverty (Chase-Lansdale, Coley, & Grining, 2001; Huston, McLoyd, & Coll, 1994). In one study, child-care centers that served high-income children delivered better-quality care than did centers that served middle- and low-income children (Phillips & others, 1994). The indices of quality (such as teacher-child ratios) in subsidized centers for the poor were fairly good, but the quality of observed teacher-child interaction was lower than in high-income centers.

What constitutes a high-quality child-care program for infants? The demonstration program developed by Jerome Kagan and his colleagues (Kagan, Kearsley, & Zelazo, 1978) at Harvard University is exemplary. The child-care center included

Careers in Child Development

Rashmi Nakhre, *Child-Care Director*

Rashmi Nakhre has two master's degrees—one in psychology, the other in child development—and is director of the Hattie Daniels Day Care Center in Wilson, North Carolina. At a recent ceremony, "Celebrating a Century of Women," Rashmi received the Distinguished Women of North Carolina Award for 1999–2000.

Rashmi first worked at the child-care center soon after she arrived in the United States 25 years ago. She says that she took the job initially because she needed the money but "ended up falling in love with my job." Rashmi has turned the Wilson, North Carolina, child-care center into a model for other centers. The Center almost closed several years after Rashmi began working there because of financial difficulties. Rashmi played a major role in raising funds not only to keep it open but to improve it. The Center provides quality child care for the children of many Latino migrant workers.

Rashmi Nakhre, working with young children at her child-care center in Wilson, North Carolina.

**National Child Care
Information Center**

**NICHD Study of
Early Child Care**

a pediatrician, a nonteaching director, and an infant-teacher ratio of 3 to 1. Teachers' aides assisted at the center. The teachers and aides were trained to smile frequently, to talk with the infants, and to provide them with a safe environment, which included many stimulating toys. No adverse effects of child care were observed in this project. More information about what to look for in a quality child-care center is presented in figure 11.10. Using such criteria, one study discovered that children who entered low-quality child care as infants were least likely to be socially competent in early childhood (less compliant, less self-controlled, less task-oriented, more hostile, and having more problems in peer interaction) (Howes, 1988). Unfortunately, children who come from families with few resources (psychological, social, and economic) are more likely to experience poor-quality child care than are children from more-advantaged backgrounds (Lamb, 1994). To read about one individual who provides quality child care to individuals from impoverished backgrounds, see the Careers in Child Development insert.

Aware of the growing use of child care, the National Institute of Child Health and Human Development (NICHD) set out to develop a comprehensive, longitudinal study (a study that follows the same individuals over time, usually several years or more) that focuses on the child-care experiences of children and their development. The study began in 1991, and data were collected on a diverse sample of almost 1,400 children and their families at 10 locations across the United States over a period of seven years. Researchers used multiple methods (trained observers, interviews, questionnaires, and testing) and measured many facets of children's development, including physical health, cognitive development, and socioemotional development. Here are some of the results of this extensive study to date (NICHD Early Child Care Network, 2001, 2002, in press):

- *Patterns of use.* There was high reliance on infant care, rapid entry into care postbirth, and considerable instability in care. By 4 months of age, nearly three-fourths of the infants had entered some form of nonmaternal child care. Almost half of the infants were cared for by a relative when they first entered care, and only 12 percent were enrolled in child-care centers. Socioeconomic factors were linked to the amount and type of care. For example, mothers with higher incomes and families that were more dependent on the mother's income placed their infants in child care at an earlier age. Mothers who believed that maternal employment has positive effects on children were more likely to place their infant in nonmaternal care for more hours. Low-income families were more likely than more affluent families to use child care, but infants from low-income families who were in child care averaged as many hours as other income groups. In the preschool years, mothers who were single, those with more education, and families with higher incomes used more hours of center care than other families. Minority families and mothers with less education used more hours of care by relatives.

- *Quality of care.* Quality of care was based on such characteristics as group size, child-adult ratio, physical environment, caregiver characteristics (such as formal education, specialized training, and child-care experience), and caregiver behavior (such as sensitivity to children). Infants from low-income families experienced lower quality of child care than infants from higher-income families. When quality of caregivers' care was high, children performed better on cognitive and language tasks, were more cooperative with their mothers during play, showed more positive and skilled interaction with peers, and had fewer behavior problems. Support was found for policies that improve state regulations for caregiver training and child-staff ratios, which were linked with higher cognitive and social competence at 54 months of age via positive caregiving by the child-care providers.

  Higher-quality child care was related to higher-quality mother-child interaction among the families that used nonmaternal care. Further, poor-quality care was related to an increase of infant insecure attachment to the mother at 15 months of age, but only when the mother was low in sensitivity and responsiveness. However, child-care quality was not linked to attachment security at 36 months of age.

- *Amount of child care.* The quantity of child care predicted some child outcomes. When children spent more hours in child care in their first three years, interactions with the mother (at 6, 15, 24, and 36 months) were less positive. Also, mothers who were more insensitive and unresponsive had children who were less likely to show secure attachment to her at 15 and 36 months. Rates of illness were higher when more hours of child care were experienced.

- *Family and parenting influences.* The results of this large national study indicated that the influence of families and parenting is not weakened by extensive child care. Parents played a significant role in helping children to regulate their emotions, which was related to positive cognitive and social outcomes through the first grade. Higher quality of family environment was associated with preschool children's ability to sustain attention and inhibit impulsive responding.

Review and Reflect: Learning Goal 5

5 Explain attachment and its development

REVIEW

- What is attachment?
- What are some individual variations in attachment?
- How are caregiving styles related to attachment classifications?
- What are some issues related to attachment?
- How do fathers fare as caregivers of infants?
- How does child care affect children?

REFLECT

- Imagine that a friend of yours is getting ready to put her baby in child care. What advice would you give to her? Do you think she should stay at home with the baby? Why or why not? What type of child care would you recommend?

Reach Your Learning Goals

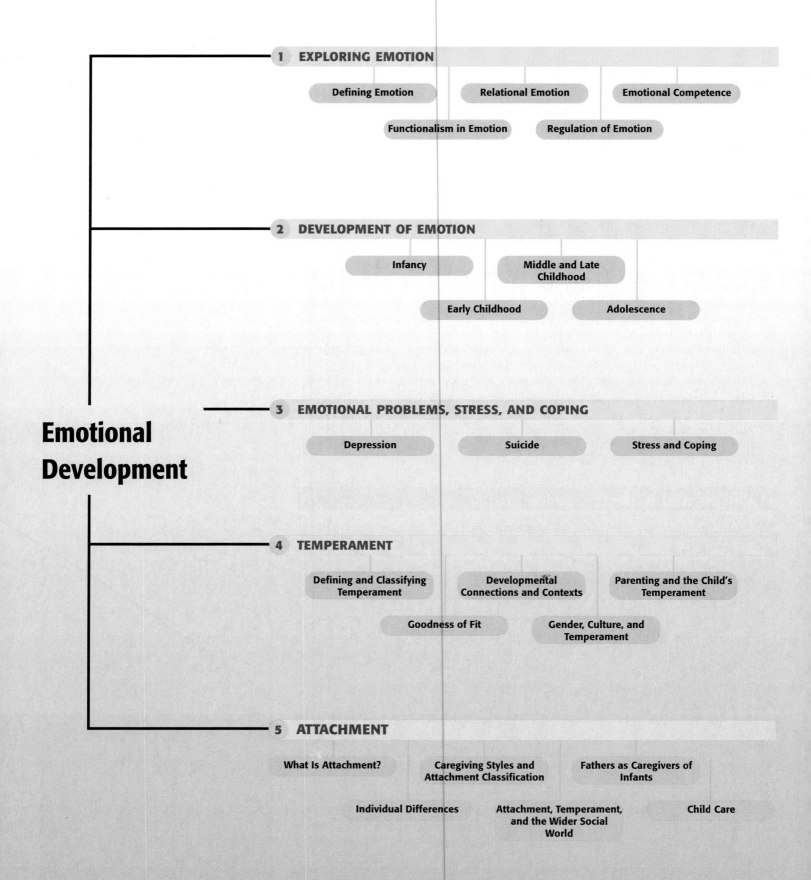

Emotional Development

1 EXPLORING EMOTION

- Defining Emotion
- Relational Emotion
- Emotional Competence
- Functionalism in Emotion
- Regulation of Emotion

2 DEVELOPMENT OF EMOTION

- Infancy
- Middle and Late Childhood
- Early Childhood
- Adolescence

3 EMOTIONAL PROBLEMS, STRESS, AND COPING

- Depression
- Suicide
- Stress and Coping

4 TEMPERAMENT

- Defining and Classifying Temperament
- Developmental Connections and Contexts
- Parenting and the Child's Temperament
- Goodness of Fit
- Gender, Culture, and Temperament

5 ATTACHMENT

- What Is Attachment?
- Caregiving Styles and Attachment Classification
- Fathers as Caregivers of Infants
- Individual Differences
- Attachment, Temperament, and the Wider Social World
- Child Care

Summary

1 Discuss basic aspects of emotion

- Emotion can be defined as feeling, or affect, that can involve physiological arousal, conscious experience, and behavioral expression. Emotions can be classified in terms of positive affectivity or negative affectivity.
- The functionalist view of emotion states that emotions are linked to contexts, often interpersonal ones. In this view, emotions derive their meaning from the individual's goals.
- The relational aspects of emotion involve parent-child relationships and peer relationships. Emotions are the first main language with which parents and infants communicate before the infant acquires speech. Children benefit from having emotion-coaching rather than emotion-dismissing parents. Emotions play an important role in whether a child's peer relations are successful or unsuccessful. Children who show effortful control of their emotions when intense situations arise get along better with their peers and are more socially competent than children who are low in emotional self-regulation.
- The ability to regulate emotions is increasingly recognized as a key aspect of development. With increasing age, children gradually shift from external sources for controlling their emotion to self-initiated sources. Also with increasing age, children are more likely to increase their use of cognitive strategies for regulating emotion, modulate their emotional arousal, become more adept at managing situations to minimize negative emotion, and choose effective ways to cope with stress.
- Becoming emotionally competent involves developing a number of skills, such as becoming aware of one's emotions, being sensitive to others' emotions, and many others. Developing these skills improves the chances that children will be able to manage their emotions more effectively, have a sense of well-being, and be resilient in the face of stress. The skills of emotional competence change developmentally.

2 Describe the development of emotion

- Two broad types of emotions are primary emotions (surprise, interest, joy, anger, sadness, fear, and disgust, which appear in the first six to eight months of life) and self-conscious emotions (empathy, jealousy, and embarrassment, which appear at about 1 ½ years of age and pride, shame, and guilt, which appear at about 2 ½ years of age). Crying is the most important mechanism newborns have for communicating with their world. Babies have at least three types of cries—basic, anger, and pain cries. Controversy swirls about whether babies should be soothed when they cry, although increasingly experts recommend immediately responding in a caring way in the first year. Two types of smiling are reflexive and social. Two fears that infants develop are stranger anxiety and separation from a caregiver (which is reflected in separation protest). Social referencing increases in the second year of life. As infants develop it is important for them to engage in emotional regulation.

- Preschoolers become more adept at talking about their own and others' emotions. Between 2 and 4 years of age, children substantially increase the number of terms they use to describe emotion and learn more about the causes and consequences of feelings. At 5 to 10 years of age, children increasingly reflect on emotions and understand that a single event can elicit different emotions in different people.
- In middle and late childhood, children increasingly understand such complex emotions as pride and shame and that more than one emotion can be expressed in a particular situation. They also increasingly take into account the events leading up to an emotional reaction, suppress and conceal their emotions, and initiate strategies to redirect their emotions.
- Early adolescence is a time when emotional highs and lows increase. It is important for adults to recognize that moodiness is a *normal* aspect of early adolescence.

3 Summarize the nature of depression, suicide, stress, and coping

- Depression is more likely to occur in adolescence than in childhood and in girls more than in boys. In childhood, the features of depression often are mixed with a broader array of behaviors than in adulthood. Bowlby's developmental view, Beck's cognitive view, and Seligman's learned helplessness view provide explanations of depression. Depression is especially prominent in women of childbearing age, and depression in parents is linked with children's adjustment problems. Depression in adolescence can be manifested in boredom, sleep problems, and eating problems.
- Suicide is the third leading cause of death in U.S. 13- to 19-year-olds. Both recent and early developmental factors may be involved in suicide.
- Lazarus believes that children's stress depends on how they cognitively appraise and interpret events. Seligman argues that an important aspect of coping with stress is whether the child is optimistic or pessimistic. Sociocultural influences, such as acculturative stress and poverty, can generate stress. Two good strategies for caregivers in helping children cope with stress are to (1) remove at least one stressor from the child's life and (2) help the child learn to use multiple coping strategies. Young children do not understand the nature of death, believing it is not final. In the middle of the elementary school years, they begin to grasp its final, irreversible nature.

4 Characterize temperament

- Temperament is an individual's behavioral style and characteristic way of emotionally responding. Developmentalists are especially interested in the temperament of infants. Chess and Thomas classified infants as (1) easy, (2) difficult, or (3) slow to warm up. Kagan believes that inhibition to the unfamiliar is an important temperament category. Recent classifications focus more on (1) positive affect and approach, (2) negative affectivity, and (3) effortful control (self-regulation).

- Goodness of fit refers to the match between a child's temperament and the environmental demands the child must cope with. Goodness of fit can be an important aspect of a child's adjustment.
- Activity level in early childhood is linked with being an outgoing young adult. In some cases, a difficult temperament in childhood is linked with adjustment problems in early adulthood.
- In one study, mothers were more responsive to the cries of irritable girls than those of irritable boys. An active temperament might be valued in some cultures (such as the United States) and not in others (such as China).
- Although research evidence is sketchy at this point in time, some general recommendations are that caregivers should (1) be sensitive to the individual characteristics of the child, (2) be flexible in responding to these characteristics, and (3) avoid negative labeling of the child.

5 Explain attachment and its development

- Attachment is a close emotional bond between the infant and caregiver. Feeding is not an important aspect of attachment, although contact comfort and trust are. Bowlby's ethological theory stresses that the caregiver and the infant instinctively trigger attachment. Attachment develops in four phases.
- Securely attached babies use the caregiver, usually the mother, as a secure base from which to explore the environment. Three types of insecure attachment are avoidant, resistant, and disorganized. Ainsworth argued that secure attachment in the first year of life is optimal for development. She created the Strange Situation, an observational measure of attachment.

- Caregivers of secure babies are sensitive to the babies' signals and are consistently available to meet their needs. Caregivers of insecure avoidant babies tend to be unavailable or rejecting. Caregivers of insecure resistant babies tend to be inconsistently available to their babies and usually are not very affectionate. Caregivers of insecure disorganized babies often neglect or physically abuse their babies.
- Some critics argue that attachment theorists have not given adequate attention to genetics and temperament. Other critics stress that they have not adequately taken into account the diversity of social agents and contexts. Cultural variations in attachment have been found, but in all cultures studied to date secure attachment is the most common classification.
- Fathers have increased their interaction with children, but they still lag far behind mothers, even when mothers are employed. The mother's role is often caregiving, the father's playful interaction. In stressful circumstances, infants often prefer their mother rather than their father.
- Child care has become a basic need of the American family. More children are in child care now than at any earlier point in history. The quality of child care is uneven, and child care remains a controversial topic. Quality child care can be achieved and seems to have few adverse affects on children. In the NICHD child-care study, infants from low-income families were found to receive the lowest quality of care. Also, higher quality of child care was linked with higher cognitive and social competence, and fewer child problems. Regardless of the type of child care, the influence of families and parenting on young children's development was not diminished. Parents especially played an important role in helping young children regulate their emotions.

Key Terms

emotion 346
positive affectivity (PA) 347
negative affectivity (NA) 347
primary emotions 350
self-conscious emotions 350
basic cry 351
anger cry 351
pain cry 351

reflexive smile 352
social smile 352
stranger anxiety 352
separation protest 352
social referencing 353
learned helplessness 356
stress 358
cognitive appraisal 359

primary appraisal 359
secondary appraisal 359
acculturation 360
temperament 363
easy child 364
difficult child 364
slow-to-warm-up child 364
goodness of fit 365

attachment 368
secure attachment 370
Strange Situation 371
insecure avoidant babies 371
insecure resistant babies 371
insecure disorganized babies 371

Key People

Nancy Eisenberg 348
Carolyn Saarni 349
John Watson 351
Mary Ainsworth and John Bowlby 351
Jacob Gewirtz 351

Reed Larson and Maryse Richards 355
Aaron Beck 356
Martin Seligman 356
Richard Lazarus 359
Michael Rutter 361

Alexander Chess and Stella Thomas 363
Jerome Kagan 364
Grazyna Kochanska 365
Theodore Wachs 366
Mary Rothbart 367

Harry Harlow 368
Erik Erikson 369
L. Alan Sroufe 371
Ross Thompson 372

Taking It to the Net

1. Catherine is conducting a class for new parents at a local clinic. What advice should Catherine give the parents about how parenting practices can affect a child's inborn temperament?

2. Peter and Rachel are adopting a 3-month-old infant. What are some practical things they can do to help ensure that their child develops a healthy attachment bond with them, in spite of not being with them in the first few months of life?

3. Veronica is anxious about choosing the best child-care center for her child. What are the main things she should consider as she visits the facilities on her list?

Connect to **www.mhhe.com/santrockcd10** to research the answers and complete these exercises.

E-Learning Tools

To help you master the material in this chapter, you'll find a number of valuable study tools on the Student CD-ROM that accompanies this book. Also visit the Online Learning Center for *Child Development,* tenth edition (**www.mhhe.com/santrockcd10**) where you'll find these additional resources:

- View video clips by key developmental psychology experts including Alan Sroufe in attachment theory.

- Build your decision-making skills by trying your hand at the parenting, nursing, and education "Scenarios" on the Online Learning Center.
- Use the interactive Prism exercises to learn more about secure attachment.

*When I say "I," I mean
something absolutely
unique not to be confused
with any other.*

—UGO BETTI
Italian Playwright, 20th Century

The Self and Identity

Chapter Outline

Learning Goals

SELF-UNDERSTANDING

What Is Self-Understanding?

Developmental Changes

1 Discuss self-understanding and its development

SELF-ESTEEM AND SELF-CONCEPT

What Are Self-Esteem and Self-Concept?

Assessment

Parent-Child Relationships

Developmental Changes

Consequences of Low Self-Esteem

Increasing Children's Self-Esteem

2 Explain self-esteem and self-concept

IDENTITY

Erikson's View

Some Contemporary Thoughts

Identity Statuses

Developmental Changes

Social Contexts

3 Describe identity and its development

The Story of a 15-Year-Old Girl's Self-Description

How do adolescents describe themselves? How would you have described yourself when you were 15 years old? What features would you have emphasized? Here is a self-portrait of one 15-year-old girl:

What am I like as a person? Complicated! I'm sensitive, friendly, outgoing, popular, and tolerant, though I can also be shy, self-conscious, and even obnoxious. Obnoxious! I'd *like* to be friendly and tolerant all of the time. That's the kind of person I *want* to be, and I'm disappointed when I'm not. I'm responsible, even studious now and then, but on the other hand, I'm a goof-off, too, because if you're too studious, you won't be popular. I don't usually do that well at school. I'm a pretty cheerful person, especially with my friends, where I can even get rowdy. At home I'm more likely to be anxious around my parents. They expect me to get all A's. It's not fair! I worry about how I probably *should* get better grades. But I'd be mortified in the eyes of my friends. So I'm usually pretty stressed-out at home, or sarcastic, since my parents are always on my case. But I really don't understand how I can switch so fast. I mean, how can I be cheerful one minute, anxious the next, and then be sarcastic? Which one is the *real* me? Sometimes, I feel phony, especially around boys. Say I think some guy might be interested in asking me out. I try to act different, like Madonna. I'll be flirtatious and fun-loving. And then everybody, I mean *everybody* else is looking at me like they think I'm totally weird. Then I get self-conscious and embarrassed and become radically introverted, and I don't know who I really am! Am I just trying to impress them or what? But I don't really care what they think anyway. I don't *want* to care, that is. I just want to know what my close friends think. I can be my true self with my close friends. I can't be my real self with my parents. They don't understand me. What do *they* know about what it's like to be a teenager? They still treat me like I'm still a kid. At least at school people treat you more like you're an adult. That gets confusing, though. I mean, which am I, a kid or an adult? It's scary, too, because I don't have any idea what I want to be when I grow up. I mean, I have lots of *ideas*. My friend Sheryl and I talk about whether we'll be stewardesses, or teachers, or nurses, veterinarians, maybe mothers, or actresses. I know I *don't* want to be a waitress or a secretary. But how do you decide all of this? I really don't know. I mean, I think about it a lot, but I can't resolve it. There are days when I wish I could just become immune to myself. (Harter, 1990, pp. 352–353)

In this chapter, we will further explore self-understanding in adolescence as well as other age periods. We will also study self-esteem and self-concept. Then, we will examine identity and its development.

1 SELF-UNDERSTANDING

What Is Self-Understanding?	Developmental Changes

What is self-understanding? When do children initially develop a self-understanding? How does self-understanding develop during the childhood and adolescent years? What is the role of perspective taking in self-understanding? We will examine each of these questions.

What Is Self-Understanding?

Self-understanding is a child's cognitive representation of the self, the substance and content of the child's self-conceptions. For example, an 11-year-old boy understands that he is a student, a boy, a football player, a family member, a video game lover, and a rock music fan. A 13-year-old girl understands that she is a middle school student, in the midst of puberty, a girl, a cheerleader, a student council member, and a movie fan. A child's self-understanding is based, in part, on the various roles and membership categories that define who children are (Harter, 1990, 1999). Though not the whole of personal identity, self-understanding provides its rational underpinnings (Damon & Hart, 1988).

Three facets of self-understanding are (1) personal memories, (2) representations of the self, and (3) theories of the self (Garcia, Hart, & Johnson-Ray, 1998). *Personal memories* are autobiographical episodes that are especially important in thoughts about oneself. These might include memories of a fight with one's parents, a day spent with a friend, a teacher saying how good one's work is, and so on.

Representations of the self include the generalized ascriptions individuals make about their selves. For example, individuals have representations of their actual selves (such as "I am big, smart, and socially awkward"), their ideal selves ("I want to be a teacher and be respected by the community"), and their past selves ("I used to be very shy").

Theories of the self enable individuals to identify which characteristics of the self are relevant, arrange these characteristics in hierarchical order of importance, and make claims about how these characteristics are related to each other. Theories of the self provide an individual with a sense of identity and a source of orientation to the world.

Developmental Changes

As children develop, their self-understanding changes. First, let's examine the development of self-understanding in infants.

Infancy Infants are not just "given" a self by their parents or the culture; rather, they find and construct selves (Garcia, Hart, & Johnson-Ray, 1998). Studying the self in infancy is difficult mainly because of infants' inability to describe with language their experiences of themselves.

Infants cannot verbally express their views on the nature of the self. They also cannot understand the complex instructions required to engage in a child developmentalist's tasks. Given these restrictions, how can researchers study infants' self-understanding? They test infants' *visual self-recognition* by presenting them with images of themselves in mirrors, pictures, and other visual media. For example, let's examine how the mirror technique works. An infant's mother puts a dot of rouge on the infant's nose. An observer watches to see how often the infant touches its nose. Next, the infant is placed in front of a mirror, and observers detect whether nose touching increases. The idea is that when the infant looks in the mirror and tries to touch or rub off the rouge, this violates the infant's self schema. The infant realizes that it is the self in the mirror but that something is not right since the real self does not have a dot of rouge on it.

In two separate investigations, in the second half of the second year of life, infants recognized their own images in the mirror and coordinated the images they saw with the actions of touching their own bodies (Amsterdam, 1968; Lewis & Brooks-Gunn, 1979) (see figure 12.1). In sum, human infants initially develop a sense of rudimentary self-understanding called self-recognition at approximately 18 months of age (Hart & Karmel, 1996; Lewis & others, 1989).

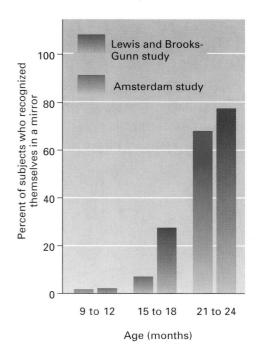

FIGURE 12.1 The Development of Self-Recognition in Infancy

The graph gives the findings of two studies in which infants of different ages showed recognition of rouge by touching, wiping, or verbally referring to it. Notice that self-recognition did not occur extensively until the second half of the second year of life.

self-understanding A child's cognitive representation of the self, the substance and content of a child's self-conceptions.

Concepts of Person and Self

Recent and Forthcoming Books on the Self

International Society for Self and Identity

Self-Development in Infancy

Early Childhood Because children can verbally communicate their ideas, research on self-understanding in childhood is not limited to visual self-recognition, as it is during infancy. Mainly through interviews, researchers have probed children's conceptions of many aspects of self-understanding, including mind and body, self in relation to others, and pride and shame in self. In early childhood, children usually conceive of the self in physical terms. Most young children conceive of the self as part of the body, which usually means the head. Young children generally confuse self, mind, and body (Broughton, 1978). For them, because the self is a body part, it can be described along many material dimensions, such as size, shape, and color. Young children distinguish themselves from others through many different physical and material attributes. Says 4-year-old Sandra, "I'm different from Jennifer because I have brown hair and she has blond hair." Says 4-year-old Ralph, "I am different from Hank because I am taller and I am different from my sister because I have a bicycle."

Researchers also believe that the *active dimension* is a central component of the self in early childhood (Keller, Ford, & Meacham, 1978). If we define the category "physical" broadly enough, we can include physical actions as well as body image and material possessions. For example, preschool children often describe themselves in terms of activities such as play. In sum, in early childhood, children often describe themselves in terms of a physical self or an active self.

Middle and Late Childhood In middle and late childhood, self-understanding increasingly shifts from defining oneself through external characteristics to defining oneself through internal characteristics. Also, elementary-school-age children are more likely to define themselves in terms of social characteristics and social comparison.

In middle and late childhood, children not only recognize differences between inner and outer states, but they are also more likely to include subjective inner states in their definition of self. In one investigation, second-grade children were much more likely than younger children to name psychological characteristics (such as preferences or personality traits) in their self-definition and less likely to name physical characteristics (such as eye color or possessions) (Aboud & Skerry, 1983). For example, 8-year-old Todd includes in his self-description, "I am smart and I am popular." Ten-year-old Tina says about herself, "I am pretty good about not worrying most of the time. I used to lose my temper but I'm better about that now. I also feel proud when I do well in school."

In addition to the increase of psychological characteristics in self-definition during the elementary school years, the *social aspects* of the self also increase at this point in development. In one investigation, elementary school children included references to social groups in their self-description (Livesly & Bromley, 1973). For example, some children referred to themselves as Girl Scouts, as Catholics, or as someone who has two close friends.

Children's self-understanding in the elementary school years also includes increasing reference to *social comparison.* At this point in development, children are more likely to distinguish themselves from others in comparative rather than in absolute terms. That is, elementary-school-age children are no longer as likely to think about what I do or do not do, but are more likely to think about what I can do *in comparison with others.* This developmental shift provides an increased tendency of establishing one's differences as an individual apart from others. In a series of studies, Diane Ruble (1983) investigated children's use of social comparison in their self-evaluations. Children were given a difficult task and then offered feedback on their performance, as well as information about the performances of other children their age. The children were then asked for self-evaluations. Children younger than 7 made virtually no reference to the information about other children's performances. However, many children older than 7 included socially comparative information in their self-descriptions.

Adolescence   The development of self-understanding in adolescence is complex and involves a number of aspects of the self (Harter, 1998, 1999). Let's examine how the adolescent's self-understanding differs from the child's.

Abstract and Idealistic   Remember from our discussion of Piaget's theory of cognitive development in chapters 2 and 7 that many adolescents begin to think in more *abstract* and *idealistic* ways. ◀ pages 35, 221 When asked to describe themselves, adolescents are more likely than children to use abstract and idealistic labels. Consider 14-year-old Laurie's abstract description of herself: "I am a human being. I am indecisive. I don't know who I am." Also consider her idealistic description of herself: "I am a naturally sensitive person who really cares about people's feelings. I think I'm pretty good-looking." Not all adolescents describe themselves in idealistic ways, but most adolescents distinguish between the real self and the ideal self.

Differentiated   Adolescents' self-understanding becomes increasingly *differentiated.* Adolescents are more likely than children to describe themselves with contextual or situational variations (Harter & others, 1998). For example, 15-year-old Amy describes herself with one set of characteristics in relation to her family and another set of characteristics in relation to her peers and friends. Yet another set of characteristics appears in self-description regarding her romantic relationship. In sum, adolescents are more likely than children to understand that one possesses different selves, depending on one's role or particular context.

The Fluctuating Self   Given the contradictory nature of the self in adolescence, it is not surprising that the self fluctuates across situations and across time (Harter, 1990). The 15-year-old girl quoted at the beginning of the chapter remarked that she could not understand how she could switch so fast—from being cheerful one moment, to being anxious the next, and then sarcastic a short time later. One researcher described the fluctuating nature of the adolescent's self with the metaphor of "the barometric self" (Rosenberg, 1986). The adolescent's self continues to be characterized by instability until the adolescent constructs a more unified theory of self, usually not until late adolescence or even early adulthood.

Contradictions Within the Self   The differentiation into multiple selves begins in early adolescence and by the middle of adolescence causes conflict and distress. In one study, Susan Harter (1986) asked seventh-, ninth-, and eleventh-graders to describe themselves. She found that the extent to which adolescents identified self-descriptive pairs of attributes as opposites in conflict with each other (ugly *and* attractive, bored *and* inquisitive, caring *and* uncaring, introverted *and* fun-loving, and so on) dramatically increased between the seventh and ninth grades. The contradictory self-descriptions declined in the eleventh grade but still were higher than in the seventh grade. Adolescents develop the cognitive ability to detect these inconsistencies in the self as they strive to construct a general theory of the self or of their personality (Harter & Monsour, 1992). In the seventh grade, adolescents don't have the ability to detect the conflicting opposites in self-descriptions (although they exist in their self-portrait). In the ninth grade, they have the cognitive ability to detect opposites, but don't have the cognitive ability to resolve the contradictions. Only in the eleventh grade are they able to integrate them. For example, older adolescents can integrate self-descriptions such as being cheerful with friends and depressed with parents, or comfortable with friends but nervous with a date.

Real and Ideal, True and False Selves   The adolescent's emerging ability to construct ideal selves in addition to actual ones can be perplexing to the adolescent. Recall from the chapter opening story how adolescents distinguish between true and false selves but often agonize about the distinction. The capacity to recognize a discrepancy between *real* and *ideal* selves represents a cognitive advance, but humanistic theorist

Know thyself, for once we know ourselves, we may learn how to care for ourselves, but otherwise we never shall.

—Socrates
Greek Philosopher, 5th Century B.C.

Carl Rogers (1950) believed that when the real and ideal selves are too discrepant, it is a sign of maladjustment. Depression can result from a substantial discrepancy between one's actual self and one's ideal self (the person one wants to be) because an awareness of this discrepancy can produce a sense of failure and self-criticism.

While, as just mentioned, some theorists consider a strong discrepancy between the ideal and real selves as maladaptive, others argue that this is not always true, especially in adolescence. For example, in one view, an important aspect of the ideal or imagined self is the **possible self,** what individuals might become, what they would like to become, and what they are afraid of becoming (Markus & Nurius, 1986). Thus, adolescents' possible selves include both what adolescents hope to be as well as what they dread they will become (Bybee & Wells, 2003; Martin, 1997). In this view, the presence of both hoped-for as well as dreaded selves is psychologically healthy, providing a balance between positive, expected selves and negative, feared selves. The attributes of future positive selves (getting into a good college, being admired, having a successful career) can direct future positive states, while attributes of future negative selves (being unemployed, being lonely, not getting into a good college) can identify what is to be avoided in the future. To read further about the important concept of multiple selves in adolescence, see the Explorations in Child Development box.

Can adolescents distinguish between their *true* and *false* selves? In one research study, they could (Harter & Lee, 1989). Adolescents are most likely to show their false self in romantic or dating situations, and with classmates; they are least likely to show their false self with close friends. Adolescents display a false self to impress others, to try out new behaviors or roles, because others force them to behave in false ways, and because others do not understand their true self. Some adolescents report that they do not like their false-self behavior, but others say that it does not bother them. Harter and her colleagues (1996) found that experienced authenticity of the self is highest among adolescents who say they receive support from their parents.

Social Comparison Some developmentalists believe that adolescents are more likely than children to use *social comparison* to evaluate themselves (Ruble & others, 1980). However, adolescents' willingness to admit that they engage in social comparison to evaluate themselves declines in adolescence because they view social comparison as socially undesirable. They think that acknowledging their social comparison motives will endanger their popularity. Relying on social comparison information in adolescence may be confusing because of the large number of reference groups. For example, should adolescents compare themselves to classmates in general? to friends? to their own gender? to popular adolescents? to good-looking adolescents? to athletic adolescents? Simultaneously considering all of these social comparison groups can be perplexing for adolescents.

Self-Conscious Adolescents are more likely than children to be *self-conscious* about and *preoccupied* with their self-understanding. As part of their self-conscious and preoccupied self-exploration, adolescents become more introspective. However, the introspection is not always done in social isolation. Sometimes, adolescents turn to their friends for support and self-clarification, obtaining their friends' opinions of an emerging self-definition. As one researcher on self-development commented, adolescents' friends are often the main source of reflected self-appraisals, becoming the social mirror into which adolescents anxiously stare (Rosenberg, 1979). This self-consciousness and self-preoccupation reflect the concept of adolescent egocentrism, which we discussed in chapter 7. ◀ **page 224**

Self-Protective In adolescence, self-understanding includes more mechanisms to *protect the self.* Although adolescents often display a sense of confusion and conflict stimulated by introspective efforts to understand themselves, they also call on mechanisms to protect and enhance the self. In protecting the self, adolescents are prone to minimize or discount their negative characteristics. For example, in Harter's inves-

possible self What an individual might become, what the person would like to become, and what the person is afraid of becoming.

Multiple Selves and Sociocultural Contexts

One of the most important shifts in the study of the self-system in the last several decades has been toward conceptualizing the self as a multidimensional framework (Harter, 1999). Differentiation of the self increases with age, so that the number of domains of the self that can be evaluated increase across the childhood, adolescence, and adult periods of development.

The increasing proliferation of selves in adolescence can vary across relationships with people, social roles, and sociocultural contexts. Researchers have found that adolescents' portraits of themselves can change depending on whether they describe themselves when they are with their mother, father, close friend, romantic partner, or peer. They also can change depending on whether they describe themselves in roles as a student, athlete, or on the job. And adolescents can create different selves depending on their ethnic and cultural background and experiences.

The multiple selves of ethnic minority youth can reflect their efforts to bridge multiple worlds (Cooper & others, 1995). Many ethnic minority youth must move between multiple contexts, some of which are populated by members of their own ethnic group, others of which are populated by members of the majority culture who might not share the values of their family of origin.

Some youth, especially those whose values are similar to those of the majority culture, move smoothly across these multiple worlds. Others, for whom there is less compatibility across cultures, might adopt strong bicultural or multicultural selves.

Hazel Markus and her colleagues (Markus & Kitayama, 1994; Markus, Mullally, & Kitayama, 1999) believe that it is important to understand how multiple selves emerge through participation in cultural practices. They argue that all selves are culture-specific selves that emerge as individuals adapt to their cultural environments. In North American contexts (especially middle-SES), individuality is promoted and maintained. North Americans, when given the opportunity to describe themselves, often provide not only portraits of their current selves but notions of their future selves as well. They also frequently show a need for having multiple selves that are stable and consistent. In Japan, multiple selves are often described in terms of relatedness to others. Self-improvement also is an important aspect of the multiple selves of many Japanese. Markus and her colleagues recognize that cultural groups are characterized by diversity but nonetheless conclude that it is helpful to understand the dominant aspects of multiple selves within a culture.

---

tigation of self-understanding, positive self-descriptions, such as *attractive, fun-loving, sensitive, affectionate,* and *inquisitive,* were more likely to be ascribed to the core of the self, indicating more importance, whereas negative self-descriptions, such as *ugly, mediocre, depressed, selfish,* and *nervous,* were more likely to be ascribed to the periphery of the self, indicating less importance (Harter, 1986).

Unconscious   In adolescence, self-understanding involves greater recognition that the self includes *unconscious,* as well as conscious, components, a recognition not likely to occur until late adolescence (Selman, 1980). That is, older adolescents are more likely than younger adolescents to believe that certain aspects of their mental experience are beyond their awareness or control.

Self-Integration   In adolescence, self-understanding becomes more *integrative,* with the disparate parts of the self more systematically pieced together, especially in late adolescence. Older adolescents are more likely to detect inconsistencies in their earlier self-descriptions as they attempt to construct a general theory of self, an integrated sense of identity.

Because the adolescent creates multiple self-concepts, the task of integrating these varying self-conceptions becomes problematic (Harter & Monsour, 1992). At the same time that adolescents are faced with pressures to differentiate the self into multiple roles, the emergence of formal operational thought presses for *integration* and the development of a consistent, coherent theory of self. These budding formal operational skills initially present a liability because they first allow adolescents to *detect* inconsistencies in the self across varying roles, only later providing the cognitive capacity to *integrate* such apparent contradictions. In the narrative that opened this chapter, the 15-year-old girl could not understand how she could be cheerful yet depressed and sarcastic, wondering "Which is the *real* me?". Researchers have found that 14- to 15-year-olds not only detect inconsistencies across their various roles (with parents, friends, and romantic partners, for example) but are much more troubled by these contradictions than younger (11- to 12-year-old) and older (17- to 18-year-old) adolescents are (Damon & Hart, 1988).

Abstract and idealistic

Differentiated

Contradictions within the self

Fluctuating

Real and ideal, true and false selves

Social comparison

Self-conscious

Self-protective

Integrative

FIGURE 12.2 Characteristics of Adolescents' Self-Understanding

perspective taking The ability to assume another person's perspective and understand his or her thoughts or feelings.

Conclusions   As we have seen, the development of self-understanding in adolescence is complex and involves a number of aspects of the self (see figure 12.2). Rapid changes that occur in the transition from childhood to adolescence result in heightened self-awareness and consciousness. This heightened self-focus leads to consideration of the self and the many changes that are occurring in it, which can produce doubt about who the self is and which facets of the self are "real" (Hart, 1996).

The Role of Perspective Taking in Self-Understanding   In Piaget's theory, which we discussed in chapters 2, "The Science of Child Development," and 7, "Cognitive Developmental Approaches," young children are egocentric.   ◀ **pages 35, 224** As they develop, they move away from this self-centeredness. These ideas of Piaget served as a foundation for the contemporary belief that perspective taking plays an important role in self-understanding. **Perspective taking** is the ability to assume another person's perspective and understand his or her thoughts and feelings.

Robert Selman (1980) has proposed a developmental theory of perspective taking that has been given considerable attention. He believes perspective taking involves a series of five stages, ranging from 3 years of age through adolescence (see figure 12.3). These stages begin with the egocentric viewpoint in early childhood and end with in-depth perspective taking in adolescence.

To study children's perspective taking, Selman interviews individual children, asking them to comment on such dilemmas as this one:

> Holly is an 8-year-old girl who likes to climb trees. She is the best tree climber in the neighborhood. One day while climbing down from a tall tree, she falls . . . but does not hurt herself. Her father sees her fall. He is upset and asks her to promise not to climb trees anymore. Holly promises.
>
> Later that day, Holly and her friends meet Shawn. Shawn's kitten is caught in a tree and can't get down. Something has to be done right away or the kitten may fall. Holly is the only one who climbs trees well enough to reach the kitten and get it down but she remembers her promise to her father. (Selman, 1976, p. 302)

Subsequently, Selman asks each child a series of questions about the dilemma, such as these:

Stage	Perspective-taking stage	Ages	Description
0	Egocentric viewpoint	3 to 5	Child has a sense of differentiation of self and other but fails to distinguish between the social perspective (thoughts, feelings) of other and self. Child can label other's overt feelings but does not see the cause-and-effect relation of reasons to social actions.
1	Social-informational perspective taking	6 to 8	Child is aware that other has a social perspective based on other's own reasoning, which may or may not be similar to child's. However, child tends to focus on one perspective rather than coordinating viewpoints.
2	Self-reflective perspective taking	8 to 10	Child is conscious that each individual is aware of the other's perspective and that this awareness influences self's and other's view of each other. Putting self in other's place is a way of judging other's intentions, purposes, and actions. Child can form a coordinated chain of perspectives but cannot yet abstract from this process to the level of simultaneous mutuality.
3	Mutual perspective taking	10 to 12	Adolescent realizes that both self and other can view each other mutually and simultaneously as subjects. Adolescent can step outside the two-person dyad and view the interaction from a third-person perspective.
4	Social and conventional system perspective taking	12 to 15	Adolescent realizes mutual perspective taking does not always lead to complete understanding. Social conventions are seen as necessary because they are understood by all members of the group (the generalized other), regardless of their position, role, or experience.

FIGURE 12.3 Selman's Stages of Perspective Taking

- Does Holly know how Shawn feels about the kitten?
- How will Holly's father feel if he finds out she climbed the tree?
- What does Holly think her father will do if he finds out she climbed the tree?
- What would you do in this situation?

By analyzing children's responses to these dilemmas, Selman (1980) concluded that children's perspective taking follows the developmental sequence described in figure 12.3.

Children's perspective taking not only can increase their self-understanding, but it can also improve their peer group status and the quality of their friendships. For example, one investigation found that the most popular children in the third and eighth grades had competent perspective-taking skills (Kurdek & Krile, 1982). Children who are competent at perspective taking are better at understanding the needs of their companions, so they likely can communicate more effectively with them (Hudson, Forman, & Brion-Meisels, 1982).

Review and Reflect: Learning Goal 1

1 Discuss self-understanding and its development

REVIEW

- What is self-understanding?
- How does self-understanding change from infancy through adolescence?

REFLECT

- If a psychologist had interviewed you at 10 and at 16 years of age, how would your self-understanding have been different?

2 SELF-ESTEEM AND SELF-CONCEPT

What Are Self-Esteem and Self-Concept?	Parent-Child Relationships	Consequences of Low Self-Esteem
Assessment	Developmental Changes	Increasing Children's Self-Esteem

Self-conception involves not only self-understanding but also self-esteem and self-concept. That is, not only do children try to define and describe attributes of the self (self-understanding), but they also evaluate these attributes (self-esteem and self-concept).

What Are Self-Esteem and Self-Concept?

Self-esteem, also referred to as self-worth or self-image, is the global evaluative dimension of the self. For example, a child might perceive that she is not merely a person but a *good* person. Of course, not all children have an overall positive image of themselves.

Self-concept refers to domain-specific evaluations of the self. Children can make self-evaluations in many domains of their lives—academic, athletic, physical appearance, and so on. In sum, self-esteem refers to global self-evaluations, self-concept to more domain-specific evaluations.

self-esteem The global evaluative dimension of the self; also called self-worth or self-image.

self-concept Domain-specific self-evaluations.

FIGURE 12.4 Evaluating Self-Esteem

These items are from a widely used measure of self-esteem, the Rosenburg Scale of Self-Esteem. The items deal with your general feelings about yourself. Place a check mark in the column that best describes your feelings about yourself:
1 = strongly agree, 2 = agree, 3 = disagree, 4 = strongly disagree.

	1	2	3	4
1. I feel that I am a person of worth, at least on an equal plane with others.				
2. I feel that I have a number of good qualities.				
3. All in all, I am inclined to feel that I am a failure.				
4. I am able to do things as well as most other people.				
5. I feel I do not have much to be proud of.				
6. I take a positive attitude toward myself.				
7. On the whole, I am satisfied with myself.				
8. I wish I could have more respect for myself.				
9. I certainly feel useless at times.				
10. At times I think I am no good at all.				

To obtain your self-esteem score, reverse your scores for items 3, 5, 8, 9, and 10. Add those scores to your scores for items 1, 2, 4, 6, and for your overall self-esteem score. Scores can range from 10 to 40. If you scored below 20, consider contacting the counseling center at your college or university for help in improving your self-esteem.

Investigators have not always made clear distinctions between self-esteem and self-concept, sometimes using the terms interchangeably or not precisely defining them (Dusek & McIntyre, 2003). As you read the remaining discussion of self-esteem and self-concept, the distinction between self-esteem as global self-evaluation and self-concept as domain-specific self-evaluation should help you to keep the terms straight. To evaluate your self-esteem, see figure 12.4.

Assessment

Measuring self-esteem and self-concept hasn't always been easy (Dusek & McIntyre, 2003). Recently, different measures have been developed to assess children and adolescents.

Susan Harter's (1985) Self-Perception Profile for Children is a revision of her original instrument, the Perceived Competence Scale for Children (Harter, 1982). The Self-Perception Profile for Children taps five specific domains of self-concept—scholastic competence, athletic competence, social acceptance, physical appearance, and behavioral conduct—plus general self-worth. Harter's scale does an excellent job of separating children's self-evaluations in different domains, and when general self-worth is assessed, questions focus on the overall self-evaluations rather than on specific domains.

The Self-Perception Profile for Children is designed to be used with third-grade through sixth-grade children. Harter also has developed a separate scale for adolescents, recognizing important developmental changes in self-perceptions. The Self-Perception Profile for Adolescents (Harter, 1989) taps eight domains—scholastic competence, athletic competence, social acceptance, physical appearance, behavioral conduct, close friendship, romantic appeal, and job competence—plus global self-worth. Thus the adolescent version has three domains not present in the children's version—job competence, romantic appeal, and close friendship.

Parent-Child Relationships

In the most extensive investigation of parent-child relationships and self-esteem, these parenting attributes were associated with boys' high self-esteem (Coopersmith, 1967):

- Expression of affection
- Concern about the child's problems
- Harmony in the home
- Participation in joint family activities
- Availability to give competent, organized help to the boys when they need it
- Setting clear and fair rules
- Abiding by these rules
- Allowing the children freedom within well-prescribed limits

Remember that these findings are correlational, and so we cannot say that these parenting attributes *cause* children's high self-esteem. Such factors as parental acceptance and allowing children freedom within well-prescribed limits probably are important determinants of children's self-esteem, but we still must say that they *are related to* rather than that they *cause* children's self-esteem, based on the available research data.

An Adolescent Talks About Self-Esteem

Exploring Self-Esteem Research

Self-Esteem Websites

Developmental Changes

In one recent study, both boys and girls had particularly high self-esteem in childhood but their self-esteem dropped considerably during adolescence (Robins & others, 2002). And the self-esteem of girls dropped about twice as much as boys' during adolescence. Other researchers have also found a more substantial drop in the self-esteem of girls than boys in adolescence (Kling & others, 1999; Major & others, 1999).

Why does self-esteem drop in adolescence, and why does it especially drop so strongly for girls? Among the reasons given for the self-esteem decline in both boys and girls are the rather intense physical changes of puberty, increased achievement demands and expectations, and inadequate support from parents and schools. Among the reasons given for gender disparity in the decline of self-esteem are the high expectations for physical attractiveness in females, which becomes more pronounced with pubertal change, and motivation for social relationships that is not rewarded by society (Crawford & Unger, 2000).

> *T*he living self has one purpose only: to come into its own fullness of being, as a tree comes into full blossom, or a bird into spring beauty, or a tiger into lustre.
>
> —D. H. LAWRENCE
> *English Author, 20th Century*

Consequences of Low Self-Esteem

For most children and adolescents, low self-esteem results only in temporary emotional discomfort (Damon, 1991). But in some children and adolescents, low self-esteem can translate into other problems (DuBois, Felner, & Brand, 1997). It has been implicated in depression, suicide, adolescent pregnancy, drug abuse, and delinquency (Crockenberg & Soby, 1989; Harter & Marold, 1992; Miller, 1988). The seriousness of the problem depends not only on the nature of the child's and adolescent's low self-esteem but on other conditions as well. When low self-esteem is compounded by difficult school transitions or family life, or by other stressful events, the child's problems can intensify (Rutter & Garmezy, 1983).

Increasing Children's Self-Esteem

Four ways children's self-esteem can be improved are through (1) identification of the causes of low self-esteem and the domains of competence important to the self, (2) emotional support and social approval, (3) achievement, and (4) coping (see figure 12.5).

Identifying children's sources of self-esteem—that is, competence in domains important to the self—is critical to improving self-esteem. Susan Harter (1990) points

FIGURE 12.5 Four Key Aspects of Improving Self-Esteem

Identifying the causes of low self-esteem and which domains of competence are important to the self

Emotional support and social approval

Achievement

Coping

out that the self-esteem enhancement programs of the 1960s, in which self-esteem itself was the target and individuals were encouraged to simply feel good about themselves, were ineffective. Rather, Harter believes that intervention must occur at the level of the *causes* of self-esteem if the individual's self-esteem is to improve significantly. Children have the highest self-esteem when they perform competently in domains that are important to them. Therefore, children should be encouraged to identify and value areas of competence.

Emotional support and social approval in the form of confirmation from others also powerfully influence children's self-esteem. Some children with low self-esteem come from conflicted families or conditions in which they experienced abuse or neglect—situations in which support was unavailable. In some cases, alternative sources of support can be implemented either informally through the encouragement of a teacher, a coach, or another significant adult or, more formally, through programs such as Big Brothers and Big Sisters. While peer approval becomes increasingly important during adolescence, both adult and peer support are important influences on the adolescent's self-esteem.

Achievement also can improve children's self-esteem (Bednar, Wells, & Peterson, 1995). For example, the straightforward teaching of real skills to children often results in increased achievement and, thus, in enhanced self-esteem. Children develop higher self-esteem because they know the important tasks to achieve goals, and they have experienced performing them or similar behaviors. The emphasis on the importance of achievement in improving self-esteem has much in common with Bandura's social cognitive concept of *self-efficacy,* which refers to individuals' beliefs that they can master a situation and produce positive outcomes.

Self-esteem also is often increased when children face a problem and try to cope with it, rather than avoid it. If coping rather than avoidance prevails, children often face problems realistically, honestly, and nondefensively. This produces favorable self-evaluative thoughts, which lead to the self-generated approval that raises self-esteem. The converse is true of low self-esteem. Unfavorable self-evaluations trigger denial, deception, and avoidance in an attempt to disavow that which has already been glimpsed as true. This process leads to self-generated disapproval as a form of feedback to the self about personal adequacy.

Review and Reflect: Learning Goal 2

2 Explain self-esteem and self-concept

REVIEW

- What are self-esteem and self-concept?
- How are self-esteem and self-concept assessed?
- What role do parent-child relationships play in self-esteem?
- When is self-esteem likely to drop developmentally? Why?
- What are the consequences of low self-esteem?
- How can children's self-esteem be increased?

REFLECT

- What behaviors would you look for when observing a child to give you an indication that a child has low or high self-esteem?

---

3 IDENTITY

- **Erikson's View**
- **Identity Statuses**
- **Social Contexts**
- **Some Contemporary Thoughts**
- **Developmental Changes**

By far the most comprehensive and provocative theory of identity development is Erik Erikson's. Some experts on adolescence consider Erikson's ideas to be the single most influential theory of adolescent development. Erikson's theory was introduced in chapter 2. page 31 Here that introduction is expanded, beginning with reanalysis of his ideas on identity. Then we examine some contemporary thoughts on identity, the four statuses of identity, developmental changes, family influences on identity, cultural and ethnic aspects of identity, and gender and identity development.

Erikson's View

Who am I? What am I all about? What am I going to do with my life? What is different about me? How can I make it on my own? Not usually considered during childhood, these questions surface as common, virtually universal, concerns during adolescence. Adolescents clamor for solutions to these questions that revolve around the concept of identity, and it was Erik Erikson (1950, 1968) who first understood how central such questions are to understanding adolescent development. That today identity is believed to be a key concept in adolescent development is a result of Erikson's masterful thinking and analysis.

Revisiting Erikson's Ideas About Identity
Identity versus identity confusion is Erikson's fifth developmental stage, which individuals experience during adolescence. At this time, adolescents examine who they are, what they are all about, and where they are going in life. Adolescents are confronted with many new roles, such as vocational and romantic roles.

identity versus identity confusion Erikson's fifth developmental stage, which individuals experience during the adolescent years. At this time, adolescents examine who they are, what they are all about, and where they are going in life.

ho are you?" said the caterpillar. Alice replied rather shyly, "I—I hardly know, sir, just at present—at least I know who I was when I got up this morning, but I must have changed several times since then."

—LEWIS CARROLL
English Writer, 19th Century

Psychosocial moratorium is Erikson's term for the gap between childhood security and adult autonomy that adolescents experience as part of their identity exploration. As adolescents explore and search their culture's identity files, they often experiment with different roles. Youth who successfully cope with these conflicting identities emerge with a new sense of self that is both refreshing and acceptable. Adolescents who do not successfully resolve this identity crisis suffer what Erikson calls identity confusion. The confusion takes one of two courses: Individuals withdraw, isolating themselves from peers and family, or they immerse themselves in the world of peers and lose their identity in the crowd.

Erikson's ideas about adolescent identity development reveal rich insights into adolescents' thoughts and feelings. Reading one or more of his original writings is worthwhile. A good starting point is *Identity: Youth and Crisis* (1968). Other works that portray identity development are *Young Man Luther* (1962) and *Gandhi's Truth* (1969)—the latter won a Pulitzer Prize.

Personality and Role Experimentation   Two core ingredients in Erikson's theory of identity development are personality and role experimentation. As indicated earlier, Erikson believes that adolescents face an overwhelming number of choices and at some point during youth enter a period of psychological moratorium. During this moratorium, they try out different roles and personalities before they reach a stable sense of self. They may want to pursue one career one month (lawyer, for example) and another career the next month (doctor, actor, teacher, social worker, or astronaut, for example). They may dress neatly one day, sloppily the next day. This personality experimentation is a deliberate effort on the part of adolescents to find out where they fit in the world.

As they gradually come to realize that they will be responsible for themselves and their own lives, adolescents search for what those lives are going to be. Many parents and other adults, accustomed to having children go along with what they say, may be bewildered or incensed by the wisecracks, the rebelliousness, and the rapid mood changes that accompany adolescence. It is important for these adults to give adolescents the time and the opportunities to explore different roles and personalities. In turn, most adolescents eventually discard undesirable roles.

"Do you have any idea who I am?"

psychosocial moratorium Erikson's term for the gap between childhood security and adult autonomy that adolescents experience as part of their identity exploration.

There are literally hundreds of roles for adolescents to try out, and probably just as many ways to pursue each role. Erikson believes that, by late adolescence, vocational roles are central to identity development, especially in a highly technological society like the United States. Youth who have been well trained to enter a workforce that offers the potential of reasonably high self-esteem will experience the least stress during the development of identity. Some youth have rejected jobs offering good pay and traditionally high social status, choosing instead to work in situations that allow them to be more genuinely helpful to their fellow humans, such as in the Peace Corps, in mental health clinics, or in schools for children from low-income backgrounds. Some youth prefer unemployment to the prospect of working at a job they feel they would be unable to perform well or at which they would feel useless. To Erikson, this attitude reflects the desire to achieve a meaningful identity through being true to oneself, rather than burying one's identity in that of the larger society.

Identity is a self-portrait composed of many pieces, including these:

- The career and work path the person wants to follow (vocational/career identity)
- Whether the person is conservative, liberal, or middle-of-the-road (political identity)
- The person's spiritual beliefs (religious identity)
- Whether the person is single, married, divorced, and so on (relationship identity)
- The extent to which the person is motivated to achieve and is intellectual (achievement, intellectual identity)
- Whether the person is heterosexual, homosexual, or bisexual (sexual identity)
- Which part of the world or country a person is from and how intensely the person identifies with his or her cultural heritage (cultural/ethnic identity)
- The kind of things a person likes to do, which can include sports, music, hobbies, and so on (interest)
- The individual's personality characteristics (such as being introverted or extraverted, anxious or calm, friendly or hostile, and so on) (personality)
- The individual's body image (physical identity)

Some Contemporary Thoughts

Contemporary views of identity development suggest several important considerations. First, identity development is a lengthy process, in many instances a more gradual, less cataclysmic transition than Erikson's term *crisis* implies (Baumeister, 1991). Second, as just indicated, identity development is extraordinarily complex (Marcia, 1989). Identity formation neither begins nor ends with adolescence. It begins with the appearance of attachment, the development of a sense of self, and the emergence of independence in infancy, and reaches its final phase with a life review and integration in old age. What is important about identity development in adolescence, especially late adolescence, is that, for the first time, physical development, cognitive development, and social development advance to the point at which the individual can sort through and synthesize childhood identities and identifications to construct a viable path toward adult maturity. Resolution of the identity issue at adolescence does not mean that identity will be stable through the remainder of life. An individual who develops a healthy identity is flexible and adaptive, open to changes in society, in relationships, and in careers (Adams, Gulotta, & Montemayor, 1992). This openness assures numerous reorganizations of identity's contents throughout the identity-achieved individual's life.

Just as there is an increasing tendency to describe the adolescent's self-system in terms of multiple selves, so have experts on adolescence begun to characterize the adolescent's identity system in terms of multiple identities (Brooks-Gunn & Graber, 1999). While identities during the adolescent years are preceded by childhood identities, central questions such as "Who am I?" and "What aspects of my

*A*s long as one keeps searching, the answers come.

—JOAN BAEZ
American Folk Singer, 20th Century

identities come out in different contexts?" are asked more frequently in the adolescent years. It is during adolescence that identities are more strongly characterized by the search for balance between the needs for autonomy and connectedness.

Identity formation does not happen neatly, and it usually does not happen cataclysmically (Kroger, 2003). At the bare minimum, it involves commitment to a vocational direction, an ideological stance, and a sexual orientation. Synthesizing the identity components can be a long and drawn-out process, with many negations and affirmations of various roles and faces. Identity development gets done in bits and pieces. Decisions are not made once and for all, but have to be made again and again. And the decisions might seem trivial at the time: whom to date, whether or not to break up, whether or not to have intercourse, whether or not to take drugs, whether or not to go to college or finish high school and get a job, which major, whether to study or whether to play, whether or not to be politically active, and so on. Over the years of adolescence, the decisions begin to form a core of what the individual is all about as a human being—what is called his or her identity.

Identity Statuses

Eriksonian researcher James Marcia (1980, 1994) believes that Erikson's theory of identity development contains four statuses of identity, or ways of resolving the identity crisis: identity diffusion, identity foreclosure, identity moratorium, and identity achievement. The extent of an adolescent's crisis and commitment are used to classify the individual according to one of the four identity statuses. **Crisis** is defined as a period of identity development during which the adolescent is exploring alternatives. Most researchers use the term *exploration* rather than *crisis*, although, in the spirit of Marcia's formulation, the term *crisis* is used here. **Commitment** is a part of identity development in which adolescents show a personal investment in what they are going to do.

The four statuses of identity are (see figure 12.6):

- **Identity diffusion,** the state adolescents are in when they have not yet experienced a crisis (that is, they have not explored meaningful alternatives) or made any commitments. Not only are they undecided about occupational and ideological choices, they are also likely to show little interest in such matters.
- **Identity foreclosure** is the state adolescents are in when they have made a commitment but not experienced a crisis. This occurs most often when parents hand down commitments to their adolescents, usually in an authoritarian way. In these circumstances, adolescents have not had adequate opportunities to explore different approaches, ideologies, and vocations on their own.
- **Identity moratorium** is the state adolescents are in when they are in the midst of a crisis but whose commitments are either absent or are only vaguely defined.
- **Identity achievement** is the state adolescents are in when they have undergone a crisis and made a commitment.

The identity status approach has been sharply criticized by some researchers and theoreticians (Blasi, 1988; Cote & Levine, 1988; Kroger, 2003; Lapsley & Power,

crisis A period of identity development during which the adolescent is choosing among meaningful alternatives.

commitment The part of identity development in which adolescents show a personal investment in what they are going to do.

identity diffusion Marcia's term for the state adolescents are in when they have not yet experienced a crisis (that is, they have not yet explored meaningful alternatives) or made any commitments.

identity foreclosure Marcia's term for the state adolescents are in when they have made a commitment but have not experienced a crisis.

identity moratorium Marcia's term for the state adolescents are in when they are in the midst of a crisis, but whose commitments either are absent or are only vaguely defined.

identity achievement Marcia's term for an adolescent's having undergone a crisis and made a commitment.

Position on Occupation and Ideology	Identity Status			
	Identity diffusion	Identity foreclosure	Identity moratorium	Identity achievement
Crisis	Absent	Absent	Present	Present
Commitment	Absent	Present	Absent	Present

FIGURE 12.6 Marcia's Four Statuses of Identity

FIGURE 12.7 Exploring Your Identity

Think deeply about your exploration and commitment in the areas listed here. For each area, check whether your identity status is diffused, foreclosed, moratorium, or achieved.

Identity Component	Identity Status			
	Diffused	Foreclosed	Moratorium	Achieved
Vocational (career)				
Political				
Religious				
Relationships				
Achievement				
Sexual				
Gender				
Ethnic/Cultural				
Intersets				
Personality				
Physical				

If you checked diffused or foreclosed for any areas, take some time to think about what you need to do to move into a moratorium identity status in those areas. How much has your identity in each of the areas changed in recent years?

1988). They believe that the identity status approach distorts and trivializes Erikson's notions of crisis and commitment. For example, Erikson's idea of commitment loses the meaning of investing oneself in certain lifelong projects and is interpreted simply as having made a firm decision or not. Others still believe that the identity status approach is a valuable contribution to understanding identity (Archer, 1989; Marica, 1994; Waterman, 1992).

To evaluate your identity in a number of different areas of development, see figure 12.7. Let's explore some examples of Marcia's identity statuses. A 13-year-old adolescent has neither begun to explore her identity in any meaningful way nor made an identity commitment, so she is *identity diffused*. An 18-year-old boy's parents want him to be a medical doctor so he is planning on majoring in premedicine in college and really has not adequately explored any other options, so he is *identity foreclosed*. Nineteen-year-old Sasha is not quite sure what life paths she wants to follow, but she recently went to the counseling center at her college to find out about different careers, so she is in *identity moratorium* status. Twenty-one-year-old Marcelo extensively explored a number of different career options in college, eventually getting his degree in science education, and is looking forward to his first year of teaching high school students, so he is *identity achieved*. Our examples of identity statuses have focused on the career dimension, but remember that the whole of identity is made up of a number of dimensions.

An alternative to Marcia's way of conceptualizing identity in terms of statuses is to emphasize how individuals process self-relevant information. Three identity processing styles are (Berzonsky, 2000):

- *Informational.* Individuals actively seek out, process, and use self-relevant information when dealing with identity issues and forming personal commitments.
- *Normative.* Individuals conform to the expectations and prescriptions of significant others.
- *Diffuse/avoidant.* Individuals deliberately avoid having to deal with personal conflicts and decisions.

Developmental Changes

In Marcia's terms, young adolescents are primarily in the identity statuses of diffusion, foreclosure, or moratorium. At least three aspects of the young adolescent's development are important in identity formation (Marcia, 1987, 1996): Young adolescents must be confident that they have parental support, must have an established sense of industry, and must be able to adopt a self-reflective stance toward the future.

Some researchers believe the most important identity changes take place in youth rather than earlier in adolescence. For example, Alan Waterman (1985, 1989, 1992) has found that from the years preceding high school through the last few years of college, there is an increase in the number of individuals who are identity achieved, along with a decrease in those who are identity diffused. College upperclassmen are more likely to be identity achieved than college freshmen or high school students are. Many young adolescents are identity diffused. These developmental changes are especially true for vocational choice. For religious beliefs and political ideology, fewer college students have reached the identity-achieved status, with a substantial number characterized by foreclosure and diffusion. Thus, the timing of identity may depend on the particular life area involved, and many college students are still wrestling with ideological commitments (Arehart & Smith, 1990; Harter, 1990).

Many identity status researchers believe that a common pattern of individuals who develop positive identities is to follow what are called "MAMA" cycles of moratorium–achievement–moratorium–achievement (Archer, 1989). These cycles may be repeated throughout life (Francis, Fraser, & Marcia, 1989). Personal, family, and societal changes are inevitable, and as they occur, the flexibility and skill required to explore new alternatives and develop new commitments are likely to enhance an individual's coping skills. Regarding commitment, Marcia (1996) believes that the first identity is just that—it is not, and should not be expected to be, the final product.

Social Contexts

Social contexts play important roles in identity. Let's examine family, culture and ethnicity, and gender to see how they are linked to identity development.

Family Influences   Parents are important figures in the adolescent's development of identity. In studies that relate identity development to parenting styles, democratic parents, who encourage adolescents to participate in family decision making, foster identity achievement. Autocratic parents, who control the adolescent's behavior without giving the adolescent an opportunity to express opinions, encourage identity foreclosure. Permissive parents, who provide little guidance to adolescents and allow them to make their own decisions, promote identity diffusion (Enright & others, 1980).

Researchers also have examined the role of individuality and connectedness in the development of identity. Developmentalist Catherine Cooper and her colleagues (Carlson, Cooper, & Hsu, 1990; Cooper & Grotevant, 1989; Grotevant & Cooper, 1985, 1998) believe that the presence of a family atmosphere that promotes both individuality and connectedness are important in the adolescent's identity development:

- **Individuality** consists of two dimensions: self-assertion—the ability to have and communicate a point of view—and separateness—the use of communication patterns to express how one is different from others.
- **Connectedness** also consists of two dimensions: mutuality—which involves sensitivity to and respect for others' views—and permeability—which involves openness to others' views. In general, Cooper's research findings reveal that identity formation is enhanced by family relationships that are both individuated, which encourages adolescents to develop their own point of view, and connected, which provides a secure base from which to explore the widening

individuality An important element in adolescent identity development. It consists of two dimensions: self-assertion, the ability to have and communicate a point of view; and separateness, the use of communication patterns to express how one is different from others.

connectedness An important element in adolescent identity development. It consists of two dimensions: mutuality, sensitivity to and respect for others' views; and permeability, openness to others' views.

social worlds of adolescence. However, when connectedness is strong and individuation weak, adolescents often have an identity foreclosure status; by contrast, when connectedness is weak, adolescents often reveal an identity confusion status (Archer & Waterman, 1994).

Stuart Hauser and his colleagues (Hauser & Bowlds, 1990; Hauser & others, 1984) also have illuminated family processes that promote the adolescent's identity development. They have found that parents who use *enabling* behaviors (such as explaining, accepting, and giving empathy) facilitate the adolescent's identity development more than do parents who use *constraining* behaviors (such as judging and devaluing). In sum, family interaction styles that give the adolescent the right to question and to be different, within a context of support and mutuality, foster healthy patterns of identity development (Harter, 1990, 1999).

Culture and Ethnicity   Erikson was especially sensitive to the role of culture in identity development. He points out that, throughout the world, ethnic minority groups have struggled to maintain their cultural identities while blending into the dominant culture (Erikson, 1968). Erikson said that this struggle for an inclusive identity, or identity within the larger culture, has been the driving force in the founding of churches, empires, and revolutions throughout history.

For ethnic minority individuals, adolescence is often a special juncture in their development (Phinney, 2000, 2003; Spencer & others, 2001). Although children are aware of some ethnic and cultural differences, most ethnic minority individuals consciously confront their ethnicity for the first time in adolescence. In contrast to children, adolescents have the ability to interpret ethnic and cultural information, to reflect on the past, and to speculate about the future.

Jean Phinney (1996) defined **ethnic identity** as an enduring, basic aspect of the self that includes a sense of membership in an ethnic group and the attitudes and feelings related to that membership. Thus, for adolescents from ethnic minority groups, the process of identity formation has an added dimension due to exposure to alternative sources of identification—their own ethnic group and the mainstream or dominant culture. Researchers have found that ethnic identity increases with age and that higher levels of ethnic identity are linked with more positive attitudes not only toward one's own ethnic group but toward members of other ethnic groups as well (Phinney, Ferguson, & Tate, 1997). Many ethnic minority adolescents have bicultural identities—identifying in some ways with their ethnic minority group, in other ways with the majority culture (Comas-Díaz, 2001; Phinney & Devich-Navarro, 1997).

The ease or difficulty with which ethnic minority adolescents achieve healthy identities depends on a number of factors (Ferrer-Wreder & others, 2002). Many ethnic minority adolescents have to confront issues of prejudice and discrimination, and barriers to the fulfillment of their goals and aspirations (Comas-Díaz, 2001).

In one investigation, ethnic identity exploration was higher among ethnic minority than among White American college students (Phinney & Alipuria, 1990). In this same investigation, ethnic minority college students who had thought about and resolved issues involving their ethnicity had higher self-esteem than did their ethnic minority counterparts who had not. In another investigation, the ethnic identity development of Asian American, African American, Latino, and White American tenth-grade students in Los Angeles was studied (Phinney,

ethnic identity An enduring, basic aspect of the self that includes a sense of membership in an ethnic group and the attitudes and feelings related to that membership.

Researcher Margaret Beale Spencer, shown here talking with adolescents, believes that adolescence is often a critical juncture in the identity development of ethnic minority individuals. Most ethnic minority individuals consciously confront their ethnicity for the first time in adolescence.

Careers in Child Development

Armando Ronquillo, *High School Counselor*

Armando Ronquillo is a high school counselor and admissions advisor at Pueblo High School in a low-income area of Tucson, Arizona. More than 85 percent of the students have a Latino background. Armando was named the top high school counselor in the state of Arizona for the year 2000.

Armando especially works with Latino students to guide them in developing a positive identity. He talks with them about their Latino background and what it's like to have a bicultural identity—preserving important aspects of their Latino heritage but also pursuing what is important to be successful in the contemporary culture of the United States.

He believes that helping them stay in school and getting them to think about the lifelong opportunities provided by a college education will benefit their identity development. Armando also works with parents to help them understand that their child going to college is doable and affordable.

Armando Ronquillo, counseling a Latina high school student about college.

> "Many ethnic minority youth must bridge "multiple worlds" in constructing their identities.
>
> —CATHERINE COOPER
> *Contemporary Psychologist, University of California at Santa Cruz*

1989). Adolescents from each of the three ethnic minority groups faced a similar need to deal with their ethnic-group identification in a predominantly White American culture. In some instances, the adolescents from the three ethnic minority groups perceived different issues to be important in their resolution of ethnic identity. For Asian American adolescents, pressures to achieve academically and concerns about quotas that make it difficult to get into good colleges were salient issues. Many African American adolescent females discussed their realization that White American standards of beauty (especially hair and skin color) did not apply to them; African American adolescent males were concerned with possible job discrimination and the need to distinguish themselves from a negative societal image of African American male adolescents. For Latino adolescents, prejudice was a recurrent theme, as was the conflict in values between their Latino culture heritage and the majority culture. To read about one individual who guides Latino adolescents in developing a positive identity, see the Careers in Child Development insert.

The contexts in which ethnic minority youth live influence their identity development (Spencer, 1999). Many ethnic minority youth in the United States live in low-income urban settings where support for developing a positive identity is absent. Many of these youth live in pockets of poverty, are exposed to drugs, gangs, and criminal activities, and interact with other youth and adults who have dropped out of school and/or are unemployed. In such settings, effective organizations and programs for youth can make important contributions to developing a positive identity.

One study focused on 60 youth organizations that involved 24,000 adolescents over a period of five years (Heath & McLaughlin, 1993). They found that these organizations were especially good at building a sense of ethnic pride in inner-city ethnic youth. Shirley Heath and Milbrey McLaughlin (1993) believe that many inner-city youth have too much time on their hands, too little to do, and too few places to go. Inner-city youth want to participate in organizations that nurture them and respond positively to their needs and interests. Organizations that perceive youth as fearful, vulnerable, and lonely, but also frame them as capable, worthy, and eager to have a healthy and productive life contribute in positive ways to the identity development of ethnic minority youth.

Today, in the United States, non-European immigrants usually develop bicultural identities. That is, they become American but also retain their ethnic identity.

The indicators of identity change are often different for each succeeding generation (Phinney, 2003). The identity of the first generation of immigrants is likely to be secure and unlikely to change considerably. They may or may not develop an "American" identity. The degree to which they begin to feel American appears to be related to learning English, developing social networks beyond their group, and becoming culturally competent in the new context. For the second generation of immigrants, an "American" identity is more secure, possibly because citizenship is granted with birth. Their ethnic identity is likely to be linked to retention of their ethnic language and social networks. For the third and later generations, the issues become more complex. Various historical, contextual, and political factors unrelated to acculturation may affect the extent to which their ethnic identity is retained. For non-European ethnic groups, racism and discrimination influence whether ethnic identity is retained.

Cultural Identity in Canada

Exploring Ethnic Identities

An Adolescent Talks About Ethnic Identity

Ethnic Identity Research

Gender   In Erikson's (1968) classic presentation of identity development, the division of labor between the sexes was reflected in his assertion that males' aspirations were mainly oriented toward career and ideological commitments, while females' were centered around marriage and childbearing. In the 1960s and 1970s researchers found support for Erikson's assertion about gender differences in identity. For example, vocational concerns were more central to the identity of males, and affiliative concerns were more important in the identity of females (LaVoie, 1976). However, in the last decade, as females have developed stronger vocational interests, these gender differences are disappearing (Waterman, 1985).

Some investigators believe that females and males go through Erikson's stages in different order. One view is that for males, identity formation precedes the stage of intimacy, while for females, intimacy precedes identity (Douvan & Adelson, 1966). These ideas are consistent with the belief that relationships and emotional bonds are more important concerns of females, while autonomy and achievement are more important concerns of males (Gilligan, 1996). In one study, the development of a clear sense of self by adolescent girls was related to their concerns about care and response in relationships (Rogers, 1987).

The task of identity exploration might be more complex for females than for males, in that females might try to establish identities in more domains than males do. In today's world, the options for females have increased and thus can at times be confusing and conflicting, especially for females who hope to successfully integrate family and career roles (Archer, 1994).

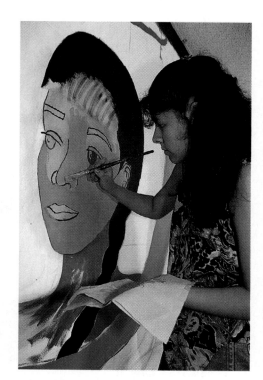

What might be some important issues for ethnic minority female adolescents to explore?

Review and Reflect: Learning Goal 3

3 Describe identity and its development

REVIEW

- What is Erikson's view of identity?
- What are some contemporary thoughts about identity?
- What are the identity statuses that can be used to classify individuals?
- What developmental changes characterize identity?
- How do the social contexts of family, culture and ethnicity, and gender influence identity?

REFLECT

- Do you think that your parents influenced your identity development? If so, how?

Reach Your Learning Goals

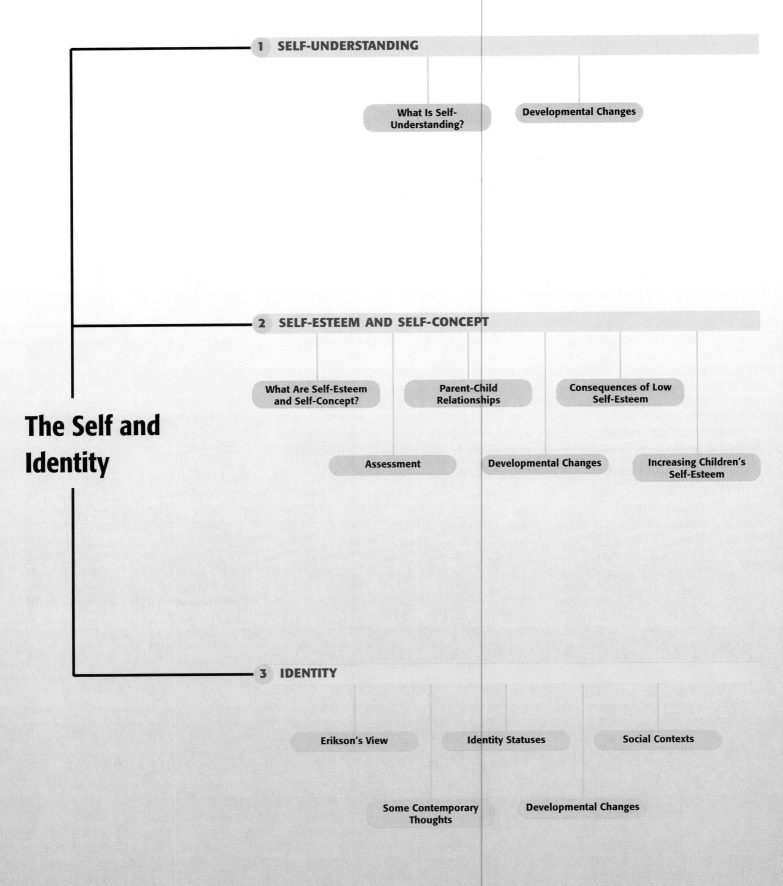

The Self and Identity

1 SELF-UNDERSTANDING

- What Is Self-Understanding?
- Developmental Changes

2 SELF-ESTEEM AND SELF-CONCEPT

- What Are Self-Esteem and Self-Concept?
- Parent-Child Relationships
- Consequences of Low Self-Esteem
- Assessment
- Developmental Changes
- Increasing Children's Self-Esteem

3 IDENTITY

- Erikson's View
- Identity Statuses
- Social Contexts
- Some Contemporary Thoughts
- Developmental Changes

Summary

1 Discuss self-understanding and its development

- Self-understanding is a child's cognitive representation of the self, the substance and content of the child's self-conceptions. It provides the rational underpinnings for identity.
- Infants develop a rudimentary form of self-recognition at approximately 18 months of age. The physical and active self becomes a part of self-understanding in early childhood. The internal self, the social self, and the socially comparative self become more prominent in middle and late childhood. Dimensions of adolescents' self-understanding include abstract and idealistic; differentiated; the fluctuating self; contradictions within the self; real and ideal, true and false selves; social comparison; self-conscious; self-protective; unconscious; and self-integration. Perspective taking is the ability to assume another person's perspective and understand his or her thoughts and feelings. Selman proposed a developmental theory of perspective taking that has five stages, ranging from 3 years of age through adolescence. The first stage in early childhood involves an egocentric viewpoint; the last stage in adolescence consists of having an in-depth perspective-taking ability.

2 Explain self-esteem and self-concept

- Self-esteem, also referred to as self-worth or self-image, is the global, evaluative dimension of the self. Self-concept refers to domain-specific evaluations of the self.
- Harter's measures assess self-evaluations in different skill domains as well as general self-worth.
- In Coopersmith's study, children's self-esteem was associated with parental acceptance and allowing children freedom within well-prescribed limits.
- Self-esteem drops in adolescence, more so for girls than boys.
- For most children, low self-esteem only translates into temporary emotional discomfort, but for others, low self-esteem can result in depression, suicide, eating disorders, and delinquency.
- Four ways to increase children's self-esteem are to (1) identify the causes of low self-esteem and which domains are important to the self, (2) provide emotional support and social approval, (3) help the child achieve, and (4) improve the child's coping skills.

3 Describe identity and its development

- Erikson argues that identity versus identity confusion is the fifth stage of the human life span, which individuals experience during adolescence. This stage involves entering a psychological moratorium between the security of childhood and the autonomy of adulthood. Personality and role experimentation are important aspects of identity development. In technological societies like those in North America, the vocational role is especially important.
- Identity development is lengthy, in many cases more gradual than Erikson implied. Identity development is extraordinarily complex and is done in bits and pieces.
- James Marcia proposed four identity statuses—identity diffusion, foreclosure, moratorium, and achievement—that are based on crisis (exploration) and commitment. Some experts believe the identity status approach oversimplifies Erickson's ideas.
- Some experts argue the main changes in identity occur in the college years rather than earlier in adolescence. College juniors and seniors are more likely to be identity achieved than freshmen or high school students, although many college students are still wrestling with ideological commitments. Individuals often follow moratorium–achievement–moratorium–achievement (MAMA) cycles in their lives.
- Parents are important figures in adolescents' identity development. Democratic parenting facilitates identity development; autocratic and permissive parenting do not. Both individuality and connectedness in family relations are related to identity development. Enabling behaviors promote identity development, constraining behaviors restrict it. Erikson is especially sensitive to culture's role in identity, underscoring that throughout the world ethnic minority groups have struggled to maintain their identities while blending into the majority culture. Adolescence is a special juncture in the identity development of ethnic minority individuals because for the first time they consciously confront their ethnic identity. In Erikson's view, adolescent males have a stronger vocational identity, adolescent females a stronger social identity involving marriage and family roles. Some researchers have found no sex differences in identity, while others argue that relationships and emotional bonds are more central to female than to male identity development.

Key Terms

self-understanding 385
possible self 388
perspective taking 390
self-esteem 391
self-concept 391

identity versus identity
    confusion 395
psychosocial moratorium 396
crisis 398
commitment 398

identity diffusion 398
identity foreclosure 398
identity moratorium 398
identity achievement 398
individuality 400

connectedness 400
ethnic identity 401

Key People

Susan Harter 387
Carl Rogers 388
Hazel Markus 389

Robert Selman 390
Erik Erikson 395
James Marcia 398

Alan Waterman 400
Catherine Cooper 400
Stuart Hauser 401

Jean Phinney 401
Shirley Heath and Milbrey
    McLaughlin 402

Taking It to the Net

1. Rita's child development teacher wants each student to depict some aspect of child development from infancy to age 6 as a chronological time line represented by descriptions or illustrations. Rita has chosen the development of the self. What behaviors at 6, 12, and 18 months, and at 2, 3, 4, 5, and 6 years of age represent milestones in self-awareness, self-concept, self-understanding, and self-esteem?

2. Thirteen-year-old Amy was adopted out of a Korean orphanage by Americans when she was 4 years old. She is now struggling with an identity crisis. Is she Korean or American? She doesn't feel that she is either. How can Amy best resolve this ethnic identity crisis?

3. Frank is going to write a paper about how boys and girls differ in their identity development. He is looking for a central theme around which to construct his paper. What are the most salient identity issues for boys that are not so salient for girls?

Connect to **www.mhhe.com/santrockcd10** to research the answers and complete these exercises.

E-Learning Tools

To help you master the material in this chapter, you'll find a number of valuable study tools on the Student CD-ROM that accompanies this book. Also visit the Online Learning Center for *Child Development*, tenth edition (**www.mhhe.com/santrockcd10**) where you'll find these additional resources:

- Build your decision-making skills by trying your hand at the parenting, nursing, and education "Scenarios" on the Online Learning Center.
- Use the interactive Prism exercises to learn more about the self and identity.

CHAPTER 13

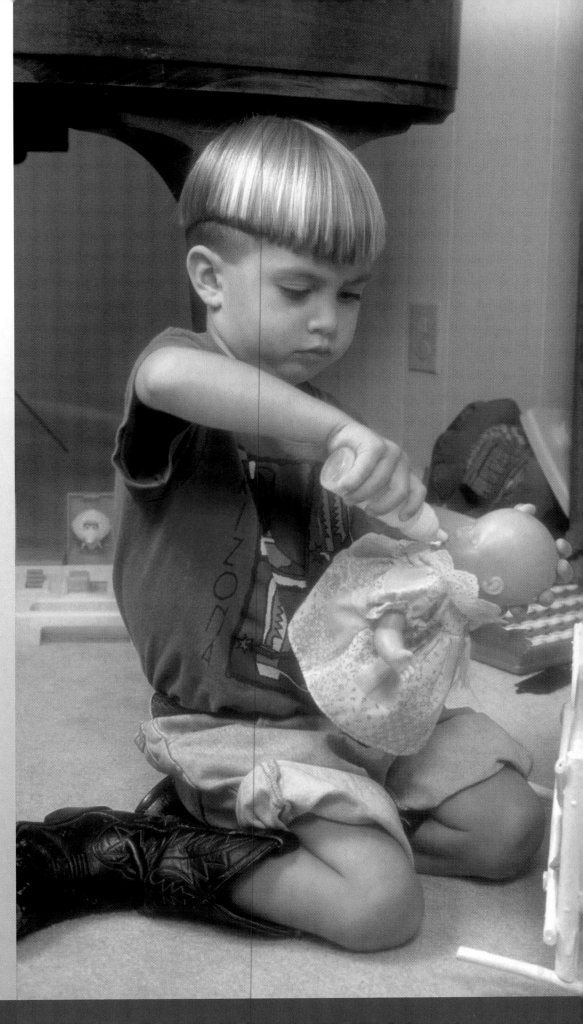

To be meek, patient, tact-
ful, modest, honorable,
brave, is not to be either
manly or womanly, but is
to be humane.

—JANE HARRISON
English Writer, 20th Century

Gender

Chapter Outline

INFLUENCES ON GENDER DEVELOPMENT

Biological Influences

Social Influences

Cognitive Influences

GENDER STEREOTYPES, SIMILARITIES, AND DIFFERENCES

Gender Stereotyping

Gender Similarities and Differences

GENDER-ROLE CLASSIFICATION

What Is Gender-Role Classification?

Androgyny and Education

Masculinity in Childhood and Adolescence

Gender-Role Transcendence

Gender in Context

DEVELOPMENTAL WINDOWS OF GENDER OPPORTUNITY AND ASYMMETRIC GENDER SOCIALIZATION

Developmental Windows

Asymmetric Gender Socialization

Learning Goals

1 Discuss the main biological, social, and cognitive influences on gender

2 Describe gender stereotyping, similarities, and differences

3 Identify how gender roles can be classified

4 Characterize developmental windows of gender opportunity and asymmetric gender socialization

The Story of Jerry Maguire: Gender, Emotion, and Caring

Gender and emotion researcher Stephanie Shields (1998) analyzed the movie *Jerry Maguire* in terms of how it reflects the role of gender in emotions and relationships. In brief, the movie is a "buddy" picture with sports agent Jerry Maguire (played by Tom Cruise) paired with two buddies: the too-short Arizona Cardinals wide receiver Rod Tidwell (played by Cuba Gooding, Jr.) and 6-year-old Ray, son of Jerry's love interest, the accountant Dorothy Boyd (played by Renée Zellweger). Through his buddies, the thinking-but-not-feeling Jerry discovers the right path by connecting to Ray's emotional honesty and African American Rod's devotion to his family. Conversely, the emotionally flamboyant and self-centered Rod, through his White buddy, Jerry, discovers that he must bring passion back to his game to be successful.

The image of nurturing and nurtured males is woven throughout the movie. Jerry's relationship with Ray, the 6-year-old, is a significant theme in the film. Through discovering a caring relationship with Ray, Jerry makes his first genuine move toward emotional maturity. The boy is the guide to the man. Chad, Ray's baby-sitter, is a good example of appropriate caring by a male.

Males are shown crying in the movie. Jerry sheds tears while writing his mission statement, when thinking about Dorothy's possible move to another city (which also means he would lose Ray), and at the success of his lone client (Rod). Rod is brought to tears when he speaks of his family. Historically, weeping, more than any emotional expression, has been associated with feminine emotion. However, it has increasingly taken on a more prominent role in the male's emotional makeup.

The movie *Jerry Maguire* reflects changes in gender roles as an increasing number of males show an interest in improving their social relationships and achieving emotional maturity. However, as we will see later in this chapter, experts on gender argue that overall females are more competent in their social relationships than males are and that large numbers of males still have a lot of room for improvement in dealing better with their emotions.

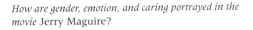

How are gender, emotion, and caring portrayed in the movie Jerry Maguire?

What exactly do we mean by gender? **Gender** refers to the psychological and sociocultural dimensions of being female or male. Two aspects of gender bear special mention: gender identity and gender role. **Gender identity** is the sense of being female or male, which most children acquire by the time they are 3 years old. A **gender role** is a set of expectations that prescribes how females and males should think, act, and feel.

1 INFLUENCES ON GENDER DEVELOPMENT

> **Biological Influences**   **Social Influences**   **Cognitive Influences**

How is gender influenced by biology? By children's social experiences? By cognitive factors?

Biological Influences

To understand biological influences, we need to consider heredity and hormones. We also will explore the theoretical views of Freud and Erikson, and the more recent view of evolutionary psychologists.

Heredity and Hormones   It was not until the 1920s that researchers confirmed the existence of human sex chromosomes, the genetic material that determines our sex. As we discussed in chapter 3, "Biological Beginnings," humans normally have 46 chromosomes arranged in pairs. ◄ **page 70** The 23rd pair may have two X-shaped chromosomes, to produce a female, or it may have both an X-shaped and a Y-shaped chromosome to produce a male.

Sex hormones are powerful chemicals that are controlled by the master gland in the brain, the pituitary. The two main classes of sex hormones are estrogens and androgens. **Estrogens,** the most important of which is estradiol, influence the development of female physical sex characteristics and help to regulate the menstrual cycle. **Androgens,** the most important of which is testosterone, promote the development of male genitals and secondary sex characteristics. They influence sexual motivation in both sexes. Androgens are produced by the adrenal glands in males and females, and by the testes in males.

In the first few weeks of gestation, female and male embryos look alike. Male sex organs start to differ from female sex organs when the Y chromosome in the male embryo triggers the secretion of androgens. Low levels of androgens in a female embryo allow the normal development of female sex organs.

To explore biological influences on gender, researchers have studied individuals who were exposed to unusual levels of sex hormones early in development because of genetic or hormonal abnormalities (Lippa, 2002):

- *Congenital adrenal hyperplasia (CAH).* Some girls have this condition that is caused by a genetic defect. Their adrenal glands enlarge and produce abnormally high levels of androgens. CAH girls, although they genetically are XX females, vary in how much their genitals look like male or female genitals. Their genitals may be surgically altered to look more like those of a typical female. Although CAH girls usually grow up to have a female gender identity, thinking of themselves as girls and women, researchers have found that they are less content with being a female and show a stronger interest in being a male than non-CAH girls (Berenbaum & Bailey, 2003; Ehrhardt, 1987; Slijper, 1984). They typically enjoy participating in rough-and-tumble play, sports, and dressing in masculine clothing, while disliking typical girl activities such as playing with dolls and wearing makeup and frilly clothes.

gender The psychological and sociocultural dimensions of being male or female.

gender identity The sense of being female or male, which most children acquire by the time they are 3 years old.

gender role A set of expectations that prescribes how females and males should think, act, and feel.

estrogens Hormones, the most important of which is estradiol, that influence the development of female physical sex characteristics and help regulate the menstrual cycle.

androgens Hormones, the most important of which is testosterone, that promote the development of male genitals and secondary sex characteristics.

- *Androgen-insensitive males.* A small number of genetic XY males do not have androgen receptors in their cells because of a genetic error. They are called androgen-insensitive males. The androgen receptors normally connect with testosterone and unless they are present, testosterone cannot affect cells. When complete androgen insensitivity is present, genetic XY males develop as females in the sense that their bodies look completely female and they develop a female gender identity. They typically are romantically and sexually attracted to males (Wisniewski & others, 2000).

- *Pelvic field defect.* A small number of newborns have a disorder called pelvic field defect, which in boys involves a missing penis. For many years, doctors usually recommended that these genetic boys be raised as girls and undergo sex reassignment surgery. They believed that a boy born without a penis could not live a normal life as a male and would adapt better if reared as a girl. The sex reassignment involved castration, which was required because they were born with testicles but not a penis. Thus, they were exposed to normal male amounts of testosterone prenatally but were castrated soon after birth. One study of pelvic field defect boys found that despite surgical reassignment and efforts by parents to rear them as girls, most of the genetically XY children insisted that they were boys (Reiner, 2001). For these XY boys, apparently normal exposure to androgens prenatally had a stronger influence on their gender identity than being castrated and raised as girls.

In another intriguing case, one of two identical twin boys lost his penis due to an errant circumcision procedure (Lippa, 2002). The twin who lost his penis was surgically reassigned to be a girl and to be reared as a girl. Bruce—the real name of the boy—became Brenda. Early reports indicated that the sex assignment had been successful, but as Brenda grew up she reported that she never really felt comfortable as a girl (Diamond & Sigmundson, 1997). As a young adult, Brenda became Bruce once again and now lives with a wife and adopted children (Colapinto, 2000).

In sum, the results from a number of genetic and hormonal studies suggest that biological factors, especially early hormonal production, play important roles in gender development (Lippa, 2002). Researchers have also found that sex hormone levels also are related to some cognitive abilities in females and males, especially spatial ability. For example, girls whose glands overproduce testosterone have spatial abilities more similar to those of the average boy than to those of the average girl (Hines, 1990). Boys whose glands underproduce testosterone, and thus are late maturing, have spatial abilities more similar to those of the average girl than to those of the average boy (Kimura, 2000).

Sex hormones are also related to aggression. Violent male criminals have above-average levels of testosterone (Dabbs & others, 1987), and professional football players have higher levels of testosterone than ministers do (Dabbs & Morris, 1990). Researchers have been able to increase the aggressiveness of animals in different species by giving them testosterone.

However, sex hormones alone, of course, do not determine such human behaviors as aggression. Later in the chapter, we will explore the environmental influences of parents, peers, and other social factors on such behaviors as aggression.

Freud and Erikson—Anatomy Is Destiny Both Sigmund Freud and Erik Erikson argued that an individual's genitals influence his or her gender behavior and, therefore, that anatomy is destiny. One of Freud's basic assumptions was that human behavior and history are directly related to reproductive processes. From this assumption arose his belief that gender and sexual behavior are essentially unlearned and instinctual. Erikson (1968) extended Freud's argument, claiming that the psychological differences between males and females stem from their anatomical differences. Erikson argued that, because of genital structure, males are more intrusive and aggressive, females more inclusive and passive. Critics of the anatomy-is-destiny view believe that experience is not given enough credit. The critics say that females and males are more free to choose their gender roles than Freud and Erikson allow. In response to the critics, Erikson modified his view, saying that females in today's world are transcending their biological heritage and correcting society's overemphasis on male intrusiveness.

Evolutionary Psychology and Gender   Evolutionary psychologists emphasize that evolutionary adaptations produced psychological sex differences (Buss, 2000).   ◀ **page 67** Evolutionary psychologists argue that women and men faced different evolutionary pressures in primeval environments when the human species was evolving and that the sexes' different roles in reproduction was the key feature that framed different adaptive problems for females and males.

To support this view of behavior, evolutionary psychologists focus on sexual selection. They suggest that sex-typed features evolved through male competition and led to a reproductive advantage for dominant males. Men sought short-term mating strategies because this allowed them to increase their reproductive advantage by fathering more children. Women also devoted more time to parenting.

Because men competed with other men for access to women, men evolved dispositions that favor violence, competition, and risk taking. Women in turn developed a preference for long-term mates who could protect and support a family. As a consequence, men strived to acquire more resources than other men in order to attract women, and women developed preferences for successful, ambitious men who could provide these resources.

Critics of the evolutionary psychology view argue that humans have the decision-making ability to change their gender behavior and therefore are not locked into the evolutionary past. They also stress that the extensive cross-cultural variation in sex differences and mate preferences provides stronger evidence for the social construction of gender differences than for an evolutionary source.

"It's a guy thing."

An Interactionist View   No one questions the presence of genetic, biochemical, and anatomical differences between the sexes. Even child developmentalists with a strong environmental orientation acknowledge that boys and girls are treated differently because of their physical differences and their different roles in reproduction. The importance of biological factors is not at issue. What is at issue is the directness or indirectness of their effects on social behavior (Lippa, 2002; Rose, 1997). For example, if a high androgen level directly influences the central nervous system, which in turn increases activity level, then the biological effect on behavior is direct. By contrast, if a child's high level of androgen produces strong muscle development, which in turn causes others to expect the child to be a good athlete and, in turn, leads the child to participate in sports, then the biological effect on behavior is indirect.

Although virtually everyone thinks that children's behavior as males or females is due to an interaction of biological and environmental factors, an interactionist position means different things to different people (Maccoby, 1998). For some, it suggests that certain environmental conditions are required before preprogrammed dispositions appear. For others, it suggests that a particular environment will have different effects, depending on the child's predispositions. For still others, it means that children shape their environments, including their interpersonal environment, and vice versa. The processes of influence and counterinfluence unfold over time. Throughout development, in this view, males and females actively construct their own versions of acceptable masculine and feminine behavior patterns.

Social Influences

Many social scientists, such as Alice Eagly (2000, 2001; Eagly & Diekman, 2003; Wood & Eagly, 2002), locate the cause of psychological sex differences not in biologically evolved dispositions but in the contrasting positions and social roles of women and men. In contemporary American society and in most cultures around the world, women have less power and status than men and control fewer resources. Women perform more domestic work than men and spend fewer hours in paid employment. Although most women are in the workforce, they receive lower pay than men and are thinly represented in the highest levels of organizations. Thus, from the perspective of social influences, gender hierarchy and sexual division of labor are important causes of sex-differentiated behavior. As women adapted to roles with less power and less status in society, they showed more cooperative, less dominant profiles than men.

Psychoanalytic and Social Cognitive Theories Two prominent theories address the way children acquire masculine and feminine attitudes and behaviors from their parents:

- The **psychoanalytic theory of gender** stems from Freud's view that the preschool child develops a sexual attraction to the opposite-sex parent. At 5 or 6 years of age, the child renounces this attraction because of anxious feelings. Subsequently, the child identifies with the same-sex parent, unconsciously adopting the same-sex parent's characteristics. However, today many child developmentalists do not believe gender development proceeds on the basis of identification, at least not in terms of Freud's emphasis on childhood sexual attraction (Callan, 2001). Children become gender-typed much earlier than 5 or 6 years of age, and they become masculine or feminine even when the same-sex parent is not present in the family.
- The **social cognitive theory of gender** emphasizes that children's gender development occurs through observation and imitation of gender behavior, and through the rewards and punishments children experience for gender-appropriate and -inappropriate behavior. Unlike identification theory, social cognitive theory argues that sexual attraction to parents is not involved in gender development. (A comparison of the psychoanalytic and social cognitive views is presented in figure 13.1.) Parents often use rewards and punishments to teach their daughters to be feminine ("Karen, you are being a good girl when you play gently with your doll") and their sons to be masculine ("Keith, a boy as big as you is not supposed to cry"). Peers also extensively reward and punish gender behavior (Lott & Maluso, 2001). And, by observing adults and peers at home, at school, in the neighborhood, and on television, children are widely exposed to a myriad of models who display masculine and feminine behavior. Critics of the social cognitive view argue that gender development is not as passively acquired as it indicates. Later, we will discuss the cognitive views of gender development, which stress that children actively construct their gender world.

Alice Eagly's Research

psychoanalytic theory of gender A theory that stems from Freud's view that preschool children develop a sexual attraction to the opposite-sex parent, then at 5 to 6 years of age renounce the attraction because of anxious feelings, subsequently identifying with the same-sex parent and unconsciously adopting the same-sex parent's characteristics.

social cognitive theory of gender This theory emphasizes that children's gender development occurs through observation and imitation of gender behavior, and through rewards and punishments they experience for gender-appropriate and -inappropriate behavior.

FIGURE 13.1 Parents Influence Their Children's Gender Development by Action and Example

Theory	Processes	Outcome
Psychoanalytic theory	Sexual attraction to opposite-sex parent at 3 to 5 years of age; anxiety about sexual attraction and subsequent identification with same-sex parent at 5 to 6 years of age	Gender behavior similar to that of same-sex parent
Social cognitive theory	Rewards and punishments of gender-appropriate and -inappropriate behavior by adults and peers; observation and initiation of models' masculine and feminine behavior	Gender behavior

Parental Influences   Once the label *girl* or *boy* is assigned by the obstetrician, virtually everyone, from parents to siblings to strangers, begins treating the infant differently (see figure 13.2).

In one study, an infant girl, Avery, was dressed in a neutral outfit of overalls and a T-shirt (Brooks-Gunn & Matthews, 1979). People responded to her differently if they thought she was a girl rather than a boy. People who thought she was a girl made comments like "Isn't she cute?" "What a sweet little, innocent thing." By contrast, people who thought the baby was a boy made remarks like "I bet he is a tough little customer. He will be running around all over the place and causing trouble in no time."

In general, parents even hope that their offspring will be a boy. In one investigation in the 1970s, 90 percent of the men and 92 percent of the women wanted their firstborn child to be a boy (Peterson & Peterson, 1973). In a more recent study, parents still preferred a boy as the firstborn child—75 percent of the men and 79 percent of the women had that preference (Hamilton, 1991).

In some countries, a male child is so preferred over a female child that many mothers will abort a female fetus after fetal testing procedures, such as amniocentesis and sonograms, that reveal the fetus' sex. For example, in South Korea, where fetal testing to determine sex is common, male births exceed female births by 14 percent, in contrast to a worldwide average of 5 percent.

Both mothers and fathers are psychologically important in children's gender development. Mothers are more consistently given responsibility for nurturance and physical care; fathers are more likely to engage in playful interaction and be given responsibility for ensuring that boys and girls conform to existing cultural norms. And whether or not they have more influence on them, fathers are more involved in socializing their sons than in socializing their daughters (Lamb, 1986). Fathers seem to play an especially important part in gender-role development—they are more likely to act differently toward sons and daughters than mothers are, and thus contribute more to distinctions between the genders (Huston, 1983).

Many parents encourage boys and girls to engage in different types of play and activities (Fagot, 1995; Fisher-Thompson & others, 1993). Girls are more likely to be given dolls to play with during childhood and, when old enough, are more likely to be assigned baby-sitting duties. Girls are encouraged to be more nurturant and emotional than boys, and their fathers are more likely to engage in aggressive play

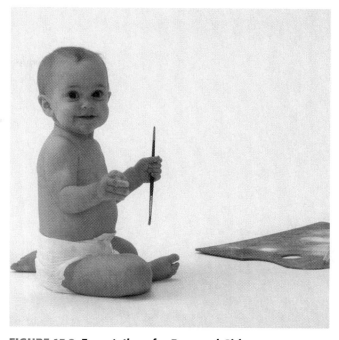

FIGURE 13.2 Expectations for Boys and Girls

First imagine that this is a photograph of a baby girl.
What expectations would you have for her?
Then imagine that this is a photograph of a baby boy.
What expectations would you have for him?

cathy®   **by Cathy Guisewite**

Cathy © 1986 Cathy Guisewite. Reprinted with permission of UNIVERSAL PRESS SYNDICATE. All Rights Reserved.

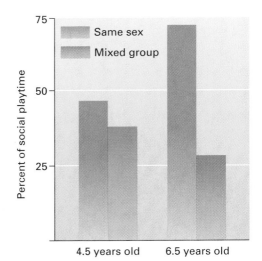

FIGURE 13.3 Developmental Changes in Percentage of Time Spent in Same-Sex and Mixed-Group Settings

Observations of children show that they are more likely to play in same-sex than mixed-sex groups. This tendency increases between 4 and 6 years of age.

with their sons than with their daughters. As adolescents increase in age, parents permit boys more freedom than girls, allowing them to be away from home and stay out later without supervision. When parents place severe restrictions on their adolescent sons, it has been found to be especially disruptive to the sons' development (Baumrind, 1989).

In recent years, the idea that parents are the critical socializing agents in gender-role development has come under fire (Huston, 1983). Parents are only one of many sources through which the individual learns gender roles. Culture, schools, peers, the media, and other family members can also influence a child's gender development. Yet it is important to guard against swinging too far in this direction because—especially in the early years of development—parents are important influences on gender development.

Peer Influences Parents provide the earliest discrimination of gender roles in development, but before long, peers join the societal process of responding to and modeling masculine and feminine behavior. Children who play in sex-appropriate activities tend to be rewarded for doing so by their peers. Those who play in cross-sexed activities tend to be criticized by their peers or left to play alone. Children show a clear preference for being with and liking same-sex peers (Buhrmester, 1993; Maccoby, 1998), and this tendency usually becomes stronger during the middle and late childhood years (Maccoby & Jacklin, 1987) (see figure 13.3). After extensive observations of elementary school playgrounds, two researchers characterized the play settings as "gender school," pointing out that boys teach one another the required masculine behavior and enforce it strictly (Luria & Herzog, 1985). Girls also pass on the female culture and mainly congregate with one another. Individual "tomboy" girls can join boys' activities without losing their status in the girls' groups, but the reverse is not true for boys, reflecting our society's greater sex-typing pressure for boys (Miracle, Miracle, & Baumeister, 2002).

Peer demands for conformity to gender role become especially intense during adolescence. While there is greater social mixing of males and females during early adolescence, in both formal groups and in dating, peer pressure is strong for the adolescent boy to be the very best male possible and for the adolescent girl to be the very best female possible.

Thus, parent-child relationships and peer relationships make important contributions to gender. To read about one individual who has made important contributions to our understanding of gender, parent-child relationships, and peer relationships, see the Careers in Child Development insert.

Schools and Teachers There are concerns that schools and teachers have biases against both boys and girls. What evidence is there that the classroom is biased against boys? Here are some factors to consider (DeZolt & Hull, 2001):

- Compliance, following rules, and being neat and orderly are valued and reinforced in many classrooms (DeZolt & Hull, 2001). These are behaviors that are typically associated with girls rather than boys.
- A large majority of teachers are females, especially in the elementary school. This may make it more difficult for boys than girls to identify with their teachers and model their teachers' behavior.
- Boys are more likely than girls to be identified as having learning problems.
- Boys are more likely than girls to be criticized.
- School personnel tend to ignore that many boys are clearly having academic problems, especially in the language arts.
- School personnel tend to stereotype boys' behavior as problematic.

What evidence is there that the classroom is biased against girls? Consider the views of Myra and David Sadker (2000):

- In a typical classroom, girls are more compliant, boys more rambunctious. Boys demand more attention, girls are more likely to quietly wait their turn. Teachers are more likely to scold and reprimand boys, as well as send boys to school authorities for disciplinary action. Educators worry that girls' tendency to be compliant and quiet comes at a cost: diminished assertiveness.

- In many classrooms, teachers spend more time watching and interacting with boys while girls work and play quietly on their own. Most teachers don't intentionally favor boys by spending more time with them, yet somehow the classroom frequently ends up with this type of gendered profile.

- Boys get more instruction than girls and more help when they have trouble with a question. Teachers often give boys more time to answer a question, more hints at the correct answer, and further tries if they give the wrong answer.

- Boys are more likely than girls to get lower grades and to be grade repeaters, yet girls are less likely to believe that they will be successful in college work.

- Girls and boys enter first grade with roughly equal levels of self-esteem. Yet by the middle school years, girls' self-esteem is significantly lower than boys' (American Association of University Women, 1992).

- When elementary school children are asked to list what they want to do when they grow up, boys describe more career options than girls do.

Thus, there is evidence of gender bias against both males and females in schools (DeZolt & Hull, 2001). Many school personnel are not aware of their gender-biased attitudes. These attitudes are deeply entrenched in and supported by the general culture. Increasing awareness of gender bias in schools is clearly an important strategy in reducing such bias.

Gender and the Media The messages carried by the media about what is appropriate or inappropriate for males and for females also are important influences on gender development (Calvert, 1999; Purcheco & Hurtado, 2001). A special concern is the way females are pictured on television. In the 1970s, it became apparent that television was portraying females as less competent than males. For example, about 70 percent of the prime-time characters were males, men were more likely to be shown in the workforce, women were more likely to be shown as housewives and in romantic roles, men were more likely to appear in higher-status jobs and in a greater diversity of occupations, and men were presented as more aggressive and constructive (Sternglanz & Serbin, 1974).

Television networks have become more sensitive to how males and females are portrayed on television shows. Consequently, many programs now focus on divorced families, cohabitation, and women in high-status roles. Yet with this shift in programming, researchers continued to find that television portrayed males as more

Careers in Child Development

Eleanor Maccoby, *Professor*

Eleanor Maccoby has been a prolific contributor to the field of child development. She obtained her undergraduate degree from the University of Washington and her doctoral degree from the University of Michigan. Eleanor then became a faculty member at Harvard University and later at Stanford University. Her research has focused on a wide range of topics involving children's socioemotional development, including gender, parent-child relationships, and peer relationships. In 1996, she was given the American Psychological Association's Gold Medal Award for Lifetime Achievement in the Science of Psychology and has been a president of the Society for Research on Child Development.

Eleanor faced the challenges of many women balancing a career and family. She commented, "When my children were young, I worked part-time so I could take care of them. . . . The balancing act is never easy. I developed a habit of getting up at 2 A.M. and working until 4 A.M. With no distractions, I managed to be quite productive. . . . I continued to work this late night shift for 20 years."

Eleanor Maccoby

competent than females (Durkin, 1985). In one investigation, young adolescent girls indicated that television occupations were more extremely stereotyped than real-life occupations were (Wroblewski & Huston, 1987).

Television directed at adolescents might be the most extreme in its portrayal of the sexes, especially of teenage girls (Beal, 1994). In one study, teenage girls were shown as primarily concerned with dating, shopping, and their appearance (Campbell, 1988). They were rarely depicted as interested in school or career plans. Attractive girls were often portrayed as "airheads" and intelligent girls as unattractive.

Another highly stereotyped form of programming specifically targeted for teenage viewers is rock music videos. What adolescents see on MTV and rock music videos is highly stereotyped and slanted toward a male audience. In music videos, females are twice as likely as in prime-time programming to be dressed provocatively, and aggressive acts are often perpetrated by females; for example, in one scene a woman pushes a man to the ground, holds him down, and kisses him. MTV has been described as a teenage boy's "dreamworld," filled with beautiful, aroused women who outnumber men, who seek out and even assault men to have sex, and who always mean yes even when they say no.

If television can communicate sexist messages and influence adolescents' gender behavior, might nonstereotyped gender messages on television reduce sexist behavior? One major effort to reduce gender stereotyping was the television series *Freestyle* (Johnston, Etteman, & Davidson, 1980; Williams, LaRose, & Frost, 1981). The series was designed to counteract career stereotypes in 9- to 12-year-olds. After watching *Freestyle,* both girls and boys were more open to nontraditional career possibilities. The benefits of *Freestyle* were greatest for students who viewed the TV series in the classroom and who participated in discussion groups about the show led by their teacher. Classroom discussion was especially helpful in altering boys' beliefs, which were initially more stereotyped than girls'.

However, in one study with 12- to 13-year-olds, the strategy of showing nonstereotyped television programming backfired (Durkin & Hutchins, 1984). The young adolescents watched sketches that portrayed people with nontraditional jobs, such as a male secretary, a male nurse, and a female plumber. After viewing the series, the adolescents still held traditional views about careers, and in some cases were more disapproving of the alternative careers than they had been before watching the TV sketches. Thus, once stereotypes are strongly in place, they are difficult to change.

Gender stereotyping also appears in the print media. Females and males are portrayed with different personalities, and perform different tasks, in children's books (Matlin, 1993). Males are described and pictured as clever, industrious, and brave. They acquire skills, earn fame and fortune, and explore. By contrast, females tend to be passive, dependent, and kind. They are more likely to cook and clean up.

In one study, 150 children's books were analyzed for gender-role content (Kortenhaus & Demarest, 1993). It was found that the frequency with which females and males are depicted in the stories has become more equal over the past 50 years. The roles played by females and males in the books have changed in a more subtle way. Girls are now being pictured in more instrumental activities (behavior that is instrumental in attaining a goal), but in the portrayals they are as passive and dependent as they were depicted as being 50 years ago! Boys are occasionally shown as passive and dependent today, but the activities they are pictured in are no less instrumental than they were 50 years ago.

Today, with effort, parents and teachers can locate interesting books in which girls and women are presented as appropriate models. And it is worth the effort.

Cognitive Influences

Developmentalists also recognize the important role that cognitive factors play in gender. Two cognitive theories of gender have been proposed:

Theory	Processes	Emphasis
Cognitive developmental theory	Development of gender constancy, especially around 6 to 7 years of age, when conservation skills develop; after children develop ability to consistently conceive of themselves as male or female, children often organize their world on the basis of gender, such as selecting same-sex models to imitate	Cognitive readiness facilitates gender identity
Gender schema theory	Sociocultural emphasis on gender-based standards and stereotypes; children's attention and behavior are guided by an internal motivation to conform to these gender-based standards and stereotypes, allowing children to interpret the world through a network of gender-organized thoughts	Gender schemas reinforce gender behavior

FIGURE 13.4 The Development of Gender-Typed Behavior According to the Cognitive Developmental and Gender Schema Theories of Gender Development

- The **cognitive developmental theory of gender** states that children's gender typing occurs after they have developed a concept of gender. Once they consistently conceive of themselves as male or female, children often organize their world on the basis of gender. In this view, children use physical and behavioral clues to differentiate gender roles and to gender-type themselves early in their development. Initially proposed by Lawrence Kohlberg (1966), this theory argues that gender development proceeds in the following way. A child realizes, "I am a girl. I want to do girl things. Therefore, the opportunity to do girl things is rewarding." Kohlberg said that gender constancy develops at about 6 or 7 years of age in concert with the development of children's conservation and categorization skills. After children consistently conceive of themselves as female or male, they begin to organize their world on the basis of gender, such as selecting same-sex models to imitate.

- **Gender schema theory** states that an individual's attention and behavior are guided by an internal motivation to conform to gender-based sociocultural standards and stereotypes. Note that a *schema* is a cognitive structure, a network of associations that organizes and guides an individual's perceptions. ◀ **page 255** A *gender schema* organizes the world in terms of female and male. Gender schema theory suggests that "gender typing" occurs when individuals are ready to encode and organize information along the lines of what is considered appropriate or typical for males and females in a society (Martin & Dinella, 2001; Martin, Ruble, & Szkrybalo, 2002; Tenenbaum & Leaper, 2002). Whereas Kohlberg's cognitive developmental theory argues that a particular cognitive prerequisite—gender constancy—is necessary for gender typing, *gender constancy* refers to the understanding that sex remains the same even though activities, clothing, and hairstyle might change (Ruble, 2000). Gender schema theory states that a general readiness to respond to and categorize information on the basis of culturally defined gender roles fuels children's gender-typing activities. A comparison of the cognitive developmental and gender schema theories is presented in figure 13.4.

Researchers have shown that the appearance of gender constancy in children is related to their level of cognitive development, especially the acquisition of conservation skills (which supports the cognitive developmental theory of gender) (Serbin & Sprafkin, 1986). However, they have also shown that young children who are pre-gender-constant have more gender-role knowledge than the cognitive developmental theory of gender predicts (which supports gender schema theory) (Carter & Levy, 1988).

The cognitive aspects of gender also involve the language children use and encounter (Hort & Leinbach, 1993). The nature of the language children hear can

cognitive developmental theory of gender In this view, children's gender-typing occurs after they have developed a concept of gender. Once they begin to consistently conceive of themselves as male or female, children often organize their world on the basis of gender.

gender schema theory According to this theory, an individual's attention and behavior are guided by an internal motivation to conform to gender-based sociocultural standards and stereotypes.

be sexist. That is, the English language contains gender bias, especially through the use of *he* and *man* to refer to everyone. For example, in one investigation, mothers and their 1- to 3-year-old children looked at popular children's books, such as *The Three Bears,* together (DeLoache, Cassidy, & Carpenter, 1987). The three bears were almost always referred to as boys: 95 percent of all characters of indeterminate gender were referred to by mothers as males.

Review and Reflect: Learning Goal 1

1 Discuss the main biological, social, and cognitive influences on gender

REVIEW

- What are some biological influences on gender development?
- What are some social influences on gender development?
- What are some cognitive influences on gender development?

REFLECT

- Which theory of gender development do you like best? What might an eclectic theoretical view of gender development be like? (You might want to review the discussion of an eclectic theoretical orientation in chapter 2.)

---

2 GENDER STEREOTYPES, SIMILARITIES, AND DIFFERENCES

Gender Stereotyping

Gender Similarities and Differences

How pervasive is gender stereotyping? What are the real differences between boys and girls?

Gender Stereotyping

Gender stereotypes are broad categories that reflect our general impressions and beliefs about females and males. How widespread is feminine and masculine stereotyping?

Stereotyping Across Cultures According to a far-ranging study of college students in 30 countries, stereotyping of females and males is pervasive (Williams & Best, 1982). Males were widely believed to be dominant, independent, aggressive, achievement-oriented, and enduring, while females were widely believed to be nurturant, affiliative, less esteemed, and more helpful in times of distress. Other research continues to find that gender stereotyping is pervasive (Best, 2001; Kite, 2001).

In a subsequent study, women and men who lived in more highly developed countries perceived themselves as more similar than women and men who lived in less developed countries (Williams & Best, 1989). In the more highly developed countries, the women were more likely to attend college and be gainfully employed. Thus, as sexual equality increases, male and female stereotypes, as well as actual behavioral differences, may diminish. In this study, the women were more likely to perceive similarity between the sexes than the men were (Williams & Best, 1989). And the sexes were perceived more similarly in the Christian than in the Muslim societies.

gender stereotypes Broad categories that reflect impressions and beliefs about what behavior is appropriate for females and males.

Stereotyping of Occupations   One area of gender stereotyping involves occupations (Liben, Bigler, & Krogh, 2001). Despite the fact that increasing numbers of men and women are now entering jobs historically associated with the other sex, many occupations in American culture remain strongly "gendered." Even young children associate different occupations with men and women and aspire to occupations that are consistent with the cultural stereotypes for their own sex (Liben, Bigler, & Krogh, 2001).

Gender Stereotyping

One study focused on reducing children's gender stereotyping (Bigler & Liben, 1990). The researchers' goal was to decrease children's stereotyping of ten occupations commonly viewed as either feminine (beautician, fashion model, flight attendant, laundromat worker, and librarian) or masculine (construction worker, dentist, farmer, firefighter, and janitor). The participants in the study were 76 children from 6 through 11 years of age. During the first week of school, they were given a pretest stereotyping measure and then randomly assigned to a week of daily 20-minute experimental- or control-group lessons on occupations. The following week, the children were given a posttest stereotyping measure.

The children in the experimental group were told that gender is irrelevant and that what's important is liking the job (construction workers must like to build things, for example) and having the skills needed for the job (construction workers must learn to drive big machines, for example). The children then were given practice problems to work. When the children gave gendered responses, the experimenter gave them corrective feedback. For example, one practice problem involved Ann driving a bulldozer. Children were told "Ann loves to build things" and "Ann knows how to drive a bulldozer." The children then were asked, "Could Ann be a construction worker?" "How do you know?" If children said, "No, she couldn't because she is a girl," they were corrected for appealing to gender in their justifications. In the control group, children were given lessons on the same occupations but with no reference to or feedback about gender.

What were the results of this experiment? In the posttest, which was given after the week of gender instruction, the experimental group gave more nonstereotyped answers not only on the ten occupations they had been studying but also on many other occupations. For example, when children in the experimental group were asked which sex could do best at occupations like firefighting and being a librarian, they were more likely to say "both men and women" than the children in the control group, who were most likely to say "Girls can't be firefighters."

Gender Similarities and Differences

Let's now examine some of the differences between the sexes, keeping in mind that (1) the differences are averages—not all females versus all males; (2) even when differences are reported, there is considerable overlap between the sexes; and (3) the differences may be due primarily to biological factors, sociocultural factors, or both. First, we will examine physical differences, and then we will turn to cognitive and socioemotional differences.

Physical Similarities and Differences   From conception on, females have a longer life expectancy than males, and females are less likely than males to develop physical or mental disorders. Estrogen strengthens the immune system, making females more resistant to infection, for example. Female hormones also signal the liver to produce more "good" cholesterol, which makes females' blood vessels more elastic than males'. Testosterone triggers the production of low-density lipoprotein, which clogs blood vessels. Males have twice the risk of coronary disease as females. Higher levels of stress hormones cause faster clotting in males, but also higher blood pressure than in females. Women have about twice the body fat of men, most concentrated around breasts and hips. In males, fat is more likely to go to the abdomen. On the average, males grow to be 10 percent taller than females.

"So according to the stereotype, you can put two and two together, but I can read the handwriting on the wall."

www.mhhe.com/santrocked10

Shortchanging Girls, Shortchanging America

Positive Expectations for Girls

War on Boys

Center for Gender Equity

If you are going to generalize about women, you will find yourself up to here in exceptions.

—DOLORES HITCHENS
American Mystery Writer, 20th Century

rapport talk The language of conversation and a way of establishing connections and negotiating relationships; more characteristic of females than of males.

report talk Talk that conveys information; more characteristic of males than of females.

Male hormones promote the growth of long bones; female hormones stop such growth at puberty.

Does gender matter when it comes to brain structure and function? Human brains are much alike, whether the brain belongs to a male or a female (Halpern, 2001). However, researchers have found some differences in the brains of males and females (Goldstein & others, 2001; Kimura, 2000) Among the differences that have been discovered are:

- One part of the hypothalamus responsible for sexual behavior is larger in men than women (Swaab & others, 2001).
- Portions of the corpus callosum—the band of tissues through which the brains' two hemispheres communicate—is larger in females than males (Le Vay, 1994).
- An area of the parietal lobe that functions in visuospatial skills is larger in males than females (Frederikse & others, 2000).
- The areas of the brain involved in emotional expression show more metabolic activity in females than males (Gur & others, 1995).

Cognitive Similarities and Differences In a classic review of gender differences, Eleanor Maccoby and Carol Jacklin (1974) concluded that males have better math and visuospatial skills (the kinds of skills an architect needs to design a building's angles and dimensions), while females have better verbal abilities. Subsequently, Maccoby (1987) revised her conclusion about several gender dimensions. She said that the accumulation of research evidence now suggests that verbal differences between females and males have virtually disappeared but that the math and visuospatial differences still exist.

Some experts in gender, such as Janet Shibley Hyde (1993; Hyde & Mezulis, 2001), believe that the cognitive differences between females and males have been exaggerated. For example, Hyde points out that there is considerable overlap in the distributions of female and male scores on math and visuospatial tasks.

In a national study by the U.S. Department of Education (2000), boys did slightly better than girls at math and science. Overall, though, girls were far superior students, and they were significantly better than boys in reading. In another recent national study, females had higher reading achievement and better writing skills than males in grades 4, 8, and 12 with the gap widening as students progressed through school (Coley, 2001).

Socioemotional Similarities and Differences Four areas of socioemotional development in which gender has been studied are relationships, aggression, emotion, and achievement.

Relationships Sociolinguist Deborah Tannen (1990) distinguishes between rapport talk and report talk:

- **Rapport talk** is the language of conversation and a way of establishing connections and negotiating relationships. Females enjoy rapport talk and conversation that is relationship-oriented more than boys do.
- **Report talk** is talk that gives information. Public speaking is an example of report talk. Males hold center stage through report talk with such verbal performances as storytelling, joking, and lecturing with information.

Tannen says that boys and girls grow up in different worlds of talk—parents, siblings, peers, teachers, and others talk to boys and girls differently. The play of boys and girls is also different. Boys tend to play in large groups that are hierarchically structured, and their groups usually have a leader who tells the others what to do and how to do it. Boys' games have winners and losers and often are the subject of arguments. And boys often boast of their skill and argue about who is best at what. In contrast, girls are more likely to play in small groups or pairs, and at the center of a girl's world is often a best friend. In girls' friendships and peer groups, intimacy is pervasive. Turn taking is more characteristic of girls' games than of boys' games. And much of the time, girls simply like to sit and talk with each other, concerned more about being liked by others than jockeying for status in some obvious way.

In sum, Tannen, like other gender experts such as Carol Gilligan, whose ideas you will read about in the chapter 14, "Moral Development," believes that girls are more relationship-oriented than boys—and that this relationship orientation should be prized as a skill in our culture more than it currently is.

Aggression One of the most consistent gender differences is that boys are more physically aggressive than girls. The difference occurs in all cultures and appears very early in children's development (White, 2001). The physical aggression difference is especially pronounced when children are provoked. Both biological and environmental factors have been proposed to account for gender differences in aggression. Biological factors include heredity and hormones. Environmental factors include cultural expectations, adult and peer models, and social agents who reward aggression in boys and punish aggression in girls.

Although boys are consistently more physically aggressive than girls, might girls show as much or more verbal aggression, such as yelling, than boys? When verbal aggression is examined, gender differences often disappear or are sometimes even more pronounced in girls (Eagly & Steffen, 1986). Girls are more likely than boys to engage in what is called *relational aggression*, which involves such behaviors as trying to make others dislike a certain child by spreading malicious rumors about the child or ignoring another child when angry at him or her (Crick & others, 2001; Underwood, 2002).

Self-Regulation of Emotion An important skill is to be able to regulate and control your emotions and behavior (Eisenberg, 2002). Males usually show less self-regulation than females, and this low self-control can translate into behavioral problems (Eisenberg, Martin, & Fabes, 1996; Eisenberg & Wang, 2003; Eisenberg & others, 2002). In one study, children's low self-regulation was linked with greater aggression, the teasing of others, overreaction to frustration, low cooperation, and inability to delay gratification (Block & Block, 1980).

Achievement For some areas of achievement, gender differences are so large they can best be described as nonoverlapping. For example, no major league baseball players are female; and 96 percent of all registered nurses are female. However, some measures of achievement-related behaviors do not reveal gender differences. For example, girls and boys show similar persistence at tasks.

With regard to school achievement, females earn better grades. For example, recent evidence suggests that boys predominate in the academic bottom half of high school classes (DeZolt & Hull, 2001). That is, although many boys perform at the average or advanced level, the bottom 50 percent academically is made up mainly of boys. Males are more likely than females to be assigned to special/remedial education classes. Females are more likely to be engaged with academic material, be attentive in class, put forth more academic effort, and participate more in class than boys are (DeZolt & Hull, 2001).

Gender Controversy Not all psychologists agree that psychological differences between females and males are rare or small. Alice Eagly (1996, 2001) stated that such a belief arose from a feminist commitment to similarity between the sexes as a route to political equality, and from piecemeal and inadequate interpretations of

www.mhhe.com/santrockcd10

Gender and Communication

> *W*hat are little boys made of?
> Frogs and snails
> and puppy dogs' tails.
> What are little girls made of?
> Sugar and spice
> And all that's nice
>
> —J.O. HALLIWELL
> *English Author, 19th Century*

relevant empirical research. Many feminists express a fear that differences between females and males will be interpreted as deficiencies in females and as biologically based, which could promote the old stereotypes that women are inferior to men (Unger & Crawford, 2000). According to Eagly, contemporary psychology has produced a large body of research that reveals that behavior is sex differentiated to varying extents and that the differences are socially induced.

Evolutionary psychologist David Buss (1995, 2000) argues that men and women differ psychologically in those domains in which they have faced different adaptive problems across their evolutionary history. In all other domains, predicts Buss, the sexes will be found to be psychologically similar. He cites males' superiority in the cognitive domain of spatial rotation. This ability is essential for hunting, in which the trajectory of a projectile must anticipate the trajectory of a prey animal as each moves through space and time. Buss also cites a sex difference in casual sex, with men engaging in this behavior more than women do. In one study, men said that ideally they would like to have more than eighteen sex partners in their lifetime, whereas women stated that ideally they would like to have only four or five (Buss & Schmitt, 1993). In another study, 75 percent of the men but none of the women approached by an attractive stranger of the opposite sex consented to a request for sex (Clark & Hatfield, 1989). Such sex differences, says Buss, are exactly the type predicted by evolutionary psychology, since multiple sexual liaisons improve the likelihood that the male will pass on his genes. A woman's contribution to the gene pool is improved by securing resources for her offspring, which is promoted more effectively by a monogamous relationship.

In sum, controversy continues over whether sex differences are rare and small or common and large. Such controversy is evidence that gender is a political issue.

Review and Reflect: Learning Goal 2

2 **Describe gender stereotyping, similarities, and differences**

REVIEW

- How extensive is gender stereotyping?
- What are some gender similarities and differences in the areas of biological, cognitive, and socioemotional development?

REFLECT

- How is your gender behavior and thinking similar or different from your mother's and grandmothers' if you are a female? How is your gender behavior and thinking different than your father's and grandfathers' if you are a male?

---

3 GENDER-ROLE CLASSIFICATION

What Is Gender-Role Classification?

Masculinity in Childhood and Adolescence

Gender in Context

Androgyny and Education

Gender-Role Transcendence

Not very long ago, it was accepted that boys should grow up to be masculine and girls to be feminine, that boys are made of "frogs and snails" and girls are made of "sugar and spice and all that's nice." Let's further explore such gender classifications of boys and girls as "masculine" and "feminine."

The following items are from the Bem Sex-Role Inventory. When taking the BSRI, a person is asked to indicate on a 7-point scale how well each of the 60 characteristics describes herself or himself. The scale ranges from 1 (never or almost never true) to 7 (always or almost always true).

FIGURE 13.5 **The Bem Sex-Role Inventory: Are You Androgynous?**

EXAMPLES OF MASCULINE ITEMS	EXAMPLES OF FEMININE ITEMS
Defends open beliefs	Does not use harsh language
Forceful	Affectionate
Willing to take risks	Loves children
Dominant	Understanding
Aggressive	Gentle

Scoring: The items are scored on independent dimensions of masculinity and feminity as well as androgyny and undifferentiate classifications.

What Is Gender-Role Classification?

In the past, a well-adjusted boy was supposed to be independent, aggressive, and powerful. A well-adjusted girl was supposed to be dependent, nurturant, and uninterested in power. The masculine characteristics were considered to be healthy and good by society; the feminine characteristics were considered undesirable.

In the 1970s, as both females and males become dissatisfied with the burdens imposed by their stereotypic roles, alternatives to femininity and masculinity were proposed. Instead of describing masculinity and femininity as a continuum in which more of one means less of the other, it was proposed that individuals could have both masculine and feminine traits. This thinking led to the development of the concept of **androgyny,** the presence of masculine and feminine characteristics in the same person (Bem, 1977; Spence & Helmreich, 1978). The androgynous boy might be assertive (masculine) and nurturant (feminine). The androgynous girl might be powerful (masculine) and sensitive to others' feelings (feminine). In one recent study it was confirmed that societal changes are leading females to be more assertive (Spence & Buckner, 2000).

Measures have been developed to assess androgyny. One of the most widely used measures is the Bem Sex-Role Inventory. To see whether your gender-role classification is masculine, feminine, or androgynous, see figure 13.5.

Gender experts, such as Sandra Bem, argue that androgynous individuals are more flexible, competent, and mentally healthy than their masculine or feminine counterparts. To some degree, though, deciding on which gender-role classification is best depends on the context involved. For example, in close relationships, feminine and androgynous orientations might be more desirable because of the expressive nature of close relationships. However, masculine and androgynous orientations might be more desirable in traditional academic and work settings because of the achievement demands in these contexts.

Androgyny

Androgyny and Education

Can and should androgyny be taught to students? In general, it is easier to teach androgyny to girls than to boys and easier to teach it before the middle school grades. For example, in one study, a gender curriculum was put in place for one year in the kindergarten, fifth, and ninth grades (Guttentag & Bray, 1976). It involved books, discussion materials, and classroom exercises with an androgynous bent. The program was most successful with the fifth-graders, least successful with the ninth-graders. The ninth-graders, especially the boys, showed a boomerang effect, in which they had more traditional gender-role attitudes after the year of androgynous instruction than before it.

androgyny The presence of masculine and feminine characteristics in the same person.

Despite such mixed findings, the advocates of androgyny programs believe that traditional sex-typing is harmful for all students and especially has prevented many girls from experiencing equal opportunity. The detractors argue that androgynous educational programs are too value-laden and ignore the diversity of gender roles in our society.

Masculinity in Childhood and Adolescence

Concern about the ways boys have been brought up in traditional ways has been called a "national crisis of boyhood" by William Pollack (1999) in his book *Real Boys*. Pollack says that although there has been considerable talk about the "sensitive male," little has been done to change what he calls the "boy code." He says that this code tells boys they should show little if any emotion as they are growing up. Too often boys are socialized to not show their feelings and act tough, says Pollack. Boys learn the boy code in many different contexts—sandboxes, playgrounds, schoolrooms, camps, hangouts—and are taught the code by parents, peers, coaches, teachers, and other adults. Pollack, as well as many others, believes that boys would benefit from being socialized to express their anxieties and concerns rather than keep them bottled up as well as to learn how to better regulate their aggression.

There also is a special concern about boys who adopt a strong masculine role in adolescence, because this is increasingly being found to be associated with problem behaviors. Joseph Pleck (1995) believes that what defines traditional masculinity in many Western cultures includes behaviors that do not have social approval but nonetheless validate the adolescent boy's masculinity. That is, in the male adolescent culture, male adolescents perceive that they will be thought of as more masculine if they engage in premarital sex, drink alcohol and take drugs, and participate in illegal delinquent activities.

Gender-Role Transcendence

Some critics of androgyny say enough is enough and that there is too much talk about gender. They believe that androgyny is less of a panacea than originally envisioned (Paludi, 2002). An alternative is **gender-role transcendence,** the view that when an individual's competence is at issue, it should be conceptualized on a personal basis rather than on the basis of masculinity, femininity, or androgyny (Pleck, 1983). That is, we should think about ourselves as people, not as masculine, feminine, or androgynous. Parents should rear their children to be competent boys and girls, not masculine, feminine, or androgynous, say the gender-role critics. They believe such gender-role classification leads to too much stereotyping.

Gender in Context

The concept of gender-role classification involves a personality trait-like categorization of a person. However, it may be helpful to think of personality in terms of person-situation interaction rather than personality traits alone. Thus, in our discussion of gender-role classification, we describe how different gender roles might be more appropriate, depending on the context, or setting, involved.

To see the importance of considering gender in context, let's examine helping behavior and emotion. The stereotype is that females are better than males at helping. However, it depends on the situation. Females are more likely than males to volunteer their time to help children with personal problems and to engage in caregiving behavior (Taylor, 2002). However, in situations in which males feel a sense of competence and involve danger, males are more likely than females to help (Eagly & Crowley, 1986). For example, a male is more likely than a female to stop and help a person stranded by the roadside with a flat tire.

www.mhhe.com/santrockcd10

Psychological Study of Males

Male Issues

Exploring Masculinity

gender-role transcendence The belief that, when an individual's competence is at issue, it should be conceptualized not on the basis of masculinity, femininity, or androgyny but, rather, on a personal basis.

Gender Roles in Iran and China

In recent decades, roles assumed by males and females in the United States have become increasingly similar—that is, androgynous. In many countries, though, gender roles have remained more gender-specific. For example, in Iran, the division of labor between Iranian males and females is dramatic: Iranian males are socialized to work in the public sphere, females in the private world of home and child rearing. The Islamic religion dictates that the man's duty is to provide for his family, the woman's to care for her family and household (Dickerscheid & others, 1988). Any deviations from this traditional gender-role orientation are severely disapproved of.

Iran is not the only country in which males and females are socialized to behave, think, and feel in strongly gender-specific ways. Kenya and Nepal are two other cultures in which children are brought up under very strict gender-specific guidelines (Munroe, Himmin, & Munroe, 1984). In the People's Republic of China, the female's status has historically been lower than the male's. The teachings of the fifth-century B.C. Chinese philosopher Confucius were used to reinforce the concept of the female as an inferior being. Beginning with the 1949 revolution in China, women began to achieve more economic freedom and more-equal status in marital relationships. However, even with the sanctions of a socialist government, the old patriarchal traditions of male supremacy in China have not been completely uprooted. Chinese women still make considerably less money than Chinese men in comparable positions, and in rural China a tradition of male supremacy still governs many women's lives.

Thus, while in China, females have made considerable strides, complete equality remains a distant objective. And in many cultures, such as Iran and other countries where the Muslim religion predominates, gender-specific behavior is pronounced, and females are not given access to high-status positions.

In China, females and males are usually socialized to behave, feel, and think differently. The old patriarchal traditions of male supremacy have not been completely uprooted. Chinese women still make considerably less money than Chinese men do, and, in rural China (such as here in the Lixian Village of Sichuan) male supremacy still governs many women's lives.

"She is emotional; he is not"—that is the master emotional stereotype. However, like differences in helping behavior, emotional differences in males and females depend on the particular emotion involved and the context in which it is displayed (Shields, 1991). Males are more likely to show anger toward strangers, especially male strangers, when they feel they have been challenged. Males also are more likely to turn their anger into aggressive action. Emotional differences between females and males often show up in contexts that highlight social roles and relationships. For example, females are more likely to discuss emotions in terms of relationships, and they are more likely to express fear and sadness.

The importance of considering gender in context is nowhere more apparent than when examining what is culturally prescribed behavior for females and males in different countries around the world (Gibbons, 2000). While there has been greater acceptance of androgyny and similarities in male and female behavior in the United States, in many countries gender roles have remained gender-specific. To read further about the cultural contexts of gender, see the Explorations in Child Development box.

Access to education for girls has improved somewhat around the world, but girls' education still lags behind boys' education. For example, according to recent UNICEF (2003) analysis of education around the world, by age 18, girls have received, on average, 4.4 years less education than boys have. This lack of education reduces their chances of developing to their future potential. Noticeable exceptions to lower participation and completion rates in education for girls occur in Western nations, Japan, and the Phillipines (Brown & Larson, 2002). Gaining advanced training or advanced degrees is higher in most countries for males (Fussell & Greene, 2002).

www.mhhe.com/santrockcd10

Gender Around the World
Gender Socialization in Six Countries

Although there are still gender gaps in most countries that favor males, evidence of increasing gender equality is appearing (Brown & Larson, 2002). For example, among upper-class families in India and Japan, fathers are assuming more child-rearing responsibilities (Stevenson & Zusho, 2002; Verma & Saraswathi, 2002). Rates of employment and career opportunities are expanding in many countries for women. Control over adolescent girls' social relationships, especially sexual and romantic relationships, is decreasing in some countries.

Review and Reflect: Learning Goal 3

3 Identify how gender roles can be classified

REVIEW

- What is gender-role classification?
- What are the effects of teaching androgyny in schools?
- What are some risks of masculinity in childhood and adolescence?
- What is gender-role transcendence?
- How can gender be conceptualized in terms of context?

REFLECT

- Several decades ago, the word *dependency* was used to describe the relational orientation of femininity. Dependency took on a negative connotation for females—for instance, that females can't take care of themselves while males can. Today, the term *dependency* is being replaced by *relational abilities*, which has more positive connotations (Caplan & Caplan, 1999). Rather than being thought of as dependent, women are now more often described as skilled in forming and maintaining relationships. Make up a list of words that you associate with masculinity and femininity. Do these words have any negative connotations for males and females? For the words that do have negative connotations, think about replacements for them that have more positive connotations.

---

4 DEVELOPMENTAL WINDOWS OF GENDER OPPORTUNITY AND ASYMMETRIC GENDER SOCIALIZATION

Developmental Windows

Asymmetric Gender Socialization

Are children more prone to forming gender roles at some points in development than at others? Are the amount, timing, and intensity of gender socialization different for girls and boys?

Developmental Windows

Do gender lessons have to be hammered into children's heads year after year? Apparently not, according to gender expert Carole Beal (1994). Instead, what girls and boys learn about gender seems to be learned quickly at certain points in development, especially when new abilities first emerge. For example, toddlers learn a lot about gender when they make their first bids for autonomy and begin to talk. Children form many ideas about what the sexes are like from about $1\frac{1}{2}$ to 3 years of age. Many parents begin to think more intensely about gender issues involving their child in the early childhood years. However, at that point children have already altered their gender behavior and learned to think of themselves as a girl or a boy. Few parents have to tell their little boys not to wear pink pants to the first grade!

Early adolescence is another transitional point that seems to be especially important in gender development. Young adolescents have to cope with the enormous changes of puberty, changes that are intensified by their expanding cognitive abilities that make them acutely aware of how they appear to others. ◀ **page 183** Relations with others change extensively as dating relationships begin and sexuality is experienced. Adolescents often cope with the stress of these changes by becoming more conservative and traditional in their gender thinking and behavior, a tendency that is heightened by media stereotypes of females and males.

Asymmetric Gender Socialization

The amount, timing, and intensity of gender socialization is different for girls and boys (Beal, 1994). Boys receive earlier and more intense gender socialization than girls do. The social cost of deviating from the expected male role is higher for boys than is the cost for girls of deviating from the expected female role, in terms of peer rejection and parental disapproval. Imagine a girl who is wearing a toy holster, bandanna, and cowboy hat, running around in the backyard pretending to herd cattle. Now imagine a boy who is wearing a flowered hat, ropes of pearls, and lipstick, pretending to cook dinner on a toy stove. Which of these do you have a stronger reaction to—the girl's behavior or the boy's? Probably the boy's. Researchers have found that "effeminate" behavior in boys elicits much more negative reactions than does "masculine" behavior in girls (Lippa, 2002).

Boys might have a more difficult time learning the masculine gender role because male models are less accessible to young children and messages from adults about the male role are not always consistent. For example, most mothers and teachers would like for boys to behave in masculine ways, but also to be neat, well-mannered, and considerate. However, fathers and peers usually want boys to behave in another way—independent and engaging in rough-and-tumble play. The mixed messages make it difficult for boys to figure out which gender role they should follow. According to Beal (1994), although gender roles have become more flexible in recent years, the flexibility has occurred more for girls than for boys. Girls can now safely be ambitious, competitive, and interested in sports, but relatively few adults are equally supportive of boys' being gentle, interested in fashion, and motivated to sign up for ballet classes.

> *W*e are born twice over; the first time for existence, the second time for life; once as human beings and later as men or as women.
>
> —JEAN-JACQUES ROUSSEAU
> *French-Born Swiss Philosopher,*
> *18th Century*

Review and Reflect: Learning Goal 4

4 Characterize developmental windows of gender opportunity and asymmetric gender socialization

REVIEW

- What are some developmental windows of gender opportunity?
- How is gender socialization asymmetric?

REFLECT

- As a parent, how would you want to relate to your children to influence their gender development? First, answer this question for a boy, then for a girl.

Reach Your Learning Goals

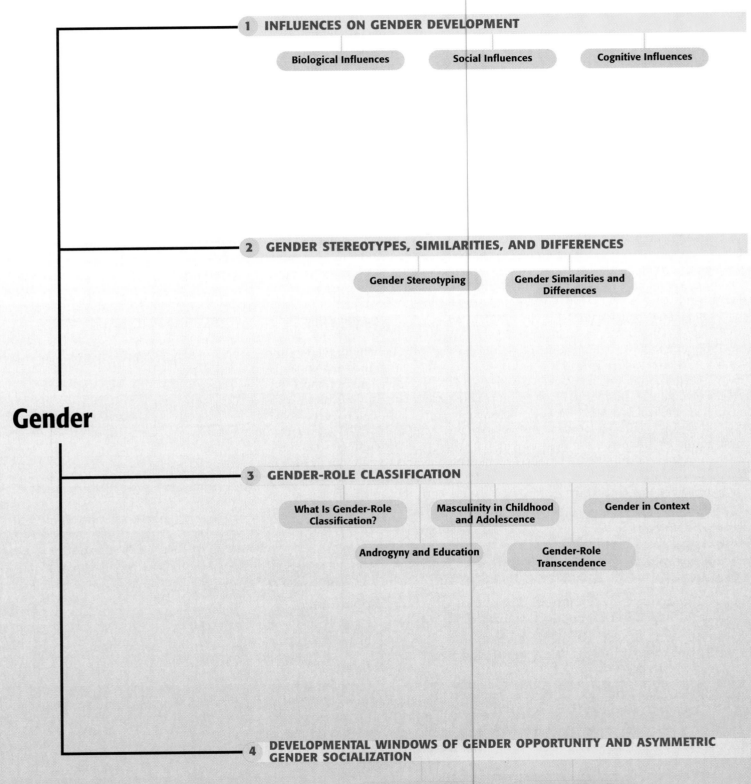

Gender

1 INFLUENCES ON GENDER DEVELOPMENT

Biological Influences   Social Influences   Cognitive Influences

2 GENDER STEREOTYPES, SIMILARITIES, AND DIFFERENCES

Gender Stereotyping   Gender Similarities and Differences

3 GENDER-ROLE CLASSIFICATION

What Is Gender-Role Classification?   Masculinity in Childhood and Adolescence   Gender in Context

Androgyny and Education   Gender-Role Transcendence

4 DEVELOPMENTAL WINDOWS OF GENDER OPPORTUNITY AND ASYMMETRIC GENDER SOCIALIZATION

Developmental Windows   Asymmetric Gender Socialization

Summary

1 Discuss the main biological, social, and cognitive influences on gender

- Gender refers to the psychological and sociocultural dimensions of being male or female. A gender role is a set of expectations that prescribes how females or males should think, act, and feel. The 23rd pair of chromosomes determines our sex. Ordinarily, females have two X chromosomes, males one X and one Y. Chromosomes determine anatomical sex differences, but culture and society strongly influence gender. The two main classes of hormones are androgens and estrogens. Researchers have found that early hormonal production is linked with later gender development. Both Freud's and Erikson's theories promote the idea that anatomy is destiny. In the evolutionary psychology view, evolutionary adaptations produced psychological sex differences that are especially present in sexual selection.

- In the social roles view, women have less power and status than men and control fewer resources. In this view, gender hierarchy and sexual division of labor are important causes of sex-differentiated behavior. Both psychoanalytic and social cognitive theories emphasize the adoption of parents' gender characteristics. Parents and other adults also might assign gender roles to children and reward or punish behavior along gender lines. Peers are especially adept at rewarding gender-appropriate behavior. Schools and teachers show biases against both boys and girls. Despite improvements, TV still portrays males as more competent than females.

- Both cognitive developmental and gender schema theories emphasize the role of cognition in gender development. Gender is present in the language children use and encounter. This language is often sexist.

2 Describe gender stereotyping, similarities, and differences

- Gender stereotypes are widespread around the world, especially emphasizing the male's power and the female's nurturance. Stereotyping of occupations is extensive.

- Physical and biological differences between males and females are substantial. Males are often better at math and visuospatial skills. However, some experts, such as Hyde, argue that cognitive differences between males and females have been exaggerated. Males are more physically aggressive and active than females, while females are often more likely to focus on social relationships. Females often are more achievement-oriented in school than males are. There is considerable controversy about how similar or different females and males are in a number of areas.

3 Identify how gender roles can be classified

- In the past, the well-adjusted male was supposed to show masculine traits, the well-adjusted female feminine traits. In the 1970s, alternatives to traditional gender roles were introduced. It was proposed that competent individuals could show both masculine and feminine traits. This thinking led to the development of the concept of androgyny, the presence of masculine and feminine traits in one individual. Gender-role measures often categorize individuals as masculine, feminine, androgynous, or undifferentiated. Most androgynous individuals are flexible and mentally healthy, although the particular context and the individual's culture also determine the adaptiveness of a gender-role orientation.

- Androgyny education programs have been more successful with females than males and more successful with children than adolescents.

- A special concern is that boys raised in a traditional manner are socialized to conceal their emotions. Some experts believe that gender-role intensification occurs in early adolescence because of increased pressure to conform to traditional gender roles. Researchers have found that problem behaviors often characterize highly masculine adolescents.

- One alternative to androgyny is gender-role transcendence, which states that there has been too much emphasis on gender and that a better strategy is to think about competence in terms of people rather than gender.

- In thinking about gender, it is important to keep in mind the context in which gender behavior is displayed. In many countries around the world, such as Iran and China, traditional gender roles are still dominant.

4 Characterize developmental windows of gender opportunity and asymmetric gender socialization

- Two especially important transition points in learning gender roles are the toddler years and early adolescence.

- The amount, timing, and intensity of gender socialization are different for boys and girls. Boys receive earlier and more intense gender socialization than girls do. Boys often have a more difficult time learning the masculine gender role because (1) male models are less accessible to boys than female models are to girls, and (2) the messages from adults about the male role are not always consistent.

Key Terms

gender 411
gender identity 411
gender role 411
estrogens 411
androgens 411

psychoanalytic theory of
  gender 414
social cognitive theory
  of gender 414

cognitive developmental
  theory of gender 419
gender schema theory 419
gender stereotypes 420

rapport talk 422
report talk 422
androgyny 425
gender-role transcendence 426

Key People

Stephanie Shields 410
Sigmund Freud 412
Erik Erikson 412
Alice Eagly 414

Myra and David Sadker 416
Eleanor Maccoby 417
Lawrence Kohlberg 419
Carol Jacklin 422

Janet Shibley Hyde 422
Deborah Tannen 422
David Buss 424
Sandra Bem 425

William Pollack 426
Joseph Pleck 426
Carole Beal 428

Taking It to the Net

1. Ellen is taking a class in gender psychology. She wants to test the theory of androgyny among her peers in her large geology lecture. She has heard that there is an online version of the test, and thinks people will feel more comfortable taking it online. She is going to try it herself, first. What conclusions can Ellen draw on the androgyny theory after taking this test?

2. Derek is the program chair for the Men's Focus Group on campus. He is planning a program on the social barriers to men being fully involved fathers. He thinks it has something to do with gender stereotypes that suggest that women are the best nurturers and caregivers. Is there some research Derek ought to share with the group?

3. Professor Lombard told the child development class to find out the current thinking on how to treat infants who are born without fully developed genitalia. She said that the old line of thinking was that these children should be surgically altered during infancy so that their genitals appear female. Are other alternatives being considered today?

Connect to **www.mhhe.com/santrockcd10** to research the answers and complete these exercises.

E-Learning Tools

To help you master the material in this chapter, you'll find a number of valuable study tools on the Student CD-ROM that accompanies this book. Also visit the Online Learning Center for *Child Development*, tenth edition (**www.mhhe.com/santrockcd10**) where you'll find these additional resources:

- Build your decision-making skills by trying your hand at the parenting, nursing, and education "Scenarios" on the Online Learning Center.
- Use the interactive Prism exercises to learn more about androgyny and the self.

It is one of the beautiful compensations of this life that no one can sincerely try to help another without helping himself.

—CHARLES DUDLEY WARNER
American Essayist, 19th Century

Moral Development

Chapter Outline

DOMAINS OF MORAL DEVELOPMENT

Moral Thought
Moral Behavior
Moral Feeling

CONTEXTS OF MORAL DEVELOPMENT

Parenting
Schools

PROSOCIAL AND ANTISOCIAL BEHAVIOR

Altruism
Juvenile Delinquency

Learning Goals

1 Discuss theories and research on moral thought, behavior, and feeling

2 Explain how parents and schools influence moral development

3 Describe the development of prosocial and antisocial behavior

The Story of Pax, the Make-Believe Planet

Can children understand such concepts as discrimination, economic inequality, affirmative action, and comparable worth? Probably not, if we use those terms, but might we be able to construct circumstances involving those concepts that they are able to understand? Phyllis Katz (1987) asked elementary-school-age children to pretend that they had taken a long ride on a spaceship to a make-believe planet called Pax. She asked for their opinions about various situations in which they found themselves. The situations involved conflict, socioeconomic inequality, and civil-political rights. For example, regarding conflict she asked them what a teacher should do when two students were tied for a prize or when they have been fighting. The economic equality dilemmas included a proposed field trip that not all students could afford, a comparable-worth situation in which janitors were paid more than teachers, and an employment situation that discriminated against those with dots on their noses instead of stripes. The rights items dealt with minority rights and freedom of the press.

The elementary school children did indeed recognize injustice and often came up with interesting solutions to problems. For example, all but two children believed that teachers should earn as much as janitors—the holdouts said teachers should make less because they stay in one room or because cleaning toilets is more disgusting and therefore deserves higher wages. Children were especially responsive to the economic inequality items. All but one thought that not giving a job to a qualified applicant who had different physical characteristics (a dotted rather than a striped nose) was unfair. The majority recommended an affirmative action solution—giving the job to the one from the discriminated-against minority. None of the children verbalized the concept of freedom of the press or seemed to understand that a newspaper has the right to criticize a mayor in print without being punished. What are our schools teaching children about democracy? Some of the courses of action suggested were intriguing. Several argued that the reporters should be jailed. One child said that, if she were the mayor being criticized, she would worry, make speeches, and say, "I didn't do anything wrong," not unlike what American presidents have done in recent years. Another said that the mayor should not put the newspaper people out of work, because that might make them print more bad things. "Make them write comics instead," he said. The children believed that poverty exists on Earth but mainly in Africa, big cities, or Vietnam. War was mentioned as the biggest problem on Earth, although children were not certain whether it is presently occurring. Other problems mentioned were crime, hatred, school, smog, and meanness. Overall, the types of rules the children believed a society should abide by were quite sensible—almost all included the need for equitable sharing of resources and work and prohibitions against aggression.

Moral development is one of the oldest topics of interest to those who are curious about human nature. In prescientific periods, philosophers and theologians heatedly debated children's moral status at birth, which they felt had important implications for how children should be reared. Today, most people have very strong opinions about acceptable and unacceptable behavior, ethical and unethical conduct, and the ways in which acceptable and ethical behaviors are to be fostered in children.

1 DOMAINS OF MORAL DEVELOPMENT

Moral Thought   **Moral Behavior**   **Moral Feeling**

Moral development involves age-related thoughts, behaviors, and feelings regarding rules, principles, and values that guide what people should do. Moral development has an *intrapersonal* dimension (a person's basic values and sense of self) and an *interpersonal* dimension (a focus on what people should do in their interactions with other people) (Walker, 1996: Walker & Pitts, 1998). The intrapersonal dimension regulates a person's activities when she or he is not engaged in social interaction. The interpersonal dimension regulates people's social interactions and arbitrates conflict. Let's now further explore some basic ideas about moral thoughts, behaviors, and feelings.

First, how do children *reason* or *think* about rules for ethical conduct? For example, consider cheating. A child can be presented with a story in which someone has a conflict about whether or not to cheat in a particular situation, such as when taking a test in school. The child is asked to decide what is appropriate for the character to do and why. The focus is on the reasoning children use to justify their moral decisions.

Second, how do children actually *behave* in moral circumstances? In our example of cheating, emphasis is on observing the child's cheating and the environmental circumstances that produced and maintained the cheating. Children might be presented with some toys and asked to select which one they believe is the most attractive. Then, the experimenter tells the young child that the particular toy selected is someone else's and is not to be played with. Observations of different conditions under which the child deviates from the prohibition or resists temptation are conducted.

Third, how does the child *feel* about the moral matters? In the example of cheating, does the child feel enough guilt to resist temptation? If children cheat, do feelings of guilt after the transgression keep them from cheating the next time they face temptation?

Moral Thought

How do children think about the standards of right and wrong? Piaget had some thoughts about this question, and so did Lawrence Kohlberg.

Piaget's Theory   Interest in how children think about moral issues was stimulated by Piaget (1932), who extensively observed and interviewed children from the ages of 4 through 12. Piaget watched children play marbles to learn how they used and thought about the game's rules. He also asked children questions about ethical issues—theft, lies, punishment, and justice, for example. Piaget concluded that children think in two distinct ways about morality, depending on their developmental maturity:

- **Heteronomous morality** is the first stage of moral development in Piaget's theory, occurring from 4 to 7 years of age. Justice and rules are conceived of as unchangeable properties of the world, removed from the control of people.
- **Autonomous morality** is the second stage of moral development in Piaget's theory, displayed by older children (about 10 years of age and older). The child becomes aware that rules and laws are created by people and that, in judging an action, one should consider the actor's intentions as well as the consequences. Children 7 to 10 years of age are in a transition between the two stages, evidencing some features of both.

www.mhhe.com/santrockcd10

Exploring Moral Development

moral development Age-related thoughts, behaviors, and feelings regarding rules, principles, and values that guide what people should do.

heteronomous morality (Piaget) The first stage of moral development in Piaget's theory, occurring from 4 to 7 years of age. Justice and rules are conceived of as unchangeable properties of the world, removed from the control of people.

autonomous morality (Piaget) The second stage of moral development in Piaget's theory, displayed by older children (about 10 years of age and older). The child becomes aware that rules and laws are created by people and that, in judging an action, one should consider the actor's intentions as well as the consequences.

Let's consider Piaget's two stages of moral development further. A heteronomous thinker judges the rightness or goodness of behavior by considering the consequences of the behavior, not the intentions of the actor. For example, the heteronomous thinker says that breaking 12 cups accidentally is worse than breaking 1 cup intentionally while trying to steal a cookie. For the moral autonomist, the reverse is true. The actor's intentions assume paramount importance. The heteronomous thinker also believes that rules are unchangeable and are handed down by all-powerful authorities. When Piaget suggested to a group of young children that new rules be introduced into the game of marbles, they resisted. They insisted that the rules had always been the same and could not be altered. In contrast, older children—who are moral autonomists—accept change and recognize that rules are merely convenient, socially agreed-upon conventions, subject to change by consensus.

The heteronomous thinker also believes in **immanent justice,** the concept that, if a rule is broken, punishment will be meted out immediately. The young child somehow believes that the violation is connected automatically to the punishment. Thus, young children often look around worriedly after committing a transgression, expecting inevitable punishment. Immanent justice also implies that if something unfortunate happens to someone it must be because the person had transgressed earlier. Older children, who are moral autonomists, recognize that punishment is socially mediated and occurs only if a relevant person witnesses the wrongdoing and that, even then, punishment is not inevitable.

Piaget argued that, as children develop, they become more sophisticated in thinking about social matters, especially about the possibilities and conditions of cooperation. Piaget believed that this social understanding comes about through the mutual give-and-take of peer relations. In the child's peer group, where others have power and status similar to the child's, plans are negotiated and coordinated, and disagreements are reasoned about and eventually settled. Parent-child relations, in which parents have the power and children do not, are less likely to advance moral reasoning, because rules are often handed down in an authoritarian way.

Remember that Piaget believed adolescents usually become formal operational thinkers. ← **page 221** Thus, they are no longer tied to immediate and concrete phenomena but are more logical, abstract, and deductive reasoners. Formal operational thinkers frequently compare the real to the ideal; create contrary-to-fact propositions; are cognitively capable of relating the distant past to the present; understand their roles in society, in history, and in the universe; and can conceptualize their own thoughts and think about their mental constructs as objects. For example, it usually is not until about the age of 11 or 12 that boys and girls spontaneously introduce concepts of belief, intelligence, and faith into their definitions of their religious identities.

Kohlberg's Theory　The most provocative view of moral development in recent years was crafted by Lawrence Kohlberg (Kohlberg, 1958, 1976, 1986). We will explore Kohlberg's concept of moral stages, influences on the Kohlberg stages, and Kohlberg's critics.

Kohlberg's Stages　Kohlberg (1927–1987) believed that moral development is primarily based on moral reasoning and unfolds in a series of stages. He arrived at his view after extensively interviewing children about moral dilemmas. In the interview, children are presented with a series of stories in which characters face moral dilemmas. Here is the most popular of the Kohlberg dilemmas:

> In Europe a woman was near death from a special kind of cancer. There was one drug that the doctors thought might save her. It was a form of radium that a druggist in the same town had recently discovered. The drug was expensive to make, but the druggist was charging ten times what the drug cost him to make. He paid $200 for the radium and charged $2,000 for a small dose of the drug. The sick woman's husband, Heinz, went to everyone he knew to borrow the money, but he could only get together

Lawrence Kohlberg, the architect of a provocative cognitive developmental theory of moral development. *What is the nature of his theory?*

immanent justice Piaget's concept that if a rule is broken, punishment will be meted out immediately.

LEVEL 1 Preconventional Level No Internalization	**LEVEL 2** Conventional Level Intermediate Internalization	**LEVEL 3** Postconventional Level Full Internalization
Stage 1 Heteronomous Morality *Children obey because adults tell them to obey. People base their moral decisions on fear of punishment.*	**Stage 3** Mutual Interpersonal Expectations, Relationships, and Interpersonal Conformity *Individuals value trust, caring, and loyalty to others as a basis for moral judgments.*	**Stage 5** Social Contract or Utility and Individual Rights *Individuals reason that values, rights, and principles undergird or transcend the law.*
Stage 2 Individualism, Purpose, and Exchange *Individuals pursue their own interests but let others do the same. What is right involves equal exchange.*	**Stage 4** Social Systems Morality *Moral judgments are based on understanding of the social order, law, justice, and duty.*	**Stage 6** Universal Ethical Principles *The person has developed moral judgments that are based on universal human rights. When faced with a dilemma between law and conscience, a personal, individualized conscience is followed.*

FIGURE 14.1 Kohlberg's Three Levels and Six Stages of Moral Development

$1,000, which is half of what it cost. He told the druggist that his wife was dying and asked him to sell it cheaper or let him pay later. But the druggist said, "No, I discovered the drug, and I am going to make money from it." So Heinz got desperate and broke into the man's store to steal the drug for his wife. (Kohlberg, 1969, p. 379)

This story is one of eleven that Kohlberg devised to investigate the nature of moral thought. After reading the story, interviewees answer a series of questions about the moral dilemma. Should Heinz have stolen the drug? Was stealing it right or wrong? Why? Is it a husband's duty to steal the drug for his wife if he can get it no other way? Would a good husband steal? Did the druggist have the right to charge that much when there was no law setting a limit on the price? Why?

From the answers interviewees gave for this and other moral dilemmas, Kohlberg hypothesized three levels of moral development, each of which is characterized by two stages. A key concept in understanding moral development is **internalization,** the developmental change from behavior that is externally controlled to behavior that is controlled by internal standards and principles. As children and adolescents develop, their moral thoughts become more internalized. Let's look further at Kohlberg's three levels of moral development (see figure 14.1).

Kohlberg's Level 1: Preconventional Reasoning   **Preconventional reasoning** is the lowest level in Kohlberg's theory of moral development. At this level, the individual shows no internalization of moral values—moral reasoning is controlled by external rewards and punishments.

- Stage 1. **Heteronomous morality** is the first stage in Kohlberg's theory. At this stage, moral thinking is often tied to punishment. For example, children and adolescents obey adults because adults tell them to obey.
- Stage 2. **Individualism, instrumental purpose, and exchange** is the second Kohlberg stage of moral development. Thus, what is right involves an equal exchange. People are nice to others so that they will be nice to them in return.

Kohlberg's Level 2: Conventional Reasoning   **Conventional reasoning** is the second, or intermediate, level in Kohlberg's theory of moral development. At this level, internalization is intermediate. Individuals abide by certain standards (internal), but they are the standards of others (external), such as parents or the laws of society.

internalization The developmental change from behavior that is externally controlled to behavior that is controlled by internal standards and principles.

preconventional reasoning The lowest level in Kohlberg's theory of moral development. The individual shows no internalization of moral values—moral reasoning is controlled by external rewards and punishment.

heteronomous morality (Kohlberg) The first stage in Kohlberg's theory. At this stage, moral thinking is often tied to punishment.

individualism, instrumental purpose, and exchange The second Kohlberg stage of moral development. At this stage, what is right involves an equal exchange.

conventional reasoning The second, or intermediate, level in Kohlberg's theory of moral development. Internalization is intermediate. Individuals abide by certain standards (internal), but they are the standards of others (external), such as parents or the laws of society.

- Stage 3. **Mutual interpersonal expectations, relationships, and interpersonal conformity** is Kohlberg's third stage of moral development. At this stage, individuals value trust, caring, and loyalty to others as a basis of moral judgments. Children and adolescents often adopt their parents' moral standards at this stage, seeking to be thought of by their parents as a "good girl" or a "good boy."
- Stage 4. **Social systems morality** is the fourth stage in Kohlberg's theory of moral development. At this stage, moral judgments are based on understanding the social order, law, justice, and duty. For example, adolescents may say that, for a community to work effectively, it needs to be protected by laws that are adhered to by its members.

Kohlberg's Level 3: Postconventional Reasoning

Postconventional reasoning is the highest level in Kohlberg's theory of moral development. At this level, morality is completely internalized and is not based on others' standards. The individual recognizes alternative moral courses, explores the options, and then decides on a personal moral code.

- Stage 5. **Social contract or utility and individual rights** is the fifth Kohlberg stage. At this stage, individuals reason that values, rights, and principles undergird or transcend the law. A person evaluates the validity of actual laws, and social systems can be examined in terms of the degree to which they preserve and protect fundamental human rights and values.
- Stage 6. **Universal ethical principles** is the sixth and highest stage in Kohlberg's theory of moral development. At this stage, the person has developed a moral standard based on universal human rights. When faced with a conflict between law and conscience, the person will follow conscience, even though the decision might involve personal risk.

How might individuals at each of the six Kohlberg stages respond to the "Heinz and the druggist" moral dilemma described earlier? Figure 14.2 provides some examples of these responses.

Kohlberg believed that these levels and stages occur in a sequence and are age related: Before age 9, most children reason about moral dilemmas in a preconventional way; by early adolescence, they reason in more conventional ways; and, by early adulthood, a small number of people reason in postconventional ways. In a 20-year longitudinal investigation, the uses of stages 1 and 2 decreased. Stage 4, which did not appear at all in the moral reasoning of the 10-year-olds, was reflected in the moral thinking of 62 percent of the 36-year-olds. Stage 5 did not appear until the age of 20 to 22 and never characterized more than 10 percent of the individuals. Thus, the moral stages appeared somewhat later than Kohlberg initially envisioned, and the higher stages, especially stage 6, were extremely elusive (Colby & others, 1983) (see figure 14.3). Recently, stage 6 was removed from the Kohlberg scoring manual but is still considered to be theoretically important in the Kohlberg scheme of moral development.

Influences on the Kohlberg Stages

Kohlberg believed that children's moral orientation unfolds as a consequence of their cognitive development. Children construct their moral thoughts as they pass from one stage to the next rather than passively accepting a cultural norm of morality. Investigators have sought to understand the factors that influence children's movement through the moral stages, among them modeling, cognitive conflict, peer relations, and perspective-taking opportunities (Turiel, 1998).

Modeling and Cognitive Conflict

Several investigators have attempted to advance individuals' levels of moral development by having a model present arguments that reflect moral thinking one stage above the individuals' established levels. These studies are based on the cognitive developmental concepts of equilibrium and conflict.

---

mutual interpersonal expectations, relationships, and interpersonal conformity Kohlberg's third stage of moral development. At this stage, individuals value trust, caring, and loyalty to others as a basis of moral judgments.

social systems morality The fourth stage in Kohlberg's theory of moral development. Moral judgments are based on understanding the social order, law, justice, and duty.

postconventional reasoning The highest level in Kohlberg's theory of moral development. Morality is completely internalized.

social contract or utility and individual rights Kohlberg's fifth stage of moral development. At this stage, individuals reason that values, rights, and principles undergird or transcend the law.

universal ethical principles The sixth and highest stage in Kohlberg's theory of moral development. Individuals develop a moral standard based on universal human rights.

Stage Description	Examples of Moral Reasoning That Support Heinz's Theft of the Drug	Examples of Moral Reasoning That Indicate That Heinz Should Not Steal the Drug
Preconventional reasoning		
Stage 1: Heteronomous morality	Heinz should not let his wife die; if he does, he will be in big trouble.	Heinz might get caught and sent to jail.
Stage 2: Individualism, purpose, and exchange	If Heinz gets caught, he could give the drug back and maybe they would not give him a long jail sentence.	The druggist is a businessman and needs to make money.
Conventional reasoning		
Stage 3: Mutual interpersonal expectations, relationships, and interpersonal conformity	Heinz was only doing something that a good husband would do; it shows how much he loves his wife.	If his wife dies, he can't be blamed for it; it is the druggist's fault. The druggist is the selfish one.
Stage 4: Social systems morality	If you did nothing, you would be letting your wife die; it is your responsibility if she dies. You have to steal it with the idea of paying the druggist later.	It is always wrong to steal; Heinz will always feel guilty if he steals the drug.
Postconventional reasoning		
Stage 5: Social contract or utility and individual rights	The law was not set up for these circumstances; taking the drug is not really right, but Heinz is justified in doing it.	You can't really blame someone for stealing, but extreme circumstances don't really justify taking the law into your own hands. You might lose respect for yourself if you let your emotions take over; you have to think about the long term.
Stage 6: Universal ethical principles	By stealing the drug, you would have lived up to society's rules, but you would have let down your conscience.	Heinz is faced with the decision of whether to consider other people who need the drug as badly as his wife. He needs to act by considering the value of all the lives involved.

FIGURE 14.2 Moral Reasoning at Kohlberg's Stages in Response to the "Heinz and the Druggist" Story

By presenting moral information slightly beyond the children's cognitive level, a disequilibrium is created that motivates them to restructure their moral thought. The resolution of the disequilibrium and conflict should be toward increased competence, but the data are mixed. In one of the pioneer studies on this topic, Eliot Turiel (1966) discovered that children prefer moral reasoning that is one stage above their current stage more than moral reasoning that is two stages above it. However, in the study, they chose one stage below their stage more often than one stage above it. Apparently, the children were motivated more by security needs than by the need to reorganize their thought to a higher level. Other studies indicate children prefer a more advanced stage over a less advanced stage (Rest, Turiel, & Kohlberg, 1969).

Since the early studies of stage modeling, a number of investigations have attempted to determine more precisely the effectiveness of various forms of stage modeling and argument (Lapsley & Quintana, 1985). The upshot of these studies is that virtually any plus-stage discussion format, for any length of time, seems to promote more advanced moral reasoning. For example, in one investigation (Walker, 1982), exposure to plus-two-stage reasoning (arguments two stages above the child's current stage of moral thought) was just as effective in advancing

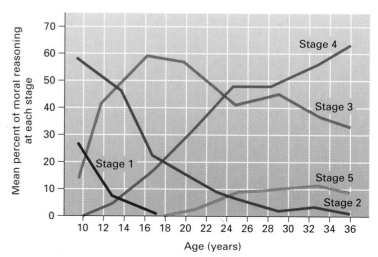

FIGURE 14.3 Age and the Percentage of Individuals at Each Kohlberg Stage

Both Piaget and Kohlberg believed that peer relations are a critical part of the social stimulation that challenges children to advance their moral reasoning. The mutual give-and-take of peer relations provides children with role-taking opportunities that give them a sense that rules are generated democratically.

moral thought as plus-one-stage reasoning. Exposure to plus-two-stage reasoning did not produce more plus-two-stage reasoning but rather, like exposure to plus-one-stage reasoning, increased reasoning at one stage above the current stage. Other research has found that exposure to reasoning only one-third of a stage higher than the individual's current level of moral thought advances that person's moral thought (Berkowitz & Gibbs, 1983). In sum, current research on modeling and cognitive conflict reveals that moral thought can be moved to a higher level through exposure to models or discussion that is more advanced than the child's level.

Peer Relations and Perspective Taking   Kohlberg believed that peer interaction is a critical part of the social stimulation that challenges children to change their moral orientation. Whereas adults characteristically impose rules and regulations on children, the mutual give-and-take in peer interaction provides children with an opportunity to take the perspective of another person and to generate rules democratically. Kohlberg stressed that perspective-taking opportunities can, in principle, be engendered by any peer group encounter. Although Kohlberg believed that such perspective-taking opportunities are ideal for moral development, he also believed that certain types of parent-child experiences can induce the child to think at more advanced levels of moral thinking. In particular, parents who allow or encourage conversation about value-laden issues promote more advanced moral thought in their children; however, many parents do not systematically provide their children with such perspective-taking opportunities. Nonetheless, in one recent study, children's moral development was related to their parents' discussion style, which involved questioning and supportive interaction (Walker & Taylor, 1991). There is an increasing emphasis on the role of parenting in moral development (Eisenberg & Valiente, 2002).

In a recent longitudinal study conducted by Lawrence Walker and his colleagues over a four-year period, both parent-child and friendship relationships were linked with children's moral maturity, as assessed by Kohlberg stories and scoring (Walker, Hennig, & Krettenauer, 2000). A general Socratic style of eliciting the other's opinion and checking for understanding (as when using appropriate probes) was effective in advancing in both parent-child and peer contexts. However, excessive information giving was associated with lower rates of moral growth, possibly being interpreted as overly opinionated lecturing. Parents provided a more cognitively stimulating environment than did children's friends, while friends engaged in more simple sharing of information.

Kohlberg's Critics   Kohlberg's provocative theory of moral development has not gone unchallenged (Gilligan, 1982, 1992; Lapsley, 1996; Rest & others, 1999). The criticisms involve the link between moral thought and moral behavior, the quality of the research, inadequate consideration of culture's role in moral development, underestimation of the care perspective, and inadequate consideration of social conventions.

www.mhhe.com/santrockcd10

Kohlberg's Theory of Moral Development
Kohlberg's Moral Dilemmas
Kohlberg's Moral Stages

Moral Thought and Moral Behavior   Kohlberg's theory has been criticized for placing too much emphasis on moral thought and not enough emphasis on moral behavior. Moral reasons can sometimes be a shelter for immoral behavior. Bank embezzlers and presidents endorse the loftiest of moral virtues when commenting about moral dilemmas, but their own behavior may be immoral. No one wants a nation of cheaters and thieves who can reason at the postconventional level. The cheaters and thieves may know what is right, yet still do what is wrong.

In evaluating the relation between moral thought and moral behavior, consider the corrupting power of rationalizations and other defenses that disengage us from self-blame; these include reconstrual of the situation, euphemistic labeling, and attribution of blame to authorities, circumstances, or victims (Bandura, 1991). One area in which a link between moral judgment and behavior has been found is where higher Kohlberg-stage reasoning acts as a buffer against criminal activity (Taylor & Walker, 1997).

Given the terrorist attacks of 09/11/01 and the continuing war on terrorism, it is intriguing to explore how heinous actions can be cloaked in a mantle of moral virtue and why that is especially dangerous. Social cognitive theorist Albert Bandura (1999, 2002) argues that people usually don't engage in harmful conduct until they have justified the morality of their actions to themselves. In this process of moral justification, immoral conduct is made personally and socially acceptable by portraying it as serving socially worthy or moral purposes. In many instances throughout history, perpetrators have twisted theology so that they see themselves as doing God's will. Bandura provides the example of Islamic extremists who mount their jihad (holy war) as self-defense against tyrannical, decadent people who they see as seeking to enslave the Islamic world.

Assessment of Moral Reasoning   Some developmentalists fault the quality of Kohlberg's research and believe that more attention should be paid to the way moral development is assessed (Boyes, Giordano, & Galperyn, 1993). For example, James Rest (1986) argued that alternative methods should be used to collect information about moral thinking instead of relying on a single method that requires individuals to reason about hypothetical moral dilemmas. Rest also said that Kohlberg's stories are extremely difficult to score. To help remedy this problem, Rest developed his own measure of moral development, called the Defining Issues Test (DIT).

The DIT attempts to determine which moral issues individuals feel are more crucial in a given situation by presenting them with a series of dilemmas and a list of definitions of the major issues involved (Kohlberg's procedure does not make use of such a list). In the dilemma of Heinz and the druggist, individuals might be asked whether a community's laws should be upheld or whether Heinz should be willing to risk being injured or caught as a burglar. They might also be asked to list the most important values that govern human interaction. They are given six stories and asked to rate the importance of each issue involved in deciding what ought to

Story Subject	Grade		
	7	9	12
	Percentage		
Alcohol	2	0	5
Civil rights	0	6	7
Drugs	7	10	5
Interpersonal relations	38	24	35
Physical saftey	22	8	3
Sexual relations	2	20	10
Smoking	7	2	0
Stealing	9	2	0
Working	2	2	15
Other	11	26	20

FIGURE 14.4 Actual Moral Dilemmas Generated by Adolescents

justice perspective A moral perspective that focuses on the rights of the individual; individuals independently make moral decisions.

care perspective The moral perspective, emphasized by Carol Gilligan, that views people in terms of their connectedness with others and emphasizes interpersonal communication, relationships with others, and concern for others.

be done. Then they are asked to list what they believe are the four most important issues. Rest argued that this method provides a more valid and reliable way to assess moral thinking than Kohlberg's method (Rest & others, 1999).

Researchers also have found that the hypothetical moral dilemmas posed in Kohlberg's stories do not match the moral dilemmas many children and adults face in their everyday lives (Walker, de Vries, & Trevethan, 1987). Most of Kohlberg's stories focus on the family and authority. However, when one researcher invited adolescents to write stories about their own moral dilemmas, the adolescents generated dilemmas that were broader in scope, focusing on friends, acquaintances, and other issues, as well as family and authority (Yussen, 1977). The adolescents' moral dilemmas also were analyzed in terms of their content. As shown in figure 14.4, the moral issue that concerned adolescents more than any other was interpersonal relationships.

Some moral development researchers believe that a valuable method is to have research participants recall and discuss real-life dilemmas from their own experience (Walker, de Vries, & Trevethan, 1987). This strategy can provide a valid assessment not only of their moral stage but also of how they interpret moral situations that are relevant to them.

Culture and Moral Development Yet another criticism of Kohlberg's view is that it is culturally biased (Banks, 1993; Fang & others, 2003; Jensen, 1995; Miller, 1991, 1995). A review of research on moral development in twenty-seven countries concluded that moral reasoning is more culture-specific than Kohlberg envisioned and that Kohlberg's scoring system does not recognize higher-level moral reasoning in certain cultural groups (Snarey, 1987). Examples of higher-level moral reasoning that would not be scored as such by Kohlberg's system are values related to communal equity and collective happiness in Israel, the unity and sacredness of all life-forms in India, and the relation of the individual to the community in New Guinea. These examples of moral reasoning would not be scored at the highest level in Kohlberg's system because they do not emphasize the individual's rights and abstract principles of justice. One study assessed the moral development of twenty adolescent male Buddhist monks in Nepal (Huebner & Garrod, 1993). The issue of justice, a basic theme in Kohlberg's theory, was not of paramount importance in the monks' moral views, and their concerns about prevention of suffering and the role of compassion are not captured by Kohlberg's theory. In sum, although Kohlberg's approach does capture much of the moral reasoning voiced in various cultures around the world, as we have just seen, there are some important moral concepts in particular cultures that his approach misses or misconstrues (Haidt, 1997).

Gender and the Care Perspective Carol Gilligan (1982, 1992, 1996) believes that relationships and connections to others are critical aspects of female development. Gilligan also has criticized Kohlberg's theory of moral development. She believes that his theory does not adequately reflect relationships and concern for others. The **justice perspective** is a moral perspective that focuses on the rights of the individual; individuals stand alone and independently make moral decisions. By contrast, the **care perspective** is a moral perspective that views people in terms of their connectedness with others and emphasizes interpersonal communication, relationships with others, and concern for others. Gilligan's theory is a care perspective.

According to Gilligan, Kohlberg greatly underplayed the care perspective in moral development. She believes that this may have happened because he was a male, because most of his research was with males rather than females, and because he used male responses as a model for his theory.

In extensive interviews with girls from 6 to 18 years of age, Gilligan and her colleagues found that girls consistently interpret moral dilemmas in terms of human relationships and base these interpretations on listening and watching other people (Gilligan, Brown, & Rogers, 1990; Gilligan & others, 2003). According to Gilligan, girls have the ability to sensitively pick up different rhythms in relationships and often are able to follow the pathways of feelings. Gilligan believes that girls reach a critical juncture in their development when they reach adolescence. Usually around 11 to 12 years of age, girls become aware that their intense interest in intimacy is not prized by the male-dominated culture, even though society values women as caring and altruistic. The dilemma is that girls are presented with a choice that makes them look either selfish or selfless. Gilligan believes that, as adolescent girls experience this dilemma, they increasingly silence their "distinctive voice."

Contextual variations influence whether adolescent girls silence their "voice." In one study, Susan Harter and her colleagues (Harter, Waters, & Whitesell, 1996) found evidence for a refinement of Gilligan's position in that feminine girls reported lower levels of voice in public contexts (at school with teachers and classmates) but not in more private interpersonal relationships with close friends and parents. However, androgynous girls reported a strong voice in all contexts. Harter and her colleagues also found that adolescent girls who buy into societal messages that females should be seen and not heard are at most risk in their development of a self. The greatest liabilities occurred for females who not only lacked a "voice" but emphasized the importance of appearance. In focusing on their outer selves, these girls face formidable challenges in meeting the punishing cultural standards of attractiveness.

A recent meta-analysis (a statistical analysis that combines the results of many different studies) cast doubt on Gilligan's claim of substantial gender differences in moral judgment (Jaffee & Hyde, 2000). In this study, no substantial overall differences in moral orientation were found between males and females. When differences occurred, they were better explained by the nature of the dilemma than by gender (for example, both males and females tended to use care reasoning when dealing with interpersonal dilemmas and justice reasoning to handle societal dilemmas).

Social Conventional Reasoning   Some theorists and researchers argue that it is important to distinguish between moral reasoning and social conventional reasoning, something they believe Kohlberg did not adequately do (Turiel, 1998; Lapsley, 1996). **Social conventional reasoning** focuses on thoughts about social consensus and convention. In contrast, moral reasoning emphasizes ethical issues. Conventional rules are created to control behavioral irregularities and maintain the social system. Conventional rules are arbitrary and subject to individual judgment. For example, not eating food with one's fingers is a social conventional rule, as is raising one's hand in class before speaking.

In contrast, moral rules are not arbitrary and determined by whim. They also are not created by social consensus. Rather, moral rules are obligatory, widely accepted, and somewhat impersonal (Turiel, 1998). Thus, rules pertaining to lying, cheating, stealing, and physically harming another person are moral rules because violation of these rules affronts ethical standards that exist apart from social consensus and convention. In sum, moral judgments involve concepts of justice, whereas social conventional judgments are concepts of social organization.

Moral Behavior

What are the basic processes that behaviorists believe are responsible for children's moral behavior? What is the nature of resistance to temptation and self-control? How do social cognitive theorists view children's moral development?

Basic Processes   Behavioral views emphasize the importance of studying children's moral behavior and its environmental determinants. The familiar processes

Carol Gilligan is shown with some of the students she has interviewed about the importance of relationships in a female's development. *What is Gilligan's view of moral development?*

In a Different Voice
Exploring Girls' Voices

social conventional reasoning Thoughts about social consensus and convention.

of reinforcement, punishment, and imitation have been invoked to explain how and why children learn certain responses and why their responses differ from one another; the general conclusions to be drawn are the same as elsewhere. When children are reinforced for behavior that is consistent with laws and social conventions, they are likely to repeat that behavior. When provided with models who behave "morally," children are likely to adopt their actions. Finally, when children are punished for "immoral" or unacceptable behaviors, those behaviors can be eliminated, but at the expense of sanctioning punishment by its very use and of causing emotional side effects for the child.

To these general conclusions are added some qualifiers. The effectiveness of reward and punishment depends on the consistency with which they are administered and the schedule (for example, continuous or partial) that is adopted. The effectiveness of modeling depends on the characteristics of the model (such as esteem or power) and the presence of symbolic codes to enhance retention of the modeled behavior.

What kind of adult moral models are children being exposed to in our society? Do such models usually do what they say? There is evidence that the adult models children are exposed to often display a double standard, with their moral thinking not always corresponding to their actions. A poll of 24,000 Americans sampled their views on a wide variety of moral issues. Eight detailed scenarios of everyday moral problems were developed to test moral decision making. A summary of the responses to these moral dilemmas is shown in figure 14.5. Consider the example of whether the person queried would knowingly buy a stolen color television set. More than 20 percent of the respondents said they would, even though 87 percent said that such an act is probably morally wrong. Further, approximately 31 percent of the adults said that, if they knew they would not get caught, they would be more likely to buy the stolen television. Although moral thought is a very important dimension of moral development, these data glaringly point out that what people believe about right and wrong does not always predict how they will act in moral situations.

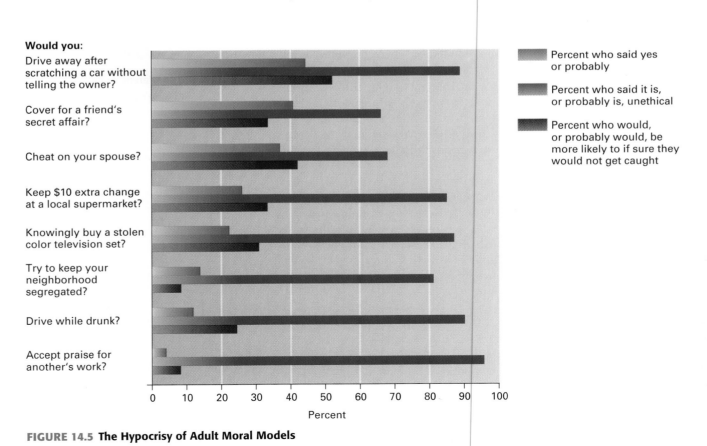

Would you:

Drive away after scratching a car without telling the owner?

Cover for a friend's secret affair?

Cheat on your spouse?

Keep $10 extra change at a local supermarket?

Knowingly buy a stolen color television set?

Try to keep your neighborhood segregated?

Drive while drunk?

Accept praise for another's work?

Percent who said yes or probably

Percent who said it is, or probably is, unethical

Percent who would, or probably would, be more likely to if sure they would not get caught

Percent

FIGURE 14.5 The Hypocrisy of Adult Moral Models

In addition to emphasizing the role of reinforcement, punishment, and imitation in determining moral behavior, behaviorists make a strong claim that moral behavior is situationally dependent. That is, from the behavioral perspective, children do not consistently display moral behavior in different situations. In a classic investigation of moral behavior, one of the most extensive ever conducted, Hugh Hartshorne and Mark May (1928–1930) observed the moral responses of 11,000 children who were given the opportunity to lie, cheat, and steal in a variety of circumstances—at home, at school, at social events, and in athletics. A completely honest or a completely dishonest child was difficult to find. Situation-specific behavior was the rule. Children were more likely to cheat when their friends put pressure on them to do so and when the chance of being caught was slim. Other analyses of the consistency of moral behavior suggest that, although moral behavior is influenced by situational determinants, some children are more likely than others to cheat, lie, and steal (Burton, 1984).

Resistance to Temptation and Self-Control   A key ingredient of moral development from the social cognitive perspective is a child's ability to resist temptation and to develop self-control (Bandura, 1986; Mischel, 1987). When pressures mount for children to cheat, lie, or steal, it is important to ask whether they have developed the ability to control themselves and to resist such temptations.

Developmentalists have invented a number of ways to investigate such temptations. In one procedure, children are shown attractive toys and told that the toys belong to someone else, who has requested that they not be touched. Children then experience social influence, perhaps in the form of a discussion of virtues about respecting other people's property or in the form of a model resisting or giving in to the temptation to play with prohibited objects. Children are left alone in the room to amuse themselves when the experimenter departs (under a pretext), announcing that he or she will return in 10 to 15 minutes. The experimenter then watches through a one-way mirror to see whether children resist or give in to the temptation to play with the toys.

There has been considerable interest in the effects of punishment on children's ability to resist temptation (Parke, 1972, 1977). For the most part, offering children cognitive rationales enhances most forms of punishment, such as reasons why a child should not play with a forbidden toy. Cognitive rationales have been more effective in getting children to resist temptation over a period of time than have strategies that do not use reasoning, such as when parents place children in their rooms without explaining the consequences for others of the children's deviant behavior.

The ability to resist temptation is closely tied to delay of gratification. Self-control is involved in both the ability to resist temptation and the ability to delay gratification. In the case of resisting temptation, children must overcome their impulses to get something that is desired but is known to be prohibited. Similarly, children must show a sense of patience and self-control in delaying gratification for a desirable future reward rather than succumbing to the immediate pressure of pursuing a smaller reward.

Considerable research has been conducted on children's self-control. Walter Mischel (1974) believes that self-control is strongly influenced by cognitive factors. Researchers have shown that children can instruct themselves to be more patient and, in the process, show more self-control. In one investigation, preschool children were asked to perform a very dull task (Mischel & Patterson, 1976). Close by was a very enticing talking mechanical clown that tried to persuade the children to play with it. The children who had been trained to say to themselves, "I'm not going to look at Mr. Clown when Mr. Clown says to look at him" were more likely to control their behavior and continue working on the dull task than were children who were not given the self-instructional strategy.

Interest in the cognitive factors in resistance to temptation, delay of gratification, and self-control reflect the increasing interest among social cognitive theorists in the ways in which such cognitions mediate the link between environmental experiences and moral behavior. Next, we will examine a view that captures this cognitive trend.

Social Cognitive Theory The **social cognitive theory of morality** emphasizes a distinction between a child's *moral competence* (the ability to perform moral behaviors) and *moral performance* (performing those behaviors in specific situations) (Mischel & Mischel, 1975). Moral competence, or acquisition of moral knowledge, depends primarily on cognitive-sensory processes; it is the outgrowth of these processes. Competencies include what children are capable of doing, what they know, their skills, their awareness of moral rules and regulations, and their cognitive ability to construct behaviors. Children's moral performance, or behavior, however, is determined by their motivation and the rewards and incentives to act in a specific moral way. Albert Bandura (1991, 1999, 2002) also believes that moral development is best understood by considering a combination of social and cognitive factors, especially those involving self-control. ◀ **page 37** Earlier, we described his views on the importance of considering a distinction between moral thinking and moral behavior, including how moral thinking can be used to justify immoral behavior.

Bandura (2002) argues that in developing a moral self, individuals adopt standards of right and wrong that serve as guides and deterrents for conduct. In this self-regulatory process, people monitor their conduct and the conditions under which it occurs, judge it in relation to moral standards, and regulate their actions by the consequences they apply to themselves. They do things that provide them satisfaction and a sense of self-worth. They often refrain from engaging in ways that violate their moral standards in order to avoid self-condemnation. Thus, self-sanctions keep conduct in line with internal standards. In Bandura's view, morality is rooted in self-regulation rather than abstract reasoning.

Not surprisingly, social cognitive theorists have been critical of Kohlberg's theory of moral development, which emphasizes abstract reasoning. Among other reasons, they believe he placed too little emphasis on moral behavior and the situational determinants of morality. However, although Kohlberg argued that moral judgment is an important determinant of moral behavior, he, like the Mischels, stressed that an individual's interpretation of both the moral and the factual aspects of a situation leads to a moral decision (Kohlberg & Candee, 1979). For example, Kohlberg mentioned that "extra-moral" factors, such as the desire to avoid embarrassment, may cause children to avoid doing what they believe to be morally right. In sum, according to both the Mischels and Kohlberg, moral action is influenced by complex factors. Overall, the findings are mixed with regard to the association of moral thought and behavior (Arnold, 1989), although in one investigation with college students, individuals with both highly principled moral reasoning and high ego strength were less likely to cheat in a resistance-to-temptation situation than were their low-principled and low-ego-strength counterparts (Hess, Lonky, & Roodin, 1985).

Moral Feeling

Think about when you do something you sense is wrong—does it affect you emotionally? Maybe you get a twinge of guilt. And when you give someone a gift, you might feel joy. Let's further explore the nature of moral feelings.

Psychoanalytic Theory In chapter 2, we discussed Sigmund Freud's psychoanalytic theory, which describes the *superego* as one of the three main structures of personality (the id and ego are the other two). ◀ **page 30** In Freud's classical psychoanalytic theory, a child's superego—the moral branch of personality—develops as the child resolves the Oedipus conflict and identifies with the same-sex parent in the early childhood years. One reason children resolve the Oedipus conflict is to alleviate the fears of losing their parents' love and of being punished for their unacceptable sexual wishes toward the opposite-sex parent. To reduce anxiety, avoid punishment, and maintain parental affection, children form a superego by identifying with the same-sex parent. Through this identification, children internalize the parent's standards of right and wrong that reflect societal prohibitions. Also, the child turns inward the hostility that was previously aimed externally at the same-sex parent.

social cognitive theory of morality The theory that distinguishes between *moral competence* (the ability to perform moral behaviors) and *moral performance* (performing those behaviors in specific situations).

This inwardly directed hostility is then experienced self-punitively (and unconsciously) as guilt. In the psychoanalytic account of moral development, self-punitiveness of guilt keeps children from committing transgressions. That is, children conform to societal standards to avoid guilt.

In Freud's view, the superego consists of two main components, the ego ideal and conscience, which promote children's development of moral feelings. The *ego ideal* is the component of the superego that involves ideal standards approved of by parents, whereas *conscience* is the component of the superego that involves behaviors disapproved of by parents. A child's ego ideal rewards the child by conveying a sense of pride and personal value when the child acts according to moral standards. The conscience punishes the child for acting immorally by making the child feel guilty and worthless. In this way, self-control replaces parental control.

In one recent study, 106 preschool children were observed in laboratory situations in which they were led to believe that they had damaged valuable objects (Kochanska & others, 2002). In these mishaps, the behavioral indicators of guilt that were coded by observers included avoiding gaze (looking away or down), body tension (squirming, backing away, hanging head down, covering face with hands), and distress (looking uncomfortable, crying). Girls expressed more guilt than boys did. Children with a more fearful temperament expressed more guilt. Children of mothers who used power-oriented discipline (such as spanking, slapping, and yelling) displayed less guilt.

Empathy Positive feelings, such as empathy, contribute to the child's moral development. Feeling **empathy** means reacting to another's feelings with an emotional response that is similar to the other's feelings (Damon, 1988). Although empathy is experienced as an emotional state, it often has a cognitive component—the ability to discern another's inner psychological states, or what we have previously called *perspective taking* (Eisenberg & others, 1991). Infants have the capacity for some purely empathic responses, but, for effective moral action, children need to learn to identify a wide range of emotional states in others and to anticipate what kinds of action will improve another person's emotional state.

What are the main milestones in children's development of empathy? According to an analysis by child developmentalist William Damon (1988), changes in empathy take place in early infancy, at 1 to 2 years of age, in early childhood, and at 10 to 12 years of age. *Global empathy* is the young infant's empathic response in which clear boundaries between the feelings and needs of the self and those of another have not yet been established. For example, one 11-month-old infant fought off her own tears, sucked her thumb, and buried her head in her mother's lap after she had seen another child fall and hurt himself. Not all infants cry every time someone else is hurt, though. Many times, an infant will stare at another's pain with curiosity. Although global empathy is observed in some infants, it does not consistently characterize all infants' behavior.

Between 1 and 2 years of age, the infant's undifferentiated feelings of discomfort at another's distress grow into more genuine feelings of concern. The infant realizes that others are independent persons in their own right, with their own unhappy feelings. The infant may sense that these unhappy feelings in others need attention and relief, but the infant cannot translate this realization into effective behavior. For example, toddlers may offer a beloved blanket or doll for comfort to an unhappy-looking adult. In one study, empathy appeared more regularly after 18 months (Lamb, 1993).

In the early childhood years, children become aware that every person's perspective is unique and that someone else may have a reaction to a situation that is different from their own. Such awareness permits the child to respond more appropriately to another's distress. For example, at the age of 6, a child may realize that, in some instances, an unhappy person may best be left alone rather than helped, or the child may learn to wait for just the right time to give comfort. In sum, at this point, children make more objective assessments of others' distress and needs.

Toward the end of the elementary school years, at about 10 to 12 years of age, children develop empathy for people who live in unfortunate circumstances.

> *W*hat is moral is what you feel good after and what is immoral is what you feel bad after.
>
> —ERNEST HEMINGWAY
> *American Author, 20th Century*

empathy Reacting to another's feelings with an emotional response that is similar to the other's feelings.

FIGURE 14.6 Damon's Description of Developmental Changes in Empathy

Age Period	Nature of Empathy
Early infancy	Characterized by global empathy, the young infant's empathic response does not distinguish between feelings and needs of self and others.
1 to 2 years of age	Undifferentiated feelings of discomfort at another's distress grow into more genuine feelings of concern, but infants cannot translate realization of other's unhappy feelings into effective action.
Early childhood	Children become aware that every person's perspective is unique and that someone else may have a different reaction to a situation. This awareness allows the child to respond more appropriately to another person's distress.
10 to 12 years of age	Children develop an emergent orientation of empathy for people who live in unfortunate circumstances—the poor, the handicapped, and the socially outcast. In adolescence, this newfound sensitivity may give a humanitarian flavor to the individual's ideological and political views.

Children's concerns are no longer limited to the feelings of particular persons in situations the child observes directly (Shorr & Shorr, 1995). Instead, children expand their concerns to the general problems of people in unfortunate situations—the poor, the handicapped, and the socially outcast, for example. This newfound sensitivity may lead to altruistic behavior by the older elementary school child and later, in adolescence, give a humanitarian flavor to the adolescent's development of ideological and political views. A summary of Damon's description of empathy development is shown in figure 14.6.

Although everyone may be capable of responding with empathy, not all individuals do. There is considerable variation in individual empathic behavior. For example, in older children and adolescents, empathic dysfunctions can contribute to antisocial behavior. Some delinquents convicted of violent crimes show a lack of feeling for their victims' distress. A 13-year-old boy convicted of violently mugging a number of elderly people, when asked about the pain he had caused for one blind woman, said, "What do I care? I'm not her" (Damon, 1988).

Not only is there individual variation in adolescents' empathy and concern about the welfare of others, but sociohistorical influences also may be involved. Over the past two decades, adolescents have shown an increased concern for personal well-being and a decreased concern for the welfare of others, especially for the disadvantaged. As shown in figure 14.7, today's college freshmen are more strongly motivated to be well-off financially and less motivated to develop a meaningful philosophy of life than were their counterparts 20 or even 10 years ago (Sax & others, 2002). Among high school seniors, increasing numbers are motivated by the opportunity to make a considerable amount of money (Bachman, Johnston, & O'Malley, 1987).

However, two values that increased during the 1960s continue to be important to today's youth: self-fulfillment and self-expression. As part of their motivation for self-fulfillment, many adolescents show great interest in their physical health and well-being. Greater self-fulfillment and self-expression can be laudable goals, but if they become the only goals, self-destruction, loneliness, or

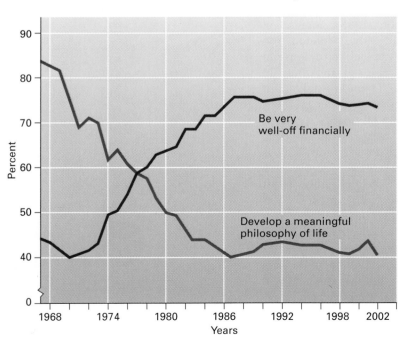

FIGURE 14.7 Changing Freshmen Life Goals, 1968–2002

In the last three decades, a significant change has occurred in freshmen students' life goals. A far greater percentage of today's college freshmen state that a "very important" life goal is to be well off financially, and far fewer state that developing a meaningful philosophy of life is a "very important" life goal.

alienation may result. Young people also need to develop a corresponding sense of commitment to others' welfare (Yates, 1995). Encouraging adolescents to have a strong commitment to others, in concert with an interest in self-fulfillment, is a major task for our nation at the beginning of the twenty-first century.

Values of American College Freshmen

The Contemporary Perspective on Emotion and Moral Development We have seen that classical psychoanalytic theory emphasizes the power of unconscious guilt in moral development but that other theorists, such as Damon, emphasize the role of empathy. Today, many child developmentalists believe that both positive feelings, such as empathy, sympathy, admiration, and self-esteem, and negative feelings, such as anger, outrage, shame, and guilt, contribute to children's moral development (Damon, 1988; Eisenberg & Fabes, 1998; Roberts & Strayer, 1996). When strongly experienced, these emotions influence children to act in accord with standards of right and wrong. Such emotions as empathy, shame, guilt, and anxiety over other people's violations of standards are present early in development and undergo developmental change throughout childhood and beyond (Damon, 1988). These emotions provide a natural base for children's acquisition of moral values, both orienting children toward moral events and motivating them to pay close attention to such events. However, moral emotions do not operate in a vacuum to build a child's moral awareness, and they are not sufficient in themselves to generate moral responsivity. They do not give the "substance" of moral regulation—the rules, values, and standards of behavior that children need to understand and act on. Moral emotions are inextricably interwoven with the cognitive and social aspects of children's development.

In one study of fifth-, eighth-, and eleventh-graders, parents were the individuals most likely to evoke guilt (Williams & Bybee, 1994). With development, guilt evoked by family members was less prevalent, but guilt engendered by girlfriends or boyfriends was more frequent. At the higher grade levels, the percentage of students reporting guilt about aggressive, externalizing behaviors declined, whereas those mentioning guilt over internal thoughts and inconsiderateness increased. Males were more likely to report guilt over externalizing behaviors, while females reported more guilt over violating norms of compassion and trust.

Review and Reflect: Learning Goal 1

1 **Discuss theories and research on moral thought, behavior, and feeling**

REVIEW

- What are Piaget's and Kohlberg's theories of moral development? How can Kohlberg's theory be evaluated? What is social conventional reasoning?
- What is involved moral behavior? What is the social cognitive theory of moral development?
- How are moral feelings related to moral development?

REFLECT

- What do you think about these circumstances?
  A man who had been sentenced to serve 10 years for selling a small amount of marijuana walked away from a prison camp after serving only six months of his sentence. Twenty-five years later he was caught. He is now in his fifties and is a model citizen. Should he be sent back to prison? Why or why not? At which Kohlberg stage should your response be placed?
  A young woman who had been in a tragic accident is "brain dead" and has been kept on life-support systems for four years without ever regaining consciousness. Should the life-support systems be removed? Explain your response. At which Kohlberg stage should your response be placed?

2 CONTEXTS OF MORAL DEVELOPMENT

Parenting	Schools

Earlier in the chapter, we saw that both Piaget and Kohlberg believed that peer relations are an important context for moral development. Children's experiences in families and schools also are important contexts for moral development.

Parenting

Both Piaget and Kohlberg held that parents do not provide any unique or essential inputs to children's moral development. They do believe that parents are responsible for providing general role-taking opportunities and cognitive conflict, but they reserve the primary role in moral development for peers. Earlier in the chapter we discussed recent research that revealed how both parents and peers contribute to children's moral maturity (Walker, Hennig, & Krettenauer, 2000). A general Socratic style of eliciting the other's opinion and checking for understanding was effective in advancing both moral maturity in both parent and peer contexts. Here we will focus more on parental discipline and its role in moral development and then draw some conclusions about parenting and moral development.

Parental Discipline   In Freud's psychoanalytic theory, the aspects of child rearing that encourage moral development are practices that instill the fears of punishment and of losing parental love. Child developmentalists who have studied child-rearing techniques and moral development have focused on parents' discipline techniques. These include love withdrawal, power assertion, and induction (Hoffman, 1970):

- **Love withdrawal** comes closest to the psychoanalytic emphasis on fear of punishment and of losing parental love. It is a discipline technique in which a parent withholds attention or love from the child, as when the parent refuses to talk to the child or states a dislike for the child. For example, the parent might say, "I'm going to leave you if you do that again" or "I don't like you when you do that."
- **Power assertion** is a discipline technique in which a parent attempts to gain control over the child or the child's resources. Examples include spanking, threatening, or removing privileges.
- **Induction** is the discipline technique in which a parent uses reason and explanation of the consequences for others of the child's actions. Examples of induction include, "Don't hit him. He was only trying to help" and "Why are you yelling at her? She didn't mean to trip you."

Moral development theorist and researcher Martin Hoffman (1970) believes that any discipline produces arousal on the child's part. Love withdrawal and power assertion are likely to evoke a very high level of arousal, with love withdrawal generating considerable anxiety and power assertion considerable hostility. Induction is more likely to produce a moderate level of arousal in children, a level that permits them to attend to the cognitive rationales parents offer. When a parent uses power assertion and love withdrawal, the child may be so aroused that, even if the parent gives accompanying explanations about the consequences for others of the child's actions, the child might not attend to them. Power assertion presents parents as weak models of self-control—as individuals who cannot control their feelings. Accordingly, children may imitate this model of poor self-control when they face stressful circumstances. The use of induction, however, focuses the child's attention

love withdrawal A discipline technique in which a parent withholds attention or love from the child.

power assertion A discipline technique in which a parent attempts to gain control over the child or the child's resources.

induction A discipline technique in which a parent uses reason and explanation of the consequences for others of the child's actions.

on the action's consequences for others, not on the child's own shortcomings. For these reasons, Hoffman (1988) believes that parents should use induction to encourage children's moral development. In research on parenting techniques, induction is more positively related to moral development than is love withdrawal or power assertion, although the findings vary according to children's developmental level and socioeconomic status. Induction works better with elementary-school-age children than with preschool children (Brody & Shaffer, 1982) and better with middle-SES than with lower-SES children (Hoffman, 1970). Older children are probably better able to understand the reasons given to them and are better at perspective taking. Some theorists believe that the internalization of society's moral standards is more likely among middle-SES than among lower-SES individuals, because internalization is more rewarding in the middle-SES culture (Kohn, 1977).

Parenting Moral Children Parental discipline does contribute to children's moral development, but there are other aspects of parenting that also play an important role, such as providing opportunities for perspective taking and modeling moral behavior and thinking. Nancy Eisenberg and her colleagues (Eisenberg & Murphy, 1995; Eisenberg & Valiente, 2002) summarized the findings from the research literature on ways in which parenting can influence children's moral development. They concluded that, in general, moral children tend to have parents who

- Are warm and supportive rather than punitive. One recent study found that maternal warmth was linked with children's empathy through the mother's positive expression of emotions (Zhou & others, 2002).
- Use inductive discipline
- Provide opportunities for the children to learn about others' perspectives and feelings
- Involve children in family decision making and in the process of thinking about moral decisions
- Model moral behaviors and thinking themselves and provide opportunities for their children to model such moral behaviors and thinking

Parents who show this configuration of behaviors likely foster the development of concern and caring about others in their children, and create a positive parent-child relationship. These parents also provide information about what behaviors are expected of the child and why, and promote an internal rather than an external sense of morality.

Schools

Schools are an important context for moral development. Moral education is hotly debated in educational circles. We will study one of the earliest analyses of moral education and then turn to some contemporary views of moral education.

The Hidden Curriculum More than 60 years ago, educator John Dewey (1933) recognized that even when schools do not have specific programs in moral education, they provide moral education through a "hidden curriculum." The **hidden curriculum** is conveyed by the moral atmosphere that is a part of every school. The moral atmosphere is created by school and classroom rules, the moral orientation of teachers and school administrators, and text materials. Teachers serve as models of ethical or unethical behavior. Classroom rules and peer relations at school transmit attitudes about cheating, lying, stealing, and consideration of others. And through its rules and regulations, the school administration infuses the school with a value system.

Character Education **Character education** is a direct approach that involves teaching students a basic moral literacy to prevent them from engaging in immoral

hidden curriculum The moral atmosphere that is part of every school.

character education A direct approach that involves teaching students a basic moral literacy to prevent them from engaging in immoral behavior and doing harm to themselves or others.

behavior and doing harm to themselves and others. The argument is that such behaviors as lying, stealing, and cheating are wrong and students should be taught this throughout their education. Every school should have an explicit moral code that is clearly communicated to students. Any violations of the code should be met with sanctions (Bennett, 1993). Instruction in specified moral concepts, like cheating, can take the form of example and definition, class discussions and role-playing, or rewarding students for proper behavior.

Some character education movements are the Character Education Partnership, the Character Education Network, the Aspen Declaration on Character Education, and the publicity campaign "Character Counts." Books that promote character education include William Bennett's (1993) *Book of Virtues* and William Damon's (1995) *Greater Expectations*.

Values Clarification Values clarification means helping people to clarify what their lives are for and what is worth working for. In this approach, students are encouraged to define their own values and understand the values of others. Values clarification differs from character education in not telling students what their values should be.

In one values clarification example, students are asked to select from among ten people the six who will be admitted to a safe shelter because a third world war has broken out (Johnson, 1990):

You work for a government agency in Washington and your group has to decide which six of the following ten people will be admitted to a small fallout shelter. Your group has only 20 minutes to make the decision. These are your choices:

- A 30-year-old male bookkeeper
- The bookkeeper's wife, who is six months pregnant
- A second-year African American male medical student who is a political activist
- A 42-year-old male who is a famous historian-author
- A Hollywood actress who is a singer and dancer
- A female biochemist
- A 54-year-old male rabbi
- A male Olympic athlete who is good in all sports
- A female college student
- A policeman with a gun

In this type of values clarification exercise, there are no right or wrong answers. The clarification of values is left up to the individual student. Advocates of values clarification say it is value-free. However, critics argue that its controversial content offends community standards. They also say that because of its relativistic nature, values clarification undermines accepted values and fails to stress right behavior.

Cognitive Moral Education Cognitive moral education is a concept based on the belief that students should learn to value things like democracy and justice as their moral reasoning develops. Kohlberg's theory has been the basis for a number of cognitive moral education programs. In a typical program, high school students meet in a semester-long course to discuss a number of moral issues. The instructor acts as a facilitator rather than as a director of the class. The hope is that students will develop more advanced notions of such concepts as cooperation, trust, responsibility, and community. Toward the end of his career, Kohlberg (1986) recognized that the moral atmosphere of the school is more important than he initially envisioned. For example, in one study, a semester-long moral education class based on Kohlberg's theory was successful in advancing moral thinking in three

www.mhhe.com/santrockcd10

Variations in Moral Education

Association for Moral Education

Moral Education in Japan

Shown here is an adolescent who has volunteered to work in the National Helpers Network. This program gives students an opportunity to participate in service learning. Among the services provided are helping with environmental concerns, improving neighborhoods, and tutoring. Students also participate in weekly seminars that encourage them to reflect on their active involvement in the community. *What are some of the possible influences of service learning on adolescent development? Should all high school or college students be required to do service learning?*

values clarification Helping people clarify what their lives are for and what is worth working for.

cognitive moral education A concept based on the belief that students should learn to value things like democracy and justice as their moral reasoning develops.

democratic schools but not in three authoritarian schools (Higgins, Power, & Kohlberg, 1983).

In our coverage of moral education, we have examined John Dewey's concept of the hidden curriculum, character education, values clarification, and cognitive moral education. As we see next, there is increasing interest in including service learning in education, especially at the secondary school level.

Service Learning **Service learning** is a form of education that promotes social responsibility and service to the community. In service learning, adolescents might engage in tutoring, help the elderly, work in a hospital, assist at a day-care center, or clean up a vacant lot to make a play area. An important goal of service learning is for adolescents to become less self-centered and more strongly motivated to help others (Hart & others, 2003; Waterman, 1997).

Service learning takes education out into the community (Levesque & Prosser, 1996; Piliavin, 2003). One eleventh-grade student worked as a reading tutor for students from low-income backgrounds with reading skills well below their grade levels. She commented that until she did the tutoring she did not realize how many students had not experienced the same opportunities that she had when she was growing up. An especially rewarding moment was when one young girl told her, "I want to learn to read like you so I can go to college when I grow up." Thus, service learning not only can benefit adolescents but also the recipients of their help.

Researchers have found that service learning benefits adolescents in a number of ways:

- Their grades improve, they become more motivated, and they set more goals (Johnson & others, 1998; Search Institute, 1995; Serow, Ciechalski, & Daye, 1990).
- Their self-esteem improves (Hamburg, 1997; Johnson & others, 1998).
- They have an improved sense of being able to make a difference for others (Search Institute, 1995).
- They become less alienated (Calabrese & Schumer, 1986).
- They increasingly reflect on society's political organization and moral order (Yates, 1995).

Required community service has increased in high schools. In one survey, 15 percent of the nation's largest school districts had such a requirement (National Community Service Coalition, 1995). Even though required community service has increased in high schools, in one survey of 40,000 adolescents, two-thirds said that they had never done any volunteer work to help other people (Benson, 1993). The benefits of service learning, both for the volunteer and the recipient, suggest that more adolescents should be required to participate in such programs.

www.mhhe.com/santrockcd10

National Service Learning Clearinghouse

The Center for the Fourth and Fifth RS Character Education Topics

Exploring Values Education

More than just about anything else, 12-year-old Katie Bell (*at bottom*) wanted a playground in her New Jersey town. She knew that other kids also wanted one so she put together a group, which generated fund-raising ideas for the playground. They presented their ideas to the town council. Her group got more youth involved. They helped raise money by selling candy and sandwiches door-to-door. Katie says, "We learned to work as a community. This will be an important place for people to go and have picnics and make new friends." Katie's advice: "You won't get anywhere if you don't try."

Review and Reflect: Learning Goal 2

2 Explain how parents and schools influence moral development

REVIEW

- How does parental discipline affect moral development? What are some effective parenting strategies for advancing children's moral development?
- What is the hidden curriculum? What are some contemporary approaches to moral education?

REFLECT

- What type of discipline did your parents use with you? What effect do you think this has had on your moral development?

service learning A form of education that promotes social responsibility and service to the community.

Service learning, which we just discussed, exemplifies positive moral behavior. Next, we explore other aspects of positive moral behavior, as well as antisocial behavior.

3 PROSOCIAL AND ANTISOCIAL BEHAVIOR

Altruism	Juvenile Delinquency

Moral development includes both positive moral behavior (prosocial behavior) and negative moral behavior (antisocial behavior) (Hart & others, 2003). Altruism is an especially important aspect of prosocial behavior, and juvenile delinquency is representative of antisocial behavior.

Altruism

Altruism is an unselfish interest in helping another person. Human acts of altruism are plentiful—the hardworking laborer who places $5 in a Salvation Army kettle; rock concerts to feed the hungry, help farmers, and fund AIDS research; and the child who takes in a wounded cat and cares for it. How do psychologists account for such acts of altruism?

Reciprocity and exchange often are involved in altruism. Reciprocity is found throughout the human world. It is present in every widely practiced religion in the world—Christianity, Judaism, Hinduism, Buddhism, and Islam. Reciprocity encourages children to do unto others as they would have others do unto them. Human sentiments are wrapped up in this reciprocity. Trust is probably the most important principle, over the long run, in altruism. Guilt surfaces if the child does not reciprocate, and anger may result if someone else does not reciprocate. Not all altruism is motivated by reciprocity and exchange, but self-other interactions and relationships help us understand altruism's nature. The circumstances most likely to involve altruism are empathic emotion for an individual in need or a close relationship between benefactor and recipient (Batson, 1989).

In addition to presenting a developmental sequence of children's empathy, which we discussed earlier, Damon (1988) has also described a developmental sequence of children's altruism, especially of sharing. Most sharing during the first three years of life is done for nonempathic reasons, such as for the fun of the social play ritual or out of mere imitation. Then, at about 4 years of age, a combination of empathic awareness and adult encouragement produces a sense of obligation on the part of the child to share with others. This obligation forces the child to share, even though the child may not perceive this as the best way to have fun. Most 4-year-olds are not selfless saints, however. Children believe they have an obligation to share but do not necessarily think they should be as generous to others as they are to themselves. Neither do their actions always support their beliefs, especially when the object of contention is coveted. What is important developmentally is that the child has developed an internal belief that sharing is an obligatory part of a social relationship and that this involves a question of right and wrong. However, a preschool child's sense of reciprocity does not constitute a moral duty but, rather, is a pragmatic means of getting one's way. Despite their shortcomings, these ideas about justice formed in early childhood set the stage for giant strides that children make in the years that follow.

By the start of the elementary school years, children genuinely begin to express more objective ideas about fairness. These notions about fairness have been used throughout history to distribute goods and to resolve conflicts. They involve the

> W ithout civic morality communities perish; without personal morality their survival has no value.
> —BERTRAND RUSSELL
> *English Philosopher, 20th Century*

altruism Unselfish interest in helping another person.

principles of equality, merit, and benevolence. *Equality* means that everyone is treated the same. *Merit* means giving extra rewards for hard work, a talented performance, or other laudatory behavior. *Benevolence* means giving special consideration to individuals in a disadvantaged condition. Equality is the first of these principles used regularly by elementary school children. It is common to hear 6-year-old children use the word *fair* as synonymous with *equal* or *same*. By the mid to late elementary school years, children also believe that equity means special treatment for those who deserve it—the principles of merit and benevolence.

Missing from the factors that guide children's altruism is one that many adults might expect to be the most influential of all: the motivation to obey adult authority figures. Surprisingly, a number of studies have shown that adult authority has only a small influence on children's sharing. For example, when Nancy Eisenberg (1982) asked children to explain their own altruistic acts, they mainly gave empathic and pragmatic reasons for their spontaneous acts of sharing. Not one of the children referred to the demands of adult authority. Parental advice and prodding certainly foster standards of sharing, but the give-and-take of peer requests and arguments provide the most immediate stimulation of sharing. Parents can set examples that children carry into peer interaction and communication, but parents are not present during all of their children's peer exchanges. The day-to-day construction of fairness standards is done by children in collaboration and negotiation with each other. Over the course of many years and thousands of encounters, children's understanding of altruism deepens. With this conceptual elaboration that involves such notions as equality, merit, benevolence, and compromise come a greater consistency and generosity in children's sharing behavior (Damon, 1988).

One study examined prosocial behavior and caring in adolescents who lived in a highly impoverished area of Camden, New Jersey (Hart & Fegley, 1995). Participants were African American and Latino adolescents who had been nominated by community leaders for demonstrating unusual commitments to care for others or the community. The highly caring adolescents were compared with a group of adolescents who had not been singled out for their caring. The caring adolescents were more likely to (1) describe themselves in terms of moral personality traits and goals, and (2) think of themselves as incorporating their ideals and parental images.

Juvenile Delinquency

What is a juvenile delinquent? What are the antecedents of delinquency? What types of interventions have been used to prevent or reduce delinquency?

What Is Juvenile Delinquency?   The term **juvenile delinquency** refers to a broad range of behaviors, ranging from socially unacceptable behavior (such as acting out in school) to status offenses (such as running away) to criminal acts (such as burglary). For legal purposes, a distinction is made between index offenses and status offenses:

- **Index offenses** are criminal acts, whether they are committed by juveniles or adults. They include such acts as robbery, aggravated assault, rape, and homicide.
- **Status offenses,** such as running away, truancy, underage drinking, sexual promiscuity, and uncontrollability, are less serious acts. They are performed by youth under a specified age, which classifies them as juvenile offenses.

States often differ in the age used to classify an individual as a juvenile or an adult. Approximately three-fourths of the states have established age 18 as a maximum for defining juveniles. Two states use age 19 as the cutoff, seven states use

juvenile delinquency A broad range of behaviors, ranging from socially unacceptable behavior (such as acting out in school) to status offenses (such as running away) to criminal acts (such as burglary).

index offenses Criminal acts, whether they are committed by juveniles or adults. They include such acts as robbery, aggravated assault, rape, and homicide.

status offenses Less serious acts (than index offenses). Status offenses include truancy, underage drinking, sexual promiscuity, and uncontrollability. They are performed by youth under a specified age, which make them juvenile offenses.

age 17, and four states use age 16. Thus, running away from home at age 17 may be an offense in some states but not others.

U.S. government statistics reveal that 8 of 10 cases of juvenile delinquency involve males (Snyder & Sickmund, 1999). Although males are still far more likely to engage in juvenile delinquency, in the last two decades there has been a greater increase in female delinquency than male delinquency (Snyder & Sickmund, 1999). For both male and female delinquents, rates for property offenses are higher than for other rates of offenses (such as toward persons, drug offenses, and public order offenses).

Arrests of adolescent males for delinquency still are much higher than for adolescent females. However, the juvenile delinquency rate of females has increased substantially in the last several decades (Office of Juvenile Justice and Prevention, 1999). This is especially true for adolescent females committing violent crimes.

Delinquency rates among African Americans, other minority groups, and lower-socioeconomic-status youth are especially high in proportion to the overall population of these groups. However, such groups have less influence over the judicial decision-making process in the United States and, therefore, may be judged delinquent more readily than their White, middle-socioeconomic-status counterparts.

Office of Juvenile Justice and Delinquency Prevention

Justice Information Center

Preventing Crime

One issue in juvenile justice is whether an adolescent who commits a crime should be tried as an adult (Steinberg & Cauffman, 2001). In one study, trying adolescent offenders as adults increased rather than reduced their crime rate (Myers, 1999). The study evaluated more than 500 violent youths in Pennsylvania, which has adopted a "get tough" policy. Although these 500 offenders had been given harsher punishment than a comparison group retained in juvenile court, they were more likely to be rearrested—and rearrested more quickly—for new offenses once they were returned to the community. This suggests that the price of short-term public safety attained by prosecuting juveniles as adults might increase the number of criminal offenses over the long run.

In addition to the legal classifications of index offenses and status offenses, many of the behaviors considered delinquent are included in widely used classifications of abnormal behavior. **Conduct disorder** is the psychiatric diagnostic category that is used when multiple behaviors occur over a six-month period. These behaviors include truancy, running away, fire setting, cruelty to animals, breaking and entering, excessive fighting, and others. When three or more of these behaviors co-occur before the age of 15, and the child or adolescent is considered unmanageable

A current special concern in low-income areas is escalating gang violence. *Why might gang violence have increased?*

or out of control, the clinical diagnosis is conduct disorder.

In sum, most children or adolescents at one time or another act out or do things that are destructive or troublesome for themselves or others. If these behaviors occur often in childhood or early adolescence, psychiatrists diagnose them as conduct disorders. If these behaviors result in illegal acts by juveniles, society labels them *delinquents.*

conduct disorder The psychiatric diagnosis category used when multiple behaviors occur over a six-month period. These behaviors include truancy, running away, fire setting, cruelty to animals, breaking and entering, excessive fighting, and others. When three or more of these behaviors co-occur before the age of 15, and the child or adolescent is considered unmanageable or out of control, the clinical diagnosis is conduct disorder.

Antecedents of Delinquency Predictors of delinquency include conflict with authority, minor covert acts that are followed by property damage and other more serious acts, minor aggression followed by fighting and violence, identity (negative identity), self-control (low degree), cognitive distortions (egocentric bias), age (early initiation), sex (male), expectations for education (low expectations, little commitment), school grades (low achievement in early grades), peer influence (heavy influence, low resistance), socioeconomic status (low), parental role (lack of monitoring, low support, and ineffective discipline), siblings (having an older sibling who is a delinquent), and neighborhood quality (urban, high crime, high mobility). A summary of these antecedents of delinquency is presented in figure 14.8.

In the Pittsburgh Youth Study, a longitudinal study focused on more than 1,500 inner-city boys, three developmental pathways to delinquency were (Loeber & Farrington, 2001; Loeber & others, 1998; Stouthamer-Loeber & others, 2002):

- *Authority conflict.* Youth on this pathway showed stubbornness prior to age 12, then moved on to defiance and avoidance of authority.
- *Covert.* This pathway included minor covert acts, such as lying, followed by property damage and moderately serious delinquency, then serious delinquency.
- *Overt.* This pathway included minor aggression followed by fighting and violence.

Antecedent	Association with Delinquency	Description
Authority conflict	High degree	Youth show stubborness prior to age 12, then become defiant of authority.
Covert acts	Frequent	Minor covert acts, such as lying, are followed by property damage and moderately serious delinquency, then serious delinquency.
Overt acts of aggression	Frequent	Minor aggression is followed by fighting and violence.
Identity	Negative identity	Erikson believes delinquency occurs because the adolescent fails to resolve a role identity.
Cognitive distortions	High degree	The thinking of delinquents is frequently characterized by a variety of cognitive distortions (such as egocentric bias, externalizing of blame, and mislabeling) that contribute to inappropriate behavior and lack of self-control.
Self-control	Low degree	Some children and adolescents fail to acquire the essential controls that others have acquired during the process of growing up.
Age	Early initiation	Early appearance of antisocial behavior is associated with serious offenses later in adolescence. However, not every child who acts out becomes delinquent.
Sex	Male	Boys engage in more antisocial behavior than girls do, although girls are more likely to run away. Boys engage in more violent acts.
Expectations for education and school grades	Low expectations and low grades	Adolescents who become delinquents often have low educational expectations and low grades. Their verbal abilities are often weak.
Parental influences	Monitoring (low), support (low), discipline (ineffective)	Delinquents often come from families in which parents rarely monitor their adolescents, provide them with little support, and ineffectively discipline them.
Sibling relations	Older delinquent sibling	Individuals with an older delinquent sibling are more likely to become delinquent.
Peer influences	Heavy influence, low resistance	Having delinquent peers greatly increases the risk of becoming delinquent.
Socioeconomic status	Low	Serious offenses are committed more frequently by lower-class males.
Neighborhood quality	Urban, high crime, high mobility	Communities often breed crime. Living in a high-crime area, which also is characterized by poverty and dense living conditions, increases the probability that a child will become a delinquent. These communities often have grossly inadequate schools.

FIGURE 14.8 The Antecedents of Juvenile Delinquency

Let's look in more detail at several other factors that are related to delinquency. Erik Erikson (1968) believes that adolescents whose development has restricted their access to acceptable social roles or made them feel that they cannot measure up to the demands placed on them may choose a negative identity. Adolescents with a negative identity may find support for their delinquent image among peers, reinforcing the negative identity. For Erikson, delinquency is an attempt to establish an identity, although it is a negative identity.

Although delinquency is less exclusively a lower-SES phenomenon than it was in the past, some characteristics of lower-SES culture can promote delinquency. The norms of many low-SES peer groups and gangs are antisocial, or counterproductive, to the goals and norms of society at large. Getting into and staying out of trouble are prominent features of life for some adolescents in low-income neighborhoods. Adolescents from low-income backgrounds may sense that they can gain attention and status by performing antisocial actions. Being "tough" and "masculine" are high-status traits for low-SES boys, and these traits are often measured by the adolescent's success in performing and getting away with delinquent acts. A community with a high crime rate also lets the adolescent observe many models who engage in criminal activities. These communities may be characterized by poverty, unemployment, and feelings of alienation toward higher-SES individuals. Quality schooling, educational funding, and organized neighborhood activities may be lacking in these communities.

Family support systems are also associated with delinquency (Feldman & Weinberger, 1994; Tolan, Gorman-Smith, & Henry, 2003). Parents of delinquents are less skilled in discouraging antisocial behavior and in encouraging skilled behavior than are parents of nondelinquents. Parental monitoring of adolescents is especially important in determining whether an adolescent becomes a delinquent (Patterson, DeBaryshe, & Ramsey, 1989). Family discord and inconsistent and inappropriate discipline are also associated with delinquency, as are sibling relations. An increasing number of studies have found that siblings can have a strong influence on delinquency (Conger & Reuter, 1996). In one recent study, high levels of hostile sibling relationships and older sibling delinquency were linked with younger sibling delinquency in both brother and sister pairs (Slomkowski & others, 2001).

Violence and Youth Youth violence is a special concern in the United States today (U.S. Department of Health and Human Services, 2001). In one study, 17 percent of U.S. high school students reported carrying a gun or other weapon the past 30 days (National Center for Health Statistics, 2000). In this same study, a smaller percentage (7 percent) reported bringing a gun or other weapon onto school property. Not all violence-related behaviors involve weapons. In this study, 44 percent of male and 27 percent of female high school students said they had been involved in one or more fights.

These factors often are present in at-risk youths and seem to propel them toward violent acts (Walker, 1998):

- Early involvement with drugs and alcohol
- Easy access to weapons, especially handguns
- Association with antisocial, deviant peer groups
- Pervasive exposure to violence in the media

Many at-risk youth also are easily provoked to rage, reacting aggressively to real or imagined slights and acting upon them, sometimes with tragic consequences. They might misjudge the motives and intentions of others toward them because of the hostility and agitation they carry (Coie & Dodge, 1998). Consequently, they frequently engage in hostile confrontations with peers and teachers. It is not unusual to find anger-prone youth issuing threats of bodily harm to others.

Oregon Social Learning Center

National Youth Gang Center

Center for the Prevention of School Violence

Lost Boys

Here are some of the Oregon Social Learning Center's recommendations for reducing youth violence (Walker, 1998):

- *Recommit to raising children safely and effectively.* This includes engaging in parenting practices that have been shown to produce healthy, well-adjusted children. Such practices include consistent, fair discipline that is not harsh or severely punitive, careful monitoring and supervision, positive family management techniques, involvement in the child's daily life, daily debriefings about the child's experiences, and teaching problem-solving strategies.
- *Make prevention a reality.* Too often lip service is given to prevention strategies without investing in them at the necessary levels to make them effective.
- *Give more support to schools, which are struggling to educate a population that includes many at-risk children.*
- *Forge effective partnerships among families, schools, social service systems, churches, and other agencies to create the socializing experiences that will provide all youth with the opportunity to develop in positive ways.*

One current program that seeks to prevent juvenile delinquency is called *Fast Track* (Dodge, 2001; Conduct Problems Prevention Research Group, 2002). High-risk children who show conduct problems at home and at kindergarten were identified. Then, during the elementary school years, the at-risk children and their families are given support and training in parenting, problem-solving and coping skills, peer relations, classroom atmosphere and curriculum, academic achievement, and home-school relations. Ten project interventionists work with the children, their families, and schools to increase the protective factors and decrease the risk factors in these areas. Thus far, results show that the intervention effectively improved parenting practices and children's problem-solving and coping skills, peer relations, reading achievement, and problem behavior at home and school during the elementary school years compared to a control of high-risk children who did not experience the intervention.

One individual whose goal is to reduce violence in adolescence and help at-risk adolescents cope more effectively with their lives is Rodney Hammond. To read about his work, see the Careers in Child Development insert.

There recently has been a rash of murders committed by adolescents, with the targets of their violence being classmates or school personnel. To read further about adolescent murderers, see the Explorations in Child Development box.

Careers in Child Development

Rodney Hammond, *Health Psychologist*

When Rodney Hammond went to college at the University of Illinois in Champaign-Urbana, he had not decided on a major. To help finance his education, he took a part-time job in a child development research program sponsored by the psychology department. In this job, he observed inner-city children in contexts designed to improve their learning. He saw firsthand the contributions psychology can make and knew then that he wanted to be a psychologist.

Rodney Hammond went on to obtain a doctorate in school and community psychology with a focus on children's development. Today, he trains psychologists at Wright State University in Ohio and directs a program funded by federal and state agencies to prevent homicide and violence among ethnic minority youth. Rodney calls himself a "health psychologist," although when he went to graduate school, training for that profession did not exist as it does now. He and his associates teach at-risk youth how to use social skills to manage conflict effectively and to recognize situations that could become violent. They have shown in their research that with this intervention many youth are less likely to become juvenile delinquents. Rodney's message to undergraduates: "If you are interested in people and problem solving, psychology is a great way to combine the two."

Rodney Hammond, counseling an adolescent girl about the risks of adolescence and how to effectly cope with them.

Why Youth Kill

In the late 1990s, a series of school shootings gained national attention. In April 1999, two Columbine High School (in Littleton, Colorado) students, Eric Harris (age 18) and Dylan Klebold (age 17), shot and killed 12 students and a teacher, wounded 23 others, and then killed themselves. In May 1998, slightly-built Kip Kinkel strode into a cafeteria at Thurston High School in Springfield, Oregon, and opened fire on his fellow students, murdering two and injuring many others. Later that day, police went to Kip's home and found his parents lying dead on the floor, also victims of Kip's violence. In 1997, three students were killed and five others wounded in a hallway at Heath High School in West Paducah, Kentucky, by a 14-year-old student. These are but three of many school shooting incidents that have occurred in recent years.

Is there any way psychologists can predict whether a youth will turn violent? It's a complex task, but they have pieced together some clues (Cowley, 1998). Violent youth are overwhelmingly male, and many are driven by feelings of powerlessness. Violence seems to infuse these youth with a sense of power. Sixteen-year-old Luke Woodham was known as a chubby nerd at his school in Pearl, Mississippi. But in the fall of 1997, he shed that image by stabbing his mother to death and shooting nine of his classmates, killing two of them. Woodham wrote in a letter, "I killed because people like me are mistreated every day. Murder is not weak and slow-witted. Murder is gutsy and daring."

Small-town shooting sprees attract attention, but there is far more youth violence in poverty-infested areas of inner cities. Urban poverty fosters powerlessness and the rage that goes with it. Living in poverty is frustrating, and many inner-city neighborhoods provide almost daily opportunities to observe violence. Many urban youth who live in poverty also lack adequate parent involvement and supervision.

University of Virginia psychologist Dewey Cornell (1998) says that many youth give clear indications of their future violence but aren't taken seriously. Cornell University psychologist James Garbarino (1999, 2001) says there is a lot of ignoring that goes on in these kinds of situations. Parents often don't want to acknowledge what might be a very upsetting reality. Harris and Klebold were members of the "Trenchcoat Mafia" clique of Columbine outcasts. The two even had made a video for a school video class the previous fall that depicted them walking down the halls at the school, shooting other students. Allegations were made that a year earlier the sheriff's department had been given information that Harris had bragged openly on the Internet that he and Klebold had built four bombs. Kip Kinkel had an obsession with guns and explosives, a history of abusing animals, and a nasty temper when crossed. When police examined his room, they found two pipe bombs, three larger bombs, and bomb-making recipes that Kip had downloaded from the Internet. Clearly, some signs were present in these students' lives to suggest some serious problems, but it is still very difficult to predict whether youth like these will actually act on their anger and sense of powerlessness to commit murder.

Garbarino (1999, 2001) has interviewed a number of youth who are killers. He concludes that nobody really knows precisely why a tiny minority of youth kill, but that it might be a lack of a spiritual center. In the youthful killers he interviewed, Garbarino often found a spiritual or emotional emptiness in which the youth sought meaning on the dark side of life.

What are some of the reasons psychologists give to explain why youth like Eric Harris kill?

Review and Reflect: Learning Goal 3

3 Describe the development of prosocial and antisocial behavior

REVIEW

- How is altruism defined? How does children's altruism develop?
- What is juvenile delinquency? What are the antecedents of delinquency? What are some factors that are involved in youth violence?

REFLECT

- As the head of a major government agency responsible for reducing delinquency in the United States, what programs would you try to implement?

> *Youth who kill often have a distorted perspective on what is right and wrong. This distorted perspective can become a self-justifying rationale for violence.*
>
> —JAMES GARBARINO
> *Contemporary Developmental Psychologist, Cornell University*

Reach Your Learning Goals

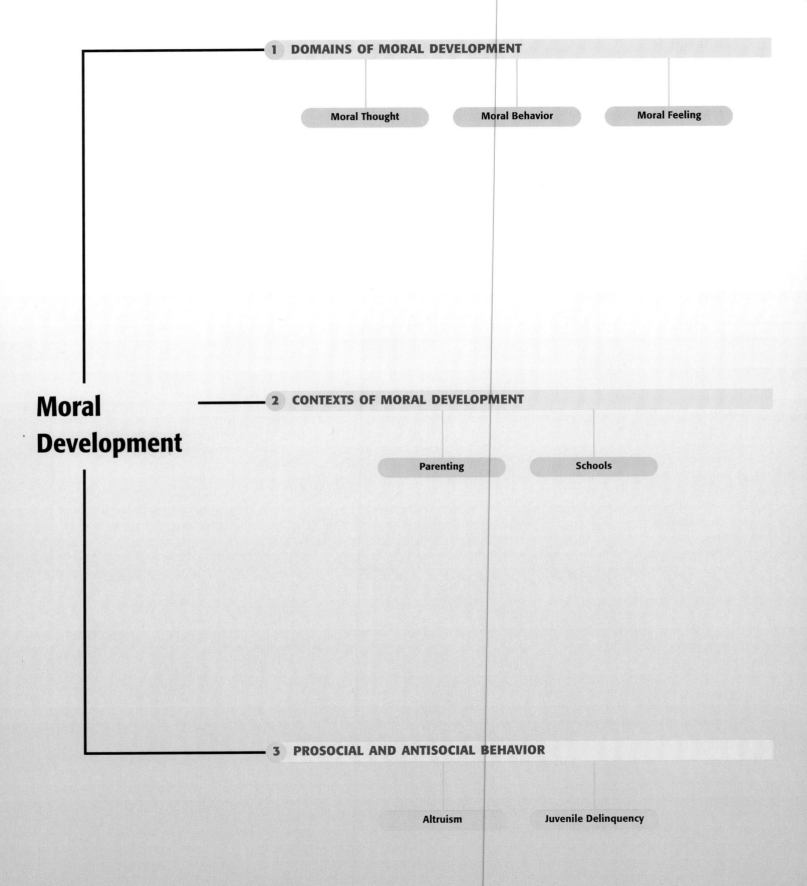

Moral Development

1 DOMAINS OF MORAL DEVELOPMENT

Moral Thought   Moral Behavior   Moral Feeling

2 CONTEXTS OF MORAL DEVELOPMENT

Parenting   Schools

3 PROSOCIAL AND ANTISOCIAL BEHAVIOR

Altruism   Juvenile Delinquency

Summary

1 Discuss theories and research on moral thought, behavior, and feeling

- The three main domains of moral development are thought, behavior, and feeling. Piaget and Kohlberg proposed major cognitive theories of moral development. Piaget distinguishes between the heteronomous morality of younger children and the autonomous morality of older children. His ideas about formal operational thought have implications for understanding adolescents' moral development. Kohlberg developed a provocative theory of moral reasoning. Kohlberg argued that moral development consists of three levels—preconventional, conventional, and postconventional—and six stages (two at each level). Increased internalization characterizes movement to levels 2 and 3. Influences on the Kohlberg stages include cognitive development, imitation and cognitive conflict, peer relations, and perspective taking. Criticisms of Kohlberg's theory involve inadequate attention to moral behavior, inadequate assessment, failure to include the care perspective, underestimation of culture's role, and inadequate consideration of social conventional reasoning. Gilligan advocates a stronger care perspective and says that early adolescence is a critical juncture in the development of girls. Social conventional reasoning involves thoughts about social consensus and convention.

- Behaviorists argue that children's moral behavior is determined by the processes of reinforcement, punishment, and imitation. Situational variability in moral behavior is stressed by behaviorists. In Hartshorne and May's classic study, considerable situational variation in moral behavior was found. Behaviorists who study children's moral behavior often examine resistance to temptation and the development of self-control. The use of rationales and self-instruction helps children to increase their self-control. Social cognitive theory emphasizes a distinction between moral competence (the ability to perform moral behaviors) and moral performance (performing those behaviors in specific situations). Social cognitive theorists believe Kohlberg gave inadequate attention to moral behavior and situational variations.

- In Freud's theory, the superego—the moral branch of personality—is one of personality's three main structures. Through identification, children internalize a parent's standards of right and wrong. Children conform to moral standards to avoid guilt. The two main components of the superego are ego ideal and conscience. Feeling empathy means reacting to another's feelings with an emotional response that is similar to the other's feelings. Empathy often has a cognitive component—perspective taking. Empathy changes developmentally. Both positive feelings (such as empathy) and negative feelings (such as guilt) contribute to children's moral development. Emotions are interwoven with the cognitive and social dimensions of moral development.

2 Explain how parents and schools influence moral development

- Parental discipline can involve love withdrawal, power assertion, or induction. Induction has been the most effective technique, especially with middle-SES children. Children's moral development is advanced when parents are warm and supportive rather than punitive, provide opportunities for their children to learn about others' perspectives and feelings, involve children in family decision making, and model moral behavior and thinking.

- Originally proposed by John Dewey, the hidden curriculum refers to the moral atmosphere of a school. Character education is a direct education approach that advocates teaching students a basic moral literacy. Values clarification focuses on helping students to clarify what their lives are for and what is worth exploring. Cognitive moral education emphasizes helping students develop such values as democracy and justice as their moral reasoning develops. Kohlberg's theory has served as the basis for a number of cognitive moral education programs. Service learning is a form of education that promotes social responsibility and service to the community. Service learning benefits youth in a number of ways.

3 Describe the development of prosocial and antisocial behavior

- Altruism is an unselfish interest in helping another person. Reciprocity and exchange are involved in altruism. Damon described a developmental sequence of altruism that highlights sharing.

- Delinquency includes a broad range of behaviors, including index offenses and status offenses. Conduct disorder is a psychiatric category often used to describe delinquent-type behavior. Predictors of delinquency include conflict with authority, minor covert acts followed by property damage and more serious acts, minor aggression followed by fighting and violence, a negative identity, low self-control, early initiation of delinquency, weak educational orientation, heavy peer influence, low parental monitoring, ineffective discipline, having an older sibling who is a delinquent, and living in an urban, high-crime area. The high rate of violence in youth is an increasing problem. Recommendations for reducing youth violence include effective parenting, prevention, support for schools, and forging effective partnerships among families, schools, and communities. Conflict resolution programs are being used in attempts to reduce youth violence.

Key Terms

moral development 437
heteronomous morality (Piaget) 437
autonomous morality (Piaget) 437
immanent justice 438
internalization 439
preconventional reasoning 439
heteronomous morality (Kohlberg) 439

individualism, instrumental purpose, and exchange 439
conventional reasoning 439
mutual interpersonal expectations, relationships, and interpersonal conformity 440
social systems morality 440
postconventional reasoning 440
social contract or utility and individual rights 440

universal ethical principles 440
justice perspective 444
care perspective 444
social conventional reasoning 445
social cognitive theory of morality 448
empathy 449
love withdrawal 452
power assertion 452

induction 452
hidden curriculum 453
character education 453
values clarification 454
cognitive moral education 454
service learning 455
altruism 456
juvenile delinquency 457
index offenses 457
status offenses 457
conduct disorder 458

Key People

Jean Piaget 437
Lawrence Kohlberg 438
James Rest 443
Carol Gilligan 444

Hugh Hartshorne and Mark May 447
Walter Mischel 447
Albert Bandura 448

Sigmund Freud 448
Martin Hoffman 452
Nancy Eisenberg 453
John Dewey 453

William Damon 456
James Garbarino 462

Taking It to the Net

1. Geraldine is giving a report on Kohlberg's theory of moral development. She is having a hard time thinking of an example of moral reasoning that would demonstrate each of the six Kohlberg stages of moral development. What examples would best demonstrate the six stages of moral development?

2. Kirk is planning to be a fifth-grade teacher. He is interested in the new approach to disciplining students that is designed to strengthen a child's character and impart moral values. How can Kirk begin to use this approach in the classroom?

3. Justin and his father are having a heated discussion over the factors that may have contributed to a young boy's shooting and killing a schoolmate. Justin thinks that the boy may have witnessed, or been a victim of, violence in his home. Justin's father says that if all people who have seen violence were themselves violent, we would all be locked up. How should Justin respond?

Connect to **www.mhhe.com/santrockcd10** to research the answers and complete these exercises.

E-Learning Tools

To help you master the material in this chapter, you'll find a number of valuable study tools on the Student CD-ROM that accompanies this book. Also visit the Online Learning Center for *Child Development,* tenth edition (**www.mhhe.com/santrockcd10**) where you'll find these additional resources:

- Build your decision-making skills by trying your hand at the parenting, nursing, and education "Scenarios" on the Online Learning Center.

Social Contexts of Development

It is not enough for parents to understand children. They must also accord children the privilege of understanding them.

—MILTON SAPIRSTEIN
American Psychiatrist and Writer, 20th Century

Parents cradle children's lives, but children's growth is also shaped by successive choirs of siblings, peers, friends, and teachers. Children's small worlds widen as they discover new refuges and new people. In the end there are but two lasting bequests that parents can leave children: one being roots, the other wings. In this section, we will study four chapters: "Families" (chapter 15), "Peers" (chapter 16), "Schools" (chapter 17), and "Culture" (chapter 18).

CHAPTER
15

There's no vocabulary for love within a family, love that's lived in but not looked at, love within the light of which all else is seen, the love within which all other love finds speech. That love is silent.

—T. S. Eliot
American-Born English Poet, 20th Century

Families

Chapter Outline

FAMILY PROCESSES

Reciprocal Socialization and the Family as a System
The Developmental Construction of Relationships
Adapting Parenting to Developmental Changes in the Child
Sociocultural and Historical Changes
The Roles of Cognition and Emotion in Family Relationships

PARENTING

The Parental Role
Parents as Managers
Parenting Styles
Punishment
Child Maltreatment
Parenting Takes Time and Effort

SIBLINGS

Sibling Relationships
Birth Order

FAMILIES AND ADOLESCENTS

Autonomy and Attachment
Parent-Adolescent Conflict

THE CHANGING FAMILY IN A CHANGING SOCIAL WORLD

Working Mothers
Effects of Divorce on Children
Stepfamilies
Gay and Lesbian Parents
Cultural, Ethnic, and Socioeconomic Variations in Families
Gender and Parenting

Learning Goals

1 Discuss family processes

2 Explain how parenting is linked to children's development

3 Identify how siblings influence children's development

4 Summarize the changes in families with adolescents

5 Characterize the changing family in a changing social world

The Story of a Mother with Multiple Sclerosis

When Shelley Schwarz (2002) and her husband David had been married four years, they decided to have children. They had two children and when they were 3 and 5 years old, Shelley was diagnosed with multiple sclerosis. Two years later, she had to quit her job as a teacher of hearing-impaired children because of her worsening condition.

By the time the children were 7 and 9 years old, it was more difficult for Shelley to prepare meals for the family by herself, so her husband David began taking over that responsibility. They also enlisted the children's help in preparing meals.

Shelley continued to take advantage of parenting classes and workshops the school offered and asked school professionals for recommendations on the best parenting books. She even started a "Mothers-of-10-Year-Olds" support group.

Parenting with multiple sclerosis had its frustrations for Shelley. Attending school functions, teacher conferences, and athletic events often presented problems because the facilities weren't always wheelchair accessible. However, Shelley felt guilty if she didn't at least try to attend these functions. She didn't want her children to think she didn't care enough to try.

When her children were 17 and 19, Shelley says that she began to relax a little. She could see how capable and independent they were becoming and that her disability had not ruined their lives. In some ways, she believes, they were better off because of her disability. They learned to trust themselves and face challenges head-on. When the time came for them to go away to college, she knew they were ready.

Shelley says she now understands that having a disability was not the worst thing in the world that could happen to a parent. What she says would be a tragedy is letting your disability interfere with your ability to stay involved in your children's lives. She comments that parenting is so much more than driving car pools, attending gymnastic meets, or baking cookies at an open house. It is loving, caring, listening, guiding, and supporting your child. It is gently consoling your child who is crying because her friends thought her haircut was ugly. It is counseling a child worried because his 12-year-old friend is drinking. It is helping a child understand relationships and what love is.

This chapter is about the many aspects of children's development in families. We will explore the best ways to parent children, sibling relationships, and the changing family in a changing social world. Along the way, we will examine such family topics as child maltreatment, working mothers, the effects of divorce on children, stepfamilies, and many others.

1 FAMILY PROCESSES

```
┌─────────────────────┐      ┌─────────────────────┐      ┌─────────────────────┐
│ Reciprocal Socialization │   │ Adapting Parenting  │     │ The Roles of Cognition │
│ and the Family      │      │ to Developmental    │      │ and Emotion in Family  │
│ as a System         │      │ Changes in the Child │     │ Relationships         │
└─────────────────────┘      └─────────────────────┘      └─────────────────────┘

        ┌───────────────────────┐      ┌───────────────────┐
        │ The Developmental     │      │ Sociocultural and │
        │ Construction of Relationships │  │ Historical Changes │
        └───────────────────────┘      └───────────────────┘
```

Among the important considerations in studying children and their families are reciprocal socialization and the family system; how children construct relationships and how such relationships influence developmental changes in the child; sociocultural and historical influences on the family; and the roles of cognition and emotion in family relationships.

Reciprocal Socialization and the Family as a System

For many years, socialization between parents and children was viewed as a one-way process: Children were considered to be the products of their parents' socialization techniques. As we see next, however, today we view parent-child interaction as reciprocal.

Reciprocal Socialization   **Reciprocal socialization** is a socialization process that is bidirectional; children socialize parents just as parents socialize children (Crouter & Booth, 2003; Patterson & Fisher, 2002). For example, the interaction of mothers and their infants is sometimes symbolized as a dance or dialogue in which successive actions of the partners are closely coordinated. This coordinated dance or dialogue can assume the form of mutual synchrony (each person's behavior depending on the partner's previous behavior), or it can be reciprocal in a more precise sense; the actions of the partners can be matched, as when one partner imitates the other or when there is mutual smiling (Cohn & Tronick, 1988).

When reciprocal socialization has been investigated in infancy, mutual gaze or eye contact has been found to play an important role in early social interaction (Fogel, Toda, & Kawai, 1988). In one investigation, the mother and infant engaged in a variety of behaviors while they looked at each other; by contrast, when they looked away from each other, the rate of such behaviors dropped considerably (Stern & others, 1977). In sum, the behaviors of mothers and infants involve substantial interconnection and synchronization. And in one investigation, synchrony in parent-child relationships was positively related to children's social competence (Harrist, 1993).

One example of parental responses to children's behavior is the elicitation of scaffolding behavior, which in turn affects the level of behavior children show in the future. **Scaffolding** refers to parental behavior that serves to support children's efforts, allowing them to be more skillful than they would if they relied only on their own abilities. Parents' efforts to time interactions in such a way that the infant experiences turn taking with the parent illustrates an early parental scaffolding behavior (Landry & others, 2002). For example, in the game peek-a-boo, mothers initially cover their babies, then remove the covering, and finally register "surprise" at the reappearance. As infants become more skilled at peek-a-boo, they do the covering and uncovering. In addition to peek-a-boo, pat-a-cake, and "so-big" are other caregiver games that exemplify scaffolding and turn-taking sequences. In one investigation, infants who had more-extensive scaffolding experiences with their parents, especially in the form of turn taking, were more likely to engage in turn taking as

Children, Youth, and Families Education and Research Network

Children, Youth, and Family Services

reciprocal socialization The process by which children socialize parents just as parents socialize them.

scaffolding Parental behavior that supports children's efforts, allowing children to be more skillful than they would be if they relied only on their own abilities.

I looked on child rearing not only as a work of love and duty but as a profession that was fully as interesting and challenging as any honorable profession in the world and one that demanded the best that I could bring to it.

—Rose Kennedy
U.S. Public Figure and
Philanthropist, 20th Century

they interacted with their peers (Vandell & Wilson, 1988). Scaffolding is not just confined to parent-infant interaction but can be used by parents to support children's efforts at any age (Stringer & Neal, 1993). For example, parents can support children's achievement-related efforts in school by modifying the amount and type of support they provide to best suit the child's level of development.

Family as a System   As a social system, the family can be thought of as a constellation of subsystems defined in terms of generation, gender, and role (Davis, 1996). Divisions of labor among family members define particular subunits, and attachments define others. Each family member is a participant in several subsystems—some dyadic (involving two people), some polyadic (involving more than two people). The father and child represent one dyadic subsystem, the mother and father another; the mother-father-child represent one polyadic subsystem, the mother and two siblings another (Piotrowski, 1997).

An organizational scheme that highlights the reciprocal influences of family members and family subsystems is shown in figure 15.1 (Belsky, 1981). As the arrows in the figure show, marital relations, parenting, and infant/child behavior can have both direct and indirect effects on each other. Researchers have become interested in how a number of indirect relationships (such as siblings with parents and grandparents with parents) might be related to the child's direct relationships with parents (Hart & others, 1997).

Marital Relationships and Parenting   As researchers have broadened their focus in families beyond just studying the parent-child relationship, an increasingly studied aspect of the family system involves the link between marital relationships and parenting (Cummings & others, 2003). For example, in one study, when marriages were less intimate and more distant during prenatal development, mothers were less sensitive, and fathers invested less time in parenting, when the infants were 3 years old (Cox & others, 1989).

The most consistent findings are that happily married parents are more sensitive, responsive, warm, and affectionate toward their children (Grych, 2002). Researchers have also found that promoting marital satisfaction often leads to good parenting. The marital relationship is an important support for parenting (Gable, Belsky, & Crnic, 1992; Kanoy & others, 2003). When parents report more intimacy and better communication in their marriage, they are more affectionate to their children (Grych, 2002). Thus, an important, if unintended, benefit of marriage enhancement programs is the improvement of parenting, and consequently healthier children. Programs that focus on parenting skills might also benefit from including attention to the participants' marriages.

The Developmental Construction of Relationships

Developmentalists have shown an increased interest in understanding how we construct relationships as we grow up (Cassidy & Shaver, 1999; Shaver, 1993). Psychoanalytic theorists have always been interested in how this process works in families. However, the current explanations of how relationships are constructed are virtually stripped of Freud's psychosexual stage terminology and also are not always confined to the first five years of life, as has been the case in classical psychoanalytic theory. Today's **developmental construction views** share the belief that as individuals grow up they acquire modes of relating to others. There are two main variations in this view, one that emphasizes continuity and stability and one that emphasizes discontinuity and change.

The Continuity View   The **continuity view** emphasizes the role that early parent-child relationships play in constructing a basic way of relating to people. These early parent-child relationships are carried forward to influence later points in development and all subsequent relationships (with peers, with friends, with teachers, and

developmental construction views Views sharing the belief that as individuals grow up, they acquire modes of relating to others. There are two main variations of this view. One emphasizes continuity and stability in relationships throughout the life span; the other emphasizes discontinuity and changes in relationships throughout the life span.

continuity view A developmental view that emphasizes the role of early parent-child relationships in constructing a basic way of relating to people throughout the life span.

with romantic partners, for example) (Ainsworth, 1979; Bowlby, 1989; Sroufe, 2002; Sroufe, Egeland, & Carlson, 1999). In its extreme form, this view states that the basic components of social relationships are laid down and shaped by the security or insecurity of parent-infant attachment relationships in the first year or two of the infant's life (remember our discussion of attachment in chapter 11). ◀ **page 370**

Close relationships with parents also are important in the child's development, because these relationships function as models or templates that are carried forward over time to influence the construction of new relationships. Clearly, close relationships do not repeat themselves in an endless fashion over the course of the child's development. And the quality of any relationship depends to some degree on the specific individual with whom the relationship is formed. However, the nature of earlier relationships that are developed over many years often can be detected in later relationships, both with those same individuals and in the formation of relationships with others at a later point in time (Gjerde, Block, & Block, 1991). Thus, the nature of parent-adolescent relationships does not depend only on what happens in the relationship during adolescence. Relationships with parents over the long course of childhood are carried forward to influence, at least to some degree, the nature of parent-adolescent relationships. And the long course of parent-child relationships also could be expected to influence, again at least to some degree, the fabric of the adolescent's peer relationships, friendships, and dating relationships.

In chapter 11, "Emotional Development," we described the longitudinal study of Alan Sroufe and his colleagues that supported the importance of continuity in development (Sroufe, 2002; Sroufe, Egeland, & Carlson, 1999). Recall that attachment history and early care were linked with peer competence in adolescence, up to 15 years after the infant assessments. For most children, there was a cascading effect in which early family relationships provided the necessary support for effectively engaging in the peer world, which in turn provided the foundation for more extensive, complex peer relationships.

The Discontinuity View

The **discontinuity view** emphasizes change and growth in relationships over time. As people grow up, they develop many different types of relationships (with parents, with peers, with teachers, and with romantic partners, for example). Each of these relationships is structurally different. With each new type of relationship, individuals encounter new modes of relating (Buhrmester & Furman, 1987; Piaget, 1932; Sullivan, 1953; Youniss, 1980). For example, Jean Piaget (1932) argued that parent-child relationships are strikingly different from children's peer relationships. Parent-child relationships, he said, are more likely to consist of parents' having unilateral authority over children. By contrast, peer relationships are more likely to consist of participants who relate to each other on a much more equal basis. In parent-child relationships, since parents have greater knowledge and authority, their children often must learn how to conform to rules and regulations laid down by parents. In this view, we use the parental-child mode when relating to authority figures (such as with teachers and experts) and when we ourselves become authority figures (when we become parents, teachers, and experts).

In contrast, relationships with peers have a different structure and require a different mode of relating to others. This more egalitarian mode is later called upon in relationships with romantic partners, friends, and coworkers. Because two peers possess relatively equal knowledge and authority (their relationship is reciprocal and symmetrical), children learn a democratic mode of relating that is based on mutual influence. With peers, children learn to formulate and assert their own opinions, appreciate the perspectives of peers, cooperatively negotiate solutions to disagreements, and evolve standards for conduct that are mutually acceptable. Because peer relationships are voluntary (rather than obligatory, as in the family), children and adolescents who fail to become skillful in the symmetrical, mutual, egalitarian, reciprocal mode of relating have difficulty being accepted by peers.

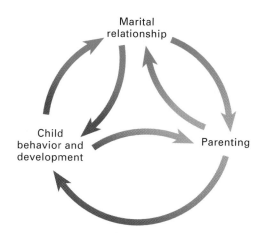

FIGURE 15.1 Interaction Between Children and Their Parents: Direct and Indirect Effects

discontinuity view A developmental view that emphasizes change and growth in relationships over time.

Evidence for the discontinuity view of relationships was found in the longitudinal study conducted by Andrew Collins and his colleagues (Collins, Hennighausen, & Sroufe, 1998). Quality of friendship interaction (based on observations of coordinated behavior, such as turn taking, sharing, eye contact, and touching, and their duration) in middle childhood was related to security with dating, and disclosure and intimacy with a dating partner, at age 16.

The discontinuity view does not deny that prior close relationships (such as with parents) are carried forward to influence later relationships, but it stresses that each new type of relationship that children and adolescents encounter (such as with peers, with friends, and with romantic partners) requires the construction of different and ever-more sophisticated modes of relating to others. In the change-and-growth view, each period of development uniquely contributes to the construction of relationship knowledge; development across the life span is not solely determined by a sensitive or critical period during infancy.

Adapting Parenting to Developmental Changes in the Child

Children change as they grow from infancy to early childhood and on through middle and late childhood and adolescence. In the view of Eleanor Maccoby (1984), a competent parent adapts to the child's developmental changes. Parents should not treat a 5-year-old the same as a 2-year-old. The 5-year-old and 2-year-old have different needs and abilities. In the first year, parent-child interaction moves from a heavy focus on routine caretaking—feeding, changing diapers, bathing, and soothing—to later include more non-caregiving activities, such as play and visual-vocal exchanges (Bornstein, 2002). During the child's second and third years, parents often handle disciplinary matters by physical manipulation: They carry the child away from a mischievous activity to the place they want the child to go to; they put fragile and dangerous objects out of reach; they sometimes spank. As the child grows older, however, parents increasingly turn to reasoning, moral exhortation, and giving or withholding special privileges. As children move toward the elementary school years, parents show them less physical affection.

Parent-child interactions during early childhood focus on such matters as modesty, bedtime regularities, control of temper, fighting with siblings and peers, eating behavior and manners, autonomy in dressing, and attention seeking (Edwards & Liu, 2002). Although some of these issues—fighting and reaction to discipline, for example—are carried forward into the elementary school years, many new issues appear by the age of 7. These include whether children should be made to perform

Calvin and Hobbes   by Bill Watterson

WHAT ASSURANCE DO I HAVE THAT YOUR PARENTING ISN'T SCREWING ME UP?

chores and, if so, whether they should be paid for them, how to help children learn to entertain themselves rather than relying on parents for everything, and how to monitor children's lives outside the family in school and peer settings.

As children move into the middle and late childhood years, parents spend considerably less time with them (Collins & Madsen, 2002). In one investigation, parents spent less than half as much time with their children aged 5 to 12 in caregiving, instruction, reading, talking, and playing as when the children were young (Hill & Stafford, 1980). This drop in parent-child interaction may be even more extensive in families with little parental education. Although parents spend less time with their children in middle and late childhood than in early childhood, parents continue to be extremely important socializing agents in their children's lives (Collins, Harris, & Susman, 1995). Children also must learn to relate to adults outside the family on a regular basis—adults who interact with the child much differently than parents do. During middle and late childhood, interactions with adults outside the family involve more formal control and achievement orientation.

Discipline during middle and late childhood is often easier for parents than it was during early childhood; it may also be easier than during adolescence. In middle and late childhood, children's cognitive development has matured to the point where it is possible for parents to reason with them about resisting deviation and controlling their behavior. By adolescence, children's reasoning has become more sophisticated, and they may be less likely to accept parental discipline. Adolescents also push more strongly for independence, which contributes to parenting difficulties (Steinberg & Silk, 2002). Parents of elementary school children use less physical discipline than do parents of preschool children. By contrast, parents of elementary school children are more likely to use deprivation of privileges, appeals directed at the child's self-esteem, comments designed to increase the child's sense of guilt, and statements indicating to the child that she is responsible for her actions.

During middle and late childhood, some control is transferred from parent to child, although the process is gradual and involves *coregulation* rather than control by either the child or the parent alone (Maccoby, 1984). The major shift to autonomy does not occur until about the age of 12 or later. During middle and late childhood, parents continue to exercise general supervision and exert control while children are allowed to engage in moment-to-moment self-regulation. This coregulation process is a transition period between the strong parental control of early childhood and the increased relinquishment of general supervision of adolescence.

During this coregulation, parents should

- monitor, guide, and support children at a distance;
- effectively use the times when they have direct contact with the child; and
- strengthen in their children the ability to monitor their own behavior, to adopt appropriate standards of conduct, to avoid hazardous risks, and to sense when parental support and contact are appropriate.

To be a competent parent, further adaptation is required as children become adolescents, which will be discussed later in the chapter. Next, we will explore another important consideration in understanding families: sociocultural and historical changes.

Sociocultural and Historical Changes

Family development does not occur in a social vacuum. Important sociocultural and historical influences affect family processes (Elder & Conger, 2000; Parke & Buriel, 1998; Rothbaum & others, 2002). Family changes may be due to great upheavals in a nation, such as war, famine, or mass immigration. Or they may be due more to subtle transitions in ways of life. The Great Depression in the early 1930s had some negative effects on families. During its height, the Depression produced economic deprivation, adult discontent, depression about living conditions, marital conflict, inconsistent child rearing, and unhealthy lifestyles—heavy drinking, demoralized attitudes, and health disabilities—especially in fathers (Elder, 1980). Subtle changes in a culture that have significant influences on the family were described by the famous anthropologist Margaret Mead (1978). The changes focus on the longevity of the elderly and the role of the elderly in the family, the urban and suburban orientation of families and their mobility, television, and a general dissatisfaction and restlessness.

Fifty years ago, the older people who survived were usually hearty and still closely linked to the family, often helping to maintain the family's existence. Today, older people live longer, which means that their middle-aged children are often pressed into a caretaking role for their parents or the elderly parents may be placed in a nursing home. Elderly parents may have lost some of their socializing role in the family during the twentieth century as many of their children moved great distances away.

Many of these family moves were away from farms and small towns to urban and suburban settings. In the small towns and farms, individuals were surrounded by lifelong neighbors, relatives, and friends. Today, neighborhood and extended-family support systems are not nearly as prevalent. Families now move all over the country, often uprooting the child from a school and peer group he or she has known for a considerable length of time. And for many families, this type of move occurs every year or two, as one or both parents are transferred from job to job.

The media and technology also play a major role in the changing family (Douglas, 2003). Many children who watch television find that parents are too busy working to share this experience with them. Children increasingly experience a world their parents are not a part of. Instead of participating in neighborhood peer groups, children come home after school and plop down in front of the television set or a computer screen. And television allows children and their families to see new ways of life. Lower-SES families can look into the family lives of middle-SES families by simply pushing a button.

Another subtle change in families has been an increase in general dissatisfaction and restlessness. The result of such restlessness and the tendency to divorce and remarry has been a hodgepodge of family structures, with far greater numbers of single-parent and stepparent families than ever before in history. Later in the chapter, we discuss such aspects of the changing social world of the child and the family in greater detail.

The Roles of Cognition and Emotion in Family Relationships

Cognitive processes are increasingly believed to be central to understanding socialization in the family (Bugental & Goodnow, 1998; Parke & Buriel, 1998). The role of cognition in family socialization comes in many forms, including parents' cognitions, beliefs, and values about their parental role, as well as how parents perceive, organize, and understand their children's behaviors and beliefs.

In one study, a link was found between mothers' beliefs and their preschool children's social problem-solving skills (Rubin, Mills, & Rose-Krasnor, 1989). Mothers who placed higher values on such skills as making friends, sharing with others, and leading or influencing other children had children who were more assertive, prosocial, and competent problem solvers.

Emotion also is increasingly viewed as central to understanding family processes (Parke & Buriel, 1998). Aspects of emotion in family processes that have been studied include the development of emotional regulation, the development of emotional production and understanding, and the role of emotion in carrying out the parental role.

Especially important in effective parenting is helping children learn to manage their emotions. Children's social competence is often linked to the emotional lives of their parents. For example, in one study, parents who displayed positive emotional expressiveness had children who were high in social competence (Boyum &

Parke, 1995). Through interactions with parents, children learn to express their emotions in socially appropriate ways.

Researchers also are finding that parental support and acceptance of children's emotions is related to children's ability to manage their emotions in positive ways (Parke & Buriel, 1998). Parental comforting of children when they experience negative emotion is linked with constructive anger reactions (Eisenberg & Fabes, 1994). Also, parental motivation to discuss emotions with their children is related to children's awareness and understanding of others' emotions (Denham, Cook, & Zoller, 1992; Dunn & Brown, 1994). In another study, fathers' acceptance and assistance with children's sadness and anger at 5 years of age was linked with children's social competence with peers at 8 years of age (Gottman, Katz, & Hooven, 1997).

Underlying much of the current research on socialization processes in families is the belief that cognition and emotion generally operate together in determining parenting practices (Dix, 1991).

Review and Reflect: Learning Goal 1

1 **Discuss family processes**

REVIEW

- What is reciprocal socialization? How can the family be viewed as a system?
- What are the two versions of the developmental construction of relationships?
- How can parenting be adapted to developmental changes in the child?
- What are some sociocultural and historical changes that have influenced the family?
- What roles do cognition and emotion play in family relationships?

REFLECT

- What do you predict will be some major changes in families in the twenty-first century?

2 PARENTING

| The Parental Role | Parenting Styles | Child Maltreatment |
| Parents as Managers | Punishment | Parenting Takes Time and Effort |

What is the parent's role in the child's development? How can parents effectively manage children's lives? What parenting styles do parents use when they interact with their children?

The Parental Role

For many adults, the parental role is well planned and coordinated with other roles in life and is developed with the individual's economic situation in mind. For others, the discovery that they are about to become parents is a startling surprise. In either event, the prospective parents may have mixed emotions and romantic illusions about having a child. Parenting consists of a number of interpersonal skills and emotional demands, yet there is little in the way of formal education for this task. Most parents learn parenting practices from their own parents—some of these practices they accept, some they discard. Husbands and wives may bring different viewpoints

CHEEVERWOOD

by Michael Fry

...ONE THING, BEFORE YOU SEND ME UP TO MY ROOM FOR THE REST OF MY LIFE... HAVE YOU READ THOSE STUDIES THAT SAY YOU SHOULD REASON WITH YOUR KIDS INSTEAD OF PUNISHING THEM?

I GUESS SHE HADN'T READ THOSE STUDIES...

CHEEVERWOOD © 1986 Michael Fry. Used by permission of Michael Fry.

of parenting practices to the marriage. Unfortunately, when methods of parents are passed on from one generation to the next, both desirable and undesirable practices are perpetuated.

The needs and expectations of parents have stimulated many myths about parenting, such as these (Okun & Rappaport, 1980):

- The birth of a child will save a failing marriage.
- As a possession or extension of the parent, the child will think, feel, and behave like the parents did in their childhood.
- Children will take care of parents in old age.
- Parents can expect respect and get obedience from their children.
- Having a child means that the parents will always have someone who loves them and is their best friend.
- Having a child gives the parents a "second chance" to achieve what they should have achieved.
- If parents learn the right techniques, they can mold their children into what they want.
- It's always the parents' fault when children fail.
- Mothers are naturally better parents than fathers.
- Parenting is an instinct and requires no training.

One career involving parenting is parent educator. To read about the work of one parent educator, see the Careers in Child Development insert.

Parents as Managers

In our discussion of the increased interest in studying the roles of cognition and emotion in family processes, we indicated that an important aspect of parenting is helping children manage their emotions. Likewise, an increasing trend in conceptualizing and researching parent-child relationships is to think of parents as managers of children's lives.

Parents can play important roles as managers of children's opportunities, as monitors of children's social relationships, and as social initiators and arrangers (Parke & Buriel, 1998). Parents serve as regulators of opportunities for social contact with peers, friends, and adults. From infancy through adolescence, mothers are more likely than fathers to have a managerial role in parenting. In infancy, this might involve taking a child to a doctor, and arranging for day care; in early childhood, it might involve a decision about which preschool the child should attend; in middle and late childhood, it might include directing the child to take a bath, to match their clothes and wear clean clothes, and to put away toys; in adolescence,

www.mhhe.com/santrockcd7o

Parenting

it could involve participating in a parent-teacher conference and subsequently managing the adolescent's homework activity.

An important aspect of the managerial role of parenting is effective monitoring of the child. This is especially important as children move into the adolescent years. Monitoring includes supervising a child's choice of social settings, activities, and friends. As we saw in chapter 14, "Moral Development," a lack of adequate parental monitoring is related to juvenile delinquency more than any other parenting factor (Patterson & Stouthamer-Loeber, 1984).

Parents have an important role in facilitating their children's development by initiating contact between their children (especially when they are young) and potential play partners. In one study, children of parents who arranged peer contacts had a larger number of playmates outside of their school than children of parents who were less active in arranging these contacts (Ladd, LeSeiur, & Profilet, 1993).

Parenting Styles

Parents want their children to grow into socially mature individuals, and they may feel frustrated in trying to discover the best way to accomplish this. Developmentalists have long searched for the ingredients of parenting that promote competent socioemotional development. For example, in the 1930s, John Watson argued that parents are too affectionate with their children. In the 1950s, a distinction was made between physical and psychological discipline. Psychological discipline, especially reasoning, was emphasized as the best way to rear a child. In the 1970s and beyond, the dimensions of competent parenting have become more precise.

Especially widespread is the view of Diana Baumrind (1971). She believes parents should be neither punitive nor aloof. Rather, they should develop rules for their children and be affectionate with them. She emphasizes four types of parenting styles:

Careers in Child Development

Janis Keyser, *Parent Educator*

Janis Keyser is a parent educator and teaches in the Department of Early Childhood Education at Cabrillo College in California. In addition to teaching college classes and conducting parenting workshops, Janis also has co-authored a book with Laura Davis (1997), *Becoming the Parent You Want to Be: A Sourcebook of Strategies for the First Five Years.*

Janis also writes as an expert on the iVillage website **(http://www.parentsplace.com)**. And she co-authors a nationally syndicated parenting column, "Growing Up, Growing Together." She is the mother of 3, stepmother of 5, grandmother of 12, and great-grandmother of 6.

Janis Keyser (*right*), conducting a session to help parents interact more effectively with their children.

- **Authoritarian parenting** is a restrictive, punitive style in which parents exhort the child to follow their directions and respect their work and effort. The authoritarian parent places firm limits and controls on the child and allows little verbal exchange. For example, an authoritarian parent might say, "You do it my way or else." Authoritarian parents also might spank the child frequently, enforce rules rigidly but not explain them, and show rage toward the child. Children of authoritarian parents are often unhappy, fearful, and anxious about comparing themselves with others, fail to initiate activity, and have weak communication skills. Sons of authoritarian parents may display and behave in aggressive ways (Hart & others, 2003).
- **Authoritative parenting** encourages children to be independent but still places limits and controls on their actions. Extensive verbal give-and-take is allowed, and parents are warm and nurturant toward the child. An authoritative parent might put his arm around the child in a comforting way and say, "You know you should not have done that. Let's talk about how you can handle the situation better next time." Authoritative parents show pleasure and support of children's constructive behavior. They also expect mature, independent,

authoritarian parenting This is a restrictive, punitive style in which the parent exhorts the child to follow the parent's directions and to respect their work and effort. Firm limits and controls are placed on the child, and little verbal exchange is allowed. This style is associated with children's socially incompetent behavior.

authoritative parenting This style encourages children to be independent but still places limits and controls on their actions. Extensive verbal give-and-take is allowed, and parents are warm and nurturant toward the child. This style is associated with children's socially competent behavior.

	Accepting, responsive	Rejecting, unresponsive
Demanding, controlling	Authoritative	Authoritarian
Undemanding, uncontrolling	Indulgent	Neglectful

FIGURE 15.2 Classification of Parenting Styles

The four types of parenting styles (authoritative, authoritarian, indulgent, and neglectful) involve the dimensions of acceptance and responsiveness on the one hand and demand and control on the other. For example, authoritative parenting involves being both accepting/responsive and demanding/controlling.

neglectful parenting A style in which the parent is very uninvolved in the child's life. It is associated with children's social incompetence, especially a lack of self-control.

indulgent parenting A style in which parents are highly involved with their children but place few demands or controls on them. This is associated with children's social incompetence, especially a lack of self-control.

and age-appropriate behavior of children. Children whose parents are authoritative are often cheerful, self-controlled and self-reliant, achievement-oriented, maintain friendly relations with peers, cooperate with adults, and cope well with stress.

- **Neglectful parenting** is a style in which the parent is very uninvolved in the child's life. Children whose parents are neglectful develop the sense that other aspects of the parents' lives are more important than they are. These children tend to be socially incompetent. Many have poor self-control and don't handle independence well. They frequently have low self-esteem, are immature, and may be alienated from the family. In adolescence, they may show patterns of truancy and delinquency.

- **Indulgent parenting** is a style of parenting in which parents are highly involved with their children but place few demands or controls on them. Such parents let their children do what they want. The result is that the children never learn to control their own behavior and always expect to get their way. Some parents deliberately rear their children in this way because they believe the combination of warm involvement and few restraints will produce a creative, confident child. However, children whose parents are indulgent rarely learn respect for others and have difficulty controlling their behavior. They might be domineering, egocentric, noncompliant, and have difficulties in peer relations.

These four classifications of parenting involve combinations of acceptance and responsiveness on the one hand and demand and control on the other (Maccoby & Martin, 1983). How these dimensions combine to produce authoritarian, authoritative, neglectful, and indulgent parenting is shown in figure 15.2.

Why is authoritative parenting likely to be the most effective style? These reasons have been given (Hart, Newell, & Olsen, 2002; Steinberg & Silk, 2002):

1. Authoritative parents establish an appropriate balance between control and autonomy, giving children opportunities to develop independence while providing the standards, limits, and guidance that children need (Reuter & Conger, 1995).

2. Authoritative parents are more likely to engage children in verbal give-and-take and allow children to express their views (Kuczynski & Lollis, 2002). This type of family discussion is likely to help children to understand social relationships and what is required for being a socially competent person.

3. The warmth and parental involvement provided by authoritative parents make the child more receptive to parental influence (Sim, 2000).

Do the benefits of authoritative parenting transcend the boundaries of ethnicity, socioeconomic status, and household composition? Although occasional exceptions to patterns have been found, the evidence linking authoritative parenting with competence on the part of the child has been found in research across a wide range of ethnic groups, social strata, cultures, and family structures (Steinberg & Silk, 2002).

Punishment

For centuries, corporal (physical) punishment, such as spanking, has been considered a necessary and even desirable method of disciplining children (Greven, 1991). Use of corporal punishment by parents is legal in every state in America, and it is estimated that 70 to 90 percent of American parents have spanked their children (Straus, 1991).

Despite the widespread use of corporal punishment, there have been surprisingly few research studies on physical punishment, and those that have been conducted are correlational (Baumrind, Larzelere, & Cowan, 2002). Clearly, it would be highly unethical to randomly assign parents to either spank or not spank their children in an experimental study. Recall that cause and effect cannot be determined in a correlational study. In one correlational study, spanking by parents was linked with children's antisocial behavior, including cheating, telling lies, being mean to others, bullying, getting into fights, and being disobedient (Strauss, Sugarman, & Giles-Sims, 1997). In a recent study of White, African American, and Latino families, spanking by parents predicted an increase in children's problems over time in all three groups (McLoyd & Smith, 2002). However, when parents showed strong emotional support of the child, the link between spanking and child problems was reduced.

A recent research review concluded that corporal punishment by parents is associated with children's higher levels of immediate compliance and aggression, and lower levels of moral internalization and mental health (Gershoff, 2002). Some critics, though, argue that the research evidence is not yet sound enough to warrant a blanket injunction against corporal punishment (Baumrind, Larzelere, & Cowan, 2002).

Here are some of the reasons why spanking or other forms of intense punishment with children should be avoided:

- When intense punishment, like yelling, screaming, or spanking is used, the adult is presenting the child with an out-of-control model for handling stressful situations. The children may imitate this aggressive, out-of-control behavior.
- Punishment can instill fear, rage, or avoidance in children. For example, spanking the child may cause the child to avoid being around the parent and fear the parent.
- Punishment tells children what not to do rather than what to do. When parents make punishing statements to children, such as "No, don't do that!" it should be accompanied by positive feedback, such as, "but why don't you try this."
- Punishment can be abusive. When parents discipline their children, they might not intend to be abusive but become so aroused when they are punishing the child that they become abusive (Baumrind, Larzelere, & Cowan, 2002).

Because of reasons such as these, a law was passed in Sweden in 1979 forbidding parents to physically punish (spank or slap, for example) when disciplining their children. The law is still in effect and since it was enacted youth rates of juvenile delinquency, alcohol abuse, rape, and suicide have dropped in Sweden (Durrant, 2000). The improved picture for Swedish youth may have occurred for other reasons, such as changing societal attitudes and opportunities for youth. Nonetheless, the Swedish experience suggests that physical punishment of children may not be necessary to improve the well-being of youth. Joining Sweden in forbidding parents to physically punish their children, these countries have also passed anti-spanking laws: Finland (1984), Denmark (1986), Norway (1987), Austria (1989), Cyprus (1994), Latvia (1998), Croatia (1999), Germany (2000), and Israel (2000).

A recent cross-cultural comparison found that individuals in the United States and Canada were among the most favorable toward corporal punishment and remembered it being used by their parents (Curran & others, 2001) (see figure 15.3). People in Sweden especially had an unfavorable attitude toward corporal punishment and were less likely than people in the other countries to remember it being used by their parents.

Most child psychologists recommend reasoning with the child, especially explaining the consequences of the child's actions for others, as the best way to handle children's misbehaviors. Time out, in which the child is removed from a setting where the child experiences positive reinforcement, can also be effective. For example, when the child has misbehaved, a parent might take away TV viewing for a specified period of time.

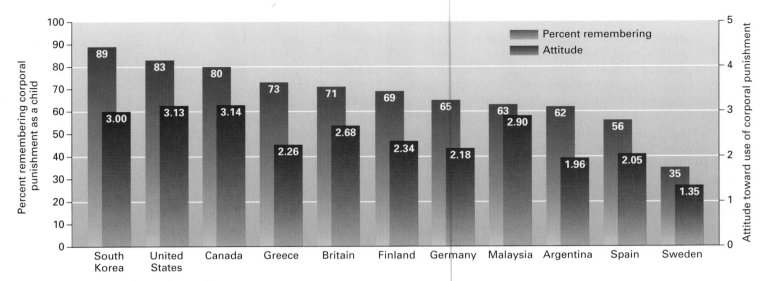

FIGURE 15.3 Corporal Punishment in Different Countries

A 5-point scale was used to assess attitudes toward corporal punishment with scores closer to 1 indicating an attitude against its use and scores closer to 5 suggesting an attitude for its use.

Child Maltreatment

Unfortunately, as we just mentioned, punishment sometimes leads to the abuse of infants and children. Child abuse is an increasing problem in the United States. Estimates of its incidence vary, but some authorities say that as many as 500,000 children are physically abused every year. Laws in many states now require doctors and teachers to report suspected cases of child abuse, yet many cases go unreported, especially those of battered infants.

Child abuse is such a disturbing circumstance that many people have difficulty understanding or sympathizing with parents who abuse or neglect their children. Our response is often outrage and anger directed at the parent. This outrage focuses our attention on parents as bad, sick, monstrous, sadistic individuals who cause their children to suffer. Experts on child abuse believe that this view is too simple and deflects attention away from the social context of the abuse and parents' coping skills. It is especially important to recognize that child abuse is a diverse condition, that it is usually mild to moderate in severity, and that it is only partially caused by the individual personality characteristics of parents (Azar, 2002; Field, 2000). The most common kind of abuser is not a raging, uncontrolled physical abuser but an overwhelmed single mother in poverty who neglects the child.

The Multifaceted Nature of Abuse Whereas the public and many professionals use the term *child abuse* to refer to both abuse and neglect, developmentalists increasingly use the term *child maltreatment* (Azar, 2002; Cicchetti, 2001). This term does not have quite the emotional impact of the term *abuse* and acknowledges that maltreatment includes several different conditions. Over 1 million children are affected by maltreatment each year, with 2,000 children killed by their caregivers (National Center on Child Abuse and Neglect, 2002). Among the different types of maltreatment are physical and sexual abuse; the fostering of delinquency; lack of supervision; medical, educational, and nutritional neglect; and drug or alcohol abuse (Bouvier, 2003; Golden, Samuels, & Southall, 2003). Approximately 54 percent of child maltreatment cases involve neglect and 23 percent involve abuse (Azar, 2002).

The Cultural Context of Abuse The extensive violence that takes place in the American culture is reflected in the occurrence of violence in the family (Azar, 2002). A regular diet of violence appears on television screens, and parents often resort to power assertion as a disciplinary technique. In China, where physical punishment is rarely used to discipline children, the incidence of child abuse is reported to be very low. In the United States, many abusing parents report that they do not have sufficient resources or help from others. This may be a realistic evaluation of the situation experienced by many low-income families, who do not have adequate preventive and supportive services.

Family Influences To understand abuse in the family, the interactions of all family members need to be considered, regardless of who actually performs the violent acts against the child (Margolin, 1994). For example, even though the father may be the one who physically abuses the child, contributions by the mother, the child, and siblings also should be evaluated. Many parents who abuse their children come from families in which physical punishment was used. These parents view physical punishment as a legitimate way of controlling the child's behavior. Physical punishment may be a part of this sanctioning.

Were parents who abuse children abused by their own parents? About one-third of parents who were abused themselves when they were young abuse their own children (Cicchetti & Toth, 1998). Thus, some, but not a majority, of parents are locked into an intergenerational transmission of abuse. Mothers who break out of the intergenerational transmission of abuse often have at least one warm, caring adult in their background, have a close, positive marital relationship, and have received therapy (Egeland, Jacobvitz, & Sroufe, 1988).

Developmental Consequences of Abuse Among the developmental consequences of child maltreatment are poor emotion regulation, attachment problems, problems in peer relations, difficulty in adapting to school, and other psychological problems (Azar, 2002; Shonk & Cicchetti, 2001). Difficulties in initiating and modulating positive and negative affect have been observed in maltreated infants (Cicchetti, Ganiban, & Barnett, 1991). Maltreated infants also may show excessive negative affect or blunted positive affect. In one recent study, 80 percent of maltreated 4- to 6-year-olds showed dysregulated emotion patterns (undercontrolled, overcontrolled, or unresponsive).

Maltreated children appear to be poorly equipped to develop successful peer relations, due to their aggressiveness, avoidance, and aberrant responses to both distress and positive approaches from peers (Bolger & Patterson, 2001; Mueller & Silverman, 1989).

Being physically abused has been linked with children's anxiety, personality problems, depression, conduct disorder, and delinquency (Maughan & Cicchetti, 2002; Shonk & Cicchetti, 2001). Later, during the adult years, maltreated children show increased violence toward other adults, dating partners, and marital partners, as well as increased substance abuse, anxiety, and depression (Malinosky-Rummell & Hansen, 1993). In sum, maltreated children are at risk for developing a wide range of problems and disorders (Bissada & Briere, 2001).

Careers in Child Development

Darla Botkin, *Marriage and Family Therapist*

Darla Botkin is a marriage and family therapist who teaches, conducts research, and engages in therapy in the area of marriage and family therapy. She is on the faculty of the University of Kentucky. Darla obtained a bachelor's degree in elementary education with a concentration in special education and then went on to receive a master's degree in early childhood education. She spent the next six years working with children and their families in a variety of settings, including day care, elementary school, and Head Start. These experiences led Darla to recognize the interdependence of the developmental settings that children and their parents experience (such as home, school, and work). She returned to graduate school and obtained a Ph.D. in family studies from the University of Tennessee. She then became a faculty member in the Family Studies program at the University of Kentucky. Completing further coursework and clinical training in marriage and family therapy, she became licensed as a marriage and family therapist in the state of Kentucky and an Approved Supervisor with the American Association for Marriage and Family Therapy.

Darla's current interests include (1) working with young children in family therapy and (2) the use of play in clinical, educational, and business settings.

Darla Botkin (*left*), conducting a family therapy session.

National Clearinghouse on Child Abuse and Neglect

Child Abuse Prevention Network

International Aspects of Child Abuse

Parenting Takes Time and Effort

In today's society, there is an unfortunate theme which suggests that parenting can be done quickly and with little or no inconvenience (Sroufe, 2000). One example of this involves playing Mozart CDs in the hope that they will enrich infants' and young children's brains. Some of these parents might be thinking "I don't have enough time to spend with my children so I'll just play these intellectual CDs and then they won't need me as much." Judith Harris' book *The Nurture Assumption* (which states that heredity and peer relations are the key factors in children's development) fits into this theme that parents don't need to spend much time with their children. Why did it become so popular? To some degree, some people who don't spend much time with their children saw it as supporting their neglect and reducing their guilt.

One-minute bedtime stories also are now being marketed successfully for parents to read to their children (Walsh, 2000). Most of these are brief summaries of longer stories. There are one-minute bedtime bear books, puppy books, and so on. These parents know it is good for them to read with their children, but they don't want to spend a lot of time doing it.

What is wrong with these quick-fix approaches to parenting? Good parenting takes a lot of time and a lot of effort. You can't do it in a minute here and a minute there. You can't do it with CDs.

Parents who do not spend enough time with their children or who have problems in child rearing can benefit from counseling and therapy. To read about the work of marriage and family counselor Darla Botkin, see the Careers in Child Development insert.

Review and Reflect: Learning Goal 2

2 Explain how parenting is linked to children's development

REVIEW

- What are some dimensions of the parental role?
- How can parents be effective managers of children?
- What are the four main styles of parenting? How are they linked to children's development?
- How does punishment affect children?
- What are some factors involved in child maltreatment? What are the developmental outcomes of child maltreatment?
- How does effective parenting involve time and effort?

REFLECT

- In our discussion of parenting, authoritative parenting was associated with children's social competence. In some cases, though, a child's parents differ in their parenting styles. Consider all four parenting styles—authoritarian, authoritative, neglectful, and indulgent—on the parts of the mother and father. A best case is when both parents are authoritative. What might be the effects on the child when one parent uses one style and the other parent uses a different style? Also, consider what style or styles of parenting your mother and father used in rearing you. What effects do you think their parenting style(s) had on your development?

So far our coverage of families has taken us through the nature of family processes, the parenting role, parents as managers of children's lives, and parenting styles. Next, we explore another important aspect of family life for many children—siblings.

3 SIBLINGS

| Sibling Relationships | Birth Order |

Sandra describes to her mother what happened in a conflict with her sister:

> We had just come home from the ball game. I sat down on the sofa next to the light so I could read. Sally, the sister, said, "Get up, I was sitting there first. I just got up for a second to get a drink." I told her I was not going to get up and that I didn't see her name on the chair. I got mad and started pushing her. Her drink spilled all over her. Then she got really mad; she shoved me against the wall, hitting and clawing at me. I managed to grab a handful of hair.

Sibling Relationships

Any of you who have grown up with siblings probably have a rich memory of aggressive, hostile interchanges. But sibling relationships also have many pleasant, caring moments (Volling, 2002; Zukow-Goldring, 2002). Children's sibling relationships include helping, sharing, teaching, fighting, and playing. Children can act as emotional supports, rivals, and communication partners (Carlson, 1995). More than 80 percent of American children have one or more siblings (brothers or sisters). Because there are so many possible sibling combinations, it is difficult to generalize about sibling influences. Among the factors to consider are the number of siblings, the ages of siblings, birth order, age spacing, the sex of siblings, and whether sibling relationships are different from parent-child relationships (Teti, 2001).

Is sibling interaction different from parent-child interaction? There is some evidence that it is. Observations indicate that children interact more positively and in more varied ways with their parents than with their siblings (Baskett & Johnson, 1982). Children also follow their parents' dictates more than those of their siblings, and they behave more negatively and punitively with their siblings than with their parents.

In some instances, siblings may be stronger socializing influences on the child than parents are (Circirelli, 1994). Someone close in age to the child—such as a sibling—may be able to understand the child's problems and communicate more effectively than parents can. In dealing with peers, coping with difficult teachers, and discussing such taboo subjects as sex, siblings may be more influential than parents in the socialization process.

Is sibling interaction the same around the world? In industrialized societies, such as the United States, the delegation of responsibility for younger siblings to older siblings tends to be carried out informally by parents. This is done primarily to give the parents freedom to pursue other activities. However, in nonindustrialized countries, such as Kenya, a much greater degree of importance is attached to the older sibling's role as a caregiver to younger siblings. In industrialized countries, the older sibling's caregiving role is often discretionary; in nonindustrialized countries, it is more obligatory (Circirelli, 1994).

Birth Order

Birth order is a special interest of sibling researchers. When differences related to birth order are found, they usually are explained by variations in interactions with parents and siblings associated with the unique experiences of being in a particular position in the family. This is especially true in the case of the firstborn child (Teti & others, 1993). The oldest child is the only one who does not have to share parental love and affection with other siblings—until another sibling comes along. An infant requires more attention than an older child; this means that the firstborn sibling

*B*ig sisters are the crab grass in the lawn of life.

—CHARLES SCHULZ, "PEANUTS"
American Cartoonist, 20th Century

now gets less attention than before the newborn arrived. Does this result in conflict between parents and the firstborn? In one research study, mothers became more negative, coercive, and restraining and played less with the firstborn following the birth of a second child (Dunn & Kendrick, 1982). Even though a new infant requires more attention from parents than does an older child, an especially intense relationship is often maintained between parents and firstborns throughout the life span. Parents have higher expectations for firstborn children than for later-born children. They put more pressure on them for achievement and responsibility. They also interfere more with their activities (Rothbart, 1971).

Birth order is also associated with variations in sibling relationships. The oldest sibling is expected to exercise self-control and show responsibility in interacting with younger siblings. When the oldest sibling is jealous or hostile, parents often protect the younger sibling. The oldest sibling is more dominant, competent, and powerful than the younger siblings. The oldest sibling is also expected to assist and teach younger siblings. Indeed, researchers have shown that older siblings are both more antagonistic—hitting, kicking, and biting—and more nurturant toward their younger siblings than vice versa (Abramovitch & others, 1986). There is also something unique about same-sex sibling relationships. Aggression and dominance occur more in same-sex relationships than in opposite-sex sibling relationships (Minnett, Vandell, & Santrock, 1983).

Given the differences in family dynamics involved in birth order, it is not surprising that firstborns and later-borns have different characteristics (Zajonc, 2001). Firstborn children are more adult-oriented, helpful, conforming, anxious, and self-controlled than their siblings. Parents give more attention to firstborns, and this is related to firstborns' nurturant behavior (Stanhope & Corter, 1993). Parental demands and high standards established for firstborns result in these children's excelling in academic and professional endeavors. Firstborns are overrepresented in *Who's Who* and Rhodes scholars, for example. However, some of the same pressures placed on firstborns for high achievement may be the reason they also have more guilt, anxiety, and difficulty in coping with stressful situations, as well as higher admission to child guidance clinics.

What is the only child like? The popular conception is that the only child is a "spoiled brat," with such undesirable characteristics as dependency, lack of self-control, and self-centered behavior. But researchers present a more positive portrayal of the only child, who often is achievement-oriented and displays a desirable personality, especially in comparison with later-borns and children from large families (Falbo & Poston, 1993; Jiao, Ji, & Jing, 1996).

So far, our consideration of birth-order effects suggests that birth order might be a strong predictor of behavior. However, an increasing number of family researchers believe that birth order has been overdramatized and overemphasized. The critics argue that, when all of the factors that influence behavior are considered, birth order itself shows limited ability to predict behavior. Consider sibling relationships alone. They vary not only in birth order but also in number of siblings, age of siblings, age spacing of siblings, and sex of siblings.

Consider also the temperament of siblings. page 363 Researchers have found that siblings' temperamental traits ("easy" and "difficult," for example), as well as differential treatment of siblings by parents, influence how siblings get along (Stocker & Dunn, 1991). Siblings with "easy" temperaments who are treated in relatively equal ways by parents tend to get along with each other the best. By contrast, siblings with "difficult" temperaments, or whose parents have given one of them preferential treatment, get along the worst.

Beyond temperament and differential treatment of siblings by parents, think about some of the other important factors in children's lives that influence their behavior beyond birth order. They include heredity, models of competency or incompetency that parents present to children on a daily basis, peer influences, school influences, socioeconomic factors, sociohistorical factors, and cultural variations. When someone says firstborns are always like this but last-borns are always like that, you now know that the person is making overly simplistic statements that do not adequately take into account the complexity of influences on a child's behavior. Keep in mind, though, that although birth order itself may not be a good predictor of children's behavior, sibling relationships and interaction are important dimensions of family processes.

Review and Reflect: Learning Goal 3

3 Identify how siblings influence children's development

REVIEW

- How can sibling relationships be characterized?
- What role does birth order play in children's development?

REFLECT

- If you grew up with a sibling, you likely showed some jealousy of your sibling and vice versa. What can parents do to help children reduce their jealousy toward a sibling?

---

4 FAMILIES AND ADOLESCENTS

Autonomy and Attachment   **Parent-Adolescent Conflict**

Some of the most important issues and questions that need to be raised about family relationships in adolescence are these: What roles do attachment and autonomy play in parent-adolescent relationships? How intense is parent-adolescent conflict?

Autonomy and Attachment

The adolescent's push for autonomy and responsibility puzzles and angers many parents. Parents see their teenager slipping from their grasp. They may have an urge to take stronger control as the adolescent seeks autonomy and responsibility. Heated emotional exchanges may ensue, with either side calling names, making threats, and doing whatever seems necessary to gain control. Parents may seem frustrated because they *expect* their teenager to heed their advice, to want to spend time with the family, and to grow up to do what is right. Most parents anticipate that their teenager will have some difficulty adjusting to the changes that adolescence brings, but few parents can imagine and predict just how strong an adolescent's desires will be to spend time with peers or how much adolescents will want to show that it is they—not their parents—who are responsible for their successes and failures.

Gender differences characterize autonomy-granting in adolescence with boys being given more independence than girls. In one recent study, this was especially true in U.S. families with a traditional gender-role orientation (Bumpus, Crouter, & McHale, 2001).

Cultural differences also characterize adolescent autonomy. In one study, U.S. adolescents sought autonomy earlier than Japanese adolescents (Rothbaum & others, 2000). In the transition to adulthood, Japanese youth are less likely to live outside the home than Americans (Hendry, 1986).

The ability to attain autonomy and gain control over one's behavior in adolescence is acquired through appropriate adult reactions to the adolescent's desire for control (Keener & Boykin, 1996). At the onset of adolescence, the average individual does not have the knowledge to make appropriate or mature decisions in all areas of life. As the adolescent pushes for autonomy, the wise adult relinquishes control in those areas in which the adolescent can make reasonable decisions but continues to guide the adolescent to make reasonable decisions in areas in which the adolescent's knowledge is more limited. Gradually, adolescents acquire the ability to make mature decisions on their own.

Recall from chapter 11, "Emotional Development," that one of the most widely used concepts regarding the socioemotional development of infants is the concept of secure or insecure attachment. ◄ **page 370** In the past decade, developmentalists also have begun to explore the role of secure attachment, and related concepts such as connectedness to parents, in adolescence (Cassidy & Shaver, 1999). They believe that secure attachment to parents in adolescence may facilitate the adolescent's social competence and well-being, as reflected in such characteristics as self-esteem, emotional adjustment, and physical health (Cooper, Shaver, & Collins, 1998). In the research of Joseph Allen and his colleagues (Allen & Hauser, 1994; Allen & others, 2002; Allen & others, 2003), securely attached adolescents had somewhat lower probabilities of engaging in problem behaviors.

Many studies that assess secure and insecure attachment in adolescence use the Adult Attachment Interview (AAI) (George, Main, & Kaplan, 1984). This measure examines an individual's memories of significant attachment relationships. Based on the responses to questions on the AAI, individuals are classified as *secure-autonomous* (which corresponds to secure attachment in infancy) or one of these three insecure categories:

- **Dismissing/avoidant attachment** is an insecure category in which individuals deemphasize the importance of attachment. This category is associated with consistent experiences of the rejection of attachment needs by caregivers. One possible outcome of dismissing/avoidant attachment is that parents and adolescents may mutually distance themselves from each other, which lessens parents' influence. In one study, dismissing/avoidant attachment was related to violent and aggressive behavior on the part of the adolescent.
- **Preoccupied/ambivalent attachment** is an insecure attachment category in which adolescents are hypertuned to attachment experiences. This is thought to occur mainly when parents are inconsistently available to the adolescent. This may result in a high degree of attachment-seeking behavior, mixed with angry feelings. Conflict between parents and adolescents in this type of attachment may be too high for healthy development.
- **Unresolved/disorganized attachment** is an insecure category in which the adolescent has an unusually high level of fear and is disoriented. This may result from such traumatic experiences as a parent's death or abuse by parents.

Secure attachment, or connectedness to parents, promotes competent peer relations and positive, close relationships outside of the family (Cassidy, 1999). In one investigation in which attachment to parents and peers was assessed, adolescents who were securely attached to parents also were securely attached to peers; those who were insecurely attached to parents also were more likely to be insecurely attached to peers (Armsden & Greenberg, 1984). There are times when adolescents reject closeness, connection, and attachment to their parents as they assert their ability to make decisions and to develop an identity. But, for the most part, the worlds of parents and peers are coordinated and connected, not uncoordinated and disconnected.

Parent-Adolescent Conflict

While attachment to parents remains strong during adolescence, the connectedness is not always smooth. Early adolescence is a time when conflict with parents escalates beyond childhood levels (Riesch & others, 2003). This increase may be due to a number of factors: the biological changes of puberty, cognitive changes involving increased idealism and logical reasoning, social changes focused on independence

Parents' and Adolescents' Expectations

Parenting Adolescents

Exploring Parent-Adolescent Relationships

dismissing/avoidant attachment An insecure attachment category in which individuals deemphasize the importance of attachment. This category is associated with consistent experiences of rejection of attachment needs by caregivers.

preoccupied/ambivalent attachment An insecure attachment category in which adolescents are hypertuned to attachment experiences. This is thought to mainly occur because parents are inconsistently available to the adolescent.

unresolved/disorganized attachment An insecure category in which the adolescent has an unusually high level of fear and is disoriented. This may result from such traumatic experiences as a parent's death or abuse by parents.

and identity, maturational changes in parents, and expectations that are violated by parents and adolescents. The adolescent compares her parents to an ideal standard and then criticizes their flaws. A 13-year-old girl tells her mother, "That is the tackiest-looking dress I have ever seen. Nobody would be caught dead wearing that." The adolescent demands logical explanations for comments and discipline. A 14-year-old boy tells his mother, "What do you mean I have to be home at 10 P.M. because it's the way we do things around here? Why do we do things around here that way? It doesn't make sense to me."

Many parents see their adolescent changing from a compliant child to someone who is noncompliant, oppositional, and resistant to parental standards. When this happens, parents tend to clamp down and put more pressure on the adolescent to conform to parental standards. Parents often expect their adolescents to become mature adults overnight, instead of understanding that the journey takes 10 to 15 years. Parents who recognize that this transition takes time handle their youth more competently and calmly than those who demand immediate conformity to adult standards. The opposite tactic—letting adolescents do as they please without supervision—is also unwise.

In one study, Reed Larson and Marsye Richards (1994) had mothers, fathers, and adolescents carry electronic pagers for a week and report their activities and emotions at random times. The result was a portrait of the hour-by-hour emotional realities lived by families with adolescents. Differences between the fast-paced daily realities lived by each family member created considerable potential for misunderstanding and conflict. Because each family member was often attending to different priorities, needs, and stressors, their realities were often out of sync. Even when they wanted to share leisure activity, their interests were at odds. One father said that his wife liked to shop, his daughter liked to play video games, and he liked to stay home. Although the main theme of this work was the hazards of contemporary life, some families with adolescents were buoyant, and their lives were coordinated.

Conflict with parents increases in early adolescence, but it does not reach the tumultuous proportions G. Stanley Hall envisioned at the beginning of the twentieth century (Holmbeck, 1996; Steinberg & Silk, 2002). Rather, much of the conflict involves the everyday events of family life, such as keeping a bedroom clean, dressing neatly, getting home by a certain time, and not talking forever on the phone. The conflicts rarely involve major dilemmas, such as drugs and delinquency.

It is not unusual to hear parents of young adolescents ask, "Is it ever going to get better?" Things usually do get better as adolescents move from early to late adolescence. Conflict with parents often escalates during early adolescence, remains somewhat stable during the high school years, and then lessens as the adolescent reaches 17 to 20 years of age. Parent-adolescent relationships become more positive if adolescents go away to college than if they stay at home and go to college (Sullivan & Sullivan, 1980).

The everyday conflicts that characterize parent-adolescent relationships may actually serve a positive developmental function. These minor disputes and negotiations facilitate the adolescent's transition from being dependent on parents to becoming an autonomous individual. For example, in one study, adolescents who expressed disagreement with their parents explored identity development more actively than did adolescents who did not express disagreement with their parents (Cooper & others, 1982). One way for parents to cope with the adolescent's push for independence and identity is to recognize that adolescence is a 10- to 15-year transitional period in the journey to adulthood, rather than an overnight accomplishment. Recognizing that conflict and negotiation can serve a positive developmental function can tone down parental hostility too. Understanding parent-adolescent conflict, though, is not simple (Conger & Ge, 1999).

In sum, the old model of parent-adolescent relationships suggested that as adolescents mature they detach themselves from parents and move into a world of autonomy apart from parents. The old model also suggested that parent-adolescent

> When I was a boy of 14, my father was so ignorant I could hardly stand to have the man around. But when I got to be 21, I was astonished at how much he had learnt in 7 years.
>
> —MARK TWAIN
> *American Writer and Humorist, 19th Century*

Old Model	New Model
Autonomy, detachment from parents; parent and peer worlds are isolated	Attachment and autonomy; parents are important support systems and attachment figures; adolescent-parent and adolescent-peer worlds have some important connections
Intense, stressful conflict throughout adolescence; parent-adolescent relationships are filled with storm and stress on virtually a daily basis	Moderate parent-adolescent conflict common and can serve a positive developmental function; conflict greater in early adolescence, especially during the apex of puberty

FIGURE 15.4 Old and New Models of Parent-Adolescent Relationships

Adolescence is like cactus.
—ANAÏS NIN
French Novelist, 20th Century

www.mhhe.com/santrockcd10

Parent-Adolescent Conflict

Families as Asset Builders

Prevention of Adolescent Problems

Reengaging Families with Adolescents

conflict is intense and stressful throughout adolescence. The new model emphasizes that parents serve as important attachment figures and support systems as adolescents explore a wider, more complex social world. The new model also emphasizes that, in most families, parent-adolescent conflict is moderate rather than severe and that the everyday negotiations and minor disputes are normal and can serve the positive developmental function of helping the adolescent make the transition from childhood dependency to adult independence (see figure 15.4).

Still, a high degree of conflict characterizes some parent-adolescent relationships. One estimate of the proportion of parents and adolescents who engage in prolonged, intense, repeated, unhealthy conflict is about one in five families (Montemayor, 1982). While this figure represents a minority of adolescents, it indicates that 4 to 5 million American families encounter serious, highly stressful parent-adolescent conflict. And this prolonged, intense conflict is associated with a number of adolescent problems—movement out of the home, juvenile delinquency, school dropout, pregnancy and early marriage, membership in religious cults, and drug abuse (Brook & others, 1990).

We have seen that parents play very important roles in adolescent development. In the National Longitudinal Study on Adolescent Health (Council of Economic Advisors, 2000) of more than 12,000 adolescents, those who did not eat dinner with a parent five or more days a week had dramatically higher rates of smoking, drinking, marijuana use, getting into fights, and early initiation of sexual activity. In another recent study, parents who played an active role in monitoring and guiding their adolescents' development were more likely to have adolescents with positive peer relations and lower drug use than parents who had a less active role (Mounts, 2002).

Review and Reflect: Learning Goal 4

4 Summarize the changes in families with adolescents

REVIEW

- What roles do autonomy and attachment play in parent-adolescent relationships?
- How extensive is parent-adolescent conflict? How does parent-adolescent conflict affect adolescent development?

REFLECT

- What was the nature of your relationship with your parents during middle school and high school? Has your relationship with your parents changed since then? Does it involve less conflict? What do you think are the most important characteristics of a competent parent of adolescents?

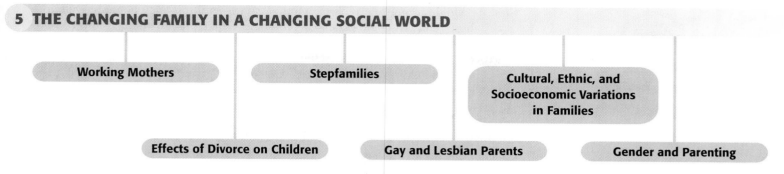

5 THE CHANGING FAMILY IN A CHANGING SOCIAL WORLD

- Working Mothers
- Stepfamilies
- Cultural, Ethnic, and Socioeconomic Variations in Families
- Effects of Divorce on Children
- Gay and Lesbian Parents
- Gender and Parenting

More children are growing up in a greater variety of family structures than ever before. Many mothers spend the greatest part of their day away from their children, even their infants. More than one of every two mothers with a child under the age of 5 is in the labor force; more than two of every three with a child from 6 to 17 years of age is. And the increasing number of children growing up in single-parent families is staggering. As shown in figure 15.5, the United States has the highest percentage of single-parent families, compared with virtually all other countries.

Working Mothers

Because household operations have become more efficient and family size has decreased in America, it is not certain that children with mothers working outside the home actually receive less attention than children in the past whose mothers were not employed. Outside employment—at least for mothers with school-age children—may simply be filling time previously taken up by added household burdens and more children. It also cannot be assumed that, if the mother did not go to work, the child would benefit from the time freed up by streamlined household operations and smaller families. Mothering does not always have a positive effect on the child. The educated, nonworking mother may overinvest her energies in her children. This can foster an excess of worry and discourage the child's independence. In such situations, the mother may give more parenting than the child can profitably handle.

Lois Hoffman (1989; Hoffman & Youngblade, 1999) believes that maternal employment is a part of modern life. It is not an aberrant aspect of it but a response to other social changes. It meets needs that cannot be met by the previous family ideal of a full-time mother and homemaker. Not only does it meet the parent's needs, but in many ways it may be a pattern better suited to socializing children for the adult roles they will occupy. This is especially true for daughters, but it is also true for sons. The broader range of emotions and skills that each parent presents is more consistent with this adult role. Just as his father shares the breadwinning role

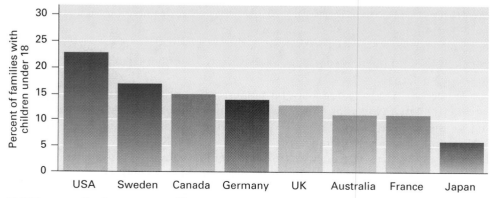

FIGURE 15.5 Single-Parent Families in Different Countries

Working Mothers

Family and the Workplace

and the child-rearing role with his mother, so the son, too, may be more willing to share these roles. The rigid gender stereotyping perpetuated by the divisions of labor in the traditional family is not appropriate for the demands that will be made on children of either sex as adults. The needs of the growing child require the mother to loosen her hold on the child. This task may be easier for the working woman, whose job is an additional source of identity and self-esteem.

Overall, in most studies, researchers have found no detrimental effects of maternal employment on children's development (Gottfried, Gottfried, & Bathurst, 2002; Hoffman & Youngblade, 1999). In specific circumstances, though, work can produce positive or negative effects on parenting. In some families, work-related stress can spill over and harm parenting. In others, a greater sense of overall well-being produced by work can lead to more positive parenting.

Further, researchers are consistently finding when a child's mother works in the first year of life it can have a negative effect on the child's later development (Belsky & Eggebeen, 1991; Hill & others, 2001). For example, a recent major longitudinal study found that the 3-year-old children of mothers who went to work before the children were 9 months old had poorer cognitive outcomes than 3-year-old children who had stayed at home with their mothers in the first nine months of the child's life (Brooks-Gunn, Han, & Waldfogel, 2002). The negative effects of working mothers were less pronounced when the mothers worked less than 30 hours a week, the mothers were more sensitive (responsive and comforting) in their caregiving, and the child care the children received outside the home was higher in quality. Thus, when mothers do go back to work in the infant's first year of life, it clearly is important that they consider how many hours they are going to work, be sensitive in their caregiving, and get the best child care they can afford.

A subset of children from working-mother families deserves further scrutiny: latchkey children. These children typically do not see their parents from the time they leave for school in the morning until about 6 or 7 P.M. They are called "latchkey" children because they are given the key to their home, take the key to school, and then use it to let themselves into the home while their parents are still at work. Latchkey children are largely unsupervised for two to four hours a day during each school week. During the summer months, they might be unsupervised for entire days, five days a week.

In one study, more than 1,500 latchkey children were interviewed (Long & Long, 1983). A slight majority of these children had had negative latchkey experiences. Some latchkey children may grow up too fast, hurried by the responsibilities placed on them. How do latchkey children handle the lack of limits and structure during the latchkey hours? Without limits and parental supervision, latchkey children find their way into trouble more easily, possibly stealing, vandalizing, or abusing a sibling. Ninety percent of the juvenile delinquents in Montgomery County, Maryland, are latchkey children. Joan Lipsitz (1983), in testifying before the Select Committee on Children, Youth, and Families, called the lack of adult supervision of children in the after-school hours one of today's major problems. Lipsitz called it the "three-to-six-o'clock problem" because it was during this time that the Center for Early Adolescence in North Carolina, when Lipsitz was director, experienced a peak of referrals for clinical help. And, in a 1987 national poll, teachers rated the latchkey children phenomenon the number one reason that children have problems in schools (Harris, 1987).

While latchkey children may be vulnerable to problems, the experiences of latchkey children vary enormously, as do the experiences of all children with working mothers (Belle, 1999). Parents need to give special attention to the ways in which their latchkey children's lives can be effectively monitored. Variations in latchkey experiences suggest that parental monitoring and authoritative parenting help the children cope more effectively with latchkey experiences, especially in resisting peer pressure (Galambos & Maggs, 1989; Steinberg, 1986). In one recent study of children in the after-school hours, unsupervised peer contact, lack of neighborhood safety, and low monitoring were linked with externalizing problems (such as acting out problems, delinquency) in children (Pettit & others, 1999). In another study, attending a formal after-school program that included academic, recreational, and remedial activities was associated with better academic achievement and social adjustment, in comparison with other types of after-school care (such as informal adult supervision or self-care) (Posner & Vandell, 1994). Researchers and policymakers recommend that after-school programs have warm and supportive staff, a flexible and relaxed schedule, multiple activities, and opportunities for positive interactions with staff and peers (Vandell & Pierce, 1999).

Effects of Divorce on Children

Divorce rates have been changing rather dramatically in the United States and many countries around the world. The U.S. divorce rate increased dramatically in the 1960s and 1970s but has declined since the 1980s. By comparison, the divorce rate in Japan increased in the 1990s (Ministry of Health, Education, and Welfare, 2002). However, the divorce rate in the United States is still much higher than in Japan and higher than most other countries as well. It is estimated that 40 percent of children born to married parents in the United States will experience their parents' divorce (Hetherington & Stanley-Hagan, 2002).

These are the questions that we will explore that focus on the effects of divorce: Are children better adjusted in intact, never-divorced families than in divorced families? Should parents stay together for the sake of their children? How much do family processes matter in divorced families? What factors are involved in the child's individual risk and vulnerability in a divorced family? What role does socioeconomic status play in the lives of children in divorced families?

Are Children Better Adjusted in Intact, Never-Divorced Families Than in Divorced Families?
Most researchers agree that children from divorced families show poorer adjustment than their counterparts in nondivorced families (Amato & Keith, 1991; Hetherington and Stanley-Hagan, 2002) (see figure 15.6). Those that have experienced multiple divorces are at greater risk.

Children in divorced families are more likely than children in nondivorced families to have academic problems, to show externalized problems (such as acting out and delinquency) and internalized problems (such as anxiety and depression), to be less socially responsible, to have less competent intimate relationships, to drop out of school, to become sexually active at an early age, to take drugs, to associate with antisocial peers, and to have low self-esteem (Conger & Chao, 1996). Nonetheless, keep in mind that a majority of children in divorced families (about 75 percent) do not have significant adjustment problems (Buchanan, 2001).

Should Parents Stay Together for the Sake of Their Children?
Whether parents should stay in an unhappy or conflicted marriage for the sake of their children is one of the most commonly asked questions about divorce, according to leading divorce researcher E. Mavis Hetherington (1999, 2000). If the stresses and disruptions in family relationships associated with an unhappy, conflictual marriage that erode the well-being of children are reduced by the move to a divorced, single-parent family, divorce may be advantageous. However, if the diminished resources and increased risks associated with divorce also are accompanied by inept parenting and sustained or increased conflict, not only between the divorced couple but also between the parents, children, and siblings, the best choice for the children would be for an unhappy marriage to be retained (Hetherington & Stanley-Hagan, 2002). These are "ifs," and it is difficult to determine how these will play out when parents either remain together in an acrimonious marriage or become divorced.

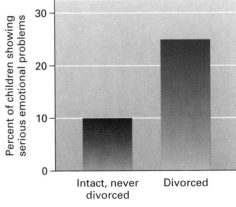

FIGURE 15.6 Divorce and Children's Emotional Problems

In Hetherington's research, 25 percent of children from divorced families showed serious emotional problems compared to only 10 percent of children from intact, never-divorced families. However, keep in mind that a substantial majority (75 percent) of the children from divorced families did not show serious emotional problems.

How Much Do Family Processes Matter in Divorced Families? Family processes matter a lot (Emery & others, 2001; Hetherington & Stanley-Hagan, 2002; Kelly, 2001). When divorced parents' relationship with each other is harmonious and when they use authoritative parenting, the adjustment of children improves (Hetherington, Bridges, & Insabella, 1998). A number of researchers have shown that a disequilibrium, which includes diminished parenting skills, occurs in the year following the divorce but that, by two years after the divorce, restabilization has occurred and parenting skills have improved (Hetherington, 1989). About one-fourth to one-third of children in divorced families, compared with 10 percent in nondivorced families, become disengaged from their families, spending as little time as possible at home and in interaction with family members (Hetherington & Jodl, 1994). This disengagement is higher for boys than girls in divorced families. However, if there is a caring adult outside the home, such as a mentor, the disengagement may be a positive solution to a disrupted, conflicted family circumstance.

What Factors Are Involved in the Child's Individual Risk and Vulnerabilty in a Divorced Family? Among the factors involved in the child's risk and vulnerability are the child's adjustment prior to the divorce, as well as the child's personality and temperament, developmental status, gender, and custody situation (Hetherington & Stanley-Hagan, 2002). Children whose parents later divorce show poorer adjustment before the breakup (Amato & Booth, 1996). When antecedent levels of problem behaviors are controlled, differences in the adjustment of children in divorced and nondivorced families are reduced (Cherlin & others, 1991).

Personality and temperament also play a role in children's adjustment in divorced families. Children who are socially mature and responsible, who show few behavioral problems, and who have an easy temperament are better able to cope with their parents' divorce. Children with a difficult temperament often have problems in coping with their parents' divorce (Hetherington, 1999).

Earlier studies reported gender differences in response to divorce, with divorce being more negative for boys than for girls in mother-custody families. However, more recent studies have shown that gender differences are less pronounced and consistent than was previously believed. Some of the inconsistency may be due to the increase in father custody, joint custody, and increased involvement of noncustodial fathers, especially in their sons' lives. One recent analysis of studies found that children in joint-custody families were better adjusted than children in sole-custody families (Bauserman, 2002). Some studies have shown that boys adjust better in father-custody families, girls in mother-custody families (Maccoby & Mnookin, 1992; Santrock & Warshak, 1979).

What Role Does Socioeconomic Status Play in the Lives of Children in Divorced Families? Custodial mothers experience the loss of about one-fourth to one-half of their predivorce income, in comparison with a loss of only one-tenth by custodial fathers (Emery, 1994). This income loss for divorced mothers is accompanied by increased workloads, high rates of job instability, and residential moves to less desirable neighborhoods with inferior schools.

Stepfamilies

Not only are parents divorcing more, they are also getting remarried more (Dunn & others, 2001). The number of remarriages involving children has grown steadily in recent years. Also, divorces occur at a 10 percent higher rate in remarriages than in first marriages (Cherlin & Furstenberg, 1994). As a result of their parents' successive marital transitions, about half of all children whose parents divorce will have a stepparent within four years of parental separation.

In some cases, the stepfamily may have been preceded by a circumstance in which the spouse died. However, by far the largest number of stepfamilies are preceded by divorce rather than death.

Children and Divorce
Divorce and Family Ties
Divorce Resources
Father Custody

Three common types of stepfamily structure are (1) stepfather, (2) stepmother, and (3) blended or complex. In stepfather families, the mother typically had custody of the children and became remarried, introducing a stepfather into her children's lives. In stepmother families, the father usually had custody and became remarried, introducing a stepmother into his children's lives. In a blended or complex stepfamily, both parents bring children from previous marriages to live in the newly formed stepfamily.

Researchers have found that children's relationships with custodial parents (mothers in stepfather families, fathers in stepmother families) are often better than with stepparents (Santrock, Sitterle, & Warshak, 1988). Also, children in simple families (stepmother, stepfather) often show better adjustment than their counterparts in complex (blended) families (Anderson & others, 1999; Hetherington & Kelly, 2002).

As in divorced families, children in stepfamilies show more adjustment problems than children in nondivorced families (Hetherington, Bridges, & Insabella, 1998; Hetherington & Kelly, 2002). The adjustment problems are similar to those in divorced children—academic problems and lower self-esteem, for example (Anderson & others, 1999). However, as with divorced children, it is important to recognize that a majority of children in stepfamilies do not have problems. In one recent analysis, 25 percent of children from stepfamilies showed adjustment problems compared to 10 percent in intact, never-divorced families (Hetherington & Kelly, 2002; Hetherington & Stanley-Hagan, 2002).

In terms of the age of the child, researchers have found that early adolescence is an especially difficult time for the formation of a stepfamily (Anderson & others, 1999). This may occur because the stepfamily circumstances exacerbate normal adolescent concerns about identity, sexuality, and autonomy.

How does living in a stepfamily influence a child's development?

Stepfamilies
Stepfamily Resources
Stepfamily Support

Gay and Lesbian Parents

Increasingly, gay and lesbian couples are creating families that include children. This is controversial to many heterosexual individuals who view a gay or lesbian family as damaging to the development of a child. Approximately 20 percent of lesbians and 10 percent of gay men are parents, most of whom have children from a heterosexual marriage that ended in a divorce (Patterson, 2002). There may be more than 1 million gay and lesbian parents in the United States today.

Diversity Among Lesbian Mothers, Gay Fathers, and Their Children
An important aspect of lesbian and gay families with children is the sexual identity of parents at the time of a child's birth or adoption (Patterson, 2002). The largest group of children with lesbian and gay parents are likely those who were born in the context of heterosexual relationships with one or both parents only later identifying themselves as gay or lesbian. Gay and lesbian parents may be single or they may have same-gender partners. In addition, lesbians and gay men are increasingly choosing parenthood through donor insemination and surrogates. Custodial arrangements also may vary.

Another issue focuses on custody arrangements for children. Many lesbian mothers and gay fathers have lost custody of their children to heterosexual spouses following divorce. For this reason, many lesbian mothers and gay fathers are noncustodial parents.

Effects on Children of Having Lesbian Mothers and Gay Fathers
Researchers have found few differences in children growing up with lesbian mothers or gay fathers and children growing up with heterosexual parents (Patterson, 2002). For example, children growing up in gay or lesbian families are just as popular with their peers, and there are no differences in the adjustment and mental health of children living in these families when they are compared with children in

What are the research findings regarding the development and psychological well-being of children raised by gay and lesbian couples?

Family Diversity

heterosexual families (Hyde & DeLamater, 2002). Also, the overwhelming majority of children growing up in a gay or lesbian family have a heterosexual orientation (Tasker & Golombok, 1997).

Cultural, Ethnic, and Socioeconomic Variations in Families

Parenting can be influenced by culture, ethnicity, and socioeconomic status. What have cross-cultural studies found about parenting?

Cross-Cultural Studies Cultures vary on a number of issues involving families, such as what the father's role in the family should be, the extent to which support systems are available to families, and the ways in which children should be disciplined (Harkness & Super, 2002). Although there are cross-cultural variations in parenting (Whiting & Edwards, 1988), in one study of parenting behavior in 186 cultures around the world, the most common pattern was a warm and controlling style, one that was neither permissive nor restrictive (Rohner & Rohner, 1981). The investigators commented that the majority of cultures have discovered, over many centuries, a "truth" that only recently emerged in the Western world—namely, that children's healthy social development is most effectively promoted by love and at least some moderate parental control.

Nonetheless, in some countries, authoritarian parenting continues to be widely practiced. In the Arab world, families today are still very authoritarian and dominated by the father's rule (Booth, 2002). In Arab countries, children are taught strict codes of conduct and family loyalty. In one recent study, Chinese mothers of preschool children reported that they used more physical coercion, more encouragement of modesty, more shaming/love withdrawal, less warmth, and less democratic participation than U.S. mothers of preschool children (Wu & others, in press).

In many countries around the world, there are trends toward greater family mobility, migration to urban areas, family members working in distant cities or countries, smaller families, fewer extended-family households, and increases in the mother's employment (Brown & Larson, 2002; Larson, Brown, & Mortimer, 2003). These trends can change the resources that are available to children. For example, in the future there may be fewer extended-family members available and decreased support and guidance for children. Also, smaller families may produce more openness and communication between parents and children.

Ethnicity Families within different ethnic groups in the United States differ in their size, structure, composition, reliance on kinships networks, and levels of income and education (Coll & Pachter, 2002; Parke & Buriel, 1998). Large and extended families are more common among minority groups than among the White majority. For example, 19 percent of Latino families have three or more children, compared with 14 percent of African American and 10 percent of White families. African American and Latino children interact more with grandparents, aunts, uncles, cousins, and more-distant relatives than do White children.

Single-parent families are more common among African Americans and Latinos than among White Americans (Weinraub, Horvath, & Gringlas, 2002). In comparison with two-parent households, single parents often have more limited resources of time, money, and energy (Gyamfi, Brooks-Gunn, & Jackson, 2001). Ethnic minority parents also are less educated and more likely to live in low-income circumstances than their White counterparts. Still, many impoverished ethnic minority families manage to find ways to raise competent children (Coll & Pachter, 2002).

Some aspects of home life can help protect ethnic minority children from injustice. The community and the family can filter out destructive racist messages, and parents can present alternative frames of reference to those presented by the majority. The extended family also can serve as an important buffer to stress (McAdoo,

2002). To read further about ethnic minority parenting, see the Explorations in Child Development box.

Socioeconomic Status   In America and most Western cultures, differences have been found in child rearing among different socioeconomic-status (SES) groups (Hoff, Laursen, & Tardif, 2002):

- Lower-SES parents (1) are more concerned that their children conform to society's expectations, (2) create a home atmosphere in which it is clear that parents have authority over children, (3) use physical punishment more in disciplining their children, and (4) are more directive and less conversational with their children.
- Higher-SES parents (1) are more concerned with developing children's initiative and delay of gratification, (2) create a home atmosphere in which children are more nearly equal participants and in which rules are discussed rather than being laid out in an authoritarian manner, (3) are less likely to use physical punishment, and (4) are less directive and more conversational with their children.

There also are socioeconomic differences in the way that parents think about education (Hoff, Laursen, & Tardif, 2002; Magnuson & Duncan, 2002). Middle- and upper-income parents more often think of education as something that should be mutually encouraged by parents and teachers. By contrast, low-income parents are more likely to view education as the teacher's job. Thus, increased school-family linkages especially can benefit students from low-income families.

Gender and Parenting

What is the mother's role in the family? The father's role? How can mothers and fathers become cooperative, effective partners in parenting?

What are some characteristics of families within different ethnic groups?

The Mother's Role   What do you think of when you hear the word *motherhood*? If you are like most people, you associate motherhood with a number of powerful images (Barnard & Solchany, 2002). For example, you might have positive images of mothers such as warm, selfless, dutiful, and tolerant (Matlin, 1993). And while most women expect that motherhood will be happy and fulfilling, the reality is that motherhood has been accorded relatively low prestige in our society. When stacked up against money, power, and achievement, motherhood unfortunately doesn't fare too well, and mothers rarely receive the appreciation they warrant. When children don't succeed or develop problems, our society has had a tendency to attribute the lack of success or the development of problems to a single source—mothers. One of psychology's most important lessons is that behavior is multiply determined. So it is with children's development—when development goes awry, mothers are not the single cause of the problems even though our society stereotypes them in this way.

The reality of motherhood today is that while fathers have increased their child-rearing responsibilities somewhat, the main responsibility for children in many families still falls on the mother's shoulders (Barnard & Martell, 1995). Mothers do far more family work than fathers do—two to three times more (Thompson & Walker, 1989). A few "exceptional" men do as much family work as their wives; in one

Acculturation and Ethnic Minority Parenting

Cynthia Garcia Coll and Lee Pachter (2002) recently described how the cultural context influences ethnic minority parenting. A summary of their views is presented here.

Ethnic minority children and their parents are expected to transcend their own cultural background and incorporate aspects of the dominant culture into their development. Young children's expectations and opportunities for acculturation (the process through which cultural adaptation and change occurs) are mainly influenced by their parents and the extended-family system. The level of family acculturation can affect parenting style by influencing expectations for children's development, parent-child interactions, and the role of the extended family. The appropriateness of caregiving practices may involve conflict or confusion between less-acculturated and more-acculturated family members. For example, in one study, the level of acculturation and maternal education were the strongest predictors of maternal-infant interaction patterns in Latino families (Perez-Febles, 1992).

In early childhood, the family's level of acculturation continues to influence caregiving practices and important decisions about day care and early childhood education. In child-care centers, school, church, and other community settings, ethnic minority children learn about the dominant culture's values and may be expected to adapt to unfamiliar cultural norms (such as being on the winning team, expressing emotions, and being responsible for one's self). For example, an African American mother might prefer to leave her children with extended-family members while she is at work because historically this has been seen as the best way to cope with an absent mother. However, this well-intentioned, culturally appropriate decision might place the child at an educational and social disadvantage relative to other children of the same age who benefit from preschool experiences that support the transition into the elementary school years.

In middle and late childhood and adolescence, disparity between the acculturation of children, their parents, and the extended family can become magnified. In adolescence, individuals often make decisions about their acculturation status more independently from their family. When immigrant adolescents choose to adopt the values of the dominant U.S. culture (such as unchaperoned dating), they often clash with parents and extended-family members who have more traditional values.

It is important to recognize the complexity and individual variation in the acculturative aspects of ethnic minority parenting. This complexity and variation involve the generation of the family members, the recency of their migration, their socioeconomic status, national origin, and many aspects of the social context of the dominant culture in which they now live (such as racial attitudes, quality of schooling, and community support groups).

study the figure was 10 percent of the men (Berk, 1985). Not only do women do more family work than men, the family work most women do is unrelenting, repetitive, and routine, often involving cleaning, cooking, child care, shopping, laundry, and straightening up. The family work most men do is infrequent, irregular, and nonroutine, often involving household repairs, taking out the garbage, and yard work. Women report that they often have to do several tasks at once, which helps to explain why they find domestic work less relaxing and more stressful than men do (Shaw, 1988).

Because family work is intertwined with love and embedded in family relations, it has complex and contradictory meanings (Villani, 1997). Many women feel that family tasks are mindless but essential. They usually enjoy tending to the needs of their loved ones and keeping the family going, even if they do not find the activities themselves enjoyable and fulfilling. Family work is both positive and negative for women. They are unsupervised and rarely criticized, they plan and control their own work, and they have only their own standards to meet. However, women's family work is often worrisome, tiresome, menial, repetitive, isolating, unfinished, inescapable, and often unappreciated. It is not surprising that men report that they are more satisfied with their marriage than women do.

In sum, the role of the mother brings with it benefits as well as limitations. Although motherhood is not enough to fill most women's entire lives, for most mothers, it is one of the most meaningful experiences in their lives (Hoffnung, 1984).

The Father's Role   The father's role has undergone major changes (Day & Lamb, 2003; Lamb, 1997; Parke, 2002). During the colonial period in America, fathers were primarily responsible for moral teaching. Fathers provided guidance and values, especially through religion. With the Industrial Revolution, the father's role changed;

he gained the responsibility as the breadwinner, a role that continued through the Great Depression. By the end of World War II, another role for fathers emerged, that of being a gender-role model. Although being a breadwinner and moral guardian continued to be important father roles, attention shifted to his role as a male, especially for sons. Then, in the 1970s, the current interest in the father as an active, nurturant, caregiving parent emerged. Rather than being responsible only for the discipline and control of older children and for providing the family's economic base, the father now is being evaluated in terms of his active, nurturant involvement with his children (Day & Lamb, 2003; Perry-Jenkins, Payne, & Hendricks, 1999).

Amount of Father Involvement   How much time do children spend with fathers? In one U.S. study, a nationally representative sample of more than 1,700 children up to 12 years of age spent an average of 2.5 hours a day with their fathers on weekdays and 6.2 hours a day on weekends (Yeung & others, 2001). For about half that time, fathers are directly engaged with their children—playing, eating, shopping, watching TV, or working together around the house. The rest of the time they are nearby or available to their children if needed. In this study, mothers still shouldered the lion's share of parenting, especially on weekdays (see figure 15.7).

Research conducted in the 1970s suggested that fathers spent about one-third as much time with their children as mothers did. In the early 1990s, that proportion had jumped to approximately 43 percent. In the more recent study just mentioned, fathers spent about 65 percent as much time with children as mothers did on weekdays and about 87 percent as much time as mothers did on weekends (Yeung & others, 2001).

In the study just described, the entire sample was drawn from intact, nondivorced families (Yeung & others, 2001). Other studies that include mother-custody single-parent families often find that fathers spend less time with children. For example, a typical finding is that American fathers spend about an average of 45 minutes a day caring for children by themselves.

Family responsibility was a major theme of the Million Man March in Washington, D.C., in 1995. Men today appear to be better fathers—when they are

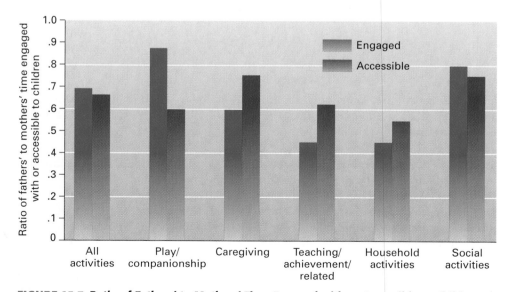

FIGURE 15.7 Ratio of Fathers' to Mothers' Time Engaged with or Accessible to Children on Weekdays

Note: A value of 1 indicates an equal contribution by mothers and fathers, value less than 1 a greater contribution by mothers. *Engaged* refers to doing an activity with the child. *Accessible* refers to the time a father is available to the child but not directly involved with him or her.

Children can significantly benefit from interaction with a caring, accessible, and dependable father who fosters a sense of trust and confidence.

around. However, too many children growing up today see little of their fathers. In 1994, 16.3 million children in the United States were living with their mothers. Forty percent of these children had not seen their father in the past year.

Impact of Fathering on Men Themselves   Variations in fathering have implications for men themselves (Parke, 2002). There typically is a decline in marital satisfaction, especially on the part of men, when a child is born (Belsky & Pensky, 1988). This decline may occur for a number of reasons, such as increased financial strain, physical demands of child care, restrictions of parenthood, and the emotional demands of new family responsibilities.

In terms of self-identity, a longitudinal study found that fatherhood was linked to men's ability to understand themselves, to understand others sympathetically, and to integrate their own feelings (Heath, 1977). Other researchers have found that involved fathering is related in positive ways to other aspects of men's lives, such as being a good spouse, a good citizen, and participating in neighborhood and community activities (Snarey, 1993).

In sum, although having a child often produces an initial decline in marital satisfaction on the part of fathers, over time involved fathering has positive effects on men's self-identity, relationship with a spouse, and community involvement.

Influence of Fathering on Children's Development Researchers have found that fathers who use an authoritative parenting style are more likely to have children with fewer externalized problems (such as acting out or being highly aggressive) and internalized problems (such as anxiety or depression) (Marsiglio & others, 2000). The positive effects of paternal involvement are not confined to childhood. One longitudinal study found that fathers' child-rearing involvement at age 5 was the strongest predictor of empathy for both men and women at 31 years of age (Koestner, Franz, & Weinberger, 1990). In further study, at age 41, men and women with better social relationships (marriage quality and extrafamilial ties—such as friendships) had experienced more paternal warmth as children (Franz, McClelland, & Weinberger, 1991).

Coparenting A dramatic increase in research on coparenting has occurred in the last two decades. The organizing theme of this research is that poor coordination, active undermining and disparagement of the other parent, lack of cooperation and warmth, and disconnection by one parenting partner—either alone or in combination with overinvolvement by the other—are conditions that place children at developmental risk (McHale & others, 2002). By contrast, parental solidarity, cooperation, and warmth show clear ties to children's prosocial behavior and competence in peer relations. For example in one study, 4-year-old children from families characterized by low levels of mutuality and support in coparenting were more likely than their classmates to show difficulties in social adjustment when observed on the playground (McHale, Johnson, & Sinclair, 1999).

When parents show cooperation, mutual respect, balanced communication, and attunement to each other's needs, this helps the child to develop positive attitudes toward both males and females (Biller, 1993; Tamis-Lemonda & Cabrera, 1999). It is much easier for working parents to cope with changing family circumstances when the mother and the father cooperate and equitably share child-rearing responsibilities. Mothers feel less stress and have more positive attitudes toward their husbands when the husband is a supportive partner.

Fathering
The Fatherhood Project
Online Resources for Fathers

Review and Reflect: Learning Goal 5

5 Characterize the changing family in a changing social world

REVIEW

- How are children influenced by working mothers?
- How does divorce affect children's development?
- What are the effects of a stepfamily on children's development?
- How do lesbian mothers and gay fathers influence children's development?
- How do culture, ethnicity, and socioeconomic status influence children's development in a family?
- What roles do mothers and fathers play in children's development? How does coparenting affect children's development?

REFLECT

- Now that you have studied many aspects of families in this chapter, imagine that you have decided to write a book on some aspect of families. What specific aspect of families would you mainly focus on? What would be the title of your book? What would be the major theme of the book?

Reach Your Learning Goals

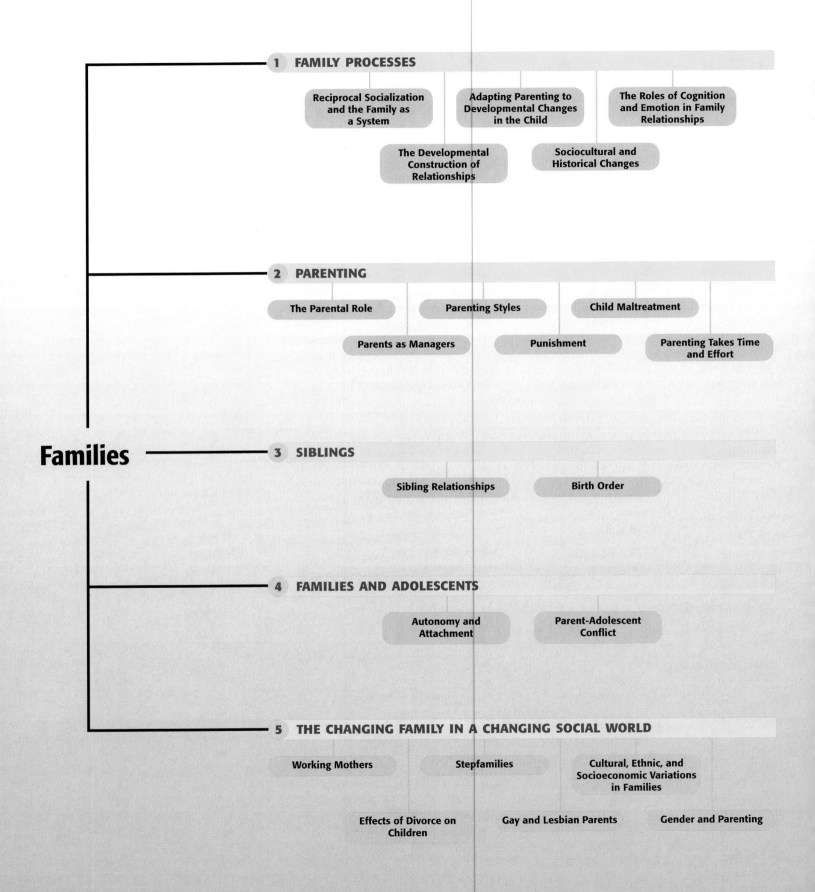

Families

1 FAMILY PROCESSES

- Reciprocal Socialization and the Family as a System
- Adapting Parenting to Developmental Changes in the Child
- The Roles of Cognition and Emotion in Family Relationships
- The Developmental Construction of Relationships
- Sociocultural and Historical Changes

2 PARENTING

- The Parental Role
- Parenting Styles
- Child Maltreatment
- Parents as Managers
- Punishment
- Parenting Takes Time and Effort

3 SIBLINGS

- Sibling Relationships
- Birth Order

4 FAMILIES AND ADOLESCENTS

- Autonomy and Attachment
- Parent-Adolescent Conflict

5 THE CHANGING FAMILY IN A CHANGING SOCIAL WORLD

- Working Mothers
- Stepfamilies
- Cultural, Ethnic, and Socioeconomic Variations in Families
- Effects of Divorce on Children
- Gay and Lesbian Parents
- Gender and Parenting

Summary

1 Discuss family processes

- Children socialize parents just as parents socialize children. Scaffolding is an important aspect of reciprocal socialization. The family is a system of interacting individuals with different subsystems—some dyadic, some polyadic. Belsky's model describes direct and indirect effects. Positive marital relations can have a positive influence on parenting.
- The developmental construction views share the belief that as individuals grow up they acquire modes of relating to others. There are two main variations within this view, one that emphasizes continuity and stability in relationships (the continuity view) and one that focuses on discontinuity and change in relationships (the discontinuity view).
- Parents need to adapt their parenting as children grow older, using less physical manipulation and more reasoning in the process. Parents spend less time in caregiving, instruction, reading, talking, and playing with children in middle childhood than earlier in the child's development. In middle and late childhood, control becomes more coregulatory.
- Changes in families may be due to great upheavals, such as war, or more subtle changes, such as television and the mobility of families.
- The role of cognition includes parents' cognitions, beliefs, and values about their parental role, as well as the way they perceive, organize, and understand their children's behaviors and beliefs. The role of emotion includes the regulation of emotion in children, the development of production and understanding of emotion in children, and emotion in carrying out the parenting role.

2 Explain how parenting is linked to children's development

- For some, the parental role is well planned and coordinated. For others, there is surprise. There are many myths about parenting, including the myth that the birth of a child will save a failing marriage.
- An increased trend is to conceptualize parents as managers of children's lives. Parents play important roles as managers of children's opportunities, in monitoring children's relationships, and as social initiators and arrangers.
- Authoritarian, authoritative, neglectful, and indulgent are the four main categories of parenting styles. Authoritative parenting is associated with socially competent child behavior more than the other styles.
- There are a number of reasons not to use physical punishment in disciplining children, and in some countries physical punishment of children has been outlawed. Intense punishment presents the child with an out-of-control model. Punishment can instill fear, rage, or avoidance in children. Punishment tells children what not to do rather than what to do. Punishment can be abusive.
- Child maltreatment is an increasing problem in the United States and is a multifaceted problem. Understanding child maltreatment requires information about the cultural context and family influences. Child maltreatment places the child at risk for a number of developmental problems.
- In today's world, too many parents do not spend enough time in parenting. Competent parenting takes time and effort.

3 Identify how siblings influence children's development

- Siblings interact with each other in more negative and less varied ways than parents and children interact.
- Birth order is related in certain ways to child characteristics, but some critics believe it has been overestimated as a predictor of child behavior.

4 Summarize the changes in families with adolescents

- Many parents have a difficult time handling the adolescent's push for autonomy. Attachment to parents increases the likelihood that the adolescent will be socially competent. Researchers increasingly are classifying as secure-autonomous and breaking down insecure attachment into different categories.
- Conflict with parents often increases in early adolescence, but this conflict is often moderate rather than severe. The increase in conflict probably serves the positive developmental functions of increasing adolescent autonomy and identity. A subset of adolescents experience high parent-adolescent conflict, and this is linked with negative outcomes for adolescents.

5 Characterize the changing family in a changing social world

- In general, in most studies, the mother's working outside the home has not had an adverse effect on children's development. However, in specific circumstances, negative effects of working mothers have been found, such as when mothers work more than 30 hours in the first year of the infant's life. Another concern involves latchkey experiences, which do not have a uniform effect on children. Parental monitoring and participation in structured activities with competent supervision are important influences on latchkey children's adjustment.
- Children in divorced families show more adjustment problems than their counterparts in nondivorced families. Whether parents should stay in an unhappy or conflicted marriage for the sake of the children is difficult to determine. Children show better adjustment in divorced families when parents' relationships with each other are harmonious and authoritative parenting is used. Factors to be considered in the adjustment of children in divorced families are adjustment prior to the divorce, personality and temperament, developmental status, gender, and custody. Income loss for divorced mothers may be linked with a number of stresses that can affect the child's adjustment.

- Like in divorced families, children in stepfamilies have more problems than their counterparts in nondivorced families. Adolescence is especially a difficult time for remarriage of parents to occur. Restabilization often takes longer in stepfamilies than in divorced families. Children have better relationships with their biological parents than their stepparents and show more problems in complex, blended families than simple ones.
- Approximately 20 percent of lesbians and 10 percent of gay men are parents. There is considerable diversity among lesbian mothers, gay fathers, and their children. Researchers have found few differences between children growing up in gay or lesbian families and children growing up in heterosexual families.
- Cultures vary on a number of issues regarding families. African American and Latino children are more likely than White American children to live in single-parent families, larger families, and families with extended connections. Higher-income families are more likely to use discipline that promotes internalization; low-income families are more likely to use discipline that encourages externalization.
- Most people associate motherhood with a number of positive images, but the reality is that motherhood is accorded a relatively low status in our society. Over time, the father's role in the child's development has evolved from moral teacher to breadwinner to gender-role model to nurturant caregiver. Fathers are much less involved in child rearing than mothers are. Coparenting has positive effects on children's development. Father-mother cooperation and mutual respect help the child to develop positive attitudes toward both males and females.

Key Terms

reciprocal socialization 473
scaffolding 473
developmental construction
   views 474

continuity view 474
discontinuity view 475
authoritarian parenting 481
authoritative parenting 481

neglectful parenting 482
indulgent parenting 482
dismissing/avoidant
   attachment 490

preoccupied/ambivalent
   attachment 490
unresolved/disorganized
   attachment 490

Key People

Jean Piaget 475
Andrew Collins 476
Eleanor Maccoby 476
Diana Baumrind 481

Joseph Allen 490
Reed Larson and Marsye
   Richards 491

G. Stanley Hall 491
Lois Hoffman 493
Joan Lipsitz 494

E. Mavis Hetherington 495
Cynthia Garcia Coll and Lee
   Pachter 500

Taking It to the Net

1. Frieda is the middle child in a family with five children. She is interested in what researchers have to say about the effect of birth order on sibling relationships. How does being a middle child contribute to the dynamics between Frieda and her brothers and sisters?

2. Mary and Peter are the parents of 13-year-old Cameron and 15-year-old Suzanne. They had heard that the adolescent years could be difficult, but they were not prepared for the constant conflict and bickering. They don't feel that they are doing a very good job as parents. Are there some guidelines that will help them restore some peace and sanity to their family?

3. Bruce and Caitlin are planning to separate and divorce. Both are miserable, and their household is like an armed camp. Unfortunately, they have three children, ages 6, 8, and 12. What should they tell the children, and how and when should they tell them?

Connect to **www.mhhe.com/santrockcd10** to research the answers and complete these exercises.

E-Learning Tools

To help you master the material in this chapter, you'll find a number of valuable study tools on the Student CD-ROM that accompanies this book. Also visit the Online Learning Center for *Child Development,* tenth edition (**www.mhhe.com/santrockcd10**) where you'll find these additional resources:

- View video clips by key developmental psychology experts including Judy Dunn on the age gap between siblings and its influence on sibling relationships, and on the influence parents have on the relationships between their children. Also see clips from Robert Emery on divorce and child development, and Laurence Steinberg on parent/adolescent conflict.

- Build your decision-making skills by trying your hand at the parenting, nursing, and education "Scenarios" on the Online Learning Center.

You are troubled at see-ing him spend his early years in doing nothing. What! Is it nothing to be happy? Is it nothing to skip, to play, to run about all day long? Never in his life will he be so busy as now.

—JEAN-JACQUES ROUSSEAU
*Swiss-Born French Philosopher,
18th Century*

Peers

Chapter Outline

Learning Goals

PEER RELATIONS

Peer Group Functions
The Distinct but Coordinated Worlds of Parent-Child and Peer Relations
The Developmental Course of Peer Relations in Childhood
Social Cognition
Peer Statuses
Bullying
Gender and Peer Relations

1 Discuss peer relations in childhood

PLAY

Play's Functions
Parten's Classic Study of Play
Types of Play
The Sociocultural Contexts of Play

2 Describe children's play

FRIENDSHIP

Friendship's Functions
Sullivan's Ideas
Intimacy and Similarity
Mixed-Age Friendships

3 Explain friendship

ADOLESCENCE, PEERS, AND ROMANTIC RELATIONSHIPS

Peer Pressure and Conformity
Cliques and Crowds
Adolescent Groups Versus Child Groups
Dating and Romantic Relationships

4 Characterize peer relations and romantic relationships in adolescence

The Stories of Young Adolescent Girls' Friends and Relational Worlds

Lynn Brown and Carol Gilligan (1992) conducted in-depth interviews of one hundred 10- to 13-year-old girls who were making the transition to adolescence. They listened to what these girls were saying about how important friends were to them. The girls were very curious about the human world they lived in and kept track of what was happening to their peers and friends. The girls spoke about the pleasure they derived from the intimacy and fun of human connection, and about the potential for hurt in relationships. They especially highlighted the importance of clique formation in their lives.

One girl, Noura, said that she learned about what it feels like to be the person that everyone doesn't like and that it was very painful. Another girl, Gail, reflected on her life over the last year and said that she was getting along better with people, probably because she was better at understanding how they think and at accepting them. A number of the girls talked about the "whitewashing" of the adolescent relational world. That is, many girls say nice and kind things to be polite but they often don't really mean them. They know the benefits of being perceived as the perfect, happy girl, at least on the surface. Suspecting that people prefer the "perfect girl," they experiment with her image and the happiness she might bring. The perfectly nice girl seems to gain popularity with other girls, and as many girls strive to become her, jealousies and rivalries break out. Cliques can provide emotional support for girls who are striving to be perfect but know they are not. One girl, Victoria, commented that some girls like her, who weren't very popular, nonetheless were accepted into a "club" with three other girls. She now felt that when she was sad or depressed she could count on the "club" for support. Though they were "leftovers" and did not get into the most popular cliques, these four girls said they knew they were liked and it felt great.

Another girl, Judy, at age 13, spoke about her interest in romantic relationships. She said that although she and her girlfriends were only 13, they wanted to be romantic. She covered her bodily desires and sexual feelings with romantic ideals. She described a girl who went out with guys and went farther than most girls would and said the girl's behavior is "disgusting." Rather than sex, Judy said she was looking for a really good relationship with a guy.

This chapter is about peers, which clearly are very important in the lives of the adolescent girls we just described. They also are very important in the lives of children. We begin the chapter by examining a number of ideas about children's peer relations, then turn to children's play. Next, we will explore the roles that friends play in children's development and conclude by discussing peer and romantic relationships in adolescence.

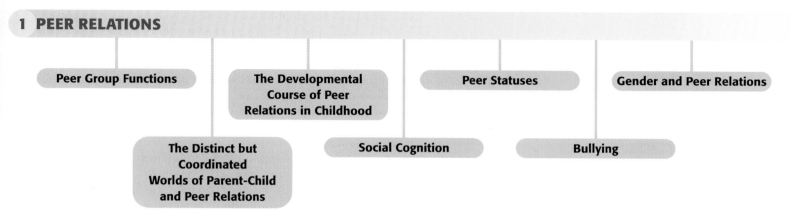

1 PEER RELATIONS

- Peer Group Functions
- The Developmental Course of Peer Relations in Childhood
- Peer Statuses
- Gender and Peer Relations
- The Distinct but Coordinated Worlds of Parent-Child and Peer Relations
- Social Cognition
- Bullying

As children grow older, peer relations consume increasing amounts of their time. What is the function of a child's peer group?

Peer Group Functions

Peers are children of about the same age or maturity level. Same-age peer interaction fills a unique role in our culture. Age grading would occur even if schools were not age graded and children were left alone to determine the composition of their own societies. One of the most important functions of the peer group is to provide a source of information and comparison about the world outside the family. Children receive feedback about their abilities from their peer group. Children evaluate what they do in terms of whether it is better than, as good as, or worse than what other children do. It is hard to do this at home because siblings are usually older or younger.

Are peers necessary for development? When peer monkeys who have been reared together are separated, they become depressed and regress socially (Suomi, Harlow, & Domek, 1970). The human development literature contains a classic example of the importance of peers in social development. Anna Freud (Freud & Dann, 1951) studied six children from different families who banded together after their parents were killed in World War II. Intensive peer attachment was observed; the children formed a tightly knit group, dependent on one another and aloof with outsiders. Even though deprived of parental care, they became neither delinquent nor psychotic.

Thus, good peer relations may be necessary for normal social development. Special concerns focus on children who are withdrawn and aggressive (Ladd, 1999). Withdrawn children who are rejected by peers and/or victimized and feeling lonely are at risk for depression. Children who are aggressive with their peers are at risk for developing a number of problems, including delinquency and dropping out of school.

As you might have detected from our discussion of peer relations thus far, peer influences can be both positive and negative (Rubin, Bukowski, & Parker, 1998). Both Jean Piaget (1932) and Harry Stack Sullivan (1953) were influential theorists who stressed that it is through peer interaction that children and adolescents learn the symmetrical reciprocity mode of relationships discussed in chapter 15. Children explore the principles of fairness and justice by working through disagreements with peers. They also learn to be keen observers of peers' interests and perspectives in order to smoothly integrate themselves into ongoing peer activities. In addition, Sullivan argued that adolescents learn to be skilled and sensitive partners in intimate relationships by forging close friendships with selected peers. These intimacy skills are carried forward to help form the foundation of later dating and marital relationships, according to Sullivan.

www.mhhe.com/santrockcd10

Peer Relations

peers Children of about the same age or maturity level.

In contrast, some theorists have emphasized the negative influences of peers on children's and adolescents' development. Being rejected or overlooked by peers leads some children to feel lonely or hostile. Further, such rejection and neglect by peers are related to an individual's subsequent mental health and criminal problems. Some theorists have also described the children's peer culture as a corrupt influence that undermines parental values and control. Further, peers can introduce adolescents to alcohol, drugs, delinquency, and other forms of behavior that adults view as maladaptive.

As you read about peers, also keep in mind that although peer experiences have important influences on children's development, those influences vary according to the way peer experience is measured, the outcomes specified, and the developmental trajectories traversed (Hartup, 1999). "Peers" and "peer group" are global concepts. These can be beneficial concepts in understanding peer influences as long as they are considered in terms of the specific type of setting or peer context in which the child participates, such as "acquaintance," "clique," "neighborhood associates," "friendship network," or "activity group." For example, one analysis of the peer group describes these aspects of the youth culture: membership crowd, neighborhood crowd, reference crowd, church crowd, sports team, friendship group, and friend (Brown, 1999).

The Distinct but Coordinated Worlds of Parent-Child and Peer Relations

What are some of the similarities and differences between peer and parent-child relationships? Children touch, smile, frown, and vocalize when they interact with both parents and peers. However, rough-and-tumble play occurs mainly with other children, not with adults, and, in times of stress, children often move toward their parents rather than toward their peers.

In addition to evaluating whether children engage in similar or dissimilar behaviors when interacting with parents and peers, it is also important to examine whether children's peer relations develop independently of parent-child relationships or are wedded to them (Hartup & Laursen, 1999). Recall our discussion of the developmental construction of relationships in chapter 15, which affords two different views. In the continuity view, early parent-child relationships strongly influence children's subsequent peer relations and friendships. By contrast, in the discontinuity view, peer relations and friendships have a more independent developmental path.

A number of theorists and researchers argue that parent-child relationships serve as emotional bases for exploring and enjoying peer relations (Ladd, 1999; Rubin, Bukowski, & Parker, 1998). In one study, the parent-child relationship history of each peer helped to predict the nature of peer interaction (Olweus, 1980) (see figure 16.1). Some boys were highly aggressive ("bullies") and other boys were the recipients of aggression ("whipping boys") throughout their preschool years. The bullies and the whipping boys had distinctive relationship histories. The bullies' parents frequently rejected them, were authoritarian, and were permissive about their sons' aggression, and the bullies' families were characterized by discord. By contrast, the whipping boys' parents were anxious and overprotective, taking special care to have their sons avoid aggression. The well-adjusted boys in the study were much less likely to be involved in aggressive peer interchanges than were the bullies and whipping boys. Their parents did not sanction aggression, and their responsive involvement with their sons promoted the development of self-assertion rather than aggression or wimpish behavior. We will further discuss bullying later in the chapter.

Parents also can model or coach their children in the ways of relating to peers (Ladd & Pettit, 2002; Updegraff, 1999). In one investigation, parents indicated they recommended specific strategies to their children regarding peer relations (Rubin & Sloman, 1984). For example, parents told their children how to mediate disputes or how to become less shy with others. They also encouraged them to be tolerant and

Rejecting, authoritarian, permissive toward aggression; discord

Anxious, overprotective parenting; take special care to avoid aggression

Bullies ⟷ Whipping boys

FIGURE 16.1 Peer Aggression and Parent-Child Relationship Histories

Children's peer behavior is influenced by their parent-child relationship histories.

to resist peer pressure. In another study, parents who frequently initiated peer contacts for their preschool children had children who were more accepted by their peers and had higher levels of prosocial behavior (Ladd & Hart, 1992).

A key aspect of peer relations can be traced to basic lifestyle decisions by parents (Cooper & Ayers-Lopez, 1985). Parents' choices of neighborhoods, churches, schools, and their own friends largely determine the pool from which their children might select possible friends. For example, the chosen schools can lead to specific grouping policies, as well as particular academic and extracurricular activities. In turn, such facts affect which students their children meet, their purpose in interacting, and eventually who become friends. For example, classrooms in which teachers encourage more cooperative peer interchanges have fewer isolates.

In sum, parent-child and peer worlds are coordinated and connected (Ladd & Pettit, 2002; Maccoby, 1996). However, they also are distinct. Earlier we indicated that rough-and-tumble play occurs mainly with other children, not in parent-child interaction. And, in times of stress, children often turn to parents, not peers, for support. Peer relations also are more likely to consist of interaction on a much more equal basis than parent-child relations. In parent-child relations, since parents have greater knowledge and authority, their children must often learn how to conform to rules and regulations laid down by parents. With peers, children learn to formulate and assert their own opinions, appreciate the perspective of peers, cooperatively negotiate solutions to disagreements, and evolve standards of conduct that are mutually acceptable.

The Developmental Course of Peer Relations in Childhood

Although we generally think of peer relations as not assuming an important role until early childhood, some researchers believe that the quality of peer interaction in infancy provides valuable information about social development (Vandell, 1985). For example, in one investigation, positive affect in infant peer relations was related to easy access to peer play groups and to peer popularity in early childhood (Howes,

1985). As increasing numbers of children attend day care, peer interaction in infancy takes on a more important developmental role.

The frequency of peer interaction, both positive and negative, picks up considerably during early childhood (Hartup, 1983). Although aggressive interaction and rough-and-tumble play increase, the *proportion* of aggressive exchanges, compared to friendly exchanges, decreases. Children tend to abandon their immature and inefficient social exchanges with age and acquire more mature ways of relating to peers.

Children spend an increasing amount of time in peer interaction during middle and late childhood and adolescence. In one investigation, children interacted with peers 10 percent of their day at age 2, 20 percent at age 4, and more than 40 percent between the ages of 7 and 11. In a typical school day, episodes with peers totaled 299 times per day (Barker & Wright, 1951).

Social Cognition

Social cognitions involve thoughts about social matters (Lewis & Carpendale, 2002). How might children's thoughts contribute to their peer relations? Three possibilities are through their perspective-taking ability, social information-processing skills, and social knowledge.

Perspective Taking As we discussed in chapter 14, "Moral Development," **perspective taking** involves taking another's point of view. ◀ **page 442** As children enter the elementary school years, both their peer interaction and their perspective-taking ability increase. Reciprocity—playing games, functioning in groups, and cultivating friendships, for example—is especially important in peer interchanges at this point in development. One of the important skills that helps elementary school children improve their peer relations is communication effectiveness. In one investigation, the communication exchanges among peers at kindergarten, first-, third-, and fifth-grade levels were evaluated (Krauss & Glucksberg, 1969). Children were asked to instruct a peer in how to stack a set of blocks. The peer sat behind a screen with blocks similar to those the other child was stacking (see figure 16.2). The kindergarten children made numerous errors in telling the peer how to duplicate the novel block stack. The older children, especially the fifth-graders, were much more efficient in communicating to a peer how to stack the blocks. They were sensitive to the communication demands of the task and were far superior at perspective taking and figuring out how they had to talk for the peer to understand them. In ele-

perspective taking The ability to assume another person's perspective and understand his or her thoughts and feelings.

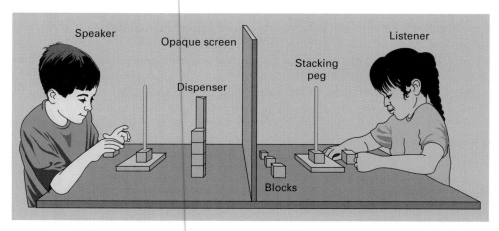

FIGURE 16.2 The Development of Communication Skills

This is an experimental arrangement of speaker and listener in the investigation of the development of communication skills.

mentary school, children also become more efficient at understanding complex messages, so the listening skills of the peer in this experiment probably helped the communicating peer as well. Other researchers have documented the link between perspective-taking skills and the quality of peer relations, especially in the elementary school years (LeMare & Rubin, 1987).

Social Information-Processing Skills Of special interest is how children process information about peer relations (Dodge, 1993). For example, a boy accidentally trips and knocks a peer's soft drink out of his hand. The peer misinterprets the encounter as hostile, which leads him to retaliate aggressively against the boy. Through repeated encounters of this kind, other peers come to perceive the aggressor as habitually acting inappropriately. Peer relations researcher Kenneth Dodge (1993) argues that children go through five steps in processing information about their social world: decoding social cues, interpreting, searching for a response, selecting an optimal response, and enacting it. Dodge has found that aggressive boys are more likely to perceive another child's actions as hostile when the child's intention is ambiguous, and when aggressive boys search for clues to determine a peer's intention, they respond more rapidly, less efficiently, and less reflectively than nonaggressive children.

Social Knowledge Social knowledge also is involved in children's ability to get along with peers. An important part of children's social life involves choosing which goals to pursue in poorly defined or ambiguous situations. Social relationship goals are also important, such as how to initiate and maintain a social bond. Children need to know what scripts to follow to get children to be their friends. For example, as part of the script for getting friends, it helps to know that saying nice things, regardless of what the peer does or says, will make the peer like the child more.

The social cognitive perspective views children who are maladjusted as lacking social cognitive skills to interact effectively with others (Rabiner & others, 1991). One investigation explored the possibility that maladjusted children do not have the social cognitive skills necessary for positive social interaction (Asarnow & Callan, 1985). Boys with and without peer adjustment difficulties were identified, and their social cognitive skills were assessed. Boys without peer adjustment problems generated more alternative solutions to problems, proposed more assertive and mature solutions, gave less-intense aggressive solutions, showed more adaptive planning, and evaluated physically aggressive responses less positively than did the boys with peer adjustment problems.

Peer Statuses

Children often think, "What can I do to get all of the kids at school to like me?" or "What's wrong with me? Something must be wrong or I would be more popular." What makes a child popular with peers? **Popular children** are frequently nominated as a best friend and are rarely disliked by their peers. Researchers have found that popular children give out reinforcements, listen carefully, maintain open lines of communication with peers, are happy, act like themselves, show enthusiasm and concern for others, and are self-confident without being conceited (Hartup, 1983).

Developmentalists have distinguished three other types of peer statuses (Wentzel & Asher, 1995):

- **Neglected children** are infrequently nominated as a best friend but are not disliked by their peers.
- **Rejected children** are infrequently nominated as someone's best friend and are actively disliked by their peers.

Social Cognition

Peer Conflicts

Aggressive Boys, Friendships, and Adjustment

popular children Children who are frequently nominated as a best friend and are rarely disliked by their peers.

neglected children Children who are infrequently nominated as a best friend but are not disliked by their peers.

rejected children Children who are infrequently nominated as a best friend and are actively disliked by their peers.

• **Controversial children** are frequently nominated both as someone's best friend and as being disliked.

The controversial peer status had not been studied until recently. In one study, girls who had a controversial peer status in the fourth grade were more likely to become adolescent mothers than were girls of other peer statuses (Underwood, Kupersmidt, & Coie, 1996). Also, aggressive girls had more children than nonaggressive girls.

Rejected children often have more serious adjustment problems than those who are neglected (Parker & Asher, 1987). For example, one recent study found that in kindergarten, rejected children were less likely to engage in classroom participation, express a desire to avoid school, and more likely to report being lonely (Buhs & Ladd, 2001). In another study, 112 fifth-grade boys were evaluated over a period of seven years until the end of high school (Kupersmidt & Coie, 1990). The best predictor of whether rejected children would engage in delinquent behavior or drop out of school later during adolescence was aggression toward peers in elementary school.

Not all rejected children are aggressive (Haselager & others, 2002; Ladd, 1999). Aggression and its related characteristics of impulsiveness and disruptiveness underlie rejection about half the time, but approximately 10 to 20 percent of rejected children are shy (Cillessen & others, 1992).

An important question to ask is how neglected children and rejected children can be trained to interact more effectively with their peers (Ladd, Buhs, & Troop, 2002). The goal of training programs with neglected children is often to help them attract attention from their peers in positive ways and to hold their attention by asking questions, by listening in a warm and friendly way, and by saying things about themselves that relate to the peers' interests. They also are taught to enter groups more effectively.

Children may need to be persuaded or motivated that these strategies work effectively and are satisfying. In some programs, children are shown videotapes of appropriate peer interaction; then they are asked to comment on them and to draw lessons from what they have seen. In other training programs, popular children are taught to be more accepting of neglected and rejected peers.

Bullying

Significant numbers of students are victimized by bullies (Espelage, Holt, & Henkel, 2003; Rigby, 2002). In one recent national survey of more than 15,000 sixth-through tenth-grade students, nearly one of every three students said that they had experienced occasional or frequent involvement as a victim or perpetrator in bullying (Nansel & others, 2001). In this study, bullying was defined as verbal or physical behavior intended to disturb someone less powerful. Boys and younger middle school students were most likely to be affected. As shown in figure 16.3, being belittled about looks or speech was the most frequent type of bullying. Children who said they were bullied reported more loneliness and difficulty in making friends, while those who did the bullying were more likely to have low grades and to smoke and drink alcohol.

To reduce bullying, teachers can follow these suggestions (Limber, 1997):

• Get older peers to serve as monitors for bullying and intervene when they see it taking place.
• Develop school-wide rules and sanctions against bullying and post them throughout the school.
• Form friendship groups for adolescents who are regularly bullied by peers.
• Incorporate the message of the antibullying program into places of worship, school, and other community activities where adolescents are involved.

Reducing Bullying

controversial children Children who are frequently nominated both as someone's best friend and as being disliked.

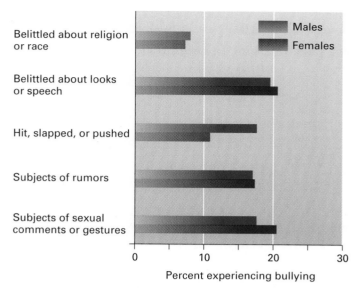

FIGURE 16.3 Bullying Behaviors Among U.S. Youth

This graph shows the type of bullying most often experienced by U.S. youth. The percentages reflect the extent to which bullied students said that they had experienced a particular type of bullying. In terms of gender, note that when they were bullied, boys were more likely to be hit, slapped, or pushed than girls were.

Gender and Peer Relations

There is increasing evidence that gender plays an important role in peer relations (Benenson & others, 2001). ← **page 416** This evidence involves the gender composition of children's groups, group size, interaction in same-sex groups, and socialization within same-sex groups (Maccoby, 1998, 2002):

- *Gender composition of children's groups.* Around the age of 3, children already show a preference to spend time with same-sex playmates. From 4 to 12 years of age, this preference for playing in same-sex groups increases, and during the elementary school years children spend a large majority of their free time with children of their own sex.
- *Group size.* From about 5 years of age onward, boys are more likely to associate together in larger clusters than girls are. Boys are more likely to participate in organized group games than girls are. In one study, same-sex groups of six children were permitted to use play materials in any way they wished (Benenson, Apostolaris, & Parnass, 1997). Girls were more likely than boys to play in dyads or triads, while boys were more likely to interact in larger groups and seek to attain a group goal.
- *Interaction in same-sex groups.* Boys are more likely than girls to engage in rough-and-tumble play, competition, conflict, ego displays, risk taking, and to seek dominance. By contrast, girls are more likely to engage in "collaborative discourse," in which they talk and act in a more reciprocal manner.
- *Socialization within same-sex groups.* One research study with preschoolers found that over the course of six months, the more time boys spent playing with other boys, the more their activity level, rough-and-tumble play, and sex-typed choices of toys and games increased, and the less time they spent near adults (Martin & Fabes, 2001). By contrast, the more time girls spent playing with girls, the lower was their aggression and activity level, the higher their choices of girl-type play and activities, and the more time they spent near adults.

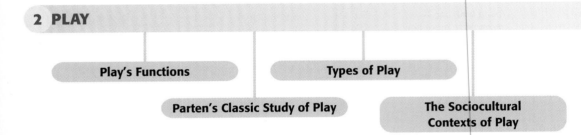

> :o: **Review and Reflect:** Learning Goal 1
>
> **1** **Discuss peer relations in childhood**
>
> **REVIEW**
> - What are the functions of peer groups?
> - How are the worlds of parents and peers distinct but coordinated?
> - What is the developmental course of peer relations in childhood?
> - How is social cognition involved in peer relations?
> - How are peer statuses related to development?
> - What is the nature of bullying?
> - How is gender involved in children's peer relations?
>
> **REFLECT**
> - Think back to your middle school/junior high and high school years. What was your relationship with your parents like? Were you securely attached or insecurely attached to them? How do you think your relationship with your parents affected your friendship and peer relations?

2 PLAY

- **Play's Functions**
- **Parten's Classic Study of Play**
- **Types of Play**
- **The Sociocultural Contexts of Play**

An extensive amount of peer interaction during childhood involves play; however, social play is but one type of play. **Play** is a pleasurable activity that is engaged in for its own sake.

Play's Functions

Play is essential to a young child's health. As today's children continue to experience pressure in their lives, play becomes even more crucial. Play increases affiliation with peers, releases tension, advances cognitive development, and increases exploration. Play increases the probability that children will converse and interact with each other. During this interaction, children practice the roles they will assume later in life.

According to Freud and Erikson, play is an especially useful form of human adjustment, helping the child master anxieties and conflicts. Because tensions are relieved in play, the child can cope with life's problems. Play permits the child to work off excess physical energy and to release pent-up tensions. **Play therapy** allows children to work off frustrations and is a medium through which therapists can analyze children's conflicts and ways of coping with them. Children may feel less threatened and be more likely to express their true feelings in the context of play.

Piaget (1962) saw play as a medium that advances children's cognitive development. At the same time, he said that children's cognitive development constrains the way they play. Play permits children to practice their competencies and acquired skills in a relaxed, pleasurable way. Piaget believed that cognitive structures need to be exercised, and play provides the perfect setting for this exercise. For example, children who have just learned to add or multiply begin to play with numbers in different ways as they perfect these operations, laughing as they do so.

play A pleasurable activity that is engaged in for its own sake.

play therapy Therapy that allows the child to work off frustrations and is a medium through which the therapist can analyze the child's conflicts and ways of coping with them. Children may feel less threatened and be more likely to express their true feelings in the context of play.

Vygotsky (1962), whose developmental theory was discussed in chapter 7, also believed that play is an excellent setting for cognitive development. He was especially interested in the symbolic and make-believe aspects of play, as when a child rides a stick as if it were a horse. For young children, the imaginary situation is real. Parents should encourage such imaginary play because it advances the child's cognitive development, especially creative thought.

Daniel Berlyne (1960) described play as exciting and pleasurable in itself because it satisfies the exploratory drive each of us possesses. This drive involves curiosity and a desire for information about something new or unusual. Play is a means whereby children can safely explore and seek out new information—something they might not otherwise do. Play encourages this exploratory behavior by offering children the possibilities of novelty, complexity, uncertainty, surprise, and incongruity.

www.mhhe.com/santrockcd10

Play

Parten's Classic Study of Play

Many years ago, Mildred Parten (1932) developed an elaborate classification of children's play. Based on observations of children in free play at nursery school, Parten arrived at these play categories:

- **Unoccupied play** is not play as it is commonly understood. The child may stand in one spot or perform random movements that do not seem to have a goal. In most nursery schools, unoccupied play is less frequent than other forms of play.
- **Solitary play** happens when the child plays alone and independently of others. The child seems engrossed in the activity and does not care much about anything else that is happening. Two- and 3-year-olds engage more frequently in solitary play than older preschoolers do.

unoccupied play Play in which the child is not engaging in play as it is commonly understood and might stand in one spot, look around the room, or perform random movements that do not seem to have a goal.

solitary play Play in which the child plays alone and independently of others.

Mildred Parten classified play into six categories. Study the photograph and determine which of her categories are reflected in the behavior of the children pictured.

*A*nd that park grew up with me; that small world widened as I learned its secret boundaries, as I discovered new refuges in its woods and jungles: hidden homes and lairs for the multitudes of imagination, for cowboys . . . and Devon-facing seashore, hoping for gold watches or the skull of a sheep or a message in a bottle to be washed up with the tide.

—DYLAN THOMAS
Welsh Poet, 20th Century

onlooker play Play in which the child watches other children play.

parallel play Play in which the child plays separately from others, but with toys like those the others are using or in a manner that mimics their play.

associative play Play that involves social interaction with little or no organization.

cooperative play Play that involves social interaction in a group with a sense of group identity and organized activity.

sensorimotor play Behavior engaged in by infants to derive pleasure from exercising their existing sensorimotor schemas.

practice play Play that involves repetition of behavior when new skills are being learned or when physical or mental mastery and coordination of skills are required for games or sports. Sensorimotor play, which often involves practice play, is primarily confined to infancy, while practice play can be engaged in throughout life.

pretense/symbolic play Play that occurs when a child transforms the physical environment into a symbol.

- **Onlooker play** takes place when the child watches other children play. The child may talk with other children and ask questions but does not enter into their play behavior. The child's active interest in other children's play distinguishes onlooker play from unoccupied play.
- **Parallel play** occurs when the child plays separately from others but with toys like those the others are using or in a manner that mimics their play. The older children are, the less frequently they engage in this type of play. However even older preschool children engage in parallel play quite often.
- **Associative play** involves social interaction with little or no organization. In this type of play, children seem to be more interested in each other than in the tasks they are performing. Borrowing or lending toys and following or leading one another in line are examples of associative play.
- **Cooperative play** consists of social interaction in a group with a sense of group identity and organized activity. Children's formal games, competition aimed at winning, and groups formed by the teacher for doing things together are examples of cooperative play. Cooperative play is the prototype for the games of middle childhood. Little cooperative play is seen in the preschool years.

Types of Play

Parten's categories represent one way of thinking about the different types of play. However, today researchers and practitioners who are involved with children's play believe other types of play are important in children's development. Whereas Parten's categories emphasize the role of play in the child's social world, the contemporary perspective on play emphasizes both the cognitive and the social aspects of play. Among the most widely studied types of children's play today are sensorimotor and practice play, pretense/symbolic play, social play, constructive play, and games (Bergen, 1988). We will consider each of these types of play in turn.

Sensorimotor and Practice Play **Sensorimotor play** is behavior that is engaged in by infants to derive pleasure from exercising their existing sensorimotor schemas. The development of sensorimotor play follows Piaget's description of sensorimotor thought, which we discussed in chapter 7. Infants initially engage in exploratory and playful visual and motor transactions in the second quarter of the first year of life. For example, at 9 months of age, infants begin to select novel objects for exploration and play, especially those that are responsive, such as toys that make noise or bounce. At 12 months of age, infants enjoy making things work and exploring cause and effect.

Practice play involves the repetition of behavior when new skills are being learned or when physical or mental mastery and coordination of skills are required for games or sports. Sensorimotor play, which often involves practice play, is primarily confined to infancy, while practice play can be engaged in throughout life. During the preschool years, children often engage in play that involves practicing various skills. While practice play declines in the elementary school years, practice play activities such as running, jumping, sliding, twirling, and throwing balls or other objects are frequently observed on the playgrounds at elementary schools.

Pretense/Symbolic Play **Pretense/symbolic play** occurs when the child transforms the physical environment into a symbol. Between 9 and 30 months of age, children increase their use of objects in symbolic play. They learn to transform objects—substituting them for other objects and acting toward them as if they were these other objects. For example, a preschool child treats a table as if it were a car and says, "I'm fixing the car," as he grabs a leg of the table.

Many experts on play consider the preschool years the "golden age" of symbolic/pretense play that is dramatic or sociodramatic in nature (Fein, 1986). This type of make-believe play often appears at about 18 months of age and reaches a peak at 4 to 5 years of age, then gradually declines.

Social Play **Social play** is play that involves interaction with peers. Parten's categories, described earlier, are oriented toward social play. Social play with peers increases dramatically during the preschool years.

Constructive Play **Constructive play** combines sensorimotor/practice repetitive activity with symbolic representation of ideas. Constructive play occurs when children engage in self-regulated creation or construction of a product or a problem solution. Constructive play increases in the preschool years as symbolic play increases and sensorimotor play decreases. In the preschool years, some practice play is replaced by constructive play. For example, instead of moving their fingers around and around in finger paint (practice play), children are more likely to draw the outline of a house or a person in the paint (constructive play). Constructive play is also a frequent form of play in the elementary school years, both in and out of the classroom. Constructive play is one of the few playlike activities allowed in work-centered classrooms. For example, having children create a play about a social studies topic involves constructive play.

A preschool "superhero" at play.

Games **Games** are activities that are engaged in for pleasure. They include rules and often competition with one or more individuals. Preschool children may begin to participate in social game play that involves simple rules of reciprocity and turn taking. However, games take on a much stronger role in the lives of elementary school children. In one study, the highest incidence of game playing occurred between 10 and 12 years of age (Eiferman, 1971). After age 12, games decline in popularity (Bergin, 1988).

In sum, play is a multidimensional, complex concept. It ranges from an infant's simple exercise of a newfound sensorimotor talent to a preschool child's riding a tricycle to an older child's participation in organized games. It is also important to note that children's play can involve a combination of the play categories we have described. For example, social play can be sensorimotor (rough-and-tumble), symbolic, or constructive.

The Sociocultural Contexts of Play

American children's freewheeling play once took place in rural fields and city streets, using equipment largely made by children themselves. Today, play is becoming confined to backyards, basements, playrooms, and bedrooms and derives much of its content from video games, television dramas, and Saturday morning cartoons (Sutton-Smith, 1985). Modern children spend a large part of their lives alone with their toys, which was inconceivable several centuries earlier. Childhood was once part of collective village life. Children did not play separately but joined adults in seasonal festivals that intruded on the work world with regularity and boisterousness.

One of the most widely debated issues in the sociocultural contexts of play is whether children from low socioeconomic groups and traditional, non-Western societies have underdeveloped skills in the imaginative and sociodramatic aspects of pretense play (Johnson, Christie, & Yawkey, 1987). Some researchers believe there are developmental deficiencies in the imaginative and sociodramatic play of children from low socioeconomic groups and traditional, non-Western societies, whereas others believe that many methodological shortcomings in this research cloud the results.

social play Play that involves social interactions with peers.

constructive play Play that combines sensorimotor/practice repetitive activity with symbolic representation of ideas. Constructive play occurs when children engage in self-regulated creation or construction of a product or a problem solution.

games Activities engaged in for pleasure that include rules and often competition with one or more individuals.

For example, many of these studies do not adequately measure socioeconomic status, do not systematically measure classroom and school variables, and in some cases do not use statistical analysis (McLoyd, 1982).

Some children may be capable of high-level imaginative play but require adult prompting and encouragement to overcome their initial shyness (Johnson, Christie, & Yawkey, 1987). Before expecting high-level play from children, teachers should determine if the children have had adequate time to become familiar with the materials and routines in their day-care center or preschool classroom. This familiarity is especially important for children whose main language is not English or for any child who comes from a home environment that is in marked contrast with the school environment.

Review and Reflect: Learning Goal 2

2 Describe children's play

REVIEW

- What are the functions of play?
- How would you describe Parten's classic study of play?
- What are the different types of play?
- How is play influenced by sociocultural contexts?

REFLECT

- Do you think most young children's lives today are too structured? Do young children have too little time to play? Explain.

---

3 FRIENDSHIP

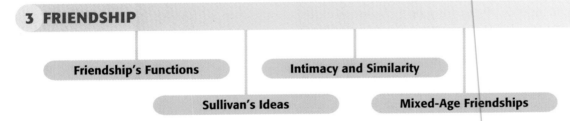

| Friendship's Functions | Intimacy and Similarity |
| Sullivan's Ideas | Mixed-Age Friendships |

The world of peers is one of varying acquaintances; children interact with some children they barely know, and with others they know well, for hours every day. It is to the latter type—friends—that we now turn.

Friendship's Functions

Friendships serve six functions (Gottman & Parker, 1987):

1. *Companionship.* Friendship provides children with a familiar partner, someone who is willing to spend time with them and join in collaborative activities.
2. *Stimulation.* Friendship provides children with interesting information, excitement, and amusement.
3. *Physical support.* Friendship provides resources and assistance.
4. *Ego support.* Friendship provides the expectation of support, encouragement, and feedback that helps children to maintain an impression of themselves as competent, attractive, and worthwhile individuals.
5. *Social comparison.* Friendship provides information about where children stand vis-à-vis others and whether children are doing okay.
6. *Intimacy/affection.* Friendship provides children with a warm, close, trusting relationship with another individual, a relationship that involves self-disclosure.

Sullivan's Ideas

Harry Stack Sullivan (1953) was the most influential theorist to discuss the importance of friendships. He argued that there is a dramatic increase in the psychological importance and intimacy of close friends during early adolescence. In contrast to other psychoanalytic theorists' narrow emphasis on the importance of parent-child relationships, Sullivan contended that friends also play important roles in shaping children's and adolescents' well-being and development. In terms of well-being, he argued that all people have a number of basic social needs, including the need for tenderness (secure attachment), playful companionship, social acceptance, intimacy, and sexual relations. Whether or not these needs are fulfilled largely determines our emotional well-being. For example, if the need for playful companionship goes unmet, then we become bored and depressed; if the need for social acceptance is not met, we suffer a lowered sense of self-worth. During adolescence, individuals increasingly depend on friends, and thus the ups and downs of experiences with friends increasingly shape adolescents' state of well-being. In particular, Sullivan believed that the need for intimacy intensifies during early adolescence, motivating teenagers to seek out close friends. He felt that, if adolescents failed to forge such close friendships, they would experience painful feelings of loneliness coupled with a reduced sense of self-worth.

Research findings support many of Sullivan's ideas. For example, adolescents report disclosing intimate and personal information to their friends more often than do younger children (Buhrmester, 1998; Buhrmester & Furman, 1987) (see figure 16.4). Adolescents also say they depend more on friends than on parents to satisfy their needs for companionship, reassurance of worth, and intimacy (Furman & Buhrmester, 1992). In one study, daily interviews with 13- to 16-year-old adolescents over a five-day period were conducted to find out how much time they spent engaged in meaningful interactions with friends and parents (Buhrmester & Carbery, 1992). Adolescents spent an average of 103 minutes per day in meaningful interactions with friends, compared with just 28 minutes per day with parents. In addition, the quality of friendship is more strongly linked to feelings of well-being during adolescence than during childhood. Teenagers with superficial friendships, or no close friendships at all, report feeling lonelier and more depressed, and they have a lower sense of self-esteem than do teenagers with intimate friendships (Yin, Buhrmester, & Hibbard, 1996). In another study, friendship in early adolescence was a significant predictor of self-worth in early adulthood (Bagwell, Newcomb, & Bukowski, 1994).

In addition to the role they play in the socialization of social competence, friendship relationships are often important sources of support (Berndt, 1999). Sullivan described how adolescent friends support one another's sense of personal worth. When close friends disclose their mutual insecurities and fears about themselves, they discover that they are not "abnormal" and that they have nothing to be ashamed of. Friends also act as important confidants that help children and adolescents work through upsetting problems (such as difficulties with parents or the breakup of romance) by providing both emotional support and informational advice. Friends can also protect "at-risk" adolescents from victimization by peers (Bukowski, Sippola, & Boivin, 1995). In addition, friends can become active partners in building a sense of identity. During countless hours of conversation, friends act as sounding boards as teenagers explore issues ranging from future plans to stances on religious and moral issues.

Willard Hartup (1996, 2000), who has studied peer relations across four decades, has concluded that children often use friends as cognitive and social resources on a regular basis. Hartup also commented that normative transitions, such as moving from elementary to middle school, are negotiated more competently by children who have friends than by those who don't. The quality of friendship is also important to consider. Supportive friendships between socially skilled individuals are developmentally advantageous, whereas coercive and conflict-ridden friendships are not (Hartup &

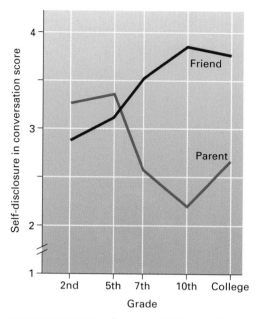

FIGURE 16.4 Developmental Changes in Self-Disclosing Conversations

Self-disclosing conversations with friends increased dramatically in adolescence while declining in an equally dramatic fashion with parents. However, self-disclosing conversations with parents began to pick up somewhat during the college years. The measure of self-disclosure involved a 5-point rating scale completed by the children and youth with a higher score representing greater self-disclosure. The data shown represent the means for each age group.

Abecassis, 2002). Being able to forgive also is important in maintaining friendships (Rose & Asher, 1999). Friendship and its developmental significance can vary from one child to another. Children's characteristics, such as temperament ("easy" versus "difficult" for example), likely influence the nature of their friendships. To read about appropriate and inappropriate strategies for making friends, see figure 16.5.

Intimacy and Similarity

In the context of friendship, *intimacy* has been defined in different ways. For example, it has been defined broadly to include everything in a relationship that makes the relationship seem close or intense. In most research studies, though, **intimacy in friendship** is defined narrowly as self-disclosure or sharing of private thoughts. Private or personal knowledge about a friend has been used as an index of intimacy (Selman, 1980; Sullivan, 1953).

The most consistent finding in the last two decades of research on adolescent friendships is that intimacy is an important feature of friendship (Berndt & Perry, 1990; Bukowski, Newcomb, & Hoza, 1987). When young adolescents are asked what they want from a friend or how they can tell someone is their best friend, they frequently say that a best friend will share problems with them, understand them, and listen when they talk about their own thoughts or feelings. When young children talk about their friendships, they rarely comment about intimate self-disclosure or

Friendships

Strategies Appropriate for Making Friends

Category	Examples
Initiate interaction	Learn about friend: ask for his or her name, age, favorite activities. Prosocial overtures: introduce self, start conversation, invite him or her to do things.
Be nice	Be nice, kind, considerate.
Show prosocial behavior	Be honest and trustworthy: tell the truth, keep promises. Be generous, sharing, cooperative.
Show respect for self and others	Respect others, have good manners: be polite and courteous. Listen to what others say. Have a positive attitude and personality: be open to others, be friendly, be funny. Be yourself. Enhance your own reputation: be clean, dress neatly, be on best behavior.
Provide social support	Be supportive: help, give advice, show you care. Engage in activities together: study or play, sit next to one another, be in same group. Enhance others: compliment them.

Strategies Inappropriate for Making Friends

Category	Examples
Be psychologically aggressive	Show disrespect, bad manners: be prejudiced and inconsiderate, use others, curse, be rude. Be exclusive, uncooperative: don't invite others to do things, ignore them, isolate them, don't share with or help them. Hurt their reputation or feelings: gossip, spread rumors, embarrass them, criticize them.
Present yourself negatively	Be self-centered: be snobby, conceited, and jealous; show off, care only about yourself. Be mean, have bad attitude or affect: be cruel, hostile, a grouch, angry all the time. Hurt own reputation: be a slob, act stupidly, throw temper tantrums, start trouble, be a sissy.
Behave antisocially	Be physically aggressive: fight, trip, spit, cause physical harm. Be verbally aggressive or controlling: yell at others, pick on them, make fun of them, call them names, be bossy. Be dishonest, disloyal: steal, cheat, tell secrets, break promises. Break school rules: skip school, drink alcohol, use drugs.

FIGURE 16.5 Appropriate and Inappropriate Strategies for Making Friends at School

intimacy in friendship Self-disclosure or the sharing of private thoughts.

mutual understanding. In one investigation, friendship intimacy was more prominent in 13- to 16-year-olds than in 10- to 13-year-olds (Buhrmester, 1990).

Are the friendships of adolescent girls more intimate than the friendships of adolescent boys? When asked to describe their best friends, girls refer to intimate conversations and faithfulness more than boys do. For example, girls are more likely to describe their best friend as "sensitive just like me" or "trustworthy just like me" (Duck, 1975). The assumption behind this gender difference is that girls are more oriented toward interpersonal relationships. Boys may discourage one another from openly disclosing their problems, as part of their masculine, competitive nature (Maccoby, 1996). Boys make themselves vulnerable to being called "wimps" if they can't handle their own problems and insecurities.

Another predominant characteristic of friendship is that, throughout the childhood and adolescent years, friends are generally similar—in terms of age, sex, ethnicity, and many other factors (Luo, Fang, & Aro, 1995). Friends often have similar attitudes toward school, similar educational aspirations, and closely aligned achievement orientations. Friends like the same music, wear the same kind of clothes, and prefer the same leisure activities (Berndt, 1982). If friends have different attitudes about schools, one of them may want to play basketball or go shopping rather than do homework. If the other friend insists on completing homework, the conflict may weaken the friendship, and the two may drift apart.

Mixed-Age Friendships

Although most adolescents develop friendships with individuals who are close to their own age, some adolescents become best friends with younger or older individuals. A common fear, especially among parents, is that adolescents who have older friends will be encouraged to engage in delinquent behavior or early sexual behavior. Researchers have found that adolescents who interact with older youths do engage in these behaviors more frequently, but it is not known whether the older youths guide younger adolescents toward deviant behavior or whether the younger adolescents were already prone to deviant behavior before they developed the friendship with the older youths (Billy, Rodgers, & Udry, 1984).

In a longitudinal study of eighth-grade girls, early-maturing girls developed friendships with girls who were chronologically older but biologically similar to them (Magnusson, 1988). Because of their associations with older friends, the early-maturing girls were more likely than their peers to engage in a number of deviant behaviors, such as being truant from school, getting drunk, and stealing. Also, as adults (26 years of age), the early-maturing girls were more likely to have had a child and were less likely to be vocationally and educationally oriented than their later-maturing counterparts. Thus, parents do seem to have reason to be concerned when their adolescents become close friends with individuals who are considerably older than they are.

Review and Reflect: Learning Goal 3

3 Explain friendship

REVIEW

- What are six functions of friendship?
- What is Sullivan's view of friendship?
- What role do intimacy and similarity play in friendship?
- What is the developmental outcome of mixed-age friendship?

REFLECT

- Examine the list of six functions of friendships at the beginning of this section. Rank order the six functions from most (1) to least (6) important as you were growing up.

4 ADOLESCENCE, PEERS, AND ROMANTIC RELATIONSHIPS

Peer Pressure and Conformity

Adolescent Groups Versus Child Groups

Cliques and Crowds

Dating and Romantic Relationships

Adolescent Peer Relationships

Peer Pressure

Peer relations play powerful roles in the lives of adolescents. When you think back to your adolescent years, many of your most enjoyable moments probably were spent with peers—on the telephone, in school activities, in the neighborhood, at dances, or just hanging out. Peer relations undergo important changes in adolescence. In childhood, the focus of peer relations is on being liked by classmates and being included in games or lunchroom conversations. Being overlooked or, worse yet, being rejected can have damaging effects on children's development that sometimes are carried forward to adolescence. Beginning in early adolescence, teenagers typically prefer to have a smaller number of friendships that are more intense and intimate than those of young children. Cliques are formed and shape the social lives of adolescents as they begin to "hang out" together. Dating and romantic relationships become important in the social lives of most older adolescents.

Peer Pressure and Conformity

Consider this statement made by an adolescent girl:

> Peer pressure is extremely influential in my life. I have never had very many friends, and I spend quite a bit of time alone. The friends I have are older. . . . The closest

*E*ach of you, individually; walkest with the tread of a fox, but collectively ye are geese.

—SOLON
Greek Statesman and Poet,
7th Century B.C.

Most adolescents conform to the mainstream standards of their peers. However, the rebellious or anticonformist adolescent reacts counter to the mainstream peer group's expectations, deliberately moving away from the actions or beliefs this group advocates.

friend I have had is a lot like me in that we are both sad and depressed a lot. I began to act even more depressed than before when I was with her. I would call her up and try to act even more depressed than I was because that is what I thought she liked. In that relationship, I felt pressure to be like her.

Conformity to peer pressure in adolescence can be positive or negative (Wall, 1993). Teenagers engage in all sorts of negative conformity behavior—for instance, they use seedy language, steal, vandalize, and make fun of parents and teachers. However, a great deal of peer conformity, such as dressing like one's friends and wanting to spend huge chunks of time with members of a clique, is not negative and reflects the desire to be involved in the peer world.

During adolescence, especially early adolescence, we conformed more to peer standards than we did in childhood. Investigators have found that, around the eighth and ninth grades, conformity to peers—especially to their antisocial standards—peaks (Berndt, 1979; Leventhal, 1994). At this point in development, an adolescent is most likely to go along with a peer to steal hubcaps off a car, draw graffiti on a wall, or steal cosmetics from a store counter.

Cliques and Crowds

Cliques and crowds assume more important roles in the lives of adolescents than children. **Cliques** are small groups that range from 2 to about 12 individuals and average about 5 to 6 individuals. The clique members are usually of the same sex and about the same age. Cliques can form because adolescents engage in similar activities, such as being in a club or on a sports team. Some cliques also form because of friendship. Several adolescents may form a clique because they have spent time with each other and enjoy each other's company. Not necessarily friends, they often develop a friendship if they stay in the clique. What do adolescents do in cliques? They share ideas, hang out together, and often develop an in-group identity in which they believe that their clique is better than other cliques.

Crowds are a larger group structure than cliques. Adolescents are usually members of a crowd based on reputation and may or may not spend much time together. Crowds are less personal than cliques. Many crowds are defined by the activities adolescents engage in (such as "jocks," who are good at sports, or "druggies," who take drugs).

In one study, crowd membership was associated with adolescent self-esteem (Brown & Lohr, 1987). The crowds included jocks (athletically oriented), populars (well-known students who led social activities), normals (middle-of-the-road students who made up the masses), druggies or toughs (known for illicit drug use or other delinquent activities), and nobodies (low in social skills or intellectual abilities). The self-esteem of the jocks and the populars was highest, whereas that of the nobodies was lowest. One group of adolescents not in a crowd had self-esteem equivalent to that of the jocks and the populars; this group was the independents, who indicated that crowd membership was not important to them. Keep in mind that these data are correlational; self-esteem could increase an adolescent's probability of becoming a crowd member, just as crowd membership could increase the adolescent's self-esteem.

Adolescent Groups Versus Child Groups

Child groups differ from adolescent groups in several important ways. The members of child groups often are friends or neighborhood acquaintances, and their groups usually are not as formalized as many adolescent groups. During the adolescent years, groups tend to include a broader array of members. In other words, adolescents other than friends or neighborhood acquaintances often are members of adolescent groups. Try to recall the student council, honor society, or football team at your junior high school. If you were a member of any of these organizations, you

I didn't belong as a kid, and that always bothered me. If only I'd known that one day my differentness would be an asset, then my early life would have been much easier.

—BETTE MIDLER
Contemporary American Actress

cliques Small groups that range from 2 to about 12 individuals and average about 5 to 6 individuals. Cliques can form because of friendship or because individuals engage in similar activities, and members usually are of the same sex and about the same age.

crowds The crowd is a larger group structure than a clique. Adolescents usually are members of a crowd based on reputation and may or may not spend much time together. Many crowds are defined by the activities adolescents engage in.

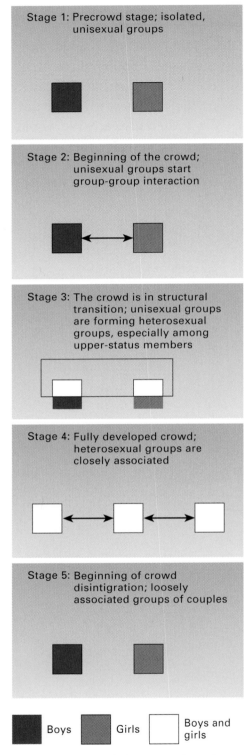

Stage 1: Precrowd stage; isolated, unisexual groups

Stage 2: Beginning of the crowd; unisexual groups start group-group interaction

Stage 3: The crowd is in structural transition; unisexual groups are forming heterosexual groups, especially among upper-status members

Stage 4: Fully developed crowd; heterosexual groups are closely associated

Stage 5: Beginning of crowd disintigration; loosely associated groups of couples

Boys   Girls   Boys and girls

FIGURE 16.6 Dunphy's Progression of Peer Group Relations in Adolescence

probably remember that they were made up of many people you had not met before and that they were a more heterogeneous group than your childhood peer groups. For example, peer groups in adolescence are more likely to have a mixture of individuals from different ethnic groups than are peer groups in childhood. To read further about ethnic minority adolescents' peer groups, see the Explorations in Child Development box on page 530. Also, in adolescent peer groups, rules and regulations are usually defined more precisely than in children's peer groups. For example, captains or leaders are often formally elected or appointed in adolescent peer groups.

A well-known observational study by Dexter Dunphy (1963) supports the notion that mixed-sex participation in groups increases during adolescence. In late childhood, boys and girls participate in small, same-sex cliques. As they move into the early adolescent years, the same-sex cliques begin to interact with each other. Gradually, the leaders and high-status members form further cliques based on mixed-sex relationships. Eventually, the newly created mixed-sex cliques replace the same-sex cliques. The mixed-sex cliques interact with each other in large crowd activities, too—at dances and athletic events, for example. In late adolescence, the crowd begins to dissolve as couples develop more-serious relationships and make long-range plans that may include engagement and marriage (see figure 16.6).

Dating and Romantic Relationships

Though many adolescent boys and girls have social interchanges through formal and informal peer groups, it is through dating that more serious contacts between the sexes occur (Bouchey & Furman, 2003; Carver, Joyner, & Udry, 2003; Florsheim, 2003; Furman & Shaffer, 2003). Adolescents spend considerable time either dating or thinking about dating, which has gone far beyond its original courtship function to become a form of recreation, a source of status and achievement, and a setting for learning about close relationships. One function of dating, though, continues to be mate selection.

Heterosexual Romantic Relationships A number of developmental changes characterize developmental changes in heterosexual dating. In one recent study, announcing that "I like someone" occurred by the sixth grade for 40 percent of the individuals sampled (Buhrmester, 2001) (see figure 16.7). However, it was not until the tenth grade that 50 percent of the adolescents had a sustained romantic relationship that lasted 2 months or longer. By their senior year, 25 percent still had not engaged in this type of sustained romantic relationship. Also, in this study, girls' early romantic involvement was linked with lower grades, less active participation in class discussion, and school-related problems. A rather large portion of adolescents in dating relationships say that their relationships have persisted 11 months or longer: 20 percent of adolescents 14 or younger, 35 percent of 15- to 16-year-olds, and almost 60 percent of 17- and 18-year-olds (Carver, Joyner, & Udry, 2003).

In their early romantic relationships, many adolescents are not motivated to fulfill attachment or even sexual needs. Rather, early romantic relationships serve as a context for adolescents to explore how attractive they are, how they should romantically interact with someone, and how all of this looks to the peer group (Brown, 1999). Only after adolescents acquire some basic competencies in interacting with romantic partners does the fulfillment of attachment and sexual needs become central functions of these relationships (Furman & Wehner, 1999).

In their early exploration of romantic relationships, today's adolescents often find comfort in numbers and begin hanging out together in heterosexual groups. Sometimes they just hang out at someone's house or get organized enough to get someone to drive them to a mall or a movie (Peterson, 1997). A special concern is early dating and "going with" someone, which is associated with adolescent pregnancy and problems at home and school (Downey & Bonica, 1997).

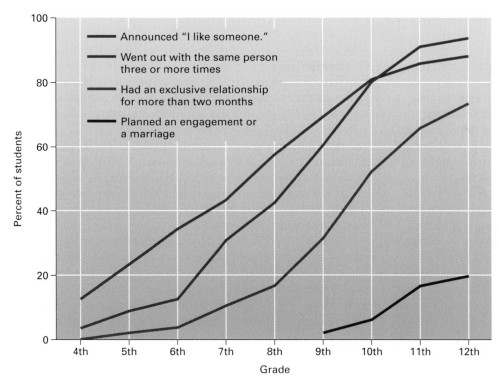

FIGURE 16.7 Age of Onset of Heterosexual Romantic Activity

In this study, announcing that "I like someone" occurred earliest, followed by going out with the same person three or more times, having an exclusive relationship for over two months, and finally planning an engagement or marriage (which characterized only a very small percentage of participants by the twelfth grade) (Buhrmester, 2001).

Yet another form of dating recently has been added. *Cyberdating* is dating over the Internet (Thomas, 1998). One 10-year-old girl posted this ad on the Net:

> Hi! I'm looking for a Cyber Boyfriend! I'm 10. I have brown hair and brown eyes. I love swimming, playing basketball, and think kittens are adorable!!!

Cyberdating is especially becoming popular among middle school students. By the time they reach high school and are able to drive, dating usually has evolved into a more traditional real-life venture. Adolescents need to be cautioned about the potential hazards of cyberdating and not really knowing who is on the other end of the computer connection.

Romantic Relationships in Sexual Minority Youth   Most research on romantic relationships in adolescence has focused on heterosexual relationships. Recently, researchers have begun to study romantic relationships in gay, lesbian, and bisexual youth (Diamond & Savin-Williams, 2003).

Most sexual minority youth have same-sex sexual experience but relatively few have same-sex romantic relationships because of limited opportunities and the social disapproval such relationships may generate from families or heterosexual peers (Diamond, 2003; Diamond, Savin-Williams, & Dubé, 1999). The importance of romance to sexual minority youth was underscored in a study which found that they rated the breakup of a current romance as their second most stressful problem, second only to disclosure of their sexual orientation to their parents (D'Augelli, 1991).

What romantic pathways do sexual minority youth follow? Let's examine three common myths about these pathways and explore how they are more variable than usually believed (Diamond, 2003):

Ethnic Minority Adolescents' Peer Relations

As ethnic minority children move into adolescence and enter schools with more heterogeneous school populations, they become more aware of their ethnic minority status (Phinney & Cobb, 1993). Ethnic minority adolescents may have difficulty joining peer groups and clubs in predominantly White schools. Similarly, White adolescents may have peer relations difficulties in predominantly ethnic minority schools. However, schools are only one setting in which peer relations take place; they also occur in the neighborhood and in the community (Jones & Gostin, 1997).

Ethnic minority adolescents often have two sets of peer relationships, one at school, the other in the community. Community peers are more likely to be from their own ethnic group in their immediate neighborhood. Sometimes, they go to the same church and participate in activities together, such as Black History Week, Chinese New Year's, or Cinco de Mayo Festival. Because ethnic group adolescents usually have two sets of peers and friends, when researchers ask about their peers and friends, questions should focus on both relationships at school and in the neighborhood and community. Ethnic minority adolescents who are social isolates at school may be sociometric stars in their segregated neighborhood. Also, because adolescents are more mobile than children, inquiries should be made about the scope of their social networks.

In one investigation the school and neighborhood friendship patterns of 292 African American and White adolescents who attended an integrated junior high school were studied (DuBois & Hirsch, 1990). Most students reported having an other-ethnic school friend, but only 28 percent of the students saw such a friend frequently outside school. Reports of an interethnic school friendship that extended to nonschool settings were more common among African American adolescents than among White adolescents and among adolescents who lived in an integrated rather than a segregated neighborhood. African American adolescents were more likely than White adolescents to have extensive neighborhood friendship networks, but African American adolescents said they talked with fewer friends during the school day.

Of special interest to investigators is the degree of peer support for an ethnic minority adolescent's achievement orientation. Some researchers argue that peers often dissuade African American adolescents from doing well in school (Fordham & Ogbu, 1986; Fuller, 1984). However, in one investigation, peer support of achievement was relatively high among Asian American adolescents, moderate among African American and Latino adolescents, and relatively low among Anglo-American adolescents (Brown & others, 1990). The low peer support of achievement among Anglo-American adolescents possibly is due to their strong individualistic, competitive, and social comparison orientation.

Adolescent peer relations take place in a number of settings—at school, in the neighborhood, and in the community, for example. Ethnic minority adolescents often have two sets of peer relationships—one at school, the other in the community. A special interest is the degree to which peers support an ethnic minority adolescent's achievement orientation.

- *Myth 1: All sexual minority youth quietly struggle with same-sex attractions in childhood, shun heterosexual dating, and gradually sense that they are gay in mid to late adolescence.* Many youth do follow this pathway but others deviate from it. For example, many adolescents have no memories of same-sex attractions during their childhood and experience more abrupt realization of their same-sex sexual attraction during late adolescence (Diamond & Savin-Williams, 2000). Also, many sexual minority youth date other-sex peers, which may help them to clarify their sexual orientation or disguise it from others (Furman, 2002).

- *Myth 2: All gay and lesbian youth only have same-sex attractions.* Researchers have found that like adults, many gay and lesbian youth experience some degree of other-sex attractions (Garofalo & others, 1999).
- *Myth 3: Adolescents who sexually desire the same sex always fall in love with the same sex.* Some youths say that their same-sex attractions are purely physical, while others claim they have more to do with emotional attachment (Savin-Williams, 1998).

In sum, there is a great deal of complexity in the romantic possibilities of sexual minority youth (Diamond, 2003). To adequately address the relational interests of sexual minority youth, we can't simply generalize from heterosexual youth and simply switch the labels. Instead, the full range of variation in sexual minority youths' sexual desires and romantic relationships for same- and other-sex partners need to be considered.

Dating Scripts **Dating scripts** are the cognitive models that guide individuals' dating interactions. In one study, first dates were highly scripted along gender lines (Rose & Frieze, 1993). The males followed a proactive dating script, the females a reactive one. The male's script involved initiating the date (asking for and planning it), controlling the public domain (driving and opening doors), and initiating sexual interaction (making physical contact, making out, and kissing). The female's script focused on the private domain (concern about appearance, enjoying the date), participating in the structure of the date established by the male (being picked up, having doors opened), and responding to his sexual overtures. These gender differences give males more power in the initial stage of a dating relationship.

In another study, male and female adolescents brought different motivations to the dating experience (Feiring, 1996). The 15-year-old girls were more likely to describe romance in terms of interpersonal qualities, the boys in terms of physical attraction. The young adolescents frequently mentioned the affiliative qualities of companionship, intimacy, and support as positive aspects of romantic relationships,

Exploring Dating

Teen Chat

What are some examples of dating scripts in adolescence?

dating scripts The cognitive models that adolescents and adults use to guide and evaluate dating interactions.

but not love and security. Also, the young adolescents described physical attraction more in terms of cute, pretty, or handsome than in sexual terms (such as being a good kisser). Possibly the failure to discuss sexual interests was due to the adolescents' discomfort in talking about such personal feelings with an unfamiliar adult.

Emotion and Romantic Relationships   The strong emotions of romantic relationships can thrust adolescents into a world in which things are turned upside down and ordinary reality recedes from view (Larson, Clore, & Wood, 1999). One 14-year-old reports that he is so in love he can't think about anything else. A 15-year-old girl is enraged by the betrayal of her boyfriend. She is obsessed with ways to get back at him. The daily fluctuations in the emotions of romantic relationships can make the world seem almost surreal. Although the strong emotions of romance can have disruptive effects on adolescents, they also provide a source for possible mastery and growth. Learning to manage these strong emotions can give adolescents a sense of competence.

Romantic relationships often are involved in an adolescent's emotional experiences (Collins, 2002). In one study of ninth- to twelfth-graders, girls gave real and fantasized heterosexual relationships as the explanation for more than one-third of their strong emotions, and boys gave this reason for 25 percent of their strong emotions (Wilson-Shockley, 1995). Strong emotions were attached far less to school (13%), family (9%), and same-sex peer relations (8%). The majority of the emotions were reported as positive, but a substantial minority (42%) were reported as negative, including feelings of anxiety, anger, jealousy, and depression. The most common trigger of the first episode of major depression in adolescence is a romantic breakup.

Sociocultural Contexts and Dating   The sociocultural context exerts a powerful influence on adolescent dating patterns and on mate selection (Booth, 2002; Stevenson & Zusho, 2002). Values and religious beliefs of people in various cultures often dictate the age at which dating begins, how much freedom in dating is allowed, whether dates must be chaperoned by adults or parents, and the roles of males and females in dating. In the Arab world, Asian countries, and South America, adults are typically highly restrictive of adolescent girls' romantic relationships.

Immigrants to the United States have brought these restrictive standards with them. For example, in the United States, Latino and Asian American cultures have more conservative standards regarding adolescent dating than the Anglo-American culture. Dating can be a source of cultural conflict for many immigrants and their families who have come from cultures in which dating begins at a late age, little freedom in dating is allowed, dates are chaperoned, and dating by adolescent girls is especially restricted.

In one recent study, Latino young adults living in the Midwestern region of the United States reflected on their socialization for dating and sexuality (Raffaelli & Ontai, 2001). Because U.S.-style dating was viewed as a violation of traditional courtship styles by most of their parents, the parents placed strict boundaries on their romantic involvement. As a result many of the Latinos described their adolescent dating experiences as filled with tension and conflict. The average age at which the girls began dating was 15.7 years with early dating experiences usually occurring without parental knowledge or permission. Over half of the girls engaged in "sneak dating."

Review and Reflect: Learning Goal 4

4 Characterize peer relations and romantic relationships in adolescence

REVIEW

- What is peer pressure and conformity like in adolescence?
- How are cliques and crowds involved in adolescent development?
- What is the nature of adolescent dating and romantic relationships?

REFLECT

- What were your peer relationships like during adolescence? What peer groups were you involved in? How did they influence your development? What were your dating and romantic relationships like in adolescence? If you could change anything about the way you experienced peer relations in adolescence, what would it be?

Reach Your Learning Goals

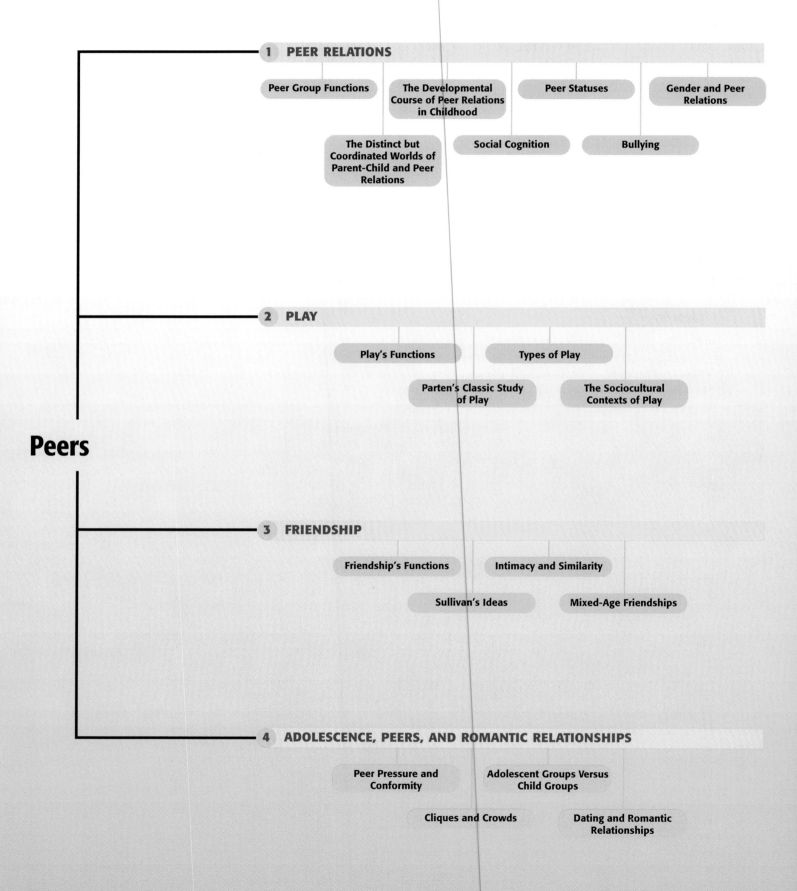

Peers

1 PEER RELATIONS

- Peer Group Functions
- The Developmental Course of Peer Relations in Childhood
- Peer Statuses
- Gender and Peer Relations
- The Distinct but Coordinated Worlds of Parent-Child and Peer Relations
- Social Cognition
- Bullying

2 PLAY

- Play's Functions
- Types of Play
- Parten's Classic Study of Play
- The Sociocultural Contexts of Play

3 FRIENDSHIP

- Friendship's Functions
- Intimacy and Similarity
- Sullivan's Ideas
- Mixed-Age Friendships

4 ADOLESCENCE, PEERS, AND ROMANTIC RELATIONSHIPS

- Peer Pressure and Conformity
- Adolescent Groups Versus Child Groups
- Cliques and Crowds
- Dating and Romantic Relationships

Summary

1 Discuss peer relations in childhood

- Peers are individuals who are at about the same age or maturity level. Peers provide a means of social comparison and a source of information about the world outside the family. Good peer relations may be necessary for normal social development. The inability to "plug in" to a social network is associated with a number of problems. Peer relations can be both positive and negative. Piaget and Sullivan stressed that peer relations provide the context for learning the symmetrical reciprocity mode of relationships. Peer relations vary according to the way peer experience is measured, the outcomes specified, and the developmental trajectories traversed.
- Children touch, smile, and vocalize when they interact with parents and peers. Healthy family relations usually promote healthy peer relations. Parents can model or coach their children in ways of relating to peers. Parents' choices of neighborhoods, churches, schools, and their own friends influence the pool from which their children might select possible friends. Rough-and-tumble play occurs mainly in peer relations rather than in parent-child relations. In times of stress, children usually turn to parents rather than peers. Peer relations have a more equal basis than parent-child relations.
- Some researchers believe that the quality of social interaction with peers in infancy provides valuable information about social development. As increasing numbers of infants have attended day care, infant peer relations have increased. The frequency of peer interaction, both positive and negative, increases in the preschool years. Children spend even more time with peers in the elementary and secondary school years.
- Perspective taking, social information-processing skills, and social knowledge are important dimensions of social cognition in peer relations.
- Popular children are frequently nominated as a best friend and are rarely disliked by their peers. Neglected children are infrequently nominated as a best friend but are not disliked by their peers. Rejected children are infrequently nominated as a best friend and are disliked by their peers. Rejected children often have more serious adjustment problems than neglected children. Controversial children are frequently nominated both as one's best friend and as being disliked by peers.
- Significant numbers of students are bullied, and this can result in problems for the victim.
- Gender is linked to peer relations in these ways: Gender composition of children's groups (from 4 to 12 years of age, preference for playing in same-sex groups increases), group size (boys' groups are larger and they participate in more organized games than girls), interaction in same-sex groups (boys are more likely to engage in rough-and-tumble play, competition, ego displays, risk taking, and dominance, while girls are more likely to engage in collaborative dis-

course), and socialization within same-sex groups (the more time boys spend playing with boys, the higher their levels of aggression and activity, while the more time girls spend playing with girls, the lower their levels of aggression and activity).

2 Describe children's play

- The functions of play include affiliation with peers, tension release, advances in cognitive development, and exploration.
- Parten examined these categories of social play: unoccupied, solitary, onlooker, parallel, associative, and cooperative.
- The contemporary perspective emphasizes both social and cognitive aspects of play. The most widely studied types of play include sensorimotor and practice play, pretense/symbolic play, social play, constructive play, and games.
- Modern children spend a large of part of their play with toys, and their play increasingly is confined to backyards, basements, playrooms, and bedrooms rather than rural fields and city streets. The form and content of children's play are influenced by cultural and socioeconomic factors.

3 Explain friendship

- The functions of friendship include companionship, stimulation, physical support, ego support, social comparison, and intimacy/affection.
- Sullivan argued that there is a dramatic increase in the psychological importance and intimacy of close friends in adolescence. Research findings support his view.
- Intimacy and similarity are two of the most common characteristics of friendships. Intimacy in friendship is much more common in adolescents than children. Friends often have similar attitudes toward school, similar educational aspirations, and so on.
- Children and adolescents who become friends with older individuals engage in more deviant behaviors than their counterparts with same-age friends. Early-maturing girls are more likely than late-maturing girls to have older friends, which can contribute to their problem behaviors.

4 Characterize peer relations and romantic relationships in adolescence

- The pressure to conform to peers is strong during adolescence, especially in eighth and ninth grade.
- Cliques and crowds assume more importance in the lives of adolescents than children. Membership in certain crowds—especially jocks and populars—is associated with increased self-esteem. Independents also show high self-esteem. Children groups are less formal, less heterogeneous, and less heterosexual than adolescent groups.
- Dating takes on added importance in adolescence, and it can have many functions. Younger adolescents often begin to hang out together in heterosexual groups. A special concern

is early dating, which is linked with developmental problems. Male dating scripts are proactive, those of females reactive. Most sexual minority youth have same-sex sexual experience but relatively few have same-sex romantic relationships. Many sexual minority youth date other-sex peers, which can help them to clarify their sexual orientation or disguise it from others. Emotions are heavily involved in adolescent dating and romantic relationships. Culture can exert a powerful influence on adolescent dating.

Key Terms

peers 511
perspective taking 514
popular children 515
neglected children 515
rejected children 515
controversial children 516

play 518
play therapy 518
unoccupied play 519
solitary play 519
onlooker play 520
parallel play 520

associative play 520
cooperative play 520
sensorimotor play 520
practice play 520
pretense/symbolic play 520
social play 521

constructive play 521
games 521
intimacy in friendship 524
cliques 527
crowds 527
dating scripts 531

Key People

Anna Freud 511
Kenneth Dodge 515
Erik Erikson 518

Sigmund Freud 518
Jean Piaget 518
Lev Vygotsky 519

Daniel Berlyne 519
Mildred Parten 519
Harry Stack Sullivan 523

Willard Hartup 523
Dexter Dunphy 528

Taking It to the Net

1. Barbara is going to lead a discussion in her child development class about peer relationships and friendships in early childhood. What should Barbara tell the class about how peer relationships develop between the ages of 3 and 6 years?

2. Darla, 13, has been living in foster homes since she was 4 years old. As a result of being abandoned by her parents and moved from foster home to foster home, she doesn't trust anyone. She is in counseling to help her adjust to her latest home and her new middle school. Her therapist brings up the importance of making and having friends, a concept alien to Darla. What does Darla need to learn in order to have a friend and be one?

3. Kristin is getting intense pressure from her friends at school to go out and drink with them. She wants to hang out with them, but has no interest in drinking. Because she can't turn to her friends to help her, she hopes her mother can give her some pointers for dealing with this pressure. What can Kristin's mother say to help?

Connect to **www.mhhe.com/santrockcd10** to research the answers and complete these exercises.

E-Learning Tools

To help you master the material in this chapter, you'll find a number of valuable study tools on the Student CD-ROM that accompanies this book. Also visit the Online Learning Center for Child Development, tenth edition (**www.mhhe.com/santrockcd10**) where you'll find these additional resources:

- View video clips by key developmental psychology experts including Alan Sroufe on attachment and peers.
- Build your decision-making skills by trying your hand at the parenting, nursing, and education "Scenarios" on the Online Learning Center.

The whole art of teaching is the art of awakening the natural curiosity of young minds.

—ANATOLE FRANCE
French Novelist, 20th Century

Schools

Chapter Outline

EXPLORING CHILDREN'S SCHOOLING

Contemporary Approaches to Children's Schooling

Schools' Changing Social Developmental Contexts

SCHOOLS AND DEVELOPMENTAL STATUS

Early Childhood Education

The Transition to Elementary School

Schools for Adolescents

SOCIOECONOMIC STATUS AND ETHNICITY IN SCHOOLS

Socioeconomic Status

Ethnicity

CHILDREN WITH DISABILITIES

Who Are Children with Disabilities?

Learning Disabilities

Attention Deficit Hyperactivity Disorder (ADHD)

Educational Issues

ACHIEVEMENT

Need for Achievement

Extrinsic and Intrinsic Motivation

Mastery Motivation

Self-Efficacy

Goal Setting, Planning, and Self-Monitoring

Ethnicity and Culture

Learning Goals

1 Discuss some approaches to children's schooling and changing social developmental contexts in schools

2 Summarize what schooling is like for children of different ages

3 Describe the roles of socioeconomic status and ethnicity in schools

4 Characterize children with disabilities and their schooling

5 Explain the development of achievement in children

The Story of Reggio Emilia's Children

The Reggio Emilia approach is an educational program for young children that was developed in the northern Italian city of Reggio Emilia. Children of single parents and children with disabilities have priority in admission; other children are admitted according to a scale of needs. Parents pay on a sliding scale based on income.

The children are encouraged to learn by investigating and exploring topics that interest them. A wide range of stimulating media and materials is available for children to use as they learn—music, movement, drawing, painting, sculpting, collages, puppets and disguises, and photography, for example.

In this program, children often explore topics in a group, which fosters a sense of community, respect for diversity, and a collaborative approach to problem solving. Two co-teachers are present to serve as guides for children. The Reggio Emilia teachers consider a project as an adventure, which can start from an adult's suggestion, from a child's idea, or from an event, such as a snowfall or something else unexpected. Every project is based on what the children say and do. The teachers allow children enough time to think and craft a project.

At the core of the Reggio Emilia approach is the image of children who are competent and have rights, especially the right to outstanding care and education (Bredekamp, 1993). Parent participation is considered essential, and cooperation is a major theme in the schools. Many early childhood education experts believe the Reggio Emilia approach provides a supportive, stimulating context in which children are motivated to explore their world in a competent and confident manner (Firlik, 1996).

In this chapter, we will examine not only early childhood education, but other aspects of schooling as children develop, such as the transition to elementary school and schools for adolescents. We also will discuss the roles that socioeconomic status and ethnicity play in schools, educational issues involving children with disabilities, and many aspects of children's achievement.

A Reggio Emilia classroom in which young children explore topics that interest them.

1 EXPLORING CHILDREN'S SCHOOLING

> **Contemporary Approaches to Children's Schooling**

> **Schools' Changing Social Developmental Contexts**

Two of the important questions we will explore regarding children's schooling are these: What are some contemporary approaches to student learning? How do the social contexts of their schools change as children age?

Contemporary Approaches to Children's Schooling

There is much controversy over what the best way is for children to learn in school. The back-to-basics movement still has strong advocates, who believe that children should mainly be taught in a **direct instruction approach,** a teacher-centered approach that is characterized by teacher direction and control, mastery of academic skills, high expectations for students' progress, and maximum time spent on learning tasks. This approach has much in common with the behavioral approach we discussed in chapter 2, "The Science of Child Development." ◀ **page 36**

In the last decade, there has been a wave of interest in constructivist approaches to school reform (Santrock, 2004). **Cognitive constructivist approaches** emphasize the child's active, cognitive construction of knowledge and understanding. Piaget's theory (discussed in chapters 2 and 7) is an example of a cognitive constructivist approach. ◀ **pages 33, 207** The implications of Piaget's theory are that teachers should provide support for students to explore their world and develop understanding. **Social constructivist approaches** focus on collaboration with others to produce knowledge and understanding. Vygotsky's theory (also discussed in chapters 2 and 7) is an example of a social constructivist approach. ◀ **pages 35, 229** The implications of Vygotsky's theory are that teachers should create many opportunities for students to learn with the teacher and with peers in co-constructing understanding (John-Steiner & Mahn, 2003).

Advocates of the cognitive and social constructivist approaches argue that the direct instruction approach turns children into passive learners and does not adequately challenge them to think in critical and creative ways. The direct instruction enthusiasts say that the constructivist approaches often do not give enough attention to the content of a discipline, such as history or science. They also say that many constructivist approaches are too relativistic and vague.

A constructivist theme is evident in what are called learner-centered principles, which move instruction away from the teacher and toward the student. Increased interest in learner-centered principles resulted in the publication of *Learner-Centered Psychological Principles: A Framework for School Reform and Redesign* (Learner-Centered Principles Work Group, 1997; Presidential Task Force on Psychology and Education, 1992; Work Group of the American Psychological Association's Board of Affairs, 1995). This statement of principles was constructed and is periodically revised by a prestigious group of scientists and educators from a wide range of disciplines and interests. The principles have important implications for the way teachers instruct students.

The fourteen learner-centered principles involve cognitive and metacognitive factors, motivational and affective factors, developmental and social factors, and individual difference factors. To read more about these learner-centered principles, see figure 17.1.

Schools' Changing Social Developmental Contexts

The social context differs at the preschool, elementary, and secondary level. The preschool setting is a protected environment, whose boundary is the classroom. In this

www.mhhe.com/santrockcd1o

National Education Research Centers

Pathways to School Improvement

APA's Learner-Centered Psychological Principles

---

direct instruction approach A teacher-centered approach that is characterized by teacher direction and control, mastery of academic material, high expectations for students' progress, and maximum time spent on learning tasks.

cognitive constructivist approaches Approaches that emphasize the child's active, cognitive construction of knowledge and understanding; Piaget's theory is an example of this approach.

social constructivist approaches Approaches that focus on collaboration with others to produce knowledge and understanding; Vygotsky's theory is an example of this approach.

FIGURE 17.1 Learner-Centered Psychological Principles

Cognitive and Metacognitive Factors

1. Nature of the Learning Process
   The learning of complex subject matter is most effective when it is an intentional process of constructing meaning and experience.

2. Goals of the Learning Process
   Successful learners, over time and with support and instructional guidance, can create meaningful, coherent representations of knowledge.

3. Construction of Knowledge
   Successful learners can link new information with existing knowledge in meaningful ways.

4. Strategic Thinking
   Successful learners can create a repertoire of thinking and reasoning strategies to achieve complex goals.

5. Thinking about Thinking
   Higher order strategies for selecting and monitoring mental operations facilitate creative and critical thinking.

6. Context of Learning
   Learning is influenced by environmental factors, including culture, technology, and instructional practices.

Motivational and Instructional Factors

7. Motivational and Emotional Influences on Learning
   What and how much is learned is influenced by the learner's motivation. Motivation to learn, in turn, is influenced by the learner's emotional states, beliefs, interests, goals, and habits of thinking.

8. Intrinsic Motivation to Learn
   The learner's creativity, higher order thinking, and natural curiosity all contribute to motivation to learn. Intrinsic (internal, self-generated) motivation is stimulated by tasks of optimal novelty and difficulty, tasks that are relevant to personal interests, and when learners are provided personal choice and control.

9. Effects of Motivation on Effort
   Acquiring complex knowledge and skills requires extended learner effort and guided practice. Without learners' motivation to learn, the willingness to exert this effort is unlikely without coercion.

Developmental and Social Factors

10. Developmental Influences on Learning
    As individuals develop, there are different opportunities and constraints for learning. Learning is most effective when development within and across physical, cognitive, and socioemotional domains is taken into account.

11. Social Influences on Learning
    Learning is influenced by social interactions, interpersonal relations, and communication with others.

Individual Difference Factors

12. Individual Differences in Learning
    Learners have different strategies, approaches, and capabilities for learning that are a function of prior experience and heredity.

13. Learning and Diversity
    Learning is most effective when differences in learners' linguistic, cultural, and social backgrounds are considered.

14. Standards and Assessment
    Setting appropriately high and challenging standards and assessing the learner as well as learning progress are integral aspects of the learning experience.

limited social setting, preschool children interact with one or two teachers, almost always female, who are powerful figures in the young child's life. The preschool child also interacts with peers in a dyadic relationship or in small groups. Preschool children have little concept of the classroom as an organized social system, although they are learning how to make and maintain social contacts and communicate their needs. The preschool serves to modify some patterns of behavior developed through family experiences. Greater self-control may be required in the preschool than earlier in development.

The classroom is still the major context for the elementary school child, although it is more likely to be experienced as a social unit than in the preschool. The network of social expression also is more complex now. Teachers and peers have a prominent influence on children during the elementary school years. The teacher symbolizes authority, which establishes the climate of the classroom, conditions of social interaction, and the nature of group functioning. The peer group becomes more salient, with increased interest in friendship, belonging, and status. And the peer group also becomes a learning community in which social roles and standards related to work and achievement are formed.

As children move into middle or junior high schools, the school environment increases in scope and complexity. The social field is the school as a whole rather than the classroom. Adolescents socially interact with many different teachers and peers from a range of social and ethnic backgrounds. Students are often exposed to a greater mix of male and female teachers. And social behavior is heavily weighted toward peers, extracurricular activities, clubs, and the community. The student in secondary school is usually aware of the school as a social system and may be motivated to conform and adapt to the system or challenge it (Minuchin & Shapiro, 1983).

Review and Reflect: Learning Goal 1

1 Discuss some approaches to children's schooling and changing social developmental contexts in schools

REVIEW

- What are the direct instruction, cognitive constructivist, and social constructivist approaches to schooling? What are the American Psychological Association's learner-centered principles?
- How do schools' social developmental contexts change?

REFLECT

- How would you characterize the approach of the schools that you attended as a child and an adolescent? Do you think your schools were effective? Explain.

---

2 SCHOOLS AND DEVELOPMENTAL STATUS

Early Childhood Education	The Transition to Elementary School	Schools for Adolescents

What is the nature of early childhood education? How do children make the transition to elementary school? What is the nature of schools for adolescents?

Early Childhood Education

There are many variations in the way young children are educated (Goelman & others, 2003). In the story that opened this chapter, you read about the Reggio Emilia program in northern Italy, a promising strategy that is receiving increased attention. First, we will explore the nature of the child-centered kindergarten, then turn our attention to Maria Montessori's approach. Next, we will examine the important concepts of developmentally appropriate and inappropriate education, followed by a discussion of what early childhood education's effects are.

The Child-Centered Kindergarten Kindergarten programs vary a great deal. Some approaches place more emphasis on young children's social development, others on their cognitive development. Some experts on early childhood education believe that the curriculum of too many of today's kindergarten and preschool programs place too much emphasis on achievement and success, putting pressure on young children too early in their development (Charlesworth, 2000; Elkind, 1988). Kindergartens were not originally intended to be factories of achievement.

In the 1840s, Friedrich Froebel's concern for quality education for young children led to the founding of the kindergarten—literally, "a garden for children." The founder of the kindergarten understood that, like growing plants, children require careful nurturing. Unfortunately, too many of today's kindergartens have forgotten the importance of careful nurturing for our nation's young children.

In the **child-centered kindergarten,** education involves the whole child and includes concern for the child's physical, cognitive, and socioemotional development. Instruction is organized around the child's needs, interests, and learning styles. Emphasis is on the process of learning rather than on what is learned. Each child follows a unique developmental pattern, and young children learn best through firsthand experiences with people and materials (Wardle, 2003). Play is extremely important in the child's total development. *Experimenting, exploring, discovering, trying out, restructuring, speaking,* and *listening* are all words that describe the activities in excellent kindergarten programs. Such programs are closely attuned to the developmental status of 4- and 5-year-old children. They are based on a state of being, not on a state of becoming.

The Montessori Approach Montessori schools are patterned after the educational philosophy of Maria Montessori (1870–1952), an Italian physician-turned-educator, who crafted a revolutionary approach to young children's education at the beginning of the twentieth century (Wentworth, 1999). Her work began in Rome with a group of children who were mentally retarded. She was successful in teaching them to read, write, and pass examinations designed for normal children. Some time later, she turned her attention to poor children from the slums of Rome and had similar success in teaching them. Her approach has since been adopted extensively in private nursery schools in the United States.

The **Montessori approach** is a philosophy of education in which children are given considerable freedom and spontaneity in choosing activities. They are allowed to move from one activity to another as they desire. The teacher acts as a facilitator rather than a director of learning. The teacher shows the child how to perform intellectual activities, demonstrates interesting ways to explore curriculum materials, and offers help when the child requests it.

Some developmentalists favor the Montessori approach, but others believe that it neglects children's social development (Chattin-McNichols, 1992). For example, while Montessori fosters independence and the development of cognitive skills, it deemphasizes verbal interaction between the teacher and child and peer interaction. Montessori's critics also argue that it restricts imaginative play and its heavy reliance on self-corrective materials may not adequately allow for creativity and learning-style flexibility (Goffin & Wilson, 2001).

Developmentally Appropriate and Inappropriate Practices in the Education of Young Children It is time for number games in a kindergarten class at the Greenbrook School in South Brunswick, New Jersey. With little prodding from the teacher, 23 5- and 6-year-old children fetch geometric puzzles, playing cards, and counting equipment from the shelves lining the room. At one round table, some young children fit together brightly colored shapes. One girl forms a hexagon out

www.mhhe.com/santrockcd10

Ask ERIC
American Educational Research Association (AERA)
Early Childhood Education
Reggio Emilia

child-centered kindergarten Education that involves the whole child by considering both the child's physical, cognitive, and social development and the child's needs, interests, and learning styles.

Montessori approach An educational philosophy in which children are given considerable freedom and spontaneity in choosing activities and are allowed to move from one activity to another as they desire.

of triangles. Other children gather around her to count up how many parts were needed to make the whole. After about half an hour, the children prepare for story time. They put away their counting equipment and sit in a circle around one young girl. She holds up a giant book about a character named Mrs. Wishywashy, who insists on giving the farm animals a bath. The children recite the whimsical lines, clearly enjoying one of their favorite stories. The hallway outside the kindergarten is lined with drawings depicting the children's own interpretations of the book. After the first reading, volunteers act out various parts of the book. There is not one bored face in the room.

This is not reading, writing, and arithmetic the way most individuals remember it. A growing number of educators and psychologists believe that preschool and young elementary school children learn best through active, hands-on teaching methods such as games and dramatic play. They know that children develop at varying rates and that schools need to allow for these individual differences (Brewer, 2004; Henninger, 1999). They also believe that schools should focus on improving children's social development, as well as their cognitive development. Educators refer to this type of schooling as **developmentally appropriate practice,** which is based upon knowledge of the typical development of children within an age span (age appropriateness), the uniqueness of the child (individual appropriateness), and cultural appropriateness. Developmentally appropriate practice contrasts with developmentally inappropriate practice, which ignores the hands-on approach to learning. Direct teaching largely through abstract paper-and-pencil activities presented to large groups of young children is believed to be developmentally inappropriate.

One of the most comprehensive documents addressing the issue of developmentally appropriate practice in early childhood programs is the position statement by the National Association for the Education of Young Children (NAEYC) (Bredekamp, 1987, 1997; NAEYC, 1986). This document represents the expertise of many of the foremost experts in the field of early childhood education. In figure 17.2, you can examine some of the NAEYC recommendations for developmentally appropriate and inappropriate practice.

One recent study, conducted by Craig Hart and his colleagues (2003), compared 182 children from five developmentally appropriate kindergarten classrooms (hands-on activities and integrated curriculum tailored to meet age group, cultural, and individual learning styles) and five developmentally inappropriate kindergarten classrooms (academic, direct instruction emphasis with extensive use of workbooks/worksheets, seatwork, and rote drill/practice activities) in a Louisiana school system. Children from the two types of classrooms did not differ in pre-K readiness, and the classrooms were balanced in terms of sex and socioeconomic status. Teacher ratings of child behavior and scores on the California Achievement Test were obtained through the third grade. Children who were in developmentally appropriate classrooms had slower growth in vocabulary, math application, and math computation. In another recent study, the academic achievement of mostly African American and Latino children who were attending Head Start was assessed in terms of whether they were in schools emphasizing developmentally appropriate or inappropriate practices (Huffman & Speer, 2000). The young children in the developmentally appropriate classrooms were more advanced in letter/word identification and showed better performance in applying problems over time. Other researchers have found support for developmentally appropriate education (Hart, Burts, & Charlesworth, 1997).

A special worry of early childhood educators is that the back-to-basics movement that has recently characterized educational reform is filtering down to kindergarten. Another worry is that many parents want their children to go to school earlier than kindergarten for the purpose of getting a "head start" in achievement.

How common are programs that use developmentally appropriate practice? Unfortunately, as few as one-third to one-fifth of all early childhood programs follow this educational strategy. Even fewer elementary schools do. Child-initiated

developmentally appropriate practice Education that focuses on the typical developmental patterns of children (age appropriateness), the uniqueness of each child (individual appropriateness), and cultural appropriateness. Such practice contrasts with developmentally inappropriate practice, which ignores the concrete, hands-on approach to learning. Direct teaching largely through abstract paper-and-pencil activities presented to large groups of young children is believed to be developmentally inappropriate.

Component	Appropriate Practice	Inappropriate Practice
Curriculum goals	Experiences are provided in all developmental areas—physical, cognitive, social, and emotional.	Experiences are narrowly focused on cognitive development without recognition that all areas of the child's development are interrelated.
	Individual differences are expected, accepted, and used to design appropriate activities.	Children are evaluated only against group norms, and all are expected to perform the same tasks and achieve the same narrowly defined skills.
	Interactions and activities are designed to develop children's self-esteem and positive feelings toward learning.	Children's worth is measured by how well they conform to rigid expectations and perform on standardized tests.
Teaching strategies	Teachers prepare the environment for children to learn through active exploration and interaction with adults, other children, and materials.	Teachers use highly structured, teacher-directed lessons almost exclusively.
	Children select many of their own activities from among a variety the teacher prepares.	The teacher directs all activity, deciding what children will do and when.
	Children are expected to be mentally and physically active.	Children are expected to sit down, be quiet, and listen or do paper-and-pencil tasks for long periods of time. A major portion of time is spent passively sitting, watching, and listening.
Guidance of socioemotional development	Teachers enhance children's self-control by using positive guidance techniques, such as modeling and encouraging expected behavior, redirecting children to a more acceptable activity, and setting clear limits.	Teachers spend considerable time enforcing rules, punishing unacceptable behavior, demeaning children who misbehave, making children sit and be quiet, and refereeing disagreements.
	Children are provided many opportunities to develop social skills, such as cooperating, helping, negotiating, and talking with the person involved to solve interpersonal problems.	Children work individually at desks and tables most of the time and listen to the teacher's directions to the whole group.

FIGURE 17.2 NAEYC Recommendations for Developmentally Appropriate and Inappropriate Education

activities, divergent questioning, and small-group instruction are the exception rather than the rule (Dunn & Kontos, 1997).

Curriculum Controversy in Early Childhood Education   Currently, there is controversy about what the curriculum for U.S. early childhood education should be (Vecchiotti, 2003). On one side are those who advocate a child-centered, constructivist approach much like that emphasized by the NAEYC along the lines of developmentally appropriate practice. On the other side are those who advocate an academic, instructivist approach. From the academic, instructivist perspective, the child is viewed as dependent on adults' instruction in the academic knowledge and skills that can serve as a foundation for later academic achievement. In the academic approach, this involves teachers directly instructing young children to learn basic academic skills, especially in reading and math.

Early childhood education expert Lillian Katz (1999) argues that both sides in this argument may be overlooking and undervaluing a third option—curriculum and teaching methods that emphasize children's *intellectual development.* Both academic and constructivist approaches endorse early childhood programs that promote young children's intellectual development. Katz' observations of large numbers of early childhood programs indicate that many of these include both academic and constructivist approaches in their effort to develop young children's intellectual competence. What many experts, such as Katz, do not advocate are academic early childhood programs that pressure young children to achieve, do not provide them with opportunities to actively construct their learning, at least in part of the curriculum, and do not also emphasize the development of socioemotional skills.

NAEYC (2002) recently addressed the dramatic increase in the use of standards regarding desired results, outcomes, or learning expectations for U.S. children. NAEYC states that these standards can be a valuable part of early education but only if early learning standards (1) emphasize significant, developmentally appropriate content and outcomes; (2) are developed through inclusive, informed processes (in all instances, experts in early childhood education should be involved in creating the standards); and (3) use implementation and assessment strategies that are ethical and appropriate for young children (assessment and accountability should be used to improve practices and services and should not be used to rank, sort, or penalize young children).

Education for Children Who Are Disadvantaged   For many years, children from low-income families did not receive any education before they entered the first grade. In the 1960s, an effort was made to try to break the cycle of poverty and poor education for young children in the United States through compensatory education. **Project Head Start** is a compensatory program designed to provide children from low-income families the opportunity to acquire the skills and experiences important for success in school. Project Head Start began in the summer of 1965, funded by the Economic Opportunity Act, and it continues to serve disadvantaged children today.

Evaluations support the positive influence of quality early childhood programs on both the cognitive and social worlds of disadvantaged young children (Anderson & others, 2003; Reynolds, 1999; Schweinhart, 1999). One high-quality early childhood education program (although not a Head Start program) is the Perry Preschool program in Ypsilanti, Michigan, a 2-year preschool program that includes weekly home visits from program personnel. In an analysis of the long-term effects of the program, as young adults the Perry Preschool children have higher high school graduation rates, more are in the workforce, fewer need welfare, crime rates are lower among them, and there are fewer teen pregnancies than in a control group from the same background who did not get the enriched early childhood education experience (Weikart, 1993).

www.mhhe.com/santrockcd10

Head Start Resources
Poverty and Learning
Early Childhood Care and Education
Around the World

Project Head Start Compensatory education designed to provide children from low-income families the opportunity to acquire the skills and experiences important for school success.

Careers in Child Development

Yolanda Garcia, *Director of Children's Services/Head Start*

Yolanda Garcia has worked in the field of early childhood education and family support for three decades. She has been the Director of the Children's Services Department for the Santa Clara, California, County Office of Education since 1980. As director, she is responsible for managing child development programs for 2,500 3- to 5-year-old children in 127 classrooms. Her training includes two master's degrees, one in public policy and child welfare from the University of Chicago and another in educational administration from San Jose State University.

Yolanda has served on many national advisory committees that have resulted in improvements in the staffing of Head Start programs. Most notably, she served on the Head Start Quality Committee that recommended the development of Early Head Start and revised performance standards for Head Start programs. Yolanda currently is a member of the American Academy of Science Committee on the Integration of Science and Early Childhood Education.

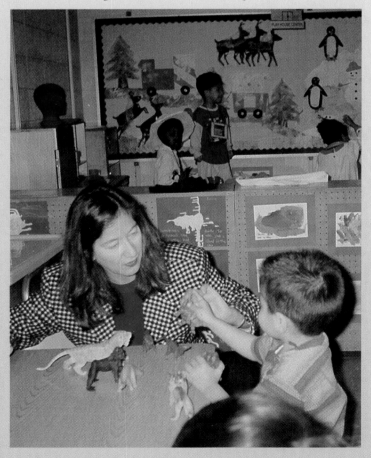

Yolanda Garcia, Director of Children's Services/Head Start, working with some Head Start children in Santa Clara, California.

One long-term investigation of early childhood education involved pooling data from eleven different early education studies that focused on children ranging in age from 9 to 19 years (Lazar, Darlington, & others, 1982). The early education models varied substantially, but all were carefully planned and executed by experts in early childhood education. Outcome measures included indicators of school competence (such as special education and grade retention), abilities (as measured by standardized intelligence and achievement tests), attitudes and values, and impact on the family. The results indicated substantial benefits of competent preschool education with low-income children on all four dimensions investigated. In sum, ample evidence indicates that well-designed and well-implemented early childhood education programs are successful with low-income children.

Although educational intervention in impoverished young children's lives is important, Head Start programs are not all created equal. One estimate is that 40 percent of the 1,400 Head Start programs are of questionable quality (Zigler & Styfco, 1994). More attention needs to be given to developing consistently high-quality Head Start programs (Bronfenbrenner, 1995).

Too many young children go to substandard early childhood programs (Morrison, 2000). In a report by the Carnegie Corporation (1996), four out of five early childhood programs did not meet quality standards. Early childhood education should encourage adequate preparation for learning, varied learning activities, trusting relationships between adults and children, and increased parental involvement (Hildebrand, Phenice, & Hines, 2000).

One individual who is strongly motivated to make Head Start a valuable learning experience for young children from disadvantaged backgrounds is Yolanda Garcia. To read about her work, see the Careers in Child Development insert.

The Effects of Early Childhood Education Because kindergarten and preschool programs are so diverse, it is difficult to make overall conclusions about their effects on children's development. Nonetheless, in one review of early childhood education's influence (Clarke-Stewart & Fein, 1983), it was concluded that children who attend preschool or kindergarten

- interact more with peers, both positively and negatively
- are less cooperative with and responsive to adults than home-reared children
- are more socially competent and mature, in that they are more confident, extraverted, assertive, self-sufficient, independent, verbally expressive, knowledgeable about the social world, comfortable in social and stressful circumstances, and better adjusted when they go to school (exhibiting more task persistence, leadership, and goal direction, for example)

- are less socially competent, in that they are less polite, less compliant to teacher demands, louder, and more aggressive and bossy, especially if the school or family supports such behavior

In sum, early childhood education generally has a positive effect on children's development, since the behaviors just mentioned—while at times negative—seem to be in the direction of developmental maturity, in that they increase as the child ages through the preschool years.

School Readiness   Educational reform has prompted considerable concern about children's readiness to enter kindergarten and first grade (Shonkoff & Phillips, 2001). National studies suggest that 40 percent of kindergarteners are not ready for first grade (Kauffman Early Education Exchange, 2002).

The concept of school readiness is based on the assumption that all children need to possess a predetermined set of capabilities before they enter school. Thus, any discussions of school readiness should consider three important factors:

- The diversity and inequity of children's early life experiences
- The wide range of variation in young children's development and learning
- The degree to which school expectations for children entering kindergarten are reasonable, appropriate, and supportive of individual differences in children

The NAEYC (1990) stresses that government officials and educators who promote universal school readiness should commit to:

- Addressing the inequities in early life experiences, so that all children have access to the opportunities that promote success in school
- Recognizing and supporting individual differences in children
- Establishing reasonable and appropriate expectations for children's capabilities on school entry

An increasing number of U.S. parents are delaying the entry of their children into the first grade with the hope that the additional year will provide their child with a competitive advantage. Borrowing the term from college athletics (in which an athlete is held out of competition for a year in hope that greater maturity and experience will produce improved performance), this strategy has been referred to as "academic redshirting." On the whole, the evidence about the short-term and long-term effects of redshirting are inconclusive (ERIC/EECE, 2002; West, Denton, & Germino-Hausken, 2000; Zill, Loomis, & West, 1997), when benefits of redshirting appear, though they typically are short-lived and may in the long term be disadvantageous (Graue & DiPerna, 2000; Spitzer, Cupp, & Parke, 1995).

A related issue involves whether a child who is not doing well in kindergarten should be held back for a second year of kindergarten rather than entering the first grade. Researchers have found that this is generally not a good strategy, resulting in lower academic achievement and self-esteem (Carlton & Winsler, 1999; Dennebaum & Kulberg, 1994).

The Transition to Elementary School

For most children, entering the first grade signals a change from being a "homechild" to being a "schoolchild"—a situation in which new roles and obligations are experienced. Children take up a new role (being a student), interact and develop relationships with new significant others, adopt

As children make the transition to elementary school, they interact and develop relationships with new and significant others. School provides them with a rich source of new ideas to shape their sense of self.

Careers in Child Development

Susan Bradburn, *Elementary School Teacher*

Susan Bradburn teaches grades 4 to 6 at West Marian Elementary School in North Carolina. She created a school museum in which students conduct research and create exhibitions. She has put her school museum concept "on wheels" by having students take carts to other classes and into the community, and she has used award money to spread the use of mobile museums to other North Carolina schools. Nicknamed "the turtle lady" because of her interest in turtles and other animals, Susan takes students on three-day field trips to Edisto Island, South Carolina, to search for fossils and study coastal ecology. Her students sell calendars that contain their original poetry and art, and they use the proceeds to buy portions of a rain forest so it won't be destroyed.

Susan Bradburn (*left*) with several students at West Marian Elementary School.

Elementary Education

new reference groups, and develop new standards by which to judge themselves. School provides children with a rich source of new ideas to shape their sense of self.

A special concern about children's early school experiences is emerging. Evidence is mounting that early schooling proceeds mainly on the basis of negative feedback. For example, children's self-esteem in the latter part of elementary school is lower than it is in the earlier part, and older children rate themselves as less smart, less good, and less hardworking than do younger ones (Blumenfeld & others, 1981).

In school as well as out of school, children's learning, like children's development, is *integrated* (NAEYC, 1988). One of the main pressures on elementary teachers has been the need to "cover the curriculum." Frequently, teachers have tried to do so by tightly scheduling discrete time segments for each subject. This approach ignores the fact that children often do not need to distinguish learning by subject area. For example, they advance their knowledge of reading and writing when they work on social studies projects; they learn mathematical concepts through music and physical education (Katz & Chard, 1989). A curriculum can be facilitated by providing learning areas in which children plan and select their activities. For example, the classroom may include a fully equipped publishing center, complete with materials for writing, illustrating, typing, and binding student-made books; a science area, with animals and plants for observation and books to study; and other similar areas. In this type of classroom, children learn reading as they discover information about science; they learn writing as they work together on interesting projects. Such classrooms also provide opportunities for spontaneous play, recognizing that elementary school children continue to learn in all areas through unstructured play, either alone or with other children.

Education experts Lillian Katz and Sylvia Chard (1989) recently described two elementary school classrooms. In one, children spent an entire morning making identical pictures of traffic lights. The teacher made no attempt to get the children to relate the pictures to anything else the class was doing. In the other class, the children were investigating a school bus. They wrote to the district's school superintendent and asked if they could have a bus parked at their school for a few days. They studied the bus, discovered the functions of its parts, and discussed traffic rules. Then, in the classroom, they built their own bus out of cardboard. The children had fun, but they also practiced writing, problem solving, and even some arithmetic. When the class had their parents' night, the teacher was ready with reports on how each child was doing. However, all the parents wanted to see was the bus because their children had been talking about it at home for weeks. Many contemporary education experts believe that this is the kind of education all children deserve. That is, they believe that children should be active, constructivist learners and taught through concrete, hands-on experience (Bonk & Cunningham, 1999). To read about the work of one teacher who uses a constructivist approach to learning, see the Careers in Child Development insert.

Schools for Adolescents

These are some of the questions regarding schools for adolescents that we will explore: What is the nature of the transition from elementary to middle or junior

The transition from elementary to middle or junior high school occurs at the same time as a number of other developmental changes. *What are some of these other developmental changes?*

high school? What are effective schools for young adolescents like? Why do adolescents drop out of school? What can be done to improve high school?

The Transition to Middle or Junior High School   The emergence of junior high schools in the 1920s and 1930s was justified on the basis of the physical, cognitive, and social changes that characterize early adolescence, as well as the need for more schools for the growing student population. Old high schools became junior high schools, and new regional high schools were built. In most systems, the ninth grade remained a part of the high school in content, although physically separated from it in a 6-3-3 system. Gradually, the ninth grade was restored to the high school, as many school systems developed middle schools that include the seventh and eighth grades, or sixth, seventh, and eighth grades. The creation of middle schools was influenced by the earlier onset of puberty in recent decades.

One worry of educators and psychologists is that junior high and middle schools have simply become watered-down versions of high schools, mimicking their curricular and extracurricular schedules. The critics argue that unique curricular and extracurricular activities reflecting a wide range of individual differences in biological and psychological development in early adolescence should be incorporated into our junior high and middle schools. The critics also stress that many high schools foster passivity rather than autonomy and that schools should create a variety of pathways for students to achieve an identity.

The transition to middle school or junior high school from elementary schools interests developmentalists because, even though it is a normative experience for virtually all children, the transition can be stressful. Why? The transition takes place at a time when many changes—in the individual, in the family, and in school—are occurring simultaneously. These changes include puberty and related concerns about body image; the emergence of at least some aspects of formal operational thought, including accompanying changes in social cognition; increased responsibility and independence in association with decreased dependency on parents; change from a small, contained classroom structure to a larger, more impersonal school structure; change from one teacher to many teachers and from a small, homogeneous set of peers to a larger, more heterogeneous set of peers; and an increased focus on achievement and performance and their assessment. This list includes a number of negative, stressful features, but there can be positive aspects to the transition. Students are more likely to feel grown up, have more subjects from which to select,

Schools for Adolescents
National Center for Education Statistics
United States Department of Education
Middle Schools

have more opportunities to spend time with peers and to locate compatible friends, and enjoy increased independence from direct parental monitoring, and they may be more challenged intellectually by academic work.

When students make the transition from elementary school to middle or junior high school, they experience the **top-dog phenomenon,** the circumstance of moving from the top position (in elementary school, being the oldest, biggest, and most powerful students in the school) to the lowest position (in middle or junior high school, being the youngest, smallest, and least powerful students in the school). Researchers who have charted the transition from elementary to middle or junior high school find that the first year of middle or junior high school can be difficult for many students (Hawkins & Berndt, 1985). For example, in one study of the transition from sixth grade in an elementary school to the seventh grade in a junior high school, adolescents' perceptions of the quality of their school life plunged in the seventh grade (Hirsch & Rapkin, 1987). In the seventh grade, the students were less satisfied with school, were less committed to school, and liked their teachers less. The drop in school satisfaction occurred regardless of how academically successful the students were.

Effective Schools for Young Adolescents What makes a successful middle school? Joan Lipsitz (1984) and her colleagues searched the nation for the best middle schools. Extensive contacts and observations were made. Based on the recommendations of education experts and observations in schools in different parts of the United States, four middle schools were chosen for their outstanding ability to educate young adolescents. What were these middle schools like? The most striking feature was their willingness and ability to adapt all school practices to their students' individual differences in physical, cognitive, and social development. The schools took seriously the knowledge we have developed about young adolescents. This seriousness was reflected in the decisions about different aspects of school life. For example, one middle school fought to keep its schedule of minicourses on Friday, so that every student could be with friends and pursue personal interests. Two other middle schools expended considerable energy on a complex school organization, so that small groups of students worked with small groups of teachers who could vary the tone and pace of the school day, depending on the students' needs. Another middle school developed an advisory scheme, so that each student had daily contact with an adult who was willing to listen, explain, comfort, and prod the adolescent. Such school policies reflect thoughtfulness and personal concern about individuals who have compelling developmental needs.

Another aspect of the effective middle schools was that early in their existence—the first year in three of the schools and the second year in the fourth school—they emphasized the importance of creating an environment that was positive for adolescents' social and emotional development. This goal was established not only because such environments contribute to academic excellence but also because social and emotional development were valued as intrinsically important in adolescents' schooling. To read about the work of one middle school teacher who provides a supportive socioemotional environment for his students, see the Careers in Child Development insert.

Recognizing that the vast majority of middle schools do not approach the excellent schools described by Joan Lipsitz (1984), in 1989 the Carnegie Foundation issued an extremely negative evaluation of our nation's middle schools. In the report, "Turning Points: Preparing American Youth for the 21st Century," the conclusion was put forth that most young adolescents attend massive, impersonal schools, learn from seemingly irrelevant curricula, trust few adults in school, and lack access to health care and counseling. Here are recommendations of the Carnegie Foundation (1989) report:

- Develop smaller "communities" or "houses" to lessen the impersonal nature of large middle schools.

top-dog phenomenon The circumstance of moving from the top position in elementary school to the lowest position in middle or junior high school.

- Lower student-to-counselor ratios from several hundred-to-1 to 10-to-1.
- Involve parents and community leaders in schools.
- Develop curricula that produce students who are literate, understand the sciences, and have a sense of health, ethics, and citizenship.
- Have teachers team teach in more flexibly designed curriculum blocks that integrate several disciplines, instead of presenting students with disconnected, rigidly separated 50-minute segments.
- Boost students' health and fitness with more in-school programs and help students who need public health care to get it.

In *Turning Points 2000* (Jackson & Davis, 2000), there was continued reliance on the recommendations set forth in *Turning Points 1989*. However, new recommendations in 2000 included teaching a curriculum grounded in rigorous academic standards, preparing all students to achieve higher standards and become lifelong learners, and involving parents and communities in supporting student learning and healthy development.

In sum, middle schools throughout the nation need a major redesign if they are to be effective in educating adolescents for becoming competent adults in the twenty-first century.

High School
Just as there are concerns about U.S. middle school education, so are there concerns about U.S. high school education (Dornbusch & Kaufman, 2001; Kaufman, 2001). Many students graduate from high school with inadequate reading, writing, and mathematical skills, including many who go on to college and have to enroll in remediation classes there. Other students drop out of high school and do not have skills that will allow them to advance in the work world.

High School Dropouts
In the last half of the twentieth century, high school dropout rates declined overall (National Center for Education Statistics, 2001). For example, in the 1940s, more than half of U.S. 15- to 24-year-olds had dropped out of school, but in 2000 this figure had decreased to only 10.9 percent. Figure 17.3 shows the trends in high school dropout rates from 1972 through 2000. Notice that the dropout rate of Latino adolescents remains precariously high (27.8 percent of 15- to 24-year-old Latino adolescents had dropped out of school in 2000). The highest dropout rate in the United States, though, occurs for Native American youth—only about 10 percent finish their high school education.

Students drop out of schools for many reasons. In one study, almost 50 percent of the dropouts cited school-related reasons for leaving school, such as not liking school or being expelled or suspended (Rumberger, 1995). Twenty percent of the dropouts (but 40 percent of the Latino students) cited economic reasons for leaving school. One-third of the female students dropped out for personal reasons, such as pregnancy or marriage.

Careers in Child Development

Mark Fodness, *Middle School Teacher*

Mark Fodness has taught seventh-grade social studies for 17 years at Bemidji Middle School in Minnesota. He says that during that time he has found it necessary to deal with numerous traumatic events that affect his students. Sometimes the tragedy is a local one, such as the death of a student, parent, or teacher. Other crises, like the Gulf War, have been national or international events.

On September 11, 2001, Mark says that he and his students encountered a new type of trauma—the terrorist attack against the United States. His students were left with many questions. "Could this be the beginning of the end of the world?" one boy asked. One girl wanted to know if her brother would have to go to war. Many students wanted to know "why?" and everyone was concerned about the future. Mark talked with his students about fear and reminded them of former U.S. President Franklin D. Roosevelt's words. "The only thing we have to fear is fear itself." Mark got students to talk about situations in which they have been afraid and found that many were most fearful when they were alone.

Over the course of the week following the terrorist attack, Mark worked with his students to answer many of their questions. He wanted his students to be empathetic to the pain and suffering caused by the tragedy. He felt that his students would be better able to handle their emotions if they could gain some sense of control. Together, Mark and his students developed a five-point plan:

1. *We want to keep those in need in our thoughts.* Students encouraged each other to remember those who perished, were wounded, were part of rescue teams, or were family members or friends of the victims.
2. *We want to help.* Students raised more than $6,000 to send to victims' families.
3. *We want to show our support.* Students designed patriotic T-shirts and sweatshirts as a way to promote their unity.
4. *We want to support our own community.* Students went out into the community and raked leaves for senior citizens on October 23, 2001.
5. *We want to appreciate diversity.* To remind students of the role of diversity in the community, Mark took his students to the Bemidji Race Relations Conference on September 28, 2001.

Mark concluded, "The recent events in our nation and in our world should all remind us in the education field that we face a challenge. We must deal with moral and ethical questions in ways that are meaningful to our students."

FIGURE 17.3 Trends in High School Dropout Rates

From 1972 through 2000, the school dropout rate for Latinos remained very high (27.8 percent of 16- to 24-year-olds in 2000). The African American dropout rate was still higher (13.1 percent) than the White non-Latino rate (6.9 percent) in 2000. The overall dropout rate declined considerably from the 1940s through the 1960s but has declined only slightly since 1972.

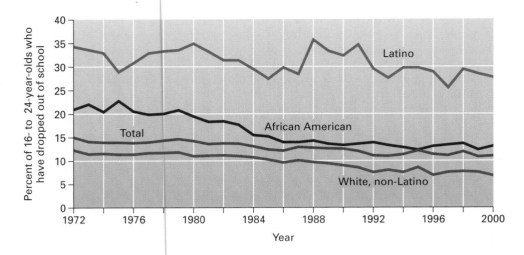

Toward Effective High Schools Many high school graduates not only are poorly prepared for college, they also are poorly prepared for the demands of the modern, high-performance workplace. In a review of hiring practices at major companies, it was concluded that many companies now have sets of basic skills they want the individuals they hire to have. These include the ability to read at relatively high levels, do at least elementary algebra, use personal computers for straightforward tasks such as word processing, solve semistructured problems in which hypotheses must be formed and tested, communicate effectively (orally and in writing), and work effectively in groups with persons of various backgrounds (Murnane & Levy, 1996).

These adolescents participate in the "I Have a Dream" (IHAD) Program, a comprehensive, long-term dropout prevention program that has been very successful. The IHAD program was created in 1981, when philanthropist Eugene Lang made an impromtu offer of college tuition to a class of graduating sixth-graders at P.S. 121 in East Harlem. Statistically, 75 percent of the students should have dropped out of school; instead, 90 percent graduated and 60 percent went on to college. Since the National IHAD Foundation was created in 1986, it has grown to number over 150 projects in 57 cities and 28 states, serving some 12,000 children. *What are some other strategies for reducing high school dropout rates?*

An increasing number of educators believe that the nation's high schools need a new mission for the twenty-first century, which addresses these problems (National Commission on the High School Senior Year, 2001):

1. More support is needed to enable all students to graduate from high school with the knowledge and skills needed to succeed in postsecondary education and careers. Many parents and students, especially those in low-income and minority communities, are unaware of the knowledge and level of skills required to succeed in postsecondary education.

2. High schools need to have higher expectations for student achievement. A special concern is the senior year of high school, which has become too much of a partytime rather than a time to prepare for one of life's most important transitions. Some students who have been accepted to college routinely ignore the academic demands of their senior year. Low academic expectations harm students from all backgrounds.

3. U.S. high school students spend too much time working in low-level service jobs. Researchers have found that when tenth-graders work more than 14 hours a week their grades drop, and when eleventh-graders work 20 or more hours a week their grades drop (Greenberger & Steinberg, 1986). At the same time, shorter, higher-quality work experiences, including community service and internships, have been shown to benefit high school students.

4. There has been too little coordination and communication across the different levels of K–12, as well as between K–12 schools and institutions of higher education.

5. At the middle and secondary school levels, every student needs strong, positive connections with adults, preferably many of them, as they explore options for school, postsecondary education, and work.

Review and Reflect: Learning Goal 2

2 **Summarize what schooling is like for children of different ages**

REVIEW

- What is the nature of early childhood education?
- What is the transition to elementary school like?
- How would you describe schools for adolescents?

REFLECT

- Might preschool be more beneficial to children from middle-income than low-income families? Why?

---

3 SOCIOECONOMIC STATUS AND ETHNICITY IN SCHOOLS

Socioeconomic Status   Ethnicity

Children from low-income, ethnic minority backgrounds have more difficulties in school than do their middle-socioeconomic-status, White counterparts. Why? Critics argue that schools have not done a good job of educating low-income, ethnic minority students to overcome the barriers to their achievement (Scott-Jones, 1995). Let's further explore the roles of socioeconomic status and ethnicity in schools.

Socioeconomic Status

Many children in poverty face problems at home and at school that present barriers to their learning (Books, 2003; Bradley & Corwyn, 2002; Phillips & others, 1999). At home, they might have parents who don't set high educational standards for them, who are incapable of reading to them, and who don't have enough money to pay for educational materials and experiences, such as books and trips to zoos and museums. They might be malnourished and live in areas where crime and violence are a way of life (Polakow, 2003; Weiss, Marcus, & Freie, 2003).

Many of the schools that children from impoverished backgrounds attend have fewer resources than do the schools in higher-income neighborhoods (Bradley & Corwyn, 2002). Schools in low-income areas are more likely to have more students with lower achievement test scores, lower graduation rates, and smaller percentages of students going to college. And they are more likely to have young teachers with less experience than do schools in higher-income neighborhoods. In some instances, though, federal aid has provided a context for improved learning in schools located in low-income areas.

Schools in low-income areas also are more likely to encourage rote learning, while schools in higher-income areas are more likely to work with children to improve their thinking skills (Spring, 1998). Thus, far too many schools in low-income neighborhoods provide students with environments that are not conducive to effective learning, and many of the schools' buildings and classrooms are old, crumbling, and poorly maintained.

Jonathan Kozol (1991) vividly described some of the problems that children of poverty face in their neighborhood and at school in *Savage Inequalities*. Following are

In his book *Savage Inequalities,* Jonathan Kozol (*above*) vividly portrayed the problems that children of poverty face in their neighborhood and at school. *What are some of these problems?*

some of his observations in one inner-city area. East St. Louis, Illinois, which is 98 percent African American, has no obstetric services, no regular trash collection, and few jobs. Seventy-five percent of its population lives on welfare of some form. Blocks upon blocks of housing consist of dilapidated, skeletal buildings. Residents breathe the chemical pollution of nearby Monsanto Chemical Company. Raw sewage repeatedly backs up into homes. Lead from nearby smelters poisons the soil. Child malnutrition and fear of violence are common. The problems of the streets spill over into the schools, where sewage also backs up from time to time. Classrooms and hallways are old and unattractive, athletic facilities inadequate. Teachers run out of chalk and paper, the science labs are 30 to 50 years out of date, and the schools' heating systems have never worked correctly. A history teacher has 110 students but only 26 books.

Kozol says that anyone who visits places like East St. Louis, even for a brief time, comes away profoundly shaken. After all, these are innocent children who have done nothing wrong. Kozol's interest was in describing what life is like in the nation's inner-city neighborhoods and schools, which are predominantly African American and Latino. However, as indicated earlier, there are many non-Latino White children who live in poverty, although they often are in suburban or rural areas. Kozol argues that many inner-city schools are still segregated, are grossly underfunded, and do not provide adequate opportunities for children to learn effectively.

One trend in antipoverty programs is to conduct two-generation intervention (McLoyd, 1998, 1999, 2000). This involves providing both services for children (such as educational day care or preschool education) and services for parents (such as adult education, literacy training, and job skill training). Recent evaluations of the two-generation programs suggest that they have more positive effects on parents than they do on children (St. Pierre, Layzer, & Barnes, 1996). Also discouraging for children is that, when the two-generation programs show benefits, they are more likely to be in the form of health benefits than cognitive gains.

Ethnicity

School segregation is still a factor in the education of children of color in the United States. Almost one-third of all African American and Latino students attend schools in which 90 percent or more of the students are from minority groups (Banks, 2002).

The school experiences of students from different ethnic groups vary considerably (Bennett, 2003; Taylor & Whittaker, 2003). African American and Latino students are much less likely than non-Latino White or Asian American students to be enrolled in academic, college preparatory programs and are much more likely to be enrolled in remedial and special education programs. Asian American students are far more likely than other ethnic minority groups to take advanced math and science courses in high school. African American students are twice as likely as Latinos, Native Americans, or Whites to be suspended from school. Ethnic minorities of color constitute the majority in 23 of the 25 largest school districts in the United States, a trend that is increasing (Banks, 2002, 2003). However, 90 percent of the teachers in America's schools are non-Latino White, and the percentage of minority teachers is projected to decrease even further in the coming years.

American anthropologist John Ogbu (1989) proposed the view that ethnic minority students are placed in a position of subordination and exploitation in the American educational system. He believes that students of color, especially African Americans and Latinos, have inferior educational opportunities, are exposed to teachers and school administrators who have low academic expectations for them, and encounter negative stereotypes of ethnic minority groups (Ogbu & Stern, 2001). In one study of middle schools in predominantly Latino areas of Miami, Latino and

White teachers rated African American students as having more behavioral problems than African American teachers rated the same students as having (Zimmerman & others, 1995).

Like Ogbu, educational psychologist Margaret Beale Spencer (1990) says that a form of institutional racism permeates many American schools. That is, well-meaning teachers, acting out of misguided liberalism, fail to challenge children of color to achieve. Such teachers prematurely accept a low level of performance from these children, substituting warmth and affection for high standards of academic success.

Here are some strategies for improving relationships among ethnically diverse students (Santrock, 2004).

- *Turn the class into a jigsaw classroom.* When Eliot Aronson was a professor at the University of Texas at Austin, the school system contacted him for ideas on how to reduce the increasing racial tension in classrooms. Aronson (1986) developed the concept of "jigsaw classroom," in which students from different cultural backgrounds are placed in a cooperative group in which they have to construct different parts of a project to reach a common goal. Aronson used the term *jigsaw* because he saw the technique as much like a group of students cooperating to put different pieces together to complete a jigsaw puzzle. How might this work? Team sports, drama productions, and music performances are examples of contexts in which students cooperatively participate to reach a common goal.
- *Use technology to foster cooperation with students from around the world.*
- *Encourage students to have positive personal contact with diverse other students.* Contact alone does not do the job of improving relationships with diverse others. For

Interview with Jonathan Kozol

Exploring Multicultural Education

Multicultural Education Resources

The Comer School Development Program

What are some positive strategies for improving interethnic relations among students in schools?

Careers in Child Development

James Comer, *Child Psychiatrist*

James Comer grew up in a low-income neighborhood in East Chicago, Indiana, and credits his parents with leaving no doubt about the importance of education. He obtained a BA degree from Indiana University. He went on to obtain a medical degree from Howard University College of Medicine, a Master of Public Health degree from the University of Michigan School of Public Health, and psychiatry training at the Yale University School of Medicine's Child Study Center. He currently is the Maurice Falk Professor of Child Psychiatry at the Yale University Child Study Center and an associate dean at the Yale University Medical School. During his years at Yale, James has concentrated his career on promoting a focus on child development as a way of improving schools. His efforts in support of healthy development of young people are known internationally.

Comer, perhaps, is best known for the founding of the School Development Program in 1968, which promotes the collaboration of parents, educators, and community to improve social, emotional, and academic outcomes for children. His concept of teamwork is currently improving the educational environment in more than 500 schools throughout America.

James Comer (*left*) is shown with some of the inner-city African American children who attend a school that became a better learning environment because of Comer's intervention. Comer is convinced that a strong, familylike atmosphere is a key to improving the quality of inner-city schools.

example, busing ethnic minority students to predominantly White schools, or vice versa, has not reduced prejudice or improved interethnic relations (Minuchin & Shapiro, 1983). What matters is what happens after children get to school. Especially beneficial in improving interethnic relations is sharing one's worries, successes, failures, coping strategies, interests, and other personal information with people of other ethnicities. When this happens, people are seen more as individuals than as a heterogeneous cultural group.

- *Encourage students to engage in perspective taking.* Exercises and activities that help students see others' perspectives can improve interethnic relations. This helps students "step into the shoes" of peers who are culturally different and feel what it is like to be treated in fair or unfair ways.

- *Help students think critically and be emotionally intelligent when cultural issues are involved.* Students who think in narrow ways are prejudiced. Students who learn to think critically and deeply about interethnic relations are likely to decrease their prejudice (Rothstein-Fisch, 2003). Becoming more emotionally intelligent includes understanding the causes of one's feelings, managing anger, listening to what others are saying, and being motivated to share and cooperate.

- *Reduce bias.* Teachers can reduce bias by displaying images of children from diverse ethnic and cultural groups, selecting play materials and classroom activities that encourage cultural understanding, helping students resist stereotyping, and working with parents.

- *View the school and community as a team to help support teaching efforts.* James Comer (1988; Comer & others, 1996) believes that a community, team approach is the best way to educate children. Three important aspects of the Comer Project for Change are (1) a governance and management team that develops a comprehensive school plan, assessment strategy, and staff development plan; (2) a mental health or school support team; and (3) a parents' program. Comer believes that the entire school community should have a cooperative rather than an adversarial attitude. The Comer program is currently operating in more than 600 schools in 26 states. To read further about Comer's work and his career, see the Careers in Child Development insert.

- *Be a competent cultural mediator.* Teachers can play a powerful role as a cultural mediator by being sensitive to racist content in materials and classroom interactions, learning more about different ethnic groups, being sensitive to children's ethnic attitudes, viewing students of color positively, and thinking of positive ways to get parents of color more involved as partners with teachers in educating children (Jones & Fuller, 2003).

3 **Describe the roles of socioeconomic status and ethnicity in schools**

REVIEW

- How do socioeconomic status and poverty influence children's schooling?
- How is ethnicity involved in children's schooling?

REFLECT

- In the context of education, are ethnic differences always negative? Come up with some differences that might be positive in U.S. classrooms.

4 CHILDREN WITH DISABILITIES

Who Are Children with Disabilities?

Learning Disabilities

Attention Deficit Hyperactivity Disorder (ADHD)

Educational Issues

Children with a disability are especially sensitive about their differentness and how it is perceived by others. Life is not always fair for children with a disability. Adjusting to school and to peers is often difficult for them.

Who Are Children with Disabilities?

Approximately 10 percent of all children in the United States receive special education or related services. Figure 17.4 shows the approximate percentages of children with various disabilities who receive special education services (U.S. Department of Education, 2000). Within this group, a little more than half have a learning disability. Substantial percentages of children also have speech or language impairments

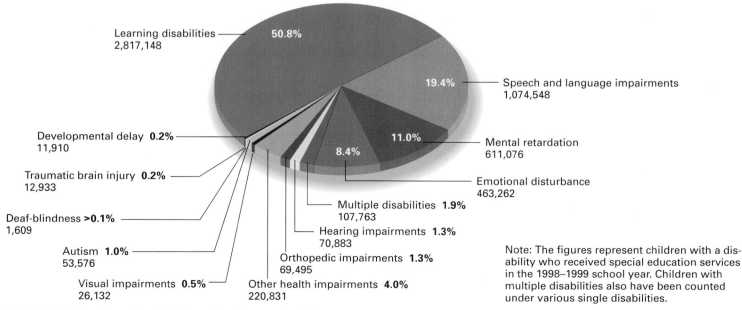

Learning disabilities — 50.8% — 2,817,148

Speech and language impairments — 19.4% — 1,074,548

Mental retardation — 11.0% — 611,076

Emotional disturbance — 8.4% — 463,262

Developmental delay 0.2% — 11,910

Traumatic brain injury 0.2% — 12,933

Deaf-blindness >0.1% — 1,609

Autism 1.0% — 53,576

Visual impairments 0.5% — 26,132

Other health impairments 4.0% — 220,831

Orthopedic impairments 1.3% — 69,495

Hearing impairments 1.3% — 70,883

Multiple disabilities 1.9% — 107,763

Note: The figures represent children with a disability who received special education services in the 1998–1999 school year. Children with multiple disabilities also have been counted under various single disabilities.

FIGURE 17.4 The Diversity of Children Who Have a Disability

(19.4 percent of those with disabilities), mental retardation (11 percent), and serious emotional disturbance (8.4 percent).

Educators now prefer to speak of "children with disabilities" rather than "disabled children" to emphasize the person, not the disability (Hallahan & Kauffman, 2003). The term *handicapping conditions* is still used to describe impediments to the learning and functioning of individuals with a disability that have been imposed by society. For example, when children who use a wheelchair do not have adequate access to a bathroom, transportation, and so on, this is referred to as a handicapping condition.

Learning Disabilities

Bobby's second-grade teacher complains that his spelling is awful. Eight-year-old Tim says reading is really hard for him, and a lot of times the words don't make much sense. Alisha has good oral language skills but has considerable difficulty in computing correct answers to arithmetic problems. Each of these students has a learning disability.

Characteristics Three criteria have mainly been used to define learning disabilities (Siegel, 2003):

- *Exclusionary criteria.* Learning disabilities are not the result of some other condition. Learning disabilities are not the result of inadequate education; the child does not have sensory deficits, such as hearing or visual impairment; the child does not have serious neurological disorders that might restrict learning; and the child does not have major socioemotional problems that might interfere with learning. The exclusionary criteria dimension is generally believed to be a reasonable aspect of a definition of learning disabilities.
- *IQ-achievement discrepancy.* There needs to be a discrepancy between potential (as measured by an IQ test) and achievement, with achievement being significantly lower than would be predicted by IQ. IQ-achievement discrepancy is a highly controversial aspect of the definition of learning disabilities. Some experts on learning disabilities believe IQ-achievement discrepancy is a key part of what a learning disability is (Lyon, 1995); others argue that the research evidence is strongly in favor of deleting this concept from the definition of a learning disability (Siegel, 1988). Criticisms focus on IQ being an inadequate assessment of children's specific cognitive skills and research not always supporting a gap between IQ and achievement as a predictor of whether a child will have a reading disability (Siegel & Himel, 1998; Toth & Siegel, 1994).
- *Specificity.* The learning problem is specific, usually confined to one or two cognitive areas. Some experts argue that the concept of a general, homogeneous group of children given the label of learning-disabled (LD) children be abandoned and the child with a learning disability be considered as part of a smaller, more specifically defined subtype (Stanovich, 1986). The two subtypes of learning disabilities that have most often been described are (1) reading disability, and (2) arithmetic disability.

After examining the research on learning disabilities, leading expert Linda Siegel (2003) recently concluded that a definition of **learning disabilities** should include these components: (1) a minimum IQ level; (2) a significant difficulty in a school-related area (especially reading and/or mathematics); and (3) exclusion of only severe emotional disorders, second-language background, sensory disabilities, and/or specific neurological deficits.

About three times as many boys as girls are classified as having a learning disability (U.S. Department of Education, 1996). Among the explanations for this gender difference are a greater biological vulnerability of boys, as well as referral bias (boys are more likely to be referred by teachers for treatment because of their disruptive, hyperactive behavior).

learning disability Includes three components: (1) a minimum IQ level, (2) a significant difficulty in a school-related area (especially reading or mathematics), and (3) exclusion of only severe emotional disorders, second-language background, sensory disabilities, and/or specific neurological deficits.

About 5 percent of all school-age children in the United States receive special education or related services because of a learning disability. In the federal classification of children receiving special education and related services, attention deficit hyperactivity disorder (ADHD) is included in the learning disabilities category. Because of the significant interest in ADHD today, we will discuss it by itself following learning disabilities.

In the past two decades, the percentage of children classified as having a learning disability has increased substantially—from less than 30 percent of all children receiving special education and related services between 1977 and 1978 to a little more than 50 percent today. Some experts say that the dramatic increase reflects poor diagnostic practices and overidentification. They believe that teachers sometimes are too quick to label children with the slightest learning problem as having a learning disability, instead of recognizing that the problem may rest in their ineffective teaching. Other experts say the increase in children being labeled with a "learning disability" is justified (Hallahan & Kauffman, 2003).

Dyslexia   The most common problem that characterizes children with a learning disability involves reading (Grigorenko, 2001). Such children especially show problems with phonological skills, which involve being able to understand how sounds and letters match up to make words. **Dyslexia** is a category that is reserved for individuals who have a severe impairment in their ability to read and spell (Eden & Moats, 2002; Olson, 2002; Thomson, 2003).

Children with a learning disability often have difficulties in handwriting, spelling, or composition. Their writing may be extremely slow, their writing products may be virtually illegible, and they may make numerous spelling errors because of their inability to match up sounds and letters.

Dyscalculia   **Dyscalculia,** also known as developmental arithmetic disorder, is a learning disability that involves difficulty in math computation. It is estimated to characterize 2 to 6 percent of U.S. elementary school children (National Center for Learning Disabilities, 2003). Researchers have found that children with math computation problems are characterized by a number of cognitive and neuropsychological deficits, including poor performance in working memory, visual perception, and visual-spatial abilities (Share, Moffitt, & Silva, 1988; Siegel & Ryan, 1988). In some cases, a child will have both a reading disability and a math disability, and there are cognitive deficits that characterize both types of disabilities, such as poor working memory (Siegel, 2003).

Diagnosis   Diagnosing whether a child has a learning disability is a difficult task. A learning disability often encompasses co-occurring conditions that can include problems in listening, concentrating, speaking, reading, writing, reasoning, math, or social interaction. Thus, individual children with a learning disability can have very different profiles. Learning disabilities often appear in association with such medical conditions as lead poisoning and fetal alcohol syndrome (American Psychiatric Association, 1994). And learning disabilities can occur with other disabilities, such as communication disorders and emotional/behavioral disorders (Polloway & others, 1997).

Intervention Strategies   Many interventions have focused on improving the child's reading ability (Lyon & Moats, 1997). For example, in one study, instruction in phonological awareness at the kindergarten level had positive effects on reading development when the children reached the first grade (Blachman & others, 1994).

Unfortunately, not all children who have a learning disability that involves reading problems have the benefit of appropriate early intervention. Most children whose reading disability is not diagnosed until the third grade or later and who receive standard interventions fail to show noticeable improvement (Lyon, 1996). However, intensive instruction over a period of time by a competent teacher can

dyslexia A category of learning disabilities involving a severe impairment in the ability to read and spell.

dyscalculia Also known as developmental arithmetic disorder, this learning disability involves difficulty in math computation.

remediate the deficient reading skills of many children (Bost & Vaughn, 2002; Strichart & Mangrum, 2002). For example, in one study, 65 severely dyslexic children were given 65 hours of individual instruction in addition to group instruction in phonemic awareness and thinking skills (Alexander & others, 1991). The intensive intervention significantly improved the dyslexic children's reading skills.

Children with severe phonological deficits that lead to poor decoding and word recognition skills respond to intervention more slowly than do children with mild to moderate reading problems (Torgesen, 1999). Also, the success of even the best-designed reading intervention depends on the training and skills of the teacher.

Disability in basic reading skills has been the most common target of intervention studies because it is the most common form of learning disability, it is identifiable, and it represents the area of learning disabilities about which there is the most knowledge (Lyon, 1996; Rittey, 2003). Interventions for other types of learning disabilities have been created but have not been extensively researched.

Improving outcomes for children with a learning disability is a challenging task and generally has required intensive intervention for even modest improvement in outcomes. However, no model program has proven to be effective for all children with learning disabilities (Terman & others, 1996).

Learning disabilities expert Linda Siegel (2003) recently provided these recommendations for helping children with learning disabilities:

- To improve word recognition skills, use a word family approach to draw attention to common word patterns (such as cat, bat, sat, fat, rat, and mat).
- Use talking books and/or textbooks on tape.
- Use high-interest, low-vocabulary books.
- Use a language experience approach, which involves dictating stories then using the words from these stories as a basis for reading vocabulary.
- Encourage children to use a word processor on a computer to help them improve their written work.
- Copying from the blackboard is difficult, so teachers should consider alternatives such as class handouts or tape recording oral lessons.
- Have children with a math computation disability use a calculator to help them with arithmetic facts and multiplication tables.

Attention Deficit Hyperactivity Disorder (ADHD)

Attention deficit hyperactivity disorder (ADHD) is a disability in which children consistently show one or more of the following characteristics over a period of time: (1) inattention, (2) hyperactivity, and (3) impulsivity. Children who are inattentive have difficulty focusing on any one thing and may get bored with a task after only a few minutes. Children who are hyperactive show high levels of physical activity, almost always seeming to be in motion. Children who are impulsive have difficulty curbing their reactions and don't do a good job of thinking before they act. Depending on the characteristics that children with ADHD display, they can be diagnosed as (1) ADHD with predominantly inattention, (2) ADHD with predominantly hyperactivity/impulsivity, or (3) ADHD with both inattention and hyperactivity/impulsivity (Whalen, 2001).

The U.S. Office of Education figures on children with a disability shown in figure 17.4 include children with ADHD in the category of children with specific learning disabilities, an overall category that comprises slightly more than one-half of all children who receive special education services. The number of children diagnosed and treated for ADHD has increased substantially, by some estimates doubling in the 1990s. The disorder occurs as much as four to nine times more in boys than in girls. There is controversy about the increased diagnosis of ADHD (Terman & others, 1996), however. Some experts attribute the increase mainly to heightened awareness of the disorder. Others are concerned that many children are being diagnosed without undergoing extensive professional evaluation based on input from multiple sources.

attention deficit hyperactivity disorder (ADHD) A disability in which children consistently show one or more of the following characteristics: (1) inattention, (2) hyperactivity, and (3) impulsivity.

Definitive causes of ADHD have not been found. For example, scientists have not been able to identify cause-related sites in the brain. However, a number of causes have been proposed, such as low levels of certain neurotransmitters (chemical messengers in the brain), prenatal abnormalities, and postnatal abnormalities (Biederman & Faraone, 2003). Heredity also may play a role, as 30 to 50 percent of children with ADHD have a sibling or parent who has the disorder (Woodrich, 1994).

Students with ADHD have a failure rate in school that is two to three times that of other students. About one-half of students with ADHD have repeated a grade by adolescence and more than one-third eventually drop out of school.

Many experts recommend a combination of academic, behavioral, and medical interventions to help students with ADHD learn and adapt more effectively (Medd, 2003; Rapport & others, 2001; Stein & Perrin, 2003; Whalen, 2001). This intervention requires cooperation and effort on the part of the parents of students with ADHD, school personnel (teachers, administrators, special educators, and school psychologists), and health-care professionals (Whalen, 2001).

About 85 to 90 percent of students with ADHD are taking stimulant medication such as Ritalin or Adderall (which has fewer side effects than Ritalin) to control their behavior (Denney, 2001). Ritalin is a stimulant and for most individuals it speeds up the nervous system and behavior. However, in many children with ADHD it has the opposite effect, slowing down their nervous system and behavior, although scientists are still not sure why these drugs work in such opposite ways for children with ADHD and those who do not have the disorder (Johnson & Leung, 2001). Researchers have found that a combination of medication (such as Ritalin) and behavior management improves the behavior of children with ADHD better than medication alone or behavior management alone (Swanson & others, 2001; Swanson & Volkow, 2002).

The use of Ritalin and other stimulants to treat ADHD continues to be controversial. Critics argue that physicians are too quick to prescribe Ritalin, especially for mild cases of ADHD, and that long-term studies of the effects of Ritalin on children with ADHD have not been conducted to determine possible negative effects.

Educational Issues

The legal requirement that schools serve all children with a disability is fairly recent. Beginning in the mid 1960s to mid 1970s, legislatures, the federal courts, and the U.S. Congress laid down special educational rights for children with disabilities. Prior to that time, most children with a disability were either refused enrollment or inadequately served by schools. In 1975, *Public Law 94-142*, the Education for All Handicapped Children Act,

Increasingly, children with disabilities are being taught in the regular classroom, as is this child with mild mental retardation.

required that all students with disabilities be given a free, appropriate public education and be provided the funding to help implement this education.

In 1990, Public Law 94-142 was renamed the *Individuals with Disabilities Education Act (IDEA)*. The IDEA spells out broad mandates for services to all children with disabilities. These include evaluation and eligibility determination, appropriate education and the individualized education plan (IEP), and the least restrictive environment (LRE) (Hardman, Drew, & Egan, 2002).

The IDEA requires that students with disabilities have an **individualized education plan (IEP),** a written statement that spells out a program that is specifically tailored for the student with a disability. In general, the IEP should be (1) related to the child's learning capacity, (2) specifically constructed to meet the child's individual needs and not merely a copy of what is offered to other children, and (3) designed to provide educational benefits.

Under the IDEA, a child with a disability must be educated in the **least restrictive environment (LRE),** which is a setting that is as similar as possible to the

individualized education plan (IEP) A written statement that spells out a program tailored to a child with a disability. The plan should be (1) related to the child's learning capacity, (2) specially constructed to meet the child's individual needs and not merely a copy of what is offered to other children, and (3) designed to provide educational benefits.

least restrictive environment (LRE) The concept that a child with a disability must be educated in a setting that is as similar as possible to the one in which children who do not have a disability are educated.

Education of Children Who Are Exceptional

Inclusion

The Council for Exceptional Children

Legal Issues and Disabilities

one in which children who do not have a disability are educated. The term **inclusion** describes the education of a child with special education needs full-time in the general school program. Not long ago, it was considered appropriate to educate children with disabilities outside the regular classroom. However, today, schools must make every effort to provide inclusion for children with disabilities (Dettmer, Dyck, & Thurston, 2002; Friend & Bursuck, 2002; Smith, 2004).

Review and Reflect: Learning Goal 4

4 **Characterize children with disabilities and their schooling**

REVIEW

- Who are children with disabilities?
- What characterizes children with learning disabilities?
- How would you describe children with attention deficit hyperactivity disorder? What kind of treatment are they typically given?
- What are some issues in educating children with disabilities?

REFLECT

- Think back to your own schooling and how children with learning disabilities or ADHD either were or were not diagnosed. Were you aware of such individuals in your classes? Were they helped by specialists? You may know one or more individuals with a learning disability or ADHD. Ask them about their educational experiences and whether they believe schools could have done a better job of helping them.

---

5 ACHIEVEMENT

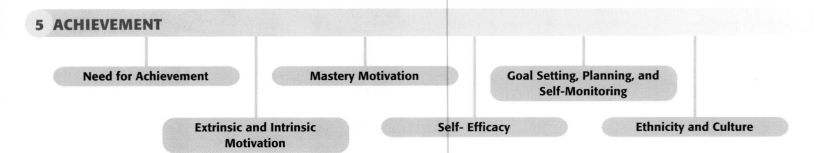

| Need for Achievement | Mastery Motivation | Goal Setting, Planning, and Self-Monitoring |

| Extrinsic and Intrinsic Motivation | Self- Efficacy | Ethnicity and Culture |

We are a species motivated to do well at what we attempt, to gain mastery over the world in which we live, to explore unknown environments with enthusiasm and curiosity, and to achieve the heights of success. We live in an achievement-oriented world, with standards that tell children success is important. The standards suggest that success requires a competitive spirit, a desire to win, a motivation to do well, and the wherewithal to cope with adversity and to persist until an objective is reached. Some developmentalists, though, believe that we are becoming a nation of hurried, "wired" people who are raising our children to become the same way— uptight about success and failure and far too worried about what we accomplish in comparison with others. It was in the 1950s that an interest in achievement began to flourish. The interest initially focused on the need for achievement.

Need for Achievement

Think about yourself and your friends for a moment. Are you more achievement-oriented than they are, or are you less so? If we were to ask you and your friends to tell stories about achievement-related themes, could we accurately determine which of you is the most achievement-oriented?

inclusion Educating a child with special education needs full-time in the regular classroom.

Some individuals are highly motivated to succeed and they expend a lot of effort, striving to excel. Other individuals are not as motivated to succeed and don't work as hard to achieve (Brophy, 1998). These two types of individuals vary in their **achievement motivation (need for achievement),** the desire to accomplish something, to reach a standard of excellence, and to expend effort to excel. David McClelland (1955) assessed achievement by showing individuals ambiguous pictures that were likely to stimulate achievement-related responses. The individuals were asked to tell a story about the picture, and their comments were scored according to how strongly they reflected achievement.

A host of studies have correlated achievement-related responses with different aspects of the individual's experiences and behavior (Winter, 2000). The findings are diverse, but they suggest that achievement-oriented individuals have a stronger hope for success than a fear of failure, are moderate rather than high or low in risk taking, and persist for appropriate lengths of time in solving difficult problems. Early research had indicated that independence training by parents promotes children's achievement, but more recent research reveals that parents, to increase achievement, need to set high standards for achievement, model achievement-oriented behavior, and reward their children for their achievements. And, in one study, the middle school students who had the highest grades were those whose parents, teachers, and schools were authoritative (Paulson, Marchant, & Rothlisberg, 1995).

Extrinsic and Intrinsic Motivation

We begin our coverage of extrinsic and intrinsic motivation by examining what they are, then turn to a number of ideas about how they work best in learning and achievement.

What Are Extrinsic and Intrinsic Motivation?

The behavioral perspective emphasizes the importance of extrinsic motivation in achievement. **Extrinsic motivation** involves doing something to obtain something else (a means to an end). Extrinsic motivation is often influenced by external incentives such as rewards and punishments. For example, a student may study hard for a test in order to obtain a good grade in the course.

While the behavioral perspective emphasizes the importance of extrinsic motivation in achievement, the cognitive perspective stresses the importance of intrinsic motivation in achievement. **Intrinsic motivation** involves the internal motivation to do something for its own sake (an end in itself). For example, another student may study hard for a test because he or she enjoys the content of the course.

Current evidence strongly favors establishing a classroom climate in which students are intrinsically motivated to learn (Hennessey & Amabile, 1998; Wigfield & Eccles, 2002). Students are more motivated to learn when they are given choices, become absorbed in challenges that match their skills, and receive rewards that have informational value but are not used for control. Praise also can enhance students' intrinsic motivation. To see why these things are so, let's first consider the intrinsic motivation of self-determination and personal choice. Then, we will examine how external rewards can either enhance or undermine intrinsic motivation. Finally, we will identify some developmental changes in intrinsic and extrinsic motivation as students move up the educational ladder.

Self-Determination and Personal Choice

One view of intrinsic motivation emphasizes self-determination (Deci, Koestner, & Ryan, 2001; Deci & Ryan, 1994). In this view, students want to believe that they are doing something because of their own will, not because of external success or rewards.

Researchers have found that students' internal motivation and intrinsic interest in school tasks increase when students have some choice and some opportunities to take personal responsibility for their learning (Stipek, 1996, 2002). For example,

achievement motivation (need for achievement) The desire to accomplish something, to reach a standard of excellence, and to expend effort to excel.

extrinsic motivation Involves doing something to obtain something else (a means to an end).

intrinsic motivation Involves the internal motivation of doing something for its own sake (an end in itself).

Calvin and Hobbes

by Bill Watterson

The reward of a thing well done is to have done it.

—RALPH WALDO EMERSON
American Poet and Essayist, 19th Century

www.mhhe.com/santrockcd10

Motivation and Achievement
Intrinsic Motivation

in one study, high school science students who were encouraged to organize their own experiments demonstrated more care and interest in laboratory classes than did their counterparts who had to follow detailed instructions and directions (Rainey, 1965).

In another study, which included mainly African American students from low-income backgrounds, teachers were encouraged to give the students more responsibility for their school program (deCharms, 1984). This consisted of opportunities to set their own goals, plan how to reach the goals, and monitor their progress toward the goals. Students were given some choice of activities to engage in and when they would do them. They also were encouraged to take personal responsibility for their behavior, including reaching the goals that they had set. Compared to a control group, students in the intrinsic motivation/self-determination group had higher achievement gains and were more likely to graduate from high school.

Extrinsic Rewards and Intrinsic Motivation In some situations, rewards can actually undermine learning. In one study, students who already had a strong interest in art spent more time drawing when they did not expect a reward than did their counterparts who also had a strong interest in art but knew they would be rewarded (Lepper, Greene, & Nisbett, 1973). Other researchers have found similar effects (Morgan, 1984).

However, classroom rewards can be useful (Cameron, 2001). Two uses are (Bandura, 1982; Deci, 1975): (1) as an incentive to engage in tasks, in which case the goal is to control the student's behavior; and (2) to convey information about mastery. When rewards convey information about mastery, students' feelings of competence are likely enhanced. An important point here is that it is not the reward itself that causes the effect but rather the offer or the expectation of the reward (Schunk, 2001). Rewards used as incentives lead to perceptions that the student's behavior was caused by the external reward and not by the student's own motivation to be competent.

To better understand the difference between using rewards to control students' behavior and using them to provide information about mastery, consider this example (Schunk, 2000). A teacher puts a reward system in place in which the more work students accomplish, the more points they will earn. Students will be motivated to work to earn points because the points can be exchanged for privileges, but the points also provide information about their capabilities. That is, the more points students earn, the more work they have accomplished. As they accumulate points, students are more likely to feel competent. In contrast, if points are provided simply for spending time on a task, the task might be perceived as a means to an end. In this case, because the points don't convey anything about capabilities, students are likely to perceive that the rewards control their behavior.

Thus, rewards that convey information about students' mastery can increase intrinsic motivation by increasing their sense of competence. However, negative feedback, such as criticism, that carries information that students are incompetent can undermine intrinsic motivation, especially if students doubt their ability to become competent (Stipek, 2002).

Developmental Shifts in Intrinsic and Extrinsic Motivation Many psychologists and educators believe that it is important for children to develop greater internalization and intrinsic motivation as they grow older. However, researchers have found that as students move from the early elementary school years to the high school years, their intrinsic motivation decreases (Harter, 1996). In one research study, the biggest drop in intrinsic motivation and largest increase in extrinsic motivation was between the sixth and seventh grade (Harter, 1981). In another study, as students moved from the sixth to the eighth grade, they increasingly said that school is boring and irrelevant (Harter, 1996). In this study, however, students who were intrinsically motivated were doing much better academically than those who were extrinsically motivated.

Why the shift toward extrinsic motivation as children move to higher grades? One explanation is that school grading practices reinforce external motivation. That is, as students get older, they lack the increasing emphasis on grades and their internal motivation drops.

Jacquelynne Eccles and her colleagues (Eccles & Midgley, 1989; Eccles & Wigfield, 2002; Wigfield, Eccles, & Pintrich, 1996) identified some specific changes in the school context that help to explain the decline in intrinsic motivation. Middle and junior high schools are more impersonal, more formal, more evaluative, and more competitive than elementary schools. Students compare themselves more with other students because they are increasingly graded in terms of their relative performance on assignments and standardized tests. The Explorations in Child Development box further explores the importance of supportive, caring teachers.

Mastery Motivation

Closely related to an emphasis on intrinsic motivation is the concept of mastery motivation. Researchers have identified mastery as one of three types of achievement orientation: mastery, helpless, and performance.

Carol Dweck and her colleagues (Dweck & Elliott, 1983; Dweck & Leggett, 1988) have found that children show two distinct responses to difficult or challenging circumstances: a mastery orientation or a helpless orientation. Children with a **mastery orientation** focus on the task rather than on their ability, have positive affect (suggesting they enjoy the challenge), and generate solution-oriented strategies that improve their performance. Mastery-oriented students often instruct themselves to pay attention, to think carefully, and to remember strategies that worked for them in the past (Anderman, Maehr, & Midgley, 1996). In contrast, children with a **helpless orientation** focus on their inadequacies, often attribute their difficulty to a lack of ability, and display negative affect (including boredom and anxiety). This orientation undermines their performance. Figure 17.6 describes some behaviors that might reflect learned helplessness.

A mastery orientation can be contrasted with a **performance orientation,** which involves being concerned with outcome rather than with process. For performance-oriented students, winning is what matters, and happiness is thought to be a result of winning. For mastery-oriented students, what matters is the sense that they are effectively interacting with their environment. Mastery-oriented students do like to win, but winning isn't as important as it is for performance-oriented students. Developing their skills is more important.

mastery orientation An orientation in which one is task-oriented and, instead of focusing on one's ability, is concerned with learning strategies.

helpless orientation An orientation in which one seems trapped by the experience of difficulty, often attributes one's difficulty to a lack of ability, and displays negative affect.

performance orientation An orientation in which one focuses on achievement outcomes; winning is what matters most, and happiness is thought to result from winning.

Explorations in Child Development

Teachers Who Care

Nel Noddings (1992, 1998, 2001) believes that students are most likely to develop into competent human beings when they feel cared for. This requires teachers to get to know students fairly well. She believes that this is difficult in large schools with large numbers of students in each class. She would have teachers remain with the same students for two to three years (voluntarily on the part of the teacher and the pupil) so that teachers would be better positioned to attend to the interests and capacities of each student (Thornton, 2001).

Researchers have found that students who feel they have supportive, caring teachers are more strongly motivated to engage in academic work than students with unsupportive, uncaring teachers (McCombs, 2001; Ryan & Deci, 2000). One researcher examined students' views of the qualities of good relationships with a teacher by asking middle school students questions such as how they knew a teacher cared about them (Wentzel, 1997). As shown in figure 17.5, attentiveness to the students as human beings was important to the students. Interestingly, students also considered teachers' instructional behaviors in evaluating how much their teachers cared about them. The students said that teachers convey that they care about their students when they make serious efforts to promote learning and have appropriately high standards.

	Teachers Who Care	Teachers Who Do *Not* Care
Teaching behaviors	Makes an effort to make class interesting, teaches in a special way	Teaches in a boring way, gets off-task, teaches while students aren't paying attention
Communication style	Talks to me, pays attention, asks questions, listens	Ignores, interrupts, screams, yells
Equitable treatment and respect	Is honest and fair, keeps promises, trusts me, tells the truth	Embarrasses, insults
Concern about individuals	Asks what's wrong, talks to me about my problems, acts as a friend, asks when I need help, takes time to make sure I understand, calls on me	Forgets my name, does nothing when I do something wrong, doesn't explain things or answer questions, doesn't try to help me

FIGURE 17.5 Students' Descriptions of Teachers Who Care

Self-Efficacy

self-efficacy The belief that one can master a situation and produce favorable outcomes.

Self-efficacy is the belief that one can master a situation and produce favorable outcomes. Albert Bandura (1997, 2001; Bandura & Locke, 2003), whose social cognitive theory we described in chapter 2, "The Science of Child Development," believes that self-efficacy is a critical factor in whether or not students achieve. ◀ **page 37** Self-efficacy has much in common with mastery motivation and intrinsic motivation. Self-efficacy is the belief that "I can"; helplessness is the belief that "I cannot" (Maddux, 2002; Stipek, 2002). Students with high self-efficacy endorse such statements as "I know that I will be able to learn the material in this class" and "I expect to be able to do well at this activity."

Dale Schunk (1991, 2001) has applied the concept of self-efficacy to many aspects of students' achievement. In his view, self-efficacy influences a student's choice of activities. Students with low self-efficacy for learning may avoid many learning tasks, especially those that are challenging. By contrast, high-self-efficacy counterparts eagerly work at learning tasks. High-self-efficacy students are more likely to expend effort and persist longer at a learning task than low-self-efficacy students.

Bandura (1997) also addressed the characteristics of efficacious schools. School leaders seek ways to improve instruction. They figure out ways to work around stifling policies and regulations that impede academic innovations. Masterful academic leadership by the principal builds teachers' sense of instructional efficacy, while in low-achieving schools, principals function more as administrators and disciplinarians.

High expectations and standards for achievement pervade efficacious schools. Teachers regard their students as capable of high

The student:

- Says "I can't"
- Doesn't pay attention to teacher's instructions
- Doesn't ask for help, even when it is needed
- Does nothing (e.g., stares out the window)
- Guesses or answers randomly without really trying
- Doesn't show pride in successes
- Appears bored, uninterested
- Is unresponsive to teacher's exhortations to try
- Is easily discouraged
- Doesn't volunteer answers to teacher's questions
- Maneuvers to get out of or to avoid work (e.g., has to go to the nurse's office)

FIGURE 17.6 Behaviors that Suggest Learned Helplessness

academic achievement, set challenging academic standards for them, and provide support to help them reach these high standards. In contrast, in low-achieving schools not much is expected academically of students, teachers spend less time actively teaching and monitoring students' academic progress, and they tend to write off a high percentage of students as unteachable (Brookover & others, 1979). Not surprisingly, students in such schools have low self-efficacy and a sense of academic futility.

Goal Setting, Planning, and Self-Monitoring

Researchers have found that self-efficacy and achievement improve when individuals set goals that are specific, proximal, and challenging (Bandura, 2001; Schunk, 2001). A nonspecific, fuzzy goal is "I want to be successful." A more concrete, specific goal is "I want to make the honor roll by the end of the semester."

Students can set both long-term (distal) and short-term (proximal) goals. It is okay for individuals to set some long-term goals, such as "I want to graduate from high school" or "I want to go to college," but they also need to create short-term goals, which are steps along the way. "Getting an A on the next math test" is an example of a short-term, proximal goal. So is "Doing all of my homework by 4 P.M. Sunday." David McNally (1990), author of *Even Eagles Need a Push,* advises that when individuals set goals and plan, they should be reminded to live their lives one day at a time. Have them make their commitments in bite-size chunks. A house is built one brick at a time, a cathedral one stone at a time. The artist paints one stroke at a time. The student should also work in small increments.

Another good strategy is for individuals to set challenging goals. A challenging goal is a commitment to self-improvement. Strong interest and involvement in activities are sparked by challenges. Goals that are easy to reach generate little interest or effort. However, goals should be optimally matched to the individual's skill level. If goals are unrealistically high, the result will be repeated failures that lower the individual's self-efficacy.

Carol Dweck (1996; Dweck & Leggett, 1988) and John Nicholls (1979) define goals in terms of immediate achievement-related focus and definition of success. For example, Nicholls distinguishes between ego-involved goals, task-involved goals, and work-avoidant goals. Individuals who have ego-involved goals strive to maximize favorable evaluations and minimize unfavorable ones. For example, ego-involved individuals focus on how smart they will look and how effectively they can outperform others. In contrast, individuals who have task-involved goals focus on mastering tasks. They concentrate on how they can do the task and what they will learn. Individuals with work-avoidant goals try to exert as little effort as possible when faced with a task.

It is not enough just to get individuals to set goals. It also is important to encourage them to plan how they will reach their goals. Being a good planner means managing time effectively, setting priorities, and being organized.

Individuals not only should plan their next week's activities but also monitor how well they are sticking to their plan. Once engaged in a task, they need to monitor their progress, judge how well they are doing on the task, and evaluate the outcomes to regulate what they do in the future (Eccles, Wigfield, & Schiefele, 1998). Researchers have found that high-achieving adolescents often are self-regulatory learners (Schunk & Zimmerman, 2001, 2003; Zimmerman, 2001). For example, high-achieving adolescents self-monitor their learning more and systematically evaluate their progress toward a goal more than low-achieving students do. Encouraging adolescents to self-monitor their learning conveys the message that adolescents are responsible for their own behavior and that learning requires active dedicated participation by the adolescent (Pintrich, 2003; Zimmerman, Bonner, & Kovach, 1996).

In sum, we have seen that a number of psychological and motivational factors influence children's achievement. Especially important in the child's ability to adapt to new academic and social pressures are achievement motivation, intrinsic motivation,

They can because they think they can.

—VIRGIL
Roman Poet, 1st Century B.C.

Mastery Motivation
Exploring Self-Efficacy
Self-Efficacy Resources

a mastery orientation and goal setting, planning, and self-regulation (Pintrich & Schunk, 2002). Next, we examine the roles of ethnicity and culture in achievement.

Ethnicity and Culture

What is the nature of achievement in ethnic minority children? How does culture influence children's achievement?

Ethnicity The diversity that exists among ethnic minority children is evident in their achievement. For example, many Asian American students have a strong academic achievement orientation, but some do not.

In addition to recognizing the diversity that exists within every cultural group in terms of their achievement, it also is important to distinguish between difference and deficiency. Too often, the achievement of ethnic minority students—especially African Americans, Latinos, and Native Americans—has been interpreted as *deficits* by middle-socioeconomic-status White standards, when they simply are *culturally different and distinct* (Jones, 1994).

At the same time, many investigations overlook the socioeconomic status of ethnic minority students. In many instances, when ethnicity *and* socioeconomic status are investigated in a study, socioeconomic status predicts achievement better than ethnicity does. Students from middle- and upper-income families fare better than their counterparts from low-income backgrounds in a host of achievement situations—for example, expectations for success, achievement aspirations, and recognition of the importance of effort (Gibbs, 1989).

Sandra Graham (1986, 1990) has conducted a number of studies that reveal not only stronger socioeconomic status than ethnic differences in achievement but also the importance of studying ethnic minority student motivation in the context of general motivational theory. Her inquiries focus on the causes that African American students give for their achievement orientation, such as why they succeed or fail. She is struck by how consistently middle-income African American students do not fit the stereotype of being unmotivated. Like their White middle-income counterparts, they have high achievement expectations and understand that failure is usually due to a lack of effort, rather than bad luck. In one recent study in which the participants were mainly ethnic minority students from low-income families, a mastery motivation classroom that provided considerable positive support was linked with students' motivation to learn to resist distractions involving emotional distress (Strobel, 2001).

A special challenge for many ethnic minority students, especially those living in poverty, is dealing with racial prejudice, conflict between the values of their group and those of the majority group, and a lack of high-achieving adults in their cultural group who can serve as positive role models (McLoyd, 2000). It also is important to consider the nature of the schools that primarily serve ethnic minority students (Eccles, Wigfield, & Schiefele, 1998; Spencer, 1999). More than one-third of all African American and almost one-third of all Latino students attend schools in the 47 largest city school districts in the United States, compared with only 5 percent of all White and 22 percent of all Asian American students. Many of these ethnic minority students come from low-income families (more than one-half are eligible for free or reduced-cost lunches). These inner-city schools are less likely than other schools to serve more advantaged populations or to offer high-quality academic support services, advanced courses, and courses that challenge students' active thinking skills. Even students who are motivated to learn and achieve may find it difficult to perform effectively in such contexts.

Cross-Cultural Comparisons In the past decade, the poor performance of American children in math and science has become well publicized. For example, in one cross-national comparison of the math and science achievement of 9- to 13-year-old students, the United States finished 13th (out of 15) in science and 15th (out of 16) in math achievement (Educational Testing Service, 1992). In this study, Korean and Taiwanese students placed first and second, respectively.

Harold Stevenson's (1995; Stevenson, Hofer, & Randel, 1999; Stevenson & others, 1990) research explores reasons for the poor performance of American students. Stevenson and his colleagues have completed five cross-cultural comparisons of students in the United States, China, Taiwan, and Japan. In these studies, Asian students consistently outperform American students. And, the longer the students are in school, the wider the gap becomes between Asian and American students—the lowest difference is in the first grade, the highest in the eleventh grade (the highest grade studied).

To learn more about the reasons for these large cross-cultural differences, Stevenson and his colleagues spent thousands of hours observing in classrooms, as well as interviewing and surveying teachers, students, and parents. They found that the Asian teachers spent more of their time teaching math than did the American teachers. For example, more than one-fourth of total classroom time in the first grade was spent on math instruction in Japan, compared with only one-tenth of the time in the U.S. first-grade classrooms. Also, the Asian students were in school an average of 240 days a year, compared with 178 days in the United States.

Asian grade schools intersperse studying with frequent periods of activities. This approach helps children maintain their attention and likely makes learning more enjoyable. Shown here are Japanese fourth-graders making wearable masks.

In addition to the substantially greater time spent on math instruction in the Asian schools than the American schools, differences were found between the Asian and American parents. The American parents had much lower expectations for their children's education and achievement than did the Asian parents. Also, the American parents were more likely to believe that their children's math achievement was due to innate ability; the Asian parents were more likely to say that their children's math achievement was the consequence of effort and training (see figure 17.7). The Asian students were more likely to do math homework than were the American students, and the Asian parents were far more likely to help their children with their math homework than were the American parents (Chen & Stevenson, 1989).

Critics of the cross-national comparisons argue that, in many comparisons, virtually all U.S. children are being compared with a "select" group of children from other countries, especially in the secondary school comparisons. Therefore, they conclude, it is no wonder that American students don't fare so well. That criticism holds for some international comparisons. However, even when the top 25 percent of students in different countries were recently compared, U.S. students moved up some, but not a lot (Mullis & others, 1998).

Review and Reflect: Learning Goal 5

5 **Explain the development of achievement in children**

REVIEW

- What is the nature of need for achievement?
- How does extrinsic motivation differ from intrinsic motivation? What role do rewards play in extrinsic and intrinsic motivation? What are some developmental changes in extrinsic and intrinsic motivation?
- How can mastery, helpless, and performance orientations be differentiated?
- What is self-efficacy, and how is it involved in achievement?
- What functions do goal setting, planning, and self-monitoring have in achievement?
- How is achievement related to ethnicity and culture?

REFLECT

- Think about several of your own past schoolmates who showed low motivation in school. Why do you think they behaved that way? What teaching strategies may have helped them?

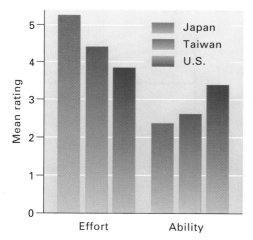

FIGURE 17.7 Mothers' Beliefs about the Factors Responsible for Children's Math Achievement in Three Countries

In one study, mothers in Japan and Taiwan were more likely to believe that their children's math achievement was due to effort rather than innate ability, while U.S. mothers were more likely to believe their children's math achievement was due to innate ability (Stevenson, Lee, & Stigler, 1986). If parents believe that their children's math achievement is due to innate ability and their children are not doing well in math, the implication is that they are less likely to think their children will benefit from putting forth more effort.

Reach Your Learning Goals

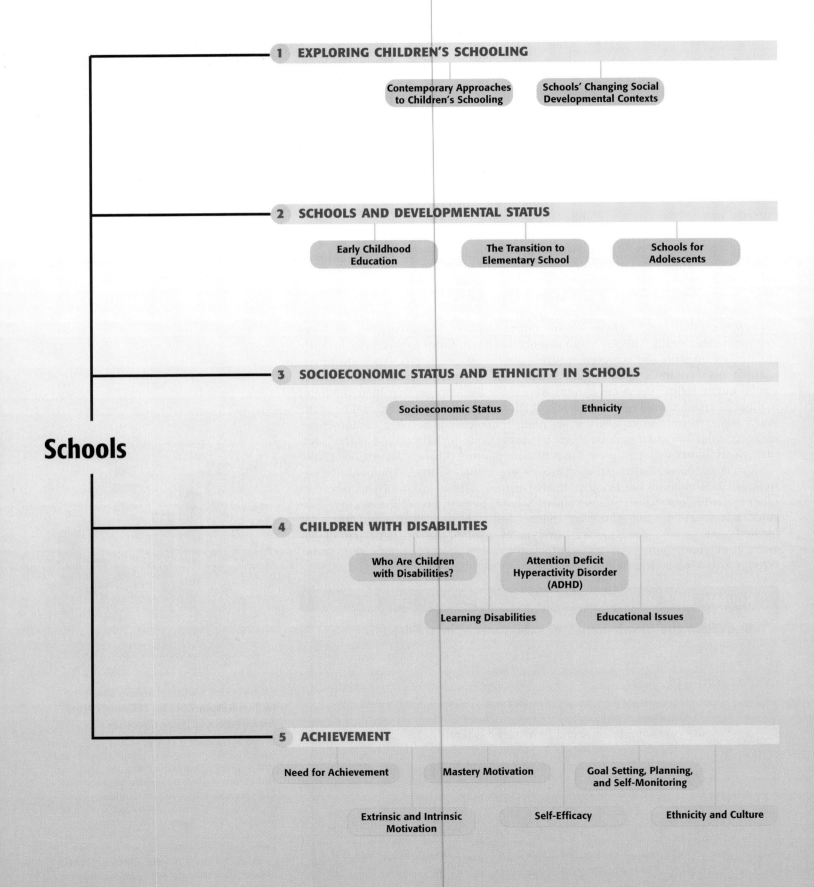

Schools

1 EXPLORING CHILDREN'S SCHOOLING

Contemporary Approaches
to Children's Schooling

Schools' Changing Social
Developmental Contexts

2 SCHOOLS AND DEVELOPMENTAL STATUS

Early Childhood
Education

The Transition to
Elementary School

Schools for
Adolescents

3 SOCIOECONOMIC STATUS AND ETHNICITY IN SCHOOLS

Socioeconomic Status

Ethnicity

4 CHILDREN WITH DISABILITIES

Who Are Children
with Disabilities?

Attention Deficit
Hyperactivity Disorder
(ADHD)

Learning Disabilities

Educational Issues

5 ACHIEVEMENT

Need for Achievement

Mastery Motivation

Goal Setting, Planning,
and Self-Monitoring

Extrinsic and Intrinsic
Motivation

Self-Efficacy

Ethnicity and Culture

Summary

1 Discuss some approaches to children's schooling and changing social developmental contexts in schools

- Contemporary approaches to student learning include the direct instruction and constructivist (cognitive and social) approaches. The direct instruction approach is a teacher-centered approach characterized by teacher direction and control. Cognitive constructivist approaches emphasize the child's active construction of knowledge and understanding. The social constructivist approaches focus on collaboration with others to produce knowledge and understanding. The American Psychological Association has proposed 14 learner-centered psychological principles to guide children's education that include cognitive and metacognitive factors, motivational and instructional factors, developmental and social factors, and individual difference factors.
- The social context differs at the preschool, elementary, and secondary level. The preschool setting is a more protected environment than the others. As children move into middle or junior high school, the school environment increases in complexity and scope. The social context now is more likely to be the entire school rather than an individual classroom.

2 Summarize what schooling is like for children of different ages

- Variations in early childhood education include the child-centered kindergarten, the Montessori approach, the Reggio Emilia approach, and developmentally appropriate and inappropriate education. Compensatory education has tried to break through the poverty cycle with programs like Project Head Start. Long-term studies reveal that model preschool programs have positive effects on children's development. It is difficult to evaluate the effects of early childhood education, but overall they appear to be positive. School readiness guidelines should include an emphasis on diversity, individual variation, and reasonable and appropriate expectations.
- A special concern is that early elementary education proceeds mainly on the basis of negative feedback to children. Many education experts believe that early elementary school children should involve active, constructivist learning.
- Middle schools have become more popular than junior high schools in recent years to coincide with puberty's earlier arrival. The transition to middle/junior high school occurs at the same time as many physical, cognitive, and socioemotional changes involved in the transition to adolescence. This transition from an elementary school to a middle or junior high school is often stressful and involves moving from being a "top dog" to the least powerful position in a school. Successful schools for young adolescents take individual differences seriously, show a deep concern for what is known about early adolescence, and stress the importance of socioemotional development at least as much as cognitive development. The Carnegie Foundation has recommended a major overhaul of America's middle schools. The overall high school dropout rate declined considerably in the last half of the twentieth century, but the dropout rates of Latino and Native American youth remain very high. A number of strategies have been proposed for improving U.S. high schools, including better support and higher expectations.

3 Describe the roles of socioeconomic status and ethnicity in schools

- Children in poverty face problems at home and at school that present barriers to their learning. Schools in low-income neighborhoods often have fewer resources, have less experienced teachers, and are more likely to encourage rote learning rather than thinking skills.
- The school experiences of students from different ethnic groups vary considerably. It is important for teachers to have positive expectations for students of color. Comer believes a community, team approach is the best way to educate children. Aronson created the jigsaw classroom to reduce racial tension.

4 Characterize children with disabilities and their schooling

- An estimated 10 percent of U.S. children receive special education or related services. Slightly more than 50 percent of these students are classified as having a learning disability (in the federal government classification, this includes attention deficit hyperactivity disorder—ADHD). The term *children with disabilities* is now used instead of the term *disabled children.*
- A learning disability includes three components: (1) a minimum IQ level, (2) a significant difficulty in a school-related area (especially reading or mathematics), and (3) exclusion of only severe emotional disorders, second-language background, sensory disabilities, and/or specific neurological deficits. Dyslexia is a category of learning disabilities involving a severe impairment in the ability to read and spell. Dyscalculia, also known as developmental arithmetic disorder, is a learning disability that involves difficulty in math computation.
- ADHD is a disability in which children consistently show problems in one or more of these areas: inattention, hyperactivity, and impulsivity. Many experts recommend a combination of academic, behavioral, and medical interventions to help students with ADHD learn and adapt more effectively.
- Beginning in the mid 1960s to mid 1970s, the educational rights for children with disabilities were laid down. In 1975, Public Law 94-142, the Education for All Handicapped Children Act, required that all children be given a free, appropriate public education. In 1990, Public Law 94-142 was renamed the Individuals with Disabilities Education Act (IDEA). An IEP consists of a written plan that spells out a program tailored to a child with a disability. The concept of

least restrictive environment, which is contained in the IDEA, states that children with disabilities must be educated in a setting that is as similar as possible to the one in which children without disabilities are educated. The term *inclusion* means educating children with disabilities full-time in the regular classroom.

5 Explain the development of achievement in children

- Achievement motivation (need for achievement) is the desire to accomplish something, to reach a standard of excellence, and to expend effort to excel. Links between parenting practices and children's achievement have been found.
- Extrinsic motivation involves doing something to obtain something else (a means to an end). Intrinsic motivation involves the internal motivation to do something for its own sake (an end in itself). Overall, most experts recommend that teachers create a classroom climate in which students are intrinsically motivated to learn. One view of intrinsic motivation emphasizes its self-determining characteristics. Giving students some choice and providing opportunities for personal responsibility increase intrinsic motivation. When rewards are used, they should convey information about task mastery rather than external control. Researchers have found that as students move from the early elementary school years to high school, their intrinsic motivation declines, especially during the middle school years.

- A mastery orientation focuses on the task rather than ability, involves positive affect, and includes solution-oriented strategies. A helpless orientation focuses on personal inadequacies, attributing difficulty to lack of ability. Negative affect (boredom or anxiety, for example) also is present. A performance orientation involves being concerned with achievement outcome rather than achievement process. Mastery orientation is the preferred achievement orientation.
- Self-efficacy is the belief that one can master a situation and produce positive outcomes. Bandura believes that self-efficacy is a critical factor in whether students will achieve. Schunk argues that self-efficacy influences a student's choice of tasks, with low-self-efficacy students avoiding many learning tasks.
- Setting specific, proximal (short-term), and challenging goals benefits students' self-efficacy and achievement. Dweck and Nicholls define goals in terms of immediate achievement-related focus and definition of success. Being a good planner means managing time effectively, setting priorities, and being organized. Self-monitoring is a key aspect of self-regulation and benefits student learning.
- Too often, researchers have characterized minority groups in terms of deficits. When studying ethnic minority children, it is important to consider their socioeconomic status. Stevenson's research has found that many Asian children outperform U.S. children in math achievement.

Key Terms

direct instruction approach 541
cognitive constructivist approaches 541
social constructivist approaches 541
child-centered kindergarten 544
Montessori approach 544

developmentally appropriate practice 545
Project Head Start 547
top-dog phenomenon 552
learning disability 560
dyslexia 561
dyscalculia 561
attention deficit hyperactivity disorder (ADHD) 562

individualized education plan (IEP) 563
least restrictive environment (LRE) 563
inclusion 564
achievement motivation (need for achievement) 565

extrinsic motivation 565
intrinsic motivation 565
mastery orientation 567
helpless orientation 567
performance orientation 567
self-efficacy 568

Key People

Maria Montessori 544
Craig Hart 545
Lillian Katz and Sylvia Chard 547, 550
Joan Lipsitz 552

Jonathan Kozol 555
John Ogbu 556
Margaret Beale Spencer 557
Eliot Aronson 557
James Comer 558

David McClelland 565
Carol Dweck 567
Nel Noddings 568
Albert Bandura 568

John Nicholls 569
Sandra Graham 570
Harold Stevenson 571

Taking It to the Net

1. Mark is going to teach high school mathematics. He has read that parents' involvement in their children's education is virtually nonexistent by the time the kids reach high school. What can Mark do as a teacher to encourage parental involvement?

2. Eight-year-old Grace has just been diagnosed with dyslexia. Her parents have no idea what causes the disorder or how to help her. What causes dyslexia? And what can be done to help Grace?

3. Karen is on a school board committee studying how the transition to middle school can decrease student motivation and lead to social and academic problems that might continue into high school. She wants to present an overview of the psychological research on this issue. What have psychologists found to be the negative roles that middle schools play in achievement and motivation?

Connect to **www.mhhe.com/santrockcd10** to research the answers and complete these exercises.

E-Learning Tools

To help you master the material in this chapter, you'll find a number of valuable study tools on the Student CD-ROM that accompanies this book. Also visit the Online Learning Center for *Child Development,* tenth edition (**www.mhhe.com/santrockcd10**) where you'll find these additional resources:

- View video clips by key developmental psychology experts including Laurence Steinberg on teachers dealing with conflict in the classroom.
- Build your decision-making skills by trying your hand at the parenting, nursing, and education "Scenarios" on the Online Learning Center.

CHAPTER 18

Our most basic common link is that we all inhabit this planet. We all breathe the same air. We all cherish our children's future.

—JOHN F. KENNEDY
United States President, 20th Century

Culture

Chapter Outline		*Learning Goals*

CULTURE AND CHILDREN'S DEVELOPMENT   **1**

What Is Culture?

The Relevance of Culture to the Study of Children

Cross-Cultural Comparisons

Discuss the role of culture in children's development

SOCIOECONOMIC STATUS AND POVERTY   **2**

What Is Socioeconomic Status?

Socioeconomic Variations in Families, Neighborhoods, and Schools

Poverty

Describe how socioeconomic status and poverty impact children's lives

ETHNICITY   **3**

Immigration

Ethnicity and Socioeconomic Status

Differences and Diversity

Prejudice, Discrimination, and Bias

Assimilation and Pluralism

America: A Nation of Blended Cultures

Explain how ethnicity is linked to children's development

TECHNOLOGY   **4**

Television

Computers and the Internet

Summarize the influence of technology on children's development

The Stories of Sonya's and Michael's Cultural Conflicts

Sonya, a 16-year-old Japanese American girl, was upset over her family's reaction to her White American boyfriend. Her parents refused to meet him and more than once threatened to disown her. Her older brothers also reacted angrily to Sonya's dating a White American, warning that they were going to beat him up. Her parents were also disturbed that Sonya's grades, above average in middle school, were beginning to drop.

Generational issues contributed to the conflict between Sonya and her family (Nagata, 1989). Her parents had experienced strong sanctions against dating Whites when they were growing up and were legally prevented from marrying anyone but a Japanese. As Sonya's older brothers were growing up, they valued ethnic pride and solidarity. The brothers saw her dating a White as "selling out" her own ethnic group. Sonya's and her family members' cultural values obviously differ.

Michael, a 17-year-old Chinese American high school student, was referred to an outpatient adolescent crisis center by the school counselor for depression and suicidal tendencies (Huang & Ying, 1989). Michael was failing several subjects and was repeatedly absent or late for school. Michael's parents were successful professionals who told the therapist that there was nothing wrong with them or with Michael's younger brother and sister, so what, they wondered, was wrong with Michael? What was wrong was that the parents expected all of their children to become doctors. They were frustrated and angered by Michael's school failures, especially since he was the firstborn son, who in Chinese families is expected to achieve the highest standards of all siblings.

The therapist underscored the importance of the parents' putting less pressure for achievement on Michael and gradually introduced more realistic expectations for Michael (who was not interested in becoming a doctor and did not have the necessary academic record anyway). The therapist supported Michael's desire not to become a doctor and empathized with the pressure he had experienced from his parents. As Michael's school attendance improved, his parents noted his improved attitude toward school and supported a continuation of therapy. Michael's case illustrates how expectations that Asian American youth will be "whiz kids" can become destructive.

Sonya's and Michael's circumstances underscore the importance of culture in understanding children's development. In this chapter, we will explore many aspects of culture, including cross-cultural comparisons of children's development, the harmful effect of poverty on children's development, the role of ethnicity in development, and how technology impacts children's lives.

1 CULTURE AND CHILDREN'S DEVELOPMENT

What Is Culture?	The Relevance of Culture to the Study of Children	Cross-Cultural Comparisons

Culture had a strong influence on the conflict Sonya and Michael experienced in their families and on their behavior outside of the family—in Sonya's case, dating; in Michael's case, school. Of course, a family's cultural background does not always produce conflict between children and other family members, but the two cases described here reveal the importance of understanding a family's cultural values, especially those of ethnic minority families.

What Is Culture?

In chapter 1, we defined **culture** as the behavior, patterns, beliefs, and all other products of a particular group of people that are passed on from generation to generation. ◀ **page 13** The products result from the interaction between groups of people and their environment over many years.

The concept of culture is broad—it includes many components and can be analyzed in many ways (Berry, 2000). Already in previous chapters we have analyzed a number of sociocultural contexts in children's development—families, peers, and schools, for example. In this chapter, we will focus on these aspects of culture, including cross-cultural comparisons, socioeconomic status and poverty, ethnicity, and technology.

Cross-cultural expert Richard Brislin (1993) described a number of characteristics of culture:

- Culture is made up of ideals, values, and assumptions about life that guide people's behavior.
- Culture consists of those aspects of the environment that people make.
- Culture is transmitted from generation to generation, with the responsibility for the transmission resting on the shoulders of parents, teachers, and community leaders.
- Culture's influence becomes noticed the most in well-meaning clashes between people from very different cultural backgrounds.
- Despite compromises, cultural values still remain.
- When their cultural values are violated or their cultural expectations are ignored, people react emotionally.
- It is not unusual for people to accept a cultural value at one point in their lives and reject it at another point. For example, rebellious adolescents and young adults might accept a culture's values and expectations after having children of their own.

The Relevance of Culture to the Study of Children

If the study of child development is to be a relevant discipline in the twenty-first century, increased attention will need to be given to the study of culture and ethnicity. The future will bring extensive contact between people from varied cultural and ethnic backgrounds (Schirato, 2003). Schools and neighborhoods can no longer be the fortresses of one privileged group whose agenda is the exclusion of those with different skin colors or different customs. Immigrants, refugees, and ethnic minority individuals increasingly refuse to become part of a homogeneous melting pot, instead requesting that schools, employers, and governments honor many of their cultural customs. Adult refugees and immigrants might find more opportunities and better-paying jobs in the United States, but their children may learn attitudes in U.S. schools that challenge traditional authority patterns in the home (Brislin, 1993).

For the most part, the study of children has been ethnocentric, emphasizing American values, especially middle-socioeconomic-status, White, male values (Matsumoto, 2000). Cross-cultural psychologists point out that many of the assumptions about contemporary ideas in fields like child development were developed in Western cultures (Triandis, 2001). One example of **ethnocentrism**—the tendency to favor one's

Cross-cultural studies involve the comparison of a culture with one or more other cultures. Shown here is a 14-year-old !Kung girl who has added flowers to her beadwork during the brief rainy season in the Kalahari desert in Botswana, Africa. Delinquency and violence occur much less frequently in the peaceful !Kung culture than in most other cultures around the world.

culture The behavior, patterns, beliefs, and all other products of a particular group of people that are passed on from generation to generation.

ethnocentrism A tendency to favor one's group over other groups.

The Web of Culture
Global Internet Communication
The Global Lab Project
Worldwide Classroom
Cross-Cultural Comparisons

own group over other groups—is the American emphasis on the individual or self. Many Eastern countries, such as Japan, China, and India, are group oriented. So is Mexican culture. Shortly, we will further discuss the individual and group emphases in cultures.

Research by American psychologist Donald Campbell and his colleagues (Brewer & Campbell, 1976; Campbell & LeVine, 1968) revealed that people in all cultures tend to

- believe that what happens in their culture is "natural" and "correct" and that what happens in other cultures is "unnatural" and "incorrect"
- perceive their cultural customs as universally valid, that is, believe that "what is good for us is good for everyone"
- behave in ways that favor their cultural group
- feel hostile toward other cultural groups

Global interdependence is no longer a matter of belief or choice. It is an inescapable reality (Schirato, 2003). Children and their parents are not just citizens of the United States, or Canada, or another country. They are citizens of the world— a world that, through advances in transportation and technology, has become increasingly interactive. By better understanding the behavior and values of cultures around the world, we may be able to interact more effectively with each other and make this planet a more hospitable, peaceful place in which to live (Matsumoto, 2000).

Cross-Cultural Comparisons

Early in this century, overgeneralizations about the universal aspects of children were made based on data and experience in a single culture—the middle-class culture of the United States (Havighurst, 1976). For example, it was believed that adolescents everywhere went through a period of "storm and stress" characterized by self-doubt and conflict. However, when anthropologist Margaret Mead visited the island of Samoa, she found that adolescents of the Samoan culture were not experiencing such stress.

Mead (1928) studied adolescents on the South Seas island of Samoa. She concluded that the basic nature of adolescents is not biological, as G. Stanley Hall envisioned, but rather sociocultural. She argued that when cultures provide a smooth, gradual transition from childhood to adulthood, which is the way adolescence is handled in Samoa, little storm and stress are associated with the period. Mead's observations of Samoan adolescents revealed that their lives were relatively free of storm and stress. Mead concluded that cultures that allow adolescents to observe sexual relations, see babies born, regard death as natural, do important work, engage in sex play, and know clearly what their adult roles will be promote a relatively stress-free adolescence. However, in cultures like the United States, in which children are considered very different from adults and where adolescence is not characterized by the aforementioned experiences, adolescence is more likely to be stressful.

More than half a century after Mead's Samoan findings, her work was criticized as being biased and error-prone (Freeman, 1983). The current criticism also states that Samoan adolescence is more stressful than Mead observed, and that delinquency appears among Samoan adolescents just as it does among Western adolescents. In the current controversy over Mead's findings, some researchers have defended Mead's work (Holmes, 1987).

As we discovered in chapter 1, **cross-cultural studies** involve the comparison of a culture with one or more other cultures. page 13 This comparison provides information about the degree to which children's development is similar, or universal, across cultures, or the degree to which it is culture-specific. The study of children has emerged in the context of Western industrialized society, with the practi-

Anthropologist Margaret Mead (*left*) with a Samoan adolescent girl. Mead found that adolescence in Samoa was relatively stress-free, although recently her findings have been challenged. Mead's observations and analysis challenged G. Stanley Hall's biological, storm-and-stress view and called attention to the sociocultural basis of adolescence.

cross-cultural studies Studies that compare a culture with one or more other cultures. Such studies provide information about the degree to which adolescent development is similar, or universal, across cultures or about the degree to which it is culture-specific.

cal needs and social norms of this culture dominating thinking about child development. Consequently, the development of children in Western cultures has evolved as the norm for all children of the human species, regardless of economic and cultural circumstances. This narrow viewpoint can produce erroneous conclusions about the nature of children. To develop a more global, cosmopolitan perspective on children, let us consider achievement behavior, individualism and collectivism, and rites of passage in different cultures.

Achievement   The United States is an achievement-oriented culture, and U.S. children are more achievement oriented than children are in many other countries. Many American parents socialize their children to be achievement oriented and independent. In one investigation of 104 societies, parents in industrialized countries like the United States placed a higher value on socializing children for achievement and independence than did parents in nonindustrialized countries like Kenya, who placed a higher value on obedience and responsibility (Bacon, Child, & Barry, 1963).

European American children are more achievement oriented than Mexican and Mexican American children are. For example, in one study, European American children were more competitive and less cooperative than their Mexican and Mexican American counterparts (Kagan & Madsen, 1972). In this study, European Americans were more likely to minimize the gains of other students when they could not reach the goals themselves. In other investigations, European American children were more individual centered, while Mexican children were more family centered (Holtzmann, 1982). Some developmentalists believe that the American culture is too achievement oriented for rearing mentally healthy children (Elkind, 1981).

While European American children are more achievement oriented than children in many other cultures, as we saw in chapter 17, they are not as achievement oriented as many Japanese, Chinese, and Asian American children (Stevenson, 1995).   page 571 For example, as a group, Asian American children demonstrate exceptional achievement patterns. Asian American children exceed the national average for high school and college graduates. Eighty-six percent of Asian Americans, compared to 64 percent of White Americans, are in some higher-education program two years after high school graduation. Clearly, education and achievement are highly valued aspirations of many Asian American children.

Individualism and Collectivism   In cross-cultural research, the search for basic traits has extended to characteristics common to whole nations. In recent years, the most elaborate search for traits has focused on the dichotomy between individualism and collectivism (Hofstede, 1980; Triandis, 1994, 2001):

- **Individualism** involves giving priority to personal goals rather than to group goals; it emphasizes values that serve the self, such as feeling good, personal distinction and achievement, and independence.
- **Collectivism** emphasizes values that serve the group by subordinating personal goals to preserve group integrity, interdependence of the members, and harmonious relationships.

Figure 18.1 summarizes some of the main characteristics of individualistic and collectivistic cultures. Many Western cultures, such as the United States, Canada,

Individualistic	Collectivistic
Focuses on individual	Focuses on groups
Self is determined by personal traits independent of groups; self is stable across contexts	Self is defined by in-group terms; self can change with context
Private self is more important	Public self is most important
Personal achievement, competition, power are important	Achievement is for the benefit of the in-group; cooperation is stressed
Cognitive dissonance is frequent	Cognitive dissonance is infrequent
Emotions (such as anger) are self-focused	Emotions (such as anger) are often relationship based
People who are the most liked are self-assured	People who are the most liked are modest, self-effacing
Values: pleasure, achievement, competition, freedom	Values: security, obedience, in-group harmony, personalized relationships
Many casual relationships	Few, close relationships
Save own face	Save own and other's face
Independent behaviors: swimming, sleeping alone in room, privacy	Interdependent behaviors: co-bathing, co-sleeping
Relatively rare mother-child physical contact	Frequent mother-child physical contact (such as hugging, holding)

FIGURE 18.1 Characteristics of Individualistic and Collectivistic Cultures

individualism Giving priority to personal goals rather than to group goals; emphasizing values that serve the self, such as feeling good, personal distinction and achievement, and independence.

collectivism Emphasizing values that serve the group by subordinating personal goals to preserve group integrity, interdependence of members, and harmonious relationships.

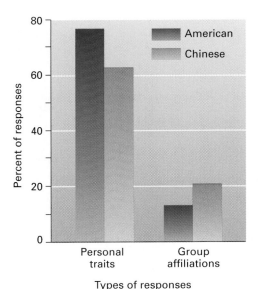

FIGURE 18.2 American and Chinese Self-Conceptions

College students from the United States and China completed 20 "I am ＿＿" sentences. Both groups filled in personal traits more than group affiliations. However, the U.S. college students more often filled in the blank with personal traits, the Chinese with group affiliations.

rites of passage Ceremonies or rituals that mark an individual's transition from one status to another, especially into adulthood.

Great Britain, and the Netherlands, are described as individualistic; many Eastern cultures, such as China, Japan, India, and Thailand, are described as collectivistic.

Many of psychology's basic tenets have been developed in individualistic cultures like the United States. Consider the flurry of *self-* terms in psychology that have an individualistic focus: for example, *self-actualization, self-awareness, self-efficacy, self-reinforcement, self-criticism, self-serving, selfishness,* and *self-doubt* (Lonner, 1988).

Researchers have found that self-conceptions are related to culture. In one study, American and Chinese college students completed 20 sentences beginning with "I am ＿＿＿" (Trafimow, Triandis, & Goto, 1991). As indicated in figure 18.2, the American college students were much more likely to describe themselves with personal traits ("I am assertive"), while the Chinese students were more likely to identify themselves by their group affiliations ("I am a member of the math club").

Critics of the Western notion of psychology point out that human beings have always lived in groups, whether large or small, and have always needed one another for survival. They argue that the Western emphasis on individualism may undermine our basic species need for relatedness (Kagitcibasi, 1988, 1995). Some social scientists believe that many problems in Western cultures are intensified by the Western cultural emphasis on individualism. Individualistic cultures have higher rates than collectivistic cultures of suicide, drug abuse, crime, teenage pregnancy, divorce, child abuse, and mental disorders. Some critics believe that the pendulum might have swung too far toward individualism in many Western cultures. Regardless of their cultural background, people need a positive sense of *self* and *connectedness to others* to develop fully as human beings.

Rites of Passage   **Rites of passage** are ceremonies or rituals that mark an individual's transition from one status to another, especially into adulthood. Some societies have elaborate rites of passage that signal the adolescent's transition to adulthood; others do not (Kottak, 2002). In many primitive cultures, rites of passage are the avenue through which adolescents gain access to sacred adult practices, knowledge, and sexuality (Sommer, 1978). These rites often involve dramatic practices intended to facilitate the adolescent's separation from the immediate family, especially the mother. The transformation usually is characterized by some form of ritual death and rebirth, or by means of contact with the spiritual world. Bonds are forged between the adolescent and the adult instructors through shared rituals, hazards, and secrets to allow the adolescent to enter the adult world. This kind of ritual provides a forceful and discontinuous entry into the adult world at a time when the adolescent is perceived to be ready for the change.

Africa, especially sub-Saharan Africa, has been the location of many rites of passage for adolescents. Under the influence of Western culture, many of the rites are disappearing today, although some vestiges remain. In locations where formal education is not readily available, rites of passage are still prevalent.

Americans do not have formal rites of passage that mark the transition from adolescence to adulthood. Some religious and social groups, however, have initiation ceremonies that indicate an advance in maturity—the Jewish bar mitzvah, the Catholic confirmation, and social debuts, for example.

School graduation ceremonies come the closest to being culturewide rites of passage in the United States. The high school graduation ceremony has become nearly universal for middle-SES adolescents and increasing numbers of adolescents from low-income backgrounds (Fasick, 1988). Nonetheless, high school graduation does not result in universal changes—many high school graduates continue to live with their parents, to be economically dependent on them, and to be undecided about career and lifestyle matters. Another rite of passage for increasing numbers of

American adolescents is sexual intercourse (Halonen & Santrock, 1999). By the end of adolescence, more than 70 percent of American adolescents have had sexual intercourse.

The absence in America of clear-cut rites of passage makes the attainment of adult status ambiguous. Many individuals are unsure whether they have reached adult status. In Texas, the age for beginning employment is 15, but many younger adolescents and even children are employed, especially Mexican immigrants. The age for driving is 16, but when emergency need is demonstrated, a driver's license can be obtained at age 15. Even at age 16, some parents might not allow their son or daughter to obtain a driver's license, believing that 16-year-olds are too young for this responsibility. The age for voting is 18, and the age for drinking has recently been raised to 21. Exactly when adolescents become adults has not been as clearly delineated in America as it has been in some primitive cultures, where rites of passage are universal.

These Congolese Koto boys painted their faces as part of a rite of passage to adulthood. *What kinds of rites of passage do American adolescents have?*

Review and Reflect: Learning Goal 1

1 **Discuss the role of culture in children's development**

REVIEW

- What is culture?
- What is the relevance of culture to the study of children?
- What are cross-cultural comparisons? Describe cross-cultural comparisons involving rites of passage.

REFLECT

- What was the achievement orientation in your family as you grew up? How did the cultural background of your parents influence this orientation?

---

2 SOCIOECONOMIC STATUS AND POVERTY

What Is Socioeconomic Status?	Socioeconomic Variations in Families, Neighborhoods, and Schools	Poverty

Many subcultures exist within countries. For example, the values and attitudes of children growing up in an urban ghetto or rural Appalachia may differ from those of children growing up in a wealthy suburb.

What Is Socioeconomic Status?

Socioeconomic status (SES) refers to the grouping of people with similar occupational, educational, and economic characteristics. Socioeconomic status implies certain inequalities. Generally, members of a society have (1) occupations that vary in prestige, and some individuals have more access than others to higher-status occupations; (2) different levels of educational attainment, and some individuals have more access than others to better education; (3) different economic resources; and (4) different levels of power to influence a community's institutions. These differences in the ability to control resources and to participate in society's rewards produce unequal opportunities for adolescents.

socioeconomic status (SES) A grouping of people with similar occupational, educational, and economic characteristics.

The number of visibly different socioeconomic statuses depends on the community's size and complexity. In most investigators' descriptions of socioeconomic status, two categories, low and middle, are used, although as many as five categories are delineated. Sometimes low socioeconomic status is described as low-income, working class, or blue collar; sometimes the middle category is described as middle-income, managerial, or white collar. Examples of low-SES occupations are factory worker, manual laborer, welfare recipient, and maintenance worker. Examples of middle-SES occupations include skilled worker, manager, and professional (doctor, lawyer, teacher, accountant, and so on).

Socioeconomic Variations in Families, Neighborhoods, and Schools

The families, schools, and neighborhoods of children have socioeconomic characteristics. Some children have parents who have a great deal of money, and who work in prestigious occupations. These children live in attractive houses and neighborhoods, and attend schools where the mix of students is primarily from middle- and upper-SES backgrounds. Other children have parents who do not have very much money and who work in less prestigious occupations. These children do not live in very attractive houses and neighborhoods, and they attend schools where the mix of students is mainly from lower-SES backgrounds. Such variations in neighborhood settings can influence children's adjustment (Leffert & Blyth, 1996). In one study, neighborhood crime and isolation were linked with low self-esteem and psychological distress in children (Bolland, 2003; Roberts, Jacobson, & Taylor, 1996).

In chapter 15, "Families," we indicated that socioeconomic differences in child rearing exist (Hoff, Laursen, & Tardif, 2002). Recall our conclusions that lower-SES parents are more concerned that their children conform to society's expectations, have an authoritarian parenting style, use physical punishment more in disciplining their children, and are more directive and less conversational with their children. By contrast, higher-SES parents are more concerned with developing children's initiative, create a home atmosphere in which children are more nearly equal participants, are less likely to use physical punishment, and are less directive and more conversational with their children.

SES differences also are involved in an important aspect of children's intellectual orientation (Chapman, 2003). Most school tasks require children to use and process language. As a part of developing language skills, students must learn to read efficiently, write effectively, and give competent oral reports. Although variations exist, one study found that students from low-SES families read less and watched television more than their middle-SES counterparts (Erlick & Starry, 1973) (see figure 18.3). Consequently, they may tend to develop weaker intellectual skills, such as reading and writing, that promote academic success. Although television involves some verbal activity, it is primarily a visual medium, which suggests that children from low-SES families prefer a visual medium over a verbal medium.

One study examined socioeconomic status, parenting, and skill-building activities in divorced families (DeGarmo, Forgatch, & Martinez, 1998). Each of three indicators of socioeconomic status—education, occupation, and income—were studied independently to determine their effects on achievement in elementary school boys. Each indicator was associated with better parenting in the divorced families. Especially noteworthy was the finding that the effects of maternal education on boys' achievement was mediated by the time the child spent reading, engaged in skill-building activities, and time not spent watching television.

Like their parents, children from low-SES backgrounds are at high risk for experiencing mental health problems (McLoyd, 1993, 1998, 2000). Social maladaptation and psychological problems, such as depression, low self-confidence, peer conflict, and juvenile delinquency, are more prevalent among children living in low-SES

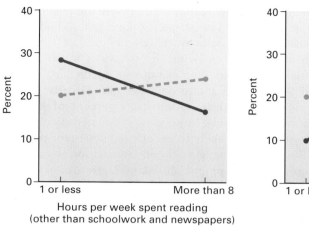
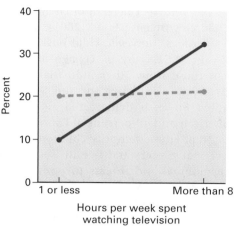

Students whose mothers had graduated from college (middle SES)
Students whose mothers had 11 or fewer years of schooling (low SES)

FIGURE 18.3 **The Reading and Television Habits of High School Students from Low- and Middle-SES Families**

families than among economically advantaged children (Gibbs & Huang, 1989). Although psychological problems are more prevalent among adolescents from low-SES backgrounds, these adolescents vary considerably in intellectual and psychological functioning. For example, a sizable portion of children from low-SES backgrounds perform well in school; some perform better than many middle-SES students. When children from low-SES backgrounds are achieving well in school, it is not unusual to find a parent or parents making special sacrifices to provide the necessary living conditions and support that contribute to school success. One study found that, although positive times occurred in the lives of ethnically diverse children growing up in poverty, many of their negative experiences were worse than those of their middle-SES counterparts (Richards & others, 1994). These adversities involved physical punishment and lack of structure at home, violence in the neighborhood, and domestic violence in their buildings.

In chapter 17, "Schools," we read about schools in low-income neighborhoods having fewer resources than schools in higher-income neighborhoods. The schools in the low-income areas also are more likely to have more students with lower achievement test scores, lower rates of graduation, and smaller percentages of students going to college (Garbarino & Asp, 1981). For example, 80 percent of urban disadvantaged students scored in the bottom half of standardized tests for reading and math. In some instances, however, federal aid to schools has provided a context for enhanced learning in low-income areas.

Poverty

In a report on the state of America's children and adolescents, the Children's Defense Fund (1992) described what life is like for all too many youth. When sixth-graders in a poverty-stricken area of St. Louis were asked to describe a perfect day, one boy said he would erase the world, then he would sit and think. Asked if he wouldn't rather go outside and play, the boy responded, "Are you kidding, out there?"

The world is a dangerous and unwelcoming place for too many of America's youth, especially those whose families, neighborhoods, and schools are low-income (Edelman, 1997; Swisher & Whitlock, 2003). Some children are resilient and cope with the challenges of poverty without any major setbacks, but too many struggle unsuccessfully (Magnuson & Duncan, 2002). Each child of poverty who reaches adulthood unhealthy, unskilled, or alienated keeps our nation from being as competent and productive as it can be (Children's Defense Fund, 1992).

Children, Youth, and Poverty

Poverty in Canada

Research on Poverty

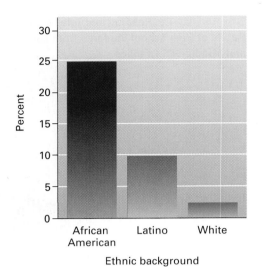

Note: A distressed neighborhood is defined by high levels (at least one standard deviation above the mean) of (1) poverty; (2) female-headed families; (3) high school dropouts; (4) unemployment; and (5) reliance on welfare.

FIGURE 18.4 Percentages of Youth Under 18 Who Are Living in Distressed Neighborhoods

In 2000, 16.2 percent of children were living in families below the poverty line (Children's Defense Fund, 2001). This is the lowest rate of poverty for children in two decades. However, child poverty rates rose in working families.

The U.S. figure of 16 percent of children living in poverty is much higher than those from other industrialized nations. For example, Canada has a child poverty rate of 9 percent and Sweden has a rate of 2 percent. Poverty in the United States is demarcated along ethnic lines. Almost 50 percent of African American and 40 percent of Latino children live in poverty. Compared with White children, ethnic minority children are more likely to experience persistent poverty over many years and live in isolated poor neighborhoods where social supports are minimal and threats to positive development abundant (Jarrett, 1995) (see figure 18.4).

Why is poverty among American children so high? Three reasons are apparent (Huston, McLoyd, & Coll, 1994): (1) economic changes have eliminated many blue-collar jobs that paid reasonably well, (2) the percentage of youth living in single-parent families headed by the mother has increased, and (3) government benefits were reduced during the 1970s and 1980s.

Poor children and their families are often exposed to poor health conditions, inadequate housing and homelessness, environmental toxins, and violent or unsupportive neighborhoods (Hill, Bush, & Roosa, 2003). Unlike income loss or unemployment due to job loss, poverty is not a homogeneous variable or distinct event. Also, unemployment, unstable work history, and income loss do not always push families into poverty.

Let's further consider some of the psychological ramifications of living in poverty. First, the poor are often powerless. In occupations, they rarely are the decision makers. Rules are handed down to them in an authoritarian manner. Second, the poor are often vulnerable to disaster. They are not likely to be given notice before they are laid off from work and usually do not have financial resources to fall back on when problems arise. Third, their range of alternatives is often restricted. Only a limited number of jobs are open to them. Even when alternatives are available, the poor might not know about them or be prepared to make a wise decision, because of inadequate education and inability to read well. Fourth, being poor means having less prestige. This lack of prestige is transmitted to children early in their lives. The child in poverty observes that many other children wear nicer clothes and live in more attractive houses.

When poverty is persistent and long-standing, it can have especially damaging effects on children. In one study, the longer children lived in families with income below the poverty line, the lower was the quality of their home environments (Garrett, Ng'andu, & Ferron, 1994). Also in this study, improvements in family income had their strongest effects on the home environments of chronically poor children. In another study, children in families experiencing both persistent and occasional poverty had lower IQs and more internalized behavior problems than never-poor children, but persistent poverty had a much stronger negative effect on these outcomes than occasional poverty did (Duncan, Brooks-Gunn, & Klebanov, 1994). Further, one recent study of more than 30,000 individuals from birth into the adult years found that the greater risk for developmental outcomes took place with persistent and accumulating socioeconomic disadvantage throughout childhood and adolescence (Schoon & others, 2002).

A special concern is the high percentage of single mothers in poverty, more than one-third of whom are in poverty, compared to only 10 percent of single fathers. Vonnie McLoyd (1998) concludes that because poor, single mothers are more distressed than their middle-SES counterparts are, they often show low support, nurturance, and involvement with their children. Among the reasons for the high poverty rate of single mothers are women's low pay, infrequent awarding of alimony payments, and poorly enforced child support by fathers. The term

feminization of poverty refers to the fact that far more women than men live in poverty. Women's low income, divorce, and the resolution of divorce cases by the judicial system, which usually leaves women with less money than they and their children need to adequately function, are the likely causes of the feminization of poverty.

One recent study documented the importance of family processes in elementary school children's social adjustment in low-income families (Mistry & others, 2002). Lower levels of economic well-being and elevated perceptions of economic pressure were linked with parenting behavior. Distressed parents reported feeling less effective and capable in disciplining their children and were observed to be less affectionate in parent-child interactions. In turn, less optimal parenting predicted lower teacher ratings of children's positive social behavior and higher ratings of behavior problems.

Some recent studies show that benefits provided to parents may have important effects on children as well. One study showed that work-based antipoverty programs for parents were linked to enhanced school performance and social behavior of children (Huston & others, 2001). In this study, wage supplements sufficient to raise family income above the poverty threshold and subsidies for child care and health insurance were given to adults who worked full-time. Positive effects were found for boys' academic achievement, classroom behavior skills, problem behaviors, and educational and occupational aspirations. Possibly the effects were more positive for boys than girls because boys have more behavioral and school-related problems to begin with.

In another recent study, an experimental welfare program in Minnesota resulted in positive outcomes for children (Gennetian & Miller, 2002). This program includes financial incentives to encourage work and mandatory participation in employment-focused activities. The program was linked with increased employment rates, decreased poverty, decreased children's problem behaviors, and improved children's school performance.

One recent trend in antipoverty programs is to conduct two-generation interventions (McLoyd, 1998). This involves providing both services for children (such as educational day care or preschool education) and services for parents (such as adult education, literacy training, and job-skill training). Recent evaluations of the two-generation programs suggest that they have more positive effects on parents than they do on children (St. Pierre, Layzer, & Barnes, 1996). Also discouraging for children is that when the two-generation programs show benefits, these are more likely to be health benefits than cognitive gains.

What happens to a dream deferred?
Does it dry up
Like a raisin in the sun?
—**Langston Hughes**
American Poet and Author, 20th Century

Review and Reflect: Learning Goal 2

2 Describe how socioeconomic status and poverty impact children's lives

REVIEW

- What is socioeconomic status?
- What are some socioeconomic variations in families, neighborhoods, and schools?
- What characterizes children living in poverty?

REFLECT

- What would you label the socioeconomic status of your family as you grew up? How do you think the SES status of your family influenced your development?

feminization of poverty The fact that far more women than men live in poverty. Women's low income, divorce, and the resolution of divorce cases by the judicial system, which usually leaves women with less money than they and their children need to adequately function, are the likely causes.

3 ETHNICITY

| Immigration | Differences and Diversity | Assimilation and Pluralism |

| Ethnicity and Socioeconomic Status | Prejudice, Discrimination, and Bias | America: A Nation of Blended Cultures |

Children live in a world that has been made smaller and more interactive by dramatic improvements in travel and communication. U.S. children live in a world that is far more diverse in its ethnic makeup than in past decades. Ninety-three languages are spoken in Los Angeles alone! With these changes have come conflicts, and concerns about what the future will bring.

Groups like the Taliban and Al Qaeda attack countries like the United States that they perceive to be too secular and materialistic. And the United States retaliates. Israelis and Palestinians bicker and fight over territory in the Middle East, each claiming religious rights to disputed land. In countries across Africa, tribal chiefs try to craft a new social order favorable to their own rule. In Germany, an increasing number of youth join the neo-Nazi movement. Some German-born citizens want an ethnic cleansing of their country; non-German-born immigrants have been beaten and killed.

In chapter 1 we defined **ethnicity** as based on cultural heritage, nationality characteristics, race, religion, and language. ◀ page 13 Nowhere are cultural changes in the United States more dramatic than in the increasing ethnic diversity of America's children.

Immigration

Relatively high rates of minority immigration are contributing to the growth in the proportion of ethnic minorities in the U.S. population (Cushner, McClelland, & Safford, 2003; McLoyd, 2000; Padillo & Perez, 2003; Phinney, 2003). Immigrants often experience stressors uncommon to or less prominent among longtime residents, such as language barriers, dislocations and separations from support networks, dual struggle to preserve identity and to acculturate, and changes in SES status (Cushner, 2003; Suarez-Orozco, 2002).

Parents and children may be at different stages of acculturation, which can produce conflict over cultural values (Roosa & others, 2002; Samaniego & Gonzales, 1999). One study examined the cultural values and intergenerational value discrepancies in immigrant (Vietnamese, Armenian, and Mexican) and nonimmigrant families (African American and European American) (Phinney, 1996). Family obligations were endorsed more by parents than adolescents in all groups, and the intergenerational value discrepancy generally increased with time in the United States.

Research increasingly shows links between acculturation and adolescent problems (Gonzales & others, 2002). For example, more acculturated Latino youth in the United States experience higher rates of conduct problems, substance abuse, and risky sexual behavior than their less-acculturated counterparts (Brook & others, 1998; Epstein, Botvin, & Diaz, 1998).

One individual who is deeply concerned about immigrant youth and conducts research to learn more about ways to help them cope with life in America is Carola Suarez-Orozco. To read about her work, see the Careers in Child Development insert.

Ethnicity and Socioeconomic Status

Much of the research on ethnic minority children has failed to tease apart the influences of ethnicity and socioeconomic status (SES). Ethnicity and SES can interact

www.mhhe.com/santrockcd10

Migration and Ethnic Relations

Immigration: Journals and Newsletter

Immigration and Ethnicity: Research Centers

Immigrant Families

I am here and you will know that I am the best and will hear me. The color of my skin or the kink of my hair or the spread of my mouth has nothing to do with what you are listening to.

—LEONTYNE PRICE
American Operatic Soprano, 20th Century

ethnicity A dimension of culture based on cultural heritage, nationality, race, religion, and language.

in ways that exaggerate the negative influence of ethnicity because ethnic minority individuals are overrepresented in the lower socioeconomic levels of American society (Coll & Pachter, 2002; Spencer & Dornbusch, 1990). Consequently, too often researchers have given ethnic explanations of child development that were largely based on socioeconomic status rather than on ethnicity. For example, decades of research on group differences in self-esteem failed to consider the socioeconomic status of African American and White American children (Hare & Castenell, 1985). When the self-esteem of African American children from low-income backgrounds is compared with that of White American children from middle-class backgrounds, the differences are often large but not informative because of the confounding of ethnicity and SES (Scott-Jones, 1995).

In chapter 1, we described a recent research study that focused on the home environments of four ethnic groups: European American, African American, Latino, and Asian American (Bradley & others, 2001). There were some ethnic differences, but the most consistent results involved poverty, which was a more powerful indicator of the type of home environment children experienced than ethnicity was.

In this study, both similarities and differences characterized the home environments of children from different ethnic groups in terms of the percentage of children who were exposed to various events and conditions. For example, about 90 percent of all mothers (regardless of ethnic group) spoke to their infants during the home visit. About 85 percent of the play environments of infants (regardless of ethnic group) appeared to be safe. Further, relatively few mothers (5 to 11 percent) restricted their preschool children during the home visit. Also, about 75 percent of the elementary school children (regardless of ethnic group) were encouraged to talk during the home visit.

However, there were some ethnic differences in the observations of home environments:

- African American mothers were less likely than the other three groups to display physical affection to their children and reported using physical punishment more.
- European American and Asian American homes were more likely than African American and Latino homes to contain materials for learning and recreation; the European American and Asian American mothers were also more likely to read to their children than the other two groups.
- Fathers were less likely to be present in the African American homes than the other three groups.

While some ethnic minority children are from middle-SES backgrounds, economic advantage does not entirely enable them to escape their ethnic minority status (Harwood & others, 2002; McAdoo, 2002; Spencer & Dornbusch, 1990). Middle-SES ethnic minority children still encounter much of the prejudice, discrimination, and bias associated with being a member of an ethnic minority group. Often characterized as a "model minority" because of their strong achievement orientation and family cohesiveness, Japanese Americans still experience stress associated with ethnic

Careers in Child Development

Carola Suarez-Orozco, *Lecturer, Researcher, and Codirector of Immigration Projects*

Carola Suarez-Orozco is a researcher and lecturer in the Human Development and Psychology area at Harvard University. She also is codirector of the Harvard Immigration Projects. She obtained her undergraduate degree (development studies) and graduate (clinical psychology) degrees from the University of California at Berkeley.

Carola has worked both in clinical and public school settings in California and Massachusetts. She currently is codirecting a five-year longitudinal study of immigrant adolescents' (coming from Central America, China, and the Dominican Republic) adaptation to schools and society. One of the courses she teaches at Harvard is on the psychology of immigrant youth. She especially believes that more research needs to be conducted on the intersection of cultural and psychological factors in the adaptation of immigrant and ethnic minority youth.

Carola Suarez-Orozco, with her husband Marcelo, who also studies the adaptation of immigrants.

minority status (Sue, 1990). Although middle-SES ethnic minority children have more resources available to counter the destructive influences of prejudice and discrimination, they still cannot completely avoid the pervasive influence of negative stereotypes about ethnic minority groups.

While not all ethnic minority families are poor, poverty contributes to the stressful life experiences of many ethnic minority children (Coll & Pachter, 2002). Vonnie McLoyd (1990) concluded that ethnic minority children experience a disproportionate share of the adverse effects of poverty and unemployment in America today. Thus, many ethnic minority children experience a double disadvantage: (1) prejudice, discrimination, and bias because of their ethnic minority status; and (2) the stressful effects of poverty.

Differences and Diversity

Historical, economic, and social experiences produce legitimate differences between various ethnic minority groups, and between ethnic minority groups and the majority White group (Halonen & Santrock, 1999). Individuals living in a particular ethnic or cultural group adapt to the values, attitudes, and stresses of that culture. Their behavior, while possibly different from your own, is, nonetheless, often functional for them. Recognizing and respecting these differences is an important aspect of getting along with others in a diverse, multicultural world. Children, like all of us, need to take the perspective of individuals from ethnic and cultural groups that are different than their own and think, "If I were in their shoes, what kind of experiences might I have had?" "How would I feel if I were a member of their ethnic or cultural group?" "How would I think and behave if I had grown up in their world?" Such perspective taking often increases empathy and understanding of individuals from ethnic and cultural groups different from one's own.

Unfortunately, the emphasis often placed by our society and science on the differences between ethnic minority groups and the White majority in the United States has been damaging to ethnic minority individuals. Ethnicity has defined who will enjoy the privileges of citizenship and to what degree and in what ways (Jones, 1994). An individual's ethnic background has determined whether the individual will be alienated, oppressed, or disadvantaged.

For too long, differences between any ethnic minority group and Whites were conceptualized as *deficits* or inferior characteristics on the part of the ethnic minority group. Indeed, research on ethnic minority groups often focused only on a group's negative, stressful aspects. For example, research on African American adolescent females invariably examined such topics as poverty, unwed mothers, and dropping out of school. These topics continue to be important areas of adolescent development much in need of research, but research on the positive aspects of African American adolescent females in a pluralistic society is also much needed and sorely neglected. The self-esteem, achievement, motivation, and self-control of children from different ethnic minority groups deserve considerable study.

The current emphasis on differences between ethnic groups underscores the strengths of various ethnic minority groups and is long overdue (Wooroffe & Spencer, 2003). For example, the extended-family support system that characterizes many ethnic minority groups is now recognized as an important factor in coping. And researchers are finding that African American males are better than Anglo-American males at nonverbal cues, multilingual/multicultural expression, improvised problem solving, and using body language in communication (Evans & Whitfield, 1988).

As we noted in chapter 1, there also is considerable diversity within each ethnic group (Banks, 2001; Cushner, 2003). Ethnic minority groups are not homogeneous; they have different social, historical, and economic backgrounds (Stevenson, 1998). For example, Mexican, Cuban, and Puerto Rican immigrants are Latinos, but they had different reasons for migrating, came from varying socioeconomic back-

*C*onsider the flowers of a garden: Though differing in kind, color, form, and shape, yet, inasmuch as they are refreshed by the waters of one spring, revived by the breath of one wind, invigorated by the rays of one sun, this diversity increases their charm and adds to their beauty. . . . How unpleasing to the eye if all the flowers and plants, the leaves and blossoms, the fruits, the branches, and the trees of that garden were all of the same shape and color! Diversity of hues, form, and shape enriches and adorns the garden and heightens its effect.

—'Abdu'l Baha
Persian Baha'i Religious Leader, 19th/20th Century

grounds in their native countries, and experience different rates and types of employment in the United States (Coll & others, 1995). The U.S. federal government now recognizes the existence of 511 *different* Native American tribes, each having a unique ancestral background with differing values and characteristics. Asian Americans include the Chinese, Japanese, Filipinos, Koreans, and Southeast Asians, each group having a distinct ancestry and language. The diversity of Asian Americans is reflected in their educational attainment: Some achieve a high level of education, while many others have no education whatsoever. For example, 90 percent of Korean American males graduate from high school, but only 71 percent of Vietnamese American males do.

Sometimes, well-meaning individuals fail to recognize the diversity within an ethnic group (Sue, 1990). For example, a sixth-grade teacher went to a human relations workshop and was exposed to the necessity of incorporating more ethnicity into her instructional planning. Since she had two Mexican American adolescents in her class, she asked them to be prepared to demonstrate to the class on the following Monday how they danced at home. The teacher expected both of them to perform Mexican folk dances, reflecting their ethnic heritage. The first boy got up in front of the class and began dancing in a typical American fashion. The teacher said, "No, I want you to dance like you and your family do at home, like you do when you have Mexican American celebrations." The boy informed the teacher that his family did not dance that way. The second boy demonstrated a Mexican folk dance to the class. The first boy was highly assimilated into the American culture and did not know how to dance Mexican folk dances. The second boy was less assimilated and came from a Mexican American family that had retained more of its Mexican heritage.

This example illustrates the diversity and individual differences that exist within any ethnic minority group. Failure to recognize diversity and individual variations results in the stereotyping of an ethnic minority group.

Prejudice, Discrimination, and Bias

Prejudice is an unjustified negative attitude toward an individual because of the individual's membership in a group. The group toward which the prejudice is directed can be made up of people of a particular ethnic group, sex, age, religion, or other detectable difference. Our concern here is prejudice against ethnic minority groups.

Many ethnic minority individuals continue to experience persistent forms of prejudice, discrimination, and bias (Scott, 2003; Sue, 1990). Ethnic minority adolescents are taught in schools that often have a middle-SES, White bias and in classroom contexts that are not adapted to ethnic minority adolescents' learning styles. They are assessed by tests that are often culturally biased and are evaluated by teachers whose appreciation of their abilities may be hindered by negative stereotypes about ethnic minorities (Spencer & Dornbusch, 1990). Discrimination and prejudice continue to be present in the media, interpersonal interactions, and daily conversations (Aboud, Mendelson, & Purdy, 2003). Crimes, strangeness, poverty, mistakes, and deterioration are often mistakenly attributed to ethnic minority individuals or foreigners.

As Asian American researcher Stanley Sue (1990) points out, people frequently have opposing views about discrimination and prejudice. On the one side are individuals who value and praise the significant strides made in civil rights in recent years, pointing to affirmative action programs as proof of these civil rights advances. On the other side are individuals who criticize American institutions, such as education, because they believe that many forms of discrimination and prejudice still characterize these institutions.

For several reasons, the "browning" of Americans portends heightened racial/ethnic prejudice and conflict, or at least sharper racial and ethnic cleavages (McLoyd, 1998). First, it is occurring against a backdrop of longstanding White privilege and an ingrained sense of entitlement and superiority among non-Latino Whites.

Jason Leonard, age 15: "I want America to know that most of us black teens are not troubled people from broken homes and headed to jail. . . . In my relationships with my parents, we show respect for each other and we have values in our house. We have traditions we celebrate together, including Christmas and Kwanzaa."

www.mhhe.com/santrockcd10

Ethnic Minority Families

African Americans

Latinos and Native Americans

Asian Americans

Prejudice

$\mathcal{P}$rejudice is the reason of fools.

—**Voltaire**
French Philosopher, 18th Century

prejudice An unjustified negative attitude toward an individual because of her or his membership in a group.

Second, the youth of today's immigrants are less likely than their counterparts in the early twentieth century to believe that they must reject the values and ways of their parents' homeland to succeed in American society. Many espouse economic, but not cultural, assimilation into mainstream society. Third, today's immigrants often settle in inner-city neighborhoods where assimilation often means joining a world that is antagonistic to the American mainstream because of its experience of racism and economic barriers.

Progress has been made in ethnic minority relations, but discrimination and prejudice still exist, and equality has not been achieved. Much remains to be accomplished.

Assimilation and Pluralism

Assimilation refers to the absorption of ethnic minority groups into the dominant group. This often means the loss of some or virtually all of the behavior and values of the ethnic minority group. Individuals who favor assimilation usually advocate that ethnic minority groups should become more American. By contrast, **pluralism** refers to the coexistence of distinct ethnic and cultural groups in the same society. Individuals who advocate pluralism usually advocate that cultural differences should be maintained and appreciated (Leong, 2000).

For many years, assimilation was thought to be the best course for American society because the mainstream was believed to be superior in many ways. Even though many individuals today reject the notion that the mainstream culture is intrinsically superior to ethnic minority cultures, the assimilation approach is currently resurfacing with a more complex face. Advocates of assimilation now often use practical and functional arguments rather than intrinsic superiority arguments to buttress their point of view. For example, they say that educational programs for immigrant children (Mexican, Chinese, and so on) should stress the learning of English as early as possible, rather than bilingual education. Their argument is that spending time on any language other than English may be a handicap, especially since a second language is not functional in the classroom. By contrast, the advocates of pluralism argue that an English-only approach reasserts the mainstream-is-right-and-best belief. Thus, responses to the ethnic minority issue of bilingual education involve a clash of fundamental values. As Sue (1990) asks, how can one argue against the development of functional skills and to some degree the support of Americanization? Similarly, how can one doubt that pluralism, diversity, and respect for different cultures are valid? Sue believes that the one-sidedness of the issue is the main problem. Advocates of assimilation often overlook the fact that a consensus may be lacking on what constitutes functional skills or that a particular context may alter what skills are useful. For example, with an increasing immigrant population, the ability to speak Spanish or Japanese may be an asset, as is the ability to interact with and collaborate with diverse ethnic groups.

Sue believes that one way to resolve value conflicts about sociocultural issues is to conceptualize or redefine them in innovative ways. For example, in the assimilation/pluralism conflict, rather than assuming that assimilation is necessary for the development of functional skills, we could focus on the fluctuating criteria of what skills are considered functional or the possibility that developing functional skills does not prevent the existence of pluralism. For instance, the classroom instructor might use multicultural examples when teaching social studies, while also discussing culturally universal and culturally specific approaches to American and other cultures.

America: A Nation of Blended Cultures

America has been and continues to be a great receiver of ethnic groups. It has embraced new ingredients from many cultures. The cultures often collide and cross-pollinate, mixing their ideologies and identities. Some of the culture of origin is retained, some of it lost, some of it mixed with the American culture. One after

assimilation The absorption of ethnic minority groups into the dominant group, which often means the loss of some or virtually all of the behavior and values of the ethnic minority group.

pluralism The coexistence of distinct ethnic and cultural groups in the same society.

Canada

Canada is a vast and diverse country with a population of approximately 27 million people. Although Canada shares a number of similarities with the United States, there are some important differences (Majhanovich, 1998; Siegel & Wiener, 1993). Canada comprises a mixture of cultures that are loosely organized along the lines of economic power. The three main Canadian cultures include:

- Native peoples, or First Nations, who were Canada's original inhabitants
- Descendants of French settlers who came to Canada during the seventeenth and eighteenth centuries
- Descendants of British settlers who came to Canada during and after the seventeenth century, or from the United States after the American Revolution in the latter part of the eighteenth century

The late nineteenth century brought three more waves of immigrants:

- From Asia, mainly China, immigrants came to the west coast of Canada in the latter part of the nineteenth and early twentieth centuries.

- From various European countries, immigrants came to central Canada and the prairie provinces during the early twentieth century and following World War II.
- From countries in economic and political turmoil (in Latin America, the Caribbean, Asia, Africa, the Indian subcontinent, the former Soviet Union, and the Middle East), immigrants have come to many different parts of Canada.

Canada has two official languages—English and French. Primarily French-speaking individuals reside mainly in Quebec; primarily English-speaking individuals reside mainly in other Canadian provinces. In addition to its English- and French-speaking populations, Canada has a large multicultural community. In three large Canadian cities—Toronto, Montreal, and Vancouver—more than 50 percent of the children and adolescents come from homes in which neither English nor French is the native language (Siegel & Wiener, 1993).

another, immigrants have come to America and been exposed to new channels of awareness and, in turn, exposed Americans to new channels of awareness. African American, Latino, Asian American, Native American, and other cultural heritages mix with the mainstream, receiving a new content and giving a new content. The ethnicity of Canadian children is discussed in the Explorations in Child Development box.

Earlier in the chapter, we saw that children in low-socioeconomic circumstances watch TV more and read less than their middle-socioeconomic-status counterparts. Next, we will explore further the roles of television and other technology in children's lives.

Review and Reflect: Learning Goal 3

3 Explain how ethnicity is linked to children's development

REVIEW

- How does immigration influence children's development?
- How are ethnicity and socioeconomic status related?
- What is important to know about differences and diversity?
- How are prejudice, discrimination, and bias involved in children's development?
- What are assimilation and pluralism? How has their emphasis changed in America?
- How is America a nation of blended cultures?

REFLECT

- No matter how well intentioned children are, their life circumstances likely have given them some prejudices. If they don't have prejudices toward people with different cultural and ethnic backgrounds, other kinds of people may bring out prejudices in them. For example, prejudices can be developed about people who have certain religious or political conventions, people who are unattractive or too attractive, people with a disability, and people in a nearby town. As a parent or teacher, how would you attempt to reduce children's prejudices?

4 TECHNOLOGY

Television	Computers and the Internet

Few cultural changes have affected children's lives in the twentieth century more than technology. These changes are likely to continue throughout the twenty-first century. We will begin our exploration of technology's influence on children's development by focusing on television and then discussing computers and the Internet.

Television

Few developments in society in the second half of the twentieth century had a greater impact on children than television (Brown & others, 2003; Murray, 2000). Many children spend more time in front of the television set than they do with their parents. Although it is only one of the many mass media that affect children's behavior, television is the most influential. The persuasive capabilities of television are staggering (Kotler, Wright, & Huston, 2001). The 20,000 hours of television watched by the time the average American adolescent graduates from high school are greater than the number of hours spent in the classroom.

Television's Many Roles   Television can have a negative influence on children's development by taking them away from homework, making them passive learners, teaching them stereotypes, providing them with violent models of aggression, and presenting them with unrealistic views of the world (Wilson, 2003). However, television can also have a positive influence on children's development by presenting motivating educational programs, increasing children's information about the world beyond their immediate environment, and providing models of prosocial behavior (Clifford, Gunter, & McAleer, 1995).

Television has been called many things, not all of them good. Depending on one's point of view, it may be a "window on the world," the "one-eyed monster," or the "boob tube." Television has been attacked as one of the reasons that scores on national achievement tests in reading and mathematics are lower now than in the past. Television, it is claimed, attracts children away from books and schoolwork. In one study, children who read printed materials, such as books, watched television less than those who did not read (Huston, Seigle, & Bremer, 1983). Furthermore, critics argue that television trains children to become passive learners; rarely, if ever, does television require active responses from the observer.

Television also is said to deceive; that is, it teaches children that problems are resolved easily and that everything always comes out right in the end. For example, TV detectives usually take only 30 to 60 minutes to sort through a complex array of clues to reveal a killer—and they *always* find the killer. Violence is a way of life on many shows. On TV it is all right for police to use violence and to break moral codes in their fight against evildoers. The lasting results of violence are rarely brought home to the viewer. A person who is injured on TV suffers for only a few seconds; in real life, the person might need months or years to recover, or might not recover at all. Yet one out of every two first-grade children says that the adults on television are like adults in real life (Lyle & Hoffman, 1972).

Sesame Street demonstrates that education and entertainment can work well together (Cole, Richman, & Brown, 2001; Fisch & Truglio, 2001). Through *Sesame Street*, children experience a world of learning that is both exciting and entertaining. *Sesame Street* also follows the principle that teaching can be accomplished both

www.mhhe.com/santrockcd10

Television and Children
Children's Television Workshop

*T*elevision is a medium of entertainment which permits millions of people to listen to the same joke at the same time, and yet remain lonesome.

—T. S. ELIOT
American-born English Poet,
20th Century

directly and indirectly. Using the direct way, a teacher might tell children exactly what they are going to be taught and then teach them. However, in real life, social skills are often communicated in indirect ways. Rather than merely telling children, "You should cooperate with others," TV can show children so that they can figure out what it means to be cooperative and what the advantages are.

The Amount of Television Children Watch   Just how much television do young children watch? They watch a lot. In the 1990s, children watched an average of 26 hours of television each week, which is more than any other activity except sleep (National Center for Children Exposed to Violence, 2001). As shown in figure 18.5, considerably more children in the United States than their counterparts in other developed countries watch television for long periods. For example, seven times as many 9-year-olds in the United States as their counterparts in Switzerland watch television more than five hours a day.

A special concern is the extent to which children are exposed to violence and aggression on television. Up to 80 percent of the prime-time shows include violent acts, including beatings, shootings, and stabbings. The frequency of violence increases on the Saturday morning cartoon shows, which average more than 25 violent acts per hour.

The Effects of Television on Aggression and Prosocial Behavior   What are the effects of television violence on children's aggression? Does television merely stimulate a child to go out and buy a *Star Wars* ray gun, or can it trigger an attack on a playmate? When children grow up, can television violence increase the likelihood that they will violently attack someone?

In one longitudinal investigation, the amount of violence viewed on television at age 8 was significantly related to the seriousness of criminal acts performed as an adult (Huesmann, 1986). In another investigation, long-term exposure to television violence was significantly related to the likelihood of aggression in 1,565 boys 12 to 17 years old (Belson, 1978). Boys who watched the most aggression on television were the most likely to commit a violent crime, swear, be aggressive in sports, threaten violence toward another boy, write slogans on walls, or break windows. These investigations are *correlational,* so we can conclude from them not that television violence causes children to be more aggressive, but only that watching television violence is *associated with* aggressive behavior. In one experiment, children were randomly assigned to one of two groups: One watched television shows taken directly from violent Saturday-morning cartoon offerings on 11 different days; the second group watched television cartoon shows with all of the violence removed (Steur, Applefield, & Smith, 1971). The children were then observed during play at

"Mrs. Horton, could you stop by school today?"

Copyright © 1981 Martha F. Campbell. Used by permission of Martha F. Campbell.

Exploring Television Violence

Children, Youth, Media, and Violence

Culture and TV Violence

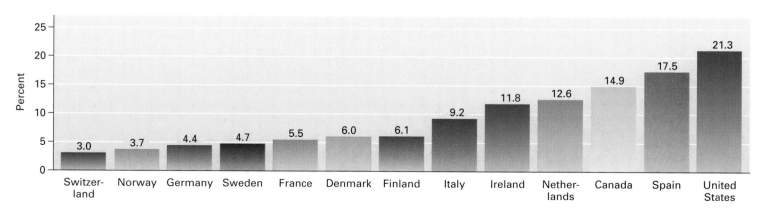

FIGURE 18.5 Percentage of 9-Year-Old Children Who Report Watching More Than Five Hours of Television per Weekday

their preschool. The preschool children who saw the TV cartoon shows with violence kicked, choked, and pushed their playmates more than the preschool children who watched nonviolent TV cartoon shows did. Because children were randomly assigned to the two conditions (TV cartoons with violence versus with no violence), we can conclude that exposure to TV violence *caused* the increased aggression in children in this investigation.

Some critics have argued that research results do not warrant the conclusion that TV violence causes aggression (Freedman, 1984). However, many experts insist that TV violence can cause aggressive or antisocial behavior in children (Anderson & Bushman, 2002; Bushman & Huesmann, 2001; Perse, 2001). Of course, television violence is not the *only* cause of aggression. There is no *one* cause of any social behavior. Aggression, like all other social behaviors, has multiple determinants (Donnerstein, 2001). The link between TV violence and aggression in children is influenced by children's aggressive tendencies and by their attitudes toward violence and monitoring of children's exposure to it.

An example of a high-risk portrayal of violence on television involves a hostile motorcycle gang that terrorizes a neighborhood. In their harassment, they kidnap a well-known rock singer. A former boyfriend of the singer then tries to rescue her. He sneaks up on the gang and shoots six of them, one at a time. Some of the gunfire causes the motorcycles to blow up. The scene ends with the former boyfriend rescuing the tied-up singer.

This violence contains all of the features that encourage aggression in adolescents. The ex-boyfriend is young and good looking, and cast as a rugged hero. His attack on the gang is shown as justifiable—the gang members are ruthless and uncontrollable, and have kidnapped an innocent woman. The "hero" is never punished or disciplined, even though it appears that he has taken the law into his own hands. Serving as the ultimate reward, the young woman proclaims her love for him after he rescues her. Also, in spite of the extensive violence in this movie, no one is shown as being seriously hurt. The focus quickly shifts away from gang members after they have been shot, and viewers do not see anyone die or suffer.

Television also can teach children that it is better to behave in positive, prosocial ways than in negative, antisocial ways (Dorr, Rabin, & Irlen, 2002; Wilson, 2001). Aimee Leifer (1973) demonstrated that television is associated with prosocial behavior in young children. She selected a number of episodes from the television show *Sesame Street* that reflected positive social interchanges. She was especially interested in situations that taught children how to use their social skills. For example, in one interchange, two men were fighting over the amount of space available to them. They gradually began to cooperate and to share the space. Children who watched these episodes copied these behaviors, and in later social situations they applied the prosocial lessons they had learned. To read about ways to make television more developmentally appropriate, see figure 18.6.

Television and Cognitive Development Children bring various cognitive skills and abilities to their television viewing experience (Rabin & Dorr, 1995). Several important cognitive shifts take place between early childhood and middle and late childhood (Wilson, 2001). Preschool children often focus on the most striking perceptual features of a TV program and are likely to have difficulty in distinguishing reality from fantasy in the portrayals. As children enter elementary school, they are better able to link scenes together and draw causal conclusions from narratives. Judgments of reality also become more accurate in older children.

How does television influence children's creativity and verbal skills? Television is negatively related to children's creativity (Williams, 1986). Also, because television is primarily a visual modality, verbal skills—especially expressive language— are enhanced more by aural or print exposure (Beagles-Roos & Gat, 1983). Educational programming for young children can promote creativity and imagination,

Developmental Issues	What Children See on TV	What Children Should See
To establish a sense of *trust and safety*	The world is dangerous; enemies are everywhere; weapons are needed to feel safe.	A world where people can be trusted and help each other, where safety and predictability can be achieved, where fears can be overcome.
To develop a sense of *autonomy with connectedness*	Autonomy is equated with fighting and weapons. Connectedness is equated with helplessness, weakness, and altruism.	A wide range of models of independence within meaningful relationships and of autonomous people helping each other.
To develop a sense of *empowerment and efficacy*	Physical strength and violence equal power and efficacy. Bad guys always return. A range of ways to have an impact are *not* shown.	Many examples of people having a positive effect on their world without violence.
To establish *gender identity*	Exaggerated, rigid gender divisions— boys are strong, violent, and save the world; girls are helpless, victimized, and irrelevant to world events.	Complex characters with wide-ranging behaviors, interests, and skills; commonalities between the sexes overlapping in what both can do.
To develop an *appreciation of diversity* among people	Racial and ethnic stereotyping. Dehumanized enemies. Diversity is dangerous. Violence against those who are different is justified.	Diverse peoples with varied talents, skills, and needs, who treat each other with respect, work out problems nonviolently, and enrich each other's lives.
To construct the foundations of *morality and social responsibility*	One-dimensional characters who are all good or all bad. Violence is the solution to interpersonal problems. Winning is the only acceptable outcome. Bad guys deserve to be hurt.	Complex characters who act responsibly and morally toward others—showing kindness and respect, working out moral problems, taking other people's points of view.
To have opportunities for *meaningful play*	Program content is far removed from children's experience or level of understanding. Toys are linked to programs promoting initiative, not to creative play.	Meaningful content to use in play, which resonates deeply with developmental needs; shows not linked to realistic toys so that children can create their own unique play.

FIGURE 18.6 A Developmental Framework for Assessing Television

possibly because it has a slower pace, and auditory and visual modalities are better coordinated (Anderson & others, 2001). Newer technologies, especially interactive television, hold promise for motivating children to learn and become more exploratory in solving problems (Singer, 1993).

In one recent longitudinal study, viewing educational programs as preschoolers was associated with a host of desirable characteristics in adolescence: getting higher grades, reading more books, placing a higher value on achievement, being more creative, and acting less aggressively (Anderson & others, 2001). These associations were more consistent for boys than girls. Figure 18.7 shows the results for boys' high school grade point average. However, girls who were more frequent viewers of violent TV programs in the preschool years had lower grades in adolescence than girls who infrequently watched violent TV programs in the preschool years.

Computers and the Internet

Culture involves change, and nowhere is that change greater than in the technological revolution today's children are experiencing with increased use of computers and the Internet. For children to be adequately prepared for tomorrow's jobs, technology needs to become an integral part of their lives (Sharp, 1999). In a poll of seventh- through twelfth-graders jointly conducted by CNN and the National Science Foundation (1997), 82 percent predicted that they would not be able to make a good living unless they have computer skills and understand other

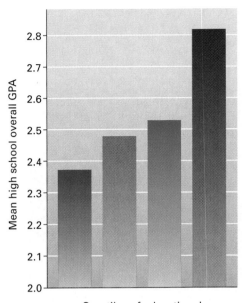

Quartiles of educational
viewing at age 5

FIGURE 18.7 Educational TV Viewing in Early Childhood and High School Grade Point Average for Boys

When boys watched more educational television (especially *Sesame Street*) as preschoolers, they had higher grade point averages in high school. The graph displays the boys' early TV viewing patterns in quartiles and the means of their grade point averages. The bar on the left is for the lowest 25 percent of boys who viewed educational TV programs, the next bar the next 25 percent, and so on, with the bar on the right for the 25 percent of the boys who watched the most educational TV shows as preschoolers.

Technology and Education

Webliography

Internet Pals

Critical Analysis of the Internet

Internet The core of computer-mediated communication. The Internet system is worldwide and connects thousands of computer networks, providing an incredible array of information adolescents can access.

e-mail Electronic mail, a valuable way to send and receive messages.

technology. The technology revolution is part of the information society in which we now live.

People are using computers to communicate today the way they used to use pens, postage stamps, and telephones. The new information society still relies on some basic nontechnological competencies: good communication skills, the ability to solve problems, thinking deeply, thinking creatively, and having positive attitudes. However, how people pursue these competencies is being challenged and extended in ways and at a speed that few people had to cope with in previous eras (Bissell, Manring, & Rowland, 1999; Collis & Sakamoto, 1996).

The Internet The **Internet** is the core of computer-mediated communication. The Internet system is worldwide and connects thousands of computer networks, providing an incredible array of information adolescents can access (Donnerstein, 2002). In many cases, the Internet has more current, up-to-date information than books.

Youth throughout the world are increasingly using the Internet, despite substantial variation in use in different countries around the world and in socioecomomic groups (Anderson, 2002). Between 1998 and 2001, the percentage of U.S. 14- to 17-year-olds using the Internet increased from 51 percent to 75 percent and the percentage of U.S. 10- to 13-year-olds increased from 39 percent to 65 percent (Kaiser Family Foundation, 2002). The most U.S. adolescents say that they teach themselves how to use the Internet (40 percent), while others learn from their parents (30 percent), friends (23 percent), and siblings (10 percent) (Kaiser Family Foundation, 2002). Only 5 percent said they learned how to use the Internet at school. Studies have found that almost 50 percent of adolescents go online every day (Kaiser Family Foundation, 2001). Among 15- to 17-year-olds, one-third use the Internet for 6 hours a week or more, 24 percent use it for 3 to 5 hours a week, and 20 percent use it for 1 hour a week or less (Woodard, 2000).

What do adolescents do when they are online? As shown in figure 18.8, **e-mail** (electronic mail, a valuable way to send and receive messages) is the most frequent Internet activity they engage in, and more than 70 percent of the adolescents who go online connect with a chat room (Kaiser Family Foundation, 2001). E-mail messages can be sent to and received from individuals as well as large numbers of people.

Special concerns have emerged about children's and adolescents' access to information on the Internet, which has been largely unregulated. Adolescents can access adult sexual material, instructions for making bombs, and other information that is inappropriate for them. Information on the Internet is not well organized or evaluated, indicating a critical need for adolescents to develop the navigational skills to sort through complex information (Anderson, 2002).

With as many as 11 million American adolescents now online, more and more of adolescent life is taking place in a landscape that is inaccessible to many parents. Many adolescents have a computer in their bedroom, and most parents don't have any idea what information their adolescents are obtaining online. Some psychologists recommend putting the computer in the family room, where adults and adolescents have more opportunities to discuss what information is being accessed online. Every Web browser records what sites users visit. With just elementary computer know-how, parents can monitor their adolescents' computer activities.

In one study, about half of parents said that being online is more positive than watching TV for adolescents (Tarpley, 2001). However, an analysis of content suggests they might be wise to be more concerned about their adolescents' use of the Internet (Donnerstein, 2002; Tarpley, 2001):

- Of the 1,000 most visited sites, 10 percent are adult sex oriented.
- Forty-four percent of adolescents have viewed an adult Internet site.

- Twenty-five percent of adolescents have visited an Internet site that promotes hate groups.
- Twelve percent have visited an Internet site where they can obtain information about how to purchase a gun.

In sum, the Internet holds a great deal of potential for increasing adolescents' educational opportunities. However, the Internet also has limitations and dangers. The Internet is a technology that needs parents to monitor and regulate adolescents' use of it (Donnerstein, 2002).

Technology and Sociocultural Diversity Technology brings with it certain social issues. A special concern is whether increased use of technology (especially computers) in homes and schools will widen the learning gap between rich and poor and male and female students (Kaiser Family Foundation, 2002). One national survey found that children and adolescents who go to school in lower-income communities spend more time with most types of media than their counterparts in wealthier neighborhoods, but were significantly less likely to use computers (Roberts & others, 1999) (see figure 18.9). There are gaps in computer availability across ethnic groups as well. A recent study found that approximately half of all African American and Latino adolescents do not use the Internet, compared with just one-fifth of non-Latino White or Asian American adolescents (U.S. Department of Commerce, 2002).

Technology and Education Technology has been a part of schooling for many decades, but until recently the technologies being used were rather simple and changed slowly. To underscore how technology in schools has changed dramatically, in 1983 there were fewer than 50,000 computers in America's schools. In 2002, there were more than 6 million! Hardly a school in America today is without at least one computer. Nearly every week, a school board approves the purchase of ten to twenty computers for improving students' writing skills, another school board approves a high school's use of Channel One (a 10-minute daily recap of news that has become controversial because it also includes 2 minutes of advertising), and another sets aside funds for a telecomputing network system that connects classrooms within a school and with different schools.

It is important to keep in mind that technology itself does not improve a child's ability to learn. A number of conditions in combination are necessary to create learning environments that adequately support students' learning. These include vision and support from educational leaders, educators who are skilled in the use of technology for learning, access to contemporary technologies, and an emphasis on the child as an active, constructivist learner (International Society for Technology in Education, 1999).

E-mail	83%
Search engine	78
Music sites	59
General research	58
Games	51
TV/movie sites	43
Chat room	42
Own Web page	38
Sports sites	35

FIGURE 18.8 Percentage of U.S. 15- to 17-Year-Olds Engaging in Different Online Activities

Note: Study conducted by telephone in fall 2001, with a national random sample of 398 15- to 17-year-olds.

Review and Reflect: Learning Goal 4

4 Summarize the influence of technology on children's development

REVIEW
- How does television influence children's development?
- What roles do computers and the Internet play in children's development?

REFLECT
- How much television did you watch as a child? What effect do you believe it has had on your development?

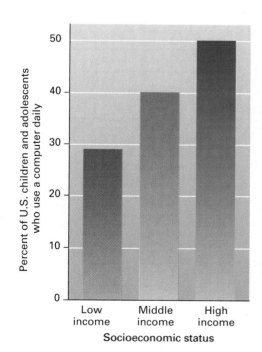

FIGURE 18.9 Daily Computer Use by Children and Adolescents in Different Socioeconomic Groups

Reach Your Learning Goals

Culture

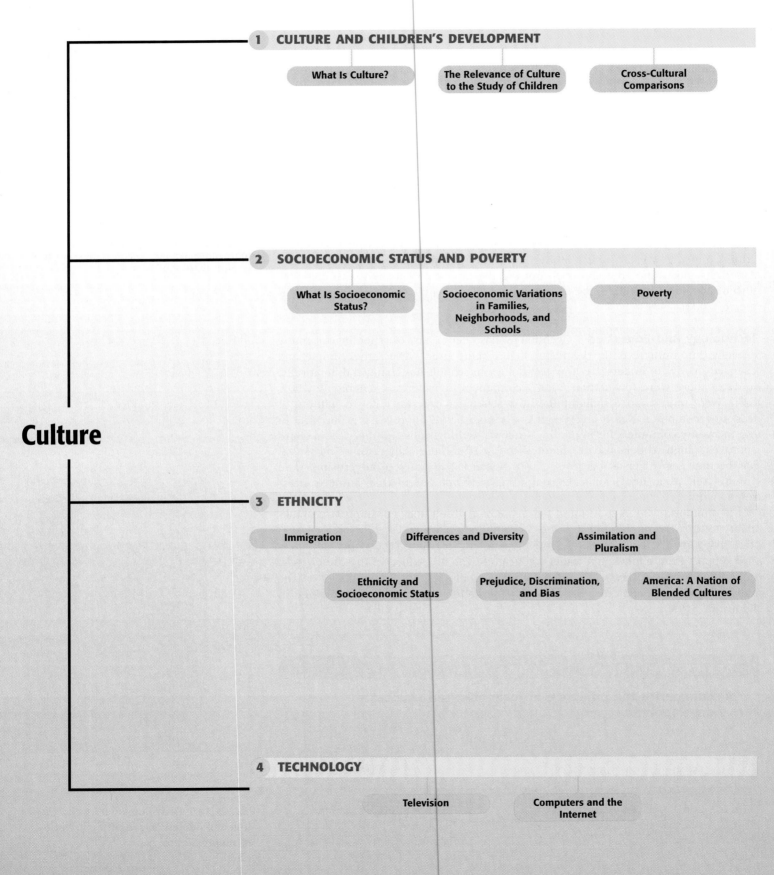

1 CULTURE AND CHILDREN'S DEVELOPMENT

- What Is Culture?
- The Relevance of Culture to the Study of Children
- Cross-Cultural Comparisons

2 SOCIOECONOMIC STATUS AND POVERTY

- What Is Socioeconomic Status?
- Socioeconomic Variations in Families, Neighborhoods, and Schools
- Poverty

3 ETHNICITY

- Immigration
- Differences and Diversity
- Assimilation and Pluralism
- Ethnicity and Socioeconomic Status
- Prejudice, Discrimination, and Bias
- America: A Nation of Blended Cultures

4 TECHNOLOGY

- Television
- Computers and the Internet

Summary

1 Discuss the role of culture in children's development

- *Culture* refers to the behavior patterns, beliefs, and all other products of a particular group of people that are passed on from generation to generation.
- If the study of children is to be a relevant discipline in the twenty-first century, there will have to be increased attention to culture.
- Cross-cultural comparisons involve the comparison of one culture with one or more other cultures, which provides information about the degree to which information is universal or culture-specific. Rites of passage are ceremonies that mark an individual's transition from one status to another, especially into adulthood. In primitive cultures, rites of passage are well-defined, but in contemporary America they are not.

2 Describe how socioeconomic status and poverty impact children's lives

- Socioeconomic status (SES) is the grouping of people with similar occupational, educational, and economic characteristics. SES often carries with it certain inequities.
- The families, neighborhoods, and schools of children have SES characteristics that are related to the child's development. Parents from low-SES families are more likely to value external characteristics and to use physical punishment than their middle-SES counterparts.
- Poverty is defined by economic hardship. The subculture of the poor is often characterized not only by economic hardship but also by social and psychological difficulties. When poverty is persistent and longlasting, it especially has adverse effects on children's development.

3 Explain how ethnicity is linked to children's development

- Ethnicity is based on cultural heritage, nationality characteristics, race, religion, and language. The immigration of families to the United States brings about a number of challenges for helping children adapt to their new culture. Parents and children may be at different stages of acculturation.
- Too often researchers have not teased apart ethnic and socioeconomic status effects when studying ethnic minority children. Although not all ethnic minority families are poor, poverty contributes to the stress of many ethnic minority families and between ethnic minority groups and the White majority.
- Recognizing differences in ethnicity is an important aspect of getting along with others in a diverse, multicultural world. Too often differences have been described as deficits on the part of ethnic minority individuals. Ethnic minority groups are not homogeneous. Failure to recognize this diversity results in stereotyping.

- Prejudice is an unjustified negative attitude toward an individual because of the individual's membership in a group. Progress has been made in ethnic minority relations, but discrimination and bias still exist.
- For many years, assimilation (the absorption of ethnic groups into the dominant group, which often means the loss of some or virtually all of the behavior and values of the ethnic minority group) was thought to be the best course for American society, but pluralism (the coexistence of distinct ethnic and cultural groups in the same society) is increasingly being advocated.
- America has been, and continues to be, a great receiver of ethnic immigrants.

4 Summarize the influence of technology on children's development

- Although television can have a negative influence on children's development by taking them away from homework, making them passive learners, teaching them stereotypes, and presenting them with unrealistic views of the world, television also can have positive influences by presenting motivating educational programs, increasing children's information beyond their immediate environment, and providing models of prosocial behavior. Children watch huge amounts of TV. Preschool children watch an average of 4 hours a day. U.S. children watch more TV than children in all other countries. Up to 80 percent of the prime-time TV shows have violent episodes. TV violence is not the only cause of children's aggression, but most experts agree that it can induce aggression and antisocial behavior. Prosocial behavior on TV is associated with increased positive behavior by children. Children's cognitive skills and abilities influence their TV viewing experiences. TV viewing is negatively related to children's verbal skills and creativity.
- Today's children are experiencing a technological revolution through the dramatic increase in the use of computers and the Internet. The Internet is the core of computer-mediated communication, and it is worldwide. A special concern is the largely unregulated aspects of the Internet that make it difficult for parents to monitor the information their children are accessing. One concern is whether increased technology will widen the gap between rich and poor, male and female students. Keep in mind that technology alone does not improve children's learning. A combination of other factors such as an emphasis on active, constructivist learning also is required.

Key Terms

culture 579
ethnocentrism 579
cross-cultural studies 580
individualism 581

collectivism 581
rites of passage 582
socioeconomic status (SES)
 583

feminization of poverty 586
ethnicity 588
prejudice 591
assimilation 592

pluralism 592
Internet 598
e-mail 598

Key People

Donald Campbell 580
Margaret Mead 580

Vonnie McLoyd 586

Stanley Sue 591

Aimee Leifer 596

Taking It to the Net

1. Jeremy is attending college in California, where he is majoring in political science. For his senior thesis he is required to choose an area of social policy and develop a legislative agenda. Based upon recent news reports about the increasing number of low- and middle-income wage earners who don't make enough money for decent housing, food, and health care for their children, he decides to make the needs of these children his priority. What types of programs should he propose for the children of these families?

2. Mrs. Bernstein thinks that she ought to involve her fourth-grade students in a dialogue about racism and prejudice, because there are several ethnic groups represented in her class.

But a colleague warned her that talking to kids about racism could backfire and actually cause prejudice. Is that possible?

3. Denise has heard about the "digital divide"—the concept that ethnic minorities and economically deprived populations are not participating in the Internet explosion. Denise is about to begin teaching third grade in an inner-city school, and she wonders if the school is likely to be as well equipped technologically as a school in a better neighborhood. What are the facts?

Connect to **www.mhhe.com/santrockcd10** to research the answers and complete these exercises.

E-Learning Tools

To help you master the material in this chapter, you'll find a number of valuable study tools on the Student CD-ROM that accompanies this book. Also visit the Online Learning Center for *Child Development*, tenth edition (**www.mhhe.com/santrockcd10**) where you'll find these additional resources:

- View video clips by key developmental psychology experts including Sandra Calvert on the impact of television violence and on how parents can help children become critical viewers.
- Build your decision-making skills by trying your hand at the parenting, nursing, and education "Scenarios" on the Online Learning Center.

Appendix *Careers in Child Development*

Some of you may be quite sure about what you plan to make your life's work. Others of you may not have decided on a major yet and are uncertain about which career path you want to follow. Each of us wants to find a rewarding career and enjoy the work we do. The field of child development offers an amazing breadth of career options that can provide extremely satisfying work.

If you decide to pursue a career in child development, what career options are available to you? There are many. College and university professors teach courses in many different areas of child development, education, family development, nursing, and medicine. Teachers impart knowledge, understanding, and skills to children and adolescents. Counselors, clinical psychologists, nurses, and physicians help parents and children of different ages to cope more effectively with their lives and well-being. Various professionals work with families to improve the quality of family functioning.

Although an advanced degree is not absolutely necessary in some areas of child development, you usually can expand your opportunities (and income) considerably by obtaining a graduate degree. Many careers in child development pay reasonably well. For example, psychologists earn well above the median salary in the United States. Also, by working in the field of child development, you can guide people in improving their lives, understand yourself and others better, possibly advance the state of knowledge in the field, and have an enjoyable time while you are doing these things.

If you are considering a career in child development, would you prefer to work with infants? Children? Adolescents? Parents? As you go through this term, try to spend some time with children of different ages. Observe their behavior. Talk with them about their lives. Think about whether you would like to work with children of this age in your life's work.

Another important aspect of exploring careers is to talk with people who work in various jobs. For example, if you have some interest in becoming a school counselor, call a school, ask to speak with a counselor, and set up an appointment to discuss the counselor's career and work. If you have an interest in becoming a nurse, think about whether you would rather work with babies, children, or adolescents. Call a hospital, ask to speak with the nursing department, and set up an appointment to talk with the nursing coordinator about a nursing career.

Something else that should benefit you is to work in one or more jobs related to your career interests while you are in college. Many colleges and universities have internships or work experiences for students who major in such fields as child development. In some instances, these opportunities are for course credit or pay; in others, they are strictly on a volunteer basis. Take advantage of these opportunities. They can provide you with valuable experiences to help you decide if this is the right career area for you and they can help you get into graduate school, if you decide you want to go.

Now we will profile a number of careers in four areas: education/research; clinical/counseling; medical/nursing/physical development; and families/relationships. These are not the only career options in child development, but they should provide you with an idea of the range of opportunities available and information about some of the main career avenues you might pursue. In profiling these careers, we will address the amount of education required, the nature of the training, and a description of the work.

EDUCATION/RESEARCH

There are numerous career opportunities in child development that involve education and/or research. These range from being a college professor to day-care director to school psychologist.

College/University Professor

Courses in child development are taught in many different programs and schools in college and universities, including psychology, education, nursing, child and family studies, social work, and medicine. A Ph.D. or master's degree almost always is required to teach in some area of child development in a college or university. Obtaining a doctoral degree usually takes four to six years of graduate work. A master's degree requires approximately two years of graduate work. The professorial job might be at a research university with one or more master's or Ph.D. programs in child development, at a four-year college with no graduate programs, or at a community college.

The training involves taking graduate courses, learning to conduct research, and attending and presenting papers at professional meetings. Many graduate students work as teaching or research assistants for professors in an apprenticeship relationship that helps them to become competent teachers and researchers. The work that college professors do includes teaching courses either at the undergraduate or graduate level (or both), conducting research in a specific area, advising students and/or directing their research, and serving on college or university committees. Some college instructors do not conduct research as part of their job but instead focus mainly on teaching. In many instances, research is most likely to be part of the job description at universities with master's and Ph.D. programs.

If you are interested in becoming a college or university professor, you might want to make an appointment with your instructor in this class on child development to learn more about his or her profession and work.

Researcher

Some individuals in the field of child development work in research positions. In most instances, they will have either a master's or Ph.D. in some area of child development. The researchers might work at a university, in some cases in a university professor's research program, in government at such agencies as the National Institute of Mental Health, or in private industry. Individuals who have full-time research positions in child development generate innovative research ideas, plan studies, carry out the research by collecting data, analyze the data, and then interpret it. Then, they will usually attempt to publish the research in a scientific journal. A researcher often works in a collaborative manner with other researchers on a project and may present the research at scientific meetings, where she or he also learns about other research. One researcher might spend much of his or her time in a laboratory while another researcher might work out in the field, such as in schools, hospitals, and so on.

Elementary or Secondary School Teacher

Becoming an elementary or secondary school teacher requires a minimum of an undergraduate degree. The training involves taking a wide range of courses with a major or concentration in education as well as completing a supervised practice-teaching internship. The work of an elementary or secondary school teacher involves teaching in one or more subject areas, preparing the curriculum, giving tests, assigning grades, monitoring students' progress, conducting parent-teacher conferences, and attending in-service workshops.

Exceptional Children (Special Education) Teacher

Becoming a teacher of exceptional children requires a minimum of an undergraduate degree. The training consists of taking a wide range of courses in education and a concentration of courses in educating children with disabilities or children who are gifted. The work of a teacher of exceptional children involves spending concentrated time with individual children who have a disability or are gifted. Among the children a teacher of exceptional children might work with are children with learning disabilities, ADHD (attention deficit hyperactivity disorder), mental retardation, or a physical disability such as cerebral palsy. Some of this work will usually be done outside of the student's regular classroom, some of it will be carried out when the student is in the regular classroom. The exceptional children teacher works closely with the student's regular classroom teacher and parents to create the best educational program for the student. Teachers of exceptional children often continue their education after obtaining their undergraduate degree and attain a master's degree.

Early Childhood Educator

Early childhood educators work on college faculties and have a minimum of a master's degree in their field. In graduate school, they take courses in early childhood education and receive supervisory training in day-care or early childhood programs. Early childhood educators usually teach in community colleges that award an associate degree in early childhood education.

Preschool/Kindergarten Teacher

Preschool teachers teach mainly 4-year-old children and kindergarten teachers primarily teach 5-year-old children. They usually have an undergraduate degree in education, specializing in early childhood education. State certification to become a preschool or kindergarten teacher usually is required. These teachers direct the educational activities of young children.

Family and Consumer Science Educator

Family and consumer science educators may specialize in early childhood education or instruct middle and high school students about such matters as nutrition, interpersonal relationships, human sexuality, parenting, and human development. Hundreds of colleges and universities throughout the United States offer two- and four-year degree programs in family and consumer science. These programs usually include an internship requirement. Additional education courses may be needed to obtain a teaching certificate. Some family and consumer educators go on to graduate school for further training, which provides a background for possible jobs in college teaching or research.

Educational Psychologist

An educational psychologist most often teaches in a college or university and conducts research in such areas of educational psychology as learning, motivation, classroom management, and assessment. Most educational psychologists have a doctorate in education, which takes four to six years of graduate work. They help train students who will take various positions in education, including educational psychology, school psychology, and teaching.

School Psychologist

School psychologists focus on improving the psychological and intellectual well-being of elementary and secondary school students. They usually have a master's or doctoral degree in school psychology. In graduate school, they take courses in counseling, assessment, learning, and other areas of education and psychology. School psychologists may work in a centralized office in a school district or in one or more schools. They give psychological tests, interview students and their parents, consult with teachers, and may provide counseling to students and their families.

CLINICAL/COUNSELING

There are a wide variety of clinical and counseling jobs that are linked with child development. These range from clinical psychologist to adolescent drug counselor.

Clinical Psychologist

Clinical psychologists seek to help people with psychological problems. They work in a variety of settings, including colleges and universities, clinics, medical schools, and private practice. Clinical psychologists have either a Ph.D. (which involves clinical and research training) or a Psy.D. degree (which only involves clinical training). This graduate training usually takes five to seven years and includes courses in clinical psychology and a one-year supervised internship in an accredited setting toward the end of the training. In most cases, they must pass a test to become licensed in a state and to call themselves a clinical psychologist. Some clinical psychologists only conduct psychotherapy, others do psychological assessment and psychotherapy, and some also do research. Clinical psychologists may specialize in a particular age group, such as children (child clinical psychologist).

Psychiatrist

Psychiatrists obtain a medical degree and then do a residency in psychiatry. Medical school takes approximately four years and the psychiatry residency another three to four years. Unlike psychologists (who do not go to medical school), psychiatrists can administer drugs to clients.

Like clinical psychologists, psychiatrists might specialize in working with children (child psychiatry) or adolescents (adolescent psychiatry). Psychiatrists might work in medical schools in teaching and research roles, in a medical clinic, or in private practice. In addition to administering drugs to help improve the lives of people with psychological problems, psychiatrists also may conduct psychotherapy.

Counseling Psychologist

Counseling psychologists go through much of the same training as clinical psychologists, although in a graduate program in counseling rather than clinical psychology. Counseling psychologists have either a master's degree or a doctoral degree. They also must go through a licensing procedure. One type of master's degree in counseling leads to the designation of licensed professional counselor. They work in the same settings as clinical psychologists, and may do psychotherapy, teach, or conduct research. In many instances, counseling psychologists do not do therapy with individuals who have a severe mental disorder. A counseling psychologist might specialize in working with children, adolescents, and/or families.

School Counselor

School counselors help identify students' abilities and interests, guide students in developing academic plans, and explore career options with students. They may help students cope with adjustment problems. They may work with students individually, in small groups, or even in a classroom. They often consult with parents, teachers, and school administrators when trying to help students with their problems. School counselors usually have a master's degree in counseling.

High school counselors advise students on choosing a major, admissions requirements for college, taking entrance exams, applying for financial aid, and on appropriate vocational and technical training. Elementary school counselors are mainly involved in counseling students about social and personal problems. They may observe children in the classroom and at play as part of their work.

Career Counselor

Career counselors help individuals to identify what the best career options are for them and guide them in applying for jobs. They may work in private industry or at a college/university. They usually interview individuals and give them vocational and/or psychological tests to help them provide students with information about appropriate careers that fit their interests and abilities. Sometimes they help individuals to create professional resumes or conduct mock interviews to help them feel comfortable in a job interview. They may create and promote job fairs or other recruiting events to help individuals obtain jobs.

Social Worker

Social workers often are involved in helping people with social or economic problems. They may investigate, evaluate, and attempt to rectify reported cases of abuse, neglect, endangerment, or domestic disputes. They can intervene in families if necessary and provide counseling and referral services to individuals and families. They have a minimum of an undergraduate degree from a school of social work that includes course work in various areas of sociology and psychology. Some social workers also have a master's or doctoral degree. They often work for publicly funded agencies at the city, state, or national level, although increasingly they work in the private sector in areas such as drug rehabilitation and family counseling.

In some cases, social workers specialize in a certain area, as is true of a medical social worker, who has a master's degree in social work (M.S.W.). This involves graduate course work and supervised clinical experiences in medical settings. A medical social worker might coordinate a variety of support services to people with a severe or long-term disability. Family care social workers often work with families who need support services.

Drug Counselor

Drug counselors provide counseling to individuals with drug-abuse problems. They may work on an individual basis with a substance abuser or conduct group therapy sessions. At a minimum, drug counselors go through an associates or certificate program. Many have an undergraduate degree in substance-abuse counseling, and some have master's and doctoral degrees. They may work in private practice, with a state or federal government agency, with a company, or in a hospital setting. Some drug counselors specialize in working with adolescents or families. Most states provide a certification procedure for obtaining a license to practice drug counseling.

MEDICAL/NURSING/PHYSICAL DEVELOPMENT

This third main area of careers in child development includes a wide range of careers in the medical and nursing areas, as well as jobs pertaining to improving some aspect of the person's physical development.

Obstetrician/Gynecologist

An obstetrician/gynecologist prescribes prenatal and postnatal care and performs deliveries in maternity cases. The individual also treats diseases and injuries of the female reproductive system. Becoming an obstetrician/gynecologist requires a medical degree plus three to five years of residency in obstetrics/gynecology. Obstetricians may work in private practice, in a medical clinic, in a hospital, or in a medical school.

Pediatrician

A pediatrician monitors infants' and children's health, works to prevent disease or injury, helps children attain optimal health, and treats children with health problems. Pediatricians have attained a medical degree and then go on to do a three- to five-year residency in pediatrics.

Pediatricians may work in private practice, in a medical clinic, in a hospital, or in a medical school. As a medical doctor, they can administer drugs to children and may counsel parents and children on ways to improve the children's health. Many pediatricians on the faculty of medical schools also teach and conduct research on children's health and diseases.

Neonatal Nurse

A neonatal nurse is involved in the delivery of care to the newborn infant. The neonatal nurse may work to improve the health and well-being of infants born under normal circumstances or be involved in the delivery of care to premature and critically ill neonates. A minimum of an undergraduate degree in nursing with a specialization in the newborn is required. This training involves course work in nursing and the biological sciences, as well as supervisory clinical experiences.

Nurse-Midwife

A nurse-midwife formulates and provides comprehensive care to selected maternity patients, cares for the expectant mother as she prepares to give birth and guides her through the birth process, and cares for the postpartum patient. The nurse-midwife also may provide care to the newborn, counsel parents on the infant's development and parenting, and provide guidance about health practices. Becoming a nurse-midwife generally requires an undergraduate degree from a school of nursing. A nurse-midwife most often works in a hospital setting.

Pediatric Nurse

Pediatric nurses have a degree in nursing that takes from two to five years to complete. Some also may go on to obtain a master's or doctoral degree in pediatric nursing. Pediatric nurses take courses in biological sciences, nursing care, and pediatrics, usually in a school of nursing. They also undergo supervised clinical experiences in medical settings. They monitor infants' and children's health, work to prevent disease or injury, and help children attain optimal health. They may work in hospitals, in schools of nursing, or with pediatricians in private practice or at a medical clinic.

Audiologist

An audiologist has a minimum of an undergraduate degree in hearing science. This includes courses and supervisory training. Audiologists assess and identify the presence and severity of hearing loss, as well as problems in balance. Some audiologists also go on to obtain a master's and/or doctoral degree. They may work in a medical clinic, with a physician in private practice, in a hospital, or in a medical school.

Speech Therapist

Speech therapists are health-care professionals who are trained to identify, assess, and treat speech and language problems. They may work with physicians, psychologists, social workers, and other health-care professionals in a team approach to helping individuals with physical or psychological problems in which speech and language are involved in the problem. Speech pathologists have a minimum of an undergraduate degree in the speech and hearing science or communications disorders area. They may work in private practice, in hospitals and medical schools, and in government agencies with individuals of any age. Some may specialize in working with children, others with the elderly, or in a particular type of speech disorder.

Genetic Counselor

Genetic counselors are health professionals with specialized graduate degrees and experience in the areas of medical genetics and counseling. Most enter the field after majoring in undergraduate school in such disciplines as biology, genetics, psychology, nursing, public health, and social work.

Genetic counselors work as members of a health-care team, providing information and support to families who have members with birth defects or genetic disorders and to families who may be at risk for a variety of inherited conditions. They identify families at risk and provide supportive counseling. They serve as educators and resource people for other health-care professionals and the public. Almost one-half work in university medical centers and another one-fourth work in private hospital settings.

FAMILIES/RELATIONSHIPS

A number of careers and jobs are available for working with families and relationship problems. These range from being a child welfare worker to a marriage and family therapist.

Child Welfare Worker

A child welfare worker is employed by the Child Protective Services Unit of each state. The child welfare worker protects the child's rights, evaluates any maltreatment the child might experience, and may have the child removed from the home if necessary. A child social worker has a minimum of an undergraduate degree in social work.

Child Life Specialist

Child life specialists work with children and their families when the child needs to be hospitalized. They monitor the child patient's activities, seek to reduce the child's stress, help the child cope effectively, and assist the child in enjoying the hospital experience as much as possible. Child life specialists may provide parent education and develop individualized treatment plans based on an assessment of the child's development, temperament, medical plan, and available social supports. Child life specialists have an undergraduate degree and they take courses in child development and education, as well as usually taking additional courses in a child life program.

Marriage and Family Therapist

Marriage and family therapists work on the principle that many individuals who have psychological problems benefit when psychotherapy is provided in the context of a marital or family relationship. Marriage and family therapists may provide marital therapy, couple therapy to individuals in a relationship who are not married, and family therapy to two or more members of a family.

Marriage and family therapists have a master's and/or doctoral degree. They go through a training program in graduate school similar to a clinical psychologist but with the focus on marital and family relationships. To practice marital and family therapy in most states it is necessary to go through a licensing procedure.

WEBSITE CONNECTIONS FOR CAREERS IN CHILD DEVELOPMENT

By going to the website for this book, www.mhhe.com/santrockcd10 you can obtain more detailed career information about the various careers in child development described in this Appendix. Go to the Web connections in the Career Appendix section, where you will read about a description of the websites. Then click on the title and you will be able to go directly to the website described. Here are the website connections:

Education/Research

Careers in Psychology
Elementary and Secondary School Teaching
Exceptional Children Teachers
Early Childhood Education
Family and Consumer Science Education
Educational Psychology
School Psychology

Clinical/Counseling

Clinical Psychology
Psychiatry
Counseling Psychology
School Counseling
Drug Counseling
Social Work

Medical/Nursing/Physical Development

Obstetrics and Gynecology
Pediatrics
Nurse-Midwife
Neonatal Nursing
Pediatric Nursing
Audiology and Speech Pathology
Genetic Counseling

Families/Relationships

Child Welfare Worker
Child Life Specialist
Marriage and Family Therapist

Glossary

A

A$\overline{\text{B}}$ error The Piagetian object-permanence concept in which an infant progressing into substage 4 makes frequent mistakes, selecting the familiar hiding place (A) rather than the new hiding place ($\overline{\text{B}}$). 212

accommodation Occurs when children adjust to new information. 34

acculturation Cultural change that results from continuous, firsthand contact between two distinctive cultural groups. Accultural stress is the negative consequence of acculturation. 360

achievement motivation (need for achievement) The desire to accomplish something, to reach a standard of excellence, and to expend effort to excel. 565

achievement tests Tests that measure what a person has learned or the skills that a person has mastered. 285

active (niche-picking) genotype-environment correlations Correlations that exist when children seek out environments they find compatible and stimulating. 85

adolescence The developmental period of transition from childhood to early adulthood, entered at approximately 10 to 12 years of age and ending at 18 to 22 years of age. 18

adolescent egocentrism The heightened self-consciousness of adolescents, which is reflected in their belief that others are as interested in them as the adolescents are in themselves, and in adolescents' sense of personal uniqueness and vulnerability. 224

adoption study A study in which investigators seek to discover whether, in behavior and psychological characteristics, adopted children are more like their adoptive parents, who provided a home environment, or more like their biological parents, who contributed their heredity. Another form of the adoption study is to compare adoptive and biological siblings. 74

affordances Opportunities for interaction offered by objects that are necessary to perform functional activities. 152

algorithms Strategies that guarantee a solution to a problem. 262

altruism Unselfish interest in helping another person. 456

amnion The life-support system that is a bag or envelope that contains a clear fluid in which the developing embryo floats. 96

androgens Hormones, the most important of which is testosterone, that promote the development of male genitals and secondary sex characteristics. 411

androgyny The presence of masculine and feminine characteristics in the same person. 425

anger cry A cry similar to the basic cry, with more excess air forced through the vocal chords (associated with exasperation or rage). 351

animism A facet of preoperational thought, the belief that inanimate objects have "life-like" qualities and are capable of action. 216

anorexia nervosa An eating disorder that involves the relentless pursuit of thinness through starvation. 178

Apgar Scale A widely used method to assess the health of newborns at one and five minutes after birth. The Apgar Scale evaluates infants' heart rate, respiratory effort, muscle tone, body color, and reflex irritability. 118

aphasia A language disorder, resulting from brain damage, that involves a loss of the ability to use words. 318

aptitude tests Tests that predict an individual's ability to learn a skill or what the individual can accomplish with training. 285

assimilation (Piaget) Occurs when children incorporate new information into their existing knowledge. 34

assimilation (culture) The absorption of ethnic minority groups into the dominant group, which often means the loss of some or virtually all of the behavior and values of the ethnic minority group. 592

associative play Play that involves social interaction with little or no organization. 520

attachment A close emotional bond between an infant and a caregiver. 368

attention Concentrating and focusing mental resources. 245

attention deficit hyperactivity disorder (ADHD) A disability in which children consistently show one or more of the following characteristics: (1) inattention, (2) hyperactivity, and (3) impulsivity. 562

authoritarian parenting This is a restrictive, punitive style in which the parent exhorts the child to follow the parent's directions and to respect work and effort. Firm limits and controls are placed on the child, and little verbal exchange is allowed. This style is associated with children's socially incompetent behavior. 481

authoritative parenting This style encourages children to be independent but still places limits and controls on their actions. Extensive verbal give-and-take is allowed, and parents are warm and nurturant toward the child. This style is associated with children's socially competent behavior. 481

automaticity The ability to process information with little or no effort. 234

autonomous morality (Piaget) The second stage of moral development in Piaget's theory, displayed by older children (about 10 years of age and older). The child becomes aware that rules and laws are created by people and that, in judging an action, one should consider the actor's intentions as well as the consequences. 437

B

basal metabolism rate (BMR) The minimum amount of energy an individual uses in a resting state. 177

basic cry A rhythmic pattern usually consisting of a cry, a briefer silence, a shorter inspiratory whistle that is higher pitched than the main cry, and then a brief rest before the next cry. 351

basic-skills-and-phonetics approach An approach that emphasizes that reading instruction should teach phonetics and its basic rules for translating written symbols into sounds. 334

Bayley Scales of Infant Development Widely used scales in assessing infant development with three main components: a Mental Scale, a Motor Scale, and a Behavior Rating Scale. 295

behavior genetics The study of the degree and nature of behavior's basis in heredity. 74

biological processes Changes in an individual's body. 17

blastocyst The inner layer of cells that develops during the germinal period. These cells later develop into the embryo. 95

bonding The formation of a close connection, especially a physical bond between parents and their newborn in the period shortly after birth. 122

brainstorming A technique in which children are encouraged to come up with creative ideas in a group, play off each other's ideas, and say practically whatever comes to mind. 301

Brazelton Neonatal Behavioral Assessment Scale A test given several days after birth to assess newborns' neurological development, reflexes, and reactions to people. 118

breech position The baby's position in the uterus that causes the buttocks to be the first part to emerge from the vagina. 113

Broca's area An area of the brain's left frontal lobe that directs the muscle movements involved in speech production. 318

bulimia nervosa An eating disorder that involves a binge-and-purge sequence on a regular basis. 179

C

canalization The process by which certain characteristics take a narrow path or developmental course. Apparently, preservative forces help to protect a person from environmental extremes. 73

care perspective The moral perspective, emphasized by Carol Gilligan, that views people in terms of their connectedness with others and emphasizes interpersonal communication, relationships with others, and concern for others. 444

case study An in-depth look at a single individual. 46

centration The focusing of attention on one characteristic to the exclusion of all others. 217

cephalocaudal pattern The sequence in which the greatest growth occurs at the top—the head—with physical growth in size, weight, and feature differentiation gradually working from top to bottom. 131

character education A direct approach that involves teaching students a basic moral literacy to prevent them from engaging in immoral behavior and doing harm to themselves or others. 453

child-centered kindergarten Education that involves the whole child by considering both the child's physical, cognitive, and social development and the child's needs, interests, and learning styles. 544

child-directed speech The kind of speech often used by adults to talk to babies and young children—in a higher pitch than normal and with simple words and sentences. 321

chromosomes Threadlike structures that come in 23 pairs, one member of each pair coming from each parent. Chromosomes contain the genetic substance DNA. 70

cliques Small groups that range from 2 to about 12 individuals and average about 5 to 6 individuals. Cliques can form because of friendship or because individuals engage in similar activities, and members usually are of the same sex and about the same age. 527

cognitive appraisal Lazarus' term for children's interpretations of events in their lives as harmful, threatening, or challenging, and their determination of whether they have the resources to effectively cope with the event. 359

cognitive constructivist approaches Approaches that emphasize the child's active, cognitive construction of knowledge and understanding; Piaget's theory is an example of this approach. 541

cognitive developmental theory of gender In this view, children's gender-typing occurs after they have developed a concept of gender. Once they begin to consistently conceive of themselves as male or female, children often organize their world on the basis of gender. 419

cognitive moral education A concept based on the belief that students should learn to value things like democracy and justice as their moral reasoning develops. 454

cognitive processes Changes in an individual's thought, intelligence, and language. 17

collectivism Emphasizing values that serve the group by subordinating personal goals to preserve group integrity, interdependence of members, and harmonious relationships. 581

commitment The part of identity development in which adolescents show a personal investment in what they are going to do. 398

concepts Categories used to group objects, events, and characteristics on the basis of common properties. 260

conduct disorder The psychiatric diagnosis category used when multiple behaviors occur over a six-month period. These behaviors include truancy, running away, fire setting, cruelty to animals, breaking and entering, excessive fighting, and others. When three or more of these behaviors co-occur before the age of 15, and the child or adolescent is considered unmanageable or out of control, the clinical diagnosis is conduct disorder. 458

connectedness An important element in adolescent identity development. It consists of two dimensions: mutuality, sensitivity to and respect for others' views; and permeability, openness to others' views. 400

conservation The idea that an amount stays the same regardless of how its container changes. 217

constructive play Play that combines sensorimotor/practice repetitive activity with symbolic representation of ideas. Constructive play occurs when children engage in self-regulated creation or construction of a product or a problem solution. 521

context The settings, influenced by historical, economic, social, and cultural factors, in which development occurs. 12

continuity view A developmental view that emphasizes the role of early parent-child relationships in constructing a basic way of relating to people throughout the life span. 474

continuity-discontinuity issue The issue regarding whether development involves gradual, cumulative change (continuity) or distinct stages (discontinuity). 20

controversial children Children who are frequently nominated both as someone's best friend and as being disliked. 516

conventional reasoning The second, or intermediate, level in Kohlberg's theory of moral development. Internalization is intermediate. Individuals abide by certain standards (internal), but they are the standards of others (external), such as parents or the laws of society. 439

convergent thinking Thinking that produces one correct answer; characteristic of the type of thinking required on traditional intelligence tests. 301

cooperative play Play that involves social interaction in a group with a sense of group identity and organized activity. 520

coordination of secondary circular reactions Piaget's fourth sensorimotor substage, which develops between 8 and 12 months of age. In this substage, several significant changes take place involving the coordination of schemes and intentionality. 210

correlation coefficient A number based on statistical analysis used to describe the degree of association between two variables. 47

correlational research A type of research whose goal is to describe the strength of the relationship between two or more events or characteristics. 46

creativity The ability to think about something in novel and unusual ways and come up with unique solutions to problems. 300

crisis A period of identity development during which the adolescent is choosing among meaningful alternatives. 398

critical period A period in which there is learning readiness. Beyond this period, learning is difficult or impossible. 319

critical thinking Thinking reflectively and productively, and evaluating the evidence. 267

cross-cultural studies Studies that compare a culture with one or more other cultures. Such studies provide information about the degree to which adolescent development is similar, or universal, across cultures or about the degree to which it is culture-specific. 13, 580

cross-sectional approach A research strategy in which individuals of different ages are compared at one time. 48

crowds The crowd is a larger group structure than a clique. Adolescents usually are members of a crowd based on reputation and may or may not spend much time together. Many crowds are defined by the activities adolescents engage in. 527

culture The behavior patterns, beliefs, and all other products of a particular group of people that are passed on from generation to generation. 13, 579

culture-fair tests Intelligence tests that are intended not to be culturally biased. 287, 579

dating scripts The cognitive models that adolescents and adults use to guide and evaluate dating interactions. 531

deprivation dwarfism A type of growth retardation caused by emotional deprivation; when children are deprived of affection, they experience stress, which alters the release of hormones by the pituitary gland. 170

descriptive research A type of research whose purpose is to observe and record behavior. 43

development The pattern of change that begins at conception and continues through the life cycle. 17

developmental construction views Views sharing the belief that as individuals grow up, they acquire modes of relating to others. There are two main variations of this view. One emphasizes continuity and stability in relationships throughout the life span; the other emphasizes discontinuity and changes in relationships throughout the life span. 474

developmental quotient (DQ) An overall developmental score that combines subscores in the motor, language, adaptive, and personal-social domains in the Gesell assessment of infants. 295

developmentally appropriate practice Education that focuses on the typical developmental patterns of children (age appropriateness), the uniqueness of each child (individual appropriateness), and cultural appropriateness. Such practice contrasts with developmentally inappropriate practice, which ignores the concrete, hands-on approach to learning. Direct teaching largely through abstract paper-and-pencil activities presented to large groups of young children is believed to be developmentally inappropriate. 545

difficult child A child who tends to react negatively and cry frequently, who engages in irregular daily routines, and who is slow to accept change. 364

direct instruction approach A teacher-centered approach that is characterized by teacher direction and control, mastery of academic material, high expectations for students' progress, and maximum time spent on learning tasks. 541

discontinuity view A developmental view that emphasizes change and growth in relationships over time. 475

dishabituation Increase in responsiveness after a change in stimulation. 245

dismissing/avoidant attachment An insecure attachment category in which individuals deemphasize the importance of attachment. This category is associated with consistent experiences of rejection of attachment needs by caregivers. 490

divergent thinking Thinking that produces many answers to the same question; characteristic of creativity. 301

DNA A complex molecule that contains genetic information. 70

doula A caregiver who provides continuous physical, emotional, and educational support to the mother before, during, and just after childbirth. 112

Down syndrome A form of mental retardation, caused by the presence of an extra or altered 21st chromosome. 78

dynamic systems theory The new perspective on motor development in infancy that seeks to explain how motor behaviors are assembled for perceiving and acting. 151

dyscalculia Also known as developmental arithmetic disorder, this learning disability involves difficulty in math computation. 561

dyslexia A category of learning disabilities involving a severe impairment in the ability to read and spell. 561

early childhood The developmental period that extends from the end of infancy to about 5 to 6 years of age, sometimes called the preschool years. 18

early-later experience issue The issue of the degree to which early experiences (especially infancy) or later experiences are the key determinants of the child's development. 20

easy child A child who is generally in a positive mood, who quickly establishes regular routines in infancy, and who adapts easily to new experiences. 364

eclectic theoretical orientation An orientation that does not follow any one theoretical approach, but rather selects from each theory whatever is considered the best in it. 41

ecological theory Bronfenbrenner's environmental systems theory that focuses on five environmental systems: microsystem, mesosystem, exosystem, macrosystem, and chronosystem. 40

ecological view The view that perception functions to bring organisms in contact with the environment and to increase adaptation.   152

egocentrism A salient feature of preoperational thought, the inability to distinguish between one's own and someone else's perspective.   215

e-mail Electronic mail, a valuable way to send and receive messages.   598

embryonic period The period of prenatal development that occurs two to eight weeks after conception. During the embryonic period, the rate of cell differentiation intensifies, support systems for the cells form, and organs appear.   95

emotion Feeling, or affect, that can involve physiological arousal, conscious experience, and behavioral expression.   346

emotional intelligence The ability to monitor one's own and others emotions and feelings, to discriminate among them, and to use this information to guide one's thinking and action.   293

empathy Reacting to another's feelings with an emotional response that is similar to the other's feelings.   449

encoding The process by which information gets into memory.   243

epigenetic view Emphasizes that development is the result of an ongoing, bidirectional interchange between heredity and environment.   86

equilibration A mechanism that Piaget proposed to explain how children shift from one stage of thought to the next. The shift occurs as children experience cognitive conflict or disequilibrium in trying to understand the world. Eventually, they resolve the conflict and reach equilibrium of thought.   208

Erikson's theory Includes eight stages of human development. Each stage consists of a unique developmental task that confronts individuals with a crisis that must be faced.   31

estrogens Hormones, the most important of which is estradiol, that influence the development of female physical sex characteristics and help regulate the menstrual cycle.   411

ethnic gloss Using an ethnic label such as African American or Latino in a superficial way that portrays an ethnic group as being more homogeneous than it really is.   56

ethnic identity A sense of membership in an ethnic group, based upon shared language, religion, customs, values, history, and race.   13, 401

ethnicity A characteristic based on cultural heritage, nationality characteristics, race, religion, and language.   13, 588

ethnocentrism A tendency to favor one's group over other groups.   579

ethology Stresses that behavior is strongly influenced by biology, is tied to evolution, and is characterized by critical or sensitive periods.   38

evocative genotype-environment correlations Correlations that exist when the child's genotype elicits certain types of physical and social environments.   85

evolutionary psychology A contemporary approach that emphasizes the importance of adaptation, reproduction, and survival of the fittest in explaining behavior.   68

expanding Restating, in a linguistically sophisticated form, what a child has said.   322

experiment A carefully regulated procedure in which one or more of the factors believed to influence the behavior being studied are manipulated while all other factors are held constant.   47

extrinsic motivation Involves doing something to obtain something else (a means to an end).   565

F

factor analysis A statistical procedure that examines various items or measures and identifies factors that are correlated with each other.   290

feminization of poverty The fact that far more women than men live in poverty. Women's low income, divorce, and the resolution of divorce cases by the judicial system, which usually leaves women with less money than they and their children need to adequately function, are the likely causes.   586

fetal alcohol syndrome (FAS) A cluster of abnormalities that appears in the offspring of mothers who drink alcohol heavily during pregnancy.   101

fetal period The prenatal period of development that begins two months after conception and lasts for seven months, on the average.   97

fine motor skills Motor skills that involve more finely tuned movements, such as finger dexterity.   146

first habits and primary circular reactions Piaget's second sensorimotor substage, which develops between 1 and 4 months of age. Infants learn to coordinate sensation and types of schemes or structures—that is, habits and primary circular reactions.   209

fragile X syndrome A disorder involving an abnormality in the X chromosome, which becomes constricted and often breaks.   78

G

games Activities engaged in for pleasure that include rules and often competition with one or more individuals.   521

gender The psychological and sociocultural dimension of being female or male.   14, 411

gender identity The sense of being female or male, which most children acquire by the time they are 3 years old.   411

gender role A set of expectations that prescribes how females and males should think, act, and feel.   411

gender-role transcendence The belief that, when an individual's competence is at issue, it should be conceptualized not on the basis of masculinity, femininity, or androgyny but, rather, on a personal basis.   411

gender schema theory According to this theory, an individual's attention and behavior are guided by an internal motivation to conform to gender-based sociocultural standards and stereotypes.   419

gender stereotypes Broad categories that reflect impressions and beliefs about what behavior is appropriate for females and males.   420

genes Units of hereditary information composed of DNA. Genes carry information that enables cells to reproduce themselves and manufacture the proteins that maintain life.   70

genetic epistemology The study of how children's knowledge changes over the course of their development.   9

genotype A person's genetic heritage; the actual genetic material.   73

germinal period The period of prenatal development that takes place in the first two weeks after conception. It includes the creation of the zygote, continued cell division, and the attachment of the zygote to the uterine wall.   95

gifted Describes individuals who have a high IQ (130 or higher) and/or superior talent for something.   299

gonads The sex glands—the testes in males and the ovaries in females.   185

goodness of fit Refers to the match between a child's temperament and the environmental demands the child must cope with.   365

grasping reflex A neonatal reflex that occurs when something touches the infant's palms. The infant responds by grasping tightly.   144

gross motor skills Motor skills that involve large muscle activities, such as walking.   146

habituation Repeated presentation of the same stimulus, which causes reduced attention to the stimulus.   245

helpless orientation An orientation in which one seems trapped by the experience of difficulty, often attributes one's difficulty to a lack of ability, and displays negative affect.   567

heritability The fraction of the variance in IQ in a population that is attributed to genetics.   303

heteronomous morality (Kohlberg) The first stage in Kohlberg's theory. At this stage, moral thinking is often tied to punishment.   437

heteronomous morality (Piaget) The first stage of moral development in Piaget's theory, occurring from 4 to 7 years of age. Justice and rules are conceived of as unchangeable properties of the world, removed from the control of people.   439

heuristics Strategies that can suggest a solution to a problem but don't guarantee a solution.   262

hidden curriculum The moral atmosphere that is part of every school.   453

horizontal décalage Piaget's concept that similar abilities do not appear at the same time within a stage of development.   220

hormones Powerful chemical substances secreted by the endocrine glands and carried through the body by the bloodstream.   185

hypothalamus A structure in the higher portion of the brain that monitors eating, drinking, and sex.   185

hypotheses Specific assumptions and predictions that can be tested to determine their accuracy.   29

hypothetical-deductive reasoning Piaget's formal operational concept that adolescents have the cognitive ability to develop hypotheses about ways to solve problems and can systematically deduce which is the best path to follow in solving the problem.   222

identity achievement Marcia's term for an adolescent's having undergone a crisis and made a commitment.   398

identity diffusion Marcia's term for the state adolescents are in when they have not yet experienced a crisis (that is, they have not yet explored meaningful alternatives) or made any commitments.   398

identity foreclosure Marcia's term for the state adolescents are in when they have made a commitment but have not experienced a crisis.   398

identity moratorium Marcia's term for the state adolescents are in when they are in the midst of a crisis, but whose commitments either are absent or are only vaguely defined.   398

identity versus identity confusion Erikson's fifth developmental stage, which individuals experience during the adolescent years. At this time, adolescents examine who they are, what they are all about, and where they are going in life.   395

imaginary audience An adolescent's belief that others are as preoccupied with her as she is.   224

immanent justice Piaget's concept that if a rule is broken, punishment will be meted out immediately.   438

inclusion Educating a child with special education needs full-time in the regular classroom.   564

index offenses Criminal acts, whether they are committed by juveniles or adults. They include such acts as robbery, aggravated assault, rape, and homicide.   457

individualism Giving priority to personal goals rather than to group goals; emphasizing values that serve the self, such as feeling good, personal distinction and achievement, and independence.   581

individualism, instrumental purpose, and exchange The second Kohlberg stage of moral development. At this stage, what is right involves an equal exchange.   439

individuality An important element in adolescent identity development. It consists of two dimensions: self-assertion, the ability to have and communicate a point of view; and separateness, the use of communication patterns to express how one is different from others.   400

individualized education plan (IEP) A written statement that spells out a program tailored to a child with a disability. The plan should be (1) related to the child's learning capacity, (2) specially constructed to meet the child's individual needs and not merely a copy of what is offered to other children, and (3) designed to provide educational benefits.   563

induction A discipline technique in which a parent uses reason and explanation of the consequences for others of the child's actions.   452

indulgent parenting A style in which parents are highly involved with their children but place few demands or controls on them. This is associated with children's social incompetence, especially a lack of self-control.   482

infancy The developmental period that extends from birth to about 18 to 24 months.   18

infinite generativity The ability to produce an endless number of meaningful sentences using a finite set of words and rules.   315

information-processing approach The approach that focuses on the ways children process information about their world—how they manipulate information, monitor it, and strategize about it.   242

information-processing theory Emphasizes that children manipulate information, monitor it, and strategize about it. Central to this approach are the processes of memory and thinking.   36

innate goodness view The idea, presented by Swiss-born philosopher Jean-Jacques Rousseau, that children are inherently good.   7

insecure avoidant babies Babies that show insecurity by avoiding the caregiver.   371

insecure disorganized babies Babies that show insecurity by being disorganized and disoriented.   371

insecure resistant babies Babies that might cling to the caregiver, then resist her by fighting against the closeness, perhaps by kicking or pushing away.   371

intelligence The ability to solve problems and to adapt to and learn from life's everyday experiences.   281

intelligence quotient (IQ) Devised by William Stern in 1912, this consists of an individual's mental age divided by chronological age multiplied by 100.   282

intermodal perception The ability to relate and integrate information about two or more sensory modalities, such as vision and hearing.   159

internalization The developmental change from behavior that is externally controlled to behavior that is controlled by internal standards and principles.   439

internalization of schemes Piaget's sixth sensorimotor substage, which develops between 18 and 24 months of age. In this substage, infants' mental functioning shifts from a purely sensorimotor plane to a symbolic plane, and they develop the ability to use primitive symbols.   210

Internet The core of computer-mediated communication. The Internet system is worldwide and connects thousands of computer networks, providing an incredible array of information adolescents can access.   598

intimacy in friendship Self-disclosure or the sharing of private thoughts.   524

intrinsic motivation Involves the internal motivation of doing something for its own sake (an end in itself).   565

intuitive thought substage The second substage of preoperational thought, occurring approximately between 4 and 7 years of age. Children begin to use primitive reasoning and want to know the answers to all sorts of questions.   217

justice perspective A moral perspective that focuses on the rights of the individual; individuals independently make moral decisions.   444

juvenile delinquency A broad range of behaviors, ranging from socially unacceptable behavior (such as acting out in school) to status offenses (such as running away) to criminal acts (such as burglary).   457

kangaroo care A way of holding a preterm infant so that there is skin-to-skin contact.   116

Klinefelter syndrome A disorder in which males have an extra X chromosome, making them XXY instead of XY.   78

kwashiorkor A condition caused by a deficiency in protein in which the child's abdomen and feet become swollen with water.   141

labeling Identifying the names of objects.   322

laboratory A controlled setting in which many of the complex factors of the "real world" are removed.   44

language A form of communication, whether spoken, written, or signed, that is based on a system of symbols.   314

language acquisition device (LAD) Chomsky's theoretical concept of a biological endowment that enables the child to detect certain language categories, such as phonology, syntax, and semantics.   319

lateralization Specialization of function in one hemisphere of the cerebral cortex or the other.   135

learned helplessness Seligman's theory of depression—that it occurs when individuals are exposed to negative experiences, especially prolonged stress or pain, over which they have no control.   356

learning disability Includes three components: (1) a minimum IQ level, (2) a significant difficulty in a school-related area (especially reading or mathematics), and (3) exclusion of only severe emotional disorders, second-language background, sensory disabilities, and/or specific neurological deficits.   560

least restrictive environment (LRE) The concept that a child with a disability must be educated in a setting that is as similar as possible to the one in which children who do not have a disability are educated.   563

longitudinal approach A research strategy in which the same individuals are studied over a period of time, usually several years or more.   48

long-term memory A type of memory that holds enormous amounts of information for a long period of time in a relatively permanent fashion.   252

love withdrawal A discipline technique in which a parent withholds attention or love from the child.   452

low birth weight infant An infant who weighs less than 5½ pounds at birth.   114

marasmus A wasting away of body tissues in the infant's first year, caused by severe protein-calorie deficiency.   141

mastery orientation An orientation in which one is task-oriented and, instead of focusing on one's ability, is concerned with learning strategies.   567

means-end analysis A heuristic in which one identifies the goal (end) of a problem, assesses the current situation, and determines what needs to be done (means) in order to attain the goal.   263

meiosis The process by which cells in the reproductive organs divide into gametes (sperm in males, eggs in females), which have half of the genetic material of the parent cell.   70

memory The retention of information over time, involving encoding, storage, and retrieval.   244

menarche A girls' first menstruation.   184

mental age (MA) An individual's level of mental development relative to others.   282

mental retardation A condition of limited mental ability in which the individual has a low IQ, usually below 70, has difficulty adapting to everyday life, and has an onset of these characteristics in the so-called developmental period.   298

metacognition Cognition about cognition, or "knowing about knowing."   243

metacognitive activity Using self-awareness to adapt to and manage strategies during problem solving and thinking.   271

metacognitive knowledge Monitoring and reflecting on one's current or recent thoughts.   271

middle and late childhood The developmental period that extends from about 6 to 11 years of age, sometimes called the elementary school years.   18

mitosis The process by which each chromosome in a cell's nucleus duplicates itself.   70

Montessori approach An educational philosophy in which children are given considerable freedom and spontaneity in choosing activities and are allowed to move from one activity to another as they desire.   544

moral development Age-related thoughts, behaviors, and feelings regarding rules, principles, and values that guide what people should do.   437

Moro reflex A neonatal startle response that occurs in reaction to a sudden, intense noise or movement. When startled, the newborn arches its back, throws its head back, and flings out its arms and legs. Then the newborn rapidly closes its arms and legs to the center of the body.   144

morphology Units of meaning involved in word formation.   315

multiple-factor theory Thurstone's theory that intelligence consists of seven primary mental abilities: verbal comprehension, number ability, word fluency, spatial visualization, associative memory, reasoning, and perceptual speed.   290

mutual interpersonal expectations, relationships, and interpersonal conformity Kohlberg's third stage of moral development. At this stage, individuals value trust, caring, and loyalty to others as a basis of moral judgments.   440

myelination A process in which nerve cells are insulated with a layer of fat cells, which increases the speed at which information travels through the nervous system.   173

natural childbirth Developed in 1914 by Dick-Read, this method attempts to reduce the mother's pain by decreasing her fear through education about childbirth and relaxation techniques during delivery.   113

naturalistic observation Observing behavior in real-world settings.   44

nature-nurture issue *Nature* refers to an organism's biological inheritance, *nurture* to environmental influences. The "nature" proponents claim biological inheritance is the most important influence on development; the "nurture" proponents claim that environmental experiences are the most important.   19

negative affectivity (NA) The range of negatively toned emotions, such as anxiety, anger, guilt, and sadness.   347

neglected children Children who are infrequently nominated as a best friend but are not disliked by their peers.   515

neglectful parenting A style in which the parent is very uninvolved in the child's life. It is associated with children's social incompetence, especially a lack of self-control.   482

neo-Piagetians Developmentalists who have elaborated on Piaget's theory, believing that children's cognitive development is more specific in many respects than he thought.   229

neuron Nerve cell that handles information processing at the cellular level.   132

nonshared environmental experiences The child's own unique experiences, both within the family and outside the family, that are not shared by another sibling. Thus, expe-riences occurring within the family can be part of the "nonshared environment."   86

normal distribution A symmetrical, bell-shaped curve with a majority of the cases falling in the middle of the possible range of scores and few scores appearing toward the extremes of the range.   283

object permanence The Piagetian term for one of an infant's most important accomplishments: understanding that objects and events continue to exist even when they cannot directly be seen, heard, or touched.   211

onlooker play Play in which the child watches other children play.   520

operations Internalized sets of actions that allow children to do mentally what before they had done physically.   215

organization Piaget's concept of grouping isolated behaviors into a higher-order, more smoothly functioning cognitive system; the grouping or arranging of items into categories.   208

organogenesis Organ formation that takes place during the first two months of prenatal development.   96

original sin view Advocated during the Middle Ages, the belief that children were born into the world as evil beings and were basically bad.   7

pain cry A sudden appearance of loud crying without preliminary moaning and a long initial cry followed by an extended period of breath holding.   351

parallel play Play in which the child plays separately from others, but with toys like those the others are using or in a manner that mimics their play.   520

passive genotype-environment correlations Correlations that occur because biological parents provide an environment that matches their own genetic tendencies, and their children inherit genetic tendencies from their parents.   85

peers Children of about the same age or maturity level.   511

perception The interpretation of what is sensed.   152

performance orientation An orientation in which one focuses on achievement outcomes; winning is what matters most, and happiness is thought to result from winning.   567

personal fable An adolescent's sense of personal uniqueness and indestructibility.   224

perspective taking The ability to assume another person's perspective and understand his or her thoughts or feelings.   390, 514

phenotype The way an individual's genotype is expressed in observable and measurable characteristics.   73

phenylketonuria (PKU) A genetic disorder in which an individual cannot properly metabolize a substance needed for production of proteins in the body. PKU is now easily detected but, if left untreated, results in mental retardation and hyperactivity.   78

phonology A language's sound system.   315

Piaget's theory States that children actively construct their understanding of the world and go through four stages of cognitive development.   33

pituitary gland An important endocrine gland that controls growth and regulates other glands.   185

placenta A life-support system that consists of a disk-shaped group of tissues in which small blood vessels from the mother and offspring intertwine.   95

play A pleasurable activity that is engaged in for its own sake.   518

play therapy Therapy that allows the child to work off frustrations and is a medium through which the therapist can analyze the child's conflicts and ways of coping with them. Children may feel less threatened and be more likely to express their true feelings in the context of play.   518

pluralism The coexistence of distinct ethnic and cultural groups in the same society.   592

popular children Children who are frequently nominated as a best friend and are rarely disliked by their peers.   515

positive affectivity (PA) The range of positive emotions, from high energy, enthusiasm, and excitement to being calm, quiet, and withdrawn.   347

possible self What an individual might become, what the person would like to become, and what the person is afraid of becoming.   388

postconventional reasoning The highest level in Kohlberg's theory of moral development. Morality is completely internalized.   440

postpartum depression Strong feelings of sadness, anxiety, or despair in new mothers that make it difficult for them to carry out daily tasks.   121

postpartum period The period after childbirth when the mother adjusts, both physically and psychologically, to the process of childbirth. This period lasts for about six weeks or until her body has completed its adjustment and returned to a near prepregnant state.   119

power assertion A discipline technique in which a parent attempts to gain control over the child or the child's resources.   452

practice play Play that involves repetition of behavior when new skills are being learned or when physical or mental mastery and coordination of skills are required for games or sports. Sensorimotor play, which often involves practice play, is primarily confined to infancy, while practice play can be engaged in throughout life.   520

pragmatics The use of appropriate conversation and knowledge of how to effectively use language in context.   316

preconventional reasoning The lowest level in Kohlberg's theory of moral development. The individual shows no internalization of moral values—moral reasoning is controlled by external rewards and punishment.   439

prejudice An unjustified negative attitude toward an individual because of her or his membership in a group.   591

prenatal period The time from conception to birth.   18

preoccupied/ambivalent attachment An insecure attachment category in which adolescents are hypertuned to attachment experiences. This is thought to mainly occur because parents are inconsistently available to the adolescents.   490

prepared childbirth Developed by French obstetrician Ferdinand Lamaze, this childbirth strategy is similar to natural childbirth but includes a special breathing technique to control pushing in the final stages of labor and a more detailed anatomy and physiology course.   113

pretense/symbolic play Play that occurs when a child transforms the physical environment into a symbol.   520

preterm infant An infant born three weeks or more before the pregnancy has reached its full term.   114

primary appraisal Lazarus' concept that individuals interpret whether an event involves harm or loss that already has occurred, a

threat that involves some future danger, or a challenge to be overcome.   359

primary circular reactions Schemes based on the infant's attempt to reproduce an interesting or pleasurable event that initially occurred by chance.   210

primary emotions Emotions that are present in humans and other animals, including surprise, interest, joy, anger, sadness, fear, and disgust; appear in first six to eight months of life.   350

problem solving Finding an appropriate way to attain a goal.   261

Project Head Start Compensatory education designed to provide children from low-income families the opportunity to acquire the skills and experiences important for school success.   547

proximodistal pattern The sequence in which growth starts at the center of the body and moves toward the extremities.   131

psychoanalytic theory Describes development as primarily unconscious and heavily colored by emotion. Behavior is merely a surface characteristic, and the symbolic workings of the mind have to be analyzed to understand behavior. Early experiences with parents are emphasized.   30

psychoanalytic theory of gender A theory that stems from Freud's view that preschool children develop a sexual attraction to the opposite-sex parent, then at 5 to 6 years of age renounce the attraction because of anxious feelings, subsequently identifying with the same-sex parent and unconsciously adopting the same-sex parent's characteristics.   414

psychosocial moratorium Erikson's term for the gap between childhood security and adult autonomy that adolescents experience as part of their identity exploration.   396

puberty A period of rapid physical maturation involving hormonal and bodily changes that occurs mainly in early adolescence.   184

R

rapport talk The language of conversation and a way of establishing connections and negotiating relationships; more characteristic of females than of males.   422

reaction range The range of possible phenotypes for each genotype, suggesting the importance of an environment's restrictiveness or richness.   73

recasting Rephrasing a statement that a child has said, perhaps turning it into a question.   322

reciprocal socialization The process by which children socialize parents just as parents socialize them.   473

reciprocal teaching A teaching method in which students take turns leading small-group discussions.   268

reflexive smile A smile that does not occur in response to external stimuli. It appears during the month after birth, usually during irregular patterns of sleep, not when the infant is in an alert state.   352

rejected children Children who are infrequently nominated as a best friend and are actively disliked by their peers.   515

reliability The extent to which a test yields a consistent, reproducible measure of performance.   286

report talk Talk that conveys information; more characteristic of males than of females.   422

reproduction The process that, in humans, begins when a female gamete (ovum) is fertilized by a male gamete (sperm).   71

retrieval Taking information out of storage.   244

rites of passage Ceremonies or rituals that mark an individual's transition from one status to another, especially into adulthood.   582

rooting reflex A newborn's built-in reaction that occurs when the infant's cheek is stroked or the side of the mouth is touched. In response, the infant turns its head toward the side that was touched, in an apparent effort to find something to suck.   144

S

scaffolding Changing the level of support over the course of a teaching session in which a more-skilled individual (teacher or more-advanced peer of the child) adjusts the amount of guidance to fit the child's current performance level.   230, 473

schema A concept or framework that already exists at a given moment in a child's mind and that provides information and provides a structure for organizing it.   207

secondary appraisal Lazarus' concept that individuals evaluate their resources and determine how effectively they can cope with an event.   359

secondary circular reactions Piaget's third sensorimotor substage, which develops between 4 and 8 months of age. Infants become more object-oriented or focused on the world, moving beyond preoccupation with the self in sensorimotor interactions.   210

secure attachment The infant uses a caregiver as a secure base from which to explore the environment. Ainsworth believes that secure attachment in the first year of life provides an important foundation for psychological development later in life.   370

self-concept Domain-specific self-evaluations.   391

self-conscious emotions Emotions that require cognition, especially consciousness; include empathy, jealousy, embarrassment, pride, shame, and guilt, appear for the first time from the middle of the second year through the middle of the third year of life.   350

self-efficacy The belief that one can master a situation and produce favorable outcomes.   568

self-esteem The global evaluative dimension of the self; also called self-worth or self-image.   391

self-regulatory learning Generating and monitoring thoughts, feelings, and behaviors to reach a goal.   272

self-understanding A child's cognitive representation of the self, the substance and content of a child's self-conceptions.   385

semantics The meanings of words and sentences.   316

sensation The product of the interaction between information and the sensory receptors—the eyes, ears, tongue, nose, and skin.   152

sensorimotor play Behavior engaged in by infants to derive pleasure from exercising their existing sensorimotor schemas.   520

sensory memory The memory system that holds information from the world in its original sensory form for only an instant.   251

separation protest An infant's distress at being separated from his or her caregiver.   352

seriation The concrete operation that involves ordering stimuli along a quantitative dimension (such as length).   220

service learning A form of education that promotes social responsibility and service to the community.   455

sexually transmitted infections (STIs) Infections that are contracted primarily through sexual contact, which is not limited to sexual intercourse. Oral-genital and anal-genital contact also can transmit STIs.   190

shape constancy Recognition that an object remains the same even though its orientation to us changes.   155

shared environmental experiences Children's common environmental experiences that are shared with their siblings, such as their parents' personalities and intellectual orientation, the family's social class, and the neighborhood in which they live.   85

short-term memory The limited-capacity memory system in which information is retained for as long as 30 seconds, unless the information is rehearsed, in which case it can be retained longer.   251

sickle-cell anemia A genetic disorder that affects the red blood cells and occurs most often in people of African descent.   79

simple reflexes Piaget's first sensorimotor substage, which corresponds to the first month after birth. The basic means of coordinating sensation and action is through reflexive behaviors, such as rooting and sucking, which infants have at birth.   209

size constancy Recognition that an object remains the same even though the retinal image of the object changes.   155

slow-to-warm-up child A child who has a low activity level, is somewhat negative, and displays a low intensity of mood.   364

small for date infant Also called a small for gestational age infant, this infant's birth weight is below normal when the length of pregnancy is considered. A small for date infant may be preterm or full-term.   114

social cognitive theory The view of psychologists who emphasize behavior, environment, and cognition as the key factors in development.   37

social cognitive theory of gender This theory emphasizes that children's gender development occurs through observation and imitation of gender behavior, and through rewards and punishments they experience for gender-appropriate and -inappropriate behavior.   414

social cognitive theory of morality The theory that distinguishes between *moral competence* (the ability to perform moral behaviors) and *moral performance* (performing those behaviors in specific situations).   448

social constructivist approaches Approaches that focus on collaboration with others to produce knowledge and understanding; Vygotsky's theory is an example of this approach.   235, 541

social contract or utility and individual rights Kohlberg's fifth stage of moral development. At this stage, individuals reason that

values, rights, and principles undergird or transcend the law.   440

social conventional reasoning Thoughts about social consensus and convention.   445

social play Play that involves social interactions with peers.   521

social policy A national government's approach to promoting the welfare of its citizens.   14

social referencing "Reading" emotional cues in others to help determine how to act in a particular situation.   353

social smile A smile in response to an external stimulus, which, early in development, typically is in response to a face.   352

social systems morality The fourth stage in Kohlberg's theory of moral development. Moral judgments are based on understanding the social order, law, justice, and duty.   440

socioeconomic status (SES) A grouping of people with similar occupational, educational, and economic characteristics.   583

socioemotional processes Changes in an individual's relationships with other people, emotions, and personality.   17

solitary play Play in which the child plays alone and independently of others.   519

standardization Involves developing uniform procedures for administering and scoring a test, as well as creating norms for the test.   286

standardized test A test with uniform procedures for administration and scoring. Many standardized tests allow a person's performance to be compared with the performance of other individuals.   45

status offenses Less serious acts (than index offenses). Status offenses include truancy, underage drinking, sexual promiscuity, and uncontrollability. They are performed by youth under a specified age, which make them juvenile offenses.   457

storage The retention of information over time.   244

Strange Situation An observational measure of infant attachment that requires the infant to move through a series of introductions, separations, and reunions with the caregiver and an adult stranger in a prescribed order.   371

stranger anxiety An infant's fear and wariness of strangers; it tends to appear in the second half of the first year of life.   352

strategy construction The process of discovering a new procedure for processing information.   243

stress The response of individuals to the circumstances and events (called stressors) that threaten them and tax their coping abilities.   358

subgoaling Setting intermediate goals that put one in a better position to reach the final goal or solution.   262

sucking reflex A newborn's built-in reaction of automatically sucking an object placed in its mouth. The sucking reflex enables the infant to get nourishment before it has associated a nipple with food.   144

sudden infant death syndrome (SIDS) A condition that occurs when an infant stops breathing, usually during the night, and suddenly dies without an apparent cause.   138

symbolic function substage The first substage of preoperational thought, occurring roughly between the ages of 2 and 4. In this substage, the young child gains the ability to represent mentally an object that is not present.   215

syntax The ways words are combined to form acceptable phrases and sentences.   316

tabula rasa view The idea, proposed by John Locke, that children are like a "blank tablet."   7

telegraphic speech The use of short and precise words without grammatical markers to communicate; it characterizes young children's two- or three-word combinations.   329

temperament An individual's behavioral style and characteristic way of emotional response.   363

teratogen From the Greek word *tera*, meaning "monster." Any agent that causes a birth defect. The field of study that investigates the causes of birth defects is called teratology.   99

tertiary circular reactions Schemes in which the infant purposely explores new possibilities with objects, continually changing what is done to them and exploring the results.   210

tertiary circular reactions, novelty, and curiosity Piaget's fifth sensorimotor substage, which develops between 12 and 18 months of age. Infants become intrigued by the variety of properties that objects possess and by the multiplicity of things they can make happen to objects.   210

theory An interrelated, coherent set of ideas that helps to explain and to make predictions.   29

theory of mind Awareness of one's own mental processes and the mental processes of others.   260

thinking Manipulating and transforming information in memory.   260

top-dog phenomenon The circumstance of moving from the top position in elementary school to the lowest position in middle or junior high school.   552

transitivity In concrete operational thought, a mental concept that underlies the ability to logically combine relations to understand certain conclusions. It focuses on reasoning about the relations between classes.   221

triarchic theory Sternberg's theory that there are three main types of intelligence: analytical, creative, and practical.   291

trophoblast The outer layer of cells that develops in the germinal period. These cells provide nutrition and support for the embryo.   95

Turner syndrome A disorder in females in which either an X chromosome is missing, making the person XO instead of XX, or the second X chromosome is partially deleted.   78

twin study A study in which the behavioral similarity of identical twins is compared with the behavioral similarity of fraternal twins.   74

two-factor theory Spearman's theory that individuals have both general intelligence (g) and a number of specific abilities (s).   289

umbilical cord A life-support system, containing two arteries and one vein, that connects the baby to the placenta.   95

universal ethical principles The sixth and highest stage in Kohlberg's theory of moral development. Individuals develop a moral standard based on universal human rights.   440

unoccupied play Play in which the child is not engaging in play as it is commonly understood and might stand in one spot, look around the room, or perform random movements that do not seem to have a goal.   519

unresolved/disorganized attachment An insecure category in which the adolescent has

an unusually high level of fear and is disoriented. This may result from such traumatic experiences as a parent's death or abuse by parents.   490

validity The extent to which a test measures what it is intended to measure.   286

values clarification Helping people clarify what their lives are for and what is worth working for.   454

Vygotsky's theory A sociocultural cognitive theory that emphasizes how culture and social interaction guide cognitive development.   35

Wernicke's area An area of the brain's left hemisphere that is involved in language comprehension.   318

whole-language approach An approach that stresses that reading instruction should parallel children's natural language learning. Reading materials should be whole and meaningful.   333

working memory A kind of mental "workbench" where information is manipulated and assembled when making decisions, solving problems, and comprehending language.   252

XYY syndrome A disorder in which males have an extra Y chromosome.   78

zone of proximal development (ZPD) Vygotsky's term for the range of tasks that are too difficult for children to master alone but that can be mastered with the guidance and assistance of adults or more highly skilled children.   230

zygote The single cell formed through fertilization.   71

References

Abbassi, V. (1998). Growth and normal puberty. *Pediatrics* (Suppl.), *102* (2) 507–511.

Abel, E. L., Kruger, M., & Burd, L. (2002). Effects of maternal and paternal age on Caucasian and Native American preterm births and birth weights. *American Journal of Perinatology, 19,* 49–54.

Aboud, F., & Skerry, S. (1983). Self and ethnic concepts in relation to ethnic constancy. *Canadian Journal of Behavioral Science, 15,* 3–34.

Aboud, F. E., Mendelson, M. J., & Purdy, K. T. (2003). Cross-race peer relations and friendship quality. *International Journal of Behavioral Development, 27,* 165–173.

Abramovitch, R., Corter, C., Pepler, D. J., & Stanhope, L. (1986). Sibling and peer interaction: A final follow-up and comparison. *Child Development, 47,* 217–229.

Abramson, L. Y., Metalsky, G. I., & Alloy, L. B. (1989). Hopelessness depression: A theory-based subtype of depression. *Psychological Bulletin, 96,* 358–372.

Acredolo, L. P., & Hake, J. L. (1982). Infant perception. In B. B. Wolman (Ed.), *Handbook of developmental psychology.* Englewood Cliffs, NJ: Prentice Hall.

Adams, G. R., Gulotta, T. P., & Montemayor, R. (Eds.). (1992). *Adolescent identity formation.* Newbury Park, CA: Sage.

Adams, R. J. (1989). Newborns' discrimination among mid- and long-wavelength stimuli. *Journal of Experimental Child Psychology, 47,* 130–141.

Adato, A. (1995, April). Living legacy? Is heredity destiny? *Life,* pp. 60–68.

Addis, A., Magrini, N., & Mastroiacovo, P. (2001). Drug use during pregnancy. *Lancet, 357,* 800.

Adler, T. (1991, January). Seeing double? Controversial twins study is widely reported, debated. *APA Monitor, 22,* 1, 8.

Adolph, K. E. (1997). Cognitive-motor learning in infant locomotion. *Monographs of the Society for Research in Child Development* (Serial No. 251).

Adolph, K. E., & Eppler, M. A. (2002). Flexibility and specificity in infant motor skill acquisition. In J. Fagan & M. Hayne (Eds.), *Progress in infancy research, Vol. 2.* Mahwah, NJ: Erlbaum.

Ahluwalia, I. B., Tessaro, I., Grumer-Strawn, L. M., MacGowan, C., & Benton-Davis, S. (2000). Georgia's breastfeeding promotion program for low-income women. *Pediatrics, 105,* E-85–E-87.

Ahn, N. (1994). Teenage childbearing and high school completion: Accounting for individual heterogeneity. *Family Planning Perspectives, 26,* 17–21.

Aiken, L. R. (2003). *Psychological testing and assessment* (11th ed.). Boston: Allyn & Bacon.

Ainsworth, M. D. S. (1979). Infant-mother attachment. *American Psychologist, 34,* 932–937.

Alan Guttmacher Institute (1998). *Teen sex and pregnancy.* New York: Author.

Alan Guttmacher Institute. (2002). Teen pregnancy: Trends and lessons learned. In *Policy analysis: Issues in brief.* New York: Author.

Alexander, A., Anderson. H., Heilman, P. C., & others. (1991). Phonological awareness training and remediation of analytic decoding deficits in a group of severe dyslexics. *Annals of Dyslexia, 41,* 193–206.

Alexander, C., Piazza, M., Mekos, D., & Valente, T. (2001). Peers, schools and cigarette smoking. *Journal of Adolescent Health, 29,* 22–30.

Allen, J. P., March, P., McFarland, C., McElhaney, K. B., Land, D. J., Jodl, K., & Peck, S. (2002). Attachment and autonomy as predictors of the development of social skills and delinquency during midadolescence. *Journal of Consulting and Clinical Psychology, 70,* 56–66.

Allen, J. P., McElhaney, K. B., Land, D. J., Kumpermine, G. P., Moore, C. W., O'Beirne-Kelly, H., & Kilmer, S. L. (2003). A secure base in adolescence: markers of attachment security in the mother-adolescent relationship. *Child Development, 74,* 292–307.

Allen, M., Brown, P., & Finlay, B. (1992). *Helping children by strengthening families.* Washington, DC: Children's Defense Fund.

Amabile, T. M. (1993). Commentary. In D. Goleman, P. Kaufman, & M. Ray, *The creative spirit.* New York: Plume.

Amabile, T. M., & Hennesey, B. A. (1992). The motivation for creativity in children. In A. K. Boggiano & T. S. Pittman (Eds.), *Achievement and motivation.* New York: Cambridge University Press.

Amato, P. R., & Booth, A. (1996). A prospective study of divorce and parent-child relationships. *Journal of Marriage and the Family, 58,* 356–365.

Amato, P. R., & Keith, B. (1991). Parental divorce and the well-being of children: A meta-analysis. *Psychological Bulletin, 110,* 26–46.

American Academy of Pediatrics. (2001). Suicide and suicide attempts in adolescence. *Pediatrics, 105,* 871–874.

American Academy of Pediatrics. (2001). *Toilet training.* Available on the World Wide Web at: http://www.aap.org/family.toil.htm.

American Academy of Pediatrics. (2001a). Health care supervision for children with Williams syndrome. *Pediatrics, 107,* 1192–1204.

American Academy of Pediatrics. (2001b). Children, adolescents, and television. *Pediatrics, 107,* 423–426.

American Academy of Pediatrics (AAP) Committee on Drugs. (1994). The transfer of drugs and other chemicals into human milk. *Pediatrics, 93,* 137–150.

American Academy of Pediatrics (AAP) Task Force on Infant Positioning and SIDS. (2000). Changing concepts of sudden infant death syndrome, *Pediatrics, 105,* 650–656.

American Academy of Pediatrics (AAP) Work Group on Breastfeeding. (1997). Breastfeeding and the use of human milk. *Pediatrics, 100,* 1035–1039.

American Association of University Women. (1992). *How schools shortchange girls: A study of major findings on girls and education.* Washington, DC: Author.

American Association on Mental Retardation, Ad Hoc Committee on Terminology and Classification. (1992). *Mental retardation* (9th ed.). Washington, DC: Author.

American Psychiatric Association. (1994). *Diagnostic and statistical manual of mental disorders* (4th ed.). Washington, DC: American Psychiatric Association.

Amsterdam, B. K. (1968). *Mirror behavior in children under two years of age.* Unpublished doctoral dissertation, University of North Carolina, Chapel Hill.

Anastasi, A., & Urbina, S. (1996). *Psychological testing* (7th ed.). Upper Saddle River, NJ: Prentice Hall.

Anderman, E. M., Maehr, M. L., & Midgley, C. (1996). Declining motivation after the transition to middle school: Schools can make a difference. Unpublished manuscript, University of Kentucky, Lexington.

Anderson, C. A., & Bushman, B. J. (2002). Human aggression. *Annual Review of Psychology* (Vol. 53). Palo Alto, CA: Annual Reviews.

Anderson, D. R., Huston, A. C., Schmitt, K., Linebarger, D. L., & Wright, J. C. (2001). Early childhood viewing and adolescent behavior: The recontact study. *Monographs of the Society for Research in Child Development, 66* (1, Serial No. 264).

Anderson, D. R., Lorch, E. P., Field, D. E., Collins, P. A., & Nathan, J. G. (1985, April). *Television viewing at home: Age trends in visual attention and time with TV.* Paper presented at the biennial meeting of the Society for Research in Child Development, Toronto.

Anderson, E., Greene, S. M., Hetherington, E. M., & Clingempeel, W. G. (1999). The dynamics of parental remarriage. In E. M. Hetherington (Ed.), *Coping with divorce, single parenting, and remarriage.* Mahwah, NJ: Erlbaum.

Anderson, L. D. (1939). The predictive value of infant tests in relation to intelligence at 5 years. *Child Development, 10,* 202–212.

Anderson, L. M., Shinn, C., Fullilove, M. T., Serimshaw, S. C., Fielding, J. E., Normand, J., & Carande-Kulis, V.G. (2003). The effectiveness of early childhood development programs: A systematic review. *American Journal of Preventive Medicine, 24 (3 Supplement),* 32–46.

Anderson, R. E. (2002). Youth and information technology. In J. T. Mortimer & R. W. Larson (Eds.), *The changing adolescent experience.* New York: Cambridge University Press.

Andrist, L. C. (2003). Media images, body dissatisfaction, and disordered eating in adolescent women. *MCN American Journal of Maternal and Child Nursing, 28,* 119–123.

Archer, S. L. (1989). The status of identity: Reflections on the need for intervention. *Journal of Adolescence, 12,* 345–359.

Archer, S. L. (Ed.). (1994). *Intervention for adolescent identity development.* Newbury Park, CA: Sage.

Archer, S. L., & Waterman, A. S. (1994). Adolescent identity development: Contextual perspectives. In C. B. Fisher & R. M. Lerner (Eds.), *Applied developmental psychology.* New York: McGraw-Hill.

Archibald, A. B., Graber, J. A., & Brooks-Gunn, J. (1999). Associations among parent-adolescent relationships, pubertal growth, dieting, and body image in young adolescent girls: A short-term longitudinal study. *Journal of Research on Adolescence, 9,* 395–415.

Archibald, S. L., Fennema-Notetine, C., Gamst, A., Riley, E. P., Mattson, S. N., & Jernigan, T. L. (2001). Brain dysmorphology in individuals with severe prenatal alcohol exposure. *Developmental Medicine and Child Neurology, 43,* 148–154.

Arehart, D. M., & Smith, P. H. (1990). Identity in adolescence: Influences on dysfunction and psychosocial task issues. *Journal of Youth and Adolescence, 19,* 63–72.

Arendt, R., Angelopoulos, J., Salvator, A., & Singer, L. (1999). Motor development of cocaine-exposed children at age two years. *Pediatrics, 103,* 86–92.

Ariès, P. (1962). *Centuries of childhood* (R. Baldrick, Trans.). New York: Knopf.

Armsden, G., & Greenberg, M. T. (1984). *The inventory of parent and peer attachment: Individual differences and their relationship to psychological well-being in adolescence.* Unpublished manuscript, University of Washington.

Arnett, J. (1990). Contraceptive use, sensation seeking, and adolescent egocentrism. *Journal of Youth and Adolescence, 19,* 171–180.

Arnold, M. L. (1989, April). *Moral cognition and conduct: A quantitative review of the literature.* Paper presented at the Society for Research in Child Development meeting, Kansas City.

Aronson, E. (1986, August). *Teaching students things they think they already know about: The case of prejudice and desegregation.* Paper presented at the meeting of the American Psychological Association, Washington, DC.

Arshad, S. H. (2001). Food allergen avoidance in primary prevention of food allergy. *Allergy, 56,* 113–116.

Asarnow, J. R., & Callan, J. W. (1985). Boys with peer adjustment problems: Social cognitive processes. *Journal of Consulting and Clinical Psychology, 53,* 80–87.

Asher, J., & Garcia, R. (1969). The optimal age to learn a foreign language. *Modern Language Journal, 53,* 334–341.

Aslin, R. N. (1987). Visual and auditory development in infancy. In J. Osofksy (Ed.), *Handbook of infant development (2nd Ed.).* New York: Wiley.

Aslin, R. N., Jusczyk, P. W., & Pisoni, D. B. (1998). Speech and auditory processing. In W. Damon (Ed.), *Handbook of child psychology, 5th Ed., Vol. 2.* New York: Wiley.

Attie, I., & Brooks-Gunn, J. (1989). Development of eating problems in adolescent girls: A longitudinal study. *Developmental Psychology, 25,* 70–79.

Azar, S. T. (2002). Parenting and child maltreatment. In M. H. Bornstein (Ed.), *Handbook of parenting* (2nd ed., Vol. 4). Mahwah, NJ: Erlbaum.

B

Bachman, J. G., Johnston, L. P., & O'Malley, P. M. (1987). *Monitoring the future.* Ann Arbor: University of Michigan, Institute of Social Research.

Bacon, M. K., Child, I. L., & Barry, H. (1963). A cross-cultural study of correlates of crime. *Journal of Abnormal and Social Psychology, 66,* 291–330.

Baddeley, A. (1990). *Human memory: Theory and practice.* Boston: Allyn & Bacon.

Baddeley, A. (1998). *Human memory* (rev. ed.). Boston: Allyn & Bacon.

Baddeley, A. (2001). *Is working memory still working?* Paper presented at the meeting of the American Psychological Association, San Francisco.

Baer, J. S., Barr, H. M., Bookstein, F. L., Sampson, P. D., & Streissguth, A. P. (1998). Prenatal alcohol exposure and family history of alcoholism in the etiology of adolescent alcohol problems. *Journal of Studies on Alcohol, 59,* 533–543.

Bagwell, C. L., Newcomb, A. F., & Bukowski, W. M. (1994, February). *Early adolescent friendship as a predictor of adult adjustment: A twelve year follow-up investigation.* Paper presented at the biennial meeting of the Society for Research on Adolescence, San Diego.

Bahado-Singh, R. O., Choic, S. J., Oz, U., Mendilciolglu, I., Rowther, M., & Persutte, W. (2003). Early second-trimester individualized estimation of trisomy 18 risk by ultrasound. *Obestetrics and Gynecology, 101,* 463–468.

Bailey, B., Forget, S., & Koren, G. (2002). Pregnancy outcome of women who failed appointments at a teratogen information service clinic. *Reproductive Toxicology, 16,* 77–80.

Baillargeon, R. (1986). Representing the existence and the location of hidden objects: Object permanence in 6- and 8-month-old infants. *Cognition, 23,* 21–41.

Baillargeon, R. (1995). The object concept revisited: New directions in the investigation of infants' physical knowledge, In C. E. Granrud (Ed.), *Visual perception and cognition in infancy.* Hillsdale, NJ: Erlbaum.

Baird, A. A., Gruber, S. A., Cohen, B. M., Renshaw, R. J., & Yureglun-Todd, D. A. (1999). MRI of the amygdala in children and adolescents. *American Academy of Child & Adolescent Psychiatry, 38,* 195–199.

Bakeman, R., & Brown, J. V. (1980). Early interaction: Consequences for social and mental development at three years. *Child Development, 51,* 437–447.

Bakker, E., Van Gool, J. D., Van Sprundel, M., Van Der Auwerea, C., & Wyndaele, J. J. (2002). Results of a questionnaire evaluating the effects of different methods of toilet training on achieving bladder control. *BJU International, 90,* 456–461.

Baltes, P. B. (2000). Life-span psychology theory. In A. Kazdin (Ed.), *Encyclopedia of psychology.* Washington, DC, & New York City: American Psychological Association and Oxford University Press.

Bandstra, E. S., Morrow, C. E., Anthony, J. C., Haynes, V. L., Johnson, A. L., Xue, L., & Audrey, Y. (2000, May). *Effects of prenatal cocaine exposure on attentional processing in children through five years of age.* Paper presented at the joint meetings of the Pediatric Academic Societies and the American Academy of Pediatrics, Boston.

Bandura, A. (1965). Influences of models' reinforcement contingencies on the acquisition of imitative responses. *Journal of Personality and Social Psychology, 1,* 589–596.

Bandura, A. (1977). *Social learning theory.* Englewood Cliffs, NJ: Prentice Hall.

Bandura, A. (1982). Self-efficacy mechanism in human agency. *American Psychologist, 37,* 122–147.

Bandura, A. (1986). *Social foundations of thought and action: A social cognitive theory.* Englewood Cliffs, NJ: Prentice Hall.

Bandura, A. (1991). Social cognitive theory of moral thought and action. In W. M. Kurtines & J. Gewirtz (Eds.), *Handbook of moral behavior and development* (Vol. 1). Hillsdale, NJ: Erlbaum.

Bandura, A. (1997). *Self-efficacy.* New York: W. H. Freeman.

Bandura, A. (1998, August). *Swimming against the mainstream: Accentuating the positive aspects of humanity.* Paper presented at the meeting of the American Psychological Association, San Francisco.

Bandura, A. (1999). Moral disengagement in the perpetuation of inhumanities. *Personality and Social Psychology Review, 3,* 193–209.

Bandura, A. (2000). Social cognitive theory. In A. Kazdin (Ed.), *Encyclopedia of psychology.* Washington, DC, & New York: American Psychological Association and Oxford University Press.

Bandura, A. (2002). Social cognitive theory. *Annual Review of Psychology* (Vol. 52). Palo Alto, CA: Annual Reviews.

Bandura, A. (2002). Selective moral disengagement in the exercise of moral agency. *Journal of Moral Education, 31,* 101–119.

Bandura, A., & Locke, E. A. (2003). Negative self-efficacy and goals revisited. *Journal of Applied Psychology, 88,* 87–99.

Banks, E. C. (1993, March). *Moral education curriculum in a multicultural context: The Malaysian primary curriculum.* Paper presented at the biennial meeting of the Society for Research in Child Development, New Orleans.

Banks, J. A. (2001). Multicultural education. In J. A. Banks & C. A. M. Banks (Eds.), *Multicultural education: Issues and perspectives.* New York: Wiley.

Banks, J. A. (2002). *Introduction to multicultural education.* Boston: Allyn & Bacon.

Banks, J. A. (2003). *Teaching strategies for ethnic studies* (7th ed.). Boston: Allyn & Bacon.

Banks, M. S., & Salapatek, P. (1983). Infant visual perception. In P. H. Mussen (Ed.), *Handbook of child psychology* (4th ed., Vol. 2). New York: Wiley.

Barker, R., & Wright, H. F. (1951). *One boy's day.* New York: Harper & Row.

Barnard, K. E., & Martell, L. K. (1995). Mothering. In M. H. Bornstein (Ed.), *Handbook of parenting* (Vol. 3). Hillsdale, NJ: Erlbaum.

Barnard, K. E., & Solchany, J. E. (2002). Mothering. In M. H. Bornstein (Ed.), *Handbook of parenting* (2nd ed., Vol. 3). Mahwah, NJ: Erlbaum.

Barnes, D. L. (2002). What midwives need to know about postpartum depression. *Midwifery Today, 61,* 18–19.

Barnett, D., Ganiban, J., & Cicchetti, D. (1999). Maltreatment, negative expressivity, and the development of type D attachments from 12 to 24 months of age. In J. I. Vondra & D. Barnett (Eds.), *Monograph of the Society for Research in Child Development, 64* (3, Serial No. 258), 97–118.

Barnett, S. B., & Maulik, D. (2001). Guidelines and recommendations for safe use of Doppler ultrasound in perinatal applications. *Journal of Maternal and Fetal Medicine, 10,* 75–84.

Baron, N. S. (1992). *Growing up with language.* Reading, MA: Addison-Wesley.

Barr, H. M., & Streissguth, A. P. (2001). Identifying maternal self-reported alcohol use associated with fetal alcohol disorders. *Alcoholism: Clinical and Experimental Research, 25,* 283–287.

Barrett, D. E., Radke-Yarrow, M., & Klein, R. E. (1982). Chronic malnutrition and child behavior: Effects of calorie supplementation on social and emotional functioning at school age. *Developmental Psychology, 18,* 541–556.

Baskett, L. M., & Johnson, S. M. (1982). The young child's interaction with parents versus siblings. *Child Development, 53,* 643–650.

Bates, A. S., Fitzgerald, J. F., Dittus, R. S., & Wollinsky, F. D. (1994). Risk factors for underimmunization in poor urban infants. *Journal of the American Medical Associations, 272,* 1105–1109.

Bates, E., & Thal, D. (1991). Associations and dissociations in language development. In J. Millder (Ed.), *Research on language disorders: A decade of progress.* Austin: Pro-Ed.

Bates, J. E. (2001). Adjustment style in childhood as a product of parenting and temperament. In T. D. Wachs & G. A. Kohnstamm (Eds.), *Temperament in context.* Mahwah, NJ: Erlbaum.

Batson, C. D. (1989). Personal values, moral principles, and the three path model of prosocial motivation. In N. Eisenberg & J. Reykowski (Eds.), *Social and moral values.* Hillsdale, NJ: Erlbaum.

Baumeister, R. F. (1991). Identity crisis. In R. M. Lerner, A. C. Petersen, & J. Brooks-Gunn (Eds.), *Encyclopedia of adolescence* (Vol. 1). New York: Garland.

Baumrind, D. (1971). Current patterns of parental authority. *Developmental Psychology Monographs, 4* (1, Pt. 2).

Baumrind, D. (1989, April). *Sex-differentiated socialization effects in childhood and adolescence*. Paper presented at the biennial meeting of the Society for Research in Child Development, Kansas City.

Baumrind, D. (1999, November). Unpublished review of J. W. Santrock's *Child development*, 9th ed. (New York: McGraw-Hill).

Baumrind, D., Larzelere, R. E., & Cowan, P. A. (2002). Ordinary physical punishment: Is it harmful? Comment on Gershoff (2002). *Psychological Bulletin, 128,* 590–595.

Bauserman, R. (2002). Child adjustment in joint-custody versus sole-custody arrangements: A meta-analytic review. *Journal of Family Psychology, 16,* 91–102.

Bayley, N. (1943). Mental growth during the first three years. In R. G. Barker, J. S. Kounin, & H. F. Wright (Eds.), *Child behavior and development*. New York: McGraw-Hill.

Bayley, N. (1969). *Manual for the Bayley Scales of Infant Development*. New York: Psychological Corporation.

Bayley, N. (1970). Development of mental abilities. In P. H. Mussen (Ed.), *Manual of child psychology* (3rd ed., Vol. 1). New York: Wiley.

Beagles-Roos, J., & Gat, I. (1983). Specific impact of radio and television on children's story comprehension. *Journal of Educational Psychology, 75,* 128–137.

Beal, C. R. (1994). *Boys and girls: The development of gender roles*. New York: McGraw-Hill.

Beardslee, W. (2002). *Out of the darkened room*. Boston: Little, Brown.

Bearison, D. J., & Dorval, B. (2002). *Collaborative cognition*. Westport, CT: Ablex.

Bechtold, A. G., Bushnell, E. W., & Salapatek, P. (1979, April.) *Infants' visual localization of visual and auditory targets*. Paper presented at the meeting of the Society for Research in Child Development, San Francisco.

Beck, A. T. (1973). *The diagnosis and management of depression*. Philadelphia: University of Pennsylvania Press.

Beck, A. T. (1993). Cognitive therapy: Past, present, and future. *Journal of Consulting and Clinical Psychology, 61,* 194–198.

Beck, C. T. (2002). Theoretical perspectives of postpartum depression and their treatment implications. *American Journal of Maternal/Child Nursing, 27,* 282–287.

Bednar, R. L., Wells, M. G., & Peterson, S. R. (1995). *Self-esteem* (2nd ed.). Washington, DC: American Psychological Association.

Begley, S. (1997). How to build a baby's brain. *Newsweek Special Issue*. Spring/Summer, 28–32.

Bell, M. A., & Fox. N. A. (1992). The relations between frontal brain electrical activity and cognitive development during infancy. *Child Development, 63,* 1142–1163.

Bell, S. M., & Ainsworth, M. D. S. (1972). Infant crying and maternal responsiveness. *Child Development, 43,* 1171–1190.

Belle, D. (1999). *The after school lives of children*. Mahwah, NJ: Erlbaum.

Bellinger, D., Leviton, A., Waternaux, C., Needleman, H., & Rabinowitz, M. (1987). Longitudinal analysis of prenatal and postnatal lead exposure and early cognitive development. *New England Journal of Medicine, 316,* 1037–1043.

Bellugi, U., & Wang, P. P. (1996). Williams syndrome: From brain to cognition. *Encyclopedia of neuroscience*. Amsterdam: Elsevier.

Belsky, J. (1981). Early human experience: A family perspective. *Developmental Psychology, 17,* 3–23.

Belsky, J., & Eggebeen, D. (1991). Early and extensive maternal employment/child care and 4–6 year-olds socioemotional development: Children of the National Longitudinal Survey of Youth. *Journal of Marriage and the Family, 53,* 1083–1099.

Belsky, J., & Pensky, E. (1988). Marital change across the transition to parenthood. In R. Palkowitz & M. B. Sussman (Eds.), *Transitions to parenthood*. New York: Haworth.

Belson, W. (1978). *Television violence and the adolescent boy*. London: Saxon House.

Bem, S. L. (1977). On the utility of alternative procedures for assessing psychological androgyny. *Journal of Consulting and Clinical Psychology, 45,* 196–205.

Bendelius, J. (2003). The nutritional challenge of genetic enzyme-deficiency syndromes. *School Nurse News, 20,* 16–17.

Benenson, J. F., Apostolaris, N. H., & Parnass, J. (1997). Age and sex differences in dyadic and group interaction. *Developmental Psychology, 33,* 538–543.

Benenson, J. F., Nicholson, C., Waite, A., Roy, R., & Simpson, A. (2001). The influence of group size on children's competitive behavior. *Child Development, 72,* 921–928.

Bennett, C. I. (2003). *Comprehensive multicultural education* (5th ed.). Boston: Allyn & Bacon.

Bennett, W. (1993). *The book of virtues*. New York: Simon & Schuster.

Benson, P. (1993). *The troubled journey*. Minneapolis: The Search Institute.

Bereiter, C., & Scardamalia, M. (1993). *Surpassing ourselves: An inquiry into the nature and implications of expertise*. Chicago: Open Court.

Berenbaum, S. A., & Bailey, J. M. (2003). Effects on gender identity of prenatal androgens and genital appearance: evidence from girls with congenital adrenal hyperplasia. *Journal of Clinical Endocrinology and Metabolism, 88,* 1102–1106.

Bergen, D. (1988). Stages of play development. In D. Bergen (Ed.), *Play as a medium for learning and development*. Portsmouth, NH: Heinemann.

Berk, S. F. (1985). *The gender factory: The apportionment of work in American households*. New York: Plenum.

Berko, J. (1958). The child's learning of English morphology. *Word, 4,* 150–177.

Berko Gleason, J. (2000). Language: An overview. In A. Kazdin (Ed.), *Encyclopedia of psychology*. Washington, DC, & New York: American Psychological Association and Oxford University Press.

Berko Gleason, J. (2002). Review of J. W. Santrock's *Life-span development,* (9th ed.). (New York: McGraw-Hill).

Berkowitz, M., & Gibbs, J. (1983). Measuring the developmental features of moral discussion. *Merrill-Palmer Quarterly, 29,* 399–410.

Berlin, L., & Cassidy, J. (2000). Understanding parenting: Contributions of attachment theory and research. In J. D. Osofsky & H. E. Fitzgerald (Eds.), *WAIMH handbook of infant mental health* (Vol. 3). New York: Wiley.

Berlyne, D. E. (1960). *Conflict, arousal, and curiosity*. New York: McGraw-Hill.

Berndt, T. J. (1979). Developmental changes in conformity to peers and parents. *Developmental Psychology, 15,* 608–616.

Berndt, T. J. (1982). The features and effects of friendships in early adolescence. *Child Development, 53,* 1447–1460.

Berndt, T. J. (1999). Friends' influence on children's adjustment. In W. A. Collins & B. Laursen (Eds.), *Relationships as developmental contexts*. Mahwah, NJ: Erlbaum.

Berndt, T. J., & Perry, T. B. (1990). Distinctive features and effects of early adolescent friendships. In R. Montemayor (Ed.), *Advances in adolescent research*. Greenwich, CT: JAI Press.

Bernier, M. O., Plu-Bureau, G., Bossard, N., Ayzac, L., Thalabard, J. C. (2000). Breastfeeding and risk of breast cancer: A metaanalysis of published studies. *Human Reproduction Update, 6*(4), 374–386.

Berry, J. (2000). Cultural foundations of human behavior. In A. Kazdin (Ed.), *Encyclopedia of psychology.* Washington, DC, and New York: American Psychological Association and Oxford University Press.

Bertenthal, B. I., Rose, J. L., & Bai, D. L. (1997). Perception-action coupling in the development of visual control of posture. *Journal of Experimental Psychology: Human Perception and Performance, 23,* 1631–1643.

Berzonsky, M. (2000, June). *A social cognitive approach to identity development: The role of identity style.* Paper presented at the meeting of the European Association for Research on Adolescence, Jena, Germany.

Best, D. (2001). Cross-cultural gender roles. In J. Worell (Ed.), *Encyclopedia of women and gender.* San Diego: Academic Press.

Best, J. W., & Kahn, J. V. (2003). *Research in education* (9th ed.). Boston: Allyn & Bacon.

Bialystok, E. (1997). Effects of bilingualism and biliteracy on children's emerging concepts of print. *Development Psychology, 33,* 429–440.

Bialystok, E. (1999). Cognitive complexity and attentional control in the bilingual mind. *Child Development, 70,* 537–804.

Bialystok, E. (2001). Metalinguistic aspects of bilingual processing. *Annual Review of Applied Linguistics, 21,* 169–181.

Biderman, J., & Faraone, S. V. (2003). Current concepts on the neurobiology of attention-deficit/hyperactivity disorder. *Journal of Attention Disorders, 6,* Supplement 1, S7–S16.

Bigler, R. S., & Liben, L. S. (1990). The role of attitudes and interventions in gender-schematic processing. *Child Development, 61,* 1440–1452.

Biller, H. B. (1993). *Fathers and families: Paternal factors in child development.* Westport, CT: Auburn House.

Billman, J. (2003). *Observation and participation in early childhood setting: A practicum guide* (2nd ed.). Boston: Allyn & Bacon.

Billy, J. O. G., Rodgers, J. L., & Udry, J. R. (1984). Adolescent sexual behavior and friendship choice. *Social Forces, 62,* 653–678.

Bissada, A., & Briere, J. (2001). Child abuse: Physical and sexual. In J. Worell (Ed.), *Encyclopedia of women and gender.* San Diego: Academic Press.

Bissell, J., Manring, A., & Rowland, V. (1999). *Cybereducator.* New York: McGraw-Hill.

Bjorklund, D. F. (2000). *Children's thinking: Developmental function and individual differences* (3rd ed.). Belmont, CA: Wadsworth.

Bjorklund, D. F., & Harnishfeger, K. K. (1987). Developmental differences in the mental effort requirements for the use of an organizational strategy in free recall. *Journal of Experimental Child Psychology, 44,* 109–125.

Bjorklund, D. F., & Pellegrini, A. D. (2002). *The origins of human nature.* New York: Oxford University Press.

Bjorklund, D. F., & Rosenbaum, K. (2000). Middle childhood: Cognitive development. In A. Kazdin (Ed.), *Encyclopedia of psychology.* Washington, DC, & New York: American Psychological Association and Oxford University Press.

Bjorklund, D. F., & Bering, J. M., (2001, April). *Evolutionary developmental psychology.* Paper presented at the meeting of the Society for Research in Child Development, Minneapolis.

Blachman, B. A., Ball, E., Black, R., & Tangel, D. (1994). Kindergarten teachers develop phoneme awareness in low-income inner-city classrooms: Does it make a difference? In B.A. Blachman (Ed.), *Reading and writing.* Mahwah, NJ: Erlbaum.

Black, J. E. (2001, April). *Complex and interactive effects of enriched experiences on brain development.* Paper presented at the meeting of the Society for Research in Child Development, Minneapolis.

Blair, C., & Ramey, C. (1996). Early intervention with low birth weight infants: The path to second generation research. In M. J. Guralnick (Ed.). *The effectiveness of early intervention.* Baltimore: Paul H. Brookes.

Blasi, A. (1988). Identity and the development of the self. In D. Lapsley & F. C. Power (Eds.), *Self, ego, and identity: Integrative approaches.* New York: Springer-Verlag.

Blickstein, I. (2003). Motherhood at or beyond the edge of reproductive age. *International Journal of Fertility and Women's Medicine, 48,* 17–24.

Block, J. (1993). Studying personality the long way. In D. Funder, R. D. Parke, C. Tomlinson-Keasey, & K. Widaman (Ed.), *Studying lives through time.* Washington, DC: American Psychological Association.

Block, J. H., & Block, J. (1980). The role of ego-control and ego-resiliency in the organization of behavior. In W. A. Collins (Ed.), *Minnesota symposium on child psychology* (Vol. 13). Minneapolis: University of Minnesota Press.

Bloom, B. (1985). *Developing talent in young people.* New York: Ballantine.

Bloom, L. (1993). *The transition from infancy to language: Acquiring the power of expression.* Cambridge, England: Cambridge University Press.

Bloom, L. (1998). Language acquisition in its developmental context. In W. Damon (Ed.), *Handbook of child psychology* (5th ed., Vol. 2). New York: Wiley.

Bloom, L., Lifter, K., & Broughton, J. (1985). The convergence of early cognition and language in the second year of life: Problems in conceptualization and measurement. In M. Barrett (Ed.), *Single word speech.* London: Wiley.

Bloom, P. (2002). *How children learn the meaning of words.* Cambridge, MA: MIT Press.

Blum, L. M. (2000). *At the breast: Ideologies of breastfeeding and motherhood in the contemporary United States.* Boston: Beacon Press.

Blumenfeld, P. C., Pintrich, P. R., Wessles, K., & Meece, J. (1981, April). *Age and sex differences in the impact of classroom experiences on self-perceptions.* Paper presented at the biennial meeting of the Society for Research in Child Development, Boston.

Blumenthal, J., Jeffries, N. O., Castellanos, F. X., Liu, H., Zidjdenbos, A., Paus, T., Evans, A. C., Rapoport, J. L., & Giedd, J. N. (1999). Brain development during childhood and adolescence: A longitudinal MRI study. *Nature Neuroscience, 10,* 861–863.

Bohlin, G., & Hagekull, B. (1993). Stranger wariness and sociability in the early years. *Infant Behavior and Development, 16,* 53–67.

Bohnhorst, B., Heyne, T., Peter, C. S., & Poets, C. F. (2002). Skin-to-skin (kangaroo) care, respiratory control, and thermoregulation. *Journal of Pediatrics, 138,* 193–197.

Bojesen, A., Juul, S., & Gravholt, C. H. (2003). Prenatal and postnatal prevalence of Klinefelter syndrome: a chance association? *Journal of Endocrinology and Metabolism, 88,* 622–626.

Bolger, K. E., & Patterson, C. J. (2001). Developmental pathways from child maltreatment to peer rejection. *Child Development, 72,* 339–351.

Bolland, J. M. (2003). Hopelessness and risk behavior among adolescents living in high-poverty inner-city neighborhoods. *Journal of Adolescence, 26,* 145–158.

Bonk, C. J., & Cunningham, D. J. (1999). Searching for learner-centered, constructivist, and sociocultural components of collaborative educational learning tools. In C. J. Bonk & K. S. King (Eds.), *Electronic collaborators.* Mahwah, NJ: Erlbaum.

Bonvillian, J. D., Orlansky, M. D., & Novack, L. L. (1983). Developmental milestones: Sign language and motor development. *Child Development, 54,* 1435–1445.

Books, S. (Ed.). (2003). *Invisible children in the society and its schools.* Mahwah, NJ: Erlbaum.

Bookstein, F. L., Streissguth, A. P., Sampson, P. D., Connor, P. D., & Barr, H. M. (2002). Corpus callosum shape and neuropsychological deficits in adult males with heavy fetal alcohol exposure. *Neuroimage, 15,* 233–251.

Booth, M. (2002). Arab adolescents facing the future: Enduring ideals and pressure to change. In B. B. Brown, R. W. Larson, & T. S. Saraswathi (Eds.), *The world's youth.* New York: Cambridge University Press.

Boring, E. G. (1950). *A history of experimental psychology.* New York: Appleton-Century-Crofts.

Borkowski, J. G., Ramey, S. L., & Bristol-Power, M. (Eds.). (2002). *Parenting and the child's world.* Mahwah, NJ: Erlbaum.

Bornstein, M. H. (2000). Unpublished review of J. W. Santrock's *Life-span development,* 8th ed. (New York: McGraw-Hill).

Bornstein, M. H. (2002). Parenting infants. In M. H. Bornstein (Ed.), *Handbook of parenting* (2nd ed., Vol. 1). Mahwah, NJ: Erlbaum.

Bornstein, M. H., & Arterberry, M. E. (1999). Perceptual development. In M. H. Bornstein & M. E. Lamb (Eds.), *Developmental psychology: An advanced textbook* (4th ed.). Mahwah, NJ: Erlbaum.

Bornstein, M. H., & Bradley, R. H. (Eds.). (2003). *Socioeconomic status, parenting, and child development.* Mahwah, NJ: Erlbaum.

Bornstein, M. H., & Krasnegor, N. A. (1989). *Stability and continuity in mental development.* Hillsdale, NJ: Erlbaum.

Bornstein, M. H., & Sigman, M. D. (1986). Continuity in mental development from infancy. *Child Development, 57,* 251–274.

Borowsky, I. W., Ireland, M., & Resnick, M. D. (2001). Adolescent suicide attempts: Risks and protectors. *Pediatrics, 107,* 485–493.

Bost, C. S., & Vaughn, S. (2002). *Strategies for teaching students with learning and behavioral problems* (5th ed.). Boston: Allyn & Bacon.

Botvin, G. J. (1999, June). *Impact of preventive interventions on protection for drug use, onset, and progression.* Paper presented at the meeting of the Society for Prevention Research, New Orleans.

Bouchard, T. J. (1995, August). *Heritability of intelligence.* Paper presented at the meeting of the American Psychological Association, New York.

Bouchard, T. J., Lykken, D. T., McGue, M., Segal, N. L., & Tellegen, A. (1990). Source of human psychological differences. The Minnesota Study of Twins Reared Apart. *Science, 250,* 223–228.

Bouchey, H. A., & Furman, W. (2003). Dating and romantic relationships in adolescence. In G. Adams & M. Berzonsky (Eds.), *Blackwell handbook of adolescence.* Malden, MA: Blackwell.

Bouvier, P. (2003). Child sexual abuse: vicious circles of fate or paths to resilience? *Lancet, 361,* 446–447.

Bower, B. (1985). The left hand of math and verbal talent. *Science News, 127,* 263.

Bower, B. (1999, March 20). Minds on the move. *Science News,* 1–5.

Bower, T. G. R. (1966). Slant perception and shape constancy in infants. *Science, 151,* 832–834.

Bower, T. G. R. (2002). Space and objects. In A. Slater & M. Lewis (Eds.), *Introduction to infant development.* New York: Oxford University Press.

Bowlby, J. (1969). *Attachment and loss* (Vol. 1). London: Hogarth Press.

Bowlby, J. (1989). *Secure and insecure attachment.* New York: Basic Books.

Boyer, K., & Diamond, A. (1992). Development of memory for temporal order in infants and young children. In A. Diamond (Ed.), *Development and neural bases of higher cognitive function.* New York: New York Academy of Sciences.

Boyes, M. C., Giordano, R., & Galperyn, K. (1993, March). *Moral orientation and interpretive contexts of moral deliberation.* Paper presented at the biennial meeting of the Society for Research in Child Development, New Orleans.

Boyum, L., & Parke, R. D. (1995). Family emotional expressiveness and children's social competence. *Journal of Marriage and the Family, 57,* 593–608.

Brabeck, M. M. (2000). Kohlberg, Lawrence. In A. Kazdin (Ed.), *Encyclopedia of psychology.* Washington, DC, & New York: American Psychological Association and Oxford University Press.

Bracken, M. B., Eskenazi, B., Sachse, K., McSharry, J., Hellenbrand, K., & Leo-Summers, L. (1990). Association of cocaine use with sperm concentration, motility, and morphology. *Fertility and Sterility, 53,* 315–322.

Bradley, R. H., & Corwyn, R. F. (2002). Socioeconomic status and child development. *Annual Review of Psychology* (Vol. 53). Palo Alto, CA: Annual Reviews.

Bradley, R. H., Corwyn, R. F., McAdoo, H. P., & Coll, C. G. (2001). The home environments of children in the United States. Part I: Variations by age, ethnicity, and poverty status. *Child Development, 72,* 1844–1867.

Bramswig, J. H. (2001). Long-term results of growth hormone therapy in Turner syndrome. *Endocrinology, 15,* 5–13.

Brazelton, T. B. (1956). Sucking in infancy. *Pediatrics, 17,* 400–404.

Brazelton, T. B. (1998, September 7). Commentary. *Dallas Morning News,* p. C2.

Brazelton, T. B., Nugent, J. K., & Lester, B. M. (1987). Neonatal behavioral assessment scale. In J. D. Osofsky (Ed.), *Handbook of infant development* (2nd ed.). New York: Wiley.

Bredekamp, S. (1987). *Developmentally appropriate practice in early childhood programs serving children from birth through age 8.* Washington, DC: National Association for the Education of Young Children.

Bredekamp, S. (1993). Reflections on Reggio Emilia. *Young Children, 49,* 13–16.

Bredekamp, S. (1997). NAEYC issues revised position statement on developmentally appropriate practice in early childhood programs. *Young Children, 52,* 34–40.

Bredekamp, S., & Rosegrant, T. (1996). *Reaching potentials* (Vol. 2). Washington, DC: National Association for the Education of Young Children.

Bremner, G. (2002). Cognitive development: Knowledge of the physical world. In A. Fogel & G. Bremner (Eds.), *Blackwell handbook of infant development.* Malden, MA: Blackwell.

Brenner, R. A., Trumble, A. C., Smith, G. S., Kessler, E. P., & Overpeck, M. D. (2001). Where children drown, 1995. *Pediatrics, 108,* 85–89.

Brent, R. L., & Fawcett, L. B. (2000, May). *Environmental causes of human birth defects: What have we learned about the mechanism, nature, and etiology of congenital malformations in the past 50 years?* Paper presented at the joint meetings of the Pediatric Academic Societies and the American Academy of Pediatrics, Boston.

Bretherton, I., Stolberg, U., & Kreye, M. (1981). Engaging strangers in proximal interaction: Infants' social initiative. *Developmental Psychology, 17,* 746–755.

Brewer, J. A. (2004). *Introduction to early childhood education.* Boston: Allyn & Bacon.

Brewer, M. B., & Campbell, D. T. (1976). *Ethnocentrism and intergroup attitudes.* New York: Wiley.

Bridges, L. J. (2003). Coping as an element of developmental well-being. In M. H. Bornstein, L. Davidson, C. L. M. Keyes, & K. A. Moore (Eds.), *Well-being.* Mahwah, NJ: Erlbaum.

Brislin, R. (1993). *Understanding culture's influence on behavior.* Fort Worth: Harcourt Brace.

Brody, G. H., & Ge, X. (2001). Linking parenting processes and self-regulation to psychological functioning and alcohol use during early adolescence. *Journal of Family Psychology, 15,* 82–94.

Brody, G. H., & Shaffer, D. R. (1982). Contributions of parents and peers to children's moral socialization. *Developmental Review, 2,* 31–75.

Brody, J. E. (1994, April 6). The value of breast milk. *The New York Times,* p. C11.

Brody, N. (2000). Intelligence. In A. Kazdin (Ed.), *Encyclopedia of psychology.* Washington, DC, & New York: American Psychological Association and Oxford University Press.

Brodzinsky, D. M., Lang, R., & Smith, D. W. (1995). Parenting adopted children. In M. H. Bornstein (Ed.), *Handbook of parenting* (Vol. 3). Hillsdale, NJ: Erlbaum.

Brodzinsky, D. M., Schechter, D. E., Braff, A. M., & Singer, L. M. (1984). Psychological and academic adjustment in adopted children. *Journal of Consulting and Clinical Psychology, 52,* 582–590.

Bronfenbrenner, U. (1986). Ecology of the family as a context for human development: Research perspectives. *Developmental Psychology, 22,* 723–742.

Bronfenbrenner, U. (1995, March). *The role research has played in Head Start.* Paper presented at the meeting of the Society for Research in Child Development, Indianapolis.

Bronfenbrenner, U. (2000). Ecological theory. In A. Kazdin (Ed.), *Encyclopedia of psychology.* Washington, DC, & New York: American Psychological Association and Oxford University Press.

Bronfenbrenner, U., & Morris, P. (1998). The ecology of developmental processes. In W. Damon (Ed.), *Handbook of child psychology* (5th ed., Vol. 1). New York: Wiley.

Brook, J. S., Brook, D. W., Gordon, A. S., Whiteman, M., & Cohen, P. (1990). The psychological etiology of adolescent drug use: A family interactional approach. *Genetic, Social, and General Psychology Monographs, 116,* 110–267.

Brook, J. S., Whiteman, M., Balka, E. B., Win, P. T., & Gursen, M. D. (1998). Drug use among Puerto Ricans: Ethnic identity as a protective factor. *Hispanic Journal of Behavioral Sciences, 20,* 241–254.

Brookover, W. B., Beady, C., Flood, P., Schweitzer, U., & Wisenbaker, J. (1979). *School social systems and student achievement: Schools make a difference.* New York: Praeger.

Brooks, J. G., & Brooks, M. G. (1993). *The case for constructivist classrooms.* Alexandria, VA: Association for Supervision and Curriculum.

Brooks, J. G., & Brooks, M. G. (2001). *The case for constructivist classrooms* (2nd ed.). Upper Saddle River, NJ: Erlbaum.

Brooks-Gunn, J., & Graber, J. A. (1999). *What's sex got to do with it? The development of health and sexual identities during adolescence.* Unpublished manuscript, Department of Psychology, Columbia University, New York City.

Brooks-Gunn, J., Han W. J., & Waldfogel, J. (2002). Maternal employment and child cognitive outcomes in the first three years of life: The NICHD Study of Early Child Care. *Child Development, 73,* 1052–1072.

Brooks-Gunn, J., Leventhal, T., & Duncan, G. (2000). Why poverty matters for young children: Implications for policy. In J. Osofsky & H. E. Fitzgerald (Eds.), *WAIMH Handbook of Infant Mental Health* (Vol. 3). New York: Wiley.

Brooks-Gunn, J., & Matthews, W. S. (1979). *He and she: How children develop their sex role identity.* Englewood Cliffs, NJ: Prentice Hall.

Brooks-Gunn, J., & Paikoff, R. (1993). "Sex is a gamble, kissing is a game": Adolescent sexuality and health promotion. In S. P. Millstein, A. C. Petersen, & E. O. Nightingale (Eds.), *Promoting the health behavior of adolescents.* New York: Oxford University Press.

Brooks-Gunn, J., & Paikoff, R. (1997). Sexuality and developmental transitions during adolescence. In J. Schulenberg, J. Maggs, & K. Hurrelmann (Eds.), *Health risks and developmental transitions during adolescence.* New York: Cambridge University Press.

Brooks-Gunn, J., & Warren, M. P. (1989). The psychological significance of secondary sexual characteristics in 9- to 11-year-old girls. *Child Development, 59,* 161–169.

Brophy, J. (1998). *Motivating students to learn.* New York: McGraw-Hill.

Broughton, J. M. (1978). Development of concepts of self, mind, reality, and knowledge. In W. Damon (Ed.), *Social cognition.* San Francisco: Jossey-Bass.

Brouwers, E. P. M., van Baar, A. L., & Pop, V. J. M. (2001). Maternal anxiety during pregnancy and subsequent infant development. *Infant Behavior & Development, 24,* 95–106.

Brown, A. L. (1990). Domain-specific principles affect learning and transfer in children. *Cognitive Science, 14,* 107–133.

Brown, A. L. (1997). Transforming schools into communities of learners. *American Psychologist, 52,* 399–409.

Brown, A. L. (1998, April). *Reciprocal teaching.* Paper presented at the meeting of the American Educational Research Association, San Diego.

Brown, A. L., & Campione, J. C. (1996). Psychological learning theory and the design of innovative environments. In L. Schauble & R. Glaser (Eds.), *Contributions of instructional innovation to understanding learning.* Mahwah, NJ: Erlbaum.

Brown, A. L., & Day, J. D. (1983). Macrorules for summarizing texts: The development of expertise. *Journal of Verbal Learning and Verbal Behavior, 22,* 1–14.

Brown, A. L., Kane, M. J., & Echols, K. (1986). Young children's mental models determine analogical transfer across problems with a common goal structure. *Cognitive Development, 1,* 103–122.

Brown, B. B. (1999). "You're going with whom?!": Peer group influences on adolescent romantic relationships. In W. Furman, B. B. Brown, & C. Feiring (Eds.), *The development of romantic relationships in adolescence.* Cambridge: Cambridge University Press.

Brown, B. B. (1999). Measuring the peer environment of American adolescents. In S. L. Friedman & T. D. Wachs (Eds.), *Measuring environment across the life span.* Washington, DC: American Psychological Association.

Brown, B. B., & Larson, R. W. (2002). The kaleidoscope of adolescence: Experiences of the world's youth at the beginning of the 21st century. In B. B. Brown, R. W. Larson, & T. S. Saraswathi (Eds.), *The world's youth.* New York: Cambridge University Press.

Brown, B. B., & Lohr, M. J. (1987). Peer-group affiliation and adolescent self-esteem: An integration of ego-identity and symbolic-interaction theories. *Journal of Personality and Social Psychology, 52,* 47–55.

Brown, B. B., Steinberg, L., Mounts, N., & Philipp, M. (1990, March). *The comparative influence of peers and parents on high school achievement: Ethnic differences.* Paper presented at the meeting of the Society for Research on Adolescence, Atlanta.

Brown, J. D., Schaffer, R., Vargas, L., & Romocki, L. S. (2003). Popular media culture and the promise of critical media literacy. In S. F. Hamilton & M. A. Hamilton (Eds.), *The youth development handbook.* Newbury Park, CA: Sage.

Brown, L. M., & Gilligan, C. (1992). *Meeting at the crossroads: Women's and girls' development.* Cambridge, MA: Harvard University Press.

Brown, R. (1973). *A first language: The early stages*. Cambridge, MA: Harvard University Press.

Brown, R. (1986). *Social psychology* (2nd ed.). New York: Free Press.

Brownlee, S. (1998, June 15). Baby talk. *U.S. News & World Report*, 48–54.

Bruce, J. M., Olen, K., & Jensen, S. J. (1999, April). *The role of emotion and regulation in social competence*. Paper presented at the meeting of the Society for Research in Child Development, Albuquerque.

Bruck, M., & Ceci, S. J. (1999). The suggestibility of children's memory. *Annual Review of Psychology, 50*, 419–439.

Bruer, J. T. (1999). *The myth of the first three years*. New York: Free Press.

Bruner, J. S. (1983). *Child talk*. New York: W. W. Norton.

Bruner, J. S. (1996). *The culture of education*. Cambridge, MA: Harvard University Press.

Buchanan, C. M. (2001, August). *Understanding the variability in children's adjustment after divorce*. Paper presented at the meeting of the American Psychological Association, San Francisco.

Budwig, N. (1993). *A developmental functionalist approach to child language*. Hillsdale, NJ: Erlbaum.

Bugental, D. B., & Goodnow, J. J. (1998). Socialization processes. In W. Damon (Ed.), *Handbook of child psychology* (5th ed., Vol. 3). New York: Wiley.

Buhrmester, D. (1990). Friendship, interpersonal competence, and adjustment in preadolescence and adolescence. *Child Development, 61*, 1101–1111.

Buhrmester, D. (1993, March). *Adolescent friendship and the socialization of gender differences in social interaction styles*. Paper presented at the biennial meeting of the Society for Research in Child Development, New Orleans.

Buhrmester, D. (1998). Need fulfillment, interpersonal competence, and the developmental contexts of early adolescent friendship. In W. M. Bukowski & A. F. Newcomb (Eds.), *The company they keep: Friendship in childhood and adolescence*. New York: Cambridge University Press.

Buhrmester, D. (2001, April). *Romantic development: Does age at which romantic involvement starts matter?* Paper presented at the meeting of the Society for Research in Child Development, Minneapolis.

Buhrmester, D., & Furman, W. (1987). The development of companionship and intimacy. *Child Development, 58*, 1101–1113.

Buhs, E. S., & Ladd, G. W. (2001). Peer rejection as an antecedent of young children's school adjustment: An examination of mediating processes. *Developmental Psychology, 37*, 550–560.

Bukowski, W. M., Newcomb, A. F., & Hoza, B. (1987). Friendship conceptions among early adolescents: A longitudinal study of stability and change. *Journal of Early Adolescence, 7*, 143–152.

Bukowski, W. M., Sippola, L. K., & Boivin, M. (1995, March). *Friendship protects "at risk" children from victimization by peers*. Paper presented at the meeting of the Society for Research in Child Development, Indianapolis.

Bumpus, M. F., Crouter, A. C., & McHale, S. M. (2001). Parental autonomy granting during adolescence: Exploring gender differences in context. *Developmental Psychology, 37*, 161–173.

Burchinal, M. R., Roberts, J. E., Nabors, L. A., & Bryant, D. M. (1996). Quality of center child care and infant cognitive and language development. *Child Development, 67*, 606–620.

Burton, R. V. (1984). A paradox in theories and research in moral development. In W. M. Kurtines & J. L. Gewirtz (Eds.), *Morality, moral behavior, and moral development*. New York: Wiley.

Bush, P. G., Mayhew, T. M., Abramovich, D. R., Aggett, P. J., Burke, M. D., & Page, K. R. (2001). Maternal cigarette smoking and oxygen diffusion across the placenta. *Placenta, 21*, 824–833.

Bushman, B. J., & Huesmann, L. R. (2001). Effects of televised violence on aggression. In D. Singer & J. Singer (Eds.), *Handbook of children and the media*. Thousand Oaks, CA: Sage.

Bushnell, I. W. R. (2001). Mother's face recognition in newborn infants: Learning and memory. *Infant and Child Development, 10*, 67–74.

Buss, D. M. (1995). Psychological sex differences: Origins through sexual selection. *American Psychologist, 50*, 164–168.

Buss, D. M. (1999). *Evolutionary psychology: The new science of the mind*. Boston: Allyn & Bacon.

Buss, D. M. (2000). Evolutionary psychology. In A. Kazdin (Ed.), *Encyclopedia of psychology*. Washington, DC, & New York: American Psychological Association and Oxford University Press.

Buss, D. M., & Schmitt, D. P. (1993). Sexual strategies theory: An evolutionary perspective on human mating. *Psychological Review, 100*, 204–232.

Butz, A. M., Pulsifer, M., Marano, N., Belcher, H., Lears, M. K., & Royall, R. (2001). Effectiveness of a home intervention for perceived child behavioral problems and parenting stress in children with in utero drug exposure. *Archives of Pediatric and Adolescent Medicine, 155*, 1029–1037.

Buzwell, S., & Rosenthal, D. (1996). Constructing a sexual self: Adolescents' sexual self-perceptions and sexual risk-taking. *Journal of Research on Adolescence, 6*, 489–513.

Bybee, J. A., & Wells, Y. A. (2003). The development of possible selves during adulthood. In J. Demick & C. Andreoletti (Eds.), *Handbook of adult development*. New York: Kluwer.

Byrnes, J. P. (2001). *Minds, brains, and learning*. New York: Guilford Press.

C

Cairns, R. B. (1983). The emergence of developmental psychology. In P. H. Mussen (Ed.), *Handbook of child psychology* (4th ed., Vol. 1). New York: Wiley.

Cairns, R. B. (1998). The making of developmental psychology.

Calabrese, R. L., & Schumer, H. (1986). The effects of service activities on adolescent alienation. *Adolescence, 21*, 675–687.

Call, J. (1955, March). *Imitative learning as a problem-solving strategy in Orangutans* (pono pygmaeus) *and three- and four-year-old human children*. Paper presented at the meeting of the Society for Research in Child Development, Indianapolis.

Callan, J. E. (2001). Gender development: Psychoanalytic perspectives. In J. Worell (Ed.), *Encyclopedia of women and gender*. San Diego: Academic Press.

Callender, E. S., Rickard, L., Rinksy-Eng, J. (2001). Knowledge and use of folic acid supplementation: A study of Colorado women whose pregnancies were affected by a fetal neural tube defect. *Clinical Investigations in Medicine, 24*, 124–128.

Calvert, S. (1999). *Children's journeys through the information age*. New York: McGraw-Hill.

Camaioni, L. (2002). Early language. In U. Goswami (Ed.), *Blackwell handbook of childhood cognitive development*. Malden, MA: Blackwell.

Cameron, J. (2001). Negative effects of reward on intrinsic motivation—a limited phenomenon. *Review of Educational Research, 71,* 29–42.

Cameron, J. R., Hansen, R., & Rosen, D. (1989). Preventing behavioral problems in infancy through temperament assessment and parental support programs. In W. B. Carey & S. C. McDevitt (Eds.), *Clinical and education applications of temperament research.* Amsterdam: Swets & Zeitlinger.

Campbell, C. Y. (1988, August 24). Group raps depiction of teenagers. *Boston Globe,* p. 44.

Campbell, D. T., & LeVine, R. A. (1968). Ethnocentrism and intergroup relations. In R. Abelson & others (Eds.), *Theories and cognitive consistency: A sourcebook.* Chicago: Rand-McNally.

Campbell, L., Campbell, B., & Dickinson, D. (1999). *Teaching and learning through multiple intelligences* (2nd ed.). Boston: Allyn & Bacon.

Campos, J. (1994, spring). The new functionalism in emotions. *SRCD Newsletter,* pp. 1, 7, 9–11, 14.

Campos, J. (2001, April). *Emotion in emotional development: Problems and prospects.* Paper presented at the meeting of the Society for Research in Child Development, Minneapolis.

Campos, J. J., Langer, A., & Krowitz, A. (1970). Cardiac responses on the visual cliff in prelocomotor human infants. *Science, 170,* 196–197.

Canfield, R. L., & Haith, M. M. (1991). Young infants' visual expectations for symmetric and asymmetric stimulus sequences. *Developmental Psychology, 27,* 198–208.

Caporael, L. R. (2001). Evolutionary psychology. *Annual Review of Psychology* (Vol. 52). Palo Alto, CA: Annual Reviews.

Capparelli, E. V., Mirocnick, M., Danker, W. M., Blanchard, S., Mofenson, L., McSherry, G. D., Gay, H., Ciupak, G., Smith, B., & Connor, J. D. (2003). Pharmacokinetics and tolerance of zidovudine in preterm infants. *Journal of Pediatrics, 142,* 47–52.

Carbonell, O. A., Alzte, G., Bustamante, M. R., & Quiceno, J. (2002). Maternal caregiving and infant security in two cultures. *Developmental Psychology, 38,* 67–78.

Carbonne, B., Tsatsarius, V., & Goffinet, F. (2001). The new tocolytics. *Gynecology, Obstetrics, and Fertility, 29,* 316–319.

Carey, L. M. (2001). *Measuring and evaluating school learning* (3rd ed.). Boston: Allyn & Bacon.

Carey, S. (1977). The child as word learner. In M. Halle, J. Bresman, & G. Miller (Eds.), *Linguistic theory and psychological reality.* Cambridge, MA: MIT Press.

Carey, S. (1988). Are children fundamentally different kinds of thinkers and learners than adults? In K. Richardson & S. Sheldon (Eds.), *Cognitive development to adolescence.* Hillsdale, NJ: Erlbaum.

Carey, S., & Gelman, R. (1991). *The epigenesis of mind.* Hillsdale, NJ: Erlbaum.

Carlson, C., Cooper, C., & Hsu, J. (1990, March). *Predicting school achievement in early adolescence: The role of family process.* Paper presented at the meeting of the Society for Research in Adolescence, Atlanta.

Carlson, K. S. (1995, March). *Attachment in sibling relationships during adolescence: Links to other familial and peer relationships.* Paper presented at the meeting of the Society for Research in Child Development, Indianapolis.

Carlton, M. P., & Winsler, A. (1999). School readiness: The need for a paradigm shift. *School Psychology Review, 28,* 338–352.

Carnegie Corporation. (1989). *Turning points: Preparing youth for the 21st century.* New York: Author.

Carnegie Corporation. (1996). *Report on education for children 3–10 years of age.* New York: Carnegie Foundation.

Carroll, J. (1993). *Human cognitive abilities.* Cambridge, England: Cambridge University Press.

Carter, D. B., & Levy, G. D. (1988). Cognitive aspects of children's early sex-role development: The influence of gender schemas on preschoolers' memories and preference for sex-typed toys and activities. *Child Development, 59,* 782–793.

Carter-Saltzman, L. (1980). Biological and sociocultural effects on handedness: Comparison between biological and adoptive families. *Science, 209,* 1263–1265.

Carver, K., Joyner, K., & Udry, J. R. (2003). National estimates of romantic relationships. In P. Florsheim (Ed.), *Adolescent romantic relations and sexual behavior: Theory, research, and practical implications.* Mahwah, NJ: Erlbaum.

Carver, L. J., & Bauer, P. J. (1999). When the event is more than the sum of its parts: Nine-month-olds' long-term ordered recall. *Memory, 7,* 147–174.

Carver, L. J, & Bauer, P. J. (2001). The dawning of a past: The emergence of long-term explicit memory in infancy. *Journal of Experimental Psychology: General, 130* (4), 726–745.

Carver, L. J., Bauer, P. J., & Nelson, C. A. (2000). Associations between infant brain activity and recall memory. *Developmental Science, 3,* 234–246.

Case, R. (1985). *Intellectual development: Birth to adulthood.* New York: Academic Press.

Case, R. (1987). Neo-Piagetian theory: Retrospect and prospect. *International Journal of Psychology, 22,* 773–791.

Case, R. (1999). Conceptual development in the child and the field: A personal view of the Piagetian legacy. In E. K. Skolnick, K. Nelson, S. A. Gelman, & P. H. Miller (Eds.), *Conceptual development.* Mahwah, NJ: Erlbaum.

Case, R., Kurland, D. M., & Goldberg, J. (1982). Operational efficiency and the growth of short-term memory span. *Journal of Experimental Child Psychology, 33,* 386–404.

Casey, B. J., Durston, S., & Fossella, J. A. (2001). Evidence for a mechanistic model of cognitive control. *Clinical Neuroscience Research, 1,* 267–282.

Casey, B. M., McIntire, D. D., Leveno, K. J. (2001). The continuing value of the Apgar score for the assessment of newborn infants. *New England Journal of Medicine, 344,* 467–471.

Caspi, A. (1998). Personality development across the life course. In W. Damon (Ed.), *Handbook of child psychology* (Vol. 3). New York: Wiley.

Cassidy, J. (1999). The nature of the child's ties. In J. Cassidy & P. Shaver (Eds.), *Handbook of attachment.* New York: Guilford.

Cassidy, J., & Shaver, P. R. (Eds.). (1999). *Handbook of attachment.* New York: Guilford Press.

Cauffman, B. E. (1994, February). *The effects of puberty, dating, and sexual involvement on dieting and disordered eating in young adolescent girls.* Paper presented at the meeting of the Society for Research on Adolescence, San Diego.

Caulfield, R. A. (2001). *Infants and toddlers.* Upper Saddle River, NJ: Prentice Hall.

Ceci, S. J. (2000). Bronfenbrenner, Urie. In A. Kazdin (Ed.), *Encyclopedia of psychology.* Washington, DC, & New York: American Psychological Association and Oxford University Press.

Ceci, S. J., & Gilstrap, L. L. (2000). Determinants of intelligence: Schooling and intelligence. In A. Kazdin (Ed.), *Encyclopedia of psychology.* Washington, DC, & New York: American Psychological Association and Oxford University Press.

Centers for Disease Control and Prevention. (2000). *HIV/AIDS surveillance report.* Atlanta: Author.

Centers for Disease Control and Prevention. (2002). *Sexually transmitted diseases.* Atlanta: Author.

Chall, J. S. (1979). The great debate: Ten years later with a modest proposal for reading stages. In L. B. Resnick & P. A. Weaver (Eds.), *Theory and practice of early reading.* Hillsdale, NJ: Erlbaum.

Chan, A., Keane, R. J., & Robinson, J. S. (2001). The contribution of maternal smoking to preterm birth, small for gestational age, and low birth weight among Aboriginal and non-Aboriginal births in South Australia. *Medical Journal of Australia, 174,* 389–393.

Chan, W. S. (1963). *A source book in Chinese philosophy.* Princeton, NJ: Princeton University Press.

Chapman, M. V. (2003). Poverty level and school performance: Using contextual and self-report measures to inform intervention. *Children and Schools, 25,* 5–17.

Charlesworth, R. (2000). *Understanding child development* (5th ed.). Albany, NY: Delmar.

Charpak, N., Guiz-Pelaez, J. G., Figueroa, Z., & Charpak, Y. (1997). Kangaroo mother versus traditional care for newborn infants ≤ 2000 grams: A randomized, controlled trial. *Pediatrics, 100,* 682–688.

Charpak, N., Guirz-Pelaez, J. G., Figueroa, Z., & Charpak, Y. (2001). A randomized, controlled trial of kangaroo mother care: Results of follow-up at 1 year of corrected age. *Pediatrics, 108,* 1072–1079.

Chase-Lansdale, P. L., Coley, R. L., & Grining, C. P. L. (2001, April). *Low-income families and child care.* Paper presented at the meeting of the Society for Research in Child Development, Minneapolis.

Chattin-McNichols, J. (1992). *The Montessori controversy.* Albany, NY: Delmar.

Chaudhry, V., Cornblath, D. R., Corse, A., Freimer, M., Simmons-O'Brien, E., & Vogelsang, G. (2002). Thalidomide-induced neuropathy. *Neurology, 59,* 1872–1875.

Chauhuri, J. H., & Williams, P. H. (1999, April). *The contribution of infant temperament and parent emotional availability to toddler attachment.* Paper presented at the meeting of the Society for Research in Child Development, Albuquerque.

Chavkin, W. (2001). Cocaine and pregnancy—time to look at the evidence. *Journal of the American Medical Association, 285,* 1626–1628.

Chen, C., & Stevenson, H. W. (1989). Homework: A cross-cultural examination. *Child Development, 60,* 551–561.

Chen, X., Hastings, P. D., Rubin, K. H., Chen, H., Cen, G., & Stewart, S. L. (1998). Childrearing attitudes and behavioral inhibition in Chinese and Canadian toddlers: A cross-cultural study. *Developmental Psychology, 34,* 677–686.

Chen, Z., & Siegler, R. S. (2000). Intellectual development in childhood. In R. J. Sternberg (Ed.), *Handbook of intelligence.* New York: Cambridge University Press.

Cheng, T. L., Fields, C. B., Brenner, R. A., Wright, J. L., Lomax, T., & Schedit, P. C. (2000). Sports injuries: An important cause of morbidity in urban youth. *Pediatrics, 105,* E32–33.

Cherlin, A. J., & Furstenberg, F. F. (1994). Stepfamilies in the United States: A reconsideration. In J. Blake & J. Hagen (Eds.), *Annual review of sociology.* Palo Alto, CA: Annual Reviews.

Cherlin, A. J., Furstenberg, F. F., Chase-Lansdale, P. L., Kiernan, K. E., Robins, P. K., Morrison, D. R., & Teitler, J. O. (1991). Longitudinal studies of effects of divorce in children in Great Britain and the United States. *Science, 252,* 1386–1389.

Chess, S., & Thomas, A. (1977). Temperamental individuality from childhood to adolescence. *Journal of Child Psychiatry, 16,* 218–226.

Chi, M. T. H. (1978). Knowledge structures and memory development. In R. S. Siegler (Ed.), *Children's thinking: What develops?* Hillsdale, NJ: Erlbaum.

Child Trends. (2000). Trends in sexual activity and contraceptive use among teens. *Child trends research brief.* Washington, DC: Author.

Child Trends. (2001). *Trends among Hispanic children, youth, and families.* Washington, DC: Author.

Children's Defense Fund. (1992). *The state of America's children, 1992.* Washington, DC: Author.

Children's Defense Fund. (2001). *A fair start.* Washington, DC: Author.

Chisholm, K. (1998). A three-year follow-up of attachment and indiscriminate friendliness in children adopted from Romanian orphanages. *Child Development, 69,* 1092–1106.

Chomsky, N. (1957). *Syntactic structures.* The Hague: Mouton.

Christian, K., Bachnan, H. J., & Morrison, F. J. (2001). Schooling and cognitive development. In R. J. Sternberg & E. L. Grigorenko (Eds.), *Environmental effects on cognitive development.* Mahwah, NJ: Erlbaum.

Christian, M. S., & Brent, R. L. (2002). Teratogen update: Evaluation of the reproductive and developmental risks of caffeine. *Teratology, 64,* 51–78.

Chun, K. M., Organista, P. B., & Marín, G. (Eds.). (2003). *Acculturation.* Washington, DC: American Psychological Association.

Chwo, M. J., Anderson, G. C., Good, M., Dowling, D. A., Shaiau, S. H., & Chu, D. M. (2002). A randomized controlled trial of early kangaroo care for preterm infants: Effects on temperature, weight, behavior, and acuity. *Journal of Nursing Research, 10,* 129–142.

Cicchetti, D. (2001). How a child builds a brain. In W. W. Hartup & R. A. Weinberg (Eds.), *Child psychology in retrospect and prospect.* Mahwah, NJ: Erlbaum.

Cicchetti, D. (2001, April). *The emergence, evolution, and future of developmental psychopathology.* Paper presented at the meeting of the Society for Research in Child Development, Minneapolis.

Cicchetti, D., & Toth, S. L. (1998). Perspectives on research and practice in developmental psychology. In W. Damon (Ed.), *Handbook of child psychology* (Vol. 4). New York: Wiley.

Cicchetti, D., Ganiban, J., & Barnett, D. (1991). Contributions from the study of high risk populations to understanding the development of emotion regulation. In J. Garber & K. Dodge (Eds.), *The development of emotion regulation and dysregulation.* New York: Cambridge University Press.

Cillessen, A. H. N., Van IJzendoorn, H. W., Van Lieshout, C. F. M., & Hartup, W. W. (1992). Heterogeneity among peer-rejected boys: Subtypes and stabilities. *Child Development, 63,* 893–905.

Circirelli, V. G. (1994). Sibling relationships in cross-cultural perspective. *Journal of Marriage and the Family, 56,* 7–20.

Clark, E. (2000). Language acquisition. In A. Kazdin (Ed.), *Encyclopedia of psychology.* Washington, DC, & New York: American Psychological Association and Oxford University Press.

Clark, R. D., & Hatfield, E. (1989). Gender differences in receptivity to sexual offers. *Journal of Psychology and Human Sexuality, 2,* 39–55.

Clark, S. D., Zabin, L. S., & Hardy, J. B. (1984). Sex, contraception, and parenthood: Experience and attitudes among urban black young men. *Family Planning Perspectives, 16,* 77–82.

Clarke-Stewart, K. A., & Fein, G. G. (1983). Early childhood programs. In P. H. Mussen (Ed.), *Handbook of child psychology* (4th ed., Vol. 2). New York: Wiley.

Clausson, B., Granath, F., Ekbom, A., Lundgren, S., Nordmark, A., Signorello, L. B., & Cnattingius, S. (2002). Effect of caffeine exposure during pregnancy on birth weight and gestational age. *American Journal of Epidemiology, 155,* 429–436.

Clifford, B. R., Gunter, B., & McAleer, J. L. (1995). *Television and children.* Hillsdale, NJ: Erlbaum.

Clifton, R. K., Morrongiello, B. A., Kulig, J. W., & Dowd, J. M. (1981). Developmental changes in auditory localization in infancy. In R. N. Aslin, J. R. Alberts, & M. R. Petersen (Eds.), *Development of perception* (Vol. 1). Orlando, FL: Academic Press.

Clifton, R. K., Muir, D. W., Ashmead, D. H., & Clarkson, M. G. (1993). Is visually guided reaching in early infancy a myth? *Child Development, 64,* 1099–1110.

Clinchy, B. M., Mansfield, A. F., & Schott, J. L. (1995, March). *Development of narrative and scientific modes of thought in middle childhood.* Paper presented at the meeting of the Society for Research in Child Development, Indianapolis.

Cnattingius, S., Bergstrom, R., Lipworth, L., & Kramer, M. S. (1998). Prepregnancy weight and the risk of adverse pregnancy outcomes. *New England Journal of Medicine, 338,* 147–152.

Cnattingius, S., Signorello, L. B., Anneren, G., Classon, B., Ekbom, A., Ljunger, E., Blot, W. J., McLaughlin, J. K., Petersson, G., Rane, A., & Granath, F. (2000). Caffeine intake and the risk of first-trimester spontaneous abortion. *New England Journal of Medicine, 343,* 1839–1845.

CNN and the National Science Foundation. (1997). *Poll on technology and education.* Washington, DC: National Science Foundation.

Cohen, G. J. (2000). *American Academy of Pediatrics guide to your child's sleep: Birth through Adolescence.* New York: Villard Books.

Cohen, L. B., & Sashon, C. H. (2003). Infant perception and cognition. In I. B. Weiner (Ed.), *Handbook of psychology, vol. 6.* New York: Wiley.

Cohn, J. F., & Tronick, E. Z. (1988). Mother-infant face-to-face interaction. Influence is bidirectional and unrelated to periodic cycles in either partner's behavior. *Developmental Psychology, 24,* 396–397.

Coie, J. D., & Dodge, K. A. (1998). Aggression and antisocial behavior. In W. Damon (Ed.), *Handbook of child psychology* (5th ed., Vol. 3). New York: Wiley.

Colapinto, J. (2000). *As nature made him.* New York: Simon & Schuster.

Colby, A., Kohlberg, L., Gibbs, J., & Lieberman, M. (1983). A longitudinal study of moral judgment. *Monographs of the Society for Research in Child Development, 48* (21, Serial No. 201).

Cole, C. F., Richman, B. A., & Brown, S. K. (2001). The world of *Sesame Street* research. In S. M. Fisch & R. T. Truglio (Eds.), *"G" is for growing: Thirty years of research on children and* Sesame Street. Mahwah, NJ: Erlbaum.

Coles, R. (1970). *Erik H. Erikson: The growth of his work.* Boston: Little, Brown.

Coley, R. (2001). *Differences in the gender gap: Comparisons across racial/ethnic groups in the United States.* Princeton, NJ: Educational Testing Service.

Coll, C. T. G., & Pachter, L. M. (2002). Ethnic and minority parenting. In M. H. Bornstein (Ed.), *Handbook of parenting* (2nd ed.). Mahwah, NJ: Erlbaum.

Coll, C. T. G., Erkut, S., Alarcon, O., Garcia, H. A. V., & Tropp, L. (1995, March). *Puerto Rican adolescents and families: Lessons in construct and instrument development.* Paper presented at the meeting of the Society for Research in Child Development, Indianapolis.

Coll, C. T. G., & Pachter, L. M. (2002). Ethnic and minority parenting. In M. H. Bornstein (ed.), *Handbook of parenting* (2nd ed., Vol. 4) Mahwah, NJ: Erlbaum.

Collins, W. A. (2002, April). *More than myth: The developmental significance of romantic relationships during adolescence.* Paper presented at the meeting of the Society for Research in Adolescence, New Orleans.

Collins, W. A., Harris, M., & Susman, A. (1995, March). Parenting during middle childhood. In M. H. Bornstein (Ed.), *Handbook of parenting* (Vol. 1). Hillsdale, NJ: Erlbaum.

Collins, W. A., Hennighausen, K. H., & Sroufe, L. A. (1998, June). *Developmental precursors of intimacy in romantic relationships: A longitudinal analysis.* Paper presented at International Conference on Personal Relationships, Saratoga Springs, NY.

Collins, W. A., Maccoby, E. E., Steinberg, L., Hetherington, E. M., & Bornstein, M. H. (2000). Contemporary research on parenting: The case for nature and nurture. *American Psychologist, 55,* 218–232.

Collins, W. A., Maccoby, E. E., Steinberg, L., Hetherington, E. M., & Bornstein, M. H. (2001). Toward nature WITH nurture. *American Psychologist, 56,* 171–173.

Collins, W. A., & Madsen, S. D. (2002). Parenting during middle childhood. In M. H. Bornstein (Ed.), *Handbook of parenting* (2nd ed., Vol. 1). Mahwah, NJ: Erlbaum.

Comas-Díaz, L. (2001). Hispanics, Latinos, or Americanos: The evolution of identity. *Cultural Diversity and Ethnic Minority Psychology, 7,* 115–120.

Comer, J. P. (1988). Educating poor minority children. *Scientific American, 259,* 42–48.

Comer, J. P., Haynes, N. M., Joyner, E. T., & Ben-Avie, M. (1996). *Rallying the whole village: The Conner process for reforming urban education.* New York: Teachers College Press.

Committee on Drugs. (2000). Use of psychoactive medication during pregnancy and possible effects on the fetus and newborn. *Pediatrics, 105,* 880–887.

Committee on Fetus and Newborn. (2000). Prevention and management of pain and stress in the newborn. *Pediatrics, 105,* 454–461.

Committee on Pediatric AIDS. (2000). Identification and care of HIV-exposed and HIV-infected infants, children, and adolescents. *Pediatrics, 106,* 149–153.

Committee on Sports Medicine and Fitness. (2000). Injuries in youth soccer: A subject review. *Pediatrics, 105,* 659–661.

Committee on Substance Abuse. (2000). Fetal alcohol syndrome and alcohol-related neurodevelopmental disorders. *Pediatrics, 106,* 258–261.

Commoner, B. (2002). Unraveling the DNA myth: The spurious foundation of genetic engineering. *Harper's Magazine, 304,* 39–47.

Compas, B. E., Connor-Smith, J. K., Saltzman, H., Thomsen, A. H., & Wadsworth, M. E. (2001). *Psychological Bulletin, 127,* 87–127.

Compas, B. E., & Grant, K. E. (1993, March). *Stress and adolescent depressive symptoms: Underlying mechanisms and processes.* Paper presented at the biennial meeting of the Society for Research in Child Development, New Orleans.

Condry, K. F., Smith, W. C., & Spelke, E. S. (2001). Development of perceptual organization. In F. Lacerda, C. von Hofsten, & M. Heimann (Eds.), *Emerging cognitive abilities in infancy.* Mahwah, NJ: Erlbaum.

Conduct Problems Prevention Research Group. (2002). Evaluation of the first

3 years of the Fast Track prevention trial with children at high risk for adolescent conduct problems. *Journal of Abnormal Child Psychology, 30,* 19–35.

Conger, R., & Reuter, M. (1996). Siblings, parents, and peers: A longitudinal study of social influences in adolescent risk for alcohol use and abuse. In G. H. Brody (Ed.), *Sibling relationships: Their causes and consequences.* Norwood, NJ: Ablex.

Conger, R. D., & Chao, W. (1996). Adolescent depressed mood. In R. L. Simons (Ed.), *Understanding differences between divorced and intact families: Stress, interaction, and child outcome.* Thousand Oaks, CA: Sage.

Conger, R. D., & Ge, X. (1999). Conflict and cohesion in parent-adolescent relations: Changes in emotional expression. In M. J. Cox & J. Brooks-Gunn (Eds.), *Conflict and cohesion in families.* Mahwah, NJ: Erlbaum.

Cook, M., & Birch, R. (1984). Infant perception of the shapes of tilted plane forms. *Infant Behavior and Child Development, 7,* 389–402.

Cooper, C., Jackson, J. F., Azmitia, M., Lopez, E., & Dunbar, N. (1995). Bridging students' multiple worlds: African American and Latino youth in academic outreach programs. In R. F. Macias & R. G. Garcia-Ramos (Eds.), *Changing schools for changing students.* Santa Barbara: University of California Linguistic Minority Research Institute.

Cooper, C. R., & Ayers-Lopez, S. (1985). Family and peer systems in early adolescence: New models of the role of relationships in development. *Journal of Early Adolescence, 5,* 9–22.

Cooper, C. R., & Grotevant, H. D. (1989, April). *Individuality and connectedness in the family and adolescent's self and relational competence.* Paper presented at the meeting of the Society for Research in Child Development, Kansas City.

Cooper, C. R., Grotevant, H. D., Moore, M. S., & Condon, S. M. (1982, August). *Family support and conflict: Both foster adolescent identity and role taking.* Paper presented at the meeting of the American Psychological Association, Washington, DC.

Cooper, M. L., Shaver, P. R., & Collins, N. L. (1998). Attachment styles, emotional regulation, and adjustment in adolescence. *Journal of Personality and Social Psychology, 74,* 1380–1397.

Coopersmith, S. (1967). *The antecedents of self-esteem.* San Francisco: W. H. Freeman.

Cornell, D. (1998, April 6). Commentary, *Newsweek,* p. 24.

Corrigan, R. (1981). The effects of task and practice on search for invisibly displaced objects. *Developmental Review, 1,* 1–17.

Corsini, R. J. (1999). *The dictionary of psychology.* Philadelphia: Brunner/Mazel.

Cosey, E. J., & Bechtel, G. A. (2001). Family support and prenatal care among unmarried African American teenage primiparas. *Journal of Community Health and Nursing, 18,* 107–114.

Cosmides, L., Tooby, J., Cronin, H., & Curry, O. (Eds.). (2003). *What is evolutionary psychology? Explaining the new science of the mind.* New Haven, CT: Yale University Press.

Cote, J. E., & Levine, C. (1988). On critiquing the identity crisis paradigm: A rejoinder to Waterman. *Developmental Review, 8,* 209–218.

Council of Economic Advisors. (2000). *Teens and their parents in the 21st century: An examination of trends in teen behavior and the role of parent involvement.* Washington, DC: Author.

Cowan, C. P., & Cowan, P. A. (2000). *When partners become parents.* Mahwah, NJ: Erlbaum.

Cowan, F., Rutherford, M., Groenendaal, F., Eken, P., Mercuri, E., Bydder, G. M., Meiners, L. C., Dubowitz, L. M., & de Vries, L. S. (2003). Origin and timing of brain lesions in term infants with neonatal encephalopathy. *Lancet, 361,* 736–742.

Cowley, G. (1998, April 6). Why children turn violent. *Newsweek,* pp. 24–25.

Cox, J. L., Holden, J. M., & Sagovsky, R. (1987). Detection of postnatal depression: Development of the 10-items Edinburgh Postnatal Depression Scale. *British Journal of Psychiatry, 150,* 782–786.

Cox, M. J., Owne, M. T., Lewis, J. M., & Henderson, V. K. (1989). Marriage, adult adjustment, and early parenting. *Child Development, 60,* 1015–1024.

Craik, F. I. M., & Lockhart, R. S. (1972). Levels of processing: A framework for memory research. *Journal of Verbal Learning and Verbal Behavior, 11,* 671–684.

Crawford, M., & Unger, R. (2000). *Women and gender* (3rd ed.). New York: McGraw-Hill.

Crick, N. R., Nelson, D. A., Morales, J. R., Cullerton-Sen, C., Casas, J. F., & Hickman, S. (2001). Relational victimization in childhood and adolescence: I hurt you through the grapevine. In J. Juvonen & S. Graham (Eds.), *Peer harassment in school: The plight of the vulnerable and victimized,* New York: Guilford.

Crnic, K. (1996). *Children, families, and stress.* Cambridge, MA: Blackwell.

Crockenberg, S. B. (1986). Are temperamental differences in babies associated with predictable differences in caregiving? In J. V. Lerner & R. M. Lerner (Eds.), *Temperament and social interaction during infancy and childhood.* San Francisco: Jossey-Bass.

Crockenberg, S., & Soby, B. (1989) Self-esteem and teenage pregnancy. In A. Mecca, N. J. Smelser, & J. Vasconcellos (Eds.), *The social importance of self-esteem.* Berkeley: University of California Press.

Cromer, R. (1987). Receptive language in the mentally retarded: Processes and diagnostic distinctions. In R. Schiefelbusch & L. Lloyd (Eds.), *Language perspectives: Acquisition, retardation, and intervention.* Baltimore: University Park Press.

Cronin, C. (2003). First-time mothers—identifying their needs, perceptions, and experiences. *Journal of Clinical Nursing, 12,* 260–267.

Crouter, A. C., & Booth, A. (Eds.). (2003). *Children's influence on family dynamics.* Mahwah, NJ: Erlbaum.

Crowley, K., Callahan, M. A., Tenenbaum, H. R., & Allen, E. (2001). Parents explain more to boys than to girls during shared scientific thinking. *Psychological Science, 12,* 258–261.

Croyle, R. T. (2000). Genetic counseling. In A. Kazdin (Ed.), *Encyclopedia of psychology.* Washington, DC, & New York: American Psychological Association and Oxford University Press.

Cullen, K. (2001). *Context and eating behavior in children.* Unpublished research, Children's Nutrition Research Center, Baylor School of Medicine, Houston.

Cummings, E. M. (1987). Coping with background anger in early childhood. *Child Development. 58,* 976–984.

Cummings, E. M., Braungar-Rieker, J. M., & Du Rocher-Schudlich, T. (2003). Emotion and personality development. In I. B. Weiner (Ed.), *Handbook of psychology, Vol. 6.* New York: Wiley.

Cummings, M. (2003). *Human heredity* (6th ed.). Belmont, CA: Wadsworth.

Curran, K., DuCette, J., Eisenstein, J., & Hyman, I. A. (2001, August). *Statistical analysis of the cross-cultural data: The third year.* Paper presented at the meeting of the American Psychological Association, San Francisco.

Curtiss, S. (1977). *Genie.* New York: Academic Press.

Cushner, K. (1999). *Human diversity in action.* New York: McGraw-Hill.

Cushner, K. H. (2003). *Human diversity in action: Developing multicultural competencies for the classroom.* New York: McGraw-Hill.

Cushner, K. H., McClelland, A., & Safford, P. (2003). *Human diversity in action: An integrative approach* (4th ed.). New York: McGraw-Hill.

Dabbs, J. M., Jr., Frady, R. I., Carr, T. S., & Besch, M. F. (1987). Saliva, testosterone, and criminal violence in young adult prison inmates. *Psychosomatic Medicine, 49,* 174–182.

Dabbs, J. M., Jr., & Morris, R. (1990). Testosterone, social class, and antisocial behavior in a sample of 4,462 men. *Psychological Science, 1,* 209–211.

Dahl, R. E. (2001). Affect regulation, brain development, and behavioral/emotional health in adolescence. *CNS Spectrums, 6,* 60–72.

Damon, W. (1988). *The moral child.* New York: Free Press.

Damon, W. (1991). Self-concept, adolescent. In R. M. Lerner, A. C. Petersen, & J. Brooks-Gunn (Eds.), *Encyclopedia of adolescence* (Vol. 2). New York: Garland.

Damon, W. (1995). *Greater expectations.* New York: Free Press.

Damon, W. (2003). Bringing in a new era in the field of youth development. In R. M. Lerner, F. Jacobs, & D. Wertlieb (Eds.), *Handbook of applied developmental psychology* (Vol. 2). Thousand Oaks, CA: Sage.

Damon, W., & Hart, D. (1988). *Self-understanding in childhood and adolescence.* New York: Cambridge University Press.

Darwin, C. (1859). *On the origin of species.* London: John Murray.

Das, J. P. (2000). Mental retardation. In A. Kazdin (Ed.), *Encyclopedia of psychology.* Washington, DC, & New York: American Psychological Association and Oxford University Press.

Dashe, J. S., Sheffield, J. S., Olscher, D. A., Tood, S. J., Jackson, G. L., & Wendel, G. D. (2002). Relationship between maternal methadone dosage and neonatal withdrawal. *Obstetrics and Gynecology, 100,* 1244–1249.

Dattilio, F. M. (Ed.). (2001). *Case studies in couple and family therapy.* New York: Guilford.

D'Augelli, A. R. (1991). Gay men in college: Identity processes and adaptations. *Journal of College Student Development, 32,* 140–146.

Davidson, D. (1996). The effects of decision characteristics on children's selective search of predecisional information. *Acta Psychologica, 92,* 263–281.

Davies, K. (2001). *Cracking the genome.* New York: Free Press.

Davis, K. (1996). *Families.* Pacific Grove, CA: Brooks/Cole.

Davis, L., & Keyser, J. (1997). *Becoming the parent you want to be.* New York: Broadway Books.

Davison, G. C., & Neale, J. M. (2001). *Abnormal psychology* (8th ed.). New York: Wiley.

Davison, K. K., & Birth, L. L. (2001). Weight status, parent reaction, and self-concept in five-year-old girls. *Pediatrics, 107,* 46–53.

Davisson, M. T., Gardiner, K., & Costa, A. C. (2001). Report of the ninth international workshop on the molecular biology of human chromosome 21 and Down syndrome. *Cytogenetic Cell Genetics, 92,* 1–22.

Daws, D. (2000). *Through the night.* San Francisco: Free Association Books.

Day, R. D., & Lamb, M. E. (2003). Conceptualizing and measuring father involvement: Pathways, problems, and progress. In R. D. Day & M. E. Lamb (Eds.), *Conceptualizing and measuring father involvement.* Mahwah, NJ: Erlbaum.

Day, R. H., & McKenzie, B. E. (1973). Perceptual shape constancy in early infancy. *Perception, 2,* 315–320.

de la Rochebrochard, E., & Thonneau, P. (2002). Paternal age and maternal age are risk factors for miscarriage: Results of a multicentre European study. *Human Reproduction, 17,* 1649–1656.

de Villiers, J. G., & de Villiers, P. A. (1999). Language development. In M. H. Bornstein & M. E. Lamb (Eds.), *Developmental psychology: An advanced textbook* (4th ed.). Mahwah, NJ: Erlbaum.

de Wolff, M. S., & van IJzendoorn, M. H. (1997). Sensitivity and attachment: A meta-analysis on parental antecedents of infant attachment. *Child Development, 68,* 571–591.

DeCasper, A. J., & Spence, M. J. (1986). Prenatal maternal speech influences newborn's perception of speech sounds. *Infant Behavior and Development, 9,* 133–150.

deCharms, R. (1984). Motivation enhancement in educational settings. In R. Ames & C. Ames (Eds.), *Research on motivation in education* (Vol. 1). Orlando: Academic Press.

Deci, E. (1975). *Intrinsic motivation.* New York: Plenum Press.

Deci, E., & Ryan, R. (1994). Promoting self-determined education. *Scandinavian Journal of Educational Research, 38,* 3–14.

Deci, E. L., Koestner, R., & Ryan, R. M. (2001). Extrinsic rewards and intrinsic motivation in education: Reconsidered once again. *Review of Educational Research, 71,* 1–28.

DeGarmo, D. S., Forgatch, M. S., & Martinez, C. R. (1998). *Parenting of divorced mothers as a link between social status and boys' academic outcomes: Unpacking the effects of SES.* Unpublished manuscript, Oregon Social Learning Center, University of Oregon, Eugene.

deHaan, M., & Nelson, C. A. (1999). Brain activity differentiates face and object processing in 6-month-old infants. *Developmental Psychology, 35,* 1113–1121.

DeLamater, J., & MacCorquodale, P. (1979). *Premarital sexuality.* Madison: University of Wisconsin Press.

DeLoache, J. S. (1984). Oh where, oh where: Memory-based searching by very young children. In C. Sophian (Ed.), *Origins of cognitive skills.* Hillsdale, NJ: Erlbaum.

DeLoache, J. S. (1989). The development of representation in young children. In H. W. Reese (Ed.), *Advances in child development and behavior* (Vol. 22, pp. 1–39). New York: Academic Press.

DeLoache, J. S. (2002). Early development of the understanding and use of symbolic artifacts. In U. Goswami (Ed.), *Blackwell handbook of childhood cognitive development.* Malden, MA: Blackwell.

DeLoache, J. S., Cassidy, D. J., & Brown, A. L. (1985). Precursors of mnemonic strategies in very young children's memory. *Child Development, 56,* 125–137.

DeLoache, J. S., Cassidy, D. J., & Carpenter, C. J. (1987). The Three Bears are all boys: Mothers' gender labeling of neutral picture book characters. *Sex Roles, 17,* 163–178.

DeLoache. J. S., Miller, K. F., & Pierroutsakos, S. L. (1997). Reasoning and problem solving. In D. Kuhn & R. S. Siegler (Eds.), *Handbook of child psychology* (5th ed., Vol. 2). New York: Wiley.

Deluca, P. (1999, April). *Does illness enhance children's understanding of the inside of the body, death, and illness contagion?* Paper presented at the meeting of the Society for Research in Child Development, Albuquerque.

DeMarie-Dreblow, D., & Miller, P. H. (1988). The development of children's strategies for selective attention: Evidence for a transitional period. *Child Development, 59,* 1504–1513.

Demetriou, A., Christou, C., Spanoudis, G., & Platsidou, M. (2002). The development of mental processing: Efficiency, working memory, and thinking. *Monographs of the Society for Research in Child Development, 67* (1, Serial No. 168).

Dempster, F. N. (1981). Memory span: Sources of individual and developmental differences. *Psychological Bulletin, 89,* 63–100.

Denham, S. A., Blair, K. A., DeMulder, E., Levitas, J., Sawyer, K., Auerbach-Major, S., & Queenan, P. (2003). Preschool emotional competence: pathway to social competence? *Child Development, 74,* 238–256.

Denham, S. A., Cook, M., & Zoller, D. (1992). Maternal emotional responsiveness to toddlers' social-emotional functioning. *Journal of Child Psychology and Psychiatry, 34,* 715–728.

Denmark, F. L., Russo, N. F., Frieze, I. H., & Eschuzur, J. (1988). Guidelines for avoiding sexism in psychological research: A report of the ad hoc committee on nonsexist research. *American Psychologist, 43,* 582–585.

Dennebaum, J. M., & Kulberg, J. M. (1994). Kindergarten retention and transition classrooms: Their relationship to achievement. *Psychology in the Schools, 31,* 5–12.

Denny, C. B. (2001). Stimulant effects in attention deficit hyperactivity disorder. *Journal of Clinical Child Psychology, 30,* 98–109.

Dettmer, P., Dyck, N., & Thurston, L. (2002). *Consultation, collaboration, and teamwork for students with special needs* (4th ed.). Boston: Allyn & Bacon.

Dewey, J. (1933). *How we think.* Lexington, MA: D.C. Heath.

Dezolt, D. M., & Hull, S. H. (2001). Classroom and school climate. In J. Worell (Ed.), *Encyclopedia of women and gender.* San Diego: Academic Press.

Diamond, A. (2001). A model system for studying the role of dopamine in the prefrontal cortex during early development in humans: Early and continuously treated phenylketonuria. In C. Nelson & M. Luciana (Eds.), *Handbook of developmental cognitive neuroscience.* Cambridge, MA: MIT Press.

Diamond, A. D. (1985). Development of the ability to use recall to guide action, as indicated by infants' performance on AB. *Child Development, 56,* 868–883.

Diamond, A. D. (1995, March). *Exciting new findings in development cognitive neuroscience.* Paper presented at the meeting of the Society for Research in Child Development, Indianapolis.

Diamond, L. (2003). Love matters: Romantic relations among sexual minority youth. In P. Florsheim (Ed.), *Adolescent romantic relations and sexual behavior.* Mahwah, NJ: Erlbaum.

Diamond, L., & Savin-Williams, R. C. (2003). The intimate relationships of sexual-minority youths. In G. Adams & M. Berzonsky (Eds.), *Blackwell handbook of adolescence.* Malden, MA: Blackwell.

Diamond, L., Savin-Williams, R. C., & Dubé, E. M. (1999). Sex, dating, passionate friendships, and romance: Intimate peer relations among lesbian, gay, and bisexual adolescents. In W. Furman, B. B. Brown, & C. Feiring (Eds.), *The development of relationships during adolescence.* New York: Cambridge University Press.

Diamond, M., & Sigmundson, H. K. (1997). Sex reassignment at birth: Long-term review and clinical implications. *Archives of Pediatric and Adolescent Medicine, 151,* 298–304.

Diaz, C. (2003). *Multicultural education in the 21st century.* Boston: Allyn & Bacon.

Dickerscheid, J. D., Schwarz, P. M., Noir, S., & El-Taliawy, T. (1988). Gender concept development of preschool-aged children in the United States and Egypt. *Sex Roles, 18,* 669–677.

Dieter, J. N., Field, T., Hernandez-Reif, M., Jones, N. A., Lecanuet, J. P., Salman, F. A., & Redzepi, M. (2001). Maternal depression and increased fetal activity. *Journal of Obstetrics and Gynecology, 21,* 468–473.

Dishion, T. (2001, April). *Understanding and preventing adolescent drug use.* Paper presented at the meeting of the Society for Research in Child Development, Minneapolis.

Dix, T. (1991). The affective organization of parenting: Adaptive and maladaptive processes. *Psychological Bulletin, 110,* 3–25.

Dodge, K. A. (1993). Social cognitive mechanisms in the development of conduct disorder and depression. *Annual Review of Psychology, 44,* 559–584.

Dodge, K. A. (2001). The science of youth violence prevention: Progressing from developmental psychopathology to efficacy to effectiveness in public policy. *American Journal of Preventive Medicine, 20,* 63–70.

Dolcini, M. M., Coh, L. D., Adler, N. E., Millstein, S. G., Irwin, C. E., Kegeles, S. M., & Stone, G. C. (1989). Adolescent egocentrism and feelings of invulnerability: Are they related? *Journal of Early Adolescence, 9,* 409–418.

Donnerstein, E. (2001). Media violence. In J. Worell (Ed.), *Encyclopedia of gender and women.* San Diego: Academic Press.

Donnerstein, E. (2002). The Internet. In V. C. Strasburger & B. J. Wilson (Eds.), *Children, adolescents, and the media.* Newbury Park, CA: Sage.

Donovan, P. (1993). *Testing positive: Sexually transmitted disease and the public health response.* New York: Alan Guttmacher Institute.

Dorn, L. D., & Lucas, F. L. (1995, March). *Do hormone-behavior relations vary depending upon the endocrine and psychological status of the adolescent?* Paper presented at the meeting of the Society for Research in Child Development, Indianapolis.

Dornbusch, S., & Kaufman, J. (2001). The social structure of the U.S. high school. In T. Urdan & F. Pajares (Eds.), *Adolescence and education.* Greenwich, CT: IAP.

Dorr, A., Rabin, B. E., & Irlen, S. (2002). Parents, children, and the media. In M. H. Bornstein (Ed.), *Handbook of parenting* (2nd ed., Vol. 5). Mahwah, NJ: Erlbaum.

Douglas, W. (2003). *Television families.* Mahwah, NJ: Erlbaum.

Douvan, E., & Adelson, J. (1966). *The adolescent experience.* New York: Wiley.

Dowda, M., Ainsworth, B. E., Addy, C. L., Saunders, R., & Riner, W. (2001). Environmental influences, physical activity, and weight status in 8- to 16-year-olds. *Archives of Pediatric and Adolescent Medicine, 155,* 711–717.

Downey, G., & Bonica, C. A. (1997, April). *Characteristics of early adolescent dating relationships.* Paper presented at the meeting of the Society for Research in Child Development, Washington, DC.

Downey, G., & Coyne, J. C. (1990). Children of depressed parents: An integrative review. *Psychological Bulletin, 108,* 50–76.

Dryfoos, J. G. (1990). *Adolescents at risk: Prevalence or prevention.* New York: Oxford University Press.

Dryfoos, J. G. (1995). Full service schools: Revolution or fad? *Journal of Research on Adolescence, 5,* 147–172.

DuBois, D. L., & Hirsch, B. J. (1990). School and neighborhood friendship patterns of Blacks and Whites in early adolescence. *Child Development, 61,* 524–536.

DuBois, D. L., Felner, R. D., & Brand, S. (1997, April). *Self-esteem profiles and adjustment in early adolescence: A two-year longitudinal study.* Paper presented at the meeting of the Society for Research in Child Development, Washington, DC.

Duck, S. W. (1975). Personality similarity and friendship choices by adolescents. *European Journal of Social Psychology, 5,* 351–365.

Duncan, G. J., Brooks-Gunn, J., & Klebanov, P. K. (1994). Economic deprivation and early childhood development. *Child Development, 65,* 296–318.

Duncker, K. (1945). On problem solving. *Psychological Monographs, 58* (Whole No. 270).

Dunkel-Schetter, C. (1998). Maternal stress and preterm delivery. *Prenatal and Neonatal Medicine, 3,* 39–42.

Dunkel-Schetter, C. (1999, August). *Is maternal stress a risk factor for adverse birth outcomes?* Paper presented at the meeting of the American Psychological Association, Boston.

Dunkel-Schetter, C., Gurung, R. A. R., Lobel, M., & Wadhwa, P. D. (2001). Stress processes in pregnancy and birth. In A. Baum, T. A. Revenson, & J. E. Singer (Eds.), *Handbook of health psychology.* Mahwah, NJ: Erlbaum.

Dunn, J., & Brown, J. (1994). Affect expression in the family, children's understanding of emotions, and their interactions with others. *Merrill-Palmer Quarterly, 40,* 120–137.

Dunn, J., Davies, L. C., O'Connor, T. G., & Sturgess, W. (2001). Family lives and friendships: The perspectives of children in step-, single-parent, and nonstep families. *Journal of Family Psychology, 15,* 272–287.

Dunn, J., & Kendrick, C. (1982). *Siblings.* Cambridge, MA: Harvard University Press.

Dunn, L., & Kontos, S. (1997). What have we learned about developmentally appropriate education? *Young Children, 52* (2), 4–13.

Dunnewold, A., & Sanford, D. G. (1994). *Postpartum survival guide.* Oakland: New Harbinger.

Dunphy, D. C. (1963). The social structure of urban adolescent peer groups. *Society, 26,* 230–246.

Durkin, K. (1985). Television and sex-role acquisition: 1. Content. *British Journal of Social Psychology, 24,* 101–113.

Durkin, K., & Hutchins, G. (1984). Challenging traditional sex role stereotypes via career education broadcasts: The reactions of young secondary school pupils. *Journal of Educational Television, 10,* 25–33.

Durrant, J. E. (2000). Trends in youth crime and well-being since the abolition of corporal punishment in Sweden. *Youth and Society, 31* (4), 437–455.

Durrant, R., & Ellis, B. (2003). Evolutionary psychology. In I. B. Weiner (Ed.), *Encyclopedia of psychology* (Vol. III). New York: Wiley.

Dusek, J. B., & McIntyre, J. G. (2003). Self-concept and self-esteem development. In G. Adams & M. Berzonsky (Eds.), *Blackwell handbook of adolescence.* Malden, MA: Blackwell.

Dweck, C. (1996). Social motivation: Goals and social-cognitive processes. In J. Juvonen & K. R. Wentzel (Eds.), *Social motivation.* New York: Cambridge University Press.

Dweck, C., & Elliott, E. (1983). Achievement motivation. In P. Mussen (Ed.), *Handbook of child psychology* (4th ed., Vol. 4). New York: Wiley.

Dweck, C., & Leggett, E. (1988). A social cognitive approach to motivation and personality. *Psychological Review, 95,* 256–273.

E

Eagle, M. (2000). Psychoanalytic theory: History of the field. In A. Kazdin (Ed.), *Encyclopedia of psychology.* Washington, DC, & New York: American Psychological Association and Oxford University Press.

Eagly, A. H. (1996). Differences between women and men. *American Psychologist, 51,* 158–159.

Eagly, A. H. (2000). Gender roles. In A. Kazdin (Ed.), *Encyclopedia of psychology.* Washington, DC, & New York: American Psychological Association and Oxford University Press.

Eagly, A. H. (2001). Social role theory of sex differences and similarities. In J. Worell (Ed.), *Encyclopedia of women and gender.* San Diego: Academic Press.

Eagly, A. H., & Crowley, M. (1986). Gender and helping behavior: A meta-analytic review of the social psychological literature. *Psychological Bulletin, 100,* 283–308.

Eagly, A. H., & Diekman, A. B. (2003). The malleability of sex differences in response to social roles. In L. G. Aspinwall & V. M. Staudinger (Eds.), *A psychology of human strengths.* Washington, DC: American Psychological Association.

Eagly A. H., & Steffen V. J. (1986). Gender and aggressive behavior: A meta-analytic review of the social psychological literature. *Psychological Bulletin, 100,* 309–330.

Eaves, L. J., & Silberg, J. L. (2003). Modulation of gene expression by genetic and environmental heterogeneity in timing of developmental milestones. *Behavior Genetics, 33,* 1–6.

Eccles, J. S. (2002, April). *Ethnicity as a context for development.* Paper presented at the meeting of the Society for Research on Adolescence, New Orleans.

Eccles, J. S., & Midgley, C. (1989). Stage-environment fit: Developmentally appropriate classrooms for young adolescents. In C. Ames & R. Ames (Eds.), *Research on motivation in education* (Vol. 3). Orlando: Academic Press.

Eccles, J. S., & Wigfield, A. (2002). Motivational beliefs, values, and goals. *Annual Review of Psychology* (Vol. 53). Palo Alto, CA: Annual Reviews.

Eccles, J. S., Wigfield, A., & Schiefele, U. (1998). Motivation to succeed. In W. Damon (Ed.), *Handbook of child psychology* (5th ed., Vol. 3). New York: Wiley.

Edelman, M. W. (1997, April). *Children, families and social policy.* Paper presented at the meeting of the Society for Research in Child Development, Washington, DC.

Eden, G. F., & Moats, L. (2002). The role of neuroscience in the remediation of students with dyslexia. *Nature Neuroscience, 5* (Suppl.), 1080–1084.

Educational Testing Service. (1992, February). *Cross-national comparison of 9–13 year olds' science and math achievement.* Princeton, NJ: Educational Testing Service.

Edwards, C. P., & Liu, W. (2002). Parenting toddlers. In M. H. Bornstein (Ed.), *Handbook of parenting* (2nd ed., Vol. 1). Mahwah, NJ: Erlbaum.

Egeland, B., Jacobvitz, D., & Sroufe, L. A. (1988). Breaking the cycle of abuse. *New Directions for Child Development, 11,* 77–92.

Eggebeen, D. J., & Knoester, C. (2001). Does fatherhood matter for men? *Journal of Marriage and the Family, 63,* 381–393.

Ehrhardt, A. A. (1987). A transactional perspective on the development of gender differences. In J. M. Reinisch, L. A. Rosenblum, & S. A. Sanders (Eds.), *Masculinity/femininity: Basic perspectives.* New York: Oxford University Press.

Ehrlich, R., Jordaan, E., Du Toit, D., Potter, P., Volmink, J., Zwarentein, M., & Weinberg, E. (2001). Household smoking and bronchial hyperresponsiveness in children with asthma. *Journal of Asthma, 38,* 239–251.

Eiferman, R. R. (1971). Social play in childhood. In R. Herron & B. Sutton-Smith (Eds.), *Child's play.* New York: Wiley.

Eiger, M. S., & Olds, S. W. (1999). *The complete book of breastfeeding* (3rd ed.). New York: Bantam.

Eisenberg, N. (Ed.). (1982). *The development of prosocial behavior.* New York: Wiley.

Eisenberg, N. (1998). Introduction. In N. Eisenberg (Ed.), *Handbook of child psychology* (5th ed., Vol. 3). New York: Wiley.

Eisenberg, N. (2001). Emotion-regulated regulation and its relation to quality of social functioning. In W. W. Hartup & R. A. Weinberg (Eds.), *Child psychology in retrospect and prospect*. Mahwah, NJ: Erlbaum.

Eisenberg, N. (2002). Prosocial behavior, empathy, and sympathy. In M. H. Bornstein, L. Davidson, C. L. M. Keyes, & K. A. Moore (Eds.), *Well-being*. Mahwah, NJ: Erlbaum.

Eisenberg, N., & Fabes, R. A. (1994). Emotional regulation and the development of social competence. In M. Clark (Ed.), *Review of personality and social psychology*. Newbury Park, CA: Sage.

Eisenberg, N., & Fabes, R. A. (1998). Prosocial development. In N. Eisenberg (Ed.), *Handbook of child psychology* (5th ed., Vol. 3). New York: Wiley.

Eisenberg, N., Fabes, R. A., Guthrie, I. K., & Reiser, M. (2002). The role of emotionality and regulation in children's social competence and adjustment. In L. Pulkkinen & A. Caspi (Eds.), *Paths to successful development*. New York: Cambridge University Press.

Eisenberg, N., Martin, C. L., & Fabes, R. A. (1996). Gender development and gender effects. In D. C. Berliner & R. C. Calfee (Eds.), *Handbook of educational psychology*. New York: Macmillan.

Eisenberg, N., & Murphy, B. (1995). Parenting and children's moral development. In M. H. Bornstein (Ed.), *Children and parenting* (Vol. 4). Hillsdale, NJ: Erlbaum.

Eisenberg, N., Shea, C. I., Carolo, G., & Knight, G. P. (1991). Empathy-related responding and cognition: A chicken and egg dilemma. In W. M. Kurtines & J. Gewirtz (Eds.), *Moral behavior and development* (Vol. 2). Hillsdale, NJ: Erlbaum.

Eisenberg, N., & Valiente, C. (2002). Parenting and children's prosocial and moral development. In M. H. Bornstein (Ed.), *Handbook of parenting* (2nd ed.). Mahwah, NJ: Erlbaum.

Eisenberg, N., & Wang, V. O. (2003). Toward a positive psychology: Social Developmental and cultural contributions. In L. G. Aspinwall & U. M. Staudinger (Eds.), *A psychology of human strengths*. Washington, DC: American Psychological Association.

Ekwo, E. E., & Moawad, A. (2000). Maternal age and preterm births in a black population. *Pediatric Perinatal Epidemiology, 2,* 145–151.

Elder, G. H. (1980). Adolescence in historical perspective. In J. Adelson (Ed.), *Handbook of adolescent psychology*. New York: Wiley.

Elder, G. H., & Conger, R. D. (2002). *Children of the land*. Chicago: University of Chicago Press.

El-Ghobashy, A. A., & West, C. R. (2003). The human sperm head: a key for successful fertilization. *Journal of Andrology, 24,* 232–238.

Elicker, J. (1996). A knitting tale: Reflections on scaffolding. *Childhood Education, 72,* 29–32.

Elkind, D. (1961). Quantity conceptions in junior and senior high school students. *Child Development, 32,* 551–560.

Elkind, D. (1976). *Child development and education: A Piagetian perspective*. New York: Oxford University Press.

Elkind, D. (1978). Understanding the young adolescent. *Adolescence, 13,* 127–134.

Elkind, D. (1981). *The hurried child*. Reading, MA: Addison-Wesley.

Elkind, D. (1988, January). Educating the very young: A call for clear thinking. *NEA Today*, pp. 22–27.

Ellis, H. C. (1987). Recent developments in human memory. In V. P. Makosky (Ed.), *The G. Stanley Hall lecture series*. Washington, DC: American Psychological Association.

Elmes, D. G., Kantowitz, B. H., & Roedinger, H. L. (2003). *Research methods in psychology* (7th ed.). Belmont, CA: Wadsworth.

Emde, R. N., Gaensbauer, T. G., & Harmon, R. J. (1976). Emotional expression in infancy: A biobehavioral study: *Psychological Issues: Monograph Series, 10* (37).

Emery, R. E. (1994). *Renegotiating family relationships*. New York: Guilford Press.

Emery, R. E., Laumann-Billings, L., Waldron, M. C., Sbarra, D. A., & Dillon, P. (2001). Child custody mediation and litigation: Custody, contact, and coparenting 12 years after initial dispute resolution. *Journal of Consulting and Clinical Psychology, 69,* 323–332.

England, L. J., Kendrick, J. S., Gargiullo, P. M., Zhniser, S. C., & Hannon, W. H. (2001). Measures of maternal tobacco exposure and infant birth weight at term. *American Journal of Epidemiology, 153,* 954–960.

Engler, A. J., Ludington-Hoe, S. M., Cusson, R. M., Adams, R., Bahnsen, M., Brumbaugh, E., Coates, P., Grief, J., McHargue, L., Ryan, D. L., Settle, M., & Williams, D. (2002). Kangaroo care: National survey of practice, knowledge, barriers, and perceptions. *American Journal of Maternal/Child Nursing, 27,* 146–153.

Englert, C. S., Berry, R., & Dunsmore, K. (2001). A case study of the apprenticeship process. *Journal of Learning Disabilities, 34,* 152–171.

Enoch, M. A., & Goldman, D. (2002). Problem drinking and alcoholism: Diagnosis and treatment. *American Family Physician, 65,* 441–448.

Enright, R. D., Lapsley, D. K., Dricas, A. S., & Fehr, L. A. (1980). Parental influence on the development of adolescent autonomy and identity. *Journal of Youth and Adolescence, 9,* 529–546.

Epstein, J. A., Botvin, G. J., & Diaz, T. (1998). Linguistic acculturation and gender effects on smoking among Hispanic youth. *Preventive Medicine, 27,* 538–589.

Erdem, A., Erdem, M., Arslan, M., Yazici, G., Eskandari, R., & Himmetogulu, O. (2002). The effects of maternal anemia and iron deficiency on fetal erythropoiesis: comparison between serum erythropoietin, hemoglobin and ferritin levels in mothers and newborns. *Journal of Maternal, Fetal, and Neonatal Medicine, 11,* 329–332.

ERIC/EECE (2002). Academic redshirting. *ERIC Clearinghouse on Elementary and Early Childhood Education,* 1–15.

Ericsson, K. A. (Ed.). (1996). *The road to excellence*. Mahwah, NJ: Erlbaum.

Ericsson, K. A., Krampe, R. T., & Tesch-Römer, C. (1993). The role of deliberate practice in the acquisition of expert performance. *Psychological Review, 100,* 363–406.

Erikson, E. H. (1950). *Childhood and society*. New York: W. W. Norton.

Erikson, E. H. (1962). *Young man Luther*. New York: W. W. Norton.

Erikson, E. H. (1968). *Identity: Youth and crisis*. New York: W. W. Norton.

Erikson, E. H. (1969). *Gandhi's truth*. New York: W. W. Norton.

Erlick, A. C., & Starry, A. R. (1973, June). *Sources of information for career decisions*. Report of Poll No. 98, Purdue Opinion Panel.

Eskenazi, B., Stapleton, A. L., Kharrazi, M., & Chee, W. Y. (1999). Associations between maternal decaffeinated and caffeinated coffee consumption and fetal growth and gestational duration. *Epidemiology, 10,* 242–249.

Espelage, D. L., Holt, M. K., & Henkel, R. R. (2003). Examination of peer-group contextual effects on aggression during early adolescence. *Child Development, 74,* 205–220.

Etaugh, C., & Bridges, J. S. (2001). *Psychology of women: A life-span perspective*. Boston: Allyn & Bacon.

Etzel, R. (1988, October). *Children of smokers*. Paper presented at the meeting of the American Academy of Pediatrics, New Orleans.

Evans, B. J., & Whitfield, J. R. (Eds.). (1988). *Black males in the United States: An annotated bibliography from 1967 to 1987.* Washington, DC: American Psychological Association.

F

Fabes, R. A., Eisenberg, N., Jones, S., Smith, M., Gutherie, I., Poulin, R., Shepard, S., & Friedman, J. (1999). Regulation, emotionality, and preschoolers' socially competent peer interactions. *Child Development, 70,* 432–442.

Fabricius, W. V., & Hagen, J. W. (1984). Use of causal attributions about recall performance to assess metamemory and predict strategic memory behavior in young children. *Developmental Psychology, 20,* 975–987.

Fagan, J. F. (1992). Intelligence: A theoretical viewpoint. *Current Directions in Psychological Science, 1,* 82–86.

Fagot, B. I. (1995). Parenting boys and girls. In M. H. Bornstein (Ed.), *Handbook of parenting* (Vol. 1). Hillsdale, NJ: Erlbaum.

Fairburn, C. G., & Harrison, P. J. (2003). Eating disorders. *Lancet, 361,* 407–416.

Falbo, T., & Poston, D. L. (1993). The academic, personality, and physical outcomes of only children in China. *Child Development, 64,* 18–35.

Famy, C., Streissguth, A. P., & Unis, A. S. (1998). Mental illness in adults with fetal alcohol syndrome or fetal alcohol effects. *American Journal of Psychiatry, 155,* 552–554.

Fang, G., Fang, F., Keller, M., & Edelstein, W. (2003). Social moral reasoning in Chinese Children: A developmental study. *Psychology in the Schools, 40,* 125–138.

Fang, J., Madhaven, S., & Alderman, M. H. (1999). Low birth weight: Race and maternal nativity—Impact of community income. *Pediatrics, 103,* e5.

Fantz, R. L. (1963). Pattern vision in newborn infants. *Science, 140,* 296–297.

Fasick, F. (1988). Patterns of formal education in high school as rites of passage. *Adolescence, 23,* 457–468.

Fein, G. G. (1986). Pretend play. In D. Görlitz & J. F. Wohlwill (Eds.), *Curiosity, imagination, and play.* Hillsdale, NJ: Erlbaum.

Feiring, C. (1996). Concepts of romance in 15-year-old adolescents. *Journal of Research on Adolescence, 6,* 181–200.

Feldhusen, J. (1999). Giftedness and creativity. In M.A. Runco & S. Pritzker (Eds.), *Encyclopedia of creativity.* San Diego: Academic Press.

Feldman, D. H. (1997, August), *Hitting middle C: Toward a more comprehensive domain for creativity research.* Paper presented at the meeting of the American Psychological Association, Chicago.

Feldman, R., & Eidelman, A. I. (2003). Skin-to-skin (Kangaroo Care) accelerates autonomic and neurobehavioral maturation in preterm infants. *Developmental Medicine and Child Neurology, 45,* 274–281.

Feldman, R., Weller, A., Sirota, L., & Eidelman, A. I. (2002). Skin-to-skin contact (kangaroo care) promotes self-regulation in premature infants: Sleep-wake cyclicity, arousal modulation, and sustained exploration. *Developmental Psychology, 38,* 194–207.

Feldman, S. S. (1999). Unpublished review of J. W. Santrock's *Adolescence,* 8th ed. (New York: McGraw-Hill).

Feldman, S. S., & Elliott, G. R. (1990). Progress and promise of research on normal adolescent development. In S. S. Feldman & G. Elliott (Eds.), *At the threshold: The developing adolescent.* Cambridge, MA: Harvard University Press.

Feldman, S. S., Turner, R., & Araujo, K. (1999). Interpersonal context as an influence on sexual timetables of youths: Gender and ethnic effects. *Journal of Research on Adolescence, 9,* 25–52.

Feldman, S. S., & Weinberger, D. A. (1994). Self-restraint as a mediator of family influences on boys' delinquent behavior: A longitudinal study. *Child Development, 65,* 195–211.

Feng, H. L. (2003). Molecular biology of male infertility. *Archives of Andrology, 49,* 19–27.

Fenson, L., Dale, P. S., Reznick, S. J., Bates, E., Thal, D. J., & Pethick, S. (1994). Variability in early communicative development. *Monographs of the Society for Research in Child Development, 60* (5, Serial No. 242).

Ferguson, D. M., Harwood, L. J., & Shannon, F. T. (1987). Breastfeeding and subsequent social adjustment in 6- to 8-year-old children. *Journal of Child Psychology and Psychiatry, 28,* 378–386.

Ferguson, D. M., Harwood, L. J., & Beautrais, A. L. (1999). Is sexual orientation related to mental health problems and suicidality in young people? *Archives of General Psychiatry, 56,* 876–880.

Fernandes, O., Sabharwal, M., Smiley, T., Pastuszak, A., Koren, G., & Einarson, T. (1998). Moderate to heavy caffeine consumption during pregnancy and relationship to spontaneous abortion and abnormal fetal growth: A meta-analysis. *Reproductive Toxicology, 12,* 435–444.

Ferrer-Wreder, L., Lorene, C. C., Kurtines, W., Briones, E., Bussell, J., Berman, S., & Arrufat, O. (2002). Promoting identity development in marginalized youth. *Journal of Adolescent Research, 17,* 168–187.

Field, A. E., Cambargo, C. A., Taylor, C. B., Berkey, C. S., Roberts, S. B., & Colditz, G. A. (2001). Peer, parent, and media influences on the development of weight concerns and frequent dieting among preadolescent and adolescent girls and boys. *Pediatrics, 107,* 54–60.

Field, T. (1990). *Infancy.* Cambridge, MA: Harvard University Press.

Field, T. (2000). Child abuse. In A. Kazdin (Ed.), *Encyclopedia of psychology.* Washington, DC, & New York: American Psychological Association and Oxford University Press.

Field, T. (2001). Massage therapy facilitates weight gain in preterm infants. *Current Directions in Psychological Science, 10,* 51–55.

Field, T. (2002). Infants' need for touch. *Human Development, 45,* 100–103.

Field, T., Schanberg, S. M., Scafidi, F., Bauer, C. R., Vega-Lahr, N., Garcia, R., Nystrom, J., & Kuhn, C. M. (1986). Tactile/kinesthetic stimulation effects on preterm neonates. *Pediatrics, 77,* 654–658.

Field, T., Seligman, S., Scafidi, F., & Schanberg, S. (1996). Alleviating posttraumatic stress in children following Hurricane Andrew. *Journal of Applied Developmental Psychology, 17,* 37–50.

Field, T. M. (1992, September). Stroking babies helps growth, reduces stress. *Brown University Child and Adolescent Behavior Letter,* pp. 1, 6.

Field, T. M. (1998). Massage therapy effects. *American Psychologist, 53,* 1270–1281.

Field, T. M., Grizzle, N., Scafidi, F., & Schanberg, S. (1996). Massage and relaxation therapies' effects on depressed adolescent mothers. *Adolescence, 31,* 903–911.

Field, T. M., Hernandez-Reif, M., Seligman, S., Krasnegor, J., & Sunshine, W. (1997). Juvenile rheumatoid arthritis: Benefits from massage therapy. *Journal of Pediatric Psychology, 22,* 607–617.

Field, T. M., Hernandez-Reif, M., Taylor, S., Quintino, O., & Burman, I. (1997). Labor pain is reduced by massage therapy. *Journal of Psychosomatic Obstetrics and Gynecology, 18,* 286–291.

Field, T. M., Lasko, D., Mundy, P., Henteleff, T., Kabat, S., Talpins, S., & Dowling, M. (1997). Brief report: Autistic children's attentiveness and responsivity improve after touch therapy. *Journal of Autism and Developmental Disorders, 27*, 333–338.

Field, T. M., Quintino, O., Hernandez-Reif, M., & Koslosky, G. (1998b). Adolescents with attention deficit hyperactivity disorder benefit from massage therapy. *Adolescence, 33*, 103–108.

Field, T. M., Woodson, R., Greenberg, R., & Cohen, D. (1982). Discrimination and imitation of facial expressions by neonates. *Science, 218*, 179–181.

Fields, R. (1998). *Drugs in perspective* (3rd ed.). New York: McGraw-Hill.

Fifer, B., & Grose-Fifer. J. (2001). Prenatal development and risk. In A. Fogel & G. Bremner (Eds.), *Blackwell handbook of infant development*. London: Blackwell.

Firlik, R. (1996). Can we adapt the philosophies and practices of Reggio Emilia, Italy, for use in American schools? *Young Children, 51*, 217–220.

Fisch, S. M., & Truglio, R. T. (Eds.). (2001). *"G" is for growing: Thirty years of research on children and* Sesame Street. Mahwah, NJ: Erlbaum.

Fischer, K. W., & Bidell, T. R. (1998). Dynamic development of psychological structures in action and thought. In W. Damon (Ed.), *Handbook of child psychology* (Vol. 1). New York: Wiley.

Fischer, K. W., & Rose, S. P. (1995, Fall). Concurrent cycles in the dynamic development of brain and behavior. *SRCD Newsletter*, pp. 3–4, 15–16.

Fisher-Thompson, D., Polinski, L., Eaton, M., & Hefferman, K. (1993, March). *Sex-role orientation of children and their parents: Relationship to the sex-typing of Christmas toys*. Paper presented at the biennial meeting of the Society for Research in Child Development, New Orleans.

Fixler, J., & Styles, L. (2002). Sickle cell disease. *Pediatric Clinics of North America, 49*, 1192–1210.

Flavell, J. H. (1980, fall). A tribute to Piaget. *Society for Research in Child Development Newsletter*, p. 1.

Flavell, J. H. (1999). Cognitive development. *Annual Review of Psychology* (Vol. 50). Palo Alto, CA: Annual Reviews.

Flavell, J. H., Beach, D. R., & Chinsky, J. M. (1966). Spontaneous verbal rehearsal in a memory task as a function of age. *Child Development, 37*, 283–289.

Flavell, J. H., Friedrichs, A., & Hoyt, J. (1970). Developmental changes in memorization processes. *Cognitive Psychology, 1*, 324–340.

Flavell, J. H., Miller, P. H., & Miller, S. A. (2002). *Cognitive development* (4th ed.). Upper Saddle River, NJ: Prentice Hall.

Fleming, J. E., Boyle, M., & Offord, D. R. (1993). The outcome of adolescent depression in the Ontario child health study follow-up. *Journal of the American Academy of Child & Adolescent Psychiatry, 32*, 28–29.

Flick, L., White, D. K., Vemulapalli, C., Stulac, B. B., & Kemp, J. S. (2001). Sleep position and the use of soft bedding during bed sharing among African American infants at increased risk for sudden infant death syndrome. *Journal of Pediatrics, 138*, 338–343.

Flohr, J. W., Atkins, D. H., Bower, T. G. R., & Aldridge, M. A. (2001, April). *Infant music preferences*. Paper presented at the meeting of the Society for Research in Child Development, Minneapolis.

Flores, D. L., & Hendrick, V. C. (2002). Etiology and treatment of postpartum depression. *Current Psychiatry Reports, 4*, 461–466.

Florsheim, P. (Ed.). (2003). *Adolescent romantic relations and sexual behavior*. Mahwah, NJ: Erlbaum.

Flynn, J. R. (1999). Searching for justice: The discovery of IQ gains over time. *American Psychologist, 54*, 5–20.

Foege, W. (2000). The power of immunization. *The progress of nations*. New York: UNICEF.

Fogel, A. (2001). *Infancy* (4th ed.). Belmont, CA: Wadsworth.

Fogel, A., Toda, S., & Kawai, M. (1988). Mother-infant face-to-face interaction in Japan and the United States: A laboratory comparison using 3-month-old infants. *Developmental Psychology, 24*, 398–406.

Ford, K., Sohn, W., & Lepkowski, J. (2001). Characteristics of adolescents' sexual partners and their association with use of condoms and other contraceptive methods. *Family Planning Perspectives, 33*, 100–105, 132.

Fordham, S., & Ogbu, J. U. (1986). Black students' school success: Coping with the burden of "acting white." *Urban Review, 18*, 176–206.

Forrest, J. D., & Singh, S. (1990). The sexual and reproductive behavior of American women, 1982–1988. *Family Planning Perspectives, 22*, 206–214.

Fountain, L., & Krulewitch, C. J. (2002). Trends in assisted reproductive technology. *Fertility and Sterility, 78*, 419–420.

Fox, B., & Hull, M. (2002). *Phonics for the teacher of reading* (8th ed.). Upper Saddle River, NJ: Merrill.

Fraga, C. G., Motchnik, P. A., Shigenaga, M. K., Helbock, H. J., Jacob, R. A., & Ames, B. N. (1991). Ascorbic acid protects against endogenous oxidative DNA damage in human sperm. *Proceedings of the National Academy of Sciences of the United States, 88*, 11003–11006.

Fraiberg, S. (1959). *The magic years*. New York: Scribner's.

Francis, J., Fraser, G., & Marcia, J. E. (1989). *Cognitive and experimental factors in moratorium-achievement (MAMA) cycles*. Unpublished manuscript, Department of Psychology, Simon Fraser University, Burnaby, British Columbia.

Frank, D. A., Augustyn, M., Knight, W. G., Pell, T., & Zuckerman, B. (2001). Growth, development, and behavior in early childhood following cocaine exposure: A systematic review. *Journal of the American Medical Association, 285*, 1613–1625.

Frank, D. A., Jacobs, R. R., Beeghly, M., Augustyn, M., Bellinger, D., Cabral, H., & Heeren, T. (2002). Level of prenatal cocaine exposure and scores on the Bayley Scales of Infant Development: Modifying effects of caregiver, early intervention, and birth weight. *Pediatrics, 110*, 1143–1152.

Franz, C. E. (1996). The implications of preschool tempo and motoric activity level for personality decades later. Reported in Caspi, A. (1998). Personality development across the life course. In W. Damon (Ed.), *Handbook of child psychology* (Vol 3). New York: Wiley, p. 337.

Franz, C. E., McClelland, D., & Weinberger, J. (1991). Childhood antecedents of conventional social accomplishment in midlife adults: A 26-year prospective study. *Journal of Personality and Social Psychology, 58*, 709–717.

Fraser, S. (Ed.). (1995). *The bell curve wars: Race, intelligence, and the future of America*. New York: Basic Books.

Frayling, T. M., & Hattersley, A. T. (2002). The role of genetic susceptibility in the association of low birth weight with type 2 diabetes. *British Medical Bulletin, 60*, 80–101.

Frederikse, M., Lu, A., Aylward, E., Barta, P., Sharma, T., & Pearlson, G. (2000). Sex differences in inferior lobule volume in schizophrenia. *American Journal of Psychiatry, 157*, 422–427.

Fredrickson, D. D. (1993). Breastfeeding research priorities, opportunities, and study criteria: What we learned from the smoking trial. *Journal of Human Lactation, 3,* 147–150.

Freedman, J. L. (1984). Effects of television violence on aggressiveness. *Psychological Bulletin, 96,* 227–246.

Freeman, D. (1983). *Margaret Mead and Samoa.* Cambridge, MA: Harvard University Press.

Freeman, K. E., & Gehl, K. S. (1995, March). *Beginnings, middles, and ends: 24-month-olds' understanding of analogy.* Paper presented at the meeting of the Society for Research in Child Development, Indianapolis.

French, S. A., Story, M., & Jeffery, R. W. (2001). Environmental influences on eating and physical activity. *Annual Review of Public Health, 22,* 309–335.

Freud, A., & Dann, S. (1951). Instinctual anxiety during puberty. In A. Freud (Ed.), *The ego and its mechanisms of defense.* New York: International Universities Press.

Freud, S. (1917). *A general introduction to psychoanalysis.* New York: Washington Square Press.

Frezzo, T. M., Rubinstein, W. S., Dunham, D., & Ormond, K.E. (2003). The genetic family history as a risk assessment tool in internal medicine. *Genetic Medicine 5,* 84–91.

Frias, J. L., & Davenport, M. L. (2003). Health supervision for children with Turner Syndrome. *Pediatrics, 111,* 692–702.

Fried, P. A., & Smith, A. M. (2001). A literature review of the consequences of prenatal marijuana exposure. An emerging theme of a deficiency in executive function. *Neurotoxicology and Teratology, 23,* 1–11.

Fried, P. A., & Watkinson, B. (1990). 36- and 48-month neurobehavioral follow-up of children prenatally exposed to marijuana, cigarettes, and alcohol. *Developmental and Behavioral Pediatrics, 11,* 49–58.

Friend, M., & Bursuck, W. D. (2002). *Including students with special needs* (3rd ed.). Boston: Allyn & Bacon.

Frye, D., Zelazo, P. D., Brooks, P. J., & Samuels, M. C. (1996). Inference and action in early causal reasoning. *Developmental Psychology, 32,* 120–131.

Fuligni, A. J., & Yoshikawa, H. (2003). Socioeconomic resources, poverty, and child development among immigrant families. In M. H. Bornstein & R. H. Bradley (Eds.), *Socioeconomic status, parenting, and child development.* Mahwah, NJ: Erlbaum.

Fuller, M. (1984). Black girls in a London comprehensive school. In M. Hammersley & P. Woods (Eds.), *Life in school: The sociology of pop culture.* New York: Open University Press.

Furman, W. (2002). The emerging field of adolescent romantic relationships. *Current Directions in Psychological Science, 11,* 177–180.

Furman, W., & Buhrmester, D. (1992). Age and sex differences in perceptions of networks of personal relationships. *Child Development, 63,* 103–115.

Furman, W., & Shaffer, L. (2003). The role of romantic relationships in adolescent development. In P. Florsheim (Ed.), *Adolescent romantic relations and sexual behavior.* Mahwah, NJ: Erlbaum.

Furman, W., & Wehner, E. A. (1999). Adolescent romantic relationships: A developmental perspective. In S. Shulman & W. A. Collins (Eds.), *New directions for child development: Adolescent romantic relationships.* San Francisco: Jossey-Bass.

Furth, H. G. (1973). *Deafness and learning: A psychosocial approach.* Belmont, CA: Wadsworth.

Furth, H. G., & Wachs, H. (1975). *Thinking goes to school.* New York: Oxford University Press.

Fussell, E., & Greene, M. E. (2002). Demographic trends affecting youth around the world. In B. B. Brown, R. W. Larson, & T. S. Saraswathi (Eds.), *The world's youth.* New York: Cambridge University Press.

G

Galambos, N. L., & Costigan, C. L. (2003). Emotional and personality development in adolescence. In I. B. Weiner (Ed.), *Handbook of psychology* (Vol. VI). New York: Wiley.

Galambos, N. L., & Maggs, J. L. (1989, April). *The after-school ecology of young adolescents and self-reported behavior.* Paper presented at the biennial meeting of the Society for Research in Child Development, Kansas City.

Gall, M. D., Borg, W. R., & Gall, J. P. (2003). *Educational research* (7th ed.). Boston: Allyn & Bacon.

Gao, Y., Elliott, M. E., & Waters, E. (1999, April). *Maternal attachment representations and support for three-year-olds' secure base behavior.* Paper presented at the meeting of the Society for Research in Child Development, Albuquerque.

Garbarino, J. (1999). *Lost boys: Why our sons turn violent and how we can save them.* New York: Free Press.

Garbarino, J. (2001). Violent children. *Archives of Pediatrics & Adolescent Medicine, 155,* 1–2.

Garbarino, J., & Asp, C. E. (1981). *Successful schools and competent students.* Lexington, MA: Lexington Books.

Garcia, E., & Willis, A. I. (2001). Framework for understanding multicultural literacies. In P. R. Schmidt & P. B. Mosenthal (Eds.), *Reconceptualizing literacy in the new age of multiculturalism and pluralism.* Greenwich, CT: IAP.

Garcia, E. E., Bravo, M. A., Dickey, L. M., Cun, K., & Sun-Irminger, X. (2002). Rethinking school reform in the context of cultural and linguistic diversity: Creating a responsive learning community. In L. Minaya-Rowe (Ed.), *Teaching training and effective pedagogy in the context of cultural diversity.* Greenwich, CT: IAP.

Garcia, L., Hart, D., & Johnson-Ray, R. (1998). What do children and adolescents think about themselves? A developmental account of self-concept development. In S. Hala, (Ed.), *The development of social cognition.* London: University College of London Press.

Garcia-Bournissen, F., Feig, D. S., & Koren, G. (2003). Maternal-fetal transport of hypoglyicaemic drugs. *Clinical Pharmacokinetics, 42,* 303–313.

Gard, J. W., Alexander, J. M., Bawdon, R. E., & Albrecht, J. T. (2002). Oxytocin preparation stability in several common intravenous solutions. *American Journal of Obstetrics and Gynecology, 186,* 496–498.

Gardner, H. (1983). *Frames of mind.* New York: Basic Books.

Gardner, H. (1993). *Multiple intelligences.* New York: Basic Books.

Gardner, H. (1998). Multiple intelligences: Myths and messages. In A. Woolfolk (Ed.), *Readings in educational psychology* (2nd ed.). Boston: Allyn & Bacon.

Gardner, H. (2001, March 13). *An education for the future.* Paper presented to the Royal Symposium, Amsterdam.

Gardner, H. (2002). The pursuit of excellence through education. In M. Ferrari (Ed.), *Learning from extraordinary minds.* Mahwah, NJ: Erlbaum.

Gardner, H. (2003). Three distinct meanings of intelligence. In R.J. Sternberg, J. Lautrey, & T. I. Lubert (Eds.), *Models of intelligence: International perspectives.* Washington, DC: American Psychological Association.

Gardner, L. I. (1972). Deprivation dwarfism. *Scientific American, 227,* 76–82.

Garmezy, N. (1993). Children in poverty: Resilience despite risk. *Psychiatry, 56,* 127–136.

Garner, D. M., & Desai, J. J. (2001). Eating disorders in children and adolescents. In J. N. Hughes, A. M. La Greca, & J. C. Conoley

(Eds.), *Handbook of psychological services for children and adolescents*. New York: Oxford University Press.

Garofalo, R., Wolf, R. C., Wissow, L. S., Woods, E. R., & Goodman, E. (1999). Sexual orientation and risk of suicide attempts among a representative sample of youth. *Archives of Pediatrics and Adolescent Medicine, 153,* 487–493.

Garrett, P., Ng'andu, N., & Ferron, J. (1994). Poverty experiences of young children and the quality of their home environments. *Child Development, 65,* 331–345.

Gazzaniga, M. S. (1986). *The social brain.* New York: Plenum.

Gazzaniga, M. S., Ivry, R. B., & Mangum, G. R. (2002). *Cognitive neuroscience* (2nd ed.). New York: W. W. Norton.

Geary, D. C., & Huffman, K. J. (2002). Brain and cognitive evolution: forms of modularity and functions of mind. *Psychological Bulletin, 128,* 667–698.

Gelfand, D. M., Teti, D. M., & Fox, C. E. R. (1992). Sources of parenting stress for depressed and nondepressed mothers of infants. *Journal of Clinical Child Psychology, 21,* 262–272.

Gelman, R. (1969). Conservation acquisition: A problem of learning to attend to relevant attributes. *Journal of Experimental Child Psychology, 7,* 67–87.

Gelman, R., & Brenneman, K. (1994). Domain specificity and cultural variation are not inconsistent. In L. A. Hirschfeld & S. Gelman (Eds.), *Mapping the mind: Domain specificity in cognition and culture*. New York: Cambridge University Press.

Gelman, R., & Williams, E. M. (1998). Enabling constraints for cognitive development and learning. In W. Damon (Ed.), *Handbook of child psychology* (5th ed., Vol. 4). New York: Wiley.

Gelman, S. A., & Opfer, J. E. (2002). Development of the animate-inanimate distinction. In U. Goswami (Ed.), *Blackwell handbook of childhood cognitive development*. Malden, MA: Blackwell.

Geltman, P. L., Brown, M. J., & Cochran, J. (2001). Lead poisoning among refugee children settled in Massachusetts, 1995 to 1999. *Pediatrics, 108,* 158–162.

Gennetian, L. A., & Miller, C. (2002). Children and welfare reform: A view from an experimental welfare program in Minnesota. *Child Development, 73,* 601–620.

George, C., Main, M., & Kaplan, N. (1984). *Attachment interview with adults.* Un-

published manuscript, University of California, Berkeley.

Gergen, P. J., Fowler, J. A., Maurer, K. R., Davis, W. W., & Overpeck, M. D. (1998). The burden of environmental tobacco smoke exposure on the respiratory health of children 2 months through 5 years of age in the United States: Third National Health and Nutrition Examination Survey, 1988 to 1994. *Pediatrics, 101,* E8.

Gershoff, E. T. (2002). Corporal punishment by parents and associated child behaviors and experiences: A meta-analysis and theoretical review. *Psychological Bulletin, 128,* 539–579.

Geschwind, N., & Behan, P. O. (1984). Laterality, hormones, and immunity. In N. Geschwind & A. M. Galaburda (Eds.), *Cerebral dominance: The biological foundations*. Cambridge, MA: Harvard University Press.

Gesell, A. (1934). *An atlas of infant behavior.* New Haven, CT: Yale University Press.

Gesell, A. L. (1928). *Infancy and human growth.* New York: Macmillan.

Gesell, A. L. (1934). *Infancy and human growth.* New York: Macmillan.

Gewirtz, J. (1977). Maternal responding and the conditioning of infant crying: Directions of influence within the attachment-acquisition process. In B. C. Etzel, J. M. LeBlanc, & D. M. Baer (Eds.), *New developments in behavioral research*. Hillsdale, NJ: Erlbaum.

Gibbons, J. L. (2000). Gender development in cross-cultural perspective. In T. Eckes & H. M. Trautner (Eds.), *The developmental social psychology of gender*. Mahwah, NJ: Erlbaum.

Gibbs, J. T. (1989). Black American adolescents. In J. T. Gibbs & L. N. Huang (Eds.), *Children of color*. San Francisco: Jossey-Bass.

Gibbs, J. T., & Huang, L. N. (1989). A conceptual framework for assessing and treating minority youth. In J. T. Gibbs & L. N. Huang (Eds.), *Children of color*. San Francisco: Jossey-Bass.

Gibson, E. J. (1969). *Principles of perceptual learning and development*. New York: Appleton-Century-Crofts.

Gibson, E. J. (1989). Exploratory behavior in the development of perceiving, acting, and the acquiring of knowledge. *Annual Review of Psychology* (Vol. 39). Palo Alto, CA: Annual Reviews.

Gibson, E. J. (2001). *Perceiving the affordances*. Mahwah, NJ: Erlbaum.

Gibson, E. J., Riccio, G., Schmuckler, M. A., Stoffregen, T. A., Rosenberg, D., & Taormina, J. (1987). Detection of the tra-

versability of surfaces by crawling and walking infants. *Journal of Experimental Psychology: Human Perception and Performance, 13,* 533–544.

Gibson, E. J., & Walk, R. D. (1960). The "visual cliff." *Scientific American, 202,* 64–71.

Gibson, J. H., Harries, M., Mitchell, A., Godfrey, R., Lunt, M., & Reeve, J. (2000). Determinants of bone density and prevalence of osteopenia among female runners in their second to seventh decades of age. *Bone, 26,* 591–598.

Gibson, J. J. (1966). *The senses considered as perceptual systems*. Boston: Houghton Mifflin.

Gibson, J. J. (1979). *The ecological approach to visual perception*. Boston: Houghton Mifflin.

Gielchinsky, Y., Rojansky, N., Fasoliotis, S. J., & Ezra, Y. (2002). Placenta accreta—summary of 10 years: A survey of 310 cases. *Placenta, 23,* 210–214.

Gilligan, C. (1982). *In a different voice*. Cambridge, MA: Harvard University Press.

Gilligan, C. (1992, May). *Joining the resistance: Girls' development in adolescence*. Paper presented at the symposium on development and vulnerability in close relationships, Montreal, Quebec.

Gilligan, C. (1996). *Minding women: Reshaping the education realm*. Cambridge, MA: Harvard University Press.

Gilligan, C. (1996). The centrality of relationships in psychological development: A puzzle, some evidence, and a theory. In G. G. Noam & K. W. Fischer (Eds.), *Development and vulnerability in close relationships*. Hillsdale, NJ: Erlbaum.

Gilligan, C., Brown, L. M., & Rogers, A. G. (1990). Psyche embedded: A place for body, relationships, and culture in personality theory. In A. I. Rabin, R. A. Zucker, R. A. Emmons, & S. Frank (Eds.), *Studying persons and lives*. New York: Springer.

Gilligan, C., Spencer, R., Weinberg, M. K., & Bertch, T. (2003). On the listening guide: A voice-centered relational model. In P. M. Camic & J. E. Rhodes (Eds.), *Qualitative research in psychology*. Washington, DC: American Psychological Association.

Gilliland, A. L. (2002). Beyond holding hands: the modern role of the professional doula. *Journal of Obstetrics, Gynecologic, and Neonatal Nursing, 31,* 762–769.

Gjerde, P. F., Block, J., & Block, J. H. (1991). The preschool family context of 18-year-olds with depressive symptoms: A prospective study. *Journal of Research on Adolescence, 1,* 63–92.

Gleason, J. B., & Ratner, N. (1998). *Psycholinguistics* (4th ed.). Ft. Worth: Harcourt Brace.

Glei, D. A. (1999). Measuring contraceptive use patterns among teenage and adult women. *Family Planning Perspectives, 31,* 73–80.

Goelman, H., Anderson, C. J., Anderson, J., Gouzaousasis, P., Kendrick, M., Kindel, A. M., Porath, M., & Koh, J. (2003). Early childhood education. In I. B. Weiner (Ed.), *Handbook of psychology, Vol. 7.* New York: Wiley.

Goffin, S. G., & Wilson, C. S. (2001). *Curriculum models and early childhood education.* Upper Saddle River, NJ: Prentice Hall.

Gojdamaschko, N. (1999). Vygotsky. In M. A. Runco & S. Pritzker (Eds.), *Encyclopedia of creativity.* San Diego: Academic Press.

Golden, M. H., Samuels, M. P., & Southall, D. P. (2003). How to distinguish between neglect and deprivational abuse. *Archives of Diseases in Childhood, 88,* 105–107.

Goldin-Meadow, S. (2000). Language: Language development, syntax, and communication. In A. Kazdin (Ed.), *Encyclopedia of psychology.* Washington, DC, & New York: American Psychological Association and Oxford University Press.

Goldsmith, H. H. (1988, August). *Does early temperament predict late development?* Paper presented at the meeting of the American Psychological Association, Atlanta.

Goldsmith, H. H., & Gottesman, I. I. (1981). Origins of variation in behavioral style: A longitudinal study of temperament in young twins. *Child Development, 52,* 91–103.

Goldstein, J. M., Seidman, L. J., Horton, N. J., Makris, N., Kennedy, D. N., Caviness, V. S., Faraone, S. V., & Tsuang, M. T. (2001). Normal sexual dimorphism of the adult human brain assessed by in vivo magnetic resonance imaging. *Cerebral Cortex, 11,* 490–497.

Goldstein-Ferber, S. (1997, April). *Massage in preterm infants.* Paper presented at the Child Development Conference, Bar-Ilan, Israel.

Goldwater, P. N. (2001). SIDS: More facts and controversies. *Medical Journal of Australia, 174,* 302–304.

Goleman, D. (1995). *Emotional intelligence.* New York: Basic Books.

Goleman, D., Kaufman, P., & Ray, M. (1993). *The creative spirit.* New York: Plume.

Golombok, S., MacCallum, F., & Goodman, E. (2001). The "test-tube" generation: Parent-child relationships and the psychological well-being of in vitro fertilization children at adolescence. *Child Development, 72,* 599–608.

Gonzales, N. A., Knight, G. P., Morgan Lopez, A., Saenz, D., & Sirolli, A. (2002). Acculturation and the mental health of Latino youths: An integration and critique of the literature. In J. M. Contreras, K. A. Kerns, & A. M. Neal-Barnett (Eds.), *Latino children and families in the United States.* Westport, CT: Greenwood.

Gonzalez-del Angel, A. A., Vidal, S., Saldan, Y., del Castillo, V., Angel, M., Macias, M., Luna, P., & Orozco, L. (2000). Molecular diagnosis of the fragile X and FRAXE syndromes in patients with mental retardation of unknown cause in Mexico. *Annals of Genetics, 43,* 29–34.

Goodman, R. A., Mercy, J. A., Loya, F., Rosenberg, M. L., Smith, J. C., Allen, N. H., Vargas, L., & Kolts, R. (1986). Alcohol use and interpersonal violence: Alcohol detected in homicide victims. *American Journal of Public Health, 76,* 144–149.

Goodstadt, L., & Ponting, C. P. (2001). Sequence variation and disease in the wake of the draft human genome. *Human Molecular Genetics, 20,* 2209–2214.

Gopnik, A., & Meltzoff, A. (1997). *Words, thoughts, and theories.* Cambridge, MA: MIT Press.

Gottfried, A. E., Gottfried, A. W., & Bathurst, K. (2002). Maternal and dual-earner employment status and parenting. In M. H. Bornstein (Ed.), *Handbook of parenting* (2nd ed., Vol. 2). Mahwah, NJ: Erlbaum.

Gottlieb, G. (1998). Normally occurring environmental and behavioral influences on gene activity: From central dogma to probabilistic epigenesis. *Psychological Review, 105,* 792–802.

Gottlieb, G. (2000). Nature and nurture theories. In A. Kazdin (Ed.), *Encyclopedia of psychology.* Washington, DC, & New York: American Psychological Association and Oxford University Press.

Gottlieb, G. (2001). Origin of species: The potential significance of early experience for evolution. In W. W. Hartup, & R. A. Weinberg (Eds.), *Child psychology in retrospect and prospect.* Mahwah, NJ: Erlbaum.

Gottlieb, G. (2002). Origin of species: The potential significance of early experience for evolution. In W. W. Hartup, & R. A. Weinberg (Eds.), *Child psychology in retrospect and prospect.* Mahwah, NJ: Erlbaum.

Gottlieb, G. (2003). *Developmental behavioral genetics and the statistical concept of interaction.* Unpublished manuscript, University of North Carolina, Chapel Hill.

Gottlieb, G., Wahlsten, D., & Lickliter, R. (1998). The significance of biology for human development: A developmental psychobiological systems view. In W. Damon (Ed.), *Handbook of child psychology* (5th ed., Vol. 1). New York: Wiley.

Gottlieb, G. L. (2001). Influence of strategy on muscle activity during impact movements. *Journal of Motor Behavior, 33,* 235–242.

Gottman, J. M., Katz, L. F., & Hooven, C. (1997). *Meta-emotion: How families communicate.* Mahwah, NJ: Erlbaum.

Gottman, J. M., & Parker, J. G. (Eds.). (1987). *Conversations of friends.* New York: Cambridge University Press.

Gould, S. J. (1981). *The mismeasure of man.* New York: W. W. Norton.

Graber, J. A., & Brooks-Gunn, J. (2001). *Co-occurring eating and depressive problems: An 8-year study of adolescent girls.* Unpublished manuscript, Center for Children and Families, Columbia University.

Graber, J. A., & Brooks-Gunn, J. (in press). "Sometimes I think that you don't like me": How mothers and daughters negotiate the transition to adolescence. In M. Cox & J. Brooks-Gunn (Eds.), *Conflict and closeness in families: Consequences for children and youth.* Mahwah, NJ: Erlbaum.

Graham, S. (1986, August). *Can attribution theory tell us something about motivation in blacks?* Paper presented at the meeting of the American Psychological Association, Washington, DC.

Graham, S. (1990). Motivation in Afro-Americans. In G. L. Berry & J. K. Asamen (Eds.), *Black students: Psychosocial issues and academic achievement.* Newbury Park, CA: Sage.

Graham, S. (1992). Most of the subjects were white and middle class. *American Psychologist, 47,* 629–637.

Grant, J. P. (1997). *The state of the world's children.* New York: UNICEF and Oxford University Press.

Grantham-McGregor, S., Ani, C., & Fernald, L. (2001). The role of nutrition in cognitive development. In R. J. Sternberg & E. L. Grigorenko (Eds.), *Environmental effects on cognitive abilities.* Mahwah, NJ: Erlbaum.

Graue, M. E., & DiPerna, J. (2000). Redshirting and early retention: Who gets the "gift of time" and what are its outcomes? *American Educational Research Journal, 37,* 509–534.

Graziano, W. G., & Tobin, R. M. (2003). Emotional regulation from infancy through adolescence. In M. H. Bornstein, L. Davidson,

C. L. M. Keyes, & K. A. Moore (Eds.), *Well-being*. Mahwah, NJ: Erlbaum.

Green, L. A., Fryer, G. E., Yawn, B. P., Lanier, D., & Dovey, S. M. (2001). The ecology of medical care revisited. *New England Journal of Medicine, 344*, 2021–2025.

Greenberger, E., & Steinberg, L. (1986). *When teenagers work: The psychological social costs of adolescent employment.* New York: Basic Books.

Greeno, J. G., Collins, A. M., & Resnick, L. (1996). Cognition and learning. In D. C. Berliner & R. C. Chafee (Eds.), *Handbook of educational psychology.* New York: Macmillan.

Greenough, W. T. (1997, April 21). Commentary in article, "Politics of biology." *U.S. News & World Report.* p. 79.

Greenough, W. T. (1999, April). *Experience, brain development, and links to mental retardation.* Paper presented at the meeting of the Society for Research in Child Development, Albuquerque.

Greenough, W. T. (2000). Brain development. In A. Kazdin (Ed.), *Encyclopedia of psychology.* Washington, DC, & New York: American Psychological Association and Oxford University Press.

Greenough, W. T. (2001, April). *Nature and nurture in the brain development process.* Paper presented at the meeting of the Society for Research in Child Development, Minneapolis.

Greenough, W. T., Klintsova, A. Y., Irvan, S. A., Galvez, R., Bates, K. E., & Weiler, I. J. (2001). Synaptic regulation of protein synthesis and the fragile X protein. *Proceedings of the National Academy of Sciences USA, 98*, 7101–7106.

Greven, P. (1991). *Spare the child: The religious roots of punishment and the psychological impact of physical abuse.* New York: Knopf.

Grigorenko, E. (2000). Heritability and intelligence. In R. J. Sternberg (Ed.), *Handbook of intelligence.* New York: Cambridge University Press.

Grigorenko, E. L. (2001). Developmental dyslexia: An update on genes, brains, and environments. *Journal of Child Psychology and Psychiatry, 42*, 91–125.

Grigorenko, E. L. (2001). The invisible danger: The impact of ionizing radiation on cognitive development and functioning. In R. J. Sternberg & E. L. Grigorenko (Eds.), *Environmental effects on cognitive abilities.* Mahwah, NJ: Erlbaum.

Grigoriadis, S., & Kennedy, S. H. (2002). Role of estrogen in the treatment of depression. *American Journal of Therapy, 9*, 503–509.

Grodzinsky, Y. (2001). The neurology of syntax: Language use without Broca's area. *Behavior and Brain Sciences, 23*, 1–21.

Grolnick, W. S., Bridges, L. J., & Connell, J. P. (1996). Emotion regulation in two-year-olds: Strategies and emotional expression in four contexts. *Child Development, 67*, 928–941.

Grossmann, K., Grossmann, K. E., Spangler, G., Suess, G., & Unzner, L. (1985). Maternal sensitivity and newborns' orientation responses as related to quality of attachment in northern Germany. In I. Bretherton & E. Waters (Eds.), Growing points of attachment theory and research. *Monographs of the Society for Research in Child Development, 50* (1–2, Serial No. 209).

Grotevant, H. D., & Cooper, C. R. (1985). Patterns of interaction in family relationships and the development of identity exploration in adolescence. *Child Development, 56*, 415–428.

Grotevant, H. D., & Cooper, C. R. (1998). Individuality and connectedness in adolescent development: Review and prospects for research on identity, relationships, and context. In E. Skoe & A. von der Lippe (Eds.), *Personality development in adolescence: A cross-national and life-span perspective.* London: Routledge.

Grotevant, H. D., & McRoy, R. G. (1990). Adopted adolescents in residential treatment: The role of the family. In D. M. Brodzinsky & M. D. Schechter (Eds.), *The psychology of adoption.* New York: Oxford University Press.

Grych, J. H. (2002). Marital relationships and parenting. In M. H. Bornstein (Ed.), *Handbook of parenting* (2nd ed., Vol. 4). Mahwah, NJ: Erlbaum.

Guilford, J. P. (1967). *The structure of intellect.* New York: McGraw-Hill.

Gunnar, M. R., & Davis, E. P. (2003). Stress and emotion in early childhood. In I. B. Weiner (Ed.), *Handbook of psychology, Vol. 6.* New York: Wiley.

Gunnar, M. R., Malone, S., & Fisch, R. O. (1987). The psychobiology of stress and coping in the human neonate: Studies of the adrenocortical activity in response to stress in the first week of life. In T. Field, P. McCabe, & N. Scheiderman (Eds.), *Stress and coping.* Hillsdale, NJ: Erlbaum.

Gur, R. C., Mozley, L. H., Mozley, P. D., Resnick, S. M., Karp, J. S., Alavi, A., Arnold, S. E., & Gur, R. E. (1995). Sex differences in regional cerebral glucose metabolism during a resting state. *Science, 267*, 528–531.

Gurwitch, R. H., Silovksy, J. F., Schultz, S., Kees, M., & Burlingame, S. (2001). *Reactions and guidelines for children following trauma/disaster.* Norman, OK: Department of Pediatrics, University of Oklahoma Health Sciences Center.

Guttentag, M., & Bray, H. (1976). *Undoing sex stereotypes: Research and resources for educators.* New York: McGraw-Hill.

Gyamfi, P., Brooks-Gunn, J., & Jackson, A. P. (2001). Associations between employment and financial and parental stress in low-income single Black mothers. In M. C. Lennon (Ed.), *Welfare, work, and well-being.* New York: Haworth.

H

Hack, M., Flannery, D. J., Schlucter, M., Cartar, L., Borawski, E., & Klein, N. (2002). Outcomes in young adulthood for very-low-birth-weight infants. *New England Journal of Medicine, 346*, 149–157.

Hahn, C. S., & DiPietro, J. A. (2001). In vitro fertilization and the family: Quality of parenting, family functioning, and child psychosocial adjustment. *Developmental Psychology, 37*, 37–48.

Hahn, D. B., & Payne, W. A. (2003). *Focus on health* (6th ed.). New York: McGraw-Hill.

Hahn, W. K. (1987). Cerebral lateralization of function: From infancy through childhood. *Psychological Bulletin, 101*, 376–392.

Haidt, J. D. (1997, April). *Cultural and class variations in the domain of morality and the morality of conventions.* Paper presented at the meeting of the Society for Research in Child Development, Washington, DC.

Haig, D. (2003). Behavioral genetics: Family matters. *Nature, 421*, 491–492.

Haith, M. H. (1991, April). *Setting a path for the 90s: Some goals and challenges in infant-sensory and perceptual development.* Paper presented at the Society for Research in Child Development, Seattle.

Haith, M. M., & Benson, J. B. (1998). Infant cognition. In W. Damon (Ed.). *Handbook of child psychology* (5th ed., Vol. 2). New York: Wiley.

Haith, M. M., Hazen, C., & Goodman, G. S. (1988). Expectation and anticipation of dynamic visual events by 3.5 month old babies. *Child Development, 59*, 467–479.

Hakuta, K. (2000). Bilingualism. In A. Kazdin (Ed.). *Encyclopedia of psychology*. Washington, DC, and New York: American Psychological Association and Oxford University Press.

Hakuta, K., Bialystok, E., & Wiley, E. (2003). Critical evidence: A test of the critical-period hypothesis for second-language acquisition. *Psychological Science, 14,* 31–38.

Hakuta, K., Butler, Y. G., & Witt, D. (2000). *How long does it take English learners to attain proficiency?* Berkeley, CA: The University of California Linguistic Minority Research Institute Policy Report 2000-1.

Hakuta, K., & Garcia, E. E. (1989). Bilingualism and education. *American Psychologist, 44,* 374–379.

Haladyna, T. M. (2002). *Essentials of standardized testing*. Boston: Allyn & Bacon.

Hale, S. (1990). A global developmental trend in cognitive processing speed. *Child Development, 61,* 653–663.

Hall, G. S. (1904). *Adolescence* (Vols. 1 & 2). Englewood Cliffs, NJ: Prentice Hall.

Hall, R. T. (2000). Prevention of premature birth: Do pediatricians have a role? *Pediatrics, 105,* 1137–1140.

Hallahan, D. P., & Kaufmann, J. M. (2003). *Exceptional learners* (9th ed.). Boston: Allyn & Bacon.

Halle, T. G. (2003). Emotional development and well-being. In M. H. Bornstein, L. Davidson, C. L. M. Keyes, & K. A. Moore (Eds.), *Well-being*. Mahwah, NJ: Erlbaum.

Halonen, J., & Santrock, J. W. (1999). *Psychology: The contexts of behavior* (3rd ed.). New York: McGraw-Hill.

Halpern, D. (2001). Sex difference research: Cognitive abilities. In J. Worell (Ed.), *Encyclopedia of women and gender*. San Diego: Academic Press.

Hamburg, D. A. (1990). *Life skills training: Preventive interventions for young adolescents*. Washington, DC: Carnegie Council on Adolescent Development.

Hamburg, D. A. (1997). Meeting the essential requirements for healthy adolescent development in a transforming world. In R. Takanishi & D. Hamburg (Eds.), *Preparing adolescents for the 21st century*. New York: Cambridge University Press.

Hamburg, D. A., Millstein, S. G., Mortimer, A. M., Nightingale, E. O., & Petersen, A. C. (1993). Adolescent health promotion in the twenty-first century: Current frontiers and future directions. In S. G. Millstein, A. C. Petersen, & E. O. Nightingale (Eds.), *Promoting the health of adolescents*. New York: Oxford University Press.

Hamilton, M. C. (1991). *Preference for sons or daughters and the sex role characteristics of potential parents*. Paper presented at the meeting of the Association for Women in Psychology, Hartford, CT.

Hand, I. L., Noble, L., McVeigh, T. J., Kim, M., & Yoon, J. J. (2001). The effects of intrauterine cocaine exposure on the respiratory status of the very low birthweight infant. *Journal of Perinatology, 6,* 372–375.

Hanson, L. A., & Korotkova, A. (2002). The role of breastfeeding in prevention of neonatal infection. *Seminars in Neonatology, 7,* 257–281.

Hanson, L. A., Korotkova, M., Haversen, L., Mattsby-Baltzer, I., Hahn-Zoric, M., Silferdal, S. A., Strandvik, B., & Telemo, E. (2002). Breastfeeding, a complex support system for the offspring. *Pediatrics International, 44,* 347–352.

Hardman, M. L., Drew, C. J., & Egan, M. W. (2002). *Human exceptionality* (7th ed.). Boston: Allyn & Bacon.

Hare, B. R., & Castenell, L. A. (1985). No place to run, no place to hide: Comparative status and future prospects of black boys. In M. B. Spencer, G. K. Brookins, & W. R. Allen (Eds.), *Beginnings: The social and affective development of black children*. Hillsdale, NJ: Erlbaum.

Harkness, S., & Super, C. M. (2002). Culture and parenting. In M. H. Bornstein (Ed.), *Handbook of parenting* (2nd ed., Vol. 2). Mahwah, NJ: Erlbaum.

Harlow, H. F. (1958). The nature of love. *American Psychologist, 13,* 673–685.

Harris, G., Thomas, A., & Booth, D. A. (1990). Development of salt taste in infancy. *Developmental Psychology, 26,* 534–538.

Harris, J. R. (1998). *The nurture assumption: Why children turn out the way they do: Parents matter less than you think and peers matter more.* New York: Free Press.

Harris, L. (1987, September 3). The latchkey child phenomena. *Dallas Morning News,* pp. 1A, 10A.

Harris, L. (1997). *A national poll of children and exercise*. Washington, DC: Lou Harris & Associates.

Harrist, A. W. (1993, March). *Family interaction styles as predictors of children's competence: The role of synchrony and nonsynchrony*. Paper presented at the biennial meeting of the Society for Research in Child Development, New Orleans.

Hart, B., & Risley, T. R. (1995). *Meaningful differences*. Baltimore: Paul H. Brookes.

Hart, C. H., Burts, D. C., & Charlesworth, R. (Eds.). (1997). *Integrated curriculum and developmentally appropriate practice: Birth to age 8*. Albany, NY: State University of New York Press.

Hart, C. H., Newell, L. D., & Olsen, S. F. (2003). Parenting skills and social-communicative competence in childhood. In J. O. Greene & B. R. Burleson (Eds.), *Handbook of communication and social interaction skill*. Mahwah, NJ: Erlbaum.

Hart, C. H., Olsen, S. F., Robinson, C. C., & Mandleco, B. L. (1997). The development of social and communicative competence in childhood: Review and a model of personal, familial, and extra-familial processes. *Communication Yearbook, 20,* 305–373.

Hart, C. H., Yang, C., Charlesworth, R., & Burts, D. C. (2003, April). *Early childhood teachers' curriculum beliefs, classroom practices, and children's outcomes: What are the connections?* Paper presented at the biennial meeting of the Society for Research in Child Development, Tampa, FL.

Hart, D. (1996). Unpublished review of J. W. Santrock's *Child development*, 8th ed. (Dubuque, IA: Brown & Benchmark).

Hart, D., Burock, D., London, B., & Atkins, R. (2003). Prosocial development, antisocial development, and moral development. In A. M. Slater & G. Bremner (Eds.), *An introduction to developmental psychology*. Malden, MA: Blackwell.

Hart, D., & Fegley, S. (1995). Prosocial behavior and caring in adolescence: Relations to self-understanding and social judgment. *Child Development, 66,* 1346–1359.

Hart, D., & Karmel, M. P. (1996). Self-awareness and self-knowledge in humans, great apes, and monkeys. In A. Russon, K. Bard, & S. Parker (Eds.), *Reaching into thought*. New York: Cambridge University Press.

Harter, S. (1981). A new self-report scale of intrinsic versus extrinsic orientation in the classroom: Motivational and informational components. *Developmental Psychology, 17,* 300–312.

Harter, S. (1982). The Perceived Competence Scale for Children. *Child Development, 53,* 87–97.

Harter, S. (1985). *Self-Perception Profile for Children*. Denver: University of Denver, Department of Psychology.

Harter, S. (1986). Processes underlying the construction, maintenance, and enhancement of the self-concept of children. In J. Suls & A. Greenwald (Eds.), *Psychological perspective on the self* (Vol. 3). Hillsdale, NJ: Erlbaum.

Harter, S. (1989). *Self-Perception Profile for Adolescents.* Denver: University of Denver, Department of Psychology.

Harter, S. (1990). Self and identity development. In S. S. Feldman & G. R. Elliott (Eds.), *At the threshold: The developing adolescent.* Cambridge, MA: Harvard University Press.

Harter, S. (1996). Teacher and classmate influences on scholastic motivation, self-esteem, and level of voice in adolescents. In J. Juvonen & K. R. Wentzel (Eds.), *Social motivation.* New York: Cambridge University Press.

Harter, S. (1998). The development of self-representations. In N. Eisenberg (Ed.), *Handbook of child psychology* (5th ed., Vol. 3). New York: Wiley.

Harter, S. (1999). *The construction of the self.* New York: Guilford Press.

Harter, S., & Lee, L. (1989). *Manifestations of true and false selves in adolescence.* Paper presented at the meeting of the Society for Research in Child Development, Kansas City.

Harter, S., & Marold, D. B. (1992). Psychological risk factors contributing to adolescent suicide ideation. In G. Noam & S. Borst (Eds.), *Child and adolescent suicide.* San Francisco: Jossey-Bass.

Harter, S., Marold, D. B., Whitesell, N. R., & Cobbs, G. (1996). A model of the effects of perceived parent and peer support on adolescent false self behavior. *Child Development, 67,* 360–374.

Harter, S., & Monsour, A. (1992). Developmental analysis of conflict caused by opposing attributes in the adolescent self-portrait. *Developmental Psychology, 28,* 251–260.

Harter, S., Waters, P., & Whitesell, N. (1996, March). *False self behavior and lack of voice among adolescent males and females.* Paper presented at the meeting of the Society for Research on Adolescence, Boston.

Harter, S., Waters, P. L., Whitesell, N. R., & Kastelic, D. (1998). Level of voice among female and male high school students: Relational context, support, and gender orientation. *Developmental Psychology, 34,* 892–901.

Harter, S., & Whitesell, N. (2001, April). *What we have learned from Columbine: The impact of self-esteem on suicidal and violent ideation among adolescents.* Paper presented at the meeting of the Society for Research in Child Development, Minneapolis.

Hartshorne, H., & May, M. S. (1928–1930). *Moral studies in the nature of character: Studies in deceit* (Vol. 1); *Studies in self-control* (Vol. 2). *Studies in the organization of character* (Vol. 3). New York: Macmillan.

Hartup, W. W. (1983). The peer system. In P. H. Mussen (Ed.), *Handbook of child psychology* (4th ed., Vol. 4). New York: Wiley.

Hartup, W. W. (1996). The company they keep: Friendships and their development significance. *Child Development, 67,* 1–13.

Hartup, W. W. (1999, April). *Peer relations and the growth of the individual child.* Paper presented at the meeting of the Society for Research in Child Development, Albuquerque.

Hartup, W. W. (2000). Middle childhood: Socialization and social context. In A. Kazdin (Ed.), *Encyclopedia of psychology.* Washington, DC, & New York: American Psychological Association and Oxford University Press.

Hartup, W. W., & Abecassis, M. (2002). Friends and enemies. In P. K. Smith & C. H. Hart (Eds.), *Blackwell handbook of childhood social development.* Malden, MA: Blackwell.

Hartup, W. W., & Laursen, B. (1999). Relationships as developmental contexts: Retrospective themes and contemporary issues. In W. Andrew Collins & B. Laursen (Eds.), *Relationships as developmental contexts.* Mahwah, NJ: Erlbaum.

Harwood, R., Leyendecker, B., Carlson, V., Asencio, M., & Miller, A. (2002). Parenting among Latino families in the U.S. In M. H. Bornstein (Ed.), *Handbook of parenting* (2nd ed.). Mahwah, NJ: Erlbaum.

Haselager, G. J. T., Cillessen, A. H. N., Van Lieshout, C. F. M., Riksen-Walraen, J. M. A., & Hartup, W. W. (2002). Heterogeneity among peer-rejected boys across middle childhood: Developmental pathways of social behavior. *Developmental Psychology, 38,* 446–456.

Hauck, F. R., Moore, C. M., Herman, S. M., Donovan, M., Kalelkar, M., Christoffel, K. K., Hoffman, H. J., & Rowley, D. (2002). The contribution of prone sleeping position to the racial disparity in sudden infant death syndrome: The Chicago Infant Mortality Study. *Pediatrics, 110,* 772–780.

Hauser, S. T., & Bowlds, M. K. (1990). Stress, coping, and adaptation. In S. S. Feldman & G. R. Elliott (Eds.), *At the threshold: The developing adolescent.* Cambridge, MA: Harvard University Press.

Hauser, S. T., Powers, S. I., Noam, G. G., Jacobson, A. M., Weisse, B., & Follansbee, D. J. (1984). Familial contexts of adolescent ego development. *Child Development, 55,* 195–213.

Hauth, J. C., & Cunningham, F. G. (2002). Vaginal breech delivery is still justified. *Obstetrics and Gynecology, 99,* 1115–1116.

Havighurst, R. J. (1976). A cross-cultural view. In J. F. Adams (Ed.), *Understanding adolescence.* Boston: Allyn & Bacon.

Hawkins, J. A., & Berndt, T. J. (1985, April). *Adjustment following the transition to junior high school.* Paper presented at the biennial meeting of the Society for Research in Child Development, Toronto.

Hay, P., & Bacaltchuk, J. (2002). Bulimia nervosa. *Clinical Evidence, 8,* 914–926.

Health Management Resources (2001). *Child health and fitness.* Boston: Author.

Heath, D. H. (1977). Some possible effects of occupation on the maturing professional man. *Journal of Vocational Behavior, 11,* 263–281.

Heath, S. B. (1989). Oral and literate traditions among Black Americans living in poverty. *American Psychologist, 44,* 367–373.

Heath, S. B., & McLaughlin, M. W. (Eds.). (1993). *Identity and inner-city youth.* New York: Teacher College Press.

Heilman, A. W., Blair, T. R., & Rupley, W. H. (2002). *Principles and practices of teaching reading* (10th ed.). Upper Saddle River, NJ: Merrill.

Hellige, J. B. (1990). Hemispheric asymmetry. *Annual Review of Psychology* (Vol. 41). Palo Alto, CA: Annual Reviews.

Hendry, J. (1986). *Becoming Japanese: The world of the preschool child.* Honolulu: University of Hawaii Press.

Hennessey. B. A., & Amabile, T. M. (1998). Reward, intrinsic motivation, and creativity. *American Psychologist, 53,* 674–675.

Henninger, M. L. (1999). *Teaching young children.* Columbus, OH: Merrill.

Hepper, P. G., Shahidullah, S., & White, R. (1990). Origins of fetal handedness. *Nature, 347,* 431.

Herrill, R., Goldberg, J., True, W. R., Ramakrishnan, V., Lyons, M., Eisen, S., & Tsuang, M. T. (1999). Sexual orientation and suicidality: A co-twin control study in adult men. *Archives of General Psychiatry, 56,* 867–874.

Herrnstein, R. J., & Murray, C. (1994). *The bell curve: Intelligence and class structure in American life.* New York: Macmillan.

Hess, L., Lonky, E., & Roodin, P. A. (1985, April). *The relationship of moral reasoning and ego strength to cheating behavior.* Paper presented at the meeting of the Society for Research in Child Development, Toronto.

Hetherington, E. M. (1989). Coping with family transitions: Winners, losers, and survivors. *Child Development, 60,* 1–14.

Hetherington, E. M. (1993). An overview of the Virginia Longitudinal Study of Divorce and Remarriage with a focus on early adolescence. *Journal of Family Psychology, 7,* 39–56.

Hetherington, E. M. (1999). Social capital and the development of youth from non-divorced, divorced, and remarried families. In W. A. Collins & B. Laursen (Eds.), *Relationships as developmental contexts.* Mahwah, NJ: Erlbaum.

Hetherington, E. M. (2000). Divorce. In A. Kazdin (Ed.), *Encyclopedia of psychology.* Washington, DC, & New York: American Psychological Association and Oxford University Press.

Hetherington, E. M., Bridges, M., & Insabella, G. M. (1998). What matters? What does not? Five perspectives on the association between marital transitions and children's adjustment. *American Psychologist, 53,* 167–184.

Hetherington, E. M., & Jodl, K. M. (1994). Stepfamilies as settings for child development. In A. Booth & J. Dunn (Eds.), *Stepfamilies: Who benefits? Who does not?* Hillsdale, NJ: Erlbaum.

Hetherington, E. M., & Kelly, J. (2002). *For better or worse: Divorce reconsidered.* New York: W. W. Norton.

Hetherington, E. M., & Stanley-Hagan, M. (2002). Parenting in divorced and remarried families. In M. H. Bornstein (Ed.), *Handbook of parenting* (2nd ed., Vol. 3). Mahwah, NJ: Erlbaum.

Hetherington, E. M., Reiss, D., & Plomin, R. (Eds.). (1994). *Separate social worlds of siblings: The impact of nonshared environment on development.* Hillsdale, NJ: Erlbaum.

Heuwinkel, M. K. (1996). New ways of learning 5 new ways of teaching. *Childhood Education, 72,* 27–31.

Hiebert, E. H., & Raphael, T. E. (1996). Psychological perspectives on literacy and extensions to educational practice. In D. C. Berliner & R. C. Calfee (Eds.), *Handbook of educational psychology.* New York: Macmillan.

Higgins, A., Power, C., & Kohlberg, L. (1983, April). *Moral atmosphere and moral judgment.* Paper presented at the biennial meeting of the Society for Research in Child Development, Detroit.

Hildebrand, V., Phenice, A., & Hines, R. P. (2000). *Knowing and serving diverse families.* Columbus, OH: Merrill.

Hill, C. R., & Stafford, F. P. (1980). Parental care of children: Time diary estimate of quantity, predictability, and variety. *Journal of Human Resources, 15,* 219–239.

Hill, J., Waldfogel, J., Brooks-Gunn, J., & Han, W. (2001, November) *Towards a better estimate of casual links in child policy: The case of maternal employment and child outcomes.* Paper presented at the Association for Public Policy Analysis and Management Fall Research Conference, Washington, DC.

Hill, J. O., & Trowbridge, F. L. (1998). Childhood obesity: Future directions and research priorities. *Pediatrics, 101,* 570–574.

Hill, N. E., Bush, K. R., & Roosa, M. W. (2003). Parenting and family socialization strategies and children's mental health: Low-income Mexican-American and European-American mothers and children. *Child Development, 74,* 189–205.

Hines, M. (1990). Gonadal hormones and human cognitive development. In J. Balthazart (Ed.), *Hormones, brain, and behavior in vertebrates.* Basel: Karger.

Hirsch, B. J., & Rapkin, B. D. (1987). The transition to junior high school: A longitudinal study of self-esteem, psychological symptomatology, school life, and social support. *Child Development, 58,* 1235–1243.

Hobel, C. J., Dunkel-Schetter, C., Roesch, S. C., Castro, L. C., & Arora, C. P. (1999). Maternal plasma corticotrophin-releasing hormone associated with stress at 20 weeks' gestation in pregnancies ending in preterm delivery. *American Journal of Obstetrics and Gynecology, 180,* S257–S263.

Hochschild, A. R. (1983). *The managed heart: Commercialization of feelings.* Berkeley, University of California Press.

Hockenberry, M. (2003). *Wong's nursing care of infants and children.* St. Louis: Mosby.

Hodges, E. A. (2003). A primer on early childhood obesity and parental influence. *Pediatric Nursing, 29,* 13–16.

Hoff, E., Laursen, B., & Tardif, T. (2002). Socioeconomic status and parenting. In M. H. Bornstein (Ed.), *Handbook of parenting* (2nd ed.). Mahwah, NJ: Erlbaum.

Hoff-Ginsberg, E. (1999). *How children use input to acquire vocabulary: Evidence from a study of individual and group differences.* Unpublished manuscript, Division of Science, Florida Atlantic University.

Hoff-Ginsberg, E., & Lerner, S. (1999, April). *The nature of vocabulary differences related to socioeconomic status at two and four years.* Paper presented at the meeting of the Society for Research in Child Development, Albuquerque.

Hoffman, L. W. (1989). Effects of maternal employment in two-parent families. *American Psychologist, 44,* 283–293.

Hoffman, L. W., & Youngblade, L. M. (1999). *Mothers at work: Effects on children's well-being.* New York: Cambridge.

Hoffman, M. L. (1970). Moral development. In P. H. Mussen (Ed.), *Manual of child psychology* (3rd ed., Vol. 2). New York: Wiley.

Hoffman, M. L. (1988). Moral development. In M. H. Bornstein & E. Lamb (Eds.), *Developmental psychology: An advanced textbook* (2nd ed.). Hillsdale, NJ: Erlbaum.

Hoffman, S., Foster, E., & Furstenberg, F. (1993). Reevaluating the costs of teenage childbearing. *Demography, 30,* 1–13.

Hoffnung, M. (1984). Motherhood: Contemporary conflict for women. In J. Freeman (Ed.), *Women: A feminist perspective* (3rd ed.). Palo Alto, CA: Mayfield.

Hofstede, G. (1980). *Culture's consequences: International differences in work-related values.* Newbury Park, CA: Sage.

Holding, S. (2002). Current state of screening for Down syndrome. *Annals of Clinical Biochemistry, 39,* 1–11.

Hollier, L. M., Harstad, T. W., Sanchez, P. J., Twickler, D. M., & Wendel, G. D. (2001). Fetal syphilis: Clinical and laboratory characteristics. *Obstetrics and Gynecology, 97,* 947–953.

Holmbeck, G. N. (1996). A model of family relational transformations during the transition to adolescence: Parent-adolescent conflict and adaptation. In J. A. Graber, J. Brooks-Gunn, & A. C. Petersen (Eds.), *Transitions through adolescence.* Hillsdale, NJ: Erlbaum.

Holmes, L. D. (1987). *Quest for the real Samoa: The Mead-Freeman controversy and beyond.* South Hadley, MA: Bergin & Garvey.

Holtzen, D. W. (2000). Handedness and professional tennis. *International Journal of Neuroscience, 105,* 101–119.

Holtzmann, W. (1982). Cross-cultural comparisons of personality development in Mexico and the United States. In D. Wagner & H. W. Stevenson (Eds.), *Cultural perspectives on child development.* San Francisco: W. H. Freeman.

Honein, M. A., Paulozzi, L. J., Mathews, T. J., Erickson, J. D., & Wong, L. Y. (2001). Impact of folic acid fortification of the U.S. food supply on the occurrence of tube defects. *Journal of the American Medical Association, 285,* 2981–2986.

Honig, A. S. (2002). Choosing child care for young children. In M. H. Bornstein (Ed.), *Handbook of parenting* (2nd ed.). Mahwah, NJ: Erlbaum.

Honzik, M. P., MacFarlane, J. W., & Allen, L. (1948). The stability of mental test performance between two and eighteen years. *Journal of Experimental Education, 17,* 309–324.

Hood, B. (1995). Gravity rules for 2- to 4-year-olds? *Cognitive Development, 10,* 577–598.

Hopkins, B. (1991). Facilitating early motor development: An intracultural study of West Indian mothers and their infants living in Britain. In J. K. Nugent, B. M. Lester, & T. B. Brazelton (Eds.), *The cultural context of infancy: Vol. 2. Multicultural and interdisciplinary approaches to parent-infant relations.* Norwood, NJ: Ablex.

Hopkins, B., & Westra, T. (1988). Maternal handling and motor development: An intracultural study. *Genetic Psychology Monographs, 14,* 377–420.

Hopkins, B., & Westra, T. (1990). Motor development, maternal expectations, and the role of handling. *Infant Behavior and Development, 13,* 117–122.

Hopkins, J. R. (2000). Erikson, E. H. In A. Kazdin (Ed.), *Encyclopedia of psychology.* Washington, DC, & New York: American Psychological Association and Oxford University Press.

Hoppu, U., Kalliomaki, M., Laiho, K., & Isolauri, E. (2001). Breast milk—immunomodulatory signals against allergenic diseases, *Allergy, 56,* 23–26.

Horne, R. S., Franco, P., Adamson, T. M., Groswasser, U., & Kahn, A. (2002). Effects of body position on sleep and arousal characteristics in infants. *Early Human Development, 69,* 25–33.

Horowitz, F. D., & O'Brien, M. (1989). In the interest of the nation: A reflective essay on the state of knowledge and the challenges before us. *American Psychologist, 44,* 441–445.

Hort, B. E., & Leinbach, M. D. (1993, March). *Children's use of metaphorical cues in gender-typing of objects.* Paper presented at the biennial meeting of the Society for Research in Child Development, New Orleans.

Hotchner, T. (1997). *Pregnancy and childbirth.* New York: Avon.

Hoving, K. L., Spender, T., Robb, K. Y., & Schulte, D. (1978). Developmental changes in visual information processing. In P. A. Ornstein (Ed.), *Memory development in children.* Hillsdale, NJ: Erlbaum.

Howard, R. W. (2001). Searching the real world for signs of rising population intelligence. *Personality and Individual Differences, 30,* 1039–1058.

Howe, M. J. A., Davidson, J. W., Moore, D. G., & Sloboda, J. A. (1995). Are there early childhood signs of musical ability? *Psychology of Music, 23,* 162–176.

Howell, C. J., Dean, T., Lucking, L., Dziedzic, K., Jones, P. W., & Johanson, R. B. (2002). Randomized study of long term outcome after epidural versus non-epidural analgesia during labor. *British Medical Journal, 352,* 357.

Howell, E. M. (2001). The impact of Medicaid expansions for pregnant women: A synthesis of the evidence. *Medical Care Research Review, 58,* 3–30.

Howes, C. (1985, April). *Predicting preschool sociometric status from toddler peer interaction.* Paper presented at the meeting of the Society for Research in Child Development, Toronto.

Howes, C. (1988, April). *Can the age of entry and the quality of infant child care predict behaviors in kindergarten?* Paper presented at the International Conference on Infant Studies, Washington, DC.

Hoyle, R. H., & Judd, C. M. (2002). *Research methods in social psychology* (7th ed.). Belmont, CA: Wadsworth.

Huang, L. N., & Ying, Y. (1989). Chinese American children and adolescents. In J. T. Gibbs & L. N. Huang (Eds.), *Children of color.* San Francisco: Jossey-Bass.

Hudson, L. M., Forman, E. R., & Brion-Meisels, S. (1982). Role-taking as a predictor of prosocial behavior in cross-age tutors. *Child Development, 53,* 1320–1329.

Huebner, A. M., & Garrod, A. C. (1993). Moral reasoning among Tibetan monks: A study of Buddhist adolescents and young adults in Nepal. *Journal of Cross-Cultural Psychology, 24,* 167–185.

Huesmann, L. R. (1986). Psychological processes promoting the relation between exposure to media violence and aggressive behavior by the viewer. *Journal of Social Issues, 42,* 125–139.

Huffman, L. R., & Speer, P. W. (2000). Academic performance among at-risk children: The role of developmentally appropriate practices. *Early Childhood Research Quarterly, 15,* 167–184.

Hughey, J. B., & Slack, C. (2001). *Teaching children to write.* Upper Saddle River, NJ: Merrill.

Hulse, G. K., O'Neill, G., Pereira, C., & Brewer, C. (2001). Obstetric and neonatal outcomes associated with maternal naltrexone exposure. *Australian and New Zealand Journal of Obstetrics and Gynecology, 41,* 424–428.

Hunsley, M., & Thoman, E. B. (2002). The sleep of co-sleeping infants when they are not co-sleeping: Evidence that co-sleeping is stressful. *Developmental Psychobiology, 40,* 14–22.

Hunt, E. (1995). *Will we be smart enough? A cognitive analysis of the coming work force.* New York: Russell Sage.

Hunt, R. R., & Ellis, H. C. (1999). *Fundamentals of cognitive psychology* (6th ed.). New York: McGraw-Hill.

Hunt, R. R., & Kelly, R. E. S. (1996). Accessing the particular from the general: The power of distinctiveness in the context of organization. *Memory and Cognition, 24,* 217–225.

Huston, A. C. (1983). Sex-typing. In P. H. Mussen (Ed.), *Handbook of child psychology* (4th ed., Vol. 4). New York: Wiley.

Huston, A. C., Duncan, G. J., Grander, R., Bos, J., McLoyd, V., Mistry, R., Crosby, D., Gibson, C., Magnuson, K., Romich, J., & Ventura, A. (2001). Work-based antipoverty programs for parents can enhance the school performance and social behavior of children. *Child Development, 72,* 318–336.

Huston, A. C., McLoyd, V. C., & Coll, C. G. (1994). Children and poverty: Issues in contemporary research. *Child Development, 65,* 275–282.

Huston, A. C., Seigle, J., & Bremer, M. (1983, April). *Family environment and television use by preschool children.* Paper presented at the Society for Research in Child Development meeting, Detroit.

Huttenlocher, J., & Cymerman, E. (1999). Unpublished data on speech syntax. Chicago: University of Chicago.

Huttenlocher, J., Haight, W., Bruk, A., Seltzer, M., & Lyons, T. (1991). Early vocabulary growth: Relation to language input and gender. *Developmental Psychology, 27,* 236–248.

Huttenlocher, J., Levine, S., & Vevea, J. (1998). Environmental input and cognitive growth: A study using time-period comparisons. *Child Development, 69,* 1012–1029.

Huttenlocher, P. R., & Dabholkar, A. S. (1997). Regional differences in synaptogenesis in human cerebral cortex. *Journal of Comparative Neurology, 37* (2), 167–178.

Hyde, J. S. (1993). Meta-analysis and the psychology of women. In F. L. Denmark & M. A. Paludi (Eds.), *Handbook on the psychology of women.* Westport, CT: Greenwood.

Hyde, J. S., & DeLamater, J. (2002). *Human Sexuality* (8th ed.). New York: McGraw-Hill.

Hyde, J. S., & Mezulis, A. H. (2001). Gender difference research: Issues and critique. In

J. Worell (Ed.), *Encyclopedia of women and gender*. San Diego: Academic Press.

Hyde, J. S., & Plant, E. A. (1995). Magnitude of psychological gender differences: Another side of the story. *American Psychologist, 50*, 159–161.

Inoff-Germain, G., Arnold, G. S., Nottelmann, E. D., Susman, E. J., Cutler, G. B., & Chrousos, G. P. (1988). Relations between hormone levels and observational measures of aggressive behavior of young adolescents in family interactions. *Developmental Psychology, 24*, 124–139.

International Society for Technology in Education. (1999). *National educational technology standards for students*. Eugene, OR: International Society for Technology in Education.

Isasa, V., Requena, A., Garcia-Velasco, J. A., Remohi, J., Pellicer, A., & Simon, C. (2003). Recombinant vs. urinary follicle-stimulating hormone in couples undergoing intrauterine insemination. A randomized study. *Journal of Reproductive Medicine, 48*, 112–118.

Izard, C. (2000). Affect. In A. Kazdin (Ed.), *Encyclopedia of psychology*. Washington, DC, & New York: American Psychological Association and Oxford University Press.

Jaakkola, J. J., Nafstad, P., & Magnus, P. (2001). Environmental tobacco smoke, parental atopy, and childhood asthma. *Environmental Health Perspectives, 109*, 579–582.

Jackson, A., & Davis, G. (2000). *Turning points 2000*. New York: Teachers College Press.

Jacob, N., Van Gestel, S., Derom, C., Theiry, E., Vernon, P., Derom, R., & Vlietinck, R. (2001). Heritability estimates of intelligence in twins: Effect of chorion type. *Behavior Genetics, 31*, 209–217.

Jacobson, J. L., & Jacobson, S. W. (2002). Association of prenatal exposure to an environmental contaminant with intellectual function in childhood. *Journal of Toxicology–Clinical Toxicology, 40*, 467–475.

Jacobson, J. L., Jacobson, S. W., Fein, G. G., Schwartz, P. M., & Dowler, J. (1984). Prenatal exposure to an environmental toxin: A test of the multiple-effects model. *Developmental Psychology, 20*, 523–532.

Jaffee, S., & Hyde, J. S. (2000). Gender differences in moral orientation: A meta-analysis. *Psychological Bulletin, 126*, 703–726.

Jaffee, S. R. (2002). Pathways to adversity in young adulthood among early childbearers. *Journal of Family Psychology, 16*, 38–49.

James, W. (1890/1950). *The principles of psychology*. New York: Dover.

Jarrett, R. L. (1995). Growing up poor: The family experiences of socially mobile youth in low-income African-American neighborhoods. *Journal of Adolescent Research, 10*, 111–135.

Jeffery, H. E., Megevand, A., Page, H., & Page, M. (2000). Why the prone position is a risk factor in sudden infant death syndrome. *Pediatrics, 104*, 263–269.

Jenkins, J. M., & Astington, J. W. (1996). Cognitive factors and family structure associated with theory of mind development in young children. *Developmental Psychology, 32*, 70–78.

Jensen, A. R. (1969). How much can we boost IQ and scholastic achievement? *Harvard Educational Review, 39*, 1–123.

Jensen, L. A. (1995, March). *The moral reasoning of orthodox and progressivist Indians and Americans*. Paper presented at the meeting of the Society for Research in Child Development, Indianapolis.

Jessor, R. (Ed.). (1998). *New perspectives on adolescent risk behavior*. New York: Cambridge University Press.

Ji, B. T., Shu, X. O., Linet, M. S., Zheng, W., Wacholde, S., Gao, Y. T., Ying, D. M., & Jin, F. (1997). Paternal cigarette smoking and the risk of childhood cancer among offspring of nonsmoking mothers. *Journal of the National Cancer Institute, 89*, 238–244.

Jiao, S., Ji, G., & Jing, Q. (1996). Cognitive development of Chinese urban only children and children with siblings. *Child Development, 67*, 387–395.

Jin, S. H., Kim, T. I., Han, D. S., Shin, S. K., & Kim, W. H. (2002). Thalidomide suppresses the interleukin 1 beta-induced NF-k-B signaling pathway in colon cancer cells. *Annals of the New York Academy of Science, 973*, 414–418.

Jinon, S. (1996). The effect of infant massage on growth of the preterm infant. In C. Yarbes-Almirante & M. De Luma (Eds.), *Increasing safe and successful pregnancy*. Amsterdam: Elsevier.

Jirtle, R. L., Sander, M., & Barrett, J. C. (2000). Genomic imprinting and environmental disease susceptibility. *Environmental Health Perspectives, 108*, 271–278.

John-Steiner, V., & Mahn, H. (2003). Sociocultural contexts for teaching and learning. In I. B. Weiner (Ed.), *Handbook of psychology, Vol. 7*. New York: Wiley.

Johnson, D. W. (1990). *Teaching out: Interpersonal effectiveness and self-actualization*. Upper Saddle River, NJ: Prentice Hall.

Johnson, J. E., Christie, J. F., & Yawkey, T. D. (1987). *Play and early childhood development*. Glenview, IL: Scott, Foresman.

Johnson, J. S., & Newport, E. L. (1991). Critical period effects on universal properties of language: The status of subjacency in the acquisition of a second language. *Cognition, 39*, 215–258.

Johnson, M. H. (2000). Infancy: Biological processes. In A. Kazdin (Ed.), *Encyclopedia of psychology*. Washington, DC, & New York: American Psychological Association and Oxford University Press.

Johnson, M. H. (2001). Functional brain development during infancy. In A. Fogel & G. Bremner (Eds.), *Blackwell handbook of infant development*. London: Blackwell.

Johnson, M. K., Beebe, T., Mortimer, J. T., & Snyder, M. (1998). Volunteerism in adolescence: A process perspective. *Journal of Research on Adolescence, 8*, 309–332.

Johnston, C., & Leung, D. W. (2001). Effects of medication, behavioral, and combined treatments on parents' and children's attributions for the behavior of children with attention-deficit hyperactivity disorder, *Journal of Consulting and Clinical Psychology, 69*, 67–76.

Johnston, J., Etteman, J., & Davidson, T. (1980). *An evaluation of "Freestyle": A television series to reduce sex-role stereotypes*. Ann Arbor: University of Michigan, Institute of Social Research.

Johnston, L. D., O'Malley, P. M., & Bachman, J. G. (1992, January 25), *Most forms of drug use decline among American high school and college students*. News release, Institute of Social Research, University of Michigan, Ann Arbor.

Johnston, L. D., O'Malley, P. M. & Bachman, J. G. (2001, December). *Monitoring the future, 2001*. Ann Arbor, MI: Institute for Social Research, University of Michigan.

Johnston, L. D., O'Malley, P. M., & Bachman, J. G. (2003). *Monitoring the future national results on adolescent drug use: Overview of key findings, 2002*. Bethesda, MD: National Institute of Drug Abuse.

Jones, D. C., & Costin, S. E. (1997, April). *The friendships of African-American and European-American adolescents*. Paper presented at the meeting of the Society for Research in Child Development, Washington, DC.

Jones, G., Riley, M., & Dwyer, T. (2000). Breastfeeding early in life and bone mass in prepubertal children: A longitudinal study. *Osteoporosis International, 11*, 146–152.

Jones, J. M. (1994). The African American: A duality dilemma? In W. J. Lonner & R. Malpass (Eds.), *Psychology and culture*. Needham Heights, MA: Allyn & Bacon.

Jones, M. C. (1965). Psychological correlates of somatic development. *Child Development, 36*, 899–911.

Jones, T. G., & Fuller, M. L. (2003). *Teaching Hispanic children*. Boston: Allyn & Bacon.

Joseph, C. L. M. (1989). Identification of factors associated with delayed antenatal care. *Journal of the American Medical Association, 81*, 57–63.

Jusczyk, P. W. (2000). *The discovery of spoken language*. Cambridge, MA: MIT Press.

Jusczyk, P. W., & Hohne, E. A. (1997). Infants' memory for spoken words. *Science, 277*, 1984–1986.

K

Kagan, J. (1984). *The nature of the child*. New York: Basic Books.

Kagan, J. (1987). Perspectives on infancy. In J. D. Osofsky (Ed.), *Handbook on infant development* (2nd ed.). New York: Wiley.

Kagan, J. (1992). Yesterday's promises, tomorrow's promises. *Developmental Psychology, 28*, 990–997.

Kagan, J. (1997). Temperament and the reactions to unfamiliarity. *Child Development, 68*, 139–143.

Kagan, J. (1998). *The power of parents*. Available on the world wide web at: http:// psychplace.com.

Kagan, J. (2000). Temperament. In A. Kazdin (Ed.), *Encyclopedia of psychology*. Washington, DC, & New York: American Psychological Association and Oxford University Press.

Kagan, J. (2002). Behavioral inhibition as a temperamental category. In R. J. Davidson, K. R. Scherer, & H. H. Goldsmith (Eds.), *Handbook of affective sciences*. New York: Oxford University Press.

Kagan, J. (2003). Biology, context, and developmental inquiry. *Annual Review of Psychology* (Vol. 54). Palo Alto, CA: Annual Reviews.

Kagan, J., & Snidman, N. (1991). Infant predictors of inhibited and uninhibited behavioral profiles. *Psychological Science, 2*, 40–44.

Kagan, J. J., Kearsley, R. B., & Zelazo, P. R. (1978). *Infancy: Its place in human development*. Cambridge, MA: Harvard University Press.

Kagan, S., & Madsen, M. C. (1972). Experimental analysis of cooperation and competition of Anglo-American and Mexican children. *Developmental Psychology, 6*, 49–59.

Kagitcibasi, C. (1988). Diversity of socialization and social change. In P. R. Dasen, J. W. Berry, & N. Sartorious (Eds.), *Health and cross-cultural psychology: Toward applications*. Newbury Park, CA: Sage.

Kagitcibasi, C. (1995). Is psychology relevant to global human development issues? Experience from Turkey. *American Psychologist, 50*, 293–300.

Kahn, A., Sawaguchi, T., Sawaguchi, A., Groswasser, J., Franco, P., Scaillet, S., Kelmanson, I., & Dan, B. (2002). Sudden infant deaths: From epidemiology to physiology. *Forensic Science International, 130* (Suppl.) S8–S20.

Kail, R. (1993, March). *The nature of global developmental change in processing time*. Paper presented at the biennial meeting of the Society for Research in Child Development, New Orleans.

Kaiser Family Foundation. (2001). *Generation Rx.com: How young people use the Internet for health information*. Menlo Park, CA: Henry J. Kaiser Family Foundation.

Kaiser Family Foundation. (2002). *Key facts: Teens online*. Menlo Park, CA: Henry J. Kaiser Family Foundation.

Kamii, C. (1985). *Young children reinvent arithmetic: Implications of Piaget's theory*. New York: Teachers College Press.

Kamii, C. (1989). *Young children continue to reinvent arithmetic*. New York: Teachers College Press.

Kammerman, S. B. (1989). Child care, women, work, and the family: An international overview of child-care services and related policies. In J. S. Lande, S. Scarr, & N. Gunzenhauser (Eds.), *Caring for children: Challenge to America*. Hillsdale, NJ: Erlbaum.

Kammerman, S. B. (2000a). Parental leave policies. *Social Policy Report of the Society for Research in Child Development, XIV* (No. 2), 1–15.

Kammerman, S. B. (2000b). From maternity to paternity child leave policies. *Journal of the Medical Women's Association, 55*, 98–99.

Kanoy, K., Ulku-Steiner, B., Cox, M., & Burchinal, M. (2003). Marital relationship and individual psychological characteristics that predict physical punishment of children. *Journal of Family Psychology, 17*, 20–28.

Kassin, S. M., Tubb, V. A., Hosch, H. M., & Memon, A. (2001). On the "general acceptance" of eyewitness testimony research. *American Psychologist, 56*, 405–416.

Katz, L. (1999). Curriculum disputes in early childhood education. *ERIC Clearinghouse on Elementary and Early Childhood Education*, Document EDO-PS-99-13.

Katz, L., & Chard, S. (1989). *Engaging the minds of young children: The project approach*. Norwood, NJ: Ablex.

Katz, P. A. (1987, August). *Children and social issues*. Paper presented at the meeting of the American Psychological Association, New York.

Kauffman Early Education Exchange (2002). *Set for success: Building a strong foundation for school readiness based on the social-emotional development of young children, 1* (No. 1). Kansas City: The Ewing Marion Kauffman Foundation.

Kaufman, P. (2001). Dropping out of school: Detours in the life course. In T. Urdan & F. Pajares (Eds.), *Adolescence and education*. Greenwich, CT: IAP.

Kaugers, A. S., Russ, S. W., & Singer, L. T. (2000, May). *Self-regulation among cocaine-exposed four-year-old children*. Paper presented at the joint meetings of the Pediatric Academic Societies and the American Academy of Pediatrics, Boston.

Kee, D. W., & Howell, S. (1988, April). *Mental effort and memory development*. Paper presented at the meeting of the American Educational Research Association, New Orleans.

Keener, D. C., & Boykin, K. A. (1996, March). *Parental control, autonomy, and ego development*. Paper presented at the meeting of the Society for Research on Adolescence, Boston.

Keeney, T. J., Cannizzo, S. R., & Flavell, J. H. (1967). Spontaneous and induced verbal rehearsal in a recall task. *Child Development, 38*, 953–966.

Keller, A., Ford, L., & Meacham, J. (1978). Dimensions of self-concept in preschool children. *Developmental Psychology, 14*, 483–489.

Kellman, P. J., & Banks, M. S. (1998). Infant visual perception. In W. Damon (Ed.), *Handbook of child psychology, 5th Ed., Vol. 2*. New York: Wiley.

Kelly, J. B. (2001). Legal and educational interventions for families in residence and contact disputes. *Australian Journal of Family Law, 15*, 92–113.

Kelm, J., Ahlhelm, F., Pape, D., Pitsch, W., & Engel, C. (2001). School sports accidents: Analysis of causes, modes, and frequencies. *Journal of Pediatric Orthopedics, 21,* 165–168.

Kennedy, H. P., Beck, C. T., & Driscoll, J. W. (2002). A light in the fog: Caring for women with postpartum depression. *Journal of Midwifery & Women's Health, 47,* 318–330.

Kennell, J. H., & McGrath, S. K. (1999). Commentary: Practical and humanistic lessons from the third world for perinatal caregivers everywhere. *Birth, 26,* 9–10.

Kenrick, D. T., Li, N. P., & Butner, J. (2003). Dynamical evolutionary psychology: individual decision rules and emergent social norms. *Psychological Review, 110,* 3–28.

Kessen, W., Haith, M. M., & Salapatek, P. (1970). Human infancy. In P. H. Mussen (Ed.), *Manual of child psychology* (3rd ed., Vol. 1). New York: Wiley.

Kiess, W., Galler, A., Reich, A., Muller, G., Kapellen, T., Deutscher, J., Raile, K., & Kratzch, J. (2001). Clinical aspects of obesity in childhood and adolescence. *Obesity Reviews, 2,* 29–36.

Kilbride, H. W., Thorstad, K. K., & Daily, D. K. (2000, May). *Preschool outcome for extremely low birth weight infants compared to their full term siblings.* Paper presented at the joint meeting of the Pediatric Academic Societies and American Academy of Pediatrics, Boston.

Kimm, S. Y., Barton, B. A., Obarzanek, E., McMahon, R. P., Kronsberg, S. S., Waclawiw, M. A., Morrison, J. A., Schreiber, G. G., Sabry, Z. I., & Daniels, S. R. (2002). Obesity development during adolescence in a biracial cohort: The NHLBI Growth and Health Study. *Pediatrics, 110,* e54.

Kimm, S. Y., & Obarzanek, E. (2002). Childhood obesity: A new pandemic of the new millenium. *Pediatrics, 110,* 1003–1007.

Kimura, D. (2000). *Sex and cognition.* Cambridge, MA: MIT Press.

Kisilevsky, B. S. (1995). The influence stimulus and subject variables on human fetal responses to sound and vibration. In J-P Lecaunet, W. P. Fifer, M. A. Krasnegor, & W. P. Smotherman (Eds.), *Fetal development.* Hillsdale, NJ: Erlbaum.

Kite, M. (2001). Gender stereotypes. In J. Worell (Ed.), *Encyclopedia of women and gender.* San Diego: Academic Press.

Klaus, M., & Kennell, H. H. (1976). *Maternal-infant bonding.* St. Louis: Mosby.

Klaus, M. H., Kennell, J. H., & Klaus, P. H. (1993). *Mothering the mother.* Reading, MA: Addison-Wesley.

Klesges, L. M., Johnson, K. C., Ward, K. D., & Barnard, M. (2001). Smoking cessation in pregnant women. *Obstetrics and Gynecological Clinics of North America, 28,* 269–282.

Kling, K. C., Hyde, J. S., Showers, C. J., & Buswell, B. N. (1999). Gender differences in self-esteem: A meta-analysis. *Psychological Bulletin, 125,* 470–500.

Klug, W. S., & Cummings, M. R. (2003). *Genetics: A molecular perspective.* Upper Saddle River, NJ: Prentice Hall.

Knecht, S., Drager, B., Deppe, M., Bobe, L., Lohmann, H., Floel, A., Ringelstein, E. B., & Henningsen, H. (2000). Handedness and hemispheric language dominance in healthy humans. *Brain, 135,* 2512–2518.

Kochanska, G. (1997). Multiple pathways to conscience for children with different temperaments: From toddlerhood to age 5. *Developmental Psychology, 33,* 228–240.

Kochanska, G., Gross, J. N., Lin, M., & Nichols, K. E. (2002). Guilt in young children: Development, determinants, and relations with a broader set of standards. *Child Development, 73,* 461–482.

Koestner, R., Franz, C., & Weinberger, J. (1990). The family origins of empathic concern: A 26-year longitudinal study. *Journal of Personality and Social Psychology, 58,* 709–717.

Kohlberg, L. (1958). *The development of modes of moral thinking and choice in the years 10 to 16.* Unpublished doctoral dissertation, University of Chicago.

Kohlberg, L. (1966). A cognitive-developmental analysis of children's sex-role concepts and attitudes. In E. E. Maccoby (Ed.), *The development of sex differences.* Palo Alto, CA: Stanford University Press.

Kohlberg, L. (1969). Stage and sequence: The cognitive-developmental approach to socialization. In D. A. Goslin (Ed.), *Handbook of socialization theory and research,* Chicago: Rand McNally.

Kohlberg, L. (1976). Moral stages and moralization: The cognitive-developmental approach. In T. Lickona (Ed.), *Moral development and behavior.* New York: Holt, Rinehart & Winston.

Kohlberg, L. (1986). A current statement on some theoretical issues. In S. Modgil & C. Modgil (Eds.), *Lawrence Kohlberg.* Philadelphia: Falmer.

Kohlberg, L., & Candee, D. (1979). *Relationships between moral judgment and moral action.* Unpublished manuscript, Harvard University.

Kolbe, L. J., Collins, J., & Cortese, P. (1997). Building the capacity of schools to improve the health of the nation. *American Psychologist, 52,* 256–265.

Koniak-Griffin, D., Lesser, J., Uman, G., & Nyamathi, A. (2003). Teen pregnancy, motherhood, and unprotected sexual activity. *Research in Nursing and Health, 26,* 4–19.

Kopp, C. B. (1992, October). *Trends and directions in studies of developmental risk.* Paper presented at the 27th Minnesota Symposium on Child Psychology, University of Minnesota, Minneapolis.

Kopp, C. B., & Neufeld, S. J. (2002). Emotional development in infancy. In R. Davidson, K. Scherer, & H. H. Goldsmith (Eds.), *Handbook of affective sciences.* New York: Oxford University Press.

Kortenhaus, C. M., & Demarest, J. (1993). Gender role stereotyping in children's literature: An update. *Sex Roles, 28,* 219–230.

Kotler, J. A., Wright, J. C., & Huston, A. C. (2001). Television use in families with children. In J. Bryant & J. A. Bryant (Eds.), *Television and the American Family.* Mahwah, NJ: Erlbaum.

Kotovsky, L., & Baillargeon, R. (1994). Calibration-based reasoning about collision events in 11-month-old infants. *Cognition, 51,* 107–129.

Kottak, C. P. (2002). *Cultural anthropology* (9th ed.). New York: McGraw-Hill.

Kozol, J. (1991). *Savage inequalities.* New York: Crown.

Kozulin, A. (2000). Vygotsky. In A. Kazdin (Ed.), *Encyclopedia of psychology.* Washington, DC, & New York: American Psychological Association and Oxford University Press.

Kramer, M. S., & others (2001). Promotion of breastfeeding intervention trial. *Journal of the American Medical Association, 285* (No. 4), 413–420.

Krauss, R. A., & Glucksberg, S. (1969). The development of communication: Competence as a function of age. *Child Development, 40,* 255–266.

Kreutzer, M., Leonard, C., & Flavell, J. H. (1975). An interview study of children's knowledge about memory. *Monographs of the Society for Research in Child Development, 40* (1, Serial No. 159).

Krimer, L. S., & Goldman-Rakic, P. S. (2001). Prefrontal microcircuits. *Journal of Neuroscience, 21,* 3788–3796.

Kroger, J. (2003). Identity development during adolescence. In G. Adams & M. Berzonsky (Eds.), *Blackwell handbook of adolescence.* Malden, MA: Blackwell.

Kuczynski, L., & Lollis, S. (2002). Four foundations for a dynamic model of parenting. In J. R. M. Gerris (Ed.), *Dynamics of parenting*. Mahwah, NJ: Erlbaum.

Kuebli, J. (1994, March). Young children's understanding of everyday emotions. *Young Children*, pp. 36–48.

Kuhl, P. K. (1993). Infant speech perception: A window on psycholinguistic development. *International Journal of Psycholinguistics, 9*, 33–56.

Kuhl, P. K. (2000). A new view of language acquisition. *Proceedings of the National Academy of Sciences, 97* (22), 11850–11857.

Kuhn, D. (1998). Afterword to Volume 2: Cognition, perception, and language. In W. Damon (Ed.), *Handbook of child psychology* (5th ed., Vol. 2). New York: Wiley.

Kuhn, D. (1999). A developmental model of critical thinking. *Educational Researcher, 28*, 26–37.

Kuhn, D. (2000). Adolescent thought processes. In A. Kazdin (Ed.), *Encyclopedia of psychology*. Washington, DC, & New York: American Psychological Association and Oxford University Press.

Kuhn, D., Amsel, E., & O'Laughlin, M. (1988). *The development of scientific thinking skills*. Orlando, FL: Academic Press.

Kuhn, D., Schauble, L., & Garcia-Mila, M. (1992). Cross-domain development of scientific reasoning. *Cognition and Instruction, 9*, 285–327.

Kulik, J. A., Bangert-Drowns, R. L., & Kulick, R. L. (1984). The effectiveness of coaching on aptitude tests. *Psychological Bulletin, 95*, 179–188.

Kumari, A. S. (2001). Pregnancy outcome in women with morbid obesity. *International Journal of Gynecology and Obstetrics, 73*, 101–107.

Kupersmidt, J. B., & Coie, J. D. (1990). Preadolescent peer status, aggression, and school adjustment as predictors of externalizing problems in adolescence. *Child Development, 61*, 1350–1363.

Kurdek, L. A., & Krile, D. (1982). A developmental analysis of the relation between peer acceptance and both interpersonal understanding and perceived social self-competence. *Child Development, 53*, 1485–1491.

Kutchinsky, B. (1992). The child sexual abuse panic. *Norsisk Sexolig, 10*, 30–42.

Kwak, H. K., Kim, M., Cho, B. H., & Ham, Y. M. (1999, April). *The relationship between children's temperament, maternal control strategies, and children's compliance*. Paper presented

at the meeting of the Society for Research in Child Development, Albuquerque.

La Greca, A. M., Silerman, W. K., Vernberg, E. M., & Roberts, M. C. (Eds.). (2002). *Helping children cope with disasters and terrorism*. Washington, DC: American Psychological Association.

Lackmann, G. M., Salzberger, U., Tollner, U., Chen, M., Carmella, S. G., & Hecht, S. S. (1999). Metabolites of a tobacco-specific carcinogen in urine from newborns. *Journal of the National Cancer Institute, 91*, 459–465.

Ladd, G., Buhs, E., & Troop, W. (2002). School adjustment and social skills training. In P. K. Smith & C. H. Hart (Eds.), *Blackwell handbook of childhood social development*. Malden, MA: Blackwell.

Ladd, G. W. (1999). Peer relationships and social competence during early and middle childhood. *Annual Review of Psychology, 50*. Palo Alto, CA: Annual Reviews.

Ladd, G. W., & Hart, C. H. (1992). Creating informal play opportunities: Are parents' and preschoolers' initiations related to children's competence with peers? *Cognitive Psychology, 28*, 1179–1187.

Ladd, G. W., LeSeiur, K., & Profilet, S. M. (1993). Direct parental influences on young children's peer relations. In S. Duck (Ed.), *Learning about relationships* (Vol. 2). London: Sage.

Ladd, G. W., & Pettit, G. S. (2002). Parenting and the development of children's peer relationships. In M. H. Bornstein (Ed.), *Handbook of parenting* (2nd ed., Vol. 5). Mahwah, NJ: Erlbaum.

Lamb, M. E. (1977). The development of mother-infant and father-infant attachments in the second year of life. *Developmental Psychology, 13*, 637–648.

Lamb, M. E. (1986). *The father's role: Applied perspectives*. New York: Wiley.

Lamb, M. E. (1994). Infant care practices and the application of knowledge. In C. B. Fisher & R. M. Lerner (Eds.), *Applied developmental psychology*. New York: McGraw-Hill.

Lamb, M. E. (1997). Fatherhood then and now. In A. Booth & A. C. Crouter (Eds.), *Men in families*. Mahwah, NJ: Erlbaum.

Lamb, M. E. (2000). The history of research on father involvement: An overview. *Marriage and Family Review, 29*, 23–42.

Lamb, M. E., Frodi, A. M., Hwant, C. P., Frodi, M., & Steinberg, J. (1982). Mother- and father-infant interaction involving play and holding in traditional and nontraditional Swedish families. *Developmental Psychology, 18*, 215–221.

Lamb, M. E., & Sternberg, K. J. (1992). Sociocultural perspectives in nonparental childcare. In M. E. Lamb, K. J. Sternberg, C. Hwang, & A. G. Broberg (Eds.), *Child care in context*. Hillsdale, NJ: Erlbaum.

Lamb, S. (1993). The beginnings of morality. In A. Garrod (Ed.), *Approaches to moral development*. New York: Teachers College Press.

Landry, S. H., Miller-Loncar, C. L., Smith, K. E., & Swank, P. R. (2002). The role of early parenting in children's development of executive processes. *Developmental Neuropsychology, 21*, 15–41.

Langer, L. L. (1991). *Holocaust testimonies: The ruins of memory*. New Haven: Yale University Press.

Langley-Evans, S. C., & Langley-Evans, A. J. (2002). Use of folic acid supplements in the first trimester of pregnancy. *Journal of the Royal Society of Health, 122*, 181–186.

Langston, W. (2002). *Research methods manual for psychology*. Belmont, CA: Wadsworth.

Lapsley, D. K. (1989). Continuity and discontinuity in adolescent social cognitive development. In R. Montemayor, G. Adams, & T. Gullota (Eds.), *Advances in adolescence research* (Vol. 2). Orlando, FL: Academic Press.

Lapsley, D. K. (1996). *Moral psychology*. Boulder, CO: Westview Press.

Lapsley, D. K., & Power, F. C. (Eds.). (1988). *Self, ego, and identity*. New York: Springer-Verlag.

Lapsley, D. K., & Quintana, S. M. (1985). Recent approaches in children's elementary moral and social education. *Elementary School Guidance and Counseling Journal, 19*, 246–251.

Larsen, R. J., & Buss, D. M. (2002). *Personality psychology: Domains of knowledge about human nature*. New York: McGraw-Hill.

Larson, R., & Lampman-Petraitis, C. (1989). Daily emotional states as reported by children and adolescents. *Child Development, 60*, 1250–1260.

Larson, R., & Richards, M. (1994). *Divergent realities: The emotional lives of mothers, fathers, and adolescents*. New York: Basic Books.

Larson, R. W., Brown, B. B., & Mortimer, J. (2003). Introduction: Globalization, societal change, and new technologies: What they mean for the future of adolescence. In R. W. Larson, B. B. Brown, & J. Mortimer (Eds.),

Adolescents' preparation for the future: Perils and promises. Malden, MA: Blackwell.

Larson, R. W., Clore, G. L., & Wood, G. A. (1999). The emotions of romantic relationships. In W. Furman, B. B. Brown, & C. Feiring (Eds), *The development of romantic relationships in adolescence.* New York: Cambridge University Press.

LaVoie, J. (1976). Ego identity formation in middle adolescence. *Journal of Youth and Adolescence, 5,* 371–385.

Lazar, L., Darlington, R., & Collaborators. (1982). Lasting effects of early education: A report from the consortium for longitudinal studies. *Monographs of the Society for Research in Child Development, 47.*

Lazarus, R. S. (1996). *Psychological stress and the coping process.* New York: McGraw-Hill.

Lazarus, R. S., & Folkman, S. (1984). *Stress, appraisal and coping.* New York: Springer.

Leadbeater, B. J. R., & Way, N. (2001). *Growing up fast.* Mahwah, NJ: Erlbaum.

Learner-Centered Principles Work Group. (1997). *Learner-centered psychological principles: A framework for school reform and redesign.* Washington, DC: American Psychological Association.

Leffert, N., & Blyth, D. A. (1996, March). *The effects of community contexts on early adolescents.* Paper presented at the meeting of the Society for Research on Adolescence, Boston.

Leger, A., Demonet, J. F., Ruff, S., Aithamon, B., Touyeras, B., Puel, M., Boulanoura, K., & Cardebat, D. (2002). Neural substrates of spoken language rehabilitation in an aphasic patient: an fMRI study. *Neuroimage, 17,* 174–183.

Lehrer, R., Schauble, L., & Petrosino, A. (2001). Reconsidering the role of the experiment in science. In K. Crowley, C. Schunn, & T. Okada (Eds.), *Designing for science.* Mahwah, NJ: Erlbaum.

Leifer, A. D. (1973). *Television and the development of social behavior.* Paper presented at the meeting of the International Society for the Study of Behavioral Development, Ann Arbor, Michigan.

LeMare, L. J., & Rubin, K. H. (1987). Perspective taking and peer interaction: Structural and developmental analyses. *Child Development, 58,* 306–315.

Lenders, C. M., McElrath, T. F., & Scholl, T. O. (2000). Nutrition in pregnancy. *Current Opinions in Pediatrics, 12,* 291–296.

Lenneberg. E. (1967). *The biological foundations of language.* New York: Wiley.

Lenoir, C. P., Mallet, E., & Calenda, E. (2000). Siblings of sudden infant death syndrome and near miss in about 30 families: Is there a genetic link? *Medical Hypotheses, 54,* 408–411.

Leong, F. T. L. (2000). Cultural pluralism. In A. Kazdin (Ed.), *Encyclopedia of psychology.* Washington, DC, & New York: American Psychological Association and Oxford University Press.

Lepper, M., Greene, D., & Nisbett, R. (1973). Undermining children's intrinsic interest with intrinsic rewards: A test of the overjustification hypothesis. *Journal of Personality and Social Psychology, 28,* 129–137.

Lerner, R. (2002). *Concepts and theories of human development* (3rd ed.). Mahwah, NJ: Erlbaum.

Lester, B. M., & Tronick, E. Z. (1990). Introduction. In B. M. Lester & E. Z. Tronick (Eds.). *Stimulation and the preterm infant: The limits of plasticity.* Philadelphia: W. B. Saunders.

Lester, B. M., Tronick, E. Z., LaGasse, L., Seifer, R., Bauer, C. R., Shankaran, S., Bada, H. S., Wright, L. L., Smeriglio, V. L., Lu, J., Finnegan, L. P., & Maza, P. L. (2002). The maternal lifestyle study: Effects of substance exposure during pregnancy on neurodevelopmental outcome in 1-month-old infants. *Pediatrics, 110,* 1182–1192.

Lester, B. (2000). Unpublished review of J. W. Santrock's *Life-span development* (8th ed.) (New York: McGraw-Hill).

Le Vay, S. (1994). *The sexual brain.* Cambridge, MA: MIT Press.

Leventhal, A. (1994, February). *Peer conformity during adolescence: An integration of developmental, situational, and individual characteristics.* Paper presented at the meeting of the Society for Research on Adolescence, San Diego.

Levesque, J., & Prosser, T. (1996). Service learning connections. *Journal of Teacher Education, 47,* 325–334.

Levran, D., Farhi, J., Nahum, H., Royburt, M., Glezerman, M., & Weissman, A. (2002). Prospective evaluation of blastocyst stage transfer vs. zygote intrafallopian tube transfer in patients with repeated implantation failure. *Fertility and Sterility, 77,* 971–977.

Levy, T. M. (Ed.). (1999). *Handbook of attachment interventions.* San Diego: Academic Press.

Lewis, C., & Carpendale, J. (2002). Social cognition. In P. K. Smith & C. H. Hart (Eds.), *Blackwell handbook of childhood social development.* Malden, MA: Blackwell.

Lewis, M. (1997). *Altering fate: Why the past does not predict the future.* New York: Guilford Press.

Lewis, M. (2002). Early emotional development. In A. Slater & M. Lewis (Eds.), *Infant development.* New York: Oxford University Press.

Lewis, M., & Brooks-Gunn, J. (1979). *Social cognition and the acquisition of the self.* New York: Plenum.

Lewis, M., & Ramsay, D. S. (1999). Effect of maternal soothing and infant stress response. *Child Development, 70,* 11–20.

Lewis, M., Sullivan, M. W., Sanger, C., & Weiss, M. (1989). Self-development and self-conscious emotions. *Child Development, 60,* 146–156.

Lewis, R. (1997). With a marble and telescope: Searching for play. *Childhood Education, 36,* 346.

Lewis, R. (2003). *Human genetics* (5th ed.). New York: McGraw-Hill.

Li, A. M., Chan, D., Wong, E., Yin J., Nelson, E. A., & Fok, T. F. (2003). The effects of obesity on pulmonary function. *Archives of Diseases in Childhood, 88,* 361–363.

Li, Z. L., Lin, H., Zhang, X. N., & Xiao, W. F. (2003). Intracytoplasmic sperm injection in cases with a history of in vitro fertilization failure. *Asian Journal of Andrology, 5,* 69–72.

Liaw, J. J. (2000). Tactile stimulation and preterm infants. *Journal of Perinatal and Neonatal Nursing, 14,* 84–103.

Liben, L. S., Bigler, R. S., & Krogh, H. R. (2001). Pink and blue collar jobs: Children's judgements of job status and job aspirations in relation to sex of worker. *Journal of Experimental Child Psychology, 79* (4), 346–363.

Lifshitz, F., Pugliese, M. T., Moses, N., & Weyman-Daum, M. (1987). Parental health beliefs as a cause of nonorganic failure to thrive. *Pediatrics, 80,* 175–182.

Lightwood, J. M., Phibbs, C. S., & Glantz, S. A. (1999). Short-term health and economic benefits of smoking cessation. *Pediatrics, 104,* 1312–1320.

Limber, S. P. (1997). Preventing violence among school children. *Family Futures, 1,* 27–28.

Limber, S. P., & Wilcox, B. L. (1996). Application of the U.N. convention on the rights of the child to the United States. *American Psychologist, 51,* 1246–1250.

Lindberg, M. A., Keiffer, J., & Thomas, S. W. (2000). Eyewitness testimony for physical abuse as a function of personal experience, development, and focus of study. *Journal of Applied Developmental Psychology, 21,* 555–591.

Lindbohm, M. (1991). Effects of paternal occupational exposure in spontaneous abortions. *American Journal of Public Health, 121,* 1029–1033.

Lippa, R. A. (2002). *Gender, nature, and nurture.* Mahwah, NJ: Erlbaum.

Lipsitz, J. (1983, October). *Making it the hard way: Adolescents in the 1980s.* Testimony presented at the Crisis Intervention Task Force, House Select Committee on Children, Youth, and Families, Washington, DC.

Lipsitz, J. (1984). *Successful schools for young adolescents.* New Brunswick, NJ: Transaction.

Litovsky, R. Y., & Ashmead, D. H. (1997). Development of binaural and spatial hearing in infants and children. In R. H. Gilkey & T. R. Anderson (Eds.), *Binaural and spatial hearing in real and virtual environments.* Mahwah, NJ: Erlbaum.

Livesly, W., & Bromley, D. (1973). *Person perception in childhood and adolescence.* New York: Wiley.

Loebel, M., & Yali, A. M. (1999, August). *Effects of positive expectancies on adjustment to pregnancy.* Paper presented at the meeting of the American Psychological Association, Boston.

Loeber, R., DeLamatre, M., Keenan, K., & Zhang, Q. (1998). A prospective replication of developmental pathways in disruptive and delinquent behavior. In R. Cairns, L. Bergman, & J. Kagan (Eds.), *Methods and models for studying the individual.* Thousand Oaks, CA: Sage.

Loeber, R., & Farrington, D. P. (Eds.). (2001). *Child delinquents: Development, intervention and service needs.* Thousand Oaks, CA: Sage.

Loftus, E. F. (1993). The reality of repressed memories. *American Psychologist, 48,* 518–537.

Loftus, E. F. (2002). Memory faults and fixes. *Issues in Science and Technology, XVIII* (No. 4), 41–50.

London, M. L., Olds, S. B., & Ladewig, P. W. (2000). *Maternal newborn nursing care* (4th ed.). Boston: Addison-Wesley.

Long, T., & Long, L. (1983). *Latchkey children.* New York: Penguin.

Lonner, W. J. (1988, October). *The introductory psychology text and cross-cultural psychology: A survey of cross-cultural psychologists.* Bellingham: Western Washington University, Center for Cross-cultural Research.

Lorenz, K. Z. (1965). *Evolution and the modification of behavior.* Chicago: University of Chicago Press.

Lott, B., & Maluso, D. (2001). Gender development: Social learning. In J. Worell (Ed.)., *Encyclopedia of women and gender.* San Diego: Academic Press.

Lowe, X., Eskenazi, B., Nelson, D. O., Kidd, S., Alme, A., & Wyrobek, A. J. (2001). Frequency of XY sperm increases with age in fathers of boys with Klinefelter syndrome. *American Journal of Human Genetics, 69,* 1046–1054.

Lubinski, D. (2000). Measures of intelligence: Intelligence tests. In A. Kazdin (Ed.), *Encyclopedia of psychology.* Washington, DC, & New York: American Psychological Association and Oxford University Press.

Ludington-Hoe, S., & Golant, S. K. (1993). *Kangaroo care: The best you can do to help your preterm baby.* New York: Bantam. Doubleday.

Ludington-Hoe, S. M., Cong, X., & Hashemi, F. (2002). Infant crying: Nature, physiologic consequences, and select interventions. *Neonatal Network, 21,* 29–36.

Luffy, R., & Grove, S. K. (2003). Examining the validity, reliability, and preference of three pediatric pain measurement tools in African-American children. *Pediatric Nursing, 29,* 54–59.

Luo, Q., Fang, X., & Aro, P. (1995, March). *Selection of best friends by Chinese adolescents.* Paper presented at the meeting of the Society for Research in Child Development, Indianapolis.

Luria, A., & Herzog, E. (1985, April). *Gender segregation across and within settings.* Paper presented at the biennial meeting of the Society for Research in Child Development, Toronto.

Lyle, J., & Hoffman, H. R. (1972). Children's use of television and other media. In E. A. Rubenstein, G. A. Comstock, & J. P. Murray (Eds.), *Television and social behavior* (Vol. 4). Washington, DC: U.S. Government Printing Office.

Lynn, R. (1996). Racial and ethnic differences in intelligence in the U.S. on the Differential Ability Scale. *Personality and Individual Differences, 26,* 271–273.

Lyon, G. R. (1995). Toward a definition of dyslexia. *Annals of Dyslexia, 45,* 3–27.

Lyon, G. R. (1996). Learning disabilities. *The Future of Children, 6* (1), 54–76.

Lyon, G. R., & Moats, L. C. (1997). Critical conceptual and methodological considerations in reading intervention research. *Journal of Learning Disabilities, 30,* 578–588.

Lyon, T. D., & Flavell, J. H. (1993). Young children's understanding of forgetting over time. *Child Development, 64,* 789–800.

M

Maas, J. B. (1998). *Power sleep.* New York: Villard Books.

Maccoby, E. E. (1984). Middle childhood in the context of the family. In *Development during middle childhood.* Washington, DC: National Academy Press.

Maccoby, E. E. (1987, November). Interview with Elizabeth Hall: All in the family. *Psychology Today,* pp. 54–60.

Maccoby, E. E. (1992). The role of parents in the socialization of children: An historical overview. *Developmental Psychology, 28,* 1006–1018.

Maccoby, E. E. (1996). Peer conflict and intrafamily conflict: Are there conceptual bridges? *Merrill-Palmer Quarterly, 42,* 165–176.

Maccoby, E. E. (1998). *The two sexes: Growing up apart, coming together.* Cambridge, MA: Harvard University Press.

Maccoby, E. E. (1999). The uniqueness of the parent-child relationship. In W. A. Collins & B. Laursen (Eds.), *Relationships as developmental contexts.* Mahwah, NJ: Erlbaum.

Maccoby, E. E. (2001, April) *Influencing policy through research.* Paper presented at the meeting of the Society for Research in Child Development, Minneapolis.

Maccoby, E. E. (2002). Gender and group process: A developmental perspective. *Current Directions in Psychological Science, 11,* 54–57.

Maccoby, E. E. (2002). Parenting effects: Issues and controversies. In J. G. Borkowski, S. L. Ramey, & M. Bristol-Power (Eds.), *Parenting and the child's world.* Mahwah, NJ: Erlbaum.

Maccoby, E. E., & Jacklin, C. N. (1974). *The psychology of sex differences.* Palo Alto, CA: Stanford University Press.

Maccoby, E. E., & Jacklin, C. N. (1987). Gender segregation in childhood. In H. W. Reese (Ed.), *Advances in child development and behavior, 20,* 239–287.

Maccoby, E. E., & Martin, J. A. (1983). Socialization in the context of the family: Parent-child interaction. In P. H. Mussen (Ed.), *Handbook of child psychology* (4th ed., Vol. 4). New York: Wiley.

Maccoby, E. E., & Mnookin, R. H. (1992). *Dividing the child: Social and legal dilemmas of custody.* Cambridge, MA: Harvard University Press.

MacDorman, M. F., Minino, A. M., Strobino, D. M., & Guyer, B. (2002). Annual summary of vital statistics—2001. *Pediatrics, 110,* 1037–1052.

MacDorman, M. F., & Singh, G. K. (1998). Midwifery care, social and medical factors, and birth outcomes in the USA. *Journal of Epidemiology and Community Health, 52,* 310–317.

MacFarlane, J. A. (1975). Olfaction in the development of social preferences in the human neonate. In *Parent-infant interaction.* Ciba Foundation Symposium No. 33. Amsterdam: Elsevier.

MacLean, W. E. (2000). Down syndrome. In A. Kazdin (Ed.), *Encyclopedia of psychology.* Washington, DC, & New York: American Psychological Association and Oxford University Press.

MacWhinney, B. (Ed.). (1999). *The emergence of language.* Mahwah, NJ: Erlbaum.

Maddux, J. (2002). The power of believing you can. In C. R. Snyder & S. J. Lopez (Eds.), *Handbook of positive psychology.* New York: Oxford University Press.

Maddux, J. E., Roberts, M. C., Sledden, E. A., & Wright, L. (1986). Developmental issues in child health psychology. *American Psychologist, 41,* 24–34.

Mader, S. S. (2002). *Human biology* (7th ed.). New York: McGraw-Hill.

Maggs, J. L., Schulenberg, J., & Hurrelmann, K. (1997). Developmental transitions in adolescence: Health promotion implications. In J. Schulenberg, J. L. Maggs, & K. Hurrelmann (Eds.), *Health risks and developmental transitions during adolescence.* New York: Cambridge University Press.

Magnuson, K. A., & Duncan, G. J. (2002). Parents in poverty. In M. H. Bornstein (Ed.), *Handbook of parenting* (2nd ed., Vol. 4). Mahwah, NJ: Erlbaum.

Magnusson, D. (1988). *Individual development from an interactional perspective: A longitudinal study.* Hillsdale, NJ: Erlbaum.

Main, M. (2000). Attachment theory. In A. Kazdin (Ed.), *Encyclopedia of psychology.* Washington, DC, & New York: American Psychological Association and Oxford University Press.

Maizels, M., Rosenbaum, D., & Keating, B. (1999). *Getting to dry: How to help your child overcome bedwetting.* Cambridge, MA: Harvard Common Press.

Majhanovich, S. (1998, April). *Unscrambling the semantics of Canadian multiculturalism.* Paper presented at the meeting of the American Educational Research Association, San Diego.

Major, B., Barr, L., Zubek, J., & Babey, S. H. (1999). Gender and self-esteem: A meta-analysis. In W. Swann & J. Langlois (Eds.), *Sexism and stereotypes in modern society: The gender science of Janet Taylor Spence.* Washington DC: American Psychological Association.

Makrides, M., Neumann, M., Simmer, K., Pater, J., & Gibson, R. (1995). Are long-chain polyunsaturated fatty acids essential nutrients in infancy? *Lancet, 345,* 1463–1468.

Malinosky-Rummell, R., & Hansen, D. J. (1993). Long-term consequences of childhood physical abuse. *Psychological Bulletin, 114,* 68–79.

Mandler, G. (1980). Recognizing: The judgment of previous occurrence. *Psychological Review, 87,* 252–271.

Mandler, J. M. (1998). Representation. In W. Damon (Ed.), *Handbook of child psychology* (5th ed., Vol. 2). New York: Wiley.

Mandler, J. M. (2000). Review of J. W. Santrock's *Life-span development,* 8th ed. New York: McGraw-Hill.

Mandler, J. M., & McDonough, L. (1995). Long-term recall in infancy. *Journal of Experimental Child Psychology, 59,* 457–474.

Mannessier, L., Alie-Daram, S., Roubinet, F., & Brossard, Y. (2000). Prevention of fetal hemolytic disease: It is time to take action. *Tranfusions in Clinical Biology, 7,* 527–532.

Mannino, D. M., Moorman, J. E., Kingsley, B., Rose, D., & Repace, J. (2001). Health effects related to environmental tobacco smoke exposure in the United States. *Archives of Pediatric and Adolescent Medicine, 155,* 36–41.

Maratsos, M. (1998). The acquisition of grammer. In D. Kuhn & R. S. Siegler (Eds.), *Handbook of child psychology* (5th ed., Vol. 2). New York: Wiley.

Marcia, J. E. (1980). Ego identity development. In J. Adelson (Ed.), *Handbook of adolescent psychology.* New York: Wiley.

Marcia, J. E. (1987). The identity status approach to the study of ego identity development. In T. Honess & K. Yardley (Eds.), *Self and identity: Perspectives across the life-span.* London: Routledge & Kegan Paul.

Marcia, J. E. (1994). The empirical study of ego identity. In H. A. Bosma, T. L. G. Graafsma, H. D. Grotevant, & D. J. De Levita (Eds.), *Identity and development.* Newbury Park, CA: Sage.

Marcia, J. E. (1996). Unpublished review of J. W. Santrock's *Adolescence,* 7th ed. Dubuque, IA: Brown & Benchmark.

Marcus, D. L., Mulrine, A., & Wong, K. (1999, September 13). How kids learn. *U.S. News & World Report,* pp. 44–50.

Margolin, L. (1994). Child sexual abuse by uncles. *Child Abuse and Neglect, 18,* 215–224.

Markowitz, M. (2000). Lead poisoning. *Pediatrics in Review, 21,* 327–335.

Markus, H. R., & Kitayama, S. (1994). The cultural construction of self and emotion: Implications for social behavior. In S. Kitayama & H. R. Markus (Eds.), *Emotion and culture.* Washington, DC: American Psychological Association.

Markus, H. R., Mullally, P. R., & Kitayama, S. (1999). *Selfways: Diversity in modes of cultural participation.* Unpublished manuscript, Department of Psychology, University of Michigan.

Markus, H. R., & Nurius, P. (1986). Possible selves. *American Psychologist, 41,* 954–969.

Marsiglio, W., Amato, P., Day, R. D., & Lamb, M. E. (2000). Scholarship on fatherhood in the 1990s and beyond. *Journal of Marriage and Family, 62,* 1173–1191.

Martin, C. L., & Dinella, L. (2001). Gender development: Gender schema theory. In J. Worell (Ed.), *Encyclopedia of women and gender.* San Diego: Academic Press.

Martin, C. L., & Fabes, R. A. (2001). The stability and consequences of young children's segregated social play. *Developmental Psychology, 37,* 431–446.

Martin, C. L., Ruble, D. N., & Szkrybalo, J. (2002). Cognitive theories of early gender development. *Psychological Bulletin, 128,* 903-933.

Martin, N. C. (1997, April). *Adolescents' possible selves and the transition to adulthood.* Paper presented at the meeting of the Society for Research in Child Development, Washington, DC.

Martinez-Pasarell, O., Nogues, C., Bosch, M., Egozcue, J., & Templado, C. (1999). Analysis of sex chromosome aneupolidy in sperm from fathers of Turner syndrome patients. *Human Genetics, 104,* 345–349.

Martorano, S. (1977). A developmental analysis of performance on Piaget's formal operations tasks. *Developmental Psychology, 13,* 666–672.

Masten, A., & Reed, A. G. (2002). Resilience in development. In C. R. Snyder & S. J. Lopez (Eds.), *The handbook of positive psychology.* New York: Oxford University Press.

Masten, A. S. (2001). Ordinary magic: Resilience processes in development. *American Psychologist, 56,* 227–238.

Masten, A. S., & Coatsworth, J. D. (1998). The development of competence in favorable and unfavorable environments. *American Psychologist, 53,* 205–220.

Matheny, A. P., & Phillips, K. (2001). Temperament and context: Correlates of home environment with temperament continuity and change. In T. D. Wachs & G. A. Kohnstamm (Eds.), *Temperament in context.* Mahwah, NJ: Erlbaum.

Mathes, P. G., & Torgesen, J. K. (1999). All children can learn to read: Critical care for the prevention of reading failure. In J. W. Miller & M. C. McKenna (Eds.), *Literacy education in the 21st century.* Mahwah, NJ: Erlbaum.

Matlin, M. W. (1993). *The psychology of women* (2nd ed.). San Diego: Harcourt Brace Jovanovich.

Matsumoto, D. (2000). *Culture and psychology: People around the world* (2nd ed.). Belmont, CA: Wadsworth.

Matsumoto, D. (Ed.). (2001). *The handbook of culture and psychology.* New York: Oxford University Press.

Matusov, E., Bell, N., & Rogoff, B. (2001, April). *Schooling as a cultural process.* Paper presented at the meeting of the Society for Research in Child Development, Minneapolis.

Maughan, A., & Cicchetti, D. (2002). Impact of child maltreatment and interadult violence on children's emotion regulation difficulties and socioemotional adjustment. *Child Development, 73,* 1525–1542.

Maurer, D., & Salapatek, P. (1976). Developmental changes in the scanning of faces by young infants. *Child Development, 47,* 523–527.

Mauro, V. P., Wood, I. C., Krushel, L., Crossin, K. L., & Edelman, G. M. (1994). Cell adhesion alters gene transcription in chicken embryo brain cells and mouse embryonal carcinoma cells. *Proceedings of the National Academy of Sciences USA, 91,* 2868–2872.

Maxon, S. (2003). Behavioral genetics. In I. B. Weiner (Ed.), *Encyclopedia of psychology* (Vol. III). New York: Wiley.

Mayer, R. E. (2003). Memory and information processes. In I. B. Weiner (Ed.), *Handbook of psychology* (Vol. VII). New York: Wiley.

McAdoo, H. P. (2002). African-American parenting. In M. H. Bornstein (Ed.), *Handbook of parenting* (2nd ed., Vol. 4). Mahwah, NJ: Erlbaum.

McCabe, M. P., & Ricciardelli, L. A. (2003). Sociocultural influences on body image and body changes among adolescent boys and girls. *Journal of Social Psychology, 143,* 5–26.

McCall, R. B., Applebaum, M. I., & Hogarty, P. S. (1973). Developmental changes in mental performance. *Monographs of the Society for Research in Child Development, 38* (Serial No. 150).

McCarty, M. E., & Ashmead, D. H. (1999). Visual control of reaching and grasping in infants. *Developmental Psychology, 35,* 620–631.

McClelland, D. C. (1955). Some social consequences of achievement motivation. In M. R. Jones (Ed.), *The Nebraska Symposium on Motivation.* Lincoln: University of Nebraska Press.

McCombs, B. L. (2001, April). *What do we know about learners and learning? The learner-centered framework.* Paper presented at the meeting of the American Educational Research Association, Seattle.

McCormick, C. B., & Pressley, M. (1997). *Educational psychology.* New York: Longman.

McCormick, M. C. (2001). Prenatal care—necessary, but not sufficient. *Health Services Research, 36,* 399–403.

McGrath, S., Kennell, J., Suresh, M., Moise, K., & Hinkley, C. (1999, May). *Doula support vs. epidural analgesia: Impact on cesarean rates.* Paper presented at the meeting of the Society for Pediatric Research, San Francisco.

McGue, M., Bouchard, T. J., Iacono, W. G., & Lykken, D. T. (1993). Behavioral genetics of cognitive ability: A life-span perspective. In R. Plomin & G. E. McClearn (Eds.), *Nature, nurture, and psychology.* Washington, DC: American Psychological Association.

McGuire, S. (2001). Are behavioral genetic and socialization research compatible? *American Psychologist, 56,* 171.

McHale, J., Johnson, D., & Sinclair, R. (1999). Family dynamics, preschoolers' family representations, and preschool peer relationships. *Early Education and Development, 10,* 373–401.

McHale, J., Khazan, I., Erera, P., Rotman, T., DeCourcey, W., & McConnell, M. (2002). Coparenting in diverse family systems. In M. H. Bornstein (Ed.), *Handbook of parenting* (2nd ed., Vol. 3). Mahwah, NJ: Erlbaum.

McHale, J. P., Luretti, A., Talbot, J., & Pouquette, C. (2001). Retrospect and prospect in the psychological study of marital and couple relationships. In J. P. McHale & W. S. Grolnick (Eds.), *Retrospect and prospect in the psychological study of families.* Mahwah, NJ: Erlbaum.

McKenna, J. J., Mosko, S. S., & Richard, C. A. (1997). Bedsharing promotes breastfeeding. *Pediatrics, 100,* 214–219.

McLoyd, V. (1990). Minority children: An introduction to the special issue. *Child Development, 61,* 263–266.

McLoyd, V. C. (1982). Social class differences in sociodramatic play: A critical review. *Developmental Review, 2,* 1–30.

McLoyd, V. C. (1993, March). *Sizing up the future: Economic stress, expectations, and adolescents' achievement motivation.* Paper presented at the biennial meeting of the Society for Research in Child Development, New Orleans.

McLoyd, V. C. (1998). Children in poverty: Development, public policy, and practice. In W. Damon (Ed.), *Handbook of child psychology* (5th ed., Vol. 4). New York: Wiley.

McLoyd, V. C. (1999). Cultural influences in a multicultural society: Conceptual and methodological issues. In A. S. Masten (Ed.), *Cultural processes in child development.* Mahwah, NJ: Erlbaum.

McLoyd, V. C. (2000). Poverty. In A. Kazdin (Ed.), *Encyclopedia of psychology.* Washington, DC, & New York: American Psychological Association and Oxford University Press.

McLoyd, V. C., & Smith, J. (2002). Physical discipline and behavior problems in African American, European American, and Hispanic children: Emotional support as a moderator. *Journal of Marriage and Family, 64,* 40–53.

McMillan, J. H. (2001). *Classroom assessment* (2nd ed.). Boston: Allyn & Bacon.

McMillan, J. H., & Wergin, J. F. (2002). *Understanding and evaluating educational research* (2nd ed.). Upper Saddle River, NJ: Prentice Hall.

McNally, D. (1990). *Even eagles need a push.* New York: Dell.

McNamara, F., & Sullivan, C. E. (2000). Obstructive sleep apnea in infants. *Journal of Pediatrics, 136,* 318–323.

McRee, J. N., & Gebelt, J. L. (2001, April). *Pubertal development, choice of friends, and adolescent male tobacco use.* Paper presented at the meeting of the Society for Research in Child Development, Minneapolis.

McVeigh, C. A., Baafi, M., & Williamson, M. (2002). Functional status after fatherhood: An Australian study. *Journal of Obstetrics, Gynecology, and Neonatal Nursing, 31,* 165–171.

Mead, M. (1928). *Coming of age in Samoa.* New York: Morrow.

Mead, M. (1978, Dec. 30–Jan. 5). The American family: An endangered species. *TV Guide,* pp. 21–24.

Medd, S. E. (2003). Children with ADHD need our advocacy. *Journal of Pediatric Health Care, 17,* 102–104.

Medin, D. L. (2000). Concepts: An overview. In A. Kazdin (Ed.), *Encyclopedia of* *psychology.* Washington, DC, & New York: American Psychological Association and Oxford University Press.

Mehler, J., Jusczyk, P. W., Lambertz, G., Halsted, N., Bertoncini, J., & Amiel-Tison, C. (1988). A precursor of language acquisition in young infants. *Cognition, 29,* 132–178.

Melamed, B. G., Roth, B., & Fogel, J. (2001). Childhood health issues across the life span. In A. Baum, T. A. Revenson, & J. E. Singer (Eds.), *Handbook of health psychology.* Mahwah, NJ: Erlbaum.

Meltzoff, A. (1995). What infant memory tells us about infantile amnesia: Long-term recall and deferred imitation. *Journal of Experimental Child Psychology, 59,* 497–515.

Meltzoff, A. N. (1988). Infant imitation and memory: Nine-month-old infants in immediate and deferred tests. *Child Development, 59,* 217–225.

Meltzoff, A. N. (2000). Learning and cognitive development. In A. Kazdin (Ed.), *Encyclopedia of psychology.* Washington, DC, & New York: American Psychological Association and Oxford University Press.

Meltzoff, A. N., & Gopnik, A. (1997). *Words, thoughts, and theories.* Cambridge, MA: MIT Press.

Meltzoff, A. N., & Moore, M. K. (1999). A new foundation for cognitive development in infancy: The birth of the representational infant. In E. K. Skolnick, K. Nelson, S. A. Gelman, & P. H. Miller (Eds.), *Conceptual development.* Mahwah, NJ: Erlbaum.

Menyuk, P., Liebergott, J., & Schultz, M. (1995). *Early language development in full-term and premature infants.* Mahwah, NJ: Erlbaum.

Mercer, J. R., & Lewis, J. F. (1978). *System of multicultural pluralistic assessment.* New York: Psychological Corporation.

Meredith, N. V. (1978). Research between 1960 and 1970 on the standing height of young children in different parts of the world. In H. W. Reece & L. P. Lipsitt (Eds.), *Advances in child development and behavior* (Vol. 12). New York: Academic Press.

Merrick, J., Aspler, S., & Schwartz, G. (2001). Should adults with phenylketonuria have diet treatment? *Mental Retardation, 39,* 215–217.

Michel, G. L. (1981). Right-handedness: A consequence of infant supine head-orientation preference? *Science, 212,* 685–687.

Michel, R. S. (2000). Toilet training. *Pediatric Review, 20,* 240–245.

Miller, B. C., Benson, B., & Galbraith, K. A. (2001). Family relationships and adolescent pregnancy risk: A research synthesis. *Developmental Review.*

Miller, B. C., Fan, X., Christensen, M., Grotevant, H. D., & von Dulmen, M. (2000). Comparisons of adopted and non-adopted adolescents in a large, nationally representative sample. *Child Development, 71,* 1458–1473.

Miller, G. A. (1981). *Language and speech.* New York: W. H. Freeman.

Miller, J. G. (1991). A cultural perspective on the morality of beneficence and interpersonal responsibility. In S. Ting-Toomey & F. Korzenny (Eds.), *International and intercultural communication annual* (Vol. 15). Newbury Park, CA: Sage.

Miller, J. G. (1995, March). *Culture, context, and personal agency: The cultural grounding of self and morality.* Paper presented at the meeting of the Society for Research in Child Development, Indianapolis.

Miller, P. H. (2001). *Theories of developmental psychology* (4th ed.). New York: Worth.

Miller, R. L. (1988). Positive self-esteem and alcohol/drug related attitudes among school children. *Journal of Alcohol and Drug Education, 33,* 26–31.

Miller-Jones, D. (1989). Culture and testing. *American Psychologist, 44,* 360–366.

Ministry of Health, Education, and Welfare. (2002). *Divorce trends in Japan.* Tokyo: Ministry of Health, Education, and Welfare.

Minnett, A. M., Vandell, D. L., & Santrock, J. W. (1983). The effects of sibling status on sibling interaction: Influence of birth order, age spacing, sex of the child, and sex of the sibling. *Child Development, 54,* 1064–1072.

Minuchin, P. P., & Shapiro, E. K. (1983). The school as a context for social development. In P. H. Mussen (Ed.), *Handbook of child psychology* (4th ed., Vol. 4). New York: Wiley.

Miracle, T. S., Miracle, A. W., & Baumeister, R. F. (2002). *Human sexuality.* Upper Saddle River, NJ: Prentice Hall.

Mischel, W. (1973). Toward a cognitive social learning reconceptualization of personality. *Psychological Review, 80,* 252–283.

Mischel, W. (1974). Process in delay of gratification. In L. Berkowitz (Ed.), *Advances in experimental social psychology* (Vol. 7). New York: Academic Press.

Mischel, W. (1987). *Personality* (4th ed.). New York: Holt, Rinehart & Winston.

Mischel, W. (1995, August). *Cognitive-affective theory of person-environment psychology.* Paper presented at the meeting of the American Psychological Association, New York City.

Mischel, W., & Mendoza-Denton, R. (2003). Harnessing willpower and social intelligence to enhance human agency potential. In L. G. Aspinwall & U. M. Staudinger (Eds.), *A psychology of human strengths.* Washington, DC: American Psychological Association.

Mischel, W., & Mischel, H. (1975, April). *A cognitive social-learning analysis of moral development.* Paper presented at the meeting of the Society for Research in Child Development, Denver.

Mischel, W., & Patterson, C. J. (1976). Substantive and structural elements of effective plans for self-control. *Journal of Social and Personality Psychology, 34,* 942–950.

Mishell, D. (2000). *2000 Yearbook of obstetrics.* St. Louis: Mosby.

Mistry, R. S., Vandewater, E. A., Huston, A. C., & McLoyd, V. C. (2002). Economic well-being and children's social adjustment: The role of family process in an ethnically diverse low-income sample. *Child Development, 3,* 935–951.

Mitchell, E. A., Stewart, A. W., Crampton, P., & Salmond, C. (2000). Deprivation and sudden infant death syndrome. *Social Science and Medicine, 51,* 147–150.

Miyake, Y., Yura, A., & Iki, M. (2003). Breastfeeding and the prevalence of symptoms of allergic disorders in Japanese adolescents. *Clinical and Experimental Allergy, 33,* 312–316.

Moely, B. E., Olson, F. A., Halwes, T. G., & Flavell, J. H. (1969). Production deficiency in young children's clustered recall. *Developmental Psychology, 1,* 26–34.

Mohan, R. M., Golding, S., & Paterson, D. J. (2001). Intermittent hypoxia improves atrial tolerance to subsequent anoxia and reduces stress protein expression. *Acta Physiology Scandinavia, 172,* 89–95.

Monk, C., Fifer, W. P., Sloan, R. P., & Myers, M. M. (2000, May). *Individual differences in fetal cardiac reactivity are associated with maternal anxiety and infant birth weight.* Paper presented at the joint meetings of the Pediatric Academic Societies and the American Academy of Pediatrics, Boston.

Montemayor, R. (1982). The relationship between parent-adolescent conflict and the amount of time adolescents spend with parents, peers, and alone. *Child Development, 53,* 1512–1519.

Moody, R. (2001). Adoption: Women must be helped to consider all options. *British Medical Journal, 323,* 867.

Moore, D. (2001). *The dependent gene.* New York: W. H. Freeman.

Moos, M. K., Bartholomew, N. E., & Lohr, K. N. (2003). Counseling in the clinical setting to prevent unintended pregnancy: An evidence-based research agenda. *Contraception, 67,* 115–132.

Morelli, G. A., Rogoff, B., Oppenheim, D., & Goldsmith, D. (1992). Cultural variation in infants' sleeping arrangements: Questions of independence. *Developmental Psychology, 28,* 604–613.

Morgan, M. (1984). Reward-induced decrements and increments in intrinsic motivation. *Review of Educational Research, 54,* 5–30.

Morris, J. K., Wald, N. J., Mutton, D. E., & Alberman, E. (2003). Comparison of models of maternal age-specific risk for Down syndrome live births. *Prenatal Diagnostics, 23,* 252–258.

Morrison, F. J., Holmes, D. L., & Haith, D. L. (1974). A developmental study of the effects of familiarity on short-term visual memory. *Journal of Experimental Child Psychology, 18,* 412–425.

Morrison, G. S. (2000). *Fundamentals of early childhood education.* Columbus, OH: Merrill.

Morrison, J., & MacKenzie, I. Z. (2003). Cesarean section on demand. *Seminars in Perinatology, 27,* 20–33.

Morrongiello, B. A., Fenwick, K. D., & Chance, G. (1990). Sound localization acuity in very young infants: An observer-based testing procedure. *Developmental Psychology, 26,* 75–84.

Mounts, N. S. (2002). Parental management of adolescent peer relationships in context: The role of parenting style. *Journal of Family Psychology, 16,* 58–69.

Moyo, N. T. (2003). Midwives and women together for the family of the world: the place of research. *Midwifery, 19,* 10–16.

Mozingo, J. N., Davis, M. W., Droppleman, P. G., & Merideth, A. (2000). "It wasn't working": Women's experiences with short-term breast feeding. *American Maternal Journal of Nursing, 25,* 120–126.

Mueller, N., & Silverman, N. (1989). Peer relations in maltreated children. In D. Cicchetti & V. Carlson (Eds.), *Child maltreatment.* New York: Cambridge University Press.

Mullis, I. V. S., Martin, M. O., Beaton, A. E., Gonzales, E. J., Kelly, D. L., & Smith, T. A. (1998). *Mathematics and science achievement in the final year of secondary school.* Chestnut Hill, MA: Boston College, TIMSS International Study Center.

Mumme, D. L., Fernald, A., & Herrera, C. (1996). Infant's responses to facial & emotional signals in a social referencing paradigm. *Child Development, 67,* 3219–3237.

Munroe, R. H., Himmin, H. S., & Munroe, R. L. (1984). Gender understanding and sex role preference in four cultures. *Developmental Psychology, 20,* 673–682.

Murnane, R. J., & Levy, F. (1996). *Teaching new basic skills.* New York: Free Press.

Murray, J. P. (2000). Media effects. In A. Kazdin (Ed.), *Encyclopedia of psychology.* Washington, DC, & New York: American Psychological Association and Oxford University Press.

Myers, D. L. (1999). *Excluding violent youths from juvenile court: The effectiveness of legislative waiver.* Doctoral dissertation, University of Maryland, College Park.

Myerson, J., Rank, M. R., Raines, F. Q., & Schnitzler, M. A. (1998). Race and general cognitive ability: The myth of diminishing returns in education. *Psychological Science, 9,* 139–142.

NAEYC. (1986). Position statement on developmentally appropriate practice in programs for 4- and 5-year-olds. *Young Children, 41,* 20–29.

NAEYC. (1988). NAEYC position statement on developmentally appropriate practices in the primary grades, serving 5- through 8-year-olds. *Young Children, 43,* 64–83.

NAEYC. (1990). NAEYC position statement on school readiness. *Young Children, 46,* 21–28.

NAEYC. (2002). *Early learning standards: Creating the conditions for success.* Washington, DC: National Association for the Education of Young Children.

Nagata, D. K. (1989). Japanese American children and adolescents. In J. T. Gibbs & L. N. Huang (Eds.), *Children of color.* San Francisco: Jossey-Bass.

Nahas, G. G. (1984). *Marijuana in science and medicine.* New York: Raven Press.

Nakamura, J., & Csikszentmihalyi, M. (2003). The motivational sources of creativity as viewed from the paradigm of positive psychology. In L. G. Aspinwall & U. M. Staudinger (Eds.), *A psychology of human strengths.* Washington, DC: American Psychological Association.

Nansel, T. R., Overpeck, M., Pilla, R., Ruan, W., Simons-Morton, B., & Scheidt, P. (2001). Bullying behaviors among U.S. youth. *Journal of the American Medical Association, 285,* 2094–2100.

Narang, A., & Jain, N. (2001). Haemolytic disease of newborn. *Indian Journal of Pediatrics, 68,* 167–172.

Nash, J. M. (1997, February 3). Fertile minds. *Time,* pp. 50–54.

National Advisory Council on Economic Opportunity. (1980). *Critical choices for the 80s.* Washington, DC: U.S. Government Printing Office.

National Assessment of Educational Progress. (2000). *Reading achievement.* Washington, DC: National Center for Education Statistics.

National Center for Addiction and Substance Abuse. (2001). *2000 teen survey.* New York: National Center for Addiction and Substance Abuse, Columbia University.

National Center for Children Exposed to Violence. (2001). *Violence and children.* New Haven, CT: National Center for Children Exposed to Violence.

National Center for Education Statistics. (2001). *Dropout rates in the United States: 2000.* Washington, DC: U.S. Department of Education.

National Center for Health Statistics. (2000). *Health United States, 1999.* Atlanta: Centers for Disease Control and Prevention.

National Center for Health Statistics. (2000). *Health United States, 2000, with adolescent health chartbook.* Bethesda, MD: U.S. Department of Health and Human Services.

National Center for Health Statistics. (2001). Causes of death. Hyattsville, MD: Department of Health and Human Services.

National Center for Health Statistics. (2002). *New CDC report tracks trends in cesarean births and VCACs during the 1990s.* Atlanta: Centers for Disease Control and Prevention.

National Center for Health Statistics. (2002). Prevalence of overweight among children and adolescents: United States 1999–2000 (Table 71). *Health United States, 2002.* Atlanta: Centers for Disease Control and Prevention.

National Center for Health Statistics. (2002). *National Vital Statistics Report: Death Statistics, Vol. 50, No. 16,* Table 1. Bethesda, MD: National Center for Health Statistics.

National Center for Learning Disabilities. (2003). *Dyscalculia.* New York: Author.

National Center on Child Abuse and Neglect. (2002). *National child abuse and neglect data system (NCANDS) summary of key findings from calendar year 2000.* Washington, DC: The Administration for Children and Families.

National Commission on the High School Senior Year. (2001). *Youth at the crossroads: Facing high school and beyond.* Washington, DC: The Education Trust.

National Community Service Coalition. (1995). *Youth volunteerism.* Washington, DC: Author.

National Institute of Drug Abuse (2001). *Marijuana.* Washington, DC: National Institutes of Health.

National Reading Panel. (2000). *Teaching children to read.* Washington, DC: National Institute of Child Health and Human Development.

National Research Council (1999). *Starting out right: A guide to promoting children's reading success.* Washington, DC: National Academy Press.

National Research Council. (1999). *How people learn.* Washington, DC: National Academic Press.

National Vital Statistics Reports. (2000). Deaths and death rates for the 10 leading causes of death in specified age groups. *National Vital Statistics Reports, 48* (No.11), Table 8.

National Vital Statistics Reports. (2001). Deaths and death rates for the 10 leading causes of death in specified age groups. *National Vital Statistics Reports, 48* (No. 11), Table 8.

Natsopoulos, D., Kiosseoglou, G., Xeroxmeritou, A., & Alevriadou, A. (1998). Do the hands talk on the mind's behalf? Differences in language between left- and right-handed children. *Brain and Language, 64,* 182–214.

Navarette, C., Martinez, I., & Salamanca, F. (1994). Paternal line of transmission in chorea of Huntington with very early onset. *Genetic Counseling, 5,* 175–178.

Negalia, J. P., Friedman, D. L., Yasui, Y., Mertens, A., Hammond, S., Stoval, S., & Donaldson, M. (2001). Second malignant neoplasms in five-year survivors of childhood cancer. *Journal of the National Cancer Institute, 93,* 618–629.

Neimark, E. D. (1982). Adolescent thought: Transition to formal operations. In B. B. Wolman (Ed.), *Handbook of developmental psychology.* Englewood Cliffs, NJ: Prentice Hall.

Neisser, U., Boodoo, G., Bouchard, T. J., Boykin, A. W., Brody, N., Ceci, S. J., Halpern, D. F., Loehlin, J. C., Perloff, R. J., Sternberg, R., & Urbina, S. (1996). Intelligence: Knowns and unknowns. *American Psychologist, 51,* 77–101.

Nelson, C. (1999). Research description. *Institute of Child Development biennial report.* Minneapolis: Institute of Child Development.

Nelson, K. (1999). Levels and modes of representation: Issues for the theory of conceptual change and development. In E. K. Skolnick, K. Nelson, S. A. Gelman, & P. H. Miller (Eds.), *Conceptual Development.* Mahwah, NJ: Erlbaum.

Neville, H., & Bavelier, D. (2002). Human brain plasticity: Evidence from sensory deprivation and altered language experience. *Progress in Brain Research, 138,* 177–188.

Newcomb, M. D., & Bentler, P. M. (1988). Substance use and abuse among children and teenagers. *American Psychologist, 44,* 242–248.

Newell, K., Scully, D. M., McDonald, P. V., & Baillargeon, R. (1989). Task constraints and infant grip configurations. *Developmental Psychobiology, 22,* 817–832.

NHANES. (2001, March). *National Health and Nutrition Examination Surveys.* Washington, DC: U.S. Department of Health and Human Services.

NICHD Early Child Care Network. (2001). Nonmaternal care and family factors in early development: An overview of the NICHD Study of Early Child Care. *Journal of Applied Developmental Psychology, 22,* 457–492.

NICHD Early Child Care Network. (2002). Structure_Process_Outcome: Direct and indirect effects of child care quality on young children's development. *Psychological Science, 13,* 199–206.

NICHD Early Child Care Network. (in press). Does amount of time spent in child care predict socioemotional adjustment during the transition to kindergarten? *Child Development.*

NICHD Early Child Care Research Network. (2000). Factors associated with fathers' caregiving activities and sensitivity with young children. *Developmental Psychology, 14,* 200–219.

Nicholls, J. G. (1979). Development of perception of own attainment and causal attribution for success and failure in reading. *Journal of Educational Psychology, 71,* 94–99.

Nichols, F. H., & Humenick, S. S. (2000). *Childbirth education* (2nd ed.). London: Harcourt International.

Nieto, S. (2002). *Language, culture, and teaching.* Mahwah, NJ: Erlbaum.

Nocentini, U., Goulet, P., Roberts, P. M., & Joanette, Y. (2001). The effects of left- versus right-hemisphere lesions on the sensitivity to intra- and interconceptual semantic relationships. *Neuropsychologia, 39,* 443–451.

Noddings, N. (1992). *The challenge to care in schools.* New York: Teachers College Press.

Noddings, N. (1998). *Teaching for continuous learning.* Paper presented at the meeting of the American Educational Research Association, San Diego.

Noddings, N. (2001). The care tradition: Beyond "add women and stir." *Theory into Practice, 40,* 29–34.

Nolan, K., Schell, L. M., Stark, A. D., & Gomez, M. I. (2002). Longitudinal study of energy and nutrient intakes for infants from low-income, urban families. *Public Health Nutrition, 5,* 405–412.

Nolen-Hoeksema, S. (2001). *Abnormal psychology* (2nd ed.). New York: McGraw-Hill.

Nolen-Hoeksema, S. (2004). *Abnormal psychology* (3rd ed.). New York: McGraw-Hill.

Nottelmann, E. D., Susman, E. J., Blue, J. H., Inoff-Germain, G., Dorn, L. D., Loriaux, D. L., Cutler, G. B., & Chrousos, G. P. (1987). Gonadal and adrenal hormone correlates of adjustment in early adolescence. In R. M. Lerner & T. T. Foch (Eds.), *Biological-psychological interactions in early adolescence.* Hillsdale, NJ: Erlbaum.

Nugent, K., & Brazelton, T. B. (2000). Preventive infant mental health: Uses of the Brazelton scale. In J. D. Osofsky & H. E. Fitzgerald (Eds.), *WAIMH Handbook of infant mental health* (Vol. 2). New York: Wiley.

Oates, J., & Lipton, M. (2003). *Teaching to change the world* (2nd ed.). New York: McGraw-Hill.

Obel, C., Olsen, J., Dalsgaard, S., Linnett, K. M., & Mick, E. (2002). Smoking and alcohol use in pregnancy. *Journal of the American Academy of Child & Adolescent Psychiatry, 41,* 1391–1393.

Obler, L. K. (1993). Language beyond childhood. In J. B. Gleason (Ed.), *The development of language* (3rd ed.). New York: Macmillan.

Oboro, V. O., & Tabowei, T. O. (2003). A randomized controlled trial of misoprostol versus oxytocin in the active management of the third stage of labor. *Journal of Obstetrics and Gynecology, 23,* 13–16.

O'Donnell, W. T., & Warren, S. T. (2003). A decade of molecular studies of fragile X syndrome. *Annual Review of Neuroscience, 25,* 315–338.

Oehninger, S. (2001). Strategies for the infertile man. *Seminars in Reproductive Medicine, 19,* 231–238.

Offer, D., Ostrov, E., Howard, K. I., & Atkinson, R. (1988). *The teenage world: Adolescents' self-image in ten countries.* New York: Plenum.

Office of Juvenile Justice and Prevention. (1999). *Juvenile offenders and victims: 1999. National Report.* Washington. DC: Author.

Ogbu, J. U. (1989, April). *Academic socialization of Black children: An inoculation against future failure?* Paper presented at the meeting of the Society for Research in Child Development, Kansas City.

Ogbu, J. U., & Stern, P. (2001). Caste status and intellectual ability. In R. J. Sternberg & E. L. Grigorenko (Eds.), *Environmental effects on cognitive abilities.* Mahwah, NJ: Erlbaum.

Ohgi, S., Fukuda, M., Moriuchi, H., Kusumoto, T., Akiyama, T., Nugent, J. K., Brazelton, T. B., Arisawa, K., Takahashi, T., & Saitoh, H. (2002). Comparison of kangaroo care and standard care: Behavioral organization, development, and temperament in healthy, low birth weight infants through 1 year. *Journal of Perinatology, 22,* 374–379.

Okagaki, L. (2000). Determinants of intelligence: Socialization of intelligence. In A. Kazdin (Ed.), *Encyclopedia of psychology.* Washington, DC, & New York: American Psychological Association and Oxford University Press.

Okun, B. F., & Rappaport, L. J. (1980). *Working with families.* North Scituate, MA: Duxbury Press.

Olson, A. L., Kemper, K. J., Kelleher, K. J., Hammond, C. S., Zuckerman, B. S., & Dietrich, A. J. (2002). Primary care pediatricians' roles and perceived responsibilities in the identification and management of maternal depression. *Pediatrics, 11,* 1169–1176.

Olson, H. C. (2000). Fetal alcohol syndrome. In A. Kazdin (Ed.), *Encyclopedia of psychology.* Washington, DC, & New York: American Psychological Association and Oxford University Press.

Olson, R. K. (2002). Dyslexia: Nature and nurture. *Dyslexia, 8,* 143–159.

Olweus, D. (1980). Bullying among schoolboys. In R. Barnen (Ed.), *Children and violence.* Stockholm: Adaemic Litteratur.

Orbanic, S. (2001). Understanding bulimia. *American Journal of Nursing, 101,* 35–41.

Osborne, L., & Pober, B. (2001). Genetics of childhood disorders: XXVII. Genes and cognition in Williams syndrome. *Journal of the Academy of Child & Adolescent Psychiatry, 40,* 732–735.

Oshio, S., Johnson, P., & Fullerton, J. (2002). The 1999–2000 task analysis of American nurse-midwifery/midwifery practice. *Journal of Midwifery and Women's Health, 47,* 35–41.

Overton, W. F., & Byrnes J. P. (1991). Cognitive development. In R. M. Lerner, A. C. Petersen, and J. Brooks-Gunn (Eds.), *Encyclopedia of adolescence* (Vol. 1). New York: Garland.

Pascali-Bonaro, D. (2002). Pregnant and widowed on September 11: The birth community reaches out. *Birth, 29,* 62–64.

Padilla, A. M., & Perez, W. (2003). Acculturation, social identity, and social cognition: A new perspective. *Hispanic Journal of Behavioral Science, 25,* 35–55.

Paikoff, R. L., Buchanan, C. M., & Brooks-Gunn, J. (1991). Hormone-behavior links at puberty, methodological links in the study of. In R. M. Lerner, A. C. Petersen, & J. Brooks-Gunn (Eds.), *Encyclopedia of adolescence.* New York: Garland.

Paivio, A. (1971). *Imagery and verbal processes.* Ft. Worth: Harcourt Brace.

Paivio, A. (1986). *Mental representations: A dual coding approach.* New York: Oxford University Press.

Paludi, M. A. (2002). *Psychology of women* (2nd ed.). Upper Saddle River, NJ: Prentice Hall.

Panchaud, C., Singh, S., Feivelson, D., & Darroch, J. E. (2000). Sexually transmitted diseases among adolescents in developed countries. *Family Planning Perspectives, 32,* 24–32.

Pang, V. O. (2001). *Multicultural education.* New York: McGraw-Hill.

Papp, C., & Papp, Z. (2003). Chorionic villus sampling and amniocentesis: what are the risks in current practice? *Current Opinions in Obstetrics and Gynecology, 15,* 159–165.

Parcel, G. S., Simons-Morton, G. G., O'Hara, N. M., Baranowski, T., Kolbe, L. J., & Bee, D. E. (1987). School promotion of healthful diet and exercise behavior: An integration of organizational change and social learning theory interventions. *Journal of School Health, 57,* 150–156.

Parke, R. D. (1972). Some effects of punishment on children's behavior. In W. W. Hartup (Ed.), *The young child* (Vol. 2). Washington, DC: National Association for the Education of Young Children.

Parke, R. D. (1977). Some effects of punishment on children's behavior—Revisited. In E. M. Hetherington & R. D. Parke (Eds.), *Readings in contemporary child psychology.* New York: McGraw-Hill.

Parke, R. D. (1995). Fathers and families. In M. H. Bornstein (Ed.), *Children and parenting* (Vol. 3). Hillsdale, NJ: Erlbaum.

Parke, R. D. (2000). Father involvement: A developmental psychology perspective. *Marriage and Family Review, 29,* 43–58.

Parke, R. D. (2001). Parenting in the new millenium. In J. P. McHale & W. S. Grolnick (Eds.), *Retrospect and prospect in the psychological study of families.* Mahwah, NJ: Erlbaum.

Parke, R. D. (2002). Fathers. In M. H. Bornstein (Ed.), *Handbook of parenting* (2nd ed., Vol. 3). Mahwah, NJ: Erlbaum.

Parke, R. D., & Buriel, R. (1998). Socialization in the family. Ethnic and ecological perspectives. In W. Damon (Ed.), *Handbook of child psychology* (5th ed., Vol. 3). New York: Wiley.

Parker, J. G., & Asher, S. R. (1987). Peer relations and later personal adjustment: Are low accepted children at risk? *Psychological Bulletin, 102,* 357–389.

Parmar, R. C., Muranjan, M. N., & Swami, S. (2002). Trisomy 21 with XYY. *Indian Journal of Pediatrics, 11,* 979–981.

Parten, M. (1932). Social play among preschool children. *Journal of Abnormal Social Psychology, 27,* 243–269.

Pasch, L. A. (2001). Confronting fertility problems. In A. Baum, T. A. Revenson, & J. E. Singer (Eds.), *Handbook of health psychology.* Mahwah, NJ: Erlbaum.

Patterson, C. J. (2002). Lesbian and gay parenthood. In M. H. Bornstein (Ed.), *Handbook of parenting* (2nd ed., Vol. 3). Mahwah, NJ: Erlbaum.

Patterson, G. R., DeBaryshe, B. D., & Ramsey, E. (1989). A developmental perspective on antisocial behavior. *American Psychologist, 44,* 329–355.

Patterson, G. R., & Fisher, P. A. (2002). Recent developments in our understanding of parenting: Bidirectional effects, causal models, and the search for parsimony. In M. H. Bornstein (Ed.), *Handbook of parenting* (2nd ed., Vol. 5). Mahwah, NJ: Erlbaum.

Patterson, G. R., & Stouthamer-Loeber, M. (1984). The correlation of family management practices and delinquency. *Child Development, 55,* 1299–1307.

Paukku, M., Quan, J., Darney, P., & Raine, T. (2003). Adolescents' contraceptive use and pregnancy history: Is there a pattern? *Obstetrics and Gynecology, 101,* 534–538.

Paulson, S. E., Marchant, G. J., & Rothlisberg, B. (1995, March). *Relations among parent, teacher, and school factors: Implications for achievement outcome in middle grade students.* Paper presented at the meeting of the Society for Research in Child Development, Indianapolis.

Pavlov, I. P. (1927). In G. V. Anrep (Trans.), *Conditioned reflexes.* London: Oxford University Press.

Peregoy, S., & Boyle, O. (2001). *Reading, writing, and learning in ESL* (3rd ed.). Boston: Allyn & Bacon.

Perez-Febles, A. M. (1992). *Acculturation and interactional styles of Latina mothers and their infants.* Unpublished honors thesis, Brown University, Providence, RI.

Perkins, D., & Tishman, S. (1997, March). Commentary in "Teaching today's pupils to think more critically." *APA Monitor,* p. 51.

Perkins, D. F., & Borden, L. M. (2003). Positive behaviors, problem behaviors, and resiliency in adolescence. In I. B. Weiner (Ed.), *Handbook of psychology* (Vol. VI). New York: Wiley.

Perry-Jenkins, M., Payne, J., & Hendricks, E. (1999, April). *Father involvement by choice or necessity: Implications for parents' well-being.* Paper presented at the meeting of the Society for Research in Child Development, Albuquerque.

Perse, E. M. (2001). *Media effects and society.* Mahwah, NJ: Erlbaum.

Peskin, E. G., & Reine, G. M. (2002). A guest editorial: What is the correct cesarean rate and how do we get there? *Obstetrical and Gynecological Survey, 57,* 189–190.

Peskin, H. (1967). Pubertal onset and ego functioning. *Journal of Abnormal Psychology, 72,* 1–15.

Petersen, A. C. (1979, January). Can puberty come any faster? *Psychology Today,* pp. 45–56.

Petersen, A. C. (1993). Creating adolescents: The role of context and process in developmental trajectories. *Journal of Research on Adolescence, 3,* 1–18.

Peterson, C. C., & Peterson, J. L. (1973). Preference for sex of offspring as a measure of change in sex attitudes. *Psychology, 10,* 3–5.

Peterson, K. S. (1997, September 3). In high school, dating is a world into itself. *USA Today,* pp. 1–2D.

Pettit, G. S., Bates, J. E., Dodge, K. A., & Meece, D. W. (1999). The impact of after-school peer contact on early adolescent externalizing problems is moderated by parental monitoring, perceived neighborhood safety, and prior adjustment. *Child Development, 70,* 768–778.

Pfeffer, C. R. (1996). *Severe stress and mental disturbance in children.* Washington, DC: American Psychiatric Press.

Pfeifer, M., Goldsmith, H. H., Davidson, R. J., & Rickman, M. (2002). Continuity and change in inhibited and uninhibited children. *Child Development, 73,* 1474–1485.

Phillips, D., Friedman, S. L., Huston, A. C., & Weinraub, M. (1999, April). *The roles of work and poverty in the lives of families with young children.* Paper presented at the meeting of the Society for Research in Child Development, Albuquerque.

Phillips, D. A., Voran, K., Kisker, E., Howes, C., & Whitebook, M. (1994). Child care for children in poverty: Opportunity or inequity? *Child Development, 65,* 472–492.

Phinney, J. S. (1989). Stages of ethnic identity development in minority group adolescents. *Journal of Early Adolescence, 9,* 34–49.

Phinney, J. S. (1996). When we talk about American ethnic groups, what do we mean? *American Psychologist, 51,* 918–927.

Phinney, J. S. (2000). Ethnic identity. In A. Kazdin (Ed.), *Encyclopedia of psychology.* Washington, DC, and New York: American Psychological Association and Oxford University Press.

Phinney, J. S. (2003). Ethnic identity and acculturation. In K. M. Chun, P. B. Organista, & G. Marín (Eds.), *Acculturation.* Washington, DC: American Psychological Association.

Phinney, J. S., & Alipuria, L. L. (1990). Ethnic identity in college students from four ethnic groups. *Journal of Adolescence, 13,* 171–183.

Phinney, J. S., & Cobb, N. J. (1993, March). *Adolescents' reasoning about discrimination: Ethnic and attitudinal predictors.* Paper presented at the biennial meeting of the Society for Research in Child Development, New Orleans.

Phinney, J. S., & Devich-Navarro, M. (1997). Variations in bicultural identification among African American and Mexican American adolescents. *Journal of Research on Adolescence, 7,* 3–32.

Phinney, J. S., Ferguson, D. L., & Tate, J. D. (1997). Intergroup attitudes among ethnic minority adolescents: A causal model. *Child Development, 68,* 955–969.

Piaget, J. (1932). *The moral judgment of the child.* New York: Harcourt Brace Jovanovich.

Piaget, J. (1952). *The origins of intelligence in children.* (M. Cook, Trans.). New York: International Universities Press.

Piaget, J. (1952a). Jean Piaget. In C. A. Murchison (Ed.), *A history of psychology in autobiography* (Vol. 4). Worcester, MA: Clark University Press.

Piaget, J. (1954). *The construction of reality in the child.* New York: Basic Books.

Piaget, J. (1962). *Play, dreams, and imitation in childhood.* New York: W. W. Norton.

Piaget, J. (1972). Intellectual evolution from adolescence to adulthood. *Human Development, 15,* 1–12.

Piaget, J., & Inhelder, B. (1969). *The child's conception of space* (F. J. Langdon & J. L. Lunger, Trans.). New York: W. W. Norton.

Pianta, R., Hamre, B., & Stuhlman, M. (2003). Relationships between teachers and children. In I. B. Weiner (Ed.), *Handbook of psychology, Vol. 7.* New York: Wiley.

Pick, H. L. (1997). Review of J. W. Santrock's *Child development,* 8th ed. (New York: McGraw-Hill).

Pillavin, J. A. (2003). Doing well by doing good: Benefits of the benefactor. In C. L. M. Keyes & J. Haidt (Eds.), *Flourishing: positive psychology and the life well lived.* Washington, DC: American Psychological Association.

Pillow, D. R., Zautra, A. J., & Sandler, I. (1996). Major life events and minor stressors: Identifying mediational links in the stress process. *Journal of Personality and Social Psychology, 70,* 381–394.

Pinker, S. (1994). *The language instinct.* New York: William Morrow.

Pintrich, P. R. (2003). Motivation and classroom learning. In I. B. Weiner (Ed.), *Handbook of psychology, Vol. 7.* New York: Wiley.

Pintrich, P. R., & Schunk, D. H. (2002). *Motivation in education* (2nd ed.). Upper Saddle River, NJ: Prentice Hall.

Piotrowski, C. C. (1997, April). *Mother and sibling triads in conflict: Linking conflict style and the quality of sibling relationships.* Paper presented at the meeting of the Society for Research in Child Development, Washington, DC.

Pittenger, D. (2003). *Behavioral research design and analysis.* New York: McGraw-Hill.

Pittman, K., Diversi, M., Irby, M., & Fabber, T. (2003). Social policy implications. In R. Larson, B. Brown, & J. Mortimer (Eds.), *Adolescents' preparation for the future: Perils and promises*. Malden, MA: Blackwell.

Plackslin, S. (2000). *Mothering the new mother: Women's feelings and needs after childbirth—A support and resource guide*. New York: Newmarket Press.

Pleck, J. H. (1983). The theory of male sex role identity: Its rise and fall, 1936–present. In M. Levin (Ed.), *In the shadow of the past: Psychology portrays the sexes*. New York: Columbia University Press.

Pleck, J. H. (1995). The gender-role strain paradigm. In R. F. Levant & W. S. Pollack (Eds.), *A new psychology of men*. New York: Basic Books.

Plomin, R. (1993, March). *Human behavioral genetics and development: An overview and update*. Paper presented at the biennial meeting of the Society for Research in Child Development, New Orleans.

Plomin, R. (1999). Genetics and general cognitive ability. *Nature, 402* (Suppl.), C25–C29.

Plomin, R., & DeFries, J. C. (1998). The genetics of abilities and disabilities. *Scientific American, 278*, 40–48.

Plomin, R., Reiss, D., Hetherington, E. M., & Howe, G. W. (1994). Nature and nurture: Contributions to measures of the family environment. *Developmental Psychology, 30*, 32–43.

Polaha, J., Warzak, W. J., & Dittmer-Memahon, K. (2002). Toilet training in primary care: Current practice and recommendations from behavioral pediatrics. *Journal of Developmental and Behavioral Pediatrics, 23*, 424–429.

Polakow, V. (2003). Homeless children and their families. In S. Books (Ed.), *Invisible children in society and its schools*. Mahwah, NJ: Erlbaum.

Polivy, J., & Herman, C. P. (2002). Causes of eating disorders. *Annual Review of Psychology* (Vol. 53). Palo Alto, CA: Annual Reviews.

Pollack, H. A. (2001). Sudden infant death syndrome, maternal smoking during pregnancy, and the cost-effectiveness of smoking cessation intervention. *American Journal of Public Health, 91*, 432–436.

Pollack, H. A., & Frohna, J. G. (2001). A competing risk model of sudden death syndrome incidence in two U.S. birth cohorts. *Journal of Pediatrics, 138*, 661–667.

Pollack, W. (1999). *Real boys*. New York: Owl Books.

Pollitt, E. P., Gorman, K. S., Engle, P. L., Martorell, R., & Rivera, J. (1993). Early supplementary feeding and cognition. *Monographs of the Society for Research in Child Development, 58* (7, Serial No. 235).

Polloway, E. A., Patton, J. R., Smith, T. E. C., & Buck, G. H. (1997). Mental retardation and learning disabilities: Conceptual and applied issues. *Journal of Learning Disabilities, 30*, 297–308.

Polychronakos, C. (2003). Impact of the human genome project on pediatric endocrinology. *Hormone Research,* 55–65.

Ponterotto, J. G., Casas, J. M., Suzuki, L. A., & Alexander, C. M. (Eds.) (2001). *Handbook of multicultural counseling*. Thousand Oaks, CA: Sage.

Poole, D. A., & Lindsey, D. S. (1996). *Effects of parents' suggestions, interviewing techniques, and age on young children's event reports*. Presented at the NATO Advanced Study Institute, Port de Bourgenay, France.

Popham, W. J. (2002). *Classroom assessment* (2nd ed.). Boston: Allyn & Bacon.

Posner, J. K., & Vandell, D. L. (1994). Low-income children's after-school care: Are there benefits of after-school programs? *Child Development, 65*, 440–456.

Potter, S. M., Zelazo, P. R., Stack, D. M., & Papageorgiou, A. N. (2000). Adverse effects of fetal cocaine exposure on neonatal auditory information processing. *Pediatrics, 105*, e40–e41.

Presidential Task Force on Psychology and Education. (1992). *Learner-centered psychological principles: Guidelines for school redesign and reform (draft)*. Washington, DC: American Psychological Association.

Pressley, M. (1983). Making meaningful materials easier to learn. In M. Pressley & J. R. Levin (Eds.), *Cognitive strategy research: Educational applications* (pp. 239–266). New York: Springer-Verlag.

Pressley, M. (1995). More about the development of self-regulation: Complex, long-term, and thoroughly social. *Educational Psychologist, 30*, 207–212.

Pressley, M. (2003). Psychology of literacy and literacy instruction. In I. B. Weiner (Ed.), *Handbook of psychology*, Vol. 7. New York: Wiley.

Pressley, M., Cariligia-Bull, T., Deane, S., & Schneider, W. (1987). Short-term memory, verbal competence, and age as predictors of imagery instructional effectiveness. *Journal of Experimental Child Psychology, 43*, 194–211.

Pressley, M., Levin, J. R., & McCormick, C. B. (1980). Young children's learning of a foreign language vocabulary: A sentence variation of the keyword. *Contemporary Educational Psychology, 5*, 22–29.

Pressley, M., Roehrig, A., Raphael, L., Solezal, S., Bohn, K., Mohan, L., Wharton-McDonald, R., Bogner, K., & Hogan, K. (2003). Teaching processes in elementary and secondary school. In I. B. Weiner (Ed.), *Handbook of psychology* (Vol. VII). New York: Wiley.

Provenzo, E. F. (2002). *Teaching, learning, and schooling in American culture: A critical perspective*. Boston: Allyn & Bacon.

Purcheco, S., & Hurtado, A. (2001). Media violence. In J. Worell (Ed.), *Encyclopedia of women and gender*. San Diego: Academic Press.

Putnam, S. P., Sanson, A. V., & Rothbart, M. K. (2002). Child temperament and parenting. In M. H. Bornstein (Ed.), *Handbook of parenting* (2nd ed.). Mahwah, NJ: Erlbaum.

Q

Quiggle, N. L., Garber, J., Panak, W. F., & Dodge, K. A. (1992). Social information processing in aggressive and depressed children. *Child Development, 63*, 1305–1320.

Qutub, M., Klapper, P., Vallely, P., & Cleator, G. (2001). Genital herpes in pregnancy: Is screening cost effective? *International Journal of STD and AIDS, 12*, 14–16.

R

Rabin, B. E., & Dorr, A. (1995, March). *Children's understanding of emotional events on family television series*. Paper presented at the meeting of the Society for Research in Child Development, Indianapolis.

Rabiner, D. L., Gordon, L., Klumb, D., & Thompson, L. B. (1991, April). *Social problem solving deficiencies in rejected children: Motivational factors and skill deficits*. Paper presented at the meeting of the Society for Research in Child Development, Seattle.

Radke-Yarrow, M., Nottlemann, E., Martinez, P., Fox, M. B., & Belmont, B. (1992). Young children of affectively ill parents: A longitudinal study of psychosocial development. *Journal of the Academy of Child & Adolescent Psychiatry, 31*, 68–77.

Raffaelli, M., & Ontai, L. (2001). "She's sixteen years old and there's boys calling over to the house": An exploratory study of sexual socialization in Latino families. *Culture, Health, and Sexuality, 3,* 295–310.

Rainey, R. (1965). The effects of directed vs. non-directed laboratory work on high school chemistry achievement. *Journal of Research in Science Teaching, 3,* 286–292.

Ramey, C. T., & Campbell, F. A. (1984). Preventive education for high-risk children: Cognitive consequences of the Carolina Abecedarian Project. *American Journal of Mental Deficiency, 88,* 515–523.

Ramey, C. T., Campbell, F. A., & Blair, C. (2001). Enhancing the life course for high-risk children: Results from the Abecedarian project. In J. Crane (Ed.), *Social programs that work.* New York: Sage.

Ramey, C. T., & Ramey, S. L. (1998). Early prevention and early experience. *American Psychologist, 53,* 109–120.

Ramey, C. T., Ramey, S. L., & Lanzi, R. G. (2001). Intelligence and experience. In R. J. Sternberg & E. I. Grigorenko (Eds.), *Environmental effects on cognitive development.* Mahwah, NJ: Erlbaum.

Ramey, S. L., & Ramey, C. T. (2000). Early childhood experiences and developmental competence. In S. Danzinger & J. Waldfogel (Eds.), *Securing the future: Investing in children from birth to college.* New York: Russell Sage Foundation.

Ramphal, C. (1962). *A study of three current problems in education.* Unpublished doctoral dissertation, University of Natal, India.

Ransjo-Arvidson, A. B., Matthiesen, A. S., Nissen, L. G., Widstrom, A. M., & Uvnas-Moberg, K. (2001). Maternal analgesia during labor disturbs newborn behavior: Effects on breastfeeding, temperature, and crying. *Birth, 28,* 5–12.

Rapport, M. D., Chung, K. M., Shore, G., & Issacs, P. (2001). A conceptual model of child psychopathology: Implications for understanding a deficit hyperactivity disorder and treatment effectiveness. *Journal of Clinical Child Psychology, 30,* 48–58.

Raudenbush, S. (2001). Longitudinal data analysis. *Annual review of psychology* (Vol. 52). Palo Alto, CA: Annual Reviews.

Raven, P. H., Johnson, G. B., Singer, S., & Loso, J. (2002). *Biology* (6th ed.). New York: McGraw-Hill.

Reid, P. T., & Zalk, S. R. (2001). Academic environments: Gender and ethnicity in U.S. higher education. In J. Worell (Ed.), *Encyclo-pedia of women and gender.* San Diego: Academic Press.

Reifman, A. (2001). Models of parenting and adolescent drinking. *American Psychologist, 56,* 170–171.

Reiner, W. G. (2001). Gender identity and sex reassignment. In L. King, B. Belman, & S. Kramer (Eds.), *Clinical pediatric urology* (3rd ed.). London: ISIS Medical.

Relier, J. P. (2001). Influence of maternal stress on fetal behavior and brain development. *Biology of the Neonate, 79,* 168–171.

Remafedi, G., Resnick, M., Blum, R., & Harris, L. (1992). The demography of sexual orientation in adolescents. *Pediatrics, 89,* 714–721.

Rest, J., Narvaez, D., Bebeau, M. J., & Thomas, S. J. (1999). *Postconventional moral thinking.* Mahwah, NJ: Erlbaum.

Rest, J. R. (1986). *Moral development: Advances in theory and research.* New York: Praeger.

Rest, J. R., Turiel, E., & Kohlberg, L. (1969). Relations between level of moral judgment and preference and comprehension of the moral judgments of others. *Journal of Personality, 37,* 225–252.

Reuter, M., & Conger, R. (1995). Antecedents of parent-adolescent disagreements. *Journal of Marriage and the Family, 57,* 435–448.

Reynolds, A. J. (1999, April). *Pathways to long-term effects in the Chicago Child-parent Center Program.* Paper presented at the meeting of the Society for Research in Child Development, Albuquerque.

Rhodes, J. E., Grossman, J. B., & Resch, N. L. (2000). Agents of change: Pathways through which mentoring relationships influence adolescents' academic adjustment. *Child Development, 71,* 1662–1671.

Ribeiro, J., Guerra, S., Pinto, A., Oliveira, J., Duarte, J., & Mota, J. (2003). Overweight and obesity in children and adolescents: Relationship with blood pressure and physical activity. *Annals of Human Biology, 30,* 203–213.

Richards, M., Suleiman, L., Sims, B., & Sedeno, A. (1994, February). *Experiences of ethnically diverse young adolescents growing up in poverty.* Paper presented at the meeting of the Society for Research on Adolescence, San Diego.

Richardson, G. A., Ryan, C., Willford, J., Day, N. L., & Goldschmidt, L. (2002). Prenatal alcohol and marijuana exposure: Effects on neuropsychological outcomes at 10 years. *Neurotoxicology and Teratology, 24,* 309–320.

Rickards, A. L., Kelly, E. A., Doyle, L. W., & Callahan, C. (2001). Cognition, academic progress, behavior, and self-concept at 14 years of very low birthweight children. *Journal of Developmental and Behavioral Pediatrics, 22,* 11–18.

Ridgeway, D., Waters, E., & Kuczaj, S. A. (1985). Acquisition of emotion-descriptive language: Receptive and productive vocabulary norms for ages 18 months to 6 years. *Developmental Psychology, 21,* 901–908.

Riesch, S. K., Gray, J., Hoefs, M., Keenan, T., Ertil, T., & Mathison, K. (2003). Conflict and conflict resolution: parent and young teen perceptions. *Journal of Pediatric Health Care, 17,* 22–31.

Rigby, K. (2002). Bullying in childhood. In P. K. Smith & C. H. Hart (Eds.), *Blackwell handbook of childhood social development.* Malden, MA: Blackwell.

Righetti-Veltema, M., Conne-Perreard, E., Bousquest, A., & Manzano, J. (2002). Postpartum depression and mother-infant relationship at 3 months old. *Journal of Affective Disorders, 70,* 291–306.

Riley, E. P., Mattson, S. N., Li, T. K., Jacobsen, S. W., Coles, C. D., Kodituwakku, P. W., Adams, C. M., & Workman, M. I. (2003). Neurobehavioral consequence of prenatal alcohol exposure: An international perspective. *Alcohol: Clinical and Experimental Research, 27,* 362–373.

Rimberg, H. M., & Lewis, R. J. (1994). Older adolescents and AIDS: Correlates of self-reported safer sex practices. *Journal of Research on Adolescence, 4,* 453–464.

Rinehart, S. D., Stahl, S. A., & Erickson, L. G. (1986). Some effects of summarization training on reading and studying. *Reading Research Quarterly, 21,* 422–438.

Rittey, C. D. (2003). Learning difficulties: what the neurologist needs to know. *Journal of Neurology and Neurological Psychiatry, 74, Supplement 1,* 30–36.

Roberts, D., Jacobson, L., & Taylor, R. D. (1996, March). *Neighborhood characteristics, stressful life events, and African-American adolescents' adjustment.* Paper presented at the meeting of the Society for Research on Adolescence, Boston.

Roberts, D. F., Foehr, U. G., Rideout, V. J., & Brodie, M. (1999). *Kids and media at the new millenium: A Kaiser Family Foundation Report.* Menlo Park, CA: The Kaiser Family Foundation.

Roberts, J. E., Burchinal, M. R., & Durham, M. (1999). Parent's report of vocabulary and grammatical development of African American preschoolers. *Child Development, 70,* 92–106.

Roberts, W., & Strayer, J. (1996). Empathy, emotional expressiveness, and prosocial behavior. *Child Development, 67,* 471–489.

Robins, R. W., Trzesniewski, K. H., Tracey, J. L., Potter, J., & Gosling, S. D. (2002). Age differences in self-esteem from age 9 to 90. *Psychology and Aging, 17,* 423–434.

Robinson, D. P., & Greene, J. W. (1988). The adolescent alcohol and drug problem: A practical approach. *Pediatric Nursing, 14,* 305–310.

Rode, S. S., Chang, P., Fisch, R. O., & Sroufe, L. A. (1981). Attachment patterns of infants separated at birth. *Developmental Psychology, 17,* 188–191.

Rodriguez, J. L., Diaz, R. M., Duran, D., & Espinosa, L. (1995). The impact of bilingual preschool education on the language development of Spanish-speaking children. *Early Childhood Research Quarterly, 10,* 475–490.

Rogers, A. (1987). *Questions of gender differences: Ego development and moral voice in adolescence.* Unpublished manuscript, Department of Education, Harvard University.

Rogers, C. R. (1950). The significance of the self regarding attitudes and perceptions. In M. L. Reymart (Ed.), *Feelings and emotions.* New York: McGraw-Hill.

Rogoff, B. (1990). *Apprenticeship in thinking.* New York: Oxford University Press.

Rogoff, B. (1998). Cognition as a collaborative process. In W. Damon (Ed.), *Handbook of child psychology* (5th ed., Vol. 2). New York: Wiley.

Rogoff, B. (2001, April). *Examining cultural processes in developmental research.* Paper presented at the meeting of the Society for Research in Child Development, Minneapolis.

Rogoff, B., Turkanis, C. G., & Bartlett, L. (Eds.) (2001). *Learning together.* New York: Oxford University Press.

Rohner, R. P., & Rohner, E. C. (1981). Parental acceptance-rejection and parental control: Cross-cultural codes. *Ethnology, 20,* 245–260.

Roosa, M. W., Dumka, L. E., Gonzales, N. A., & Knight, G. P. (2002). Cultural/ethnic issues and the prevention scientist in the 21st century. *Prevention & Treatment, 5,* 1–13.

Rose, A. A., Feldman, J. F., McCarton, C. M., & Wolfson, J. (1988). Information processing in seven-month-old infants as a function of risk status. *Child Development, 59,* 589–603.

Rose, A. J., & Asher, S. R. (1999, April). *Seeking and giving social support within a friendship.* Paper presented at the meeting of the Society for Research in Child Development, Albuquerque.

Rose, H. A. (1997, April). *Bringing biology back in: A biopsychosocial model of gender development.* Paper presented at the meeting of the Society for Research in Child Development, Washington, DC.

Rose, J. L., & Bertenthal, B. I. (1995). A longitudinal study of the visual control of posture in infancy. In B. G. Bardy, R. J. Bootsma, & Y. Guiard (Eds.), *Studies in perception and action* (pp. 251–253). Mahwah, NJ: Erlbaum.

Rose, L. C., & Gallup, A. M. (2000). The 32nd annual Phi Delta Kappa/Gallup Poll of the public's attitudes toward the public schools. *Phi Delta Kappan, 82* (No. 10) 41–58.

Rose, S., & Frieze, I. R. (1993). Young singles' contemporary dating scripts. *Sex Roles, 28,* 499–509.

Rosenberg, M. (1979). *Conceiving the self.* New York: Basic Books.

Rosenberg, M. (1986). Self-concept from middle childhood through adolescence. In J. Suls & A. G. Greenwald (Eds.), *Psychological perspective on the self* (Vol. 3). Hillsdale, NJ: Erlbaum.

Rosenblith, J. F. (1992). *In the beginning* (2nd ed.). Newbury Park, CA: Sage.

Rosenblum, G. D., & Lewis, M. (2003). Emotional development in adolescence. In G. Adams & M. Berzonsky (Eds.), *Blackwell handbook of adolescence.* Malden, MA: Blackwell.

Rosentein, D., & Oster, H. (1988). Differential facial responses to four basic tastes in newborns. *Child Development, 59,* 1555–1568.

Rosenthal, R., & Jacobsen, I. (1968). *Pygmalion in the classroom.* Fort Worth: Harcourt Brace.

Rosenzweig, M. (2000). Ethology. In A. Kazdin (Ed.), *Encyclopedia of psychology.* Washington, DC, & New York: American Psychological Association and Oxford University Press.

Rosenzweig, M. R. (1969). Effects of heredity and environment on brain chemistry, brain anatomy, and learning ability in the rat. In M. Monosevitz, G. Lindzey, & D. D. Thiessen (Eds.), *Behavioral genetics.* New York: Appleton-Century-Crofts.

Rosnow, R. I., & Rosenthal, R. (1996). *Beginning behavioral research* (2nd ed.). Upper Saddle River, NJ: Prentice Hall.

Rosnow, R. L. (1995). Teaching research ethics through role-playing and discussion. In M. E. Ware & D. E. Johnson (Eds.), *Demonstrations and activities in teaching psychology* (Vol. 1). Mahwah, NJ: Erlbaum.

Rotenstein, D. (2001, January 7). Commentary. *Parade Magazine,* p. 12.

Roth, J., & Brooks-Gunn, J. (2000). What do adolescents need for healthy development? Implications for youth policy. *Social Policy Report, 14* (1), 3–19.

Rothbart, M. K. (1999, April). *Developing a model for the study of temperament.* Paper presented at the meeting of the Society for Research in Child Development, Albuquerque.

Rothbart, M. K., & Bates, J. E. (1998). Temperament. In W. Damon (Ed.). *Handbook of child psychology* (5th ed., Vol. 3). New York: Wiley.

Rothbart, M. K., & Putnam, S. P. (2002). Temperament and socialization. In L. Pulkkinen & A. Caspi (Eds.), *Paths to successful development.* New York: Cambridge University Press.

Rothbart, M. L. K. (1971). Birth order and mother-child interaction, *Dissertation Abstracts, 27,* 45–57.

Rothbaum, F., Pott, M., Azuma, H., Miyake, K., & Weisz, J. (2000). The development of close relationships in Japan and the United States: Paths of symbiotic harmony and generative tension. *Child Development, 71,* 1121–1142.

Rothbaum, F., Rosen, K., Ujiie, T., & Uchida, N. (2002). Family system theory, attachment theory, and culture. *Family Processes, 41,* 328–350.

Rothstein-Fisch, C. (Ed.) (2003). *Readings for bridging cultures.* Mahwah, NJ: Erlbaum

Rovee-Collier, C. (1987). Learning and memory in children. In J. D. Osofsky (Ed.), *Handbook of infant development* (2nd ed.). New York: Wiley.

Rovee-Collier, C. (2002). Infant learning and memory. In U. Goswami (Ed.), *Blackwell handbook of childhood cognitive development.* Malden, MA: Blackwell.

Rovira, M. T., Antorn, M. T., Paya, A., Castellanos, E., Mur, A., & Carreras, R. (2001). Human immunodeficiency virus infection in pregnant women, transmission, and zidovudine therapy. *European Journal of Obstetrics, Gynecology, and Reproductive Biology, 97,* 46–49.

Rowe, D. C. (2001). The nurture assumption persists *American Psychologist, 56,* 168–169.

Rowe, D. C. (2002). What twin and adoption studies reveal about parenting. In J. G.

Borkowski, S. L. Ramey, & M. Bristol-Power (Eds.), *Parenting and the child's world*. Mahwah, NJ: Erlbaum.

Rowe, S. M., & Wertsch, J. V. (2002). Vygotsky's model of cognitive development. In U. Goswami (Ed.), *Blackwell handbook of child development*. Malden, MA: Blackwell.

Rubin, D. H., Krasilnikoff, P. A., Leventhal, J. M., Weile, B., & Berget, A. (1986, August 23). Effect of passive smoking on birthweight. *The Lancet*, 415–417.

Rubin, K. H., Bukowski, W., & Parker, J. G. (1998). Peer interactions, relationships, and groups. In N. Eisenberg (Ed.), *Handbook of child psychology* (5th ed., Vol. 3). New York: Wiley.

Rubin, K. H., Mills, R. S. L., & Rose-Krasnor, L. (1989). Maternal beliefs and children's competence. In B. Schneider, G. Attili, J. Nadel, & R. Weissberg (Eds.), *Social competence in developmental perspective*. Amsterdam: Kluwer Academic.

Rubin, Z., & Mitchell, C. (1976). Couples research as couples counseling. *American Psychologist, 31*, 17–25.

Rubin, Z., & Sloman, J. (1984). How parents influence their children's friendships. In M. Lewis (Ed.), *Beyond the dyad*. New York: Plenum.

Ruble, D. (1983). The development of social comparison processes and their role in achievement-related self-socialization. In E. Higgins, D. Ruble, & W. Hartup (Eds.), *Social cognitive development: A social-cultural perspective*. New York: Cambridge University Press.

Ruble, D. N. (2000). Gender constancy. In A. Kazdin (Ed.), *Encyclopedia of psychology*. Washington, DC, and New York: American Psychological Association and Oxford University Press.

Ruble, D. N., Boggiano, A. K., Feldman, N. S., & Loebl, J. H. (1980). Developmental analysis of the role of social comparison in self-evaluation. *Developmental Psychology, 16*, 105–115.

Rumberger, R. W. (1995). Dropping out of middle school: A multilevel analysis of students and schools. *American Education Research Journal, 3*, 583–625.

Rusak, B., Robertson, H. A., Wisden, W., & Hunt, S. P. (1990). Light pulses that shift rhythms induce gene expression in the suprachiasmatic nucleus. *Science, 248*, 1237–1240.

Russell, S. T., & Joyner, K. (2001). Adolescent sexual orientation and suicide risk: Evidence from a national study. *American Journal of Public Health, 91*, 1276–1281.

Russo, N. F. (1990). Overview: Forging research priorities for women's mental health. *American Psychologist, 45*, 368–374.

Rutter, M. (1979). Protective factors in children's response to stress and disadvantage. In M. W. Kent & J. E. Rolf (Eds.), *Primary prevention in psychopathology* (Vol. 3). Hanover, NH: University of New Hampshire Press.

Rutter, M. (2002). Nature, nurture, and development: From evangelism through science toward policy and practice. *Child Development, 73*, 1–21.

Rutter, M., & Garmezy, N. (1983). Developmental psychopathology. In P. H. Mussen (Ed.), *Handbook of child psychology* (4th ed., Vol. 4). New York: Wiley.

Ryan, A. S. (1997). The resurgence of breastfeeding in the United States. *Pediatrics, 99*, E-12.

Ryan, A. S., Wenjun, Z., & Acosta, A. (2002). Breastfeeding continues to increase into the new millennium. *Pediatrics, 110*, 1103–1109.

Ryan, R., & Deci, E. (2000). Self-determination theory and the facilitation of intrinsic motivation, social development, and well-being. *American Psychologist, 55*, 68–78.

Ryan-Finn, K. D., Cauce, A. M., & Grove, K. (1995, March). *Children and adolescents of color: Where are you? Selection, recruitment, and retention in developmental research*. Paper presented at the meeting of the Society for Research in Child Development, Indianapolis.

Rymer, R. (1992). *Genie*. New York: HarperCollins.

Saarni, C. (1999). *The development of emotional competence*. New York: Guilford Press.

Saarni, C. (2000). Emotional competence: A developmental perspective. In R. Bar-On & J. D. Parker (Eds.), *The handbook of emotional intelligence*. San Francisco: Jossey-Bass.

Saarni, C. (2002). Unpublished review of J. W. Santrock's *Life-span development*, 10th ed. (New York: McGraw-Hill).

Sadker, D. M. P., & Sadker, D. M. (2000). *Teachers, schools, and society* (5th ed.). New York: McGraw-Hill.

Sadker, M. P., & Sadker, D. M. (2003). *Teachers, schools, and society* (6th ed.). New York: McGraw-Hill.

Sagan, C. (1977). *The dragons of Eden*. New York: Random House.

Salkind, N. J. (2003). *Exploring research* (5th ed.). Upper Saddle River, NJ: Prentice Hall.

Salovey, P., & Mayer, J. D. (1990). Emotional intelligence. *Imagination, Cognition, and Personality, 9*, 185–211.

Samaniego, R. Y., & Gonzales, N. A. (1999). Multiple mediators of the effects of acculturation status on delinquency for Mexican American adolescents. *American Journal of Community Psychology, 27*, 189–210.

Samour, P. Q., Helm, K. K., & Lang, C. E. (Eds.). (2000). *Handbook of pediatric nutrition* (2nd ed.). Aspen, CO: Aspen.

Samuels, M., & Samuels, N. (1996). *New well pregnancy book*. New York: Fireside.

Sanson, A., & Rothbart, M. K. (1995). Child temperament and parenting. In M. H. Bornstein (Ed.), *Handbook of parenting* (Vol. 4). Hillsdale, NJ: Erlbaum.

Santiago-Delefosse, M. J., Delefosse, J., & Oderic, J. M. (2002). Piaget and Vygotsky: Three positions on child thought and language. *Theory and Psychology, 12*, 723–747.

Santrock, J. W. (2002). *Life-span development* (8th ed.). New York: McGraw-Hill.

Santrock, J. W. (2004). *Educational psychology* (2nd ed.). New York: McGraw-Hill.

Santrock, J. W., Sitterle, K. A., & Warshak, R. A. (1988). Parent-child relationships in stepfather families. In P. Bronstein & C. P. Cowan (Eds.), *Fatherhood today: Men's changing roles in the family*. New York: Wiley.

Santrock, J. W., & Warshak, R. A. (1979). Father custody and social development in boys and girls. *Journal of Social Issues, 35*, 112–125.

Sarigiani, P. A., & Petersen, A. C. (2000). Adolescence: Puberty and biological maturation. In A. Kazdin (Ed.), *Encyclopedia of psychology*. Washington, DC, & New York: American Psychological Association and Oxford University Press.

Sauls, D. J. (2002). Effects of labor support on mothers, babies, and birth outcomes. *Journal of Obstetric, Gynecologic, and Neonatal Nursing, 31*, 733–741.

Savin-Williams, R. C. (1998). *". . . And then I became gay": Young men's stories*. New York: Routledge.

Savin-Williams, R. C. (2001). A critique of research on sexual minority youths. *Journal of Adolescence, 24*, 5–13.

Savin-Williams, R. C. (2001). *"Mom, dad, I'm gay."* Washington, DC: American Psychological Association.

Sax, G. (1997). *Principles of educational and psychology measurement* (4th ed.). Belmont, CA: Wadsworth.

Sax, L. J., Lindholm, J. A., Astin, A. W., Korn, W. S., & Mahoney, K. M. (2002). *The American college freshman: national norms for fall 2002.* Los Angeles: Higher Education Research Institute, UCLA.

Scarr, S. (1984, May). Interview. *Psychology Today.* pp. 59–63.

Scarr, S. (1993). Biological and cultural diversity: The legacy of Darwin for development. *Child Development, 64,* 1333–1353.

Scarr, S. (2000). Day care. In A. Kazdin (Ed.), *Encyclopedia of Psychology.* Washington, DC, & New York: American Psychological Association and Oxford University Press.

Scarr, S., & Weinberg, R. A. (1980). Calling all camps! The war is over. *American Sociological Review, 45,* 859–865.

Scarr, S., & Weinberg, R. A. (1983). The Minnesota adoption studies: Genetic differences and malleability. *Child Development, 54,* 253–259.

Schachter, S. C., & Ransil, B. J. (1996). Handedness distributions in nine professional groups. *Perceptual and Motor Skills, 82,* 51–63.

Schacter, D. L. (2001). *The seven sins of memory.* Boston: Houghton Mifflin.

Schaffer, H. R. (1996). *Social development.* Cambridge, MA: Blackwell.

Schauble, L. (1996). The development of scientific reasoning in knowledge-rich contexts. *Developmental Psychology, 32,* 102–119.

Schirato, T. (2003). *Understanding globalization.* Newbury Park, CA: Sage.

Schlegel, M. (2000). All work and play. *Monitor on Psychology, 31* (No. 11), 50–51.

Schmidt, P. R., & Mosenthal, P. B. (Eds.). (2001). *Reconceptualizing literacy in the new age of multiculturalism and pluralism.* Greenwich, CT: IAP.

Schneider, B. H., Atkinson, L., & Tardif, C. (2001). Child-parent attachment and children's peer relations: A quantitative review. *Developmental Psychology, 37,* 86–100.

Schneider, W. (2002). Memory development in children. In U. Goswami (Ed.), *Blackwell handbook of childhood cognitive development.* Malden, MA: Blackwell.

Schneider, W., & Bjorklund, D. F. (1998). Memory. In W. Damon (Gen. Ed.), and D. Kuhn, & R. S. Siegler (Vol. Eds.), *Handbook of child psychology: Vol. 2. Cognition, perception, and language.* New York: Wiley.

Schneider, W., & Pressley, M. (1997). *Memory development from 2 to 20* (2nd ed.). Mahwah, NJ: Erlbaum.

Schnorr, T. M., & others. (1991). Video-display terminals and the risk of spontaneous abortion. *New England Journal of Medicine, 324,* 727–733.

Schoendorf, K. C., & Kiely, J. L. (1992). Relationship of sudden infant death syndrome to maternal smoking during and after pregnancy. *Pediatrics, 90,* 905–908.

Schoon, I., Bynner, J., Joshi, H., Parsons, S., Wiggins, R. D., & Sacker, A. (2002). The influence of context, timing, and duration of risk experiences for the passage from childhood to midadulthood. *Child Development, 73,* 1486–1504.

Schrag, S. G., & Dixon, R. L. (1985). Occupational exposure associated with male reproductive dysfunction. *Annual Review of Pharmacology and Toxicology, 25,* 467–592.

Schroeder, C. S., & Gordon, B. N. (2002). *Assessment and treatment of childhood problems* (2nd ed.). New York: Guilford Press.

Schulpis, K. H., Tsakiris, S., Karikas, G. A., Moukas, M., & Behrakis, P. (2003). Effect of diet on plasma total antioxidant status in phenylketonuric patients. *European Journal of Clinical Nutrition, 57,* 383–387.

Schultz, R. T., Grelotti, D. J., & Pober, B. (2001). Genetics of childhood disorders: XXVI. Williams syndrome and brain-behavior relationships. *Journal of the American Academy of Child & Adolescent Psychiatry, 40,* 606–609.

Schum, T. R., McAuliffe, T. L., Simms, M. D., Walter, J. A., Lewis, M., & Pupp, R. (2001). Factors associated with toilet training in the 1990s. *Ambulatory Pediatrics, 1,* 79–86.

Schunk, D. H. (1991). Self-efficacy and academic motivation. *Educational Psychologist, 25,* 71–86.

Schunk, D. H. (2000). *Theories of learning* (3rd ed.). Upper Saddle River, NJ: Prentice Hall.

Schunk, D. H. (2001). Social cognitive theory and self-regulated learning. In B. J. Zimmerman & D. H. Schunk (Eds.), *Self-regulated learning and achievement* (2nd ed.). Mahwah, NJ: Erlbaum.

Schunk, D. H., & Zimmerman, B. J. (Eds.). (2001). *Self-regulated learning and academic achievement.* Mahwah, NJ: Erlbaum.

Schunk, D. H., & Zimmerman, B. J. (2003). Self-regulation and learning. In I. B. Weiner (Ed.), *Handbook of psychology.* New York: Wiley.

Schwartz, D., & Mayaux, M. J. (1982). Female fecundity as a function of age: Results of artificial insemination in nulliparous women with azoospermic husbands. *New England Journal of Medicine, 306,* 304–306.

Schwartz, M. B., & Puhl, R. (2003). Childhood obesity: a societal problem to solve. *Obesity Review, 4,* 57–71.

Schwarz, S. P. (2002). A mother's story. Available at http://www.makinglifeeasier.com/article3.html.

Schweinhart, L. J. (1999, April). *Generalizing from High/Scope longitudinal studies.* Paper presented at the meeting of the Society for Research in Child Development, Albuquerque.

Schwitzer, A. M., Rodriquez, L. E., Thomas, C., & Salami, L. (2001). The eating disorders NOS profile among college women. *Journal of American College Health, 49* 157–166.

Scott, L. D. (2003). The relation of racial identity and racial socialization to coping with discrimination among African American adolescents. *Journal of Black Studies, 33,* 520–538.

Scott-Jones, D. (1995, March). *Incorporating ethnicity and socioeconomic status in research with children.* Paper presented at the meeting of the Society for Research in Child Development, Indianapolis.

Scribner, S. (1977). Modes of thinking and ways of speaking: Culture and logic reconsidered. In P. N. Johnson-Laird & P. C. Wason (Eds.), *Thinking: Readings in cognitive science.* New York: Cambridge University Press.

Search Institute. (1995). *Barriers to participation in youth programs.* Unpublished manuscript, the Search Institute, Minneapolis.

Seligman, M. E. P. (1975). *Learned helplessness.* San Francisco: W. H. Freeman.

Seligman, M. E. P. (1995). *The optimistic child.* Boston: Houghton Mifflin.

Selman, R. L. (1976). Social-cognitive understanding. In T. Lickona (Ed.), *Moral development and behavior.* New York: Holt, Rinehart & Winston.

Selman, R. L. (1980). *The growth of interpersonal understanding.* New York: Academic Press.

Semba, R. D., & Neville, M. C. (1999). Breastfeeding, mastitis, and HIV transmission: Nutritional implication. *Nutrition Review, 57,* 146–153.

Serbin, L. A., & Sprafkin, C. (1986). The salience of gender: The process of sex-typing in three- to seven-year-old children. *Child Development, 57,* 1188–1209.

Serow, R. C., Ciechalski, J., & Daye, C. (1990). Students as volunteers. *Urban Education, 25,* 157–168.

Serpell, R. (2000). Culture and intelligence. In A. Kazdin (Ed.), *Encyclopedia of psychology.* Washington, DC, & New York: American Psychological Association and Oxford University Press.

Share, D. L., Moffitt, T. E., & Silva, P. A. (1988). Factors associated with arithmetic-and-reading disability and specific arithmetic disability. *Journal of Learning Disabilities, 21,* 313–321.

Sharma, A. R., McGue, M. K., & Benson, P. I. (1996, March). *The emotional and behavioral adjustment of United States adopted adolescents.* Paper presented at the meeting of the Society for Research on Adolescent Development, Boston.

Sharma, A. R., McGue, M. K., & Benson, P. L. (1996). The emotional and behavioral adjustment of adopted adolescents: Part I: Age at adoption. *Children and Youth Services Review, 18,* 101–114.

Sharma, A. R., McGue, M. K., & Benson, P. L. (1998). The psychological adjustment of United States adopted adolescents and their nonadopted siblings. *Child Development, 69,* 791–802.

Sharma, V. (2002). Pharmacotherapy of postpartum depression. *Expert Opinions on Pharmacotherapy, 3,* 1421–1431.

Sharp, V. (1999). *Computer education for teachers* (3rd ed.). New York: McGraw-Hill.

Shatz, M., & Gelman, R. (1973). The development of communication skills: Modifications in the speech of young children as a function of the listener. *Monographs of the Society for Research in Child Development, 38* (Serial No. 152).

Shaughnessy, J. J., Zechmeister, E. B., & Zechmeister, J. S. (2003). *Research methods in psychology* (6th ed.). New York: McGraw-Hill.

Shaver, P. R. (1993, March). *Where do adult romantic attachment patterns come from?* Paper presented at the biennial meeting of the Society for Research in Child Development, New Orleans.

Shaw, G. M. (2001). Adverse human reproductive outcomes and electromagnetic fields. *Bioelectromagnetics, 5* (Suppl.), S5–S18.

Shaw, S. M. (1988). Gender differences in the definition and perception of household labor. *Family Relations, 37,* 333–337.

Shields, S., & Eyssell, K. M. (2001). History of the study of gender psychology. In J. Worell (Ed.), *Encyclopedia of women and gender.* San Diego: Academic Press.

Shields, S. A. (1991). Gender in the psychology of emotion: A selective research review. In K. T. Strongman (Ed.), *International review of studies on emotion.* New York: Wiley.

Shields, S. A. (1998, August). *What Jerry Maguire can tell us about gender and emotion.* Paper presented at the meeting of the International Society for Research on Emotions, Wurzburg, Germany.

Shiffrin, R. M. (1996). Laboratory experimentation on the genesis of expertise. In K. A. Ericsson (Ed.), *The road to excellence.* Mahwah, NJ: Erlbaum.

Shiono, P. H., & Behrman, R. E. (1995, spring). Low birth weight: Analysis and recommendations. *Future of Children, 5* (1), 4–18.

Shonk, S. M., & Cicchetti, D. (2001). Maltreatment, competency deficits, and risk for academic and behavioral maladjustment. *Developmental Psychology, 37,* 3–17.

Shonkoff, J., & Phillips, D. (2001). *From neurons to neighborhoods: The science of early childhood development.* Washington, DC: National Academy Press.

Shorr, D. N., & Schorr, C. J. (1995, March). *Children's perceptions of kindness and anonymity in others' helping.* Paper presented at the meeting of the Society for Research in Child Development, Indianapolis.

Siegel, L. S. (1988). Evidence that IQ scores are irrelevant to the definition and analysis of reading disability. *Canadian Journal of Psychology, 42,* 202–215.

Siegel, L. S. (2003). Learning disabilities. In I. B. Weiner (Ed.), *Handbook of psychology,* (Vol. VI). New York: Wiley.

Siegel, L. S., & Himel, N. (1998). Socioeconomic status, age and the classification of dyslexic and poor readers: Further evidence of the irrelevancy of IQ to reading disability. *Dyslexia, 4,* 90–104.

Siegel, L. S., & Ryan, E. B. (1988). Development of grammatical sensitivity, phonological, and short-term memory skills in normally achieving and learning disabled children. *Developmental Psychology, 24,* 28–37.

Siegel, L. S. & Ryan, E. B. (1989). The development of working memory in normally achieving and subtypes of learning disabled children. *Child Development, 60,* 973–980.

Siegel, L. S., & Wiener, J. (1993, Spring). Canadian special education policies: Children with disabilities in a bilingual and multicultural society. *Social Policy Report, Society for Research in Child Development, 7,* 1–16.

Siegler, R. (2001). Cognition, instruction, and the quest for meaning. In S. M. Carver & D. Klahr (Eds.), *Cognition and Instruction.* Mahwah, NJ: Erlbaum.

Siegler, R. S. (1976). Three aspects of cognitive development. *Cognitive Psychology, 8,* 481–520.

Siegler, R. S. (1998). *Children's thinking* (3rd ed.). Upper Saddle River, NJ: Prentice Hall.

Siegler, R. S. (2001). Children's discoveries and brain-damaged patients' rediscoveries. In J. L. McClelland & R. J. Siegler (Eds.), *Mechanisms of cognitive development.* Mahwah, NJ: Erlbaum.

Sigman, M., Cohen, S. E., & Beckwith, L. (2000). Why does infant attention predict adolescent intelligence? In D. Muir & A. Slater (Eds.), *Infant development: Essential readings.* Malden, MA: Blackwell.

Signore, C. (2001). Rubella. *Primary Care Update in Obstetrics and Gynecology, 8,* 133–137.

Silverstein, L. B. (2001). Father and families. In J. P. McHale & W. S. Grolnick (Eds.), *Retrospect and prospect in the psychological study of families.* Mahwah, NJ: Erlbaum.

Sim, T. (2000). Adolescent psychosocial competence: The importance and role of regard for parents. *Journal of Research on Adolescence, 10,* 49–64.

Simmons, R. G., & Blyth, D. A. (1987). *Moving into adolescence.* Hawthorne, NY: Aldine.

Simons, J., Finlay, B., & Yang, A. (1991). *The adolescent and young adult fact book.* Washington, DC: Children's Defense Fund.

Simons-Morton, B., Haynie, D. L., Crump, A. D., Eitel, P., & Saylor, K. E. (2001). Peer and parent influences on smoking and drinking among early adolescents. *Health Education and Behavior, 28,* 95–107.

Singer, D. G. (1993). Creativity of children in a changing world. In G. L. Berry & J. K. Asamen (Eds.), *Children and television: Images in a changing sociocultural world.* Newbury Park, CA: Sage.

Singer, L. T., Arendt, R., Fagan, J., Minnes, S., Salvator, A., Bolek, T., & Becker, M. (1999). Neonatal visual information processing in cocaine-exposed and nonexposed infants. *Infant Behavior and Development, 22,* 1–15.

Singh, S., Wulf, D., Samara, R., & Cuca, Y. P. (2000). Gender differences in the timing of first intercourse: Data from 14 countries. *International Family Planning Perspectives, 26,* 21–28, 43.

Skinner, B. F. (1938). *The behavior of organisms: An experimental analysis.* New York: Appelton-Century-Crofts.

Skinner, B. F. (1975). *Verbal behavior.* New York: Appleton-Century-Crofts.

Slater, A. (2001). Visual perception. In A. Fogel & G. Bremner (Eds.), *Blackwell handbook of infant development.* London: Blackwell.

Slater, A., Field, T., & Hernandez-Reif, M. (2002). The development of the senses. In A. Slater & M. Lewis (Eds.), *Introduction to infant development.* New York: Oxford University Press.

Slater, A., Morison, V., & Somers, M. (1988). Orientation discrimination and cortical function in the human newborn. *Perception, 17,* 597–602.

Slijper, F. M. E. (1984). Androgens and gender role behavior in girls with congenital adrenal hyperplasia (CAH). *Progress in Brain Research, 61,* 417–422.

Slobin, D. (1972, July). Children and language: They learn the same way around the world. *Psychology Today,* 71–76.

Slomkowski, C., Rende, R., Conger, K. J., Simons, R. L., & Conger, R. D. (2001). Sisters, brothers, and delinquency: Social influence during early and middle adolescence. *Child Development, 72,* 271–283.

Smit, E. M. (2002). Adopted children: core issues and unique challenges. *Journal of Child and Adolescent Psychiatric Nursing, 15,* 143–150.

Smith, D. (2004). *Introduction to special education, 5th Ed.* Boston: Allyn & Bacon.

Smith, L., & Hattersley, J. (2000). *The smart guide to preventing SIDS.* New York: Smart.

Smith, L. M., Chang L., Yonekura, M. L., Gilbride, K., Kuo, J., Poland, R. E., Walot, I., & Ernst, T. (2001). Brain proton magnetic resonance spectroscopy and imaging in children exposed to cocaine in utero. *Pediatrics, 107,* 227.

Smolak, L., & Striegel-Moore, R. (2001). Body image concerns. In J. Worell (Ed.), *Encyclopedia of women and gender.* San Diego: Academic Press.

Snarey, J. (1987, June). A question of morality. *Psychology Today,* pp. 6–8.

Snarey, J. (1993). *How fathers care for the next generation.* Cambridge, MA: Harvard University Press.

Snow, C. (1999). Social perspectives on the emergence of language. In B. MacWhinney (Ed.), *The emergence of language.* Mahwah, NJ: Erlbaum.

Snyder, H. N., & Sickmund, M. (1999, October). *Juvenile offenders and victims: 1999 national report.* Washington, DC: National Center for Juvenile Justice.

Sommer, B. B. (1978). *Puberty and adolescence.* New York: Oxford University Press.

Soong, W. T., Chao, K. Y., Jang, C. S., & Wang, J. D. (1999). Long-term effect of increased lead absorption on intelligence of children. *Archives of Environmental Health, 54,* 297–301.

Sophian, C. (1985). Perseveration and infants' search: A comparison of two- and three-location tasks. *Developmental Psychology, 21,* 187–194.

Sorokin, P. (2002). New agents and future directions in biotherapy. *Clinical Journal of Oncological Nursing, 6,* 19–24.

Sowter, B., Doyle, L. W., Morley, C. J., Altmann, A., & Halliday, J. (1999). Is sudden infant death syndrome still more common in very low birth weight infants in the 1990s? *Medical Journal of Australia, 171,* 411–413.

Spandorfer, S. D., Goldstein, J., Navarro, J., Veeck, L., Davis, O. K., & Rosenwaks, Z. (2003). Difficult embryo transfer has a negative impact on the outcome of in vitro fertilization. *Fertility and Sterility, 79,* 654–655.

Spear, H. J., & Kulbok, P. A. (2001). Adolescent health behaviors and related factors: A review. *Public Health Nursing, 18,* 82–93.

Spearman, C. E. (1927). *The abilities of man.* New York: Macmillan.

Spelke, E. S. (1979). Perceiving bimodally specified events in infancy. *Developmental Psychology, 5,* 626–636.

Spelke, E. S. (1991). Physical knowledge in infancy: Reflections on Piaget's theory. In S. Carey & R. Gelman (Eds.), *The epigenesis of mind: Essays on biology and cognition.* Hillsdale, NJ: Erlbaum.

Spelke, E. S., & Newport, E. L. (1998). Nativism, empiricism, and the development of knowledge. In W. Damon (Ed.), *Handbook of child psychology* (5th ed., Vol. 2). New York: Wiley.

Spelke, E. S., & Owsley, C. J. (1979). Intermodal exploration and knowledge in infancy. *Infant Behavior and Development, 2,* 13–28.

Spence, J. T., & Buckner, C. E. (2000). Instrumental and expressive traits, trait stereotypes, and sexist attitudes: What do they signify? *Psychology of Women Quarterly, 24,* 44–62.

Spence, J. T., & Helmreich, R. (1978). *Masculinity and feminity: Their psychological dimensions.* Austin: University of Texas Press.

Spence, M. J., & DeCasper, A. J. (1987). Prenatal experience with low-frequency maternal voice sounds influences neonatal perception of maternal voice samples. *Infant Behavior and Development, 10,* 133–142.

Spencer, M. B. (1990). Commentary in Spencer, M. B., & Dornbusch, S. Challenges in studying ethnic minority youth. In S. S. Feldman & G. R. Elliott (Eds.), *At the threshold: The developing adolescent.* Cambridge, MA: Harvard University Press.

Spencer, M. B. (1999). Social and cultural influences on school adjustment: The application of an identity-focused cultural ecological perspective. *Educational Psychologist, 34,* 43–57.

Spencer, M. B., & Dornbusch, S. M. (1990). Challenges in studying minority youth. In S. S. Feldman & G. R. Elliott (Eds.), *At the threshold: The developing adolescent.* Cambridge, MA: Harvard University Press.

Spencer, M. B., Noll, E., Stoltzfuz, J., & Harpalani, V. (2001). Identity and school adjustment: Revisiting the "acting white" assumption. *Educational Psychologist, 36,* 21–30.

Spitzer, S., Cupp, R., & Parke, R. D. (1995). School entrance age, social acceptance, and self-perceptions in kindergarten and the first grade. *Early Childhood Research Quarterly, 10,* 433–450.

Spring, J. (1998). *The intersection of cultures.* New York: McGraw-Hill.

Springer, S. P., & Deutsch, G. (1985). *Left brain, right brain.* San Francisco: Freeman.

Sroufe, L. A. (2000, Spring). The inside scoop on child development: Interview. *Cutting through the hype.* Minneapolis: College of Education and Human Development, University of Minnesota.

Sroufe, L. A. (2002). From infant attachment to promotion of adolescent autonomy. In J. G. Borkowski, S. L. Ramey, & M. Bristol-Power (Eds.), *Parenting and the child's world.* Mahwah, NJ: Erlbaum.

Sroufe, L. A., Egeland, B., & Carlson, E. A. (1999). One social world: The integrated development of parent-child and peer relationships. In W. A. Collins & B. Laursen (Eds.), *Minnesota symposium on child psychology* (Vol. 31). Mahwah, NJ: Erlbaum.

Sroufe, L. A., & Waters, E. (1976). The ontogenesis of smiling and laughter: A perspective on the organization of development in infancy. *Psychological Review, 83,* 173–198.

Sroufe, L. A., Waters, E., & Matas, L. (1974). Contextual determinants of infant affectional response. In M. Lewis & L. Rosenblum (Eds.), *Origins of fear*. New York: Wiley.

St. Pierre, R., Layzer, J., & Barnes, H. (1996). *Regenerating two-generation programs.* Cambridge, MA: Abt Associates.

Stahl, S. (2002, January). *Effective reading instruction in the first grade.* Paper presented at the Michigan Reading Recovery conference, Dearborn.

Stanhope, L., & Corter, C. (1993, March). *The mother's role in the transition to siblinghood.* Paper presented at the biennial meeting of the Society for Research in Child Development, New Orleans.

Stanovich, K. E. (1986). Cognitive processes and the reading problems of learning disabled children: Evaluating the assumption of specificity. In J. Torgesen & B. Wong (Eds.), *Psychological and educational perspectives on learning disabilities*. Orlando, FL: Academic Press.

Stattin, H., & Magnusson, D. (1990). *Pubertal maturation in female development: Paths through life* (Vol. 2). Hillsdale, NJ: Erlbaum.

Stearns, S. C. (2002). A cross-cultural analysis of the behavior of women and men: implications for the origins of sex differences. *Psychological Bulletin, 128,* 699–727.

Stein, M. T., & Perrin, J. M. (2003). Diagnosis and treatment of ADHD in school-age children in primary care settings: a synopsis of the AAP practice guidelines. *Pediatric Review, 24,* 92–98.

Steinberg, L. D. (1986). Latchkey children and susceptibility to peer pressure: An ecological analysis. *Developmental Psychology, 22,* 433–439.

Steinberg, L., & Cauffman, E. (2001). Adolescents as adults in court. *Social Policy Report of the Society for Research in Child Development, XV* (No. 4), 1–13.

Steinberg, L., & Levine, A. (1997). *You and your adolescent* (2nd ed.). New York: HarperCollins.

Steinberg, L., & Silk, J. S. (2002). Parenting adolescents. In M. Bornstein (Ed.), *Handbook of parenting* (2nd ed., Vol. 1). Mahwah, NJ: Erlbaum.

Steiner, J. E. (1979). Human facial expressions in response to taste and smell stimulation. In H. Reese & L. Lipsitt (Eds.), *Advances in child development and behavior* (Vol. 13). New York: Academic Press.

Steiner, M., Dunn, E., & Born, L. (2003). Hormones and mood: from menarche to menopause and beyond. *Journal of Affective Disorders, 74,* 67–83.

Stern, D. N., Beebe, B., Jaffe, J., & Bennett, S. L. (1977). The infant's stimulus world during social interaction: A study of caregiver behaviors with particular reference to repetition and timing. In H. R. Schaffer (Ed.), *Studies in mother-infant interaction*. London: Academic Press.

Sternberg, R. J. (1986). *Intelligence applied.* Fort Worth: Harcourt Brace.

Sternberg, R. J. (1994, December). Commentary. *APA Monitor,* p. 22.

Sternberg, R. J. (1997). *Successful intelligence.* New York: Simon & Schuster.

Sternberg, R. J. (1999). Intelligence. In M. A. Runco & S. Pritzker (Eds.), *Encyclopedia of creativity.* San Diego: Academic Press.

Sternberg, R. J. (2003a). Contemporary theories of intelligence. In I. B. Weiner (Ed.), *Handbook of psychology* (Vol. VII). New York: Wiley.

Sternberg, R. J. (2003b). Driven to despair: Why we need to redefine the concept and measurement of intelligence. In L. G. Aspinwall & U. M. Staudinger (Eds.), *A psychology of human strengths*. Washington, DC: American Psychological Association.

Sternberg, R. J., & Ben-Zeev T. (2001). *Complex cognition.* New York: Oxford University Press.

Sternberg, R. J., & Grigorenko, E. L. (Eds.). (2001). *Environmental effects on cognitive abilities*. Mahwah, NJ: Erlbaum.

Sternberg, R. J., Lautrey, J., & Lubert, T. I. (Eds.). (2003). *Models of intelligence: International perspectives*. Washington, DC: American Psychological Association.

Sternglanz, S. H., & Serbin, L. A. (1974). Sex-role stereotyping in children's television programming. *Developmental Psychology, 10,* 710–715.

Steur, F. B., Applefield, J. M., & Smith, R. (1971). Televised aggression and interpersonal aggression of preschool children. *Journal of Experimental Child Psychology, 11,* 442–447.

Stevenson, H. C. (1998). Raising safe villages: Cultural-ecological factors that influence the emotional adjustment of adolescents. *Journal of Black Psychology, 24,* 44–59.

Stevenson, H. G. (1995, March). *Missing data: On the forgotten substance of race, ethnicity, and socioeconomic classifications.* Paper presented at the meeting of the Society for Research in Child Development, Indianapolis.

Stevenson, H. G., Lee, S., & Stigler, J. W. (1986). Mathematics achievement of Chinese, Japanese, and American children. *Science, 231,* 693–699.

Stevenson, H. W. (1995). Mathematics achievement of American students: First in the world by 2000? In C. A. Nelson (Ed.), *Basic and applied perspectives in learning, cognition, and development*. Minneapolis: University of Minnesota Press.

Stevenson, H. W. (2000). Middle childhood: Education and schooling. In A. Kazdin (Ed.), *Encyclopedia of psychology*. Washington, DC, & New York: American Psychological Association and Oxford University Press.

Stevenson, H. W., Hofer, B. K., & Randel, B. (1999). *Middle childhood: Education and schooling.* Unpublished manuscript, Dept. of Psychology, University of Michigan, Ann Arbor.

Stevenson, H. W., Lee, S., Chen, C., Stigler, J. W., Hsu, C., & Kitamura, S. (1990). Contexts of achievement. *Monograph of the Society for Research in Child Development, 55* (Serial No. 221).

Stevenson, H. W. & Zusho, A. (2002). Adolescence in China and Japan: Adapting to a changing environment. In B. B. Brown, R. W. Larson, & T. S. Saraswathi (Eds.), *The world's youth.* New York: Cambridge University Press.

Stice, E. (2002). Risk and maintenance factors for eating pathology. *Psychological Bulletin, 128,* 825–848.

Stipek, D. J. (1996). Motivation and instruction. In D. C. Berliner & R. C. Calfee (Eds.), *Handbook of educational psychology.* New York: Macmillan.

Stipek, D. J. (2002). *Motivation to learn* (4th ed.). Boston: Allyn & Bacon.

Stocker, C., & Dunn, J. (1990). Sibling relationships in adolescence: Links with friendships and peer relationships. *British Journal of Developmental Psychology, 8,* 227–244.

Stocker, C., & Dunn, J. (1991). Sibling relationships in adolescence. In R. M. Lerner, A. C. Petersen, & J. Brooks-Gunn (Eds.), *Encyclopedia of adolescence* (Vol. 2). New York: Garland.

Stouthamer-Loeber, M., Loeber, R., Wei, E., Farrington, D. P., & Wikstrom, P. H. (2002). Risk and promotive effects in the explanation of persistent serious delinquency in boys. *Journal of Consulting and Clinical Psychology, 70,* 111–123.

Strahan, D. B. (1983). The emergence of formal operations in adolescence. *Transcendence, 11,* 7–14.

Strass, P. (2002). Postpartum depression support. *Canadian Nurse, 98,* 25–28.

Straus, M. A. (1991). Discipline and deviance: Physical punishment of children and violence and other crimes in adulthood. *Social Problems, 38,* 133–154.

Straus, M. A., Sugarman, D. B., & Giles-Sims, J. (1997). Spanking by parents and subsequent antisocial behavior of children. *Archives of Pediatric and Adolescent Medicine, 151,* 761–767.

Strauss, R. S. (2001). Environmental tobacco smoke and serum vitamin C levels in children. *Pediatrics, 107,* 540–542.

Streissguth, A. P., Martin, D. C., Sandman, B. M., Kirchner, G. L., & Darby, B. L. (1984). Intrauterine alcohol and nicotine exposure: Attention and reaction time in four-year-old children. *Developmental Psychology, 20,* 533–543.

Strichart S. S., & Mangrum, C. T. (2002). *Teaching study skills and strategies to students with learning disabilities, attention deficit disorders, or special needs* (3rd ed.). Boston: Allyn & Bacon.

Striegel-Moore, R. H., Silberstein, L. R., & Rodin, J. (1993). The social self in bulimia nervosa: Public self-consciousness, social anxiety, and perceived fraudulence. *Journal of Abnormal Psychology, 102,* 297–303.

Stringer, S., & Neal, C. (1993, March). *Scaffolding as a tool for assessing sensitive and contingent teaching: A comparison between high- and low-risk mothers.* Paper presented at the biennial meeting of the Society for Research in Child Development, New Orleans.

Strobel, K. R. (2001, April). *Successful outcomes for at-risk youth.* Paper presented at the meeting of the American Educational Research Association, Seattle.

Suárez-Orozco, C. (2002). Afterword: Understanding and serving the children of immigrants. *Harvard Educational Review, 71,* 579–589.

Sue, S. (1990, August). *Ethnicity and culture in psychological research and practice.* Paper presented at the meeting of the American Psychological Association, Boston.

Sullivan, H. S. (1953). *The interpersonal theory of psychiatry.* New York: W. W. Norton.

Sullivan, K., & Sullivan, A. (1980). Adolescent-parent separation. *Developmental Psychology, 16,* 93–99.

Suomi, S. J., Harlow, H. F., & Domek, C. J. (1970). Effect of repetitive infant-infant separations of young monkeys. *Journal of Abnormal Psychology, 76,* 161–172.

Super, C., & Harkness, S. (1997). The cultural structuring of child development. In J. W. Berry, Y. H. Poortinga, & J. Pandey (Eds.), *Handbook of cross-cultural psychology: Vol. 2. Theory and method.* Boston: Allyn & Bacon.

Susman, E. J., Murowchick, E., Worrall, B. K., & Murray, D. A. (1995, March). *Emotionality, adrenal hormones, and context interactions during puberty and pregnancy.* Paper presented at the meeting of the Society for Research in Child Development, Indianapolis.

Sutton-Smith, B. (1985, October). The child at play. *Psychology Today,* pp. 64–65.

Swaab, D. F., Chung, W. C., Kruijver, F. P., Hofman, M. A., & Ishunina, T. A. (2001). Structural and functional sex differences in the human hypothalamus. *Hormones and Behavior, 40,* 93–98.

Swanson, J. M., & others (2001). Clinical relevance of the primary findings of MTA: Success rates based on severity of ADHD and ODD symptoms at the end of treatment. *Journal of the American Academy of Child and Adolescent Psychiatry, 40,* 168–179.

Swanson, J. M., & Volkow, N. D. (2002). Pharmacokinetic and pharmacodynamic properties of stimulants: Implications for the design of new treatments for ADHD. *Behavior and Brain Research, 130,* 73–80.

Sweet, M. P., Hodgman, J. E., Pena, I., Barton, L., Pavlova, Z., & Ramanathan, R. (2003). Two-year outcome of infants weighing 600 grams or less at birth and born 1994 through 1998. *Obstetrics and Gynecology, 101,* 18–23.

Swisher, R., & Whitlock, J. (2003). How neighborhoods matter for youth development. In S. F. Hamilton & M. A. Hamilton (Eds.), *The youth development handbook.* Newbury Park, CA: Sage.

T

Taddio, A., Katz, J., Ilersich, A. L., & Koren, G. (1997). Effect of neonatal circumcision on pain response during subsequent routine vaccination. *Lancet, 349,* 599–603.

Tager-Flusberg, H. (Ed.). (1994). *Constraints on language acquisition.* Mahwah, NJ: Erlbaum.

Takahashi, K. (1990). Are the key assumptions of the "Strange Situation" procedure universal? A view from Japanese research. *Human Development, 33,* 23–30.

Tamis-LeMonda, C. S., & Cabrera, N. (1999). Perspectives on father involvement: Research and policy. *Social Policy Report, Society for Research in Child Development, 13* (No. 2), 1–25.

Tannen, D. (1990). *You just don't understand!* New York: Ballantine.

Tappan, M. B. (1998). Sociocultural psychology and caring psychology: Exploring Vygotsky's "hidden curriculum." *Educational Psychologist, 33,* 23–33.

Tarpley, T. (2001). Children, the Internet, and other new technologies. In D. Singer & J. Singer (Eds.), *Handbook of children and the media.* Thousand Oaks, CA: Sage.

Tasker, F. L., & Golombok, S. (1997). *Growing up in a lesbian family: Effects on child development.* New York: Guilford.

Taylor, H. G., Klein, N., & Hack, M. (1994). Academic functioning in 750 gm birthweight children who have normal cognitive abilities: Evidence for specific learning disabilities. *Pediatric Research 35,* 289A.

Taylor, J. H., & Walker, L. J. (1997). Moral climate and the development of moral reasoning: The effects of dyadic discussions between young offenders. *Journal of Moral Education, 26,* 21–43.

Taylor, L. S., & Whittaker, C. R. (2003). *Bridging multiple worlds.* Boston: Allyn & Bacon.

Taylor, M. J., Denbow, M. L., Duncan, K. R., Overton, T. G., & Fisk, N. M. (2000). Antenatal factors at diagnosis that predict outcome in twin-twin transfusion syndrome. *American Journal of Obstetrics and Gynecology, 183,* 1023–1028.

Taylor, S. E. (2002). *The tending instinct.* New York: Times Books.

Tenenbaum, H. R., Callahan, M., Alba-Speyer, C., & Sandoval, L. (2002). Parent-child science conversations in Mexican descent families: Educational background, activity, and past experience as moderators. *Hispanic Journal of Behavioral Sciences, 24,* 225–248.

Tenenbaum, H. R., & Leaper, C. (2002). Are parents' gender schemas related to their children's gender-related cognitions? *Developmental Psychology, 38,* 615–630.

Tercyak, K. P., Johnson, S. B., Roberts, S. E., & Cruz, A. Z. (2001). Psychological response to prenatal genetic counseling and amniocentesis. *Patient Educational Counseling, 43,* 73–84.

Terman, D. L., Larner, M. B., Stevenson, C. S., & Behrman, R. E. (1996). Special education for students with disabilities: Analysis and recommendations. *Future of Children, 6* (1), 4–24.

Terman, L. (1925). *Genetic studies of genius. Vol. I: Mental and physical traits of a thousand gifted children.* Stanford, CA: Stanford University Press.

Terr, L. C. (1988). What happens to early memories of trauma? *Journal of the American Academy of Child and Adolescent Psychiatry, 27*, 96–104.

Terry, W. S. (2003). Learning and memory (2nd ed.). Boston: Allyn & Bacon.

Teti, D. (2001). Retrospect and prospect in the psychological study of sibling relationships. In J. P. McHale & W. S. Grolnick (Eds.), *Retrospect and prospect in the psychological study of families.* Mahwah, NJ: Erlbaum.

Teti, D. M., Sakin, J., Kucera, E., Caballeros, M., & Corns, K. M. (1993, March). *Transitions to siblinghood and security of firstborn attachment: Psychosocial and psychiatric correlates of changes over time.* Paper presented at the biennial meeting of the Society for Research in Child Development, New Orleans.

Tetreault, M. K. T. (1997). Classrooms for diversity: Rethinking curriculum and pedagogy. In J. A. Banks & C. A. Banks (Eds.), *Multicultural education* (3rd ed.). Boston: Allyn & Bacon.

Tharp, R. G. (1994). Intergroup differences among Native Americans in socialization and child cognition: An erthogenetic analysis. In P. M. Greenfield & R. Cocking (Eds.). *Cross-cultural roots of minority child development.* Mahwah, NJ: Erlbaum.

Tharp, R. G., & Gallimore, R. (1988). *Rousing minds to life: Teaching, learning, and schooling in social context.* New York: Cambridge University Press.The development of social and communicative competence in childhood: Review and a model of personal, familial, and extra-familial processes. *Communication Yearbook, 20*, 305–373.

Thelen, E. (1995). Motor development: A new synthesis. *American Psychologist, 50*, 79–95.

Thelen, E. (2000). Perception and motor development. In A. Kazdin (Ed.), *Encyclopedia of psychology.* Washington, DC, & New York: American Psychological Association and Oxford University Press.

Thelen, E. (2001). Dynamic mechanisms of change in early perceptual-motor development. In J. L. McClelland & R. S. Siegler (Eds.), *Mechanisms of cognitive development.* Mahwah, NJ: Erlbaum.

Thomas, A., & Chess, S. (1991). Temperament in adolescence and its functional significance. In R. M. Lerner, A. C. Petersen, & J. Brooks-Gunn (Eds.), *Encyclopedia of adolescence* (Vol. 2). New York: Garland.

Thomas, K. (1998, November 4). Teen cyberdating is a new wrinkle for parents, too. *USA Today*, p. 9D.

Thompson, J. L., & Hansen, L. A. (2003). Thalidomide dosing in patients with relapsed or refractory multiple myeloma. *Annals of Pharmacotherapy, 37*, 571–576.

Thompson, L., & Walker, A. J. (1989). Gender in families: Women and men in marriage, work, and parenthood. *Journal of Marriage and the Family, 51*, 845–871.

Thompson, P. M., Giedd, J. N., Woods, R. P., MacDonald, D., Evans, A. C., & Toga, A. W. (2000). Growth patterns in the developing brain detected by using continuum mechanical tensor maps. *Nature, 404*, 190–193.

Thompson, R. (2000). Early experience and socialization. In A. Kazdin (Ed.), *Encyclopedia of psychology.* Washington, DC, & New York: American Psychological Association and Oxford University Press.

Thompson, R. A. (1994). Emotion regulation: A theme in search of a definition. *Monographs of the Society for Research in Child Development, 59* (Serial No. 240), 2–3.

Thompson, R. A., Easterbrooks, M. A., & Walker, L. (2003). Social and emotional development in infancy. In I. B. Weiner (Ed.), *Handbook of psychology, Vol. 6.* New York: Wiley.

Thompson, R. A., & Nelson, C. A. (2001). Developmental science and the media. *American Psychologist, 56*, 5–15.

Thomson, M. (2003). Monitoring dyslexics' intelligence and attainments: A follow-up study. *Dyslexia, 9*, 3–17.

Thornton, S. J. (2001, April). *Caring and competence: Nel Noddings' curriculum thought.* Paper presented at the meeting of the American Educational Reseach Association, Seattle.

Thorton, A., & Camburn, D. (1989). Religious participation and sexual behavior and attitudes. *Journal of Marriage and the Family, 49*, 117–128.

Thurstone, L. L. (1938). *Primary mental abilities.* Chicago: University of Chicago Press.

Timins, J. K. (2001). Radiation during pregnancy. *New Jersey Medicine, 98*, 29–33.

Tinsley, B. J., Finley, K. A., & Ortiz, R. V. (1999, April). *Parental eating socialization in middle childhood: A multi-ethnic perspective.* Paper presented at the meeting of the Society for Research in Child Development, Albuquerque.

Tolan, P. H., Gorman-Smith, D., & Henry, D. B. (2003). The developing ecology of urban males' youth violence. *Developmental Psychology, 39*, 274–291.

Tomlinson-Keasey, C. (1972). Formal operations in females from 11 to 54 years of age. *Developmental Psychology, 6*, 364.

Torgesen, J. K. (1999) Reading disabilities. In R. Gallimore, L. P. Bernheimer, D. L. MacMillan, D. L. Speece, & S. Vaughn (Eds.), *Developmental perspectives on children with learning disabilities.* Mahwah, NJ: Erlbaum.

Toth, G., & Siegel, L. S. (1994). A critical evaluation of the IQ-achievement discrepancy based definition of dyslexia. In K. P. van den Bos, L. S. Siegel, D. J. Bakker, & D. L. Share (Eds.), *Current directions in dyslexia research.* Lisse, The Netherlands: Swets & Zeitlinger.

Tough, S. C., Newburn-Cook, C., Johnston, D. W., Svenson, L. W., Rose, S., & Belik, J. (2002). Delayed childbearing and its impact on population rate changes in lower birth weight, multiple birth, and preterm delivery. *Pediatrics, 109*, 399–403.

Trafimow, D., Triandis, H. C., & Goto, S. G. (1991). Some tests of the distinction between the private and collective self. *Journal of Personality and Social Psychology, 60*, 649–655.

Trappe, R., Laccone, F., Cobilanschi, J., Meins, M., Huppke, P., Hanefeld, F., & Engel, W. (2001). MECP2 mutations in sporadic cases of Rett syndrome are almost exclusively of paternal origin. *American Journal of Human Genetics, 68*, 1093–1101.

Trasler, J. (2000). Paternal exposures: Altered sex ratios. *Teratology, 62*, 6–7.

Trasler, J. M., & Doerksen, T. (2000, May). *Teratogen update: Paternal exposure-reproductive risks.* Paper presented at the joint meeting of the Pediatric Academic Societies and American Academy of Pediatrics, Boston.

Treffers, P. E., Eskes, M., Kleiverda, G., & van Alten, D. (1990). Home births and minimal medical interventions. *Journal of the American Medical Association, 246*, 2207–2208.

Trehub, S. E., Schneider, B. A., Thorpe, L. A., & Judge, P. (1991). Observational measures of auditory sensitivity in early infancy. *Developmental Psychology, 27*, 40–49.

Triandis, H. C. (1994). *Culture and social behavior.* New York: McGraw-Hill.

Triandis, H. C. (2001). Individualism and collectivism. In D. Matsumoto (Ed.), *Handbook of culture and psychology.* New York: Oxford University Press.

Trimble, J. E. (1989, August). *The enculturation of contemporary psychology.* Paper presented at the meeting of the American Psychological Association, New Orleans.

Troiano, R. P., & Flegal, K. M. (1998). Overweight children and adolescents: Description, epidemiology, and demographics. *Pediatrics, 101*, 497–504.

Troisi A., Moles, A., Panepuccia, L., Lo Russo, D., Palla, G., & Scucchi, S. (2002). Serum cholesterol levels and mood symptoms in the postpartum period. *Psychiatry Research, 109,* 213–219.

Tsigos, C., & Chrousos, G. P. (2002). Hypothalamic-pituitary-adrenal axis, neuroendocrine factors, and stress. *Journal of Psychosomatic Research, 53,* 865–871.

Tubman, J. G., & Windle, M. (1995). Continuity of difficult temperament in adolescence: Relations with depression, life events, family support, and substance abuse. *Journal of Youth and Adolescence, 24,* 133–152.

Tulving, E. (2000). Concepts of memory. In E. Tulving & F. I. M. Craik (Eds.), *The Oxford handbook of memory.* New York: Oxford University Press.

Turecki, S., & Tonner, L. (1989). *The difficult child.* New York: Bantam.

Turiel, E. (1966). An experimental test of the sequentiality of developmental stages in the child's moral judgments. *Journal of Personality and Social Psychology, 3,* 611–618.

Turiel, E. (1998). The development of morality. In N. Eisenberg (Ed.), *Handbook of child psychology* (5th ed., Vol. 3). New York: Wiley.

Tyring, S. K., Baker, D., & Snowden, W. (2002). Valcyclovir for herpes simplex virus infection: Long-term safety and sustained efficacy after 20 years' experience with acyclovir. *Journal of Infectious Diseases, 186* (Suppl. 1), S40–S46.

U.S. Department of Commerce. (2002). *A nation online: How Americans are expanding their use of the Internet.* Washington, DC: Author.

U.S. Department of Education. (1996). *Number and disabilities of children and youth served under IDEA.* Washington, DC: Office of Special Education Programs, Data Analysis System.

U.S. Department of Education. (2000). *To assure a free and appropriate public education of all children with disabilities.* Washington, DC: U.S. Office of Education.

U.S. Department of Education. (2000). *Trends in educational equity for girls and women.* Washington, DC: Author.

U.S. Department of Energy. (2001). *The human genome project.* Washington, DC: Author.

U.S. General Accounting Office. (1987, September). *Prenatal care: Medicaid recipients and uninsured women obtain insufficient care.* A report to the Congress of the United States, HRD-97-137. Washington, DC: GAO.

U.S. Department of Health and Human Services. (2001). *Youth violence.* Rockville, MD: Author.

Udipi, S. A., Ghugre, P., & Antony, U. (2000). Nutrition in pregnancy and lactation. *Journal of the Indian Medical Association, 98,* 548–557.

Underwood, M. (2002). Sticks and stones and social exclusion: Aggression among boys and girls. In P. K. Smith & C. H. Hart (Eds.), *Blackwell handbook of childhood social development.* Malden, MA: Blackwell.

Underwood, M. K., Kupersmidt, J. B., & Coie, J. D. (1996). Childhood peer sociometric status and aggression as predictors of adolescent childbearing. *Journal of Research on Adolescence, 6,* 201–223.

Unger, R., & Crawford, M. (2000). *Women and gender* (4th ed.). New York: McGraw-Hill.

UNICEF. (2001). *UNICEF statistics: Low birthweight.* Geneva: Author.

UNICEF. (2002). *The state of the world's children 2002: Leadership.* Geneva: UNICEF.

UNICEF. (2003). *State of the world's children: 2003.* Geneva: UNICEF.

Updegraff, K. A. (1999, April). *Mothers' and fathers' involvement in adolescents' peer relationships: Links to friendship adjustment and peer competence.* Paper presented at the meeting of the Society for Research in Child Development, Albuquerque.

Uyanik, M., Bumin, G., & Kayihan, H. (2003). Comparison of different therapy approaches in children with Down syndrome. *Pediatrics International, 45,* 68–73.

Valencia, R. R., & Suzuki, L. A. (2001). *Intelligence testing and minority students.* Thousand Oaks, CA: Sage.

Valsiner, J. (2000). Cultural psychology. In A. Kazdin (Ed.), *Encyclopedia of psychology.* Washington, DC, & New York: American Psychological Association and Oxford University Press.

Van Beveren, T. T. (2003). *Prenatal development and the newborn.* Unpublished manuscript, University of Texas at Dallas, Richardson.

Vandell, D. L. (1985, April). *Relationship between infant-peer and infant-mother interactions:*

What have we learned? Paper presented at the meeting of the Society for Research in Child Development, Toronto.

Vandell, D. L., & Pierce, K. M. (1999, April). *Can after-school programs benefit children who live in high-crime neighborhoods?* Paper presented at the meeting of the Society for Research in Child Development, Albuquerque.

Vandell, D. L., & Wilson, K. S. (1988). Infants' interactions with mother, sibling, and peer: Contrasts and relations between interaction systems. *Child Development, 48,* 176–186.

van den Boom, D. C. (1989). Neonatal irritability and the development of attachment. In G. A. Kohnstamm, J. E. Bates, & M. K. Rothbart (Eds.), *Temperament in childhood.* New York: Wiley.

van IJzendoorn, M. H., & Kroonenberg, P. M. (1988). Cross-cultural patterns of attachment: A meta-analysis of the Strange Situation. *Child Development, 59,* 147–156.

Vargas, L., & Koss-Chiono, J. (1999). *Working with Latino youth.* San Francisco: Jossey-Bass.

Venter, J. C. (2003). A part of the human genome sequence. *Science, 299,* 1183-1184.

Ventura, S. J., Martin, J. A., Curtin, S. C., & Mathews, T. J. (1997, June 10). *Report of final natality statistics, 1995.* Washington, DC: National Center for Health Statistics.

Ventura, S. J., Mosher, W. D., Curtin, S. C., Abma, J. C., & Henshaw, S. (2001). Trends in pregnancy rates for the United States, 1976–1997: An update. *National Vital Statistics Reports, 49,* 1–9.

Verklan, M. T. (2002). Physiological variability during transition to extrauterine life. *Critical Care Nursing Quarterly, 24,* 41–56.

Verma, S., & Saraswathi, T. S. (2002). Adolescence in India: Street urchins or Silicon Valley millionaires? In B. B. Brown, R. W. Larson, & T. S. Saraswathi (Eds.), *The world's youth.* New York: Cambridge University Press.

Vicari, S., Bellucci, S., & Carlesimo, G. A. (2001). Procedural learning deficit in children with Williams syndrome. *Neuropsychologia, 39,* 665–677.

Vidaeff, A. C., & Yeomans, E. R. (2002). Vaginal breech delivery is no longer justified. *Obstetrics and Gynecology, 100,* 1038.

Vidal, F. (2000). Piaget's theory. In A. Kazdin (Ed.), *Encyclopedia of psychology.* Washington, DC, & New York: American Psychological Association and Oxford University Press.

Villiani, S. L. (1997). *Motherhood at the crossroads.* New York: Plenum.

Volling, B. L. (2002). Sibling relationships. In M. H. Bornstein, L. Davidson, C. L. M. Keyes, & K. A. Moore (Eds.), *Well-being*. Mahwah, NJ: Erlbaum.

Vreugdenhil, H. J., Llijper, F. M., Mulder, P. G., & Weisglas-Kuperus, N. (2002). Effects of perinatal exposure to PCBs and dioxins on play behavior in Dutch children at school age. *Environmental Health Perspectives, 110,* A593–A591.

Vurpillot, E. (1968). The development of scanning strategies and their relation to visual differentiation. *Journal of Experimental Child Psychology, 6,* 632–650.

Vygotsky, L. S. (1962). *Thought and language.* Cambridge, MA: MIT Press.

Wachs, T. D. (1994). Fit, context and the transition between temperament and personality. In C. Halverson, G. Kohnstamm, & R. Martin (Eds.), *The developing structure of personality from infancy to adulthood.* Hillsdale, NJ: Erlbaum.

Wachs, T. D. (2000). *Necessary but not sufficient.* Washington, DC: American Psychological Association.

Wachs, T. D., & Kohnstamm, G. A. (Eds.). (2001). *Temperament in context.* Mahwah, NJ: Erlbaum.

Waddington, C. H. (1957). *The strategy of the genes.* London: Allen & Son.

Wagner, R. K. (1997). Intelligence, training, and employment. *American Psychologist, 52,* 1059–1069.

Wagner, R. K., & Sternberg, R. J. (1986). Tacit knowledge and intelligence in the everyday world. In R. J. Sternberg & R. K. Wagner (Eds.), *Practical intelligence.* Cambridge, England: Cambridge University Press.

Wahlsten, D. (2000). Behavioral genetics. In A. Kazdin (Ed.), *Encyclopedia of psychology.* Washington, DC, & New York: American Psychological Association and Oxford University Press.

Walden, T. (1991). Infant social referencing. In J. Garber & K. Dodge (Eds.), *The development of emotional regulation and dysregulation.* New York: Cambridge University Press.

Walker, H. (1998, May 31). Youth violence: Society's problem. *Eugene Register Guard,* p. 1C.

Walker, L. (1982). The sequentiality of Kohlberg's stages of moral development. *Child Development, 53,* 1130–1136.

Walker, L. J. (1996). Unpublished review of J. W. Santrock's *Child Development,* 8th ed. (New York: McGraw-Hill).

Walker, L. J., de Vries, B., & Trevethan, S. D. (1987). Moral stages and moral orientation in real-life and hypothetical dilemmas. *Child Development, 58,* 842–858.

Walker, L. J., Hennig, K. H., & Krettenauer, T. (2000). Parent and peer contexts for children's moral reasoning development. *Child Development, 71,* 1033–1048

Walker, L. J., & Pitts, R. C. (1998). Naturalistic conceptions of moral maturity. *Developmental Psychology, 34,* 403–419.

Walker, L. J., & Taylor, J. H. (1991). Family interaction and the development of moral reasoning. *Child Development, 62,* 264–283.

Wall, J. A. (1993, March). *Susceptibility to antisocial peer pressure in Mexican-American adolescents in relation to acculturation.* Paper presented at the biennial meeting of the Society for Research in Child Development, New Orleans.

Walsh, L. A. (2000, Spring). The Inside scoop on child development: Interview. *Cutting through the hype.* Minneapolis: College of Education & Human Development, University of Minnesota.

Wang, X., Zuckerman, B., Kaufman, G., Pearson, C., Wang, G., Chen, C., Wise, P., Bauchner, H., & Xu, X. (2000, May). *Maternal cigarette smoking, genetic susceptibility, and birthweight.* Paper presented at the joint meeting of the Pediatric Academic Societies and the American Academy of Pediatrics, Boston.

Ward, B. M., Lambert, S. B., & Lester, R. A. (2001). Rubella vaccination in prenatal and postnatal women: Why not use MMR? *Medical Journal of Australia, 174,* 311–312.

Wardle, F. (2003). *Introduction to special education.* Boston: Allyn & Bacon.

Warrick, P. (1992, March 1). The fantastic voyage of Tanner Roberts. *Los Angeles Times,* pp. E1, 12–13.

Warshak, R. A. (2001). Personal communication, Department of Psychology, University of Texas at Dallas, Richardson.

Wartenburger, I., Heekeren, H. R., Abutalebi, J., Cappa, S. F., Villringer, A., & Perani, D. (2003). Early setting of grammatical processing in the bilingual brain. *Neuron, 37,* 159–170.

Washington, R. L., & others. (2001). Organized sports for children and adolescents. *Pediatrics, 107,* 1459–1462.

Watemberg, N., Silver, S., Harel, S., & Lerman-Sagie, T. (2002). Significance of microencephaly among children with developmental abilities. *Journal of Child Neurology, 17,* 117–122.

Waterman, A. S. (1985). Identity in the context of adolescent psychology. In A. S. Waterman (Ed.), *Identity in adolescence: Processes and contents.* San Francisco: Jossey-Bass.

Waterman, A. S. (1989). Curricula interventions for identity change: Substantive and ethical considerations. *Journal of Adolescence, 12,* 389–400.

Waterman, A. S. (1992). Identity as an aspect of optimal psychological functioning. In G. R. Adams, T. P. Gullotta, & R. Montemayor (Eds.), *Adolescent identity formation.* Newbury Park, CA: Sage.

Waterman, A. S. (1997). An overview of service-learning and the role of research and evaluation in service-learning programs. In A. S. Waterman (Ed.), *Service learning.* Mahwah, NJ: Erlbaum.

Waters, E. (2001, April). *Perspectives on continuity and discontinuity in relationships.* Paper presented at the meeting of the Society for Research in Child Development, Minneapolis.

Watras, J. (2002). *The foundations of educational curriculum and diversity: 1565 to the present.* Boston: McGraw-Hill.

Watson, J. B. (1928). *Psychological care of infant and child.* New York: W.W. Norton.

Watson, J. B., & Rayner, R. (1920). Conditioned emotional reactions. *Journal of Experimental Psychology, 3,* 1–14.

Watts, D. H., Brown, Z. A., Money, D., Selke, S., Huang, M. L., Sacks, S. L., & Corey, L. (2003). A double-blind, randomized, placebo-controlled trial of acycolivir in late pregnancy for the reduction of herpes simplex virus shedding and cesarean delivery. *American Journal of Obstetrics and Gynecology, 188,* 836–843.

Weeks, A. D., & Mirembe, F. M. (2002). The retained placenta—new insights into an old problem. *European Journal of Obstetrics, Gynecology, and Reproductive Biology, 102,* 109–110.

Weikart, D. P. (1993). [Long-term positive effects in the Perry Preschool Head Start program]. Unpublished data, High Scope Foundation, Ypsilanti, MI.

Weincke, J. K., Thurston, S. W., Kelsey, K. T., Varkonyi, A., Wain, J. C., Mark, E. J., & Christiani, D. C. (1999). Early age at smoking initiation and tobacco carcinogen DNA damage in the lung. *Journal of the National Cancer Institute, 91,* 614–619.

Weiner, I. B. (1980). Psychopathology in adolescence. In J. Adelson (Ed.), *Handbook of adolescent psychology*. New York: Wiley.

Weinraub, M., Horvath, D. L., & Gringlas, M. B. (2002). Single parenthood. In M. H. Bornstein (Ed.), *Handbook of parenting* (2nd ed., Vol. 3). Mahwah, NJ: Erlbaum.

Weis, L., Marcus, W., & Freie, C. (2003). Living with violence: Housed and homeless women and children talk. In S. Books (Ed.), *Invisible children in society and schools*. Mahwah, NJ: Erlbaum.

Weiss, R. E. (2001). *Pregnancy and birth: Rh factor in pregnancy*. Available on the Internet at: http://www.about.com

Weiss, S. M. (2000). Health psychology: History of the field. In A. Kazdin (Ed.), *Encyclopedia of psychology*. Washington, DC, & New York: American Psychological Association and Oxford University Press.

Weissberg, R. P., & Greenberg, M. T. (1998). School and community competence-enhancement and prevention programs. In W. Damon (Ed.), *Handbook of child psychology* (5th ed., Vol. 4). New York: Wiley.

Weizmann, F. (2000). Bowlby, John. In A. Kazdin (Ed.), *Encyclopedia of psychology*. Washington, DC, & New York: American Psychological Association and Oxford University Press.

Welch, R. A., Blessed, W. B., & Lacoste, H. (2003). Five-year experience with midsemester amniocentesis performed by a single group of obstetrician-gynecologists at a community hospital. *American Journal of Obstetrics and Gynecology, 188,* 600–601.

Wellman, H. (2000). Early childhood. In A. Kazdin (Ed.), *Encyclopedia of psychology*. Washington, DC, & New York: American Psychological Association and Oxford University Press.

Wellman, H. M. (2002). Understanding the psychological world: Developing a theory of mind. In U. Goswami (Ed.), *Blackwell handbook of childhood cognitive development*. Malden, MA: Blackwell.

Wellman, H. M., Cross, D., & Watson, J. (2001). Meta-analysis of theory-of-mind development: The truth about false belief. *Child Development, 72,* 655–684.

Wellman, H. M., Ritter, R., & Flavell, J. H. (1975). Deliberate memory behavior in the delayed reactions of very young children. *Developmental Psychology, 11,* 780–787.

Wentworth, R. A. L. (1999). *Montessori for the millennium*. Mahwah, NJ: Erlbaum.

Wentzel, K. (1997). Student motivation in middle school: The role of perceived pedagog-ical caring. *Journal of Educational Psychology, 89,* 411–419.

Wentzel, K. R., & Asher, S. R. (1995). The academic lives of neglected, rejected, popular, and controversial children. *Child Development, 66,* 754–763.

Wertheimer, M. (1945). *Productive thinking*. New York: Harper.

West, J., Denton, K., & Germino-Hausken, E. (2000). *America's kindergarteners*. Washington, DC: National Center for Education Statitistics.

Whalen, C. K. (2001). ADHD treatment in the 21st century: Pushing the envelope. *Journal of Clinical Child Psychology, 30,* 136–140.

White, B., Castle, P., & Held, R. (1964). Observations on the development of visually directed reaching. *Child Development, 35,* 349–364.

White, J. W. (2001). Aggression and gender. In J. Worell (Ed.), *Encyclopedia of women and gender*. San Diego: Academic Press.

White, S. H. (1995, March). *The children's cause: Some early organizations*. Paper presented at the meeting of the Society for Research in Child Development, Indianapolis.

Whiting, B. B., & Edwards, C. P. (1998). *Children of different worlds*. Cambridge, MA: Harvard University Press.

Whitley, B. E. (2002). *Principles of research in behavioral science* (2nd ed.). New York: McGraw-Hill.

Whitman, T. L., Borkowski, J. G., Keogh, D. A., & Weed, K. (2001). *Interwoven lives*. Mahwah, NJ: Erlbaum.

Wickelgren, I. (1999). Nurture helps to mold able minds. *Science, 283,* 1832–1834.

Wigfield, A., & Eccles, J. S. (Eds.). (2002). *Development of achievement motivation*. San Diego: Academic Press.

Wigfield, A., Eccles, J. S., & Pintrich, P. R. (1996). Development between the ages of 11 and 25. In D. C. Berliner & R. C. Calfee (Eds.), *Handbook of educational psychology*, New York: Macmillan.

Wilfond, B. S. (1999, May). *Genetic testing in children: Ethics issues of research and clinical practice*. Paper presented at the meeting of the Society for Pediatric Research, San Francisco.

Willatts, P. (1990). The stage IV infant's solution of problems requiring the use of supports. *Infant Behavior and Development, 7,* 125–134.

Williams, C., & Bybee, J. (1994). What do children feel guilty about? Developmental and gender differences. *Developmental Psychology, 30,* 617–623.

Williams, C. R. (1986). *The impact of television: A natural experiment in three communities*. New York: Academic Press.

Williams, F., LaRose, R., & Frost, F. (1981). *Children, television, and sex role stereotyping*. New York: Praeger.

Williams, J. E., & Best, D. L. (1982). *Measuring sex stereotypes: A thirty-nation study*. Newbury Park, CA: Sage.

Williams, J. E., & Best, D. L. (1989). *Sex and psyche: Self-concept viewed cross-culturally*. Newbury Park, CA: Sage.

Wilson, B. (2001, April). *The role of television in children's emotional development and socialization*. Paper presented at the meeting of the Society for Research in Child Development, Minneapolis.

Wilson, C. C. (2003). *Racism, sexism, and the media*. Newbury Park, CA: Sage.

Wilson, J. F. (2003). *Biological foundations of human behavior*. Belmont, CA: Wadsworth.

Wilson, R. M., Hall, M. A., Leu, D. J., & Kinzer, C. K. (2001). *Phonics, phonemic awareness, and word analysis for teachers* (7th ed.). Upper Saddle River, NJ: Merrill.

Wilson, W. J., & Neckerman, K. M. (1986). Poverty and family structure: The widening gap between evidence and public policy issues. In S. Danziger & D. Weinberg (Eds.), *Fighting poverty*. Cambridge, MA: Harvard University Press.

Wilson-Shockley, S. (1995). *Gender differences in adolescent depression: The contribution of negative affect*. M.S. Thesis, University of Illinois at Urbana-Champaign.

Windle, M., & Windle, R. C. (2003). Alcohol and other substance use and abuse. In G. R. Adams & M. Berzonsky (Eds.), *Blackwell handbook of adolescence*. Malden, MA: Blackwell.

Windle, W. F. (1940), *Physiology of the human fetus*. Philadelphia: W. B. Saunders.

Winne, P. H. (1997). Experimenting to bootstrap self-regulated learning. *Journal of Educational Psychology, 89,* 397–410.

Winne, P. H. (2001). Self-regulated learning viewed from models of information processing. In B. J. Zimmerman & D. H. Schunk (Eds.), *Self-regulated learning and academic achievement*. Mahwah, NJ: Erlbaum.

Winner, E. (1986, August). Where pelicans kiss seals. *Psychology Today*, pp. 24–35.

Winner, E. (1996). *Gifted children: Myths and realities*. New York: Basic Books.

Winner, E. (2000). The origins and ends of giftedness. *American Psychologist, 55,* 159–169.

Winsler, A., Diaz, R. M., Espinosa, L., & Rodriquez, J. L. (1999). When learning a second language does not mean losing the first: Bilingual language development in low-income, Spanish-speaking children attending bilingual preschool. *Child Development, 70,* 349–362.

Winsler, A., Diaz, R. M., & Montero, I. (1997). The role of private speech in the transition from collaborative to independent task performance in young children. *Early Childhood Research Quarterly, 12,* 59–79.

Winter, D. G. (2000). Achievement motivation. In A. Kazdin (Ed.), *Encyclopedia of psychology.* Washington, DC, & New York: American Psychological Association and Oxford University Press.

Wintre, M. G., & Vallance, D. D. (1994). A developmental sequence in the comprehension of emotions: Intensity, multiple emotions, and valence. *Developmental Psychology, 30,* 509–514.

Wisniewski, A. B., Migeon, C. J., Meyer-Bahlburg, H. F. L., Gearhart, J. P., Berkovitz, G. D., Brown, T. R., & Money, J. (2000). Complete androgen insensitivity syndrome: Long-term medical, surgical, and psychosexual outcome. *The Journal of Clinical Endocrinology and Metabolism, 85,* 2664–2669.

Witkin, H. A., Mednick, S. A., Schulsinger, R., Bakkestrom, E., Christiansen, K. O., Goodenbough, D. R., Hirchhorn, K., Lunsteen, C., Owen, D. R., Philip, J., Ruben, D. B., & Stocking, M. (1976). Criminality in XYY and XXY men. *Science, 193,* 547–555.

Wong, D. L. (2002). *Maternal Child Nursing Care.* (6th ed.). St. Louis: Mosby.

Wong, D. L., Hockenberry-Eaton, M., Wilson, D., Winkelstein, M. L., & Schwartz, P. (2001). *Wong's essentials of pediatric nursing* (6th ed.). St. Louis: Mosby.

Wong, D. L., Perry, S. E., & Hockenberry, M. (2001). *Maternal child nursing care* (2nd ed.). St. Louis: Mosby.

Wood, W., & Eagly, A. H. (2002). A cross-cultural analysis of the behavior of women and men: Implications for the origins of sex differences. *Psychological Bulletin, 128,* 699–727.

Woodard, E. (2000). *Media in the Home 2000: The Fifth Annual Survey of Parents and Children.* Philadelphia: The Annenberg Public Policy Center.

Woodrich, D. L. (1994). *Attention-deficit hyperactivity disorder: What every parent should know.* Baltimore: Paul H. Brookes.

Woodroffe, A., & Spencer, M. (2003). Culturally and ethnically diverse communities: Building blocks for working relationships. *Child Welfare, 82,* 169–184.

Woodward, A. L., & Markman, E. M. (1998). Early word learning. In D. Kuhn & R. S. Siegler (Eds.), *Handbook of child psychology* (5th ed., Vol. 2). New York: Wiley.

Work Group of the American Psychological Association's Board of Educational Affairs. (1995). *Learner-centered psychological principles: A framework for school redesign and reform (draft).* Washington, DC: American Psychological Association.

World Health Organization. (2000). *The world health report.* Geneva: Author.

World Health Organization. (2000 February 2). *Adolescent health behavior in 28 countries.* Geneva: Author.

Worobey, J., & Belsky, J. (1982). Employing the Brazelton scale to influence mothering: An experimental comparison of three strategies. *Developmental Psychology, 18,* 736–743.

Wright, M. R. (1989). Body image satisfaction in adolescent girls and boys. *Journal of Youth and Adolescence, 18,* 71–84.

Wroblewski, R., & Huston, A. C. (1987). Televised occupational stereotypes and their effects on early adolescents: Are they changing? *Journal of Early Adolescence, 7,* 283–297.

Wu, P., Robinson, C. C., Yang, C., Hart, C. H., Olsen, S. F., Porter, C. L., Jin, S., Wo, J., & Wu, X. (in press). Similarities and differences in mothers' parenting of preschoolers in China and the United States. *International Journal of Behavioral Development.*

Xu, F., & Carey, S. E. (1995, March). *Surprising failures in ten-month-old infants' object representation.* Paper presented at the meeting of the Society for Research in Child Development, Indianapolis.

Yates, M. (1995, March). *Community service and political-moral discussions among Black urban adolescents.* Paper presented at the meeting of the Society for Research in Child Development, Indianapolis.

Yeung, W. J., Sandberg, J. F., Davis-Kean, P. E., & Hofferth, S. L. (2001). Children's time with fathers in intact families. *Journal of Marriage and Family, 63,* 136–154.

Yin, Y., Buhrmester, D., & Hibbard, D. (1996, March). *Are there developmental changes in the influence of relationships with parents and friends on adjustment during early adolescence?* Paper presented at the meeting of the Society for Research on Adolescence, Boston.

Young, D. (2001). The nature and management of pain: What is the evidence? *Birth, 28,* 149–151.

Young, K. T. (1990). American conceptions of infant development from 1955 to 1984: What the experts are telling parents. *Child Development, 61,* 17–28.

Young, S. K., & Shahinfar, A. (1995, March). *The contributions of maternal sensitivity and child temperament to attachment status at 14 months.* Paper presented at the meeting of the Society for Research in Child Development, Indianapolis.

Youniss, J. (1980). *Parents and peers in the social environment: A Sullivan Piaget perspective.* Chicago: University of Chicago Press.

Yu, V. Y. (2000). Developmental outcome of extremely preterm infants. *American Journal of Perinatology, 17,* 57–61.

Yussen, S. R. (1977). Characteristics of moral dilemmas written by adolescents. *Developmental Psychology, 13,* 162–163.

Zeskind, P. S., Gingras, J. L., Campbell, K. D., & Donnelly, K. (1999, April). *Prenatal cocaine exposure disrupts fetal autonomic regulation.* Paper presented at the meeting of the Society for Research in Child Development, Albuquerque.

Zeskind, P. S., Klein, L., & Marshall, T. R. (1992). Adults' perceptions of experimental modifications of durations and expiratory sounds in infant crying. *Developmental Psychology, 28,* 1153–1162.

Zhou, Q., Eisenberg, N., Losoya, S. H., Fabes, R. A., Reiser, M., Gutherie, I. K., Murphy, B. C., Cumberland, A. J., & Shepard, S. A. (2002). The relations of parental warmth and expressiveness to children's empathy-related responding and social functioning: A longitudinal study. *Child Development, 73,* 893–915.

Zigler, E. F., & Hall, N. W. (2000). *Child development and social policy.* Boston: McGraw-Hill.

Zigler, E. F., & Styfco, S. J. (1994). Head Start: Criticisms in a constructive context. *American Psychologist, 49,* 127–132.

Zill, N., Loomis, L., & West, J. (1997). *The elementary school performance and adjustment of children who enter kindergarten late or repeat kindergarten.* Washington, DC: National Center for Education Statistics.

Zimmerman, B. J. (2001). Developing self-fulfilling cycles of academic regulation: An analysis of exemplary instructional models. In D. H. Schunk & B. J. Zimmerman (Eds.), *Self-regulated learning and academic achievement.* Mahwah, NJ: Erlbaum.

Zimmerman, B. J., Bonner, S., & Kovach, R. (1996). Developing self-regulated learners. Washington, DC: American Psychological Association.

Zimmerman, B. J., & Schunk, D. H. (Eds.). (2001). *Self-regulated learning and academic achievement.* Mahwah, NJ: Erlbaum.

Zimmerman, R. S., Khoury, E., Vega, W. A., Gill, A. G., & Warheit, G. J. (1995). Teacher and student perceptions of behavior problems among a sample of African American, Hispanic, and non-Hispanic White students. *American Journal of Community Psychology, 23,* 181–197.

Zoppi, M. A., Ibba, R. M., Putzolu, M., Floris, M., & Monni, K. G. (2001). Nuchal translucency and the acceptance of invasive prenatal chromosomal diagnosis in women aged 35 and older. *Obstetrics and Gynecology, 97,* 916–920.

Zukow-Goldring, P. (2002). Sibling caregiving. In M. H. Bornstein (Ed.), *Handbook of parenting* (2nd ed., Vol. 3). Mahwah, NJ: Erlbaum.

Zvara, A., Hackler, L., Nagy, Z. B., Micsik, T., & Puskas, L. S. (2003). New molecular methods for classification, diagnosis, and therapy prediction of hematological malignancies. *Pathology and Oncology Research, 8,* 231–240.

Credits

Photo Credits

Section Openers

1: © Francisco Cruz/SuperStock; 2: © Petit Format/Nestle/Photo Researchers; 3: © CORBIS CD 4: © Explorer/Photo Researchers; 5: © David Young-Wolff/Photo Edit

Chapter 1

Opener: © Francisco Cruz/SuperStock; p. 6 (top & bottom): © AP/Wide World Photos; 1.1: Photo: © Erich Lessing/Art Resource, NY/Painting by A.I.G. Velasquez, Infanta Margarita Teresa in white garb, Kunsthistorische Museum, Vienna, Austria; 1.2: © Archives of the History of American Psychology; p. 11: © Luis Vargas; p. 12: National Association for the Education of Young Children, Robert Maust/Photo Agora; p. 13: © Nancy Agostini; p. 15: Courtesy of Marian Wright Edelman, The Children's Defense Fund, photograph by Rick Reinhard; p. 16: © Felicia Martinez/Photo Edit; 1.6 (left to right): Courtesy of Landrum Shettles; © Chromosohn Media, Inc./The Image Works; © John Santrock; © CORBIS website; © James L. Shaffer; p. 21: © PhotoDisc/Getty website

Chapter 2

Opener: © Ray Stott/The Image Works; p. 30: © Bettmann/CORBIS; p. 31: © Sarah Putnam/Index Stock; p. 34: © Yves deBraine/Black Star/Stock Photo; p. 35: A.R. Lauria/Dr. Michael Cole, Laboratory of Human Cognition, University of California, San Diego; p. 37: © Bettmann/CORBIS; p. 38: Courtesy of Stanford University; p. 39: © Nina Leen/TimePix; p. 41: Courtesy of Urie Bronfenbrenner; 2.6: Pavlov: © CORBIS; Freud: © Bettmann/CORBIS; Piaget: © Yves deBraine/Black Star/Stock Photo; Vygotsky: A.R. Lauria/Dr. Michael Cole, Laboratory of Human Cognition, University of California, San Diego; Skinner: © Harvard University News Office; Erikson: © UPI/Bettmann/CORBIS; Bandura: Courtesy of Stanford University News Service; Bronfenbrenner: Courtesy of Urie Bronfenbrenner; p. 44: © Richard T. Nowitz/Photo Researchers; p. 46: © Paul Popper Ltd; p. 51: © McGraw-Hill Higher Education, photographer John Thoeming; p. 55: © Pam Reid; p. 56 (top): © Kevin Fleming/CORBIS; p. 56 (bottom): © Ed Honowitz/Stone/Getty Images

Chapter 3

Opener: © Tom Rosenthal/SuperStock; p. 66: © Enrico Ferorelli; 3.2: © Sundstroem/Gamma;

p. 76: © Andrew Eccles; p. 78: © 1989 Joel Gordon Photography; p. 79: © Andrew Eccles/Outline; p. 80: © Holly Ishmael; p. 81: © J. Pavlovsky/Sygma/CORBIS; p. 83: © Ambassador/Sygma/CORBIS; p. 87: © 1999 Joel Gordon

Chapter 4

Opener: Photo Lennart Nilsson/Albert Bonniers Forlag AB., *A Child Is Born*, Dell Publishing Company.; p. 96: © David Young-Wolff/Photo Edit; 4.3 (top): Photo Lennart Nilsson/Albert Bonniers Forlag AB., *A Child Is Born*, Dell Publishing Company; (middle & bottom): © Petit Format/Nestle Science Source/Photo Researchers; 4.5: Courtesy of Ann Streissguth from A.P. Streissguth et al., "Teratogenic Effects of Alcohol in Humans and Laboratory Animals" in *Science*, 209(18): 353–361, 1980; p. 102: © John Chiasson/Liaison Agency/Getty Images; p. 103: © R.I.A./Gamma; p. 105: © Betty Press/Woodfin Camp; p. 106: © 1990 Alan Reininger/Contact Press Images; p. 107: © Rachel Thompson; p. 108 (left): © Charles Gupton/Stock Boston; (right): © Viviane Moos; p. 110: © SIU/Peter Arnold, Inc.; p. 112: © Nancy Devore/Anthro-Photo; p. 113: © Linda Pugh; p. 114: © Charles Gupton/Stock Boston; p. 116: © Kangaroo Foundation, Bogota, Colombia; p. 117: © Dr. Tiffany Field; 4.10: © Stephen Marks, Inc./The Image Bank/Getty Images; p. 120: © Michael Newman/Photo Edit; p. 122: © Tony Schanuel Photography

Chapter 5

Opener: © George Disario/The Stock Market/CORBIS; 5.5: © 1999 Kenneth Jarecke/Contact Press Images; 5.7: © A. Glauberman/Photo Researchers; 5.8ab: Courtesy of Dr. Harry T. Chugani, Children's Hospital of Michigan; 5.9a: © David Grugin Productions, Inc. Reprinted by permission.; 5.9b: Image courtesy of Dana Boatman, Ph.D., Department of Neurology, Johns Hopkins University, reprinted with permission from *The Secret Life of the Brain*, Joseph Henry Press; p. 140: © Vol. DV251 Digital Vision/Getty Images; p. 141 (top): Courtesy of Barbara Deloin; (bottom): © Bob Dammrich/The Image Works; p. 142: Courtesy of The Hawaii Family Support Center, Healthy Start Program; p. 143: Courtesy of T. Berry Brazelton; 5.13 (left & right): © Dr. Karen Adolph, New York University; p. 149 (top): © Michael Greenlar/The Image Works; p. 149 (bottom): © Frank Baily Studios; 5.15: © Judith Canty/Stock Boston;

p. 151: Courtesy of Esther Thelen; p. 153: © James Kilkelly; 5.16 (all): Courtesy of Dr. Charles Nelson; 5.17: © David Linton; 5.19: © Dr. Bruce Hood, University of Bristol, England; 5.20: © Enrico Ferorelli; 5.21a: © Michael Siluk; 5.21b: Dr. Melanie Spence, University of Texas; 5.22: © Jean Guichard/Sygma/CORBIS; 5.23 (all): From D. Rosenstein and H. Oster, "Differential Facial Responses to Four Basic Tastes in Newborns" in *Child Development*, Vol. 59, 1988. Copyright © Society For Research in Child Development, Inc.

Chapter 6

Opener: © Eyewire Vol. EP049/Getty Images; p. 168: © Joe McNally; p. 169: © The Image Works; p. 170: © Bob Daemmrich/Stone/Getty Images; p. 172: © Vol. EP078/Eyewire/Getty Images; p. 179: © Tony Freeman/Photo Edit; p. 182: Courtesy of Sharon McLeod; p. 189: © Lawrence Migdale/Stock Boston; p. 191: Courtesy of Lynn Blankinship; 6.16a: © Mark Richard/Photo Edit; 6.16b: Courtesy of National Institute of Drug Abuse; p. 197: © M. Regine/The Image Bank/Getty Images

Chapter 7

Opener: © Richard Hutchings/Photo Researchers; p. 207: © Yves deBraine/Black Star/Stock Photo; 7.1 (left & right): © Doug Goodman/Photo Researchers; 7.4: © Denise Marcotte/Index Stock; 7.8: © Paul Fusco/Magnum Photos; 7.10: © Owen Franken/Stock Boston; 7.12: © Richard Hutchings/Photo Researchers; p. 222: © David Young-Wolff/Photo Edit; 7.13: © Paul Conklin; p. 224: © Stewart Cohen/Stone/Getty Images; p. 227: © Archives Jean Piaget, Université de Genève, Switzerland; p. 228 (top): © Archives Jean Piaget, Université de Genève, Switzerland; (bottom): © M & E Bernheim/Woodfin Camp; 7.14: © Elizabeth Crews/The Image Works; p. 230: © James Wertsch/Washington University; p. 231: © David Young-Wolff/Photo Edit; p. 233: © Bob Daemmrich/The Image Works; 7.15 (left): A.R. Lauria/Dr. Michael Cole, Laboratory of Human Cognition, University of California, San Diego; 7.15 (right): © 1999 Yves deBraine/Black Star/Stock Photo

Chapter 8

Opener: © Spencer Grant/Photo Edit; p. 246: © Paul Conklin/Photo Edit; p. 258: © 1999 James Kamp; p. 262: © Nita Winter Photography; p. 266 (top): Courtesy of Judy DeLoache;

Text and Line Art Credits

Chapter 16

Figure 16.3 From Nansel et al., 2001, "Bullying Behavior Among U.S. Youth," *Journal of the American Medical Association*, 285, 2094–2100. **Figure 16.5** From John Santrock, *Child Development*, 9th Edition. Copyright © 2001 The McGraw-Hill Companies. Reproduced with permission of The McGraw-Hill Companies. **Figure 16.6** From Dexter C. Dunphy, "The Social Structure of Urban Adolescent Peer Groups," *Sociometry*, Vol. 26, 1963. American Sociological Association, Washington, DC. **Figure 16.7** "Age of Onset of Romantic Activity," from "Romantic Development: Does Age at Which Romantic Involvement Starts Matter?" by Duane Buhrmester, April 2001, paper presented at the meeting of the Society for Research in Child Development, Minneapolis, MN. Reprinted with permission.

Chapter 17

Figure 17.1 From "Learner-Centered Principles Work Group," *Learner-Centered Psychological Principles: A Framework for School Redesign and Reform*, 1997. Found at www.apa.org/ed/lcp.html. Copyright © 1997 by the American Psychological Association. Reprinted with permission. **Figure 17.2** From "Position Statement on Developmentally Appropriate Practice in Programs for 4 and 5 Year Olds," *Young Children*, 41, 23–27. Copyright © 1986 National Association for the Education of Young Children. Used by permission of the National Association for the Education of Young Children. **Figure 17.5** From K. Wentzel, 1997, "Student Motivation in Middle School: The Role of Perceived Pedagogical Caring," *Journal of Educational Psychology*, 89, 411–419. Copyright © 1997 by the American Psychological Association. Adapted with permission. **Figure 17.6** From Deborah Stipek, *Motivation to Learn: Integrating Theory and Practice*, 4th Edition. Published by Allyn & Bacon, Boston, MA. Copyright © 2002 by Pearson Education. Reprinted by permission of the publisher.

Chapter 18

Figure 18.1 From Harry C. Triandis, *Making Basic Texts in Psychology More Culture-Inclusive and Culture-Sensitive*. Used by permission of the University of Illinois Press. **Figure 18.5** From D.F. Robitaille and R.A. Garden, *The IEA Study of Mathematics II: Contexts and Outcomes of School Mathematics*. Copyright © 1989 D. F. Robitaille and R. A. Garden. Reprinted by permission of the authors. **Figure 18.6** From Diane Levin and Nancy Carlsson, "Developmentally Appropriate Television: Putting Children First," *Young Children*, 49, July 1994, p. 43. Reprinted with permission from the National Association for the Education of Young Children.

Name Index

Note: Page numbers in *italics* indicate figures and illustrations.

A

AAP. *See* American Academy of Pediatrics
Abbassi, V., 185
Abecassis, M., 523–524
Abel, E. L., 106
Abma, J. C., 191
Aboud, F., 386
Aboud, F. E., 591
Abramovich, D. R., 101
Abramovitch, R., 488
Abramson, L. Y., 356
Abutalebi, J., 318
Acosta, A., 140
Acredolo, L. P., 158
Adams, C. M., 101
Adams, G. R., 397
Adams, R., 116
Adams, R. J., 153
Adamson, T. M., 138
Adato, A., 76
Addis, A., 99
Addy, C. L., 178
Adelson, J., 403
Adler, N. E., 225
Adler, T., 66
Adolph, K. E., 147, *147*, 153
Aggett, P. J., 101
Ahlhelm, F., 180
Ahluwalia, I. B., 140
Ahn, N., 191
Aiken, L. R., 45, 286
Ainsworth, B. E., 178
Ainsworth, M. D. S., 351, 370, *370*, 372, 475
Aithamon, B., 318
Akiyama, T., 117
Alan Guttmacher Institute, 189, 190, 191
Alarcon, O., 591
Alavi, A., 422
Alba-Speyer, C., 45
Alberman, E., 78
Albrecht, J. T., 112
Alderman, M. H., 115
Aldridge, M. A., 158
Alevriadou, A., 172
Alexander, A., 562
Alexander, C., 194
Alexander, C. M., 56
Alexander, J. M., 112
Alie-Daram, S., 103
Alipuria, L. L., 401
Allen, E., 45, *45*
Allen, J. P., 490
Allen, L., 296
Allen, M., 142
Allen, N. H., 193

Alloy, L. B., 356
Alme, A., 78
Altmann, A., 138
Alzte, G., 371
Amabile, T. M., 302, 565
Amato, P. R., 495, 496, 503
American Academy of Pediatrics (AAP), 143, 324, 335, 358
American Academy of Pediatrics (AAP) Committee on Drugs, 140
American Academy of Pediatrics (AAP) Task Force on Infant Positioning and SIDS, 137, 138
American Academy of Pediatrics (AAP) Work Group on Breastfeeding, 140
American Association of University Women, 417
American Association on Mental Retardation, 298
American Psychiatric Association, 561
Ames, B. N., 107
Amiel-Tison, C., 158
Amsel, E., 270
Amsterdam, B. K., 385
Anastasi, A., 288
Anderman, E. M., 567
Anderson, C. A., 596
Anderson, C. J., 543
Anderson, D. R., 246, 597
Anderson, E., 497
Anderson, G. C., 116–117
Anderson, H., 562
Anderson, J., 543
Anderson, L. D., 296
Anderson, L. M., 547
Anderson, R. E., 598
Andrist, L. C., 179
Angel, M., 72
Angelopoulos, J., 102
Ani, C., 141
Anneren, G., 101
Anthony, J. C., 102
Antony, U., 105
Antorn, M. T., 105
Apostolaris, N. H., 517
Applebaum, M. I., 297
Applefield, J. M., 595
Araujo, K., 189
Archer, S. L., 399, 400, 401, 403
Archibald, A. B., 178
Archibald, S. L., 101
Arehart, D. M., 400
Arendt, R., 102
Ariès, P., 7
Arisawa, K., 117
Armsden, G., 490
Arnett, J., 225
Arnold, G. S., 185
Arnold, M. L., 448
Arnold, S. E., 422
Aro, P., 525
Aronson, E., 557
Arora, C. P., 106

Arrufat, O., 401
Arshad, S. H., 140
Arslan, M., 81
Arterberry, M. E., 160
Asarnow, J. R., 515
Asencio, M., 589
Asher, J., 337
Asher, S. R., 515, 516, 524
Ashmead, D. H., 149
Asp, C. E., 585
Aspler, S., 79
Astin, A. W., 450
Astington, J. W., 261
Atkins, D. H., 158
Atkins, R., 455, 456
Atkinson, L., 371
Atkinson, R., 196
Attie, I., 178
Audrey, Y., 102
Auerbach-Major, S., 349
Augustyn, M., 102
Ayers-Lopez, S., 513
Aylward, E., 422
Ayzac, L., 140
Azar, S. T., 484, 485
Azmitia, M., 389
Azuma, H., 477

B

Baafi, M., 122
Babey, S. H., 393
Bacaltchuk, J., 179
Bachman, J. G., 192, *192*, 193, 194, 195, 450
Bachnan, H. J., 305
Bacon, M. K., 581
Bada, H. S., 102
Baddeley, A., 252
Baer, J. S., 101
Bagwell, C. L., 523
Bahado-Singh, R. O., 81
Bahnsen, M., 116
Bai, D. L., 146
Bailey, B., 99
Bailey, J. M., 411
Baillargeon, R., 150, 211, 212, 213, 214
Baird, A. A., 173
Bakeman, R., 123
Baker, D., 104
Bakker, E., 143
Bakkestrom, E., 78
Balka, E. B., 588
Baltes, P. B., 18, 20
Bandstra, E. S., 102
Bandura, A., 37, 38, 44, 69, 320, 443, 447, 448, 566, 568, 569
Bangert-Drowns, R. L., 286

Banks, E. C., 444
Banks, J. A., 13, 556, 590
Banks, M. S., 153
Baranowski, T., 175
Barker, R., 514
Barnard, K. E., 499
Barnard, M., 102
Barnes, D. L., 121
Barnes, H., 556, 587
Barnett, D., 372, 485
Barnett, S. B., 103
Baron, N. S., 323
Barr, H. M., 101
Barr, L., 393
Barrett, D. E., 141
Barrett, J. C., 72
Barry, H., 581
Barta, P., 422
Bartholomew, N. E., 190
Bartlett, L., 231
Barton, B. A., 178, 179
Barton, L., 114
Baskett, L. M., 487
Bates, A. S., 108
Bates, E., 327, 330
Bates, J. E., 364, 365, 495
Bates, K. E., 87
Bathurst, K., 11, 494
Batson, C. D., 456
Bauchner, H., 101
Bauer, C. R., 10, 102, 117
Bauer, P. J., 253
Baumeister, R. F., 397, 416
Baumrind, D., 87, 416, 481, 483
Bauserman, R., 496
Bavelier, D., 132
Bawdon, R. E., 112
Bayley, N., 141, 295, 296
Beach, D. R., 247
Beady, C., 569
Beagles-Roos, J., 596
Beal, C. R., 418, 428, 429
Beardslee, W., 357
Bearison, D. J., 235
Beaton, A. E., 571
Beautrais, A. L., 358
Bebeau, M. J., 443, 444
Bechtel, G. A., 108
Bechtold, A. G., 159
Beck, A. T., 356, 357
Beck, C. T., 121
Becker, M., 102
Beckwith, L., 297
Bednar, R. L., 394
Bee, D. E., 175
Beebe, B., 473
Beebe, T., 455
Beeghly, M., 102
Begley, S., 136
Behan, P. O., 172
Behrakis, P., 79
Behrman, R. E., 107, 115, 562
Belcher, H., 102
Belik, J., 106
Bell, M. A., 135
Bell, N., 234
Bell, S. M., 351
Belle, D., 494
Bellinger, D., 102, 103
Bellucci, S., 324
Bellugi, U., 324
Belmont, B., 357
Belsky, J., 119, 474, 494, 502
Belson, W., 595
Bem, S. L., 425

Ben-Avie, M., 558
Bendelius, J., 79
Benenson, J. F., 517
Bennett, C. I., 556
Bennett, S. L., 473
Bennett, W., 454
Benson, B., 189
Benson, J. B., 228
Benson, P., 455
Benson, P. I., 83
Bentler, P. M., 194
Benton-Davis, S., 140
Ben-Zeev, T., 255
Bereiter, C., 263
Berenbaum, S. A., 411
Bergen, G., 520, 521
Berget, A., 107
Bergstrom, R., 105
Bering, J. M., 68
Berk, S. F., 500
Berkey, C. S., 178
Berko, J., 330, 330
Berko Gleason, J., 315, 322, 328, 332
Berkovitz, G. D., 412
Berkowitz, M., 442
Berlin, L., 371–372
Berlyne, D. E., 519
Berman, S., 401
Berndt, T. J., 523, 524, 525, 527, 552
Bernier, M. O., 140
Berry, J., 579
Berry, R., 231
Bertch, T., 445
Bertenthal, B. I., 146
Bertoncini, J., 158
Berzonsky, M., 399
Besch, M. F., 412
Best, D., 420
Best, D. L., 420
Best, J. W., 45
Bialystok, E., 314, 320, 336, 337
Bidell, T. R., 134
Biderman, J., 563
Bigler, R. S., 421
Biller, H. B., 503
Billman, J., 44
Billy, J. O. G., 525
Birth, L. L., 177
Bissada, A., 485
Bissell, J., 598
Bjorklund, D. F., 36, 67, 68, 244, 250, 252, 272
Black, J. E., 136
Blair, C., 115, 304
Blair, K. A., 349
Blair, T. R., 334
Blanchard, S., 105
Blasi, A., 398
Blessed, W. B., 81
Blickstein, I., 106
Block, J., 366, 423, 475
Block, J. H., 423, 475
Bloom, B., 255, 300
Bloom, L., 327, 328, 329, 332
Bloom, P., 330
Blot, W. J., 101
Blue, J. H., 185
Blum, L. M., 139
Blum, R., 188
Blyth, D. A., 187, 584
Bobe, L., 172
Boggiano, A. K., 388
Bogner, K., 271
Bohlin, G., 352

Bohn, K., 271
Bohnhorst, B., 116
Boivin, M., 523
Bojesen, A., 78
Bolek, T., 102
Bolger, K. E., 12, 485
Bolland, J. M., 584
Bonica, C. A., 528
Bonk, C. J., 550
Bonner, S., 273, 569
Bonvillian, J. D., 214
Boodoo, G., 303
Books, S., 555
Bookstein, F. L., 101
Booth, A., 473, 496
Booth, D. A., 159
Booth, M., 498, 532
Borawski, E., 114
Borden, L. M., 197
Borg, W. R., 54
Boring, E. G., 207
Borkowsky, J. G., 11, 191
Born, L., 185
Bornstein, M. H., 10, 21, 87, 160, 297, 364, 476
Borowsky, I. W., 358
Bos, J., 587
Bosch, M., 72
Bossard, N., 140
Bost, C. S., 562
Botvin, G. J., 196, 588
Bouchard, T. J., 66, 303
Bouchey, H. A., 528
Boulanoura, K., 318
Bousquest, A., 121
Bouvier, P., 484
Bower, B., 151, 172
Bower, T. G. R., 154, 158
Bowlby, J., 20, 39, 351, 352, 356, 368, 369, 372, 475
Bowlds, M. K., 401
Boyer, K., 253
Boyes, M. C., 443
Boykin, A. W., 303
Boykin, K. A., 489
Boyle, M., 357
Boyle, O., 336
Boyum, L., 478–479
Brabeck, M. M., 55
Bracken, M. B., 82
Bradley, R. H., 10, 14, 555, 589
Braff, A. M., 83
Bramswig, J. H., 78
Brand, S., 393
Braungart-Reiker, J. M., 354
Bravo, M. A., 336
Bray, H., 425
Brazelton, T. B., 87, 117, 118, 145
Bredekamp, S., 335, 540, 545
Bremer, M., 594
Bremner, G., 211
Brenneman, K., 229
Brenner, R. A., 180
Brent, R. L., 99, 101
Bretherton, I., 352
Brewer, C., 103
Brewer, J. A., 545
Brewer, M. B., 580
Bridges, J. S., 55
Bridges, L. J., 353, 361
Bridges, M., 496, 497
Briere, J., 485
Briones, E., 401
Brion-Meisels, S., 391
Brislin, R., 579
Bristol-Power, M., 11
Brodie, M., 599

Brody, G. H., 195, 453
Brody, J. E., 140
Brody, N., 293, 294, 303, 306, 307
Brodzinsky, D. M., 83
Bromley, D., 386
Bronfenbrenner, U., 40, *40*, 41, 548
Brook, D. W., 492
Brook, J. S., 492, 588
Brookover, W. B., 569
Brooks, J. G., 267
Brooks, M. G., 267
Brooks, P. J., 270
Brooks-Gunn, J., 175, 178, 185, 187, 188, 191, 361, 385, 397, 415, 494, 498, 586
Brophy, J., 565
Brossard, Y., 103
Broughton, J., 328
Broughton, J. M., 225, 386
Brouwers, E. P. M., 106
Brown, A. L., 248, 265, 268, 272
Brown, B. B., 427, 428, 498, 512, 527, 528, 530
Brown, J., 479
Brown, J. D., 594
Brown, J. V., 123
Brown, L. M., 445, 510
Brown, M. J., 181
Brown, P., 142
Brown, R., 320, 322
Brown, S. K., 594
Brown, T. R., 412
Brown, Z. A., 104
Brownlee, S., 327
Bruce, J. M., 346
Bruck, M., 259
Bruer, J. T., 21
Bruk, A., 132
Brumbaugh, E., 116
Bruner, J. S., 269, 322, 323
Bryant, D. M., 374
Buchanan, C. M., 185, 495
Buck, G. H., 561
Buckner, C. E., 425
Budwig, N., 330
Bugental, D. B., 478
Buhrmester, D., 189, 416, 475, 523, 525
Buhs, E. S., 516
Bukowski, W. M., 511, 512, 523, 524
Bumin, G., 78
Bumpus, M. F., 489
Burchinal, M. R., 331, 374, 474
Burd, L., 106
Buriel, R., 477, 478, 479, 480, 498
Burke, M. D., 101
Burlingame, S., 362
Burman, I., 117
Burock, D., 455, 456
Bursuck, W. D., 564
Burton, R. V., 447
Burts, D. C., 481, 545
Bush, K. R., 586
Bush, P. G., 101
Bushman, B. J., 596
Bushnell, E. W., 159
Bushnell, I. W. R., 155
Buss, D. M., 68, 413, 424
Bussell, J., 401
Bustamante, M. R., 371
Buswell, B. N., 393
Butler, Y. G., 336
Butner, J., 68
Butz, A. M., 102
Buzwell, S., 188
Bybee, J., 451
Bybee, J. A., 388
Bydder, G. M., 110

Bynner, J., 586
Byrnes, J. P., 172, 223

C

Caballeros, M., 487
Cable News Network (CNN), 597
Cabral, H., 102
Cabrera, N., 503
Cairns, R. B., 8, 9
Calabrese, R. L., 455
Calenda, E., 138
Call, J., 266
Callahan, C., 114
Callahan, M. A., 45, *45*
Callan, J. E., 414
Callan, J. W., 515
Callender, E. S., 105
Calvert, S., 417
Camaioni, L., 328
Cambargo, C. A., 178
Camburn, D., 188
Cameron, J., 566
Cameron, J. R., 367
Campbell, B., 290
Campbell, C. Y., 418
Campbell, D. T., 580
Campbell, F. A., 304
Campbell, K. D., 102
Campbell, L., 290
Campione, J. C., 268
Campos, J., 347
Campos, J. J., 156
Candee, D., 448
Canfield, R. L., 156
Cannizzo, S. R., 248
Caporael, L. R., 68
Cappa, S. F., 318
Capparelli, E. V., 105
Carande-Kulis, V. G., 547
Carbonell, O. A., 371
Carbonne, B., 112
Cardebat, D., 318
Carey, L. M., 286
Carey, S., 226, 260, 330
Carey, S. E., 212
Cariligia-Bull, T., 249
Carlesimo, G. A., 324
Carlson, C., 400
Carlson, E. A., 20, 371, 475
Carlson, K. S., 487
Carlson, V., 589
Carlton, M. P., 549
Carmella, S. G., 101
Carnegie Corporation, 548, 552
Carolo, G., 449
Carpendale, J., 514
Carpenter, C. J., 420
Carr, T. S., 412
Carreras, R., 105
Carroll, J., 294
Cartar, L., 114
Carter, D. B., 419
Carter-Saltzman, L., 172
Carver, K., 528
Carver, L. J., 253
Casas, J. F., 423
Casas, J. M., 56
Case, R., 229, 251, 252
Casey, B. M., 118, 132, 174
Caspi, A., 365
Cassidy, D. J., 248, 420
Cassidy, J., 371–372, 474, 490

Castellanos, E., 105
Castellanos, F. X., 173
Castenell, L. A., 589
Castle, P., 149
Castro, L. C., 106
Cauce, A. M., 56
Cauffman, B. E., 178
Cauffman, E., 458
Caulfield, R. A., 101
Caviness, V. S., 422
Ceci, S. J., 41, 259, 303, 305
Cen, G., 366
Centers for Disease Control and Prevention, 105, 190, 191
Chall, J. S., 333
Chan, A., 114
Chan, D., 177
Chan, W. S., 21
Chance, G., 158
Chang, L., 102
Chang, P., 123
Chao, K. Y., 181
Chao, W., 495
Chapman, M. V., 584
Chard, S., 550
Charlesworth, R., 481, 544, 545
Charpak, N., 116
Charpak, Y., 116
Chase-Lansdale, P. L., 375, 496
Chattin-McNichols, J., 544
Chaudhry, V., 100
Chauhuri, J. H., 372
Chavkin, W., 102
Chee, W. Y., 101
Chen, C., 101, 571
Chen, H., 366
Chen, M., 101
Chen, X., 366
Chen, Z., 36
Cheng, T. L., 180
Cherlin, A. J., 496
Chess, S., 363, 365
Chi, M. T. H., 254
Child, I. L., 581
Children's Defense Fund, 585, 586
Child Trends, 190, 191
Chinsky, J. M., 247
Chisholm, K., 83
Cho, B. H., 367
Choic, S. J., 81
Chomsky, N., 318, 319, *319*, 322
Christensen, M., 83
Christian, K., 305
Christian, M. S., 101
Christiani, D. C., 194
Christiansen, K. O., 78
Christie, J. F., 521, 522
Christoffel, K. K., 139
Christou, C., 252
Chrousos, G. P., 121, 185
Chrousos, J. P., 185
Chu, D. M., 116–117
Chun, K. M., 13
Chung, K. M., 563
Chung, W. C., 422
Chwo, M. J., 116–117
Cicchetti, D., 136, 372, 484, 485
Ciechalski, J., 455
Cilessen, A. H. N., 516
Circirelli, V. G., 487
Ciupak, G., 105
Clark, E., 330
Clark, R. D., 424
Clark, S. D., 189
Clarke-Stewart, K. A., 548

Clarkson, M. G., 149
Classon, B., 101
Clausson, B., 101
Cleator, G., 104
Clifford, B. R., 594
Clifton, R. K., 149, 159
Clinchy, B. M., 270
Clingempeel, W. G., 497
Clore, G. L., 532
Cnattingius, S., 101, 105
CNN (Cable News Network), 597
Coates, P., 116
Coatsworth, J. D., 16
Cobb, N. J., 530
Cobbs, G., 388
Cobilanschi, J., 72
Cochran, J., 181
Coh, L. D., 225
Cohen, B. M., 173
Cohen, D., 266
Cohen, G. J., 137
Cohen, L. B., 152, 154
Cohen, P., 492
Cohen, S. E., 297
Cohn, J. F., 473
Coie, J. D., 460, 516
Colapinto, J., 412
Colby, A., 440
Colditz, G. A., 178
Cole, C. F., 594
Coles, C. D., 101
Coles, R., 28
Coley, R., 422
Coley, R. L., 375
Coll, C. T. G., 14, 375, 498, 500, 586, 589, 590, 591
Collins, A. M., 35
Collins, J., 176
Collins, N. L., 490
Collins, P. A., 246
Collins, W. A., 87, 476, 477, 532
Comas-Díaz, L., 401
Comer, J. P., 558
Committee on Drugs, 100
Committee on Fetus and Newborn, 111
Committee on Pediatric AIDS, 105
Committee on Sports Medicine and Fitness, 180
Committee on Substance Abuse, 101
Commoner, B., 76, 77
Compas, B. E., 357, 362
Condon, S. M., 491
Condry, K. F., 159
Conduct Problems Prevention Research Group, 461
Cong, X., 117
Conger, K. J., 460
Conger, R. D., 460, 477, 482, 491, 495
Connell, J. P., 353
Conne-Perreard, E., 121
Connor, J. D., 105
Connor, P. D., 101
Connor-Smith, J. K., 362
Cook, M., 479
Cooper, C., 389, 400
Cooper, C. R., 400, 491, 513
Cooper, M. L., 490
Coopersmith, S., 393
Corey, L., 104
Cornblath, D. R., 100
Cornell, D., 462
Corns, K. M., 487
Corrigan, R., 211, 212
Corse, A., 100
Corsini, R. J., 13
Corter, C., 488
Cortese, P., 176

Corwyn, R. F., 14, 555, 589
Cosey, E. J., 108
Cosmides, L., 67, 68
Costa, A. C., 78
Costigan, C. L., 355
Costin, S. E., 530
Cote, J. E., 398
Council of Economic Advisors, 492
Cowan, C. P., 122
Cowan, F., 110
Cowan, P. A., 122, 483
Cowley, G., 462
Cox, J. L., 121
Cox, M., 474
Cox, M. J., 474
Coyne, J. C., 357
Craik, F. I. M., 248
Crampton, P., 139
Crawford, M., 393, 424
Crick, N. R., 423
Crnic, K., 360
Crockenberg, S. B., 366, 393
Cromer, R., 325
Cronin, C., 139
Cronin, H., 67, 68
Crosby, D., 587
Cross, D., 261, *261*
Crossin, K. L., 77
Crouter, A. C., 473, 489
Crowley, K., 45, *45*
Crowley, M., 426
Croyle, R. T., 78
Crump, A. D., 195
Cruz, A. Z., 81
Csikszentmihalyi, M., 301
Cuca, Y. P., 189
Cullen, K., 177
Cullerton-Sen, C., 423
Cumberland, A. J., 453
Cummings, E. M., 347, 354
Cummings, M., 69
Cummings, M. R., 75
Cun, K., 336
Cunningham, D. J., 550
Cunningham, F. G., 113
Cupp, R., 549
Curran, K., 484
Curry, O., 67, 68
Curtin, S. C., 111, 191
Curtiss, S., 319
Cushner, K., 46
Cushner, K. H., 13, 588, 590
Cusson, R. M., 116
Cutler, G. B., 185
Cymerman, E., 331

Dabbs, J. M., Jr., 412
Dabholkar, A. S., 132, 133
Dahl, R. E., 174
Daily, D. K., 114
Dale, P. S., 330
Dalsgaard, S., 101
Damon, W., 197, 385, 389, 393, 449, 450, 451, 454, 456, 457
Dan, B., 138
Daniels, S. R., 178, 179
Danker, W. M., 105
Dann, S., 511
Darby, B. L., 101
Darlington, R., 548

Darney, P., 190
Darroch, J. E., 190
Darwin, C., 67
Das, J. P., 298
Dashe, J. S., 103
Dattilio, F. M., 46
D'Augelli, A. R., 529
Davenport, M. L., 78
Davidson, D., 247
Davidson, J. W., 300
Davidson, R. J., 364
Davidson, T., 418
Davies, K., 75
Davies, L. C., 496
Davis, E. P., 353
Davis, G., 553
Davis, K., 474
Davis, M. W., 140
Davis, O. K., 82
Davis, W. W., 175
Davis-Kean, P. E., 501
Davison, C. G., 178, 179
Davison, K. K., 177
Davisson, M. T., 78
Daws, D., 137
Day, J. D., 272
Day, N. L., 102
Day, R. D., 500, 503
Daye, C., 455
Dean, T., 112
Deane, S., 249
DeBaryshe, B. D., 460
DeCasper, A. J., 157, 158
deCharms, R., 566
Deci, E. L., 565, 566, 568
DeCourcey, W., 503
DeFries, J. C., 84, 86, 87
DeGarmo, D. S., 584
deHaan, M., 134
DeLamater, J., 188, 498
DeLamatre, M., 459
de la Rochebrochard, E., 107
del Castillo, V., 72
Delefosse, J., 232
DeLoache, J. S., 248, 265, 420
Deluca, P., 175
Demarest, J., 418
DeMarie-Dreblow, D., 248
Demetriou, A., 252
Demonet, J. F., 318
Dempster, F. N., 251, *251*
DeMulder, E., 349
Denbow, M. L., 115
Denham, S. A., 349, 479
Denmark, F. L., 55
Dennebaum, J. M., 549
Denney, C. B., 563
Denton, K., 549
Deppe, M., 172
Derom, C., 74
Derom, R., 74
Desai, J. J., 178
Dettmer, P., 564
Deutsch, G., 172
Deutscher, J., 177
Devich-Navarro, M., 401
de Villiers, J. G., 326
de Villiers, P. A., 326
deVries, B., 444
de Vries, L. S., 110
Dewey, J., 267, 453
de Wolff, M. S., 370
Dezolt, D. M., 416, 417, 423
Diamond, A., 173, 174, 253

Diamond, A. D., 212, 213
Diamond, L., 529, 531
Diamond, M., 412
Diaz, C., 13
Diaz, R. M., 232, 336
Diaz, T., 588
Dickerscheid, J. D., 427
Dickey, L. M., 336
Dickinson, D., 290
Diekman, A. B., 414
Dieter, J. N., 106
Dietrich, A. J., 121
Dillon, P., 496
Dinella, L., 419
DiPerna, J., 549
DiPietro, J. A., 83
Dishion, T., 195
Dittmer-Memahon, K., 143
Dittus, R. S., 108
Diversi, M., 15
Dix, T., 479
Dixon, R. L., 103
Dodge, K. A., 356, 460, 461, 495, 515
Doerksen, T., 107
Dolcini, M. M., 225
Domek, C. J., 511
Donaldson, M., 181
Donnelly, K., 102
Donnerstein, E., 596, 598, 599
Donovan, M., 139
Donovan, P., 190
Dorn, L. D., 185
Dornbusch, S., 553
Dornbusch, S. M., 589, 591
Dorr, A., 596
Dorval, B., 235
Douglas, W., 478
Douvan, E., 403
Dovey, S. M., 113
Dowd, J. M., 159
Dowda, M., 178
Dowler, J., 104
Dowling, D. A., 116–117
Dowling, M., 117
Downey, G., 357, 528
Doyle, L. W., 114, 138
Drager, B., 172
Drew, C. J., 563
Dricas, A. S., 400
Driscoll, J. W., 121
Droppleman, P. G., 140
Dryfoos, J. G., 176, 189, 191, 195
Duarte, J., 178
Dubé, E. M., 529
DuBois, D. L., 393, 530
Dubowitz, L. M., 110
DuCette, J., 484
Duck, S. W., 525
Dumka, L. E., 588
Dunbar, N., 389
Duncan, G., 361
Duncan, G. J., 499, 585, 586, 587
Duncan, K. R., 115
Duncker, K., 265
Dunham, D., 80
Dunkel-Schetter, C., 106
Dunn, E., 185
Dunn, J., 348, 479, 488, 496
Dunn, L., 547
Dunnewold, A., 122
Dunphy, D. C., 528
Dunsmore, K., 231
Duran, D., 336
Durham, M., 331

Durkin, K., 417, 418
DuRocher-Schudlich, T., 354
Durrant, J. E., 483
Durrant, R., 67, 74
Durston, S., 132, 174
Dusek, J. B., 392
Du Toit, D., 181
Dweck, C., 567, 569
Dwyer, T., 140
Dyck, N., 564
Dziedzic, K., 112

E

Eagle, M., 31
Eagly, A. H., 307, 414, 423, 424, 426
Easterbrooks, M. A., 371, 373
Eaton, M., 415
Eaves, L. J., 74
Eccles, J. S., 13, 565, 567, 569, 570
Echols, K., 265
Edelman, G. M., 77
Edelman, M. W., 15, 585
Edelstein, W., 444
Eden, G. F., 561
Educational Testing Service, 570
Edwards, C. P., 476, 498
Egan, M. W., 563
Egeland, B., 20, 371, 475, 485
Eggebeen, D., 494
Eggebeen, D. J., 373
Egozcue, J., 72
Ehrhardt, A. A., 411
Ehrlich, R., 181
Eidelman, A. I., 116, 118
Eiferman, R. R., 521
Eiger, M. S., 140
Einarson, T., 101
Eisen, S., 358
Eisenberg, N., 348, 353, 364, 423, 442, 449, 451, 453, 457, 479
Eisenstein, J., 484
Eitel, P., 195
Ekbom, A., 101
Eken, P., 110
Ekwo, E. E., 106
Elder, G. H., 477, 478
El-Ghobashy, A. A., 82
Elicker, J., 232
Elkind, D., 217, 219, 224, 225, 226, 544, 581
Elliott, E., 567
Elliott, G. R., 196
Elliott, M. E., 371
Ellis, B., 67, 74
Ellis, H. C., 248, 249
Elmes, D. G., 44
El-Taliawy, T., 427
Emde, R. N., 352
Emery, R. E., 496
Engel, C., 180
Engel, W., 72
England, L. J., 114
Engle, P. L., 142
Engler, A. J., 116
Englert, C. S., 231
Enoch, M. A., 101
Enright, R. D., 400
Epstein, J. A., 588
Erdem, A., 81
Erdem, M., 81
Erera, P., 503
ERIC/EECE, 549

Erickson, J. D., 105
Erickson, L. G., 272
Ericsson, K. A., 255, 300
Erikson, E. H., 31, 32, 46, 369, 395, 396, 397, 401, 403, 412, 460
Erkut, S., 591
Erlick, A. C., 584
Ernst, T., 102
Ertil, T., 490
Eschuzur, J., 55
Eskandari, R., 81
Eskenazi, B., 78, 82, 101
Eskes, M., 111
Espelage, D. L., 516
Espinosa, L., 336
Etaugh, C., 55
Etteman, J., 418
Etzel, R., 175, 181
Evans, A. C., 173
Evans, B. J., 590
Eyssell, K. M., 55
Ezra, Y., 96

F

Faber, T., 15
Fabes, R. A., 348, 364, 423, 451, 453, 479, 517
Fabricius, W. V., 248
Fagan, J., 102
Fagan, J. F., 295
Fagot, B. I., 415
Fairburn, C. G., 179
Falbo, T., 488
Famy, C., 101
Fan, X., 83
Fang, F., 444
Fang, G., 444
Fang, J., 115
Fang, X., 525
Fantz, R. L., 153, 154, *154*
Faraone, S. V., 422, 563
Farhi, J., 82
Farrington, D. P., 459
Fasoliotis, S. J., 96
Fawcett, L. B., 99
Fegley, S., 457
Feher, L. A., 400
Feig, D. S., 96
Fein, G. G., 104, 520, 548
Feiring, C., 531
Feivelson, D., 190
Feldhusen, J., 299
Feldman, D. H., 299
Feldman, J. F., 74
Feldman, N. S., 388
Feldman, R., 116, 118
Feldman, S. S., 188, 189, 191, 196, 460
Felner, R. D., 393
Feng, H. L., 82
Fennema-Notetine, C., 101
Fenson, L., 330
Fenwick, K. D., 158
Ferguson, D. L., 401
Ferguson, D. M., 140, 358
Fernald, A., 353
Fernald, I., 141
Fernandes, O., 101
Ferrer-Wreder, L., 401
Ferron, J., 586
Field, A. E., 178
Field, D. E., 246
Field, T. M., 10, 106, 116, 117, 154, 155, 245, 266, 484

Fielding, J. E., 547
Fields, C. B., 180
Fields, R., 107
Fifer, B., 102
Fifer, W. P., 105
Figueroa, Z., 116
Finlay, B., 142, 182
Finley, K. A., 175
Finnegan, L. P., 102
Firlik, R., 540
Fisch, R. O., 123, 158
Fisch, S. M., 594
Fischer, K. W., 134
Fisher, P. A., 473
Fisher-Thompson, D., 415
Fisk, N. M., 115
Fitzgerald, J. F., 108
Fixler, J., 79
Flannery, D. J., 114
Flavell, J. H., 207, 228, 243, 247, 248, 250, 261, 270, 271
Flegal, K. M., 177
Fleming, J. E., 357
Flick, L., 139
Floel, A., 172
Flohr, J. W., 158
Flood, P., 569
Flores, D. L., 121
Floris, M., 81
Florsheim, P., 528
Flynn, J. R., 305
Foege, W., 183
Foehr, U. G., 599
Fogel, A., 101, 473
Fogel, J., 10
Fok, T. F., 177
Folkman, S., 361
Follansbee, D. J., 401
Ford, K., 190
Ford, L., 386
Fordham, S., 530
Forgatch, M. S., 584
Forget, S., 99
Forman, E. R., 391
Forrest, J. D., 190
Fossella, J. A., 132, 174
Foster, E., 191
Fountain, L., 82
Fowler, J. A., 175
Fox, B., 334
Fox, C. E. R., 357
Fox, M. B., 357
Fox, N. A., 135
Frady, R. I., 412
Fraga, C. G., 107
Fraiberg, S., 148
Francis, J., 400
Franco, P., 138
Frank, D. A., 102
Franz, C. E., 365, 503
Fraser, G., 400
Fraser, S., 307
Frayling, T. M., 99
Frederikse, M., 422
Fredrickson, D. D., 140
Freedman, J. L., 596
Freeman, D., 580
Freeman, K. E., 265
Freie, C., 555
Freimer, M., 100
French, S. A., 178
Freud, A., 511
Freud, S., 30
Frezzo, T. M., 80

Frias, J. L., 78
Fried, P. A., 101, 102
Friedman, D. L., 181
Friedman, J., 348
Friedman, S. L., 555
Friedrichs, A., 271
Friend, M., 564
Frieze, I. H., 55
Frieze, I. R., 531
Frodi, A. M., 373
Frodi, M., 373
Frohna, J. G., 139
Frost, F., 418
Frye, D., 270
Fryer, G. E., 113
Fukuda, M., 117
Fuligni, A. J., 13
Fuller, M., 530
Fuller, M. L., 558
Fullerton, J., 111
Fullilove, M. T., 547
Furman, W., 475, 523, 528, 531
Furstenberg, F., 191
Furstenberg, F. F., 496
Furth, H. G., 220, 326
Fussell, E., 427

G

Gaensbauer, T. G., 352
Galambos, N. L., 355, 494
Galbraith, K. A., 189
Gall, J. P., 54
Gall, M. D., 54
Galler, A., 177
Gallimore, R., 234
Gallup, A. M., 45
Galperyn, K., 443
Galvez, R., 87
Gamst, A., 101
Ganiban, J., 372, 485
Gao, Y., 371
Gao, Y. T., 107
Garbarino, J., 462, 585
Garber, J., 356
Garcia, E., 336
Garcia, E. E., 336
Garcia, H. A. V., 591
Garcia, L., 385
Garcia, R., 10, 117, 337
Garcia-Bournissen, F., 96
Garcia-Mila, M., 270
Garcia-Velasco, J. A., 82
Gard, J. W., 112
Gardiner, K., 78
Gardner, H., 280, 281, 290, 293, 301
Gardner, L. I., 170
Gargiullo, P. M., 114
Garmezy, N., 16, 393
Garner, D. M., 178
Garofalo, R., 531
Garrett, P., 586
Garrod, A. C., 444
Gat, I., 596
Gay, H., 105
Gazzaniga, M. S., 318
Ge, X., 195, 491
Gearhart, J. P., 412
Geary, D. C., 68
Gebelt, J. L., 193
Gehl, K. S., 265
Gelfand, D. M., 357

Gelman, R., 218, 219, 229, 260, 332
Gelman, S. A., 216
Geltman, P. L., 181
Gennetian, L. A., 587
George, C., 490
Gergen, P. J., 175
Germino-Hausken, E., 549
Gershoff, E. T., 483
Geschwind, N., 172
Gesell, A. L., 8, 151, 295
Gewirtz, J., 351
Ghugre, P., 105
Gibbons, J. L., 427
Gibbs, J., 440, 442
Gibbs, J. T., 287, 570, 585
Gibson, C., 587
Gibson, E. J., 152, 153, 156, *156*, 214
Gibson, J. H., 140
Gibson, J. J., 152
Gibson, R., 140
Giedd, J. N., 173
Gielchinsky, Y., 96
Gilbride, K., 102
Giles-Sims, J., 483
Gill, A. G., 557
Gilligan, C., 55, 403, 443, 444, 445, *445*, 510
Gilliland, A. L., 112
Gilstrap, L. L., 305
Gingras, J. L., 102
Giordano, R., 443
Gjerde, P. F., 475
Glantz, S. A., 102
Gleason, J. B., 323
Glei, D. A., 190
Glezerman, M., 82
Glucksberg, S., 514
Godfrey, R., 140
Goelman, H., 543
Goffin, S. G., 544
Goffinet, F., 112
Gojdamaschko, N., 235
Golant, S. K., 116
Goldberg, J., 252, 358
Golden, M. H., 484
Golding, S., 110
Goldin-Meadow, S., 326
Goldman, D., 101
Goldman-Rakic, P. S., 174
Goldschmidt, L., 102
Goldsmith, D., 137
Goldsmith, H. H., 364, 365
Goldstein, J., 82
Goldstein, J. M., 422
Goldstein-Ferber, S., 10
Goldwater, P. N., 138
Goleman, D., 291, 293, 302
Golombok, S., 83, *83*, 498
Gomez, M. I., 141
Gonzales, E. J., 571
Gonzales, N. A., 588
Gonzalez-del Angel, A. A., 72
Good, M., 116–117
Goodenbough, D. R., 78
Goodman, E., 83, *83*, 531
Goodman, G. S., 156
Goodman, R. A., 193
Goodnow, J. J., 478
Goodstadt, L., 75
Gopnik, A., 214, 326
Gordon, A. S., 492
Gordon, B. N., 357
Gordon, L., 515
Gorman, K. S., 142
Gorman-Smith, D., 460

Gosling, S. D., 393
Goto, S. G., 582
Gottesman, I. I., 365
Gottfried, A. E., 11, 494
Gottfried, A. W., 11, 494
Gottlieb, G., 20, 74, 77, 86
Gottman, J. M., 348, 479, 522
Gould, S. J., 69
Goulet, P., 319
Gouzaousasis, P., 543
Graber, J. A., 178, 188, 397
Graham, S., 55, 570
Granath, F., 101
Grander, R., 587
Grant, J. P., 130, 141
Grant, K. E., 357
Grantham-McGregor, S., 141
Graue, M. E., 549
Gravholt, C. H., 78
Gray, J., 490
Graziano, W. G., 348
Green, L. A., 113
Greenberg, M. T., 10, 16, 490
Greenberg, R., 266
Greenberger, E., 554
Greene, D., 566
Greene, J. W., 192
Greene, M. E., 427
Greene, S. M., 497
Greeno, J. G., 35
Greenough, W. T., 87, 134, 136
Grelotti, D. J., 325
Greven, P., 482
Grief, J., 116
Grigorenko, E. L., 87, 103, 303, 304, 561
Grigoriadis, S., 121
Gringlas, M. B., 498
Grining, C. P. L., 375
Grizzle, N., 117
Grodzinsky, Y., 319
Groenendaal, F., 110
Grolnick, W. S., 353
Grose-Fifer, J., 102
Gross, J. N., 449
Grossman, J. B., 12
Grossmann, K., 372
Grossmann, K. E., 372
Grosswasser, U., 138
Groswasser, J., 138
Grotevant, H. D., 83, 400, 491
Grove, K., 56
Grove, S. K., 79
Gruber, S. A., 173
Grumer-Strawn, L. M., 140
Grych, J. H., 474
Guerra, S., 178
Guilford, J. P., 301
Guiz-Pelaez, J. G., 116
Gulotta, T. P., 397
Gunnar, M. R., 158, 353
Gunter, B., 594
Gur, R. C., 422
Gur, R. E., 422
Gursen, M. D., 588
Gurung, R. A. R., 106
Gurwitch, R. H., 362
Gutherie, I. K., 348, 364, 423, 453
Guttentag, M., 425
Guyer, B., 114
Gyamfi, P., 498

H

Hack, M., 114, 115
Hackler, L., 75
Hagekull, B., 352
Hagen, J. W., 248
Hahn, C. S., 83
Hahn, D. B., 10
Hahn, W. K., 135
Hahn-Zoric, M., 139
Haidt, J. D., 444
Haig, D., 72
Haight, W., 132
Haith, D. L., 251
Haith, M. H., 153
Haith, M. M., 145, 156, 228
Hake, J. L., 158
Hakuta, K., 314, 320, 336, 337
Haladyna, T. M., 286
Hale, S., 252
Hall, G. S., 9, 355
Hall, M. A., 334
Hall, N. W., 10, 15
Hall, R. T., 114
Hallahan, D. P., 298, 560, 561
Halle, T. G., 347, 348
Halliday, J., 138
Halonen, J., 583, 590
Halpern, D., 422
Halpern, D. F., 303
Halsted, N., 158
Halwes, T. G., 250
Ham, Y. M., 367
Hamburg, D. A., 176, 455
Hamilton, M. C., 415
Hammond, C. S., 121
Hammond, S., 181
Hamre, B., 329, 335
Han, D. S., 100
Han, W., 494
Han, W. J., 494
Hand, I. L., 102
Hanefeld, F., 72
Hannon, W. H., 114
Hansen, D. J., 485
Hansen, L. A., 100
Hansen, R., 367
Hanson, L. A., 139, 140
Hardman, M. L., 563
Hardy, J. B., 189
Hare, B. R., 589
Harel, S., 114
Harkness, S., 137, 372, 498
Harlow, H. F., 368, 511
Harmon, R. J., 352
Harnishfeger, K. K., 250
Harpalani, V., 401
Harries, M., 140
Harris, G., 159
Harris, J. R., 87, *87*, 486
Harris, L., 179, 188, 494
Harris, M., 477
Harrison, P. J., 179
Harrist, A. W., 473
Harstad, T. W., 104
Hart, B., 321, 324, 331
Hart, C. H., 474, 481, 482, 498, 513, 545
Hart, D., 385, 389, 390, 455, 456, 457
Harter, S., 358, 384, 385, 387, 388, 389, 392, 393, 394, 400, 401, 445, 567
Hartshorne, H., 447
Hartup, W. W., 87, 512, 514, 515, 516, 523–524
Harwood, L. J., 140

Harwood, R., 589
Haselager, G. J. T., 516
Hashemi, F., 117
Hastings, P. D., 366
Hatfield, E., 424
Hattersley, A. T., 99
Hattersley, J., 138
Hauck, F. R., 139
Hauser, S. T., 401
Hauth, J. C., 113
Haversen, L., 139
Havighurst, R. L., 580
Hawkins, J. A., 552
Hay, P., 179
Haynes, N. M., 558
Haynes, V. L., 102
Haynie, D. L., 195
Hazen, C., 156
Heath, D. H., 502
Heath, S. B., 231, 402
Hecht, S. S., 101
Heekeren, H. R., 318
Heeren, T., 102
Hefferman, K., 415
Heilman, A. W., 334
Heilman, P. C., 562
Helbock, H. J., 107
Held, R., 149
Hellenbrand, K., 82
Hellige, J. B., 319
Helm, K. K., 139
Helmreich, R., 425
Henderson, V. K., 474
Hendrick, V. C., 121
Hendricks, E., 501
Hendry, J., 489
Henkel, R. R., 516
Hennessey, B. A., 302, 565
Hennig, K. H., 442, 452
Hennighausen, K. H., 476
Henninger, M. L., 545
Henningsen, H., 172
Henry, D. B., 460
Henshaw, S., 191
Henteleff, T., 117
Hepper, P. G., 172
Herman, C. P., 177
Herman, S. M., 139
Hernandez-Reif, M., 106, 117, 154, 155, 245
Herrera, C., 353
Herrill, R., 358
Herrnstein, R. J., 306, *306*
Herzog, E., 416
Hess, L., 448
Hetherington, E. M., 10, 41, 86, 87, 365, 495, *495*, 496, 497
Heuwinkel, M. K., 226
Heyne, T., 116
Hibbard, D., 523
Hickman, S., 423
Hiebert, E. H., 335
Higgins, A., 455
Hildebrand, V., 548
Hill, C. R., 477
Hill, J., 494
Hill, J. O, 178
Hill, N. E., 586
Himel, N., 560
Himmetogulu, O., 81
Himmin, H. S., 427
Hines, M., 412
Hines, R. P., 548
Hinkley, C., 112
Hirchhorn, K., 78

Hirsch, B. J., 530, 552
Hobel, C. J., 106
Hochschild, A. R., 354
Hockenberry, M., 111, 170
Hockenberry-Eaton, M., 181
Hodges, E. A., 178
Hodgman, J. E., 114
Hoefs, M., 490
Hofer, B. K., 571
Hoff, E., 499, 584
Hofferth, S. L., 501
Hoff-Ginsberg, E., 331
Hoffman, H. J., 139
Hoffman, H. R., 594
Hoffman, L. W., 493, 494
Hoffman, M. L., 452, 453
Hoffman, S., 191
Hoffnung, M., 500
Hofman, M. A., 422
Hofstede, G., 581
Hogan, K., 271
Hogarty, P. S., 297
Hohne, E. A., 327–328
Holden, J. M., 121
Holding, S., 106
Hollier, L. M., 104
Holmbeck, G. N., 491
Holmes, D. L., 251
Holmes, L. D., 580
Holt, M. K., 516
Holtzen, D. W., 172
Holtzmann, W., 581
Honein, M. A., 105
Honig, A. S., 11
Honzik, M. P., 296
Hood, B., 155–156
Hooven, C., 348, 479
Hopkins, B., 149
Hopkins, J. R., 32, 33
Hoppu, U., 140
Horne, R. S., 138
Horowitz, F. D., 15
Hort, B. E., 419
Horton, N. J., 422
Horvath, D. L., 498
Horwood, L. J., 358
Hosch, H. M., 258
Hotchner, T., 112
Hoving, K. L., 251
Howard, K. I., 196
Howard, R. W., 305
Howe, G. W., 365
Howe, M. J. A., 300
Howell, C. J., 112
Howell, E. M., 108
Howell, S., 248
Howes, C., 375, 376, 513–514
Hoyle, R. H., 44, 54
Hoyt, J., 271
Hoza, B., 524
Hsu, C., 571
Hsu, J., 400
Huang, L. N., 287, 578, 585
Huang, M. L., 104
Hudson, L. M., 391
Huebner, A. M., 444
Huesmann, L. R., 595, 596
Huffman, K. J., 68
Huffman, L. R., 545
Hughey, J. B., 335
Hull, M., 334
Hull, S. H., 416, 417, 423
Hulse, G. K., 103
Humenick, S. S., 107
Hunsley, M., 138

Hunt, E., 294
Hunt, R. R., 248, 249
Hunt, S. P., 77
Huppke, P., 72
Hurrelmann, K., 175
Hurtado, A., 417
Huston, A. C., 375, 415, 416, 418, 555, 586, 587,
    594, 597
Hutchins, G., 418
Huttenlocher, J., 132, 331
Huttenlocher, P. R., 132, 133
Hwant, C. P., 373
Hyde, J. S., 55, 307, 393, 422, 445, 498
Hyman, I. A., 484

I

Iacono, W. G., 303
Ibba, R. M., 81
Iki, M., 140
Ilersich, A. L., 158
Inhelder, B., 215
Inoff-Germain, G., 185
Insabella, G. M., 496, 497
International Society for Technology in Education, 599
Irby, M., 15
Ireland, M., 358
Irlen, S., 596
Irvan, S. A., 87
Irwin, C. E., 225
Isasa, V., 82
Ishunina, T. A., 422
Isolauri, E., 140
Issacs, P., 563
Ivry, R. B., 318
Izard, C., 346

J

Jaakkola, J. J., 181
Jacklin, C. N., 416, 422
Jackson, A., 553
Jackson, A. P., 498
Jackson, G. L., 103
Jackson, J. F., 389
Jacob, N., 74
Jacob, R. A., 107
Jacobs, R. R., 102
Jacobsen, I., 288
Jacobsen, S. W., 101
Jacobson, A. M., 401
Jacobson, J. L., 104
Jacobson, L., 584
Jacobson, S. W., 104
Jacobvitz, D., 485
Jaffe, J., 473
Jaffee, S., 445
Jaffee, S. R., 191
Jain, N., 103
James, W., 153
Jang, C. S., 181
Jarrett, R. L., 586
Jeffery, H. E., 138
Jeffery, R. W., 178
Jeffries, N. O., 173
Jenkins, J. M., 261
Jensen, A. R., 303, 306
Jensen, L. A., 444
Jensen, S. J., 346
Jernigan, T. L., 101
Jessor, R., 175

Ji, B. T., 107
Ji, G., 488
Jiao, S., 488
Jin, F., 107
Jin, S., 498
Jin, S. H., 100
Jing, Q., 488
Jinon, S., 10
Jirtle, R. L., 72
Joanette, Y., 319
Jodl, K. M., 490, 496
Johanson, R. B., 112
Johnson, A. L., 102
Johnson, C., 563
Johnson, D., 503
Johnson, D. W., 454
Johnson, G. B., 67
Johnson, J. E., 521, 522
Johnson, K. C., 102
Johnson, M. H., 135, 136
Johnson, M. K., 455
Johnson, P., 111
Johnson, S., 336, *337*
Johnson, S. B., 81
Johnson, S. M., 487
Johnson-Ray, R., 385
John-Steiner, V., 541
Johnston, D. W., 106
Johnston, J., 418
Johnston, L. D., 192, *192*, 193, 194, 195
Johnston, L. P., 450
Jones, D. C., 530
Jones, G., 140
Jones, J. M., 570, 590
Jones, M. C., 187
Jones, N. A., 106
Jones, P. W., 112
Jones, S., 348
Jones, T. G., 558
Jordaan, E., 181
Joseph, C. L. M., 108
Joshi, H., 586
Joyner, E. T., 558
Joyner, K., 358, 528
Judd, C. M., 44, 54
Judge, P., 157
Jusczyk, P. W., 158, 327–328
Juul, S., 78

K

Kabat, S., 117
Kagan, J., 20, 73, 87, 352, 364, 366, 372, 375
Kagan, S., 581
Kagitcibasi, C., 582
Kahn, A., 138
Kahn, J. V., 45
Kail, R., 252
Kaiser Family Foundation, 598, 599
Kalelkar, M., 139
Kalliomaki, M., 140
Kamii, C., 227
Kammerman, S. B., 374
Kane, M. J., 265
Kanoy, K., 474
Kantowitz, B. H., 44
Kapellen, T., 177
Kaplan, N., 490
Karikas, G. A., 79
Karmel, M. P., 385
Karp, J. S., 422
Kassin, S. M., 258
Kastelic, D., 387

Katz, J., 158
Katz, L., 547, 550
Katz, L. F., 348, 479
Katz, P. A., 436
Kauffman Early Education Exchange, 549
Kauffman, J. M., 298
Kaufman, G., 101
Kaufman, J., 553
Kaufman, P., 291, 302, 553
Kaugers, A. S., 102
Kawai, M., 473
Kayihan, H., 78
Keane, R., 114
Kearsley, R. B., 352, 375
Keating, B., 143
Kee, D. W., 248
Keelnan, T., 490
Keenan, K., 459
Keener, D. C., 489
Keeney, T. J., 248
Kees, M., 362
Kegeles, S. M., 225
Keiffer, J., 259
Keith, B., 495
Kelleher, K. J., 121
Keller, A., 386
Keller, M., 444
Kelly, D. L., 571
Kelly, E. A., 114
Kelly, J., 10, 497
Kelly, J. B., 496
Kelly, R. E. S., 249
Kelm, J., 180
Kelmanson, I., 138
Kelsey, K. T., 194
Kemp, J. S., 139
Kemper, K. J., 121
Kendrick, C., 488
Kendrick, J. S., 114
Kendrick, M., 543
Kennedy, D. N., 422
Kennedy, H. P., 121
Kennedy, S. H., 121
Kennell, H. H., 123
Kennell, J. H., 112, 122
Kenrick, D. T., 68
Keogh, D. A., 191
Kessen, W., 145
Kessler, E. P., 180
Kharrazi, M., 101
Khazan, I., 503
Khoury, E., 557
Kidd, S., 78
Kiely, J. L., 101
Kiernan, K. E., 496
Kiess, W., 177
Kilbride, H. W., 114
Kilmer, S. L., 490
Kim, M., 102, 367
Kim, T. I., 100
Kim, W. H., 100
Kimm, S. Y., 177, 178, 179, 180
Kimura, D., 412, 422
Kindel, A. M., 543
Kingsley, B., 181
Kinzer, C. K., 334
Kiosseoglou, G., 172
Kirchner, G. L., 101
Kisilevsky, B. S., 157
Kisker, E., 375
Kitamura, S., 571
Kitayama, S., 389
Kite, M., 420
Klapper, P., 104
Klaus, M., 123

Klaus, M. H., 112
Klaus, P. H., 112
Klebanov, P. K., 586
Klein, L., 351
Klein, N., 114, 115
Klein, R. E., 141
Kleiverda, G., 111
Klesges, L. M., 102
Kling, K. C., 393
Klintsova, A. Y., 87
Klug, W. S., 75
Klumb, D., 515
Knecht, S., 172
Knight, G. P., 449, 588
Knight, W. G., 102
Knoester, C., 373
Kochanska, G., 365, 449
Kodituwakku, P. W., 101
Koestner, R., 503, 565
Koh, J., 543
Kohlberg, L., 55, 419, 437, 438, *438*, 439, 440, *441*, 442, 448, 454, 455
Kohnstamm, G. A., 364
Kolbe, L. J., 175, 176
Kolts, R., 193
Koniak-Griffin, D., 191
Kontos, S., 547
Kopp, C. B., 114, 353
Koren, G., 96, 99, 101, 158
Korn, W. S., 450
Korotkova, A., 139, 140
Kortenhaus, C. M., 418
Koslosky, G., 117
Koss-Chiono, J., 11
Kotler, J. A., 594
Kotovsky, L., 213
Kottak, C. P., 582
Kovach, R., 273, 569
Kozol, J., 555, 556, *556*
Kozulin, A., 35, 230, 232
Kramer, M. S., 105, 140
Krampe, R. T., 255, 300
Krasilnikoff, P. A., 107
Krasnegor, J., 117
Krasnegor, N. A., 297
Kratzch, J., 177
Krauss, R. A., 514
Krettenauer, T., 442, 452
Kreutzer, M., 271
Kreye, M., 352
Krile, D., 391
Krimer, L. S., 174
Kroger, J., 398
Krogh, H. R., 421
Kronsberg, S. S., 178, 179
Kroonenberg, P. M., 372, *372*
Krowitz, A., 156
Kruger, M., 106
Kruijver, F. P., 422
Krulewitch, C. J., 82
Krushel, L., 77
Kucera, E., 487
Kuczaj, S. A., 354
Kuczynski, L., 482
Kuebli, J., 353, 354
Kuhl, P. K., 327, *327*
Kuhn, C. M., 10, 117
Kuhn, D., 214, 268, 270, 271
Kulberg, J. M., 549
Kulbok, P. A., 175
Kulig, J. W., 159
Kulik, J. A., 286
Kulik, R. L., 286
Kumari, A. S., 105
Kuo, J., 102

Kupermine, G. P., 490
Kupersmidt, J. B., 516
Kurdek, L. A., 391
Kurland, D. M., 252
Kurtines, W., 401
Kusumoto, T., 117
Kwak, H. K., 367

L

Laccone, F., 72
Lackmann, G. M., 101
Lacoste, H., 81
Ladd, G. W., 12, 481, 511, 512, 513, 516
Ladewig, P. W., 140
LaGasse, L., 102
La Greca, A. M., 362
Laiho, K., 140
Lamb, M. E., 21, 123, 373, 376, 415, 500, 503
Lamb, S., 449
Lambert, S. B., 104
Lambertz, G., 158
Lampman-Petraitis, C., 355
Land, D. J., 490
Landry, S. H., 473
Lang, C. E., 139
Lang, R., 83
Langer, A., 156
Langer, L. L., 257
Langley-Evans, A. J., 105
Langley-Evans, S. C., 105
Langston, W., 44
Lanier, D., 113
Lanzi, R. G., 304
Lapsley, D. K., 225, 398–399, 400, 440, 443, 445
Larner, M. B., 562
LaRose, R., 418
Larsen, R. J., 68
Larson, R., 355, *355*, 491
Larson, R. W., 427, 428, 498, 532
Larzelere, R. E., 483
Lasko, D., 117
Laumann-Billings, L., 496
Laursen, B., 499, 584
Lautrey, J., 281
LaVoie, J., 403
Layzer, J., 556, 587
Lazar, L., 548
Lazarus, R. S., 361
Leadbeater, B. J. R., 191
Leaper, C., 419
Learner-Centered Principles Work Group, 541
Lears, M. K., 102
Lecanuet, J. P., 106
Lee, L., 388
Lee, S., 571, *571*
Leffert, N., 584
Leger, A., 318
Leggett, E., 567, 569
Lehrer, R., 270
Leifer, A. D., 596
Leinbach, M. D., 419
LeMare, L. J., 515
Lenders, C. M., 106
Lenneberg, E., 319, 325
Lenoir, C. P., 138
Leonard, C., 271
Leong, F. T. L., 592
Leo-Summers, L., 82
Lepkowski, J., 190
Lepper, M., 566
Lerman-Sagie, T., 114
Lerner, R., 8

Lerner, S., 331
LeSeiur, K., 481
Lesser, J., 191
Lester, B., 109
Lester, B. M., 102, 115, 118
Lester, R. A., 104
Leu, D. J., 334
Leung, D. W., 563
Le Vay, S., 422
Leveno, K. J., 118
Leventhal, A., 527
Leventhal, J. M., 107
Leventhal, T., 361
Levesque, J., 455
Levin, J. R., 249
Levine, A., 355
Levine, C., 398
LeVine, R. A., 580
Levine, S., 331
Levitas, J., 349
Leviton, A., 103
Levran, D., 82
Levy, F., 554
Levy, G. D., 419
Levy, T. M., 372
Lewis, C., 514
Lewis, J. F., 287
Lewis, J. M., 474
Lewis, M., 143, 350, 352, 355, 372, 385
Lewis, R., 71, 72, 78, 302
Lewis, R. J., 190
Leyendecker, B., 589
Li, A. M., 177
Li, N. P., 68
Li, T. K., 101
Li, Z. L., 82
Liaw, J. J., 115
Liben, L. S., 421
Lickliter, R., 77, 86
Liebergott, J., 329
Lieberman, M., 440
Lifshitz, F., 139
Lifter, K., 328
Lightwood, J. M., 102
Limber, S. P., 15, 516
Lin, H., 82
Lin, M., 449
Lindberg, M. A., 259
Lindbohm, M., 107
Lindholm, J. A., 450
Lindsey, D. S., 259
Linebarger, D. L., 597
Linet, M. S., 107
Linnett, K. M., 101
Lippa, R. A., 411, 412, 413, 429
Lipsitz, J., 494, 552
Lipton, M., 12
Lipworth, L., 105
Liu, H., 173
Liu, W., 476
Livesly, W., 386
Ljunger, E., 101
Llijper, F. M., 103
Lobel, M., 106
Locke, E. A., 568
Lockhart, R. S., 248
Loebel, M., 106
Loeber, R., 459
Loebl, J. H., 388
Loehlin, J. C., 303
Loftus, E. F., 259
Lohmann, H., 172
Lohr, K. N., 190
Lohr, M. J., 527
Lollis, S., 482

Lomax, T., 180
London, B., 455, 456
London, M. L., 140
Long, L., 494
Long, T., 494
Lonky, E., 448
Lonner, W. J., 582
Loomis, L., 549
Lopez, E., 389
Lorch, E. P., 246
Lorene, C. C., 401
Loriaux, D. L., 185
Lo Russo, D., 121
Loso, J., 67
Losoya, S. H., 453
Lott, B., 414
Lowe, X., 78
Loya, F., 193
Lu, A., 422
Lu, J., 102
Lubert, T. I., 281
Lubinski, D., 294
Lucas, F. L., 185
Lucking, L., 112
Ludington-Hoe, S. M., 116, 117
Luffy, R., 79
Luna, P., 72
Lundgren, S., 101
Lunsteen, C., 78
Lunt, M., 140
Luo, Q., 525
Luretti, A., 373
Luria, A., 416
Lykken, D. T., 66, 303
Lyle, J., 594
Lynn, R., 306
Lyon, G. R., 560, 561, 562
Lyon, T. D., 271
Lyons, M., 358
Lyons, T., 132

Maas, J. B., 138
McAdoo, H. P., 14, 498–499, 589
McAleer, J. L., 594
McAuliffe, T. L., 143
McCabe, M. P., 186
McCall, R. B., 297
MacCallum, F., 83, *83*
McCarton, C. M., 74
McCarty, M. E., 149
McClelland, A., 588
McClelland, D., 503
McClelland, D. C., 565
Maccoby, E. E., 11, 86, 87, 347, 373, 413, 416, 422, 476, 477, 482, 496, 513, 517, 525
McCombs, B. L., 568
McConnell, M., 503
McCormick, C. B., 249, 271
McCormick, M. C., 107
MacCorquodale, P., 188
MacDonald, D., 173
McDonald, P. V., 150
McDonough, L., 253
MacDorman, M. F., 111, 114
McElhaney, K. B., 490
McElrath, T. F., 106
McFarland, C., 490
MacFarlane, J. A., 158, *158*
MacFarlane, J. W., 296
MacGowan, C., 140

McGrath, S., 112
McGrath, S. K., 122
McGue, M. K., 66, 83, 303
McGuire, S., 84
McHale, J., 503
McHale, J. P., 373
McHale, S. M., 489
McHargue, L., 116
Macias, M., 72
McIntire, D. D., 118
McIntyre, J. G., 392
McKenna, J. J., 137
MacKenzie, I. Z., 113
McLaughlin, J. K., 101
McLaughlin, M. W., 402
MacLean, W. E., 78
McLoyd, V. C., 13, 361, 375, 483, 522, 556, 570, 584, 586, 587, 588, 590, 591
McMahon, R. P., 178, 179
McMillan, J. H., 43, 286
McNally, D., 569
McNamara, F., 138
McRee, J. N., 193
McRoy, R. G., 83
McSharry, J., 82
McSherry, G. D., 105
McVeigh, C. A., 122
McVeigh, T. J., 102
MacWhinney, B., 320
Maddux, J., 568
Maddux, J. E., 175
Mader, S. S., 86
Madhaven, S., 115
Madsen, M. C., 581
Madsen, S. D., 477
Maehr, M. L., 567
Maggs, J. L., 175, 494
Magnum, G. R., 318
Magnus, P., 181
Magnuson, K. A., 499, 585, 587
Magnusson, D., 187, 525
Magrini, N., 99
Mahn, H., 541
Mahoney, K. M., 450
Main, M., 371, 490
Maizels, M., 143
Majhanovich, S., 593
Major, B., 393
Makrides, M., 140
Makris, N., 422
Malinosky-Rummell, R., 485
Mallet, E., 138
Malone, S., 158
Maluso, D., 414
Mandleco, B. L., 474
Mandler, G., 250
Mandler, J. M., 214, 253
Mangrum, C. T., 562
Mannessier, L., 103
Mannino, D. M., 181
Manring, A., 598
Mansfield, A. F., 270
Manzano, J., 121
Marano, N., 102
Maratsos, M., 316
March, P., 490
Marchant, G. J., 565
Marcia, J. E., 398, 399, 400
Marcus, D. L., 134
Marcus, W., 555
Margolin, L., 485
Marín, G., 13
Mark, E. J., 194
Markman, E. M., 328
Markowitz, M., 103

Markus, H. R., 388, 389
Marold, D. B., 388, 393
Marshall, T. R., 351
Marsiglio, W., 503
Martell, L. K., 499
Martin, C. L., 419, 423, 517
Martin, D. C., 101
Martin, J. A., 111, 482
Martin, M. O., 571
Martin, N. C., 388
Martinez, C. R., 584
Martinez, I., 72
Martinez, P., 357
Martinez-Pasarell, O., 72
Martorano, S., 225
Martorell, R., 142
Masten, A. S., 16
Mastroiacovo, P., 99
Matas, L., 352
Matheny, A. P., 365
Mathes, P. G., 335
Mathews, T. J., 105, 111
Mathison, K., 490
Matlin, M. W., 418, 499
Matsumoto, D., 13, 579, 580
Matthews, W. S., 415
Matthiesen, A. S., 112
Mattsby-Baltzer, I., 139
Mattson, S. N., 101
Matusov, E., 234
Maughan, A., 485
Maulik, D., 103
Maurer, D., 155
Maurer, K. R., 175
Mauro, V. P., 77
Maxon, S., 74
May, M. S., 447
Mayaux, M. J., 106
Mayer, J. D., 293
Mayer, R. E., 256, 268
Mayhew, T. M., 101
Maza, P. L., 102
Meacham, J., 386
Mead, M., 478, 580, *580*
Medd, S. E., 563
Medin, D. L., 260
Mednick, S. A., 78
Meece, D. W., 495
Meece, J., 550
Megevand, A., 138
Mehler, J., 158
Meiners, L. C., 110
Meins, M., 72
Mekos, D., 194
Melamed, B. G., 10
Meltzoff, A. N., 213, 214, 228, 266, *266*, 267, 326
Memon, A., 258
Mendelson, M. J., 591
Mendilcioglu, I., 81
Mendoza-Denton, R., 348
Menyuk, P., 329
Mercer, J. R., 287
Mercuri, E., 110
Mercy, J. A., 193
Meredith, N. V., 169
Merideth, A., 140
Merrick, J., 79
Mertens, A., 181
Metalsky, G. I., 356
Meyer-Bahlburg, H. F. L., 412
Mezulis, A. H., 55, 307, 422
Michel, G. L., 172
Michel, R. S., 143
Mick, E., 101
Micsik, T., 75

Midgley, C., 567
Migeon, C. J., 412
Miller, A., 589
Miller, B. C., 83, 189
Miller, C., 587
Miller, G. A., 330
Miller, J. G., 444
Miller, K. F., 265
Miller, P. H., 29, 48, 228, 243, 248, 261, 270
Miller, R. L., 393
Miller, S. A., 228, 243, 261, 270
Miller-Jones, D., 287
Miller-Loncar, C. L., 473
Mills, R. S. L., 478
Millstein, S. G., 176, 225
Minino, A. M., 114
Ministry of Health, Education, and Welfare, 495
Minnes, S., 102
Minnett, A. M., 488
Minuchin, P. P., 543, 558
Miracle, A. W., 416
Miracle, T. S., 416
Mirembe, F. M., 96
Mirocnick, M., 105
Mischel, H., 448
Mischel, W., 37, 348, 447, 448
Mishell, D., 111
Mistry, R. S., 587
Mitchell, A., 140
Mitchell, C., 53
Mitchell, E. A., 139
Miyake, K., 477
Miyake, Y., 140
Mnookin, R. H., 496
Moats, L. C., 561
Moawad, A., 106
Moely, B. E., 250
Mofenson, L., 105
Moffitt, T. E., 561
Mohan, L., 271
Mohan, R. M., 110
Moise, K., 112
Moles, A., 121
Money, D., 104
Money, J., 412
Monk, C., 105
Monni, K. G., 81
Monsour, A., 387, 389
Montemayor, R., 397, 492
Montero, I., 232
Moody, R., 83
Moore, C. M., 139
Moore, C. W., 490
Moore, D., 76, 77
Moore, D. G., 300
Moore, M. K., 267
Moore, M. S., 491
Moorman, J. E., 181
Moos, M. K., 190
Morales, J. R., 423
Morelli, G. A., 137
Morgan, M., 566
Morgan Lopez, A., 588
Morison, V., 245, *245*
Moriuchi, H., 117
Morley, C. J., 138
Morris, J. K., 78
Morris, P., 40, 41
Morris, R., 412
Morrison, D. R., 496
Morrison, F. J., 251, 305
Morrison, G. S., 548
Morrison, J., 113
Morrison, J. A., 178, 179
Morrongiello, B. A., 158, 159

Morrow, C. E., 102
Mortimer, A. M., 176
Mortimer, J., 498
Mortimer, J. T., 455
Mosenthal, P. B., 335
Moses, N., 139
Mosher, W. D., 191
Mosko, S. S., 137
Mota, J., 178
Motchnik, P. A., 107
Moukas, M., 79
Mounts, N., 530
Mounts, N. S., 492
Moyo, N. T., 111
Mozingo, J. N., 140
Mozley, L. H., 422
Mozley, P. D., 422
Mueller, N., 485
Muir, D. W., 149
Mulder, P. G., 103
Mullally, P. R., 389
Muller, G., 177
Mullis, I. V. S., 571
Mulrine, A., 134
Mumme, D. L., 353
Mundy, P., 117
Munroe, R. H., 427
Munroe, R. L., 427
Mur, A., 105
Muranjan, M. N., 78
Murnane, R. J., 554
Murowchick, E., 185
Murphy, B., 453
Murphy, B. C., 453
Murray, C., 306, *306*
Murray, D. A., 185
Murray, J. P., 594
Mutton, D. E., 78
Myers, D. L., 458
Myers, M. M., 105
Myerson, J., 307

N

Nabors, L. A., 374
NAEYC. *See* National Association for the Education of Young Children
Nafstad, P., 181
Nagata, D. K., 578
Nagy, Z. B., 75
Nahas, G. G., 107
Nahum, H., 82
Nakamura, J., 301
Nansel, T. R., 516
Narang, A., 103
Narvaez, D., 443, 444
Nash, J. M., 136
Nathan, J. G., 246
National Advisory Council on Economic Opportunity, 361
National Assessment of Educational Progress, 334
National Association for the Education of Young Children (NAEYC), 375, 545, *546*, 547, 549, 550
National Center for Addiction and Substance Abuse, 195
National Center for Children Exposed to Violence, 595
National Center for Education Statistics, 553
National Center for Health Statistics, 114, 178, *178*, 357, 358, 460
National Center for Learning Disabilities, 561
National Center on Child Abuse and Neglect, 484
National Commission on the High School Senior Year, 554
National Community Service Coalition, 455
National Institute of Drug Abuse, 102

National Reading Panel, 334
National Research Council, 254, 329
National Science Foundation, 597
National Vital Statistics Reports, 180, *181*, 182, 358
Natsopoulos, D., 172
Navarette, C., 72
Navarro, J., 82
Neal, C., 474
Neale, J. M., 178, 179
Neckerman, K. M., 361
Needleman, H., 103
Negalia, J. P., 181
Neimark, E. D., 225
Neisser, U., 303
Nelson, C. A., 133, 134, *134*, 253
Nelson, D. A., 423
Nelson, D. O., 78
Nelson, E. A., 177
Nelson, K., 214
Neufeld, S. J., 353
Neumann, M., 140
Neville, H., 132
Neville, M. C., 105
Newburn-Cook, C., 106
Newcomb, A. F., 523, 524
Newcomb, M. D., 194
Newell, K., 150
Newell, L. D., 482
Newport, E. L., 214, 336, *337*
Ng'andu, N., 586
NHANES, 177
NICHD Early Child Care Network, 376
NICHD Early Child Care Research Network, 373
Nicholls, J. G., 569
Nichols, F. H., 107
Nichols, K. E., 449
Nicholson, C., 517
Nieto, S., 336
Nightingale, E. O., 176
Nisbett, R., 566
Nissen, L. G., 112
Noam, G. G., 401
Noble, L., 102
Nocentini, U., 319
Noddings, N., 568
Nogues, C., 72
Noir, S., 427
Nolan, K., 141
Nolen-Hoeksema, S., 355, 356
Noll, E., 401
Nordmark, A., 101
Normand, J., 547
Nottelmann, E. D., 185
Nottleman, E., 357
Novack, L. L., 214
Nugent, J. K., 117, 118
Nugent, K., 118
Nurius, P., 388
Nyamathi, A., 191
Nystrom, J., 10, 117

Oates, J., 12
Obarzanek, E., 177, 178, 179, 180
Obel, C., 101
O'Bierne-Kelly, H., 490
Obler, L. K., 319
Oboro, V. O., 112
O'Brien, M., 15
O'Connor, T. G., 496
Oderic, J. M., 232

O'Donnell, W. T., 72
Oehninger, S., 82
Offer, D., 196
Office of Juvenile Justice and Prevention, 458
Offord, D. R., 357
Ogbu, J. U., 307, 530, 556
O'Hara, N. M., 175
Ohgi, S., 117
Okagaki, L., 304
Okun, B. F., 480
O'Laughlin, M., 270
Olds, S. B., 140
Olds, S. W., 140
Olen, K., 346
Oliveira, J., 178
Olscher, D. A., 103
Olsen, J., 101
Olsen, S. F., 474, 482, 498
Olson, A. L., 121
Olson, F. A., 250
Olson, H. C., 101
Olson, R. K., 561
Olweus, D., 512
O'Malley, P. M., 192, *192*, 193, 194, 195, 450
O'Neill, G., 103
Ontai, L., 533
Opfer, J. E., 216
Oppenheim, D., 137
Orbanic, S., 179
Organista, P. B., 13
Orlansky, M. D., 214
Ormond, K. E., 80
Orozco, L., 72
Ortiz, R. V., 175
Osborne, L., 324
Oshio, S., 111
Oster, H., 159
Ostrov, E., 196
Overpeck, M., 516
Overpeck, M. D., 175, 180
Overton, T. G., 115
Overton, W. F., 223
Owen, D. R., 78
Owne, M. T., 474
Owsley, C. J., 159
Oz, U., 81

Pachter, L. M., 498, 500, 589, 590
Padilla, A. M., 588
Page, H., 138
Page, K. R., 101
Page, M., 138
Paikoff, R. L., 185, 187, 191
Paivio, A., 249
Palla, G., 121
Paludi, M. A., 55, 426
Panak, W. F., 356
Panchaud, C., 190
Panepuccia, L., 121
Pang, V. O., 14
Papageorgiou, A. N., 102
Pape, D., 180
Papp, C., 81
Papp, Z., 81
Parcel, G. S., 175
Parke, R. D., 373, 447, 477, 478–479, 480, 498, 500, 502, 549
Parker, J. G., 511, 512, 516, 522
Parmar, R. C., 78
Parnass, J., 517

Parsons, S., 586
Parten, M., 519, 520
Pascali-Bonaro, D., 112
Pasch, L. A., 82
Pastuszak, A., 101
Pater, J., 140
Paterson, D. J., 110
Patterson, C. G., 497
Patterson, C. J., 12, 447, 485
Patterson, G. R., 460, 473, 481
Patton, J. R., 561
Paukku, M., 190
Paulozzi, L. J., 105
Paulson, S. E., 565
Paus, T., 173
Pavlov, I. P., 37
Pavlova, Z., 114
Paya, A., 105
Payne, J., 501
Payne, W. A., 10
Pearlson, G., 422
Pearson, C., 101
Peck, S., 490
Pell, T., 102
Pellegrini, A. D., 67, 68
Pellicer, A., 82
Pena, I., 114
Pensky, E., 502
Pepler, D. J., 488
Perani, D., 318
Peregoy, S., 336
Perez, W., 588
Perez-Febles, A. M., 500
Periera, C., 103
Perkins, D., 268
Perkins, D. F., 197
Perloff, R. J., 303
Perrin, J. M., 563
Perry, S. E., 111
Perry, T. B., 524
Perry-Jenkins, M., 501
Perse, E. M., 596
Persutte, W., 81
Peskin, E. G., 113
Peskin, H., 187
Peter, C. S., 116
Petersen, A. C., 176, 184, 187
Peterson, C. C., 415
Peterson, J. L., 415
Peterson, K. S., 528
Peterson, S. R., 394
Petersson, G., 101
Pethick, S., 330
Petrosino, A., 270
Pettit, G. S., 12, 495, 512, 513
Pfeffer, C. R., 360
Pfeifer, M., 364
Phenice, A., 548
Phibbs, C. S., 102
Philip, J., 78
Philipp, M., 530
Phillips, D., 549, 555
Phillips, D. A., 375
Phillips, K., 365
Phinney, J. S., 13, 401, 402, 530, 588
Piaget, J., 28, 34, 206, 207, 209, 214, 215, 225, 437, 438, 475, 511, 518
Pianta, R., 329, 335
Piazza, M., 194
Pick, H. L., 160
Pierce, K. M., 474, 495
Pierroutsakos, S. L., 265
Pilla, R., 516
Pillavin, J. A., 455

Pillow, D. R., 360
Pinker, S., 318
Pinto, A., 178
Pintrich, P. R., 272, 550, 567, 569, 570
Piotrowski, C. C., 474
Pitsch, W., 180
Pittenger, D., 44
Pittman, K., 15
Pitts, R. C., 437
Plackslin, S., 120
Plant, E. A., 55
Platsidou, M., 252
Pleck, J. H., 426
Plomin, R., 84, 86, 87, 184, 255, 365
Plu-Bureau, G., 140
Pober, B., 324, 325
Poets, C. F., 116
Pointing, C. P., 75
Polaha, J., 143
Polakow, V., 555
Poland, R. E., 102
Polinski, L., 415
Polivy, J., 177
Pollack, H. A., 139
Pollack, W., 426
Pollitt, E. P., 142
Polloway, E. A., 561
Polychronakos, C., 75
Ponterotto, J. G., 56
Poole, D. A., 259
Pop, V. J. M., 106
Popham, W. J., 287
Porath, M., 543
Porter, C. L., 498
Posner, J. K., 495
Poston, D. L., 488
Pott, M., 477
Potter, J., 393
Potter, P., 181
Potter, S. M., 102
Poulin, R., 348
Pouquette, C., 373
Power, C., 455
Power, F. C., 398–399
Powers, S. I., 401
Presidential Task Force on Psychology and Education, 541
Pressley, M., 249, 271, 272, 329, 335
Profilet, S. M., 481
Prosser, T., 455
Provenzo, E. F., 287
Puel, M., 318
Pugliese, M. T., 139
Puhl, R., 178
Pulsifer, M., 102
Pupp, R., 143
Purcheco, S., 417
Purdy, K. T., 591
Puskas, L. S., 75
Putnam, S. P., 366, 367
Putzolu, M., 81

Q

Quan, J., 190
Queenan, P., 349
Quiceno, J., 371
Quiggle, N. L., 356
Quintana, S. M., 440
Quintino, O., 117
Qutub, M., 104

R

Rabin, B. E., 596
Rabiner, D. L., 515
Rabinowitz, M., 103
Radke-Yarrow, M., 141, 357
Rafaelli, M., 533
Raile, K., 177
Raine, T., 190
Raines, F. Q., 307
Rainey, R., 566
Ramakrishnan, V., 358
Ramanathan, R., 114
Ramey, C., 115
Ramey, C. T., 132, 304
Ramey, S. L., 11, 132, 304
Ramphal, C., 305
Ramsay, D. S., 352
Ramsey, E., 460
Randel, B., 571
Rane, A., 101
Rank, M. R., 307
Ransil, B. J., 172
Ransjo-Arvidson, A. B., 112
Raphael, L., 271
Raphael, T. E., 335
Rapkin, B. D., 552
Rapoport, J. L., 173
Rappaport, L. J., 480
Rapport, M. D., 563
Ratner, N., 323
Raudenbush, S., 48
Raven, P. H., 67
Ray, M., 291, 302
Rayner, R., 37
Redzepi, M., 106
Reed, M-G., 16
Reeve, J., 140
Reich, A., 177
Reid, P. T., 55
Reifman, A., 195
Reine, G. M., 113
Reiner, W. G., 412
Reiser, M., 364, 423, 453
Reiss, D., 86, 365
Relier, J. P., 105
Remafedi, G., 188
Remohi, J., 82
Rende, R., 460
Renshaw, R. J., 173
Repace, J., 181
Requena, A., 82
Resch, N. L., 12
Resnick, L., 35
Resnick, M., 188
Resnick, M. D., 358
Resnick, S. M., 422
Rest, J. R., 440, 443, 444
Reuter, M., 460, 482
Reynolds, A. J., 547
Reznick, S. J., 330
Rhodes, J. E., 12
Ribeiro, J., 178
Ricciardelli, L. A., 186
Riccio, G., 153
Richard, C. A., 137
Richards, M., 585
Richards, M. H., 355, 355, 491
Richardson, G. A., 102
Richman, B. A., 594
Rickard, L., 105
Rickards, A. L., 114
Rickman, M., 364

Rideout, V. J., 599
Ridgeway, D., 354
Riesch, S. K., 490
Rigby, K., 516
Righetti-Beltema, M., 121
Riksen-Walraen, J. M. A., 516
Riley, E. P., 101
Riley, M., 140
Rimberg, H. M., 190
Rinehart, S. D., 272
Riner, W., 178
Ringelstein, E. B., 172
Rinsky-Eng, J., 105
Risley, T. R., 321, 324, 331
Ritter, R., 248
Rittey, C. D., 562
Rivera, J., 142
Robb, K. Y., 251
Roberts, D., 584
Roberts, D. F., 599
Roberts, J. E., 331, 374
Roberts, M. C., 175, 362
Roberts, P. M., 319
Roberts, S. B., 178
Roberts, S. E., 81
Roberts, W., 451
Robertson, H. A., 77
Robins, P. K., 496
Robins, R. W., 393
Robinson, C. C., 474, 498
Robinson, D. P., 192
Robinson, J. S., 114
Rode, S. S., 123
Rodgers, J. L., 525
Rodin, J., 179
Rodriguez, J. L., 336
Rodriquez, L. E., 179
Roedinger, H. L., 44
Roehrig, A., 271
Roesch, S. C., 106
Rogers, A., 403
Rogers, A. G., 445
Rogers, C. R., 388
Rogoff, B., 35, 137, 231, 234, 235, 268, 305
Rohner, E. C., 498
Rohner, R. P., 498
Rojansky, N., 96
Romich, J., 587
Romocki, L. S., 594
Roodin, P. A., 448
Roosa, M. W., 586, 588
Rose, A. A., 74
Rose, A. J., 524
Rose, D., 181
Rose, H. A., 413
Rose, J. L., 146
Rose, L. C., 45
Rose, S., 106, 531
Rose, S. P., 134
Rosegrant, T., 335
Rose-Krasnor, L., 478
Rosen, D., 367
Rosen, K., 477, 489
Rosenbaum, D., 143
Rosenbaum, K., 36
Rosenberg, D., 153
Rosenberg, M., 387, 388
Rosenberg, M. L., 193
Rosenblith, J. F., 149, 246
Rosenblum, G. D., 355
Rosenstein, D., 159
Rosenthal, D., 188
Rosenthal, R., 288
Rosenwaks, Z., 82

Rosenzweig, M., 135
Rosenzweig, M. R., 38
Rosnow, R. I., 288
Rosnow, R. L., 54
Rotenstein, D., 178
Roth, B., 10
Roth, J., 175
Rothbart, M. K., 364, 366, 367
Rothbart, M. L. K., 488
Rothbaum, F., 477, 489
Rothlisberg, B., 565
Rothstein-Fisch, C., 558
Rotman, T., 503
Roubinet, F., 103
Rovee-Collier, C., 245, 253
Rovira, M. T., 105
Rowe, D. C., 74, 85, 86
Rowe, S. M., 235
Rowland, V., 598
Rowley, D., 139
Rowther, M., 81
Roy, R., 517
Royall, R., 102
Royburt, M., 82
Ruan, W., 516
Ruben, D. B., 78
Rubin, D. H., 107
Rubin, K. H., 366, 478, 511, 512, 515
Rubin, Z., 53, 512
Rubinstein, W. S., 80
Ruble, D., 386
Ruble, D. N., 388, 419
Ruff, S., 318
Rumberger, R. W., 553
Rupley, W. H., 334
Rusak, B., 77
Russ, S. W., 102
Russell, S. T., 358
Russo, N. F., 55, 361
Rutherford, M., 110
Rutter, M., 19, 21, 361, 393
Ryan, A. S., 140
Ryan, C., 102
Ryan, D. L., 116
Ryan, E. B., 252, *252*, 561
Ryan, R., 568
Ryan, R. M., 565
Ryan-Finn, K. D., 56
Rymer, R., 319

S

Saarni, C., 349, 353, 354, 355, 362, 364
Sabharwal, M., 101
Sabry, Z. I., 178, 179
Sachse, K., 82
Sacker, A., 586
Sacks, S. L., 104
Sadker, D. M., 12, 416
Sadker, M. P., 12, 416
Saenz, D., 588
Safford, P., 588
Sagovsky, R., 121
St. Pierre, R., 556, 587
Saitoh, H., 117
Sakin, J., 487
Salamanca, F., 72
Salami, L., 179
Salapatek, P., 145, 153, 155, 159
Salday, Y., 72
Salkind, N. J., 29
Salman, F. A., 106
Salmond, C., 139

Salovey, P., 293
Saltzman, H., 362
Salvator, A., 102
Salzberger, U., 101
Samaniego, R. Y., 588
Samara, R., 189
Samour, P. Q., 139
Sampson, P. D., 101
Samuels, M., 113
Samuels, M. C., 270
Samuels, M. P., 484
Samuels, N., 113
Sanchez, P. J., 104
Sandberg, J. F., 501
Sander, M., 72
Sandler, I., 360
Sandman, B. M., 101
Sandoval, L., 45
Sanford, D. G., 122
Sanger, C., 385
Sanson, A., 367
Sanson, A. V., 366
Santiago-Delefosse, M. J., 232
Santrock, J. W., 18, 488, 496, 497, 541, 557, 583, 590
Saraswathi, T. S., 428
Sarigiani, P. A., 187
Sashon, C. H., 152, 154
Sauls, D. J., 111
Saunders, R., 178
Savin-Williams, R. C., 188, 358, 529, 531
Sawaguchi, A., 138
Sawaguchi, T., 138
Sawyer, K., 349
Sax, G., 286, 288
Sax, L. J., 450
Saylor, K. E., 195
Sbarra, D. A., 496
Scafidi, F., 10, 117
Scaillet, S., 138
Scardamalia, M., 263
Scarr, S., 11, 73, 74, 84, 86, 287, 307, 374
Schacter, D. L., 244, 253, 257
Schacter, S. C., 172
Schaffer, H. R., 369
Schaffer, R., 594
Schanberg, S., 117
Schanberg, S. M., 10, 117
Schauble, L., 270
Schechter, D. E., 83
Schedit, P. C., 180
Scheidt, P., 516
Schell, L. M., 141
Schiefele, U., 569, 570
Schirato, T., 579, 580
Schlegel, M., 262
Schlucter, M., 114
Schmidt, P. R., 335
Schmitt, D. P., 424
Schmitt, K., 597
Schmuckler, M. A., 153
Schneider, B. A., 157
Schneider, B. H., 371
Schneider, W., 244, 249, 251, 271, 272
Schnitzler, M. A., 307
Schnorr, T. M., 104
Schoendorf, K. C., 101
Scholl, T. O., 106
Schoon, I., 586
Schott, J. L., 270
Schrag, S. G., 103
Schreiber, G. G., 178, 179
Schroeder, C. S., 357
Schulenberg, J., 175
Schulpis, K. H., 79
Schulsinger, R., 78

Schulte, D., 251
Schultz, M., 329
Schultz, R. T., 325
Schultz, S., 362
Schum, T. R., 143
Schumer, H., 455
Schunk, D. H., 272, 566, 568, 569, 570
Schwartz, D., 106
Schwartz, G., 79
Schwartz, M. B., 178
Schwartz, P., 181
Schwartz, P. M., 104
Schwarz, P. M., 427
Schwarz, S. P., 472
Schweinhart, L. J., 547
Schweitzer, U., 569
Schwitzer, A. M., 179
Scott, L. D., 591
Scott-Jones, D., 589
Scribner, S., 224
Scucchi, S., 121
Scully, D. M., 150
Search Institute, 455
Sedeno, A., 585
Segal, N. L., 66
Seidman, L. J., 422
Seifer, R., 102
Seligman, M. E. P., 356, 359, 361
Seligman, S., 117
Selke, S., 104
Selman, R. L., 389, 390, 391, 524
Seltzer, M., 132
Semba, R. D., 105
Serbin, L. A., 417, 419
Serimshaw, S. C., 547
Serow, R. C., 455
Serpell, R., 305
Settle, M., 116
Shaffer, D. R., 453
Shaffer, L., 528
Shahidullah, S., 172
Shahinfar, A., 372
Shaiau, S. H., 116–117
Shankaran, S., 102
Shannon, F. T., 140
Shapiro, E. K., 543, 558
Share, D. L., 561
Sharma, A. R., 83
Sharma, T., 422
Sharma, V., 121
Sharp, V., 597
Shatz, M., 332
Shaughnessy, J. J., 48
Shaver, P. R., 474, 490
Shaw, G. M., 103
Shaw, S. M., 500
Shea, C. I., 449
Sheffield, J. S., 103
Shepard, S., 348
Shepard, S. A., 453
Shields, S., 55
Shields, S. A., 410, 427
Shiffrin, R. M., 255
Shigenaga, M. K., 107
Shin, S. K., 100
Shinn, C., 547
Shiono, P. H., 107, 115
Shonk, S. M., 485
Shonkoff, J., 549
Shore, G., 563
Shorr, C. J., 450
Shorr, D. N., 450
Showers, C. J., 393
Shu, X. O., 107
Sickmund, M., 458

Siegel, L. S., 252, *252*, 560, 561, 562, 593
Siegle, J., 594
Siegler, R. S., 36, 242, 243, 251, 263, *263*, 264, 272
Sigman, M., 297
Sigman, M. D., 297
Sigmundson, H. K., 412
Signore, C., 104
Signorello, L. B., 101
Silberg, J. L., 74
Silberstein, L. R., 179
Silerman, W. K., 362
Silferdal, S. A., 139
Silk, L. S., 477, 482, 491
Silovsky, J. F., 362
Silva, P. A., 561
Silver, S., 114
Silverman, N., 485
Silverstein, L. B., 373
Sim, T., 482
Simmer, K., 140
Simmons, R. G., 187
Simmons-O'Brien, E., 100
Simms, M. D., 143
Simon, C., 82
Simons, J., 182
Simons, R. L., 460
Simons-Morton, B., 195, 516
Simons-Morton, G. G., 175
Simpson, A., 517
Sims, B., 585
Sinclair, R., 503
Singer, D. G., 597
Singer, L., 102
Singer, L. M., 83
Singer, L. T., 102
Singer, S., 67
Singh, G. K., 111
Singh, S., 189, 190
Sippola, L. K., 523
Sirolli, A., 588
Sirota, L., 118
Sitterle, K. A., 497
Skerry, S., 386
Skinner, B. F., 37, 320
Slack, C., 335
Slater, A., 152, 153, 154, 155, 245, *245*
Sledden, E. A., 175
Slijper, F. M. E., 411
Sloan, R. P., 105
Slobin, D., 328
Sloboda, J. A., 300
Sloman, J., 512
Slomkowski, C., 460
Smeriglio, V. L., 102
Smiley, T., 101
Smit, E. M., 83
Smith, A. M., 102
Smith, B., 105
Smith, D., 564
Smith, D. W., 83
Smith, G. S., 180
Smith, J., 483
Smith, J. C., 193
Smith, K. E., 473
Smith, L., 138
Smith, L. M., 102
Smith, M., 348
Smith, P. H., 400
Smith, R., 595
Smith, T. A., 571
Smith, T. E. C., 561
Smith, W. C., 159
Smolak, L., 178
Snarey, J., 444, 502
Snidman, N., 20, 364

Snow, C., 320
Snowden, W., 104
Snyder, H. N., 458
Snyder, M., 455
Soby, B., 393
Sohn, W., 190
Solchany, J. E., 499
Solezal, S., 271
Somers, M., 245, *245*
Sommer, B. B., 582
Soong, W. T., 181
Sophian, C., 212
Sorokin, P., 100
Southall, D. P., 484
Sowter, B., 138
Spandorfer, S. D., 82
Spangler, G., 372
Spanoudis, G., 252
Spear, H. J., 175
Spearman, C. E., 289
Speer, P. W., 545
Spelke, E. S., 156, 159, 214
Spence, J. T., 425
Spence, M. J., 157, 158
Spencer, M., 590
Spencer, M. B., 401, 402, 557, 570, 589, 591
Spencer, R., 445
Spender, T., 251
Spitzer, S., 549
Sprafkin, C., 419
Spring, J., 555
Springer, S. P., 172
Sroufe, L. A., 20, 123, 352, 371, 372, 475, 476, 485, 486
Stack, D. M., 102
Stafford, F. P., 477
Stahl, S., 334
Stahl, S. A., 272
Stanhope, L., 488
Stanley-Hagan, M., 495, 496, 497
Stanovich, K. E., 560
Stapleton, A. L., 101
Stark, A. D., 141
Starry, A. R., 584
Stattin, H., 187
Stearns, S. C., 73
Steffen, V. J., 423
Stein, M. T., 563
Steinberg, J., 373
Steinberg, L., 87, 355, 458, 477, 482, 491, 530, 554
Steinberg, L. D., 494
Steiner, J. E., 158
Steiner, M., 185
Stern, D. N., 473
Stern, P., 307, 556
Sternberg, K. J., 21
Sternberg, R. J., 87, 255, 281, 291, 292, 293, 294, 301, 303, 304, 306
Sternglanz, S. H., 417
Steur, F. B., 595
Stevenson, C. S., 562
Stevenson, H. C., 590
Stevenson, H. G., 56, *571*, 581
Stevenson, H. W., 13, 428, 532, 571
Stewart, A. W., 139
Stewart, S. L., 366
Stice, E., 178
Stigler, J. W., 571, *571*
Stipek, D. J., 565, 567, 568
Stocker, C., 348, 488
Stocking, M., 78
Stoffregen, T. A., 153
Stolberg, U., 352
Stoltzfuz, J., 401
Stone, G. C., 225

Story, M., 178
Stouthamer-Loeber, M., 459, 481
Stoval, S., 181
Strahan, D. B., 225
Strandvik, B., 139
Strass, P., 121
Straus, M. A., 482, 483
Strauss, R. S., 181
Strayer, J., 451
Streissguth, A. P., 101
Strichart, S. S., 562
Striegel-Moore, R. H., 178, 179
Stringer, S., 474
Strobel, K. R., 570
Strobino, D. M., 114
Stuhlman, M., 329, 335
Stulac, B. B., 139
Sturgess, W., 496
Styfco, S. J., 15, 548
Styles, L., 79
Suárez-Orozco, C., 13, 588
Sue, S., 590, 591, 592
Suess, G., 372
Sugarman, D. B., 483
Suleiman, L., 585
Sullivan, A., 491
Sullivan, C. E., 138
Sullivan, H. S., 475, 511, 523, 524
Sullivan, K., 491
Sullivan, M. W., 385
Sun-Irminger, X., 336
Sunshine, W., 117
Suomi, S. J., 511
Super, C. M., 137, 372, 498
Suresh, M., 112
Susman, A., 477
Susman, E. J., 185
Sutton-Smith, B., 521
Suzuki, L. A., 56
Svenson, L. W., 106
Swaab, D. F., 422
Swami, S., 78
Swank, P. R., 473
Swanson, J. M., 563
Sweet, M. P., 114
Swisher, R., 585
Szkrybalo, J., 419

T

Tabowei, T. O., 112
Taddio, A., 158
Tager-Flusberg, H., 319
Takahashi, K., 372
Takahashi, T., 117
Talbot, J., 373
Talpins, S., 117
Tamis-Lemonda, C. S., 503
Tannen, D., 422, 423
Taormina, J., 153
Tappan, M. B., 230
Tardif, C., 371
Tardif, T., 499, 584
Tarpley, T., 598
Tasker, F. L., 498
Task Force on Infant Positioning and SIDS (AAP), 137, 138
Tate, J. D., 401
Taylor, C. B., 178
Taylor, H. G., 115
Taylor, J. H., 442, 443
Taylor, L. S., 556
Taylor, M. J., 115

Taylor, R. D., 584
Taylor, S., 117
Taylor, S. E., 426
Teitler, J. O., 496
Telemo, E., 139
Tellegen, A., 66
Templado, C., 72
Tenenbaum, H. R., 45, *45*, 419
Tercyak, K. P., 81
Terman, D. L., 562
Terman, L., 299
Terr, L. C., 257
Terry, W. S., 255
Tesch-Römer, C., 255, 300
Tessaro, I., 140
Teti, D. M., 357, 487
Tetreault, M. K. T., 55
Thal, D. J., 327, 330
Thalabard, J. C., 140
Tharp, R. G., 233, 234
Theiry, E., 74
Thelen, E., 146, 151, 160
Thoman, E. B., 138
Thomas, A., 159, 363, 365
Thomas, C., 179
Thomas, K., 529
Thomas, S. J., 443, 444
Thomas, S. W., 259
Thompson, J. L., 100
Thompson, L., 499
Thompson, L. B., 515
Thompson, P. M., 173
Thompson, R., 371, 373
Thompson, R. A., 133, 353, 371, 373
Thomsen, A. H., 362
Thomson, M., 561
Thonneau, P., 107
Thornton, S. J., 568
Thorpe, L. A., 157
Thorstad, K. K., 114
Thorton, A., 188
Thurston, L., 564
Thurston, S. W., 194
Thurstone, L. L., 290
Timins, J. K., 103
Tinsley, B. J., 175
Tishman, S., 268
Tobin, R. M., 348
Toda, S., 473
Toga, A. W., 173
Tolan, P. H., 460
Tollner, U., 101
Tomlinson-Keasey, C., 225
Tonner, L., 367
Tooby, J., 67, 68
Tood, S. J., 103
Torgesen, J. K., 335, 562
Toth, G., 560
Toth, S. L., 485
Tough, C. S., 106
Touyeras, B., 318
Tracey, J. L., 393
Trafimow, D., 582
Trappe, R., 72
Trasler, J. M., 107
Treffers, P. E., 111
Trehub, S. E., 157
Trevethan, S. D., 444
Triandis, H. C., 579, 581, 582
Trimble, J. E., 56
Troiano, R. P., 177
Troisi, A., 121
Tronick, E. Z., 102, 115, 473
Troop, W., 516

Tropp, L., 591
Trowbridge, F. L., 178
True, W. R., 358
Truglio, R. T., 594
Trumble, A. C., 180
Trzesniewski, K. H., 393
Tsakiris, S., 79
Tsatsarius, V., 112
Tsigos, C., 121
Tsuang, M. T., 358, 422
Tubb, V. A., 258
Tubman, J. G., 195
Tulving, E., 253
Turecki, S., 367
Turiel, E., 440, 445
Turkanis, C. G., 231
Turner, R., 189
Twickler, D. M., 104
Tyring, S. K., 104

U

Uchida, N., 477, 489
Udipi, S. A., 105
Udry, J. R., 525, 528
Ujie, T., 477, 489
Ulku-Steiner, B., 474
Uman, G., 191
Underwood, M. K., 423, 516
Unger, R., 393, 424
UNICEF, 114, *115*, 182, 183, 427
Unis, A. S., 101
Unzner, L., 372
Updegraff, K. A., 512
Urbina, S., 288, 303
U.S. Department of Commerce, 599
U.S. Department of Education, 422, 559, 560
U.S. Department of Energy, 75, 76
U.S. Department of Health and Human Services, 460
U.S. General Accounting Office, 108
Uvnas-Moberg, K., 112
Uyanik, M., 78

V

Valencia, R. R., 46
Valente, T., 194
Valiente, C., 442, 453
Vallance, D. D., 354
Vallely, P., 104
Valsiner, J., 13
van Alten, D., 111
van Baar, A. L., 106
Van Beveren, T. T., 111
Vandell, D. L., 488, 495, 513
van den Boom, D. C., 367
Van Der Auwerea, C., 143
Vandewater, E. A., 587
Van Gestel, S., 74
Van Gool, J. D., 143
Van IJzendoorn, H. W., 516
van IJzendoorn, M. H., 370, 372, *372*
Van Lieshout, C. F. M., 516
Van Sprundel, M., 143
Vargas, L., 11, 193, 594
Varkonyi, A., 194
Vaughn, S., 562
Veeck, L., 82
Vega, W. A., 557
Vega-Lahr, N., 10, 117

Vemulapalli, C., 139
Venter, J. C., 75
Ventura, A., 587
Ventura, S. J., 111, 191
Verklan, M. T., 109
Verma, S., 428
Vernberg, E. M., 362
Vernon, P., 74
Vevea, J., 331
Vicari, S., 324
Vidaeff, A. C., 113
Vidal, F., 34
Vidal, S., 72
Villani, S. L., 500
Villringer, A., 318
Vlietinck, R., 74
Vogelsang, G., 100
Volkow, N. D., 563
Volling, B. L., 487
Volmink, J., 181
von Dulmen, M., 83
Voran, K., 375
Vreugdenhil, H. J., 103
Vurpillot, E., 247, *247*
Vygotsky, L. S., 35, 230, 232, 519

W

Wacholde, S., 107
Wachs, H., 220
Wachs, T. D., 364, 365, 366
Waclawiw, M. A., 178, 179
Waddington, C. H., 73
Wadhwa, P. D., 106
Wadsworth, M. E., 362
Wagner, R. K., 294
Wahlsten, D., 74, 77, 86
Wain, J. C., 194
Waite, A., 517
Wald, N. J., 78
Walden, T., 353
Waldfogel, J., 494
Waldron, M. C., 496
Walk, R. D., 156, *156*
Walker, A. J., 499
Walker, H., 460, 461
Walker, L., 371, 373, 440
Walker, L. J., 437, 442, 443, 444, 452
Wall, J. A., 527
Walot, I., 102
Walsh, L. A., 486
Walter, J. A., 143
Wang, G., 101
Wang, J. D., 181
Wang, P. P., 324
Wang, V. O., 423
Wang, X., 101
Ward, B. M., 104
Ward, K. D., 102
Wardle, F., 544
Warheit, G. J., 557
Warren, M. P., 185
Warren, S. T., 72
Warrick, P., 94
Warshak, R. A., 84, 496, 497
Wartenburger, I., 318
Warzak, W. J., 143
Washington, R. L., 180
Watemberg, N., 114
Waterman, A. S., 399, 400, 401, 403, 455
Waternaux, C., 103
Waters, E., 21, 352, 354, 371

Waters, P., 445
Waters, P. L., 387
Watkinson, B., 101
Watras, J., 287
Watson, J., 261, *261*
Watson, J. B., 9, 37, 139, 351
Watts, D. H., 104
Way, N., 191
Weed, K., 191
Weeks, A. D., 96
Wehner, E. A., 528
Wei, E., 459
Weikart, D. P., 547
Weile, B., 107
Weiler, I. J., 87
Weinberg, E., 181
Weinberg, M. K., 445
Weinberg, R. A., 74, 86, 307
Weinberger, D. A., 460
Weinberger, J., 503
Weincke, J. K., 194
Weiner, I. B., 356
Weinraub, M., 498, 555
Weis, L., 555
Weisglas-Kuperus, N., 103
Weiss, M., 385
Weiss, R. E., 103
Weiss, S. M., 10
Weissberg, R. P., 10, 16
Weisse, B., 401
Weissman, A., 82
Weisz, J., 477
Weizmann, F., 369
Welch, R. A., 81
Weller, A., 118
Wellman, H. M., 248, 261, *261*
Wells, M. G., 394
Wells, Y. A., 388
Wendel, G. D., 103, 104
Wenjun, Z., 140
Wentworth, R. A. L., 544
Wentzel, K., 568
Wentzel, K. R., 515
Wergin, J. F., 43
Wertheimer, M., 267
Wertsch, J. V., 235
Wessles, K., 550
West, C. R., 82
West, J., 549
Westra, T., 149
Weyman-Daum, M., 139
Whalen, C. K., 562, 563
Wharton-McDonald, R., 271
White, B., 149
White, D. K., 139
White, J. W., 423
White, R., 172
White, S. H., 8
Whitebook, M., 375
Whiteman, M., 492, 588
Whitesell, N., 358, 445
Whitesell, N. R., 387, 388
Whitfield, J. R., 590
Whiting, B. B., 498
Whitley, B. E., 46, 54
Whitlock, J., 585
Whitman, T. L., 191
Whittaker, C. R., 556
Wickelgren, I., 304
Widstrom, A. M., 112
Wiener, J., 593
Wigfield, A., 565, 567, 569, 570
Wiggins, R. D., 586
Wikstrom, P. H., 459
Wilcox, B. L., 15

Wiley, E., 314, 320, 337
Wilfond, B. S., 76
Willatts, P., 263
Willford, J., 102
Williams, C., 451
Williams, C. R., 596
Williams, D., 116
Williams, E. M., 229
Williams, F., 418
Williams, J. E., 420
Williams, P. H., 372
Williamson, M., 122
Willis, A. I., 336
Wilson, B., 596
Wilson, C. C., 594
Wilson, C. S., 544
Wilson, D., 181
Wilson, J. F., 67, 70
Wilson, K. S., 474
Wilson, R. M., 334
Wilson, W. J., 361
Wilson-Shockley, S., 532
Win, P. T., 588
Windle, M., 195
Windle, R. C., 195
Windle, W. F., 158
Winkelsein, M. L., 181
Winne, P. H., 272
Winner, E., 216, 299, 300
Winsler, A., 232, 336, 549
Winter, D. G., 565
Wintre, M. G., 354
Wisden, W., 77
Wise, P., 101
Wisenbaker, J., 569
Wisniewski, A. B., 412
Wissow, L. S., 531
Witkin, H. A., 78
Witt, D., 336
Wo, J., 498
Wolf, R. C., 531
Wolfson, J., 74
Wollinsky, F. D., 108
Wong, D. L., 111, 170, 181
Wong, E., 177
Wong, K., 134
Wong, L. Y., 105
Wood, G. A., 532
Wood, I. C., 77
Wood, W., 414
Woodard, E., 598
Woodrich, D. L., 563
Woodroffe, A., 590
Woods, E. R., 531
Woods, R. P., 173
Woodson, R., 266
Woodward, A. L., 328
Work Group of the American Psychological Association's Board of Affairs, 541
Workman, M. I., 101
World Health Organization, 176, 190
Worobey, J., 119
Worrall, B. K., 185
Wright, H. F., 514
Wright, J. C., 594, 597
Wright, J. L., 180
Wright, L., 175
Wright, L. L., 102
Wright, M. R., 186
Wroblewski, R., 418
Wu, P., 498
Wu, X., 498
Wulf, D., 189
Wyndaele, J. J., 143
Wyrobek, A. J., 78

Xeroxmeritou, A., 172
Xiao, W. F., 82
Xu, F., 212
Xu, X., 101
Xue, L., 102

Yali, A. M., 106
Yang, A., 182
Yang, C., 481, 498
Yasui, Y., 181
Yates, M., 451, 455
Yawkey, T. D., 521, 522
Yawn, B. P., 113
Yazici, G., 81
Yeomans, E. R., 113
Yeung, W. J., 501
Yin, J., 177
Yin, Y., 523
Ying, D. M., 107
Ying, Y., 578
Yonekura, M. L., 102
Yoon, J. J., 102
Yoshikawa, H., 13
Young, D., 112
Young, K. T., 140
Young, S. K., 372
Youngblade, L. M., 493, 494
Youniss, J., 475
Yu, V. Y., 114
Yura, A., 140
Yureglun-Todd, D. A., 173
Yussen, S. R., 444

Zabin, L. S., 189
Zalk, S. R., 55
Zautra, A. J., 360
Zechmeister, E. B., 48
Zechmeister, J. S., 48
Zelazo, P. D., 270
Zelazo, P. R., 102, 352, 375
Zeskind, P. S., 102, 351
Zhang, Q., 459
Zhang, X. N., 82
Zheng, W., 107
Zhniser, S. C., 114
Zhou, Q., 453
Zidjdenbos, A., 173
Zigler, E. F., 10, 15, 548
Zill, N., 549
Zimmerman, B., 273
Zimmerman, B. J., 272, 569
Zimmerman, R. S., 557
Zoller, D., 479
Zoppi, M. A., 81
Zubek, J., 393
Zuckerman, B., 101, 102
Zuckerman, B. S., 121
Zukow-Goldring, P., 487
Zusho, A., 428, 532
Zuzuki, L. A., 46
Zvara, A., 75
Zwarentein, M., 181

Subject Index

Note: page numbers in *italics* indicate figures or illustrations and their captions.

A

AAI (Adult Attachment Interview), 490
AAP (American Academy of Pediatrics), 138
Abecedarian Intervention Program, 304, *304*
AB error, 212–213
Ability tests, 288–289
Abnormalities, 77–80
　chromosome abnormalities, 76, 77, 77–78, 106
　gene-linked, 78–80, *79*
Abstract self-understanding, 387
Abstract thought, 221, 222
"Academic redshirting," 549
Accessibility to children, parental, 501, *501*
Accidents
　adolescent deaths due to, 182
　children's deaths due to, 180–181, *181*
Accommodation, 34, 208, 224, 225
Acculturation, 360, 500, 588
Accutane, teratology of, 100
Achievement, 574
　cross-cultural comparisons of, 570–571, *571,* 581
　ethnicity and, 570, 581
　expectations for, 554
　extrinsic and intrinsic motivation, 565–567
　gender differences in, 422, 423
　goal setting and, 569–570
　high-achieving adolescents, 569
　IQ-achievement discrepancy, 560
　mastery motivation and, 567, *568*
　need for, 564–565
　peer support of, 530
　in school, 564–571
　self-efficacy and, 568–569
　self-esteem and, 394
　self-regulatory learning and, 272
　socioeconomic variations in, 584
Achievement motivation, 565
Achievement tests, 285, 545
Active dimension of self, 386
Active genotype-environment correlations, 85, *85*
Adaptive behavior, 67, 68–69
Adderall, 563
ADHD (attention deficit hyperactivity disorder), 561, 562–563
Adjustment problems
　divorce and, 495, *495,* 496, 497
　social cognitive skills and, 515
Adolescence, 18, *19,* 199–200, 580
　acculturation, 500
　autonomy and attachment, 489–490
　brain in, 173–174
　causes of death in, 182, 357–358, 379
　cliques and crowds, 526, 527
　contraceptive use during, 189–190

developing sexual identity, 188, 529–531
developmental window in, 429
emotional development in, 355, *355*
empathy in, 450–451
exercise in, 179–180, *180*
families and, 489–492, 505
formal operational stage, 221–226, 438
health and, 175–176, 182, 199
identity formation during, 397–398
managerial role of parents and, 481
need for intimacy in, 523, *523*
parent-adolescent conflict, 490–492, *492*
parent-child interactions in, 477
peers and, 526–532
problems during. *See* Adolescent problems
progression of sexual behaviors, 188–189
puberty, 183–184, *184*
self-descriptions in, 384
self-understanding in, 387–390
sexuality in, 187–191
social contexts of high school, 543
sociocultural contexts of, 580
stepfamilies and, 497
use of elaboration in, 249
weight in, 186
　See also Adolescents
Adolescent egocentrism, 224–225
Adolescent groups, 527–528, *528*
Adolescent problems
　alcohol use, 193
　child maltreatment and, 485
　cigarette smoking, 193–194, *194*
　depression, 357
　eating disorders, *178,* 178–179
　intervention programs, 195–196
　moodiness, 355
　parent-adolescent conflict and, 490–492, *492*
　pregnancy, *190,* 190–191
　risk of sexual problems, 189
　romantic relationships, 528–531, *529*
　sexually transmitted infections, 190, 191
　substance use and abuse, *192,* 192–195, *193*
　suicide, 182, 357–358, 379
　See also Adolescence; Adolescents
Adolescent relational world, 510
Adolescents
　contemporary, 196–197
　detachment from parents, 491–492, *492*
　families and, 489–492, 497, 505
　high-achieving, 569
　school and, 550–555
　second-language learning by, 337, *337*
　television directed at, 418
　transition to middle school, 551–552
　See also Adolescence; Adolescent problems
Adoption, 83–84
Adoption studies, 74
Adrenaline, childbirth and, 110–111
Adult Attachment Interview (AAI), 490

Adulthood, 68, 365, *366*
Adults
　gender role socialization by, 429
　as role models, 269
　second-language learning by, 336–337, *337*
Affective communication, 347–348
Affordances, 152–153
African Americans, 13
　achievement and, 570
　altruism, 457
　girls, risks of obesity, 178, *178,* 179
　girls, standards of beauty, 402
　high school dropout rate, *554*
　home environments, 589
　incidence of sickle-cell anemia in, 79, *79*
　incidence of SIDS among, 139
　intelligence testing and, 306, 307
　interethnic friendships, 530
　intrinsic motivation in, 566
　juvenile delinquency, 458
　schools attended, 556
　stress and, 361
　vocabulary development in, 331
　See also Culture; Ethnicity; Ethnic minorities
Afterbirth, 110
After-school programs, 495
Aggression
　birth order and, 488
　effects of television on, 595–596
　gender differences in, 423, 427
　sex hormones and, 412
　See also Violence
AIDS, 105, 183, 190
Ainsworth Strange Situation, 370, *370,* 371
Air-Crib, 37
Alcohol, 101, *101,* 193, 561
Algorithms, in problem solving, 262
Alpha-fetoprotein (AFT) blood test, 81
Alternate forms reliability, 286
Altruism, 456–457
Altruistic behavior, 450, 456
American Academy of Pediatrics (AAP), 138
American culture
　as blended culture, 592–593
　"browning" of Americans, 591–592
　child abuse and, 484–485
　Internet and, 598–599, *599*
　White American culture, 402
American Heart Association, 177
American Pediatric Association (APA), 140
American Psychological Association (APA), 54, 303, 417
Amniocentesis, 81
Amnion, 96
Amygdala, 173–174
Analgesia, for childbirth, 112
Analogies, in solving problems, 265–266
Anal stage, 30, *31*
Analytical intelligence, 291, 292
Anatomy as destiny, 412–413

Androgen-insensitive males, 412
Androgens, 411, 412
Androgyny
    education and, 425–426
    moral development and, 445
    relationships and, 425
Anesthesia, 112, 158
Anger cry, 351
Animism, 216
Anorexia nervosa, 178–179
Anoxia, 110
Antibiotics, teratology of, 100
Antidepressants, teratology of, 100
Antipoverty programs, 556, 587
Antisocial behavior, 450, 457–463, 465
Antispanking laws, 483–484
Anxiety, maternal, effects on fetus, 106
APA (American Pediatric Association), 140
APA (American Psychological Association), 54, 303, 417
Apgar Scale, 118, *118*
Aphasia, 318
Aptitude tests, 285
Asian Americans, 13
    achievement orientation, 581
    diversity among, 591
    expectations of, 578
    home environments, 589
    schools attended, 556
    stress and, 360, 589–590
Aspen Declaration on Character Education, 454
Assessment
    cultural, in health care, 108
    of infants, 296, *296*
    of moral reasoning, 443–444, *444*
    multicultural (SOMPA), 287–288
    neonatal, *118*, 118–119, 295
    ongoing, 227
    of self-esteem, 392
Assimilation, 34, 224, 225
    diversity and, 591
    in Piaget's theory, 207–208
    pluralism and, 592
Associative play, 520
Asymmetric gender socialization, 429
Athletic ability, 255
Attachment, 380
    adolescent autonomy and, 489–490
    bonding, 122–123
    caregiving styles and, 371–372
    child-care and, 374–377, *375*
    emotional development and, 368–377
    ethological theory of, 369–370
    fathers as caregivers and, 373–374
    feeding and, 367–368
    individual differences in, *370*, 370–371
    nature of, 368–370, *369*
    research in, 367–368, *368*, *370*, 371
    social world and, *372*, 372–373
Attachment theory, 39
Attention, 245–247
    decrement and recovery, 297
    developmental changes in, 246–247, *247*
    habituation and dishabituation, *245*, 245–246
Attention deficit hyperactivity disorder (ADHD), 561, 562–563
Attention-focusing strategies, 246
Attention-getting behavior, 224
Audiology, careers in, A–6
Auditory-visual relations, in newborns, 159
Authoritarian parenting, 481
Authoritative parenting, 481–482, 494–495, 503
Authority, obedience to, 457
Authority conflict, delinquency and, 459
Autocratic parents, 400

Automaticity, 243
Autonomous morality, 437, 438
Autonomy, adolescence and, 489–490
Autonomy *versus* shame and doubt, 32, *32*
AZT (zidovudine), 105

Babbling, 326–327
Babinski reflex, *145*
"Baby blues," 121
Baby talk, 321
Balance scale problem, *263*, 263–265, *264*
Baldwin, James Mark, 8, 9
Bandura, Albert, 37, 38, *38*
"Barometric self," 387
Basal metabolism rate (BMR), 177
Basic cry, 351
Basic-skills-and-phonetics approach, 333–334
Bayley Scales of Infant Development, 295, 296
Beethoven, Ludwig van, 290
Behavioral theories, 36, 37, *42*
    evaluation of, 38
    of language development, 320
    Pavlov's theory, 37
    Skinner's operant conditioning, *37*, 37
Behavior genetics, 74
Behavior management, medical, 563
Bell, Alexander Graham, 314
Bell, Katie, *455*
The Bell Curve: Intelligence and Class Structure in American Life (Herrnstein & Murray), 306, *306*
Bem Sex-Role Inventory, 425, *425*
Benevolence, 457
Bias
    cultural, in intelligence testing, 287–288, *288*, 306–307
    ethnicity and, 589, 591–592
    gender bias, 54–55, 285, 416–417, 419–420
    reducing, 558
    in research, minimizing, 54–57
Bickford, Laura, 242
Big Brothers/Big Sisters programs, 394
Bilingual education, 336, 592
Bilingualism, 336–337, *337*, 339
Binet, Alfred, 8, 282, *282*
Binet intelligence tests, 282–283, *283*, 289
Binge-and-purge eating, 179
Binge drinking, 193
Biological evolution, 318
Biological factors, 64–89
    example of, 66–67
    in gender development, 411–413
    genetic foundations, 69–80
    heredity-environment interaction, 84–87
    in language development, 318–320, 339
    reproductive challenges, 81–84
Biological prewiring, 319
Biological processes, 17, *18*
Birth control pill, 190
Birthing centers, 111
Birth order, 487–489
Birth process. *See* Childbirth
Blankinship, Lynn, 191, *191*
Blastocyst, 95, *96*
Blending, 334
Blinking reflex, 144, *145*
Blood type, incompatibility in, 103
"Blooming and pruning," 132–133, *133*
BMR (basal metabolism rate), 177
Bodily-kinesthetic skills, 290
Body mass, puberty and, 184
Bonding, postpartum, 122–123

Book of Virtues (Bennett), 454
Botkin, Darla, 485, *485*, 486
Bottlefeeding, 130, *139*, 139–140
"Boy code," 426
Boys
    bullying and, 516, *517*
    classroom bias against, 416
    early and late maturation, 187, *188*
    effects of divorce on, 496
    effects of educational television on, 597, *598*
    friendships, 525
    gender socialization of, 429
    Latino, risks of obesity, 178, *178*
    with learning disabilities, 560
    self-esteem in, 393
Bradburn, Susan, 550, *550*
Bradley method of childbirth, 113
Brain
    changes in neurons, 173
    cognitive development and, 174, *174*
    development of, 132–134, *132–134*
    early experience and, 135–136, *136*
    gender differences in, 422
    growth in childhood, 172–173, *173*
    growth in infancy, *132*, 132–136
    handedness and, 172
    lobes and hemispheres, 134–135, *135*, 319, *319*
    maturation of, 253
    role in language development, 318–319, *319*
    role in language processing, 135, 172, 319, *319*
    structures of, 173–174, *174*
Brain-scanning techniques, 173
Brainstorming, 301
Brazelton, T. Berry, 142, 143, *143*
Brazelton Neonatal Behavioral Assessment Scale, 118–119, 295
Breastfeeding
    bottlefeeding contrasted, 130, *139*, 139–140
    kangaroo care and, 116
Breech position, 113
Broca, Paul, 315
Broca's area, 318, *319*
Bronfenbrenner, Urie, 40–41, *41*
"Browning" of Americans, 591–592
Bulimia nervosa, 179
Bullying, 512, *513*, 516, *517*

Caffeine, teratology of, 101
CAH (congenital adrenal hyperplasia), 411
California Achievement Test, 545
Calorie requirements, 177, *177*
Canalization, 73–74
Cancer
    as leading cause of death, *181*, 181–182, *183*
    leukemia in children, 182, *183*
Career counseling, careers in, A–5
Careers in child development, A–1—A–8
    clinical and counseling jobs, A–4—A–5
    education and research, 589, *589*, A–1—A–4
    family and relationship counseling, A–7—A–8
    health professionals, A–5—A–7
    Internet information on, A–8
Caregivers
    attachment and, 371–372
    fathers as, 373–374
    games, 473–474
    language development and, 320
    safety and, 175
    soothing crying infants, 351–352
Care perspective, 444–445

Caretaking role, 478
Case studies, 46
Casual sex, 424
Causation
    correlation differentiated, 46, 47, 52
    infant understanding of, 213, 213
Centration, 217
Cephalocaudal growth pattern, 131, 131
Cerebral cortex, 134–135, 135
Cesarean delivery, 113–114
Change mechanisms, 243
Channel One, 599
"Character Counts," 454
Character education, 453–454
Character Education Network, 454
Character Education Partnership, 454
Chat rooms, 598
Child abuse. See Child maltreatment
Childbirth, 109–119, 125
    birth process, 109–114
    description of, 94
    effects of stress on, 106
    low birth weight infants, 114–118, 115, 116
    measures of neonatal health and responsiveness, 118,
        118–119
    methods of delivery, 112–114
    prenatal development and, 92–126
    setting and attendants, 111–112
    stages of, 110, 110
    strategies for, 111–114
    transition to newborn, 110–111
    See also Postpartum period
Child care
    day care, federal funding for, 15
    emotional development and, 374–377, 375
    government policies, 374
    high-quality programs, 375, 375–376, 377
Child-care directors, 376, 376
Child-centered kindergarten, 544
Child development, 4–23
    culture and, 578–583, 601
    developmental process and periods, 17–19
    history of, 7–16
    issues in, 19–21
    research in, 43–51, 52
    resilience and competence, 16, 16
    science of, 26–59
    social policy and, 14–15
Child development theories, 29–42, 42, 43
    behavioral theories, 36, 37, 37, 38, 320
    cognitive theories. See Cognitive developmental
        approaches; Cognitive theories
    eclectic theoretical orientation, 41–42
    ecological theory, 40, 40–41
    ethological theory, 38–40, 369–370
    evolutionary theory, 67–69, 89
    psychoanalytic theories. See Psychoanalytic theories
    social cognitive theory. See Social cognitive theory
Child-directed speech, 321
Child groups, 517, 527–528, 528
Childhood
    brain growth in, 172–173, 173
    contemporary concerns, 10–14
    depression in, 356
    health in, 174–183, 199
    historical views of, 7, 7–8
    modern study of, 8, 8–9
    motor development in, 170–172
    physical growth in, 169–170, 199
    See also Early childhood; Middle and late childhood
Child labor laws, 15
Child life specialists, 182, 182, A–7
Child maltreatment
    cultural context of, 484–485
    developmental consequences of, 485

family influences, 485
    nature of, 484
    repressed memories and, 259, 259
    violence and, 484–485
Child psychiatry, 558
Child-rearing leave, 374
Children's Defense Fund, 15, 15
Children with disabilities, 559–564
    ADHD, 561, 562–563
    deaf children, 325–326, 327
    demographics of, 559, 559–560
    educational issues, 563–564
    learning disabilities, 560–562, 573–574
Child welfare work, careers in, A–7
Chlamydia, 190
Chorionic villus sampling, 81
Chromosome abnormalities, 77, 77–78
    Down syndrome. See Down syndrome
    sex chromosome abnormalities, 78
Chromosomes, 70, 70
Chronological age, mental age and, 282
Chronosystem, 40, 41
Chunking, 249, 254
Cigarette smoking
    by adolescents, 193–194, 194
    effects on fetus, 101–102, 107
    exposure to, illness and, 181
    SIDS and, 101, 139
"Circular reactions," 210
Circumcision, 158, 412
Classical conditioning, 37
Classification, 220, 220
Classrooms
    cognitive apprenticeship in, 231
    FCL classrooms, 268–269
    gender bias in, 416–417
    jigsaw classroom, 269, 557
    multiple intelligences in, 290–291
    Project Spectrum, 280, 291
    as setting of exploration, 227
    triarchic intelligence in, 292
Clinical child psychology, careers in, 11, 11
Cliques, 510, 526, 527
"Club drugs," 192
Cocaine, effects on fetus, 102
Cognition
    adolescent, variations in, 225–226
    cognitive processes, 17, 18
    language and, 324–326, 325, 339
    role in families, 478
    self-control and, 447
    social cognition, 514–515
    stress and, 358–359, 360
Cognitive appraisal, 359
Cognitive apprenticeship, 230, 231, 231
Cognitive conflict, 440–442
Cognitive constructivist approaches, 541
Cognitive development
    bilingualism and, 336
    brain and, 174, 174
    gender and, 422
    moral development and, 440–443
    play and, 518–519
    television and, 596–597, 598
Cognitive developmental approaches, 33–35, 34,
    204–238
    information-processing approach compared, 243–244
    Piaget's theory, 207–229, 237
    Vygotsky's theory. See Vygotsky's theory
Cognitive developmental theory of gender, 419, 419
Cognitive frameworks, 207, 209, 228
Cognitive influences, on gender development,
    418–420, 419
Cognitive moral education, 454–455

Cognitive processes, 17, 18
Cognitive schema, 356
Cognitive skills, 135, 335
Cognitive strategies, 348
Cognitive theories, 33–36, 42
    evaluation of, 36
    information-processing theory, 36, 242–244, 275
    Piaget's theory, 33–35, 34
    of reading, 334
    Vygotsky's theory. See Vygotsky's theory
Collaborative gene, 75–77
Collaborative learning, 268
Collectivism, individualism and, 581, 581–582, 582
College students, 195, 284–285, 400
Color vision, 153
Columbine High School shootings, 462, 462
Comer, James, 558, 558
Comer Project for Change, 558, 558
Commitment, 398
Communication skills, 514, 514–515
Community, SES in, 584
Community-school partnerships, 558
Community service, 455, 455
Companionship, friendship and, 522
Competence
    competence enhancement, 16
    emotional, 349
    estimates of, 228
    measures of, 392
    moral, 448
    social. See Social competence
Computers
    cultural change and, 597–598
    in FCL classrooms, 269
    parental monitoring of use, 598–599, 599
Concepts, 260
    formation of, 260–261
    theory of mind and, 260–261, 261
Conceptual development, in infancy, 214
Concrete operational stage, 34, 35
Concrete operational thought, 220, 220–221, 221
Condoms, 190
Conduct disorder, 458
Confidentiality, 54
Conformity, 416, 440, 441, 526–527
Congenital adrenal hyperplasia (CAH), 411
Connectedness, 400–401
Conscience, 449
Conservation, 217–219, 220, 229
Conservation tasks, 217, 217–218, 218
Constraining behaviors, 401
Constructive play, 521
Constructivist approaches, 226–227, 235
    cognitive constructivist approach, 541
    to learning, 550
    social constructivist approach, 235, 541
Content knowledge, 254, 254–255
Context, 12
Continuity-discontinuity issue, 20, 20
Continuity view of family, 474–475
Contraceptives, 189–190
Control group, 47–48, 48
Controversial children, 515
Conventional reasoning, 439–440, 441
Convergent thinking, 301
Conversation, language acquisition and, 323
Cooing, 326
Cooperative play, 520
Coordination of secondary circular reactions, 210
Coparenting, 503
Coping
    cognitive appraisal and, 359
    with death of parent or sibling, 362–363
    emotion regulation and, 353

self-esteem and, 394–395
stress and, 358–363
Coregulation, 477
Corporal punishment, 482–484, *483*
Corpus callosum, 422
Correlational research, 46–47, *47*, 52, 595
Correlation coefficient, 47
Corticotrophin-releasing hormone (CRH), 106
Coughing reflex, 144
Counseling psychology, careers in, A–4
Covert pathway to delinquency, 459
Creative intelligence, 291, 292
Creativity
    intelligence and, 300–302
    stimulation of, 301–302
    television and, 596–597
CRH (corticotrophin-releasing hormone), 106
Crisis, 398
Criterion validity, 286
Critical period, 38, 319–320
Critical thinking, 242, 267–269, 558
Cross-age teaching, 232, 268–269
Cross-classification, 229
Cross-cultural studies, 13, 580–583
    of achievement, 570–571, *571*, 581
    of contemporary adolescents, 196
    of families, 498
    individualism and collectivism, *581*, 581–582, *582*
    of intelligence, 305–306
    of rites of passage, 582–583, *583*
Cross-sectional approach, 48
"Cross-talk" sessions, 269
Crowds, 527
Crying, 326
Cue-dependent forgetting, 257
Cultural assessment, in health care, 108
Cultural bias, in IQ testing, 287–288, *288*, 306–307
Cultural conflict, 578
Cultural diversity, 590–591, 593
Cultural-familial retardation, 298–299
Cultural mediation, 558
Culture, 13, 576–601
    achievement and, 570–571, *571*, 581
    adolescent autonomy and, 489
    adolescent dating and, 532–533
    American. *See* American culture
    attachment and, *372*, 372–373
    beliefs about pregnancy, 108–109
    biological factors and, 69
    childbirth practices, 112, *112*
    child development and, 578–583, 601
    child maltreatment and, 484–485
    computers and Internet, 529, 597–599
    cross-cultural comparisons, 580–583
    culture conflicts, 578
    families, neighborhoods, and schools, 498, 584–585, *585*
    formal operational thought and, 224
    gender and, 420, 427
    gross motor skills and, 148–149, *149*
    handling "tools" of, 231
    language rules and, 317
    moral development and, 444
    nature and characteristics of, 579
    poverty and, 585–587, *586*
    preferences for infant's sex and, 415, *415*
    prenatal development and, 108–109
    relevance of, 579–580
    role in identity formation, 401–403
    role of television in, 594–597
    self-concept and, 582, *582*
    separation protest and, 352, *352*
    sibling relationships and, 487
    sleeping practices, 137

as social context, 401, 402–403
socioeconomic status and, 583–584
stages of development and, 229
standardized tests and, 46
study of children and, 579–580
technology and, 594–599
temperament and, 366–367
See also Developing countries; Ethnicity
Culture-fair tests, 287
Curanderos, 109
Cyberdating, 529
Cystic fibrosis, 79, *79*

D

Dahmer, Jeffrey, 6, *6*
Daily hassles, 359–360
Darwin, Charles, 8, 9
Dating, 528
    cultural conflict about, 578
    cyberdating, 529
    sociocultural contexts of, 532–533
Dating scripts, 531–532
Davidson, Richard, 76
Day care. *See* Child care
Deaf children, language acquisition in, 325–326, 327
Death
    causes of, 180–183, *181*
    coping with, 362–363
    SIDS, 101, 138–139
Debriefing, 54
Decay theory, 257
Deception, in research, 54
Declarative memory, 252, 253, *253*
Deep processing, 248
Deferred imitation, 267
Defining Issues Test (DIT), 443
Deliberate practice, expertise and, 254–255
Deloin, Barbara, 141, *141*
Democratic mode, in relationships, 475
Democratic parents, 400
Deoxyribonucleic acid (DNA), 70, *70*, 77
Dependent variable, 47
Depression, 379
    in adolescence, 357
    in childhood, 356
    in parents, 356–357
    postpartum, measures of, 121
Deprivation dwarfism, 170
Deprived environment, 136, *136*
Depth perception, 156, *156*
Descriptive research, 43–46
    case studies, 46
    observation, 43–45, *45*
    standardized tests, 45–46
    survey and interview, 45
Developing countries
    AIDS in, 190
    breastfeeding in, 130
    childhood illness in, 182–183
    gross motor skill development, 149
    low birth weight infants in, 114
    malnutrition in, 140–142
    sibling relationships in, 487
    See also Culture
Development, 17
Developmental changes
    in attention, 246–247, *247*
    consequences of child abuse, 485
    emotional development, 350, *351*
    in identity, 400
    metacognition and, 271

parenting and, 476–477
in self-esteem, 393
Developmental construction views, 474–476
    continuity view, 474–475
    discontinuity view, 475–476
Developmentally appropriate practice, 544–545, *546*, 547
Developmental problems, 114–115
Developmental psychology, 55
    careers in, 262, *262*
    evolutionary, 68–69
Developmental quotient (DQ), 295
Developmental windows, 428–429
Dewey, John, 455
Diabetes, 79, *79*
Dialogue, in scaffolding, 230
Diaphragm, 190
Diarrhea, 182
Dick-Read, Grantley, 113
Differentiated self-understanding, 387
Difficult child, 364, 367
Diffuse/avoidant processing style, 399
Direct instruction approach, 541
Disability, parenting and, 472
Discipline, 452–453, 476, 477
Discontinuity, in development, 20
Discontinuity view, of family, 475–476
Dishabituation, *245*, 245–246
Dismissing/avoidant attachment, 490
Displacement, 331
Distinctiveness of memory code, 249
DIT (Defining Issues Test), 443
Divergent thinking, 301
Divorce
    effects on children, 495–496
    stepfamilies and, 496–497
Divorce rate, 495
Dizygotic twins, 74
DNA (deoxyribonucleic acid), 70, *70*, 77
Domain-specific mechanisms, 68
Dominant genes, 71, *71*
Dominant-recessive genes principle, 71, *71*
Dose, teratology and, 99
Doula, 112
Down syndrome, 76, 77, 78, *78*, 299
    age of parents and, 106, 107
    language development, 324
DQ (developmental quotient), 295
Drinking age, 583
Driver's license, obtaining, 583
Drug abuse. *See* Substance use and abuse
Drug counseling, careers in, A–5
Drug therapy, for depression, 357
Dwarfism, 107, 170
Dynamic systems theory, 151
Dyscalculia, 561
Dyslexia, 561

E

Early childhood, 18, *19*
    acculturation, 500
    attention and, 246
    brain and, 173
    emotional development in, 353–354, *354*
    empathy in, 449
    fine motor skills, 171–172
    gross motor skills, 170–171
    illness in, 175, 180–181, *181*
    language development in, 329–332
    moral development in, 436
    parent-child interactions in, 476–477

physical growth in, 169–170
pretense/symbolic play in, 520–521
regulation of emotion in, 348
rehearsal in, 248
safety hazards, 175
self-understanding in, 386
sharing in, 456
sports participation in, 168, *168*
view of death, 362–363
Early childhood education, 543–550, 573
   careers in, A–3
   child-centered kindergarten, 544
   curriculum controversy in, 547
   developmentally appropriate practice, 544–545, *546*, 547
   for disadvantaged children, 547–548
   effects of, 548–549
   Montessori approach, 544
   school readiness and, 549
   transition to elementary school, 549–550
   See also Schools
Early-experience doctrine, 20
Early-later experience issue, 20–21
Early maturation, 187, *187*, 525
Easy child, 364
Eating behaviors
   in adolescence, 176
   nutritional needs and, 139
   obesity and, 177–178
Eating disorders
   in adolescence, *178*, 178–179
   anorexia nervosa, 178–179
   bulimia nervosa, 179
Eclectic theoretical orientation, 41–42, *42*
Ecological theory, *40*, 40–41, *42*, 152–153
Economic Opportunity Act of 1965, 547
Ecstasy, *193*
Ectoderm, 95
Edelman, Marian Wright, 15, *15*
Edinburgh Postnatal Depression Scale, 121
Education
   access to, for girls, 427
   androgyny and, 425–426
   bilingual education, 336, 592
   careers in, 589, *589*, A–1—A–4
   character education, 453–454
   of children with disabilities, 563–564
   cognitive moral education, 454–455
   contemporary concerns, 12
   life science and life skills education, 176
   Piaget's theory and, 226–227
   socioeconomic status and, 499
   special education services, 559, *559*
   standards-based, 547
   technology and, 599
   Vygotsky's theory and, 232–234
   See also Early Childhood education; Schools
Educational psychology, careers in, 55, A–3
Educational television, 594–595, 596, 597, *598*
Educational Testing Service, 285
Education for All Handicapped Children Act of 1975, 563
Education supervision, careers in, 300, 301, *301*
EEG (electroencephalogram), 134
"Effeminate" behavior, 429
Effortful control, 364
Egalitarian mode, in relationships, 475
Ego, 30
Egocentric viewpoint, *390*
Egocentrism, 215, 224–225
Ego ideal, 449
Ego-involved goals, 569
Ego support, friendship and, 522
Eight intelligences theory, 290–291

Elaboration, encoding and, 248–249, *249*
Electroencephalogram (EEG), 134
Elementary school
   KEEP program, 233–234
   language development and, 332
   physical growth during, 170
   Piagetian classroom, 227
   school readiness and, 549
   social contexts, 543
   transition to, 549–550
   See also Classrooms; Education
Elementary school teaching, careers in, 550, *550*, A–2
E-mail, 598
Embryo, 95
Embryonic period, 95–97
Emerson, Ralph Waldo, 315
Emotion, 346–350, 379
   defining, 346–347
   emotional competence, 349
   family processes and, 478–479
   functionalism in, 347
   gender and, 427
   regulation of, 348–349
   relational, 347–348
   role in families, 478–479
   romantic relationships and, 532
   self-conscious emotions, 350, *351*
   self-presentation of, 355
Emotional adjustment, divorce and, 495, *495*, 496, 497
Emotional competence, 349
Emotional development, 344–380
   in adolescence, 355, *355*
   attachment and, 368–377
   crying, 351–352
   early changes, 350, *351*
   in early childhood, 353–354, *354*
   emotion regulation and coping, 353
   fathering, 346
   fear, 352, *352*
   in infancy, 350–353
   in middle and late childhood, 354
   smiling, 352
   social referencing, 353
   temperament and, 363–368
   See also Emotion; Emotional problems
Emotional intelligence, 293, 558
Emotional problems, 356–363, 379–380
   depression, 356–357
   stress and coping, 358–363
   suicide, 182, 357–358, 379
Emotional states
   effects on fetus, 105–106
   postpartum adjustments, 120–122, *121*
Emotional stereotypes, 427
Emotional support, 394
Emotion-coaching parents, 348
Emotion-dismissing parents, 348
Emotion regulation, 348–349, 366
   cognitive strategies for, 348
   coping and, 353
   effortful control, 364
   family and, 478–479
   gender and, 423
   social competence and, 354
Empathy, 449–451, *450*
Employment
   age for beginning, 583
   in high school, 554
   working mothers, 493–495
   See also Careers in child development; *specific careers*
Enabling behaviors, 401
Encoding, 243
   attention and, 245–247
   deep processing and, 248

   elaboration and, 248–249, *249*
   image construction in, 249, *249*
   in memory, 244–250
   organization in, 249–250
   rehearsal and, 247–248, 249
Endoderm, 95
Energy needs, 177, *177*
Engagement with children, 501, *501*
Environment
   brain development and, 135–136
   cultural-familial retardation and, 298–299
   deprived, brain activity and, 136, *136*
   development of grasping and, 149–151
   enrichment programs, 115
   genotype-environment correlations, 85, *85*
   goodness of fit and, 365
   heredity and. *See* Heredity-environment interaction
   influence on intelligence, 304–305, *305*
   language development and, 320–322, *321*
   stimulation of creativity, 301–302
   temperament and, 367
Environmental experiences, 19
Environmental hazards, *103*, 103–104
Environmental stimulation, 115–116
Epidural block, 112
Epigenetic view, 86, *86*
Episodic memory, 252, *253*, 253–254
Equality, 457
Equilibration, 208
Erikson, Erik Homberger, 28, 30, *31*, 41, 46, 411, 413, 518
Erikson's theory, 31–33, *32*, *42*, 395–397, 399
Eskimos, incidence of SIDS among, 139
Estradiol, 185
Estrogens, 121, 411, 421
Ethical research, 53–54
Ethics guidelines, 54
Ethnic gloss, 56–57
Ethnic identity, 13, 401
Ethnicity, 13, 601
   achievement and, 570, 581
   assimilation and pluralism, 592
   blended cultures and, 592–593
   differences and diversity, 590–591
   diversity within groups, 590–591
   families and, 498–499, 500
   immigration and, 588
   intelligence and, *283*, 306–307
   poverty and, 13
   prejudice, discrimination, and bias, 589, 591–592
   research on, 14
   role in identity formation, 401–403
   schools and, 556–558
   as social context, 401–402
   socioeconomic status and, 588–590
   See also Culture
Ethnic minorities
   interethnic friendships, 530
   multiple selves and, 389
   negative stereotypes of, 556–557
   peer relations, 530, *530*
   research bias and, 55–57
   standardized tests and, 46
   See also specific ethnic groups
Ethnic minority parenting, 500
Ethnocentrism, 579–580
Ethological theory, 38–40, *42*, 369–370
Ethology, 38
Evocative genotype-environment correlations, 85, *85*
Evolution, biological, 318
Evolutionary psychology, 67–69
   developmental, 68–69
   evaluating, 69
   gender and, 413

Evolutionary theory, 67–69, 89
  adaptive behavior, 67, 68–69
  natural selection, 67
Exclusionary criteria for learning disabilities, 560
Exercise, 179–180, *180*
  in adolescence, 179–180, *180*
  inadequate, obesity and, 178
Exosystem, *40*, 41
Expanding strategy, 322
Experience sampling method, 355, *355*
Experimental group, 47–48, *48*
Experimental research, 47–48, *48*
Experiments, 47
Expertise
  content knowledge and, 254, *254*
  practice and, 254–255
Explicit memory, 253, *253*
Exploratory behavior, 227, 519
Extended families, ethnicity and, 498, 500
Extended "juvenile" period, 68
"Extra-moral" factors, in morality, 448
Extrinsic motivation, 565, 567
Extrinsic rewards, 566–567
Eye contact, 473, 476

Facilitation, in education, 227
Factor analysis, 290
Factual knowledge, 271
Fagan Test of Infant Intelligence, 295–296
Fairness, 456–457
False beliefs, 261, *261*
False self, true self and, 388
Families, 470–506
  adolescents and, 489–492
  contemporary concerns, 10–12
  culture and, 498
  developmental construction views, 474–476
  discontinuity view of, 475–476
  effects of divorce, 495–496
  ethnicity and, 498–499, 500
  extended families, 498, 500
  family processes, 473–479, 496, 505
  gay and lesbian parents, 497–498
  influences on child care, 377
  influences on child maltreatment, 485
  influences on identity, 400–401
  intervention programs for, 142, *142*
  juvenile delinquency and, 460
  marital relationships, 474
  one-parent families. *See* Single-parent families
  reciprocal socialization in, 473–474
  research on, 12
  roles of cognition and emotion in, 478–479
  sibling relationships, 487–489
  as social context, 400–401
  social world and, *493*, 493–503
  sociocultural and historical changes, 477–478, 505–506
  socioeconomic status and, 499, 584–585
  stepfamilies, 496–497
  as systems, 474, *475*
  work in, done by women, 499–500
  working mothers, 493–495
  See also Parenting; Parents
Family and consumer science education, careers in, 191, *191*, A–3
Family leave, 374
Family tree task, 220, *220*
Family work, done by women, 499–500
FAS (fetal alcohol syndrome), 101, *101*, 561

Fast Track program, 461
Fathering, 346
Fathers
  in African American homes, 589
  as caregivers, 373–374
  child development and, 503
  gender development and, 415–416
  impact of fathering on men, 502–503
  involvement with children, *501*, 501–502
  paternal factors in fetal development, 107
  postpartum adjustments, 121
  role of, 500–503
  See also Men
FCL (Fostering a Community of Learners), 268–269
Fear, in infants, 352, *352*
Feedback, 263
Feeding, attachment and, 367–368
Feminists, controversy over gender, 423–424
Feminization of poverty, 586–587
Fetal alcohol syndrome (FAS), 101, *101*, 561
Fetal period, 97–98, *98*
Fetus, ability to hear, 157
Field, Tiffany, 117, *117*
Fine motor skills
  in early childhood, 171
  in infancy, 146, 149–151, *150*
  in middle and late childhood, 171–172
First habits and primary circular reactions, 209–210
First words, 328, *328*
"Flashbacks," 258
"Flashbulb" memories, 257
Flexible thinking, 302
Flynn effect, 305
Fodness, Mark, 553
Folic acid, need for, 105
Forgetting, 257
Formal operational stage, *34*, 35
Formal operational thought, 221–226, 438
  adolescent egocentrism, 224–225
  characteristics of, 221–224, *223*
  early and late, 225
  middle school and, 551
  variations in cognition and, 225–226
Fostering a Community of Learners (FCL), 268–269
"Fourth trimester," 119
Fragile X syndrome, 72, *77*, 78
Fraternal (dizygotic) twins, 74
Frederick II, Holy Roman Emperor, 326
Freestyle (TV series), 419
Freud, Sigmund, 8, 9, 29, *30*, 206, 368, 411–414, 448, 518
Freud's theory, 30–31, *31*, 42
Friendship interaction, 476
Friendships, 522–525, 535
  functions of, 522
  interethnic, 530
  intimacy and similarity in, 524–525
  making friends, strategies for, 524, *524*
  mixed-age, 525
  neighborhood networks, 530, *530*
  Sullivan's views of, *523*, 523–524, *524*
Froebel, Friedrich, 544
Frontal lobe, 135, *135*, 253, 318–319, *319*
Functionalist view of emotion, 347

g (general intelligence), 293, 294
Gallamore, Suellen, 76, *76*
Galton, Sir Francis, 282
Games, 473–474, 521
Gamete intrafallopian transfer (GIFT), 82
Gandhi, Mohandas (Mahatma), 46

Gandhi's Truth (Erikson), 396
Garcia, Yolanda, 548, *548*
Gardner's theory of intelligences, 290–291
Gay and lesbian parents, 497–498
Gender, 14, 411
  asymmetric gender socialization, 429
  autonomy-granting and, 489
  body perception and, 187
  controversy over, 423–424
  culture and, 420, 427
  depression and, 357
  differences in aggression and, 423, 427
  emotion and, 427
  evolutionary psychology and, 413
  feelings of guilt and, 449
  helping behavior and, 426
  instrumental activities and, 418
  media portrayals of, 417–418
  moral development and, 444–445
  parenting and, 499–503
  peer relations and, 517
  performance on IQ tests and, 307
  response to divorce and, 496
  as social context, 403
  suicide and, 358
  temperament and, 366
  theories of, 414, *414*, 419, *419*
  See also Boys; Girls; Men; Women
Gender bias
  in classroom, 416–417
  in language, 419–420
  minimizing, 54–55
  in SAT test, 285
Gender constancy, 419
Gender curricula, 425–426
Gender development, 408–431
  anatomy as destiny, 412–413
  asymmetric gender socialization, 429
  biological influences on, 411–413
  cognitive influences on, 418–420, *419*
  developmental windows, 428–429
  evolutionary psychology, 413
  gender-role classification and, 424–428
  heredity and hormones, 411–412
  influence of schools and teachers, 416–417
  interactionist view of, 413
  media influence on, 417–418
  nurturing males, 410
  parental influences on, *415*, 415–416
  peer influences on, 416, *416*
  psychoanalytic theory of, 414, *414*
  similarities and differences in, 421–424
  social cognitive theory of, 414, *414*
  social influences on, 414–418
  stereotyping, 420–421
Gender equality, increasing, 428
Gender (sexual) identity, 188, 411, 529–531
Gender-role classification, 424–428
  androgyny and education, 425–426
  defined, 425, *425*
  gender in context, 426–428
  gender-role transcendence, 426
  masculinity, 426
Gender roles, 373–374, 411, 427
Gender-role transcendence, 426
Gender schema theory of gender, 419, *419*
Gender socialization, asymmetric, 429
Gender-specific behavior, 414, *414*, 427, *427*
Gender stereotypes, 323, 420–421
Gene-linked abnormalities, 78–80, *79*
General intelligence (*g*), 293, 294
"Generational forgetting," 192–193
Generational issues, 578
Generativity *versus* stagnation, *32*, 32–33

Genes, 70, *70*
Genetic counseling, 76, 80, *80*
  careers in, A–7
Genetic disorders
  androgen-insensitive males, 412
  congenital adrenal hyperplasia, 411
  malignant hyperthermia, 76
  pelvic field defect, 412
Genetic epistemology, 9
Genetic factors, in puberty, 184
Genetic foundations, 69–80, 89
  abnormalities, 77–80
  behavior genetics, 74
  collaborative gene, 75–77
  genes, 70, *70*
  meiosis, 70–71
  mitosis, 70
  molecular genetics, 74–75, *75*
  principles of genetics, 71–74
Genetic health risks, 75, *75*
Genetic imprinting, 72
Genetic principles, 71–74
  canalization, 73–74
  dominant-recessive genes, 71, *71*
  genetic imprinting, 72
  polygenic inheritance, 72–73
  reaction range, 73
  sex-linked genes, 72, *72*
Genetic susceptibility, 99
"Genie," 46, 314, 319–320, *320*
Genital herpes, 190
Genital stage, 31, *31*
Genotype, 73, 86
German measles (rubella), 104
Germinal period, 95, *96*
Gesell, Arnold, *8*, 8–9
Gestures, 326
"Get tough" policy, on delinquency, 458
GIFT (gamete intrafallopian transfer), 82
Giftedness, 299–300
Gilligan, Carol, 423
Girls
  access to education, 427
  African American, 178, *178*, 179, 402
  care perspective in, 444–445
  classroom bias against, 416–417
  dating scripts, 531
  early and late maturation, 187, *188*
  eating disorders in, *178*, 178–179
  gender socialization of, 429
  intimate friendships in, 525
  juvenile delinquency, 458
  relational aggression and, 423
  self-esteem in, 393
  "tomboy" girls, 416
Global empathy, 449
Global interdependence, 580
Goal setting, achievement and, 569
Gonads, 185
Gonorrhea, 190
Goodness of fit, 365
Grammar, 332–333
Grasping, 149–151
Grasping reflex, 144–145, *145*
Great Depression, 477–478
Greater Expectations (Damon), 454
Gross motor skills, 146–149
  culture and, 148–149, *149*
  in early childhood, 170–171
  fitness classes and, 148
  in middle and late childhood, 170–171
  milestones in, 147–148, *148*
  posture, 146
  walking, 146–147, *147*

Group intelligence testing, 283–285
Guilt, 449, 451
Gymnastics, 168, *168*

H

Habits, 209–210
Habituation, *245*, 245–246
Hall, G. Stanley, 8, 9, 491, 580
Hammond, Rodney, 461, *461*
Handedness, 172
Hand-eye coordination, 212
Handicapping conditions, 560
Harris, Eric, 462, *462*
Hawaii Family Support/Healthy Start Program, 142, *142*
Head Start program, 15, 545, 547–548, *548*
Health
  in adolescence, 175–176, 182, 199
  in childhood, 174–183, 199
  cigarette smoking and, 193–194, *194*
  developmental perspective of, 175–176
  exercise, 179–180, *180*
  genetic health risks, 75, *75*
  illness and. *See* Illness
  intellectual health, 227
  lifestyles and, 10
  mental health problems, 584–585, 586
  neonatal, measures of, *118*, 118–119
  nutrition and obesity, 176–179, *177*
  poverty and, 181, 586
  sports, 180
  STIs. *See* Sexually transmitted infections
  substance use and abuse, *192*, 192–195, *193*
Health care, 108
Health psychology, careers in, 461, *461*
Hearing, in infancy, *157*, 157–158
Heat, effects on fetus, 104
Height
  in early childhood, 169–170
  growth in infancy, 132
  pubertal growth spurt, 185–186, *186*
"Heinz and the drug" dilemma, 438–439, 443–444
Helping behavior, 426
Helpless orientation, 567
Hemispheres of brain, 135, *135*, 172, 319, *319*
Hemophilia, 72, 76, 79, *79*
Heredity
  intelligence and, *303*, 303–304
  polygenic inheritance, 72–73
  role in gender development, 411–412
  role in temperament, 365
  X-linked inheritance, 72
Heredity-environment interaction, 84–87, 89
  conclusions about, 86–87
  correlations, 84–85, *85*
  epigenetic view of, 86, *86*
  shared and nonshared experiences, 85–86
Heroin, effects on fetus, 103
Heteronomous morality, 437, 438, 439, *441*
Heuristics, in problem solving, 262
Hidden curriculum, 453
Hierarchical networks, 255
High-quality child-care programs, *375*, 375–376, 377
High school, 553–555, 573
  dropouts, 553, *554*
  drug use in, 195
  effectiveness of, 554–555
  social contexts, 543
  violence in, 462, *462*
High school counseling, careers in, 402
High Scope Foundation, 196
Historical influences on family, 477–478

HIV (human immunodeficiency virus), 190
Home childbirth, 111
Homicide, 182
Homosexuality, 188
  adolescent romantic relationships, 529–531
  gay and lesbian parents, 497–498
  myths about, 530–531
  suicide and, 358
Horizontal décalage, 220
Hormones
  androgens, 411, 412
  estrogens, 121, 411, 421
  growth-related, 169–170
  postpartum production of, 120
  puberty and, 185, *185*
  sex hormones, 411–412, 421–422
  teratology, 100
  testosterone, 185, 412, 421
Hospitals, 123
Hubbard, Jerry, *79*
Human Genome Project, 75, 76
Human immunodeficiency virus (HIV), 190
Humor, 347
Huxley, Aldous, 268
Hypothalamus, 185, 422
Hypotheses, 29
Hypothetical-deductive reasoning, 222–223

I

ICSI (intracytoplasmic sperm injection), 82
Id, 30
IDEA (Individuals with Disabilities Education Act of 1990), 563
Idealistic self-understanding, 387
Ideal self, real self and, 387–388
Identical (monozygotic) twins, 74
Identity: Youth and Crisis (Erikson), 396
Identity achievement, 398, *398*, 399
Identity development, 382–405
  changes in, 400
  contemporary views of, 397–398
  Erikson's view of, 395–397
  ethnicity and, 13, 401–403
  family influences on, 400–401
  gender and, 403
  identity formation, 395–403
  personality and role experimentation, 396–397
  role of culture and ethnicity, 401–403
  self-esteem and self-concept, 391–395
  self-understanding, 384–391
  social contexts of, 400–403
Identity diffusion, 398, *398*, 399
Identity foreclosure, 398, *398*, 399
Identity moratorium, 398, *398*, 399
Identity statuses, *398*, 398–399, *399*
Identity *versus* identity confusion, 32, *32*, 395–396
IEP (individualized education plan), 563
"I Have a Dream" (IHAD) Program, *554*
Illness, 180–183, 199
  in adolescence, 182
  in developing countries, 182–183
  in early childhood, 175, 180–181, *181*
  in middle and late childhood, 181–182, *183*
  See also Health; *specific diseases*
Image construction, memory and, 249, *249*
Imaginary audience, 224
Imaginative play, 522
Imitation, by infants, *266*, 266–267
Immigration, 588
Imminent justice, 438
Implantation, 95, *96*

Implicit memory, 253, *253*
Imprinting, 38–39, *39*
Inclusion, 564
Incompatible blood types, 103
Independent variable, 47
In-depth perspective taking, *390*
Index offenses, 457
Individual differences
    in adolescent cognition, 225–226
    in attachment, *370*, 370–371
    effective schools and, 552
    in emotion regulation, 349
    in formal operational thought, 223–224
    in intelligence, 281
    in puberty, 186
Individualism, collectivism and, *581*, 581–582, *582*
Individualism, instrumental purpose, and exchange, 439, *441*
Individuality, 300, 367, 400
Individualized education plan (IEP), 563
Individuals with Disabilities Education Act (IDEA) of 1990, 563
Induction, 452–453
Indulgent parenting, 482
Industrialized nations, poverty in, 586, *586*
Industry *versus* inferiority, 32, *32*
Infancy, 18, *19*
    conceptual development in, 214
    developmental transformations, 294–297
    emotional development in, 350–353
    empathy in, 449
    growth in, 131–143
    handedness in, 172
    imitation in, *266*, 266–267
    intelligence testing in, 295–296
    language development in, 323, *323*, 326–329
    maternal employment during, 494
    means-end analysis in, 263
    motor development in, 144–151
    physical development in, 128–163
    regulation of emotion in, 348
    self-understanding in, 385, *385*
    sensorimotor stage. *See* Sensorimotor thought
    sensory and perceptual development, 152–161, 163, 214
    stability of intelligence in, 296–297
Infant assessment specialists, 296, *296*
Infantile amnesia, 253
Infants
    assessment of, *118*, 118–119, 295–296, *296*
    crying, soothing of, 351–352
    cultural preferences for gender, 415, *415*
    fear in, 352
    understanding of causation, 213, *213*
    use of imitation in problem solving, *266*, 266–267
    See also Low birth weight infants
Infectious diseases, effects on fetus, 104–105
Infertility, 81–83, *82, 83*
Infinite generativity, 315
Information processing, 240–276
    information-processing approach, 242–244
    memory. *See* Memory
    metacognition, 270–273
    skills in, peer relations and, 515
    styles of, 399
    thinking. *See* Thinking
Information-processing approach, 36, 242–244, 275
    cognitive developmental approach compared, 243–244
    processes, 242–243
Information-processing tasks, 297
Informed consent, 54
Inhibition, 366

Inhibition to the unfamiliar, 364
Initiative *versus* guilt, 32, *32*
Innate goodness view, 7
Inner speech, 232
Insecure avoidant babies, 371–372
Insecure disorganized babies, 371, 372
Insecure resistant babies, 371, 372
Institute of Social Research, 194
Institutional racism, 557
Instrumental activities, 418
Integrated learning, 550
Integrity *versus* despair, *32*, 33
Intellectual carefulness, 268
Intellectual curiosity, 268
Intellectual development, 547
Intellectual health, 227
Intelligence, 278–310
    Abecedarian Intervention Program, 304, *304*
    creativity and, 300–302
    cross-cultural comparisons of, 305–306
    developmental transformations, 294–297
    emotional intelligence, 293, 558
    environmental influences on, 304–305, *305*
    ethnic comparisons of, *283*, 306–307
    extremes of, 298–302, 309–310
    giftedness, 299–300
    group comparisons of, 305–307
    heritability of, *303*, 303–304
    information-processing tasks and, 297
    mental retardation, *298*, 298–299, *299*
    multiple intelligence theories, 280, 289–294, 309
    nature of, 281
    Project Spectrum, 280, 291
    stability and change in, 296–297
    testing. *See* Intelligence testing
Intelligence quotient (IQ), 282
Intelligence testing, 8, 281–289, 309
    approaches to, 282–285
    aptitude and achievement tests, 285
    Binet tests, 282–283, *283*, 289
    criteria for tests, 285–287
    cultural bias in, 287–288, *288*, 306–307
    Fagan Test of Infant Intelligence, 295–296
    group tests, 283–285
    infant testing, 295–296
    performance, gender and, 307
    predictive ability of, 294
    reliability in, 286
    role of gender in, 307
    Scholastic Aptitude Test, 281, 284
    standardization of, 286–287, *287*
    Stanford-Binet tests, 45, 283, *283*, 296, 299, *305*
    use and misuse of tests, 288–289
    validity in, 286
    Wechsler scales, 283, *284*
Intentionality, 210
Interactionist view
    of gender, 413
    of language development, 322–324
Interaction with peers. *See* Peer relations
Interference theory, 257
Intermodal perception, 159
Internalization, 439
Internalization of schemes, 210–211
Internet, 529, 598–599, *599*, A–8
Interpersonal skills, 290
Intervention programs
    Abecedarian Intervention Program, 304, *304*
    for adolescents, successful, 195–196
    for families, 142, *142*
Intervention strategies
    for learning disabilities, 561–562
    two-generation intervention, 556, 587
Interviewing, 45

Intimacy
    in friendship, 522, 524–525
    need for, in adolescence, 523, *523*
Intimacy skills, 511
Intimacy *versus* isolation, 32, *32*
Intracytoplasmic sperm injection (ICSI), 82
Intrapersonal skills, 290
Intrauterine insemination (IUI), 82
Intrinsic motivation, 565, 566–567
Intuitive thought substage, 216–219, *216–219*
In vitro fertilization (IVF), 82, *83*
Involution, 120
IQ (intelligence quotient), 282
IQ-achievement discrepancy, 560
IQ scores, 74, 296–297, 307
Ishmael, Holly, 80, *80*
IUI (intrauterine insemination), 82
IVF (in vitro fertilization), 82, *83*
iVillage website, 481

J

James, William, 257
Jerry Maguire (film), 410, *410*
Jigsaw classroom, 269, 557
Jones, Sterling, 300, 301, *301*
Jordan, Michael, 255
Junior high school. *See* Middle school
Junta, Thomas, 180
Justice perspective, 444
Juvenile delinquency, 457–461
    among latchkey children, 494
    antecedents of, 458–460, *459*
    lack of parental monitoring and, 481, 494–495
    nature of, 457–458
    violence, 460–461, 462, *462*

K

Kamehameha Elementary Education Program (KEEP), 233–234
Kangaroo care, 116–118
Kaufman Assessment Battery for Children, *116*
KEEP (Kamehameha Elementary Education Program), 233–234
Keller, Helen, 314
Key School, 291, *291*
Keyser, Janis, 481, *481*
Kindergarten, 544, 549
Kinkel, Kip, 462
Kissing, 189
Klebold, Dylan, 462
Klinefelter syndrome, *77*, 78
Knowledge, 271
    collaborative nature of, 35
    content knowledge, *254*, 254–255
    social knowledge, peers and, 515
Kohlberg, Lawrence, 55, 438, *438*
Kohlberg's theory of moral development, 438–440
    conventional reasoning, 439–440
    critics of, 443–445
    modeling and cognitive conflict, 440–442
    peer relations and, 442–443
    postconventional reasoning, 440, *441*
    preconventional reasoning, 439
    stages in, 438–439, *439*
Kwashiorkor, 141, *141*

L

Labeling strategy, 322
Laboratory, 44
LAD (language acquisition device), 319, 322
Lamaze, Ferdinand, 113
Language, 314–315
  cognition and, 324–326, *325*, 339
  gender bias in, 419–420
  handedness and, 172
  morphology, 315–316, 329–330
  phonology, 315
  pragmatics, 316–317, 331–332
  rules of, culture and, 317
  rule systems for, 315–317, *317*, 339
  semantics, 316, 330–331
  sensitivity to sounds of, 158
  sign language, 327
  syntax, 316, 330
  thought and, 232
  "universal linguists," 327, *327*
Language acquisition device (LAD), 319, 322
Language acquisition support system (LASS), 323
Language comprehension, 327, 329, *329*
Language development, 312–339
  babbling and vocalizations, 326–327
  behavioral and environmental influences, 320–322, *321*
  bilingualism, 336–337, *337*, 339
  biological influences on, 318–320, 339
  brain's role in, 318–319, *319*
  critical period for, 319–320
  in deaf children, 325–326, 327
  in early childhood, 329–332
  evolution and, 318
  first words, 328, *328*
  grammar, 332–333
  in infancy, 323, *323*, 326–329
  interactionist view of, 322–324
  in middle and late childhood, 332–335
  nature of language, 314–317
  parental facilitation of, 323, *323*
  "prewiring," 319
  process of, 326–336
  production and comprehension, 329, *329*
  reading, writing, and literacy, 333–335
  second-language learning, 316, 336–337, *337*
  socioeconomic status and, 321, *321*, 324, 331
  sound recognition, *327*, 327–328
  two-word utterances, 328–329
  vocabulary, 328, 330–331, 332
Language processing, 135, 172, 319, *319*
Language production, 329, *329*
Lap reading, 335
LASS (language acquisition support system), 323
Latchkey children, 494–495
Late maturation, 187, *187*
Latency stage, 31, *31*
Lateralization, 135, *135*
Later-experience doctrine, 20–21
Latinos, 13
  achievement and, 570, 581
  adolescent dating, 533
  altruism, 457
  boys, risks of obesity, 178, *178*
  diversity among, 590–591
  ethnic identity, 402
  high school dropout rate, 553, *554*
  Mexican Americans, 109
  schools attended, 556
  stress and, 360, 361
LD (learning-disabled) children, 560
Lead, effects on fetus, 103

Lead poisoning, 181, 561
Learned helplessness, 356, 567, *568*
Learner-centered principles, 541, *542*
Learning disabilities, 559, *559*, 573–574
  characteristics of, 560–561
  diagnosis of, 561
  intervention strategies, 561–562
  in low birth weight infants, 115
Learning-disabled (LD) children, 560
Least restrictive environment (LRE), 563–564
Leonard, Jason, *591*
Leukemia, in children, 182, *183*
Levels of processing theory, 248
Lewis, Jim, 66, *66*
Life events, 359–360
Life science education, 176
Life skills education, 176
Lifestyles, health and, 10
Literacy, 231, 335
"Little Albert" experiments, 37
Locke, John, 7
Locomotor experience, 147, *147*
Logical reasoning, 221, 222
Longitudinal approach, 48–49, *49, 50*
Long-term goals, 569
Long-term memory, 252
  network theories, 255
  schema theories, 255–256
"Looking chamber," 154, *154*
Lorenz, Konrad, 38–39, *39*, 99
Love withdrawal, 452
Low birth weight infants, 114–118, *115, 116*
  enrichment programs for, 115
  kangaroo care and, 116–118
  level of stimulation and, 115–116
  massaging, 116, 117, *117*
  maternal age and, 106
  SIDS and, 138
Low self-esteem, consequences of, 393
LRE (least restrictive environment), 563–564

M

MA (mental age), 282
McCaughey septutplets, *83*
Maccoby, Eleanor, 417, *417*
McLeod, Sharon, 182, *182*
Macrosystem, *40*, 41
Magnetic resonance imaging (MRI), 134, 173
Malignant hyperthermia (MH), 76
Malnutrition, in infancy, 140–142
"MAMA" cycles, 400
Managed-care organizations, 112
Managerial role of parents, 480–481
Marasmus, 141
Marchese, Janet, 78
Marfan's syndrome, 107
Marijuana, 102–103
Marital relationships
  divorce and, 495
  parenting and, 474
  remarriage, 496–497
Marriage and family therapy, 485, *485*
  careers in, A–7—A–8
Martin, Laura, 269, *269*
Masculinity, 426
Massage therapy, for infants, 10, 116, 117, *117*
Mastery, 169, 567, *568*
Mastery orientation, 567
Maternal age, effects on fetus, 106–107
Maternal blood tests, 81
Maternity leave, 374

Mathematics skills, 290, 422, 571, *571*
Mead, Margaret, 580, *580*
Means-end analysis, 262–263
Measles, 182–183
Media
  electronic. *See* Television
  family and, 478
  fashion image, 179
  portrayals of gender, 417–418
  reports of research in, 52
Meiosis, 70, 71
Memory, 244–258, 275
  content knowledge, 254–256
  contents of, 252–254, *253*
  declarative and procedural, 252, 253, *253*
  encoding, 244–250
  episodic, 252, *253*, 253–254
  explicit and implicit, 253, *253*
  "flashbulb" memories, 257
  forgetting, 257
  nature of, 244, *245*
  personal memories, 385
  personal trauma and, 257–258
  repressed memories, 258, 259, *259*
  retrieval, *256*, 256–257
  semantic, 252, *253*, 254
  storage, 250–256
Memory time frames, 250–252
  long-term memory, 252, 255–256
  sensory memory, 251
  short-term memory, *251*, 251–252, *252*
Men
  causes of infertility in, 82
  impact of fathering on, 502–503
  nurturing, 410, *410*
Menarche, 184, 186
Mental age (MA), 282
Mental health problems, 584–585, 586
Mental retardation, 76, *298*, 298–299, *299*
  cultural-familial, 298–299
  Down syndrome. *See* Down syndrome
  organic, 298
Mental rotation abilities, 251, *252*
Mentoring, research on, 12
Merit, 457
Mesoderm, 95
Mesosystem, *40*, 40
Metacognition, 243, 270–273, 275–276
  developmental changes and, 271
  in formal operational stage, 222
  self-regulatory learning, 272–273, *273*
  strategies in, 271–272
Metacognitive activity, 271
Metacognitive knowledge, 271
Meta-knowing skills, 271
MH (malignant hyperthermia), 76
Microsystem, *40*, 40
Middle and late childhood, 18, *19*
  acculturation, 500
  attention and, 246–247
  brain development, 173
  emotional development in, 354
  empathy in, 449–450
  fine motor skills, 171–172
  gross motor skills, 170–171
  illness in, 181–182, *183*
  increased organization in, 250
  language development in, 332–335
  parent-child interactions in, 477
  physical growth in, 170
  scientific thinking in, 270
  self-understanding in, 386
  stress in, 361–362
  use of elaboration in, 249, *249*

Middle school, 573
　bullying in, 516
　effectiveness of, 552–553
　life science and life skills education in, 176
　social contexts, 543
　transition to, 551–552
Middle school teachers, 553
Midwife, *108*, 111
Million Man March, 501
Minnesota Study of Twins Reared Apart, 66–67, 74
Mitosis, 70, 71
Mixed-age friendships, 525
Mixed-sex peer groups, 528
Modeling
　adults as role models, 269
　experiments in, 44
　of gender behavior, 414, *414*
　of moral behavior, 446, *446*, 453
　of moral thinking, 440–442
　of optimism, 359
　of self-regulatory learning, 273, *273*
Molecular genetics, 74–75, *75*
Monitoring the Future Study, 192, *192*
Monozygotic twins, 74
Montessori, Maria, 543, 544
Montessori approach, 544
Moodiness, 355
Moral behavior, 445–448, 465
　altruistic, empathy and, 450, 456
　basic processes in, 445–447, *446*
　emphasis on, 443
　modeling of, 446, *446*, 453
　resistance to temptation, 447
　roles of reward and punishment, 446–447
　social cognitive theory of, 448
Moral competence, 448
Moral development, 434–465
　altruism, 456–457
　cognitive development and, 440–443
　contemporary perspective of, 449–451, *450*
　gender and, 444–445
　juvenile delinquency and, 457–461
　Kohlberg's theory. *See* Kohlberg's theory of moral
　　development
　moral behavior and, 445–448
　moral feeling and, 448–451
　moral thought and, 437–445
　Piaget's theory, 437–438
　psychoanalytic theories, 448–449, 452
　recognizing injustice, 436
　role of parents in, 442–443, 448–449, 452–453
　role of schools in, 453–455
Moral development theory, 55
Moral dilemmas, 438–439, 443–444, *444*
Moral feeling, 448–451, 465
　empathy and, 449–451, *450*
　psychoanalytic theory of, 448–449
Morality
　autonomous, 437, 438
　"extra-moral" factors in, 448
　heteronomous, 437, 438, 439, *441*
　social cognitive theory of, 448
　social systems morality, 440, *441*
　social understanding and, 438
Moral performance, 448
Moral thought, 437–445, 465
　assessment of moral reasoning, 443–444, *444*
　cognitive conflict and, 440–442
　critics of Kohlberg's theory, 440–445
　Kohlberg's theory, 438–440
　modeling of, 440–442
　Piaget's theory, 437–438
　social conventional reasoning, 445
Moro reflex, 144, *145*

Morpheme, 315
Morphology, 315–316, *317*, 329–330
Mothers
　age of, effects on fetus, 106–107
　attachment to, 373
　managerial role of, 480–481
　maternal factors in fetal development, 104–107
　role of, 499–500
　talkativeness of, vocabulary and, 331
　working mothers, 493–495
　See also Women
Motivation
　developmental shifts in, 567
　extrinsic and intrinsic, 565–567
　mastery motivation, 567, *568*
　practice and, 255
　rewards and, 566–567
　self-determination and personal choice, 565–566
　self-motivation, 300, 302
Motor development
　in childhood, 170–172
　dynamic systems theory of, 151
　fine motor skills. *See* Fine motor skills
　gross motor skills. *See* Gross motor skills
　handedness, 172
　in infancy, 144–151, 163
　perceptual-motor coupling, 159–161
　reflexes, 144–145, *145*
Motor recognition, 214
Motor vehicle accidents, 181, 182
"Moving room" experiment, 146
Mozart, Wolfgang Amadeus, 255
MRI (magnetic resonance imaging), 134, 173
MTV, 418
Multiple births, 83, *83*
Multiple-factor theory, 290
Multiple identities, in adolescence, 397–398
Multiple intelligences approach, 280, 289–294, 309
　emotional intelligence, 293
　evaluating, 293, *293*
　Gardner's theory of, 290–291
　general intelligence (*g*), 294
　multiple-factor theory of, 290
　Sternberg's triarchic theory, 291–292
　two-factor theory of, 289–290
Multiple sclerosis, 472
Musical ability, 255, 290, 291
Mutual interpersonal expectations, relationships, and
　interpersonal conformity, 440, *441*
Mutual perspective taking, *390*
Myelination, 132, 173
Myelin sheath, 132, *132*

N

NA (negative affectivity), 347, 364
NAEYC (National Association for the Education of
　Young Children), 335, 545, *546*, 547
Nakhre, Rashmi, 376, *376*
National Association for the Education of Young
　Children (NAEYC), 335, 545, *546*, 547
National Helpers Network, *454*
National IHAD Foundation, *554*
National Institute of Child Health and Human Develop-
　ment (NICHD), 376
National Longitudinal Study on Adolescent Health, 492
Native Americans, 13
　achievement and, 570
　diversity among, 591
　high school dropout rate, 553
　stress and, 360
Natural childbirth, 113

Naturalistic observation, 44–45
Naturalist skills, 290
Natural language acquisition, 322
Natural selection, 67
Nature-nurture issue, 19, 79
Nechita, Alexandra, 300
Need for achievement, 565
Negative affectivity (NA), 347, 364
Negative correlation, 47
Negative feedback, 550
Negative feelings, 451
Negative influences of peers, 512
Neglected children, 515, 516
Neglectful parenting, 482
Neighborhood friendship networks, 530, *530*
Neighborhoods, 584, *586*
Neonatal nursing, careers in, A–6
Neonates. *See* Newborns
Neo-Piagetians, 229
Network theories, 255
Neural tube, 96
Neurons, 132, *132*, 173
Neurotransmitters, 173
Newborns
　habituation in, 245, *245*
　measures of health and responsiveness, *118*,
　　118–119, 295
　temperament of, 364–365
　transition of fetus to, 110–111
New Connections program, 296
Newton, Sir Isaac, 299
NICHD (National Institute of Child Health and Human
　Development), 376
Niche-picking genotype-environment correlations,
　85, *85*
Nicotine, effects on fetus, 101–102
Nonprescription drugs, 101
Nonshared environmental experiences, 86
Noradrenaline, 110–111
Normal distribution, 283, *283*
Normative comparisons, 323
Normative processing style, 399
Norms, 286–287
Nurse-midwifery, careers in, A–6
The Nurture Assumption (Harris), 87, *87*, 486
Nutrition, 176–179, *177*
　breastfeeding v. bottlefeeding, *139*, 139–140
　eating behavior and, 139
　effects on fetus, 105
　energy needs, 176–179, *177*
　malnutrition in infancy, 140–142
　obesity, 177–178
　physical growth and, 139–142
　puberty and, 184
　teratology and, 105
　See also Eating disorders

O

Obesity
　eating behaviors and, 177–178
　effects on fetus, 105
　nutrition and, 176–179, *177*
　risks of, 178, *178*, 179
Object permanence, *211*, 211–213, *212*
Objects, perception of, 155–156
Observation, 43–45, *45*
　in descriptive research, 43–45, *45*
　direct observation, *8*, 8–9
　models of gender behavior, 414, *414*
　naturalistic, 44–45
　Piaget's theory and, 206, 213–214

Obstetrics/gynecology, careers in, A–6
Occipital lobe, 135, *135*
Occupations
    gender stereotyping and, 421
    See also Careers in child development; Employment
Ochoa, Gregory, 287
Oedipus complex, 31
Oldest child, 487–488
"One-minute bedtime stories," 486
One-parent families. *See* Single-parent families
Onlooker play, 520
Only child, 488
On the Origin of Species (Darwin), 67
Open-mindedness, 268
Operant conditioning, 37, *37*
Operations, 215
Optimistic children, 359, *360*
Oral satisfaction, 367
Oral stage, 30, *31*
Oregon Social Learning Center, 461
Organic retardation, 298
Organization, 208, 249–250
Organogenesis, 96–97
Original sin view, 7
Outcome measures, 548
Overcontrol, 302
Overextension, 328
Overt pathway to delinquency, 459
Oxytocics, 112

P

PA (positive affectivity), 347
Pain cry, 351
Pain relief, for childbirth, 112
Pain sensation, in infancy, 158
Parallel play, 520
Parent-adolescent conflict, 490–492, *492*
Parental leave, 374
Parental role, 479–480
Parent-child interactions, 476–477
Parent-child relationships
    continuity view of, 474–475
    emotion and, 347–348
    moral development and, 442–443
    parent-adolescent conflict, 490–492, *492*
    peer relations compared, 512–513, *513*
    self-esteem and, 393
    synchrony in, 473
Parent education, careers in, 481, *481*
Parenting, 479–486, 505
    child maltreatment and, 484–485
    coparenting, 503
    developmental changes and, 476–477
    with disabilities, 472
    ethnic minority parenting, 500
    fitness for, 11
    gender and, 499–503
    managerial role, 480–481
    marital relationship and, 474
    moral development and, 452–453, 465
    myths about, 480
    parental role, 479–480
    punishment and, 482–484, *483*
    styles of, 481–482, *482*
    temperament and, 367
    time and effort involved, 486
    violence and, 461
    See also Families; Parents
Parenting programs, prepackaged, 367
Parents
    accessible to children, 501, *501*
    adolescent detachment from, 491–492, *492*

age of, Down syndrome and, 106, 107
    death of, coping with, 362–363
    depression in, 356–357
    differential treatment by, 488–489
    discipline by, 452–453
    emotion and, 348
    facilitation of language development, 323, *323*
    feelings of guilt and, 451
    gay and lesbian, 497–498
    gay and lesbian parents, 497–498
    influence on gender development, *415*, 415–416
    influences on child care, 377
    monitoring by, delinquency and, 481, 494–495
    monitoring computer use, 598–599, *599*
    prevention of drug abuse and, 195
    role in child development, 87, *87*
    role in moral development, 442–443, 448–449,
        452–453
Parietal lobe, 135, *135*, 422
Passing, 188
Passive genotype-environment correlations, 85, *85*
Paternity leave, 374
Pavlov, Ivan, 36, 37
Pavlov's theory, 37
PCBs, effects on fetus, 103–104
Pediatric medicine, careers in, 143, A–6
Pediatric nursing, careers in, 141, A–6
Peer groups
    child groups v. adolescent groups, 527–528, *528*
    ethnic minority youth and, 530, *530*
    group functions, 511–512
    mixed-sex groups, 528
    same-sex groups, 517
Peer pressure, conformity and, 416, 526–527
Peer relations, 475, 511–518, 535
    bullying, 512, *513*, 516, *517*
    child maltreatment and, 485
    developmental course of, 513–514
    emotion and, 348
    friendship interaction, 476
    gender and, 517
    information-processing skills and, 515
    moral development and, 442–443
    parent-child relations compared, 512–513, *513*
    peer statuses and, 515–516
    perspective taking and, 442–443
    positive personal contact, 557–558
    in preschool, 542–543
    reciprocal socialization, *514*, 514–515
    research on, 12
    same-sex groups, 517
    social cognition and, 514–515
    social development and, 511
    training in, 516
Peers, 508–536
    adolescence and, 510, 526–532
    cliques and crowds, 527
    conformity to, 526–527
    ethnic minority youth, 530, *530*
    friendships, 522–525
    influence on gender development, 416, *416*
    influence on moral development, 452
    negative influences of, 512
    play and. *See* Play
    prevention of drug abuse and, 195
    relations with. *See* Peer relations
    romantic relationships, 528–533, 535–536
    same-sex, preference for, 416, *416*
Peer statuses, 515–516
Peer teachers, 232, 268–269
Pelvic field defect, 412
Penis, missing, 412
Perceived Competence Scale for Children, 392
Perception, 152

Perceptual constancy, 154–156, *155, 156*
Perceptual development
    ecological view of, 152–153
    hearing, *157*, 157–158
    in infancy, 152–161, 163, 214
    intermodal perception, 159
    pain, 158
    perception, 152
    perceptual-motor coupling, 159–161
    smell, 158, *158*
    taste, 158–159, *159*
    touch, 158
    visual. *See* Visual perception
Perceptual-motor coupling, 159–161
Performance orientation, 567
Perinatal nursing, careers in, 113, *113*
Periods of development, 18, *19*
Permissive parents, 400
Perry, Nora, 209
Perry Preschool, 196, 547
Personal choice, motivation and, 565–566
Personal fable, 224–225
Personality, 396–397
Personal memories, 385
Perspective taking, 449, 558
    peer relations and, 442–443
    in self-understanding, *390*, 390–391
Pessimistic children, 359, *360*
PET (positron emission tomography) scans, 134
Petting, 189
Phallic stage, 31, *31*
Phenotype, 73
Phenylketonuria (PKU), 78–79, *79*
Phoneme, 315
Phonological instruction, 561–562
Phonology, 315, *317*
Physical adjustments, postpartum, 120
Physical fitness classes, dangers of, 148
Physical growth, 166–200
    of brain. *See* Brain
    in childhood, 169–170, 199
    gender similarities in, 421–422
    Healthy Start program, 142, *142*
    height and weight, 132
    infancy, 131–143, 163
    in infancy, 128–163
    motor development. *See* Motor development
    nutrition and, 139–142
    patterns of, *131*, 131–132, 169–170
    sleep and, 137–139
    toilet training and, 143
Physical support, friendship and, 522
Piaget, Jean, 9, 29, 41, *207, 227, 228, 267*, 294
Piaget's theory, 33–35, *34, 42*, 207–229, 237
    application to education, 226–227
    concrete operational thought, *220*, 220–221, *221*
    criticisms of, 228–229
    evaluation of, 227–229
    formal operational thought, 221–226
    of moral development, 437–438
    preoperational thought, 214–219
    role of observation in, 206, 213–214
    sensorimotor thought, 209–214
    stages, 209–226
    theory and processes, 207–208
    Vygotsky's theory compared, 234–235, *235*
Picasso, Pablo, 216, 301
Pitch, 157
Pittsburgh Youth Study, 459
Pituitary gland, 185
PKU (phenylketonuria), 78–79, *79*
Placenta, 95–96, *97*
Planfulness of attention, 246–247, *247*
Planning and strategy, 268

Plath, Sylvia, 299
Play, 518–522, 535
  in child-centered kindergarten, 544
  functions of, 518–519
  games, 473–474, 521
  gender development and, 415–416
  gender differences in, 422–423
  as preparation for adulthood, 68
  research on, *519*, 519–520
  rough-and-tumble, 514
  sociocultural contexts of, 521–522
  types of, 520–521
Playful thinking, 302
Play therapy, 518
Pluralism, assimilation and, 592
Polson, Donene, 233
Polygenic inheritance, 72–73
Popular children, 515
Positive affect and approach, 364
Positive affectivity (PA), 347
Positive correlation, 47
Positive feelings, 451
Positive prenatal development, 109
Positron emission tomography (PET) scans, 134
Possible self, 388
Postconventional reasoning, 440, *441*
Postpartum period, 119–123, 125–126
  bonding during, 122–123
  described, 119–120
  emotional adjustments in, 120–122, *121*
  physical adjustments in, 120
Post-traumatic stress disorder, 258
Postural control, 146
Poverty
  Abecedarian Intervention Program, 304, *304*
  antipoverty programs, 556, 587
  as barrier to learning, 555
  child care and, 375
  cocaine use and, 102
  culture and, 585–587, *586*
  ethnicity and, 13
  family and, 498
  feminization of, 586–587
  health and, 181, 586
  home environment and, 589
  identity and, 402
  sexual problems and, 189
  socioeconomic status and, 585–587, *586*, 601
  violence and, 462
Power assertion, 452
Practical intelligence, 291, 292
Practice, 254–255, 272
Practice play, 520, 521
Pragmatics, 316–317, *317*, 331–332
Precocity, 299–300
Preconventional reasoning, 439, *441*
Prefrontal cortex, 133–134, 174, *174*
Pregnancy
  adolescent, rates of, *190*, 190–191
  cultural beliefs about, 108–109
  maternal age and, 106
  See also Childbirth; Postpartum period; Prenatal development
Prejudice, discrimination, and bias, 589, 591–592
Prenatal care, 107–108
Prenatal development, 95–109, 125
  birth and, 92–126
  course of, 95–98
  culture and, 108–109
  embryonic period, 95–97
  fetal period, 97–98, *98*
  germinal period, 95, *96*
  positive, 109
  prenatal care and, 107–108

sex hormones and, 411–412
  teratology and, 99–107, *100*
Prenatal diagnostic tests, 81, *81*
Prenatal period, 18, *19*
Preoccupied/ambivalent attachment, 490
Preoperational stage, *34*, 35
Preoperational thought, 214–219
  intuitive thought substage, 216–219, *216–219*
  symbolic function substage, *215*, 215–216, *216*
Prepared childbirth, 113
Preschools
  intelligence testing, 283
  Perry Preschool, 196, 547
  social contexts, 541–543
Prescription drugs, 99–100
Pretense/symbolic play, 520–521
Preterm infants, 114
  bonding in, 122–123
  research on, 10
  See also Low birth weight infants
Primacy effect, 257
Primary (cognitive) appraisal, 359
Primary circular reactions, 210
Primary emotions, 350
Print media, gender portrayals in, 418
Private, 232
Problem behaviors, masculine role and, 426
Problem solving, 261–267
  balance scale problem, *263*, 263–265, *264*
  developing strategies, 261–263
  evaluating solutions, 263
  finding and framing problems, 261
  infant imitation in, *266*, 266–267
  rethinking and redefining, 263
  using analogies, 265–266
  using rules, *263*, 263–265, *264*
  using scale models, 265–266
Problem-solving skills, 478
Problem-solving strategy, 361
Procedural memory, 252, 253, *253*
Processing speed, 251–252
Project Head Start, 15, 545, 547–548, *548*
Project Spectrum, 280, 291
Prosocial behavior, 456–457, 465, 596, *597*
Proximodistal growth pattern, 131–132
"Pruning," 132–133, *133*
Psychiatry, careers in, 122, A–4
Psychoactive drugs, 101–102
Psychoanalytic theories, 30–33
  Erikson's psychosocial theory, 31–33, *32*, *42*
  evaluation of, 33
  Freud's theory, 30–31, *31*, *42*
  of gender, 414, *414*
  of moral development, 448–449, 452
Psychological adjustments
  divorce and, 495
  postpartum, 120–122, *121*
  during puberty, 186–187
Psychology, careers in
  clinical child psychology, 11, *11*
  clinical psychology, 122, A–4
  counseling psychology, A–4
  developmental psychology, 262, *262*
  educational psychology, 55, A–3
  health psychology, 461, *461*
  school psychologists, A–3—A–4
Psychometrists, 285
Psychosexual theory, 30–31, *31*
Psychosocial moratorium, 396
Psychosocial stages, 31
Psychosocial theory
  Erikson's theory, 31–33, *32*, *42*
  identity formation, 395–396, 399
Psychotherapy, for depression, 357

Puberty, 183–184, *184*, 199
  body image and, 186–187
  early and late maturation, 187, *188*
  height and weight, 185–186, *186*
  hormonal changes, 185, *185*
  individual variations in, 186
  pubertal growth spurt, 185–186, *186*
  schooling and, 551
  sexuality and, 187–191
  sexual maturation, 186, *187*
Pugh, Linda, 113, *113*
Punishment
  child maltreatment, 484–485
  corporal punishment, 482–484, *483*

Questionnaires, 8
Questions, 219

Race, 13
Racism, institutional, 557
Radiation, effects on fetus, 103
Rage, in at-risk youth, 460
Rain Man (film), 290
Random assignment, 48
Rapid eye movement (REM) sleep, 137, *138*
Rapport talk, 422
Rationalizations, 443
Raven Progressive Matrices Test, 287, *288*
"Raves," 192
Reaching, 149
Reaction range, 73
"Readiness approach" to toilet training, 143
Reading
  approaches to, 333–334, *334*
  comprehension, working memory and, 262
  developmental model of, 333
  lap reading, 335
  problems with, 231
  socioeconomic variations in, 584, *585*
Real-life moral dilemmas, 444, *444*
Real self, ideal self and, 387–388
Reasoning
  logical reasoning, 221, 222
  moral reasoning, assessment of, 443–444, *444*
  scientific reasoning, 270
  social conventional reasoning, 445
  training in, 229
  in young children, *216*, 217
  See also Kohlberg's theory of moral development
Reasoning with child, punishment and, 484
Recall, 257
Recasting strategy, 322
Recency effect, 257
Recessive genes, 71, *71*
Reciprocal socialization
  in families, 473–474
  in peer relations, *514*, 514–515
Reciprocal teaching, 268–269
Recognition, 257
"Recovered memories," 259, *259*
Reflexes, in infancy, 144–145, *145*
Reflexive smile, 352
Reframing, 362
Reggio Emilia approach, 540, *540*, 543
Regulation of emotion. *See* Emotion regulation
Rehbein, Michael, 46, 136, *136*

Rehearsal, 247–248, 249
Reid, Pamela Trotman, 55, *55*, 57
Rejected children, 515, 516
Relational aggression, 423
Relational emotion, 347–348
Relationships
　androgyny and, 425
　attachment and, 490
　discontinuity view of, 475–476
　gender differences in, 422–423
　gender roles and, 425
Relaxation techniques, 120
Reliability, of intelligence tests, 286
Remarriage, 496–497
REM sleep, 137, *138*
Report talk, 422
Repressed memories, 258, 259, *259*
Reproduction, 71
　adoption, 83–84
　challenges in, 81–84, 89
　infertility and, 81–83, *82, 83*
　prenatal diagnostic tests, 81, *81*
Research, 10, 12, 14, 43–51, 52
　in attachment, 367–368, *368, 370*, 371
　bias in, 54–57
　careers in, 589, *589*, A–1—A–4
　descriptive, 43–46
　direct observation, *8*, 8–9
　ethical, 53–54
　media reporting of, 52
　on play, *519*, 519–520
　on problem solving, *263*, 263–265, *264*
　rights of participants, 53–54
　specialization in, 269, *269*
　study of children, culture and, 579–580
　time span of, 48–49, *49, 50*
　See also Cross-cultural studies
Research bias, 54–57
　cultural and ethnic, 55–57
　gender bias, 54–55
Research centers, 8
Research journals, 49–51
Research methods
　case studies, 46
　correlational research, 46–47, *47*, 595
　cross-sectional approach, 48
　experience sampling method, 355, *355*
　experimental, 47–48, *48*
　interviewing, 45
　longitudinal approach, 48–49, *49, 50*
　observation. *See* Observation
　questionnaires, 8
　standardized tests, 45–46
　theory and, 49, *50*
Resilience, 16, *16*
Resistance to temptation, 447
Respiratory problems, 101, 181
Retention in grade, 549
Retrieval, 244–255, *256*, 256–257
Reversibility of thought, 218–219, 220
Reward and punishment
　moral behavior and, 446–447
　in parenting, 482–484, *483*
　self-control and, 447
Rh factor, 103
RhoGAM, 103
Ribonucleic acid (RNA), 76
Risky behaviors, adolescent, 189, 191
Ritalin, 563
Rites of passage, 582–583, *583*
RNA (ribonucleic acid), 76
RNA editing, 76
Rock music videos, 418
Role experimentation, 396–397

Romantic relationships, 510, 528–533, 535–536
　dating scripts, 531–532
　emotion and, 532
　heterosexual, 528–529, *529*
　homosexual and bisexual, 529–531
　sociocultural contexts, 532–533
Ronquillo, Armando, 402, *402*
Rooming-in arrangements, 123
Rooting reflex, 144, *145*, 209
Roseanne, 259
Rosenburg Scale of Self-Esteem, *392*
Rousseau, Jean-Jacques, 7
Royal, Jennifer, *258*
Rubella (German measles), 104
Rule assessment approach, 264–265
Rules, using, in problem solving, *263*, 263–265, *264*

S

s (specific intelligences), 293
Safe sex practices, 190
Safety hazards, in early childhood, 175
Same-sex parent, 448–449
Same-sex peers
　group interactions, 517
　preference for, 416, *416*
Sanford, Diane, 122, *122*
Santrock, John, 296
SAT (Scholastic Aptitude Test), 45, 172, 281, 284
Savage Inequalities (Kozol), 555–556
Scaffolding, 230, 232, 473–474
Scale models, use in problem solving, 265–266
Schemas, 207, 209, 228
　gender schemas, 419, *419*
　negative cognitive schema, 356
Schema theories
　gender schema theory, 419, *419*
　in long-term memory, 255–256
Scholastic Aptitude Test (SAT), 45, 172, 281, 284
School counseling, careers in, A–4—A–5
School Development Program, 558
Schooling
　contemporary approaches to, 541, *542*, 573
　effects on intelligence, 305
　puberty and, 551
School psychology, careers in, A–3—A–4
School readiness, 549
Schools, 538–574
　achievement in. *See* Achievement
　for adolescents, 550–555
　after-school programs, 495
　character education, 453–454
　children with disabilities and, 559–564
　cognitive moral education, 454–455
　critical thinking and, 267–268
　cultural conflict about, 578
　developmental status and, 543–555
　efficacious, characteristics of, 568–569
　elementary. *See* Elementary school
　ethnicity and, 556–558
　gender curricula, 425–426
　grading practices, 567
　graduation ceremonies, 582
　hidden curriculum, 453
　interethnic friendships, 530
　life science and life skills education, 176
　middle. *See* Middle school
　Reggio Emilia approach, 540, *540*, 543
　role in gender development, 416–417
　role in moral development, 453–455, 465
　secondary. *See* High school
　service learning, *454*, 455

social development contexts, 541–543
　socioeconomic status and, 555–556, 573
　socioeconomic variations in, 585
　traditional v. collaborative, 233–234
　values clarification, 454
　See also Early childhood education; Education；
　　Schooling
Schwe, Helen, 262, *262*
Science museum education, 269, *269*
Scientific method, 29
Scientific reasoning, 270
Scientific thinking, 270
Scripts, 256
Secondary (cognitive) appraisal, 359
Secondary circular reactions, 210
Second-language learning, 316, 336–337, *337*
Secure attachment, 370
Secure-autonomous individuals, 490
Segmentation, 334
Seizures, 136
Selective attention, 247
Self
　active dimensions of, 386
　fluctuating, 387
　multiple selves, 389
　real v. ideal, 387–388
　theories of, 385
Self-concept, 391, 582, *582*
Self-conscious emotions, 350, *351*
Self-conscious evaluative emotions, 350, *351*
Self-consciousness, 388
Self-control, 447
Self-descriptions, 384, 489
Self-determination, 565–566
Self-disclosure, 523, *523*, 524
Self-efficacy, 394, 568–569
Self-esteem, 391–395
　assessment of, 392
　classroom bias and, 417
　crowd membership and, 527
　increasing, 393–395, *394*
　low, consequences of, 393
　negative feedback and, 550
　SES and, 589
Self-esteem enhancement programs, 394
Self-expression, 450–451
Self-fulfillment, 450–451
Self-identity, fatherhood and, 502
Self-integration, 389
Self-modification, 243
Self-motivation, 300, 302
Self-Perception Profile for Adolescents, 392
Self-Perception Profile for Children, 392
Self-protectiveness, 388–389
Self-reflective perspective taking, *390*
Self-regulation, 364, 448
Self-regulatory learning, 272–273, *273*, 569
Self-representations, 385
Self-soothing, 353
Self-understanding, 384–391
　in adolescence, 387–390
　characteristics of, 390, *390*
　in early childhood, 386
　in infancy, 385, *385*
　in middle and late childhood, 386
　nature of, 385
　perspective taking in, *390*, 390–391
Semantic memory, 252, *253*, 254
Semantics, 316, *317*, 330–331
Sensation, 152
Sense of invincibility, 225
Sense of mastery, 169
Sensorimotor play, 520
Sensorimotor stage, 34, *34*

Sensorimotor thought, 209–214
  causality and, 213, *213*
  conceptual development and, 214
  evaluating sensorimotor stage, 213–214
  object permanence and, *211*, 211–213, *212*
  perceptual development and, 214
  understanding physical reality, 211–213
Sensory development
  in infancy, 152–161, 163
  sensation, 152
Sensory memory, 251
Separation protest, 352, *352*
Serial position effect, 256, *256*
Seriation, 220–221
Service learning, *454*, 455
SES. *See* Socioeconomic status
Sesame Street, 594–595, 596, *598*
Sex, 14
Sex hormones, 411–412, 421–422
Sex-linked genes, 72, *72*
Sex reassignment surgery, 412
Sexton, Anne, 299
Sexual (gender) identity, 188, 411, 529–531
Sexual intercourse, 120, 189, 582–583
Sexuality
  developing sexual identity, 188
  progression of sexual behaviors, 188–189
  puberty and, 187–191
Sexually transmitted infections (STIs)
  in adolescence, 190, 191
  effects on fetus, 104–105
Sexual maturation, 186, *187*
Sexual orientation, 188
Sexual selection, 413
Sexual stereotypes, 323
Shape constancy, 155
Shared environmental experiences, 85–86
Shared sleeping, 137–138
Sharing, 456, 476
Shaw, George Bernard, 11
Short-term goals, 569
Short-term memory, *251*, 251–252, *252*
Shyness, 364
Siblings, 505
  birth order and, 487–489
  death of, coping with, 362–363
  sibling relationships, 487
Sickle-cell anemia, 79, *79*
Sign language, 327
Similarity in friendship, 525
Simon, Theophile, 282
Simple reflexes, 209
Sims, Bob, 76
Sims, Mary, 76
Single-parent families, 10–11, 493, *493*
  ethnicity and, 498
  poverty and, 586–587
Sitting, 146
Situation-specific behavior, 447
Size constancy, 155
Skinner, B. F., 36, 37, *37*
Skinner's operant conditioning, 37, *37*
Sleep, 137–139
  depression and, 357
  REM sleep, 137, *138*
  shared sleeping, 137–138
Sleep apnea, SIDS and, 138
Slow-to-warm-up child, 364
Small for date infants, 114
Smell, in infancy, 158
Smiling, 352
Snellen chart, 153
Social adjustment, 299, 495
Social approval, self-esteem and, 394

Social aspects of self, 386
Social cognition, peer relations and, 514–515
Social cognitive theory, 36, 37–38, *38*, 42
  of gender, 414, *414*
  of morality, 448
Social comparison, 386, 388, 522
Social competence
  attachment and, 371
  emotional competence, 349
  emotion regulation and, 354
  importance of friendships, 523
  private speech and, 232
  romantic relationships and, 528
Social constructivist approach, 235, 541
Social contexts, 400–403
  culture and ethnicity, 401–403
  family influences, 400–401
  gender, 403
  of peer relations, 512
  schools, 541–543
Social contract or utility and individual rights, 440, *441*
Social conventional reasoning, 445
Social development
  Montessori approach and, 544
  peer relations and, 511
  schools and, 541–543
Social influences, on gender development, 414–418
Social-informational perspective taking, *390*
Social mobility, of family, 478, 498
Social play, 521
Social policy, 14–15
Social referencing, 353
Social roles of women, 414–418
Social smile, 352
Social support, 195
Social systems, family as, 474, *475*
Social systems morality, 440, *441*
Social thinking, 224–225
Social understanding, morality and, 438
Social work, careers in, A–5
Social world
  attachment and, *372*, 372–373
  families and, *493*, 493–503
Society, adolescent sexuality and, 188
Sociocultural cognitive theory, 33, 35
Sociocultural contexts
  of adolescence, 580
  of child maltreatment, 484–485
  contemporary concerns, 12–14
  of dating, 532–533
  of language development, 322–324
  of play, 521–522
  self and, 389
  of stress, 360–361
Sociocultural diversity, technology and, 599, *599*
Sociocultural influences, on family, 477–478, 505–506
Socioeconomic status (SES), 601
  Abecedarian Intervention Program, 304, *304*
  divorce and, 496
  ethnicity and, 588–590
  families and, 499, 584–585
  intelligence testing and, 307
  juvenile delinquency and, 460
  language development and, 321, *321*, 324, 331
  mental health problems and, 584–585, 586
  moral development and, 453
  nature of, 583–584
  physical growth and, 169–170
  poverty and, 585–587, *586*, 601
  pretense play and, 521–522
  schools and, 555–556, 573
  sexual problems and, 189
Socioemotional development, 422–423
Socioemotional processes, 17, *18*

Sociohistorical influences, 450
Socrates, 299
Solitary play, 519
SOMPA (System of Multicultural Pluralistic Assessment), 287–288
Sounds
  memory for, 261
  sound localization, 157–158
  sound recognition, *327*, 327–328
Spanking, 483–484
Spatial skills, 290, 307
Special education services, careers in, 559, *559*, A–3
Specific intelligences (s), 293
Specificity of learning, 147, *147*
Specificity of learning disability, 560
Speech style, 332
Speech therapy, careers in, A–7
Spelling, development of, 334–335
Spina bifida, 79, *79*, 80
Spinal cord, formation of, 96
Sports, 168, *168*, 180
Springer, Jim, 66, *66*
Stages, evaluation of, 228–229
Standardized tests, 45–46, 286–287, *287*
Standards-based education, 547
Stanford-Binet intelligence tests, 45, 283, *283*, 296, 299, *305*
Status offenses, 457
Stepfamilies, 496–497
Stepping reflex, *145*
Stereotyping
  emotional stereotypes, 427
  gender stereotypes, 420–421
  intelligence tests and, 288
  negative, of ethnic minorities, 556–557
  traditional family and, 494
Stern, William, 282
Stimulant medications, 563
Stimulation, friendship and, 522
STIs. *See* Sexually transmitted infections
Storage, 244
"Storm and stress" in adolescence, 355
Stranger anxiety, 352
Strange Situation, 370, *370*, 371
Strategic knowledge, 271
Strategy construction, 243
Strategy instruction, 272
Stress, 358–363, 379
  cognitive factors in, 358–359, *360*
  culture and, 360, 361, 589–590
  of death, coping with, 362–363
  effects on fetus, 105–106
  life events and daily hassles, 359–360
  in middle and late childhood, 361–362
  post-traumatic stress disorder, 258
  poverty and, 590
  sociocultural factors in, 360–361
  tolerance for, 372
  transition to middle school and, 551–552
Stress hormones, 116
Suarez-Orozco, Carola, 588, 589, *589*
Subgoaling, in problem solving, 262
Substance use and abuse
  in adolescence, *192*, 192–195, *193*
  alcohol use, 101, *101*, 193, 561
  cigarette smoking, 193–194, *194*
  roles of parents and peers, 194–195
  See also specific drugs
Sucking reflex, 144, 145, *145*, 209–210
Sudden infant death syndrome (SIDS), 138–139
  nicotine and, 101, 139
  sleeping practices and, 137–138
Suggestion, vulnerability to, 259
Suicide, 182, 357–358, 379

Sullivan's theory of friendships, *523*, 523–524, *524*
Superego, 30, 448
Supplementary feeding, in infancy, 142
Surveys, 45
Swimming reflex, *145*
Symbolic activity, 214, 216, *216*
Symbolic function substage, *215*, 215–216, *216*
Symbols, 210, 265–266, 314
Synapses, 132, *133*, 173
Syntax, 316, *317*, 330
Syphilis, effects on fetus, 104
System of Multicultural Pluralistic Assessment (SOMPA), 287–288

T

Tabula rasa view, 7
Tamayo, Salvador, 337
Task-involved goals, 569
Taste, in infancy, 158–159, *159*
Tay-Sachs disease, 79, *79*
Ta Yü (Chinese emperor), 283
Teachers
    caring, 568, *568*
    as cultural mediators, 558
    "labeling" LD children, 561
    peer teachers, 232, 268–269
    reducing bullying, 516
    role in gender development, 416–417
Teaching, 233, 553
    careers in, 550, *550*, A–2
    child-centered kindergarten, 544
    cross-age teaching, 232, 268–269
    developmentally appropriate practice, 544–545, *546*, 547
    Montessori approach, 544
Technology, 594–599, 601
    computers and Internet, 269, 529, 597–599, *599*
    education and, 599
    family and, 478
    school improvement and, 557
    sociocultural diversity and, 599, *599*
    television, 594–597
Telegraphic speech, 329
Television, 594–597
    amount watched, 595, *595*
    cognitive development, 595–596, *597*
    educational television, 594–595, 596, 597, *598*
    links to obesity, 179
    literacy and, 335
    portrayals of gender, 417–418
    roles of, 594–595
    socioeconomic variations in watching, 584, *585*
    See also Media
Temperament, 379–380
    birth order and, 488
    defining and classifying, 363–365
    developmental connections, 365–366, *366*
    emotional development and, 363–368
    gender, culture and, 366–367
    goodness of fit, 365
    parenting and, 367
    response to divorce and, 496
Temporal lobe, 135, *135*
Teratogen, 99
Teratology, 99–107, *100*
    of alcohol, 101, *101*, 561
    of cocaine, 102
    environmental hazards, *103*, 103–104
    of heroin, 103
    incompatible blood types, 103
    infectious diseases, 104–105

of marijuana, 102–103
maternal factors, 104–107
of nicotine, 101–102
nutrition and, 105
paternal factors, 107
prescription and nonprescription drugs, 99–101
psychoactive drugs, 101–102
stress and, 105–106
Terman, Lewis, 282
Terrorism
    dealing with concerns, 553
    moral behavior and, 443
    stress and, 362
Tertiary circular reactions, 210
Tertiary circular reactions, novelty, and curiosity, 210
Testosterone, 185, 412, 421
Tetanus, 182–183
Thalidomide, 100
Theories of self, 385
Theory(ies), 29
    research methods and, 49, *50*
    See also specific theories
Theory of mind, 260–261, *261*
Thinking, 260–270, 275, 301, 302
    forming concepts, 260–261
    as information processing, 243
    moral development and, 437–445, 465
    nature of, 260
    problem solving, 261–267
    scientific thinking, 270
    social thinking, 224–225
    thinking critically, 242, 267–269, 558
Thinking critically, 242, 267–269, 558
Thompson, Rachel, 107, *107*
Three mountains task, 215, *215*
Thumb sucking, 145, 353
Time limits, in intelligence testing, 288
Time of exposure, teratology and, 99
Time span of research, 48–49
    cross-sectional approach, 48
    longitudinal approach, 48–49, *49*, *50*
Toddlers
    emotion regulation in, 353
    language development, 323
    mobility of, 147–148
    problem solving, 265–266
Toilet training, 143
"Tomboy" girls, 416
Tonic neck reflex, *145*
Top-dog phenomenon, 552
Touch, in infancy, 158
Touching, 476
Toxic wastes, effects on fetus, 103
Traditional learning, 268
Transitivity, 221
Traumatic memory, 257–258
Triarchic theory of intelligence, 291–292
Trimesters, prenatal, 97–98, *98*
Trophoblast, 95
True self, false self and, 388
Trust *versus* mistrust, 32, *32*, 369
Turner syndrome, 77, 78
Turning Points reports, 553
Turn taking, 473–474, 476
Twin studies, 74
    of heritability of intelligence, 303, *303*
    Minnesota Study of Twins Reared Apart, 66–67, 74
Two-factor theory, 289–290
Two-generation intervention, 556, 587
Two-word utterances, 328–329

U

Ultrasound sonography, 81, *81*
Umbilical cord, 95–96, *97*, 111
Unconscious self, 389
Underextension, 328
UNICEF, 15, 130
Universal ethical principles, 440, *441*
"Universal linguists," 327, *327*
University professors, careers as, 417, *417*, A–2
Unoccupied play, 519
Unresolved/disorganized attachment, 490
U.S. Office of Education, 562

V

Validity of intelligence tests, 286
Values clarification, 454
Van Beveren, Toosje Thyssen, 296, *296*
van Gogh, Vincent, 299
Vargas, Luis, 10, 11, *11*
Variables, 47
Verbal skills, 290, 307
    gender and, 422
    television and, 596
Vernix caseosa, 111
Verougstraete, Wendy, 324
Violence
    child abuse and, 484–485
    stress and, 361
    on television, 594, 595–596
    youth and, 460–461, 462, *462*
    See also Aggression
Violence prevention, 461
Visual acuity, 153, *154*
Visual expectations, 156–157
Visual images, memory for, 261
Visual perception
    auditory-visual relations in newborns, 159
    color vision, 153
    depth perception, 156, *156*
    in infancy, 153–157
    perceptual constancy, 154–156, *155*, *156*
    self-movement and, 146
    visual acuity, 153, *154*
    visual expectations, 156–157
    visual preferences, 153–154, *154*
Visual self-recognition, 385, *385*
Visuospatial skills, 172, 422
Vitamin C, 181
Vocabulary, 330–331, 332
Vocabulary spurt, 328
Vocalizations, 326–327
Voting age, 583
Vygotsky, Lev, 30, *35*, 41, 230, *230*
Vygotsky's theory, 33, 35, *42*, 206, 229–235, 237–238
    application to education, 232–234, 541
    language and thought, 232
    Piaget's theory compared, 234–235, *235*
    scaffolding, 230, 232, 473–474
    zone of proximal development, 230, *230*, 232, 233

W

Walker, Alice, 6, *6*
Walking, in infancy, 146–147, *147*
War on Poverty programs, 15
Watson, John B., 36, 37, 481
Wavy Gravy, 302

Weaning, early, malnutrition and, 140–141
Wechsler, David, 283, 289
Wechsler Adult Intelligence Scale III (WAIS-III), 283
Wechsler Intelligence Scale for Children—III (WISC-III), 283, *284*
Wechsler Preschool and Primary Scale of Intelligence (WPPSI), 283
Wechsler scales, 283, *284*
Weight
    in adolescence, 186
    in early childhood, 169
    growth in infancy, 132
    See also Eating disorders; Low birth weight infants; Obesity
Weikart, David, 196
Welfare programs, 587
Wernicke's area, 318, *319*
"Whipping boys," 512, *513*
Whites
    female, anorexia in, 179
    intelligence testing and, 306
    White American culture, 402
Whole-language approach to reading, 333–334
Whooping cough, 182–183

Wild Boy of Aveyron, 314
Williams, Tennessee, 244
Williams syndrome, 324–325, *325*
Women
    causes of infertility in, 82
    family work done by, 499–500
    feminization of poverty, 586–587
    social roles of, 414–418
    See also Mothers
Woodham, Luke, 462
Work-avoidant goals, 569
Working (short-term) memory, *251*, 251–252, *252*
Working mothers, 493–495
World Health Organization, 130
Writing, development of, 334–335
"Wugs," 330, *330*

X-linked inheritance, 72
XYY syndrome, *77*, 78

Yawning reflex, 144
Young Man Luther (Erikson), 396
Youth organizations, 502

Zhang Liyin, 168, *168*
Zidovudine (AZT), 105
ZIFT (zygote intrafallopian transfer), 82
Zone of proximal development (ZPD), 230, *230*, 232, 233
Zygote, 71, 95
Zygote intrafallopian transfer (ZIFT), 82